SOCIAL SECURITY LEGISLATION 2023/24

VOLUME II: UNIVERSAL CREDIT, STATE PENSION CREDIT AND THE SOCIAL FUND

SOCIAL SECURITY LEGISLATION 2023/24

General Editor
Nick Wikeley, M.A. (Cantab)

VOLUME II:
UNIVERSAL CREDIT, STATE PENSION CREDIT AND THE SOCIAL FUND

Commentary By

John Mesher, B.A., B.C.L. (Oxon), LL.M. (Yale)
Retired Judge of the Upper Tribunal
Emeritus Professor of Law,
University of Sheffield

Tom Royston, M.A. (Cantab)
Barrister

Nick Wikeley, M.A. (Cantab)
Judge of the Upper Tribunal,
Emeritus Professor of Law,
University of Southampton

Consultant Editor
Child Poverty Action Group

SWEET & MAXWELL

 THOMSON REUTERS

Published in 2023 by Thomson Reuters, trading as Sweet & Maxwell.
Thomson Reuters is registered in England & Wales, Company
No.1679046. Registered Office and address for service: 5 Canada Square,
Canary Wharf, London, E14 5AQ.

For further information on our products and services, visit
http://www.sweetandmaxwell.co.uk

Typeset by Servis Filmsetting Ltd, Stockport, Cheshire
Printed and bound by CPI Group (UK) Ltd, Croydon, CR0 4YY

A CIP catalogue record for this book is available
from the British Library

ISBN (print): 978-0-414-115484
ISBN (e-book): 978-0-414-115507
ISBN (print and e-book): 978-0-414-115491

For orders and enquiries,
go to: *http://www.tr.com/uki-legal-contact*; Tel: 0345 600 9355.
Crown Copyright material is reproduced with permission of the
Controller of HMSO and the King's Printer for Scotland.

CHILD POVERTY ACTION GROUP

The Child Poverty Action Group ("CPAG") is a charity, founded in 1965, which campaigns for the relief of poverty in the UK. It has a particular reputation in the field of welfare benefits law derived from its legal work, publications, training and parliamentary and policy work, and is widely recognised as the leading organisation for taking test cases on social security law.

CPAG is therefore ideally placed to act as Consultant Editor to this five-volume work—**Social Security Legislation**. CPAG is not responsible for the detail of what is contained in each volume, and the authors' views are not necessarily those of CPAG. The Consultant Editor's role is to act in an advisory capacity on the overall structure, focus and direction of the work.

For more information about CPAG, its rights and policy publications or training courses, its address is 30 Micawber Street, London, N1 7TB (telephone: 020 7837 7979—website: *http://www.cpag.org.uk*).

FOREWORD

These volumes provide a comprehensive and up-to-date compilation of social security legislation along with expert commentaries, which makes them an indispensable reference work for the judiciary and all those involved in social security proceedings. I am grateful to the authors of these latest volumes and to Sweet and Maxwell for their continued commitment to producing them each year. I commend this latest new edition, which provides essential information and guidance in this complex field of law and jurisprudence.

Judge Kate Markus KC
Chamber President of the First-tier Tribunal,
Social Entitlement Chamber

PREFACE

Universal Credit, State Pension Credit and the Social Fund is Volume II of the series *Social Security Legislation 2023/24*. The companion volumes are Hooker, Mesher, Mitchell, Ward and Wikeley, Volume I: *Non-Means Tested Benefits*; Rowland and Ward, Volume III: *Administration, Adjudication and the European Dimension*; and Hooker, Mitchell, Rowland and Wikeley, Volume IV: *HMRC-administered Social Security Benefits and Scotland*; plus Mesher, Poynter and Wikeley, Volume V: *Income Support and the Legacy Benefits 2021/22* as up-dated in the Cumulative Supplement located at the end of the present volume. The "year" in the title refers to the tax/ contribution year and indicates the period the books, including the subsequent Supplement, are designed to cover.

Each of the volumes in the series provides a legislative text, clearly showing the form and date of amendments, up to date to April 10, 2023, with explanatory commentary. The commentary sometimes includes references to later case law as well as to later administrative guidance and to expected legislative changes.

We again draw the attention of readers to the substantial restructuring of the five volumes that took place in 2021. A separate Note on Restructuring the *Social Security Legislation* series follows this Preface. We urge all readers, and especially seasoned readers of these Volumes (who may now not find material where they expected it to be), to read that Note. It explains the process of restructuring the series to reflect the fact that universal credit has now become the default working-age means-tested benefit for new claims in the social security system. This has resulted in some re-ordering of material across the volumes to provide readers with a clear and coherent explanation (at least so far as we can) of the various social security benefits. A specific part of the process from 2022/23 onwards is that no new edition of Volume V has been published. Instead, Cumulative up-dating Supplements have been and will be produced both in the mid-year general Supplement and at the end of each main Volume II. The latest version, incorporating all changes down to April 10, 2023, appears at the end of this book. A separate Preface to that Cumulative Supplement contains further explanation. Readers are therefore advised not to dispose of their copies of the 2021/22 Volume V, which will in the future most probably only be up-dated by way of such Supplements.

The present volume covers the three current Department for Work and Pensions means-tested benefits: universal credit, state pension credit and social fund payments for maternity and funeral expenses and for cold weather and winter fuel. The primary legislation relevant to all those benefits is in Part I and the regulations are in Parts II (universal credit), III (state pension credit) and IV (social fund). Part V covers the current provisions on persons subject to immigration control as relevant to those benefits. The relevant provisions on claims and payments and on decisions and appeals are now to be found in Volume III of this series, *Administration,*

Adjudication and the European Dimension, as for other benefits. The operative Commencement Orders for the Welfare Reform Act 2012 are to be found in Volume V of this series, *Income Support and the Legacy Benefits 2021/22*, as up-dated in the Cumulative Supplements. Those Orders now have primary relevance to the abolition of legacy benefits for new claims and to savings provisions. Provisions restricted to those living in Scotland and administered by the Scottish Ministers are covered in Volume IV of this series. Housing benefit, as administered by local authorities, is not covered by this series: see *CPAG's Housing Benefit and Council Benefit Legislation*.

The position has now been reached where it is impossible to make a new claim for any of the so-called "legacy" means-tested benefits replaced by universal credit: income support, income-based jobseeker's allowance, income-related employment and support allowance, housing benefit for those under pension age, child tax credit and working tax credit. Someone of working age not already in receipt of a legacy benefit whose income is insufficient now has only universal credit as a choice for a means-tested benefit to claim. The pilot for "managed migration", the transfer of existing recipients of legacy benefits at the behest of the DWP was postponed on the onset of the Covid-19 pandemic, but the process has now restarted in an expanding number of areas under the Universal Credit (Transitional Provisions) (Amendment) Regulations 2022, beginning with claimants receiving only tax credits in 2023/24 and moving on in 2024/25 to those receiving tax credits in combination with another legacy benefit and to income support, old style JSA and housing benefit recipients. But the migration of old style ESA recipients is not scheduled to be completed until 2028.

This edition includes the 2022 and 2023 Social Security (Additional Payments) Acts, on "cost of living" payments. Among the many amendments to secondary legislation since the last edition are significant changes to the Loans for Mortgage Interest Regulations 2017, a series of amendments to reg.99(6) of the Universal Credit Regulations 2013 on when full "conditionality" can be applied to claimants who are in work, through the raising of the so-called administrative earnings threshold and flawed provisions aimed at disregarding the amount of payments made in consequence of the Bereavement Benefits (Remedial) Order 2023.

There has been the usual process of expansion, refinement and correction of explanatory commentary, to take account not only of legislative amendment, but also of new Upper Tribunal and court decisions, as well as the emergence of practical problems. For instance, court decisions discussed include *Guest v Guest* [2022] UKSC 27 (on proprietary estoppel remedies in the context of the calculation of capital) and *Commissioners of HMRC v Murphy* [2022] EWCA Civ 1112 (on profit from employment in the context of the calculation of earned income). The many Upper Tribunal decisions considered include that of the three-judge panel in *SSWP v AT (UC)* [2022] UKUT 330 (AAC) (on the continuing effect of the Charter of Fundamental Rights of the European Union on the right to reside rules – under appeal to the Court of Appeal) and *JN v SSWP (UC)* [2023] UKUT 49 (on the effect pre-November 16, 2020 of the Court of Appeal's declaration in *Johnson* in look-alike cases of monthly-paid claimants).

We renew our thanks for the flexibility and forbearance of the publishers and for a great deal of help from a number of sources. Those include in particular the Child Poverty Action Group as advisory editor to this series in this 40th anniversary year of the publication of the ancestor of Volumes II and V in the form of Mesher, *CPAG's Supplementary Benefit Legislation Annotated*, which would never have got off the ground without the Group's support. We remain grateful for this assistance in our task of providing an authoritative reflection on and critique of the current state of the law. Users of the series, and its predecessor works, have over the years contributed considerably to their effectiveness by providing valuable comments on our commentary, or pointing out where the text of some provision has been omitted in error, or become garbled, or not been brought fully up to date. In providing such feedback, users of the work have helped to shape the content and ensure the accuracy of our material, and for that we continue to be grateful. That is all the more important given the major restructuring that has taken place. We therefore hope that users of the work will continue to provide such helpful input and feedback. Please write to the General Editor of the series, Professor Nick Wikeley, c/o School of Law, University of Southampton, Highfield, Southampton SO17 1BJ, email: *njw@soton. ac.uk*, and he will pass on any comments received to the appropriate commentator.

Our gratitude also goes to the President of the Social Entitlement Chamber of the First-tier Tribunal and her colleagues there for continuing the now long tradition of help and encouragement in our endeavours.

August 2023

John Mesher
Tom Royston
Nick Wikeley

NOTE ON RESTRUCTURING THE *SOCIAL SECURITY LEGISLATION* SERIES

The advent of Universal Credit (UC) has changed the landscape of the modern social security system and especially the role of the previous 'legacy' means tested benefits. The phased introduction of UC has presented a major challenge to commentators such as ourselves. To start with, our response was simply to prepare a stand-alone separate Volume in the series, namely (in previous years) *Volume V: Universal Credit*. However, the existing mapping of social security benefits across the five volumes has become increasingly difficult to sustain as UC has become the default means-tested benefit across the country rather than in selected postcode areas. Indeed, we did not anticipate that a five Volume series would continue indefinitely, but our plans for restructuring the whole series have been repeatedly delayed over recent years in keeping with the protracted roll out of UC itself. Last year, however, we begun the process of restructuring the series to reflect the 'new normal' in social security provision. In doing so we have sought to combine both intellectual coherence and practical utility in our treatment of the various aspects of the benefits system.

The principal change in the series is that the arrangement of material as between Volumes II and V has been fundamentally re-organised to reflect the default position for today's means-tested benefits, namely that new claimants applying for a means tested benefit claim UC and not one of the legacy benefits. Accordingly, the main change in the series is that most of the UC material has been moved from Volume V to Volume II. The legislative material and commentary on Income Support and income-based Jobseeker's Allowance (or old-style JSA) has made the reverse journey from Volume II to Volume V. At the same time, and as part of this rationalisation, the income-related Employment and Support Allowance (or old style ESA) material has been transferred from Volume I over to Volume V so that it sits alongside the other legacy benefits. Volume V was last published in 2021/22 and readers needing to refer to legislation concerning those benefits and to the commentary upon it should keep a copy of that edition, to which there is an up-dating supplement within Volume II of this year's edition.

As a result, Volume II has been renamed *Universal Credit, State Pension Credit and the Social Fund* while Volume V has been retitled *Income Support and the Legacy Benefits*. Thus, Volume II deals with UC and the other current means tested benefits for new claimants (pension credit and the social fund), while Volume V covers Income Support, old-style ESA and JSA, the UC Commencement Orders and other legacy issues (including immigration status and right to reside). The restructuring has therefore principally affected Volumes II and V in the series. There have, however, been knock on consequences for the other three Volumes.

So far as Volume I is concerned, and as already noted, old-style ESA material has been moved from Volume I to Volume V so that it sits with the other legacy benefits. However, as part of the process of ensuring all non means tested benefits are grouped together in Volume I, the material covering the new-style JSA (a contributory benefit) has been transferred to Volume I from Volume II, so joining new-style ESA in Volume I. For the convenience of readers, Volume I also includes a new Part covering limited capability for work and limited capability for work-related activity for old-style ESA cases.

So far as Volume III is concerned, the contents have been re-organised and re-ordered to reflect the post-Brexit realities, and so are arranged thus: Part I: Social Security Statutes, Part II: Social Security Regulations, Part III: Tribunals, Part IV: Human Rights and Part V: The European Dimension.

So far as Volume IV is concerned, Parts I to XII are essentially as before, covering tax credits and HMRC-administered social security benefits, with the addition of a new Part XI dealing with the Tax-Free Childcare Regulations. However, new Parts XIII and XIV bring together in one place the existing material relating exclusively to the Scottish social security system and previously found in Volumes II and III. In recognition of this reorganisation, and putting to one side theological arguments about whether tax credits are social security benefits, the Volume has been retitled as *Volume IV: HMRC-administered Social Security Benefits and Scotland.* In due course, the replacement of tax credits by universal credit will result in further changes to this Volume.

CONTENTS

PART I
STATUTES

PART II
UNIVERSAL CREDIT: REGULATIONS

PART IIA
UNIVERSAL CREDIT: REGULATIONS

Contents

PART IIB
TRANSITIONAL AND SAVINGS PROVISIONS

PART III
STATE PENSION CREDIT REGULATIONS

PART IV
THE SOCIAL FUND

Contents

PART V
PERSONS SUBJECT TO IMMIGRATION CONTROL

SUPPLEMENT MATERIAL TO VOLUME V

USING THIS BOOK: AN INTRODUCTION TO LEGISLATION AND CASE LAW

Introduction

This book is not a general introduction to, or general textbook on, the law relating to social security but it is nonetheless concerned with both of the principal sources of social security law—*legislation* (both primary and secondary) and *case law*. It sets out the text of the most important legislation, as currently in force, and then there is added commentary that refers to the relevant case law. Lawyers will be familiar with this style of publication, which inevitably follows the structure of the legislation.

This note is designed primarily to assist readers who are not lawyers to find their way around the legislation and to understand the references to case law, but information it contains about how to find social security case law is intended to be of assistance to lawyers too.

Primary legislation

Primary legislation of the United Kingdom Parliament consists of *Acts of Parliament* (also known as *Statutes*). They will have been introduced to Parliament as *Bills*. There are opportunities for Members of Parliament and peers to debate individual clauses and to vote on amendments before a Bill is passed and becomes an Act (at which point the clauses become sections). No tribunal or court has the power to disapply, or hold to be invalid, an Act of Parliament, although, until December 31, 2020, that could be done if it was inconsistent with European Union law.

An Act is known by its "short title", which incorporates the year in which it was passed (e.g. the Social Security Contributions and Benefits Act 1992), and is given a chapter number (abbreviated as, for instance, "c.4" indicating that the Act was the fourth passed in that year). It is seldom necessary to refer to the chapter number but it appears in the running headers in this book.

Each *section* (abbreviated as "s." or, in the plural, "ss.") of an Act is numbered and may be divided into *subsections* (abbreviated as "subs." and represented by a number in brackets), which in turn may be divided into *paragraphs* (abbreviated as "para." and represented by a lower case letter in brackets) and *subparagraphs* (abbreviated as "subpara." and represented by a small roman numeral in brackets). Subparagraph (ii) of para.(a) of subs. (1) of s.72 will usually be referred to simply as "s.72(1)(a)(ii)". Upper case letters may be used where additional sections or subsections are inserted by amendment and additional lower case letters may be used where new paragraphs and subparagraphs are inserted. This accounts for the rather ungainly s.109B(2A)(aa) of the Social Security Administration Act 1992.

Sections of a large Act may be grouped into a numbered *Part*, which may even be divided into *Chapters*. It is not usual to refer to a Part or a Chapter unless referring to the whole Part or Chapter.

Where a section would otherwise become unwieldy because it is necessary to include a list or complicated technical provisions, the section may simply refer to a *Schedule* at the end of the Act. A Schedule (abbreviated as "Sch.") may be divided into paragraphs and subparagraphs and further divided into heads and subheads. Again, it is usual to refer simply to, say, "para.23(3)(b)(ii) of Sch.3". Whereas it is conventional to speak of a section *of* an Act, it is usual to speak of a Schedule *to* an Act.

Secondary legislation

Secondary legislation (also known as *subordinate legislation* or *delegated legislation*) is made by *statutory instrument* in the form of a set of *Regulations* or a set of *Rules* or an *Order*. The power to make such legislation is conferred on ministers and other persons or bodies by Acts of Parliament. To the extent that a statutory instrument is made beyond the powers (in Latin, *ultra vires*) conferred by primary legislation, it may be held by a tribunal or court to be invalid and ineffective. Secondary legislation must be laid before Parliament. However, most secondary legislation is not debated in Parliament and, even when it is, it cannot be amended although an entire statutory instrument may be rejected.

A set of Regulations or Rules or an Order has a name indicating its scope and the year it was made and also a number, as in the Social Security (Disability Living Allowance) Regulations 1991 (SI 1991/2890) (the 2890th statutory instrument issued in 1991). Because there are over a thousand statutory instruments each year, the number of a particular statutory instrument is important as a means of identification and it should usually be cited the first time reference is made to that statutory instrument.

Sets of Regulations or Rules are made up of individual *regulations* (abbreviated as "reg.") or *rules* (abbreviated as "r." or, in the plural, "rr."). An Order is made up of *articles* (abbreviated as "art."). Regulations, rules and articles may be divided into paragraphs, subparagraphs and heads. As in Acts, a set of Regulations or Rules or an Order may have one or more Schedules attached to it. The style of numbering used in statutory instruments is the same as in sections of, and Schedules to, Acts of Parliament. As in Acts, a large statutory instrument may have regulations or rules grouped into Parts and, occasionally, Chapters. Statutory instruments may be amended in the same sort of way as Acts.

Scottish legislation

Most of the social security legislation passed by the United Kingdom Parliament applies throughout Great Britain, i.e. in England, Wales and Scotland, but a separate Scottish social security system is gradually being developed and relevant legislation is included in Volume IV in this series. Acts of the Scottish Parliament are similar to Acts of the United Kingdom Parliament and Scottish Statutory Instruments are also similar to their United Kingdom counterparts. One minor difference is that "schedule" usually has a lower case "s" and references are to a schedule *of* an Act, rather than *to* an Act.

Northern Ireland legislation

Most of the legislation set out in this series applies only in Great Britain, social security not generally being an excepted or reserved matter in relation to Northern Ireland. However, Northern Irish legislation—both primary legislation, most relevantly in the form of *Orders in Council* (which, although statutory instruments, had the effect of primary legislation in Northern Ireland while there was direct rule from Westminster and still do when made under the Northern Ireland (Welfare Reform) Act 2015) and *Acts of the Northern Ireland Assembly*, and subordinate legislation, in the form of *statutory rules*—largely replicates legislation in Great Britain so that much of the commentary in this book will be applicable to equivalent provisions in Northern Ireland legislation. Although there has latterly been a greater reluctance in Northern Ireland to maintain parity with Great Britain, one example of which led to some delay in enacting legislation equivalent to the Welfare Reform Act 2012, this is usually resolved politically by, for instance, the allocation of funds to allow the effects of some of the changes to be mitigated in Northern Ireland while the broad legislative structure remains similar.

European Union legislation

European Union primary legislation is in the form of the *Treaties* agreed by the Member States. Relevant subordinate legislation is in the form of *Regulations*, adopted to give effect to the provisions of the Treaties, and *Directives*, addressed to Member States and requiring them to incorporate certain provisions into their domestic laws. Directives are relevant because, where a person brings proceedings against an organ of the State, as is invariably the case where social security is concerned, that person may rely on the Directive as having direct effect if the Member State has failed to comply with it. Treaties, Regulations and Directives are divided into *Articles* (abbreviated as "Art.").

While the United Kingdom was a Member State of the European Union, United Kingdom legislation that was inconsistent with European Union legislation had to be disapplied. The United Kingdom ceased to be a Member State on January 31, 2020, but the effect of the European Union (Withdrawal Act) 2018, as amended in 2020, is that, with very limited exceptions, European Union law continued to apply in the United Kingdom during the implementation period ending on December 31, 2020. After that date, European Union law remains relevant only to the extent that United Kingdom legislation so provides. For instance, the 2018 Act, as amended, provides for the enforcement of the Withdrawal Agreement, under which rights acquired by individuals before the end of the implementation period may be retained.

Finding legislation in this book

If you know the name of the piece of legislation for which you are looking, use the list of contents at the beginning of each volume of this series which lists the pieces of legislation contained in the volume. That will give you the paragraph reference to enable you to find the beginning of the piece of legislation. Then, it is easy to find the relevant section, regulation, rule, article or Schedule by using the running headers on the right hand pages. If you do not know the name of the piece of legislation, you will probably need to use the index at the end of the volume in order to find the relevant paragraph number but will then be taken straight to a particular provision.

The legislation is set out as amended, the amendments being indicated by numbered sets of square brackets. The numbers refer to the numbered entries under the heading "AMENDMENTS" at the end of the relevant section, regulation, rule, article or Schedule, which identify the amending statute or statutory instrument. Where an Act has been consolidated, there is a list of "DERIVATIONS" identifying the provisions of earlier legislation from which the section or Schedule has been derived.

As regards the European Union, United Kingdom legislation concerned with the consequences of the United Kingdom's withdrawal is set out in Part V of Volume III in this series, together with relevant extracts from the Withdrawal Agreement and the Social Security Protocol to the Trade and Cooperation Agreement. Following the extracts from the Withdrawal Agreement is up-dating commentary on the European Union legislation that is set out in Part III of the 2020-21 edition of Volume III. Readers are encouraged to retain that volume so as to be able to find the main text of relevant European Union legislation there.

Finding other legislation

United Kingdom legislation and legislation made by the legislatures in Scotland, Wales and Northern Ireland may now be found on *http://www.legislation.gov.uk* in both its original form and (usually) its amended form. Northern Ireland social security legislation may also be found at *https://www.communities-ni.gov.uk/services/law-relating-social-security-northern-ireland-blue-volumes*. European Union legislation may be found at *https://eur-lex.europa.eu/homepage.html*.

Interpreting legislation

Legislation is written in English (or, at least, there is an official English version) and generally means what it says. However, languages being complicated, more than one interpretation is often possible. Most legislation itself contains definitions. Sometimes these are in the particular provision in which a word occurs but, where a word is used in more than one place, any definition will appear with others. In an Act, an interpretation section is usually to be found towards the end of the Act or of the relevant Part of the Act. In a statutory instrument, an interpretation provision usually appears near the beginning of the statutory instrument or the relevant Part of it. In the more important pieces of legislation in this series, there is included after every section, regulation, rule, article or Schedule a list of "DEFINITIONS", showing where definitions of words used in the provision are to be found.

However, not all words are statutorily defined and there is in any event more to interpreting legislation than merely defining its terms (see the note to s.3(1) of the Tribunals, Courts and Enforcement Act 2007 in Part III of Volume III of this series). Decision-makers and tribunals need to know how to apply the law in different types of situations. That is where case law comes in.

Case law and the commentary in this book

In deciding individual cases, courts and tribunals interpret the relevant law and incidentally establish legal principles. Decisions on questions of legal principle of the superior courts and appellate tribunals are said to be binding on decision-makers and the First-tier Tribunal, which means that decision-makers and the First-tier Tribunal must apply those principles. Thus the judicial decisions of the superior courts and appellate tribunals form part of the law. The commentary to the legislation in this series, under the heading "GENERAL NOTE" after a section, regulation, rule, article or Schedule, refers to this *case law*.

Most case law regarding social security benefits is in the form of decisions of the Upper Tribunal (Administrative Appeals Chamber), to which the functions of the former Social Security Commissioners and Child Support Commissioners in Great Britain were transferred on November 3, 2008. However, decisions of those Commissioners remain relevant, as are decisions of the Commissioners who still sit in Northern Ireland.

The commentary in this series is not itself binding on any decision-maker or tribunal because it is merely the opinion of the author. It is what is actually said in the legislation or in the judicial decision that is important. The legislation is set out in this series, but it will generally be necessary to look elsewhere for the precise words used in judicial decisions. The way that decisions are cited in the commentary enables that to be done.

The reporting of decisions of the Upper Tribunal and Commissioners

A few of the most important decisions of the Administrative Appeals Chamber of the Upper Tribunal are selected to be "reported" each year in the Administrative Appeals Chamber Reports (AACR), using the same criteria as were formerly used for reporting Commissioners' decisions in Great Britain. The selection is made by an editorial board of judges and decisions are selected for reporting only if they are of general importance and command the assent of at least a majority of the relevant judges. The term "reported" simply means that they are published in printed form as well as on the Internet (see *Finding case law*, below) with headnotes (i.e. summaries) and indexes, but reported decisions also have a greater precedential status than ordinary decisions (see *Judicial precedent* below).

A handful of Northern Ireland Commissioners' decisions are also selected for reporting in the Administrative Appeals Chamber Reports each year, the selection being made by the Chief Social Security Commissioner in Northern Ireland.

Citing case law

As has been mentioned, much social security case law is still to be found in decisions of Social Security Commissioners and Child Support Commissioners, even though the Commissioners have now effectively been abolished in Great Britain.

Reported decisions of Commissioners were known merely by a number or, more accurately, a series of letters and numbers beginning with an "R". The type of benefit in issue was indicated by letters in brackets (e.g. "IS" was income support, "P" was retirement pension, and so on) and the year in which the decision was selected for reporting or, from 2000, the year in which it was published as a reported decision, was indicated by the last two digits, as in *R(IS) 2/08*. In Northern Ireland there was a similar system until 2009, save that the type of benefit was identified by letters in brackets after the number, as in *R 1/07 (DLA)*.

Unreported decisions of the Commissioners in Great Britain were known simply by their file numbers, which began with a "C", as in *CIS/2287/2008*. The letters following the "C" indicated the type of benefit in issue in the case. Scottish and, at one time, Welsh cases were indicated by a "S" or "W" immediately after the "C", as in *CSIS/467/2007*. The last four digits indicated the calendar year in which the case was registered, rather than the year it was decided. A similar system operated in Northern Ireland until 2009, save that the letters indicating the type of benefit appeared in brackets after the numbers and, from April 1999, the financial year rather than the calendar year was identified, as in *C 10/06-07 (IS)*.

Decisions of the Upper Tribunal, of courts and, since 2010, of the Northern Ireland Commissioners are generally known by the names of the parties (or just two of them in multi-party cases). In social security and some other types of cases, individuals are anonymised through the use of initials in the names of decisions of the Upper Tribunal and the Northern Ireland Commissioners. Anonymity is much rarer in the names of decisions of courts. In this series, the names of official bodies are also abbreviated in the names of decisions of the Upper Tribunal and the Northern Ireland Commissioners (e.g. "SSWP" for the Secretary of State for Work and Pensions, "HMRC" for Her/His Majesty's Revenue and Customs, "CMEC" for the Child Maintenance and Enforcement Commission, "DSD" for the Department for Social Development in Northern Ireland and "DC" for the Department for Communities in Northern Ireland). Since 2010, such decisions have also been given a "flag" in brackets to indicate the subject matter of the decision, which in social security cases indicates the principal benefit in issue in the case. Thus, the name of one universal credit case is *SSWP v AJ (UC)*.

Any decision of the Upper Tribunal, of a court since 2001 or of a Northern Ireland Commissioner since 2010 that has been intended for publication has also given a neutral citation number which enables the decision to be more precisely identified. This indicates, in square brackets, the year the decision was made (although in relation to decisions of the courts it sometimes merely indicates the year the number was issued) and also indicates the court or tribunal that made the decision (e.g. "UKUT" for the Upper Tribunal (which sits in Great Britain for social security purposes but throughout the United Kingdom for some others), "UT" for the separate Upper Tribunal for Scotland, "NICom" for a Northern Ireland Commissioner, "EWCA Civ" for the Civil Division of the Court of Appeal in England and Wales, "NICA" for the Court of Appeal in Northern Ireland, "CSIH" for the Inner House of the Court of Session (in Scotland), "UKSC" for the Supreme Court and so on). A number is added so that the reference is unique and finally, in the case of the Upper Tribunal or the High Court in England and Wales, the relevant chamber of the Upper Tribunal or the relevant division or other part of the High Court is identified (e.g. "(AAC)" for the Administrative Appeals Chamber, "(Admin)" for the Administrative Court and so on). Examples of decisions of the Upper Tribunal and a Northern Ireland Commissioner with their neutral citation numbers are *SSWP v AJ (UC)* [2020] UKUT 48 (AAC) and *AR v DSD (IB)* [2010] NICom 6.

If the case is reported in the Administrative Appeals Chamber Reports or another series of law reports, a reference to the report usually follows the neutral citation number. Conventionally, this includes either the year the case was decided (in round brackets) or the year in which it was reported (in square brackets), followed by the volume number (if any), the name of the series of reports (in abbreviated form, so see the Table of Abbreviations at the beginning of each volume of this series) and either the page number or the case number. However, before 2010, cases reported in the Administrative Appeals Chamber Reports or with Commissioners' decisions were numbered in the same way as reported Commissioners' decisions. *Abdirahman v Secretary of State for Work and Pensions* [2007] EWCA Civ 657; [2008] 1 W.L.R. 254 (also reported as *R(IS) 8/07*) is a Court of Appeal decision, decided in 2007 but reported in 2008 in volume 1 of the Weekly Law Reports at page 254 and also in the 2007 volume of reported Commissioners' decisions. *NT v SSWP* [2009] UKUT 37 (AAC); *R(DLA) 1/09* is an Upper Tribunal case decided in 2009 and reported in the Administrative Appeals Chamber Reports in the same year. *Martin v Secretary of State for Work and Pensions* [2009] EWCA Civ 1289; [2010] AACR 9 is a decision of the Court of Appeal that was decided in 2009 and was the ninth decision reported in the Administrative Appeals Chamber Reports in 2010.

It is usually necessary to include the neutral citation number or a reference to a series of reports only the first time a decision is cited in any document. After that, the name of the case is usually sufficient.

All decisions of the Upper Tribunal that are on their website have neutral citation numbers. If you wish to refer a tribunal or decision-maker to a decision of the Upper Tribunal that does not have a neutral citation number, contact the office of the Administrative Appeals Chamber (*adminappeals@ justice.gov.uk*) who will provide a number and add the decision to the website.

Decision-makers and claimants are entitled to assume that judges of both the First-tier Tribunal and the Upper Tribunal have immediate access to reported decisions of Commissioners or the Upper Tribunal and they need not provide copies, although it may sometimes be helpful to do so. However, where either a decision-maker or a claimant intends to rely on an unreported decision, it will be necessary to provide a copy of the decision to the judge and other members of the tribunal. A copy of the decision should also be provided to the other party before the hearing because otherwise it may be necessary for there to be an adjournment to enable that party to take advice on the significance of the decision.

Finding case law

The extensive references described above are used so as to enable people easily to find the full text of a decision. Most decisions of any significance since the late 1990s can be found on the Internet.

Decisions of the Upper Tribunal may be found at *https://www.gov.uk/ administrative-appeals-tribunal-decisions*. The link from that page to "decisions made in 2015 or earlier" leads also to decisions of the Commissioners in Great Britain. This includes reported decisions since 1991 and other decisions considered likely to be of interest to tribunals and tribunal users since about 2000, together with a few older decisions. Decisions of Commissioners in Northern Ireland may be found on *https://iaccess.commu nities-ni.gov.uk/NIDOC*.

The Administrative Appeals Chamber Reports are also published by the Stationery Office in bound volumes which follow on from the bound volumes of Commissioners' decisions published from 1948.

Copies of decisions of the Administrative Appeals Chamber of the Upper Tribunal or of Commissioners that are otherwise unavailable may be obtained from the offices of the Upper Tribunal (Administrative Appeals Chamber) or, in Northern Ireland, from the Office of the Social Security and Child Support Commissioners.

Decisions of a wide variety of courts and tribunals in the United Kingdom may be found on the free website of the British and Irish Legal Information Institute, *http://www.bailii.org*. It includes all decisions of the Supreme Court and provides fairly comprehensive coverage of decisions given since about 1996 by the House of Lords and Privy Council and most of the higher courts in England and Wales, decisions given since 1998 by the Court of Session and decisions given since 2000 by the Court of Appeal and High Court in Northern Ireland. Some earlier decisions have been included, so it is always worth looking and, indeed, those decisions dating from 1873 or earlier and reported in the English Reports may be found through a link to *http://www.commonlii.org/uk/cases/EngR/*. Since 2022, decisions of the Upper Tribunal, the Employment Appeal Tribunal and most courts that sit in England and Wales are also to be found on The National Archives' website at *caselaw.nationalarchives.gov.uk/structured_search*. However, courts and tribunals that sit only in Wales, Scotland or Northern Ireland are not included there. Decisions of the Upper Tribunal for Scotland and of Scottish courts can be found at *https://www.scotcourts.gov.uk*.

Decisions of the Court of Justice of the European Union are all to be found at *https://curia.europa.eu*.

Decisions of the European Court of Human Rights are available at *https://www.echr.coe.int*.

Most decisions of the courts in social security cases, including decisions of the Court of Justice of the European Union on cases referred by United Kingdom courts and tribunals, are reported in the Administrative Appeals Chamber Reports or with the reported decisions of Commissioners and may therefore be found on the same websites and in the same printed series of reported decisions. So, for example, *R(I) 1/00* contains Commissioner's decision *CSI/12/1998*, the decision of the Court of Session upholding the Commissioner's decision and the decision of the House of Lords in *Chief Adjudication Officer v Faulds*, reversing the decision of the Court of Session. The most important decisions of the courts can also be found in the various series of law reports familiar to lawyers (in particular, in the *Law Reports*, the *Weekly Law Reports*, the *All England Law Reports*, the *Public and Third Sector Law Reports*, the *Industrial Cases Reports* and the *Family Law Reports*) but these are not widely available outside academic or other law libraries, or subscription-based websites. See the Table of Cases at the beginning of each volume of this series for all the places where a decision mentioned in that volume is reported.

If you know the name or number of a decision and wish to know where in a volume of this series there is a reference to it, use the Table of Cases or the Table of Commissioners' Decisions 1948–2009 in the relevant volume to find the paragraph(s) where the decision is mentioned.

Judicial precedent

As already mentioned, decisions of the Upper Tribunal, the Commissioners and the higher courts in Great Britain become case law because they set binding precedents which must be followed by decision-makers and the First-tier Tribunal in Great Britain. This means that, where the Upper Tribunal, Commissioner or court has decided a point of legal principle, decision-makers and appeal tribunals must make their decisions in conformity with the decision of the Upper Tribunal, Commissioner or court, applying the same principle and accepting the interpretation of the law contained in the decision. So a decision of the Upper Tribunal, a Commissioner or a superior court explaining what a term in a particular regulation means, lays down the definition of that term in much the same way as if the term had been defined in the regulations themselves. The decision may also help in deciding what the same term means when it is used in a different set of regulations, provided that the term appears to have been used in a similar context.

Only decisions on points of law set precedents that are binding and, strictly speaking, only decisions on points of law that were necessary to the overall conclusion reached by the Upper Tribunal, Commissioner or court are binding. Other parts of a decision (which used to be known as obiter dicta) may be regarded as helpful guidance but need not be followed if a decision-maker or the First-tier Tribunal is persuaded that there is a better approach. It is particularly important to bear this in mind in relation to older decisions of Social Security Commissioners because, until 1987, most rights of appeal to a Commissioner were not confined to points of law.

Where there is a conflict between precedents, a decision-maker or the First-tier Tribunal is generally free to choose between decisions of equal status. For these purposes, most decisions of the Upper Tribunal and decisions of Commissioners are of equal status. However, a decision-maker or First-tier Tribunal should generally prefer a reported decision to an unreported one unless the unreported decision was the later decision and the Commissioner or Upper Tribunal expressly decided not to follow the earlier reported decision. This is simply because the fact that a decision has been reported shows that at least half of the relevant judges of the Upper Tribunal or the Commissioners agreed with it at the time. A decision of a Tribunal of Commissioners (i.e. three Commissioners sitting together) or a decision of a three-judge panel of the Upper Tribunal must be preferred to a decision of a single Commissioner or a single judge of the Upper Tribunal.

A single judge of the Upper Tribunal will normally follow a decision of a single Commissioner or another judge of the Upper Tribunal, but is not bound to do so. A three-judge panel of the Upper Tribunal will generally follow a decision of another such panel or of a Tribunal of Commissioners, but similarly is not bound to do so, whereas a single judge of the Upper Tribunal will always follow such a decision.

Strictly speaking, the Northern Ireland Commissioners do not set binding precedent that must be followed in Great Britain but their decisions are relevant, due to the similarity of the legislation in Northern Ireland, and are usually regarded as highly persuasive with the result that, in practice, they are generally given as much weight as decisions of the Great Britain Commissioners. The same approach is taken in Northern Ireland to decisions of the Upper Tribunal on social security matters and to decisions of the Great Britain Commissioners. Similarly, the Upper Tribunal and the Upper Tribunal for Scotland are likely to find each other's decisions persuasive where the issues are the same, or similar.

Decisions of the superior courts in Great Britain and Northern Ireland on questions of legal principle are almost invariably followed by decision-makers, tribunals and the Upper Tribunal, even when they are not strictly binding because the relevant court was in a different part of the United Kingdom or exercised a parallel – but not superior – jurisdiction.

Decisions of the Court of Justice of the European Union come in two parts: the Opinion of the Advocate General and the decision of the Court. It is the decision of the Court which is binding. The Court is assisted by hearing the Opinion of the Advocate General before itself coming to a conclusion on the issue before it. The Court does not always follow its Advocate General. Where it does, the Opinion of the Advocate General often elaborates the arguments in greater detail than the single collegiate judgment of the Court. Within the European Union, courts and tribunals must apply decisions of the Court of Justice of the European Union, where relevant to cases before them, in preference to other authorities binding on them. This is no longer so in the United Kingdom, but it will still be necessary for courts and tribunals in the United Kingdom to take account of such decisions when issues of European Union law are relevant, and they are arguably bound by a decision of the Court of Justice on the interpretation of the Citizens' Rights provisions of the Withdrawal Agreement.

The European Court of Human Rights in Strasbourg is quite separate from the Court of Justice of the European Union in Luxembourg and serves a different purpose: interpreting and applying the European Convention on Human Rights, which is incorporated into United Kingdom law by the Human Rights Act 1998. Since October 2, 2000, public authorities in the United Kingdom, including courts, Commissioners, tribunals and decision-makers have been required to act in accordance with the incorporated provisions of the Convention, unless statute prevents this. They must take into account the Strasbourg case law and are required to interpret domestic legislation, so far as it is possible to do so, to give effect to the incorporated Convention rights. Any court or tribunal may declare secondary legislation incompatible with those rights and, in certain circumstances, invalidate it. Only the higher courts can declare a provision of primary legislation to be incompatible with those rights, but no court, tribunal or Upper Tribunal can invalidate primary legislation. The work of the Strasbourg Court and the impact of the Human Rights Act 1998 on social security are discussed in the commentary in Part IV of Volume III of this series.

See the note to s.3(2) of the Tribunals, Courts and Enforcement Act 2007 in Part III of Volume III of this series for a more detailed and technical consideration of the rules of precedent.

Other sources of information and commentary on social security law

For a comprehensive overview of the social security system in Great Britain, CPAG's *Welfare Benefits and Tax Credits Handbook*, published annually each spring, is unrivalled as a practical introduction from the claimant's viewpoint.

From a different perspective, the Department for Work and Pensions publishes the 14-volume *Decision Makers' Guide* and the newer *Advice for Decision Making*, which covers personal independence payment, universal credit and the "new" versions of Jobseeker's Allowance and Employment and Support Allowance (search for the relevant guide by name at *https://www.gov.uk* under the topic "Welfare"). Similarly, His Majesty's Revenue and Customs publish manuals relating to tax credits, child benefit and guardian's allowance, which they administer, see *https://www.gov.uk/government/collections/hmrc-manuals*. (Note that the *Child Benefit Technical Manual* also covers guardian's allowance.) These guides and manuals are extremely useful but their interpretation of the law is not binding on tribunals and the courts, being merely internal guidance for the use of decision-makers.

There are a number of other sources of valuable information or commentary on social security case law: see in particular publications such as the *Journal of Social Security Law*, CPAG's *Welfare Rights Bulletin*, *Legal Action* and the *Adviser*. As far as online resources go there is little to beat *Rightsnet* (*https://www.rightsnet.org.uk*). This site contains a wealth of resources for people working in the welfare benefits field but of special relevance in this context are Commissioners'/Upper Tribunal Decisions section of the "Toolkit" area and also the "Briefcase" area which contains summaries of the decisions (with links to the full decisions). Sweet and Maxwell's online subscription service *Westlaw* is another valuable source (*https://legalsolutions.thomsonreuters.co.uk/en/products-services/westlaw-uk.html*), as is LexisNexis Lexis (*https://www.lexisnexis.co.uk*).

Conclusion

The internet provides a vast resource but a search needs to be focused. Social security schemes are essentially statutory and so in Great Britain the legislation which is set out in this series forms the basic structure of social security law. However, the case law shows how the legislation should be interpreted and applied. The commentary in this series should point the way to the case law relevant to each provision and the Internet can then be used to find it where that is necessary.

CHANGE OF NAME FROM DEPARTMENT OF SOCIAL SECURITY TO DEPARTMENT FOR WORK AND PENSIONS

The Secretaries of State for Education and Skills and for Work and Pensions Order 2002 (SI 2002/1397) makes provision for the change of name from the Department of Social Security to Department for Work and Pensions. Article 9(5) provides:

"(5) Subject to article 12 [which makes specific amendments], any enactment or instrument passed or made before the coming into force of this Order shall have effect, so far as may be necessary for the purposes of or in consequence of the entrusting to the Secretary of State for Work and Pensions of the social security functions, as if any reference to the Secretary of State for Social Security, to the Department of Social Security or to an officer of the Secretary of State for Social Security (including any reference which is to be construed as such as reference) were a reference to the Secretary of State for Work and Pensions, to the Department for Work and Pensions or, as the case may be, to an officer of the Secretary of State for Work and Pensions."

CHANGES IN TERMINOLOGY CONSEQUENT UPON THE ENTRY INTO FORCE OF THE TREATY OF LISBON

The Treaty of Lisbon (Changes in Terminology) Order 2011 (SI 2011/1043) (which came into force on April 22, 2011) makes a number of changes to terminology used in primary and secondary legislation as a consequence of the entry into force of the Treaty of Lisbon on December 1, 2009. The Order accomplishes this by requiring certain terms in primary and secondary legislation to be read in accordance with the requirements of the Order. No substantive changes to the law are involved.

The changes are somewhat complex because of the different ways in which the term "Community" is used, and the abbreviations "EC" or "EEC" are used. References to the "European Community", "European Communities", "European Coal and Steel Communities", "the Community", "the EC" and "the EEC" are generally to be read as references to the "European Union".

The following table shows the more common usages involving the word "Community" in the first column which are now to be read in the form set out in the second column:

Original term	To be read as
Community treaties	EU treaties
Community institution	EU institution
Community instrument	EU instrument
Community obligation	EU obligation
Enforceable Community right	Enforceable EU right
Community law, or European Community law	EU law
Community legislation, or European Community legislation	EU legislation
Community provision, or European Community provision	EU provision

Provision is also made for changes to certain legislation relating to Wales in the Welsh language.

Relevant extracts from the Order can be found in Volume III, *Administration, Adjudication and the European Dimension*.

THE MARRIAGE (SAME SEX COUPLES) ACT 2013

The Marriage (Same Sex Couples) Act 2013 (c.30) provides in s.3 and Schs 3 and 4 that the terms "marriage", "married couple" and being "married" in existing and future legislation in England and Wales are to be read as references to a marriage between persons of the same sex. The same approach is taken to any legislation about couples living together as if married. This is subject to certain specified exclusions contained in Sch.4, and in any Order providing for a contrary approach to be taken.

Schedule 2 to The Marriage (Same Sex Couples) Act 2013 (Consequential and Contrary Provisions and Scotland) Order 2014 (SI 2014/560) contains a substantial list of contrary provisions to s.11(1) and (2) and paras 1 to 3 of Sch.3 to the 2013 Act. Most of these relate to specific enactments, but note that Pt 2 of the Schedule provides that s.11(1) and (2) do not apply to "EU instruments". This term is defined in Sch.1 to the European Communities Act 1972 (as amended) as "any instrument issued by an EU institution". It refers mainly to regulations, directives, decisions, recommendations and opinions issued by the institutions.

TABLE OF CASES

Table of Cases

Table of Cases

TABLE OF SOCIAL SECURITY COMMISSIONERS' DECISIONS

TABLE OF ABBREVIATIONS USED IN THIS SERIES

1975 Act	Social Security Act 1975
1977 Act	Marriage (Scotland) Act 1977
1979 Act	Pneumoconiosis (Workers' Compensation) Act 1979
1986 Act	Social Security Act 1986
1996 Act	Employment Rights Act 1996
1998 Act	Social Security Act 1998
2002 Act	Tax Credits Act 2002
2004 Act	Gender Recognition Act 2004
2006 Act	Armed Forces Act 2006
2008 Act	Child Maintenance and Other Payments Act 2008
2013 Act	Marriage (Same Sex Couples) Act 2013
2014 Act	Marriage and Civil Partnership (Scotland) Act 2014
A1P1	Art.1 of Protocol 1 to the European Convention on Human Rights
AA	Attendance Allowance
AA 1992	Attendance Allowance Act 1992
AAC	Administrative Appeals Chamber
AACR	Administrative Appeals Chamber Reports
A.C.	Law Reports, Appeal Cases
A.C.D.	Administrative Court Digest
Admin	Administrative Court
Admin L.R.	Administrative Law Reports
Administration Act	Social Security Administration Act 1992
Administration Regulations	Statutory Paternity Pay and Statutory Adoption Pay (Administration) Regulations 2002
AIP	assessed income period
All E.R.	All England Reports
All E.R. (E.C.)	All England Reports (European Cases)
AMA	Adjudicating Medical Authorities
AO	Adjudication Officer
AOG	*Adjudication Officers Guide*
art.	article
Art.	Article
ASD	Autistic Spectrum Disorder
ASPP	Additional Statutory Paternity Pay
A.T.C.	Annotated Tax Cases

Table of Abbreviations used in this Series

Attendance Allowance Regulations	Social Security (Attendance Allowance) Regulations 1991
AWT	All Work Test
BA	Benefits Agency
Benefits Act	Social Security Contributions and Benefits Act 1992
B.H.R.C.	Butterworths Human Rights Cases
B.L.G.R.	Butterworths Local Government Reports
Blue Books	*The Law Relating to Social Security*, Vols 1–11
B.P.I.R.	Bankruptcy and Personal Insolvency Reports
B.T.C.	British Tax Cases
BTEC	Business and Technology Education Council
B.V.C.	British Value Added Tax Reporter
B.W.C.C.	Butterworths Workmen's Compensation Cases
c.	chapter
C	Commissioner's decision
C&BA 1992	Social Security Contributions and Benefits Act 1992
CAA 2001	Capital Allowances Act 2001
CAB	Citizens Advice Bureau
CAO	Chief Adjudication Officer
CB	Child Benefit
CBA 1975	Child Benefit Act 1975
CBJSA	Contribution-Based Jobseeker's Allowance
C.C.L. Rep.	Community Care Law Reports
CCM	HMRC *New Tax Credits Claimant Compliance Manual*
C.E.C.	European Community Cases
CERA	cortical evoked response audiogram
CESA	Contribution-based Employment and Support Allowance
CFF payment	Children's Funeral Fund payment
CFS	chronic fatigue syndrome
Ch.	Chancery Division Law Reports; Chapter
Citizenship Directive	Directive 2004/38/EC of the European Parliament and of the Council of April 29, 2004
CJEC	Court of Justice of the European Communities
CJEU	Court of Justice of the European Union
CJRS	Coronavirus Job Retention Scheme
Claims and Payments Regulations	Social Security (Claims and Payments) Regulations 1987
Claims and Payments Regulations 1979	Social Security (Claims and Payments) Regulations 1979
Claims and Payments Regulations 2013	Universal Credit, Personal Independence Payment, Jobseeker's Allowance and Employment and Support Allowance (Claims and Payments) Regulations 2013

Table of Abbreviations used in this Series

CM	Case Manager
CMA	Chief Medical Adviser
CMEC	Child Maintenance and Enforcement Commission
C.M.L.R.	Common Market Law Reports
C.O.D.	Crown Office Digest
COLL	*Collective Investment Schemes Sourcebook*
Community, The	European Community
Computation of Earnings Regulations	Social Security Benefit (Computation of Earnings) Regulations 1978
Computation of Earnings Regulations 1996	Social Security Benefit (Computation of Earnings) Regulations 1996
Consequential Provisions Act	Social Security (Consequential Provisions) Act 1992
Contributions and Benefits Act	Social Security Contributions and Benefits Act 1992
Contributions Regulations	Social Security (Contributions) Regulations 2001
COPD	chronic obstructive pulmonary disease
Coronavirus SEISS	Coronavirus Self-Employed Income Support Scheme
CP	Carer Premium; Chamber President
CPAG	Child Poverty Action Group
CPR	Civil Procedure Rules
Cr. App. R.	Criminal Appeal Reports
CRCA 2005	Commissioners for Revenue and Customs Act 2005
Credits Regulations 1974	Social Security (Credits) Regulations 1974
Credits Regulations 1975	Social Security (Credits) Regulations 1975
Crim. L.R.	Criminal Law Review
CRU	Compensation Recovery Unit
CSA 1995	Children (Scotland) Act 1995
CSIH	Inner House of the Court of Session (Scotland)
CSM	Child Support Maintenance
CS(NI)O 1995	Child Support (Northern Ireland) Order 1995
CSOH	Outer House of the Court of Session (Scotland)
CSPSSA 2000	Child Support, Pensions and Social Security Act 2000
CTA	Common Travel Area
CTA 2009	Corporation Tax Act 2009
CTA 2010	Corporation Tax Act 2010
CTB	Council Tax Benefit
CTC	Child Tax Credit
CTC Regulations	Child Tax Credit Regulations 2002
CTF	child trust fund
CTS	Carpal Tunnel Syndrome

DAC	Directive 2011/16/ EU (Directive on administrative co-operation in the field of taxation)
DAT	Disability Appeal Tribunal
dB	decibels
DCA	Department for Constitutional Affairs
DCP	Disabled Child Premium
Decisions and Appeals Regulations 1999	Social Security Contributions (Decisions and Appeals) Regulations 1999
Dependency Regulations	Social Security Benefit (Dependency) Regulations 1977
DfEE	Department for Education and Employment
DHSS	Department of Health and Social Security
Disability Living Allowance Regulations	Social Security (Disability Living Allowance) Regulations
DIY	do it yourself
DLA	Disability Living Allowance
DLA Regs 1991	Social Security (Disability Living Allowance) Regulations 1991
DLAAB	Disability Living Allowance Advisory Board
DLADWAA 1991	Disability Living Allowance and Disability Working Allowance Act 1991
DM	Decision Maker
DMA	Decision-making and Appeals
DMG	*Decision Makers' Guide*
DMP	Delegated Medical Practitioner
DP	Disability Premium
DPT	diffuse pleural thickening
DPTC	Disabled Person's Tax Credit
DRO	Debt Relief Order
DSD	Department for Social Development (Northern Ireland)
DSM IV; DSM-5	Diagnostic and Statistical Manual of Mental Disorders of the American Psychiatric Association
DSS	Department of Social Security
DTI	Department of Trade and Industry
DWA	Disability Working Allowance
DWP	Department for Work and Pensions
DWPMS	Department for Work and Pensions Medical Service
EAA	Extrinsic Allergic Alveolitis
EAT	Employment Appeal Tribunal
EC	European Community
ECHR	European Convention on Human Rights
ECJ	European Court of Justice
E.C.R.	European Court Reports

ECSC	European Coal and Steel Community
ECSMA	European Convention on Social and Medical Assistance
EEA	European Economic Area
EEC	European Economic Community
EESSI	Electronic Exchange of Social Security Information
E.G.	Estates Gazette
E.G.L.R.	Estates Gazette Law Reports
EHC plan	education, health and care plan
EHIC	European Health Insurance Card
EHRC	European Human Rights Commission
E.H.R.R.	European Human Rights Reports
EL	employers' liability
E.L.R	Education Law Reports
EMA	Education Maintenance Allowance
EMP	Examining Medical Practitioner
Employment and Support Allowance Regulations	Employment and Support Allowance Regulations 2008
EPS	extended period of sickness
Eq. L.R.	Equality Law Reports
ERA	evoked response audiometry
ERA scheme	Employment, Retention and Advancement scheme
ES	Employment Service
ESA	Employment and Support Allowance
ESA Regs 2008	Employment and Support Allowance Regulations 2008
ESA Regs 2013	Employment and Support Allowance Regulations 2013
ESA Regulations	Employment and Support Allowance Regulations 2008
ESA WCAt	Employment and Support Allowance Work Capability Assessment
ESA(IR)	income-related employment and support allowance
ESC	employer supported childcare
ESE Scheme	Employment, Skills and Enterprise Scheme
ESE Regulations	Jobseeker's Allowance (Employment, Skills and Enterprise Scheme) Regulations 2011
ESES	Employment, Skills and Enterprise Scheme
ESES Regulations	Jobseeker's Allowance (Employment, Skills and Enterprise Scheme) Regulations 2011
ETA 1973	Employment and Training Act 1973
ETA(NI) 1950	Employment and Training Act (Northern Ireland) 1950
ETS	European Treaty Series

Table of Abbreviations used in this Series

EU	European Union
Eu.L.R.	European Law Reports
EWCA Civ	Civil Division of the Court of Appeal (England and Wales)
EWHC Admin	Administrative Court, part of the High Court (England and Wales)
FA 1993	Finance Act 1993
FA 1996	Finance Act 1996
FA 2004	Finance Act 2004
Fam. Law	Family Law
FAS	Financial Assistance Scheme
F.C.R.	Family Court Reporter
FEV	forced expiratory volume
FIS	Family Income Supplement
FISMA 2000	Financial Services and Markets Act 2000
F.L.R.	Family Law Reports
FME	further medical evidence
F(No.2)A 2005	Finance (No.2) Act 2005
FOTRA	Free of Tax to Residents Abroad
FRAA	flat rate accrual amount
FRS Act 2004	Fire and Rescue Services Act 2004
FSCS	Financial Services Compensation Scheme
FTT	First-tier Tribunal
General Benefit Regulations 1982	Social Security (General Benefit) Regulations 1982
General Regulations	Statutory Shared Parental Pay (General) Regulations 2014
GMCA	Greater Manchester Combined Authority
GMFRA	Greater Manchester Fire and Rescue Authority
GMP	Guaranteed Minimum Pension
GMWDA	Greater Manchester Waste Disposal Authority
GNVQ	General National Vocational Qualification
GP	General Practitioner
GRA	Gender Recognition Act 2004
GRB	Graduated Retirement Benefit
GRP	Graduated Retirement Pension
HB	Housing Benefit
HB (WSP) R (NI) 2017	Housing Benefit (Welfare Social Payment) Regulations (Northern Ireland) 2017
HBRB	Housing Benefit Review Board
HCA	Homes and Communities Agency
HCD	House of Commons Debates
HCP	healthcare professional
HCV	Hepatitis C virus
Health Service Act	National Health Service Act 2006

Health Service (Wales) Act	National Health Service (Wales) Act 2006
HIV	Human Immunodeficiency Virus
HL	House of Lords
H.L.R.	Housing Law Reports
HMIT	Her Majesty's Inspector of Taxes
HMRC	Her Majesty's Revenue and Customs
HMSO	Her Majesty's Stationery Office
HO	Home Office
Hospital In-Patients Regulations 1975	Social Security (Hospital In-Patients) Regulations 1975
HP	Health Professional
HPP	Higher Pensioner Premium
HRA 1998	Human Rights Act 1998
H.R.L.R.	Human Rights Law Reports
HRP	Home Responsibilities Protection
HSE	Health and Safety Executive
IAC	Immigration and Asylum Chamber
IAP	Intensive Activity Period
IB	Incapacity Benefit
IB PCA	Incapacity Benefit Personal Capability Assessment
IB Regs	Social Security (Incapacity Benefit) Regulations 1994
IB Regulations	Social Security (Incapacity Benefit) Regulations 1994
IB/IS/SDA	Incapacity Benefits Regime
IBJSA	Income-Based Jobseeker's Allowance
IBS	Irritable Bowel Syndrome
ICA	Invalid Care Allowance
I.C.R.	Industrial Cases Reports
ICTA 1988	Income and Corporation Taxes Act 1988
IFW Regulations	Incapacity for Work (General) Regulations 1995
IH	Inner House of the Court of Session
I.I.	Industrial Injuries
IIAC	Industrial Injuries Advisory Council
IIDB	Industrial Injuries Disablement Benefit
ILO	International Labour Organization
ILR	indefinite leave to remain
Imm. A.R.	Immigration Appeal Reports
Incapacity for Work Regulations	Social Security (Incapacity for Work) (General) Regulations 1995
Income Support Regulations	Income Support (General) Regulations 1987
Income Support General Regulations	Income Support (General) Regulations 1987
IND	Immigration and Nationality Directorate of the Home Office

I.N.L.R.	Immigration and Nationality Law Reports
I.O.	Insurance Officer
IPPR	Institute of Public Policy Research
IRESA	Income-Related Employment and Support Allowance
I.R.L.R.	Industrial Relations Law Reports
IS	Income Support
IS Regs	Income Support Regulations
IS Regulations	Income Support (General) Regulations 1987
ISA	Individual Savings Account
ISBN	International Standard Book Number
ITA 2007	Income Tax Act 2007
ITEPA 2003	Income Tax, Earnings and Pensions Act 2003
I.T.L. Rep.	International Tax Law Reports
I.T.R.	Industrial Tribunals Reports
ITS	Independent Tribunal Service
ITTOIA 2005	Income Tax (Trading and Other Income) Act 2005
IVB	Invalidity Benefit
IW (General) Regs	Social Security (Incapacity for Work) (General) Regulations 1995
IW (Transitional) Regs	Incapacity for Work (Transitional) Regulations
Jobseeker's Allowance Regulations	Jobseeker's Allowance Regulations 1996
Jobseeker's Regulations 1996	Jobseeker's Allowance Regulations 1996
JSA	Jobseeker's Allowance
JSA 1995	Jobseekers Act 1995
JSA (NI) Regulations	Jobseeker's Allowance (Northern Ireland) Regulations 1996
JSA (Transitional) Regulations	Jobseeker's Allowance (Transitional) Regulations 1996
JSA Regs 1996	Jobseeker's Allowance Regulations 1996
JSA Regs 2013	Jobseeker's Allowance Regulations 2013
JSA(IB)	income-based jobseeker's allowance
JS(NI)O 1995	Jobseekers (Northern Ireland) Order 1995
J.S.S.L.	Journal of Social Security Law
J.S.W.L.	Journal of Social Welfare Law
K.B.	Law Reports, King's Bench
L.& T.R.	Landlord and Tenant Reports
LCW	limited capability for work
LCWA	Limited Capability for Work Assessment
LCWRA	limited capability for work-related activity
LDEDC Act 2009	Local Democracy, Economic Development and Construction Act 2009
LEA	local education authority
LEL	Lower Earnings Limit
LET	low earnings threshold

L.G. Rev.	Local Government Review
L.G.L.R.	Local Government Reports
L.J.R.	Law Journal Reports
LRP	liable relative payment
L.S.G.	Law Society Gazette
Luxembourg Court	Court of Justice of the European Union (also referred to as CJEC and ECJ)
MA	Maternity Allowance
MAF	Medical Assessment Framework
MAN	Mandatory Activity Notification
Maternity Allowance Regulations	Social Security (Maternity Allowance) Regulations 1987
MDC	Mayoral development corporation
ME	myalgic encephalomyelitis
Medical Evidence Regulations	Social Security (Medical Evidence) Regulations 1976
MEN	Mandatory Employment Notification
Mesher and Wood	*Income Support, the Social Fund and Family Credit: the Legislation* (1996)
M.H.L.R.	Mental Health Law Reports
MHP	mental health problems
MIF	minimum income floor
MIG	minimum income guarantee
Migration Regulations	Employment and Support Allowance (Transitional Provisions, Housing Benefit and Council Tax Benefit (Existing Awards) (No.2) Regulations 2010
MP	Member of Parliament
MRSA	methicillin-resistant Staphylococcus aureus
MS	Medical Services
MWA Regulations	Jobseeker's Allowance (Mandatory Work Activity Scheme) Regulations 2011
MWAS Regulations	Jobseeker's Allowance (Mandatory Work Activity Scheme) Regulations 2011
NCB	National Coal Board
NDPD	Notes on the Diagnosis of Prescribed Diseases
NHS	National Health Service
NI	National Insurance
N.I..	Northern Ireland Law Reports
NICA	Northern Ireland Court of Appeal
NICom	Northern Ireland Commissioner
NICs	National Insurance Contributions
NINO	National Insurance Number
NIRS 2	National Insurance Recording System
N.L.J.	New Law Journal
NMC	Nursing and Midwifery Council
Northern Ireland Contributions and	Social Security Contributions and Benefits

Benefits Act	(Northern Ireland) Act 1992
N.P.C.	New Property Cases
NRCGT	non-resident capital gains tax
NTC Manual	Clerical procedures manual on tax credits
NUM	National Union of Mineworkers
NUS	National Union of Students
OCD	obsessive compulsive disorder
Ogus, Barendt and Wikeley	A. Ogus, E. Barendt and N. Wikeley, *The Law of Social Security* (1995)
Old Cases Act	Industrial Injuries and Diseases (Old Cases) Act 1975
OPB	One Parent Benefit
O.P.L.R.	Occupational Pensions Law Reports
OPSSAT	Office of the President of Social Security Appeal Tribunals
Overlapping Benefits Regulations	Social Security (Overlapping Benefits) Regulations 1975
P	retirement pension case
P. & C.R.	Property and Compensation Reports
para.	paragraph
Pay Regulations	Statutory Paternity Pay and Statutory Adoption Pay (General) Regulations 2002; Statutory Shared Parental Pay (General) Regulations 2014
PAYE	Pay As You Earn
PC	Privy Council
PCA	Personal Capability Assessment
PCC	Police and Crime Commissioner
PD	Practice Direction; prescribed disease
PENP	post-employment notice pay
Pens. L.R.	Pensions Law Reports
Pensions Act	Pension Schemes Act 1993
PEP	Personal Equity Plan
Persons Abroad Regulations	Social Security Benefit (Persons Abroad) Regulations 1975
Persons Residing Together Regulations	Social Security Benefit (Persons Residing Together) Regulations 1977
PIE	Period of Interruption of Employment
PILON	pay in lieu of notice
Pilot Scheme Regulations	Universal Credit (Work-Related Requirements) In Work Pilot Scheme and Amendment Regulations 2015
PIP	Personal Independence Payment
P.I.Q.R.	Personal Injuries and Quantum Reports
Polygamous Marriages Regulations	Social Security and Family Allowances (Polygamous Marriages) Regulations 1975
PPF	Pension Protection Fund

Prescribed Diseases Regulations	Social Security (Industrial Injuries) (Prescribed Diseases) Regulations 1985
PSCS	Pension Service Computer System
PSED	Public Sector Equality Duty
Pt	Part
PTA	pure tone audiometry
P.T.S.R.	Public and Third Sector Law Reports
PTWR 2000	Part-time Workers (Prevention of Less Favourable Treatment) Regulations 2000
PVS	private and voluntary sectors
Q.B.	Queen's Bench Law Reports
QBD	Queen's Bench Division
QCS Board	Quality Contract Scheme Board
QEF	qualifying earnings factor
QYP	qualifying young person
r.	rule
R	Reported Decision
R.C.	Rules of the Court of Session
REA	Reduced Earnings Allowance
reg.	regulation
RIPA	Regulation of Investigatory Powers Act 2000
RMO	Responsible Medical Officer
rr.	rules
RR	reference rate
RSI	repetitive strain injury
RTI	Real Time Information
R.V.R.	Rating & Valuation Reporter
s.	section
S	Scottish Decision
SAP	Statutory Adoption Pay
SAPOE Regulations	Jobseeker's Allowance (Schemes for Assisting Persons to Obtain Employment) Regulations 2013
SAWS	Seasonal Agricultural Work Scheme
SAYE	Save As You Earn
SB	Supplementary Benefit
SBAT	Supplementary Benefit Appeal Tribunal
SBC	Supplementary Benefits Commission
S.C.	Session Cases
S.C. (H.L.)	Session Cases (House of Lords)
S.C. (P.C.)	Session Cases (Privy Council)
S.C.C.R.	Scottish Criminal Case Reports
S.C.L.R.	Scottish Civil Law Reports
Sch.	Schedule
SDA	Severe Disablement Allowance

SDP	Severe Disability Premium
SEC	Social Entitlement Chamber
SEISS	Self-Employed Income Support Scheme
SEN	special educational needs
SERPS	State Earnings Related Pension Scheme
ShPP	statutory shared parental pay
ShPP Regulations	Statutory Shared Parental Pay (General) Regulations 2014
SI	Statutory Instrument
SIP	Share Incentive Plan
S.J.	Solicitors Journal
S.J.L.B.	Solicitors Journal Law Brief
SLAN	statement like an award notice
S.L.T.	Scots Law Times
SMP	Statutory Maternity Pay
SMP (General) Regulations 1986	Statutory Maternity Pay (General) Regulations 1986
SPC	State Pension Credit
SPC Regulations	State Pension Credit Regulations 2002
SPCA 2002	State Pension Credit Act 2002
SPL Regulations	Shared Parental Leave Regulations 2014
SPP	Statutory Paternity Pay
ss.	sections
SS (No.2) A 1980	Social Security (No.2) Act 1980
SSA 1975	Social Security Act 1975
SSA 1977	Social Security Act 1977
SSA 1978	Social Security Act 1978
SSA 1979	Social Security Act 1979
SSA 1981	Social Security Act 1981
SSA 1986	Social Security Act 1986
SSA 1988	Social Security Act 1988
SSA 1989	Social Security Act 1989
SSA 1990	Social Security Act 1990
SSA 1998	Social Security Act 1998
SSAA 1992	Social Security Administration Act 1992
SSAC	Social Security Advisory Committee
SSAT	Social Security Appeal Tribunal
SSCBA 1992	Social Security Contributions and Benefits Act 1992
SSCB(NI)A 1992	Social Security Contributions and Benefits (Northern Ireland) Act 1992
SSCPA 1992	Social Security (Consequential Provisions) Act 1992
SSD	Secretary of State for Defence
SSHBA 1982	Social Security and Housing Benefits Act 1982

SSHD	Secretary of State for the Home Department
SSI	Scottish Statutory Instrument
SS(MP)A 1977	Social Security (Miscellaneous Provisions) Act 1977
SSP	Statutory Sick Pay
SSP (General) Regulations	Statutory Sick Pay (General) Regulations 1982
SSPA 1975	Social Security Pensions Act 1975
SSPP	statutory shared parental pay
SSWP	Secretary of State for Work and Pensions
State Pension Credit Regulations	State Pension Credit Regulations 2002
S.T.C.	Simon's Tax Cases
S.T.C. (S.C.D.)	Simon's Tax Cases: Special Commissioners' Decisions
S.T.I.	Simon's Tax Intelligence
STIB	Short-Term Incapacity Benefit
subpara.	subparagraph
subs.	subsection
T	Tribunal of Commissioners' Decision
T.C.	Tax Cases
TCA 1999	Tax Credits Act 1999
TCA 2002	Tax Credits Act 2002
TCC	Technology and Construction Court
TCEA 2007	Tribunals, Courts and Enforcement Act 2007
TCGA 1992	Taxation of Chargeable Gains Act 2002
TCTM	*Tax Credits Technical Manual*
TEC	Treaty Establishing the European Community
TENS	transcutaneous electrical nerve stimulation
TEU	Treaty on European Union
TFC	tax-free childcare
TFEU	Treaty on the Functioning of the European Union
TIOPA 2010	Taxation (International and Other Provisions) Act 2010
TMA 1970	Taxes Management Act 1970
T.R.	Taxation Reports
Transfer of Functions Act	Social Security Contributions (Transfer of Functions etc.) Act 1999
Tribunal Procedure Rules	Tribunal Procedure (First-tier Tribunal)(Social Entitlement Chamber) Rules 2008
UB	Unemployment Benefit
UC	Universal Credit
UC Regs 2013	Universal Credit Regulations 2013
UCITS	Undertakings for Collective Investments in Transferable Securities
UKAIT	UK Asylum and Immigration Tribunal
UKBA	UK Border Agency of the Home Office

Table of Abbreviations used in this Series

UKCC	United Kingdom Central Council for Nursing, Midwifery and Health Visiting
UKFTT	United Kingdom First-tier Tribunal Tax Chamber
UKHL	United Kingdom House of Lords
U.K.H.R.R.	United Kingdom Human Rights Reports
UKSC	United Kingdom Supreme Court
UKUT	United Kingdom Upper Tribunal
UN	United Nations
Universal Credit Regulations	Universal Credit Regulations 2013
URL	uniform resource locator
USI Regs	Social Security (Unemployment, Sickness and Invalidity Benefit) Regulations 1983
USI Regulations	Social Security (Unemployment, Sickness and Invalidity Benefit) Regulations 1983
UT	Upper Tribunal
VAT	Value Added Tax
VCM	vinyl chloride monomer
Vol.	Volume
VWF	Vibration White Finger
W	Welsh Decision
WCA	Work Capability Assessment
WCAt	limited capability for work assessment
WFHRAt	Work-Focused Health-Related Assessment
WFI	work-focused interview
WFTC	Working Families Tax Credit
Wikeley, Annotations	N. Wikeley, "Annotations to Jobseekers Act 1995 (c.18)" in *Current Law Statutes Annotated* (1995)
Wikeley, Ogus and Barendt	Wikeley, Ogus and Barendt, *The Law of Social Security* (2002)
W.L.R.	Weekly Law Reports
WLUK	Westlaw UK
Workmen's Compensation Acts	Workmen's Compensation Acts 1925 to 1945
WP	Widow's Pension
WPS	War Pensions Scheme
WRA 2007	Welfare Reform Act 2007
WRA 2009	Welfare Reform Act 2009
WRA 2012	Welfare Reform Act 2012
W-RA Regulations	Employment and Support Allowance (Work-Related Activity) Regulations 2011
WRAAt	Work-Related Activity Assessment
WRPA 1999	Welfare Reform and Pensions Act 1999
WRP(NI)O 1999	Welfare Reform and Pensions (Northern Ireland) Order 1999
WRWA 2016 / WR&WA 2016	Welfare Reform and Work Act 2016

Table of Abbreviations used in this Series

WSP (LCP) R (NI) 2016	Welfare Supplementary Payment (Loss of Carer Payments) Regulations (Northern Ireland) 2016
WSP (LDRP) R (NI) 2016	Welfare Supplementary Payment (Loss of Disability-Related Premiums) Regulations (Northern Ireland) 2016
WSPR (NI) 2016	Welfare Supplementary Payment Regulations (Northern Ireland) 2016
WTC	Working Tax Credit
WTC Regulations	Working Tax Credit (Entitlement and Maximum Rate) Regulations 2002

PART I

STATUTES

Social Security Contributions and Benefits Act 1992

(1992 c.4)

SECTIONS REPRODUCED

PART VIII

THE SOCIAL FUND

138. Payments out of the social fund. 1.1

Payments out of the social fund

[¹**138.**—(1) There may be made out of the social fund, in accordance with this Part of this Act—

(a) Payments of prescribed amounts, whether in respect of prescribed items or otherwise, to meet, in prescribed circumstances, maternity expenses and funeral expenses; and

(b) ... *[Omitted as relating solely to the discretionary social fund.]*]

(2) Payments may also be made out of that fund, in accordance with this Part of this Act, of a prescribed amount or a number of prescribed amounts to prescribed descriptions of persons, in prescribed circumstances, to meet expenses for heating, which appear to the Secretary of State to have been or to be likely to be incurred in cold weather.

(3) ... *[Omitted as relating solely to the discretionary social fund.]*

(4) In this section "prescribed" means specified in or determined in accordance with regulations.

[²(4A) This section has effect in or as regards Scotland as if—

(a) references in subsections (1)(a) and (2) to the making of payments out of the social fund were to the making of payments by the Scottish Ministers,

(b) the reference in subsection (2) to the Secretary of State were to the Scottish Ministers, and

(c) the reference in subsection (4) to regulations were to regulations made by the Scottish Ministers.

(4B) Where regulations are made by the Scottish Ministers under this section—

(a) sections 175(2) and (7) and 176 do not apply, and

(b) the regulations are subject to the negative procedure (see section 28 of the Interpretation and Legislative Reform (Scotland) Act 2010).

(4C) The power to make an Order in Council under section 30(3) of the Scotland Act 1998 is exercisable for the purposes of this section as it is exercisable for the purposes of that Act.]

(5) ... *[Omitted as relating solely to the discretionary social fund.]*

AMENDMENTS

1. Social Security Act 1998 s.70 (April 5, 1999).

3

2. Scotland Act 2016 s.23(5) (May 17, 2017 for the purpose of making regulations: see SI 2017/405 reg.2(b)(iii). The amendment will not come into force for other purposes until April 1, 2022: see SI 2017/405 reg.3 as substituted by SI 2019/1438 reg.2).

GENERAL NOTE

Subsection (1)(a)

1.2   Subsection (1)(a) is re-enacted by s.70(1)(a) of the SSA 1998 with effect from April 5, 1999. This part of the social fund scheme was originally brought into operation in April 1987 to enable payments to be made for maternity and funeral expenses. These are made under the ordinary system of adjudication and under regulations required to be made by subs.(1)(a). They are not subject to any budget. See the Social Fund Maternity and Funeral Expenses (General) Regulations 2005. The death grant and the maternity grant, formerly payable under the Social Security Act 1975, were abolished (1986 Act ss.38 and 41) and the provisions for maternity and funeral expenses under the supplementary benefit regulations were removed in April 1987 (General Regulations regs 13–15).

Subsection (1)(a) does little more than provide the framework for the detailed entitlement set out in the General Regulations. See s.78(4) of the SSAA 1992 on the recovery of funeral payments from the estate of the deceased.

New restrictions on payments for funeral expenses were introduced on June 5, 1995 and there was further clarification and tightening-up of the rules on April 7, 1997 (see regs 7 and 7A of the General Regulations and the notes to those regulations). Note also the changes introduced on November 17, 1997.

Subsection (2)

1.3   Although the predecessor of this subsection was in force from April 1988, the regulations it required were not in place until November 7, 1988 (Social Fund Cold Weather Payments (General) Regulations 1988). The form of the scheme, as embodied in the 1988 Regulations, has been amended several times. The current form does not require a separate claim to be made for a severe weather payment. As for maternity and funeral expenses, the decisions are made by decision-makers, with appeals to a tribunal, and are not subject to any budget.

See also the notes to the Social Fund Winter Fuel Payment Regulations 2000.

Subsections (4A)–(4C)

1.4   These subsections make provision for the operation of the social fund in Scotland.

Immigration and Asylum Act 1999

(1999 c.33)

SECTION REPRODUCED

PART VI

SUPPORT FOR ASYLUM-SEEKERS

Exclusions

115.   Exclusion from benefits.   1.5

Exclusion from benefits

115.—(1) No person is entitled [¹⁰ to universal credit under Part 1 of   1.6
the Welfare Reform Act 2012 or] to income-based jobseeker's allowance
under the Jobseekers Act 1995 [⁴ or to state pension credit under the State
Pension Credit Act 2002] [⁶ or to income-related allowance under Part 1 of
the Welfare Reform Act 2007 (employment and support allowance)] [⁹ or to
personal independence payment] or to—
   (a) attendance allowance,
   (b) severe disablement allowance,
   (c) [¹carer's allowance],
   (d) disability living allowance,
   (e) income support,
   (f) [²...]
   (g) [²...]
   (h) a social fund payment,
[⁷ (ha) health in pregnancy grant;]
   (i) child benefit,
   (j) housing benefit, [⁸ ...]
   (k) [⁸ ...]
under the Social Security Contributions and Benefits Act 1992 while he is
a person to whom this section applies.

(2) [*Omitted as relating solely to Northern Ireland*]

(3) This section applies to a person subject to immigration control unless
he falls within such category or description, or satisfies such conditions, as
may be prescribed.

(4) Regulations under subsection (3) may provide for a person to be treated
for prescribed purposes only as not being a person to whom this section applies.

(5) In relation to [⁷ health in pregnancy grant or] [³ child benefit], "prescribed" means prescribed by regulations made by the Treasury.

(6) In relation to the matters mentioned in subsection (2) (except so far
as it relates to [⁷ health in pregnancy grant or] [³ child benefit]), "prescribed" means prescribed by regulations made by the Department.

(7) Section 175(3) to (5) of the Social Security Contributions and
Benefits Act 1992 (supplemental powers in relation to regulations) applies
to regulations made by the Secretary of State or the Treasury under subsection (3) as it applies to regulations made under that Act.

(8) Sections 133(2), 171(2) and 172(4) of the Social Security Contributions and Benefits (Northern Ireland) Act 1992 apply to regulations made by the Department under subsection (3) as they apply to regulations made by the Department under that Act.

(9) "A person subject to immigration control" means a person [[11] . . .] who—

(a) requires leave to enter or remain in the United Kingdom but does not have it;

(b) has leave to enter or remain in the United Kingdom which is subject to a condition that he does not have recourse to public funds;

(c) has leave to enter or remain in the United Kingdom given as a result of a maintenance undertaking; or

(d) has leave to enter or remain in the United Kingdom only as a result of paragraph 17 of Schedule 4.

(10) "Maintenance undertaking", in relation to any person, means a written undertaking given by another person in pursuance of the immigration rules to be responsible for that person's maintenance and accommodation.

AMENDMENTS

1. Regulatory Reform (Carer's Allowance) Order 2002 (SI 2002/1457) art.2(1) and Sch. para.3(c) (April 1, 2003).
2. Tax Credits Act 2002 s.60 and Sch.6 (April 8, 2003).
3. Tax Credits Act 2002 s.51 and Sch.4 paras 20–21 (February 26, 2003).
4. State Pension Credit Act 2002 s.4(2) (October 6, 2003).
5. State Pension Credit Act (Northern Ireland) 2002 s.4(2) (October 6, 2003).
6. Welfare Reform Act 2007 Sch.3 para.19 (October 27, 2008).
7. Health and Social Care Act 2008 s.138 (January 1, 2009).
8. Welfare Reform Act 2012 s.147 and Sch.1 Pt 1 (April 1, 2013).
9. Welfare Reform Act 2012 s.91 and Sch.9 para.44 (April 8, 2013).
10. Welfare Reform Act 2012 s.31 and Sch.2 para.54 (April 29, 2013).
11. Immigration and Social Security Co-ordination (EU Withdrawal) Act 2020 (Consequential, Saving, Transitional and Transitory Provisions) (EU Exit) Regulations 2020 (SI 2020/1309) reg.12(1) and (7) (December 31, 2020 at 11.00pm) (subject to the saving provided for by regs 3(4), 4(5) and 12(1)(i) of the Citizens' Rights (Application Deadline and Temporary Protection) (EU Exit) Regulations 2020 (SI 2020/1209): see Vol.V).

GENERAL NOTE

1.7   See the notes to the Social Security (Immigration and Asylum) Consequential Amendments Regulations 2000 (Part V below).

Paragraph 17 of Sch.4 to the Act was repealed on April 1, 2003 by Sch.9 para.1 of the Nationality, Immigration and Asylum Act 2002 but the reference to the repealed provision in s.115(9)(d) has not itself been repealed. *EE v City of Cardiff (HB)* [2018] UKUT 418 (AAC) holds that by virtue of s.17(2) of the Interpretation Act 1978, that reference should now be construed as a reference to ss.3C(1) and (2)(b) of the Immigration Act 1971 which was inserted into that Act by the 2002 Act (but not as a reference to the former s.3D of that Act). However, while *EE* appears to bind first-tier tribunals, query whether it is correctly decided: s.3C of the Immigration Act 1971 is not identically worded to para.17 of Sch.4 and it is questionable whether it really can be treated as a "re-enactment" such as to engage s.17(2) of the Interpretation Act 1978. If *EE* were wrong, a person with s.3C leave would continue to be eligible for benefit if they had been eligible before their non-s.3C leave expired.

Health in Pregnancy Grants were abolished for women who reached the 25th week of their pregnancy on or after January 1, 2011: see s.3(2) of the Savings Accounts and Health in Pregnancy Grant Act 2010. However, s.115(1)(ha) has not been repealed to reflect that circumstance.

State Pension Credit Act 2002

(2002 c.16)

21.   Enactments repealed.
22.   Short title, commencement and extent.

SCHEDULES

Schedules 1–3 [*omitted.*]

INTRODUCTION AND GENERAL NOTE

1.9   The prime purpose of this Act, embodied in ss.1–17, was to set the framework for the state pension credit that has been available to people aged 60 and over as from October 6, 2003. The Labour Government elected in 1997 set out its initial proposals in *A New Contract for Welfare: Partnership in Pensions* (Cm.4179, 1998). This led to the introduction of stakeholder pensions under Pt I of the Welfare Reform and Pensions Act 1999, with effect from April 2001, as a new option for private pension provision for those on moderate incomes.

So far as the poorest pensioners were concerned, the Government at that time resisted demands from its own backbenchers and supporters to restore the link between the state retirement pension and increases in average earnings. Instead, the value of income support for pensioners was dramatically increased and that benefit relabelled as the minimum income guarantee (or "MIG") for that client group. This had the effect of increasing the gap between the (higher) MIG entitlement and the (lower) basic state retirement pension respectively for a single pensioner. The disparity increased from £5.75 in April 1998 (when the basic pension represented 92 per cent of the MIG rate) to £22.65 by April 2002 (by which time the basic pension had fallen to 77 per cent of the MIG level). This exacerbated the longstanding problem that pensioners with small amounts of private incomes on top of their state retirement pension saw no benefit from such thrift as any such income is deducted pound-for-pound under income support rules.

The proposal for a pension credit was first canvassed in a DSS consultation paper in November 2000 (DSS, *The Pension Credit: a consultation paper,* Cm.4900), which was followed by the publication of a further paper entitled *The Pension Credit: the government's proposals* (DWP, 2001). The pension credit both continues the previous income support arrangements (or MIG) for pensioners in a modified form and provides some reward for those with small private incomes. Thus the state pension credit comprises two quite distinct elements. The first is the "guarantee credit", which is intended to provide a minimum level of income to those aged 60 or over. This replaces the MIG, the marketing name for income support for pensioners. The second is the "savings credit", which is designed to provide an additional form of income for pensioners from the age of 65 who have low or modest private incomes (e.g. an occupational pension and/or income from savings) in addition to the basic state retirement pension.

1.10   Section 1 specifies the common conditions for access to the pension credit, whilst ss.2 and 3 respectively stipulate the extra conditions which must be satisfied in order to qualify for either or both of the guarantee credit and the savings credit. The common conditions for state pension credit in s.1 are that the claimant is in Great Britain and has reached the qualifying age (set at the pensionable age for women). Note also that in *EC v Secretary of State for Work and Pensions* [2010] UKUT 93 (AAC); [2010] AACR 39 it was held that state pension credit is a special non-contributory benefit within art.10a of Regulation 1408/71 (see now art.70 of Regulation 883/2004) and so is payable only to those living in Great Britain. In addition, s.4 includes a number of exclusions from entitlement to the pension credit and s.5 confirms that a claimant's resources must be aggregated with those of their partner.

The calculation of the guarantee credit entitlement under s.2 essentially works in the same way as the income support scheme. There are, however, two important differences in the substantive rules of entitlement to the guarantee credit when contrasted with those that apply to income support. Income support is not available to those who work for 16 hours or more a week and is subject to an upper capital limit. Neither rule applies to state pension credit.

The savings credit under s.3, comprising the second potential element in the state pension credit, is an entirely novel form of benefit. It works in the opposite way to the traditional means-test which applies for the purposes of income support. Previously a pensioner who had a small private income over and above the state retirement pension saw their MIG or income support reduced pound-for-pound by any such income. In contrast, the savings credit provides a small weekly supplement to reward those with modest savings or private incomes. Section 3 sets out the two extra criteria for the award of the savings credit (in addition to the common rules contained in s.1 for the pension credit as a whole).

As originally enacted in the 2002 Act, the first of these was simply that the claimant (or their partner) was at least 65. This condition was radically altered by the Pensions Act 2014. As from the start date for the new state pension (April 6, 2016), s.3 as amended now provides that the savings credit element of state pension credit is only payable (from the savings credit qualifying age) to those who had already reached pensionable age before that date.

The second is effectively a complicated mathematical formula which is translated into text form. This can only really be understood by following the example provided in the annotation to s.3. Its effect is to provide a small savings credit of up to £15.94 a week at 2023/24 rates for a single pensioner for those with incomes which are just above the MIG level. 1.11

The other important difference from the previous arrangements, at least as the state pension credit scheme was originally enacted, concerns the duration of awards of any pension credit (of either type) and the effects of change in circumstances. Income support is a weekly benefit and any changes in circumstances (e.g. in the amount of an occupational pension) must be reported to the DWP. Where the pension credit is awarded, the Secretary of State had to specify an "assessed income period" (s.6), which will typically be for five years (s.9). The statutory assumption under s.7(4) is that the claimant's income will then remain constant throughout this period, subject to any deemed increases of a foreseeable and regular nature, such as the arrangements for indexation of any occupational or other private pension (e.g. in line with the Retail Price Index); see also s.10. The remarkable effect of these provisions was that where the claimant received a windfall increase during the period of the award, any such increases were disregarded (s.7(5)) and accordingly did not give rise to any obligation to report such a change to the Department. In the event that the pensioner's income fell, a fresh assessment could be applied for (s.8).

However, in the 2013 Spending Round the Government announced the abolition of the assessed income period in state pension credit cases from April 2016, a change effected by the Pensions Act 2014 (ss.28, 29 and Sch.12 paras 88–91). As a result, in future any change in retirement income will need to be reported to the Department when it occurs, triggering a review and a change in benefit award where appropriate.

The remaining provisions of the Act which relate to the state pension credit are of a supplementary nature. Section 11 introduces Sch.1, which applies the social security claims, decisions and appeals procedures to the state pension credit. Section 12 makes special provision for the few polygamous marriages that may fall within the ambit of the new scheme whilst s.13 enables the Secretary of State to make regulations governing transitional arrangements. Section 14 introduces Sch.2, which makes minor and consequential amendments. Sections 15–17 provide definitions of a number of key terms, such as "income" (s.15) and "retirement pension income" (s.16), as well as other general expressions (s.17), but also grant the Secretary of State extensive regulation-making powers to provide further definitions of certain terms. The relevant regulations, also in this volume (see paras 3.1, et seq.), are the State Pension Credit Regulations 2002 (SI 2002/1792), as amended. 1.12

The final point to note about the state pension credit is a matter of nomenclature. Throughout the 2002 Act the new benefit is referred to as the *state* pension credit. This formula is required because s.29 of the Welfare Reform and Pensions Act 1999 makes provision for the creation of "pension credits" as a mechanism for effecting pension sharing on divorce. This Act, therefore, could not describe the benefit simply as the pension credit. However, the benefit is known as the *state* pension credit purely for the purposes of statutory drafting. The Department's publicity material describes the benefit as pension credit *simpliciter*. For the reasons explained in the General Note to s.3, the "savings credit", one of the constituent elements in the pension credit, is itself something of a misnomer, as it is not merely a credit on savings. State pension credit has nothing whatsoever to do with the working tax credit and the child tax credit which were introduced in April 2003 by the Tax Credits Act 2002 (see Vol. IV in this series). Those *tax* credits are administered by HRMC; the state pension credit remains firmly in the province of the DWP and its Pension, Disability and Carers Service, the Department's operational arm which now has responsibility for all pensions matters. See further N. Wikeley, "State Pension Credit: completing the pensions jigsaw?" (2004) 11 *Journal of Social Security Law* 12.

The independent Pensions Commission pointed out that maintaining existing indexation rules for pension credit and the basic state retirement pension respectively would lead to a steady extension of means-testing of pensioners over time. It estimated that by 2050 over 70 per cent of all pensioners would be subject to means-tested withdrawal of either the state second pension or their private pension income: *Pensions Commission, A New Pension Settlement for the Twenty-First Century – The Second Report of the Pensions Commission* (November 2005), p.142.

1.13 Major changes to the state pension regime were made by the Pensions Act 2014, coming into force with effect from April 6, 2016. Pensioners who had already reached state pension age as at that date will continue to be entitled to the state pension under the previous rules. However, 'new' pensioners will now qualify for the new single tier state pension. One of the main principles of the reform was that the new state pension is to be set above the basic level of means-tested support. Thus whereas the standard minimum guarantee under the state pension credit scheme is £201.05 in 2023/24, the starting rate for the new state pension is £203.85.

See also s.142 of the Pensions Act 2008, which enables the Secretary of State to make regulations to supply social security information about state pension credit recipients to energy suppliers (or persons providing services to the energy suppliers or the Secretary of State). These provisions also authorise energy suppliers to share their customer information with the Secretary of State or a service provider, so as to enable either the Secretary of State or a third party to match DWP and energy supplier data to identify the relevant state pension credit recipients. The intention is to identify those persons who are eligible for financial assistance towards their electricity bill in accordance with a support scheme established under arrangements made between the Secretary of State and electricity suppliers. See further the Disclosure of State Pension Credit Information (Warm Home Discount) Regulations 2011 (SI 2011/1830) as amended by the Warm Home Discount (Miscellaneous Amendments) Regulations 2021 (SI 2021/667), the Warm Home Discount (England and Wales) Regulations 2022 (SI 2022/772) and the Warm Home Discount (Scotland) Regulations 2022 (SI 2022/1073).

Note that the State Pension Credit (Coronavirus) (Electronic Claims) (Amendment) Regulations 2020 (SI 2020/456) amended the Claims and Payments Regulations, with effect from May 4, 2020, so as to allow electronic claims to be made for pension credit. Owing to the impact of the Covid-19 outbreak in Great Britain, an online digital platform was developed to provide claimants with an additional route for claiming (and thereby to ease the operational impacts of the pandemic, given the pressure on the DWP's telephony system). Regulation 2 of the 2020 Regulations accordingly amended reg.4ZC of, and para.2 of Sch.9ZC to, the Claims and Payments Regulations to permit the use of an electronic communication in connection with a claim for pension credit. The use of an electronic communication by claimants must be in accordance with a direction of the Secretary of State. These directions are available online at: *https://www.gov.uk/government/publications/ the-social-security-electronic-communications-directions* [Accessed 1 April 2023].

Commencement

The Act received the Royal Assent on June 25, 2002. Sections 19, 20 and 22 came   1.14
into effect on that date (s.22(2)). Other provisions come into effect as the Secretary
of State may order (s.22(3)). The State Pension Credit Act 2002 (Commencement
No.1) Order 2002 (SI 2002/1691 (c.51)) provided that July 2, 2002 was the day
appointed for the coming into force of the regulation making powers under ss.1 to 7,
9 and 11–17 (except for certain provisions in s.14). The relevant regulations are the
State Pension Credit Regulations 2002 (SI 2002/1792, as amended), which came
into force on October 6, 2003.

The final Commencement Order was the State Pension Credit Act 2002
(Commencement No.5) and Appointed Day Order 2003 (SI 2003/1766 (c.75)).
This brought into force on October 6, 2003 all those provisions of the Act which
were not already in force and appointed that day as the "appointed day" for the
purposes of s.13 of the Act (transitional provisions).

Note also that s.34 and Sch.4 of the Welfare Reform Act 2012 have prospectively
amended the 2002 Act to create a new credit within state pension credit to cover
housing costs. This is intended to provide support for people who have reached the
qualifying age for state pension credit (or for couples where both members have
reached the qualifying age) once housing benefit is no longer available following
the full introduction of universal credit. In particular, the new s.3A (inserted by
Welfare Reform Act 2012 s.34 and Sch.4 paras 1 and 4 as amended by s.20(8)
of the Welfare Reform and Work Act 2016), sets out the conditions of entitlement
to the new housing credit and provides the powers to set out the structure of the
housing credit in regulations. There are also a number of consequential amendments. However, s.3A and these other amendments introduced by the Welfare
Reform Act 2012 have yet to be brought into force, and so are not included in this
edition.

State pension credit: entitlement and amount

Entitlement

1.—(1) A social security benefit to be known as state pension credit shall   1.15
be payable in accordance with the following provisions of this Act.

(2) A claimant is entitled to state pension credit if—

(a) he is in Great Britain;

(b) he has attained the qualifying age; and

(c) he satisfies—

(i) the condition in section 2(1) (guarantee credit); or

(ii) the conditions in section 3(1) and (2) (savings credit).

(3) A claimant who is entitled to state pension credit is entitled—

(a) to a guarantee credit, calculated in accordance with section 2, if he
satisfies the condition in subsection (1) of that section, or

(b) to a savings credit, calculated in accordance with section 3, if he satisfies the conditions in subsections (1) and (2) of that section,

(or to both, if he satisfies both the condition mentioned in paragraph
(a) and the conditions mentioned in paragraph (b)).

(4) Subsections (2) and (3) are subject to the following provisions of this Act.

(5) Regulations may make provision for the purposes of this Act—

(a) as to circumstances in which a person is to be treated as being or not
being in Great Britain; or

(b) continuing a person's entitlement to state pension credit during
periods of temporary absence from Great Britain.

(6) In this Act "the qualifying age" means—
(a) in the case of a woman, pensionable age; or
(b) in the case of a man, the age which is pensionable age in the case of a woman born on the same day as the man.

DEFINITIONS

"claimant"—see s.17(1).
"entitled"—*ibid.*
"guarantee credit"—*ibid.*
"pensionable age"—*ibid.*
"the qualifying age"—see subs.(6).
"regulations"—see s.17(1).
"savings credit"—*ibid.*

GENERAL NOTE

1.16   This section sets out the entitlement criteria for the state pension credit. The conditions laid down by this section are the common entitlement rules. These are that the claimant is in Great Britain (subs.(2)(a); see further subs.(5)) and has reached the qualifying age (subs.(2)(b), as defined by subs.(6)). Note also *EC v Secretary of State for Work and Pensions* [2010] UKUT 93 (AAC); [2010] AACR 39, where it was held that state pension credit is a special non-contributory benefit within art.10a of Regulation 1408/71 (now art.70 of Regulation 883/2004) which is payable only to those living in Great Britain. In addition, a claimant must satisfy either or both of the additional rules relating to eligibility for the guarantee credit (s.2) and the savings credit (s.3) (see subs.(2)(c)). The guarantee credit replaced the MIG (or, in other words, income support) for the pensioner population. The calculation of the guarantee credit itself works in the same way as the MIG and is designed to bring a pensioner's income up to a minimum threshold, which for 2023/24 is £201.05 for a single claimant and £306.85 for a couple. The savings credit, which may be payable additionally to or independently of the guarantee credit, seeks to provide a reward for those pensioner claimants who have a modest private income over and above the basic state retirement pension. A claimant's entitlement thus comprises either or both such components, depending on which conditions are met (subs.(3)). These requirements are obviously subject to the remaining provisions of the Act (subs.(4)).

Subsection (2)(a)

1.17   In *NB v Secretary of State for Work and Pensions (SPC)* [2013] UKUT 266 (AAC), an overpayment appeal, Judge Wright held that living on a British registered boat outside UK territorial waters was not being "in Great Britain" for the purpose of s.1(2)(a) (following *R(IS) 8/06*). However, the claimant will have been in Great Britain for any period that he was either on land in the UK or on his boat when in UK waters, and the tribunal erred in law in not enquiring into this aspect. Remitting the appeal to a new tribunal, the Judge directed it to consider whether the temporary absence rule applied for any period (which provides that a claimant will continue to be entitled to SPC for 13 weeks while not in Great Britain if the period of absence is unlikely to exceed 52 weeks and he continues to satisfy the other conditions of entitlement; see reg.3).
     For detailed discussion of the position of persons subject to immigration control, see Part V of this Volume.

Subsection (5)

1.18   This power enables regulations to make further provision in respect to the residence requirement. See further State Pension Credit Regulations 2002 (SI 2002/1792) regs 2 and 3, requiring pension credit claimants to be habitually resident, although they may retain their entitlement for up to 13 weeks during a period of temporary absence abroad.

Subsection (6)

This definition of "qualifying age" must be read together with the definition of   1.19
"pensionable age" in s.17(1). Its effect is that the qualifying age for both men and
women is the pensionable age for women. From the 1940s until 2010 the state
pension age was 65 for men and 60 for women. The Pensions Act 1995 (s.126 and
Sch.4) originally provided for the increase from 60 to 65 in the state pension age
for women to be phased in over the period from April 2010 to 2020. However, the
Coalition Government brought forward the Pensions Act 2011 (see s.1) to acceler-
ate the latter part of this timetable, so that the pensionable age for women reached
65 in November 2018. The reason for this change was the overall increase in life
expectancy since the timetable was last revised. It had also initially been intended
that the equalised pensionable age for men and women would then rise to 66 by
April 2020. However, because of concerns expressed about the impact on women
born in March 1954, who would see their pensionable age increase by as much as
two years as a result, it decided that this should happen over a slightly longer period,
with the uniform state pension age reaching 66 in October 2020. See further the
report by the House of Commons Work and Pensions Committee, *Communication
of state pension age changes*, Seventh Report of 2015/16, HC 899). Note that the
Pensions Act 2014 also includes provision to bring forward the increase in the
common state pension age to 67 to between 2026 and 2028.

The basic requirement under subs.(2)(a) is that a pension credit claimant must
have reached this qualifying age; this is also sufficient for entitlement to the guarantee credit under s.2. However, a claimant must actually be 65 (or their partner must
be) in order to claim the savings credit (s.3(1)). The Government's justification for
this distinction was that "the age of 65 is the first point at which we judge that the
savings credit can be fairly and equally paid to ensure that we are not open to legal
challenge in respect of gender equality" (Ms M. Eagle MP, Parliamentary Under-
Secretary for Work and Pensions, Standing Committee A, col.104). Thus retired
single women aged between 60 and 64 may claim the guarantee credit but not the
savings credit, even though they may have a small private income. Women of this age
who are members of a married or unmarried couple may claim the savings credit if
their partner is aged 65 or over, and so may see some benefit from private savings.

In a number of recent decisions the Upper Tribunal has dealt with some of the
difficult evidential issues associated with proof of age. In the first, *LS v SSWP
(SPC)* [2014] UKUT 249 (AAC), the issue was whether the claimant, the wife of a
Gurkha, was born on January 1, 1951 or some other date in 1951. Judge Williams
in the Upper Tribunal held that the tribunal had failed to apply the correct standard
of proof (balance of probabilities) and to consider all the relevant evidence. Similar
issues arose in *SW v SSWP (SPC)* [2016] UKUT 163 (AAC), where the claimant, who had originally obtained an Ethiopian passport showing her date of birth
to be January 1, 1963, subsequently became a naturalized British citizen, her UK
passport again showing her date of birth to be January 1, 1963. She later claimed
pension credit, stating that her true date of birth was May 23, 1950. The DWP
decision-maker and the First-tier Tribunal decided the passport(s) showed the
correct date of birth and concluded the claimant was not eligible for pension credit
on age grounds. The claimant's explanation, amongst other matters, was that she
had obtained her Ethiopian passport at a time when she was travelling to Qatar for
domestic work, and had been advised that she would not find employment if she
was aged over 30, and so a false date had been used. Judge Hemingway allowed the
claimant's appeal and, tasking into account all the evidence, re-made the decision,
holding that the claimant had indeed reached the qualifying age. In doing so, Judge
Hemingway made the following more general observations:

"41. ...There is the question of whether the documents are forgeries, the original
tribunal of course thought they were, and I am quite prepared to accept that it
is possible to obtain fraudulent documents in Ethiopia just as, of course, it is
possible to obtain fraudulent documents, in the right circumstances, I imagine

in pretty much every country in the world. There may, of course, be significant variations in the ease with which fraudulent but apparently genuine documents might be obtained. It seems to me that where an allegation of fraud is being made by a party then it will be necessary for the asserting party to prove it to the requisite standard which, here, is a balance of probabilities. Here, though, I cannot see that the respondent did actually submit to the tribunal that the documents were forged. It also seems to me that it will seldom be necessary for a tribunal to reach a definitive view as to whether a document is forged or not. Rather, the inquiry should be directed more as to whether any weight can be attached to the documents provided by a claimant having regard to the evidence as a whole and a claimant's general credibility. There may also be other reasons, irrespective of the veracity of any allegation as to forgery, as to why documents cannot be accorded weight. In this case I have decided, whilst I do not on balance find the appellant to be dishonest, that the documents cannot be accorded weight because of the lack of any evidence and information concerning the existence of or accuracy of record keeping on the part of the church or the relevant government department responsible for issuing birth certificates. So, as it turns out, the documents assist neither the appellant nor the respondent."

Guarantee credit

1.20

2.—(1) The condition mentioned in section 1(2)(c)(i) is that the claimant—
(a) has no income; or
(b) has income which does not exceed the appropriate minimum guarantee.
(2) Where the claimant is entitled to a guarantee credit, then—
(a) if he has no income, the guarantee credit shall be the appropriate minimum guarantee; and
(b) if he has income, the guarantee credit shall be the difference between the appropriate minimum guarantee and his income.
(3) The appropriate minimum guarantee shall be the total of—
(a) the standard minimum guarantee; and
(b) such prescribed additional amounts as may be applicable.
(4) The standard minimum guarantee shall be a prescribed amount.
(5) The standard minimum guarantee shall be—
(a) a uniform single amount in the case of every claimant who is a member of a [¹ couple]; and
(b) a lower uniform single amount in the case of every claimant who is not a member of [¹ a couple].
(6) Regulations may provide that, in prescribed cases, subsection (3) shall have effect with the substitution for the reference in paragraph (a) to the standard minimum guarantee of a reference to a prescribed amount.
(7) Where the claimant is severely disabled, there shall be included among the additional amounts prescribed under subsection (3)(b) an amount in respect of that circumstance.
(8) Where—
(a) the claimant is entitled to an allowance under section 70 of the Contributions and Benefits Act, or
(b) if the claimant is a member of a [¹ couple], the other member of the couple is entitled to such an allowance,
there shall be included among the additional amounts prescribed under subsection (3)(b) an amount in respect of that circumstance.

14

(9) Except for the amount of the standard minimum guarantee, the powers conferred by this section to prescribe amounts include power to prescribe nil as an amount.

AMENDMENT

1. Civil Partnership Act 2004 s.254 and Sch.24 paras 140 and 141 (December 5, 2005).

DEFINITIONS

"appropriate minimum guarantee"—see subs.(3) and s.17(1).
"claimant"—see s.17(1).
"Contributions and Benefits Act"—*ibid.*
"couple"—*ibid.*
"entitled"—*ibid.*
"guarantee credit"—*ibid.*
"income"—*ibid.*
"prescribed"—*ibid.*
"regulations"—*ibid.*
"standard minimum guarantee"—see subss.(4) and (5) and s.17(1).

GENERAL NOTE

This section sets out the extra condition (further to the common conditions in s.1) **1.21** which a pension credit claimant must satisfy in order to be entitled to the guarantee credit (which replaced the MIG, or income support, for pensioners). The extra condition is that the claimant either has no income or has an income which does not exceed the "appropriate minimum guarantee" (subs.(1)). "Income" is defined in accordance with ss.15 and 16 (and see State Pension Credit Regulations 2002 (SI 2002/1792 Pt III)); but note also that the claimant's income is to be aggregated with that of any partner (s.5). The "appropriate minimum guarantee" is equivalent to the applicable amount in the income support scheme. It therefore comprises the "standard minimum guarantee" and other prescribed amounts (subs.(3)). The former is a standard prescribed amount (subss.(4) and (5)) which for 2023/24 is £201.05 for a single person and £306.85 for a couple (State Pension Credit Regulations 2002 (SI 2002/1792) reg.6(1)). The other prescribed amounts mirror the premiums in the income support scheme. Specific provision is made for two particular types of extra prescribed amounts under subs.(3)(b), namely for those who are severely disabled (subs.(7); this is based on SSCBA 1992 s.135(5)) and for those who are entitled to a carer's allowance under SSCBA 1992 s.70 (subs.(8)). The extra amounts under subs.(3)(b) also include other elements, e.g. prescribed sums for owner-occupiers as regards their housing costs (see generally State Pension Credit Regulations 2002 (SI 2002/1792) Schs I and II).

The Secretary of State also has the power to substitute a prescribed amount for the uniform standard minimum guarantee (subs.(6)). This only has effect for the purpose of calculating the appropriate minimum guarantee for that person under subs.(3)(a), which is then based on the prescribed amount plus any other prescribed additional amounts. It does not, therefore, affect the standard minimum guarantee for other purposes in the Act, most notably the assessment of the maximum savings credit under s.3(7). This power has been inserted to enable a different rate to be applied where the claimant (or their partner) remains in hospital for more than 52 weeks. The previous regime provided for "hospital downrating" to apply after six weeks in hospital, but the Government initially increased this period to 13 weeks and then subsequently to 52 weeks by the Social Security (Hospital In-Patients and Miscellaneous Amendments) Regulations 2003 (SI 2003/1195); see now State Pension Credit Regulations 2002 (SI 2002/1792) Sch.III para.2.

The Secretary of State also has the power, taking subss. (6) and (9) together, to prescribe nil as the amount of the standard minimum guarantee in subs.(3)(a). The wording of subs.(9) is not entirely clear, but its import (when read with subs.(6)) appears to be that nil can be prescribed as the amount of the standard minimum guarantee under subs.(3)(a) but not as the rate of the normal standard minimum guarantee under subss.(4) and (5). This enables a nil amount to be specified for prisoners and members of religious orders who are fully maintained by their orders (both being groups who are currently excluded from income support; see now State Pension Credit Regulations 2002 (SI 2002/1792) reg.6(2) and (3) and *Scott v Secretary of State for Work and Pensions* [2011] EWCA Civ 103; [2011] AACR 23).

Three important differences with the rules governing entitlement to income support should be noted. First, there is no provision in the Act for a "16-hour rule" in the state pension credit scheme. Thus, unlike those of working age who claim income support or jobseeker's allowance, pensioners are not disentitled if they work 16 hours or more a week. Secondly, there is no upper capital limit for the pension credit (see further s.15); moreover the deemed rate of return by virtue of the tariff income rule is halved (State Pension Credit Regulations 2002 (SI 2002/1792) reg.15(6)). Finally, the traditional weekly means-test for income support was not originally replicated in the arrangements for the pension credit; instead the typical award was made for an "assessed income period" of five years (see further s.7). However, assessed income periods were abolished by the Pensions Act 2014 with effect from April 2016.

Savings credit

1.22   **3.**—[¹ (1) The first of the conditions mentioned in section 1(2)(c)(ii) is that the claimant—

    (a) has attained pensionable age before 6 April 2016 and has attained the age of 65 (before, on or after that date), or

    (b) is a member of a couple, the other member of which falls within paragraph (a).]

(2) The second of the conditions mentioned in section 1(2)(c)(ii) is that—

    (a) the claimant's qualifying income exceeds the savings credit threshold; and

    (b) the claimant's income is such that, for the purposes of subsection (3), amount A exceeds amount B.

(3) Where the claimant is entitled to a savings credit, the amount of the savings credit shall be the amount by which amount A exceeds amount B.

(4) For the purposes of subsection (3)—

"amount A" is the smaller of—

    (a) the maximum savings credit; and

    (b) a prescribed percentage of the amount by which the claimant's qualifying income exceeds the savings credit threshold; and

"amount B" is—

    (a) a prescribed percentage of the amount (if any) by which the claimant's income exceeds the appropriate minimum guarantee; or

    (b) if there is no such excess, nil.

(5) Where, by virtue of regulations under section 2(6), the claimant's appropriate minimum guarantee does not include the standard minimum guarantee, regulations may provide that the definition of "amount B" in subsection (4) shall have effect with the substitution for the reference in paragraph (a) to the appropriate minimum guarantee of a reference to a prescribed higher amount.

(2002 c.16 s.3)

(6) Regulations may make provision as to income which is, and income which is not, to be treated as qualifying income for the purposes of this section.

(7) For the purposes of this section—

"the savings credit threshold" is such amount as may be prescribed;

"the maximum savings credit" is a prescribed percentage of the difference between—

(a) the standard minimum guarantee; and

(b) the savings credit threshold.

(8) Regulations may prescribe descriptions of persons in whose case the maximum savings credit shall be taken to be nil.

AMENDMENT

1. Pensions Act 2014 s.23 and Sch.12 Pt 3 para.89 (April 6, 2016).

DEFINITIONS

"appropriate minimum guarantee"—see ss.2(3) and 17(1).
"claimant"—see s.17(1).
"couple"—*ibid.*
"entitled"—*ibid.*
"income"—*ibid.*
"maximum savings credit"—see subs.(7).
"prescribed"—see s.17(1).
"regulations"—*ibid.*
"savings credit"—*ibid.*
"savings credit threshold"—see subs.(7).
"standard minimum guarantee"—ss.2(4) and (5) and 17(1).

GENERAL NOTE

This section sets out the extra conditions (further to the common conditions in s.1) which a pension credit claimant must satisfy in order to be entitled to the savings credit. A claimant may be entitled to the savings credit even if he or she is not entitled to the guarantee credit (s.1(3)). In order to qualify for a savings credit there are two additional requirements that must be satisfied.

The first, as originally enacted, was that the claimant (or their partner) was at least 65. This stood in contrast to the eligibility conditions for guarantee credit, for which the qualifying age was (and remains) the pensionable age for women as specified in the common criteria for pension credit (ss.1(2)(a) and (6)). However, as a result of amendments made by the Pensions Act 2014 (fully in force from April 6, 2016), there is no longer access to the savings credit element for those claimants reaching state pension age on or after that date *unless* they are a member of a couple where the other member reached state pension age before April 6, 2016 (known as "a mixed-age couple"; see further s.3ZA). The policy justification for this change is that whereas the previous basic state pension was set below the level of the standard minimum guarantee in pension credit, the new state pension is set at a level above that threshold, so removing the problem that the savings credit was designed to address. See further the State Pension Credit Regulations 2002 (SI 2002/1792) reg.7A. The policy was first announced in the new state pension green and white papers (DWP, "A State Pension for the 21st Century", Cm 8053, April 2011, Ch.3 and "The single-tier pension: a simple foundation for saving", Cm 8528, January 2013, Ch.4).

The second additional condition is more complex. The claimant's "qualifying income" (including that of their partner: see further ss.5, 15 and 16 and State Pension Credit Regulations 2002 (SI 2002/1792) reg.9) must exceed the "savings

1.23

17

credit threshold" and must be such that "amount A exceeds Amount B" (subs. (2)), the difference being the amount of savings credit entitlement (subs.(3)). The complexity is the inevitable consequence of the draftsman's attempt to reduce an arithmetical calculation into comprehensible prose. The good news is that this formula does not require the same skills in advanced algebra as did the original child support scheme.

1.24 The term "savings credit" is itself something of a misnomer, as will be seen from the examples discussed below. The savings credit is not a credit that is payable simply because a pensioner has savings, e.g. in a bank account. Rather, it is a supplement that is payable to pensioners who have small amounts of private income, whether in the form of an occupational or other private pension or indeed by way of income which is generated from savings.

Note, however, that now the Pensions Act 2014 (Sch.12 para.89) is in force the savings credit element of pension credit will in future only be payable to those who have reached state pension age before April 6, 2016 (however, a younger individual may still qualify in future if they are a member of a couple and their partner qualifies).

Subsection (1)

1.25 See further the annotation to s.1(6). Note also that the words "the age of 65" in subs.(1) will be replaced by the expression "pensionable age" but that this amendment will only take effect from April 6, 2024 (Pensions Act 2007 s.13 and Sch.8 para.44).

Subsections (2)–(4)

1.26 The additional condition in subs.(2) can be understood better if it is broken down into its four constituent terms: qualifying income, the savings credit threshold and amounts A and B respectively, although the component parts of these terms also require further definition.

Qualifying income

1.27 The expression "qualifying income" is further defined by regulations (subs.(6): see State Pension Credit Regulations 2002 (SI 2002/1792) regs 15–18). The claimant's qualifying income includes those elements of their income which arise from contributions to the National Insurance scheme (e.g. the basic state retirement pension and any additional pension such as SERPS) and from their own private provision (e.g. an occupational pension or income from capital). After considerable debate, the government announced that income from work is to be treated in the same way as income from an occupational pension or savings. The term "income" is further defined by ss.15 and 16, and such income must be aggregated with that of any partner (s.5).

Savings credit threshold

1.28 The "savings credit threshold" is "such amount as may be prescribed" (subs.(7)). This threshold for 2023/24 is £174.49 for a single person and £277.12 for a couple (State Pension Credit Regulations 2002 (SI 2002/1792) reg.7(2)). This means that pensioners whose qualifying income is less than this level, even though they have, e.g. a small occupational pension or income from savings, are unable to claim the savings credit. This is likely to be the case with those women who are not entitled to a full retirement pension because of gaps in their contributions records. Thus these women pensioners may claim the guarantee credit to bring their income up to the appropriate minimum guarantee under s.2, but see no extra benefit for their thrift as their combined income from other sources does not exceed the basic retirement pension.

Furthermore, Government policy since the April 2012 uprating has been to increase the pension credit minimum guarantee and to fund this increase for the very poorest pensioners by restricting eligibility to the savings credit. In April 2011 the maximum weekly award of savings credit was £20.52 for a single person and £27.09 for a couple. However, raising the savings credit threshold has the effect of both reducing the numbers of pensioners eligible for the savings credit and reducing

18

the maximum weekly savings credit payable. As a result the maximum savings credit, available to the slightly better off pensioners, has been squeezed further to £15.94 for a single person and £17.84 for a couple for 2023/24.

Amount A

"Amount A" is the *smaller* of the "maximum savings credit" and "a prescribed percentage of the amount by which the claimant's qualifying income exceeds the savings credit threshold" (subs.(4)). The "maximum savings credit" is a prescribed percentage (60 per cent: State Pension Credit Regulations 2002 (SI 2002/1792) reg.7(1)(a)) of the difference between the standard minimum guarantee and the savings credit threshold (subs.(7)). By this stage (if not before) the reader of these annotations might appreciate a simple algebraic notation. An example may therefore assist.

For 2023/24 the maximum savings credit is 60 per cent of the difference between the standard minimum guarantee (£201.05 for a single person, £306.85 for a couple) and the savings credit threshold (£174.49 for a single person and £277.12 for a couple). The difference for a single person is thus £26.56, of which 60 per cent is £15.94. For a couple the difference is £29.73, of which 60 per cent is £17.84. The maximum savings credit is accordingly £15.94 for single claimants and £17.84 for couples.

This figure must then be compared with a second figure representing "a prescribed percentage of the amount by which the claimant's qualifying income exceeds the savings credit threshold". In this context the prescribed percentage is also 60 per cent (State Pension Credit Regulations 2002 (SI 2002/1792) reg.7(1)(b)). The savings credit threshold, which used to be aligned with the basic Category A state retirement pension, is now higher and for 2023/24 is £174.49 for a single person and £277.12 for a couple. The "qualifying income" is to be calculated in accordance with ss.15 and 16 and with regulations under subs.(6) (see also above). If a single claimant's qualifying weekly income is £184.49, comprising the basic state retirement pension and a small occupational pension, then this second figure is £6 (being 60 per cent of the difference between £184.49 and £174.49). As £6 is less than £15.94 in this scenario, Amount A is the former, i.e. £6.

Amount B

Amount B is "a prescribed percentage of the amount (if any) by which the claimant's income exceeds the appropriate minimum guarantee" or, if there is no such excess, nil (subs.(4)). The prescribed percentage in this calculation is 40 per cent in this instance, not 60 per cent (State Pension Credit Regulations 2002 (SI 2002/1792) reg.7(1)(c)). It is also important to note that in this calculation the reference is to the claimant's income, not their qualifying income (which may be a lower figure). The appropriate minimum guarantee is defined by s.2(3) and represents the previous minimum income guarantee for pensioners. Let us assume that in the scenario under discussion the claimant's appropriate minimum guarantee consists of the standard minimum guarantee (i.e. there are no extra sums equivalent to further premiums) and is £201.05 in 2023/24. In this example the claimant's income (£184.49) is clearly less than the appropriate minimum guarantee (£201.05) and so amount B must be nil.

In the hypothetical case set out above, amount A is £6 and amount B is nil. We have already established that the claimant's qualifying income (£184.49) exceeds the savings credit threshold (£174.49) and so subs.(2)(a) is met. As amount A exceeds amount B, the requirement in subs.(2)(b) is also satisfied. Assuming that the claimant (or partner) is over 65, this means that both conditions for the award of the savings credit are fulfilled. The amount of the savings credit in such a case is the amount by which amount A exceeds amount B, namely £6 (subs.(3)).

If, however, a single pensioner's total income and qualifying income in 2023/24 is say £201.05, e.g. comprising the state retirement pension and an occupational pension, then amount A is £15.94. This figure is both the maximum savings credit, i.e. a figure which is both 60 per cent of the difference between the standard

1.29

1.30

minimum guarantee and the savings credit threshold and 60 per cent of the amount by which this individual's qualifying income exceeds the savings credit threshold. In such a scenario the claimant's income is the same as the appropriate minimum guarantee and so amount B is nil. The excess of amount A over amount B is therefore £15.94 and this sum is payable by way of a savings credit under subs.(3). The pensioner's income is thus £216.99 (retirement pension and occupational pension together with £15.94 savings credit), whereas under the previous arrangements there would have been no entitlement to income support, leaving such a pensioner in the same position as a pensioner claimant whose sole income was the state retirement pension.

Once a pensioner's income starts to exceed the appropriate minimum guarantee, then the way in which amounts A and B are defined is such that the claimant's entitlement to the savings credit is gradually withdrawn as their income increases. A further simple example will suffice. Assume that a single pensioner's total weekly income is £212.49, comprising the state retirement pension and an occupational pension. On these facts amount A is the smaller of the maximum savings credit (£15.94) and 60 per cent of the amount by which the claimant's income (£212.49) exceeds the savings credit threshold (£174.49). The latter figure is £22.80 (60 per cent of the difference, being £38.00). As this obviously is more than £15.94, amount A will be £15.94. Amount B is 40 per cent of the amount by which the claimant's income (and again, for the purposes of exposition, we assume that income and qualifying income are identical) exceeds the appropriate minimum guarantee (i.e. £201.05). The difference between those two figures in this example is £11.44, of which 40 per cent is £4.58. Both the conditions set out in subs.(2) are therefore satisfied, and so the claimant's savings credit is the amount by which amount A (£15.94) exceeds amount B (£4.58), namely £11.36. The claimant, on this scenario, thus has a final income of £223.85; £212.49 by way of retirement pension and occupational pension topped up by £11.36 savings credit). Thus, the value of the savings credit will gradually diminish as the claimant's combined income from other sources rises.

Subsection (5)

1.31   Section 2(6) enables the Secretary of State to provide for a different rate for the guarantee credit to be applied in place of the standard minimum guarantee where the claimant (or their partner) remains in hospital for more than 52 weeks. If this same principle were to be carried over into the calculation of the savings credit, the effect would be that amount B would be much higher and might well exceed amount A, which would extinguish any entitlement to the savings credit by virtue of subs.(3). This provision allows regulations to be made to provide for a higher figure to be stipulated in place of the reference to the appropriate minimum guarantee in the definition of amount B. This will reduce amount B and accordingly increase the likelihood that amount A will exceed amount B and so result in the savings credit being payable (State Pension Credit Regulations 2002 (SI 2002/1792) Sch.III para.2).

Subsection (8)

1.32   This power enables a nil amount to be specified as the maximum savings credit for prisoners and members of religious orders who are fully maintained by their orders. This mirrors the power under s.2(9) and reflects the fact that both groups who are currently excluded from income support (see State Pension Credit Regulations 2002 (SI 2002/1792) reg.7(3)).

[¹ Power to limit savings credit for certain mixed-age couples

1.33   **3ZA.**—(1) Regulations may provide that, in prescribed cases, a person who is a member of a mixed-age couple is not entitled to a savings credit.

(2) For example, the regulations could provide that a member of a mixed-age couple is not entitled to a savings credit unless—

(a) the person has been awarded a savings credit with effect from a day before 6 April 2016 and was entitled to a savings credit immediately before that date, and

(b) the person remained entitled to state pension credit at all times since the beginning of 6 April 2016.

(3) In this section "mixed-age couple" means a couple (whenever formed) one member of which had attained pensionable age before 6 April 2016 and the other had not.]

AMENDMENT

1. Pensions Act 2014 s.23 and Sch.12 Pt 3 para.90 (July 7, 2015).

DEFINITIONS

"mixed-age couple"—subs.(3).
"couple"—see s.17(1).
"entitled"—*ibid.*
"pensionable age"—*ibid.*
"prescribed"—*ibid.*
"savings credit—*ibid.*

GENERAL NOTE

The first requirement for entitlement to the savings credit element of pension credit, as originally enacted, was that the claimant (or their partner) was at least 65 (s.3(1)). However, as a result of amendments made by the Pensions Act 2014, there is no longer access to the savings credit element for those claimants reaching state pension age on or after April 6, 2016 unless they are a member of a couple where the other member reached state pension age *before* that date (known as "a mixed-age couple"). This section provides for entitlement to the savings credit to be so restricted and defines what is meant by a "mixed-age couple". The policy justification for this change is that whereas the previous basic state pension was set below the level of the standard minimum guarantee in pension credit, the new state pension is set at a level (just) above that threshold, so removing the problem that the savings credit was designed to address. See further the State Pension Credit Regulations 2002 (SI 2002/1792) reg.7A.   1.34

Exclusions

4.—(1) A claimant is not entitled to state pension credit if he is a member of a [¹ couple] the other member of which is entitled to state pension credit.   1.35

[²(1A) A claimant is not entitled to state pension credit if he is a member of a couple the other member of which has not attained the qualifying age.]

(2) In section 115(1) of the Immigration and Asylum Act 1999 (c.33) (exclusion of certain persons from benefits) in the words preceding paragraph (a), after "Jobseekers Act 1995" insert "or to state pension credit under the State Pension Credit Act 2002".

(3) Where the amount payable by way of state pension credit would (apart from this subsection) be less than a prescribed amount, it shall not be payable except in prescribed circumstances.

AMENDMENTS

1. Civil Partnership Act 2004 s.254 and Sch.24 para.140 (December 5, 2005).
2. Welfare Reform Act 2012 s.31 and Sch.2 para.64 (May 15, 2019).

Definitions

"claimant"—see s.17(1).
"couple"—*ibid.*
"entitled"—*ibid.*
"prescribed"—*ibid.*

General Note

Subsection (1)

1.36 Only one member of a married or unmarried couple is entitled to the pension credit, so preventing double provision from public funds (subs.(1), modelled on SSCBA 1992 s.134(2)).

Subsection (1A)

1.37 As from May 15, 2019, a claimant is not entitled to pension credit (or to pension age housing benefit) if they are a member of the couple and their partner has not reached the qualifying age. Such a couple is known as a "mixed-age couple" (but this term has a different definition to that which continues to apply for the purpose of the savings credit—on which see ss.3(1) and 3ZA). A mixed age couple for the purpose of subs.(1A) may be eligible to claim universal credit instead. However, if the younger partner was entitled to income support, income-based JSA or income-related ESA, then they may be able to keep that entitlement with the other person as their partner. Alternatively, the younger member may assume responsibility for an income-based JSA joint-claim for both of them. Note also that the normal rules on the three-month time limit for claiming pension credit apply (Claims and Payments Regulations, reg.19(2) (and (3)(i)). As a result, claims that were made on or before August 13, 2019 can be backdated to before the rule change so long as the claimant meets the entitlement conditions as they stood on the earlier date. Conversely, advance claims could be made for up to four months before a person reaches the qualifying age, but subject to the changes effective from May 15, 2019 (Claims and Payments Regulations, reg.13D(1)).

There are savings provisions in art.4 of the Welfare Reform Act 2012 (Commencement No. 31 and Savings and Transitional Provisions and Commencement No. 21 and 23 and Transitional and Transitory Provisions (Amendment)) Order 2019 (SI 2019/37)—see Part I above and also Vol.V in this series. The savings provisions mean that the exclusion of mixed-age couples from pension credit entitlement does not apply. So, their effect is that a member of a mixed-age couple who was entitled to pension credit (or housing benefit or both benefits) on May 14, 2019 continues to be so entitled on or after May 15, 2019 (art.4(1)). However, the savings provisions cease to apply on or after May 15, 2019 to a member of a mixed-age couple when that person is not entitled to pension credit (or pension age housing benefit) as part of the same mixed-age couple (art.4(2)). At that point, the usual alternative benefit will be universal credit.

The High Court has ruled that the exclusion of mixed-age couples from pension credit is neither discriminatory nor in breach of the public sector equality duty (PSED): see *R. (on the application of Prichard) v SSWP* [2020] EWHC 1495 (Admin), where the claimant was due to reach state pension age on July 6, 2020, but his wife would not do so for a further six years. As a result of the changes outlined above, the couple would have to continue to claim working-age benefits until 2026 and would be £65,000 worse off than they would have been had the changes not been made. Both the claimant and his wife had serious illnesses and were in receipt of disability benefits. The couple would be classed as a "no-conditionality mixed-age couple" as the claimant was over pension age and his wife received carer's allowance (and so she would not be subject to any work-related requirements). On the application for judicial review, Laing J held that the Secretary of State had had appropriate regard to the relevant equality needs under the PSED (see further Equality Act

2010, s.149). She further held that the policy in question, in its application to no-conditionality mixed-age couples, was not manifestly without reasonable foundation. It followed that "the differential treatment of which the claimant complains is not a breach of article 14 (whether read with article 8 or with A1P1), and, therefore, that the 2019 Order, which provides for the commencement of paragraph 64 of the 2012 Act (and by that route, of section 4(1A) of the SPCA) is not incompatible with the claimant's Convention rights" (at [136]).

Subsection (2)

The general exclusion of persons who are "subject to immigration control" from access to the benefits system is extended to the pension credit scheme (subs.(2); for the limited exceptions to the rule in s.115 of the Immigration and Asylum Act 1999, see the Social Security (Immigration and Asylum) Consequential Amendments Regulations 2000 (SI 2000/636)). On the meaning of "residence" in that context see *CPC/1035/2005*. Commissioner Jacobs held there that "in its ordinary meaning a person does not have to be physically present at a place in order to be resident there. Whether a person is or is not resident in a particular place during a period of physical absence depends on a calculus consisting of the duration and circumstances of the absence" (para.14). On the facts of that case it was held that three prolonged periods of absence in Pakistan— each period being for more than one year—meant that the claimant had not remained "resident" in the UK.   1.38

The concept of a 'person subject to immigration control' may require careful analysis of the basis upon which a person is lawfully in the UK. In *SJ v SSWP (SPC)* [2016] AACR 17 the claimant had originally entered the UK as a sponsored visitor, subject to a maintenance undertaking. She then applied for indefinite leave to remain ("ILR") in the UK as a dependant of her adult daughter, who was settled here. The Home Office ("HO") refused the application. The First-tier Tribunal (Immigration and Asylum Chamber) allowed her appeal under both the Immigration Rules (para.317) and under art.8 ECHR human rights grounds. The HO then granted the claimant ILR. The DWP refused the claimant's subsequent pension credit claim on the basis that she was still in the UK within five years of the original maintenance undertaking. The Upper Tribunal, distinguishing *R(PC) 1/09*, rejected the Appellant's argument that she had ILR on art.8 grounds, free of the maintenance undertaking given under the Rules. It followed she was a person subject to immigration control and not entitled to pension credit.

Note that all British citizens have a right of abode under the Immigration Act 1971. As a result, British citizens cannot be regarded as sponsored immigrants or be barred for that reason from access to public funds such as state pension credit (*R(PC) 2/07*).

Subsection (3)

Provision is also made to set a minimum threshold for payment of the pension credit. Entitlement of less than 10 pence a week is not payable, unless it can be combined with another benefit (subs.(3)), modelled on SSCBA 1992 s.134(4); see State Pension Credit Regulations 2002 (SI 2002/1792) reg.13).   1.39

Aggregation

Income and capital of claimant, spouse, etc.

5.—Where the claimant is a member of a [¹ couple], the income and capital of the other member of the couple shall, except in prescribed circumstances, be treated for the purposes of this Act as income and capital of the claimant.   1.40

AMENDMENT

1. Civil Partnership Act 2004 s.254 and Sch.24 para.140 (December 5, 2005).

DEFINITIONS

"capital"—see s.17(1).
"claimant"—*ibid.*
"couple"—*ibid.*
"income"—*ibid.*
"prescribed"—*ibid.*

GENERAL NOTE

1.41   This section provides for the aggregation of the income and capital resources of the claimant and his or her partner, irrespective of marital status or sexual orientation. This is in line with standard means-tested benefit principles. Indeed, this provision is closely modelled on SSCBA 1992 s.136(1). The definition requires that the partners are living in the same household. For special cases where persons are treated as either being or not being members of the same household, see State Pension Credit Regulations 2002 (SI 2002/1792) reg.5.

Retirement provision

Duty to specify assessed income period [² for pre-6 April 2016 awards]

1.42   **6.**—(1) In any case falling within subsection (3) or (4) [² where the relevant decision takes effect before 6 April 2016], the Secretary of State shall, on the making of the relevant decision, specify a period as the assessed income period, unless prevented by subsection (2).

(2) The Secretary of State is prevented from specifying a period as the assessed income period under subsection (1)—

(a) if the relevant decision takes effect at a time when an assessed income period is in force in the case of the claimant by virtue of a previous application of this section; or

(b) in such other circumstances as may be prescribed.

(3) The first case is where—

(a) the Secretary of State determines the amount of a claimant's income for the purposes of a decision relating to state pension credit;

(b) the decision is a decision under section 8(1), 9 or 10 of the Social Security Act 1998 (c.14) (decisions on claims etc, and decisions revising or superseding decisions);

(c) the decision takes effect on or after—

(i) the day on which the claimant attains the age of 65; or

(ii) if earlier, in a case where the claimant is a member of a [¹ couple], the day on which the other member of the couple attains that age; and

(d) the decision is not to the effect that the claimant is not entitled to state pension credit.

(4) The second case is where—

(a) the amount of the claimant's income is determined on, or for the purposes of, an appeal against a decision that the claimant is not entitled to state pension credit;

24

(b) on the appeal, it is decided that the claimant is entitled to state pension credit; and

(c) the decision takes effect as mentioned in subsection (3)(c).

(5) In this section "the relevant decision" means—

(a) so far as relating to the first case, the decision mentioned in subsection (3)(a);

(b) so far as relating to the second case, the decision on appeal mentioned in subsection (4)(b).

(6) This section is subject to section 9.

(7) This section and sections 7 to 10 shall be construed as one.

AMENDMENTS

1. Civil Partnership Act 2004 s.254 and Sch.24 para.140 (December 5, 2005).
2. Pensions Act 2014 s.28(1) (April 6, 2016).

DEFINITIONS

"assessed income period"—see s.17(1).
"claimant"—*ibid.*
"couple"—*ibid.*
"entitled"—*ibid.*
"income"—*ibid.*
"prescribed"—*ibid.*
"the relevant decision"—see subs.(5).

GENERAL NOTE

When making a decision before April 2016 that a person is entitled to the pension credit, the Secretary of State was required to specify an "assessed income period" in relation to the claimant (subs.(1)). Such a decision could be made in the first instance by the Secretary of State (subs.(3)) or following an appeal (subs.(4)). The Secretary of State was prevented from so doing where an assessed income period was currently in force (subs.(2)(a)). For circumstances prescribed under subs.(2)(b), see State Pension Credit Regulations 2002 (SI 2002/1792) reg.10(1). The significance of the "assessed income period" was that it was used as the basis for a long-term award of the pension credit (see s.7). It should also be noted that this section was subject to s.9 (see subs.(6)), which specifies that the "assessed income period" was normally five years, and that ss.7–10 "shall be construed as one" (subs (7)). 1.43

Note, however, that now s.28 of the Pensions Act 2014 is in force assessed income periods are being phased out as from April 2016. As a result, any change in retirement income will in future need to be reported to the Department when it occurs, triggering a review and change in benefit award where appropriate. Thus s.28(3) expressly provides that "Regulations under section 9(5) of the State Pension Credit Act 2002 may in particular be made for the purpose of phasing out, on or after 6 April 2016, any remaining assessed income period that is 5 years or shorter than 5 years". See now the amendments to reg.12 of the State Pension Credit Regulations 2002 (SI 2002/1792).

Fixing of claimant's retirement provision for assessed income period

7.—(1) This section applies where, pursuant to section 6(1), the Secretary of State on the making of the relevant decision specifies a period as the assessed income period. 1.44

(2) This section has effect for the purpose of determining, as at any time in the assessed income period—

(a) the claimant's entitlement to state pension credit; or

(b) the amount of state pension credit to which the claimant is entitled.

(3) Where the claimant's income, as determined for the purposes of the relevant decision, includes an amount (the "assessed amount") in respect of an element of the claimant's retirement provision, the amount of that element as at any time in the assessed income period shall be taken to be the assessed amount as for the time being varied in accordance with regulations under subsection (4).

(4) The assessed amount shall be deemed, except in prescribed circumstances—

(a) to increase, or

(b) in the case of income from capital, to increase or decrease,

on such date or dates and by such amounts as may be prescribed.

(5) Where it is determined for the purposes of the relevant decision that the claimant's income does not include any, or any further, elements of retirement provision, the claimant's income throughout the assessed income period shall be taken not to include those elements.

(6) For the purposes of this Act "retirement provision" means income of any of the following descriptions—

(a) retirement pension income, other than benefit under [² Part 1 of the Pensions Act 2014 or] the Contributions and Benefits Act;

(b) income from annuity contracts (other than retirement pension income);

(c) income from capital;

and an "element" of a person's retirement provision is income of any of those descriptions from a particular source;

[¹ (d) PPF periodic payments.]

(7) For the purposes of this section, regulations may make provision—

(a) for treating income of any particular description as income of another description; or

(b) for treating income from different sources as income from the same source.

(8) Nothing in subsections (3) to (5) prevents the revision under section 9 of the Social Security Act 1998 (c.14) of the relevant decision or of any earlier or later decision under section 10 of that Act.

(9) This section is subject to section 8.

AMENDMENTS

1. Pensions Act 2004 (PPF Payments and FAS Payments) (Consequential Provisions) Order 2006 (SI 2006/343) art.3(1) (February 14, 2006).

2. Pensions Act 2014 s.23 and Sch.12 Pt 1 paras 42 and 43 (April 6, 2016).

DEFINITIONS

"assessed amount"—see subs.(3).

"assessed income period"—see s.17(1).

"capital"—*ibid.*

"claimant"—*ibid.*

"Contributions and Benefits Act"—*ibid.*

"element"—see subs.(6) and s.17(1).

"entitled"—see s.17(1).

"income"—*ibid.*

"regulations"—*ibid.*
"relevant decision"—see s.6(5).
"retirement pension income"—see ss.16 and 17(1).
"retirement provision"—see s.7(6) and s.17(1).

GENERAL NOTE

This provision is the key to understanding how the pension credit scheme funda-   **1.45**
mentally differs from other means-tested benefits in terms of the usual requirement
to report changes in income during the period of an award. Once the Secretary of
State has specified the "assessed income period" under s.6 (which is typically five
years: s.9(1)), this has the effect of fixing the "assessed amount" derived from the
claimant's "retirement provision" (effectively their income: see subs.(6)) for the duration of that period (subs.(3)). This assessed amount is subject to deemed increases or
decreases (reflecting, e.g. the terms of a claimant's pension arrangements, such as a
cost-of-living increase) (subs.(4); for further detail on this, see State Pension Credit
Regulations 2002 (SI 2002/1792) reg.10(2)–(7)). Any further elements of retirement
provision which are acquired at some later date within the assessed income period are
then disregarded (subs.(5)). Such changes accordingly need not be reported during
the lifetime of the award. Even if the changes deemed under subs.(4) work in favour
of the claimant (i.e. their actual increase is more than the deemed increase), the effect
of subs.(3) is that there is no overpayment and no need to report the change.

The implications of this radical change were spelt out by Mr Ian McCartney MP,
the then Minster for Pensions:

"Let us be clear about this: if a pensioner wins the lottery in the second week of
his or her assessed income period, the increase in capital, be it £10 or £1 million,
will not be reflected in the pension credit entitlement until the end of the assessed
income period—in four years and 50 weeks' time . . . We can live with ignoring a
few individuals' good fortune for the sake of simplification for the overwhelming
majority of pensioners". (Standing Committee A, cols 166 and 184.)

But if the claimant actually loses out, in that the deemed increase is more than their
actual increase, a new decision can be sought (s.8(1)). The normal powers to effect a
revision of an initial decision under s.9 of the SSA 1998 remain in place (subs.(8)).

The Minister's statement to the Standing Committee about the lottery winner was   **1.46**
considered by Commissioner Levenson in *CPC/0206/2005*. The claimant disclosed
in her claim that she was moving into sheltered accommodation and her house was
on the market. An official decided that its value should be disregarded for the time
being, but noted that this decision would change in the event of sale. However,
the Secretary of State then awarded pension credit for a five-year assessed income
period. Later the claimant reported that her house had been sold. Commissioner
Levenson observed that the Minister's statement did not cover a case such as this,
where the issue was "what the Secretary of State should do if it is known that a large
amount of capital is likely to be on its way" (para.10). The Commissioner held that
the original decision should be revised for official error and replaced with an award
which did not specify an assessed income period ("AIP"). That decision was then
subject to supersession for the change of circumstances in the receipt of the proceeds of sale. According to the Commissioner:

"23. It seems to me that the concept of 'error' involves more than merely taking a
decision that another decision maker with the same information would not take,
but is not limited to (although it includes, subject to the statutory exceptions) a
public law or any other error of law. Other than that it is not helpful (and could be
misleading) to go beyond the words of the regulation. On the facts of the present
case, though, I take the view that no Secretary of State or decision maker acting
reasonably could have imposed a 5 year AIP. It was already known that number
8 was up for sale and that it would realise a sum of several tens of thousands of

pounds (even if the exact amount was not known) and a view had already been taken that the progress of the sale should be monitored. In these respects the position was very different from that of a lottery winner who, at the time of the decision on the claim, had done no more than buy a ticket."

See also the decision of Commissioner Rowland in *CPC/1928/2005*, discussed in the note to s.9, below.

Fresh determinations increasing claimant's entitlement

1.47   **8.**—(1) Subsections (3) to (5) of section 7 do not prevent the making of fresh determinations as to the elements, or any of the elements, or the amount of any of the elements, of the claimant's retirement provision as at any time during the assessed income period, if—

    (a) the fresh determinations are for the purpose of making a decision under section 10 of the Social Security Act 1998 (c.14) ("the new decision");

    (b) the new decision increases the amount of state pension credit to which the claimant is entitled; and

    (c) the increase is in whole or in part the result of the fresh determinations (taken as a whole).

(2) The conditions in paragraphs (b) and (c) of subsection (1) shall be taken to be satisfied if—

    (a) the new decision reduces the amount of state pension credit to which the claimant is entitled; but

    (b) the reduction is less than it would have been apart from the fresh determinations (taken as a whole).

(3) Where a fresh determination is made by virtue of subsection (1), then, as respects the part of the assessed income period that begins with the day on which the new decision takes effect, subsections (3) to (5) of section 7 shall have effect in accordance with the fresh determination, instead of the determination which it replaces, but as if—

    (a) the fresh determination were (and the determination which it replaces were not) a determination for the purposes of the relevant decision;

    (b) any assessed amount resulting from the fresh determination were not subject to variation under subsection (4) of that section at any time before the day on which the new decision takes effect; and

    (c) the claimant's income, as determined for the purposes of the relevant decision, were constituted accordingly.

DEFINITIONS

    "assessed income period"—see ss.9(1) and 17(1).
    "claimant"—see s.17(1).
    "element"—*ibid.*
    "entitled"—*ibid.*
    "income"—*ibid.*
    "retirement provision"—see ss.7(6) and 17(1).

GENERAL NOTE

1.48   The presumption under s.7 is that the assessment of the claimant's "retirement provision" will remain unchanged during the typical five-year award of pension credit, subject to the usual uprating. However, a fresh determination can be made by way of a supersession decision within the assessed income period to increase the claimant's entitlement. This will not affect the assessed income period (subs.(1)). The assessed income period can also continue where the effect of the supersession decision is to reduce entitlement to the pension credit, but the reduction is less than it would otherwise have been because of the recalculation of some other element of the claimant's income (subs.(2)). Where a supersession decision is made, the remaining elements of the retirement provision are treated as unchanged for the rest of the assessed income period (subs.(3)). See also State Pension Credit Regulations 2002 (SI 2002/1792) reg.11.

Duration of assessed income period

9.—[² (1) An assessed income period shall (subject to the following subsections) be—

    (a) in the case of a claimant who is under the age of 75 on the day on which the relevant decision takes effect, the period of 5 years beginning with that day;

    (b) in the case of a claimant who is aged 75 or over on that day, an indefinite period beginning with that day.]

(2) If the Secretary of State considers that the particulars of the claimant's retirement provision as determined for the purposes of the relevant decision are not likely, after taking account of any assumed variations under subsection (3), to be typical of the claimant's retirement provision throughout the period of 12 months beginning with the day on which that decision takes effect—

    (a) he need not specify a period under section 6(1); and

    (b) if he does so, [² shall specify a period that is shorter than 5 years] (but beginning as mentioned in subsection (1)).

(3) It shall be assumed for the purposes of subsection (2) that the same variations fall to be made in relation to the amount of an element of the claimant's retirement provision as determined for the purposes of the relevant decision as would fall to be made under section 7(4) if an assessed income period were to be specified in accordance with subsection (1).

(4) An assessed income period shall, except in prescribed circumstances, end at any time at which—

    (a) the claimant becomes a member of a [¹ couple];

    (b) the claimant ceases to be a member of a [¹ couple];

    (c) the claimant attains the age of 65; or

    (d) in a case where the claimant is a member of a [¹ couple], the other member of the couple attains the age of 65.

(5) Regulations may prescribe further times at which, or circumstances in which, an assessed income period shall end.

[² (6) Where—

    (a) an assessed income period is brought to an end [³, on or after 6 April 2009 but before 6 April 2014,] by the expiry of a period of 5 years or more, and

    (b) the claimant is aged 80 or over at that time,

the assessed income period shall be treated as not ending at that time but, subject to subsection (4) and provision made under subsection (5), as continuing indefinitely.]

AMENDMENTS

    1. Civil Partnership Act 2004 s.254 and Sch.24 para.140 (December 5, 2005).

    2. Pensions Act 2008 s.105 (April 6, 2009).

    3. Pensions Act 2014, s.29(2)(b) (May 14, 2014).

1.49

DEFINITIONS

"assessed income period"—see subs.(1) and s.17(1).
"claimant"—see s.17(1).
"couple"—*ibid.*
"element"—*ibid.*
"prescribed"—*ibid.*
"regulations"—see s.17(1).
"relevant decision"—see s.6(5).
"retirement provision"—see ss.7(6) and 17(1).

GENERAL NOTE

1.50   The normal rule is that the "assessed income period" for the purposes of an award of the pension credit is five years (subs.(1)). Throughout this period the claimant's "retirement provision" (see s.7), i.e. their standard income during retirement, is treated as remaining the same, subject only to uprating in line with inflation. This is in contrast to the requirement that claimants of other means-tested benefits report any changes in income which affect their benefit entitlement. However, if the Secretary of State takes the view that the claimant's retirement provision as assessed is not likely to be typical of their actual income over the next 12 months, a period shorter than five years may be specified (subs.(2)). Foreseeable increases in income on retirement (e.g. in line with inflation) are not treated as making the assessment atypical (subs.(3)). Whatever its initial duration, an assessed income period terminates if the claimant becomes a member of a couple, separates from their partner or reaches 65 (or any partner does so) (subs.(4)). Further circumstances which will result in the termination of an assessed income period, as prescribed under subs.(5), are specified in the State Pension Credit Regulations 2002 (SI 2002/1792) reg.12.

In *CPC/1928/2005* the claimant applied for pension credit, having moved into rented property with her husband and having put their house up for sale. Pension credit was awarded with a seven-year assessed income period and without taking account of the capital value of the house. On April 22, 2004 the claimant's husband moved permanently to a care home. On May 19, 2004 the couple received the proceeds of sale in respect of their former home. The Secretary of State became aware of these facts later made a supersession decision on the basis that the claimant should be treated as a single person from April 22, 2004 and should be regarded as having additional capital representing half the proceeds of sale as from May 19, 2004. The tribunal disallowed the claimant's appeal. Commissioner Rowland, dismissing the claimant's further appeal, held that the tribunal had reached the correct conclusion, albeit for the wrong reasons. On these facts, with sale to be anticipated within a few months, no assessed income period should have been set. Moreover, "Where a substantial sum is expected on an uncertain date, not setting an assessed income period will generally be preferable to setting a short one, in the absence of other considerations such as likely minor variations of other income that the decision-maker considers should be ignored" (para.11). See also the decision of Commissioner Levenson in *CPC/0206/2005*, discussed in the note to s.7, above.

Subsection (5)

1.51   Note that now s.28(3) of the Pensions Act 2014 provides that regulations made under this provision "may in particular be made for the purpose of phasing out, on or after 6 April 2016, any remaining assessed income period that is 5 years or shorter than 5 years."

Subsection (6)

1.52   Subsection (6) was a transitional provision and was originally thought to be necessary only until April 6, 2014. It was therefore repealed from that date by the Pensions Act 2008 (ss.105(6) and 149(2)(c) and (4)). That repeal left some doubt about whether existing assessed income periods under subs.(6) would remain in place after April 6, 2014. Section 29 of the Pensions Act 2014 was therefore enacted to remove the doubt by ensuring that existing indefinite assessed income periods governed by s.9(6) remained in place on or after that date. Section 29(2)(a) accordingly repealed s.105(6) of the Pensions Act 2008 and treated it as never having had effect while s.29(2)(b) amended the restored version of subs.(6) in the terms indicated in the statutory text above.

Effect of variations under section 7(4)

10.—(1) This section applies where—   1.53
  (a) an assessed income period is in force; and
  (b) there is an alteration in an element of the claimant's retirement provision which affects the computation of the amount of state pension credit to which the claimant is entitled.
(2) Where, as a result of the alteration, the amount of state pension credit to which the claimant is entitled is increased or reduced, then, as from the commencing date, the amount of state pension credit payable in the case of the claimant shall be the increased or reduced amount, without any further decision of the Secretary of State (and the award of state pension credit shall have effect accordingly).
(3) Where, notwithstanding the alteration, the claimant continues on and after the commencing date to be entitled to the same amount of state pension credit as before, the award shall continue in force accordingly.
(4) In this section—
"alteration" means a variation in the amount of an element of the claimant's retirement provision in accordance with regulations under section 7(4);
"commencing date", in relation to an alteration, means the date on which the alteration comes into force.

DEFINITIONS

"alteration"—see subs.(4).
"assessed income period"—see s.17(1).
"claimant"—*ibid.*
"commencing date"—see subs.(4).
"element"—see s.17(1).
"entitled"—*ibid.*
"regulations"—*ibid.*
"retirement provision"—*ibid.*

GENERAL NOTE

Section 7(4) provides for the assessed amount of a claimant's retirement provi-   1.54
sion to be increased or decreased during the assessed income period. This provision deals with the consequences of such a change (subs.(1)). Subsection (2) allows the amount of the pension credit payable to be increased or decreased accordingly without the need for a further decision by the Secretary of State. If the level of the award remains the same, the award continues in force unaffected (subs.(3)). See also State Pension Credit Regulations 2002 (SI 2002/1792) reg.11.

Miscellaneous and supplementary

Administration

11.—Schedule 1 shall have effect and in that Schedule—   1.55

Part 1 makes amendments to Part 1 of the Administration Act (claims for, and payments and general administration of, benefit);

Part 2 makes amendments to Part 1 of the Social Security Act 1998 (c.14) (decisions and appeals); and

Part 3 makes miscellaneous and supplementary provision.

<small>DEFINITION</small>

"the Administration Act"—see s.17(1).

<small>GENERAL NOTE</small>

1.56 This section introduces Sch.1 to the Act. This makes amendments to the SSAA 1992 and the SSA 1998 which are designed to apply the normal social security rules for claims, decisions and appeals to the state pension credit scheme.

Polygamous marriages

1.57 **12.**—(1) This section applies to any case where—

(a) a person ("the person in question") is a husband or wife by virtue of a marriage entered into under a law which permits polygamy;

(b) either party to the marriage has for the time being any spouse additional to the other party; and

(c) the person in question, the other party to the marriage and the additional spouse are members of the same household.

(2) Regulations under this section may make provision—

(a) as to the entitlement of the person in question to state pension credit;

(b) as to any guarantee credit or savings credit to which that person is entitled;

(c) for prescribing a different amount as the standard minimum guarantee in the case of the person in question;

(d) in a case where the person in question is the claimant, for treating the income and capital of the other party and of the additional spouse as income and capital of the person in question.

(3) Any such regulations may provide—

(a) that prescribed provisions shall apply instead of prescribed provisions of this Act; or

(b) that prescribed provisions of this Act shall not apply or shall apply subject to prescribed modifications or adaptations.

(4) Except in relation to the amount of the standard minimum guarantee, any power to prescribe amounts by virtue of this section includes power to prescribe nil as an amount.

<small>DEFINITIONS</small>

"capital"—see s.17(1).
"claimant"—*ibid.*
"entitled"—*ibid.*
"guarantee credit"—*ibid.*
"income"—*ibid.*
"prescribed"—*ibid.*
"regulations"—*ibid.*
"savings credit"—*ibid.*
"standard minimum guarantee"—*ibid.*

GENERAL NOTE

This section makes special provision for claimants who are parties to polygamous marriages. See also State Pension Credit Regulations 2002 (SI 2002/1792) reg.8 and Sch.III para.1.

1.58

Transitional provisions

13.—(1) The Secretary of State may by regulations make such transitional provision, consequential provision or savings as he considers necessary or expedient for the purposes of, or in connection with—

1.59

(a) the coming into force of any of the state pension credit provisions of this Act; or

(b) the operation of any enactment repealed or amended by any of those provisions during any period when the repeal or amendment is not wholly in force.

(2) The provision that may be made by regulations under this section includes in particular—

(a) provision for a person who attains or has attained the qualifying age on or before the appointed day and who immediately before that day is entitled to income support—

(i) to be treated as having been awarded on, and with effect as from, that day state pension credit of an amount specified in or determined in accordance with the regulations; or

(ii) to be treated as having made a claim for state pension credit; and

(b) provision for an assessed income period under section 6 of such length as may be specified in or determined in accordance with the regulations (which may be longer than the maximum period provided for by section 9(1)) to have effect in the case of a person who attains or has attained the qualifying age on or before the appointed day.

(3) In this section—

"the appointed day" means such day as the Secretary of State may by order appoint;

"the state pension credit provisions of this Act" means this Act other than section 18.

DEFINITIONS

"the appointed day"—see subs.(3).
"the qualifying age"—see s.1(6).
"regulations"—see s.17(1).
"the state pension credit provisions of this Act"—see subs.(3).

GENERAL NOTE

This section enables regulations to be made governing the transitional arrangements for the introduction of the pension credit. The scheme came into force on October 6, 2003 (the "appointed day": see State Pension Credit Act 2002 (Commencement No.5) and Appointed Day Order 2003 (SI 2003/1766 (c.75)) and all claims made before October 2004 were backdated to October 2003 (see State Pension Credit (Consequential, Transitional and Miscellaneous Provisions) Regulations 2002 (SI 2002/3019 reg.38(4))).

For the text of regs 36–38 and full commentary on reg.38, see the 2012/13 edition of this Volume, paras 4.170–4.173.

1.60

Minor and consequential amendments

1.61   **14.**—Schedule 2 (which makes minor and consequential amendments relating to state pension credit) shall have effect.

GENERAL NOTE

1.62   This section introduces Sch.2 to the Act, which makes a series of minor and consequential amendments to the SSCBA 1992, the SSAA 1992 and other statutes.

Interpretation of state pension credit provisions

Income and capital

1.63   **15.**—(1) In this Act "income" means income of any of the following descriptions—
  (a) earnings;
  (b) working tax credit;
  (c) retirement pension income;
  (d) income from annuity contracts (other than retirement pension income);
  (e) prescribed social security benefits (other than retirement pension income and state pension credit);
  (f) foreign social security benefits of any prescribed description;
  (g) a war disablement pension or war widow's or widower's pension;
  (h) a foreign war disablement pension or foreign war widow's or widower's pension;
  (i) income from capital;
  (j) income of any prescribed description.
  (2) Regulations may provide that a person's capital shall be deemed to yield him income at a prescribed rate.
  (3) Income and capital shall be calculated or estimated in such manner as may be prescribed.
  (4) A person's income in respect of any period shall be calculated in accordance with prescribed rules.
  (5) The rules may provide for the calculation to be made by reference to an average over a period (which need not consist of or include the whole or any part of the period concerned).
  (6) Circumstances may be prescribed in which—
  (a) a person is treated as possessing capital or income which he does not possess;
  (b) capital or income which a person does possess is to be disregarded;
  (c) income is to be treated as capital; or
  (d) capital is to be treated as income.
  (7) Subsections (2) to (6) have effect for the purposes of this Act.

DEFINITIONS

  "capital"—see s.17(1).
  "earnings"—*ibid.*
  "foreign social security benefits"—*ibid.*
  "foreign war disablement pension"—*ibid.*
  "foreign war widow's or widower's pension"—*ibid.*
  "income"—see subs.(1).

"prescribed"—see s.17(1).
"regulations"—*ibid.*
"retirement pension income"—see s.16(1).
"social security benefits"—see s.17(1).
"war disablement pension"—*ibid.*
"war widow's or widower's pension"—*ibid.*
"working tax credit"—*ibid.*

GENERAL NOTE

The term "income" is given a very broad definition in subs.(1) for the purposes of the pension credit scheme. In particular, the Secretary of State has the power under subs.(1)(e) to specify which social security benefits count as income (see State Pension Credit Regulations 2002 (SI 2002/1792) reg.15(1), (3) and (4); and for foreign social security benefits see ibid., reg.15(2)). The Secretary of State may also extend the definition of income to include "income of any prescribed description" (subs.(1)(j)). This latter power has been used to include less commonly found forms of income that some pensioners have (e.g. maintenance payments); see State Pension Credit Regulations 2002 (SI 2002/1792 reg.15(5)). However, neither s.15 nor reg.15 seem to include as assessable income for state pension credit purposes regular payments of income from a benevolent institution (e.g. the Royal British Legion) or from a family member: see *AMS v SSWP (PC) (final decision)* [2017] UKUT 381 (AAC); [2018] AACR 27 at para.13. In *R(PC)3/08* the Commissioner ruled that the 2002 Act adopts the ordinary meanings of income and capital.

1.64

Relevant authorities on the meaning of income (*Leeves v Chief Adjudication Officer (R(IS) 5/99), R(IS) 4/01, Chandler v Secretary of State for Work and Pensions* [2007] EWCA Civ 1211 and *CH/1672/2007* were analysed by Judge Farbey QC in *BL v SSWP (SPC)* [2018] UKUT 4 (AAC), where she drew the following conclusions:

"30. From these authorities, the following propositions may be derived. The term 'income' in sections 15 and 16 of the State Pension Credit Act 2002 should be given its natural and ordinary meaning. Any qualification of, or restriction on, the ordinary meaning may be justified only by reference to the particular statutory context. The meaning is not to be determined by reference to other welfare benefits in other legislative contexts. Case law relating to other benefits may not, therefore, provide the correct approach.
31. Income includes not only money paid to a recipient but also money paid to a person's order or instruction. There is no principled reason to distinguish between money paid directly by A to C at B's instruction and money paid by A to B which B then forwards to C. In each case, B is in control of the money and directs or chooses where it goes.
32. It will generally be useful to consider not only whether a claimant has taken possession of funds but also whether he has practical power to treat the funds as his income. Following *Leeves*, above, money which is subject to a certain and immediate obligation of repayment will not count as income.
33. Cases will be fact sensitive: the tribunal must consider all relevant evidence relating to the funds in question and the precise nature of the payment or transaction in question. If the tribunal has applied the meaning of income in its ordinary sense and based its decision on relevant evidence, its decision is not likely to be impugned by the Upper Tribunal whose jurisdiction is limited to errors of law."

In *BL v SSWP (SPC)* itself the appeal related to money which the claimant had paid to his wife from his Standard Life pension. The couple had separated in 1991. Under a written separation agreement drawn up by lawyers, the claimant had undertaken to make monthly maintenance payments to his wife. From 2001 he directed monthly payments to her from the Standard Life pension. Judge Farbey QC upheld the FTT's finding that the payments remained the claimant's income within s.15(1) as they were under his control.

1.65   There is, however, no upper capital limit for the purposes of entitlement to the pension credit. Instead, capital is deemed, by regulations made under subs.(2), to have an assumed rate of return for the purposes of assessing entitlement to both forms of the pension credit. This rate is set at £1 for every £500 (or part thereof) in excess of the threshold of £10,000: see State Pension Credit Regulations 2002 (SI 2002/1792) reg.15(6)–(8). Any capital below this threshold is disregarded. The net result is that pensioners are treated markedly more favourably than those persons of working age in receipt of means-tested benefits, who are subject both to the capital rule and to a harsher tariff income rule on capital below that threshold.

Note that for the purposes of claiming housing benefit, pension credit claimants receiving the guarantee credit have the whole of their capital and income disregarded (see the Housing Benefit (Persons who have attained the qualifying age for state pension credit) Regulations 2006 (SI 2006/214) reg.26). For claimants receiving solely the savings credit, the local authority is required to use the DWP's calculations for claimants' capital and income, see *ibid.*, reg.27. For these reasons it is important that a tribunal reaching a decision on the amount of capital or income in a pension credit case should specify the amount of such capital or income in the Decision Notice.

The extensive powers contained in subss.(3)–(6) replicate those which apply to means-tested benefits by virtue of SSCBA 1992 ss.136(3)–(5). In *R(PC)3/08* the Commissioner observed that the powers in subs.(6) indicate "that income and capital are separate and mutually exclusive categories (even if the boundary line might sometimes be fuzzy)" (para.21).

Retirement pension income

1.66   **16.**—(1) In this Act "retirement pension income" means any of the following—

[⁶ (za) a state pension under Part 1 of the Pensions Act 2014 or under any provision in Northern Ireland which corresponds to that Part;]

(a) a Category A or Category B retirement pension payable under sections 43 to 55 of—
   (i) the Contributions and Benefits Act; or
   (ii) the Social Security Contributions and Benefits (Northern Ireland) Act 1992 (c.7);

[⁷ (b) a shared additional pension payable under—
   (i) section 55A of either of those Acts, or
   (ii) section 55AA of the Contributions and Benefits Act or any corresponding provision under the law of Northern Ireland;]

(c) graduated retirement benefit payable under section 62 of either of those Acts;

(d) a Category C or Category D retirement pension payable under section 78 of either of those Acts;

(e) age addition payable under section 79 of either of those Acts;

(f) income from an occupational pension scheme or a personal pension scheme;

(g) income from an overseas arrangement;

(h) income from a retirement annuity contract;

(i) income from annuities or insurance policies purchased or transferred for the purpose of giving effect to rights under a personal pension scheme or an overseas arrangement;

(j) income from annuities purchased or entered into for the purpose of discharging liability under—
   (i) section 29(1)(b) of the Welfare Reform and Pensions Act 1999 (c.30) (pension credits on divorce); or

    (ii) Article 26(1)(b) of the Welfare Reform and Pensions (Northern Ireland) Order 1999 (SI 1999/3147 (NI 11)) (corresponding provision for Northern Ireland).

[¹ [⁵ (k) any sum payable by way of pension under section 5 of the Civil List Act 1837 or section 7 of the Civil List Act 1952;]

[² (l) any payment, other than a payment ordered by a court or made in settlement of a claim, made by or on behalf of a former employer of a person on account of the early retirement of that person on grounds of ill-health or disability];

[³ (m) any payment made at regular intervals under an equity release scheme];

[⁴ (n) any payment made under the Financial Assistance Scheme Regulations 2005].

(2) The Secretary of State may by regulations amend subsection (1); and any such regulations may—

    (a) add to or vary the descriptions of income for the time being listed in that subsection; or

    (b) remove any such description from that subsection.

(3) In this section—

"overseas arrangement" has the meaning given by section 181(1) of the Pension Schemes Act 1993 (c.48);

"retirement annuity contract" means a contract or scheme approved under Chapter 3 of Part 14 of the Income and Corporation Taxes Act 1988 (c.1).

AMENDMENTS

    1. State Pension Credit Regulations 2002 (SI 2002/1792) reg.16 (October 6, 2003).

    2. State Pension Credit (Consequential, Transitional and Miscellaneous Provisions) (No.2) Regulations 2002 (SI 2002/3197) reg.2 and Sch. para.3 (October 6, 2003).

    3. Social Security (Housing Benefit, Council Tax Benefit, State Pension Credit and Miscellaneous Amendments) Regulations 2004 (SI 2004/2327) reg.7(4) (October 4, 2004).

    4. State Pension Credit (Amendment) Regulations 2005 (SI 2005/3205) reg.2(3) (December 18, 2005).

    5. Sovereign Grant Act 2011 s.14 and Sch.1 para.32 (April 1, 2012).

    6. Pensions Act 2014 s.23 and Sch.12 Pt 1 paras.42 and 44 (April 6, 2016).

    7. Pensions Act 2014 s.15 and Sch.11 para.15 (April 6, 2016).

DEFINITIONS

"the Contribution and Benefits Act"—see s.17(1).
"occupational pension scheme"—*ibid.*
"overseas arrangement"—see subs.(3).
"personal pension scheme"—*ibid.*
"regulations"—see s.17(1).
"retirement annuity contract"—see subs.(3).

GENERAL NOTE

    This section provides a comprehensive definition of the term "retirement pension income" for the purposes of this Act (subs.(1)). The extensive list includes both social security benefits paid to pensioners as well as various forms of private income received by pensioners. The Secretary of State may by regulations add to, vary or remove any of the descriptions so listed (subs.(2); see further State

1.67

Pension Credit Regulations 2002 (SI 2002/1792) reg.16). This power provides the necessary flexibility to accommodate other social security benefits or private financial products for pensioners that may become available in the future. But it also includes the power to remove matters listed in subs.(1).

Judge Williams analysed the definition of "overseas arrangement" in subs.(3) in *SSWP v JK* [2009] UKUT 55 (AAC) and rejected the Secretary of State's argument that all foreign state pensions should necessarily be taken into account for the purposes of the assessed income period. On the facts, the claimant's Irish state pension was an "overseas arrangement" and had therefore to be left out of account. The remedy for the Secretary of State to deal with any perceived unfairness was to set either no assessed income period or a short one. However, reg.6 of the Social Security (Miscellaneous Amendments) (No.2) Regulations 2010 (SI 2010/641) amended the relevant regulations with effect from April 13, 2010 with the intention of reversing the effect of *SSWP v JK*.

Other interpretation provisions

1.68 **17.**—(1) In this Act—

"the Administration Act" means the Social Security Administration Act 1992 (c.5);

"assessed income period" shall be construed in accordance with sections 6 and 9;

"appropriate minimum guarantee" shall be construed in accordance with section 2(3);

"capital" shall be construed in accordance with section 15;

"claimant" means a claimant for state pension credit;

"the Contributions and Benefits Act" means the Social Security Contributions and Benefits Act 1992 (c.4);

[5 "couple" means—

    (a) two people who are married to, or civil partners of, each other and are members of the same household; or

    (b) two people who are not married to, or civil partners of, each other but are living together [6 as if they were a married couple or civil partners] otherwise than in prescribed circumstances;]

"earnings" has the same meaning as in Parts 1 to 5 of the Contributions and Benefits Act (see sections 3(1) and 112, and the definition of "employment" in section 122, of that Act);

"element", in relation to the claimant's retirement provision, shall be construed in accordance with section 7(6);

"entitled", in relation to state pension credit, shall be construed in accordance with—

    (a) this Act,

    (b) section 1 of the Administration Act (entitlement to be dependent on making of claim, etc.), and

    (c) section 27 of the Social Security Act 1998 (c.14) (restrictions on entitlement to benefit in certain cases of error),

(and, in relation to any other benefit within the meaning of section 1 of the Administration Act or section 27 of the Social Security Act 1998, in accordance with that section or (as the case may be) both of those sections in addition to any other conditions relating to that benefit);

"foreign social security benefit" means any benefit, allowance or other payment which is paid under the law of a country outside the United Kingdom and is in the nature of social security;

"foreign war disablement pension" means any retired pay, pension, allowance or similar payment granted by the government of a country outside the United Kingdom—

(a) in respect of disablement arising from forces' service or war injury; or

(b) corresponding in nature to any retired pay or pension to which [¹section 641 of the Income Tax (Earnings and Pensions) Act 2003] applies;

"foreign war widow's or widower's pension" means any pension, allowance or similar payment granted to a [² widow, widower or surviving civil partner] by the government of a country outside the United Kingdom—

(a) in respect of a death due to forces' service or war injury; or

(b) corresponding in nature to a pension or allowance for a [² widow, widower or surviving civil partner] under any scheme mentioned in [¹section 641(1)(e) or (f) of the Income Tax (Earnings and Pensions) Act 2003];

"guarantee credit" shall be construed in accordance with sections 1 and 2;

"income" shall be construed in accordance with section 15;

[² . . .]

"occupational pension scheme" has the meaning given by section 1 of the Pension Schemes Act 1993 (c.48);

"pensionable age" has the meaning given by the rules in paragraph 1 of Schedule 4 to the Pensions Act 1995 (c.26) (equalisation of pensionable ages for men and women);

"personal pension scheme" means a personal pension scheme—

(a) as defined in section 1 of the Pension Schemes Act 1993; or

(b) as defined in section 1 of the Pension Schemes (Northern Ireland) Act 1993 (c.49);

[⁴ "PPF periodic payments" means—

(a) any periodic compensation payments made in relation to a person, payable under the pension compensation provisions as specified in section 162(2) of the Pensions Act 2004 or Article 146(2) of the Pensions (Northern Ireland) Order 2005 (the pension compensation provisions); or

(b) any periodic payments made in relation to a person, payable under section 166 of the Pensions Act 2004 or Article 150 of the Pensions (Northern Ireland) Order 2005 (duty to pay scheme benefits unpaid at assessment date etc.);]

"prescribed" means specified in, or determined in accordance with regulations;

"the qualifying age" has the meaning given by section 1(6);

"regulations" means regulations made by the Secretary of State;

"retirement pension income" shall be construed in accordance with section 16;

"retirement provision" shall be construed in accordance with section 7(6);

"savings credit" shall be construed in accordance with sections 1 and 3;

"social security benefits" means benefits payable under the enactments relating to social security in any part of the United Kingdom;

"standard minimum guarantee" shall be construed in accordance with section 2(3) to (5) and (9);

[² . . .]

"war disablement pension" means—

    (a) any retired pay, pension or allowance granted in respect of disablement under powers conferred by or under—

        (i) the Air Force (Constitution) Act 1917 (c.51);

        (ii) the Personal Injuries (Emergency Provisions) Act 1939 (c.82);

        (iii) the Pensions (Navy, Army, Air Force and Mercantile Marine) Act 1939 (c.83);

        (iv) the Polish Resettlement Act 1947 (c.19); or

        (v) Part 7 or section 151 of the Reserve Forces Act 1980 (c.9); or

    (b) without prejudice to paragraph (a), any retired pay or pension to which [1 any of paragraphs (a) to (f) of section 641(1) of the Income Tax (Earnings and Pensions) Act 2003] applies;

"war widow's or widower's pension" means—

    (a) [2 any widow's, widower's or surviving civil partner's] pension or allowance granted in respect of a death due to service or war injury and payable by virtue of any enactment mentioned in paragraph (a) of the definition of "war disablement pension"; or

    (b) a pension or allowance for a [2 widow, widower or surviving civil partner] granted under any scheme mentioned in [1section 641(1)(e) or (f) of the Income Tax (Earnings and Pensions) Act 2003];

"working tax credit" means a working tax credit under the Tax Credits Act 2002 to which a person is entitled whether alone or jointly with another.

[3(1A) [5 . . .]

(2) Regulations may make provision for the purposes of this Act—

    (a) as to circumstances in which persons are to be treated as being or not being members of the same household;

    (b) as to circumstances in which persons are to be treated as being or not being severely disabled.

(3) The following provisions of the Contributions and Benefits Act, namely—

    (a) section 172 (references to Great Britain or United Kingdom to include reference to adjacent territorial waters, etc.), and

    (b) section 173 (meaning of attaining an age, etc.), shall apply for the purposes of this Act as they apply for the purposes of that Act.

AMENDMENTS

1. Income Tax (Earnings and Pensions) Act 2003 Sch.6 para.263 (October 6, 2003).

2. Civil Partnership Act 2004 s.254 and Sch.24 para.142 (December 5, 2005).

3. Civil Partnership Act 2004 s.254 and Sch.24 para.143 (December 5, 2005).

4. Pensions Act 2004 (PPF Payments and FAS Payments) (Consequential Provisions) Order 2006 (SI 2006/343) art.3(2) (February 14, 2006).

5. Marriage (Same Sex Couples) Act 2013 (Consequential and Contrary Provisions and Scotland) Order 2014 (SI 214/560) art.2 and Sch.1 para.28 (March 13, 2014).

6. Civil Partnership (Opposite-sex Couples) Regulations 2019 (SI 2019/1458) reg.41(a) and para.22 of Sch.3, Part 1 (December 2, 2019).

GENERAL NOTE

1.69   This is the general definition section for the Act. For definitions of "income" and "retirement pension income", see ss.15 and 16 respectively.

In *CPC/3891/2004* Commissioner Mesher followed his earlier decision in *CIS/1720/2004* and confirmed that a decision simply that a claimant is "living together as husband and wife" is not in itself a decision which gives rise to a right of appeal. Such a decision is merely a "building block" for an outcome decision which would affect entitlement to benefit and so be capable of appeal under Social Security Act 1998 s.12(1). Accordingly a tribunal has no jurisdiction to make a substantive decision on such a "building block" decision as there is no appeal properly before it.

18.—*[Omitted.]*

[¹ **Pilot schemes**

18A.— 1.70
(1) Any regulations to which this subsection applies may be made so as to have effect for a specified period not exceeding 12 months.
(2) Subject to subsection (3), subsection (1) applies to—
(a) regulations made under this Act, and
(b) regulations made under section 1 or 5 of the Administration Act.
(3) Subsection (1) only applies to regulations if they are made with a view to ascertaining whether their provisions will—
(a) make it more likely that persons who are entitled to claim state pension credit will do so;
(b) make it more likely that persons who are entitled to claim state pension credit will receive it.
(4) Regulations which, by virtue of subsection (1), are to have effect for a limited period are referred to in this section as a "pilot scheme".
(5) A pilot scheme may, in particular—
(a) provide for a relevant provision not to apply, or to apply with modifications, for the purposes of the pilot scheme, and
(b) make different provision for different cases or circumstances.
(6) For the purposes of subsection (5)(a), a "relevant provision" is—
(a) any provision of this Act, and
(b) section 1 of the Administration Act.
(7) A pilot scheme may provide that no account is to be taken of any payment made under the pilot scheme in considering a person's—
(a) liability to tax,
(b) entitlement to benefit under an enactment relating to social security (irrespective of the name or nature of the benefit), or
(c) entitlement to a tax credit.
(8) A pilot scheme may provide that its provisions are to apply only in relation to—
(a) one or more specified areas or localities;
(b) one or more specified classes of person;
(c) persons selected—
(i) by reference to prescribed criteria, or
(ii) on a sampling basis.
(9) A pilot scheme may make consequential or transitional provision with respect to the cessation of the scheme on the expiry of the specified period.
(10) A pilot scheme may be replaced by a further pilot scheme making the same or similar provision.
(11) The power of the Secretary of State to make regulations which, by virtue of this section, are to have effect for a limited period is exercisable only with the consent of the Treasury.]

AMENDMENT

1. Welfare Reform Act 2009 s.27(2) (November 12, 2009).

GENERAL NOTE

1.71   This section makes provision for a pilot scheme to test ways in which state pension credit entitlement may be calculated and paid in order to increase the number of eligible persons receiving the credit. See also s.142 of the Pensions Act 2008, which permits data sharing between the Secretary of State and energy suppliers (and see further the Disclosure of State Pension Credit Information (Warm Home Discount) Regulations 2011 (SI 2011/1830)). The pilot scheme was extended until March 31, 2018 and then for a further three years until March 31, 2021 (see Warm Home Discount (Miscellaneous Amendments) Regulations 2018 (SI 2018/909)). It was then extended for a further year until March 31, 2022 (see Warm Home Discount (Miscellaneous Amendments) Regulations 2021 (SI 2021/667)). The scheme has now been extended until March 31, 2026—see the Warm Home Discount (England and Wales) Regulations 2022 (SI 2022/772) and to similar effect the Warm Home Discount (Scotland) Regulations 2022 (SI 2022/1073).

Regulations and orders

1.72   **19.**—(1) Subject to the following provisions of this section, subsections (1), (2) to (5) and (10) of section 175 of the Contributions and Benefits Act (regulations and orders etc) shall apply in relation to any power conferred on the Secretary of State by any provision of this Act to make regulations or an order as they apply in relation to any power conferred on him by that Act to make regulations or an order, but as if for references to that Act (other than references to specific provisions of it) there were substituted references to this Act.

(2) A statutory instrument containing (whether alone or with other provisions) the first regulations under—

(a) section 2(3)(b), (4) or (6),

(b) section 3(4), (5), (6), (7) or (8),

(c) section 4(3),

(d) section 12, or

(e) section 15(1)(e), (f) or (j), (2), (3), (4) or (6),

shall not be made unless a draft of the instrument has been laid before, and approved by a resolution of, each House of Parliament.

[¹ (2A) A statutory instrument containing regulations which, by virtue of section 18A, are to have effect for a limited period shall not be made unless a draft of the instrument has been laid before, and approved by a resolution of, each House of Parliament.]

(3) A statutory instrument—

(a) which contains regulations under this Act (whether alone or with other provisions), and

(b) which is not subject to any requirement that a draft of the instrument be laid before, and approved by a resolution of, each House of Parliament,

shall be subject to annulment in pursuance of a resolution of either House of Parliament.

AMENDMENT

1. Welfare Reform Act 2009 s.27(3) (November 12, 2009).

DEFINITIONS

"the Contribution and Benefits Act"—see s.17(1).
"regulations"—*ibid.*

GENERAL NOTE

This section applies the usual regulation-making powers for social security benefits under SSCBA 1992 s.175 to the pension credit scheme (subs.(1)). The first regulations made under the various powers listed in subs.(2) were subject to the affirmative procedure. Other regulations remain subject to the usual negative resolution procedure (subs.(3)).   1.73

Financial provisions

20.—(1) There shall be paid out of money provided by Parliament—   1.74
(a) any sums payable by way of state pension credit;
(b) any expenditure incurred by the Secretary of State or other government department under or by virtue of this Act; and
(c) any increase attributable to this Act in the sums payable out of money so provided under any other Act.
(2) There shall be paid into the Consolidated Fund any increase attributable to this Act in the sums which under any other Act are payable into that Fund.

Enactments repealed

21.—The enactments specified in Schedule 3 to this Act are repealed to the extent there specified.   1.75

GENERAL NOTE

Schedule 3 to the Act made a small number of minor repeals to existing social security legislation which appeared to be unconnected with the introduction of the pension credit.   1.76

Short title, commencement and extent

22.—(1) This Act may be cited as the State Pension Credit Act 2002.   1.77
(2) This section and sections 19 and 20 come into force on the passing of this Act.
(3) Except as provided by subsection (2), this Act shall come into force on such day as the Secretary of State may by order appoint; and different days may be so appointed for different purposes.
(4) Any order under this section may make such transitional provision as appears to the Secretary of State to be necessary or expedient in connection with the provisions brought into force by the order.
(5) Any amendment or repeal made by this Act has the same extent as the enactment to which it relates (unless otherwise provided).
(6) Subject to that, this Act extends to England and Wales and Scotland only.

GENERAL NOTE

For the reasons explained in the Introduction and General Note, although this Act is to be known as the State Pension Credit Act 2002 (subs.(1)), the credit itself is described in official literature as the pension credit. This section (along with ss.19 and 20) came into force on Royal Assent (June 25, 2002) (subs.(2)).   1.78

Welfare Reform Act 2012

SCHEDULES

1.79   **Sch.1. to Sch.3.** *[Omitted.]*

Welfare Reform Act 2012

(2012 c.5)

ARRANGEMENT OF SECTIONS

PART 1

UNIVERSAL CREDIT

CHAPTER 1

ENTITLEMENT AND AWARDS

Introductory

1.80   1.   Universal credit
       2.   Claims

Entitlement

       3.   Entitlement
       4.   Basic conditions
       5.   Financial conditions
       6.   Restrictions on entitlement

Awards

       7.   Basis of awards
       8.   Calculation of awards

Elements of an award

       9.   Standard allowance
      10.   Responsibility for children and young persons
      11.   Housing costs
      12.   Other particular needs or circumstances

CHAPTER 2

CLAIMANT RESPONSIBILITIES

Introductory

      13.   Work-related requirements: introductory
      14.   Claimant commitment

44

CHAPTER 3

SUPPLEMENTARY AND GENERAL

1.81

Regulations

PART 5

SOCIAL SECURITY: GENERAL

Benefit cap

PART 7

FINAL

SCHEDULES

An Act to make provision for universal credit and personal independence payment; to make other provision about social security and tax credits; to make provision about the functions of the registration service, child support maintenance and the use of jobcentres; to establish the Social Mobility and Child Poverty Commission and otherwise amend the Child Poverty Act 2010; and for connected purposes.

[8th March 2012]

GENERAL NOTE

1.84   Part 1 of the Welfare Reform Act 2012 ("WRA 2012") and the associated schedules to that Act establish a social security benefit known as universal credit, set out the underlying structure of that benefit and confer regulation-making powers that allow the Secretary of State for Work and Pensions to make more detailed rules.

The (ongoing) introduction of universal credit is the biggest change to the social security system since the abolition of supplementary benefit and its replacement with income support ("IS") by the Social Security Act 1986. It replaces four social security benefits (IS, housing benefit ("HB"), income-based jobseeker's allowance ("JSA(IB)"), and income-related employment and support allowance ("ESA(IR)")) and two tax credits (child tax credit ("CTC") and working tax credit ("WTC")). (The Department for Work and Pensions ("DWP") often refers to the benefits and tax credits that are to be replaced as the "legacy benefits", but this volume some-times describes them as "existing benefits"). When the transfer to universal credit is complete it will technically be the *only* means-tested, non-contributory benefit for people of working age (albeit that its conceptual elegance, as well as the practical simplicity for claimants, is spoiled by the fact that child benefit, technically non-means-tested, is in substance means-tested; and that council tax reduction, techni-cally not a benefit, is in substance a benefit).

To understand why it has been felt necessary to make such complete overhaul of the benefits system, it is necessary to set out in greater detail what the problems with the existing benefits were perceived to be and how universal credit was intended to solve them. After that, this note will discuss the slow introduction of the new benefit (and the extent to which the delay may have made matters worse rather than better) and conclude with a summary of how universal credit is structured.

The problem: complexity and disincentives to work

Before the introduction of universal credit began, people of working age who needed to claim benefit because they were not working (or, though working, were not earning enough to meet their basic needs) had to choose from a complex array of benefits some of which complemented each other and others of which were mutually exclusive.

Those who were able to work, but could not find a job, generally had to claim JSA, entitlement to which was either "contribution-based", or "income-based" which was a euphemism for "means-tested". Those who could not work because they were prevented from doing so by illness or disability claimed ESA, which again could be contributory or "income-related". Those who could not be expected to work for other reasons (e.g., because they were caring for a young child or for a disabled person) could claim IS, entitlement to which was based on a means-test and had no contributory component.

The three benefits listed above were administered by the DWP and included ele-ments to help meet a claimant's housing costs if (broadly speaking) the claimant was an owner-occupier. However, for claimants who rented their homes, help for housing costs was provided by a fourth benefit, housing benefit ("HB") which was administered by local authorities.

Moreover, ESA(IR) and—except in a limited class of transitional cases—JSA(IB) and IS were "adults only" benefits. For claimants whose families included children or "qualifying young persons" (people aged between 16 and 20 who are in educa-tion or training) state help for the cost of feeding, clothing and bringing up the child or qualifying young person was provided by HM Revenue & Customs ("HMRC") through two further benefits, child benefit and CTC.

Finally, people working more than 16 hours a week were excluded from IS, JSA(IB) and ESA(IR). However, they could sometimes claim WTC, which was not open to anyone working fewer than 16 hours a week. HB had no hours rule (although, of course, the more hours a person worked, the more likely their claim might fail on income grounds).

The complexity of that system, in which a claimant with children living in rented property might have to claim four different benefits from three different agencies was further aggravated by the fact entitlement to tax credits was normally calculated with respect to, and paid over, an entire tax year whereas entitlement to IS, JSA(IB), ESA(IR) and HB was calculated weekly and usually paid fortnightly or, in the case of HB, four-weekly or monthly. It was often difficult to ensure that the two different cal-culation and payment systems meshed together properly, not least because the mecha-nisms for sharing information between the DWP, HMRC and local authorities were

1.85

less than perfect. The whole system operated against the background that a mistake, whether by the claimant or the administering authority, could result in an overpayment, leaving the claimant in debt, often for hundreds or thousands of pounds.

The old system had the further effect of providing financial disincentives to work at certain levels of income. Under the means-tests for IS, JSA(IB) and ESA(IR) only relatively small amounts of earnings were ignored. Claimants whose earnings exceeded those "disregards" had their benefits reduced penny for penny by the amount of the excess and therefore derived no further benefit from their earnings until they earned enough to lose entitlement to benefit altogether.

This is not the place for a detailed discussion of the poverty trap. An example should suffice to make the point.

> During 2023/24, a single claimant, call her Jane, aged over 25 on the basic rate of JSA(IB) receives £84.80 per week. Jane's weekly earnings disregard is £5.00. Suppose she does one hour's work a week at the national minimum wage of £10.42 per hour. The first £5 of those earnings is disregarded but her JSA(IB) is reduced by £5.42 (the amount by which £10.42 exceeds £5) to £79.38. Jane's total weekly income is thus £89.80 (£10.42 in earnings plus JSA(IB) of £79.38). Now, suppose Jane increases her working hours to eight per week. Her weekly earnings are now £83.36 (£10.42 × 8) but her earnings disregard is still £5. Therefore, her weekly entitlement to JSA(IB) is reduced by £78.36 (£83.36–£5.00) from £84.80 to £6.44, giving her a total weekly income of £89.80 (£83.36 in earnings plus £6.44 in JSA(IB)). In short, Jane's income remains exactly the same whether she works one hour per week or eight. It is only once she works nine hours a week, taking her post-disregard earnings to £88.78 (£93.78–£5.00) and losing entitlement to JSA(IB) altogether, that Jane begins to be better off. And at that stage, if she is in rented accommodation, she is likely to lose 65 pence in HB for each additional pound that she earns. She will also lose entitlement to "passported" advantages such as automatic free prescriptions, which will provide a further disincentive to work.

The solution: universal credit

1.86   Universal credit is designed to get rid of both the problems outlined above by simplifying the social security system and ensuring that claimants will always be better off in work.

Simplification

1.87   The simplification of the system is to be achieved by abolishing IS, JSA(IB), ESA(IR) HB, CTC and WTC and replacing them with universal credit. As universal credit is administered and paid by the DWP, the effect will be to end the role of local authorities in the administration of cash working-age social security benefits and to restrict the role of HMRC to the administration of child benefit and guardian's allowance.

However, the simultaneous decision to replace council tax benefit with local council tax reduction schemes means that local authorities do still have an important role in social security adjudication, but now under a host of local schemes rather than a single national structure. Further, local authorities have come to play increasingly significant role in administering discretionary support, such as discretionary housing payments, for claimants whose needs are not adequately met by benefits available by right.

In the new system, as noted above, child benefit continues unaffected and two new benefits, confusingly called "jobseeker's allowance" and "employment and support allowance"—and referred to as "new style" JSA and ESA to distinguish them from the older, identically–named, "old style" benefits—are paid without any means-test, but for limited periods, to those who meet the contribution conditions.

Nevertheless, the new structure is undoubtedly simpler than the system it replaces.

The aim of simplification has, however, been frustrated by the decision to phase universal credit in over a period of many years. That decision is entirely understandable, given the new benefit's reliance on information technology. It would have been a recipe for disaster for universal credit to be introduced on a general basis before it had been established in pilot areas that it could be properly administered.

However, the effect of a phased introduction is that the two systems continue to co-exist, so that what has been achieved is not a simplification of the benefits system but a significant complication. During the transition, universal credit is not a *replacement* benefit but an *additional* benefit.

Moreover, it is inherent in the design of universal credit that it overlaps with each of the older benefits it is eventually intended to replace. That overlap means that, in addition to the complication of the old and new systems existing side-by-side (including having two different and mutually exclusive benefits both called JSA and two called ESA), it is also necessary to have legislation defining which set of rules applies to any particular claimant at any given time. That legislation is now to be found first, in the Universal Credit (Transitional Provisions) Regulations 2014 ("the 2014 Regulations") and, second, in a series of Commencement Orders that, even by the high standards set by past social security legislation, are bewilderingly complex.

If that were not enough, the procedures by which universal credit was introduced meant that, at least in relation to some issues, the benefit existed for a period in two forms with different substantive rules: see *Introduction of universal credit* below.

As a final complication, the need to devote departmental resources to the introduction of universal credit appears to have delayed the extension of the housing costs element of state pension credit (SPC) to cover rent and other payments made by those who are not owner-occupiers. Further, even claimants who have become subject to the universal credit rules may still claim HB if they live in "exempt accommodation" (see the definition in Sch.1, para.1 to the Universal Credit Regulations, below). The effect is that local authorities will need to retain their benefits departments—and incur the associated costs and overheads that might otherwise have been saved—to deal with claims for HB from those who are above working age and in exempt accommodation.

Challenges of transition

All of that might not matter if the transition from the old system to the new had been relatively swift. It had originally been envisaged that all households would have moved to UC by the end of 2017: DWP, *Iain Duncan Smith sets out next steps for moving claimants onto Universal Credit* (November 1, 2011). However, that has not transpired. The DWP's report *Completing the move to Universal Credit: Learning from the Discovery Phase* (January 10, 2023), published almost a decade after UC was introduced, noted that there were still 2.5 million households receiving legacy benefit. (In comparison there were about 4.9 million households receiving UC: DWP, *Universal Credit statistics: 29 April 2013 to 12 January 2023* (February 14, 2023), para.5.)

The Secretary of State intends, ultimately, to move all legacy benefit recipients onto universal credit by a process known as "managed migration". But virtually all UC claims so far have been either (i) brand new benefit claims; or (ii) the result of claimants' own decisions to end legacy benefits to claim UC; or (iii) the consequence of existing claimants undergoing a change of circumstances which ends their existing award (sometimes known as "natural migration").

The Universal Credit (Managed Migration Pilot and Miscellaneous Amendments) Regulations 2019 (SI 2019/1152) allowed for up to 10,000 people to experimentally undergo "managed moves" onto universal credit from legacy benefit. The managed migration legislation itself is in Pt 4 of the Universal Credit (Transitional Provisions) Regulations 2014; the 10,000 person limitation was imposed by reg.2 of SI 2019/1152.

A pilot scheme began in Harrogate in July 2019, but as of January 2020, only 13 people had actually moved to universal credit [HC Deb (January 27, 2020), vol.670

1.88

col.521], and operation of the scheme was suspended altogether upon the outbreak of coronavirus.

On November 8, 2021, the Secretary of State announced that the Harrogate scheme would not be resumed, and that a plan was "still in preparation, on resuming the managed move to universal credit" [HC Deb (November 8, 2021), vol.703 col.8]. The Secretary of State subsequently removed the 10,000 limit on managed moves, through reg.10 of the Universal Credit (Transitional Provisions) Amendment Regulations 2022 (SI 2022/752), so can in principle now complete the process without further legislative change. The policy which will underpin that process is emerging as this volume goes to press.

DWP's most recent estimate is that the managed migration of "legacy" benefit claimants to UC will be completed in 2028/29: *Autumn Statement 2022* (CP 751, November 2022), para.5.15. Therefore, even assuming no further delay, instead of taking four years as originally planned, the process will have taken 16 years.

The slow pace of the transition so far means that, for un-migrated existing working age claimants, the benefits system continues to be as described in the opening paragraphs of this introduction: they will continue to deal with up to three different authorities and to be subject to disincentives to work from the poverty trap.

The slow pace of the transition is also significant because it means that "natural migration" from legacy benefits to UC has become a much more significant part of the process than originally anticipated. And the Secretary of State has experienced a number of court defeats about the treatment of certain sub-groups in that category, in which some claimants can be substantially worse off on UC than on their previous benefits: *R. (TP, AR & SXC) v Secretary of State for Work and Pensions* [2020] EWCA Civ 37; [2020] P.T.S.R. 1785; *R. (TD) v Secretary of State for Work and Pensions* [2020] EWCA Civ 618; *R. (TP) v Secretary of State for Work and Pensions* [2022] EWHC 123 (Admin). In all three cases the courts decided that there was unlawfully discriminatory treatment of affected groups, contrary to s.6 of the Human Rights Act 1998.

Incentivising work

1.89   Although the universal credit scheme embodies political judgments about what claimants should be required to do in return for their benefit with which it is possible to disagree, progress has been made towards eliminating the poverty trap.

If we return to the example given above and suppose that, instead of claiming JSA, Jane had been eligible to claim universal credit, then her basic entitlement to universal credit (ignoring housing costs as we did implicitly in the JSA example) would be her "maximum amount" which would consist of the modified standard allowance (see the commentary to reg.36 of the Universal Credit Regulations) for a single person aged at least 25, namely £368.74 per month. That equates to £85.09 per week (£368.74 × 12 ÷ 52). Jane then begins to work one hour a week at the minimum wage of £10.42 per hour. In an average month she would earn £45.15 (£10.42 × 52 ÷ 12). From April 2016, Jane no is longer entitled to a work allowance (i.e. because she does not have responsibility for a child or qualifying young person and does not have limited capability for work). There would therefore be no equivalent of the £5 weekly disregard in the JSA calculation. However, under universal credit, from November 2021, only 55% of Jane's earnings will be deducted from the maximum amount, not the full amount of her (undisregarded) earnings as in JSA. In cash terms, the deduction is £24.83 (£45.15 × 55%) giving a monthly universal credit award of £343.91 (£368.74–£24.83), equivalent to £79.36 per week (£343.91 × 12 ÷ 52). Jane's equivalent weekly income is therefore £89.78 (£79.36 in universal credit + £10.42 in earnings). Jane is therefore £4.69 (£89.78–£85.09) per week better off as a result of working one hour a week. At that very low level of work, she is no better off than she would be on JSA (indeed, very slightly worse off). However, not many people work for just 1 hour a week and the more work Jane does, the more the universal credit rules begin to operate in her favour. If Jane works eight hours a week (at which level, it will be remembered, her combined weekly earnings and benefit under JSA would still have been £89.80, the same as if she had worked for just one hour), the equivalent weekly income from universal credit and earnings is £122.60 (£85.09 + (£10.42 × 8 × 0.45)).

In addition to the different earned income rules, simple and effective support with childcare costs was also intended to play a significant role in UC incentivising work. However, as the Spring Budget 2023 recorded, "Currently, only around 13% of households eligible for the childcare element in Universal Credit claim it. The current offer means parents on Universal Credit in work [are] paid in monthly arrears. This presents an issue for many low-income families who struggle to find the funds to pay for their childcare upfront." That budget announced plans to "make sure [claimants] have support with childcare costs upfront when they need it rather than in arrears" and also to increase the Universal Credit childcare cost maximum amounts to £951 for one child and £1,630 for two children: *Spring Budget 2023* (HC 1183, March 15, 2023), paras 3.53–3.55. (With effect from 28 June 2023, those policy changes have now been given effect by the Universal Credit (Childcare) (Amendment) Regulations 2023 (SI 593/2023), reg.2. See also ADM Memo 12/23. Those regulations post-date the cut-off point for this edition so are not incorporated in the main text.)

Introduction of universal credit

Universal credit raises two transitional issues. The first is whether a person making a fresh claim for benefit is free to claim IS/HB/JSA/ESA or whether he or she must now claim universal credit. The second is in what circumstances existing recipients of IS/HB/JSA/ESA will be moved from those benefits to universal credit.

Fresh claims

The process of introducing universal credit was begun by the Universal Credit (Transitional Provisions) Regulations 2013 ("the 2013 Regulations"). The text of those Regulations (which have now been revoked) is set out on pp.305-354 of Vol.V of the 2013/14 edition. In summary, they provided that claimants may (and must) claim universal credit rather than IS/JSA/ESA if, at the time their claim was made or treated as made, they resided in one of the "relevant districts" and were either in the Pathfinder Group or had formerly been jointly entitled to universal credit as a member of a former couple. The relevant districts were postcode areas linked to particular Jobcentres and specified in the various Commencement Orders (see Pt IV below). The extension of universal credit proceeded by issuing further Commencement Orders that widened the geographical scope of the rules by adding further "relevant districts".

Membership of the Pathfinder Group was governed by regs 4-12 of the 2013 Regulations (pp.312-323 of Vol.V of the 2013/14 edition). The criteria for membership of the Pathfinder Group were so narrowly drawn that it, in summary, it only included single, adult, British citizens who would otherwise have had to claim JSA. The issues that were likely to give rise to disputes were narrower still because any claimant whose circumstances were likely to give rise to complications had been excluded from the Pathfinder Group and therefore had to continue to claim IS/JSA/ESA. Unsurprisingly in those circumstances, the initial experience of the Social Entitlement Chamber of the First-tier Tribunal was that universal credit appeals were overwhelmingly about backdating and the imposition of sanctions.

The 2013 Regulations were revoked by the 2014 Regulations with effect from June 16, 2014. Nothing equivalent to the former Pathfinder conditions appeared in the 2014 Regulations. Instead, a policy decision was taken that new "Gateway conditions" would be specified in Commencement Orders. This approach gave the government flexibility to vary those conditions for different areas, or to include no Gateway conditions at all.

That flexibility was used to establish two different models for the implementation of universal credit. From November 11, 2014, the No.20 Commencement Order

1.90

1.91

(see Vol.V) allowed (and required) claimants who lived in a small area of the SM5 postcode in the London Borough of Sutton to claim universal credit without having to satisfy the Gateway conditions. On the same day, the Universal Credit (Digital Service) Amendment Regulations 2014 (SI 2014/2887) came into force and made substantive changes to the Universal Credit Regulations, that only apply in what are described as "digital service" areas. At that time, the SM5 2 postcode area was the only such area. However, subsequent Commencement Orders have expanded the areas covered by the digital service and further statutory instruments (SI 2014/3225 and SI 2015/1647) have introduced additional amendments to the Universal Credit Regulations that only apply in such areas.

In keeping with its long-standing institutional reluctance to call anything by its correct statutory name, the DWP referred to digital service areas as "full service" areas and distinguished them from the areas in which the Gateway conditions still applied by referring to the latter as "live service" areas.

The distinction reflected the fact that, during this period, universal credit was administered using two separate and incompatible IT systems, depending on whether the claimant lived in a full/digital service area or a live service area.

Once the rules for universal credit were in force on at least a live service basis (i.e., for claimants who satisfied the Gateway Conditions) throughout Great Britain, the further roll-out of universal credit consisted of a process of "de-gatewayfication": instead of Commencement Orders extending universal credit to new geographical areas by prescribing additional relevant districts, they converted existing live service areas to full/digital service areas by revoking the Gateway conditions in those areas. That process ended on December 12, 2018, since when, it is not normally possible to make a fresh claim for a "legacy benefit". The significant remaining exception is the continuing availability of housing benefit to people over pension age, and to people in "specified" or "temporary" accommodation. The exception is made by reg.6A of the Universal Credit (Transitional Provisions) Regulations 2014 SI 2014/1230. For the definitions of "specified" and "temporary" accommodation see Sch.1 paras 3A–3B of the Universal Credit Regulations. (In summary, "specified" accommodation refers to "supported living" type arrangements, while "temporary" accommodation is what gets provided at the interim stage of discharge of a homelessness duty under the Housing Act 1996.)

Existing claimants

1.92 At the time of going to press, the most recent statement of the Department's policy was a ministerial statement dated March 28, 2023 (UIN HCWS678). It indicated that managed migration currently remains in a pilot phase, with published statistics covering only a few hundred claimants. But the Minister gave details about imminent next steps. He stated

> "Through 2023/24, our focus will be on notifying households that receive tax credits only [that they must claim UC], increasing volumes incrementally each month. As we move into 2024/25, all cases with tax credits (including those on both Employment Support Allowance and tax credits), all cases on Income Support and Jobseeker's Allowance (Income Based) and all Housing Benefit cases (including combinations of these benefits) will be required to move to Universal Credit… the Government is delaying the managed migration of claimants on income-related Employment Support Allowance (except for those receiving Child Tax Credit) to Universal Credit [to 2026–29]."

The legal basis for managed migration can currently be found in Part 4 of the Universal Credit (Transitional Provisions) Regulations 2014 (SI 2014/1230) as substituted with effect from July 24, 2019 by reg.3(7) of the Universal Credit (Managed Migration Pilot and Miscellaneous Amendments) Regulations 2019 (SI 2019/1152) and further amended with effect from July 25, 2022 by the Universal Credit (Transitional Provisions) Amendment Regulations 2022 (SI 2022/752). Migration is commenced by the Secretary of State issuing a "migration notice" under the substituted reg.44 to a person who is entitled to an award of an existing benefit. The notice must inform that person that all awards of any existing benefits to which they are entitled are to terminate and that they will need to make a claim for universal credit. It must also specify a day ("the deadline day") by which a claim for universal credit must be made. If no universal credit claim is made by the deadline day (which the Secretary of State can change to a later day: see reg.45) then all awards of any existing benefits to which the person is entitled terminate on the deadline day (except for awards of housing benefit, which terminate two weeks later: see reg.46). Under reg.46(3) and (4), a claimant who does not claim universal credit by the deadline day can retrieve the situation by claiming before "the final deadline", which is the day that would be the last day of the first assessment period in relation to an award commencing on the deadline day.

Unlike "natural migration", managed migration gives entitlement to transitional protection, so that claimants should not receive less in benefit immediately after the move to universal credit than they were receiving immediately before. Substituted regs 48-57 of the Transitional Provisions Regulations 2014 contain detailed rules on how the transitional protection operates.

The structure of Universal Credit

Almost any general proposition about social security law will be subject to qualifications and exceptions. Failing to note those qualifications and exceptions risks giving an unhelpfully approximate explanation of how the structure is meant to work. However, dealing with them in full risks obscuring the view of the wood by concentrating on the trees. The purpose of this Note is to give the big picture.

There is never any substitute for looking at the actual words of the legislative text. Until they have checked both that text and the commentary to it, readers should assume that everything in this introduction is subject to unstated exceptions, particularly when such exceptions are implied by the use of words such as "normally" and "usually".

The legal structure of the universal credit scheme is as follows. As already noted, the benefit is established by Pt 1 of the Welfare Reform Act 2012 ("WRA 2012" or "the Act") and by the Schedules to that Act that are given effect by provisions in Pt 1. The Act has subsequently been amended by the Welfare Reform and Work Act 2016 ("WR&WA 2016"). As is common in social security law, the Act sets out the structure of the scheme and confers extensive powers on the Secretary of State to make regulations prescribing matters of detail. The main regulations are the Universal Credit Regulations 2013 ("the Universal Credit Regulations" or "the Regulations"), but there are others including the 2014 Regulations and regulations dealing with claims and payments, and decisions and appeals, for universal credit, personal independence payment ("PIP"), new style JSA and new style ESA.

Universal credit is a non-contributory, means-tested, working age, social security benefit. That means that it is not "universal". With very limited exceptions, people who are not of working age are excluded from entitlement, as are (with no exceptions) those who do not satisfy the means-test. Moreover, as is the case with all non-contributory benefits, the rules contain residence and presence conditions (including a right to reside test) which exclude those who are felt not have a legitimate connection with Great Britain or who have been absent from the UK for an extended period.

In addition, the fact that universal credit is a social security benefit means that it is not "credit" in the sense in which that word is used in ordinary speech. As with the child tax credit and working tax credit which preceded it, universal credit is a *payment*, made as a matter of legal right to those who meet the conditions of entitlement, not a *loan* to tide claimants over a period of reduced income. With the sole exception of the hardship payments made to those who have been sanctioned, universal credit that has been correctly paid does not have to be repaid.

1.93

Couples

1.94   One of the basic principles of universal credit is that it cannot usually be claimed by one member of a couple: WRA 2012 s.2(1) provides that a claim for universal credit may only be made a single person or by members of a couple jointly. It is implicit that any award of universal credit made on a joint claim will be a joint award to both members of the couple.

The basic conditions

1.95   Entitlement to universal credit depends upon satisfying both the "basic conditions" and the "financial conditions" set out in the Act (WRA 2012, s.3(1)). Where a joint claim is made, those conditions must usually be satisfied by both members of the couple (WRA 2012, s.3(2)).

The basic conditions are set out in s.4(1) of the Act. They are that the claimant:

- must be at least 18 years old;
- must not have reached the qualifying age for SPC (which is now pensionable age);
- is in Great Britain;
- is not receiving education; and
- has accepted a claimant commitment.

The last three of those conditions are further defined, or partially defined, in regulations. For example, a person who does not have a right to reside in the UK is treated as not being habitually resident here and hence as not being "in Great Britain": see reg.9 of the Universal Credit Regulations. All of those conditions are subject to exceptions which are specified in regulations. In addition, a person who meets the basic conditions cannot acquire entitlement to universal credit if he or she falls within the restrictions specified in s.6 of the Act and reg.19 of the Regulations.

It should be noted that it is not a condition of entitlement to universal credit that any claimant should be, or should not be, in remunerative work. The only way in which work affects universal credit is through the income that is earned from undertaking it.

The financial conditions

1.96   The financial conditions are set out in s.5 of the Act. They are that

- the claimant's capital (or, for couples, joint capital) is not greater than a prescribed amount (fixed at £16,000 ever since 2013 by reg.18 of the Regulations); and that
- the claimant's income (or, for couples, joint income) is "such that, if the claimant were entitled to universal credit, the amount payable would not be less than any prescribed minimum" (currently fixed at one penny by reg.17 of the Regulations).

As is discussed above and below, entitlement to universal credit reduces as a claimant's income increases. The effect of the convoluted wording quoted in the second bullet point above is that if, as a result of that reduction, the amount of universal credit payable would be less than one penny (i.e., nil), the financial conditions are not satisfied. In other words, one cannot be entitled to universal credit at a nil rate.

As would be expected, the calculation of a claimant's income and capital are the subject of detailed provisions in the Regulations.

Assessment periods

1.97   Universal credit is a monthly benefit. Entitlement is normally assessed by reference to the claimant's circumstances during an "assessment period", which is defined by

WRA 2012 s.7(2) and reg.21(1) of the Regulations as "a period of one month beginning with the first date of entitlement and each subsequent period of one month during which entitlement subsists". That entitlement is then normally paid monthly in arrears after the end of the assessment period to which the payment relates (see reg.47 of the Universal Credit, Personal Independence Payment, Jobseeker's Allowance and Employment and Support Allowance (Claims and Payments) Regulations 2013).

The potential hardship which could result from a long wait between claim and payment is in principle mitigated by large-scale availability of advance payments on account under reg.5 of the Social Security (Payments on Account of Benefit) Regulations 2013 (SI 2013/383). About 60% of UC claimants receive an advance payment on account, generally within a matter of days of making their claim, on the basis that it is "likely" they will be entitled to UC: NAO, *Rolling Out Universal Credit* (HC 1123, June 2018), para.2.8. The Secretary of State had taken the position that certain claimants are in principle ineligible as a class for advances (in particular, those without a national insurance number) on the basis that it can not ever in such cases be said that it was "likely" they would ultimately be entitled; but in *Bui v Secretary of State for Work and Pensions* [2023] EWCA Civ 566 (May 25, 2023) the Court of Appeal decides that approach to be unlawful; any claimant is entitled to an individual decision on whether they are "likely" to qualify; any claimant can in principle be eligible for an advance. (The Secretary of State has applied to the Supreme Court for permission to appeal.)

Calculation of entitlement to universal credit

Under s.8(1) of the Act, the amount of an award of universal credit is the balance of the "maximum amount" less "the amounts to be deducted".   **1.98**

The amount so calculated will normally be reduced by the "benefit cap" (see below) if the claimant's total entitlement to specified social security benefits would otherwise exceed the amount of the cap.

The maximum amount

The maximum amount is a monthly amount. It is conceptually equivalent to the weekly "applicable amount" used in the calculation of entitlement to IS, JSA(IB) and   **1.99** ESA(IR). It is the total of the standard allowance (equivalent to the personal allowances for IS/JSA/ESA) established by WRA 2012, s.9 and reg.36 of the Regulations, and any of the following amounts to which the claimant is (or the joint claimants are) entitled:

- the child element

  Under WRA 2012, s.10 and regs.24 & 36 of the Regulations, an amount is allowed for each child or qualifying young person for whom a claimant is responsible, up to (subject to exceptions and transitional savings) a maximum of two children or qualifying young persons. A challenge to the compatibility with Convention rights of the two-child limit was rejected by the Supreme Court in *R. (SC, CB and 8 children) v Secretary of State for Work and Pensions* [2021] UKSC 26; [2022] A.C. 223.

  An additional amount is allowed for each child or qualifying young person who is entitled to disability living allowance ("DLA") or PIP. The amount is higher if entitlement is to the highest rate of the care component of DLA or the enhanced rate of the daily living component of PIP or if the child or qualifying young person is registered blind.

- the housing costs element

  The housing costs element is payable under WRA 2012, s.11 and regs 25 & 26 of, and Schs 1-5 to the Regulations. The rules are summarised below.

- the LCWRA element

  This is payable where the claimant has limited capability for work-related activity. It is equivalent to, but paid at a considerably higher rate than, the support component of ESA (see WRA 2012, s.12 and regs 27(1)(b) & 36 of the Regulations). The former LCW element (equivalent to the former work-related activity component of ESA) was abolished with effect from April 3, 2017 and is now only payable to claimants with transitional protection.

● the carer element

This is equivalent to, and is paid at approximately the same rate as, the carer premium for IS/JSA/ESA (see WRA 2012, s.12 and regs 29 & 36 of the Regulations). To qualify, a claimant must satisfy the conditions of entitlement to carer's allowance other than having earnings below the prescribed limit and making a claim for that benefit (see regs 30(1) & (2) of the Regulations).

● the childcare costs element

The childcare costs element is 85% of the charges incurred by a claimant for relevant childcare (defined in reg.35 of the Regulations) subject to a maximum of £646.35 pcm for one child or £1,108.04 pcm for two or more children (regs 34(1) and 36) and also to anti-abuse rules in reg.34(2). To qualify, a claimant must satisfy both the work condition (reg. 32) and the childcare costs condition (reg.33).

The childcare costs element is not subject to the benefits cap (reg. 81(1)(b) and (2)).

The amounts of the standard allowance and the various elements are specified in a table that forms part of reg.36 of the Regulations.

The amounts to be deducted

1.100   Once the maximum amount has been ascertained, it is necessary to calculate the amounts to be deducted from it. By WRA 2012, s.8(3) & reg.22 of the Universal Credit Regulations, those amounts are:

● All the claimant's, or the claimants' combined, *unearned* income;

● Either (where the claimant does not have responsibility for a child or qualifying young person and does not have limited capability for work) 55% of his or her *earned* income; or

● (where the claimant has responsibility for a child or qualifying young person or has limited capability for work) 55% of the amount by which the claimant's, or the claimants' combined, *earned* income exceeds the work allowance.

The "work allowance" is what is described in IS/HB/JSA/ESA as an "earnings disregard". There are two rates, which are specified in a table that forms part of reg.22. The higher work allowance of £631.00 is applicable if the award of universal credit does not include the housing costs element: otherwise the lower work allowance of £379.00 applies.

Until April 2016, all claimants with earned income had work allowances, but, as indicated above, work allowances are now only available when the claimant (or at least one joint claimant) has responsibility for a child or qualifying young person or has limited capability for work. In addition, some of the pre-April 2016 allowances were higher than is now the case. For some claimants who have responsibility for a child, the reduction in the work allowances were at least partially offset by the April 2016 increases in the maximum rates of the childcare costs elements (reg.36 of the Regulations) and the percentage of relevant childcare charges that is eligible to be met by universal credit (reg.34). The maximum increase in the child care costs element was £114.06 per month for one child and £192.54 for two or more children, By contrast, the higher work allowance for a single person with children was cut by £337 from £734 to £397 (now £631 in 2023/24).

In fairness, the cuts in the lower work allowance are considerably less than in the higher allowance (and it is likely that many claimants who have responsibility for a child or qualifying young person will have housing costs and so only be eligible for the lower allowance). So the combined effect of the cut in the work allowance and the increase in the childcare costs element will often be a modest increase in entitlement to universal credit.

Those adjustments were made at the cost of a swingeing reduction in work incentives for able-bodied, childless claimants.

Calculation of income

Earned income

Employees

The treatment of the earned income of employees is another new feature of the universal credit scheme and one of the areas in which the benefit depends heavily upon the efficient operation of information technology. Most employers are now obliged to submit their PAYE returns to HMRC online and on a monthly basis under the "Real-Time Information" system. The idea is that that PAYE information should then be used to calculate the claimant's entitlement to universal credit for that month. If the system works, it has the advantage that claimants need not report fluctuations in their earnings (and therefore need not fear having to repay overpayments if they omit to do so). The possibility of treating earned income in this way was the main reason for establishing universal credit as a monthly, rather than weekly, benefit and for providing that payment should be in arrears after the end of the assessment period.

1.101

For those advantages to accrue, the way in which earnings from employment are calculated are different from those for IS/HB/JSA/ESA. First, earnings are to be based on the actual amount received by the claimant during the assessment period (see reg.54(1)). Then, reg.55 defines "earned income" by reference to the income tax definition. Finally reg.61 provides that where the claimant's employer is a "Real Time Information employer", the information on which the Secretary of State bases his calculation of earned income is to be the information reported by that employer through the PAYE system and the claimant is normally treated as having received those earnings in the same assessment period as the Secretary of State received the information: see *Secretary of State for Work and Pensions v Johnson* [2020] EWCA Civ 778; [2020] P.T.S.R. 1872.

As was recognised in *Johnson*, the rigidity of that rule can lead to unintuitive outcomes where—whether because of what the Court in *Johnson* referred to as "the non-banking day salary shift", or because the claimant is paid four weekly rather than monthly—a claimant receives two payments of salary in the same assessment period. The rules for the non-banking day salary shift (in which a monthly payment due on a weekend or Bank Holiday is paid early), that were declared to be irrational in *Johnson*, were changed prospectively from November 16, 2020 by the substitution of a new regulation 61 which allows the reallocation of payments from one assessment period to another where the claimant is paid monthly. In another case, *Pantellerisco*, the High Court had also found to be irrational the way in which the incomes of claimants paid four weekly are calculated (for the purposes of reg.82). But in *Secretary of State for Work and Pensions v Pantellerisco* [2021] EWCA Civ 1454; [2021] P.T.S.R. 1922 the Court of Appeal reversed that decision. Further, in *Secretary of State for Work and Pensions v LM* [2023] UKUT 72 (AAC) the Upper Tribunal decides that the logic of the *Pantellerisco* decision applies also to fortnightly-paid claimants. The fluctuations produced by the Regulations in calculating the earned income of non-monthly paid claimants may indeed sometimes be unintuitive, and may individually produce hard results, but the regulations are not in that respect irrational.

With effect from April 11, 2018 the new reg.54 introduces the rule that if a claimant's earned income (whether as an employee or as a self-employed person) is more than sufficient to wipe out entitlement to UC for an assessment period, the amount of the excess ("surplus earnings") is to be taken into account on any new claims within the following six months. There are complex provisions, with a potential to confuse claimants, for the erosion of surplus earnings within that six months by the making of claims that do not result in any entitlement. However, the practical effect of those provisions has hitherto been very considerably reduced by an annual Determination of the Secretary of State every year since then to "temporarily" make the threshold for surplus earnings £2,500 per month rather than £300. The most recent Determination was dated March 20, 2023 and extends that position to April 2024.

The self-employed

1.102   The principle in reg.54(1) of the Universal Credit Regulations that earnings are to be taken as the actual amount received by the claimant during the assessment period also applies to self-employed earnings. Under reg.57(2), a person's self-employed earnings in respect of an assessment period are to be calculated by taking that person's "gross profits" (defined by reg.57(3) as "the actual receipts in [the assessment] period less any deductions for expenses allowed under regulation 58 or 59") and then deducting any payments of income tax and Class 2 and 4 national insurance contributions actually made to HMRC in that period and any "relievable pension contributions made" (as defined in s.188 of the Finance Act 2004, i.e., contributions to a registered pension scheme for which tax relief is available). Regs 58 & 59 establish an exhaustive list of the expenses that can be deducted. In particular, reg.59 provides for flat rate deductions for business mileage and the use of the claimant's home for business purposes.

Where a claimant would otherwise be subject to all work-related requirements—or is only exempt from all work-related requirements because their earnings exceed the earnings threshold (see below)—self-employed earnings are subject to a "minimum income floor" (see regs 62-64). The minimum income floor is usually an amount representing the person's "individual threshold" (see below) converted to a monthly figure and subjected to a notional deduction to reflect the tax and national insurance contributions payable on that level of self-employed earnings. Except during a start-up period (reg.63) self-employed claimants whose earnings in any assessment period are less than their minimum income floor are treated as having earnings equal to that floor.

The operation of the minimum income floor is affected from April 2018 by the "surplus earnings" rule (see above). That, and the general calculations, is also affected from the same date by the new provision (reg.57A and amendments to reg.57) for "unused losses" in past (but not pre-April 2018) assessment periods to be set against profits in the current assessment period.

Unearned income

1.103   Unearned income is deducted from the maximum amount without any disregard or taper. However, in contrast to the rules for IS/JSA/ESA and working-age HB, not all types of unearned income fall within the definition. Those that do are set out in reg.66 of the Universal Credit Regulations and include:

- retirement pension income;
- certain social security benefits (including "new style" JSA and ESA);
- spousal maintenance payments;
- student income (e.g., student loans and grants: see reg.68);
- payments under permanent health insurance policies and certain mortgage protection policies;
- income from (non-retirement) annuities and from trusts unless disregarded as compensation for personal injury (regs 75 & 76);
- income treated as the yield from capital under reg.72 (see below);
- miscellaneous income that is taxable under Part 5 of Income Tax (Trading and Other Income) Act 2005;

Unearned income is calculated as a monthly amount but—in contrast to earned income—does not necessarily represent the amount actually received by the claimant in the assessment period for which the award is made. Regulation 73 contains detailed rules for converting unearned income (other than student income) received in respect of periods other than a month into a monthly equivalent. Student income has its own detailed rules, which are set out in regs 69-71.

Treatment of capital

Capital is relevant to universal credit entitlement in two ways. First, there is a maximum capital limit of £16,000 for both single and joint claimants (see reg.18 of the Universal Credit Regulations). Claimants who have capital in excess of that limit do not satisfy the first financial condition (see WRA 2012 s.5) and are therefore not entitled to benefit. Second, claimants with capital of more than £6,000 but less than £16,000 are treated as receiving an amount of unearned income equal to an "assumed yield" on that income. Reg.72 of the Universal Credit Regulations provides that that assumed yield is to be £4.35 per assessment period for each £250 (or part thereof). Readers who are familiar with IS/HB/JSA/ESA will recognise the "tariff income" rule under a different name. 1.104

The calculation of capital is governed by regs.45-50. By reg.46(1) and (2), the whole of a claimant's capital (other than his or her personal possessions) is to be taken into account unless it is treated as income under regs 46(3) and (4) or disregarded under reg. 48 and Sch.10. The valuation rules closely follow those for IS/HB/JSA/ESA and reg.50 contains a notional capital rule which is similar, though not identical, to that for the older working age benefits.

The benefit cap

Awards of universal credit are subject to the "benefit cap" established by ss.96-97 of the Act and regs 78-83 of the Universal Credit Regulations. This means that, subject to limited exceptions, if an award of universal credit would lead to the claimant's total entitlement to social security benefits exceeding the level of the cap then the amount of universal credit that the claimant would otherwise be awarded for the assessment period is reduced by the amount of the excess. 1.105

Until 2023 the benefit cap rates had not been changed, or even reviewed, since its rates were inserted into s.96 of the Act in 2016. But in April 2023 they were up-rated in line with the level of annual increase to other benefit levels. The Government has not stated whether this is intended to mark a new annual approach, or a one-off.

The cap is fixed at four different levels. If the claimant is (or joint claimants are) resident in Greater London, the cap is £25,323 per annum—equivalent to £486.98 per week—for joint claimants or those responsible for a child or qualifying young person and £16,967 per annum—£326.29 per week—for other claimants. If the claimant is (or joint claimants are) not resident in Greater London, the equivalent levels are £22,020 per annum and £14,753 per annum (£423.46 per week and £283.71 per week). The higher levels in Greater London are intended to reflect the higher cost of accommodation in the capital. The childcare costs element of universal credit is not subject to the cap and the cap does not apply at all if the universal credit award contains the LCWRA element; if a claimant is receiving certain other benefits including new style ESA with the support component, industrial injuries disablement benefit and attendance allowance; or if any member of the household is receiving DLA or PIP.

Housing costs

Section 8(2)(c) of the Act provides that the maximum amount is to include "any amount included under s.11 (housing costs)". Section 11(1) says that an award of universal credit must include "an amount in respect of any liability of a claimant to make payments in respect of the accommodation they occupy as their home". By s.11(2), the accommodation must be in Great Britain and must be residential accommodation but need not be self-contained. The remainder of s.11 confers powers for the Secretary of State to make regulations, which have been used to make regs 25 and 26 of, and Schs 1-5 to, the Universal Credit Regulations. 1.106

Regulation 25 establishes three conditions for eligibility, the "payment condition", the "liability condition" and the "occupation condition" (see reg.25(5)(b)).

The payment condition (reg.25(1)(a) and (2) is that payments must be rent payments (as defined in Sch.1, paras.2 and 3), owner-occupier payments (Sch.1, paras.4-6) or service charges payments (Sch.1, para.7). Until April 5, 2018, owner-occupiers were, in some circumstances, entitled to an amount of housing costs in respect of the interest on their mortgages or on loans taken out for repairs and improvements. However, from April 6, 2016 such housing costs have been replaced with loans under the Loans for Mortgage Interest Regulations 2017 (SI 2017/725): see below. As a result the only UC housing costs still payable to owner-occupiers are those in respect of service charges.

The inclusion of rent payments was a major change. Previously help with rent was given through HB which was administered by local authorities rather than the DWP. Many—but not all—of the rules about rental payments are similar to those for HB.

The liability condition (reg.25(1)(b) and (3)) is that the claimant (or either joint claimant) must either be liable to make the payments on a commercial basis, or treated as liable to make the payments (Pt 1 of Sch.2) and must not be treated as not liable to make the payments (Pt 2 of Sch.2).

The occupation condition (reg.25(1)(c) and (4)) is that the claimant must normally be treated as occupying the accommodation as his or her home (Pt 1 of Sch.3) and not be treated as not occupying it (Pt 2 of Sch.3)

The rules for the calculation of the housing costs element are set out in Schs 4 (for renters) and 5 (for the residual housing costs payable to owner occupiers).

Claimant responsibilities and the claimant commitment

The claimant commitment

1.107   Under s.4(1)(e) of the Act, it is a basic condition of entitlement to universal credit that the claimant "has accepted a claimant commitment". By s.14, a claimant commitment is "a record of a claimant's responsibilities in relation to an award of universal credit" and is to include a record of the requirements with which the claimant must comply, any prescribed information, and any other information the Secretary of State considers it appropriate to include. However, the claimant commitment does not itself impose requirements on the claimant and the condition that the clamant should accept it appears to have been included so that there is no doubt about what requirements have, in fact, been imposed. Any failure to comply with a requirement is dealt with by a sanction rather than by ending entitlement to benefit.

Claimant responsibilities

Work-related requirements

1.108   Section 13(1) of the Act empowers the Secretary of State "to impose work-related requirements with which claimants must comply". There are four different types of work-related requirement:

- the work-focused interview requirement (WRA 2012 s.15)

  As its name suggests, this is a "requirement that a claimant participate in one or more work-focused interviews as specified by the Secretary of State".

- the work preparation requirement (WRA 2012 s.16)

  This is a "requirement that a claimant take particular action specified by the Secretary of State for the purpose of making it more likely in the opinion of the Secretary of State that the claimant will obtain paid work (or more paid work or better-paid work)". Section 16(3) gives the following examples of actions that the Secretary of State may specify:
  - o attending a skills assessment;
  - o improving personal presentation;

  o participating in training;
  o participating in an employment programme;
  o undertaking work experience or a work placement;
  o developing a business plan;
  o any prescribed action.

In addition any claimant with limited capability for work may also be required to participate in a work-focused health-related assessment.

- work search requirements (WRA 2012 s.17 and reg.95)

There are two of these. The first is that a claimant must take all reasonable action for the purpose of obtaining paid work (or more paid work or better-paid work). The second is that he or she must also take any particular action specified by the Secretary of State for that purpose. Section 17(3) gives the following examples of actions that the Secretary of State may specify

  o carrying out work searches;
  o making applications;
  o creating and maintaining an online profile;
  o registering with an employment agency;
  o seeking references;
  o any prescribed action.

Under reg.95, claimants are treated as not having complied with the first work search requirement unless they have spent at least the "expected number of hours each week minus any relevant deductions" taking action to obtain paid work unless the Secretary of State is satisfied that the claimant has taken all reasonable action for that purpose despite having spent fewer hours taking action.

Reg.88 provides that the expected number of hours is 35 per week unless the claimant has caring responsibilities or is physically or mentally impaired and the Secretary of State agrees to a lesser number of hours. Reg.95(2) specifies that relevant deductions means the total of any time agreed by the Secretary of State for the claimant to carry out paid work, voluntary work, a work preparation requirement, or voluntary work preparation in that week or to deal with temporary childcare responsibilities, a domestic emergency, funeral arrangements or other temporary circumstances.

- work availability requirements (WRA 2012 s.18 and reg.96)

This is a requirement that the claimant be available for work which is defined as "able and willing immediately to take up paid work (or more paid work or better-paid work)".

The work-related requirements which may be imposed on a claimant depend on which of the following groups the claimant falls into—

- Claimants subject to no work-related requirements (WRA 2012 s.19 and regs 89-90);

These include claimants with limited capability for work and work-related activity, claimants with regular and substantial caring responsibilities for a severely disabled person, and claimants who are the responsible carer for a child under the age of 1, claimants who have reached the qualifying age for state pension credit; pregnant women within 11 weeks of the expected date of confinement and new mothers within 15 weeks of the birth, recent adopters, certain claimants in education and foster parents of children under 1.

Claimants also fall within this group if they are in work and their earnings equal or exceed the threshold that applies to them. For most people that threshold will be the amount they would earn if they worked for their expected number of hours (usually 35 per week) at the minimum wage converted to a monthly figure. At current rates, that threshold is £1,580.00 (£10.42 × 35 × 52 ÷ 12 rounded down) for those aged 23 or over. Lower thresholds apply to those aged less than 23, those who would otherwise be subject to the work-focused interview requirement only, or the work preparation requirement only, and apprentices. Couples have a joint threshold that applies to their combined weekly earnings.

- Claimants subject to the work-focused interview requirement only (WRA 2012 s.20 and reg.91);

   This group comprises the responsible carers of children who are aged 1 or more but are under 3 and certain foster parents and others caring for children.

- Claimants subject to the work-focused interview and work preparation requirements only (WRA 2012 s.21 and reg.91A);

   This group comprises claimants who have limited capability for work, but do not also have limited capability for work-related activity, or are responsible carers of children aged 3 or 4.

- Claimants subject to all work-related requirements (WRA 2012 s.22 and reg.92).

   This group comprises every claimant who is not in any of the other groups. The Secretary of State *must* impose the work search requirement and the work availability requirement on everyone in this group and *may* also impose the work-focused interview requirement and a work preparation requirement.

- A Claimant can be exempted from the work search requirements and work availability requirements while in a variety of circumstances prescribed by reg.99 of the 2013 Regulations. The most important of those is reg.99(6) (the "administrative earnings threshold"), which exempts a person earning more than a prescribed amount. Until September 2022 this was set only just above legacy benefit personal allowance levels, but from that point it increased twice in quick succession and since January 2023 has exempted only those single claimants with earnings equivalent to NMW work for at least 15 hours per week, and those in couples where the combined earnings equal at least 24 hours per week.

Reg.98 establishes special rules for the victims of domestic violence.

Connected requirements

1.109   Under s.23 of the Act, the Secretary of State may also impose a "connected requirement". There are three of these. First, claimants may be required to participate in an interview in connection with a work-related requirement. Second, they may be required to provide evidence to verify that they have complied with work-related requirements that have been imposed on them. Finally, they may be required to report specified changes in their circumstances which are relevant to work-related requirements.

Sanctions

1.110   It is not a condition of entitlement to universal credit that claimants should comply with requirements imposed by the Secretary of State under the provisions summarised above. Instead, compliance is enforced by the imposition of sanctions under which the amount of universal credit payable is reduced. Under regs 110-111 of the Universal Credit Regulations, the maximum reduction is the amount of the standard allowance applicable to the award of universal credit for the assessment period that is being considered or, where the sanction has only been imposed on one of two joint claimants, half the amount of that standard allowance.

There are four levels of sanction.

Higher-level sanctions are imposed under s.26 of the Act, which specifies that various actions or omissions by the claimant are to be "sanctionable failures". The definition of each of those failures is technical but, in broad terms, higher-level sanctions apply where, for no good reason, a claimant fails to undertake a work placement or apply for a vacancy when required to do so; fails to take up an offer of paid work; ceases work or loses pay voluntarily or through misconduct (whether before or after claiming universal credit). The sanction period is fixed by reg.102 of the Universal Credit Regulations. Again the rules are technical but for adults who commit a sanctionable failure during the currency of a claim, the length of the sanction period depends upon whether there has been a previous sanctionable failure within the previous 365 days (including the date of the failure that led to the imposition of the current sanction). If not, then the sanction period is 91 days. If there was one previous sanctionable failure within the period, it is 182 days. The sanction period for a third or subsequent sanctionable failure within the 365 day period was originally 1095 days (3 years) but was reduced to 182 days with effect from November 27, 2019. Shorter periods apply if the claimant was under 18 when the sanctionable failure occurred or in the case of a failure that occurred before the claim for universal credit. Reg.102 is subject to reg.113 which specifies a number of circumstances in which a sanctionable failure does not result in a reduction of universal credit.

Medium-level sanctions, low-level sanctions and *lowest-level sanctions* are imposed under s.27 of the Act. That section provides that it is to be a sanctionable failure for a claimant to fail, for no good reason, to comply with a work-related requirement or a connected requirement unless that failure would also be a sanctionable failure under s.26, in which case the higher-level sanction applies. The level of sanction that such a failure attracts is prescribed in regs.103-105. The regulations themselves do not say so but it is important to remember that, by virtue of s.27, each of the failures discussed below is only sanctionable if it occurred for no good reason. Moreover, regs.103-105 are subject to reg.113 which specifies a number of circumstances in which a sanctionable failure does not result in a reduction of universal credit.

A failure to take all reasonable action to obtain paid work in breach of a work search requirement under s.17(1)(a) or a failure to comply with a work availability requirement attracts a medium-level sanction under reg.103. The sanction period is 28 days for the first such failure in any 365 day period and 91 days for a second or subsequent failure in that period.

Reg.104 provides that low-level sanctions apply to claimants who are subject to the work preparation requirement or to all work-related requirements and who have failed to comply with a work-focused interview requirement, a work preparation requirement, or a connected requirement, or failed to take a particular action specified by the Secretary of State to obtain work in breach of a work search requirement. The sanction lasts until 7, 14 or 28 days (depending on the number of previous such failures in the preceding 65 days) after the claimant complies with the requirement, or has a change of circumstances so that he or she is not longer subject to any work-related requirements, or the requirement is withdrawn, or the award of universal credit ends. Again, the period for 16 and 17 year-olds is shorter.

Lowest-level sanctions are governed by reg.105. They apply to claimants who are subject to the work-focused interview requirement only (i.e., under WRA 2012, s.20) and who fail to comply with that requirement. The sanction continues until the claimant complies with the requirement, or has a change of circumstances so that he or she is no longer subject to any work-related requirements, or the award of universal credit ends.

When deciding whether there has been a previous sanctionable failure within the 365 day period, failures occurring in the 14 days immediately preceding the failure in question are disregarded (reg.101(4)).

The total of all outstanding sanction periods in relation to a particular claimant, cannot exceed 1095 days (reg.101(3)).

Under reg.109, a sanction terminates (irrespective of the length of the unexpired sanction period) if, since the most recent sanction was imposed, the claimant has been in paid work for six months (not necessarily consecutively) and during each of those months his or her earnings were equal to or exceeded the applicable threshold (see above).

Regulations provide for the date on which the sanction period is to begin. Where a claimant is subject to more than one sanction, they run consecutively (reg.101(2)).

Where a 100% sanction has been imposed (but not where there has been a 40% reduction), the Secretary of State must make a hardship payment under WRA 2012, s.28 in the (very limited) circumstances prescribed by regs 115-118. Under reg.119, hardship payments are usually recoverable in accordance with s.71ZH of the Social Security Administration Act 1992. However, any hardship payment ceases to be recoverable if, since the last date on which the award of universal credit was subject to a sanction, the claimant (or the joint claimants) has (or have) been in paid work for six months (not necessarily consecutively) and during each of those months his or her earnings (or their joint earnings) were equal to or exceeded the applicable threshold (see above).

PART 1

UNIVERSAL CREDIT

CHAPTER 1

ENTITLEMENT AND AWARDS

Introductory

1.111 **Universal credit**

1.—(1) A benefit known as universal credit is payable in accordance with this Part.

(2) Universal credit may, subject as follows, be awarded to—

(a) an individual who is not a member of a couple (a "single person"), or

(b) members of a couple jointly.

(3) An award of universal credit is, subject as follows, calculated by reference to—

(a) a standard allowance;

(b) an amount for responsibility for children or young persons;

(c) an amount for housing; and

(d) amounts for other particular needs or circumstances.

DEFINITIONS

"child"—see s.40.
"couple"—see ss.39 and 40.

GENERAL NOTE

1.112 Part 1 of the Welfare Reform Act 2012 ("WRA 2012") contains the provisions and confers regulation-making powers in relation to universal credit. Universal credit is to be the new means-tested, non-contributory benefit for people of working age. It replaces income support, income-based jobseeker's allowance (JSA), income-related employment and support allowance (ESA), housing benefit, working tax credit and child tax credit. Thus it will be paid to people both in and out of work. State pension credit will continue for people who are over the qualifying age for state pension credit— see s.4(4), which applies the definition of "the qualifying age" for state pension credit in s.1(6) of the State Pension Credit Act 2002 (see Vol.II in this series) for the purposes of universal credit. ESA and JSA will also continue but as contributory benefits only.

Note that "a person who is subject to immigration control" is not entitled to universal credit (Immigration and Asylum Act 1999, s.115, as amended by WRA 2012, Sch.2, para.54 with effect from April 29, 2013).

Initially universal credit was introduced only for people in the "pathfinder group" and only on an extremely limited geographical basis. See the Introduction and the General Note at the beginning of Part IV of this Volume for a summary of the process by which universal credit has been "rolled out" on a national basis.

As usual, Part 1 creates the legislative framework and the detail is to be found in the Universal Credit Regulations 2013 (SI 2013/376)—on which see Pt III of this Volume.

Subsection (2)

This provides that in the case of a couple awards are to be made to the couple jointly. Note the definition of "claimant" in s.40, which states that "claimant" in Pt 1 of the Act means "a single claimant or each of joint claimants".   1.113

Subsection (3)

Depending on the claimant's (or claimants') circumstances, an award of universal credit will include a standard allowance (see s.9 and reg.36 of the Universal Credit Regulations), an amount for children and young persons for whom the claimant is responsible (see s.10 and regs 24 and 36 of the Universal Credit Regulations), housing costs (see s.11 and regs 25–26 of, and Schs 1–5 to, the Universal Credit Regulations) and an amount for "other particular needs or circumstances" (see s.12 and regs 23(2) and 27–35 of, and Schs 6–9 to, the Universal Credit Regulations). Note that although subs.(3)(b) refers to an amount for children and young persons, in the case of the latter, s.10 restricts this to "qualifying young persons". For who counts as a "qualifying young person" see s.40 and reg.5 of the Universal Credit Regulations.   1.114

Claims

2.—(1) A claim may be made for universal credit by—   1.115
  (a) a single person; or
  (b) members of a couple jointly.
(2) Regulations may specify circumstances in which a member of a couple may make a claim as a single person.

DEFINITIONS

"claim"—see s.40.
"couple"—see ss.39 and 40.
"single person"—see s.40.

GENERAL NOTE

In the case of a couple, claims for universal credit are to be made jointly. This does not apply in prescribed circumstances (subs.(2)). On subs.(2), see reg.3(3) of the Universal Credit Regulations and note reg.3(4)-(6).   1.116

For the rules for claims for universal credit see the Universal Credit, Personal Independence Payment, Jobseeker's Allowance and Employment and Support Allowance (Claims and Payments) Regulations 2013 (SI 2013/380) in Vol.III. Generally a claim for universal credit has to be made online. Note reg.6 (claims not required for entitlement to universal credit in certain cases).

Entitlement

Entitlement

3.—(1) A single claimant is entitled to universal credit if the claimant meets—   1.117
  (a) the basic conditions; and
  (b) the financial conditions for a single claimant.

(2) Joint claimants are jointly entitled to universal credit if—

(a) each of them meets the basic conditions; and

(b) they meet the financial conditions for joint claimants.

DEFINITIONS

"claim"—see s.40.
"claimant"—*ibid.*
"joint claimants"—*ibid.*
"single claimant"—*ibid.*

GENERAL NOTE

1.118   This sets out the general conditions of entitlement to universal credit. A single claimant has to meet all of the basic conditions (see s.4) and the financial conditions (i.e., the means-test) (see s.5). In the case of joint claimants, both of them have to meet all of the basic and the financial conditions. Note, however, s.4(2) which allows for regulations to provide for exceptions from any of these conditions, either in the case of a single claimant, or one or both joint claimants.

Basic conditions

1.119   **4.**—(1) For the purposes of section 3, a person meets the basic conditions who—

(a) is at least 18 years old;

(b) has not reached the qualifying age for state pension credit;

(c) is in Great Britain;

(d) is not receiving education; and

(e) has accepted a claimant commitment.

(2) Regulations may provide for exceptions to the requirement to meet any of the basic conditions (and, for joint claimants, may provide for an exception for one or both).

(3) For the basic condition in subsection (1)(a) regulations may specify a different minimum age for prescribed cases.

(4) For the basic condition in subsection (1)(b), the qualifying age for state pension credit is that referred to in section 1(6) of the State Pension Credit Act 2002.

(5) For the basic condition in subsection (1)(c) regulations may—

(a) specify circumstances in which a person is to be treated as being or not being in Great Britain;

(b) specify circumstances in which temporary absence from Great Britain is disregarded.

(c) modify the application of this Part in relation to a person not in Great Britain who is by virtue of paragraph (b) entitled to universal credit.

(6) For the basic condition in subsection (1)(d) regulations may—

(a) specify what "receiving education" means;

(b) specify circumstances in which a person is to be treated as receiving or not receiving education.

(7) For the basic condition in subsection (1)(e) regulations may specify circumstances in which a person is to be treated as having accepted or not accepted a claimant commitment.

DEFINITIONS

"claim"—see s.40.
"claimant"—*ibid.*
"joint claimants"—*ibid.*

GENERAL NOTE

Subsection (1) lists the basic conditions that have to be satisfied for entitlement   1.120
to universal credit. Subsection (2) allows for regulations to provide for exceptions
from any of these conditions, either in the case of a single claimant, or one or both
joint claimants.

Subsection (1)(a)
The minimum age for entitlement to universal credit is generally 18. However,   1.121
under subs.(3) regulations can provide for a lower age in certain cases. See reg.8 of
the Universal Credit Regulations for the cases where the minimum age is 16.

Subsection (1)(b)
This subsection excludes the possibility that a person could be entitled to both   1.122
state pension credit and universal credit by providing that no person who has
reached "the qualifying age for state pension credit" will meet the basic conditions
for universal credit. But note subs.(2) and see reg.3(2) of the Universal Credit
Regulations. The effect of reg.3(2) is that a couple may still be entitled to universal
credit even if one member is over the qualifying age for state pension credit, provided that the other member of the couple is under that age.
Subsection (4) applies the definition of "the qualifying age" for state pension
credit in s.1(6) of the State Pension Credit Act 2002 (see Part I of this volume) for
the purposes of universal credit. The effect of that definition is that the qualifying age
for state pension credit for both men and women is the pensionable age for women.

Subsection (1)(c)
It is a basic condition of entitlement to universal credit that the person is in Great   1.123
Britain. Note subs.(5) under which regulations may treat a person as being or not
being in Great Britain (see reg.9 of the Universal Credit Regulations for when a
person is treated as not being in Great Britain, and reg.10 on Crown servants and
armed forces) and may provide for the circumstances in which temporary absence
from Great Britain is ignored (see reg.11).

Subsection (1)(d)
A person must not be "receiving education" to be eligible for universal credit.   1.124
For the regulations made under subs.(6) see regs 12–14 of the Universal Credit
Regulations.

Subsection (1)(e)
The concept of a claimant commitment as a condition of receiving benefit is an   1.125
important part of the underlying policy behind the Government's social security
reforms. See s.14 below and the notes to that section. Note that the condition is met
merely by having accepted the most up-to-date version of the claimant commitment.
Further, in *FO v SSWP* (UC) [2022] UKUT 56 (AAC) at paras 14 and 15, Judge
Wikeley expressed no disagreement with the Secretary of State's assertion that where
a UC award is in place and the Secretary of State wants to update the claimant commitment, a claimant's failure to engage, while potentially sanctionable, is not a basis
for ending the award because the existing claimant commitment will remain in force
(but see the notes to reg.15 of the Universal Credit Regulations, 2.54).
A failure to comply with the claimant commitment does not entail any breach of
subs.(1)(e), nor is that in itself any ground for a sanction, although sanctions may
be imposed for failures to comply with work-related and connected requirements
that are recorded in the claimant commitment and other legal consequences may
follow from failures to carry out other obligations. Under subs.(7) regulations may
specify the circumstances in which a person can be treated as having accepted or not
accepted a claimant commitment—see reg.15 of the Universal Credit Regulations.
In addition, subs.(2) allows regulations to provide exceptions to the requirement to
meet any basic condition.

That power has been exercised in relation to the condition of having accepted a claimant commitment in reg.16, which may have been of particular importance during the 2020 coronavirus outbreak, when "conditionality" was suspended for three months from March 30, 2020. Since there was no new legislation to lift the operation of s.4(1)(e) during that period, in contrast to the position on the work search and work availability requirements (see the notes to ss.17 and 18), allowing entitlement on new claims without s.4(1)(e) being met appears to be the key to not imposing those requirements. Regulation 16(b) (exceptional circumstances make it unreasonable to expect the claimant to accept a claimant commitment) could clearly be applied (see further in the notes to reg.16). For existing claimants, who had already accepted a commitment, the work search and work availability requirements were expressly lifted. For other requirements, there were to be no sanctions imposed for failing to comply and/or a flexibility in reviewing requirements over the telephone.

On July 1, 2020 it was announced in Parliament (Under-Secretary of State, Mims Davies,WQ 62431) that from that date the requirement for universal credit claimants (among others) to accept a claimant commitment was being reintroduced.The commitments of existing claimants would be reviewed and up-dated as capacity allowed. It appears that the reintroduction for new claimants was also to be phased in.

Note that the new style Jobseekers Act 1995 (Vol.I of this series) does not allow regulations to provide exceptions to the requirement to meet the conditions of entitlement in s.1(2), including that of having accepted a claimant commitment (s.1(2) (b)), so that reg.8 of the JSA Regulations 2013 appears not to have been validly made. Nor does the new style Welfare Reform Act 2007 (on new style ESA) in relation to the conditions of entitlement in s.1(3), including that of having accepted a claimant commitment (s.1(3)(aa)), so that reg.45 of the ESA Regulations 2013 appears not to have been validly made.

Subsection (5)

1.126
It is worthy of note that this superficially innocuous provision is relied on in regulations to authorise many of the practical restrictions on migrants' access to universal credit, under reg.9 of the Universal Credit Regulations. "Persons subject to immigration control" are separately excluded by s.115(9) of the Immigration and Asylum Act 1999. But there are many migrants—especially EU nationals with pre-settled status—who have a grant of leave to be in the UK, and are not excluded from access to public funds under the terms of their leave. There does not appear to be any case law analysing whether a power to "specify circumstances in which a person is to be treated as … not being in Great Britain" can authorise indefinitely excluding a person who is in fact here and has a positive right to be here.

Financial conditions

1.127
5.—(1) For the purposes of section 3, the financial conditions for a single claimant are that—
- (a) the claimant's capital, or a prescribed part of it, is not greater than a prescribed amount, and
- (b) the claimant's income is such that, if the claimant were entitled to universal credit, the amount payable would not be less than any prescribed minimum.

(2) For those purposes, the financial conditions for joint claimants are that—
- (a) their combined capital, or a prescribed part of it, is not greater than a prescribed amount, and
- (b) their combined income is such that, if they were entitled to universal credit, the amount payable would not be less than any prescribed minimum.

DEFINITIONS

"claim"—see s.40.
"claimant"—*ibid.*
"joint claimants"—*ibid.*
"prescribed"—*ibid.*
"single claimant"—*ibid.*

GENERAL NOTE

This section contains the means-test for universal credit. Both the capital and the   **1.128**
income condition have to be met. For joint claimants it is their combined capital and
their combined income that counts (subs.(2)).

Capital

The capital limit for universal credit for both a single claimant and joint claimants   **1.129**
is £16,000 (see reg.18(1) of the Universal Credit Regulations). The limit has not
altered since the inception of the universal credit scheme, or indeed since 2006 for
other means-tested benefits (see the notes to reg.18). Note that where a claimant
who is a member of a couple makes a claim as a single person (see reg.3(3) of the
Universal Credit Regulations for the circumstances in which this may occur) the
capital of the other member of the couple counts as the claimant's (reg.18(2)).

Thus the capital limit for universal credit is the same as for income support,
income-based JSA, income-related ESA and housing benefit. There is no capital
limit for working tax credit and child tax credit.

Since having capital not exceeding the prescribed limit is a condition of entitlement under s.3(1)(b) it must be the case that the burden of showing that that is so
rests on the claimant. That principle had been accepted for other income-related
benefits where there was more of an argument that the capital limit operated as
an exclusion and so might be for the Secretary of State to show (see the notes to
s.134(1) of the SSCBA 1992 in Vol.V of this series). That would be in accord with
the principle in *Kerr v Department for Social Development* [2004] UKHL 23; [2004] 1
W.L.R. 1372, also reported as *R 1/04 (SF)*, in which Baroness Hale emphasised that
the process of adjudication for social security benefits is a co-operative one in which
both the Department and the claimant should play their part, according to who is
likely to have the necessary information available, and that normally it ought not
to be necessary to resort to more formal concepts such as the burden of proof. So,
in *MB v Royal Borough of Kensington and Chelsea (HB)* [2011] UKUT 321 (AAC),
the answer to the claimant's argument that it was for the Council to show that she
had a beneficial interest in the capital at issue was that it was she who had exclusive
knowledge about the purchase of the property in question and the mortgage payments and thus it was her responsibility to marshal what evidence she could to show
that, although she was the legal owner, she was not the sole beneficial owner of the
property. Similarly, once it is accepted that a claimant possessed or received an asset,
the burden is on them to show that they no longer possess it (*R(SB) 38/85* and see
the notes to reg.50(1) of the Universal Credit Regulations).

The amount of a claimant's capital is quite likely to vary during the course of an
assessment period. What if it exceeds £16,000 (or some lower figure relevant to the
assumed yield from capital rule in reg.72 of the Universal Credit Regulations) at the
beginning of the period, but has fallen below the limit by the end of the period, or
vice versa? It is generally assumed that, since the basic rule on the date on which a
supersession on the ground of change of circumstances takes effect is the first day
of the assessment period in which the change occurred (Decisions and Appeals
Regulations 2013 Sch.1 para.20), whatever is the case at the end of the assessment
period is to be taken as having been so since the first day of the period and thus
governs the outcome. That, however, seems a fragile basis for what would seem to
be a fundamental step in the calculation of entitlement.

For the rules on calculating capital see regs 45–50 and 75–77 of, and Sch 10 to, the Universal Credit Regulations.

Income

1.130
The effect of subs.(1)(b) in the case of a single claimant and subs.(2)(b) in the case of joint claimants is that there will be no entitlement to universal credit if the amount payable is less than the minimum amount. The minimum amount is 1p (see reg.17 of the Universal Credit Regulations and note reg.6(1) on rounding). Thus it is possible for a person to be entitled to universal credit of 1p.

Note that where a claimant who is a member of a couple makes a claim as a single person (see reg.3(3) of the Universal Credit Regulations for the circumstances in which this may occur) the combined income of the couple is taken into account when calculating an award (reg.22(3)(a)).

Any income of a child is not taken into account.

See also the regulation-making powers as regards the calculation of capital and income in para.4 of Sch.1.

Restrictions on entitlement

1.131
6.—(1) Entitlement to universal credit does not arise—

(a) in prescribed circumstances (even though the requirements in section 3 are met);

(b) if the requirements in section 3 are met for a period shorter than a prescribed period.

(c) for a prescribed period at the beginning of a period during which those requirements are met.

(2) A period prescribed under subsection (1)(b) or (c) may not exceed seven days.

(3) Regulations may provide for exceptions to subsection (1)(b) or (c).

DEFINITION

"prescribed"—see s.40.

GENERAL NOTE

1.132
This enables regulations to be made which provide that a person will not be entitled to universal credit: (i) even though they meet the basic and financial conditions (subs.(1)(a)); (ii) if they meet those conditions for seven days or less (subs.(1)(b) and subs.(2)); or (iii) for a period of seven days or less at the beginning of a period during which those conditions are met (subs.(1)(c) and subs.(2)).

The power conferred by subs.(1)(a) has been exercised to make reg.19 of the Universal Credit Regulations and that conferred by subs.(1)(c) to make reg.19A. No regulations have yet been made under subs.(1)(b).

Awards

Basis of awards

1.133
7.—(1) Universal credit is payable in respect of each complete assessment period within a period of entitlement.

(2) In this Part an "assessment period" is a period of a prescribed duration.

(3) Regulations may make provision—

(a) about when an assessment period is to start;

(b) for universal credit to be payable in respect of a period shorter than an assessment period;

(c) about the amount payable in respect of a period shorter than an assessment period.

(4) In subsection (1) "period of entitlement" means a period during which entitlement to universal credit subsists.

GENERAL NOTE

See the commentary to reg.21 of the Universal Credit Regulations.   1.134

Calculation of awards

8.—(1) The amount of an award of universal credit is to be the balance of—   1.135
  (a) the maximum amount (see subsection (2)), less
  (b) the amounts to be deducted (see subsection (3)).
(2) The maximum amount is the total of—
  (a) any amount included under section 9 (standard allowance);
  (b) any amount included under section 10 (responsibility for children and young persons);
  (c) any amount included under section 11 (housing costs), and
  (d) any amount included under section 12 (other particular needs or circumstances).
(3) The amounts to be deducted are—
  (a) an amount in respect of earned income calculated in the prescribed manner (which may include multiplying some or all earned income by a prescribed percentage), and
  (b) an amount in respect of unearned income calculated in the prescribed manner (which may include multiplying some or all unearned income by a prescribed percentage).
(4) In subsection (3)(a) and (b) the references to income are—
  (a) in the case of a single claimant, to income of the claimant, and
  (b) in the case of joint claimants, to combined income of the claimants.

DEFINITIONS

"claim"—see s.40.
"claimant"—*ibid.*
"joint claimants"—*ibid.*
"prescribed"—*ibid.*
"single claimant"—*ibid.*

GENERAL NOTE

See the commentary to reg.22 of the Universal Credit Regulations.   1.136

Elements of an award

Standard allowance

9.—(1) The calculation of an award of universal credit is to include an amount by way of an allowance for—   1.137
  (a) a single claimant, or
  (b) joint claimants.
(2) Regulations are to specify the amount to be included under subsection (1).
(3) Regulations may provide for exceptions to subsection (1).

DEFINITIONS

"claim"—see s.40.
"claimant"—*ibid.*

GENERAL NOTE

1.138   See the commentary to regs 23 and 36 of the Universal Credit Regulations.

Responsibility for children and young persons

1.139   **10.**—(1) The calculation of an award of universal credit is to include an amount for each child or qualifying young person for whom a claimant is responsible.

[¹ (1A) But the amount mentioned in subsection (1) is to be available in respect of a maximum of two persons who are either children or qualifying young persons for whom a claimant is responsible.]

(2) Regulations may make provision for the inclusion of an additional amount [¹ for each] child or qualifying young person [¹ for whom a claimant is responsible who] is disabled.

(3) Regulations are to specify, or provide for the calculation of, amounts to be included under subsection (1) or (2).

(4) Regulations may provide for exceptions to subsection (1) [¹ or (1A)].

(5) In this Part, "qualifying young person" means a person of a prescribed description.

AMENDMENT

1. Welfare Reform and Work Act 2016 s.14(1)-(4) (April 6, 2017).

DEFINITIONS

"child"—see s.40.
"disabled"—*ibid.*

GENERAL NOTE

1.140   See the commentary to regs 24 and 36 of the Universal Credit Regulations.

Housing costs

1.141   **11.**—(1) The calculation of an award of universal credit is to include an amount in respect of any liability of a claimant to make payments in respect of the accommodation they occupy as their home.

(2) For the purposes of subsection (1)—

(a) the accommodation must be in Great Britain;

(b) the accommodation must be residential accommodation;

(c) it is immaterial whether the accommodation consists of the whole or part of a building and whether or not it comprises separate and self-contained premises.

(3) Regulations may make provision as to—

(a) what is meant by payments in respect of accommodation for the purposes of this section [¹ ...];

(b) circumstances in which a claimant is to be treated as liable or not liable to make such payments;

(c) circumstances in which a claimant is to be treated as occupying or not occupying accommodation as their home (and, in particular, for temporary absences to be disregarded);

(d) circumstances in which land used for the purposes of any accommodation is to be treated as included in the accommodation.

(4) Regulations are to provide for the determination or calculation of any amount to be included under this section.

(5) Regulations may—

(a) provide for exceptions to subsection (1);

(b) provide for inclusion of an amount under this section in the calculation of an award of universal credit—

(i) to end at a prescribed time, or

(ii) not to start until a prescribed time.

AMENDMENT

1. Welfare Reform and Work Act 2016 s.20(9) (April 6, 2018).

DEFINITIONS

"claim"—see s.40.
"claimant"—*ibid.*
"prescribed"—*ibid.*

GENERAL NOTE

This provides for an award of universal credit to include an amount in respect   **1.142**
of the claimant's (or claimants') liability to make payments in respect of the accommodation they occupy as their home. It could cover payments both by people who are renting their homes and by owner occupiers (as well as service charges), though in fact universal credit provides support only with rent and service charges. Owner occupier payments are addressed through a separate loans scheme (see ss.18–21 of the Welfare Reform and Work Act 2016, and the Loans for Mortgage Interest Regulations 2017 in Pt IIA of this volume).

Under subs.(2), the accommodation must be residential accommodation and must be in Great Britain. It can be the whole or part of a building and need not comprise separate and self-contained premises.

For the rules relating to housing costs see regs 25–26 of, and Schs 1–5 to, the Universal Credit Regulations.

Other particular needs or circumstances

12.—(1) The calculation of an award of universal credit is to include   **1.143**
amounts in respect of such particular needs or circumstances of a claimant as may be prescribed.

(2) The needs or circumstances prescribed under subsection (1) may include—

(a) [1 . . .]

(b) the fact that a claimant has limited capability for work and work-related activity;

(c) the fact that a claimant has regular and substantial caring responsibilities for a severely disabled person.

(3) Regulations are to specify, or provide for the determination or calculation of, any amount to be included under subsection (1).

(4) Regulations may—

(a) provide for inclusion of an amount under this section in the calculation of an award of universal credit—

(i) to end at a prescribed time, or

(ii) not to start until a prescribed time;

(b) provide for the manner in which a claimant's needs or circumstances are to be determined.

AMENDMENT

1. Welfare Reform and Work Act 2016 s.16 (April 3, 2017).

DEFINITIONS

"claim"—see s.40.
"claimant"—*ibid.*
"limited capability for work"—*ibid.*
"prescribed"—*ibid.*
"work"—*ibid.*

GENERAL NOTE

1.144   Section 12(2)(a) identified having limited capability for work as one of the needs or circumstances which "may" be prescribed. It was repealed when the LCW element was removed from the Universal Credit Regulations.

Section 12(2)(b) is carried into the regulations as one of the prescribed needs or circumstances (regs 27–28 of the Universal Credit Regulations), as is s.12(2)(c) (regs 29–30). The only prescribed need or circumstance not specifically foreshadowed in s.12 is childcare costs provision (regs 31–35).

See further the commentary to regs 27–36 of the Universal Credit Regulations.

CHAPTER 2

CLAIMANT RESPONSIBILITIES

Introductory

Work-related requirements: introductory

1.145   **13.**—(1) This Chapter provides for the Secretary of State to impose work-related requirements with which claimants must comply for the purposes of this Part.

(2) In this Part "work-related requirement" means—
(a) a work-focused interview requirement (see section 15);
(b) a work preparation requirement (see section 16);
(c) a work search requirement (see section 17);
(d) a work availability requirement (see section 18).

(3) The work-related requirements which may be imposed on a claimant depend on which of the following groups the claimant falls into—
(a) no work-related requirements (see section 19);
(b) work-focused interview requirement only (see section 20);
(c) work-focused interview and work preparation requirements only (see section 21);
(d) all work-related requirements (see section 22).

GENERAL NOTE

1.146   The remaining sections of this Chapter of the WRA 2012 in the main set out what sort of work-related requirements can be imposed on which universal credit claimants, as well as the system for imposing sanctions (reductions in benefit) on claimants for failure to comply with those requirements. Although s.13(1) refers only to work-related requirements as defined in ss.15–18, s.23 allows the Secretary of State to require a claimant to participate in an interview for various related purposes and to provide information and evidence. A failure to comply with a requirement under s.23 can lead to a sanction under s.27(2)(b) in the same way as can a failure to comply with any work-related requirement under s.27(2)(a). Section 14 contains rules about the "claimant commitment", acceptance of which is a condition of entitlement under s.4(1)(e).

There is a handy summary of the sanctions framework in Chapter 47 of CPAG's *Welfare Benefits and Tax Credits Handbook* (2023/24 edn).

It was noted in paras 17 and 18 of *S v SSWP (UC)* [2017] UKUT 477 (AAC) that s.13(1) means that a work-related requirement can only come into being when it has been *imposed* by the Secretary of State (under the duty in s.22). See the discussion in the notes to s.14 for the important implications for the effect in law of the standard terms of claimant commitments.

Note that if a claimant is entitled to both universal credit and new style JSA, reg.5 of the JSA Regulations 2013 provides that no work-related requirements can be imposed under the new style JSA regime (ss.6B-6G of the new style Jobseekers Act 1995) and that the provisions for reduction of JSA on sanctions under ss.6J and 6K of that Act do not apply. See the annotations to reg.5 in Vol.I of this series for discussion of the consequences and of a proposal for change in the indefinite future, and the notes to reg.111 of and Sch.11 to the Universal Credit Regulations. There is an equivalent provision in reg.42 of the ESA Regulations 2013 in relation to new style ESA.

Claimant commitment

14.—(1) A claimant commitment is a record of a claimant's responsibilities in relation to an award of universal credit. 1.147

(2) A claimant commitment is to be prepared by the Secretary of State and may be reviewed and updated as the Secretary of State thinks fit.

(3) A claimant commitment is to be in such form as the Secretary of State thinks fit.

(4) A claimant commitment is to include—
(a) a record of the requirements that the claimant must comply with under this Part (or such of them as the Secretary of State considers it appropriate to include),
(b) any prescribed information, and
(c) any other information the Secretary of State considers it appropriate to include.

(5) For the purposes of this Part a claimant accepts a claimant commitment if, and only if, the claimant accepts the most up-to-date version of it in such manner as may be prescribed.

DEFINITIONS

"claimant"—see s.40.
"prescribed"—*ibid.*

GENERAL NOTE

Under s.4(1)(e) the final basic condition of entitlement is that the claimant has accepted a claimant commitment. Section 14 defines the nature of a claimant commitment and there are further provisions in regs 15 and 16 of the Universal Credit Regulations. Where a claim has to be made jointly by both members of a couple, both are claimants and subject to this condition, as illustrated by *FO v SSWP (UC)* [2022] UKUT 56 (AAC) (see the notes to reg.15). 1.148

See the notes to s.4(1)(e) and reg.16 for the position during the 2020/21 coronavirus outbreak, as well as the notes on the work search and work availability requirements. It appears that at least for the period from March 30, 2020 to June 30, 2020 the power to award entitlement without having met the basic condition of having accepted a claimant commitment was invoked. On July 1, 2020 it was announced in Parliament (Under-Secretary of State, Mims Davies, WQ 62431) that from that date the requirement for universal credit claimants (among others) to accept a claimant commitment was being reintroduced. The commitments of existing claimants would be reviewed and up-dated as capacity allowed. It appears that the reintroduction for new claimants was also to be phased in. The answer stressed that claimant commitments agreed or reviewed from July 1, 2020 would have to be reasonable for the "new normal" and acknowledge the reality of a person's local jobs market and personal circumstances.

Note that the condition is met merely by having accepted the most up-to-date version of the claimant commitment, as discussed below. A failure to comply with the claimant commitment does not entail any breach of s.4(1)(e), nor is that in itself any ground for a sanction, although sanctions may be imposed for failures to comply with work-related and connected requirements that are recorded in the claimant commitment and other legal consequences may follow from failures to carry out other obligations.

It is an important element of the universal credit scheme, in contrast to the schemes that it has replaced, that the acceptance of the claimant commitment is a condition of entitlement for all categories of claimant, not merely those who would previously have been within the ambit of old style JSA. However, for those other categories the commitment can only be a much more generalised statement of responsibilities (see below), since the application of "conditionality" in the full sense to the claimant's personal circumstances will not be in issue.

Subsections (1) and (2) define a claimant commitment as a record prepared by the Secretary of State (in such form as he thinks fit: subs.(3)) of a claimant's responsibilities in relation to an award of universal credit. In particular, by subs.(4)(a), the record is to include the requirements that the particular claimant must comply with under the WRA 2012. These will in the main be work-related and connected requirements (see ss.15-25). However, in relation to those with limited capability for work or work-related activity the requirements will include those to provide information or evidence and to submit to a medical examination (s.37(5)-(7) and regs 43 and 44 of the Universal Credit Regulations). Work-related requirements can sometimes be to take specific action (e.g. to participate in a particular interview under s.15 or to take particular action to improve prospects of paid work under s.16 or to obtain paid work under s.17), although often the specification of such action by the Secretary of State will take place outside the claimant commitment (see the discussion in *JB v SSWP (UC)* [2018] UKUT 360 (AAC), detailed near the end of the notes to s.14). Nonetheless, the document will need to be detailed and closely related to the claimant's circumstances as they are from time to time. As such, it may be subject to frequent change, although there is a discretion in subs.(4) (a) to omit requirements if appropriate. The process of review and updating under subs.(2) appears to be completely informal, in stark contrast to the process for variation of a jobseeker's agreement under s.10 of the old style Jobseekers Act 1995, so can accommodate that. Each updating will trigger a new requirement to accept the most up-to-date version. Subsection (4)(b) requires the record to contain any prescribed information. Regulations have not as yet prescribed any such information. Subsection (4)(c) requires the record to contain any other information (note, information, not a further requirement) that the Secretary of State considers appropriate. For the claimant commitment to serve the basic purpose discussed below, that information must at least include information about the potential consequences under the Act of receiving a sanction for failure to carry out a requirement.

Since subs.(4) is, though, not an exhaustive statement of what a claimant commitment can contain, merely a statement of elements that it must contain, there is no reason why other responsibilities in relation to an award of universal credit cannot also be recorded, along with any appropriate accompanying information, although the perceived need to include subs.(4)(c) could be argued to cast doubt on that conclusion. For instance, the general obligations under regs 38 and 44 of the Claims and Payments Regulations 2013 to supply information and evidence in connection with an award and to notify changes of circumstances should probably be recorded, as it is in the example mentioned below.

Very limited exceptions from the application of the basic condition in s.4(1)(e) are set out in reg.16 of the Universal Credit Regulations. The WRA 2012 does not seek to define what is meant by acceptance of a claimant commitment beyond the provision in subs.(5) that it must be the most up-to-date version that has been accepted in such manner as prescribed in regulations. Regulation 15 of the Universal Credit Regulations provides for the time within which and the manner in which the claimant commitment must be accepted, but says nothing about what accepting the commitment entails in substance. In practice, the normal method specified under reg.15 is via a "To Do" action placed on the claimant's electronic journal, where a button must be clicked to indicate acceptance (Williams, Lack of commitment?, *Welfare Rights Bulletin 274* (February 2020) p.4).

Since the commitment is the record of the particular claimant's responsibilities as **1.149** imposed by or under the legislation itself it does not seem that acceptance can mean much more than an acknowledgement of its receipt or possibly also that the claimant understands the implications of the requirements set out. There can be no question of a claimant having to express any agreement with the justice or reasonableness of the requirements, let alone of the policy behind universal credit. Nor does acceptance seem to involve any personal commitment to carrying out the stated requirements, despite the language used in the example mentioned below. A failure to comply with any requirement imposed by the Secretary of State is a matter for a potential sanction under ss.26 or 27, not for a conclusion that the basic condition of entitlement in s.4(1)(e) is no longer met. There is no direct sanction for a failure to comply with a requirement just because it is included in the claimant commitment, nor does such a failure show that the claimant commitment has ceased to be accepted in the sense suggested above.

However, this distinction may be of little significance in practice, since inclusion in the claimant commitment appears to be a sufficient means of notifying a claimant of the imposition of a requirement (see s.24(4) below) and a failure for no good reason to comply with any work-related requirement attracts a sanction under s.27(2) at the least. For instance, if the Secretary of State acting under s.17(2)(b) (work search requirement) specifies in the claimant commitment an impossibly large or internally inconsistent number of actions per week, then a failure to carry out the actions is at least prima facie a sanctionable failure and the question of whether what was specified was unreasonable would appear to be relevant only to "good reason" (though see the further discussion in the notes to ss.26 and 27). It is not like the actively seeking employment condition in old style JSA where, whatever was set out in a jobseeker's agreement, the fundamental test was whether claimants had in any week taken such steps as they could reasonably have been expected to have done to have the best prospects of securing employment.

Despite the incontrovertible nature of the legal framework, official sources continue to describe an essential feature of the claimant commitment as being that it and its conditionality requirements have been agreed by the claimant. See the DWP's statement of the aim of conditionality and sanctions set out in para.10 of the House of Commons Work and Pensions Committee's report of November 6, 2018 on *Benefit Sanctions* (HC 995 2017-19) and the Committee's own description of the claimant commitment as recording "the actions a [...] claimant has agreed to undertake as a condition of receiving their benefit". Even the Social Security Advisory Committee's March 19, 2019 call for evidence on the operation of the claimant commitment in universal credit for those subject to all work-related requirements talked of the commitment setting out what a claimant has agreed to do to prepare for work, or to increase their earnings if they are already working, and what will happen if a claimant fails to meet the agreed responsibilities. It might not matter much if such terminology is restricted to policy discussions. No doubt, for the sort of reasons mentioned below, it will always be better if the requirements set out in the claimant commitment have been worked out after a full and co-operative discussion with the work coach and the claimant agrees that the requirements are realistic and achievable. But there is evidence that the approach has infected the standard terms of claimant commitments, with consequent problems in ascertaining whether the legal requirements for the imposition of sanctions have been made out (see the discussion below of the standard terms and of the decision in *JB v SSWP (UC)* [2018] UKUT 360 (AAC)).

Chapter J1 of *Advice for Decision Making* says that the claimant commitment is generated as the result of a conversation with the claimant (para.J1010) and that claimants who fall into the all work-related requirements group or the work preparation group will need to have a discussion with a work coach before a claimant commitment can be drawn up and accepted. Claimant commitments for claimants not in either of those groups may be accepted as part of the normal claims process (para.J1011). The meaning of that last phrase is not entirely clear, but may refer to those groups of claimants on whom it is clear from the outset that no personalised requirements will be imposed. There is a recognition that claimants may well not feel able to accept on the spot at a first interview with an adviser (now called a work coach) the full range of requirements set out in the claimant commitment, so that if the claimant declines to accept the document then, a "cooling-off period" of a maximum of seven days must be allowed for reconsideration (para. J1010). The legislative basis for this is under reg.15(1) of the Universal Credit Regulations, which provides that s.4(1)(e) is to be treated as satisfied from the outset when the claimant commitment is accepted within such period after the making of the claim as the Secretary of State specifies. It must in law be open to a work coach, depending on the particular circumstances, to specify a longer period or to alter the period initially specified. See the notes to reg.15 for further discussion of the dates on which claimant commitments are deemed to be accepted and of the point at which a claimant commitment is formally presented to a claimant for acceptance.

1.150   Work requirements are supposed to be set through a one-to-one relationship between work coach and claimant, enabling the development of a good understanding of the claimant's circumstances, so that the work coach can best help the claimant find work (see the DWP's evidence to the Work and Pensions Committee in para.87 of the report above). However, the Committee received evidence that many claimant commitments were "generic" in nature, failing to take account of individual circumstances, and that "easements" (i.e. circumstances in which in accordance with regulations the requirement in question could be lifted or modified) were insufficiently used. Taking the view that it was unrealistic for claimants to know the rules about when easements could apply or for them to pour out the details of their personal lives at each meeting, the Committee recommended that the DWP develop a standard set of questions that work coaches routinely ask claimants when developing their claimant commitments, as well as improve the information available to claimants on easements. The DWP's response (House of Commons Work and Pensions Committee, *Benefit Sanctions: Government Response* (HC 1949 2017-19, February 11, 2019, paras 55-65) was that current training, guidance and monitoring of work coaches involved standard key questions to identify things like caring responsibilities, health conditions and other complex circumstances that could impact ability to meet requirements. Additional easements were said to be more specific and sensitive, so should not be presented as if they would apply to the majority of claimants. Instead, a new information package on easements to be provided at the start of the claim was to become available in Spring 2019.

Thus, when it was announced (Parliamentary answer, Under-Secretary of State, Mims Davies, WQ 62431) that from July 1, 2020 the requirement for universal credit claimants (among others) to accept a claimant commitment was being reintroduced, it was stressed that claimant commitments agreed or reviewed from that date would have to be reasonable for the "new normal" and acknowledge the reality of a person's local jobs market and personal circumstances. That must entail an increased focus on "easements", but doubts have been expressed about the practicality of that when the length of meetings was being restricted, at least initially, to 30 minutes (now increased to 50 minutes a week: see the notes to reg.97(4) and (5) of the Universal Credit Regulations). Paragraph 4.31 of the September 2022 *Growth Plan 2022* (CP 743) said that the Government would be strengthening the universal credit sanctions regime to set clear expectations, including applying for jobs, attending interviews or increasing hours, but it was left unclear exactly what that was to entail or whether any legislative change was envisaged. It is not known whether the plan, such as it was, has survived the change of administration.

The Social Security Advisory Committee's (SSAC's) September 2019 study on *The effectiveness of the claimant commitment in Universal Credit* (Occasional Paper No.21) contains much interesting information on policy and the practical operation of the claimant commitment, without addressing the mismatch suggested above with the legal framework. It puts forward, within the overarching principle that the process of developing a commitment for a particular claimant should be reasonable and based on evidence of what works to help people move into sustained employment, five principles for the effectiveness of a commitment for a claimant in the intensive work search regime. It should be accessible, clear, tailored to the needs of each claimant, accepted by both parties and the claimant should have the right information. The SSAC identified many examples of good practice by work coaches, but also examples of failure to meet those principles, especially on the tailoring to individual needs and circumstances.

The notion of the claimant commitment is in many ways at the heart of what "conditionality" is meant to achieve under universal credit. It looks on its face to be an expression of what Charles Reich in his classic essay *The New Property* (1964) 73 Yale Law Journal 733 called "the New Feudalism". The universal credit claimant not only has, as the price of securing entitlement to the benefit, to accept a defined status that involves the giving up of some rights normally enjoyed by ordinary citizens, but appears to have to undertake some kind of oath of fealty by accepting a commitment to the feudal duties of that status. However, in reality the claimant commitment is a much more prosaic, and more sensible, thing. In its interesting paper *Universal Credit and Conditionality* (Social Security Advisory Committee Occasional Paper No. 9, 2012) the SSAC reported research findings that many claimants of current benefits subject to a sanctions regime did not understand what conduct could lead to a sanction, how the sanctions system worked (some not even realising that they had been sanctioned) and in particular what the consequences of a sanction would be on current and future entitlement. Paragraph 3.12 of the paper states:

> "The lessons to be learned from the research ought to be relatively straightforward to implement, although providing the appropriate training for a large number of Personal Advisers may present a considerable challenge:
>
> - claimants need to have the link between conditionality and the application of sanctions fully explained at the start of any claim
> - clear and unambiguous communication about the sanctions regime between advisers and claimants is vital at the start of any claim and must form a key element in the Claimant Commitment
> - claimants need to know when they are in danger of receiving a sanction and to be told when a sanction has been imposed, the amount and the duration
> - claimants need to know what actions they have to take to reverse a sanction—the process and consequences of re-compliance."

If one of the main aims of conditionality, of encouraging claimants to avoid behaviour that would impede a possible return to or entry into work and thus reducing the incidence of the imposition of sanctions or of more severe sanctions, is to be furthered, it therefore makes sense to build into the system a requirement to set out each claimant's responsibilities and the consequences of not meeting them in understandable terms. However, as the SSAC suggests, the nature of the personal interaction between personal advisers, now known as work coaches, and claimants may be much more important than a formal written document in getting over the realities of the situation and in encouraging claimants to take steps to avoid or reduce dependence on benefit.

1.151   A similar line of thought seems to be behind what was set out in paras 65 and 66 of the joint judgment of Lords Neuberger and Toulson in *R (on the application of Reilly and Wilson) v Secretary of State for Work and Pensions* [2013] UKSC 68; [2014] 1 A.C. 453, in relation to the JSA regime, after noting the serious consequence of imposing a requirement to engage in unpaid work on a claimant on pain of discontinuance of benefits:

> "65.   Fairness therefore requires that a claimant should have access to such information about the scheme as he or she may need in order to make informed and meaningful representations to the decision-maker before a decision is made. Such claimants are likely to vary considerably in their levels of education and ability to express themselves in an interview at a Jobcentre at a time when they may be under considerable stress. The principle does not depend on the categorisation of the Secretary of State's decision to introduce a particular scheme under statutory powers as a policy: it arises as a matter of fairness from the Secretary of State's proposal to invoke a statutory power in a way which will or may involve a requirement to perform work and which may have serious consequences on a claimant's ability to meet his or her living needs.
> 66.   Properly informed claimants, with knowledge not merely of the schemes available, but also of the criteria for being placed on such schemes, should be able to explain what would, in their view, be the most reasonable and appropriate scheme for them, in a way which would be unlikely to be possible without such information. Some claimants may have access to information downloadable from a government website, if they knew what to look for, but many will not. For many of those dependent on benefits, voluntary agencies such as Citizens Advice Bureaus play an important role in informing and assisting them in relation to benefits to which they may be entitled, how they should apply, and what matters they should draw to the attention of their Jobcentre adviser."

These principles were discussed by the Court of Appeal in *SSWP v Reilly and Hewstone* and *SSWP v Jeffrey and Bevan* [2016] EWCA Civ 413; [2017] Q.B. 657; [2017] AACR 14 in relation to Mr Bevan's cross-appeal against the decision of the three-judge panel of the Upper Tribunal in *SSWP v TJ (JSA)* [2015] UKUT 56 (AAC). There was a detailed description and discussion of the decision in *TJ* in the 2015/16 edition of what was then Vol.II of this series (notes to the Jobseekers (Back to Work Schemes) Act 2013), which need not be repeated here in the light of the Court of Appeal's decision. The Upper Tribunal had concluded, in the terms of its own summary in para.13(vi), that in the case of schemes which were mandatory both at the stages of referral onto them and once on them, no basis could be identified on which *meaningful* representations could be made prior to the decision to refer, in the sense of those representations being able to affect the decision to refer. In the 2015/16 edition of Vol.II there was some criticism of the Upper Tribunal's use of the word "mandatory" in this context.

The Court of Appeal first held that the Upper Tribunal had been right on the particular facts of Mr Bevan's case (where his complaint was that he could not afford the bus fare to attend the appointment given, so needed payment in advance rather than a refund) to find that it would have made no difference to what he would have said to the provider about the fares if he had known about what *The Work Programme Provider Guidance* issued by the DWP said about ability to use transportation.

So far as the Upper Tribunal's general guidance is concerned, the Court said this in para.172 about the submission that the Upper Tribunal had erred in saying that there was no scope for making representations in connection with a decision to refer a claimant to the Work Programme since referral was mandatory:

"We do not believe that that is a fair reading of what the Tribunal said; and if it is properly understood there does not seem to be any dispute of principle between the parties. The Tribunal was not laying down any absolute rule. The Secretary of State's policy, embodied in the guidance, is that referral to the Programme should be automatic (ignoring the specified exceptions) if the criteria are met. All that the Tribunal was doing was to point out that, that being so, any representations would have to address the question why he should depart from the policy; and that it was not easy to see what such representations might be. That seems to us an obvious common sense observation, particularly since referral to the Work Programme does not as such involve any specific obligation: see para.151 above. But it does not mean that there could never be such cases, and indeed para.224 is expressly addressed to that possibility. The Tribunal did not depart from anything that the Supreme Court said in [*Reilly and Wilson*]. It was simply considering its application in the particular circumstances of referral to the Work Programme."

The Court considered that in the real world application of the prior information duty was unlikely to be important at the point of initial referral to the Work Programme under the old style JSA legislation, as claimants were unlikely to object at that stage, before any specific requirements were imposed. Problems were likely to emerge when particular requirements were imposed on claimants that they considered unreasonable or inappropriate. The Upper Tribunal had appeared to say in para.249 of its decision that there was little or no scope for the operation of the duty at that stage. The Court of Appeal says this in paras 177 and 178:

"177. Mr de la Mare [counsel for Mr Bevan] submitted that that is wrong. If it is indeed what the Tribunal meant, we agree. So also does Ms Leventhal [counsel for the Secretary of State], who explicitly accepted in her written submissions that 'the requirements of fairness continue to apply after referral'. In principle, JSA claimants who are required, or who it is proposed should be required, under the Work Programme to participate in a particular activity should have sufficient information to enable them to make meaningful representations about the requirement – for example, that the activity in question is unsuitable for them or that there are practical obstacles to their participation. The fact that participation is mandatory if the requirement is made is beside the point: the whole purpose of the representations, and thus of the claimant having the relevant information to be able to make them, is so that the provider may be persuaded that the requirement should <u>not</u> be made, or should be withdrawn or modified.

178. However we should emphasise that the foregoing is concerned with the position in principle. It is quite another matter whether the Work Programme as operated in fact fails to give claimants such information. The Secretary of State's evidence before the Tribunal was that the relevant guidance in fact provides for them to be very fully informed. We have already referred to the Tribunal's findings about the information given at the referral interview. But it was also the evidence that at the initial interview with the provider post-referral, which is designed to find out how the claimant can be best supported, and in the subsequent inter-actions between claimant and provider claimants are supposed to be given both information and the opportunity to make representations. Whether in any particular case there has nevertheless been a failure to give information necessary to enable the claimant to make meaningful representations will have to be judged on the facts of the particular case. Tribunals will no doubt bear in mind the point made in [*Reilly and Wilson*] that it is important not to be prescriptive about how

any necessary information is provided: see para.74 of the judgment of Lord Neuberger and Lord Toulson."

It is understood that Mr Bevan, who had been represented by CPAG, abandoned the possibility of applying for permission to appeal to the Supreme Court against the Court of Appeal's decision, having been unable to obtain legal aid. The Supreme Court refused Mr Hewstone's application for permission to appeal on the ground that it did not raise a point of law that deserved consideration at that point, as the outcome would not have affected the position of the parties to the case. That was because the claimants had succeeded on the point on art.6 of the ECHR and had only been seeking a declaration of incompatibility with the ECHR. The judges did indicate, though, that the issue whether the 2013 Act breached art.1 of Protocol 1 of the ECHR might deserve consideration in another case in which its resolution could affect the outcome.

A remedial Order, the Jobseekers (Back to Work Schemes Act 2013) (Remedial) Order 2020 (SI 2020/1085), was eventually approved by Parliament, after many convolutions described in the notes to the 2020/21 edition, to come into effect on October 3, 2020. The Order inserts new ss.1A and 1B into the 2013 Act, designed to resolve the limited incompatibility with art.6 of the ECHR held by the Court of Appeal in the restricted number of old style JSA cases affected. See the notes to the 2013 Act in Vol.V of this series.

In relation to the universal credit scheme, there might well be scope therefore for the application of the general principle of fairness at the stage of the application of a work-related or connected requirement and at the stage of specification of particular actions or activities. However, the process of discussion leading to the drawing up of a claimant commitment and its notification of the requirements imposed, as described above, certainly gives full opportunity for the provision of sufficient information to enable claimants to make meaningful representations about the content of the claimant commitment and to decide whether or not to accept initially and to make meaningful representations and decisions about taking particular specified actions further down the line. But the crucial questions in any appeals will most likely be, as suggested in para.178 of *Jeffrey and Bevan*, how the process was actually carried out in the particular case in question.

In *NM v SSWP (JSA)* [2016] UKUT 351 (AAC) Judge Wright held, as eventually conceded by the Secretary of State, that the inability to show that relevant DWP guidance had been considered before the claimant was given notice to participate in a Mandatory Work Activity scheme meant either that the claimant should not have been referred to the scheme (because the officer either would have followed the guidance or could have been persuaded to do so on representations from the claimant) or that he had good reason for not participating in the scheme. The appeal related to a sanction for failing to participate, through behaviour on the scheme. The guidance, in something called *Mandatory Work Activity Guidance* or *Operational Instructions– Procedural Guidance–Mandatory Work Activity–January 2012*, was relevant because at the time it instructed that claimants should not be considered for referral to Mandatory Work Activity if, among other circumstances, they were currently working (paid or voluntary). The claimant had been volunteering in a Sue Ryder shop, which he had to give up to attend the required scheme as a volunteer in a Salvation Army shop. The Secretary of State submitted that the guidance had since been changed to introduce an element of discretion about referral of claimants doing voluntary work. Judge Wright held that this would not excuse a failure by an officer of the Secretary of State to consider his own guidance or, on any appeal, a failure to provide the guidance to a First-tier Tribunal in accordance with the principles of natural justice.

Judge Wright has since emphasised some important elements of the application of the prior information duty, that should serve to rein in an over-enthusiastic use of the principle in some First-tier Tribunals, but only when properly placed in context. In *SSWP v SD (JSA)* [2020] UKUT 39 (AAC) he stressed, by reference both to the

Supreme Court in *Reilly and Wilson* and the Court of Appeal in *Reilly and Hewstone* and *Jeffrey and Bevan*, that even if there has been a breach of the duty at the stage of initial referral to the Work Programme the notice of referral would only be invalidated if the breach was material. In the particular case, the claimant had never objected to his referral and his appeal against a sanction for failing to participate by non-attendance at a notified appointment was solely based on the ground that he had previously been told not to attend by his work coach. The tribunal, which had raised and sought evidence on the prior information point on its own initiative, failed to explain why it considered any breach of the duty material. In substituting a decision the judge rejected any unfairness in the referral to the Work Programme and rejected on the evidence the claimant's contention about the appointment.

In *SSWP v CN (JSA)* [2020] UKUT 26 (AAC), the claimant's sole ground of appeal against a sanction for failing to participate in the Work Programme by not attending an appointment was that she had never failed to keep an appointment (i.e. implicitly that she could not have received the notice of the appointment and/or had good cause under the regulations then in force). The tribunal allowed her appeal on the ground that the bundle did not contain a copy of the notice referring her to the Work Programme (i.e. the WP05) so that it was not satisfied that she had properly been notified of the requirement to participate. The tribunal appeared to think that that issue was one "raised by the appeal" within s.12(8)(a) of the SSA 1998, which it manifestly was not as the Secretary of State's submission in the bundle was that there was no dispute that the claimant was referred to the Work Programme. Nor did it give any explanation, if it had exercised its discretion under s.12(8)(a) to consider the issue, as to why it did so and how it was clearly apparent from the evidence so as to be capable of being dealt with under that discretion. Even if those hurdles had been overcome, the Secretary of State had not been given a fair opportunity to deal with the point. It is not necessary for the Secretary of State in all sanctions cases to provide evidence in the appeal bundle that *all* preconditions for the imposition of the sanction are satisfied. It depends what issues have been put in dispute in the appeal. Having therefore set the tribunal's decision aside, the judge substituted a decision finding on the evidence that the claimant had received the letter notifying her of the appointment in question.

The judge's statement that the Secretary of State need not in all sanctions cases provide evidence in the appeal bundle to support the satisfaction of all the preconditions to imposing a sanction must be read in the light of the approach in *SSWP v DC (JSA)* [2017] UKUT 464 (AAC), reported as [2018] AACR 16, and *PO'R v DFC (JSA)* [2018] NI Com 1. There it was said that the Secretary of State should in all cases involving a failure to participate in some scheme or interview where notice of certain details of the scheme etc. was required to be given, as well as notice of date, time and place, include in the appeal bundle a copy of the appointment letter, whether the claimant had raised any issue as to the terms of the letter or not. That was on the basis that unrepresented claimants could not be expected to identify technical issues about the validity of notices and it could not be predicted what particular issues might arise in the course of an appeal. If the letter was not included in the initial bundle, the decisions approved the action of tribunals in directing its production as a proper exercise of their inquisitorial jurisdiction. That exercise must rest on a use of the discretion in s.12(8)(a) to consider issues not raised by the appeal. The resolution of the approaches is no doubt that whenever a tribunal exercises that discretion it must do so consciously and explain why it has done so in any statement of reasons, and give the Secretary of State a fair opportunity to produce the document(s). It may be that an adequate explanation is to be found more readily when it is a notice of a specific appointment is in issue rather than an initial reference to a scheme.

A sample claimant commitment has been produced by the DWP in response to a freedom of information request (available at *https://www.gov.uk/government/publications/foi-query-universal-credit-claimant-commitment-example* (accessed January 27, 2014), or through a link in the universal credit part of the discussion forum on the

Rightsnet website). The document puts things in terms of what the claimant says he or she will do. It is suggested above that that is not quite what the legislation requires, but there is obviously a tension with an attempt to use everyday and simple language. Nevertheless, the document is long and complicated. In the sample, there is no attempt to specify the precise length of the sanction that would be imposed for a failure for no good reason (the document says "without good reason") to comply with a requirement, but the maximum possible duration is included, plus the words "up to". It is arguable that this information is insufficiently precise.

No more recent sample claimant commitment has become publicly available. However, examples that have emerged in tribunal documents display the same fundamental defects and, it is submitted, a misunderstanding of the DWP's own legislation. The emphasis is on what claimants commit themselves to doing, in terms of finding and taking work and the actions and activities involved, rather than making any record of the requirements imposed on them under the legislation. Examples would be "I will be available to attend a job interview immediately [and to] start work immediately", "I will normally spend 35 hours per week looking and preparing for work" and "I will also attend and take part in appointments with my adviser when required". Thus, it appears that claimant commitments in themselves may fail to carry out the duty in s.14(3)(a) to record "the requirements that the claimant must comply with" under Part I of the WRA 2012. As noted in paras 17 and 28 of *S v SSWP (UC)* [2017] UKUT 477 (AAC) (see the introductory part of the note to s.26), s.13(1) means that a work-related requirement only comes into being when imposed by the Secretary of State and s.22(2) requires the Secretary of State to impose a work search requirement and a work availability requirement on claimants who are not exempted from those requirements (with a discretion to impose a work-focused interview requirement and/or a work preparation requirement on non-exempt claimants). Requirements must be *imposed*, with notification required by s.24(4), not merely undertaken by claimants.

In *JB v SSWP (UC)* [2018] UKUT 360 (AAC) the claimant was made subject to a sanction under s.27(2)(a) of the WRA 2012 for failing for no good reason to comply with a work-related requirement under s.15 (work-focused interview requirement). He had failed to attend an appointment with an adviser on January 12, 2017, saying later that he had thought that the appointment was for the next day and later still that he did not attend because of health issues.

The First-tier Tribunal found that the claimant had signed and agreed a claimant commitment on October 27, 2016 that included a requirement to attend and take part in appointments with advisers when required and had been notified at a previous appointment of the requirement to attend on January 12, 2017. In fact the provision before the tribunal was "I will attend and take part in appointments with my adviser when required". The tribunal rejected his argument that he had had good reason for failing to attend. However, the claimant commitment supplied in evidence by the SSWP was not signed or dated and contained a provision for action to be taken by September 20, 2016. It was therefore improbable that the document in the papers had been notified to the claimant on October 27, 2016 and the SSWP had not supplied any other evidence of what claimant commitment had been accepted and what requirements might have been notified in it. Accordingly, although the unrepresented claimant had not raised the issue of whether he had been properly notified of the requirement to attend the particular appointment, the tribunal went wrong in law by proceeding on the basis that a claimant commitment agreed by the claimant on October 27, 2016 imposed a work-related requirement to attend a work-focused interview. Nor had the SSWP put forward coherent evidence of what had been said at an earlier appointment. The written submission relied on an attendance on June 1, 2016, which did not work because the universal credit claim began on September 7, 2016. The appointment history showed a "work-focused review" on December 21, 2016, but there was no evidence of any notification then of a future appointment. There could be no reliance on any presumption of regularity because there was no evidence of a general practice or "script" of what claimants are told at appointments about the need to attend work-focused interviews. Although it was implicit in the claimant's position that he knew of the appointment on January 12, 2017, a sanction could only be imposed if there had been proper notification of the requirement in question and the SSWP had failed to show that. The case was remitted to a new tribunal for rehearing, as it was fair (the issue not having been raised until an Upper Tribunal judge gave permission to appeal), to allow the SSWP an opportunity to produce further evidence.

Judge Poole QC therefore did not need to decide whether the terms of the claimant commitment in the papers were capable of constituting a notification of a requirement to participate in work-focused interviews when notified of appointments. However, she did make interesting observations on that and other wider issues. The SSWP had submitted that the standard terms of claimant commitments were prepared so that claimants could understand them, but were clear and imperative, and that in the context of a system including sanctions claimants and advisers knew that when they were requested to attend interviews it was obligatory to turn up. Judge Poole did not in so many words either accept or reject that submission, but her observations indicate that it could only be accepted subject to heavy qualifications.

In her introductory discussion of the legal principles, the judge stressed that while the universal credit legislation gave the SSWP considerable flexibility, the flip side of that was that in sanctions cases the SSWP had to be able to evidence the imposition of the requirement in question. The more informal the means of communication to a claimant the more efficient its recording systems will have to be, so that copies can be produced in cases of appeal. Her opinions on the wider issues were set out as follows in para.29:

> "29.1 The UC legislation is deliberately drafted to leave a degree of flexibility for the SSWP, and permits multiple methods of communication to claimants (paragraphs 16 and 17 above). There is a flexibility in the manner and means of notification. Given this legislative intention, it would be inappropriate for the Upper Tribunal to set out particular requirements for wording of notifications, or the means by which this is done.
>
> 29.2 In cases where the issue arises, the key matter for tribunals to consider is whether fair notice has been given, having regard to all the communications between the SSWP and the claimant (paragraphs 18 – 20 above). What tribunals need to do is look at the evidence produced by the SSWP, in the context in which it arises, together with any evidence taken from the claimant, and ask the question: does the evidence show that the substance of the relevant requirement and consequences of non-compliance were notified to the claimant? The answer to this question will turn on the particular circumstances of a case.
>
> 29.3 There is a virtue in plain English, and in couching notifications about what a claimant has to do in terms that claimants can readily understand. The Upper Tribunal Judge who granted permission raised the issue of whether requirements should be spelled out expressly and not left to implication. In my view it is not necessary that there is reproduction of statutory wording or reference to particular section or regulation numbers, or indeed any prescribed form of wording. *What is important is the substance. In this case the question was whether it could fairly be said, on the totality of the evidence, that the claimant had been notified of an obligation to attend a work-focused interview and the consequences of non-compliance.* [emphasis added by editor]
>
> 29.4 Unless the only evidence bearing on the imposition of a requirement in a sanctions case is the claimant commitment, it is artificial to focus on the sufficiency of the precise terms of the claimant commitment. This is because requirements can be imposed in various ways, including by a combination of documents (paragraph 20 above). Indeed, in this case the SSWP does not maintain that the wording in the claimant commitment of itself imposed a work-related requirement to attend a work-focused interview on 12 January 2017. Where a claimant commitment is part of the evidence, general reference to 'appointments' in the

claimant commitment seems to me to be a sensible shorthand way of conveying a need to attend meetings but leaving flexibility to impose requirements at a later stage under either Section 15 or Section 23 of the 2012 Act. I also consider the passages set out in paragraph 26 above about sanctions for not meeting requirements, giving detail of how payments are cut, and sanctions for not meeting requirements. So where the claimant commitment has been notified, then those requirements have to be considered in conjunction with other evidence before the tribunal bearing on communication to the claimant of requirements and consequences of non-compliance. This can include, for example, later appointment cards, texts about appointments, and verbal communications at interview. It seems to me that when considering the efficacy of verbal communication, although the SSWP's record keeping will be key, it is permissible to take into account a regular pattern of interviews. For example, a claimant may have been asked at interview to come back for the same sort of interview two weeks later. The claimant's experience from earlier interviews may be relevant to whether they have been informed of the substance of a requirement and consequences of non-compliance. Further, while intimation of date, time and place of appointment is a necessary component of intimation, that will be insufficient of itself unless linked in some way to notification to a claimant of a requirement to attend and consequences of non-compliance. The overall point is that tribunals have to consider not only the wording of the claimant commitment, but of all the evidence bearing on whether the substance of the relevant requirement and consequences of non-compliance were notified to the claimant.

29.5 [Deals with some of the consequences of the differences between the powers in s.15 and s.23 of the WRA 2012]."

That overall approach may not be too difficult to apply if the DWP takes on board at all levels the lessons of *JB* and routinely maintains and provides to tribunals clear and consistent records of the requirements imposed on claimants. However, if the familiar lazy assumptions exemplified in *JB* continue (or appear in older cases from before a hoped-for change of practice), a sharper focus may be necessary on how to resolve the tensions between some of the principles canvassed in para.29 in the circumstances of individual cases. For instance, at a broad level it might continue wrongly to be assumed that, if what is done (e.g. in the drafting of the standard form of terms in claimant commitments) is sensible in policy terms, the actual terms of the relevant legislation have been complied with. At a more grassroots level, there might well continue to be a failure to realise the need to provide tribunals with copies of all the evidence beyond the claimant commitment necessary to show the imposition of the requirement in question and the consequences of non-compliance. In either case, it might become necessary to address directly the effect of the standard form of terms in the claimant commitment. As well as the provision about appointments in issue in *JB*, drafted in terms of what the claimant said he would do rather than in terms of the imposition of a requirement, other standard provisions take the same form (see the examples given above from the sample claimant commitment). It is submitted that the principle expressed at the end of para.29.3 (and in earlier paragraphs) of *JB* that the test is whether the evidence shows that the claimant has been notified of an obligation becomes primary and that there is a fundamental difference between a commitment being undertaken by a claimant and a requirement being imposed by the SSWP.

In para.34 of *JB*, Judge Poole mentions two documents produced to the Upper Tribunal by the SSWP, of potential relevance in the rehearing. One was a computer printout recording the signing, acceptance and issue of a claimant commitment on September 13, 2016, together with something called a "claimant pack". The other was a standard form document headed "Your meeting plan" with spaces for entering dates, times and contacts of next meeting, with a warning on the back that missing meetings without rearranging in advance risks a sanction. According to the SSWP, the meeting plan document is issued with the "commitment pack", which the judge noted might or might not be the same thing as the "claimant pack". Such documents, in particular a complete copy of the claimant or commitment pack, might well be relevant in future cases, but only if properly put into evidence before tribunals. It is also understood that a leaflet "About Sanctions" is routinely uploaded to a claimant's electronic journal early in the course of an award.

Quite rigorous guidance has been issued to decision-makers in the universal credit context in Memo ADM 5/19. It in general emphasises the necessity for the SSWP to be able, in order to show that any failure to comply with a requirement is sanctionable, to evidence that the requirement has been imposed and that the claimant has been properly been informed of the substance of the requirement and the consequences of non-compliance. The Memo accepts that evidence other than the claimant commitment will be crucial and that copies of all relevant communications will need to be included in any appeal papers to found a notification by a combination of means. Paragraph 7 states that:

"it is expected that the SSWP will produce to a tribunal, as a minimum, copies of
1. the claimant commitment
2. any appointment letters ((for example, standard notification letters used for referring to employment programmes such as sbwa [sector based work academy], WHP [Work and Health Programme] etc)
3. records of telephone or electronic communications (for example, a copy of the relevant 'to-do' or journal notes)
4. internal electronic records (for example, a copy of the sanctions information screen)
5. any other relevant documents (for example a copy of the relevant ALP [Action List Prompt]) that shows the imposition of any work-related requirement and the consequences of non-compliance to the claimant."

Paragraph 14 says rather oddly that the ordinary meaning of "substance" is "to specify the intended purpose or subject matter". The meaning surely is not so restricted, but the Memo emphasises that where interviews are concerned the claimant must be told the purpose of the interview and the reason for it. There is now more comprehensive guidance in the section on Public Law Principles of Fairness in Ch.K1 of the ADM.

In para.29 of *S v SSWP (UC)* [2017] UKUT 477 (AAC), the judge accepted that if the Secretary of State failed to carry out the s.22(2) duty, the claimant should not bear the consequences of that (which must entail that the requirement(s) in question had not been imposed and there could be no sanction for failing to comply).

In *S*, it was said that the imposition of the work search requirement was not in issue, but the evidence to support that conclusion was not spelled out. The decision should not therefore be taken as any endorsement of a view that terms of a claimant commitment like that in *S* would be sufficient in themselves to impose work-related requirements on a claimant. Nor should the language used by Judge Jacobs in *SP v SSWP (UC)* [2018] UKUT 227 (AAC), where he talked of a claimant having to make a commitment, in that case about attendance at work-focused interviews, and about the standard term in the claimant commitment not becoming effective until made specific by a notification of the date, time and place of a particular interview by the Secretary of State. The issue in the case was whether the claimant had received the letter notifying him of the interview. Nothing in the decision undermines the principle that work-related requirements must be *imposed* and that on any sanction appeal the Secretary of State must provide evidence of such an imposition (compare the approach in *SSWP v DC (JSA)* [2017] UKUT 464 (AAC), reported as [2018] AACR 16, to the need for evidence of appointment letters to attend schemes under s.17A of the old style Jobseekers Act 1995 and in *MB v SSWP (PIP)* [2018] UKUT 213 (AAC) to the need for evidence of a requirement to attend and participate in a consultation under regulation 9 of the Social Security (Personal Independence Payment) Regulations 2013).

There is some difficulty in working out what remedies a claimant would have who disagrees with the imposition of a requirement included in the claimant commitment. If the claimant declines to accept the Secretary of State's form of the record, at the outset of the claim or as later reviewed and up-dated, then any initial disallowance of the claim or subsequent supersession of an awarding decision would be appealable. However, it is not clear whether such an appeal could succeed on the basis that a requirement in fact included in the claimant commitment should not have been imposed under the conditions in ss.19–24. If the requirement was one whose imposition was prohibited by the legislation and the claimant was prepared to accept everything else in the document, it is submitted that it could properly be concluded that the condition in s.4(1)(e) had been satisfied (compare the approach of Judge Rowland in *CJSA/1080/2002* and *GM v SSWP (JSA)* [2014] UKUT 57 (AAC) in holding that a claimant was to be accepted as satisfying a condition of attendance at a Jobcentre when he had in fact not attended after being informed that he was not entitled to JSA so that attendance was pointless: see further the notes to reg.23 of the JSA Regulations 1996 in Vol.V). If it was a matter of the Secretary of State's discretion under s.22(3), the result might be different. A claimant who accepts a claimant commitment under protest about some requirement may no doubt request the Secretary of State not to impose the challenged requirement and in consequence to review the claimant commitment. However, it appears that the claimant cannot appeal directly either against the imposition of the requirement or the content of the claimant commitment or against a refusal by the Secretary of State to remove a requirement and to review the claimant commitment. See the discussion in the note to s.24 below, which would apply equally to any of the kinds of decision mentioned. None of them are "outcome" decisions.

Work-related requirements

Work-focused interview requirement

1.152   **15.**—(1) In this Part a "work-focused interview requirement" is a requirement that a claimant participate in one or more work-focused interviews as specified by the Secretary of State.

(2) A work-focused interview is an interview for prescribed purposes relating to work or work preparation.

(3) The purposes which may be prescribed under subsection (2) include in particular that of making it more likely in the opinion of the Secretary of State that the claimant will obtain paid work (or more paid work or better-paid work).

(4) The Secretary of State may specify how, when and where a work-focused interview is to take place.

DEFINITION

"claimant"—see s.40.

GENERAL NOTE

1.153   This section defines what a "work-focused interview" is and makes the related requirement "participation" in the interview. This is for the purposes of ss.20–22, and in particular s.20, which applies the requirement to participate in such an interview to the great majority of claimants within the general work-seeking ambit, although on a discretionary basis. Note the circumstances specified in and under s.19 in which no work-related requirement may be imposed.

Under subss.(2) and (3) regulations must prescribe the purposes, relating to work or work preparation, for which an interview may be required. The prescription, in very wide terms, is in reg.93 of the Universal Credit Regulations. "Paid work" is not defined in the Act, but when that phrase is used in reg.93 the definition in reg.2 will apply (see the note to reg.93). The Secretary of State is allowed under subss.(1) and (4) to specify how, when and where the interview is to take place, so that there is no straightforward limit on the number or frequency of the interviews that may be specified, or on the persons who may conduct the interview. The interviews must of course properly be for one of the purposes prescribed in reg.93. The requirement to participate in an interview cannot be used for punitive purposes or simply as a means of control of a claimant. No doubt it is also to be implied that only rational requirements may be imposed, so that a specification of two interviews in different places at the same time or so that they could not practicably be coordinated could be disregarded (see the approach of Judge Rowland in *GM v SSWP (JSA)* [2014] UKUT 57 (AAC): notes to s.14 above). Rationality would also require that what was specified should not be incompatible with other requirements, in particular the work search and work availability requirements where there is no discretion under s.22(2) about their imposition. Thus a claimant could not validly be required to attend so many interviews that it made it impossible to take work search actions for the hours specified under s.17, unless there was a corresponding reduction in the s.17 requirements. These are rather extreme examples, which it is hoped would not arise in practice. Because, as discussed in the notes to s.24, there is no right of appeal against an imposition of a work-related or connected requirement as such, the issues will normally arise in the course of challenges to or appeals against removal of entitlement for failing to accept a claimant commitment containing the requirement(s) in questions or against reductions in benefit following a sanction for non-compliance. The main focus in the latter case may be on whether the claimant had a good reason for not complying with the requirement, but sight should not be lost of whether there had been non-compliance with the requirement as properly interpreted (see below).

However, there may also often be questions whether a requirement has in fact been imposed. There appear to be two stages. The Secretary of State may indicate in general that a claimant will be required to participate in interviews (although see the notes to s.14 for serious doubts whether the current standard form of claimant commitment achieves that result). But the requirement under subs.(1) appears not to arise, in the sense of a requirement that the claimant can comply with or fail to comply with for sanctions purposes, until the Secretary of State has specified the particular interview or interviews under subs.(4) and probably (although subs.(1) is not entirely clear) that the claimant participate. See the notes to s.14 for extensive discussion of the decision in *JB v SSWP (UC)* [2018] UKUT 360 (AAC) on the evidence that the SSWP needs to produce to show that a requirement to participate in a s.15 interview has been imposed and the guidance given to decision-makers in Memo ADM 5/19. Paragraph 6 of *JB* states that it is a condition precedent of imposing any sanction under s.27(2)(a) that the claimant was subject to the work-related requirement in issue, thus confirming the approach in para.29 of *S v SSWP (UC)* [2017] UKUT 477 (AAC) that if a specific requirement has not been imposed by the SSWP, no sanction can follow.

SP v SSWP (UC) [2018] UKUT 227 (AAC) is consistent with such a two-stage approach, but see the discussion in the notes to s.14 for how the language used should not be taken as contrary to the argument made there about evidence of the imposition of a requirement.

JB was endorsed and applied in *KG v SSWP (UC)* [2020] UKUT 307 (AAC). Before the Upper Tribunal the Secretary of State accepted that the available evidence did not show that the claimant had been properly notified of the requirement to take part in the particular telephone interview with his work coach, so that no sanction could be applied under s.27. The documents were ambiguous as to whether the interview was under s.15 or s.23 (connected requirements) and what issues the claimant was told were to be investigated, and left it unclear whether he had been adequately informed of the consequences of non-compliance.

Specification must necessarily imply communication to the claimant in time to attend the interview.

There is no requirement that the specification under subs.(4) of how, when and where an interview is to take place should be in writing or in other permanent form. However, good practice, plus the potential need for acceptable evidence of the existence and terms of the specification in the light of the principle that the claimant should in sanctions cases be given the benefit of any doubt that might reasonably arise (*DL v SSWP (JSA)* [2013] UKUT 295 (AAC)), must surely point to the need for written or computer records to be kept and to be available to the claimant for reference. Arguably, the "prior information duty" (see the notes to s.14 for detailed discussion) would require that information about the purpose of the particular interview be given in the specification. Arguably also, in accordance with the approach in *SSWP v DC (JSA)* [2017] UKUT 464 (AAC), reported as [2018] AACR 16, and *PO'R v DFC (JSA)* [2018] NI Com 1, a copy of the appointment letter should be included in the Secretary of State's submission on any appeal against a sanction for failing to comply with a requirement to participate in the interview. There it was said that the Secretary of State should in all cases involving a failure to participate in some scheme or interview where notice of certain details of the scheme etc was required to be given, as well as notice of date, time and place, include in the appeal bundle a copy of the appointment letter, whether the claimant had raised any issue as to the terms of the letter or not. That was on the basis that unrepresented claimants could not be expected to identify technical issues about the validity of notices and it could not be predicted what particular issues might arise in the course of an appeal. If the letter was not included in the initial bundle, the decisions approved the action of tribunals in directing its production as a proper exercise of their inquisitorial jurisdiction. That exercise must, if the claimant has not taken the point, rest on a use of the discretion in s.12(8)(a) of the SSA 1998 to consider issues not raised by the appeal. The resolution with the approach in *SSWP v SD (JSA)* [2020] UKUT 39 (AAC) and *SSWP v CN (JSA)* [2020] UKUT 26 (AAC) (see the notes to s.14) is no doubt that whenever a tribunal exercises that discretion it must do so consciously and explain why it has done so in any statement of reasons, and give the Secretary of State a fair opportunity to produce the document(s). It may be that an adequate explanation is to be found more readily when it is a notice of a specific appointment that is in issue rather than an initial reference to a scheme.

Note that the requirement, as now for both old style and new style JSA, is not attendance at an interview at the specified time and date, but participation in it. This would appear to mean that a claimant can be required to participate in an interview over the telephone, providing that that manner of conducting it has been specified under subs.(4). In an ambiguous (so far as JSA is concerned) Parliamentary answer on 24 November 2015 (UIN 17005), the Minister of State Priti Patel said:

> "Under JSA, claimants are not sanctioned for failing to answer their telephone. In Universal Credit, claimants who have a prearranged telephone interview with their Work Coach, and who fail to participate without good reason, can be referred for a sanction decision."

There is no further provision about what participating in a work-focused interview entails. It must at least entail turning up at the place and time specified, although the decision of Judge Knowles in *SA v SSWP (JSA)* [2015] UKUT 454 (AAC) (see the notes to s.27 for full discussion) would indicate that tribunals should consider, in cases where the claimant arrives not very late, whether it is proportionate to the nature of all the circumstances to regard that as a failure to participate in an interview. There were all sorts of mitigating circumstances in *SA*, that may well not be present in other cases. See *SN v SSWP (JSA)* [2018] UKUT 279 (AAC), detailed in the notes to s.26(2)(a) and 27(2)(a), for discussion of what might amount to a failure to participate (in that case in a mandatory work activity scheme and involving conduct before the scheme started) and the expression in para.45 of some doubt about the result in *SA*.

The requirement to participate must also extend to making some meaningful contribution to the interview, but the limits will probably not be established until there have been some more sanctions appeals in JSA or universal credit that reach the Upper Tribunal. Behaviour that leads to the premature termination of the interview may well amount to a failure to participate (see the facts of *DM v SSWP (JSA)* [2015] UKUT 67 (AAC) in the notes to s.27(2)(b)). There may, though, in cases of uncooperative claimants or heavy-handed officials or a combination, be difficult questions about when an interview has ceased to exist, so that subsequent behaviour cannot be relevant to whether there has been a failure to participate (see *PH v SSWP (ESA)* [2016] UKUT 119 (AAC) on failing to submit to a medical examination).

It was recognised in *CS v SSWP (JSA)* [2019] UKUT 218 (AAC), detailed in the notes to s.26(2)(a), that it was legitimate for a scheme provider to require a person attending to verify their identity before starting a scheme, so that a refusal to do so would usually amount to a failure to participate in the scheme. The same principle could apply to an interview, but the particular issues that arose in *CS*, to do with a scheme provider external to the DWP, are unlikely to arise if it is an interview with a work coach or other adviser that has been notified.

A failure for no good reason to comply with any work-related requirement is sanctionable under s.27(2)(a). That is the context in which what amounts to a failure to comply will be identified, as well as what might amount to a good reason for non-compliance. For instance, there appear to be no provisions prescribing the length of notice of an interview to be given or how far a claimant can be required to travel, but there could plainly be a good reason for failing to comply with unreasonable requirements, especially if the claimant had attempted in advance to draw any problem with attendance to the Secretary of State's attention. Claimants who are found not in fact to have been aware of an interview must have a good reason for failing to comply, whether or not the requirement is said to have been imposed in such circumstances (*SP v SSWP (UC)* [2018] UKUT 227 (AAC)).

Note that under s.23(1) the Secretary of State is empowered to require a claimant to attend an interview relating to the imposition of a work-related requirement on the claimant or assisting the claimant to comply with a requirement.

Work preparation requirement

16.—(1) In this Part a "work preparation requirement" is a requirement that a claimant take particular action specified by the Secretary of State for the purpose of making it more likely in the opinion of the Secretary of State that the claimant will obtain paid work (or more paid work or better-paid work).

1.154

(2) The Secretary of State may under subsection (1) specify the time to be devoted to any particular action.

(3) Action which may be specified under subsection (1) includes in particular—

(a) attending a skills assessment;
(b) improving personal presentation;
(c) participating in training;
(d) participating in an employment programme;
(e) undertaking work experience or a work placement;
(f) developing a business plan;
(g) any action prescribed for the purpose in subsection (1).

(4) In the case of a person with limited capability for work, the action which may be specified under subsection (1) includes taking part in a work-focused health-related assessment.

(5) In subsection (4) "work-focused health-related assessment" means an assessment by a health care professional approved by the Secretary of State which is carried out for the purpose of assessing—

    (a) the extent to which the person's capability for work may be improved by taking steps in relation to their physical or mental condition, and

    (b) such other matters relating to their physical or mental condition and the likelihood of their obtaining or remaining in work or being able to do so as may be prescribed.

(6) In subsection (5) "health care professional" means—

    (a) a registered medical practitioner,

    (b) a registered nurse,

    (c) an occupational therapist or physiotherapist registered with a regulatory body established by an Order in Council under section 60 of the Health Act 1999, or

    (d) a member of such other profession regulated by a body mentioned in section 25(3) of the National Health Service Reform and Health Care Professions Act 2002 as may be prescribed.

DEFINITIONS

"claimant"—see s.40.
"limited capability for work"—*ibid.*

GENERAL NOTE

1.155   This section defines "work preparation requirement" for the particular purposes of ss.21 and 22. The requirement is to take particular action specified by the Secretary of State for the purpose of making it more likely that the claimant will obtain paid work or obtain more or better-paid such work. If a specific requirement has not been imposed, then no sanction can follow (*S v SSWP (UC)* [2017] UKUT 477 (AAC) para.29). See the notes to s.14 for extensive discussion of the decision in *JB v SSWP (UC)* [2018] UKUT 360 (AAC) on the evidence that the SSWP needs to produce to show that a requirement (in that case to participate in a s.15 interview) has been imposed and the guidance given to decision-makers in Memo ADM 5/19. Paragraph 6 of *JB* states that it is a condition precedent of imposing any sanction under s.27(2)(a) that the claimant was subject to the work-related requirement in issue, thus confirming the approach in para.29 of *S*.

Subsection (3) gives a non-exhaustive list of actions that may be specified, including under para.(g) any action prescribed in regulations. No regulations have as yet been made under para.(g). The list is in fairly broad terms, not further defined in the legislation, even "employment programme". The sorts of activities required do not themselves have to be paid, so long as they can legitimately be related to the purpose of improving prospects of obtaining paid work or more or better paid work (see below and the notes to s.26(2)(a)). So unpaid work experience or placements (e.g. as an intern) or voluntary work can be made mandatory. See the notes to s.15 above for the need for the co-ordination with the practical application of other work-related or connected requirements for the specification of any particular work preparation requirement to be rational.

The Secretary of State has a discretion under ss.21 and 22(3) whether to impose a work preparation requirement in any particular case. It appears that the requirement therefore cannot arise until the Secretary of State has specified the particular action, so that general statements in a claimant commitment about normally spending 35 hours a week looking and preparing for work (even if they could be regarded as *imposed* by the Secretary of State: see the notes to s.14) would not be enough in themselves. Also note the circumstances specified in and under s.19 in which no work-related requirement may be imposed.

The Secretary of State may under subs.(2) specify the time to be devoted to any particular action, but in practice this is likely to be less controversial than the similar power in s.17(2) in relation to a work search requirement. However, the DWP appears to use a default maximum of 16 expected hours per week, subject to "tailoring" for the claimant's individual circumstances, for someone subject only to the work preparation regime (Guidance on expected hours deposited in House of Commons Library: collected on the Rightsnet website). Subsections (4)–(6) allow the application of a particular requirement to take part in a work-focused health-related assessment to claimants with limited capability for work (only claimants who also have limited capability for work-related activity being exempted from all work-related requirements under s.19(2)(a)). Paragraph 15 of *JS v SSWP (ESA)*; [2013] UKUT 635 (AAC) suggests that if a claimant is patently not going to be able to obtain work at any stage or is already in a suitable apprenticeship or placement no action could make it more likely that work or more work would be obtained, so that no action could be legitimately specified.

There is no requirement that the specification under subss.(1) and (2) of the particular action to be taken and the time to be devoted to it should be in writing or in other permanent form. However, good practice, plus the potential need for acceptable evidence of the existence and terms of the specification in the light of the principle that the claimant should in sanctions cases be given the benefit of any doubt that might reasonably arise (*DL v SSWP (JSA)* [2013] UKUT 295 (AAC)), must surely point to the need for written or computer records to be kept and to be available to the claimant for reference. See *NM v SSWP (JSA)* [2016] UKUT 351 (AAC), discussed in para.1.151 above, for circumstances in which failure to consider relevant DWP guidance about the circumstances in which there should or should not be referral to a scheme, with sufficient information to the claimant to allow the making of meaningful representations, undermines the applicability of any sanction for failure to comply with a requirement. The principles of natural justice require that the terms of the relevant guidance be provided to a tribunal on any appeal.

Arguably, the "prior information duty" (see the notes to s.14 for detailed discussion) would require that information about the purpose of the particular course, programme, placement etc. be given in the specification. Arguably also, in accordance with the approach in *SSWP v DC (JSA)* [2017] UKUT 464 (AAC), reported as [2018] AACR 16, and *PO'R v DFC (JSA)* [2018] NI Com 1, a copy of the appointment letter should be included in the Secretary of State's submission on any appeal against a sanction for failing to comply with a requirement under s.16. There it was said that the Secretary of State should in all cases involving a failure to participate in some scheme or interview where notice of certain details of the scheme etc. was required to be given, as well as notice of date, time and place, include in the appeal bundle a copy of the appointment letter, whether the claimant had raised any issue as to the terms of the letter or not. That was on the basis that unrepresented claimants could not be expected to identify technical issues about the validity of notices and it could not be predicted what particular issues might arise in the course of an appeal. If the letter was not included in the initial bundle, the decisions approved the action of tribunals in directing its production as a proper exercise of their inquisitorial jurisdiction. That exercise must, if the claimant has not taken the point, rest on a use of the discretion in s.12(8)(a) of the SSA 1998 to consider issues not raised by the appeal. The resolution with the approach in *SSWP v SD (JSA)* [2020] UKUT 39 (AAC) and *SSWP v CN (JSA)* [2020] UKUT 26 (AAC) (see the notes to s.14) is no doubt that whenever a tribunal exercises that discretion it must do so consciously and explain why it has done so in any statement of reasons, and give the Secretary of State a fair opportunity to produce the document(s). It may be that an adequate explanation is to be found more readily when it is a notice of a specific appointment that is in issue rather than an initial reference to a scheme.

A failure for no good reason by a claimant subject to all work-related requirements to comply with a requirement under this heading to undertake a work placement of a prescribed description (i.e. the Mandatory Work Activity Scheme: reg.114 of the Universal Credit Regulations) is sanctionable under s.26(2)(a) (higher-level sanctions). The scheme has not operated after April 2016. Outside that limited category, failure for no good reason to comply with any work-related requirement is sanctionable under s.27(2)(a). That is the main context in which there will be exploration of what action can be said to make it more likely that the claimant will obtain paid work or more or better-paid work, since the addition of the Secretary of State's opinion in subs.(1) will not be allowed to take away the power of tribunals to reach their own conclusions on that matter. What amounts to a failure to comply will also be identified, as well as what might amount to a good reason for non-compliance. The issue may also arise in challenges to the removal of entitlement following a failure to accept a claimant commitment containing a disputed work preparation requirement (see the notes to s.14).

Note that under s.23(1) the Secretary of State is empowered to require a claimant to participate in an interview relating to the imposition of a work-related requirement on the claimant or assisting the claimant to comply with a requirement. Under s.23(3) he can require the provision of information and evidence for the purpose of verifying compliance and that the claimant confirm compliance in any manner.

Work search requirement

1.156

17.—(1) In this Part a "work search requirement" is a requirement that a claimant take—

(a) all reasonable action, and

(b) any particular action specified by the Secretary of State,

for the purpose of obtaining paid work (or more paid work or better-paid work).

(2) The Secretary of State may under subsection (1)(b) specify the time to be devoted to any particular action.

(3) Action which may be specified under subsection (1)(b) includes in particular—

(a) carrying out work searches;

(b) making applications;

(c) creating and maintaining an online profile;

(d) registering with an employment agency;

(e) seeking references;

(f) any action prescribed for the purpose in subsection (1).

(4) Regulations may impose limitations on a work search requirement by reference to the work to which it relates; and the Secretary of State may in any particular case specify further such limitations on such a requirement.

(5) A limitation under subsection (4) may in particular be by reference to—

(a) work of a particular nature,

(b) work with a particular level of remuneration,

(c) work in particular locations, or

(d) work available for a certain number of hours per week or at particular times,

and may be indefinite or for a particular period.

DEFINITION

"claimant"—see s.40.

GENERAL NOTE

Temporary Coronavirus Provisions

The last of the temporary coronavirus provisions relevant to the work search requirement expired on November 12, 2020. See previous editions of this volume for the details.

This section defines "work search requirement" for the particular purpose of s.22, under which the requirement must be imposed on all claimants except those exempted by s.19, 20 or 21. See the notes to s.14 for discussion of whether the current standard terms of claimant commitments are sufficient in themselves to *impose* such a requirement. It is a requirement that a claimant take both all reasonable action (subs.(1)(a)) and any particular action specified by the Secretary of State (subs.(1)(b)) for the purpose of obtaining paid work or more or better-paid work. "Paid work" is not defined in the Act, nor is it defined in regulations for the specific purpose of ss.17 and 22. However, under the power in s.25, regs 94 and 95 of the Universal Credit Regulations deem the work search requirement not to have been complied with in certain circumstances and make references to "paid work". For those purposes, the definition in reg.2 will apply, i.e. work done for payment or in expectation of payment, excluding work for a charity or voluntary organisation, or as a volunteer, in return for expenses only. Regulation 87 adds nothing to the terms of s.17 itself. Thus it appears that both self-employment and employment can be considered both under the reg.2 definition and under the ordinary meaning of the phrase "paid work" and that voluntary work or unpaid internships or work placements are excluded. According to the then Minister of State Esther McVey (House of Commons written answers April 2, 2014 and September 1, 2014) guidance to Jobcentre Plus staff is that, in contrast to the position for JSA, universal credit claimants can be mandated to apply for vacancies for zero hours contracts. At the time it appeared not to matter whether there was an exclusivity clause in the contract or not, but such clauses were made unenforceable from May 26, 2015 by the new s.27A of the Employment Rights Act 1996. There will be a question in challenges to and appeals against sanctions decisions whether claimants have a good reason for not complying with a requirement to search for zero hours contracts.

Subsections (4) and (5) allow regulations to impose limitations on the kind of work search which can be required and also allow the Secretary of State to specify further limitations. Regulation 97 contains the prescribed limitations, in terms of hours of work for carers and those with a disability, of the maximum time for travel to and from work and of the type of work recently undertaken. See the notes to reg.97. There appears to be no limitation on the number of hours a week that work could involve while still falling for consideration, apart from in the cases of the particular categories of claimant identified in reg.97(2). Note also that reg.99 exempts claimants from the work search requirement in a variety of individual circumstances that would make the carrying out of any work search impracticable. See the notes to reg.99 for the details. The circumstances include several to do with care of children, the carrying out of various worthwhile activities, unfitness for work for short and (subject to conditions) more extended periods and, particularly important to the structure of universal credit, where earnings are at a defined level. Regulation 98 exempts recent victims of domestic violence for a fixed period.

What is "all reasonable action" under subs.(1)(a) for the purpose of obtaining paid work within any applicable limitations is obviously in general a matter of judgment. That includes a judgment about what counts as "action" and about the significance of any potential action that has not been taken. The actions mentioned in subs.(3) might be a starting point, but other things could plainly count, such as carrying out research into the job market or potential for self-employment. No doubt just sitting and thinking falls the other side of the line, but can often form an essential element of the hours devoted to some more active action. Subsection (3) does not include in its list accepting an offer of suitable work. However, it could certainly be argued that a claimant who failed to accept such an offer had failed to take all reasonable action for the purpose of obtaining paid work. A medium-level sanction could then follow under s.27(2)(a) if the failure was for no good reason unless the case fell within s.26(2)(c) (failing for no good reason to comply with a work availability requirement by taking up an offer of paid work). There is a certain artificiality to the s.26(2)(c) sanction (see the notes to that section) but no doubt in practice decision-makers will prefer to use that provision first in a case where an offer of work has not been taken up. If for any reason that provision does not apply, it can be argued that s.27(2)(a) and s.17(1)(a) should be considered in addition. It seems very unlikely that in practice the Secretary of State would ever be in a position to specify under sub.(1) that a claimant should accept a particular offer of paid work.

Regulation 95 of the Universal Credit Regulations deems a claimant not to have complied with the requirement unless quite stringent conditions about the weekly hours devoted to work search are satisfied. See the notes to reg.95 and remember that the sanctions in s.26(4)(a), in relation to having, before claiming universal credit, failed to take up an offer of paid work, and s.27(2)(a) can only be imposed when there was no good reason for the failure to comply. But note that the two alternative conditions in reg.95(1)(a) of spending at least the "expected hours" under reg.88 (starting point, 35) per week or of taking all reasonable action though for fewer than the expected hours are logically of equal status. A rigid approach that claimants are in general expected to devote 35 hours a week to work search is likely to lead into error. It is also arguable that if a claimant shows, say, that they have spent 35 hours on work search action in a week, they should only be regarded as not having taken all reasonable action in that week if that action does not give them the best prospects of obtaining work (reg.95(1)(b)). Paragraph 15 of *JS v SSWP (ESA)* [2013] UKUT 635 (AAC) suggests that if a claimant is patently not going to be able to obtain work at any stage or is already in a suitable apprenticeship or placement no action could make it more likely that work or more work would be obtained, so that no action could be legitimately specified.

1.159   The particular action that can be specified by Secretary of State under subs.(1) (b) can, by subs.(3), include a number of actions, including those prescribed in regulations. No relevant regulation has yet been made. The list includes, at (c), creating and maintaining an online profile. That was relied on by the DWP to support requiring claimants to create a public profile and a public CV in Universal Jobmatch. There is helpful guidance on this in Memo ADM 15/16 of June 2016, which recognised that claimants could not be mandated to do that or create an email account from day one of their claim, merely encouraged, and that mandation was not to follow until the claimant had had an initial work search interview with a work coach. The requirement was not to be imposed unless the benefits of Universal Jobmatch had been explained, its use was reasonable in the claimant's individual circumstances (including health, learning problems, whether English was a second language, lack of appropriate literacy and numeracy skills), the claimant had access to the internet (including at a Jobcentre) and the cookies fact sheet had been issued. From May 14, 2018 Universal Jobmatch has been replaced by the Find a job service, run by Adzuna. Paragraphs K5171 – K5209 of the ADM apply effectively the same approach to Find a job. Paragraphs K5174 and K5175 explain the differences between Universal Jobmatch and the new service.

Particular vacancies could also be notified to a claimant within Universal Jobmatch and a requirement to apply notified through the claimant commitment. A failure for no good reason to comply with such a requirement leads to a higher-level sanction under s.26(2)(b). Memo ADM 15/16 suggests that if a claimant subject to such a sanction has also failed to take all reasonable action for the purposes of obtaining paid work by not applying for enough notified vacancies, there can also be a medium-level sanction under s.27(2)(a). However, it is arguable that an imposition of the medium-level sanction in those circumstances would contravene s.27(3) (no s.27 sanction if failure is also a s.26 sanctionable failure).

Where a claimant has been required to apply for a particular vacancy, reg.94 of the Universal Credit Regulations deems the work search requirement not to have been complied with where the claimant fails to participate in an interview offered in connection with the vacancy.

There is no requirement that the specification under subss.(1)(b), (2) and (3) of the particular actions to be taken and the time to be devoted to them should be in writing or in other permanent form. However, good practice, plus the potential need for acceptable evidence of the existence and terms of the specification in the light of the principle that the claimant should in sanctions cases be given the benefit of any doubt that might reasonably arise (*DL v SSWP (JSA)* [2013] UKUT 295 (AAC)), must surely point to the need for written or computer records to be kept and to be available to the claimant for reference. See the notes to ss.14 and 16 for the potential application of the "prior information duty" in requiring the claimant to be given an opportunity to make informed and meaningful representations about the actions proposed to be specified before they are imposed.

Note that under s.23(1) the Secretary of State is empowered to require a claimant to participate in an interview relating to the imposition of a work-related requirement on the claimant or assisting the claimant to comply with a requirement. Under s.23(3) he can require the provision of information and evidence for the purpose of verifying compliance and that the claimant confirm compliance in any manner. A failure for no good reason to comply with any of those connected requirements is also sanctionable under s.27(2)(b).

Work availability requirement

18.—(1) In this Part a "work availability requirement" is a requirement that a claimant be available for work.   1.160

(2) For the purposes of this section "available for work" means able and willing immediately to take up paid work (or more paid work or better-paid work).

(3) Regulations may impose limitations on a work availability requirement by reference to the work to which it relates; and the Secretary of State may in any particular case specify further such limitations on such a requirement.

(4) A limitation under subsection (3) may in particular be by reference to—
(a) work of a particular nature,
(b) work with a particular level of remuneration,
(c) work in particular locations, or
(d) work available for a certain number of hours per week or at particular times,
and may be indefinite or for a particular period.

(5) Regulations may for the purposes of subsection (2) define what is meant by a person being able and willing immediately to take up work.

DEFINITION

"claimant"—see s.40.

GENERAL NOTE

Temporary Coronavirus Provisions
The last of the temporary coronavirus provisions relevant to the work availability requirement expired on November 12, 2020. See previous editions of this volume for the details.   1.161

This section defines "work availability requirement" for the particular purpose of s.22, under which the requirement must be imposed on all claimants except   1.162

those exempted by s.19, 20 or 21. See the notes to s.14 for discussion of whether the current standard terms of claimant commitments are sufficient in themselves to *impose* such a requirement. It requires in general that a claimant be able and willing immediately to take up paid work, or more or better-paid work. "Paid work" is not defined in the Act, nor is it defined in regulations for the specific purpose of ss.18 and 22. However, under the power in s.25, reg.96 of the Universal Credit Regulations deems the work availability requirement not to have been complied with in certain circumstances and to have been satisfied in other circumstances and makes references to "paid work". For those purposes, the definition in reg.2 will apply, i.e. work done for payment or in expectation of payment, excluding work for a charity or voluntary organisation, or as a volunteer, in return for expenses only. Regulation 87 adds nothing to the terms of s.18 itself. Thus it appears that willingness to take up both self-employment and employment can be considered. Under the ordinary meaning of the phrase "paid work" it would seem that voluntary work or unpaid internship or work placements are excluded (but see s.16 on work preparation).

For some suggestions as to a common sense approach to "immediately", in the specific context of reg.7 of the JSA Regulations 1996, see Simon Brown LJ in *Secretary of State for Social Security v David*, reported in *R(JSA) 3/01*, at paras 25 and 26:

> "That 'immediately' means within a very short space of time indeed is clear not only from the word itself but also from regulation 5 which provides for exceptions to this requirement in the case of those with caring responsibilities or engaged in voluntary work (who need only be willing and able to take up employment on 48 hours' notice) and certain others engaged in providing a service (who get 24 hours' notice). No doubt the requirement for immediate availability allows the claimant time to wash, dress and have his breakfast, but strictly it would seem inconsistent with, say, a claimant's stay overnight with a friend or relative, or attendance at a weekend cricket match, or even an evening at the cinema (unless perhaps he had left a contact number and had not travelled far).
>
> 26. In these circumstances, claimants ought clearly to be wary of entering into an agreement which offers unrestricted availability throughout the entire week, day and night, weekdays and weekends."

Subsections (3) and (4) allow regulations to impose limitations on the kind of work for which a claimant can be required to be available and also allow the Secretary of State to specify further limitations. Regulation 97 contains the prescribed limitations, in terms of hours of work for carers and those with a disability, of the maximum time for travel to and from work and of the type of work recently undertaken. See the notes to reg.97. There appears to be no limitation on the number of hours a week that work could involve while still falling for consideration, apart from in the cases of the particular categories of claimant identified in reg.97(2).

Although reg.97 refers to limitations as to the nature of work, e.g. where the claimant has a physical or mental impairment (reg.97(5)) and where the claimant has previously carried out work of a particular nature (reg.97(3)), those provisions apply both to the work search requirement under reg.17 and the work availability requirement. It appears that, for consistency, the question of the nature of work or level of remuneration that a claimant is prepared to accept must be assessed primarily by reference to the content of the s.17 requirement, since s.18 contains no further conditions on those matters. Since the fundamental requirement in s.17 is to take all reasonable action for the purpose of obtaining paid work or more or better-paid work, with the requirement to take any particular action specified by the Secretary of State necessarily restricted to actions that are reasonable, the same standard must be applied in so far as s.18 involves asking what kind of work and what level of remuneration the claimant is prepared to accept.

Subsection (5) allows regulations to define what is meant in subs.(1) by being able and willing immediately to take up work. Regulation 99(1)(b) of the Universal Credit Regulations uses this power to provide that claimants in any of the circumstances set out in reg.99(3), (4), (4A) or (5) are regarded as being available for work if able and willing to take up paid work or attend an interview immediately after the relevant circumstance ceases to apply. See also the provisions of reg.99(2B) with (5A) and reg.99(2C) with (5B). Regulation 96(1) deems the work availability requirement not to be complied with if the claimant is not able and willing immediately to attend an interview in connection with finding paid work. Regulation 96(2) to (5) defines circumstances in which carers, those doing voluntary work and those in paid employment are to be treated as having complied with the requirement, where it is accepted that some longer notice than "immediately" is needed. Those provisions can only apply subject to any modifications to the availability requirement made by reg.99. Regulation 98 prevents the imposition of any work-related requirement on recent victims of domestic violence.

It is notable, by contrast with the position that will be familiar to many readers   **1.163** from old style JSA and, before it, unemployment benefit, that being available for work is not a condition of entitlement to universal credit, failure to satisfy which means that there can be no entitlement to benefit at all, although it is a condition of entitlement under s.4(1)(e) to accept a claimant commitment that should record the requirement. Instead, a failure to comply with the work availability requirement, if imposed on a claimant, is merely a potential basis for a sanction under ss.26 or 27. Under s.26(2)(c) a higher-level sanction can be imposed if a claimant fails for no good reason to comply by not taking up an offer of paid work, though that can only be by showing a failure to meet the general availability requirement. Section 27(2)(a) allows the imposition of a medium-level sanction for a failure for no good reason to comply with any work-related requirement.

Note that under s.23(1) the Secretary of State is empowered to require a claimant to participate in an interview relating to the imposition of a work-related requirement on the claimant or assisting the claimant to comply with a requirement. Under s.23(3) he can require the provision of information and evidence for the purpose of verifying compliance and that the claimant confirm compliance in any manner. A failure for no good reason to comply with any of those connected requirements is also sanctionable under s.27(2)(b).

Application of work-related requirements

Claimants subject to no work-related requirements

19.—(1) The Secretary of State may not impose any work-related   **1.164** requirement on a claimant falling within this section.

(2) A claimant falls within this section if—

(a) the claimant has limited capability for work and work-related activity,

(b) the claimant has regular and substantial caring responsibilities for a severely disabled person,

(c) the claimant is the responsible carer for a child under the age of 1, or

(d) the claimant is of a prescribed description.

(3) Regulations under subsection (2)(d) may in particular make provision by reference to one or more of the following—

(a) hours worked;

(b) earnings or income;

(c) the amount of universal credit payable.

(4) Regulations under subsection (3) may—

    (a) in the case of a claimant who is a member of the couple, make provision by reference to the claimant alone or by reference to the members of the couple together;

    (b) make provision for estimating or calculating any matter for the purpose of the regulations.

(5) Where a claimant falls within this section, any work-related requirement previously applying to the claimant ceases to have effect.

(6) In this Part "responsible carer", in relation to a child means—

    (a) a single person who is responsible for the child, or

    (b) a person who is a member of a couple where—

        (i) the person or the other member of the couple is responsible for the child, and

        (ii) the person has been nominated by the couple jointly as responsible for the child.

DEFINITIONS

"claimant"—see s.40.
"limited capability for work"—*ibid.*
"limited capability for work-related activity"—*ibid.*
"regular and substantial caring responsibilities"—*ibid.*
"severely disabled"—*ibid.*
"work-related requirement"—see ss.40 and 13(2).

GENERAL NOTE

1.165
    The default position in s.22 is that a claimant is, unless falling within ss.19–21, to be subject to all work-related requirements, i.e. the work search and work availability requirements, with the optional additions of a work-focused interview and/or a work preparation requirement. Section 19 defines the circumstances in which no work-related requirement at all may be imposed. Under reg.98 of the Universal Credit Regulations, made under s.24(5) below, recent victims of domestic violence must be free of any work-related requirement for a period of 13 weeks, subject to an extension for a further 13 weeks in relation to the work search and work availability requirements for responsible carers of children (reg.98(1A)). Where a claim has to be made jointly by both members of a couple, both are claimants and it must be asked separately whether work-related requirements can be imposed on each. Note that a claimant who cannot, by virtue of s.19, have any work-related requirement imposed may nevertheless be required by the Secretary of State under s.23(1)(a) to participate in an interview relating to the possible imposition of any such requirement.

Subsection (2)

1.166
    Three categories are specifically identified in subs.(2)(a)–(c). Others can, and have been, prescribed in regulations (subss.(2)(d) and (3)–(4)):

    (a) Claimants who have limited capability for work and for work-related activity cannot have any work-related requirement imposed. Once claimants who currently qualify for employment and support allowance (ESA) fall within the ambit of universal credit, limited capability will be tested in essentially the same way as for ESA. Note that claimants who do not fall within s.19(2)(a) are exempted from the application of the work search and work availability requirements if they have limited capability for work, but not limited capability for work-related activity (s.21(1)(a)). Under reg.99 of the Universal Credit Regulations claimants who are unfit for work (not further defined) and provide prescribed evidence cannot have the work search requirement imposed and have the work availability requirement modified, for limited periods. See the notes to reg.99 for the details of the various permutations of circumstances covered.

(b) Claimants who have regular and substantial caring responsibilities for a severely disabled person cannot have any work-related requirement imposed. Although s.40 allows the meaning of "regular and substantial caring responsibilities" and "severely disabled person" to be prescribed separately in regulations, reg.30 of the Universal Credit Regulations defines the two phrases in combination in terms of meeting the conditions of entitlement to carer's allowance, disregarding the earnings conditions. There seems no reason why that should not be valid. The test is therefore, in brief, that the person cared for is entitled to attendance allowance, at least the middle rate of the care component of disability living allowance or Scottish child disability payment, the standard or enhanced rate of the daily living component of personal independence payment or Scottish adult disability payment, or armed forces independence payment and that the carer devotes at least 35 hours per week to caring for such a person. But note that by virtue of reg.30(3) anyone who derives any earnings from the caring is excluded from the definition. See the extension in reg.89(1)(b) of the Universal Credit Regulations, under para.(d) below.

(c) Claimants who are the responsible carer for a child under the age of one cannot have any work-related requirement imposed. By subs.(6) a responsible carer is a person who is responsible for a child or, for couples, either partner nominated jointly provided one is responsible for the child. Regulation 4 of the Universal Credit Regulations, made under para.5 of Sch.1 to the WRA 2012, sets out how responsibility is to be determined. See the notes to reg.4. See ss.20(1)(a) and 21(1)(aa) for children aged one and two respectively.

(d) Regulations 89 and 90 of the Universal Credit Regulations set out the additional categories of claimant who cannot have any work-related requirement imposed. Regulation 90 covers the special rules needed by virtue of the special characteristic of universal credit as both an in-work and an out-of-work benefit. It thus exempts claimants whose earnings are of an amount at least equal to a threshold figure, calculated by reference to the national minimum wage and differing weekly hours for different groups of claimants. That in most cases produces a relatively high figure. For claimants with earnings below that threshold, see the effect of reg.99 on the work search and work availability requirements.

Regulation 89 covers more general categories. Regulation 89(1)(b) allows in some claimants who do not quite meet the conditions of subs.(2)(b). Regulation 89(1)(d) and (f) allow in some claimants who do not quite meet the conditions of subs.(2)(c). Regulation 89(1)(a) applies to claimants who have reached the qualifying age for state pension credit, i.e. state pension age. Regulation 89(1)(c) brings in women for shortish periods before and after confinement. Regulation 89(1)(e) brings in some claimants in education.

Claimants subject to work-focused interview requirement only

20.—(1) A claimant falls within this section if—

(a) the claimant is the responsible carer for a child who is aged [[1]1], or

(b) the claimant is of a prescribed description.

(2) The Secretary of State may, subject to this Part, impose a work-focused interview requirement on a claimant falling within this section.

(3) The Secretary of State may not impose any other work-related requirement on a claimant falling within this section (and, where a claimant falls within this section, any other work-related requirement previously applying to the claimant ceases to have effect).

1.167

AMENDMENT

1. Welfare Reform and Work Act 2016 s.17(1)(a) (April 3, 2017).

DEFINITIONS

"claimant"—see s.40.
"responsible carer"—see ss.40 and 19(6).
"work-focused interview requirement"—see ss.40 and 15(1).
"work-related requirement"—see ss.40 and 13(2).

GENERAL NOTE

1.168　The default position in s.22 is that a claimant is, unless falling within ss.19–21, to be subject to all work-related requirements, i.e. the work search and work availability requirements, with the optional additions of a work-focused interview and/or a work preparation requirement. Section 20 defines the circumstances in which a claimant who does not fall within s.19 (no work-related requirements), that condition applying because the discretion in para.(2) is subject to the rest of Pt I of the Act, can have a work-focused interview requirement, but not any other requirement, imposed. If the conditions of s.20(1) are met, there is a discretion whether actually to impose the work-focused interview requirement (subs.(2) may) and there is no statutory limit on the frequency of interviews that can be required. Where a claim has to be made jointly by both members of a couple, both are claimants and it must be asked separately whether work-related requirements can be imposed on each. Note that under s.23 the Secretary of State may require a claimant to participate in an interview for purposes relating to the imposition of any work-related requirement, verifying compliance with any work-related requirement or assisting the claimant's compliance with any work-related requirement. They may also require the reporting of relevant changes of circumstances.

Note that a claimant falls within s.19 (no work-related requirements) if any of the provisions of reg.89 or 90 of the Universal Credit Regulations apply (s.19(2)(d)), e.g. where the conditionality earnings threshold in reg.90 is met, so that the s.20 requirement cannot then be imposed. Though do not forget the power in s.23(1) to require a claimant to participate in an interview for certain specified purposes, which is not a work-related requirement". A claimant whose employed earnings (combined such earnings for couples) do not meet that threshold but equal or exceed the "administrative earnings threshold" under the "light touch regime" of reg.99(6) remain potentially subject to the imposition of the work-focused interview requirement, but in practice are apparently only required to attend work search interviews in the first and eighth weeks on the regime.

See s.24 for the process of imposing a requirement.

Section 19(1)(c) exempts responsible carers (defined in s.19(6)) of children under the age of one from all work-related requirements (and there are slight extensions in reg.89 of the Universal Credit Regulations). So no further protection is needed where a child is under the age of one. The scope of the protection given by s.20 to limit the permissible work-related requirements that can be imposed on a claimant has been narrowed considerably since April 2013. Initially, in combination with reg.91(1), subs.(1)(a) applied where the child in question was aged less than five. In April 2014, the crucial age was reduced to three, but with some further protection under s.21(1)(b) in combination with a new reg.91A for responsible carers of children aged three or four, who could not have any work-related requirements other than the work-focused interview or work preparation requirement imposed. The April 2017 amendments limit subs.(1)(a) to responsible carers of a child aged one (not under or over that age) and take away the power to prescribe any different age in regulations. As a result, reg.91(1), which had carried out the prescription previously required by subs.(1)(a), has been revoked. The further protection under s.21(1) has been limited to responsible carers of children aged two (subs.(1)(aa)) and reg.91A has been revoked.

Under s.20(1)(b), reg.91(2) continues to extend the effect of the provision to responsible foster carers of any child aged from one to 15 and to certain categories of foster parents and "friend and family carers". It seems anomalous that "ordinary" responsible carers should be treated less favourably then those groups, but no challenge under the Human Rights Act 1998 on the ground of discrimination could lead to any finding that the amendments were invalid, since they were all carried out by primary legislation.

The nature of the requirement and the purposes of the interview are defined in s.15 and reg.93 of the Universal Credit Regulations.

Claimants subject to work preparation requirement

21.—(1) A claimant falls within this section if the claimant does not fall   1.169
within section 19 or 20 and—

(a) the claimant has limited capability for work,

[¹ (aa) the claimant is the responsible carer for a child who is aged 2,] or

(b) the claimant is of a prescribed description.

(2) The Secretary of State may, subject to this Part, impose a work preparation requirement on a claimant falling within this section.

(3) The Secretary of State may also, subject to this Part, impose a work-focused interview requirement on a claimant falling within this section.

(4) The Secretary of State may not impose any other work-related requirement on a claimant falling within this section (and, where a claimant falls within this section, any other work-related requirement previously applying to the claimant ceases to have effect).

(5) [¹ . . .]

AMENDMENT

1. Welfare Reform and Work Act 2016 s.17(1) (April 3, 2017).

DEFINITIONS

"claimant"—see s.40.
"limited capability for work"—see ss.40 and 37(1).
"prescribed"—see s.40.
"responsible carer"—see ss.40 and 19(6).
"work preparation requirement"—see ss.40 and 16(1).
"work-focused interview requirement"—see ss.40 and 15(1).
"work-related requirement"—see ss.40 and 13(2).

GENERAL NOTE

The default position in s.22 is that a claimant is, unless falling within ss.19–21,   1.170
to be subject to all work-related requirements, i.e. the work search and work availability requirements, with the optional additions of a work-focused interview and/or a work preparation requirement. Section 21 defines the circumstances in which a claimant who does not fall within ss.19 or 20 (no work-related requirements or work-focused interview requirement only) can have a work preparation requirement and, under subs.(3), a work-focused interview requirement, but not any other requirement, imposed. Under s.23(1) the Secretary of State is empowered to require a claimant to attend an interview relating to the imposition of a work-related requirement, verifying compliance with any work-related requirement or assisting the claimant's compliance with any work-related requirement. He may also require the reporting of relevant changes of circumstances. Where a claim has to be made jointly by both members of a couple, both are claimants and it must be asked separately whether work-related requirements can be imposed on each.

Note that a claimant falls within s.19 (no work-related requirements) if any of the provisions of reg.89 or 90 of the Universal Credit Regulations apply (s.19(2)(d)), e.g. where the conditionality earnings threshold in reg.90 is met, so that no requirement of either kind can then be imposed under s.21. A claimant whose employed earnings (combined such earnings for couples) do not meet that threshold but equal or exceed the "administrative earnings threshold" under the "light touch regime" of reg.99(6) remain potentially subject to the imposition of the work-focused interview and work preparation requirement, but in practice are apparently only required to attend work search interviews in the first and eighth weeks on the regime.

See s.24 for the process of imposing a requirement. Note that there is a discretion ("may") to impose the requirement if the conditions are met.

Initially, the only claimants covered by s.21 were those with limited capability for work (but not limited capability for work-related activity, which would take the claimant into s.19(2)(a)) under subs.(1)(a), because no regulations had been made under subs.(1)(b). The duty in subs.(5) to make regulations did not arise in practice because any claimant who was the responsible carer for a child aged three or four fell within s.20(1)(b) by virtue of reg.91(1) of the Universal Credit Regulations as they stood at the time. In the period from April 6, 2014, when the crucial age under s.20(1)(a) was reduced to three, a prescription became necessary, which produced a new reg.91A. With effect from April 3, 2017 and the restriction of the effect of s.20(1)(a) to children aged one (and not under or over that age), the protection of s.21 has been limited to responsible carers of a child aged two (and not under or over that age). The former duty in subs.(5) to make regulations in certain circumstances has been removed and reg.91A has been revoked.

The nature of the work preparation requirement is defined in s.16.

Claimants subject to all work-related requirements

1.171   **22.**—(1) A claimant not falling within any of sections 19 to 21 falls within this section.

(2) The Secretary of State must, except in prescribed circumstances, impose on a claimant falling within this section—

(a) a work search requirement, and

(b) a work availability requirement.

(3) The Secretary of State may, subject to this Part, impose either or both of the following on a claimant falling within this section—

(a) a work-focused interview requirement;

(b) a work preparation requirement.

DEFINITIONS

"claimant"—see s.40.
"prescribed"—*ibid.*
"work availability requirement"—see ss.40 and 18(1).
"work preparation requirement"—see ss.40 and 16(1).
"work search requirement"—see ss.40 and 17(1).
"work-focused interview requirement"—see ss.40 and 15(1).

GENERAL NOTE

Temporary Coronavirus Provisions
1.172   The last of the temporary coronavirus provisions relevant to the imposition of work-related requirements expired on November 12, 2020. See previous editions of this volume for the details.

1.173   This section sets out the default position that a claimant of universal credit is, unless falling within ss.19–21, to be subject to all work-related requirements, i.e. the work search and work availability requirements, with the optional additions of a work-focused interview and/or a work preparation requirement. Note that a claimant falls within s.19 (no work-related requirements) if any of the provisions of reg.89 or 90 of the Universal Credit Regulations apply (s.19(2)(d)), e.g. where the earnings threshold in reg.90 is met, so that no work-related requirement of kind can then be imposed under s.22. Under s.23(1) the Secretary of State is empowered to require a claimant to attend an interview relating to the imposition of a work-related requirement, to the verification of compliance or to assisting the claimant to comply with a requirement. By contrast with other provisions, where this section applies the work search and work availability requirements *must*, subject to the exceptions prescribed in regs 98 and 99 of the Universal Credit Regulations, be imposed (subs.(2)), but there is a discretion about the other requirements (subs.(3)). See the notes to ss.19–21 for the circumstances in which either no or only some work-related requirements may be imposed. The content of the requirements is set out in ss.15–18 and associated regulations. Where a claim has to be made jointly by both members of a couple, and both are claimants it must be asked separately whether work-related requirements can be imposed on each. See s.24 for the process of imposing a requirement.

See the notes to s.14 for discussion of *JB v SSWP (UC)* [2018] UKUT 360 (AAC) and the question whether the current standard terms of claimant commitments (e.g. in the form of provisions like "I will also attend and take part in appointments with my adviser when required", "I will be available to attend a job interview immediately [and to] start work immediately" or "I will normally spend 35 hours per week looking and preparing for work") are sufficient in themselves to carry out the duty in s.22(1) and the power in s.22(2) to impose the specified work-related requirements. The judge considered that that question would rarely arise in practice and that what was important was whether consideration of all the evidence produced by the SSWP of communications to the claimant showed that the substance of the requirement in issue and the consequences of non-compliance had been properly notified to the claimant. In para.29 of *S v SSWP (UC)* [2017] UKUT 477 (AAC), the judge accepted that, if the SSWP failed to carry out the s.22(1) duty, the claimant should not bear the consequences of that (which must entail that the requirement(s) in question had not been imposed and there could be no sanction for failing to comply). That approach has in effect been confirmed in para.6 of *JB*, where it was said to be a condition precedent of the imposition of a sanction under s.27(2)(a) that the claimant was subject to the work-related requirement in question. See also the notes to ss.13, 14 and 24.

Work-related requirements: supplementary

Connected requirements

23.—(1) The Secretary of State may require a claimant to participate in an interview for any purpose relating to—   **1.174**

    (a) the imposition of a work-related requirement on the claimant;

    (b) verifying the claimant's compliance with a work-related requirement;

    (c) assisting the claimant to comply with a work-related requirement.

(2) The Secretary of State may specify how, when and where such an interview is to take place.

(3) The Secretary of State may, for the purpose of verifying the claimant's compliance with a work-related requirement, require a claimant to—

    (a) provide to the Secretary of State information and evidence specified by the Secretary of State in a manner so specified;

    (b) confirm compliance in a manner so specified.

(4) The Secretary of State may require a claimant to report to the Secretary of State any specified changes in their circumstances which are relevant to—

(a) the imposition of work-related requirements on the claimant;

(b) the claimant's compliance with a work-related requirement.

DEFINITIONS

"claimant"—see s.40.
"work-related requirement"—see ss.40 and 13(2).

GENERAL NOTE

1.175   This section gives the Secretary of State power to require a claimant to do various things related to the imposition of work-related requirements, verifying compliance and assisting claimants to comply: to participate in an interview (subss.(1) and (2)); for the purpose of verifying compliance, to provide specified information and evidence or to confirm compliance (subs.(3)); or to report specified changes in a claimant's circumstances relevant to the imposition of or compliance with requirements. Note that the permitted purposes of an interview under subs.(1) do not include discussion of the drawing up or review of a claimant commitment as such. However, discussion of whether a work-related requirement should be imposed and what its content should be, which would then be recorded in a claimant commitment, would be included.

The requirements under s.23 do not fall within the meaning of "work-related requirement", but there is a separate ground of sanction under s.27(2)(b) for failing for no good reason to comply with them, but only for claimants subject to all work-related requirements or to the work preparation requirement (see reg.104(1) of the Universal Credit Regulations in conjunction with regs 102, 103 and 105). The Secretary of State is allowed under subs.(2) to specify how, when and where any interview under subs.(1) is to take place, so that there is no straightforward limit on the number or frequency of the interviews that may be specified, or on the persons who may conduct the interview. The interviews must of course properly be for one of the purposes specified in subs.(1). The requirement to participate in an interview cannot be used for punitive purposes or simply as a means of control of a claimant. The requirement, as now for new style JSA, is not attendance at an interview at the specified time and date, but participation in it. This would appear to mean that a claimant can be required to participate in an interview over the telephone, providing that that manner of conducting it has been specified under subs.(2). In an ambiguous (so far as JSA is concerned) Parliamentary answer on 24 November 2015 (UIN 17005), the Minister of State Priti Patel said:

"Under JSA, claimants are not sanctioned for failing to answer their telephone. In Universal Credit, claimants who have a prearranged telephone interview with their Work Coach, and who fail to participate without good reason, can be referred for a sanction decision."

JB v SSWP (UC) [2018] UKUT 360 (AAC) (see the notes to ss.14 and 15) was endorsed and applied in *KG v SSWP (UC)* [2020] UKUT 307 (AAC). Before the Upper Tribunal the Secretary of State accepted that the available evidence did not show that the claimant had been properly notified of the requirement to take part in the particular telephone interview with his work coach, so that no sanction could be applied under s.27. The documents were ambiguous as to whether the interview was under s.15 (work-focused interview requirement) or s.23 and what issues the claimant was told were to be investigated, and left it unclear whether he had been adequately informed of the consequences of non-compliance.

There is no further provision about what participating in an interview entails. It must at least entail turning up at the place and time specified, although the decision of Judge Knowles in *SA v SSWP (JSA)* [2015] UKUT 454 (AAC) (see the notes to s.27 for full discussion) would indicate that tribunals should consider, in cases where the claimant arrives not very late, whether it is proportionate to the nature of all the circumstances to regard that as a failure to participate in an interview. There were all sorts of mitigating circumstances in *SA*, that may well not be present in other cases. See *SN v SSWP (JSA)* [2018] UKUT 279 (AAC), detailed in the notes to ss.26(2)(a) and 27(2)(a), for discussion of what might amount to a failure to participate (in that case in a mandatory work activity scheme) and the expression in para.45 of some doubt about the result in *SA*.

The requirement to participate must also extend to making some meaning-ful contribution to the interview, but the limits will probably not be established until some more sanctions appeals in JSA or universal credit reach the Upper Tribunal. Behaviour that leads to the premature termination of the interview may well amount to a failure to participate (see the facts of *DM v SSWP (JSA)* [2015] UKUT 67 (AAC) in the notes to s.27(2)(b)). There may, though, in cases of uncooperative claimants or heavy-handed officials or a combination, be dif-ficult questions about when an interview has ceased to exist, so that subsequent behaviour cannot be relevant to whether there has been a failure to participate (see *PH v SSWP (ESA)* [2016] UKUT 119 (AAC) on failing to submit to a medical examination).

It was recognised in *CS v SSWP (JSA)* [2019] UKUT 218 (AAC), detailed in the notes to s.26(2)(a), that it was legitimate for a scheme provider to require an attender to verify their identity before starting a scheme, so that a refusal to do so would usually amount to a failure to participate in the scheme. The same principle could apply to an interview, but the particular issues that arose in *CS*, to do with a scheme provider external to the DWP, are unlikely to arise if it is an interview with a work coach or other adviser that has been notified.

The compulsory imposition of a sanction for failure for no good reason to report specified changes in circumstances, to provide specified information and evidence or to confirm compliance with a work-related requirement is a new departure.

See s.24 for the process of imposing a requirement.

Imposition of requirements

24.—(1) Regulations may make provision—   1.176
   (a) where the Secretary of State may impose a requirement under this Part, as to when the requirement must or must not be imposed;
   (b) where the Secretary of State may specify any action to be taken in relation to a requirement under this Part, as to what action must or must not be specified;
   (c) where the Secretary of State may specify any other matter in relation to a requirement under this Part, as to what must or must not be specified in respect of that matter.

   (2) Where the Secretary of State may impose a work-focused interview requirement, or specify a particular action under section 16(1) or 17(1) (b), the Secretary of State must have regard to such matters as may be pre-scribed.

   (3) Where the Secretary of State may impose a requirement under this Part, or specify any action to be taken in relation to such a requirement, the Secretary of State may revoke or change what has been imposed or specified.

   (4) Notification of a requirement imposed under this Part (or any change to or revocation of such a requirement) is, if not included in the claimant commitment, to be in such manner as the Secretary of State may determine.

   (5) Regulations must make provision to secure that, in prescribed circum-stances, where a claimant has recently been a victim of domestic violence—

(a) a requirement imposed on that claimant under this Part ceases to have effect for a period of 13 weeks, and

(b) the Secretary of State may not impose any other requirement under this Part on that claimant during that period.

(6) For the purposes of subsection (5)—

(a) "domestic violence" has such meaning as may be prescribed;

(b) "victim of domestic violence" means a person on or against whom domestic violence is inflicted or threatened (and regulations under subsection (5) may prescribe circumstances in which a person is to be treated as being or not being a victim of domestic violence);

(c) a person has recently been a victim of domestic violence if a pre-scribed period has not expired since the violence was inflicted or threatened.

DEFINITIONS

"claimant"—see s.40.
"work-focused interview requirement"—see ss.40 and 15(1).

GENERAL NOTE

1.177   This section contains a variety of powers and duties in relation to the imposi-tion by the Secretary of State of either a work-related requirement or a connected requirement under s.23. It makes the imposition of a requirement and the notifi-cation to the claimant a moderately formal process, which raises the question of whether the decision of the Secretary of State to impose a requirement is a decision that is appealable to a First-tier Tribunal under s.12(1) of the SSA 1998, either as a decision on a claim or award or one which falls to be made under the WRA 2012 as a "relevant enactment" (s.8(1)(a) and (c) of the SSA 1998). However, if it is a decision not made on a claim or award, it is not covered in Sch.3 to the SSA 1998 (or in Sch.2 to the Decisions and Appeals Regulations 2013 (see Vol.III of this series)), so could not be appealable under that heading. The discussion in the note to s.12(1) of the SSA 1998 in Vol.III would indicate that, since the imposition of a requirement is not an "outcome" decision determining entitlement or payability of universal credit or the amount payable, it is not appealable under s.12(1)(a) as a decision on a claim or award or as a decision on another basis.

Thus, it appears that a direct challenge to the imposition of any particular require-ment, including any element specified by the Secretary of State, and/or its inclusion in a claimant commitment under s.14 of this Act, can only be made by way of judicial review in the High Court, with the possibility of a discretionary transfer to the Upper Tribunal. Otherwise, a challenge by way of appeal appears not be possible unless and until a reduction of benefit for a sanctionable failure is imposed on the claimant for a failure to comply with a requirement. It must therefore be arguable that in any such appeal the claimant can challenge whether the conditions for the imposition of the requirement in question were met, with the result that, if that challenge is success-ful, the sanction must be removed. That appears to have been the assumption of the Supreme Court in *R. (on the application of Reilly and Wilson) v Secretary of State for Work and Pensions* [2013] UKSC 68; [2014] 1 A.C. 453. In para.29 of their judgment, Lords Neuberger and Toulson mentioned without any adverse comment Foskett J's holding at first instance that a consequence of a breach of a regulation requiring a claimant to be given notice of a requirement to participate in a scheme was that no sanctions could lawfully be imposed on the claimants for failure to participate in the scheme. Paragraph 6 of *JB v SSWP (UC)* [2018] UKUT 360 (AAC) states that it is a condition precedent of imposing any sanction under s.27(2)(a) that the claimant was subject to the work-related requirement in issue, thus confirming the approach in para.29 of *S v SSWP (UC)* [2017] UKUT 477 (AAC) that if a specific require-ment has not been imposed by the SSWP no sanction can follow.

Subsection (1)

Regulation 99 of the Universal Credit Regulations is made in part under para.(a), reg.98 on domestic violence falling more specifically under subs.(5) and (6). No regulations appear to have been made under paras (b) and (c).   **1.178**

Subsection (2)

No regulations appear to have been made under this provision.   **1.179**

Subsection (3)

The inclusion of this express power to revoke or change any requirement, or any specification of action, is an indication of the formality entailed in the imposition of a requirement. However, there appears to be no restriction on the circumstances in which the Secretary of State may carry out such a revocation or change, subject of course to the legislative conditions being met for whatever the new position is. A mere change of mind without any change in circumstances or mistake or error as to the existing circumstances will do.   **1.180**

Subsection (4)

There is serious doubt whether the standard terms currently used in universal credit claimant commitments are sufficient in themselves to impose any work-related requirements (see the notes to s.14 for extensive discussion of the effect of the decision in *JB v SSWP (UC)* [2018] UKUT 360 (AAC)). If they are not, the necessity for notification by some other means, as allowed by subs.(4), becomes more important. It is necessarily implied in subs.(4) in conjunction with ss.13(1) and 22 that claimants are not subject to a work-related requirement if the Secretary of State has not notified them of its imposition: see para.29 of *S v SSWP (UC)* [2017] UKUT 477 (AAC), *SP v SSWP (UC)* [2018] UKUT 227 (AAC) and now para.6 of *JB* (above)). Careful consideration will need to be given by tribunals to what evidence of imposition by the Secretary of State and notification to the claimant has been put before them.   **1.181**

JB was endorsed and applied in *KG v SSWP (UC)* [2020] UKUT 307 (AAC). Before the Upper Tribunal the Secretary of State accepted that the available evidence did not show that the claimant had been properly notified of the requirement to take part in the particular telephone interview with his work coach, so that no sanction could be applied under s.27. The documents were ambiguous as to whether the interview was under s.15 (work-focused interview requirement) or s.23 (connected requirements) and what issues the claimant was told were to be investigated, and left it unclear whether he had been adequately informed of the consequences of non-compliance.

It is plainly arguable that no work-related or connected requirement can be imposed unless the claimant has received sufficient information about the requirement to enable them to make meaningful representations about whether the requirement should be imposed or not (the "prior information duty"). That duty stems from principles stated by the Supreme Court in *Reilly and Wilson* (above) and elaborated by the Court of Appeal in *Secretary of State for Work and Pensions v Reilly and Hewstone* and *Secretary of State for Work and Pensions v Jeffrey and Bevan* [2016] EWCA Civ 413; [2017] Q.B. 657; [2017] AACR 14. See the discussion in the notes to s.14, especially for points about when any breach of the duty might be material and when issues about the duty arise on appeals. If the process for the production of claimant commitments as described in the notes to s.14 is followed, there should be ample opportunity for the giving of sufficient information, although what happened in practice in individual cases will be what matters.

This provision allows the Secretary of State to notify the claimant of the imposition of any requirement, if not included in a claimant commitment under s.14, in any manner. Thus, it may be done orally (or presumably even through the medium of mime), but it is a necessary implication that a requirement must be notified to the claimant. That in turn implies that, whatever the manner of notification, the content must be such as is reasonably capable of being understood by the particular claimant with the characteristics known to the officer of the Secretary of State (so perhaps the medium of mime will not do after all). Less flippantly, this principle may be important for claimants with sensory problems, e.g. hearing or vision difficulties. The expectation of course is that the requirements imposed under the Act will be included in the claimant commitment, one of whose aims is to ensure that claimants know and understand what is being required of them and the potential consequences of failing to comply. That expectation may not in practice have been fulfilled. However, it is clear in law that the validity of a requirement is not dependent on inclusion in the claimant commitment. There is no such express condition and under s.14(4)(a) the Secretary of State is only under a duty to record in the claimant commitment such of the requirements under the Act as he considers it appropriate to include. It may be that the fact that a requirement is not recorded in the claimant commitment could be put forward as part of an argument for there having been a good reason for failing to comply with the requirement.

Subsections (5) and (6)

1.182   The duty to make regulations providing that no work-related requirement or connected requirement under s.23 may be imposed for a period of 13 weeks on a claimant who has recently been a victim of domestic violence is partially carried out in reg.98 of the Universal Credit Regulations. Most of the meat is in the regulation, including the definition of "domestic violence", which has been amended since April 2013. See the note to reg.98 for the details. However, subs.(6)(b) does define "victim" to include not just those on whom domestic violence is inflicted but also those against whom it is threatened.

Regulation 98 appears to be defective in that it applies only to work-related requirements, which in accordance with the definition in s.13(2) do not include connected requirements under s.23. Thus the duty in subs.(5) in relation to any requirement under Part 1 of the Act has not been fulfilled in relation to connected requirements. That defect cannot affect the application of reg.98 to work-related requirements.

Compliance with requirements

1.183   **25.** Regulations may make provision as to circumstances in which a claimant is to be treated as having—

(a) complied with or not complied with any requirement imposed under this Part or any aspect of such a requirement, or

(b) taken or not taken any particular action specified by the Secretary of State in relation to such a requirement.

GENERAL NOTE

1.184   Under subs.(a) regulations may deem a claimant either to have or not to have complied with any work-related requirement or connected requirement under s.23 in particular circumstances. Regulations 94–97 of the Universal Credit Regulations make use of this power, mainly in treating claimants as not having complied. No regulations appear to have been made as yet under subs.(b).

Reduction of benefit

Higher-level sanctions

1.185   **26.**—(1) The amount of an award of universal credit is to be reduced in accordance with this section in the event of a failure by a claimant which is sanctionable under this section.

(2) It is a failure sanctionable under this section if a claimant falling within section 22—

(a) fails for no good reason to comply with a requirement imposed by the Secretary of State under a work preparation requirement to undertake a work placement of a prescribed description;

(b) fails for no good reason to comply with a requirement imposed by the Secretary of State under a work search requirement to apply for a particular vacancy for paid work;

(c) fails for no good reason to comply with a work availability requirement by not taking up an offer of paid work;

(d) by reason of misconduct, or voluntarily and for no good reason, ceases paid work or loses pay.

(3) It is a failure sanctionable under this section if by reason of misconduct, or voluntarily and for no good reason, a claimant falling within section 19 by virtue of subsection (3) of that section ceases paid work or loses pay so as to cease to fall within that section and to fall within section 22 instead.

(4) It is a failure sanctionable under this section if, at any time before making the claim by reference to which the award is made, the claimant—

(a) for no good reason failed to take up an offer of paid work, or

(b) by reason of misconduct, or voluntarily and for no good reason, ceased paid work or lost pay,

and at the time the award is made the claimant falls within section 22.

(5) For the purposes of subsections (2) to (4) regulations may provide—

(a) for circumstances in which ceasing to work or losing pay is to be treated as occurring or not occurring by reason of misconduct or voluntarily;

(b) for loss of pay below a prescribed level to be disregarded.

(6) Regulations are to provide for—

(a) the amount of a reduction under this section;

(b) the period for which such a reduction has effect, not exceeding three years in relation to any failure sanctionable under this section.

(7) Regulations under subsection (6)(b) may in particular provide for the period of a reduction to depend on either or both of the following—

(a) the number of failures by the claimant sanctionable under this section;

(b) the period between such failures.

(8) Regulations may provide—

(a) for cases in which no reduction is to be made under this section;

(b) for a reduction under this section made in relation to an award that is terminated to be applied to any new award made within a prescribed period of the termination;

(c) for the termination or suspension of a reduction under this section.

DEFINITIONS

"claimant"—see s.40.
"prescribed"—*ibid.*
"work availability requirement"—see ss.40 and 18(1).
"work preparation requirement"—see ss.40 and 16(1).
"work search requirement"—see ss.40 and 17(1).

GENERAL NOTE

Sections 26–28 set up a very similar structure of sanctions leading to reductions in the amount of universal credit to that already imposed in the new ss.19–20 of the old style Jobseekers Act 1995 substituted by the WRA 2012 and in operation from October 22, 2012 (see Vol.V of this series). The similarity is in the creation

1.186

111

of higher-level sanctions, here under s.26, and of medium, low and lowest-level sanctions, here under s.27, and in the stringency of the periods and the amount of reductions to be imposed, in particular for higher-level sanctions. See the discussion in the notes to s.19 of the old style Jobseekers Act 1995 in Vol.V. There are even more similarities to the structure of sanctions in ss.6J and 6K of the new style Jobseekers Act 1995, also introduced by the WRA 2012 and only in operation in relation to claimants to whom the universal credit provisions have started to apply. In all three places the maximum length of a higher-level sanction was initially three years, a very considerable increase on the previous position. On May 9, 2019, following a report of November 6, 2018 by the House of Commons Work and Pensions Committee on *Benefit Sanctions* (HC 995 2017–19), the Secretary of State (Amber Rudd) made a written statement to Parliament (HCWS1545) including the following:

"I have reviewed my Department's internal data, which shows that a six-month sanction already provides a significant incentive for claimants to engage with the labour market regime. I agree with the Work and Pensions Select Committee that a three-year sanction is unnecessarily long and I feel that the additional incentive provided by a three-year sanction can be outweighed by the unintended impacts to the claimant due to the additional duration. For these reasons, I have now decided to remove three year sanctions and reduce the maximum sanction length to six months by the end of the year."

That decision was implemented, subject to qualification, in relation to universal credit by the amendment to reg.102 of the Universal Credit Regulations with effect from November 27, 2019 (see below).

Paragraph 4.31 of the September 2022 *Growth Plan 2022* (CP 743) said that the government would be strengthening the universal credit sanctions regime to set clear expectations, including applying for jobs, attending interviews or increasing hours, but it was left unclear exactly what that was to entail or whether any legislative change was envisaged. It is not known whether the plan, such as it was, has survived the change of administration. Paragraph 4.148 of the *Spring Budget 2023* (HC 1183) stated that the government would strengthen the way that the universal credit sanctions regime was applied by automating part of the process, to reduce error rates, and provide additional training to work coaches to enable them to apply sanctions more effectively, including for claimants who do not look for or take up employment. It has since been clarified (Written answer of March 28, 2023 by Guy Opperman, Minister for Employment) that the automation is only to be of the initial creation of referral forms for work coaches when a mandatory appointment is missed, not of decision-making or the application of the sanctions regime.

For a summary of past government reactions to official reports and studies on the effectiveness or fairness of sanctions regimes see pp.210–11 of the 2021/22 edition of Vol.V of this series. More recently, a letter dated June 15, 2022 from the Chair of the House of Commons Work and Pensions Committee, Sir Stephen Timms, to the then Secretary of State, noted that the Committee's 2018 report on *Benefit Sanctions* had recommended that the Department "urgently evaluate the effectiveness of reforms to welfare conditionality" and that the government had accepted the recommendation, saying that it would focus its evaluation on "whether the sanctions regime within Universal Credit is effective at supporting claimants to search for work". Some research was carried out, but the DWP after initial equivocation declined to publish a report, saying that it did not adequately cover the deterrent effect of the sanctions regime. The draft report on the *Impact of Benefit Sanctions on Employment Outcomes* was eventually published on April 6, 2023 after a ruling by the Information Commissioner's Office.

The Public Law Project published a distinctly critical report, *Benefit Sanctions: A Presumption of Guilt*, on July 20, 2022.

There are some differences in the wording of otherwise similar provisions made by different parts of the WRA 2012, which will be noted below. The sanctions framework is limited to the operation of work-related and connected requirements, so that universal credit claimants who fall outside that ambit cannot be sanctioned (although other consequences might follow failure to comply with some requirements). That result is secured through the general restriction of the application of s.26 to claimants who are subject to all work-related requirements under s.22 (except under subs.(3)) and through the scope of s.27 being limited to failures to comply with work-related or connected requirements.

The test of being subject to all work-related requirements is applied at the date of the sanctionable failure (or award of universal credit for pre-claim failures) and it does not in general affect the continuing operation of the sanction if the claimant ceases to be so subject. The reduction rate drops from 100% of the standard allowance to nil if the claimant begins to have limited capability for work and work-related activity (Universal Credit Regulations, reg.111(3)). The reduction rate drops to 40% if the claimant comes within s.19 (no work-related requirements) because of certain caring responsibilities for children under one (reg.111(2)). The DWP rejected the Work and Pensions Committee's recommendation in its report on *Benefit Sanctions* (above) that sanctions be cancelled when a claimant ceased to be subject to the requirement that led to the sanction (House of Commons Work and Pensions Committee, *Benefit Sanctions: Government Response* (HC 1949 2017-19, February 11, 2019, paras 49-51). It was said that that would undermine the incentive effect of the sanctions and that the mitigations in reg.111 were adequate. Note also the termination of a reduction when the claimant has been in paid work at least a weekly rate of 35 times the hourly national minimum wage for 26 weeks (reg.109).

Note the important provision in reg.5 of the JSA Regulations 2013 that, if a claimant is entitled to both universal credit and new style JSA, no work-related requirements can be imposed under the new style JSA regime (ss.6B-6G of the new style Jobseekers Act 1995) and that the provisions for reduction of JSA on sanctions under ss.6J and 6K of that Act do not apply. See the annotations to reg.5 in Vol. I of this series for discussion of the consequences. That note shows that the issues arising from the rule have been raised with the DWP by the Social Security Advisory Committee, but that it is currently unlikely that any changes will be made in the near future, as the DWP has higher priorities for legislative amendments. The equivalent provision for new style ESA purposes is reg.42 of the ESA Regulations 2013.

The central concept under these provisions is of a "sanctionable failure", which under s.26(1) (subject to reg.113 of the Universal Credit Regulations), and s.27(1), is to lead to a reduction in the amount of an award of universal credit. For higher-level sanctions under s.26, the reduction for most adult claimants initially was in brief of 100 per cent of the claimant's individual standard allowance for 91 days for a first higher-level failure, 182 days for a second such failure (or a new style ESA or JSA failure) within a year and 1095 days for a third or subsequent such failure within a year. However, the amendment with effect from November 27, 2019 has changed the period in the third category to 182 days. That is in fulfilment of Amber Rudd's undertaking noted above. Regulation 5(3) of the amending Regulations made the transitional provision that, where an award of universal credit was subject to a 1095-day reduction under s.26 as at November 27, 2019, that reduction was to be terminated where the award had been reduced for at least 182 days.

It must, though, be noted that there has been no amendment to reg.101(3) of the Universal Credit Regulations, which imposes a 1095-day limit on the total outstanding reduction period that is allowed. Because by virtue of reg.101(2) reduction periods under universal credit (as for new style JSA, but not old style JSA) run consecutively, the result is still that a claimant subject to a series of higher-level sanctions, each individually limited to 182 days, may be subject to a continuous reduction of benefit for up to 1095 days. The precise words of Amber Rudd's pledge set out above may thus have been carried out, but the effect is not as comprehensive as may have been thought.

There is no discretion under either ss.26 or 27 as to whether or not to apply a reduction if the conditions are met and no discretion under the regulations as to the amount and period of the reduction as calculated under the complicated formulae there. Regulation 113 of the Universal Credit Regulations, made under ss.26(8)(a) and 27(9)(a), sets out circumstances in which no reduction is to be made for a sanctionable failure. There is also provision for hardship payments under s.28.

As a matter of principle, a claimant has to be able, in any appeal against a reduction in benefit on the imposition of a sanction, to challenge whether the conditions for the imposition of sanction were met. See the note to s.24.

It has recently been stated that the Secretary of State need not in all sanctions cases provide evidence in the appeal bundle to support the satisfaction of all the preconditions to imposing a sanction, but that principle must be properly understood in context. In *SSWP v CN (JSA)* [2020] UKUT 26 (AAC), the claimant's sole ground of appeal against a sanction for failing to participate in the Work Programme by not attending an appointment was that she had never failed to keep an appointment (i.e. implicitly that she could not have received the notice of the appointment and/or had good cause under the regulations then in force). The tribunal allowed her appeal on the ground that the bundle did not contain a copy of the notice referring her to the Work Programme (i.e. the WP05) so that it was not satisfied that she had properly been notified of the requirement to participate. The tribunal appeared to think that that issue was one "raised by the appeal" within s.12(8)(a) of the SSA 1998, which it manifestly was not as the Secretary of State's submission in the bundle, not challenged by the claimant, was that there was no dispute that the claimant was referred to the Work Programme. Nor did it give any explanation, if it had exercised its discretion under s.12(8)(a) to consider the issue nonetheless, as to why it did so and how it was clearly apparent from the evidence so as to be capable of being dealt with under that discretion. Even if those hurdles had been overcome, the Secretary of State had not been given a fair opportunity to deal with the point. What evidence it was necessary for the Secretary of State to provide in the appeal bundle depended what issues have been put in dispute in the appeal. Having therefore set the tribunal's decision aside, Judge Wright substituted a decision finding on the evidence that the claimant had received the letter notifying her of the appointment in question.

The same approach was applied in *SSWP v SD (JSA)* [2020] UKUT 39 (AAC). There, the tribunal had raised and sought evidence on its own initiative on the issue whether the "prior information duty" (on which see the notes to s.14) had been satisfied at the stage of initial referral to the Work Programme, which the claimant had never challenged. As well as the s.12(8)(a) problem, the tribunal had failed to explain why, even if there was a breach of the duty at that stage, the breach was material. In substituting a decision the judge rejected any unfairness in the referral to the Work Programme and rejected on the evidence the claimant's contention about the appointment.

That view of what evidence must be provided in the appeal bundle as to satisfaction of the preconditions to imposing a sanction must be read in the light of the approach in *SSWP v DC (JSA)* [2017] UKUT 464 (AAC), reported as [2018] AACR 16, and *PO'R v DFC (JSA)* [2018] NI Com 1. There it was said that the Secretary of State should in all cases involving a failure to participate in some scheme or interview where notice of certain details of the scheme etc was required to be given, as well as notice of date, time and place, include in the appeal bundle a copy of the appointment letter, whether the claimant had raised any issue as to the terms of the letter or not. That was on the basis that unrepresented claimants could not be expected to identify technical issues about the validity of notices and it could not be predicted what particular issues might arise in the course of an appeal. If the letter was not included in the initial bundle, the decisions approved the action of tribunals in directing its production as a proper exercise of their inquisitorial jurisdiction. That exercise must rest on a use of the discretion in s.12(8)(a) to consider issues not raised by the appeal. The resolution of the approaches is no doubt that whenever a tribunal exercises that discretion it must do so consciously and explain why it has done so in any statement of reasons, and give the Secretary of State a fair opportunity to produce the document(s). It may be that an adequate explanation is to be found more readily when it is a notice of a specific appointment is in issue rather than an initial reference to a scheme. See also para.6 of *JB v SSWP (UC)* [2018] UKUT 360 (AAC), detailed in the notes to s.14.

Another important concept is that of a "good reason" for the conduct or failure to comply with a requirement under the WRA 2012. Most of the definitions of sanctionable failures in ss.26 and 27 incorporate the condition that the failure was "for no good reason". Paragraph 8 of Sch.1 to the Act allows regulations to prescribe circumstances in which a claimant is to be treated as having or as not having a good reason for an act or omission and to prescribe matters that are or are not to be taken into account in determining whether a claimant has a good reason. No regulations have been made under this power. There is no equivalent to reg.72 of the JSA Regulations 1996 (but the problem dealt with there is covered for universal credit by the allowance of limitations on work search and work availability requirements). The House of Commons Work and Pensions Committee (in para.111 of its report on *Benefit Sanctions*, above) recommended that regulations be introduced containing a non-exhaustive list of circumstances that could constitute good reason. The DWP (paras 66-69 of *Benefit Sanctions: Government Response*, above) rejected that recommendation as undermining flexibility, while noting that a list of good reasons is available in the DMG and on GOV.uk (the link provided in the response is to chapter K2 of the ADM for universal credit).

Thus, the concept of "good reason" remains an open-ended one, no doubt requiring consideration of all relevant circumstances but also containing a large element of judgment according to the individual facts of particular cases. The amount and quality of information provided to the claimant in the claimant commitment or otherwise about responsibilities under the WRA 2012 and the consequences of a failure to comply will no doubt be relevant, especially in the light of the approach of the Supreme Court in paras 65 and 66 of *R (on the application of Reilly and Wilson) v Secretary of State for Work and Pensions* [2013] UKSC 68; [2014] 1 A.C. 453 and of the Court of Appeal in *SSWP v Reilly and Hewstone* and *SSWP v Jeffrey and Bevan* [2016] EWCA Civ 413; [2017] Q.B. 657; [2017] AACR 14 (see the notes to s.14 above). Probably, in addition, as in the previously familiar concept of "just cause", a balancing is required between the interests of the claimant and those of the community whose contributions and taxes finance the benefit in question. See the discussion below in relation to subs.(4) and voluntarily and for no good reason ceasing paid work or losing pay.

1.187

In *SA v SSWP (JSA)* [2015] UKUT 454 (AAC), a decision on s.19A(2)(c) of the old style Jobseekers Act 1995 and failing to carry out a jobseeker's direction, Judge Knowles accepted the Secretary of State's submission that in determining whether a good reason had been shown for the failure all the circumstances should be considered and that the question was whether those circumstances would have caused a reasonable person (with the characteristics of the claimant in question) to act as the claimant did. Expressing the approach in such terms tends to point away from the notion of a balance.

However, there is a potentially significant difference in wording. In ss.26 and 27 and in ss.6J and 6K of the new style Jobseekers Act 1995 the condition is that the claimant fails "for no good reason", not that the claimant acts or omits to act "without a good reason". It may eventually be established that these two phrases have the same meaning, but in the ordinary use of language the phrase "for no good reason" carries a suggestion that something has been done or not done capriciously or arbitrarily, without any real thought or application of reason. It could therefore be argued that it is easier for a claimant to show that they did not act for no good reason and on that basis that the balancing of interests mentioned above could not be applicable. It would be enough that the claimant acted or failed to act rationally in the light of his or her own interests. It can of course be objected that such an argument fails to give the proper weight to the identification of what is a good reason and that it would seem contrary to the overall policy of the legislation if it was much easier to escape a universal credit sanction than an old style JSA sanction. On the other hand, it can be asked why Parliament chose to use a different phrase for the purposes of universal credit sanctions than "without a good reason" when the latter phrase could have fitted happily into ss.26 and 27. It is to be hoped that the ambiguity will eventually be resolved in decisions of the Upper Tribunal or the courts.

One of the points raised when permission to appeal to the Upper Tribunal was given in *S v SSWP (UC)* [2017] UKUT 477 (AAC) was whether "for no good reason" has any different meaning from "without a good reason". In para.54 Judge Mitchell expresses the view that there is no material difference and that both phrases refer to the absence of a good reason. However, the point made in the previous paragraph about a possible difference in meaning may not yet have been conclusively rejected, as it is not clear that in the particular circumstances of *S* it would have mattered which was adopted.

The case actually decides only a relatively short point about the meaning of "for no good reason" in ss.26 and 27 of the WRA 2012. The First-tier Tribunal had said that the claimant's professed ignorance of the effect of work (including part-time work) on his universal credit entitlement could not amount to a good reason for failing to undertake all reasonable work search action because ignorance of the law was no defence. On the claimant's appeal to the Upper Tribunal the Secretary of State accepted that, by analogy with the well-established case law on good cause for a delay in claiming, ignorance of the law was capable of constituting a good reason. The judge agreed that the tribunal had erred in law, but concluded that the error was not material because the only proper conclusion on the evidence was that the claimant could reasonably have been expected to raise with his work coach or other DWP official any concerns or confusions over the financial implications on his universal credit award of taking any of the sorts of work he had agreed to search for. Thus, even on the correct approach the claimant did not have a good reason for what the tribunal had concluded was a failure under s.27(2)(a).

It may also be that the analogy with good cause (indeed in para.57 the judge said that "good reason" expressed the same concept as "good cause" but in more modern language) is misleading or at least incomplete. That is because when considering good cause for a delay in claiming there is no difficulty in adopting the general meaning approved in *R(SB) 6/83* of some fact that, having regard to all the circumstances (including a claimant's state of health and the information that he had or might have obtained), would probably have caused a reasonable person of the same age and experience to act or fail to act as the claimant had done. It was in that context that the principle that a reasonable ignorance or mistaken belief as to rights could constitute good cause was established. But the question there is what a reasonable person could be expected to do to secure an advantage to them in the form of the benefit claimed late. In the context of universal credit sanctions, the notion of reasonableness carries a distinctly different force. So where the work search requirement under s.17(1)(a) to take all reasonable action to obtain paid work is concerned, reasonableness must be based on what level of activity the community that funds universal credit is entitled to expect from a claimant as a condition of receipt of the benefit. Similar, although not necessarily identical, factors are present in relation to the other work-related requirements and the sanctions for voluntarily and for no good reason ceasing work or losing pay. Although all personal circumstances are relevant, the notion of a balance between those circumstances and the claimant's proper responsibilities is not captured by the traditional concept of "good cause". The better analogy would seem to be with "just cause" as used in unemployment benefit and in old style JSA before the 2012 amendments. The adoption of the "good cause" approach in relation to claimed ignorance of rights in *S* cannot be taken as excluding such an approach. The full meaning of "for no good reason" remains to be worked out.

Subsections (2)–(4) set out what can be a sanctionable failure for the purposes of s.26 and higher-level sanctions. All except subs.(3) are restricted to claimants who are at the time of the sanctionable failure or the imposition of the sanction subject to all work-related requirements under s.22. Thus, claimants excused from all work-related requirements under s.19 (e.g. those with limited capability for work and work-related activity or with specified caring responsibilities) or from some element of such requirements under s.20 or 21 cannot be subject to higher level sanctions. They can be subject to s.27 sanctions. Subsections (5)–(8) give regulation-making powers.

Subsection (2)

(a) It is a higher-level sanctionable failure for a claimant subject to all work-related requirements to fail for no good reason (on which see the note above) to comply with a work preparation requirement under s.16 to undertake a work placement of a description prescribed in regulations. Regulation 114(1) of the Universal Credit Regulations prescribes Mandatory Work Activity as a work placement for the purposes of this provision (although the scheme has ceased to operate after April 2016) and reg.114(2) in its substituted form gives sufficient details of the scheme to satisfy the requirement in subs.(2)(a) to give a description and not just a label (the problem identified by the Court of Appeal in relation to the then state of the JSA legislation in *R (on the application of Reilly and Wilson) v Secretary of State for Work and Pensions* [2013] EWCA Civ 66; [2013] 1 W.L.R. 2239), as approved by the Supreme Court ([2013] UKSC 68; [2014] 1 A.C.453). That was decided in relation to s.17A(1) of the old style Jobseekers Act 1995 and reg.2 of the Jobseeker's Allowance (Mandatory Work Activity Scheme) Regulations 2011 (where the description of the scheme is in substance the same as in reg.114) by Hickinbottom J in *R (Smith) v Secretary of State for Work and Pensions* [2014] EWHC 843 (Admin). That conclusion and the judge's reasoning was in essence endorsed by the Court of Appeal on the claimant's appeal ([2015] EWCA Civ 229).

1.188

Before undertaking a Mandatory Work Activity scheme could have become a work preparation requirement it must have been specified for the claimant in question by or on behalf of the Secretary of State and meet the condition of improving the particular claimant's work prospects. As the particular scheme and the potential application of subs.(2)(a) has been defunct for some years, cases on such specification and what amounts to a failure to participate in a scheme or a good reason for such a failure are discussed elsewhere in these notes.

(b) It is a higher-level sanctionable failure for a claimant subject to all work-related requirements to fail for no good reason (on which see the note above) to comply with a work search requirement under s.17 to apply for a particular vacancy for paid work. It would seem that for there to have been a requirement to apply for a particular vacancy the taking of that action must have been specified by or on behalf of the Secretary of State under s.17(1)(b). It appears that scheme providers can be authorised persons under s.29 to act on behalf of the Secretary of State to "mandate" claimants to apply for a particular vacancy or to accept it if offered (see note 3 to ADM para.K3051), though failing to accept the offer cannot lead to a sanction under subs.(2)(b), only under subs.(2)(c) by showing a failure to be available for work. See the note to s.17 for discussion of the meaning of "paid work", the notification of vacancies through Universal Jobmatch or the Find a job service and requirements to apply for vacancies in the claimant commitment. It appears in the nature of the word "vacancy" that it is for employment as an employed earner, or possibly some form of self-employment that is closely analogous to such employment, e.g. through an agency.

In *MT v SSWP (JSA)* [2016] UKUT 72 (AAC) doubts were expressed whether failure to register with an employment agency could fall within the equivalent provision for old style JSA (s.19(2)(c) of the old style Jobseekers Act 1995), at least without evidence of some specific vacancy. It is not entirely clear whether a vacancy has actually to exist at the time that the Secretary of State specifies that the claimant is to apply for it or whether it is enough that a vacancy is about to arise at that point (compare the terms of s.19(2)(c)). It may be that it is enough that the requirement is conditional on the post becoming open for applications before the next meeting with the work coach, but the "failure" cannot take place until applications are possible. And the claimant must have been given sufficient information about the vacancy in order to have been able to make meaningful representations at the time about whether the requirement should be imposed (see notes to s.14 for discussion of the "prior information duty"). Some doubt was expressed in *CJSA/4179/1997* whether the offer of a "trial" as a part-time car washer properly fell within s.19(2) (c). It was suggested that if it did not, the case should have been considered under s.19(2)(d) (neglect to avail oneself of a reasonable opportunity of employment), to which there is no direct equivalent in the universal credit legislation (see the notes to para.(c) below). But if applying for or accepting the offer of the trial had been specified by the Secretary of State as a work search action under s.17, failure to comply for no good reason would be a sanctionable failure under s.27(2)(a) of the WRA 2012.

There is no express provision that the vacancy is for work that is suitable for the claimant in question. However, plainly the question of suitability would be relevant to the issue of whether a claimant had no good reason for failing to apply for the vacancy, even in the absence of the decisions in *PL v DSD (JSA)* [2015] NI Com 72 (followed and applied in *PO'R v DFC (JSA)* [2018] NI Com 1). There, the Chief Commissioner for Northern Ireland approved and applied the obiter suggestion of Judge Ward in *PL v SSWP (JSA)* [2013] UKUT 227 (AAC) (on the pre-October 2012 form of the Great Britain legislation) that, in deciding whether claimants had good cause for failing to avail themselves of a reasonable opportunity of a place on a training scheme or employment programme, a tribunal erred in law, where the circumstances raised the issue, in failing to consider the appropriateness of the particular scheme or programme to the particular claimant in the light of their skills and experience and previous attendance on any placements. Judge Ward's suggestion had been that the test was whether the claimant had reasonably considered that what was provided would not help him. It seems likely that a similar general approach will be taken to the issue of "good reason" under s.26(2)(b) and the appropriateness of the vacancy in question, as also suggested in *MT* (above). It may though still need to be sorted out how far the issue turns on the claimant's subjective view, within the bounds of reasonableness, in the light of the information provided at the time, as against a tribunal's view of the appropriateness of the situation in employment. The Chief Commissioner made no comment in *PL* on the treatment of the claimant's refusal to complete and sign forms with information about criminal convictions and health, that the First-tier Tribunal had found were reasonably required by the training provider as part of its application process for the scheme, as a failure by the claimant to avail himself of a reasonable opportunity of a place on the training scheme. Regulation 113(1)(a) of the Universal Credit Regulations prevents any reduction in benefit being made when the vacancy was because of a strike arising from a trade dispute. According to the then Minister of State Esther McVey (House of Commons written answers April 2, 2014 and September 1, 2014) the instruction to Jobcentre Plus staff not to mandate claimants to apply for zero hours contracts applies only to JSA, not universal credit. However, again, and even though exclusivity clauses have been made unenforceable from May 26, 2015 by the new s.27A of the Employment Rights Act 1996, the suitability of such a contract for the particular claimant will certainly be relevant to the issue of no good reason.

Failure to apply for a vacancy no doubt encompasses an outright refusal to apply and also behaviour that is "tantamount to inviting a refusal by the employer to engage [the claimant]" (*R(U) 28/55*, para.7). In that case the claimant had presented himself for an interview for a job as a parcel porter in what the employer had described as a dirty and unshaven state, as a result of which he was not engaged. The Commissioner accepted that on the employer's evidence the claimant had neglected to avail himself of a reasonable opportunity of suitable employment. There is no reason why that general approach should not also apply in the present context.

It has long been accepted that a refusal or failure to complete an unobjectionable application form can amount to a failure to apply (see *R(U) 32/52* and

CJSA/2692/1999). As Commissioner Howell noted in para.5 of *CJSA/4665/2001* there will be cases:

"where the way a claimant completes or spoils a job application will be unsatisfactory and unfit to put in front of any employer so as to prevent it counting as a genuine application at all, so that he or she will have 'failed to apply': it is all a question of fact."

In *CJSA/4665/2001* itself, though, the Employment Service had refused to pass on otherwise properly completed application forms because the claimant had included criticisms of the Service and of government training initiatives. The Commissioner held that in the absence of any evidence that employers had been or would have been put off from considering the claimant by his comments or of any evidence of an intention to spoil his chances it had not been shown that he had failed to apply for the vacancies. A similar approach has been taken by Commissioner Rowland in a case in which the claimant disputed the necessity of including a photograph with the application form (*CJSA/2082/2002* and *CJSA/5415/2002*). As the employment officer did not have clear information from the employer contrary to the claimant's contention and had not tested the matter by submitting a form without a photograph, the sanction should not have been applied.

See the notes to para.(a) above for further discussion of good reason. Apart from the suitability and location of the work, personal, domestic and financial circumstances might be relevant. No doubt, as in the past, conscientious or religious objections would need particularly careful consideration. For instance, in *R(U) 2/77* (on neglect to avail) the claimant's sincerely held objection on what he described as moral grounds to joining a trade union were held to make to make an opportunity of employment unsuitable and unreasonable (and see *R(U) 5/71* for a case where a more intellectual conviction against joining a teachers' registration scheme did not have that effect). For a further example on its own facts (and no more than that) of a potential good reason for not applying for a vacancy, see *GR v SSWP (JSA)* [2013] UKUT 645 (AAC), where it was held that a claimant with a genuine fear that prevented him going to the town where a course was to take place had good cause (under reg.7 of the Jobseeker's Allowance (Employment, Skills and Enterprise Scheme) Regulations 2011) for failing to participate in the scheme.

In *KB v SSWP (UC)* [2019] UKUT 408 (AAC) the claimant failed to apply for a vacancy (as a barista) as she had agreed with her work coach to do. She said that she had later concluded that there was no point in applying, as she was temperamentally unsuited to the employer's requirements (she did not have "a passion for coffee" and was an introvert). The judge suggests that, in the absence of any further consultation with the work coach about the matter, there could not be a good reason for the failure. Although there was a misguided emphasis by the Secretary of State and the First-tier Tribunal on what the claimant agreed to do in her claimant commitment, there was no dispute that the Secretary of State had, through the work coach, "required" her to take the specified action of applying for the vacancy by, after discussion, saving the details to her Universal Jobmatch account.

Regulation 94 of the Universal Credit Regulations deems a claimant not to have complied with a requirement to apply for a particular vacancy for paid work where the claimant fails to participate in an interview offered in connection with the vacancy. Participation must at least entail turning up at the place and time for the interview, although the decision of Judge Knowles in *SA v SSWP (JSA)* [2015] UKUT 454 (AAC) (see the notes to s.27 for full discussion) would indicate that tribunals should consider, in cases where the claimant arrives not very late, whether it is proportionate to the nature of all the circumstances to regard that as a failure to participate in an interview. There were all sorts of mitigating circumstances in *SA*, that may well not be present in other cases. Participation must also extend to making some meaningful contribution to the interview, but the limits will probably not be established until there have been some more sanctions appeals to the Upper Tribunal. Behaviour that leads to the premature termination of the interview may well amount to a failure to participate (see the facts of *DM v SSWP (JSA)* [2015] UKUT 67 (AAC) in the notes to s.27(2)(b)). There may, though, in cases of unco-operative claimants or heavy-handed officials or a combination, be difficult questions about when an interview has ceased to exist, so that subsequent behaviour cannot be relevant to whether there has been a failure to participate (see *PH v SSWP (ESA)* [2016] UKUT 119 (AAC) on failing to submit to a medical examination).

See *SN v SSWP (JSA)* [2018] UKUT 279 (AAC) and *CS v SSWP (JSA)* [2019] UKUT 218 (AAC), detailed in the notes to s.27(2)(a), for further helpful discussion of what might amount to a failure to participate (in those cases in a mandatory work activity scheme and a work programme scheme) and the expression in para.45 of *SN* of some doubt about the result in *SA*.

Where non-compliance with the requirement to apply for a vacancy is constituted by failure to participate in an interview, good reason must extend to good reason for that failure to participate. There appear to be no provisions prescribing the length of notice of an interview to be given or how far a claimant can be required to travel, but there could plainly be a good reason for failing to comply with unreasonable require-ments, especially if the claimant had attempted in advance to draw any problem with attendance to the attention of the Secretary of State or the potential employer.

(c) It is a higher-level sanctionable failure for a claimant subject to all work-related requirements to fail for no good reason (on which see the note above) to comply with a work availability requirement under s.18 by not taking up an offer of paid work. See the note to s.17 for discussion of the meaning of "paid work". Since the require-ment under s.18 is in the very general terms of being able and willing immediately to take up paid work, the relevance of not taking up an offer can only be in revealing an absence of such ability or willingness. Therefore, both any limitations under reg.97 of the Universal Credit Regulations on the kinds of paid work that a claimant must be able and willing to take up immediately and the provisions of reg.96(2)–(5) on when a claimant is deemed to have complied with the requirement despite not being able to satisfy the "immediately" condition must be taken into account in determin-ing whether a claimant has failed to comply with the requirement.

There is case law on what might amount to refusing or failing to accept a situation in employment that is vacant or about to become vacant (under s.19(2)(c) of the old style Jobseekers Act 1995) that may still be relevant, subject to possible differences between that test and not taking up an offer of paid work. Accepting an offer but then telling lies which caused the employer to withdraw it was treated as refusal in a Northern Ireland decision (*R 6/50 (UB)*). In *CSU/7/1995* the claimant accepted the offer of a job of a lampshade maker at a wage of £79 per week, having been informed of the vacancy by the Employment Service. But she changed her mind and did not start the job because the wage was too low to meet her commitments. The tribunal decided that since she did accept the offer of employment, the equivalent of s.19(2)(c) did not operate to disqualify her from receiving unemployment benefit. However, the Commissioner held that although, normally, acceptance of an offer of a situation would be tantamount to accepting the situation it could not have been intended that it would be possible to defeat the operation of the legislation by an acceptance in theory but a repudiation in practice. The claimant had not "accepted the situation" within the meaning of the legislation.

See also *CJSA/4179/1997* in which the claimant was offered a "trial" as a part-time car washer. The tribunal dealt with the case under s.19(2)(c) of the old style Jobseekers Act 1995, but the Commissioner expressed doubt as to whether the "trial" was an offer of a "situation in any employment". The tribunal should have investigated what the trial involved. If that provision did not apply, the equivalent of s.19(2)(d) (neglect to avail oneself of a reasonable opportunity of employment) should then have been considered. There is no equivalent of s.19(2)(d) in s.26. However, it may be that even a "trial", if remunerated, is an offer of paid work.

Presumably a claimant escapes a sanction under this head by showing either a good reason for not accepting the particular offer, if that offer is compatible with the availability requirements currently imposed by the Secretary of State, or a good reason why those requirements should have been different in some way. See the notes to para.(b) above and the cases mentioned there for discussion of the relevance of the suitability of the work in question for the particular claimant. See also reg.113(1)(a) of the Universal Credit Regulations excluding reductions in benefit on consideration of vacancies due to strikes arising from trade disputes.

(d) It is a higher-level sanctionable failure for a claimant subject to all work-related requirements to cease paid work or lose pay by reason of misconduct or voluntarily and for no good reason (on which see the notes above). Since by definition the claimant must, if already subject to s.22, have an award of universal credit, this sanction can only apply to those claimants who are entitled to the benefit while in work. See the note to s.17 for discussion of the meaning of "paid work". See the note to subs.(4) below for discussion of the meanings of "misconduct" and "voluntarily and for no good reason", as well as of the implications of fixed and severe sanctions for losing pay apparently no matter what the amount of loss, subject to the exception from reductions in benefit in reg.113(1)(g) of the Universal Credit Regulations (earnings have not fallen below the level set in reg.99(6)). See the further exceptions in reg.113(1)(b) (trial periods in work where the claimant attempts hours additional to a limitation under ss.17(4) or 18(3)); (c) (voluntarily ceasing paid work or losing pay because of a strike); (d) (voluntarily ceasing paid work or losing pay as a member of the regular or reserve forces); and (f) (volunteering for redundancy or lay-off or short-time).

Subsection (3)

This provision applies to claimants with an award of universal credit who are   1.189
subject to no work-related requirements under s.19(2)(d) because reg.90 of the
Universal Credit Regulations, made under the specific powers in s.19(3), applies s.19
where the claimant's earnings equal or exceed the individual threshold, called by the
DWP the conditionality earnings threshold. If the claimant ceases the paid work from
which those earnings are derived or loses pay so that the earnings are then below the
individual threshold, either by reason of misconduct or voluntarily and for no good
reason (on which see the note above), and does not fall within either s.20 or 21, a
higher-level sanction is to be imposed. See the note to subs.(4) below for discussion
of the meanings of "misconduct" and "voluntarily and for no good reason". The
exception in reg.113(1)(g) of the Universal Credit Regulations (earnings have not
fallen below the level set in reg.99(6)) cannot by definition apply if this provision
applies. If reg.99(6) (monthly earnings equal or exceed the (lower) administrative
earnings threshold calculated by reference to specified hours at national minimum
wage level) applies to the new level of earnings, no work search requirement can be
imposed and the claimant therefore does not fall within s.22 (subject to all work-
related requirements). In that case, subs.(3) cannot apply under its own terms and
no exception is needed. If, as part of the ongoing process of working out an acceptable approach to in-work conditionality by subjecting claimants to pilot schemes
under the Universal Credit (Work-Related Requirements) In Work Pilot Scheme and
Amendment Regulations 2015 (see the notes to reg.99(6) and (6A) of the Universal
Credit Regulations for discussion), entitlement is to be determined on the basis that
reg.99(6) does not exist, then the terms of the exception in reg.113(1)(g) cannot
apply either. A very slight decrease in earnings could, in a marginal case, have the
effect identified in subs.(3), yet (no regulations having been made under subs.(5)(b))
the full force of the higher-level sanction must be imposed. It may be that in such
circumstances it will be correspondingly easier for a claimant to show that a voluntary loss of pay was not "for no good reason". These issues will have to be worked out
during the operation of the in-work conditionality pilot schemes mentioned above,
which apparently expose claimants subject to them to very severe sanctions rules,
although the DWP has stated that sanctions will be applied for failures to comply
with in-work requirements under a pilot scheme "in the last resort" (see the notes

to reg.99(6) and (6A)). See also the further exceptions in reg.113(1)(c) (voluntarily ceasing paid work or losing pay because of a strike); (d) (voluntarily ceasing paid work or losing pay as a member of the regular or reserve forces); and (f) (volunteering for redundancy or applying for a redundancy payment after lay-off or short-time).

Subsection (4)

1.190   Where a claimant has an award of universal credit and is subject to all work-related requirements under s.22 it is a higher-level sanctionable failure if before making the claim relevant to the award the claimant for no good reason failed to take up an offer of paid work (para.(a)) or by reason of misconduct or voluntarily and for no good reason ceased paid work or lost pay (para.(b)). A practical limit to how far back before the date of claim such action or inaction can be to lead to a reduction of benefit is set by regs 102(4) and 113(1)(e) of the Universal Credit Regulations. If the gap between the action or inaction and the date of claim is longer than or equal to the period of the reduction that would otherwise be imposed, there is to be no reduction. Thus a lot depends on whether it is a first, second or subsequent "offence" within a year. These two grounds of sanction are the most similar to the familiar JSA grounds now in s.19(2)(a), (b) and (c) of the old style Jobseekers Act 1995.

Under para.(a), see the discussion in the note to subs.(2)(c), but note that this sanction applies to any offer of paid work. Therefore, all questions of whether the work is suitable for the claimant and whether or not it was reasonable for the claimant not to take it up will have to be considered under the "no good reason" condition. See the introductory part of the note to this section for the meaning of that phrase as compared with "without a good reason".

Under para.(b), it would appear that misconduct and voluntarily ceasing work will have the same general meaning as misconduct and leaving employment voluntarily for the purposes of old style JSA and, before it, unemployment benefit, on which see the extensive discussion below. The scope of the sanction has to be wider to take account of the nature of universal credit. Ceasing paid work certainly has a significantly wider meaning than losing employment as an employed earner if it encompasses self-employment in addition, as suggested in the note to s.17. The notion of ceasing paid work seems in itself wider than that of losing employment and to avoid difficulties over whether suspension from work without dismissal and particular ways of bringing a contract of employment to an end are covered. But remember that under reg.113(1)(f) of the Universal Credit Regulations a reduction cannot be applied on the ground of voluntarily ceasing work where the claimant has volunteered for redundancy or has claimed a redundancy payment after being subject to lay-off or short-time working, although the action remains a sanctionable failure. See also the exceptions for voluntarily ceasing paid work or losing pay because of a strike arising from a trade dispute or as a member of the regular or reserve forces (reg.113(1)(c) and (d)).

1.191   The other particularly significant widening of the scope of the sanction as compared with those in old style JSA is in the application of this and the similar sanctions under previous subsections to losing pay as well as to ceasing paid work. This is necessary, both in relation to circumstances before the date of claim and later, because it is possible for a claimant to be entitled to universal credit while still in paid work. If the earnings from the work are below the amount of the claimant's work allowance (if and as applicable according to circumstances) they are disregarded in the calculation of any award (see reg.22(1)(b) of the Universal Credit Regulations). If they exceed that amount, 55 per cent of the excess is taken into account as income to be set against the maximum amount of universal credit. If a claimant does not have a work allowance, 55 per cent of earnings are taken into account.

There are also the rules, under s.19(2)(d) and (3), in reg.90 of the Universal Credit Regulations making a claimant subject to no work-related conditions if earnings are at least equal to an individual threshold (in the standard case the National Minimum Wage for 35 hours per week, with lesser hours used in defined circumstances), the conditionality earnings threshold. The sanction regime under subs.(4)

can only apply when at the time of the award in question the claimant is subject to all work-related requirements under s.22 and so cannot be receiving earnings at or above that individual threshold. Subsection (3) above deals with the situation where during the course of an award of universal credit a claimant moves from having earnings at least equal to the individual threshold to a situation where the earnings are lower than that threshold. For loss of pay, short of the ceasing of work, prior to the date of claim to trigger the application of the sanction under subs.(3) it must be within a fairly narrow limit. To bring the claimant within the scope of s.22 the loss of pay must leave earnings below the individual threshold and also below the (lower) administrative earnings threshold in reg.99(6), which exempts claimants from the work search requirement.

Old style JSA authority on losing employment through misconduct and universal credit
As explained above, the authority built up in unemployment benefit and old style JSA remains highly relevant to universal credit sanctions for ceasing paid work or losing pay by reason of misconduct. Possible points of difference will be noted below. **1.192**
"*Loses employment as an employed earner*". This concept was not confined to dismissal, but could also embrace persons claiming benefit while suspended from work for misconduct (*R(U) 10/71*) and the person who accepts the chance to resign rather than be dismissed as a result of their misconduct (*R(U) 2/76*, where the claimant used a company car without permission to give driving lessons and was found at home in the bath when he should have been out selling). In *CU/56/1989*, Commissioner Heggs, dealing with a situation in which the claimant had been allowed to resign rather than be dismissed, noted in para.7: **1.193**

"In Decision *R(U) 17/64* it was held that 'loss of employment' is a more comprehensive phrase than 'leaving voluntarily' because loss of employment may result either from voluntarily leaving or from dismissal. In considering whether employment has been lost through misconduct, therefore, it is not always necessary to determine categorically whether the claimant left voluntarily or was dismissed. In the present case the tribunal, in my view, correctly concluded that the claimant lost his employment through misconduct."

The claimant had been allowed to resign rather than be dismissed after he had been caught eating company products (pies) at his workplace in violation of a general prohibition on eating company products in the production area. He had previously violated this rule and been warned about his conduct. He had also received a final written warning that future misconduct would result in his summary dismissal. Unfortunately, the SSAT decision was erroneous in law because it contained no explanation of why the claimant's admitted conduct constituted misconduct.

The notion of ceasing paid work in s.26 cannot be any narrower than that of losing employment, if not wider in encompassing any route to ceasing work, quite apart from the addition of the category of losing pay as a result of misconduct. That seems to open up the possibility of a sanction for someone in part-time work who remains in that employment, but is disciplined and subjected to deductions from earnings or given reduced hours of work by reason of misconduct. There is definitely a wider application through the use of the term "paid work", which would apply to self-employment as well as employment and avoids some of the other problems about the meaning of "employment" in old style JSA (see the notes to s.19(2)(a) of the old style Jobseekers Act 1995 in Vol.V of this series).

"*Through misconduct*". The term in s.26 is "by reason of", but there is nothing to indicate that any difference of substance was intended. The old style JSA principle was that the loss of employment must be brought about because of the claimant's misconduct, not anyone else's. Any contrary reading would be absurd and unjust and contrary to the aim of penalising "voluntary unemployment". **1.194**

Where there were several reasons for the loss of employment, the claimant's misconduct did not need to be the sole cause of the loss of employment so long as it was a contributory cause, a necessary element in bringing about the loss (*R(U) 1/57; R(U) 14/57; CU/34/92*). Suggestions that it had to be the main cause in order to ground disqualification read too much into *R(U) 20/59*, where the Commissioner's statement that misconduct (trouble with the police) was there the main cause seems to be no more than a finding of fact in that particular case in which the multiple cause point was not really an issue.

1.195   *The meaning and scope of misconduct.* "Misconduct" has never been statutorily defined. Case law offers such definition as there is. The term has to be interpreted in a common-sense manner and applied with due regard to the circumstances of each case (*R(U) 24/56; R(U) 8/57*, para.6). It is narrower than unsatisfactory conduct (*R 124/51 (UB)*). Misconduct is "conduct which is causally but not necessarily directly connected with the employment, and having regard to the relationship of employer and employee and the rights and duties of both, can fairly be described as blameworthy, reprehensible and wrong" (*R(U) 2/77*, para.15). The Commissioner, in para.6, saw nothing wrong with a tribunal's description of it as an indictment of the claimant's character as an employee. A useful test, particularly where the conduct in question occurred away from work, would be: was the claimant's blameworthy, reprehensible or wrong conduct such as would cause a reasonable employer to dispense with their services on the ground that, having regard to this conduct they were not a fit person to hold that appointment (*R(U) 7/57*, para.6).

The act or omission alleged to constitute misconduct need not have been deliberate or intentional, although such might often be the case. Misconduct can consist in carelessness or negligence, but there it is necessary to discriminate between that type and degree of carelessness which may have to be put up with in human affairs, and the more deliberate or serious type of carelessness which justifies withholding benefit because the claimant has lost their employment through their own avoidable fault. In *R(U) 8/57* the claimant, a manager of a branch pharmacy, was dismissed for "negligence in the discharge of responsible duties" when a number of cash shortages were discovered over a period of weeks. Serious carelessness could legitimately be inferred and his disqualification was upheld, notwithstanding his acquittal on a charge of embezzlement arising out of the same situation. A claimant who acts on a genuine misunderstanding cannot properly be said to be guilty of misconduct; the behaviour cannot there be described as "blameworthy, reprehensible and wrong" (*CU/122/92*, para.6, citing *R(U) 14/56*).

Where the conduct grounding the loss of employment might be regarded as whistleblowing (public interest disclosure) the public interest disclosure provisions in the Employment Rights Act 1996 (ss.43A–43L, 47B and 103) should be considered, since the question of whether the disclosure was a protected one is relevant to the question of whether the conduct was blameworthy, reprehensible and wrong. Judge Mesher so held in *AA v SSWP (JSA)* [2012] UKUT 100 (AAC), reported as [2012] AACR 42 (see especially paras 10–15). There it had been appropriate for the claimant School Manager to refer concerns about the head teacher's expenses claim to the appropriate LEA officer and probably to the school governors. However, the misconduct found by the disciplinary panel and grounding the dismissal (the "loss of employment") was his disclosure to several other employees to whom, under the legislation, it was not reasonable to disclose the matter. So that, while the tribunal had erred in law by not considering the public interest disclosure provisions, that error was not material. Note that with effect from June 25, 2013, s.43B(1) of the Employment Rights Act has been amended to add the specific condition that the worker reasonably believes that the disclosure is made in the public interest (see *Chesterton Global Ltd v Nurmohamed* [2017] EWCA Civ 979; [2018] I.C.R. 731). In *Kilraine v Wandsworth LBC* [2018] EWCA Civ 1436; [2018] I.C.R. 1850 it is clarified that, to qualify, a disclosure must in its context have sufficient factual content to count as a disclosure of "information".

Misconduct which occurred before the claimant took up the employment, the loss of which by reason of the misconduct is under consideration, cannot ground a sanction: see *R(U) 26/56*, where an accountant was dismissed when his employers learned of a conviction for fraud which occurred before he commenced employment with them. There, both the conduct and its consequences (the criminal conviction) occurred before the employment was taken up. *R(U) 1/58* applied the same principle where the conduct occurred before the taking-up of the employment, but the consequences came after its commencement. There a civil engineer and buyer was awaiting trial for certain acts committed before he entered the employment. By agreement with his employer he ceased work pending the result of the trial. On conviction, he simply did not return to the employment. Nor, however, was he pressed to do so. The Commissioner held that "acts or omissions occurring before the commencement of the employment do not constitute 'misconduct'" (at para.4), citing *R(U) 26/56*, so the only matter remaining was the issue of voluntary leaving without just cause. The leaving was not voluntary: "he merely anticipated a decision by his employers to dispense with his services; he was not altogether a free agent when deciding or agreeing not to attend further at his place of business" (at paras 5 and 6). So, to refer to a case of interest notified to the authors, an SSAT was correct in holding that a van driver, dismissed after conviction of a drink-driving offence and disqualification from driving, could not be disqualified from benefit because the conduct constituting the offence had taken place before he took up the employment in question, even though the conviction came after he had done so.

It may perhaps be arguable that the authority discussed in the previous paragraph depended to an extent on an adoption (whether explicit or implicit) of the "causal theory" of unemployment benefit disqualifications, that the primary object was not to penalise the claimant, but more to discourage avoidable claims against the fund from which benefit was paid. As it was put in *R(U) 20/64*, the "basic purpose of unemployment benefit is to provide against the misfortune of unemployment happening against a person's will". Thus there was a responsibility on a claimant to do what was reasonable to avoid becoming a burden on the fund that could only arise once the claimant became employed. The causal theory was in the past bolstered by the limitation of the period of disqualification to a maximum of six weeks, after which time it was said that the primary cause of continued unemployment was the state of the labour market, rather than the claimant's act of misconduct or leaving employment voluntarily or whatever. Now that the sanctions regime gives every appearance of imposing penalties, with more extensive periods of exclusion from benefit possible (even though now reduced from their peak), it might be argued that it is irrelevant to whether such penalties are deserved or not that the misconduct occurred before the claimant started the employment that was later lost. However, it is submitted that to constitute misconduct an act still has to be "blameworthy" in the context of the employment relationship and that there cannot be blameworthiness in that sense if the person has not yet taken up the employment in question.

The causal connection with the employment need not be direct (*R(U) 2/77*, para.15), though there the refusal to join a union in a closed shop was found not to be misconduct. The conduct need not have taken place at work or in working hours, though cases where it did will be common. In *R(U) 1/71* the Chief Commissioner upheld the disqualification of a local authority parks' gardener dismissed for an act of gross indecency with another man, away from work and out of working hours (although apparently not in private within the meaning of s.1 of the Sexual Offences Act 1967), but reduced the period of disqualification to one week (an option not available under the current legislation). The Commissioner said in para.10:

> "If a person loses his employment by reason of misconduct which has a sufficient connection with the employment it may not matter that it was committed outside the employment. Common examples are those of the man employed as a motor vehicle driver who loses his licence as a result of his driving outside his employment and is disqualified from driving: there is an obvious link between the misconduct and the work. [See, e.g. *R(U) 7/57* and *R(U) 24/64*.] Similarly a person who commits offences of dishonesty outside his work may be disqualified . . ., since most employers regard a thief as unsuitable to have about their premises. [See, e.g. *R(U) 10/53*.]" (Case references added by annotator)

Sexual offences outside the employment were said by the Commissioner in para.11 to present considerable difficulty but could rank as misconduct in special circumstances where they could be said to have something to do with the employment:

"The commercial traveller's case [*CU/381/51*] is a good instance. The employers may well have thought that there was a real danger that when visiting houses trying to sell ribbons, probably to women who might often be alone in the house, the claimant might attempt some sort of liberties. Further, there are some employments where the employer has a legitimate interest in the conduct of employees even outside the employment. One example may be that of a person who holds a special position, e.g. a school teacher. Another may be that of an employee of a government department or a local authority, who rightly feel that their employees should maintain a high standard of conduct at all times."

In *R(U) 1/71* itself, even though the claimant did not work in public parks, the Commissioner, in a case he thought close to the line, was not prepared to overturn the tribunal's view that the claimant had lost his employment through misconduct, though substantially reducing the period of disqualification. Modern sensibilities might make the assessment of such circumstances more complex. On the one hand, there is a widespread feeling that no opprobrium should attach to the acts involved in the offence concerned. On the other, there is perhaps a more widespread feeling than in the past that actions and opinions outside employment are relevant to whether that employment should continue.

1.196   *Examples of misconduct.* Apart from those already noted, instances have been: persistent absenteeism without permission (*R(U) 22/52, R(U) 8/61*); unauthorised absence through ill health and/or domestic circumstances when coupled with failure to notify the employer (*R(U) 23/58; R(U) 11/59*); repeated unauthorised absence to seek work more suited to the claimant's state of health in circumstances in which the claimant gave the employer no reasons for his absences and he had received previous warnings about his conduct (*R(U) 8/61*); overstaying a holiday without permission (*R(U) 2/74; R(U) 11/59*). Theft from fellow workers at a works' social function has been held to be misconduct (*R(U) 10/53*). So has offensive behaviour to fellow employees, consisting of obscene language and an element of what would now be termed sexual harassment (suggestive remarks to and, in their presence, about female colleagues) (*R(U) 12/56*). By analogy, one would today expect many other types of abuse and discrimination to be capable of constituting misconduct. Recklessly or knowingly making false allegations about superiors or colleagues can be misconduct, and where a false criminal charge is so laid it would plainly be misconduct (*R(U) 24/55*, para.13), but it was not enough to prove misconduct to show that the employee's charge of assault by his supervisor had been dismissed in the magistrates' court (*ibid*). Refusal to obey a reasonable instruction in line with the claimant's contract of employment (e.g. a refusal to work overtime) has been held to be misconduct (*R(U) 38/58*), even where obeying the instruction would conflict with trade union policies (*R(U) 41/53*). However, disobedience of such an order due to a genuine misunderstanding has been held not to constitute misconduct (*R(U) 14/56*), and not every breach of every trivial rule would suffice (*R(U) 24/56*). And, of course, the claimant can legitimately refuse to obey instructions not contractually stipulated for without its constituting misconduct (*R(U) 9/59; R 9/60 (UB)*). Where an employee was dismissed for refusing to join a trade union as part of a closed-shop arrangement negotiated after his employment commenced, he did not lose his job through misconduct (*R(U) 2/77*).

1.197   *Establishing misconduct, matters of proof and the duties of the statutory authorities; decision-makers, First-tier Tribunals and the Upper Tribunal.* The Secretary of State (decision-maker) bears the onus of proof of establishing misconduct, and it must be clearly proved by the best available evidence. As a general rule, of course, hearsay evidence can be accepted by the statutory authorities, but particularly where a claimant is charged with misconduct and disputes the facts that are alleged to constitute it, "it is desirable that the most direct evidence of those facts should be adduced, so that the allegations may be properly tested" (*R(U) 2/60*, para.7).

Officers of the Secretary of State now have extensive powers to require employers to provide information (see, e.g. ss.109A and 109B of the SSAA 1992) and First-tier Tribunals have power to summons witnesses and/or require them to produce documents and answer questions (reg.16 of the Tribunal Procedure (First-tier Tribunal) (Social Entitlement Chamber) Rules 2008: Vol.III of this series). Nevertheless, the use of such powers is often considered out of proportion if, say, an employer is reluctant to supply much detail on request and it may be difficult to get to the truth of the matter. In some cases the statutory authorities may be able to have regard to what has happened in other legal or disciplinary proceedings arising out of the same situation now said to show misconduct. Where such proceedings are pending one option in difficult cases where the available evidence about the relevant conduct conflicts would be to postpone a decision on the "sanctionable failure" issue until the outcome of such proceedings as are pending is known. There is no obligation to await their outcome (*R(U) 10/54* and see *AA v SSWP (JSA)* [2012] AACR 42, above), and one must always keep in view the relationship between those proceedings and the precise issues before new style JSA tribunals.

Another option would be to try to resolve the matter by weighing and comparing the evidence available (e.g. does the tribunal believe the direct evidence given by a claimant it has seen and questioned and how does that compare with the indirect and/ or hearsay evidence in any written material from the employer or others which is relied on by the decision-maker) and ultimately, where doubts persist, allow the matter to be settled by application of the rules on onus of proof. It would presumably be open to the decision-maker to revise or supersede the tribunal's decision if new material facts came to light in the course of those other proceedings. The other legal proceedings could be criminal proceedings, court proceedings for breach of contract, or complaints of unfair dismissal heard in employment tribunals. Disciplinary proceedings may take place before a much wider variety of bodies. An important issue is what is the relationship to the decision-making task of the JSA decision-makers and tribunals, of decisions given by these other bodies on a matter relevant to the claimant's case?

While in varying degrees decisions given by such bodies certainly can constitute relevant evidence for the statutory authorities, they are not, legally speaking, conclusive of the outcome before the universal credit authorities, who are duty bound to make up their own minds as to what constitutes misconduct grounding reduction of benefit, irrespective of the conclusions reached by employers, the courts or other tribunals or disciplinary bodies (*R(U) 10/54*, para.6; *R(U) 2/74*, para.15). The other proceedings do not deal with the exact issue dealt with by the universal credit decision-makers and tribunals. For example, a motoring conviction as a private motorist which did not attract a ban from driving would not necessarily constitute misconduct warranting the disqualification of a lorry-driver who had been sacked by their employer as a result. It would depend on the nature of the conduct constituting the offence: the claimant might be able to show that notwithstanding the conviction their conduct was not "blameworthy" (*R(U) 22/64*, para.6). It must be remembered too that the standard of proof of guilt in criminal cases is proof beyond reasonable doubt, a higher standard than that applicable here—proof on the balance of probabilities. So an acquittal on a criminal charge arising out of the conduct now said to constitute misconduct does not necessarily preclude a finding of misconduct. Thus in *R(U) 8/57*, where the manager of the branch pharmacy was acquitted of embezzlement in relation to the cash shortages, he nonetheless lost his employment through misconduct since his inadequate supervision of staff amounted to serious carelessness.

Similarly, there are important differences between proceedings before First-tier Tribunals on the one hand, and unfair dismissal proceedings in the employment tribunal on the other. In unfair dismissal, while the employee's conduct is relevant, the main issue before the employment tribunal concerns the employer's behaviour in consequence. Before the tribunals dealing with universal credit, in contrast, the emphasis is more on the employee's conduct, although that of the employer is also relevant. The issues of losing employment through misconduct and of ceasing paid work by reason of misconduct entail consideration of what is fair between claimant and the other contributors to the insurance fund and not simply what is fair as between employer and employee. Commissioners stressed that social security tribunals when dealing with misconduct cases should not express their decisions in such terms as fair or unfair dismissal or proper or improper dismissal. The onus of proof in employment tribunal proceedings may not be the same on relevant issues as it is in proceedings before those universal credit tribunals. Equally, while the issue before universal credit tribunals is one of substance, the employment tribunal can find a dismissal unfair on procedural grounds. Hence, while the decision of the employment tribunal is conclusive of the matters it had to decide, it does not conclude anything in proceedings before universal credit decision-makers and tribunals, and its findings of fact are not binding on them, even where some of the facts before the employment tribunals are identical with facts relevant to the universal credit proceedings:

> "There will, therefore, be cases where a claimant succeeds before an [employment] tribunal on the unfair dismissal question, but the relevant adjudicating authority has decided that disqualification [from benefit] must be imposed by reason of misconduct, and vice versa." (per Commissioner Rice in *CU/90/1988*, para.4)

The findings of fact in the employment tribunal are, however, cogent evidence on which universal credit decision-makers and tribunals can act (*CU/17/1993*), since it may well be that with both employer and employee present and examined by the employment tribunal, a judicial authority presided over by a lawyer, reaching its deliberate findings of fact after due inquiry, it is better placed than the universal credit decision-makers and tribunals to fully investigate the facts of the matter. But the universal credit decision-makers and tribunals are not bound to decide the facts in the same way as the employment tribunal (*R(U) 2/74*, paras 14 and 15 and see generally on the relationship between the two sets of proceedings: *R(U) 4/78* and *R(U) 3/79*).

For similar reasons of ability to obtain and to probe evidence, decisions of the criminal courts on matters relevant to the case before universal credit decision-makers and tribunals are entitled to great respect. Thus, where it is clear that a criminal court has decided the identical issue which the claimant needs to reopen before the judicial authorities (First-tier or Upper Tribunal) in order to succeed in their appeal, the decision of that court is likely in practice to have considerable weight before those authorities. The approach in *R(U) 24/55* that in such circumstances the benefit authorities must, save in exceptional cases, treat a conviction by a criminal court as conclusive proof that the act or omission constituting the offence did occur seems now to have been generally rejected. Even that approach would not have prevented a claimant from seeking to explain or give further information on the circumstances of the offence and, in any event, allowed for a more direct challenge in exceptional cases. Nor would it prevent argument on the legal inferences to be drawn in the misconduct context from the fact of the criminal act or omission. A more flexible approach was taken in *R(S) 2/80*, where the Commissioner held that the fact of a conviction would have a bearing in benefit appeals, once it had been shown to be relevant to the benefit issue in question, because of the burden of proof in criminal cases, but that the burden would then in the benefit appeal shift to the claimant to show that they were nonetheless entitled to the benefit in question. In *AM v SSWP (DLA)* [2013] UKUT 94 (AAC) Judge Mark considered that *R(S) 2/80* was wrongly decided if it was intended to refer to the legal burden of proof rather than the evidential burden. In that case, as well as in *Newcastle City Council v LW (HB)* [2013] UKUT 123 (AAC) and *KL v SSWP (DLA)* [2015] UKUT 222 (AAC), the same judge appears to endorse even more flexibility. The criminal conviction is not conclusive as res judicata before the benefit authorities. Then it would depend on whether it was an abuse of process for the claimant to attempt to re-argue an issue of fact that was a necessary part of the criminal conviction. But in sanctions appeal cases claimants would not be caught by the principle that it is an abuse of process for a person to use civil proceedings to attack a criminal conviction, because they are not in a position analogous to a plaintiff, but are defending themselves against the imposition of a penalty by the Secretary of State. Then in considering whether the administration of justice would be brought into disrepute it would all depend on the circumstances, including if new or convincing evidence has come to light, whether the claimant pleaded guilty in the criminal proceedings (and if so, why) and whether the particular expertise of the specialist tribunal leads to a re-evaluation of the legal findings and inferences. See para.1.96 of Vol.III of this series and Buchanan-Smith, *Bound or Unrestrained: Social Security Tribunals, Res Judicata and Abuse of Process* (2022) 29 J.S.S.L. 129, where it is suggested, with some justice, that this area is ripe for some authoritative resolution by the Upper Tribunal of the confusing case law.

It has always been for the person relying on it to prove the fact of a conviction, and it is preferably done through official certification (*R(U) 24/64*).

Where the decisions of disciplinary bodies (which may well examine a wide range of witnesses) are concerned, it appears that although never binding on universal credit decision-makers and tribunals, they are entitled to an increasing degree of respect the more their proceedings approximate to proceedings in a court of law. Thus a finding by a chief constable after police disciplinary proceedings was cogent evidence that the claimant had committed particular acts (*R(U) 10/63*), but a decision by a hospital management committee, the precise reasons for which were not disclosed to the Commissioner, was not so regarded (*R(U) 7/61*).

Whether the concern is with decisions of the courts, of employment tribunals or disciplinary proceedings, it is submitted that crucial questions for universal credit decision-makers and tribunals will be: what was the decision; by what sort of body, how, by what process, and on what sort(s) of evidence was the decision made; and how closely does the matter involved in that decision relate to that before the universal credit decision-makers and tribunals? But where the other decision is from a prima facie cogent source and is properly proved by one party, a tribunal need not go behind that decision unless the other party comes forward with sufficient evidential or legal argument. See also the discussion in the notes to s.3 of the Tribunals, Courts and Enforcement Act 2007 under the heading Relying on decisions of other bodies in Vol.III of this series.

Old style JSA authority on leaving voluntarily without just cause and voluntarily and **1.198**
for no good reason ceasing paid work or losing pay

As explained above, the authority built up in unemployment benefit and old style JSA remains highly relevant to universal credit sanctions for voluntarily and with no good reason ceasing paid work or losing pay. Possible points of difference will be noted below.

Note at the outset the protections given by reg.113 of the Universal Credit Regulations (made under s.26(8)(a)) from reductions in benefit when there has been a sanctionable failure under s.26. Those particularly relevant to voluntarily and for no good reason ceasing paid work or losing pay are as follows. Regulation 113(1)(b) protects current claimants, in relation to s.26(2)(d) only, not s.26(4), whose work search and availability requirements are limited to a certain number of weekly hours and who take up paid work for extra hours for a trial period. There is to be no reduction of benefit if they voluntarily cease that paid work or lose pay. There is no protection when such ceasing is a pre-claim failure, but there might always be, as also in cases covered by reg.113(1)(b), good reason for ending a trial period of employment so that there is not in fact a sanctionable failure (see further below). Regulation 113(1)(c) protects anyone voluntarily ceasing paid work or losing pay because of a strike arising from a trade dispute. Regulation 113(1)(d) protects anyone voluntarily ceasing work as a member of the regular or reserve forces. Regulation 113(1)(f) protects anyone who has voluntarily ceased paid work either (i) because of redundancy after volunteering or agreeing to be dismissed; or (ii) on an agreed date without being dismissed following an agreement on voluntary redundancy or under this head or (iii) when laid off or kept on short time. See the notes to reg.113 for more details.

Section 26(2)(d), (3) and (4)(b) refers to voluntarily ceasing any paid work, so that there is now no need to consider the possible limitations in the meaning of "employment" in s.19(2)(b) of the old style Jobseekers Act 1995. It would appear that self-employment as well as any form of employment is covered. Paragraph K3274 of the ADM says that a claimant cannot be subject to a sanction for voluntarily and for no good reason ceasing paid work or misconduct if the work was under a zero hours contract if the contract contains an exclusivity clause (that the person cannot work for another employer). Such clauses were made ineffective with effect from May 26, 2015 (Employment Rights Act 1996, s.27A). Paragraph K3275 says that from then on the application of sanctions is not excluded. It is hard to see the legal basis for the pre-May 2015 guidance. Ceasing any employment would appear to bring the legislation into play, although the terms of the contract might contribute to a good reason for ceasing the work.

In *CJSA/3304/1999*, Commissioner Levenson considered the case of someone who had left employment A for unspecified reasons, then found employment with employer B, from which he was dismissed, and only then claimed JSA. The tribunal allowed the claimant's appeal against preclusion of payment founded on his having voluntarily left employment A without just cause. The Commissioner upheld the tribunal, saying that payment could only be precluded where a claim for benefit had been made and only "in respect of the employment immediately preceding the claim" (at para.16). Insofar as *R(U) 13/64* might be thought to say otherwise, the Commissioner, drawing support from Commissioner Goodman in para.9 of *CU/64/1994*, declined to follow it. The issue does not really arise under s.26(2)(d), but in relation to s.26(4)(b) on pre-claim failures it may be arguable that the reference to "at any time before making the claim" reverses the effect of *CJSA/3304/1999*. However, as noted above, regs 102(4) and 113(1)(e) of the Universal Credit Regulations set a practical limit to how far back a voluntary ceasing of work can be relevant.

The extension of the sanction to voluntarily losing pay is necessary because of the possibility of entitlement while doing a substantial amount of paid work. It theoretically opens a wide range of potential sanctions. The extension applies equally to potential pre-claim circumstances as to those arising during the course of an award. There will be a great many situations in which a claimant (pre-claim or during an award) loses pay in a way that could be regarded as voluntary (e.g. a person on a zero hours contract opting for fewer hours of work in one week than previously). The power in s.26(5)(b) to make regulations providing for the disregard of loss of pay below a prescribed level has not been exercised. Nor is there any discretion to shorten the prescribed periods for reduction of benefit (minimum, 91 days) in proportion to the gravity of the "offence" if the conditions for application of a s.26 higher-level sanction are met. In those circumstances, it must be arguable that trivial or disproportionately small losses of pay are to be ignored (compare *SA v SSWP (JSA)* [2015] UKUT 454 (AAC) on turning up late for a course). Even so, a great deal of weight will be put on what is a "good reason" for losing pay and also on common sense in not referring trivial situations to a decision-maker for determination.

In the discussion below references to ceasing paid work should be taken to include losing pay unless there is some specific point of difference that needs to be identified.

1.199   *Onus of proof.* Those who assert that the claimant left employment or ceased paid work and did so voluntarily must prove it. Once done, it was clear that under the "without just cause" test the onus passed to the claimant to prove on the balance of probabilities that they had just cause for so leaving (*R(U) 20/64(T)*). The use of the formula "voluntarily and for no good reason" could be argued to make showing the absence of good reason part of what the Secretary of State has to prove. However, there is no evidence of an intention to make such a radical change. And it would be contrary to the approach in principle demanded by *Kerr v Department for Social*

Development [2004] UKHL 23; [2004] 1 W.L.R. 1372; *R 1/04 (SF)*, putting emphasis on who is in a better position to supply information on any particular issue in a co-operative process, rather than formal concepts of onus of proof. The claimant will in the great majority of cases be the person best placed to come forward with an explanation of their reasons for ceasing paid work. It is assumed below that the onus of showing, on the balance of probabilities, that they had a good reason lies on the claimant. See the detailed discussion of good reason below.

"*Voluntarily leaves*". The commonest case of voluntarily leaving was when the claimant of their own accord handed in their notice or otherwise terminated their contract of employment. Indeed, in many cases there would be no dispute about this aspect of the case; the real issue was that of "just cause" or "good reason". The same will apply to voluntarily ceasing paid work. But voluntarily leaving also embraced other means by which employment was lost. So the actors who threatened to leave unless certain demands were met and were then treated by their employers as having given notice left voluntarily *(R(U) 33/51)*. It was still voluntarily leaving where the employment ended because the employer refused to accept the claimant's withdrawal of notice *(R(U) 27/59)*. It could also embrace in limited instances cases where the loss of employment took the form of a dismissal brought about by conduct of the claimant which would inevitably lead to termination of the employment *(R(U) 16/52; R(U) 2/54, R(U) 9/59, R(U) 7/74)*, but such situations had to be looked at with caution and restraint *(R(U) 2/77)*. Thus, in *R(U) 16/52* the claimant's appointment was conditional on her completing a satisfactory medical. She refused to undergo X-ray examination and was given notice. The Commissioner stated as a general rule of unemployment insurance law that if a person deliberately and knowingly acts in a way that makes it necessary for his employer to dismiss him, he may be regarded as having left his employment voluntarily. But another Commissioner later made clear in *R(U) 7/74* that "this would normally require a finding that the employee had acted, or was threatening to act, in a manner involving a deliberate repudiation of his contract of employment". So in that case an employee whose written terms of employment made no reference to a requirement to work overtime, did not leave voluntarily when he was dismissed for refusing to work overtime (cf. *R(U) 9/59*). Similarly, dismissal of an existing employee for refusal to join a trade union when a closed shop agreement was negotiated was not voluntary leaving *(R(U) 2/77)*. Nor was dismissal for refusing for good reason to pay a trade union subscription *(R(U) 4/51)*. Leaving was not voluntary where the claimant who departed had no effective choice but to quit, e.g. because dismissal appeared inevitable *(R(U) 1/58*: cf. *R(U) 2/76)*. That appears to be in line with the employment law principle of "constructive dismissal", though perhaps with a wider scope because of the focus on the voluntariness of the ceasing of work rather than on whether the claimant was dismissed or not. It is submitted that the "general rule of unemployment insurance law" invoked in *R(U) 16/52* should be taken, with the qualifications mentioned above, to apply the question of whether a claimant has voluntarily ceased paid work even when it was the employer who terminated the contract of employment.

In *R(U) 1/96*, Commissioner Goodman considered the case of a female nursery assistant who gave her employer four weeks' notice, was prepared to work out those weeks, but whose employer, after an unsuccessful attempt to persuade her to stay on, told her to leave after two days. The Commissioner considered and applied *CU/155/50* and *R(U) 2/54* so as to reject the argument that the claimant had not left voluntarily but had been dismissed (and could therefore only be disqualified if misconduct could be proved). He regarded *British Midland Airways v Lewis* [1978] I.C.R. 782 (a decision of the Employment Appeal Tribunal in the context of dismissal under labour legislation) as not laying down "any categorical proposition of law" but as merely being a decision on the facts of that case, and continued:

"In my view the ruling in *CU/155/50* and *R(U) 2/54* that there is a voluntary leaving applies equally, whether it is a case of an employer not allowing an employee to

1.200

work out his or her notice or whether it is a case of actual notice to leave given first by the employee, followed by a notice of termination given during the currency of the employee's notice by the employer. In the latter case, once the employee has given in his notice to leave it is a unilateral termination of the employment contract and cannot be withdrawn without the consent of the employer (*Riordan v War Office* [1959] 1 W.L.R. 1046). It follows that in the present case, when the claimant gave her four weeks notice in on Wednesday December 9, 1992 she had herself terminated the employment and thereby left it voluntarily. Even if what the employer did on Friday December 11, 1992 can be construed as giving in a counter-notice requiring her to leave on that day and not to work out her four weeks notice, that does not, in my view, alter the fact that the effective termination of the employment was a voluntary leaving by the claimant." (at para.12)

Taking early retirement could constitute voluntarily leaving (*R(U) 26/51*, *R(U) 20/64*, *R(U) 4/70*, *R(U) 1/81*). Even where a schoolteacher retired three years early in response to the generalised encouragement to take early retirement offered to teachers in his position by his local education authority, which further certified that his retirement was in the interests of the efficient discharge of the education authority's functions, it was still voluntarily leaving (*Crewe v Social Security Commissioner* [1982] 2 All E.R. 745 CA, Appendix to *R(U) 3/81*). However, in *R(U) 1/83* the Commissioner distinguished *Crewe* and held that a civil servant who acceded to his employer's specific request that he retire early should not be regarded as having left his employment voluntarily. Now, for universal credit, reg.113(1)(f) prevents there being any reduction in benefit whenever a claimant is dismissed for redundancy after volunteering or agreeing to be dismissed or ceases work on an agree date in pursuance of a voluntary redundancy agreement. That would appear to exempt claimants on the *Crewe* side of the line. The voluntary ceasing of work, if for no good reason, would remain a sanctionable failure but, importantly for purposes of calculating the period of reduction for future sanctionable failures, not a "sanctionable failure giving rise to a higher-level sanction" (reg.102(2) of the Universal Credit Regulations). For early retirement cases not saved by reg.113, the fine distinction between the *Crewe* type of case and those of the type considered in *R(U) 1/83* may still be important. In *CSU/22/94*, Commissioner Mitchell applied *R(U) 1/83* in favour of a claimant (a principal teacher) who had been pressured by his employers to accept an early retirement package, in a context in which his only alternative was to accept a lower status position, albeit one without loss of income (being placed on a long-term supply teacher basis). That alternative was one which "a teacher of the claimant's experience and standing could not reasonably be expected to accept" (at para.5). The decision thus stresses the need for tribunals carefully to consider whether the claimant can be said to have left voluntarily before moving on to the "for no good reason" aspect.

1.201   *"For no good reason"*. There is no definition of "good reason" in the WRA 2012, just as there was none of "just cause" or "good cause" in previous legislation dealing with disqualification from benefit or preclusion of payment of JSA and none of "good reason" in the old style JSA amendments to put the test in terms of "without a good reason" from October 2012. When those amendments were introduced there was some expression of an intention that "good reason" would be applied in the same way as the predecessor terms. See the beginning of this note on s.26 as a whole for discussion of the possible (just) difference between "without a good reason" and "for no good reason", of whether, despite the views expressed in *S v SSWP UC)* [2017] UKUT 477 (AAC), the proper analogy in the context of voluntarily ceasing work is with "just cause" as explained below, rather than with "good cause", and for the government's rejection of proposals for regulations to set out a non-exhaustive list of circumstances that could constitute good reasons. It is therefore still necessary to examine the case law authority on "just cause" when that was the test for unemployment benefit and old style JSA before considering the "no good reason" test.

That case law avoided laying down hard and fast rules for all circumstances, but most significantly "just cause" was regarded as requiring a balancing of the interests of the claimant with those of the community of fellow contributors to the National Insurance Fund. It was not a matter simply of what was in the best interests of the claimant, or of what was just as between employee and employer, or of what was in the public interest generally. To establish that they did not leave without just cause (that phraseology giving the proper emphasis) claimants had to show that in leaving they acted reasonably in circumstances that made it just that the burden of their unemployment should be cast on the National Insurance Fund (*Crewe v Social Security Commissioner* [1982] 2 All E.R. 745 per Slade LJ at 752; per Donaldson LJ at 750–751, explaining *R(U) 20/64(T)*, para.8; per Lord Denning MR at 749). Was what the claimant did right and reasonable in the context of the risk of unemployment? Was the voluntary leaving such as to create an unreasonable risk of unemployment, bearing in mind that there may be circumstances that leave a person no reasonable alternative but to leave employment (per Donaldson LJ at 750)? Establishing just cause may well be a heavier burden than showing "good cause" (per Slade LJ at 751). In *R(U) 4/87*, Commissioner Monroe stated that "the analogy with insurance seems now the paramount criterion of just cause" (para.8). His examination of decisions on the matter led him "to think that in general it is only where circumstances are such that a person has virtually no alternative to leaving voluntarily that he will be found to have had just cause for doing so, rather as a person who throws his baggage overboard to make room in the lifeboat can claim on his baggage insurance" (para.9).

There is therefore a faint suggestion in the earlier authority that there may be some difference in the ordinary use of language between "good cause" and "just cause". It may also be arguable that the formula "with no good reason" shifts the focus away from the notion of a balance between the interests of the claimant and those of the community of contributors to the fund from which benefit is paid towards more emphasis on the interests of the claimant. That would make it easier for a claimant to avoid the imposition of a sanction. In *SA v SSWP (JSA)* [2015] UKUT 454 (AAC), a decision on s.19A(2)(c) of the old style Jobseekers Act 1995 and failing to carry out a jobseeker's direction, Judge Knowles accepted the Secretary of State's submission that in determining whether a good reason had been shown for the failure all the circumstances should be considered and that the question was whether those circumstances would have caused a reasonable person (with the characteristics of the claimant in question) to act as the claimant did. Expressing the approach in such terms tends to point away from the notion of a balance.

In *S v SSWP (UC)* [2017] UKUT 477 (AAC), however, a similar approach was taken. The First-tier Tribunal had said that the claimant's professed ignorance of the effect of work (including part-time work) on his universal credit entitlement could not amount to a good reason for failing to undertake all reasonable work search action (thus leading to a sanction under s.27(2)(a)) because ignorance of the law was no defence. On the claimant's appeal to the Upper Tribunal the Secretary of State accepted that, by analogy with the well-established case law on good cause for a delay in claiming, ignorance of the law was capable of constituting a good reason. There was reference to the general meaning approved in *R(SB) 6/83* of some fact that, having regard to all the circumstances (including a claimant's state of health and the information that he had or might have obtained), would probably have caused a reasonable person of the same age and experience to act or fail to act as the claimant had done. Judge Mitchell agreed that the tribunal had erred in law, but concluded that the error was not material because the only proper conclusion on the evidence was that the claimant could reasonably have been expected to raise with his work coach or other DWP official any concerns or confusions over the financial implications on his universal credit award of taking any of the sorts of work he had agreed to search for. Thus, even on the correct approach the claimant did not have a good reason for what the tribunal had concluded was a failure under s.27(2)(a). The statements discussed below about the analogy of "good reason" with "good cause" were thus not necessary to the decision.

It is submitted that the analogy with good cause in *S* and in *SA* (indeed in para.57 of *S* the judge said that "good reason" expressed the same concept as "good cause" but in more modern language) is misleading in the present context or at least incomplete. That is because when considering good cause for a delay in claiming there is no difficulty in adopting the general meaning approved in *R(SB) 6/83*. It was in that context that the principle that a reasonable ignorance or mistaken belief as to rights could constitute good cause was established. But the question there is what a reasonable person could be expected to do to secure an advantage to them in the form of the benefit claimed late. In the context of universal credit and JSA sanctions, the notion of reasonableness carries a distinctly different force. So when considering what circumstances could justify a voluntary ceasing of work, it is submitted that the notion of a good reason must still be based on whether it is reasonable to place the burden of the claimant's unemployment on the community that funds universal credit and new style JSA. Although many personal circumstances will be relevant, the notion of a balance between those circumstances and the claimant's proper responsibilities is not captured by the traditional concept of "good cause" in the context of delay in claiming. The better analogy would seem to be with "just cause" as used in unemployment benefit and in old style JSA before the 2012 amendments (or with "good cause" as used in some of those provisions). The adoption of the "good cause" approach in relation to claimed ignorance of rights in S cannot be taken as excluding such an approach to s.26(2)(d) and (4)(b). The full meaning of "for no good reason" in this context remains to be worked out.

Accordingly, reference to authority based on the notion of a balance and reasonableness in the sense adopted above remains valuable.

Whether the claimant succeeds in discharging the burden of showing a good reason depends essentially on all the circumstances of the case, including the reasons for leaving and such matters as whether they had another job to go to, whether before they left they had made reasonable inquiries about other work or its prospects, or whether there were in their case good prospects of finding other work. Such elements should not be considered in water-tight compartments (*R(U) 20/64(T)*, para.9). The previous claims record is not directly relevant (*R(U) 20/64(T)*) para.18). In *R(U) 4/87* Commissioner Monroe, following para.10 of *R(U) 3/81* (approved in *Crewe*), ruled as remote from and irrelevant to the just cause issue long-term considerations prayed in aid by the claimant who had "urged that his leaving had in the long run actually benefited the national insurance fund, in that he had made available a vacancy for someone who would otherwise have continued unemployed, and that he was now earning more so that he was paying higher contributions" (at para.10). Such factors had nothing to do with the issue of being forced to leave.

In *CU/048/90*, Commissioner Sanders considered the appeal of a claimant who had, as a result of his employer's attitude, become dissatisfied with his employment and had sought alternative employment by circulating his curriculum vitae to 30 companies. During interviews with Barclays Bank he was given the impression that his application for a particular post would be successful, and he resigned from his employment. In the event he was not offered the post. Commissioner Sanders considered the correct approach to "just cause" to be that set out in *R(U) 4/87* (para.9). He thought that the "circumstances have to be very demanding before a claimant can establish just cause for leaving" (para.3). It seemed to the Commissioner "that in the circumstances of the case the claimant had reason to leave because he thought he was not progressing in his career" but took the view "that the circumstances were not so pressing as to justify his leaving, from an unemployment benefit point of view, before he had secured the job with Barclays Bank even though he had been led to believe that his application for that job would be successful". He agreed with the SSAT that the claimant did not have just cause for leaving voluntarily and had to be disqualified.

In some cases, probably rare in practice, an actual promise of immediate suitable new employment (which then falls through after the employment was left or the start of which is delayed) might afford just cause in the absence of any other justificatory circumstances (*R(U) 20/64(T)*, para.17; *Crewe* per Donaldson LJ, para.750). However, there was no rule of law saying that just cause cannot be established where the claimant leaves without another job to go to. Indeed, in *R(U) 20/64(T)* a Tribunal of Commissioners suggested that there could be circumstances in the claimant's personal or domestic life which become so pressing that they justify leaving employment "without regard to the question of other employment" (para.12) and they cited as illustrations *R(U) 14/52*, *R(U) 19/52* and *R(U) 31/59*, all noted below. Equally, it was clearly established that some feature of the claimant's existing employment may justify leaving it immediately without any regard to the question of other employment (para.11) and here the Commissioners quoted as instances *CU 248/49*, *R(U) 15/53*, *R(U) 38/53* and *R(U) 18/57*, also considered below. But there had to be some urgency in the matter and, as regards the latter class of case, the circumstances had to be so pressing that it would not be reasonable to expect the claimant to take such steps before leaving as were open to them to resolve the grievance connected with work through the proper channels of existing grievance procedures. *CU/106/1987* made it clear that a tribunal could not merely rely on the Secretary of State's (decision-maker's) suggestion that there would be such a grievance procedure in the circumstances of the claimant's employment. It was wrong in law to take account of a suggested grievance procedure to reject the claimant's appeal without having proper findings of fact as to its actual existence. One would equally have thought that a tribunal should also consider whether any procedure found to exist could cover the claimant's complaint and whether it was reasonable in the circumstances to expect the claimant to have resort to it.

A simple desire to change jobs was not usually enough to warrant putting the burden of one's unemployment on the Fund. Nor did moving house without more constitute just cause; it depended on the reasons for the move (*R(U) 20/64(T)*, para.15). Rather than approaching the just cause issue from the angle of considering it necessary for the claimant to be assured of suitable alternative employment, unless there were circumstances justifying them in leaving without it (the approach in *R(U) 14/52*), the Commissioners in *R(U) 20/64(T)* preferred a different perspective. They preferred to look: (1) at whether the reasons for leaving themselves amounted to just cause (i.e. leaving aside the matter of alternative employment or its prospects); and (2) where the reasons did not of themselves establish just cause to then consider whether the "promises or prospects of other employment may be effective as an additional factor which may help the claimant establish just cause. For example, where a man almost establishes just cause [in relation to, e.g. pressing personal or domestic circumstances] the fact that he has a promise or prospects of other employment may serve to tip the scale in his favour . . . In considering these matters of course the strength of his chances of employment and the gap, if any, likely to occur between the two employments must be taken into account" (para.17).

The Commissioners stated:

> "that it is impossible to lay down any period of time representing a gap between employments, or any degree of probability of fresh employment which will give an automatic answer to the question whether the claimant has shown just cause for leaving. We think that there is a distinction between on the one hand, having suitable employment to go to, as where there is an actual promise of employment, and having only prospects of employment on the other. It may be reasonable to expect a claimant who has only prospects to take some steps before leaving, such as communicating with the employment exchange to see whether his prospects cannot be made more certain."

A number of cases concerning, on the one hand, grievances about existing employment and, on the other, personal or domestic circumstances, can usefully be quoted as instances in which just cause was established, and it may be useful to note in contrast a number of examples in each category where it was not, subject to the importance of looking to the precise circumstances of each and every case and not regarding factual decisions as legal precedents.

1.202 (i) *Grievances about work.* In *R(U) 15/53* a piece-worker who lost his job when he refused to accept a substantial reduction in earnings thrust on him by his employer had just cause for leaving. In *R(U) 38/53* the claimant left after subjection to pressure to join a trade union and was able to establish just cause; it would have been intolerable if he had to remain. In *R(U) 18/57* an apprentice ordered to do work clearly outside the scope of his apprenticeship had only the options of doing as he was told or leaving immediately. In choosing the latter he had just cause. It may be now that working under a zero hours contract, especially when it was still legally possible for an exclusivity clause to be enforceable, could contribute towards a good reason for ceasing the employment (and see the guidance mentioned above under "such employment"). But mere failure to get on with colleagues (*R(U) 17/54*) or strained relations with one's employer (*R(U) 8/74*) has been held not enough. Not feeling oneself capable of the work, where one's employer was satisfied, was unlikely to be enough without clear medical evidence of that fact (*R(U) 13/52*), but leaving employment during a probationary period because the claimant considered himself unsuited to the work and that it was unfair to his employer to continue training him was more generously treated in *R(U) 3/73*.

Indeed, in *CU/43/87* Commissioner Davenport said that "a person who is experimenting in trying a new line of work should not lightly be penalised if that experiment fails". People should be encouraged to try new types of employment where work in their usual field is not available:

"It must be recognised that in such circumstances a person may find that he cannot stay in his employment and it may be that he is reasonable in leaving that employment, whereas a person who had more experience in the field in question would not be held to have acted reasonably if he gave up the employment. Not everyone finds that new and unfamiliar employment is such that she or he can reasonably stay in it." (At para.7)

CU/90/91 further illustrates that claimants who left employment as unsuitable after a trial period could have just cause for doing so and be protected from preclusion of payment without having to rely on the time-limited "trial period" concept found in the old style JSA legislation. Commissioner Hallett stated:

"It is clear from the evidence, which I accept, that the claimant took the job with Fords (which would have been permanent) on trial, conditionally on his being able to obtain accommodation in the area. It is well-settled in social security unemployment law that claimants should be encouraged to take jobs on trial and that if, after trial, the job proves unsuitable, they do have just cause for leaving. It is in the interests of the national insurance fund, and of public policy, to encourage persons to obtain employment and not penalise them if, after fair trial, the job proves unsuitable." (At para.10)

The claimant had just cause for leaving. There is no such well-settled principle applying to leaving a job taken, not on trial, but as a "stop-gap" pending something better turning up (*R(U) 40/53*; *CJSA/63/2007*, para.15).

1.203 (ii) *Personal or domestic circumstances.* In *R(U) 14/52* the claimant had just cause for leaving his job in order to be with his elderly and sick wife who lived alone. It was not possible for her to move to live with him so as to be near enough to his work. He also thought his chances of employment would be good in his wife's area, but there was little evidence in the case of searching inquiries about those prospects. In *R(U) 19/52* the claimant, who left her job to move with her service-man husband to a new posting, likely to be more than short-term, had just cause. Had the posting been short-term, however, she would have had to make inquiries about job prospects in the new area before leaving. See further *R(U) 4/87* and *CU/110/1987*. In *CU/110/1987* the claimant's service-man husband received telephone notice of posting to Germany on February 14, 1986. He went there on March 1, 1986. On February 14, the claimant gave the one week's notice required under her contract of employment and ceased work on February 21, claiming benefit the next day. She had to be available to vacate the married quarters in Aldershot from March 1. However, she did not join her husband in Germany until March 25, since repairs were needed to the married quarters there. Commissioner Monroe held that in those circumstances she had just cause for leaving when she did, rather than later. That, rather than whether she should have left at all, was the real issue in the case, since in the Commissioner's view it could hardly be said that she did not have just cause to leave (whenever she could) to join her husband in Germany. She was not to be disqualified from benefit. Actual entitlement to benefit, however, would turn on the unresolved matter of her availability for work. On the issue of availability in that context, see *R(U) 2/90(T)*. In *R(U) 31/59* the reason for leaving was the move to a new home, too far from the job, because the existing home (two small attic rooms) was wholly unsuitable for the claimant's family. By contrast, in *R(U) 6/53* the 21-year-old woman who left her job to move with her rather strict parents to a new area did not have just cause; it was reasonable to expect her to live alone, at least until she could find work in the new area. In *CJSA/2507/2005*, Commissioner Williams applied Commissioner Monroe's statement at para.9 of *R(U) 4/87*, quoted in 1.199 above, to dismiss the 28-year-old claimant's appeal against a tribunal-imposed three week disqualification for voluntary leaving (the decision-maker had imposed eight weeks). He had left to join his fiancée and get married, but had no job to go to. The three-week disqualification represented the period up to the marriage. The Commissioner also noted the need to treat with some caution decisions on this area which are 50 years' old, reflecting a very different job market and attitudes to married women, and given when appeal to the Commissioners covered fact and law.

Leaving for a financial advantage, e.g. to draw a marriage gratuity only payable on resignation (*R(U) 14/55*), or to take early retirement, even where this was encouraged by the employer and might be said to be in the public interest in terms of opening the way for younger teachers and promoting the efficiency of the education service, has been held not to rank as just cause (*Crewe v Social Security Commissioner* [1982] 2 All E.R. 745; *R(U) 26/51*; *R(U) 23/59*; *R(U) 20/64(T)*; *R(U) 4/70*; *R(U) 1/81*). However, if "good reason" has different nuances of meaning from "just cause", as discussed above, that might justify more emphasis on what was reasonable in the claimant's own interests. Further, it may be that a different approach is justified where a claimant leaves a job to avoid hardship rather than to pursue extra money (as suggested in *CJSA/1737/2014*, where one of the claimant's arguments was that the cost of travel to and from work was prohibitive).

Note the significant assistance, discussed above, that may be provided by reg.113(1)(f) of the Universal Credit Regulations in cases of voluntary redundancy, although that provision only prevents a reduction in benefit rather than making the voluntary ceasing of paid work not a sanctionable failure.

Subsection (5)
Regulations may deem ceasing work or losing pay not to be by reason of misconduct or voluntarily in certain circumstances and may provide that loss of pay below a prescribed level is to be disregarded. No such regulations have been made. Regulation 113 of the Universal Credit Regulations is made under the powers in subs.(8)(a) and only affects whether a reduction in benefit is to be imposed, not whether there is or is not a sanctionable failure.   **1.204**

Subsections (6) and (7)
See regs 101 and 106—111 of the Universal Credit Regulations for the amount and period of the reduction in benefit under a higher-level sanction. The three-year limit is imposed in subs.(6)(b) and cannot be extended in regulations.   **1.205**

Subsection (8)
Under para.(a), see reg.113 of the Universal Credit Regulations. Under para.(b), see reg.107. Under para.(c), see regs 108 and 109.   **1.206**

Other sanctions

1.207   **27.**—(1) The amount of an award of universal credit is to be reduced in accordance with this section in the event of a failure by a claimant which is sanctionable under this section.

(2) It is a failure sanctionable under this section if a claimant—

(a) fails for no good reason to comply with a work-related requirement;

(b) fails for no good reason to comply with a requirement under section 23.

(3) But a failure by a claimant is not sanctionable under this section if it is also a failure sanctionable under section 26.

(4) Regulations are to provide for—

(a) the amount of a reduction under this section, and

(b) the period for which such a reduction has effect.

(5) Regulations under subsection (4)(b) may provide that a reduction under this section in relation to any failure is to have effect for—

(a) a period continuing until the claimant meets a compliance condition specified by the Secretary of State,

(b) a fixed period not exceeding 26 weeks which is—

(i) specified in the regulations, or

(ii) determined in any case by the Secretary of State, or

(c) a combination of both.

(6) In subsection (5)(a) "compliance condition" means—

(a) a condition that the failure ceases, or

(b) a condition relating to future compliance with a work-related requirement or a requirement under section 23.

(7) A compliance condition specified under subsection (5)(a) may be—

(a) revoked or varied by the Secretary of State;

(b) notified to the claimant in such manner as the Secretary of State may determine.

(8) A period fixed under subsection (5)(b) may in particular depend on either or both the following—

(a) the number of failures by the claimant sanctionable under this section;

(b) the period between such failures.

(9) Regulations may provide—

(a) for cases in which no reduction is to be made under this section;

(b) for a reduction under this section made in relation to an award that is terminated to be applied to any new award made within a prescribed period of the termination;

(c) for the termination or suspension of a reduction under this section.

DEFINITIONS

"claimant"—see s.40.
"work-related requirement"—see ss.40 and 13(2).

GENERAL NOTE

1.208   See the introductory part of the note to s.26 for the general nature of the universal credit sanctions regime under ss.26 and 27 and for discussion of the meaning of "for no good reason". Section 27(1) and (2) requires there to be a reduction, of the amount and period set out in regulations, wherever the claimant has failed for no good reason to comply with any work-related requirement or a connected requirement under s.23. There is no general discretion whether or not to apply the prescribed deduction, but that is subject first to the rule in subs.(3) that if a failure is sanctionable under s.26 (and therefore subject to the higher-level regime) it is not to be sanctionable under s.27 and to the rules in reg.113 of the Universal Credit Regulations about when a reduction is not to be applied although there is a sanctionable failure (none of which currently apply to s.27). While the power and duty under subs.(4) for regulations to provide for the amount and period of the reduction to be imposed is in fact more open-ended than that in s.26(6), because it does not have the three-year limit, subss.(5)–(7) introduce the specific power (that does not of course have to be used) for regulations to provide for the period of the reduction for a particular sanctionable failure to continue until the claimant meets a "compliance condition" (subs.(6)) or for a fixed period not exceeding 26 weeks specified in regulations or determined by the Secretary of State or a combination of both. The 26-week limit in subs.(5)(b) appears not to have any decisive effect because a longer period could always be prescribed under subs.(4)(b), unless "may" is to be construed as meaning "may only".

In practice, the powers have been used in the Universal Credit Regulations to set up a structure of medium-level (reg.103), low-level (reg.104) and lowest-level (reg.105) sanctions. See the notes to those regulations for the details.

The medium-level sanction applies only to failures to comply with a work search requirement under s.17(1)(a) to take all reasonable action to obtain paid work etc. or to comply with a work availability requirement under s.18(1). A failure to comply with a work search requirement under s.17(1)(b) to apply for a particular vacancy attracts a higher-level sanction under s.26(2)(b) if the claimant is subject to all work-related requirements. The reduction period under reg.103 is 28 days for a first "offence" and 91 days for a second "offence" or subsequent offence within a year of the previous failure (7 and 14 days for under-18s).

The low-level sanction under reg.104 applies where the claimant is subject either to all work-related requirements under s.22 or to the work preparation requirement under s.21 and fails to comply with a work-focused interview requirement under s.15(1), a work preparation requirement under s.16(1), a work search requirement under s.17(1)(b) to take any action specified by the Secretary of State or a connected requirement in s.23(1), (3) or (4). Note that this is the sanction that applies to a failure for no good reason to report specified changes in circumstances (s.23(4)) or to provide specified information and evidence (s.23(3)) as well as to failure to participate in an interview. The reduction period under reg.104 lasts until the claimant complies with the requirement in question, comes within s.19 (no work-related requirements), a work preparation requirement to take particular action is no longer imposed or the award terminates, plus seven days for a first "offence", 14 days for a second "offence" within a year of the previous failure and 28 days for a third or subsequent "offence" within a year (plus seven days in all those circumstances for under-18s). 1.209

The lowest-level sanction under reg.105 applies where a claimant is subject to s.20 and fails to comply with a work-focused interview requirement. The reduction period under reg.105 lasts until the claimant complies with the requirement, comes within s.19 (no work-related requirements), a work preparation requirement to take particular action is no longer imposed or the award terminates.

For the purposes of regs 104 and 105, "compliance condition" is defined in subs.(6) to mean either a condition that the failure to comply ceases or a condition relating to future compliance. A compliance condition may be revoked or varied by the Secretary of State, apparently at will, and may be (not must be) notified to the claimant in such manner as the Secretary of State might determine (subs. (7)). But under regs 104 and 105 a compliance condition has to be "specified" by the Secretary of State. On the one hand, it is difficult to envisage it being decided that the Secretary of State can specify such a condition to himself, rather than to the claimant. On the other hand, it is difficult to envisage it being decided that a claimant who has in fact complied with a requirement has not met a compliance condition merely because the Secretary of State failed to give proper notice of the condition. It appears that during the 2020 coronavirus outbreak any contact by the claimant with the DWP was treated as compliance with any condition, thus bringing that part of the reduction period to an end.

The test of being subject to the work-related requirement in question is applied at the date of the sanctionable failure and it does not in general affect the continuing operation of the sanction if the claimant ceases to be so subject. The reduction rate drops from 100% of the standard allowance to nil if the claimant begins to have limited capability for work and work-related activity (Universal Credit Regulations, reg.111(3)). The reduction rate drops to 40% if the claimant comes within s.19 (no work-related requirements) because of certain caring responsibilities for children under one (reg.111(2)). The DWP rejected the House of Commons Work and Pensions Committee's recommendation in its report of November 6, 2018 on *Benefit Sanctions* (HC 995 2017-19) that sanctions be cancelled when a claimant ceased to be subject to the requirement that led to the sanction (House of Commons Work and Pensions Committee, *Benefit Sanctions: Government Response* (HC 1949 2017-19, February 11, 2019, paras 49 - 51). It was said that that would undermine the incentive effect of the sanctions and that the mitigations in reg.111 were adequate. Note also the termination of a reduction when the claimant has been in paid work at a weekly rate of 35 times the hourly national minimum wage for 26 weeks (reg.109).

1.210   Regulation 113 of the Universal Credit Regulations, made in part under subs.(9)(a), prescribes circumstances in which no reduction is to be made for a sanctionable failure under s.27 as well as s.26, but none of the circumstances covered seem relevant to s.27.

Under para.(b) of subs.(9), see reg.107. Under para.(c), see regs 108 and 109.

One of the most common grounds of sanction under s.27(2)(a), given the demise of the Mandatory Work Activity Scheme covered by s.26(2)(a), is the failure to comply with a work-related requirement to participate in an interview under s.15 (work-focused interview requirement) or s.17 and reg.94 of the Universal Credit Regulations (work search requirement: applying for particular vacancies and interviews). There is a separate power in s.23 to require a claimant to participate in an interview for any purpose relating to the imposition of a work-related requirement on a claimant, verification of compliance with work-related requirements or assisting a claimant to comply. Failure to comply attracts a sanction under s.27(2)(b). Many work preparation requirements (s.16) and other work-related requirements involve attendance and/or participation in various courses, assessments, training programmes etc, often provided by third parties contracted to the DWP. All of those areas raise similar questions about whether the requirement and the specification of what the claimant is to do has been properly notified, about what is involved in "participation" and about what could amount to a good reason for failure to comply. Similar issues were raised in relation to requirements to participate in various schemes under s.17A of the old style Jobseekers Act 1995.

For a sanction to be applied, the relevant work requirement must have been imposed in accordance with the legislation and been made enforceable where necessary by specification of a particular appointment and an obligation to attend and participate. See the notes to s.14 for the general principles, in particular the general guidance and application to the specific facts in *JB v SSWP (UC)* [2018] UKUT 360 (AAC), and to s.15 for other points on interviews. This will often involve a two-stage process, although in the case of s.15 or s.23 (connected requirements) interviews, it would appear, as pointed out by Judge Jacobs in *SP v SSWP (UC)* [2018] UKUT 227 (AAC), that even if a general obligation to attend interviews is mentioned in the claimant commitment the requirement does not become enforceable until a particular interview has been specified. Thus in *JB*, the evidence that the DWP produced to the First-tier Tribunal did not show notification of the specific interview in which it was said that the claimant had failed to participate. But Judge Poole QC stressed in para.29 the flexibility given by the legislation in permitting multiple methods of communication with claimants, such that it would be inappropriate for the Upper Tribunal to set out particular requirements for the wording of notifications or for methods used. She stated in para.29.3:

"What is important is the substance. In this case the question was whether it could fairly be said, on the totality of the evidence, that the claimant had been notified of an obligation to attend a work-focused interview and the consequences of non-compliance."

In *SP* Judge Jacobs also suggested that it is inherent in the nature of notification that it cannot be effective unless and until it is received. However, he did not have to rely on that proposition in dealing with a case where the claimant's evidence was that an appointment letter was not delivered until after the time of the appointment. That was because, even if notification were regarded as having been given, there was necessarily a good reason for not participating in an interview when the claimant was not aware of the appointment.

Sometimes the question of satisfaction of those legislative requirements becomes entangled with the question of whether the public law duty of fairness, often described as the "prior information duty" in the current context, has been fulfilled. Thus, in *KG v SSWP (UC)* [2020] UKUT 360 (AAC) not only did the documents in evidence fail to show whether the interview in question was required under the equivalent of s.15 or s.23, but they failed to show that the claimant had been informed what issues were to be investigated in the interview and of the consequences of non-compliance. And in *JB* the importance of notifying the claimant of the consequences of non-compliance seemed to stem from the duty of fairness rather than from the legislative obligation to go beyond mere notification of date, time and place of appointment to communicate a requirement to attend and participate. The prior information duty is considered in detail in the notes to s.14.

See also the decision in *NM v SSWP (JSA)* [2016] UKUT 351 (AAC), where Judge Wright held, as eventually conceded by the Secretary of State, that the inability to show that relevant DWP guidance had been considered before the claimant was given notice to participate in a Mandatory Work Activity scheme meant either that the claimant should not have been referred to the scheme (because the officer either would have followed the guidance or could have been persuaded to do so on representations from the claimant) or that he had good reason for not participating in the scheme. The appeal related to a sanction for failing to participate, through behaviour on the scheme. The guidance, in something called Mandatory Work Activity Guidance or Operational Instructions–Procedural Guidance–Mandatory Work Activity–January 2012, was relevant because at the time it instructed that claimants should not be considered for referral to Mandatory Work Activity if, among other circumstances, they were currently working (paid or voluntary). The claimant had been volunteering in a Sue Ryder shop, which he had to give up to attend the required scheme as a volunteer in a Salvation Army shop. The Secretary of State submitted that the guidance had since been changed to introduce an element of discretion about referral of claimants doing voluntary work. Judge Wright held that this would not excuse a failure by an officer of the Secretary of State to consider his own guidance or, on any appeal, a failure to provide the guidance to a First-tier Tribunal in accordance with the principles of natural justice.

The necessity for a sufficiently specific requirement to have been imposed does not necessarily mean that the DWP in the case of an appeal must, either in the response to the appeal in the bundle of documents or at a hearing, produce a full paper-trail. It all depends on what issues have been raised by the appeal or have been legitimately raised by the tribunal.

In *SSWP v CN (JSA)* [2020] UKUT 26 (AAC), the claimant's sole ground of appeal against a sanction for failing to participate in the Work Programme by not attending an appointment was that she had never failed to keep an appointment (i.e. implicitly that she could not have received the notice of the appointment and/or had good cause under the regulations then in force). The tribunal allowed her appeal on the ground that the bundle did not contain a copy of the notice referring her to the Work Programme (i.e. the WP05) so that it was not satisfied that she had properly been notified of the requirement to participate. The tribunal appeared to think that that issue was one raised by the appeal within s.12(8)(a) of the SSA 1998, which it manifestly was not as the Secretary of State's submission in the bundle, unchallenged by the claimant, was that there was no dispute that the claimant was referred to the Work Programme. Nor did it give any explanation, if it had exercised its discretion under s.12(8)(a) to consider the issue, of why it did so and how it was clearly apparent from the evidence so as to be capable of being dealt with under that discretion. Even if those hurdles had been overcome, the Secretary of State had not been given a fair opportunity to deal with the point. It is not necessary for the Secretary of State in all sanctions cases to provide evidence in the appeal bundle that all preconditions for the imposition of the sanction are satisfied. It depends what issues have been put in dispute in the appeal. Having therefore set the tribunal's decision aside, Judge Wright substituted a decision finding on the evidence that the claimant had received the letter notifying her of the appointment in question.

The judge's statement that the Secretary of State need not in all sanctions cases provide evidence in the appeal bundle to support the satisfaction of all the preconditions to imposing a sanction must, though, be read in the light of the approach in *SSWP v DC (JSA)* [2017] UKUT 464 (AAC), reported as [2018] AACR 16, and *PO'R v DFC (JSA)* [2018] NI Com 1. There it was said that the Secretary of State should in all cases involving a failure to participate in some scheme or interview where notice of certain details of the scheme etc. was required to be given, as well as notice of date, time and place, include in the appeal bundle a copy of the appointment letter, whether the claimant had raised any issue as to the terms of the letter or not. That was on the basis that unrepresented claimants could not be expected to identify technical issues about the validity of notices and it could not be predicted what particular issues might arise in the course of an appeal. If the letter was not included in the initial bundle, the decisions approved the action of tribunals in directing its production as a proper exercise of their inquisitorial jurisdiction. That exercise must rest on a use of the discretion in s.12(8)(a) to consider issues not raised by the appeal. The resolution of the approaches is no doubt that whenever a tribunal exercises that discretion it must do so consciously and explain why it has done so in any statement of reasons, and give the Secretary of State a fair opportunity to produce the document(s). It may be that an adequate explanation is to be found more readily when it is a notice of a specific appointment that is in issue rather than an initial reference to a scheme.

DC concerned two sanctions imposed in August 2013 for failures, without good cause, to participate in a Scheme as required under reg.4 of the Jobseekers Allowance (Employment, Skills and Enterprise Schemes) Regulations 2011 (SI 2011/917) in June and August 2012. By August 2013, the Regulations had been revoked, but continued to apply in relation to failures to participate that occurred while they were in force. For the same reason, the sanctions provisions in reg.8 (revoked with effect from October 22, 2012) applied in *DC*, rather than s.19A of the old style Jobseekers Act 1995.

The first appeal (in relation to August 2012) raised the issue of the effect of the Secretary of State's being unable to provide to the First-tier Tribunal, as directed, a copy of the appointment letter known as a Mandatory Activity Notification (MAN) sent or handed to the claimant in respect of the appointment that he failed to attend. The tribunal had allowed the claimant's appeal on the basis that the Secretary of State had failed to show that the claimant had been properly notified in accordance with the conditions in reg.4(2). In concluding that there was no error of law in that, Judge Rowland held that this was not a matter of the drawing of adverse inferences, but of the Secretary of State simply having failed to come forward with evidence on a matter on which the burden of proof was on him. Although there was evidence before the tribunal that the claimant had been given an appointment letter, that evidence did not go beyond showing the date and time of the appointment. It did not show where the claimant was to attend or what other information was provided and how it was expressed. The judge rejected the Secretary of State's submission relying on the presumption of regularity and the "inherent probabilities". Although the tribunal could, using its specialist experience, properly have concluded that the letter had contained enough information to make it effective, it was not bound to do so, given that it is not unknown for documents to be issued in an unapproved form or to use language that is not intelligible to an uninitiated recipient. The judge agreed with the tribunal that a copy of the appointment letter should have been in the tribunal bundle: a decision-maker might be able to rely on the presumption of regularity, but on an appeal (where it is not known what issues may eventually emerge) a copy of the letter should be provided. Much the same approach was taken by the Chief Commissioner in Northern Ireland in *PO'R*, where it was said that the tribunal there should not have decided against the claimant without having adjourned to obtain a copy of the appointment letter.

If a copy of the appointment letter was not in the bundle, then Judge Rowland's view was that a tribunal could, using its inquisitorial jurisdiction in an area where unrepresented claimants in particular could not be expected to identify such technical points, properly exercise its discretion under s.12(8)(a) of the SSA 1998 to direct that a copy be provided. It would not be fair to decide the case against the Secretary of State without giving that opportunity to provide the evidence. But where, as in *DC*, the evidence directed was not provided, the tribunal could properly conclude that the Secretary of State had failed to come forward with evidence on a matter on which the burden of proof was on him. There is therefore no formal incompatibility with the decision of Judge Wright in *CN*, although there was less emphasis there on the inquisitorial role of the tribunal. If there were any incompatibility, the fact that *DC* is a reported decision would point to its being preferred.

Judge Rowland accepted that the tribunal in *DC* had erred in law in deciding against the Secretary of State on the authorisation point (discussed below) without giving him an opportunity to provide relevant evidence, but that error was not material as, even if there was evidence that the provider was authorised to issue reg.4 notices, the tribunal would have been entitled to allow the claimant's appeal on the basis of the lack of necessary evidence that an effective notice had been given.

The second appeal (in relation to June 2012) raised the issue of whether the tribunal had been entitled to conclude that the Secretary of State had not shown that the Scheme provider in question had been authorised under reg.18 of the ESES Regulations to give reg.4 notices when he was unable to produce a copy of a letter of authorisation. Judge Rowland held that the tribunal had gone wrong in law. Regulation 18 did not specify the form in which authorisation had to be given (nor does s.29 of the WRA 2012 or s.6L of the new style Jobseekers Act 1995 on delegation and contracting out), so that it was a matter of fact and degree. Authority could be found to exist in evidence as to the conduct of those concerned, including what they have said and written over a period. The tribunal did not consider that possibility, raised by the provider acting as though authorised and the Secretary of State asserting that authority had been given. The judge went on to re-make the decision òn the appeal. It had emerged that, by an administrative mistake, no formal letter of authority had ever been issued, but the existence of a contract between the Secretary of State and the main contractor for the sub-contractor to act in the area in question and a draft authorisation letter was sufficient to satisfy reg.18. He found that the claimant had been properly notified and had not shown good cause for his failure to participate, so that a sanction was to be imposed. On close analysis of reg.8 the sanction was to be for four weeks, rather than the 26 that had originally been imposed.

Even though the literal legislative requirements of notification have been satisfied, it may be that the claimant has not been "properly" notified because of a material breach of the public law duty of fairness or more specifically the prior information duty. See the extensive discussion of that in the notes to s.14.

Many of the requirements that can give rise to sanctions under s.27 involve undertaking or participating in interviews, courses, assessments, programmes etc that that have a specified start time. Participation must in general involve at least turning up at the right time and place and also making some meaningful contribution to whatever is involved. Behaviour that leads to the premature termina-tion of the interview or course may well amount to a failure to participate (see the facts of *DM v SSWP (JSA)* [2015] UKUT 67 (AAC) where the claimant was asked to leave a session that he was said to be disrupting by asking questions and heckling (but see the discussion below about good reasons for failing to comply with require-ments and the suitability of courses etc). There may, though, in cases of uncoop-erative claimants or heavy-handed officials or a combination, be difficult questions whether an interview or course has ceased to exist. Behaviour after the interview or course has ceased to exist cannot be evidence of a failure to participate, in contrast to behaviour before it starts (see *SN* below).

In *SA v SSWP (JSA)* [2015] UKUT 454 (AAC) the claimant, who had hearing difficulties and wore a hearing aid in one ear, was directed by an employment officer to attend and complete a CV writing course with Learn Direct two days later from 11.15 a.m. to 12.15 p.m. He was given a letter to confirm the time and date. The claimant arrived at 11.25 a.m. and was told that he was too late and so had been deemed to have missed his appointment. He immediately went to the Jobcentre Plus office to rebook an appointment for the course and explained that he had misheard the time for the appointment as 11.50, the time that he normally signed on. A fixed four-week sanction for failing, without a good reason, to carry out a reasonable jobseeker's direction was imposed. On appeal the claimant said that at the meeting with the employment officer he had not been wearing his hearing aid and that he had not thought to check the time of the appointment on the letter as he genuinely thought that it was the same as his two previous appoint-ments. The First-tier Tribunal regarded it as clear that the direction had been reasonable and that the claimant had failed to comply with it, so that the sole ques-tion was whether he had had a good reason for the failure. On that question, the tribunal concluded that, although the error was genuine, that did not in itself give him a good reason and that he had failed to take reasonable steps to confirm the time of the appointment and dismissed his appeal. In setting aside the tribunal's decision and substituting her own decision reversing the imposition of the sanction (as had been suggested by the Secretary of State), Judge Knowles held that the tri-bunal had erred in law by failing to consider the question of whether the claimant had failed to comply with the direction. In the substituted decision, she concluded that, the claimant not having refused to carry out the direction and taking into account that his error was genuine and that he took immediate steps to rebook, it was disproportionate to treat his late arrival in isolation as amounting to a failure to comply with the direction. That can only be regarded as a determination on the particular facts that does not constitute any sort of precedent to be applied as a matter of law in other cases. The outcome may have reflected an understandable desire in a deserving case to get around the absence of any scope for varying the fixed period of four weeks for a sanction under s.19A of the old style Jobseekers Act 1995 for a "first offence". However, there could have been nothing unreason-able about a conclusion that arriving 10 minutes after the beginning of a course that only lasted for an hour amounted to a failure to comply with a direction to attend and complete the course, no matter how genuine the error that led to the late arrival.

SN v SSWP (JSA) [2018] UKUT 279 (AAC) discusses, from para.42 onwards, what can amount to a failure to participate in a scheme (at a time when the con-sequent sanction was under reg.8 of the MWAS Regulations, rather than s.19(2) (e) of the old style Jobseekers Act 1995). It confirms that conduct of the claimant related to the ordinary requirements of the work activity in question leading to the termination of their placement can amount to a failure to participate. In particular, it is held in paras 59-62 that actions before the start of the scheme can be relevant. In *SN* the claimant was required to work for four weeks as a retail assistant in a charity shop. As found by Upper Tribunal Judge Wright in substituting a decision on the appeal, the claimant visited the shop about a week before the placement was due to start, to find out what would be entailed. During the visit he used offensive language to one member of staff and about the nature of the work involved, that were unreasonable in any work setting. He attended at the shop at the specified time for the start of the placement, but, as the representative of the programme provider was not to arrive for about 20 minutes, retired to a changing cubicle to sit down, took off his shoes and appeared to go to sleep. When the representative arrived, the deputy manager of the shop told him that the claimant would not be allowed to work there in view of his earlier offensive conduct. The judge concludes that the combination of the claimant's behaviour on the earlier visit and his attitude of antagonism and lack of interest on the first day of the placement meant that he had failed to meet the notified requirements for participation in the scheme. There was no good cause for the failure to participate. Some doubt is expressed in para.45 about the result in *SA*.

In *CS v SSWP (JSA)* [2019] UKUT 218 (AAC) Judge Hemingway accepted that it was legitimate for a scheme provider to require an attender to verify their identity before starting the scheme, so that a refusal to do so would usually amount to a failure to participate in the scheme. However, in the particular case the claimant had declined to verify various items of information about him appearing on a computer screen, largely because of misguided views about the effect of the Data Protection Act 1998, but also because of concerns about the security of social security information held by scheme providers. The judge held that the tribunal had erred in law by failing to make findings of fact about whether the claimant had been offered the opportunity to verify his identity by other means, e.g. by producing a passport or driving licence or other document in addition to the appointment letter that he had already produced. In the absence of such findings the tribunal had not been entitled to conclude that the claimant had refused to confirm his identity rather than merely refused to confirm it by the method initially put forward by the scheme provider. It might in other cases be relevant to enquire what the appointment letter or other documents do or do not say about confirming identity.

Claimants who are found not in fact to have been aware of an interview must have a good reason for failing to comply, whether or not the requirement is said to have been imposed in such circumstances (*SP v SSWP (UC)* [2018] UKUT 227 (AAC)).

See the notes to s.26 for general discussion of what might be a good reason and in particular for the suggestion that in the present context, if any analogy is to be drawn with previous authority, it should not be with the concept of "good cause" for a late claim, but with "just cause" for leaving employment voluntarily or with "good cause" under the pre-2012 form of s.19 of the old style Jobseekers Act 1995. It would seem that on any appeal, if the Secretary of State has proved on the balance of probabilities that there had been a failure to comply with a work-related or connected requirement, the practical burden would fall on the claimant of showing on the balance of probabilities that they have a good reason for the failure. That would be in accord with the principle demanded by *Kerr v Department for Social Development* [2004] UKHL 23; [2004] 1 W.L.R. 1372; *R 1/04 (SF)*, putting emphasis on who is in a better position to supply information on any particular issue in a co-operative process, rather than formal concepts of onus of proof. The claimant will in the great majority of cases be the person best placed to come forward with an explanation of their reasons for failing to comply with the requirement in question.

It appears to be accepted that the suitability of whatever it is that the claimant has been required to do is relevant to whether there is a good reason for not complying with the requirement. In *PL v DSD (JSA)* [2015] NI Com 72 (followed and applied in *PO'R v DFC (JSA)* [2018] NI Com 1), the Chief Commissioner for Northern Ireland has approved and applied the obiter suggestion of Judge Ward in *PL v SSWP (JSA)* [2013] UKUT 227 (AAC) (on the pre-October 2012 form of the Great Britain legislation) that, in deciding whether claimants have good cause for failing to avail themselves of a reasonable opportunity of a place on a training scheme or employment programme, a tribunal erred in law, where the circumstances raised the issue, in failing to consider the appropriateness of the particular scheme or programme to the particular claimant in the light of their skills and experience and previous attendance on any placements. Judge Ward's suggestion had been that the test was whether the claimant had reasonably considered that what was provided would not help him. It seems likely that a similar general approach will be taken to the issue of "good reason" under s.27(2) and the appropriateness of the activity in question. It may though still need to be sorted out how far the issue turns on the claimant's subjective view, within the bounds of reasonableness, in the light of the information provided at the time, as against a tribunal's view of the appropriateness of the activity. There may also be difficult questions in circumstances where what has been required seems quite reasonable and suitable and fairly imposed, but what is provided when the claimant attends turns out to be something different and of no assistance in the claimant's particular case, as in *DM v SSWP (JSA)* [2015] UKUT 67 (AAC) below. In such circumstances, does the claimant have a good reason for not participating in the activity at all, perhaps after raising queries with the provider, or are they, to escape sanction, obliged to sit through to the end?

DM was a case on jobseekers directions under s.19A(2)(c) of the old style Jobseekers Act 1995, but with insights relevant to universal credit. The claimant was directed to attend and participate in a group information session for work programme returnees that it was said would enable him to improve his chances of employment in several ways. Judge Rowley apparently accepted the claimant's evidence that the course turned out to be about the sanctions regime. After he was asked to leave before the end because he was said to be disrupting the course by asking questions and heckling, he was sanctioned for failing to carry out a reasonable jobseeker's direction by not fully participating in the session. The judge was able to dispose of the case on the basis that the direction was not reasonable in the absence of any evidence of how the group information session would have assisted the particular claimant to find employment or have improved his prospects of becoming employed and in the absence of evidence that the administrative guidance that directions should be personalised and appropriate to the individual claimant had been applied. Thus she did not have to grapple with the question of whether the claimant had had a good reason for failing to comply with the direction. That question may well arise in cases where the imposition of the requirement in question and a failure to comply cannot be challenged.

In *DH v SSWP (JSA)* [2016] UKUT 355 (AAC), a case about the Jobseeker's Allowance (Schemes for Assisting Persons to Obtain Employment) Regulations 2013 SI 2013/3196 (see Vol.V of this series), it was held that the First-tier Tribunal erred in law in apparently dismissing the claimant's objections to attending a Work Programme run by a particular provider (on the grounds that staff of the company concerned had lied in a police statement and in court about whether travel expenses had been refunded to him and had bullied him) as, even if true, irrelevant to whether he had a good reason for failing to comply with requirements to participate. The tribunal had said that the claimant's remedies were to contact the police and to use appropriate complaints procedures, not to refuse to attend interviews or courses. The judge asked the rhetorical question in para.20 of what could amount to good reason if such matters did not. The circumstances are to be distinguished from those in *R(JSA) 7/03*, not mentioned in *DH*, where the claimant's objection was a generalised, though principled, one to the involvement of private companies in the provision of such schemes, rather than to specific aspects of the particular provider. The Commissioner held that that was not a "conscientious" objection under special provisions then in reg.73 of the JSA Regulations 1996 and did not amount to good cause for failing to carry out a direction to enroll in a Jobplan workshop, because his state of mind did not exist as a fact independently of his refusal to attend the workshop. It was not like having a particular fear of carrying out some activity that would be involved in the course or being in the location involved (on which see *GR v SSWP (JSA)* [2013] UKUT 645 (AAC) in the notes to s.26).

Hardship payments

28.—(1) Regulations may make provision for the making of additional   1.211
payments by way of universal credit to a claimant ("hardship payments")
where—
  (a) the amount of the claimant's award is reduced under section 26 or
      27, and
  (b) the claimant is or will be in hardship.
  (2) Regulations under this section may in particular make provision as
to—
  (a) circumstances in which a claimant is to be treated as being or not
      being in hardship;
  (b) matters to be taken into account in determining whether a claimant
      is or will be in hardship;
  (c) requirements or conditions to be met by a claimant in order to
      receive hardship payments;
  (d) the amount or rate of hardship payments;
  (e) the period for which hardship payments may be made;
  (f) whether hardship payments are recoverable.

DEFINITION

"claimant"—see s.40.

GENERAL NOTE

The provision of hardship payments is an important part of the sanctions regime   1.212
for universal credit. The payments are to be made by way of universal credit.
However, it will be seen that s.28, first, does not require the making of provision
for hardship payments in regulations and, second, gives almost complete freedom
in how any regulations define the conditions for and amounts of payments. The
provisions made are in regs 115–119 of the Universal Credit Regulations, which
contain stringent conditions and a restricted definition of "hardship", which nevertheless retains a number of subjective elements. Payments are generally recoverable, subject to exceptions. See the notes to those regulations for the details and
the relevant parts of Ch.52 of CPAG's *Welfare benefits and tax credits handbook
2023/2024* for helpful explanations and examples. There seems to be no reason
why a decision of the Secretary of State to make or not to make hardship payments
on an application under reg.116(1)(c) should not be appealable to a First-tier
Tribunal.

Administration

Delegation and contracting out

29.—(1) The functions of the Secretary of State under sections 13 to 25   1.213
may be exercised by, or by the employees of, such persons as the Secretary
of State may authorise for the purpose (an "authorised person").
  (2) An authorisation given by virtue of this section may authorise the
exercise of a function—
  (a) wholly or to a limited extent;
  (b) generally or in particular cases or areas;
  (c) unconditionally or subject to conditions.
  (3) An authorisation under this section—
  (a) may specify its duration;
  (b) may be varied or revoked at any time by the Secretary of State;

(c) does not prevent the Secretary of State or another person from exercising the function to which the authorisation related.

(4) Anything done or omitted to be done by or in relation to an authorised person (or an employee of that person) in, or in connection with, the exercise or purported exercise of the function concerned is to be treated for all purposes as done or omitted to be done by or in relation to the Secretary of State or (as the case may be) an officer of the Secretary of State.

(5) Subsection (4) does not apply—

(a) for the purposes of so much of any contract made between the authorised person and the Secretary of State as relates to the exercise of the function, or

(b) for the purposes of any criminal proceedings brought in respect of anything done or omitted to be done by the authorised person (or an employee of that person).

(6) Where—

(a) the authorisation of an authorised person is revoked, and

(b) at the time of the revocation so much of any contract made between the authorised person and the Secretary of State as relates to the exercise of the function is subsisting, the authorised person is entitled to treat the contract as repudiated by the Secretary of State (and not as frustrated by reason of that revocation).

DEFINITION

"person"—see Interpretation Act 1978, Sch.1.

GENERAL NOTE

1.214   This section allows the Secretary of State to authorise other persons (which word in accordance with the Interpretation Act 1978 includes corporate and unincorporated associations, such as companies) and their employees to carry out any of his functions under ss.13–25. Any such authorisation will not in practice cover the making of regulations, but may well (depending on the extent of the authorisations given) extend to specifying various matters under those sections. The involvement of private sector organisations, operating for profit, in running various schemes within the scope of the benefit system is something that claimants sometimes object to. Such a generalised objection, even if on principled grounds, is unlikely to amount in itself to a good reason for failing to engage with a scheme in question (although see the discussion in the note to s.26 on whether "for no good reason" has a restricted meaning). An objection based on previous experience with the organisation concerned or the nature of the course may raise more difficult issues. See also the discussion in *R(JSA) 7/03* plus *CSJSA/495/2007* and *CSJSA/505/2007*.

In *DH v SSWP (JSA)* [2016] UKUT 355 (AAC), an old style JSA case under the Jobseeker's Allowance (Schemes for Assisting Persons to Obtain Employment) Regulations 2013, it was held that the First-tier Tribunal erred in law in apparently dismissing the claimant's objections to attending a Work Programme run by a particular provider (on the grounds that staff of the company concerned had lied in a police statement and in court about whether travel expenses had been refunded to him and had bullied him) as, even if true, irrelevant to whether he had a good reason for failing to comply with requirements to attend. The tribunal had said that the claimant's remedies were to contact the police and to use appropriate complaints procedures, not to refuse to attend interviews or courses. The judge asked the rhetorical question in para.20 what could amount to good reason if such matters did not. The circumstances are to be distinguished from those in *R(JSA) 7/03*, not mentioned in *DH*, where the claimant's objection was a generalised one to the involvement of private companies in the provision of such schemes.

CHAPTER 3

SUPPLEMENTARY AND GENERAL

Supplementary and consequential

Supplementary regulation-making powers

30. Schedule 1 contains supplementary regulation-making powers.　　1.215

Supplementary and consequential amendments

31. Schedule 2 contains supplementary and consequential amendments.　　1.216

Power to make supplementary and consequential provision etc.

32.—(1) The appropriate authority may by regulations make such conse-　　1.217
quential, supplementary, incidental or transitional provision in relation to
any provision of this Part as the authority considers appropriate.

(2) The appropriate authority is the Secretary of State, subject to subsection (3).

(3) The appropriate authority is the Welsh Ministers for—

(a) provision which would be within the legislative competence of the
National Assembly for Wales were it contained in an Act of the
Assembly;

(b) provision which could be made by the Welsh Ministers under any
other power conferred on them.

(4) Regulations under this section may amend, repeal or revoke any
primary or secondary legislation (whenever passed or made).

Universal credit and other benefits

Abolition of benefits

33.—(1) The following benefits are abolished—　　1.218

(a) income-based jobseeker's allowance under the Jobseekers Act 1995;

(b) income-related employment and support allowance under Part 1 of
the Welfare Reform Act 2007;

(c) income support under section 124 of the Social Security Contributions
and Benefits Act 1992;

(d) housing benefit under section 130 of that Act;

(e) council tax benefit under section 131 of that Act;

(f) child tax credit and working tax credit under the Tax Credits Act
2002.

(2) In subsection (1)—

(a) "income-based jobseeker's allowance" has the same meaning as in
the Jobseekers Act 1995;

(b) "income-related employment and support allowance" means an
employment and support allowance entitlement to which is based on
section 1(2)(b) of the Welfare Reform Act 2007.

(3) Schedule 3 contains consequential amendments.

DEFINITIONS

"income-related employment and support allowance"—see subs(2)(b).
"income-based jobseeker's allowance"—see subs.(2)(a).

GENERAL NOTE

Subsection (1)

1.219   The purpose of this provision is simple enough. Sub-section (1) provides for the abolition of income-based JSA, income-related ESA, income support, housing benefit, council tax benefit, child tax credit and working tax credit. The implementation of this section is much less straightforward. Council tax benefit was abolished in favour of localised schemes from April 2013. As a general rule abolition of the other benefits will only happen when all claimants have been transferred to universal credit. See now the Welfare Reform Act 2012 (Commencement No.34 and Commencement No.9, 21, 23, 31 and 32 and Transitional and Transitory Provisions (Amendment)) Order 2022 (SI 2022/302).

    This sub-section is modelled on the drafting of s.1(3) of the Tax Credits Act (TCA) 2002, which provided for the abolition of e.g. the personal allowances for children in the income support and income-based JSA schemes. Section 1(3) of the TCA 2002 has never been fully implemented. The fate of subs.(1) here remains to be seen.

Subsection (3)

1.220   This introduces Sch.3, which makes consequential amendments relating to the abolition of these benefits. Those changes remove references in other legislation to contributory ESA or JSA, as these will be unnecessary once ESA and JSA are contributory benefits only, and update references to other legislation which has been amended.

Universal credit and state pension credit

1.221   **34.** Schedule 4 provides for a housing element of state pension credit in consequence of the abolition of housing benefit by section 33.

GENERAL NOTE

1.222   This section, which is not yet in force, provides for a new housing credit element of state pension credit to replace housing benefit for claimants above the qualifying age for state pension credit. In its original form under the SPCA 2002, state pension credit was made up of two elements: the guarantee credit (performing the same function as income support used to) and the savings credit (providing a small top-up for those claimants with modest savings). Schedule 4 amends the SPCA 2002 to create a new third credit to cover housing costs. This will provide support for people who have reached the qualifying age for state pension credit (or for couples where both members have reached the qualifying age) once housing benefit is no longer available following the introduction of universal credit.

Universal credit and working-age benefits

1.223   **35.** Schedule 5 makes further provision relating to universal credit, jobseeker's allowance and employment and support allowance.

GENERAL NOTE

1.224   This section (and Sch.5) deals with the inter-relationship between universal credit, JSA and ESA. After the introduction of universal credit, ESA and JSA will continue to be available but only as contributory benefits.

Migration to universal credit

1.225   **36.** Schedule 6 contains provision about the replacement of benefits by universal credit.

GENERAL NOTE

1.226   This section gives effect to Sch.6, which makes provision relating to the replacement of the benefits that will be abolished under s.33, as well as any other prescribed benefits, and the consequential migration (or transfer) of claimants to universal credit.

General

Capability for work or work-related activity

37.—(1) For the purposes of this Part a claimant has limited capability for work if—

    (a) the claimant's capability for work is limited by their physical or mental condition, and

    (b) the limitation is such that it is not reasonable to require the claimant to work.

(2) For the purposes of this Part a claimant has limited capability for work-related activity if—

    (a) the claimant's capability for work-related activity is limited by their physical or mental condition, and

    (b) the limitation is such that it is not reasonable to require the claimant to undertake work-related activity.

(3) The question whether a claimant has limited capability for work or work-related activity for the purposes of this Part is to be determined in accordance with regulations.

(4) Regulations under this section must, subject as follows, provide for determination of that question on the basis of an assessment (or repeated assessments) of the claimant.

(5) Regulations under this section may for the purposes of an assessment—

    (a) require a claimant to provide information or evidence (and may require it to be provided in a prescribed manner or form);

    (b) require a claimant to attend and submit to a medical examination at a place, date and time determined under the regulations.

(6) Regulations under this section may make provision for a claimant to be treated as having or not having limited capability for work or work-related activity.

(7) Regulations under subsection (6) may provide for a claimant who fails to comply with a requirement imposed under subsection (5) without a good reason to be treated as not having limited capability for work or work-related activity.

(8) Regulations under subsection (6) may provide for a claimant to be treated as having limited capability for work until—

    (a) it has been determined whether or not that is the case, or

    (b) the claimant is under any other provision of regulations under subsection (6) treated as not having it.

(9) Regulations under this section may provide for determination of the question of whether a claimant has limited capability for work or work-related activity even where the claimant is for the time being treated under regulations under subsection (6) as having limited capability for work or work-related activity.

DEFINITIONS

    "claim"—see s.40.
    "claimant"—*ibid.*
    "limited capability for work"—*ibid.*
    "prescribed"—*ibid.*
    "work search requirement"—*ibid.*

1.227

1.228   If a person has limited capability for work (LCW) or LCW and limited capability for work-related activity (LCWRA), this is relevant to universal credit in three ways. First, at least so far as LCWRA is concerned, it affects the amount of the award of universal credit (see ss.1(3)(d) and 12(2)(a) and (b) and regs 27–28 and 36 of the Universal Credit Regulations). Secondly, it determines the work-related requirements that can be imposed. Under s.19(1) and (2)(a) no work-related requirements can be imposed on a claimant who has limited capability for work and work-related activity and under s.21(1)(a) a claimant who has limited capability for work (and who does not fall within s.19 or 20) is only subject to the work preparation requirement. Thirdly, it enables the application of the appropriate work allowance (see s. 8(3)(a) and reg. 22 of the Universal Credit Regulations).

This section contains provisions that are broadly equivalent to those in ss.1(4), 2(5), 8 and 9 of the Welfare Reform Act 2007. Thus the question of whether a person has limited capability for work or limited capability for work and work-related activity, is determined in the same way as for ESA.

In relation to subs.(7), note also the regulation-making power in para.8 of Sch.1.

Information

1.229   **38.** Information supplied under Chapter 2 of this Part or section 37 is to be taken for all purposes to be information relating to social security.

Couples

1.230   **39.**—[¹ ² (1) In this Part "couple" means—
   (a) two people who are married to, or civil partners of, each other and are members of the same household; or
   (b) two people who are not married to, or civil partners of, each other but are living together [³ as if they were a married couple or civil partners].]
   (2) [¹ ² . . .]
   (3) For the purposes of this section regulations may prescribe—
   (a) circumstances in which the fact that two persons are [¹ ² married] or are civil partners is to be disregarded;
   (b) circumstances in which [¹ ² two people are to be treated as living together [³ as if they were a married couple or civil partners]];
   (c) circumstances in which people are to be treated as being or not being members of the same household.

1. Marriage (Same Sex Couples) Act 2013 (Consequential and Contrary Provisions and Scotland) Order 2014 (SI 2014/560) art.2 and Sch.1, para.36 (March 13, 2014). This amendment extended to England and Wales only.

2. Marriage and Civil Partnership (Scotland) Act 2014 and Civil Partnership Act 2004 (Consequential Provisions and Modifications) Order 2014 (SI 2014/3229) art.29 and Sch.5, para.20 (December 16, 2014). This amendment extended to Scotland only. However, as it was in the same terms as the amendment made in England and Wales by SI 2014/560 (see above), the effect is that the law is now the same throughout Great Britain.

3. Civil Partnership (Opposite-sex Couples) Regulations 2019 (SI 2019/1458) reg.41(a) and Sch.3 Pt 1 para.35 (December 2, 2019).

1.231   See the commentary to reg.3 of the Universal Credit Regulations.

Interpretation of Part 1

40. In this Part—   1.232
"assessment period" has the meaning given by section 7(2);
"child" means a person under the age of 16;
"claim" means claim for universal credit;
"claimant" means a single claimant or each of joint claimants;
"couple" has the meaning given by section 39;
"disabled" has such meaning as may be prescribed;
"joint claimants" means members of a couple who jointly make a claim
   or in relation to whom an award of universal credit is made;
"limited capability for work" and "limited capability for work-related
   activity" are to be construed in accordance with section 37(1) and (2);
"prescribed" means specified or provided for in regulations;
"primary legislation" means an Act, Act of the Scottish Parliament or Act
   or Measure of the National Assembly for Wales;
"qualifying young person" has the meaning given in section 10(5);
"regular and substantial caring responsibilities" has such meaning as
   may be prescribed;
"responsible carer", in relation to a child, has the meaning given in
   section 19(6);
"secondary legislation" means an instrument made under primary legislation";
"severely disabled" has such meaning as may be prescribed;
"single claimant" means a single person who makes a claim for universal
   credit or in relation to whom an award of universal credit is made as a
   single person;
"single person" is to be construed in accordance with section 1(2)(a);
"work" has such meaning as may be prescribed;
"work availability requirement" has the meaning given by section
   18(1);
"work preparation requirement" has the meaning given by section 16(1);
"work search requirement" has the meaning given by section 17(1);
"work-focused interview requirement" has the meaning given by section
   15(1);
"work-related activity", in relation to a person, means activity which makes
   it more likely that the person will obtain or remain in work or be able to
   do so;
"work-related requirement" has the meaning given by section 13(2).

Regulations

Pilot schemes

41.—(1) Any power to make—   1.233
(a) regulations under this Part,
(b) regulations under the Social Security Administration Act 1992 relat-
    ing to universal credit, or
(c) regulations under the Social Security Act 1998 relating to univer-
    sal credit, may be exercised so as to make provision for piloting
    purposes.
(2) In subsection (1), "piloting purposes", in relation to any provision,
means the purposes of testing—

    (a) the extent to which the provision is likely to make universal credit simpler to understand or to administer,

    (b) the extent to which the provision is likely to promote—

        (i) people remaining in work, or

       (ii) people obtaining or being able to obtain work (or more work or better-paid work), or

    (c) the extent to which, and how, the provision is likely to affect the conduct of claimants or other people in any other way.

(3) Regulations made by virtue of this section are in the remainder of this section referred to as a "pilot scheme".

(4) A pilot scheme may be limited in its application to—

    (a) one or more areas;

    (b) one or more classes of person;

    (c) persons selected—

        (i) by reference to prescribed criteria, or

       (ii) on a sampling basis.

(5) A pilot scheme may not have effect for a period exceeding three years, but—

    (a) the Secretary of State may by order made by statutory instrument provide that the pilot scheme is to continue to have effect after the time when it would otherwise expire for a period not exceeding twelve months (and may make more than one such order);

    (b) a pilot scheme may be replaced by a further pilot scheme making the same or similar provision.

(6) A pilot scheme may include consequential or transitional provision in relation to its expiry.

GENERAL NOTE

1.234   This section was brought into force for all purposes on September 15, 2014 by art.6 of the Welfare Reform Act 2012 (Commencement No. 19 and Transitional and Transitory Provisions and Commencement No. 9 and Transitional and Transitory Provisions (Amendment)) Order 2014 (SI 2014/2321).

      This important provision is similar to that in s.29 of the Jobseekers Act 1995. It contains the power to pilot changes in regulations across particular geographical areas and/or specified categories of claimants for up to three years, although this period can be extended, or the pilot scheme can be replaced by a different pilot scheme making the same or similar provision (subs.(5)). The power can only be exercised in relation to the types of regulation listed in subs.(1) and with a view to assessing whether the proposed changes are likely to make universal credit simpler to understand or administer, to encourage people to find or remain in work (or more or better-paid work) or "to affect the conduct of claimants or other people in any other way" (subs.(2)). Regulations made under this section are subject to the affirmative resolution procedure (s.43(4)). On past experience in relation to JSA, it seems likely that this power will be exercised on a fairly regular basis.

Regulations: general

1.235   **42.**—(1) Regulations under this Part are to be made by the Secretary of State, unless otherwise provided.

(2) A power to make regulations under this Part may be exercised—

    (a) so as to make different provision for different cases or purposes;

    (b) in relation to all or only some of the cases or purposes for which it may be exercised.

(3) Such a power includes—

(a) power to make incidental, supplementary, consequential or transitional provision or savings;

(b) power to provide for a person to exercise a discretion in dealing with any matter.

(4) Each power conferred by this Part is without prejudice to the others.

(5) Where regulations under this Part provide for an amount, the amount may be zero.

(6) Where regulations under this Part provide for an amount for the purposes of an award (or a reduction from an award), the amount may be different in relation to different descriptions of person, and in particular may depend on—

(a) whether the person is a single person or a member of couple.

(b) the age of the person.

(7) Regulations under section 11(4) or 12(3) which provide for the determination or calculation of an amount may make different provision for different areas.

Definitions

"couple"—see ss.39 and 40.
"single person"—see s.40.
"work"—*ibid.*

Regulations: procedure

43.—(1) Regulations under this Part are to be made by statutory instrument.

1.236

(2) A statutory instrument containing regulations made by the Secretary of State under this Part is subject to the negative resolution procedure, subject as follows.

(3) A statutory instrument containing the first regulations made by the Secretary of State under any of the following, alone or with other regulations, is subject to the affirmative resolution procedure—

(a) section 4(7) (acceptance of claimant commitment);

(b) section 5(1)(a) and (2)(a) (capital limits);

(c) section 8(3) (income to be deducted in award calculation);

(d) section 9(2) and (3) (standard allowance);

(e) section 10(3) and (4) (children and young persons element);

(f) section 11 (housing costs element);

(g) section 12 (other needs and circumstances element);

(h) section 18(3) and (5) (work availability requirement);

(i) section 19(2)(d) (claimants subject to no work-related requirements);

(j) sections 26 and 27 (sanctions);

(k) section 28 (hardship payments);

(l) paragraph 4 of Schedule 1 (calculation of capital and income);

(m) paragraph 1(1) of Schedule 6 (migration), where making provision under paragraphs 4, 5 and 6 of that Schedule.

(4) A statutory instrument containing regulations made by the Secretary of State by virtue of section 41 (pilot schemes), alone or with other regulations, is subject to the affirmative resolution procedure.

(5) A statutory instrument containing regulations made by the Secretary of State under this Part is subject to the affirmative resolution procedure if—

(a) it also contains regulations under another enactment, and

(b) an instrument containing those regulations would apart from this section be subject to the affirmative resolution procedure.

(6) For the purposes of subsections (2) to (5)—

(a) a statutory instrument subject to the "negative resolution procedure" is subject to annulment in pursuance of a resolution of either House of Parliament;

(b) a statutory instrument subject to the "affirmative resolution procedure" may not be made unless a draft of the instrument has been laid before, and approved by resolution of, each House of Parliament.

(7) A statutory instrument containing regulations made by the Welsh Ministers under section 32 may not be made unless a draft of the instrument has been laid before, and approved by resolution of, the National Assembly for Wales.

DEFINITIONS

"child"—see s.40.
"claim"—*ibid.*
"claimant"—*ibid.*
"work"—*ibid.*
"work availability requirement"—*ibid.*

PART 5

SOCIAL SECURITY: GENERAL

Benefit cap

Benefit cap

1.237

96.—(1) Regulations may provide for a benefit cap to be applied to the welfare benefits to which a single person or couple is entitled.

(2) For the purposes of this section, applying a benefit cap to welfare benefits means securing that, where a single person's or couple's total entitlement to welfare benefits in respect of the reference period exceeds the relevant amount, their entitlement to welfare benefits in respect of any period of the same duration as the reference period is reduced by an amount up to or equalling the excess.

(3) In subsection (2) the "reference period" means a period of a prescribed duration.

(4) Regulations under this section may in particular—

(a) make provision as to the manner in which total entitlement to welfare benefits for any period, or the amount of any reduction, is to be determined;

(b) make provision as to the welfare benefit or benefits from which a reduction is to be made;

(c) provide for exceptions to the application of the benefit cap;

(d) make provision as to the intervals at which the benefit cap is to be applied;

(e) make provision as to the relationship between application of the benefit cap and any other reduction in respect of a welfare benefit;

(f) provide that where in consequence of a change in the relevant amount, entitlement to a welfare benefit increases or decreases, that increase or decrease has effect without any further decision of the Secretary of State;

(g) make supplementary and consequential provision.

[¹ (5) Regulations under this section may make provision for determining the "relevant amount" for the reference period applicable in the case of a single person or couple by reference to the annual limit applicable in the case of that single person or couple.

(5A) For the purposes of this section the "annual limit" is—

(a) [² £25,323 or £16,967], for persons resident in Greater London;

(b) [² £22,020 or £14,753], for other persons.

(5B) Regulations under subsection (5) may—

(a) specify which annual limit applies in the case of—
    (i) different prescribed descriptions of single person;
    (ii) different prescribed descriptions of couple;

(b) define "resident" for the purposes of this section;

(c) provide for the rounding up or down of an amount produced by dividing the amount of the annual limit by the number of periods of a duration equal to the reference period in a year.]

(6) [¹ . . .]

(7) [¹ . . .]

(8) [¹ . . .]

(9) Regulations under this section may not provide for any reduction to be made from a welfare benefit—

(a) provision for which is within the legislative competence of the Scottish Parliament;

(b) provision for which is within the legislative competence of the National Assembly for Wales;

(c) provision for which is made by the Welsh Ministers, the First Minister for Wales or the Counsel General to the Welsh Assembly Government.

(10) In this section—

"couple" means two persons of a prescribed description;

"prescribed" means prescribed in regulations;

"regulations" means regulations made by the Secretary of State;

"single person" means a person who is not a member of a couple;

"welfare benefit" [¹ means—

(a) bereavement allowance (see section 39B of the Social Security Contributions and Benefits Act 1992),

(b) child benefit (see section 141 of the Social Security Contributions and Benefits Act 1992),

(c) child tax credit (see section 1(1)(a) of the Tax Credits Act 2002),

(d) employment and support allowance (see section 1 of the Welfare Reform Act 2007), including income-related employment and support allowance (as defined in section 1(7) of the Welfare Reform Act 2007),

(e) housing benefit (see section 130 of the Social Security Contributions and Benefits Act 1992),

(f) incapacity benefit (see section 30A of the Social Security Contributions and Benefits Act 1992),

(g) income support (see section 124 of the Social Security Contributions and Benefits Act 1992),

(h) jobseeker's allowance (see section 1 of the Jobseekers Act 1995), including income-based jobseeker's allowance (as defined in section 1(4) of the Jobseekers Act 1995),

(i) maternity allowance under section 35 or 35B of the Social Security Contributions and Benefits Act 1992,

(j) severe disablement allowance (see section 68 of the Social Security Contributions and Benefits Act 1992),

(k) universal credit,

(l) widow's pension (see section 38 of the Social Security Contributions and Benefits Act 1992),

(m) widowed mother's allowance (see section 37 of the Social Security Contributions and Benefits Act 1992), or

(n) widowed parent's allowance (see section 39A of the Social Security Contributions and Benefits Act 1992).

(11) [¹ . . .]

AMENDMENTS

1. Welfare Reform and Work Act 2016 s.8(1)-(5) (assessment periods beginning on or after November 7, 2016: see SI 2016/910).

2. Benefit Cap (Annual Limit) (Amendment) Regulations 2023 (SI 2023/335) reg.2 (assessment periods beginning on or after April 10, 2023).

GENERAL NOTE

1.238   See the commentary to regs 78–83 of the Universal Credit Regulations.

[¹ Benefit cap: review

1.239   **96A.**—(1) The Secretary of State must at least once [² every five years] review the sums specified in section 96(5A) to determine whether it is appropriate to increase or decrease any one or more of those sums.

(2) The Secretary of State may, at any other time the Secretary of State considers appropriate, review the sums specified in section 96(5A) to determine whether it is appropriate to increase or decrease any one or more of those sums.

(3) In carrying out a review, the Secretary of State must take into account—

(a) the national economic situation, and

(b) any other matters that the Secretary of State considers relevant.

(4) After carrying out a review, the Secretary of State may, if the Secretary of State considers it appropriate, by regulations amend section 96(5A) so as to increase or decrease any one or more of the sums specified in section 96(5A).

(5) Regulations under subsection (4) may provide for amendments of section 96(5A) to come into force—

(a) on different days for different areas;

(b) on different days for different cases or purposes.

(6) Regulations under subsection (4) may make such transitional or transitory provision or savings as the Secretary of State considers necessary or expedient in connection with the coming into force of any amendment made by regulations under subsection (4).

(7) Regulations under subsection (6) may in particular—

(a) provide for section 96(5A) to have effect as if the amendments made by regulations under subsection (4) had not been made, in relation to such persons or descriptions of persons as are specified in the regulations or generally, until a time or times specified in a notice issued by the Secretary of State;

(b) provide for the Secretary of State to issue notices under paragraph (a) specifying different times for different persons or descriptions of person;

(c) make provision about the issuing of notices under paragraph (a), including provision for the Secretary of State to issue notices to authorities administering housing benefit that have effect in relation to persons specified, or persons of a description specified, in the notices.

(8) Section 176 of the Social Security Administration Act 1992 (consultation with representative organisations) does not apply in relation to regulations under subsection (4).

(9) [² ...]

AMENDMENT

1. Welfare Reform and Work Act 2016 (c.7) s.9(1) (November 7, 2016).
2. Dissolution and Calling of Parliament Act 2022 (c.11) Sch.1 para.21(b) (March 24, 2022).

GENERAL NOTE

A difficulty with s.96A(1)–(2) is that the provisions are not accompanied by any obligation to publish the outcome of a review unless it results in a change to the cap levels. That omission obstructs the ability of an external observer to know whether the requirement to conduct five-yearly reviews is being complied with. In July 2022 a minister informed Parliament that there had not ever been a review of benefit cap levels under s.96A(1): PQ UIN 27503, July 4, 2022. Then, in November 2022 the Government announced that it had decided to raise the cap levels in 2023 (implying that it had at some point after July 2022 conducted a review): Autumn Statement 2022 (CP 751, November 2022), para.2.47. It follows that the s.96A(1) duty will next require a review at some point between July and November 2027—unless the Secretary of State meanwhile chooses to conduct a review, which would restart the clock. 1.240

Benefit cap: supplementary

97.—(1) Regulations under section 96 [³ or 96A] may make different provision for different purposes or cases. 1.241

(2) Regulations under section 96 [³ or 96A] must be made by statutory instrument.

(3) [² ...]

(4) A statutory instrument containing [² ...] regulations under section 96 is subject to annulment in pursuance of a resolution of either House of Parliament.

[³ (4A) A statutory instrument containing regulations under section 96A may not be made unless a draft of the instrument has been laid before, and approved by a resolution of, each House of Parliament.]

(5) [¹ ...]

(6) In Schedule 2 to the Social Security Act 1998 (decisions against which no appeal lies) after paragraph 8 there is inserted—

"Reduction on application of benefit cap

8A A decision to apply the benefit cap in accordance with regulations under section 96 of the Welfare Reform Act 2012."

AMENDMENTS

1. Welfare Reform and Work Act 2016 s.9(6) (March 16, 2016).
2. Welfare Reform and Work Act 2016 s.8(6) (assessment periods beginning on or after November 7, 2016: see SI 2016/910).
3. Welfare Reform and Work Act 2016 s.9(2)-(5) (November 7, 2016).

GENERAL NOTE

1.242   See the commentary to regs 78–83 of the Universal Credit Regulations.

PART 7

FINAL

Repeals

1.243   **147.** *[Omitted]*

Financial provision

1.244   **148.** There shall be paid out of money provided by Parliament—
(a) sums paid by the Secretary of State by way of universal credit or personal independence payment;
(b) any other expenditure incurred in consequence of this Act by a Minister of the Crown or the Commissioners for Her Majesty's Revenue and Customs;
(c) any increase attributable to this Act in the sums payable under any other Act out of money so provided.

Extent

1.245   **149.**—(1) This Act extends to England and Wales and Scotland only, subject as follows.
(2) The following provisions extend to England and Wales, Scotland and Northern Ireland—
(a) section 32 (power to make consequential and supplementary provision: universal credit);
(b) section 33 (abolition of benefits);
(c)–(f) *[Omitted]*
(g) this Part, excluding Schedule 14 (repeals).

(3) *[Omitted]*

(4) Any amendment or repeal made by this Act has the same extent as the enactment to which it relates.

Commencement

150.—(1) The following provisions of this Act come into force on the day on which it is passed— 1.246

    (a)–(e) *[Omitted]*

    (f) this Part, excluding Schedule 14 (repeals).

(2) *[Omitted]*

(3) The remaining provisions of this Act come into force on such day as the Secretary of State may by order made by statutory instrument appoint.

(4) An order under subsection (3) may—

    (a) appoint different days for different purposes;

    (b) appoint different days for different areas in relation to—

        (i) any provision of Part 1 (universal credit) or of Part 1 of Schedule 14;

        (ii)–(iii) *[Omitted]*

        (iv) section 102 (consideration of revision before appeal);

    (c) make such transitory or transitional provision, or savings, as the Secretary of State considers necessary or expedient.

Short title

151. This Act may be cited as the Welfare Reform Act 2012. 1.247

SCHEDULES

Section 30

SCHEDULE 1

UNIVERSAL CREDIT: SUPPLEMENTARY REGULATION-MAKING POWERS

Entitlement of joint claimants

    1. Regulations may provide for circumstances in which joint claimants may be entitled to universal credit without each of them meeting all the basic conditions referred to in section 4. 1.248

Linking periods

    2. Regulations may provide for periods of entitlement to universal credit which are separated by no more than a prescribed number of days to be treated as a single period.

Couples

    3.—(1) Regulations may provide—

        (a) for a claim made by members of a couple jointly to be treated as a claim made by one member of the couple as a single person (or as claims made by both members as single persons);

        (b) for claims made by members of a couple as single persons to be treated as a claim made jointly by the couple.

    (2) Regulations may provide—

        (a) where an award is made to joint claimants who cease to be entitled to universal credit as such by ceasing to be a couple, for the making of an award (without a claim) to either or each one of them—

            (i) as a single person, or

            (ii) jointly with another person;

(b) where an award is made to a single claimant who ceases to be entitled to universal credit as such by becoming a member of a couple, for the making of an award (without a claim) to the members of the couple jointly;

(c) for the procedure to be followed, and information or evidence to be supplied, in relation to the making of an award under this paragraph.

Calculation of capital and income

4.—(1) Regulations may for any purpose of this Part provide for the calculation or estimation of—

(a) a person's capital,

(b) a person's earned and unearned income, and

(c) a person's earned and unearned income in respect of an assessment period.

(2) Regulations under sub-paragraph (1)(c) may include provision for the calculation to be made by reference to an average over a period, which need not include the assessment period concerned.

(3) Regulations under sub-paragraph (1) may—

(a) specify circumstances in which a person is to be treated as having or not having capital or earned or unearned income;

(b) specify circumstances in which income is to be treated as capital or capital as earned income or unearned income;

(c) specify circumstances in which unearned income is to be treated as earned, or earned income as unearned;

(d) provide that a person's capital is to be treated as yielding income at a prescribed rate;

(e) provide that the capital or income of one member of a couple is to be treated as that of the other member.

(4) Regulations under sub-paragraph (3)(a) may in particular provide that persons of a prescribed description are to be treated as having a prescribed minimum level of earned income.

(5) In the case of joint claimants the income and capital of the joint claimants includes (subject to sub-paragraph (6)) the separate income and capital of each of them.

(6) Regulations may specify circumstances in which capital and income of either of joint claimants is to be disregarded in calculating their joint capital and income.

Responsibility for children etc

1.249

5.—(1) Regulations may for any purpose of this Part specify circumstances in which a person is or is not responsible for a child or qualifying young person.

(2) Regulations may for any purpose of this Part make provision about nominations of the responsible carer for a child (see section 19(6)(b)(ii)).

Vouchers

6.—(1) This paragraph applies in relation to an award of universal credit where the calculation of the amount of the award includes, by virtue of any provision of this Part, an amount in respect of particular costs which a claimant may incur.

(2) Regulations may provide for liability to pay all or part of the award to be discharged by means of provision of a voucher.

(3) But the amount paid by means of a voucher may not in any case exceed the total of the amounts referred to in sub-paragraph (1) which are included in the calculation of the amount of the award.

(4) For these purposes a voucher is a means other than cash by which a claimant may to any extent meet costs referred to in sub-paragraph (1) of a particular description.

(5) A voucher may for these purposes—

(a) be limited as regards the person or persons who will accept it;

(b) be valid only for a limited time.

Work-related requirements

7.—Regulations may provide that a claimant who—

(a) has a right to reside in the United Kingdom under the EU Treaties, and

(b) would otherwise fall within section 19, 20 or 21,is to be treated as not falling within that section.

Good reason

1.250

8.—Regulations may for any purpose of this Part provide for—

(a) circumstances in which a person is to be treated as having or not having a good reason for an act or omission;

(b) matters which are or are not to be taken into account in determining whether a person has a good reason for an act or omission.

DEFINITIONS

"assessment period"—see s.40 and s.7(2).
"child"—see s.40.
"claim"—*ibid.*
"claimant"—*ibid.*
"couple"—see ss.39 and 40.
"joint claimants"—see s.40.
"prescribed"—*ibid.*
"single claimant"—*ibid.*
"single person"—*ibid.*

Section 31

SCHEDULE 2

UNIVERSAL CREDIT: AMENDMENTS

[Omitted]

Section 33

SCHEDULE 3

ABOLITION OF BENEFITS: CONSEQUENTIAL AMENDMENTS

Social Security Contributions and Benefits Act 1992 (c.4)

1. The Social Security Contributions and Benefits Act 1992 is amended as follows. **1.251**
2. In section 22 (earnings factors), in subsections (2)(a) and (5), for "a contributory" there is substituted "an".
3. In section 150 (interpretation of Part 10), in subsection (2), in the definition of "qualifying employment and support allowance", for "a contributory allowance" there is substituted "an employment and support allowance".

Social Security Administration Act 1992 (c.5)

4. The Social Security Administration Act 1992 is amended as follows. **1.252**
5. In section 7 (relationship between benefits), in subsection (3), for "subsections (1) and (2)" there is substituted "subsection (1)".
6. In section 73 (overlapping benefits), in subsections (1) and (4)(c), for "a contributory" there is substituted "an".
7. In section 159B (effect of alterations affecting state pension credit), for "a contributory", wherever occurring, there is substituted "an".
8. In section 159D (as inserted by Schedule 2 to this Act) (effect of alterations affecting universal credit), for "a contributory", wherever occurring, there is substituted "an".

Immigration and Asylum Act 1999 (c.33)

9. In the Immigration and Asylum Act 1999, in section 115 (exclusion from benefits of **1.253**
persons subject to immigration control)—
    (a) in subsection (1), after paragraph (ha) there is inserted "or";
    (b) in subsection (2)(b) for "(a) to (j)" substitute "(a) to (i)".

Child Support, Pensions and Social Security Act 2000 (c.19)

10. The Child Support, Pensions and Social Security Act 2000 is amended as follows. **1.254**
11. (1) Section 69 (discretionary financial assistance with housing) is amended as
follows.
    (2) In subsection (1)—

(a) for "relevant authorities" there is substituted "local authorities";

(b) in paragraph (a), the words from "housing benefit" to "both," are repealed.

(3) In subsection (2)—

(a) in paragraph (b), for "relevant authority" there is substituted "local authority";

(b) in paragraph (e), for "relevant authorities" there is substituted "local authorities";

(c) in paragraphs (f), (g) and (h), for "relevant authority" there is substituted "local authority".

(4) In subsection (5), for "relevant authorities" there is substituted "local authorities".

(5) In subsection (7), for the definition of "relevant authority" there is substituted—

""local authority" has the meaning given by section 191 of the Social Security Administration Act 1992."

12.(1) Section 70 (grants towards cost of discretionary housing payments) is amended as follows.

(2) In subsection (1), after "payments" there is inserted "("grants")".

(3) For subsection (2) there is substituted—

"(2)The amount of a grant under this section shall be determined in accordance with an order made by the Secretary of State with the consent of the Treasury."

(4) In subsection (8)—

(a) for the definition of "relevant authority" there is substituted—

""local authority" has the same meaning as in section 69;";

(b) the definition of "subsidy" is repealed.

13. After section 70 there is inserted—

"70A. Payment of grant

1.255

(1) A grant under section 70 shall be made by the Secretary of State in such instalments, at such times, in such manner and subject to such conditions as to claims, records, certificates, audit or otherwise as may be provided by order of the Secretary of State with the consent of the Treasury.

(2) The order may provide that if a local authority has not complied with the conditions specified in it within such period as may be specified in it, the Secretary of State may estimate the amount of grant under section 70 payable to the authority and employ for that purpose such criteria as he considers relevant.

(3) Where a grant under section 70 has been paid to a local authority and it appears to the Secretary of State that—

(a) the grant has been overpaid, or

(b) there has been a breach of any condition specified in an order under this section, he may recover from the authority the whole or such part of the payment as he may determine.

(4) Without prejudice to the other methods of recovery, a sum recoverable under this section may be recovered by withholding or reducing subsidy.

(5) An order under this section may be made before, during or after the end of the period to which it relates.

(6) In this section "local authority" has the same meaning as in section 69.

(7) Section 70(5) to (7) applies to orders under this section."

1.256

14. [¹ ...]

Social Security Fraud Act 2001 (c.11)

1.257

15. The Social Security Fraud Act 2001 is amended as follows.

16. In section 6B (loss of benefit for conviction etc), in subsection (5), for "to (10)" there is substituted "and (8)".

17. In section 7 (loss of benefit for repeated conviction etc), in subsection (2), for "to (5)" there is substituted "and (4A)".

18. In section 11 (regulations), in subsection (3)(c), for the words from "section" to the end there is substituted "section 6B(5A) or (8), 7(2A) or (4A) or 9(2A) or (4A)".

Commissioners for Revenue and Customs Act 2005 (c.11)

1.258

19. The Commissioners for Revenue and Customs Act 2005 is amended as follows.

20. In section 5 (initial functions), in subsection (1), after paragraph (a) there is inserted "and".

21. In section 44 (payment into Consolidated Fund), in subsection (3), after paragraph (b) there is inserted "and".

Welfare Reform Act 2007 (c. 5)

22. The Welfare Reform Act 2007 is amended as follows.   1.259

23. In section 1 (employment and support allowance), in subsection (3)(d), at the end there is inserted "and".

24. In section 2 (amount of contributory allowance), in subsection (1), for "In the case of a contributory allowance, the amount payable" there is substituted "The amount payable by way of an employment and support allowance".

25.(1) Section 27 (financial provisions) is amended as follows.

(2) In subsection (1), for the words from "so much of" to the end there is substituted "any sums payable by way of employment and support allowance".

(3) In subsection (3), for "contributory" there is substituted "employment and support".

26. In each of the following provisions, for "a contributory allowance" there is substituted "an employment and support allowance"
    (a) section 1A(1), (3), (4), (5) and (6) (as inserted by section 51 of this Act);
    (b) section 1B(1) (as inserted by section 52 of this Act);
    (c) section 3(2)(d);
    (d) section 18(4);
    (e) section 20(2), (3)(a), (b) and (c), (4), (5)(a), (b) and (c), (6), (7)(a), (b) and (c);
    (f) in Schedule 1, paragraphs 1(5)(d) and 3(2)(a);
    (g) in Schedule 2, paragraphs 6 and 7(2)(d).

Corporation Tax Act 2009 (c. 4)

27. The Corporation Tax Act 2009 is amended as follows.   1.260

28. In section 1059 (relief relating to SME R&D: total amount of company's PAYE and NICs liabilities), in subsection (5) after "sick pay" there is inserted "or".

29. In section 1108 (relief relating to vaccine research etc: total amount of company's PAYE and NICs liabilities), in subsection (5) after "sick pay" there is inserted "or".

AMENDMENT

1. Finance Act 2019, s.33(2)(c)(viii)(a) (April 1, 2020).   1.261

GENERAL NOTE

The amendments contained in this Schedule to other primary legislation fall into   1.262
two main categories.

First, and for the most part, the amendments are consequential upon the abolition of income support, housing benefit, council tax benefit, child tax credit, working tax credit and the income-based forms of ESA and JSA. So, for example, references in other Acts to "a contributory employment and support allowance" are changed to "an employment and support allowance". This is because, after the full implementation of universal credit, the only form of ESA which will be available will be a contributory allowance.

The second category of amendments concerns those made to the Child Support, Pensions and Social Security Act 2000. These amend the provisions relating to discretionary housing payments and are consequential on the abolition of council tax benefit and housing benefit.

Section 34

SCHEDULE 4

HOUSING CREDIT ELEMENT OF STATE PENSION CREDIT

PART 1

AMENDMENTS TO STATE PENSION CREDIT ACT 2002

State Pension Credit Act 2002 (c.16)

1. The State Pension Credit Act 2002 is amended as follows.   1.263

2. In section 1 (entitlement), in subsection (2)(c), at the end there is inserted "or (iii) the conditions in section 3A(1) and (2) (housing credit)."

3. In that section, in subsection (3)—

(a) after paragraph (b)   there is inserted "or

(c) to a housing credit, calculated in accordance with section 3A, if he satisfies the conditions in subsections (1) and (2) of that section,";

(b) for the words from "(or to both)" to the end there is substituted "(or to more than one of them, if he satisfies the relevant conditions)".

4. After section 3 there is inserted—

"3A. Housing credit

1.264

(1) The first of the conditions mentioned in section 1(2)(c)(iii) is that the claimant is liable to make payments in respect of the accommodation he occupies as his home.

(2) The second of the conditions mentioned in section 1(2)(c)(iii) is that the claimant's capital and income are such that the amount of the housing credit payable (if he were entitled to it) would not be less than a prescribed amount.

(3) Where the claimant is entitled to a housing credit, the amount of the housing credit shall be an amount calculated in or determined under regulations (which may be zero).

(4) For the purposes of subsection (1)—

(a) the accommodation must be in Great Britain;

(b) the accommodation must be residential accommodation;

(c) it is immaterial whether the accommodation consists of the whole or part of a building and whether or not it comprises separate and self-contained premises.

(5) Regulations may make provision as to—

(a) the meaning of "payments in respect of accommodation" for the purposes of this section (and, in particular, as to the extent to which such payments include mortgage payments;

(b) circumstances in which a claimant is to be treated as liable or not liable to make such payments;

(c) circumstances in which a claimant is to be treated as occupying or not occupying accommodation as his home (and, in particular, for temporary absences to be disregarded);

(d) circumstances in which land used for the purposes of any accommodation is to be treated as included in the accommodation.

(6) Regulations under this section may make different provision for different areas."

5. In section 7 (fixing of retirement provision for assessed income period), at the end there is inserted—

"(10) Regulations may prescribe circumstances in which subsection (3) does not apply for the purposes of determining the amount of a housing credit to which the claimant is entitled."

6. In section 12 (polygamous marriages), in subsection (2)(b), after "savings credit" there is inserted "or housing credit".

7. In section 17 (interpretation), in subsection (1), after the definition of "guarantee credit" there is inserted—""housing credit" shall be construed in accordance with sections 1 and 3A;".

8. In Schedule 2 (consequential amendments etc), paragraph 9(5)(a) is repealed.

PART 2

AMENDMENTS TO OTHER ACTS

Social Security Administration Act 1992 (c. 5)

1.265

9. The Social Security Administration Act 1992 is amended as follows.

10. In section 5 (regulations about claims and payments) in subsection (6), before "subsection" there is inserted "or housing credit (within the meaning of the State Pension Credit Act 2002)".

11. [¹ ...].

12. (1)Section 122F (supply by rent officers of information) is amended as follows.

(2) In subsection (3)(a) at the end of the words in brackets there is inserted "or housing credit".

(3) In subsection (4) at the end there is inserted "or housing credit".

(4) After that subsection there is inserted—

"(5) In this section "housing credit" has the same meaning as in the State Pension Credit Act 2002".

Housing Act 1996 (c.52)

13.(1) Section 122 of the Housing Act 1996 (rent officers) is amended as follows.   **1.266**
(2) In the heading, at the end there is inserted "and housing credit".
(3) In subsection (1), at the end there is inserted "or housing credit (within the meaning of the State Pension Credit Act 2002)".

Child Support, Pensions and Social Security Act 2000 (c.19)

14. In section 69 of the Child Support, Pensions and Social Security Act 2000 (discretionary   **1.267**
financial assistance with housing), in subsection (1)(a), after "universal credit" there is inserted
"or housing credit (within the meaning of the State Pension Credit Act 2002)".

AMENDMENT

1. Welfare Reform and Work Act 2016 s.20(11)(f)(ii) (April 6, 2018).

GENERAL NOTE

Schedule 4 (which at the time of writing is still not yet in force) amends the State   **1.268**
Pension Credit Act 2002 to create a new type of credit within state pension credit
to cover housing costs. This will provide support for people who qualify for state
pension credit once housing benefit is no longer available. In November 2022, the
Government announced that the movement of pensioners from housing benefit to
housing credit (and therefore the commencement of Sch.4) would be delayed to
2028/29: Autumn Statement 2022 (CP 751, November 2022), para.5.14.
The key provision is para.4, which inserts a new s.3A into the SPCA 2002. This
provision sets out the conditions of entitlement to the housing credit (subss.(1) and
(2)); it also provides the power to set out the manner in which the housing credit is
to be calculated or determined in regulations (subs.(3)). The policy intention is that
claimants will be entitled to broadly the same amount of support under the housing
credit as they would previously have been entitled to by way of housing benefit.
Subsection (5) of new s.3A simply adds detail to the power in subs.(3) by listing a
number of specific matters in respect of which regulations may be made. Subsection
(6) provides that regulations may make different provision for different areas. The
underlying aim is to ensure that persons in different but abutting areas may be
treated in a different manner depending on the circumstances obtaining in that area
(e.g. to reflect different local taxation applied by different local authorities).
The other provision of note is para.5, which inserts a new s.7(10) into the SPCA
2002. Section 7 provides for assessed income periods in state pension credit, during
which a person's retirement provision as assessed at the start of the period is taken
to be the same throughout the period. The power exists in s.6(2)(b) to prescribe
circumstances in which an assessed income period may not be set. The new s.7(10)
provides that regulations may prescribe circumstances in which a person's retirement provision is not taken to be the same throughout the assessed income period
for the purposes of determining the amount of housing credit to which a person is
entitled. This power is inserted in order to replicate the current position in respect of
housing benefit, which does not operate a system based on assessed income periods.

Section 35

SCHEDULE 5

UNIVERSAL CREDIT AND OTHER WORKING-AGE BENEFITS

General

1.(1) In this Schedule "relevant benefit" means—   **1.269**
  (a) jobseeker's allowance, or
  (b) employment and support allowance.

(2) In this Schedule "work-related requirement" means—
  (a) a work-related requirement within the meaning of this Part,
  (b) a work-related requirement within the meaning of the Jobseekers Act 1995, or
  (c) a work-related requirement within the meaning of Part 1 of the Welfare Reform Act 2007.

(3) In this Schedule "sanction" means a reduction of benefit under—
  (a) section 26 or 27,
  (b) section 6J or 6K of the Jobseekers Act 1995, or
  (c) section 11J of the Welfare Reform Act 2007.

Dual entitlement

1.270 2. (1) Regulations may make provision as to the amount payable by way of a relevant benefit where a person is entitled to that benefit and universal credit.

(2) Regulations under sub-paragraph (1) may in particular provide for no amount to be payable by way of a relevant benefit.

(3) Regulations may, where a person is entitled to a relevant benefit and universal credit—
  (a) make provision as to the application of work-related requirements;
  (b) make provision as to the application of sanctions.

(4) Provision under sub-paragraph (3)(a) includes in particular—
  (a) provision securing that compliance with a work-related requirement for a relevant benefit is to be treated as compliance with a work-related requirement for universal credit;
  (b) provision disapplying any requirement on the Secretary of State to impose, or a person to comply with, a work-related requirement for a relevant benefit or universal credit.

(5) Provision under sub-paragraph (3)(b) includes in particular—
  (a) provision for the order in which sanctions are to be applied to awards of relevant benefit and universal credit;
  (b) provision to secure that the application of a sanction to an award of a relevant benefit does not result in an increase of the amount of an award of universal credit.

Movement between working-age benefits

1.271 3. Regulations may provide—
  (a) in a case where a person ceases to be entitled to universal credit and becomes entitled to a relevant benefit, for a sanction relating to the award of universal credit to be applied to the award of the relevant benefit;
  (b) in a case where a person ceases to be entitled to a relevant benefit and becomes entitled to universal credit, for a sanction relating to the award of the relevant benefit to be applied to the award of universal credit;
  (c) in a case where a person ceases to be entitled to one relevant benefit and becomes entitled to the other, for a sanction relating to the award of the former to apply to the award of the latter.

Hardship payments

1.272 4. Regulations under section 28 (hardship payments) may be made in relation to a person whose award of universal credit is reduced by virtue of regulations under paragraph 2(3)(b) or 3(b) as in relation to a person whose award is reduced under section 26 or 27.

Earnings tapers

1.273 5. In section 4 of the Jobseekers Act 1995 (amount payable by way of a jobseeker's allowance), in subsection (1)(b)—
  (a) after "making" there is inserted—
"(i) deductions in respect of earnings calculated in the prescribed manner (which may include multiplying some or all earnings by a prescribed percentage), and
  (b) "earnings," (before "pension payments") is repealed.

6. (1) Section 2 of the Welfare Reform Act 2007 (amount of contributory allowance) is amended as follows.

(2) In subsection (1)(c), after "making" there is inserted—

"(i) deductions in respect of earnings calculated in the prescribed manner (which may include multiplying some or all earnings by a prescribed percentage), and

(3) At the end there is inserted—

"(6) In subsection (1)(c)(i) the reference to earnings is to be construed in accordance with sections 3, 4 and 112 of the Social Security Contributions and Benefits Act 1992."

DEFINITIONS

"relevant benefit"—para.1(1)

"sanction"—para.1(3)

"work-related requirement"—para.1(2)

GENERAL NOTE

Schedule 5 makes provision to allow the Secretary of State to prescribe details of the relationship between universal credit on the one hand and ESA and JSA on the other. At the time of writing only paras 1-3 inclusive are in force; paras 4-6 are yet to be brought into force.   **1.274**

Paragraph 2

In certain circumstances claimants may meet the conditions of entitlement to both universal credit and JSA or ESA (as contributory benefits only). Paragraph 2 enables the Secretary of State to make provision as to the amount of contributory benefit payable where a person is entitled to both a contributory benefit and universal credit. According to the Department, Memorandum from the Department for Work and Pensions, *Welfare Reform Bill, as brought from the House of Commons on 16 June 2011*, House of Lords Select Committee on Delegated Powers and Regulatory Reform (at para.166):   **1.275**

"It is intended that the power will in particular be used to:

a) specify whether, in cases where the claimant might be entitled to both universal credit and either ESA or JSA, the claimant will be paid to only universal credit, or only the contributory benefit, or to both.

b) make provision in relation to cases where a claimant might be able to choose which benefit to claim, in the event of them being potentially entitled to both.

c) provide for exceptions, if appropriate, from the general rule.

d) prescribe how work-related requirements are to apply in such cases.

e) set out, if sanctions are applicable, which benefit is to be reduced first (in a case where a claimant is receiving both), what limitations any reductions are subject to, and to provide, if appropriate, that the application of a sanction to one benefit does not increase payment of the other."

Paragraph 3

Paragraph 3(a) and (b) allows for regulations to provide that where a person is entitled to universal credit and has their award reduced by a sanction, and then becomes entitled to JSA or ESA, the sanction can be applied to the new JSA or ESA award. This is obviously designed to ensure that claimants cannot avoid a sanction simply because they move between universal credit and JSA or ESA. Paragraph 3(c) makes similar provision for regulations to provide that sanctions imposed on claimants entitled to JSA or ESA can be applied to a subsequent award of the other benefit.   **1.276**

Paragraph 4

This allows for regulations made under s.28 (hardship payments) to apply to a person whose universal credit award is reduced by virtue of either para.2(3)(b) or 3(b) above. Section 28 only allows for universal credit hardship payments to be made to claimants who have their universal credit award reduced under ss.26 or 27,   **1.277** and so para.4 allows for claimants whose awards are reduced under other provisions to also be eligible for universal credit hardship payments.

Paragraph 5

1.278   This amendment to s.4 of the Jobseekers Act 1995 creates a power which allows the Secretary of State to deduct earnings which have been calculated in a prescribed manner, which may include multiplying some or all of the earnings by a prescribed percentage. The intention is to make provision for the amount of benefit payable to be tapered as earnings increase and to allow for some earnings to be disregarded before the taper is applied.

Paragraph 6

1.279   This amends s.2 of the Welfare Reform Act 2007, and has similar effect on provision for the calculation of earnings in ESA as does para.(5) in relation to JSA.

Section 36

Schedule 6

Migration to Universal Credit

General

1.280   1.(1) Regulations may make provision for the purposes of, or in connection with, replacing existing benefits with universal credit.
(2) In this Schedule "existing benefit" means—
(a)   a benefit abolished under section 33(1);
(b)   any other prescribed benefit.
(3) In this Schedule "appointed day" means the day appointed for the coming into force of section 1.

Claims before the appointed day

1.281   2. (1) The provision referred to in paragraph 1(1) includes—
(a)   provision for a claim for universal credit to be made before the appointed day for a period beginning on or after that day;
(b)   provision for a claim for universal credit made before the appointed day to be treated to any extent as a claim for an existing benefit;
(c)   provision for a claim for an existing benefit made before the appointed day to be treated to any extent as a claim for universal credit.
(2) The provision referred to in paragraph 1(1) includes provision, where a claim for universal credit is made (or is treated as made) before the appointed day, for an award on the claim to be made in respect of a period before the appointed day (including provision as to the conditions of entitlement for, and amount of, such an award).

Claims after the appointed day

1.282   3. (1) The provision referred to in paragraph 1(1) includes—
(a)   provision permanently or temporarily excluding the making of a claim for universal credit after the appointed day by—
(i)   a person to whom an existing benefit is awarded, or
(ii)   a person who would be entitled to an existing benefit on making a claim for it;
(b)   provision temporarily excluding the making of a claim for universal credit after the appointed day by any other person;
(c)   provision excluding entitlement to universal credit temporarily or for a particular period;
(d)   provision for a claim for universal credit made after the appointed day to be treated to any extent as a claim for an existing benefit;
(e)   provision for a claim for an existing benefit made after the appointed day to be treated to any extent as a claim for universal credit.
(2) The provision referred to in paragraph 1(1) includes provision, where a claim for universal credit is made (or is treated as made) after the appointed day, for an award on the claim to be made in respect of a period before the appointed day (including provision as to the conditions of entitlement for, and amount of, such an award).

Awards

4.(1) The provision referred to in paragraph 1(1) includes— **1.283**
 (a) provision for terminating an award of an existing benefit;
 (b) provision for making an award of universal credit, with or without application, to a person whose award of existing benefit is terminated.
(2) The provision referred to in sub-paragraph (1)(b) includes—
 (a) provision imposing requirements as to the procedure to be followed, information to be supplied or assessments to be undergone in relation to an award by virtue of that sub-paragraph or an application for such an award;
 (b) provision as to the consequences of failure to comply with any such requirement;
 (c) provision as to the terms on which, and conditions subject to which, such an award is made, including—
  (i) provision temporarily or permanently disapplying, or otherwise modifying, conditions of entitlement to universal credit in relation to the award;
  (ii) provision temporarily or permanently disapplying, or otherwise modifying, any requirement under this Part for a person to be assessed in respect of capability for work or work-related activity;
 (d) provision as to the amount of such an award;
 (e) provision that fulfilment of any condition relevant to entitlement to an award of an existing benefit, or relevant to the amount of such an award, is to be treated as fulfilment of an equivalent condition in relation to universal credit.
(3) Provision under sub-paragraph (2)(d) may secure that where an award of universal credit is made by virtue of sub-paragraph (1)(b)—
 (a) the amount of the award is not less than the amount to which the person would have been entitled under the terminated award, or is not less than that amount by more than a prescribed amount;
 (b) if the person to whom it is made ceases to be entitled to universal credit for not more than a prescribed period, the gap in entitlement is disregarded in calculating the amount of any new award of universal credit.

Work-related requirements and sanctions

5.(1) The provision referred to in paragraph 1(1) includes— **1.284**
 (a) provision relating to the application of work-related requirements for relevant benefits;
 (b) provision relating to the application of sanctions.
(2) The provision referred to in sub-paragraph (1)(a) includes—
 (a) provision that a claimant commitment for a relevant benefit is to be treated as a claimant commitment for universal credit;
 (b) provision that a work-related requirement for a relevant benefit is treated as a work-related requirement for universal credit;
 (c) provision for anything done which is relevant to compliance with a work-related requirement for a relevant benefit to be treated as done for the purposes of compliance with a work-related requirement for universal credit;
 (d) provision temporarily disapplying any provision of this Part in relation to work-related requirements for universal credit.
(3) The provision referred to in sub-paragraph (1)(b) includes—
 (a) provision for a sanction relevant to an award of a relevant benefit to be applied to an award of universal credit;
 (b) provision for anything done which is relevant to the application of a sanction for a relevant benefit to be treated as done for the purposes of the application of a sanction for universal credit;
 (c) provision temporarily disapplying any provision of this Part in relation to the application of sanctions.
(4) In this paragraph—
"relevant benefit" means—
 (a) jobseeker's allowance,
 (b) employment and support allowance, and
 (c) income support;
"work-related requirement" means—
 (a) for universal credit, a work-related requirement within the meaning of this Part;
 (b) for jobseeker's allowance, a requirement imposed—
  (i) by virtue of regulations under section 8 or 17A of the Jobseekers Act 1995,

(ii) by a jobseeker's direction (within the meaning of section 19A of that Act),
(iii) by virtue of regulations under section 2A, 2AA or 2D of the Social Security Administration Act 1992, or
(iv) by a direction under section 2F of that Act;
  (c) for employment and support allowance, a requirement imposed—
    (i) by virtue of regulations under section 8, 9, 11, 12 or 13 of the Welfare Reform Act 2007,
    (ii) by a direction under section 15 of that Act,
    (iii) by virtue of regulations under section 2A, 2AA or 2D of the Social Security Administration Act 1992, or
    (iv) by a direction under section 2F of that Act;
  (d) for income support, a requirement imposed—
    (i) by virtue of regulations under section 2A, 2AA or 2D of the Social Security Administration Act 1992, or
    (ii) by a direction under section 2F of that Act;
"sanction" means a reduction of benefit under—
  (a) section 26 or 27 above,
  (b) section 19, 19A or 19B of the Jobseekers Act 1995,
  (c) section 11, 12 or 13 of the Welfare Reform Act 2007, or
  (d) section 2A, 2AA or 2D of the Social Security Administration Act 1992.

Tax credits

1.285   6. In relation to the replacement of working tax credit and child tax credit with universal credit, the provision referred to in paragraph 1(1) includes—
  (a) provision modifying the application of the Tax Credits Act 2002 (or of any provision made under it);
  (b) provision for the purposes of recovery of overpayments of working tax credit or child tax credit (including in particular provision for treating overpayments of working tax credit or child tax credit as if they were overpayments of universal credit).

Supplementary

1.286   7. Regulations under paragraph 1(1) may secure the result that any gap in entitlement to an existing benefit (or what would, but for the provisions of this Part, be a gap in entitlement to an existing benefit) is to be disregarded for the purposes of provision under such regulations.

DEFINITIONS

    "appointed day"—see para.1(3).
    "existing benefit"—see para.1(2).
    "relevant benefit"—see para.5(4).
    "sanction"—*ibid.*
    "work-related requirement"—*ibid.*

GENERAL NOTE

1.287   Schedule 6 contains regulation-making powers to make provision in connection with replacing the existing means-tested benefits system with universal credit, and more particularly with the "migration" of claimants from one benefit to the other. Regulations made under this Schedule were subject to the affirmative resolution procedure where the power in para.1(1) was used in a way described in paras.4, 5 or 6 for the first time. This Schedule is fully in force (and has been since July 18, 2019: Welfare Reform Act 2012 (Commencement No.33) Order 2019 (SI 2019/1135), art.2).

Paragraph 1
1.288   The principal such regulations are the Transitional Provisions Regulations 2014.

Paragraph 2
1.289   Regulations may specify when a claim can be treated as a claim for an existing benefit and when a claim can be treated as a claim for universal credit. For example,

regulations may provide that a claim for an existing benefit made before the day that universal credit comes into effect, but for a period beginning after universal credit is introduced, (i.e. people making advance claims), can be treated as a claim for universal credit.

Paragraph 3

Regulations may provide that after the appointed day (i.e. the day universal credit is introduced), existing benefits cannot be claimed (see Transitional Provisions Regulations 2014 regs 5 and 6). Regulations can also provide for a claim to universal credit to be treated as a claim for existing benefit. This might be used where e.g. a claimant's benefit is backdated to a period before universal credit was introduced. Regulations may also provide that these cases may be awarded universal credit on terms, which match wholly or partly, the existing benefit.

1.290

Paragraph 4

Regulations may make provision for the "migration" of existing claimants onto universal credit. Such migration may be voluntary or mandatory. Regulations can prescribe the timing, conditions, kind and amount of any such entitlement to universal credit which was previously an award for an existing benefit. As regards para.4(1), see further the Transitional Provisions Regulations 2014.

1.291

Paragraph 5

This makes provision for the continuity of both work-related requirements and sanctions; see further especially regs 30–34 of the Transitional Provisions Regulations 2014 as regards sanctions.

1.292

Paragraph 6

The Secretary of State may, through regulations, modify any provision of the Tax Credits Act 2002 (or regulations) as necessary for the purposes of transferring people from working tax credit and child tax credit to universal credit. This power may be used to align certain tax credit rules more closely with universal credit to facilitate the transition process (para.(a)). Paragraph 6 also makes it clear that over-payments of tax credits can, through the transitional regulations, be treated as over-payments of universal credit (para.(b)). See further regs 11-12A of the Transitional Provisions Regulations 2014.

1.293

Welfare Reform and Work Act 2016

(2016 c.7)

Sections Reproduced

Welfare benefits

1.294

Final

34   Power to make consequential provision

An Act to make provision about reports on progress towards full employment and the apprenticeships target; to make provision about reports on the effect of certain support for troubled families; to make provision about life chances; to make provision about the benefit cap; to make provision about social security and tax credits; to make provision for loans for mortgage interest and other liabilities; and to make provision about social housing rents.
[March 16, 2016]

GENERAL NOTE

1.295   Sections 8-21 of, and Schedule 1 to, this Act are of potential relevance to entitlement to social security benefits and tax credits. They have been reproduced below to the extent that they are in force, do not make amendments that have been reproduced in the text of other legislation in this work, and have not been reproduced in other volumes.

Sections 1-7 concern social policy, section 22 governs an aspect of social security administration that cannot give rise to an appeal and sections 23-33 make provision about social housing rents. They are therefore beyond the scope of this work.

Welfare benefits

Benefit cap

1.296   **8.**—(1)-(7) *[Omitted]*
(8) Regulations made by the Secretary of State may make such transitional or transitory provision or savings as the Secretary of State considers necessary or expedient in connection with the coming into force of subsections (1) to (6).
(9) Regulations under subsection (8) may in particular—
(a) provide for section 96 to have effect as if the amendments made by subsections (2) to (5) and (7) had not been made, in relation to such persons or descriptions of persons as are specified in the regulations or generally, until a time or times specified in a notice issued by the Secretary of State;
(b) provide for the Secretary of State to issue notices under paragraph (a) specifying different times for different persons or descriptions of person;
(c) make provision about the issuing of notices under paragraph (a), including provision for the Secretary of State to issue notices to authorities administering housing benefit that have effect in relation to persons specified, or persons of a description specified, in the notices.
(10) Section 176 of the Social Security Administration Act 1992 (consultation with representative organisations) does not apply in relation to regulations under subsection (8).
(11) Regulations under subsection (8) must be made by statutory instrument.

(12) A statutory instrument containing regulations under subsection (8) is subject to annulment in pursuance of a resolution of either House of Parliament.

GENERAL NOTE

Section 8 was brought into force on March 16, 2016 for the purpose of making regulations (s.36(3)(a)), and on November 7, 2016 for all purposes (SI 2016/910, reg.2(1)). It extends to England, Wales and Scotland (s.35(3)). Subss.(1)-(6) amend WRA 2012 ss.96 and 97 (above) and subs.(7) revokes Pensions Act 2014 Sch.12 para.52. The regulation-making powers conferred by subs.(8)-(12) have been exercised to make the Benefit Cap (Housing Benefit and Universal Credit) (Amendment) Regulations 2016 (SI 2016/909).

1.297

Changes to child element of universal credit

14.—(1)-(5) *[Omitted]*

1.298

(6) The Secretary of State may by regulations make such transitional or transitory provision or savings as the Secretary of State considers necessary or expedient in connection with the coming into force of this section.

(7) Regulations under subsection (6) must be made by statutory instrument.

(8) A statutory instrument containing regulations under subsection (6) is subject to annulment in pursuance of a resolution of either House of Parliament.

GENERAL NOTE

Subss.(1)-(5), which amend Welfare Reform Act 2012 s.10 and Universal Credit Regulations, reg.24 came into force on April 6, 2017 (see SI 2017/111 reg.4). The other sub-sections came into force on February 8, 2017 (see SI 2017/111 reg.2(a)). The section as a whole extends to England and Wales and Scotland (s.35(3)(c)).

1.299

The regulation-making powers in subss.(6)-(8) have been used to make the Social Security (Restrictions on Amounts for Children and Qualifying Young Persons) Amendment Regulations 2017 (SI 2017/376) which amend Universal Credit Regulations, regs 2 and 24 and introduce new regs 24A and 24B and a new Sch.12 into those Regulations: see the commentary to regs 24-24B below.

Loans for mortgage interest etc

Loans for mortgage interest etc

18.—(1) The Secretary of State may by regulations provide for loans to be made in respect of a person's liability to make owner-occupier payments in respect of accommodation occupied by the person as the person's home.

1.300

(2) The regulations may make provision about eligibility to receive a loan under the regulations.

(3) Regulations under subsection (2) may in particular require that a person—

(a) is entitled to receive income support, income-based jobseeker's allowance, income-related employment and support allowance, state pension credit or universal credit;

(b) has received such a benefit for a period prescribed by the regulations.

(4) The regulations may make provision about the liabilities in respect of which a loan under the regulations may be made.

(5) Regulations under subsection (4) may in particular provide that a loan under the regulations may only be made if, and to the extent that, a person's liability to make owner-occupier payments was incurred for purposes prescribed by the regulations.

(6) Regulations under subsection (4) may in particular make provision about—

(a) determining or calculating the amount of a person's liabilities;

(b) the maximum amount of a person's liabilities in respect of which a loan under the regulations may be made.

(7) The regulations may—

(a) make provision about determining or calculating the amount that may be paid by way of loan under the regulations;

(b) require that a loan under the regulations be secured by a mortgage of or charge over a legal or beneficial interest in land or, in Scotland, by a heritable security.

(8) The regulations may define "owner-occupier payment".

(9) Regulations under this section may make different provision for different purposes.

(10) Regulations under this section must be made by statutory instrument.

(11) A statutory instrument containing regulations under this section is subject to annulment in pursuance of a resolution of either House of Parliament.

GENERAL NOTE

1.301   This section (and ss.19 & 21 below) came into force on April 3, 2017 (SI 2017/111 reg.3(d)-(f)). Section 20, which repeals and amends primary legislation governing mortgage interest support for IS, income-based JSA, SPC, income-related ESA and universal credit, came into force on July 27, 2018 (sub-ss (2)-(7) and (10): see SI 2017/802) and April 6, 2018 (sub-ss (1), (8)-(9) and (11): see SI 2018/438). All four sections extend to England and Wales and Scotland (s.35(3)(g)).

Taken together, ss.18, 19 and 21 confer powers on the Secretary of State to make regulations which replace the housing costs element for owner-occupiers under Universal Credit Regulations, reg.25(2) and Sch.5 (and the equivalent payments under IS Regulations, Sch.3; Jobseeker's Allowance Regulations 1996, Sch.2; SPC Regulations, Sch.2; and ESA Regulations, Sch.6) with repayable loans.

The Loans for Mortgage Interest Regulations 2017 (SI 2017/725) were made on July 5, 2017. They were fully in force, subject to limited transitional provision, by April 6, 2018. They make repayable loans available to eligible persons, and amend reg.25 of and Sch.1 to the Universal Credit Regulations 2013 (SI 2013/376), as well as regulations relating to various legacy benefits, to remove provision for owner-occupier housing costs payments. Significant amendments were made with effect from April 3, 2023 by the Loans for Mortgage Interest (Amendment) Regulations 2023 (SI 2023/226) (see Part IIA below). The key changes are a reduction in the waiting period from nine to three months, and abolition of the rule preventing claimants with earned income from obtaining these loans.

Section 18: further provision

1.302   **19.**—(1) This section makes further provision about regulations under section 18.

(2) The regulations may make provision about—

(a) circumstances in which a person is to be treated as liable or not liable to make owner-occupier payments;

(b) circumstances in which a person is to be treated as occupying or not occupying particular accommodation as a home.

(3) The regulations may include—

(a) provision about applying for a loan;

(b) provision requiring a person to satisfy requirements prescribed by the regulations before a loan may be made under the regulations, including requirements about receiving financial advice;

(c) provision about entering into an agreement (which may contain such terms and conditions as the Secretary of State thinks fit, subject to what may be provided in the regulations);

(d) provision about the time when, and manner in which, a loan must be repaid;

(e) provision about other terms upon which a loan is made;

(f) provision about the payment of interest, including provision prescribing or providing for the determination of the rate of interest;

(g) provision enabling administrative costs to be charged;

(h) provision about adding administrative costs to the amount of a loan;

(i) provision about accepting substituted security.

(4) The regulations may make provision—

(a) requiring that, in circumstances prescribed by the regulations, money lent in respect of a person's liability to make owner-occupier payments—

    (i) is paid directly to the qualifying lender;

    (ii) is applied by the qualifying lender towards discharging the person's liability to make owner-occupier payments;

(b) for the costs of administering the making of payments to qualifying lenders to be defrayed, in whole or in part, at the expense of the qualifying lenders, whether by requiring them to pay fees prescribed by the regulations, by deducting and retaining such part as may be prescribed by the regulations of the amounts that would otherwise be paid to them or otherwise;

(c) for requiring a qualifying lender, in a case where by virtue of paragraph (b) the amount paid to the lender is less than it would otherwise have been, to credit against the liability in relation to which the amount is paid the amount of the difference (in addition to the payment actually made);

(d) for enabling a body which, or person who, would otherwise be a qualifying lender to elect not to be regarded as a qualifying lender for the purposes of this section (other than this paragraph);

(e) for the recovery from any body or person—

    (i) of any sums paid to that body or person by way of payment under the regulations that ought not to have been so paid;

    (ii) of any fees or other sums due from that body or person by virtue of paragraph (b);

(f) for cases where the same person is liable to make owner-occupier payments under more than one agreement to make such payments.

(5) The regulations may provide for the Secretary of State to make arrangements with another person for the exercise of functions under the regulations.

(6) The regulations may include—

(a) provision requiring information and documents to be provided;

(b) provision authorising the disclosure of information.

(7) The bodies and persons who are "qualifying lenders" for the purposes of this section are—

(a) a deposit taker;

(b) an insurer;

(c) a county council, a county borough council, a district council, a London Borough Council, the Common Council of the City of London or the Council of the Isles of Scilly;

(d) a council constituted under section 2 of the Local Government etc. (Scotland) Act 1994;

(e) a new town corporation;

(f) other bodies or persons prescribed by regulations under section 18.

(8) In this section—

"deposit taker" means—

(a) a person who has permission under Part 4A of the Financial Services and Markets Act 2000 to accept deposits, or

(b) an EEA firm of the kind mentioned in paragraph 5(b) of Schedule 3 to that Act which has permission under paragraph 15 of that Schedule (as a result of qualifying for authorisation under paragraph 12 of that Schedule) to accept deposits;

"insurer" means—

(a) a person who has permission under Part 4A of the Financial Services and Markets Act 2000 to effect and carry out contracts of insurance, or

(b) an EEA firm of the kind mentioned in paragraph 5(d) of Schedule 3 to that Act which has permission under paragraph 15 of that Schedule (as a result of qualifying for authorisation under paragraph 12 of that Schedule) to effect and carry out contracts of insurance.

(9) The definitions of "deposit taker" and 'insurer" in this section must be read with—

(a) section 22 of the Financial Services and Markets Act 2000;

(b) any relevant order under that section;

(c) Schedule 2 to that Act.

GENERAL NOTE

1.303   See the General note to s.18 above.

Consequential amendments

1.304   **20.** *[Not reproduced]*

GENERAL NOTE

1.305   The amendments made by s.20 have been reproduced at the appropriate places in the text of this, and the other volumes.

Transitional provision

1.306   **21.**—(1) Regulations made by the Secretary of State may make such transitional or transitory provision or savings as the Secretary of State considers necessary or expedient in connection with the coming into force of sections 18 to 20.

(2) The regulations may include provision for temporarily excluding the making of a loan under regulations under section 18 after the coming into force of sections 18 to 20.

(3) Regulations under subsection (2) may in particular—

(a) provide for a temporary exclusion to continue until a time or times specified in a notice issued by the Secretary of State;

(b) enable the Secretary of State to issue notices under paragraph (a) specifying different times for different persons or descriptions of person.

(4) The regulations may include provision for enabling assistance with payments in respect of accommodation occupied as a home to be given by means of a qualifying benefit after the coming into force of sections 18 to 20 (including where the making of loans is temporarily excluded).

(5) Regulations under subsection (4) may in particular—

(a) provide for legislation that has been repealed or revoked to be treated as having effect;

(b) provide for assistance by means of a qualifying benefit to continue until a time or times specified in a notice issued by the Secretary of State;

(c) enable the Secretary of State to issue notices under paragraph (b) specifying different times for different persons or descriptions of person.

(6) In this section "qualifying benefit" means income support, income-based jobseeker's allowance, income-related employment and support allowance, state pension credit or universal credit.

(7) Regulations under this section may make different provision for different areas, cases or purposes.

(8) Regulations under this section must be made by statutory instrument.

(9) A statutory instrument containing regulations under this section is subject to annulment in pursuance of a resolution of either House of Parliament.

GENERAL NOTE

See the General note to s.18 above.   **1.307**

Final

Power to make consequential provision

34.—(1) The Secretary of State may by regulations make such amend-   **1.308**
ments and revocations of subordinate legislation (whenever made) as appear to the Secretary of State to be necessary or expedient in consequence of any provision of this Act.

(2) In this section "subordinate legislation" has the same meaning as in the Interpretation Act 1978.

(3) Regulations under this section must be made by statutory instrument.

(4) A statutory instrument containing regulations under this section is subject to annulment in pursuance of a resolution of either House of Parliament.

The Social Security (Additional Payments) Act 2022

(2022 c.38)

An Act to make provision about additional payments to recipients of means-tested benefits, tax credits and disability benefits.

[June 28, 2022]

1.309

ARRANGEMENT OF SECTIONS

GENERAL NOTE

1.310
This Act implements part of the package of measures announced by the Chancellor of the Exchequer on May 26, 2022 in response to the increasing cost of living crisis. The package included (i) an expansion of the Energy Bills Support Scheme, providing £400 to every household, without repayments; (ii) a one-off cost of living payment of £300, paid through the Winter Fuel Payment scheme; (iii) additional funding for the Household Support Fund, administered by local authorities; (iv) extra support for those on certain means-tested benefits in the form of a one-off cost of living payment of £650, payable in two instalments; and (v) a further £150 disability cost of living payment paid to those in receipt of eligible disability benefits. The Act makes provision for the latter two measures ((iv) and (v)). The Act was introduced in the House of Commons on June 15, 2022 on a fast-track procedure and received Royal Assent less than a fortnight later on June 28, 2022.

See also, on the same model, the Social Security (Additional Payments) Act 2023, which implements part of the package of further measures announced on November 17, 2022.

Means-tested additional payments: main payments

1.311
1.—(1) The Secretary of State must secure that—
  (a) a single payment of £326 is made to any person who has a qualifying entitlement to a social security benefit in respect of 25 May 2022 (the first "qualifying day"), and
  (b) a single payment of £324 is made to any person who has a qualifying entitlement to a social security benefit in respect of the second qualifying day.
(2) HMRC must secure that—
  (a) a single payment of £326 is made to any person who has a qualifying entitlement to child tax credit or working tax credit, but not to a social security benefit, in respect of 25 May 2022, and

   (b) a single payment of £324 is made to any person who has a qualifying entitlement to child tax credit or working tax credit, but not to
a social security benefit, in respect of the second qualifying day.
  (3) The social security benefits are—

   (a) universal credit under the Welfare Reform Act 2012 or the Welfare
Reform (Northern Ireland) Order 2015 (S.I. 2015/2006 (N.I. 1));

   (b) state pension credit under the State Pension Credit Act 2002 or
the State Pension Credit Act (Northern Ireland) 2002;

   (c) an income-based jobseeker's allowance under the Jobseekers
Act 1995 or the Jobseekers (Northern Ireland) Order 1995 (S.I.
1995/2705 (N.I. 15));

   (d) an income-related employment and support allowance under Part
1 of the Welfare Reform Act 2007 or Part 1 of the Welfare Reform
Act (Northern Ireland) 2007;

   (e) income support under section 124 of the Social Security
Contributions and Benefits Act 1992 or section 123 of the Social
Security Contributions and Benefits (Northern Ireland) Act 1992.

  (4) The second qualifying day is such day, not later than 31 October
2022, as may be specified by the Secretary of State in regulations.

  (5) Regulations under subsection (4) may specify a day before the regulations come into force.

  (6) In this section, and in sections 2 to 4, references to a "person" are to
an individual or to a couple (but not to each member of a couple separately).

DEFINITIONS

   "person"—see subs.(6).
   "HMRC"—see s.9(1).
   "a qualifying day"—see s.9(2).
   "the second qualifying day"—see s.9(1).
   "social security benefit"—see s.9(1).

GENERAL NOTE

   This section provides for means-tested additional payments to be paid to eligible persons in two tranches. These additional payments are the "main payments"
(see the heading to the regulation) to distinguish them from the "disability additional payments" made under section 5. The payments are not mutually exclusive.
Subsection (1) deals with payments by the Secretary of State to social security
claimants while subsection (2) makes parallel provision for payments by HMRC
to recipients of tax credits. The Act does not in terms give all such claimants a
direct entitlement to an additional payment (nor does it provide for claims for such
payments to be made). Instead, a duty is imposed on the Secretary of State (and
HMRC) to make such payments to those claimants who have a "qualifying entitlement", i.e. a right to at least one of the specified means-tested social security benefits or tax credits (see subs.(3) and s.2).

Subs. (1)

   This subsection requires the Secretary of State to make two means-tested additional payments of £326 and £324 respectively to an eligible person (but see subs.
(6) on what is meant by a "person", which stipulates that a "person" is an individual
or a couple but not each member of a couple separately). Eligibility depends on
having a "qualifying entitlement" (on which see s.2) to a "social security benefit"
(as listed in subs.(3)) in respect of either one or both of two dates, being the "first
qualifying day" and the "second qualifying day" in turn. The "first qualifying day"

1.312

1.313

is May 25, 2022 (see subs.(1)(a)) while the "second qualifying day" has since been fixed by regulations as September 25, 2022 (see subs.(4)).

The one-off payment of £650 was split into two payments with two eligibility windows to ensure that people who became claimants of relevant means-tested benefits by autumn 2022 will receive assistance even if they did not qualify for the first instalment earlier in the year. The qualifying days were both announced after they had passed (and so a claimant's eligibility or not was already determined) to limit the risk of fraud. Thus, the first qualifying day was fixed as the day before the cost of living package was announced. The slightly uneven split of the total £650 payment was also an anti-fraud measure.

Subs.(2)

1.314   This subsection makes parallel provision to subs.(1) for working tax credit and child tax credit claimants, with the duty to make means-tested additional payments at the two dates being imposed on HMRC. But see also s.4 below.

Subs.(3)

1.315   This subsection lists the relevant social security benefits that can generate a "qualifying entitlement" for the purposes of subs.(1). In short, they are universal credit, state pension credit and the means-tested legacy benefits, albeit with the exception of housing benefit. The thinking is that those on means-tested income-replacement benefits are most likely to struggle with the sharply rising cost of living. Claimants who only receive housing benefit have been excluded because of the difficulty (or impossibility) of the DWP and HMRC identifying such individuals, as local authorities deal with housing benefit claims. Some of these individuals may benefit from the discretionary Household Support Fund administered by local authorities. Claimants who qualify only for contributory benefits are likewise excluded. Note that state pension credit is a relevant social security benefit irrespective of whether it comprises the guarantee element or the savings credit or both variants of state pension credit.

Subss.(4) and (5)

1.316   The second qualifying day was September 25, 2022 (see Social Security Additional Payments (Second Qualifying Day) Regulations 2022 (SI 2022/1011) reg.2).

Qualifying entitlements

1.317   **2.**—(1) A person has a qualifying entitlement to a social security benefit in respect of a qualifying day if—

    (a) in respect of universal credit, the person is entitled to a payment of at least 1p in respect of an assessment period ending during the period of one month ending with the qualifying day;

    (b) in respect of state pension credit, an income-based jobseeker's allowance, an income-related employment and support allowance or income support, the person is entitled to a payment of at least 1p in respect of any day during the period of one month ending with the qualifying day.

(2) A person has a qualifying entitlement to child tax credit or working tax credit in respect of a qualifying day if—

    (a) where the qualifying day is 25 May 2022, the person receives a payment or has an award of the credit in question in the period beginning with 26 April 2022 and ending with 25 May 2022;

    (b) where the qualifying day is the second qualifying day, the person receives a payment or has an award of the credit in question in the period of one month ending with the second qualifying day, and, in either case, the payment or award of the credit in question is of at least £26 or HMRC expects the person to receive total payments or have an award of the credit in question of at least £26 in respect of the tax year 2022-23.

(3) References in this section to a person receiving a payment or having an award do not include payments received or awards made as a result of fraud.

DEFINITIONS

"HMRC"—see s.9(1).
"a qualifying day"—see s.9(2).
"the second qualifying day"—see s.9(1).
"social security benefit"—see s.9(1).
"tax year 2022-2023"—see s.9(1).

GENERAL NOTE

This section defines what is meant by a "qualifying entitlement" to a relevant social security benefit (subs.(1)) or tax credit (subs.(2)) by reference to a qualifying day. These definitions reflect the minimum amounts of benefits and tax credits payable – see e.g. Universal Credit Regulations 2013 (SI 2013/376) reg.17 and Tax Credits (Income Thresholds and Determination of Rates) Regulations 2002 (SI 2002/2008) reg. 9. Payments received or awards made as a result of fraud do not count for the purposes of a "qualifying entitlement" (subs.(3)).   **1.318**

Subs. (1)
The definition of a "qualifying entitlement" differs depending on whether universal credit or one of the other social security benefits is involved. This reflects the different structures of universal credit and other benefits respectively. Thus, for universal credit the test is whether "the person is entitled to a payment of at least 1p in respect of an assessment period ending during the period of one month ending with the qualifying day" (subs.(1)(a)). It follows that a claimant with an assessment period running from the 30th of one month to the 29th of the next month would have to have been entitled in the assessment period ending on April 29, 2022. Entitlement in the assessment period ending on May 29, 2022 would not qualify as that assessment period does not end "during the period of one month ending with the qualifying day" (May 25, 2022). This is so even though that assessment period would have covered the great majority of days in the month ending on May 25, 2022. More straightforwardly, claimants of other relevant social security benefits must just have an entitlement of at least 1p. in the month preceding the relevant qualifying day (subs.(1)(b)).   **1.319**

Subs. (2)
Tax credit recipients must have had an entitlement in respect of one day in the month before the relevant qualifying day and have a payment or an award for the tax year 2022/23 of at least £26.   **1.320**

Applicable benefits or tax credits

3.—(1) Where a person has a qualifying entitlement to universal credit and to another social security benefit in respect of a qualifying day, the benefit by reference to which the means-tested additional payment in respect of the qualifying day is to be made is universal credit (if the payment is made under section 1(1)).   **1.321**

(2) Where a person has a qualifying entitlement to child tax credit and to working tax credit in respect of a qualifying day, the tax credit by reference to which the means-tested additional payment in respect of the qualifying day is to be paid is child tax credit (if the payment is made under section 1(2)).

DEFINITIONS

"means-tested additional payment"—see s.9(1).
"a qualifying day"—see s.9(2).
"social security benefit"—see s.9(1).

GENERAL NOTE

1.322   Claimants may have a qualifying entitlement to both universal credit and another social security benefit in respect of the period of a month ending with the same qualifying day (e.g. where they move from one benefit to universal credit). In such a case the means-tested additional payment is paid by reference to the universal credit entitlement, which takes precedence (subs.(1)). In the same way, where both child tax credit (CTC) and working tax credit (WTC) are in payment, the child tax credit entitlement takes priority (subs.(2)). So, for example if CTC and WTC are paid to different members of the same couple, the additional payment will be made to the CTC recipient.

Means-tested additional payments: final payments

1.323   **4.**—(1) HMRC must secure that a single payment of £326 is made to any person who—

   (a) receives a payment or has an award of child tax credit or working tax credit in respect of the period beginning with 26 April 2022 and ending with 25 May 2022,

   (b) is not entitled to a payment under section 1(1)(a) or (2)(a), and

   (c) receives total payments or has an award of the credit in question of at least £26 in respect of the tax year 2022-23.

(2) HMRC must secure that a single payment of £324 is made to any person who—

   (a) receives a payment or has an award of child tax credit or working tax credit in respect of the period of one month ending with the second qualifying day,

   (b) is not entitled to a payment under section 1(1)(b) or (2)(b), and

   (c) receives total payments or has an award of the credit in question of at least £26 in respect of the tax year 2022-23.

(3) Where a person is entitled to a payment under this section by reference to child tax credit and working tax credit, the tax credit by reference to which the payment is to be made is child tax credit.

(4) References in this section to a person receiving a payment or having an award do not include payments received or awards made as a result of fraud.

DEFINITIONS

"HMRC"—see s.9(1).
"the second qualifying day"—see s.9(1).
"tax year 2022–2023"—see s.9(1).

This is a fall-back provision for tax credits claimants who did not qualify for an   1.324
additional payment under s.1(1) or s.1(2) above. It applies to claimants who have
an award or payments of tax credits of at least £26 for the 2022/23 tax year and
who have an award or payments of CTC or WTC for the month from April 26,
2022 to May 25, 2022. HMRC must pay them the first additional payment if they
have not already otherwise received it (subs.(1)). The same principle applies with
the necessary modification for the dates involved for the second additional payment
(subs.(2)). The second qualifying day was September 25, 2022 (see Social Security
Additional Payments (Second Qualifying Day) Regulations 2022 (SI 2022/1011)
reg.2). Where both CTC and WTC are in payment, CTC takes precedence as under
s.3(2) (see subs.(3)). As with s.2(3), payments made because of fraud do not count
(subs.(4)).

Disability additional payments

5.—(1) The Secretary of State must secure that a single payment of   1.325
£150 (a "disability additional payment") is made to each individual who is
entitled to a payment of a disability benefit that is payable in respect of 25
May 2022.
  (2) The disability benefits are—
    (a) a disability living allowance under section 71 of the Social Security
        Contributions and Benefits Act 1992 or section 71 of the Social
        Security Contributions and Benefits (Northern Ireland) Act 1992;
    (b) a personal independence payment under the Welfare Reform Act
        2012 or Part 5 of the Welfare Reform (Northern Ireland) Order
        2015;
    (c) an attendance allowance under section 64 of the Social Security
        Contributions and Benefits Act 1992 or section 64 of the Social
        Security Contributions and Benefits (Northern Ireland) Act
        1992;
    (d) a constant attendance allowance under section 104 of the Social
        Security Contributions and Benefits Act 1992 or section 104 of
        the Social Security Contributions and Benefits (Northern Ireland)
        Act 1992;
    (e) an adult disability payment under the Disability Assistance for
        Working Age People (Scotland) Regulations 2022 (S.S.I. 2022/54);
    (f) a child disability payment under the Disability Assistance for
        Children and Young People (Scotland) Regulations 2021 (S.S.I.
        2021/174);
    (g) an armed forces independence payment under article 24A of
        the Armed Forces and Reserve Forces (Compensation Scheme)
        Order 2011 (S.I. 2011/517);
    (h) a constant attendance allowance under—
        (i) article 14 or 43 of the Personal Injuries (Civilians) Scheme
            1983 (S.I. 1983/686);
        (ii) article 8 of the Naval, Military and Air Forces etc. (Disablement
            and Death) Service Pensions Order 2006 (S.I. 2006/606);
    (i) a mobility supplement under—
        (i) article 25A or 48A of the Personal Injuries (Civilians) Scheme
            1983;
        (ii) article 20 of the Naval, Military and Air Forces etc. (Disablement
            and Death) Service Pensions Order 2006.

(3) Where an indi vidual is entitled to a payment of more than one disability benefit that is payable in respect of 25 May 2022, the benefit by reference to which the disability additional payment is to be made is the first benefit in the list in subsection (2) to which the individual is entitled.

DEFINITIONS

"disability additional payment"—see subs.(1) and s.9(1).
"disability benefit"—see s.9(1).

GENERAL NOTE

1.326   The one or two means-tested additional payments may be supplemented by a single disability additional payment made under this section, amounting to £150. The Secretary of State must make such payments to claimants who were entitled to a qualifying payment of a prescribed disability benefit in respect of May 25, 2022 (subs.(1)). The relevant disability benefits are those listed in subs.(2). Those listed in subs.(2)(a)–(d) are the responsibility of the DWP or its Northern Ireland equivalent. Those in subs.(2)(e)–(f) are paid by the Scottish government, while the benefits in subs.(g)–(i) are administered by the Secretary of State for Defence (or on his behalf by the Veterans UK). Given these disparate responsibilities, the Act makes provision for data-sharing (see s.7).

Administration of additional payments

1.327   **6.**—(1) For all purposes relating to the administration of an additional payment, any provision applying in relation to a social security benefit, child tax credit, working tax credit or disability benefit by reference to which that payment is made is to apply in relation to that payment as if that payment were a payment or award of the social security benefit, child tax credit, working tax credit or disability benefit in question.

(2) The provision applied by subsection (1)—

    (a) includes provision relating to overpayments and recovery, and appeals relating to overpayments and recovery (but not provision relating to appeals or reviews about entitlement to the social security benefit, tax credit or disability benefit in question), and

    (b) is subject to any necessary modifications.

(3) Subsection (1) has effect in relation to a payment made in purported compliance with a duty under section 1 [¹,4 or 5] as if that payment were the additional payment which it purported to be.

(4) Subsection (1) (including as it has effect as a result of subsection (3)) is subject to regulations made by the Secretary of State, the Treasury or HMRC under subsection (5).

(5) The Secretary of State, the Treasury or HMRC may by regulations make provision, in relation to additional payments or payments purporting to be additional payments, applying or disapplying, with or without modifications, any provision applying in relation to a social security benefit, child tax credit, working tax credit or a disability benefit.

(6) The regulations may make provision having effect from the day on which this Act comes into force.

AMENDMENT

1. Social Security (Additional Payments) Act 2003 s.9 (1) and (2) (June 28, 2022).

DEFINITIONS

"additional payment"—see s.9(1).
"disability benefit"—see s.9(1).
"HMRC"—see s.9(1).

GENERAL NOTE

Note that there is no provision in the Act for anyone to make a claim for a means-tested additional payment. As a result, there is also no provision for the Secretary of State to make a decision under s.8(1)(a) of the Social Security Act 1998. In the same way it follows that the usual mechanism of revisions, supersessions and appeals does not apply. Instead, s.1 simply imposes a duty on the Secretary of State and HMRC to make payments to eligible individuals.   1.328

Subs. (1)

This provision applies the relevant administrative provisions relating to the qualifying benefit to the new additional payment. This method has been adopted so that the additional payments can be administered in the same manner and subject to the same rules as those which apply to a claimant's existing benefit entitlement (e.g. by payment to the same bank account as the qualifying benefit).   1.329

Subs. (2)

The provision made under subs.(1) includes provision relating to overpayment and benefit recovery procedures. This reflects the fact that different rules govern overpayment and benefit recovery procedures for different social security benefits and tax credits. This does not include provisions relating to appeals or reviews, there being no decision as such on entitlement to an additional payment to be appealed. See further the Tax Credits Act 2002 (Additional Payments Modification and Disapplication) Regulations 2022 (SI 2022/1208).   1.330

Cooperation etc between the Secretary of State and HMRC

7.—(1) The Secretary of State and HMRC must cooperate in exercising   1.331
their functions in relation to additional payments.

(2) Section 3 of the Social Security Act 1998 (use of information) has effect—

(a) in relation to HMRC as it has effect in relation to the Secretary of State, and

(b) as if, in subsection (1A), the reference to social security included additional payments.

(3) Section 127 of the Welfare Reform Act 2012 (information-sharing between Secretary of State and HMRC) has effect as if—

(a) functions of HMRC conferred by or under this Act were HMRC functions within the meaning of that section, and

(b) functions of the Secretary of State conferred by or under this Act were departmental functions within the meaning of that section.

(4) Section 34 of the Scotland Act 2016 (information-sharing between the Secretary of State and the Scottish Ministers) has effect as if, in subsection (7), the reference to social security in the definition of "social security function" included additional payments.

(5) Subsection (6) applies where—

(a) the Secretary of State or HMRC make a payment to a person in purported compliance with a duty in section 1 or 4,

(b) the person was entitled to receive an additional payment of an amount equal to that payment under a different duty in section 1 or 4 ("the applicable duty"), and

(c) the person does not receive the additional payment to which they are entitled under the applicable duty.

(6) The payment made in purported compliance with a duty in section 1 or 4 is to be treated as if it had been made in accordance with the applicable duty (and, accordingly, the payment is not recoverable on the grounds that it was not made in compliance with a duty in section 1 or 4).

DEFINITIONS

"additional payment"—see s.9(1).
"the applicable duty"—subs.(5)(b).
"HMRC"—see s.9(1).

GENERAL NOTE

1.332   This section provides for data-sharing between the DWP, HMRC and the Secretary of State for Defence (given his role in administering the benefits itemised at s.5(2)(g)–(i)) along with the relevant authorities in Northern Ireland and Scotland.

Payments to be disregarded for the purposes of tax and social security

1.333   **8.**—No account is to be taken of an additional payment in considering a person's—

(a) liability to tax,

(b) entitlement to benefit under an enactment relating to social security (irrespective of the name or nature of the benefit), or

(c) entitlement to a tax credit.

DEFINITION

"additional payment"—see s.9(1).

GENERAL NOTE

1.334   Additional payments under this Act are disregarded for the purposes of liability to income tax (para.(a)) and entitlement to social security benefits (para. (b)) and tax credits (para.(c)). So far as entitlement to social security benefits is concerned, the usual drafting technique to provide for a disregard for such forms of capital or income other than earnings is by way of a regulation (see e.g. Universal Credit Regulations 2013 (SI 2013/376) reg.76) or Schedule (see e.g. Income Support (General) Regulations 1987 (SI 1987/1967), Sch.9). However, the fact that entitlement to additional payments is directly governed by primary legislation has allowed a different and all purposes route to a statutory disregard to be adopted.

Interpretation

1.335   **9.**—(1) In this Act—

"additional payment" means a means-tested additional payment or a disability additional payment;

"disability additional payment" has the meaning given by section 5(1);

"disability benefit" means a benefit listed in section 5(2);

"HMRC" means the Commissioners for Her Majesty's Revenue and Customs;

"means-tested additional payment" means a payment under section 1 or 4;

"the second qualifying day" means the day specified in regulations under section 1(4);

"social security benefit" means a benefit listed in section 1(3);

"the tax year 2022–23" means the period beginning with 6 April 2022 and ending with 5 April 2023.

(2) In this Act—

    (a) references to "a qualifying day" are to—

        (i) 25 May 2022, or

        (ii) the day specified in regulations under section 1(4);

    (b) references to child tax credit or working tax credit are to child tax credit or working tax credit under the Tax Credits Act 2002.

Regulations

10.—(1) A power to make regulations under any provision of this Act includes power to make—

    (a) consequential, supplementary, incidental, transitional or saving provision;

    (b) different provision for different purposes.

(2) Regulations under this Act are to be made by statutory instrument.

(3) A statutory instrument containing regulations under this Act is subject to annulment in pursuance of a resolution of either House of Parliament.

Extent, commencement and short title

11.—(1) This Act extends to England and Wales, Scotland and Northern Ireland.

(2) This Act comes into force on the day on which it is passed.

(3) This Act may be cited as the Social Security (Additional Payments) Act 2022.

GENERAL NOTE

The Act received Royal Assent on June 28, 2022.

1.336

1.337

1.338

The Social Security (Additional Payments) Act 2023

(2023 Ch.7)

An Act to make provision about additional payments to recipients of means-tested benefits, tax credits and disability benefits.

[March 23, 2023]

ARRANGEMENT OF SECTIONS

1.339

GENERAL NOTE

1.340   This Act is modelled on the Social Security (Additional Payments) Act 2022 and implements part of the package of further measures announced on November 17, 2022 to assist in tackling the cost of living crisis. The 2023 Act provides for payments of up to £900 (in three instalments) to households in receipt of eligible means-tested social security benefits or tax credits at a total cost to the Exchequer of around £7.5 billion in 2023/24. The Government estimates that some 8 million benefit units (defined as a single adult or a married or cohabiting couple and any dependent children) are expected to receive the first £301 cost of living payment. The 2023 Act also makes provision for disability additional payments of £150.

Means-tested additional payments

Means-tested additional payments: main payments

1.341   **1.**—(1) The Secretary of State must secure that—

(a) a single payment of £301 is made to any person who has a qualifying entitlement to a social security benefit in respect of the first qualifying day,

(b) a single payment of £300 is made to any person who has a qualifying entitlement to a social security benefit in respect of the second qualifying day, and

(c) a single payment of £299 is made to any person who has a qualifying entitlement to a social security benefit in respect of the third qualifying day.

(2) HMRC must secure that—

(a) a single payment of £301 is made to any person who has a qualifying entitlement to child tax credit or working tax credit, but not to a social security benefit, in respect of the first qualifying day,

(b) a single payment of £300 is made to any person who has a qualifying entitlement to child tax credit or working tax credit, but not to a social security benefit, in respect of the second qualifying day, and

(c) a single payment of £299 is made to any person who has a qualifying entitlement to child tax credit or working tax credit, but not to a social security benefit, in respect of the third qualifying day.

(3) The social security benefits are—

(a) universal credit under the Welfare Reform Act 2012 or the Welfare Reform (Northern Ireland) Order 2015 (S.I. 2015/2006 (N.I. 1));

(b) state pension credit under the State Pension Credit Act 2002 or the State Pension Credit Act (Northern Ireland) 2002;

(c) an income-based jobseeker's allowance under the Jobseekers Act 1995 or the Jobseekers (Northern Ireland) Order 1995 (S.I. 1995/2705 (N.I. 15));

(d) an income-related employment and support allowance under Part 1 of the Welfare Reform Act 2007 or Part 1 of the Welfare Reform Act (Northern Ireland) 2007;

(e) income support under section 124 of the Social Security Contributions and Benefits Act 1992 or section 123 of the Social Security Contributions and Benefits (Northern Ireland) Act 1992.

(4) The first qualifying day is such day, not later than 30 April 2023, as may be specified by the Secretary of State in regulations.

(5) Regulations under subsection (4) may specify a day before this Act or the regulations are in force.

(6) The second qualifying day is such day, not later than 31 October 2023, as may be specified by the Secretary of State in regulations.

(7) The third qualifying day is such day, not later than 29 February 2024, as may be specified by the Secretary of State in regulations.

(8) Regulations under subsections (6) and (7) may specify a day before the regulations are in force.

(9) In this section, and in sections 2 to 4, references to a "person" are to an individual or to a couple (but not to each member of a couple separately).

GENERAL NOTE

This section is modelled on s.1 of the 2022 Act. The first qualifying day (see subs.(4)) is February 25, 2023: see the Social Security Additional Payments (First Qualifying Day) Regulations 2023 (SI 2023/361).

1.342

Qualifying entitlements: social security benefits

2.—(1) A person has a qualifying entitlement to a social security benefit in respect of a qualifying day if—

1.343

(a) in respect of universal credit, the person is entitled to a payment of at least 1p in respect of an assessment period ending during the period of one month ending with the qualifying day;

(b) in respect of state pension credit, an income-based jobseeker's allowance, an income-related employment and support allowance or income support, the person is entitled to a payment of at least 1p in respect of any day during the period of one month ending with the qualifying day.

(2) For the purposes of subsection (1)(b), a person is considered to be entitled to a payment irrespective of whether that payment is not payable as a result of—

(a) regulation 13 of the State Pension Credit Regulations 2002 (S.I. 2002/1792);

(b) regulation 13 of the State Pension Credit Regulations (Northern Ireland) 2003 (S.R. (N.I.) 2003 No.28);

(c) regulation 87A of the Jobseeker's Allowance Regulations 1996 (S.I. 1996/207);

(d) regulation 87A of the Jobseeker's Allowance Regulations (Northern Ireland) 1996 (S.R. (N.I.) 1996 No.198);

(e) regulation 26(4) or 26C(6) of the Social Security (Claims and Payments) Regulations 1987 (S.I. 1987/1968);

(f) regulation 26(4) or 26C(6) of the Social Security (Claims and Payments) Regulations (Northern Ireland) 1987 (S.R. (N.I.) 1987 No.465).

GENERAL NOTE

1.344   Section 2(1) mirrors s.2(1) of the 2022 Act. Section 2(2) ensures entitlement to additional payments is retained even where payment of the relevant means-tested benefit is withheld because of the de minimis rule.

Qualifying entitlements: tax credits

1.345   **3.**—(1) A person has a qualifying entitlement to child tax credit or working tax credit in respect of a qualifying day if HMRC makes a payment to the person of the credit in question in respect of a day falling within the period of one month ending with that qualifying day (the "qualifying period").

(2) References in this section to HMRC making a payment do not include—

(a) a payment made under regulation 10 of the Tax Credits (Payments by the Commissioners) Regulations 2002 (S.I. 2002/2173), where the person to whom HMRC has made the payment would not be entitled to that payment if their entitlement were assessed on any day during the qualifying period, or

(b) a payment made as a result of fraud.

Applicable benefits or tax credits

1.346   **4.**—(1) Where a person has a qualifying entitlement to more than one social security benefit in respect of a qualifying day, the benefit by reference to which the means-tested additional payment in respect of the qualifying day is to be paid is the first benefit in the list in section 1(3) to which the person has a qualifying entitlement (if the payment is made under section 1(1)).

(2) Where a person has a qualifying entitlement to child tax credit and to working tax credit in respect of a qualifying day, the tax credit by reference to which the means-tested additional payment in respect of the qualifying day is to be paid is child tax credit (if the payment is made under section 1(2)).

GENERAL NOTE

1.347   See the General Note to s.3 of the 2022 Act.

Disability additional payments

Disability additional payments

1.348   **5.**—(1) The Secretary of State must secure that a single payment of £150 (a "disability additional payment") is made to each individual who is entitled to a payment of a disability benefit that is payable in respect of the disability additional payment day.

(2) The disability benefits are—

(a) a disability living allowance under section 71 of the Social Security Contributions and Benefits Act 1992 or section 71 of the Social Security Contributions and Benefits (Northern Ireland) Act 1992;

(b) a personal independence payment under the Welfare Reform Act 2012 or Part 5 of the Welfare Reform (Northern Ireland) Order 2015 (S.I. 2015/2006 (N.I. 1));

(c) an attendance allowance under section 64 of the Social Security Contributions and Benefits Act 1992 or section 64 of the Social Security Contributions and Benefits (Northern Ireland) Act 1992;

(d) a constant attendance allowance under section 104 of the Social Security Contributions and Benefits Act 1992 or section 104 of the Social Security Contributions and Benefits (Northern Ireland) Act 1992;

(e) an adult disability payment under the Disability Assistance for Working Age People (Scotland) Regulations 2022 (S.S.I. 2022/54) or the Disability Assistance for Working Age People (Transitional Provisions and Miscellaneous Amendment) (Scotland) Regulations 2022 (S.S.I. 2022/217);

(f) a child disability payment under the Disability Assistance for Children and Young People (Scotland) Regulations 2021 (S.S.I. 2021/174);

(g) an armed forces independence payment under article 24A of the Armed Forces and Reserve Forces (Compensation Scheme) Order 2011 (S.I. 2011/517);

(h) a constant attendance allowance under—
  (i) article 14 or 43 of the Personal Injuries (Civilians) Scheme 1983 (S.I. 1983/686);
  (ii) article 8 of the Naval, Military and Air Forces etc. (Disablement and Death) Service Pensions Order 2006 (S.I. 2006/606);

(i) a mobility supplement under—
  (i) article 25A or 48A of the Personal Injuries (Civilians) Scheme 1983;
  (ii) article 20 of the Naval, Military and Air Forces etc. (Disablement and Death) Service Pensions Order 2006 (S.I. 2006/606).

(3) The disability additional payment day is such day, not later than 30 June 2023, as may be specified by the Secretary of State in regulations.

(4) Regulations under subsection (3) may specify a day before the regulations are in force.

(5) Where an individual is entitled to a payment of more than one disability benefit that is payable in respect of the disability additional payment day, the benefit by reference to which the disability additional payment is to be made is the first benefit in the list in subsection (2) to which the individual is entitled.

GENERAL NOTE

This is in essentially the same terms as s.5 of the 2022 Act.

1.349

Administration of additional payments

1.350   **6.**—(1) For all purposes relating to the administration of an additional payment, any provision applying in relation to a social security benefit, child tax credit, working tax credit or disability benefit by reference to which that payment is made is to apply in relation to that payment as if that payment were a payment of the social security benefit, child tax credit, working tax credit or disability benefit in question.

(2) The provision applied by subsection (1)—

(a) includes provision relating to overpayments and recovery, and appeals relating to overpayments and recovery (but not provision relating to appeals or reviews about entitlement to the social security benefit, tax credit or disability benefit in question), and

(b) is subject to any necessary modifications.

(3) Subsection (1) has effect in relation to a payment made in purported compliance with a duty in section 1 or 5 as if that payment were the additional payment which it purported to be.

(4) Subsection (1) (including as it has effect as a result of subsection (3)) is subject to regulations made by the Secretary of State, the Treasury or HMRC under subsection (5).

(5) The Secretary of State, the Treasury or HMRC may by regulations make provision, in relation to additional payments or payments purporting to be additional payments, applying or disapplying, with or without modifications, any provision applying in relation to a social security benefit, child tax credit, working tax credit or disability benefit.

(6) The regulations may make provision having effect from the day on which this Act comes into force.

GENERAL NOTE

1.351   See the commentary to s.6 of the 2022 Act.

Cooperation etc between the Secretary of State and HMRC

1.352   **7.**—(1) The Secretary of State and HMRC must cooperate in exercising their functions in relation to additional payments.

(2) Section 3 of the Social Security Act 1998 (use of information) has effect—

(a) in relation to HMRC as it has effect in relation to the Secretary of State, and

(b) as if, in subsection (1A), the reference to social security included additional payments.

(3) Section 127 of the Welfare Reform Act 2012 (information-sharing between Secretary of State and HMRC) has effect as if—

(a) functions of HMRC conferred by or under this Act were HMRC functions within the meaning of that section, and

(b) functions of the Secretary of State conferred by or under this Act were departmental functions within the meaning of that section.

(4) Section 34 of the Scotland Act 2016 (information-sharing between the Secretary of State and the Scottish Ministers) has effect as if, in subsection (7), the reference to social security in the definition of "social security function" included additional payments.

(5) Subsection (6) applies where—

    (a) the Secretary of State or HMRC make a payment to a person in purported compliance with a duty in section 1,

    (b) the person was entitled to receive an additional payment of an amount equal to that payment under a different duty in section 1 ("the applicable duty"), and

    (c) the person does not receive the additional payment to which they are entitled under the applicable duty.

(6) The payment made in purported compliance with a duty in section 1 is to be treated as if it had been made in accordance with the applicable duty (and, accordingly, the payment is not recoverable on the grounds that it was not made in compliance with a duty in section 1).

GENERAL NOTE

This mirrors s.7 of the 2022 Act.   1.353

Payments to be disregarded for the purposes of tax and social security

8.—No account is to be taken of an additional payment in considering a person's—   1.354

    (a) liability to tax,

    (b) entitlement to a benefit under an enactment relating to social security (irrespective of the name or nature of the benefit), or

    (c) entitlement to a tax credit.

GENERAL NOTE

This provision is in the same terms as s.8 of the 2022 Act.   1.355

Amendments to other legislation

9.—(1) In the Social Security (Additional Payments) Act 2022, in section 6(3), for "or 4" substitute ", 4 or 5".   1.356

(2) The amendment made by subsection (1) is to be treated as having come into force on 28 June 2022.

(3) The Tax Credits Act 2002 (Additional Payments Modification and Disapplication) Regulations 2022 (S.I. 2022/1208) are amended in accordance with subsections (4) and (5).

(4) In paragraph (2) of regulation 1—

    (a) for "payments" substitute "a payment";

    (b) at the end insert "or section 1(2) of the Social Security (Additional Payments) Act 2023."

(5) In regulation 6, after "2022" insert ", a payment made under section 1(2) of the Social Security (Additional Payments) Act 2023,".

(6) The amendments made by subsections (4) and (5) are to be treated as if they had been made by regulations made under sections 6(5) and (6) and 11(1) of this Act.

Final provisions

Interpretation

1.357 **10.**—(1) In this Act—

"additional payment" means a means-tested additional payment or a disability additional payment;

"disability additional payment" has the meaning given by section 5(1);

"the disability additional payment day" means the day specified in regulations under section 5(3);

"disability benefit" means a benefit listed in section 5(2);

"the first qualifying day" means the day specified in regulations under section 1(4);

"HMRC" means the Commissioners for His Majesty's Revenue and Customs;

"means-tested additional payment" means a payment under section 1;

"the second qualifying day" means the day specified in regulations under section 1(6);

"social security benefit" means a benefit listed in section 1(3);

"the third qualifying day" means the day specified in regulations under section 1(7).

(2) In this Act—

  (a) references to "a qualifying day" are to—

    (i) the first qualifying day specified in regulations under section 1(4),

    (ii) the second qualifying day specified in regulations under section 1(6),

    (iii) the third qualifying day specified in regulations under section 1(7);

  (b) references to child tax credit or working tax credit are to child tax credit or working tax credit under the Tax Credits Act 2002.

Regulations

1.358 **11.**—(1) A power to make regulations under any provision of this Act includes power to make—

  (a) consequential, supplementary, incidental, transitional or saving provision;

  (b) different provision for different purposes.

(2) Regulations under this Act are to be made by statutory instrument.

(3) A statutory instrument containing regulations under this Act is subject to annulment in pursuance of a resolution of either House of Parliament.

Extent, commencement and short title

1.359 **12.**—(1) This Act extends to England and Wales, Scotland and Northern Ireland.

(2) This Act comes into force on the day on which it is passed.

(3) This Act may be cited as the Social Security (Additional Payments) Act 2023.

GENERAL NOTE

1.360 The Act received Royal Assent on March 23, 2023.

PART II

UNIVERSAL CREDIT: REGULATIONS

PART IIA

UNIVERSAL CREDIT REGULATIONS

The Universal Credit Regulations 2013

(SI 2013/376)

Made on February 25, 2013 by the Secretary of State for Work and Pensions in exercise of the powers conferred by sections 2(2), 4(2), (3), (5), (6) and (7), 5, 6(1)(a) and (3), 7(2) and (3), 8(3), 9(2) and (3), 10(2) to (5), 11(3) to (5), 12(1), (3) and (4), 14(5), 15(2), 17(3) and (4), 18(3) and (5), 19(2)(d), (3) and (4), 20(1), 22(2), 24(1), (5) and (6), 25, 26(2)(a), (6) and (8), 27(4), (5), (9), 28, 32(1), 37(3) to (7), 39(3)(a), 40, 96 and 97 of, and paragraphs 1, 4, 5 and 7 of Schedule 1 and paragraphs 2 and 3 of Schedule 5 to, the Welfare Reform Act 2012; a draft having been laid before Parliament in accordance with section 43(3) of the Welfare Reform Act 2012 and approved by a resolution of each House of Parliament; and without the instrument having been referred to the Social Security Advisory Committee because it contains only regulations made by virtue of or consequential on Part 1 and sections 96 and 97 of, and Schedules 1 and 5 to, the Welfare Reform Act 2012 and is made before the end of the period of 6 months beginning with the coming into force of those provisions.

2.1

[April 29, 2013, but see the introductory General Note to WRA 2012]

ARRANGEMENT OF REGULATIONS

PART 1

INTRODUCTION

2.2

PART 2

ENTITLEMENT

Part 3

Awards

Part 4

Elements of An Award

Part 5

Capability for Work or Work-Related Activity

Part 6

Calculation of Capital and Income

Chapter 1

Capital

CHAPTER 2

EARNED INCOME

CHAPTER 3

UNEARNED INCOME

CHAPTER 4

MISCELLANEOUS

PART 7

THE BENEFIT CAP

PART 8

CLAIMANT RESPONSIBILITIES

CHAPTER 1

WORK-RELATED REQUIREMENTS

CHAPTER 2

SANCTIONS

CHAPTER 3

HARDSHIP

SCHEDULES

Part 1

Introduction

Citation and commencement

2.4   **1.**—These Regulations may be cited as the Universal Credit Regulations 2013 and come into force on 29th April 2013.

General Note

2.5   Although the Regulations come into force on April 29, 2013, they do not apply to all claimants. See further the Universal Credit (Transitional Provisions) Regulations 2014, the commencement orders in Pt V of Vol.V of this series and the introductory General Note to the WRA 2012 in Pt I of this volume.

Interpretation

2.6   **2.**—In these Regulations—
"the Act" means the Welfare Reform Act 2012;
[⁸ . . .]
[² "adopter" has the meaning in regulation 89(3)(a);]
[¹⁸ "adult disability payment" has the meaning given in regulation 2 of the Disability Assistance for Working Age People (Scotland) Regulations 2022;]
"attendance allowance" means—
   (a) an attendance allowance under section 64 of the Contributions and Benefits Act;
   (b) an increase of disablement pension under section 104 or 105 of that Act (increases where constant attendance needed and for exceptionally severe disablement);
   (c) [³ . . .]
   (d) a payment by virtue of article 14, 15, 16, 43 or 44 of the Personal Injuries (Civilians) Scheme 1983 or any analogous payment;
   (e) any payment based on the need for attendance which is paid as an addition to a war disablement pension;
   [¹(f) armed forces independence payment under the Armed Forces and Reserve Forces (Compensation Scheme) Order 2011;]
"bereavement allowance" means an allowance under section 39B of the Contributions and Benefits Act;
[⁶ "blind" means certified as severely sight impaired or blind by a consultant ophthalmologist;]
"care leaver" has the meaning in regulation 8;
"carer's allowance" means a carer's allowance under section 70 of the Contributions and Benefits Act;
"carer element" has the meaning in regulation 29;
[¹⁷ "child disability payment" has the meaning given in regulation 2 of the DACYP Regulations;]
"childcare costs element" has the meaning in regulation 31;
"child element" has the meaning in regulation 24;
"close relative", in relation to a person, means—
   (a) a parent, parent-in-law, son, son-in-law, daughter, daughter-in-law, step-parent, step-son, step-daughter, brother or sister; and

(b) if any of the above is a member of a couple, the other member of the couple;

"confinement" has the meaning in regulation 8;

"Contributions and Benefits Act" means the Social Security Contributions and Benefits Act 1992;

"course of advanced education" has the meaning in regulation 12;

[[17] "the DACYP Regulations" means the Disability Assistance for Children and Young People (Scotland) Regulations 2021;]

"disability living allowance" means an allowance under section 71 of the Contributions and Benefits Act;

"earned income" has the meaning in Chapter 2 of Part 6;

"EEA Regulations" means the [[14] Immigration (European Economic Area) Regulations 2016] [[16] and references to the EEA Regulations are to be read with Schedule 4 to the Immigration and Social Security Co-ordination (EU Withdrawal) Act 2020 (Consequential, Saving, Transitional and Transitory Provisions) Regulations 2020.]

"employment and support allowance" means an allowance under Part 1 of the Welfare Reform Act 2007 as amended by Schedule 3 and Part 1 of Schedule 14 to the Welfare Reform Act 2012 (removing references to an income-related allowance);

[[4] "enactment" includes an enactment comprised in, or an instrument made under, an Act of the Scottish Parliament or the National Assembly of Wales;]

"ESA Regulations" means the Employment and Support Allowance Regulations 2013;

"expected number of hours per week" has the meaning in regulation 88;

"foster parent" means—

(a) in relation to England, a person with whom a child is placed under the Fostering Services Regulations 2011;

(b) in relation to Wales, a person with whom a child is placed under the Fostering Services (Wales) Regulations 2003;

(c) in relation to Scotland, a foster carer or kinship carer with whom a child is placed under the Looked After Children (Scotland) Regulations 2009;

"grant" has the meaning in regulation 68;

"health care professional" means (except in regulation 98)—

(a) a registered medical practitioner;

(b) a registered nurse; or

(c) an occupational therapist or physiotherapist registered with a regulatory body established by Order in Council under section 60 of the Health Act 1999;

"housing costs element" has the meaning in regulation 25;

"individual threshold" has the meaning in regulation 90(2);

"industrial injuries benefit" means a benefit under Part 5 of the Contributions and Benefits Act;

"ITEPA" means the Income Tax (Earnings and Pensions) Act 2003;

"jobseeker's allowance" means an allowance under the Jobseekers Act 1995 as amended by Part 1 of Schedule 14 to the Act (removing references to an income-based allowance);

"local authority" means—

(a) in relation to England, a county council, a district council, a parish council, a London borough council, the Common Council of the City of London or the Council of the Isles of Scilly;

(b) in relation to Wales, a county council, a county borough council or a community council;

(c) in relation to Scotland, a council constituted under section 2 of the Local Government etc. (Scotland) Act 1994;

[20 "local welfare provision" means occasional financial or other assistance given by a local authority, the Scottish Ministers or the Welsh Ministers, or a person authorised to exercise any function of, or provide a service to, them, to or in respect of individuals for the purpose of—

(a) meeting, or helping to meet, an immediate short term need—

    (i) arising out of an exceptional event, or exceptional circumstances; and

    (ii) that requires to be met in order to avoid a risk to the well-being of an individual; or

(b) enabling individuals to establish or maintain a settled home, where those individuals have been or, without the assistance, might otherwise be—

    (i) in prison, hospital, a residential care establishment or other institution; or

    (ii) homeless or otherwise living an unsettled way of life;]

[12 "LCWRA element" has the meaning in regulation 27;]

"looked after by a local authority" in relation to a child or young person means a child or young person who is looked after by a local authority within the meaning of section 22 of the Children Act 1989 [10, section 17(6) of the Children (Scotland) Act 1995 or section 74 of the Social Services and Well-being (Wales) Act 2014];

"maternity allowance" means a maternity allowance under section 35 [5 or 35B] of the Contributions and Benefits Act;

"Medical Evidence Regulations" means the Social Security (Medical Evidence) Regulations 1976;

[9 "monthly earnings" has the meaning in regulation 90(6);]

"national insurance contribution" means a contribution under Part 1 of the Contributions and Benefits Act;

[11 "National Minimum Wage Regulations" means the National Minimum Wage Regulations 2015;]

"[8 ...] statutory paternity pay" means [8 ...] statutory paternity pay under Part 12ZA of the Contributions and Benefits Act;

"paid work" means work done for payment or in expectation of payment and does not include being engaged by a charitable or voluntary organisation, or as a volunteer, in circumstances in which the payment received by or due to be paid to the person is in respect of expenses;

"partner" means (except in regulation 77) the other member of a couple;

"personal independence payment" means an allowance under Part 4 of the Welfare Reform Act 2012;

"prisoner" means—

(a) a person who is detained in custody pending trial or sentence upon conviction or under a sentence imposed by a court; or

(b) is on temporary release in accordance with the provisions of the Prison Act 1952 or the Prisons (Scotland) Act 1989, other than a person who is detained in hospital under the provisions of the Mental Health Act 1983 or, in Scotland, under the provisions of the Mental Health (Care and Treatment) (Scotland) Act 2003 or the Criminal Procedure (Scotland) Act 1995;

"qualifying young person" has the meaning in regulation 5;

"redundancy" has the meaning in section 139(1) of the Employment Rights Act 1996;

[6 ...]

"regular and substantial caring responsibilities for a severely disabled person" has the meaning in regulation 30;

"relevant childcare" has the meaning in regulation 35;

"responsible for a child or qualifying young person" has the meaning in regulation 4;

"statutory adoption pay" means a payment under Part 12ZB of the Contributions Benefits Act;

"statutory maternity pay" means a payment under Part 12 of the Contributions and Benefits Act;

[15 "statutory parental bereavement pay" means statutory parental bereavement pay payable in accordance with Part 12ZD of the Contributions and Benefits Act;]

[7 "statutory shared parental pay" means statutory shared parental pay payable in accordance with Part 12ZC of the Contributions and Benefits Act;]

"statutory sick pay" means a payment under Part 11 of the Contributions and Benefits Act;

[13 "step-parent", in relation to a child or qualifying young person ("A"), means a person who is not A's parent but—

(a) is a member of a couple, the other member of which is a parent of A, where both are responsible for A; or

(b) was previously a member of a couple, the other member of which was a parent of A, where immediately prior to ceasing to be a member of that couple the person was, and has since continued to be, responsible for A.]

"student loan" has the meaning in regulation 68;

"terminally ill" means suffering from a progressive disease where death in consequence of that disease can reasonably be expected within [19 12 months];

"total outstanding reduction period" has the meaning in regulation 101(5);

"trade dispute" has the meaning in section 244 of the Trade Union and Labour Relations (Consolidation) Act 1992;

"unearned income" has the meaning in Chapter 3 of Part 6;

"war disablement pension" means any retired pay, pension or allowance payable in respect of disablement under an instrument specified in section 639(2) of ITEPA;

[1 ...]

"widowed mother's allowance" means an allowance under section 37 of the Contributions and Benefits Act;

"widowed parent's allowance" means an allowance under section 39A of the Contributions and Benefits Act;

"widow's pension" means a pension under section 39 of the Contributions and Benefits Act.

AMENDMENTS

1. Armed Forces and Reserve Forces Compensation Scheme (Consequential Provisions: Subordinate Legislation) Order 2013 (SI 2013/591) art.7 and Sch., para.54 (April 8, 2013).

2. Universal Credit (Miscellaneous Amendments) Regulations 2013 (SI 2013/803) reg.2(1) and (2) (April 29, 2013).

3. Social Security (Miscellaneous Amendments) (No.2) Regulations 2013 (SI 2013/1508) reg.3(1) and (2) (October 29, 2013).

4. Universal Credit and Miscellaneous Amendments Regulations 2014 (SI 2014/597) reg.2(1) and (2) (April 28, 2014).

5. Social Security (Maternity Allowance) (Miscellaneous Amendments) Regulations 2014 (SI 2014/884) reg.6(1) (May 18, 2014).

6. Universal Credit and Miscellaneous Amendments (No.2) Regulations 2014 (SI 2014/2888) reg.3(1)(a) (Assessment periods beginning on or after November 26, 2014).

7. Shared Parental Leave and Statutory Shared Parental Pay (Consequential Amendments to Subordinate Legislation) Order 2014 (SI 2014/3255) art.28(1) and (2)(c) (December 31, 2014).

8. Shared Parental Leave and Statutory Shared Parental Pay (Consequential Amendments to Subordinate Legislation) Order 2014 (SI 2014/3255) art.28(1) and (2)(a) and (b) (April 5, 2015). The amendments are subject to the transitional provision in art.35 (see below).

9. Universal Credit and Miscellaneous Amendments Regulations 2015 (SI 2015/1754) reg.2 (Assessment periods beginning on or after November 4, 2015).

10. Universal Credit (Care Leavers and Looked After Children) Amendment Regulations 2016 (SI 2016/543) reg.2(1) and (2) (May 26, 2016).

11. Social Security (Jobseeker's Allowance, Employment and Support Allowance and Universal Credit) (Amendment) Regulations 2016 (SI 2016/678) reg.5(1) and (2) (July 25, 2016).

12. Employment and Support Allowance and Universal Credit (Miscellaneous Amendments and Transitional and Savings Provisions) Regulations 2017 (SI 2017/204) reg. 4(1) and (2) (April 3, 2017).

13. Social Security (Restrictions on Amounts for Children and Qualifying Young Persons) Amendment Regulations 2017 (SI 2017/376) reg.2(1) and (2) (April 6, 2017).

14. Social Security (Income-related Benefits) (Updating and Amendment) (EU Exit) Regulations 2019 (SI 2019/872) reg.8(1) and (2) (May 7, 2019).

15. Parental Bereavement Leave and Pay (Consequential Amendments to Subordinate Legislation) Regulations 2020 (SI 2020/354) reg.28(1) and (2) (April 6, 2020).

16. Immigration and Social Security Co-ordination (EU Withdrawal) Act 2020 (Consequential, Saving, Transitional and Transitory Provisions) (EU Exit) Regulations 2020 (SI 2020/1309) reg.75(1) and (2) (December 31, 2020 at 11.00 pm).

17. Social Security (Scotland) Act 2018 (Disability Assistance for Children and Young People) (Consequential Modifications) Order 2021 (SI 2021/786) Sch.11 para.2 (July 26, 2021).

18. Social Security (Disability Assistance for Working Age People) (Consequential Amendments) Order 2022 (SI 2022/177) reg.13(2) (March 21, 2022).

19. Universal Credit and Employment and Support Allowance (Terminal Illness) (Amendment) Regulations 2022 (SI 2022/460) reg.2(1) (April 4, 2022).

20. Universal Credit (Local Welfare Provision Disregard) (Amendment) Regulations 2022 (SI 2022/448) reg.2 (May 4, 2022).

DEFINITIONS

"child"—see WRA 2012 s.40.
"couple"—see WRA 2012 ss.39 and 40.

"disabled"—see WRA 2012 s.40.
"qualifying young person"—see WRA 2012 ss.40 and 10(5).
"work"—see WRA 2012 s.40.

GENERAL NOTE

Most of these definitions are either self-explanatory, or references to definitions in other regulations, or discussed in the commentary to the regulations where the defined terms are used. A number are similar to terms defined for the purposes of IS, JSA and ESA: see further the commentary to reg.2(1) of the ESA Regulations 2008 and to reg.2(1) of the IS Regulations and reg.1(2) of the JSA Regulations 1996 in Vol.V.   2.7

The Benefit Unit

Couples

3.—(1) This regulation makes provision in relation to couples, including cases where both members of a couple may be entitled to universal credit jointly without each of them meeting all the basic conditions referred to in section 4 of the Act (see paragraph (2)) and cases where a person whose partner does not meet all the basic conditions [¹ or is otherwise excluded from entitlement to universal credit] may make a claim as a single person (see paragraph (3)).   2.8

(2) A couple may be entitled to universal credit as joint claimants where—

(a) one member does not meet the basic condition in section 4(1)
   (b) (under the qualifying age for state pension credit) if the other member does meet that condition; or

(b) one member does not meet the basic condition in section 4(1)(d) (not receiving education) and is not excepted from that condition if the other member does meet that condition or is excepted from it.

(3) A person who is a member of a couple may make a claim as a single person if the other member of the couple—

(a) does not meet the basic condition in section 4(1)(a) (at least 18 years old) and is not a person in respect of whom the minimum age specified in regulation 8 applies;

(b) does not meet the basic condition in section 4(1)(c) (in Great Britain);

(c) is a prisoner; [¹ . . .]

(d) is a person other than a prisoner in respect of whom entitlement does not arise by virtue of regulation 19 (restrictions on entitlement) [; or

(e) is a person to whom section 115 of the Immigration and Asylum Act 1999 (exclusion from benefits) applies,]

and regulations 18 (capital limit), 36 (amount of elements) and 22 (deduction of income and work allowance) provide for the calculation of the award in such cases.

(4) Where two people are parties to a polygamous marriage, the fact that they are husband and wife is to be disregarded if—

(a) one of them is a party to an earlier marriage that still subsists; and

(b) the other party to that earlier marriage is living in the same household,

and, accordingly, the person who is not a party to the earlier marriage may make a claim for universal credit as a single person.

(5) In paragraph (4) "polygamous marriage" means a marriage during which a party to it is married to more than one person and which took place under the laws of a country which permits polygamy.

(6) Where the claimant is a member of a couple, and the other member is temporarily absent from the claimant's household, they cease to be treated as a couple if that absence is expected to exceed, or does exceed, 6 months.

DEFINITIONS

"claim"—see WRA 2012 s.40.
"claimant"—*ibid.*
"prisoner"—see reg.2 as modified by SI 2020/409.
"single person"—see WRA 2012 ss.40 and 1(2)(a).
"couple"—see WRA 2012 ss.39 and 40.

AMENDMENT

1. Universal Credit (Consequential, Supplementary, Incidental and Miscellaneous Provisions) Regulations 2013 (SI 2013/630) reg.8(1) and (2) (April 29, 2013).

GENERAL NOTE

2.9   This regulation is the first of four under the sub-heading, "The Benefit Unit". That phrase is used extensively in departmental guidance (e.g., Chapter E2 of ADM) but is not defined anywhere in WRA 2012 or these Regulations. The Department intends the phrase to mean all the people in a given household who may, or must, be included in a claim for universal credit. That is consistent with these Regulations because identifying those people is also the subject-matter of regs 3–5 inclusive, which appear under the sub-heading.

It is not generally possible for a person who is a member of a couple to claim, or be awarded, universal credit as a single person. By s.2(1) WRA 2012, members of a couple must claim jointly and by s.1(2) any award of benefit is made jointly to both members of the couple. Further, under s.3(2)(a), the basic conditions of entitlement must be met by both members of the couple and, by ss.3(2)(b) and 5(2), whether or not they satisfy the financial conditions is assessed by reference to their combined income and capital.

It is therefore important for claimants to know whether or not they are members of a couple. The word is defined by s.39(1) and (2) WRA 2012 in terms which follow the standard definition for income-related benefits (e.g., in s.137 SSCBA 1992). It covers:

- two people who are married to each other (whether they are of different sexes or the same sex), or are civil partners of each other, and are members of the same household; and

- two people who are not married to, or civil partners of, each other but are living together as a married couple

see further the commentary to reg.2(1) of the IS Regulations in Vol.V. Note also the commentary to para.(6) below as regards temporary absence.

Paragraph (2)

2.10   Under s.4(2) WRA 2012, the Secretary of State has a general power to make regulations which provide for exceptions to the requirement to meet any of the basic conditions for universal credit. In the case of joint claimants, that power can be used to make an exception for one or both of them. Similarly, WRA 2012 Sch.1, para.1 empowers the Secretary of State to make regulations providing for circumstances in which joint claimants may be entitled to universal credit without each of them meeting all the basic conditions referred to in s.4. Those powers have been exercised to make para.(2) (among other regulations).

Under s.4(1)(b) it is a basic condition for universal credit that a person should not have reached the qualifying age for SPC (as defined in s.4(4) and s.1(6) SPCA 2002). However, under para.2(a) a couple may be jointly entitled to universal credit if one member is over that age, as long as the other member is under it. In those circumstances, the couple may be better off if the older member claims SPC. That will depend on a number of circumstances, the most important of which are likely to be whether either member has housing costs or is responsible for a child or qualifying young person. The universal credit rules include a 55% taper for earned income and, in some cases, a "work allowance" (see reg.22) which may well be more generous than the equivalent rules for SPC. However, for universal credit, owner occupiers who have earned income get a higher work allowance but do not get any amount for housing costs as part of universal credit (see para.4 of Sch.5), whereas, under SPC housing costs are paid. A couple where one member is over SPC age, and the other is not, should therefore seek advice about which benefit to claim.

Under s.4(1)(d), it is a basic condition for universal credit that a person should not be "receiving education". For the definition of that phrase, see regs 12 and 13. Note also that by s.4(2) and reg.14 some people are exempt from the condition imposed by s.4(1)(b). The effect of para.(2)(b) is that a couple may be jointly entitled to universal credit even though one member is receiving education (and does not fall within reg.14) as long as the other member is not receiving education (or does fall within reg.14).

Note that couples who fall within para.(2) must still claim universal credit jointly. The exceptions are from the requirement that both should meet the basic conditions, not the requirement for a joint claim.

Paragraph (3)

By contrast, a member of a couple who falls within para.(3) may claim universal   2.11
credit as a single person.

The paragraph is made under s.3(2) WRA 2012 which empowers the Secretary of State to make regulations that "specify circumstances in which a member of a couple may make a claim as a single person". There is no express power to make regulations which disapply the requirement in s.1(2) that universal credit must be awarded jointly where the claimants are members of a couple. However, it is implicit that a member of a couple who may lawfully *claim* universal credit as a single person may also lawfully be *awarded* benefit in that capacity.

Under para.(3) a member of a couple may claim universal credit as a single person if the other member:

- is aged less than 18 (and is not a person who is entitled to claim universal credit from the age of 16 under reg.8): para.(3)(a);

- is not in Great Britain for the purposes of s.4(1)(c) WRA 2012 (see reg.9): para.(3)(b);

- is a prisoner (as defined in reg.2 as modified by SI 2020/409): para.(3)(c).

  (Note that, under reg.19(2), certain prisoners retain entitlement to the housing costs element of universal credit during the first six months of their sentence. However, para.(3)(c) applies whenever the other member of the couple is a prisoner. There is no additional requirement, as there is under para.(3)(d)—which also covers people who fall within reg.19—that the other member of the couple should be excluded from entitlement by that regulation. The implication is that the member of the couple who is not in prison can immediately make a claim as a single person.)

- is a member of a religious order or serving a sentence of imprisonment detained in hospital and excluded from entitlement to universal credit by reg.19: para.(3)(d); or

- is a person subject to immigration control who is excluded from entitlement to benefit under s.115 Immigration and Asylum Act 1999 (see above: para. (3)(e)).

There are special rules for calculating entitlement under claims made by virtue of para.(3). Under reg.36(3) the claimant's maximum amount is calculated using the standard allowance for a single claimant. However, under reg.22(3) the couple's combined income is taken into account when calculating the income to be deducted from that amount. and, under reg.18(2), the claimant's capital is treated as including the capital of the other member of the couple.

Note that the restricted standard allowance under reg.36(3) only applies to a member of a couple who claims as a single person under para.(3). It does *not* affect claims by those who are able to make a joint claim by virtue of para.(2).

Under reg.9(1) of the Claims and Payments Regulations 2013, if a person who is a member of a couple but is entitled to claim as a single person under para.(3), instead makes a joint claim, that claim is treated as made by that person as a single person.

Paragraphs (4) and (5)

2.12   Paragraphs (4) and (5) apply to those in a polygamous marriage. "Polygamous marriage" is defined by para.(5) as "a marriage during which a party to it is married to more than one person and which took place under the laws of a country which permits polygamy". That definition could clearer. A possible interpretation is that once a party to the marriage has been married to more than one person, the marriage is to be treated as polygamous for as long as it lasts (i.e., because it is a marriage "during which" there were, at least for a period, more than two members). However, it is suggested that in the context of the regulation of the whole, that interpretation is not correct. The use of the present tense ("is married") and the provisions made by para.(4)—which can only apply if the marriage has more than two members—indicate that the head (a) of the definition is to be read as meaning that a marriage is polygamous *during any period in which* a party to it is married to more than one person. In other words, the definition preserves the distinction, which applies elsewhere in social security law, between a marriage that is actually polygamous and one that is only potentially polygamous, so that where neither party is actually married to more than one person, the marriage is not polygamous for universal credit purposes.

For the definition to apply, the party who is married to more than one person must be legally married to them under the law of England and Wales or the law of Scotland (as the case may be). This can raise complex issues of private international law: see further the commentary to the Social Security and Family Allowances (Polygamous Marriages) Regulations 1975 (SI 1975/561) in Vol.I and s.4 of Ch.17 of Dicey, Morris & Collins *The Conflict of Laws* 16th edn (Sweet & Maxwell, London, 2022).

The effect of para.(4) is that where a marriage is actually polygamous, and at least three members of that marriage live in the same household, the parties to the earlier or earliest marriage are treated as a couple and all other members of the marriage may make a claim for universal credit as a single person. Where such member of the marriage actually makes a joint claim with another member, that claim is treated as a claim made by that member as a single person (reg.9(2) and (3) of the Claims and Payments Regulations 2013).

Paragraph (6)

2.13   At first sight, the drafting of para.6 is puzzling. It seems to draw a distinction between the member of the couple who is "the claimant" who, it is implied, is the head of "the claimant's household" and that person's partner who is "the other member", when, as noted above, the structure of universal credit is that if a claim is to be made by a member of a couple, *both* parties must normally be *joint* claimants. However, WRA 2012, s.40, defines "claimant" as including "each of joint claimants". Therefore, the effect of para.(6) is that when either member of the couple is temporarily absent from the household, they cease to be treated as a couple if the absence is expected to last, or actually lasts, for more than six months.

Relationship formation and breakdown

TCA 2002 s.3, which requires couples to make a joint claim for tax credits, contains an express provision (s.3(4)), that entitlement to tax credits ceases if the claim was made by a couple and the members of that couple split up ("could no longer make a joint claim") or if, in the case of a single claim, the claimant becomes a member of a couple ("could no longer make a single claim"). By contrast, WRA 2012 does not include any such provision relating to universal credit. Various provisions in these Regulations and of the Claims and Payments Regulations 2013 *assume* that a joint award comes to an end when a couple separate and that an award to a single claimant ends if the claimant becomes a member of a couple. However, it is not permissible to interpret primary legislation on the basis of assumptions made in the secondary legislation made under it. It is more persuasive that the same assumption is made by WRA 2012, Sch.1, para.3(2), but even that paragraph empowers the Secretary of State to make regulations about what happens *if* an award of universal credit comes to an end because of a relationship change, rather than saying that is automatically the case. **2.14**

One can argue that it is inherent in the concept of a joint award to a couple, that it should come to an end if that couple no longer exists. But if that is the case, why was it felt necessary to make express provision for the situation in TCA 2002? And, when one thinks about it further, it becomes less and less clear why—in the absence of any provision equivalent to s.3(4) TCA 2002—ceasing to be a couple, or becoming one, should not be treated like any other change of circumstances, like a change of address, or a change in the amount of income or capital, rather than as a change which brings the award of benefit to an end irrespective of the circumstances of the claimants after that change. The rules in reg.9(6)-(8) and (10) of the Claims and Payments Regulations (which dispense with the need for a fresh claim where people who have been awarded universal credit become, or cease to be, members of a couple) and reg.21(3)-(3B) (under which new awards of universal credit in such cases adopt the assessment periods of the old awards) mean that, in practice, that will often be the effect of relationship formation and breakdown, even though, formally, the regulations assume that a previous entitlement to universal credit comes to an end in such circumstances.

When a person is responsible for a child or qualifying young person

4.—(1) Whether a person is responsible for a child or qualifying young person for the purposes of Pt 1 of the Act and these Regulations is determined as follows. **2.15**

(2) A person is responsible for a child or qualifying young person who normally lives with them.

(3) But a person is not responsible for a qualifying young person if the two of them are living as a couple.

(4) Where a child or qualifying young person normally lives with two or more persons who are not a couple, only one of them is to be treated as responsible and that is the person who has the main responsibility.

(5) The persons mentioned in paragraph (4) may jointly nominate which of them has the main responsibility but the Secretary of State may determine that question—

(a) in default of agreement; or

(b) if a nomination or change of nomination does not, in the opinion of the Secretary of State, reflect the arrangements between those persons.

(6) [¹ Subject to regulation 4A,] a child or qualifying young person is to be treated as not being the responsibility of any person during any period when the child or qualifying young person is—

(a) looked after by a local authority; or

(b) a prisoner,

[¹ . . .]

(7) Where a child or qualifying young person is temporarily absent from a person's household the person ceases to be responsible for the child or qualifying young person if—

(a) the absence is expected to exceed, or does exceed, 6 months; or

(b) the absence is from Great Britain and is expected to exceed, or does exceed, one month unless it is in circumstances where an absence of a person for longer than one month would be disregarded for the purposes of regulation 11(2) or (3) (medical treatment or convalescence or death of close relative etc.).

DEFINITIONS

"the Act"—see reg.2.
"child"—see WRA 2012 s.40.
"couple"—see WRA 2012 ss.39 and 40.
"looked after by a local authority"—see reg.2.
"qualifying young person"—see WRA 2012 s.40 and 10(5) and regs 2 and 5.

AMENDMENT

1. Social Security (Miscellaneous Amendments) (No.2) Regulations 2013 (SI 2013/1508) reg.3(1) and (3) (July 29, 2013).

GENERAL NOTE

2.16   Whether or not a claimant is responsible for a child or qualifying young person is relevant to their maximum amount under Pt 4, to the level of any work allowance under reg.22 and to the imposition of work-related requirements under Pt 8.

Paragraphs (1)–(5)

2.17   The general rule is that a person is responsible for a child or qualifying young person who normally lives with them (para.(2)) unless (in the case of a qualifying young person) the two of them are living together as a couple (para.(3)).

Where a child or qualifying young person normally lives with two people who are a couple, both members of the couple are responsible for him or her (because that is the effect of para.(2) and no other rule applies).

However, where he or she lives with two or more persons who are not a couple, only one of them is to be treated as responsible and that is the person who has the main responsibility for him or her (para.(4)). In those circumstances, the people with whom the child or qualifying young person lives may agree which of them has the main responsibility. However, the Secretary of State may overrule that agreement, if in his opinion, it does not reflect the arrangements those people have made (i.e., for the care of the child or qualifying young person) (para.(5)(b)). The Secretary of State may also decide who has main responsibility if the people with whom the child or qualifying young person lives do not agree who has the main responsibility (para.(5)(a)).

The application of para.(4) was considered by the Upper Tribunal (Judge Wikeley) in *MC v SSWP (UC)* [2018] UKUT 44 (AAC). In that case, the claimant was the father of a daughter who—to put the matter neutrally—stayed overnight and took her meals at her godparent's home for 12 days a fortnight. She did so to facilitate her attendance at a college near the godparent's house. However, the daughter spent every other weekend with the claimant and he contributed the cost of her keep and was responsible for all other aspects of her upbringing. Judge Wikeley rejected Departmental guidance to the effect that "a child or qualifying young person normally lives with a person where they spend more time with that person than anyone else" in favour of a "more holistic approach" in which the proportion of time spent living with an adult was a factor to be taken into consideration but was not necessarily determinative. Paras (2) and (4) established a two-stage test for first identifying who the child or young person normally lives with, and then ascribing main responsibility if more than one adult is involved. On the facts of *MC*, Judge Wikeley decided that the daughter was "normally living" with both her father and her godparent but that her father had main responsibility for her. As far as the "normally lives with" limb of the two-stage test is concerned, it should be applied with a focus on the *quality* rather than *quantification* of the normality. As regards main responsibility, Judge Wikeley took the view that the guidance at paragraph F1065 of *Advice for decision makers* is "a good starting point". That guidance is in the following terms:

"If the DM [decision maker] is required to determine who has main responsibility they should note that main responsibility is not defined in regulations and should be given the meaning of the person who is normally answerable for, or called to account for the child or young person. In determining who has the main responsibility for a child or young person consideration should be given to:
1. Who the child normally lives with
2. Who makes day to day decisions about the child's welfare including, for example, arranging and taking them to visits to the doctor or dentist or enrolling and taking the child to and from school?
3. Who provides the child with clothing, shoes, toiletries and other items needed for daily use?
4. Who is the main contact for the child's school, doctor and dentist?
5. Who cares for the child when the child is ill?
This list should not be considered exhaustive."

Judge Wikeley also endorsed the approach recommended by Judge Jacobs in *PG v HMRC and NG (TC)* [2016] UKUT 216 (AAC); [2016] AACR 45. That decision relates to child tax credit. However, the statutory test is similar.

Paragraph (6)
Children or qualifying young persons who are being looked after by a local authority or are prisoners (as defined in reg.2) are treated as not being the responsibility of any person. The effect is that the child or qualifying young person is disregarded for the purposes of reg.22, Pt 4 and Pt 8 even if he or she normally lives with the claimant or claimants.   **2.18**

However, para.(6) is subject to reg.4A, so that the child or qualifying young person is not treated as not being the responsibility of any person during any period in which he or she is being looked after by a local authority and either:

- his or her absence is "in the nature of a planned short term break, or is one of a series of such breaks, for the purpose of providing respite for the person who normally cares for" him or her; or

- (though being formally looked after by a local authority) the child or qualifying young person is placed with, or continues to live with, their parent or a person who has parental responsibility for them. For the definition of parental responsibility, see reg.4A(2).

Paragraph (7)
Paragraph 7 deals with the temporary absence of a child or qualifying young person from a claimant's (or the claimants') household. In those circumstances, the person who was previously responsible for the child or qualifying young person ceases to be so as soon as the absence is expected to exceed six months or if, unexpectedly,   **2.19**

it actually exceeds six months (para.7(a)). That period is reduced to one month if the child or qualifying young person is also absent from Great Britain unless that absence would be disregarded under reg.11(1) by virtue of reg.11(2) or (3).

[¹ Responsibility for children looked after by a local authority

2.20   **4A.**—(1) There is excluded from regulation 4(6)(a)—

(a) any period which is in the nature of a planned short term break, or is one of a series of such breaks, for the purpose of providing respite for the person who normally cares for the child or qualifying young person;

(b) any period during which the child or qualifying young person is placed with, or continues to live with, their parent or a person who has parental responsibility for them.

(2) For the purposes of this regulation, a person has parental responsibility if they are not a foster parent and—

(a) in England and Wales, they have parental responsibility within the meaning of section 3 of the Children Act 1989; or

(b) in Scotland, they have any or all of the legal responsibilities or rights described in sections 1 or 2 of the Children (Scotland) Act 1995.]

AMENDMENT

1. Social Security (Miscellaneous Amendments) (No.2) Regulations 2013 (SI 2013/1508) reg.3(1) and (4) (July 29, 2013).

DEFINITIONS

"child"—see WRA 2012 s.40.
"qualifying young person"—see WRA 2012 ss.40 and 10(5) and regs 2 and 5.
"looked after by a local authority"—see reg.2.
"local authority"—*ibid*.

GENERAL NOTE

2.21   See the general note to reg.4(6) above.

Meaning of "qualifying young person"

2.22   **5.**—(1) A person who has reached the age of 16 but not the age of 20 is a qualifying young person for the purposes of Part 1 of the Act and these Regulations—

(a) up to, but not including, the 1st September following their 16th birthday; and

(b) up to, but not including, the 1st September following their 19th birthday, if they are enrolled on, or accepted for, approved training or a course of education—

(i) which is not a course of advanced education,

(ii) which is provided at a school or college or provided elsewhere but approved by the Secretary of State, and

(iii) where the average time spent during term time in receiving tuition, engaging in practical work or supervised study or taking examinations exceeds 12 hours per week.

(2) Where the young person is aged 19, they must have started the education or training or been enrolled on or accepted for it before reaching that age.

(3) The education or training referred to in paragraph (1) does not include education or training provided by means of a contract of employment.

218

(4) "Approved training" means training in pursuance of arrangements made under section 2(1) of the Employment and Training Act 1973 or section 2(3) of the Enterprise and New Towns (Scotland) Act 1990 which is approved by the Secretary of State for the purposes of this regulation.

(5) A person who is receiving universal credit, an employment and support allowance or a jobseeker's allowance is not a qualifying young person.

MODIFICATION

With effect from June 16, 2014, reg. 5 is modified by reg. 28 of the Universal Credit (Transitional Provisions) Regulations 2014 (SI 2014/1230) (see Pt IV of this book). The modification applies where a person who would otherwise be a "qualifying young person" within the meaning of reg. 5 is entitled to an "existing benefit" (namely income-based JSA, income-related ESA, income support, housing benefit, child tax credit or working tax credit: see reg.2(1) of SI 2014/1230). The modifications are (i) that such a person is not a qualifying young person for the purposes of the Universal Credit Regulations, and (ii) that reg. 5(5) applies as if, after "a person who is receiving" there were inserted "an existing benefit (within the meaning of the Universal Credit (Transitional Provisions) Regulations 2014),".

DEFINITIONS

"employment and support allowance"—see reg.2.
"jobseeker's allowance"—*ibid.*

GENERAL NOTE

Under s.8(2)(b) and s.10(1) WRA 2012 the calculation of an award of universal credit includes an amount for a qualifying young person for whom the claimant is responsible. Regulation 5 defines who is a qualifying young person. The definition is similar to that which applies for the purposes of child benefit (see by way of comparison regs 3, 7 and 8 of the Child Benefit (General) Regulations 2006 in Vol.IV of this series) but not quite. In particular, the concept of "terminal date" has gone.

2.23

Under reg.5, a person who is aged 16 or over but under 20 counts as a qualifying young person:

(i) up to (but not including) the 1st September following their 16th birthday if they are aged 16; or

(ii) up to (but not including) the 1st September following their 19th birthday if they are aged 16–19 and has been accepted for (or has enrolled on) approved training (defined in para.(4)) or non-advanced education at a school or college (or elsewhere as approved by the Secretary of State; note that in the case of education provided other than at a school or college there is no requirement that the qualifying young person must have been receiving such education before they became 16, as there is for child benefit (see reg.3(3) of the 2006 Regulations in Vol.IV of this series and *JH v HMRC (CHB)* [2015] UKUT 479 (AAC)). In the case of a course of education at least 12 hours on average a week must be spent on tuition, practical work, supervised study or examinations. Meal breaks and unsupervised study are not included. *R(F) 1/93* held that "supervised study" (in reg.5 of the Child Benefit Regulations 1976) "would normally be understood to import the presence or close proximity of a teacher or tutor". If the person is aged 19, they must have started (or been accepted for or enrolled on) the education or training before reaching 19. The education or training must not be provided as part of a contract of employment.

But note that if a person is receiving universal credit, new style ESA or new style JSA in their own right, they cannot be a qualifying young person (para.(5)). Note also the modification to para.(5) in reg. 28 of SI 2014/1230 referred to above, which has the effect that if the person is receiving income-based JSA, income-related ESA, income support, housing benefit, child tax credit or working tax credit they are not a qualifying young person.

See also reg.12(1) which provides that if a person is a qualifying young person they are regarded as receiving education and so will not meet the basic condition in s.4(1)(d) WRA 2012 (unless they come within one of the exceptions to this requirement in reg.14).

Rounding

2.24   **6.**—(1) Where the calculation of an amount for the purposes of these Regulations results in a fraction of a penny, that fraction is to be disregarded if it is less than half a penny and otherwise it is to be treated as a penny.

[¹ (1A) Where the calculation of an amount for the purposes of the following [³ provisions] results in a fraction of a pound, that fraction is to be disregarded—

[² (za) regulation 82(1)(a) (exceptions – earnings);]
(a) regulation 90 (claimants subject to no work-related requirements – the earnings thresholds); and
(b) regulation 99(6) (circumstances in which requirements must not be imposed) [³[⁴ . . .] and
(c) [⁴ . . .].]

(2) This regulation does not apply to the calculation in regulation 111 (daily rate for a reduction under section 26 or 27 of the Act).

AMENDMENTS

1. Universal Credit and Miscellaneous Amendments Regulations 2015 (SI 2015/1754), reg.4 (November 4, 2015, or in the case of existing awards, the first assessment period beginning on or after November 4, 2015).

2. Universal Credit (Benefit Cap Earnings Exception) Amendment Regulations 2017 (SI 2017/138) reg.2(2) (April 1, 2017).

3. Universal Credit (Housing Costs Element for claimants aged 18 to 21) (Amendment) Regulations 2017 (SI 2017/252) reg.2(2) (April 1, 2017).

4. Universal Credit and Jobseeker's Allowance (Miscellaneous Amendments) Regulations 2018 (SI 2018/1129) reg.3(2) (December 31, 2018).

DEFINITION
"the Act"—see reg.2.

PART 2

ENTITLEMENT

Introduction

2.25   **7.** This Part contains provisions about—
(a) the requirement to meet the basic conditions in section 4 of the Act, including exceptions from that requirement;
(b) the maximum amount of capital and the minimum amount of universal credit for the financial conditions in section 5 of the Act; and

(c) cases where no entitlement to universal credit arises even if the basic conditions and the financial conditions are met.

DEFINITION

"the Act"—see reg.2.

Minimum age

Cases where the minimum age is 16

8.—(1) For the basic condition in section 4(1)(a) of the Act (at least 18 years old), the minimum age is 16 years old where a person—   2.26
   (a) has limited capability for work;
   (b) is awaiting an assessment under Part 5 to determine whether the person has limited capability for work and has a statement given [2...] in accordance with the Medical Evidence Regulations which provides that the person is not fit for work;
   (c) has regular and substantial caring responsibilities for a severely disabled person;
   (d) is responsible for a child;
   (e) is a member of a couple the other member of which is responsible for a child or a qualifying young person (but only where the other member meets the basic conditions in section 4 of the Act);
   (f) is pregnant, and it is 11 weeks or less before her expected week of confinement, or was pregnant and it is 15 weeks or less since the date of her confinement; or
   (g) is without parental support (see paragraph (3)).
   (2) Sub-paragraphs (c), (f) and (g) of paragraph (1) do not include any person who is a care leaver.
   (3) For the purposes of paragraph (1)(g) a young person is without parental support where that person is not being looked after by a local authority and—
   (a) has no parent;
   (b) cannot live with their parents because—
       (i) the person is estranged from them, or
       (ii) there is a serious risk to the person's physical or mental health, or that the person would suffer significant harm if the person lived with them; or
   (c) is living away from their parents, and neither parent is able to support the person financially because that parent—
       (i) has a physical or mental impairment,
       (ii) is detained in custody pending trial or sentence upon conviction or under a sentence imposed by a court, or
       (iii) is prohibited from entering or re-entering Great Britain.
   (4) In this regulation—
   "parent" includes any person acting in the place of a parent;
   "care leaver" means—
   (a) in relation to England [1 ...], an eligible child for the purposes of paragraph 19B of Schedule 2 to the Children Act 1989 or a relevant child for the purposes of section 23A of that Act;

[¹ (b) in relation to Scotland, a person under the age of 18 who—
   (i) is looked after by a local authority; or
   (ii) has ceased to be looked after by a local authority but is a person to whom a local authority in Scotland is obliged to provide advice and assistance in terms of section 29(1) of the Children (Scotland) Act 1995 or a person who is being provided with continuing care under section 26A of that Act,
   and who, since reaching the age of 14 has been looked after by a local authority for a period of, or periods totalling, 3 months or more (excluding any period where the person has been placed with a member of their family);
(c) in relation to Wales, a category 1 young person or category 2 young person within the meaning of section 104(2) of the Social Services and Well-being (Wales) Act 2014.]
"confinement" means—
(a) labour resulting in the birth of a living child; or
(b) labour after 24 weeks of pregnancy resulting in the birth of a child whether alive or dead,
   and where a woman's labour begun on one day results in the birth of a child on another day she is to be taken to be confined on the date of the birth.

Amendments

1. Universal Credit (Care Leavers and Looked After Children) Amendment Regulations 2016 (SI 2016/543) reg.2(3) (May 26, 2016).
2. Social Security (Medical Evidence) and Statutory Sick Pay (Medical Evidence) (Amendment) (No.2) Regulations 2022 (SI 2022/630) reg.4(3)(a) (July 1, 2022).

Definitions

"the Act"—see reg.2.
"child"—see WRA 2012, s.40.
"limited capability for work"—see WRA 2012, ss.40 and 37(1).
"local authority"—see reg.2.
"looked after by a local authority"—*ibid.*
"Medical Evidence Regulations"— *ibid.*
"qualifying young person"—see regs 2 and 5.
"regular and substantial caring responsibilities"—see WRA 2012, s.40 and reg.30.
"responsible for a child or qualifying young person"—see reg.4.

General Note

2.27   One of the basic conditions for entitlement to universal credit is that the claimant must be at least 18 years old (s.4(1)(a) WRA 2012). Regulation 8 provides for the exceptions to that rule.

Under para.(1) a person aged 16 or 17 (who satisfies the other basic conditions) can qualify for universal credit if they:
(a) have limited capability for work; or
(b) are waiting for a work capability assessment and have submitted a medical certificate stating that they are not fit for work; or
(c) have "regular and substantial caring responsibilities for a severely disabled person" (see reg.30), but not if they are a "care leaver" (defined in para. (4)); or
(d) are responsible for a child (see reg.4 for when a person is responsible for a child); or

(e) are a member of a couple and the other member satisfies the basic conditions and is responsible for a child or a qualifying young person (see reg.5 for who counts as a qualifying young person); or

(f) are pregnant and it is 11 weeks or less before their expected week of confinement (defined in para.(4)), or was pregnant and it is 15 weeks or less since the date of confinement, but not if they are a care leaver; or

(g) are "without parental support" (defined in para.(3)), but not if they are a care leaver.

In relation to the definition of "care leaver", for who is an "eligible child" for the purposes of para.19B of Sch.2 to the Children Act 1989 or a "relevant child" for the purposes of s.23A of that Act, or a "category 1 young person" or "category 2 young person" within the meaning of s.104(2) of the Social Services and Well-being (Wales) Act 2014, see the Children (Leaving Care) Act 2000 and the notes to that Act in Vol.V of this series.

A care leaver who is aged 16 or 17 is not entitled to a housing costs element for rent payments (see Sch.4, para.4) But note that a person aged 18-21, who was a care leaver before they became 18, is exempt from the "shared accommodation rate" for renters (see para.29(2) of Sch.4).   **2.28**

On para.(1)(g), a young person is "without parental support" if they are not being looked after by a local authority and come within one of the categories listed in para.(3). These categories are similar to those in reg.13(2)(c), (d) and (e) of the Income Support Regulations (see the notes to those provisions in Vol.V of this series). Note the definition of "parent" in para.(4). On para.(3) (b)(ii), para.E1055 of ADM gives examples of "serious risk" as: (i) having a brother or sister who is a drug addict, which poses a risk to the young person who is exposed to the drugs at the parental home; (ii) having a history of mental illness which is made worse by the parent's attitude; or (iii) suffering from chronic bronchitis, which is made worse by the damp conditions of the parent's home.

Note that under reg.3(3)(a) a person who is a member of a couple (and is either 18 or over or falls within para.(1)) but whose partner is under 18 and does not fall within para.(1) can claim universal credit as a single person.

A person is not normally eligible for universal credit if they are receiving education (see s.4(1)(d) WRA 2012). However, see reg.14 for the exceptions.

In Great Britain

Persons treated as not being in Great Britain

9.—(1) For the purposes of determining whether a person meets the basic condition to be in Great Britain, except where a person falls within paragraph (4), a person is to be treated as not being in Great Britain if the person is not habitually resident in the United Kingdom, the Channel Islands, the Isle of Man or the Republic of Ireland.   **2.29**

(2) A person must not be treated as habitually resident in the United Kingdom, the Channel Islands, the Isle of Man or the Republic of Ireland unless the person has a right to reside in one of those places.

(3) For the purposes of paragraph (2), a right to reside does not include a right which exists by virtue of, or in accordance with—

(a) regulation 13 of the EEA Regulations [5 . . .]; [2 . . .]

[2 (aa) regulation 14 of the EEA Regulations(3), but only in cases where the right exists under that regulation because the person is–

    (i) a qualified person for the purposes of regulation 6(1) of those Regulations as a jobseeker; or

    (ii) a family member (within the meaning of regulation 7 of those Regulations) of such a jobseeker; [³ ...]]

  (b) [³ regulation 16] of the EEA Regulations, but only in cases where the right exists under that regulation because [³ the person] satisfies the criteria in [³ regulation 16(5)] of those Regulations [⁵ ...] [³; or]

[³ (c) a person having been granted limited leave to enter, or remain in, the United Kingdom under the Immigration Act 1971 by virtue of—

    (i) Appendix EU to the immigration rules made under section 3(2) of that Act; or [⁶ ...]

    (ii) being a person with a Zambrano right to reside as defined in Annex 1 of Appendix EU to the immigration rules made under section 3(2) of that Act]; [⁶; or]

    [⁶ (iii) having arrived in the United Kingdom with an entry clearance that was granted under Appendix EU (Family Permit) to the immigration rules made under section 3(2) of that Act.]

[⁴ (3A) Paragraph (3)(c)(i) does not apply to a person who—

  (a) has a right to reside granted by virtue of being a family member of a relevant person of Northern Ireland; and

  (b) would have a right to reside under the EEA Regulations if the relevant person of Northern Ireland were an EEA national, provided that the right to reside does not fall within paragraph (3)(a) or (b)]

(4) A person falls within this paragraph if the person is—

[⁷ (za) a person granted leave in accordance with the immigration rules made under section 3(2) of the Immigration Act 1971, where such leave is granted by virtue of—

    (i) the Afghan Relocations and Assistance Policy; or

    (ii) the previous scheme for locally-employed staff in Afghanistan (sometimes referred to as the ex-gratia scheme);

(zb) a person in Great Britain not coming within sub-paragraph (za) or (e)[⁸ ...] who left Afghanistan in connection with the collapse of the Afghan government that took place on 15th August 2021;]

[⁸ (zc) a person in Great Britain who was residing in Ukraine immediately before 1st January 2022, left Ukraine in connection with the Russian invasion which took place on 24th February 2022 and—

    (i) has been granted leave in accordance with immigration rules made under section 3(2) of the Immigration Act 1971; [⁹ ...]

    (ii) has a right of abode in the United Kingdom within the meaning given in section 2 of that Act;] [⁹ or

    (iii) does not require leave to enter or remain in the United Kingdom in accordance with section 3ZA of that Act;]]

  (a) a qualified person for the purposes of regulation 6 of the EEA Regulations as a worker or a self-employed person;

  (b) a family member of a person referred to in sub-paragraph (a) [⁴ ...];

  (c) a person who has a right to reside permanently in the United Kingdom by virtue of regulation 15(1)(c), (d) or (e) of the EEA Regulations;

[⁴ (ca) a family member of a relevant person of Northern Ireland, with a right to reside which falls within paragraph (3)(c)(i), provided that the relevant person of Northern Ireland falls within paragraph (4)(a), or would do so but for the fact that they are not an EEA national;]

[⁵ (cb) a frontier worker within the meaning of regulation 3 of the Citizens'
   Rights (Frontier Workers) (EU Exit) Regulations 2020;
   (cc) a family member of a person referred to in sub-paragraph (cb), who
   has been granted limited leave to enter, or remain in, the United
   Kingdom by virtue of Appendix EU to the immigration rules made
   under section 3(2) of the Immigration Act 1971;]
   (d) a refugee within the definition in Article 1 of the Convention relating
   to the Status of Refugees done at Geneva on 28th July 1951, as
   extended by Article 1(2) of the Protocol relating to the Status of
   Refugees done at New York on 31st January 1967;
[¹(e) a person who has been granted, or who is deemed to have been
   granted, leave outside the rules made under section 3(2) of the
   Immigration Act 1971 [⁸ . . .]
   (f) a person who has humanitarian protection granted under those
   rules; or
   (g) a person who is not a person subject to immigration control within
   the meaning of section 115(9) of the Immigration and Asylum Act
   1999 and who is in the United Kingdom as a result of their deportation, expulsion or other removal by compulsion of law from another
   country to the United Kingdom.
[⁴ (5) In this regulation—
"EEA national" has the meaning given in regulation 2(1) of the EEA
   Regulations;
"family member" has the meaning given in regulation 7(1)(a), (b) or
   (c) of the EEA Regulations, except that regulation 7(4) of the EEA
   Regulations does not apply for the purposes of paragraphs (3A) and
   (4)(ca);
"relevant person of Northern Ireland" has the meaning given in Annex 1
   of Appendix EU to the immigration rules made under section 3(2) of
   the Immigration Act 1971.]

AMENDMENTS

1. Social Security (Miscellaneous Amendments) (No.2) Regulations 2013 (SI
2013/1508) reg.3(1) and (5) (October 29, 2013).
2. Universal Credit (EEA Jobseekers) Amendment Regulations 2015 (SI
2015/546) reg.2 (June 10, 2015).
3. Social Security (Income-related Benefits) (Updating and Amendment) (EU
Exit) Regulations 2019 (SI 2019/872) reg.8(1) and (3) (May 7, 2019).
4. Social Security (Income-Related Benefits) (Persons of Northern Ireland—
Family Members) (Amendment) Regulations 2020 (SI 2020/683), reg.8 (August
24, 2020).
5. Immigration and Social Security Co-ordination (EU Withdrawal) Act
2020 (Consequential, Saving, Transitional and Transitory Provisions) (EU Exit)
Regulations 2020 (SI 2020/1309) reg.75(1) and (3) (December 31, 2020 at 11.00
pm).
6. Immigration (Citizens' Rights etc.) (EU Exit) Regulations 2020 (SI 2020/1372)
reg.25 (immediately after December 31, 2020 at 11.00 pm).
7. Social Security (Habitual Residence and Past Presence) (Amendment)
Regulations 2021 (SI 2021/1034) reg.3 (September 15, 2021).
8. Social Security (Habitual Residence and Past Presence) (Amendment)
Regulations 2022 (SI 2022/344) reg.3 (March 22, 2022).
9. Social Security (Habitual Residence and Past Presence) (Amendment) (No.2)
Regulations 2022 (SI 2022/990), reg.2 (October 18, 2022).

DEFINITION

"EEA Regulations"—see reg.2.

GENERAL NOTE

2.30   Under s.4(1)(c) WRA 2012, it is a basic condition of entitlement to universal credit that the claimant is "in Great Britain" and s.4(5)(a) empowers the Secretary of State to make regulations specifying "circumstances in which a person is to be treated as being, or not being, in Great Britain". Regulation 9 is made under that power. The general rule (para.(1)) is that to be "in Great Britain" a person must be habitually resident in the United Kingdom, the Channel Islands, the Isle of Man or the Republic of Ireland. Apart from people who fall within para.(4), everyone who is not so habitually resident is treated as not being in Great Britain.

The habitual residence test in para.(1) is supplemented by para.(2) which establishes an ancillary right to reside test: no-one may treated as habitually resident in the United Kingdom, the Channel Islands, the Isle of Man or the Republic of Ireland for universal credit purposes unless the person has a right to reside in one of those places, other than a right to reside specified in para.(3).

Following the UK's exit from the EU, the right to reside test only affects EEA nationals with "pre-settled" status under the EU Settlement Scheme (EUSS) in Appendix EU to the Immigration Rules. EEA nationals who wish to continue to live in the UK after December 31, 2020 (technically at 11.00 pm on that date) must apply under the EUSS by June 30, 2021 (subject to limited provision for late applications) or lose their former rights under EU law.

Applicants who can satisfy the Home Office that they meet the criteria in paras EU11 or EU12 of the Appendix, and that they should not be refused on grounds of suitability (paras EU15 and EU16), will be given indefinite leave to remain (also known in this context as "settled status"). Those who have been granted settled status have a right to reside in the UK that counts for the purposes of all income-related benefits: para.(3)(c) does not affect them (because they have not been granted *limited* leave to enter or remain, within that paragraph).

Applicants who do not qualify for settled status (and who are not refused altogether) will be given limited leave to remain for five years (also known as "pre-settled status") if they meet the criteria in para.EU14. Those with pre-settled status may apply for settled status as soon as they meet the criteria in paras EU11 or EU12. That right of residence counts for immigration purposes, but the effect of para.(3)(c)(i) is that it does not count for the purposes of the right to reside test (unless they fall within para.(3A)). However, some of the rights of those with pre-settled status under the former Immigration (European Economic Area) Regulations 2016 are preserved and modified by SI 2020/1309: see the under the heading, *The United Kingdom's withdrawal from the European Union*, in the General Note to those Regulations in Part VII of Vol.V. Those modified rights of residence do potentially count for the purposes of the right to reside test, unless they fall within the other provisions of para.(3).

In *R. (Fratila) v Secretary of State for Work and Pensions* [2021] UKSC 53; [2022] P.T.S.R. 448, the Supreme Court allowed the appeal by the Secretary of State against a decision of the Court of Appeal which had found reg.9(3)(c)(i) unlawfully discriminatory contrary to art.18 of the TFEU for treating EU nationals with pre-settled status differently to UK nationals. The judgment of the Court of Appeal had become unsustainable following the decision of the CJEU, in *CG v Department for Communities* (C-709/20, July 15, 2021) [2021] 1 W.L.R. 5919, that such a provision is not contrary to art.18 of the TFEU, or Directive 2004/38.

However, what the Supreme Court elected not to address (since it was a new point, which would have required new evidence) was the implications for the domestic Regulations of what had also been said in *CG* about the Charter of Fundamental Rights of the European Union (the Charter). The Court of Justice had stated:

"[93] ... [Where] a Union citizen resides legally, on the basis of national law, in the territory of a Member State other than that of which he or she is a national, the national authorities empowered to grant social assistance are required to check that a refusal to grant such benefits based on that legislation does not expose that citizen, and the children for which he or she is responsible, to an actual and current risk of violation of their fundamental rights, as enshrined in Articles 1, 7 and 24 of the Charter. Where that citizen does not have any resources to provide for his or her own needs and those of his or her children and is isolated, those authorities must ensure that, in the event of a refusal to grant social assistance, that citizen may nevertheless live with his or her children in dignified conditions. In the context of that examination, those authorities may take into account all means of assistance provided for by national law, from which the citizen concerned and her children are actually entitled to benefit."

Important unanswered questions arising from *CG* were:

- whether the Charter has any ongoing application, since the end of the transition period in December 2020, for EU nationals resident in the UK on the basis of pre-settled status; and

- what if any substantive or procedural requirements are imposed on the Secretary of State by the obligation to "check" that Charter rights will not be breached.

In *SSWP v AT (UC)* [2022] UKUT 330 (AAC), in response to the first issue, a three-judge panel of the UT decided that the Charter does continue to confer enforceable rights on individuals. In response to the second question, it held that in order for reg.9(3)(c)(i) of the Universal Credit Regulations 2013 to be compatible with the UK's enforceable Withdrawal Agreement obligations, the Secretary of State had to be satisfied in individual cases that a claimant's right to reside in dignity was not breached. In AT's own case, her dignity right was breached by a period of time living on very meagre resources in a hostel with her small child, having fled domestic violence, dependent on charity, the local authority having declined to give significant support. As a result, reg.9(3)(c)(i) had to be disapplied in her case, with the effect that she was entitled to UC.

The Secretary of State appealed to the Court of Appeal; judgment is awaited.

Note the special rules for family members of a "relevant person of Northern Ireland" in paras.(3A) and (4)(ca). That phrase is defined by Annex 1 of Appendix EU to the Immigration Rules as:

"a person who:
 (a) is:
   (i) a British citizen; or
   (ii) an Irish citizen; or
   (iii) a British citizen and an Irish citizen; and
 (b) was born in Northern Ireland and, at the time of the person's birth, at least one of their parents was:
   (i)   a British citizen; or
   (ii) an Irish citizen; or
   (iii) a British citizen and an Irish citizen; or
   (iv) otherwise entitled to reside in Northern Ireland without any restriction on their period of residence"

For the "Zambrano right to reside" referred to in para.(3)(c)(ii), see under the heading, *Carers of British citizens*, in the General Note to reg.16 of the former Immigration (European Economic Area) Regulations 2016 in Part VII of Vol.V of this series.

Habitual residence

2.31   The requirement to be habitually resident only applies to the claimant, not to a partner or dependant.

"Habitual residence" is not defined in the regulation but case law since 1994 has established that, except in cases where EU citizens are exercising their transitional rights (see Vol.V), to be habitually resident in the CTA, a claimant must:

- have a settled intention to reside here; and

- have been "[resident] in fact for a period that shows that the residence has become 'habitual' and . . . will or is likely to continue to be habitual"

see *Nessa v Chief Adjudication Officer* [1999] 1 W.L.R. 1937; [1999] 4 All E.R. 677, HL (also reported as *R(IS) 2/00*). Whether that legal test is satisfied so that a person is habitually resident is a question of fact to be decided by reference to all the circumstances in each case (*Re J*).

2.32   The period of residence that is necessary is usually referred to as the "appreciable period" in accordance with the use of that phrase by Lord Bridge of Harwich in *Re J (A Minor) (Abduction: Custody Rights)* [1990] 2 A.C. 562; [1990] 2 All E.R. 961 HL:

> "In considering this issue it seems to me to be helpful to deal first with a number of preliminary points. The first point is that the expression 'habitually resident' . . . is nowhere defined. It follows, I think, that the expression is not to be treated as a term of art with some special meaning, but is rather to be understood according to the ordinary and natural meaning of the two words which it contains. The second point is that the question whether a person is or is not habitually resident in a specified country is a question of fact to be decided by reference to all the circumstances of any particular case. The third point is that there is a significant difference between a person ceasing to be habitually resident in country A, and his subsequently becoming habitually resident in country B. A person may cease to be habitually resident in country A in a single day if he or she leaves it with a settled intention not to return to it but to take up long-term residence in country B instead. Such a person cannot, however, become habitually resident in country B in a single day. An appreciable period of time and a settled intention will be necessary to enable him or her to become so. During that appreciable period of time the person will have ceased to be habitually resident in country A but not yet have become habitually resident in country B. The fourth point is that, where a child of J.'s age is in the sole lawful custody of the mother, his situation with regard to habitual residence will necessarily be the same as hers."

Habitual residence is not the same as domicile (*R(U) 8/88*). It is possible to be habitually resident in more than one country although it is unusual (*R(IS) 2/00*, para.20); it is also possible to be habitually resident in none.

Habitual residence can continue during absences of long or short duration.

The increasing complexity of reg.9(4) chronicles the legislator's Sisyphean attempts to avoid the hardships which would be caused by a blanket application of the habitual residence test. A further recent example is the Social Security (Habitual Residence and Past Presence) (Amendment) Regulations 2023 (SI 2023/532), exempting people who fled Sudan following violence in April 2023. (In force from May 15, 2023, those regulations post-date the cut-off point for this edition so are not shown in the main text.)

The habitual residence test dates from 1994, when it was the primary immigration-related gateway to benefit entitlement. That is no longer the case. Partly that is due to s.115 Immigration and Asylum Act 1999, which excludes "persons subject to immigration control" from entitlement to most benefits. Partly it is due to the rigours (since 2004) of the "right to reside" test, textually incorporated into the habitual residence test, but operating conceptually distinctly.

It might be questioned whether the requirement to have actual "habitual residence" in itself continues to serve its originally intended purpose. It was a measure to combat "benefit tourism", but few foreign nationals making a temporary trip to the UK are likely to enter with a right of residence conferring entitlement to receive public funds.

"Settled intention" and "appreciable period of time"

The two limbs of the habitual residence test, a settled intention and an appreciable period of time, are difficult to analyse separately. This is because the two are closely linked: the overall question is whether "in all the circumstances, including the settledness of the person's intentions as to residence, the residence has continued for a sufficient period for it to be said to be habitual" *(R(IS) 2/00)*. So, if there is a doubt about the claimant's intention to reside in the UK, it may require a longer period of residence to resolve that doubt. Similarly, where a person's circumstances are such that s/he clearly intends to make a home in the UK, it may be possible to say that s/he has become habitually resident after a relatively short period of time. There is thus no minimum "appreciable period": the length of the period required will depend upon all the circumstances of the individual case.

The intention to reside here does not need to be permanent or indefinite. It can be for a limited period. To be resident a person had to be seen to be making a "genuine home for the time being" here but it need not be his only home or a permanent one *(R(IS) 6/96)*. (Actual residence in two places is perfectly possible: *R(IS) 9/99*.) Some of the relevant factors in judging intention will include the reason for coming (or returning) here, the location of his/her possessions and family, where s/he has previously worked, the length and purpose of any absence from the UK, etc.

If the claimant's intention is conditional, e.g. on benefit being awarded, this is not a settled intention to stay *(CIS/12703/1996)*.

The leading case on the requirement for an appreciable period is the decision of the House of Lords in *Nessa* [1999] 1 W.L.R. 1937. Mrs Nessa came to the UK in August 1994, aged 55. She had previously lived all her life in Bangladesh. Her father-in-law, in whose house she had been living, had died and she had come to the UK for the emotional support of her late husband's brother and his family. Her husband had lived and worked in the UK until his death in 1975 and she had a right of abode here. She claimed income support in September 1994.

The Commissioner *(R(IS) 2/00)* and a majority of the Court of Appeal followed *Re J* and held that in order to establish habitual residence it was necessary for a claimant not only to have been in the UK voluntarily, and for settled purposes, but also to have fulfilled those conditions for an appreciable period of time. However, the Court of Appeal considered that the appreciable period need not be particularly long. The dissenting judge (Thorpe LJ) considered that Lord Brandon's comments in *Re J* were clearly obiter and that an appreciable period was not an essential ingredient of habitual residence. In his view the adjective "habitual" ensured that "the connection [to the country] is not transitory or temporary but enduring and the necessary durability can be judged prospectively in exceptional cases".

Mrs Nessa appealed again to the House of Lords which unanimously upheld the majority in the Court of Appeal. Lord Slynn of Hadley, with whom all the other judges agreed, reviewed the authorities discussed above and stated:

> "With the guidance of these cases it seems to me plain that as a matter of ordinary language a person is not habitually resident in any country unless he has taken up residence and lived there for a period. . . . If Parliament had intended that a person seeking to enter the United Kingdom or such a person declaring his intention to settle here is to have income support on arrival, it could have said so. It seems to me impossible to accept the argument at one time advanced that a person who has never been here before who says on landing, 'I intend to settle in the United Kingdom' and who is fully believed is automatically a person who is habitually resident here. Nor is it enough to say I am going to live at X or with Y. He must show residence in fact for a period which shows that the residence has become 'habitual' and, as I see it, will or is likely to continue to be habitual."

2.33

2.34

Lord Slynn did accept that there might be "special cases where the person concerned is not coming here for the first time, but is resuming an habitual residence previously had . . . On such facts the Adjudication Officer may or of course may not be satisfied that the previous habitual residence has been resumed. This position is quite different from that of someone coming to the United Kingdom for the first time." Although *Swaddling* (see below) was cited by Lord Slynn as one example of this type of case the exception seems to be considerably narrower than the principle of Community law established by that case, namely that the length of residence in a Member State could not be regarded as an intrinsic element of the concept of habitual residence where a claimant comes within Regulation 1408/71. Lord Slynn appears to be saying no more than that in some cases it will be possible to say on the facts that a returning resident is merely resuming a habitual residence which has already been established. The reference to the possibility that the AO (now decision-maker) "may not be satisfied" clearly indicates that this will not always be the case and that some returning residents will need to re-establish habitual residence by living in the CTA for a period of time.

How long is the appreciable period?

2.35   Lord Slynn's opinion also contains interesting observations on how long the appreciable period of time should be. Whilst recognising that the period is not fixed and "may be longer where there are doubts", he also stated that "it may be short" and quoted with approval the statement of Butler Sloss LJ in *Re F (A Minor) (Child Abduction)* [1994] F.L.R. 548, at 555 that "A month can be . . . an appreciable period of time". He also agreed with the Commissioner that there were factors which indicated that habitual residence had been established in Mrs Nessa's case, "even by the date of the tribunal hearing *or as I see it, even earlier*" (emphasis added). At the date of her tribunal hearing on December 6, 1994, Mrs Nessa had been in the UK for 15 weeks.

It must be stressed that the House of Lords clearly regarded this issue as one to be determined by tribunals on the facts of individual cases; however the view of the Commissioner in *R(IS)* 6/96 that the establishment of habitual residence would normally require residence of at least some months must now be read in the light of Lord Slynn's comments.

As the issue of what is an "appreciable period" is one of fact and degree, and the decisions highlighted by Commissioners for wider circulation normally concern issues of law, there are few public examples of how the Commissioners approach that issue when exercising their discretion under s.14(8)(a) of SSA 1998. However, post-*Nessa* examples can be found in *CIS/1304/1997* and *CJSA/5394/1998* and in *CIS/376/2002*, all of which involved returning residents.

2.36   In the former decision, guidance was given that in a typical case tribunals should conduct a three-stage enquiry into: (i) the circumstances in which the claimant's earlier habitual residence was lost; (ii) the links between the claimant and the UK while abroad; and (iii) the circumstances of his return to the UK. So, for example, if the claimant's departure from the UK was temporary (albeit long-term) or conditional or if habitual residence was lost only as a result of events which occurred after the claimant's departure, those would be factors favouring a resumption of habitual residence immediately on return. On the facts of those appeals, the Commissioner held that the claimants, both British nationals who—as was accepted—had previously been habitually resident here, but had lost that habitual residence during an extended period of absence abroad, nevertheless resumed their previous habitual residence on the very day of their return to Britain. The relevant extracts from *CIS/1304/1997* and *CJSA/5394/1998* were reissued as an Appendix to *CIS/4474/2003* (see below).

By contrast the claimant in *CIS/376/2002*, a naturalised British citizen who had worked in Britain for many years but had spent no more than 11 months here in the five years before the claims for benefit which were under consideration, was held not to have become habitually resident immediately. Commissioner Howell Q.C. accepted the tribunal's finding that although the claimant had been habitually resident in the past he had ceased to be so over that five-year period, but rejected the tribunal's doubts about whether he had a settled intention to remain here. On that basis, the Commissioner held that the claimant had not been resident for an appreciable period of time when his claim for IS was made (some three days after his arrival) but had become habitually resident by the date of the decision on that claim approximately five weeks later. In reaching his decision the Commissioner denied the possibility that a claimant who had lost his or her habitual residence could resume it immediately without first being present for an appreciable period of time. He stated (at para.12):

"Everything therefore depends on what counts as an 'appreciable period' of resumed residence in this context so that his residence in the United Kingdom can be said to have become established as habitual . . . As has been said many times in the cases where judges from the House of Lords down to more humble levels have had to struggle with the meaning of this expression, this is ultimately a question of fact and degree, depending on the individual circumstances of each case, and there are no hard and fast rules to apply. For a returning citizen of this country coming back to live here again after a period of residence overseas . . . the period may be short: as little as a month or so. But it is not zero or minimal, since even a returning expatriate may change his plans again and there is therefore at least some space of time after actual arrival when one simply has to wait and see."

The issue of the length of the appreciable period was also considered by the Commissioner in *CIS/4474/2003*. The Commissioner also noted that the approach taken by Commissioners to that issue had developed since *R(IS) 6/96* and gave the following guidance:

"19. What is an appreciable period depends on the circumstances of the particular case. But I agree with the Secretary of State that in the general run of cases the period will lie between one and three months. *I would certainly require cogent reasons from a tribunal to support a decision that a significantly longer period was required*" (emphasis added).

In *R(IS) 7/06*, the Commissioner indicated his broad agreement with *CIS/ 4474/2003*:   **2.37**

"I am content to accept that, where a claimant is likely to remain in the United Kingdom permanently or for a substantial period of time, the conventional period that must have elapsed between his arrival and his establishing habitual residence is between one month and three months. However, those are not rigid limits. In an exceptional case, a person with a right of abode in the United Kingdom who, although not falling within the scope of regulation 21(3)(d), has been forced to flee another country and is nonetheless able to show a settled intention to remain in the United Kingdom might be accepted as habitually resident after less than a month of residence. Perhaps less exceptionally, a person with no ties to the United Kingdom and making no effort to become established here despite a vague intention to remain might be found not to be habitually resident in the United Kingdom until considerably longer than three months had elapsed."

However, disagreement with that approach was expressed in *CIS/1972/2003* (at para.14):

"I comment only that I have seen tribunals decide on shorter periods than a month and longer periods than three months without being appealed, or appealed successfully. Too much should not be read into the facts of individual decisions or, I suggest, trends in the small number of—usually difficult—cases that Commissioners come to decide on the facts. It does not help when Commissioners' decisions are used to play a forensic game (for it is no more than that) of finding the longest, or the shortest, period endorsed by a Commissioner and then claiming some general rule from it. Parliament could have set a specific time limit. It did not. Advisors cannot seek certainty where it does not exist."

That disagreement was echoed by the Tribunal of Commissioners in *CIS/2559/2005*. The Commissioners stated that:

"The relevant period of residence required to support evidence of intention is not, in our view, something which can be reduced to a tariff. In so far as the decision of Mr Commissioner Jacobs in *CIS/4474/2003* can be interpreted to the contrary, we take a different view."

2.38 It is suggested that the approach in *CIS/4474/2003* and *R(IS) 7/06* (a reported decision that was subsequently upheld by the Court of Appeal) is to be preferred. Although it is accepted that no two cases are identical and that the decision must always be one of fact and degree in an individual case, justice as between claimants in similar situations requires that there should be some consistency in decision-making: that the appreciable periods of time required by different decision makers, tribunals and Commissioners should at least be "in the same ball park". In the early days of the test, the periods chosen varied wildly from case to case: at that time, many decision-makers—and some tribunals—would have required an appreciable period of at least a year and sometimes more on the facts of *Nessa*, whereas the Commissioner and Lord Slynn considered that Mrs Nessa had become habitually resident in approximately three months or less. In such circumstances, recognising the existence of a conventional period does not involve the imposition of a tariff as long as the period is applied flexibly in each individual case. As Commissioner Jacobs has subsequently said (in *CJSA/1223/2006* and *CJSA/1224/2006*):

"I respectfully agree with the Tribunal of Commissioners in *CIS/2559/2005* . . . that: 'The relevant period of residence required to support evidence of intention is not, in our view, something which can be reduced to a tariff.' I do not understand why the Tribunal thought that my comments might be interpreted as setting a tariff and counsel could not suggest how they might have been so understood. I remain of the view that for most cases an appreciable period is likely to be between one and three months. [Counsel for the Secretary of State] told me that that was the experience of decision-makers and he was not instructed to argue otherwise".

It is suggested that Commissioner Jacobs was surely correct to express the point in *CIS/4474/2003* as being about reasoning: a tribunal may be justified in giving a decision that is outside the normal range of decisions given by tribunals generally, but if so, it should be prepared to explain why.

For an analysis of the process involved in fixing an appreciable period, see *CJSA/1223/2006* and *CJSA/1224/2006*. That decision emphasises the importance of looking at the steps taken by the claimant to integrate him- or herself into the UK during that period.

Viability

2.39 Another issue that has vexed the application of the habitual residence test over the years is that of viability. The starting point is *R(IS) 6/96*, the first Commissioner's decision on the habitual residence test. The Commissioner in that case held that the "appreciable period of time" should be a period which showed "a settled and viable pattern of living here as a resident". Thus the practicality of a person's arrangements for residence had to be considered. In determining whether the plans were viable, the possibility of claiming income support had to be left out of account (although this did not mean that there must be no conceivable circumstances in which a person might need to resort to income support). In reliance on that decision, some decision-makers and tribunals took the view that many people from abroad could never become habitually resident because the mere fact that they had claimed income support showed that their residence was not viable in the sense required by the Commissioner. The requirement of viability certainly contributed towards the phenomenon of very long appreciable periods in the early days of the test that has been referred to above.

However, the law has developed since *R(IS) 6/96*. The Commissioner in *Nessa (R(IS) 2/00)* disagreed with *R(IS) 6/96* to the extent that the viability of a person's residence in the UK, either generally or with or without assistance from public funds, was only one relevant factor among others, to be given the appropriate weight according to the circumstances. In his view *R(IS) 6/96* should not be read as imposing an additional condition that only residence without resort to IS or public assistance was relevant to the *Re J* test.

The approach that whether the claimant's residence in the UK is viable without recourse to public funds is only one factor and not by itself decisive was followed in *CIS/1459/1996* and *CIS/16097/1996*. And in *CIS/4474/2003*, the Commissioner warns against the danger of overemphasising viability as a factor:

"16. The danger of overemphasising viability is this. A claimant needs to establish habitual residence in order to claim an income-related benefit. A claim would not be necessary if the claimant has a guaranteed source of funds sufficient for survival. The danger is that the only claimants who can establish habitual residence will be those who have sufficient access to funds not to need it. That cannot be right. Habitual residence is a test of entitlement, not a bar to entitlement. It must be applied in a way that allows for the possibility of a claimant establishing both habitual residence and an entitlement to income support."

Crown servants and members of Her Majesty's forces posted overseas

10.—(1) The following persons do not have to meet the basic condition to be in Great Britain—   2.40

  (a) a Crown servant or member of Her Majesty's forces posted overseas;

  (b) in the case of joint claimants, the partner of a person mentioned in sub-paragraph (a) while they are accompanying the person on that posting.

(2) A person mentioned in paragraph (1)(a) is posted overseas if the person is performing overseas the duties of a Crown servant or member of Her Majesty's forces and was, immediately before their posting or the first of consecutive postings, habitually resident in the United Kingdom.

(3) In this regulation—

"Crown servant" means a person holding an office or employment under the Crown; and

"Her Majesty's forces" has the meaning in the Armed Forces Act 2006.

DEFINITIONS

"joint claimants"—see WRA 2012 s.40.
"partner"—see reg.2.

GENERAL NOTE

Under s.4(1)(c) WRA 2012, it is a basic condition of entitlement to universal credit that the claimant is "in Great Britain". However s.4(2) empowers the Secretary of State to make regulations that "provide for exceptions to the requirement to meet any of the basic conditions". Regulation 10 is made under that power.   2.41

Crown Servants and members of Her Majesty's forces who are posted overseas (as defined in para.(2)) do not have to meet the basic condition to be in Great Britain.

Neither does the partner of such a Crown Servant or member of Her Majesty's forces, if a joint claim for universal credit is made. However, as it seems probable that a Crown Servant or member of Her Majesty's forces who has been posted overseas will be in full-time work, many such joint claims seem likely to fail on the basis that the financial conditions are not met.

By para.(3), the phrase "Her Majesty's forces" has the meaning in the Armed Forces Act 2006. However, that phrase is not defined in that Act except to the extent that ""Her Majesty's forces" . . . do not include any Commonwealth force" (see s.374). "Commonwealth force" is defined by the same section as meaning "a force of a Commonwealth country".

Temporary absence from Great Britain

2.42

11.—(1) A person's temporary absence from Great Britain is disregarded in determining whether they meet the basic condition to be in Great Britain if—

   (a) the person is entitled to universal credit immediately before the beginning of the period of temporary absence; and
   (b) either—
      (i) the absence is not expected to exceed, and does not exceed, one month, or
      (ii) paragraph (3) or (4) applies.

(2) The period of one month in paragraph (1)(b) may be extended by up to a further month if the temporary absence is in connection with the death of—

   (a) the person's partner or a child or qualifying young person for whom the person was responsible; or
   (b) a close relative of the person, or of their partner or of a child or qualifying young person for whom the person or their partner was responsible,

and the Secretary of State considers that it would be unreasonable to expect the person to return to Great Britain within the first month.

(3) This paragraph applies where the absence is not expected to exceed, and does not exceed, 6 months and is solely in connection with—

   (a) the person undergoing—
      (i) treatment for an illness or physical or mental impairment by, or under the supervision of, a qualified practitioner, or
      (ii) medically approved convalescence or care as a result of treatment for an illness or physical or mental impairment, where the person had that illness or impairment before leaving Great Britain; or
   (b) the person accompanying their partner or a child or qualifying young person for whom they are responsible for treatment or convalescence or care as mentioned in sub-paragraph (a).

(4) This paragraph applies where the absence is not expected to exceed, and does not exceed, 6 months and the person is—

   (a) a mariner; or
   (b) a continental shelf worker who is in a designated area or a prescribed area.

(5) In this regulation—

"continental shelf worker" means a person who is employed, whether under a contract of service or not, in a designated area or a prescribed area in connection with any activity mentioned in section 11(2) of the Petroleum Act 1998;

"designated area" means any area which may from time to time be designated by Order in Council under the Continental Shelf Act 1964 as an area within which the rights of the United Kingdom with respect to the seabed and subsoil and their natural resources may be exercised;

"mariner" means a person who is employed under a contract of service either as a master or member of the crew of any ship or vessel, or in any other capacity on board any ship or vessel where—

(a) the employment in that other capacity is for the purposes of that ship or vessel or its crew or any passengers or cargo or mails carried by the ship or vessel; and

(b) the contract is entered into in the United Kingdom with a view to its performance (in whole or in part) while the ship or vessel is on its voyage;

"medically approved" means certified by a registered medical practitioner;

"prescribed area" means any area over which Norway or any member State [¹ ...] exercises sovereign rights for the purpose of exploring the seabed and subsoil and exploiting their natural resources, being an area outside the territorial seas of Norway or such member State, or any other area which is from time to time specified under section 10(8) of the Petroleum Act 1998;

"qualified practitioner" means a person qualified to provide medical treatment, physiotherapy or a form of treatment which is similar to, or related to, either of those forms of treatment.

AMENDMENT

1. Social Security (Amendment) (EU Exit) Regulations 2019 (SI 2019/128) reg.4 and Sch, para.11 (December 31, 2020 at 11.00 pm).

DEFINITIONS

"child"—see WRA 2012 s.40.
"close relative"—see reg.2.
"partner"—*ibid.*
"prescribed"—see WRA 2012 s.40.
"responsible for a child or qualifying young person"—see regs 2, 4 and 4A.
"qualifying young person"—see WRA 2012 s.40 and 10(5) and regs 2 and 5.

GENERAL NOTE

Under s.4(1)(c) WRA 2012, it is a basic condition of entitlement to universal credit that the claimant is "in Great Britain". However s.4(5)(b) and (c) empowers the Secretary of State to make regulations that specify circumstances in which temporary absence from Great Britain is disregarded (subs.(5)(b)) and modify the application of WRA 2012 in relation to a person who is not in Great Britain but who is entitled to universal credit by virtue of subs.(5)(b) (subs.(5)(c)). Regulation 11 is made under the former power.

2.43

Paragraphs (1) and (2)

The general rule is that a person who is entitled to universal credit retains that entitlement during a temporary absence—for whatever reason—that is not expected to exceed one month and does not in fact exceed that period (para.(1)(b)(i)). By para. (1)(a), there must be an existing entitlement to universal credit for the rule to apply. It might therefore have been thought that it is not possible to claim universal credit for the first time while temporarily absent abroad. However, note that the Secretary of State's guidance for decision makers, *Going Abroad* (<*https://data.parliament.uk/ DepositedPapers/Files/DEP2023-0365/070_Going_Abroad_V8-0.pdf*>) states at p.2:

"If the claimant is abroad when they make a claim for Universal Credit but return within the first assessment period, they will be awarded Universal Credit from the date of declaration..."

The one-month period in para.(1)(b)(i) can be extended by up to a further month in the circumstances set out in para.(2)(a) and (b) if the Secretary of State considers it would be unreasonable to expect the person to return home during the first month.

Paragraphs (3) and (4)

2.44   The one-month period in para.(1)(b)(i) is also extended to six months if either para.(3) or para.(4) applies. Those paragraphs are not subject to the condition that the Secretary of State should consider that it would be unreasonable to expect the person to return home sooner.

Paragraph (3) permits an extended temporary absence for medical treatment, physiotherapy, or a treatment that is similar to either of those forms of treatment, or medically approved convalescence in the circumstances set out in para.(3)(a) and (b). Note the definitions of "medically approved" and "qualified practitioner" in para.(5). The phrase, "registered medical practitioner" is further defined by para.1 of Sch.1 Interpretation Act 1978 as meaning "a fully registered person within the meaning of the Medical Act 1983 who holds a licence to practise under that Act."

Paragraph (4) permits an extended temporary absence for a "mariner" and a "continental shelf worker" who is in a "designated area" or a "prescribed area". All four of those terms are defined in para.(5). The definition of "mariner" is self-explanatory. The definition of "continental shelf worker" is more technical but, to summarise, it means a person working on an oil or gas rig in a specified area. Readers are referred to the Continental Shelf Act 1964, the Petroleum Act 1998 and the Orders in Council made under those Acts for further details of the areas concerned.

2.45   Note that paras (2) and (3) are also relevant to the question whether a person remains responsible for a child or qualifying young person during the temporary absence of that child or qualifying young person: see the commentary to reg.4(7) above.

Receiving education

Meaning of "receiving education"

2.46   **12.**—[¹ (1) This regulation applies for the basic condition in section 4(1)(d) of the Act (not receiving education).

(1A) A qualifying young person is to be treated as receiving education, unless the person is participating in a [² relevant training scheme]

(1B) In paragraph (1A) [² "relevant training scheme" means—

(a) a traineeship, or

(b) a course or scheme which—

  (i) comprises education or training designed to assist a claimant to gain the skills needed to obtain paid work (or more paid work or better-paid work);

  (ii) is attended by a claimant falling within section 22 of the Act as a work preparation requirement or as voluntary work preparation, and

  (iii) the claimant has been referred to by the Secretary of State;]

"traineeship" means a course which—

(a) is funded (in whole or in part) by, or under arrangements made by, the—

  (i) Secretary of State under section 14 of the Education Act 2002, or

  (ii) Chief Executive of [² Education and Skills Funding];

(b) lasts no more than 6 months;

(c) includes training to help prepare the participant for work and a work experience placement; and

(d) is open to persons who on the first day of the course have reached the age of 16 but not 25;]

(2) [¹ Except in circumstances where paragraph (1A) applies] "receiving education" means—

    (a) undertaking a full-time course of advanced education; or

    (b) undertaking any other full-time course of study or training at an educational establishment for which a student loan or grant is provided for the person's maintenance.

(3) In paragraph (2)(a) "course of advanced education" means—

    (a) a course of study leading to—

        (i) a postgraduate degree or comparable qualification,

        (ii) a first degree or comparable qualification,

        (iii) a diploma of higher education,

        (iv) a higher national diploma; or

    (b) any other course of study which is of a standard above advanced GNVQ or equivalent, including a course which is of a standard above a general certificate of education (advanced level), or above a Scottish national qualification (higher or advanced higher).

(4) A claimant who is not a qualifying young person and is not undertaking a course described in paragraph (2) is nevertheless to be treated as receiving education if the claimant is undertaking a course of study or training that is not compatible with any work-related requirement imposed on the claimant by the Secretary of State.

AMENDMENTS

1. Social Security (Traineeships and Qualifying Young Persons) Amendment Regulations 2015 (SI 2015/336) reg.4 (March 27, 2015).

2. Social Security (Qualifying Young Persons Participating in Relevant Training Schemes) (Amendment) Regulations 2017 (SI 2017/987) reg.4 (November 6, 2017).

DEFINITIONS

"claimant"—see WRA 2012 s.40.

"qualifying young person"—see WRA 2012 ss.40 and 10(5) and regs 2 and 5.

GENERAL NOTE

It is a condition of entitlement to universal credit that the person is not receiving education (s.4(1)(d) WRA 2012) (but see reg.14 for the exceptions to this rule).   **2.47**

Note that a couple may be entitled to universal credit as joint claimants even where one member of the couple is receiving education (and does not come within reg.14), provided that the other member is not receiving education, or comes within reg.14 (see reg.3(2)(b)).

Regulation 12 defines who counts as receiving education. Firstly, a qualifying young person (see reg.5 for who is a qualifying young person) is deemed to be receiving education, unless they are participating in a relevant training scheme (para.(1A)). "Relevant training scheme" is defined in para.(1B) as either a traineeship (further defined in para.(1B)) or certain courses or schemes as defined therein. Where someone is participating in a relevant training scheme as so defined they will not count as receiving education for the purposes of s.4(1)(d).

If para.(1A) does not apply, receiving education means being on a full-time course of advanced education (defined in para.(3)) or on another full-time course of study or training at an educational establishment for which a student loan or grant is provided for the person's maintenance (para.(2)). But in addition a claimant will also be treated as receiving education if they are on a course of study or training that is not compatible with the work-related requirements imposed on them (para.(4)).

Paragraph (2)(a)

2.48   The meaning of "undertaking a full-time course of advanced education" under reg.12(2)(a) was in issue in *BK v SSWP (UC)* [2022] UKUT 73 (AAC), where Upper Tribunal Judge Rowley ruled as follows:

"19. The following propositions may be gleaned from the jurisprudence:
   a. Whether or not a person is undertaking a full-time course is a question of fact for the tribunal having regard to the circumstances in each particular case (*R/SB 40/83* at [13]; *R(SB) 41/83* at [12]). Parameters have been set, as appear below:
   b. The words 'full-time' relate to the course and not to the student. Specifically, they do not permit the matter to be determined by reference to the amount of time which the student happens to dedicate to their studies (*R/SB 40/83* at [14,15]; *R(SB) 2/91* at [7]; *R(SB) 41/83* at [11]).
   c. Evidence from the educational establishment as to whether or not the course is full-time is not necessarily conclusive, but it ought to be accepted as such unless it is inconclusive on its face, or is challenged by relevant evidence which at least raises the possibility that it ought to be rejected (*R/SB 40/83* at [18]), and any evidence adduced in rebuttal should be weighty in content (*R/SB 41/83* at [12]). See also *Flemming v Secretary of State for Work and Pensions* [2002] EWCA Civ 641, [2002] 1 WLR 2322 at [21]–[22] and [38]; and *Deane v Secretary of State for Work and Pensions* [2010] EWCA Civ 699, [2011] 1 WLR 743 where the Court of Appeal repeated an earlier statement in *Flemming* that:

   '38 … A tribunal of fact should, I think be very slow to accept that a person expects or intends to devote – or does, in fact, devote – significantly less time to the course than those who have conduct of the course expect of him, and very slow to hold that a person who is attending a course considered by the educational establishment to be a part-time course is to be treated as receiving full-time education because he devotes significantly more time than that which is expected of him…'

   d. If the course is offered as full-time course, the presumption is that the recipient is in full-time education. There may be exceptions to the rule, such where a student is granted exemptions from part of the course: *Deane* [51]."

Paragraph (3)

2.49   The definition of "course of advanced education" in reg.12(3) is the same as the definition in reg.61(1) of the Income Support Regulations (see Vol.V in this series). "Full-time" is not defined.

See reg.13 for when a person is regarded as being on a course.

Meaning of "undertaking a course"

2.50   **13.**—(1) For the purposes of these Regulations a person is to be regarded as undertaking a course of education [¹, study] or training—

   (a) throughout the period beginning on the date on which the person starts undertaking the course and ending on the last day of the course or on such earlier date (if any) as the person finally abandons it or is dismissed from it; or
   (b) where a person is undertaking a part of a modular course, for the period beginning on the day on which that part of the course starts and ending—
      (i) on the last day on which the person is registered as undertaking that part, or
      (ii) on such earlier date (if any) as the person finally abandons the course or is dismissed from it.

(2) The period referred to in paragraph (1)(b) includes—

(a) where a person has failed examinations or has failed to complete successfully a module relating to a period when the person was undertaking a part of the course, any period in respect of which the person undertakes the course for the purpose of retaking those examinations or completing that module; and

(b) any period of vacation within the period specified in paragraph (1)(b) or immediately following that period except where the person has registered to attend or undertake the final module in the course and the vacation immediately follows the last day on which the person is to attend or undertake the course.

(3) In this regulation "modular course" means a course which consists of two or more modules, the successful completion of a specified number of which is required before a person is considered by the educational estab-lishment to have completed the course.

(4) A person is not to be regarded as undertaking a course for any part of the period mentioned in paragraph (1) during which the following condi-tions are met—

(a) the person has, with the consent of the relevant educational estab-lishment, ceased to attend or undertake the course because they are ill or caring for another person;

(b) the person has recovered from that illness or ceased caring for that person within the past year, but not yet resumed the course; and

(c) the person is not eligible for a grant or student loan.

AMENDMENT

1. Universal Credit (Consequential, Supplementary, Incidental and Miscellaneous Provisions) Regulations 2013 (SI 2013/630) reg.38(3) (April 29, 2013).

DEFINITIONS

"grant"—see regs 2 and 68(7).
"student loan"—*ibid.*

GENERAL NOTE

Paragraphs (1) to (3) of reg.13 reproduce the rules in reg.61(2) to (4) of the Income Support Regulations. See the notes to reg.61 in Vol.V of this series.

Paragraph (4) is similar to the provision in reg.1(3D) and (3E) of the JSA Regulations 1996 (see Vol.V in this series). The person must have recovered from the illness or their caring responsibilities must have ended within the past year for para.(4) to apply (see para.(4)(b)). See further *RVS v SSWP (ESA)* [2019] UKUT 102 (AAC), a decision on a similar provision in reg.17 of the ESA Regulations 2008; however, note that the ESA Regulations 2008 do not have a provision equivalent to para. (4).

2.51

Exceptions to the requirement not to be receiving education

14.—[[1](1)] A person does not have to meet the basic condition in s.4(1)(d) of the Act (not receiving education) if—

(a) the person—

(i) is undertaking a full- time course of study or training which is not a course of advanced education,

(ii) is under the age of 21, or is 21 and reached that age whilst undertaking the course, and

(iii) is without parental support (as defined in regulation 8(3));

2.52

[¹[² (b) the person is entitled to attendance allowance, disability living allowance, child disability payment [³, adult disability payment] or personal independence payment and, on a date before the date on which the person starts receiving education—

    (i) it has been determined that the person has limited capability for work or limited capability for work and work-related activity on the basis of an assessment under Part 5 or under Part 4 or 5 of the ESA Regulations; or

    (ii) the person is treated as having limited capability for work under Schedule 8 or limited capability for work and work-related activity under Schedule 9;]

(c) the person is responsible for a child or a qualifying young person;

(d) the person is a single person and a foster parent with whom a child is placed;

(e) the person is a member of a couple, both of whom are receiving education, and the other member is—

    (i) responsible for a child or qualifying young person, or

    (ii) a foster parent with whom a child is placed; or

(f) the person—

    (i) has reached the qualifying age for state pension credit, and

    (ii) is a member of a couple the other member of which has not reached that age.

[¹(2) [² ...]]

AMENDMENTS

1. Universal Credit (Exceptions to the Requirement not to be receiving education) (Amendment) Regulations 2020 (SI 2020/827) reg.2 (August 5, 2020).

2. Universal Credit (Exceptions to the Requirement not to be receiving Education) (Amendment) Regulations 2021 (SI 2021/1224) reg.2 (December 15, 2021).

3. Social Security (Disability Assistance for Working Age People) (Consequential Amendments) Order 2022 (SI 2022/177) Part 2 art.13(3) (March 21, 2022).

DEFINITIONS

"the Act"—see reg.2.
"adult disability payment"—*ibid.*
"attendance allowance"—*ibid.*
"child"—see WRA 2012 s.30.
"child disability payment"—see reg.2.
"couple"—see WRA 2012 ss.39 and 40.
"course of advanced education"—see regs 2 and 12.
"disability living allowance"—see reg.2.
"foster parent"—*ibid.*
"personal independence payment"—*ibid.*
"qualifying young person"—see WRA 2012 ss.40 and 10(5) and regs 2 and 5.
"qualifying age for state pension credit"—see WRA 2012 s.4(4), SPCA 2002 s.1(6).

GENERAL NOTE

2.53   This regulation sets out the exceptions to the rule in s.4(1)(d) WRA 2012 that a person must not be receiving education. Note that most student funding will count as income—see regs 68–71. If a person who comes within reg.14 has student income in relation to the course that they are undertaking which is taken into account in the calculation of their universal credit award, they will not have any work requirements (see reg.89(1)(e)(ii)).

The following are exempt from the condition in s.4(1)(d):

- a person who is on a course which is not a course of advanced education (see reg.12(3) for what counts as a course of advanced education) and who is under 21 (or is 21 and reached that age while on the course) and who is "without parental support" (see reg.8(3) for who counts as without parental support) (para.(a)). Such a person will have no work requirements (see reg.89(1)(e)(i));

- a person who has limited capability for work (see reg.39(1)) and who is entitled to disability living allowance, personal independence payment, child disability payment, adult disability payment, attendance allowance or armed forces independence payment (see the definition of "attendance allowance" in reg.2 which includes armed forces independence payment) (para.(b));

- a person who is responsible for a child or qualifying young person (para.(c));

- a single person who is a foster parent with whom a child is placed (para.(d));

- a member of a couple, both of whom are receiving education, whose partner is responsible for a child or qualifying young person or is a foster parent with whom a child is placed (para.(e)); or

- a member of a couple who has reached the qualifying age for state pension credit but whose partner is below that age (para.(f)). Note that a person who falls within reg.13(4) is not regarded as undertaking a course and so is not treated as receiving education (see reg.12(2)). Note also that a couple may be entitled to universal credit as joint claimants even where one member of the couple is receiving education (and does not come within this regulation), provided that the other member is not receiving education, or comes within this regulation (see reg.3(2)(b)).

This regulation has been subject to both case law and substantial amendment. The original amendments made by the Universal Credit (Exceptions to the Requirement not to be receiving education) (Amendment) Regulations 2020 (SI 2020/827) were a response to the litigation in *R. (Kauser and JL) v Secretary of State for Work and Pensions* CO/987/2020. In those proceedings, the High Court (Fordham J) issued a declaration that under the previous law the Secretary of State had breached (what was then) reg.14(b) when read with regs 38 and 39(1)(a), in failing to determine whether the claimants had limited capability for work; and in failing to conduct a work capability assessment *before* deciding the claimants' entitlement to universal credit. The Order making the declaration in *R. (Kauser and JL) v SSWP* is available on Rightsnet at *https://www.rightsnet.org.uk/pdfs/CO_987_2020.pdf*.

A challenge to the amended reg.14(1)(b), as inserted by the 2020 amending regulations, and requiring a student to have an assessment of limited capability for work and work-related activity before making an application for universal credit, was unsuccessful in *R. (Kays) v Secretary of State for Work and Pensions* [2022] EWHC 167 (Admin). Furthermore, the Court of Appeal dismissed an appeal by the claimant against the decision of Swift J. The unsuccessful grounds of appeal were that (1) the decision to make the 2020 Regulations without consultation was irrational; (2) the 2020 Regulations achieved their purpose in an irrational and arbitrary way; (3) the purpose of those regulations was irrational and discriminatory; and (4) the respondent had not had due regard to the public sector equality duty: see *R. (Kays) v Secretary of State for Work and Pensions* [2022] EWCA Civ 1593. On May 23, 2023, the Supreme Court refused permission to appeal from that decision.

Meanwhile reg.14(1)(b) was amended for a second time by the 2021 amending regulations. This latter amendment was designed to put beyond doubt that a person who is entitled to one of the designated disability benefits must have been determined to have limited capability for work (LCW) *before* the person starts undertaking a course of education. This amendment was intended to close off a "workaround" whereby an existing disabled student, who does not have a pre-existing LCW determination, could make a claim to new-style (contributory) employment and support allowance in order to be referred for a work capability assessment so that, if the person is subsequently determined to have LCW, they could then claim and be entitled to universal credit—an outcome contrary to the policy intent.

Accepting a claimant commitment

Claimant commitment—date and method of acceptance

2.54   **15.**—(1) For the basic condition in section 4(1)(e) of the Act, a person who has accepted a claimant commitment within such period after making a claim as the Secretary of State specifies is to be treated as having accepted that claimant commitment on the first day of the period in respect of which the claim is made.

(2) In a case where an award may be made without a claim, a person who accepts a claimant commitment within such period as the Secretary of State specifies is to be treated as having accepted a claimant commitment on the day that would be the first day of the first assessment period in relation to the award in accordance with regulation 21(3) [¹or (3A)].

(3) The Secretary of State may extend the period within which a person is required to accept a claimant commitment or an updated claimant commitment where the person requests that the Secretary of State review—

(a) any action proposed as a work search requirement or a work availability requirement; or

(b) whether any limitation should apply to those requirements,

and the Secretary of State considers that the request is reasonable.

(4) A person must accept a claimant commitment by one of the following methods, as specified by the Secretary of State—

(a) electronically;

(b) by telephone; or

(c) in writing.

AMENDMENT

1. Income Support (Digital Service) Amendment Regulations 2014 (SI 2014/2887) reg.3(1)(a) (November 26, 2014).

DEFINITIONS

"claimant commitment"—see WRA 2012 s.14(1)
"work availability requirement"—see WRA 2012 ss.40 and 18(1)
"work search requirement"—see WRA 2012 ss.40 and 17(1)

GENERAL NOTE

2.55   By virtue of s.4(1)(e) of the WRA 2012 it is one of the basic conditions for making an award of universal credit that a claimant, including each of joint claimants, has accepted a claimant commitment, the meaning of which is then set out in s.14. See that provision and its annotations for the nature of a claimant commitment (i.e. a record of the claimant's responsibilities under the WRA 2012) and what is entailed in accepting such a record. There are exceptions from the basic condition in reg.16 below. Regulation 15 deals with the time within which and the method by which a claimant commitment must be accepted. The relevant regulation-making powers for reg.15 are in s.14(5) of the WRA 2012, which requires the most up-to-date version of a claimant commitment to be accepted "in such manner as may be prescribed", and in s.4(7), which allows regulations to specify circumstances in which a person is to be treated as having or as not having accepted a claimant commitment.

Note that, before there can be a question of acceptance, a claimant commitment must have been prepared on behalf of the Secretary of State and offered for acceptance. A claimant should not be found to have failed to satisfy the basic condition in s.4(1)(e) merely by failing to attend and participate in what is called a commitments interview with a work coach.

However, the effect of such a failure is difficult to work out, especially if the interview is on a new claim. In general, such a failure to participate, for no good reason, whether in relation to an interview under s.15 of the WRA 2012 (work-focused interview requirement) or under s.23(1) (connected requirements), is a matter for a sanction under s.27(2), not for a decision that there is no entitlement to universal credit. But a claimant cannot be allowed to stymie the process of drawing up a claimant commitment into a form in which it can be accepted or not accepted by refusing to take part in that process. It would not appear proper in such circumstances for the work coach to prepare a generic commitment recording work requirements that had not been identified through consideration of the claimant's individual circumstances and present that formally to the claimant for acceptance or otherwise. However, it is suggested that, once the question of any good reason for failing to participate in the interview has been explored, possibly after a second appointment has been offered, a decision could properly be made that the claimant is not entitled to universal credit from the outset by reason of failing to satisfy the basic condition in s.4(1)(e). The claimant will not have accepted a claimant commitment and on a new claim it is as a matter of principle for the claimant to show satisfaction of the basic conditions. Chapter J1 of *Advice for decision making* does not seem to deal with this scenario.

By contrast, that chapter does deal in some detail with the situation where a claimant has accepted a claimant commitment, so has an award of universal credit, and there is a question of review of some work-related requirement recorded in that current version. J1031 says that a requirement to accept the most up-to-date version of the claimant commitment (see s.14(5) of the WRA 2012) does not necessarily require participation in an interview to discuss, review and ask the claimant to accept the revised commitment, but that the public law principles of fairness must be met when notifying the claimant of the requirement to accept any new commitments and of the consequences of failing to do so. If the claimant attends the interview and the work coach draws up a revised commitment, the claimant can accept then or be given a "cooling-off period", usually of seven days, in which to do so (during which entitlement continues by virtue of the acceptance of the existing version). If the claimant does not attend the interview or participate in substance, this guidance is currently given in J1034 and J1036:

J1034 Taking part in an interview can be set as a requirement for the claimant even if taking part in an interview is not included on the current claimant commitment. The claimant **must** be separately and correctly informed of the date, time and place of the appointment, the reasons for the interview and the consequences of failing to take part in that appointment.

"J1036 If the claimant

1. fails to attend the interview the DM will consider a sanction (see Note 1) or

2. takes part in the interview but fails or refuses to accept the new commitments at the end of the cooling off period the DM will end the award of UC (see Note 2).

Note 1: There is no legal basis to consider ending the award of UC for not having a new claimant commitment since the previous claimant commitment still applies, but requirements can be set outside of the claimant commitment to take part in an interview, if it is reasonable to do so. Any failure to comply with a requirement to participate in a commitments review for no good reason, i.e. they fail to attend the interview, is a sanctionable failure and not reason to suspend or terminate the award of UC. The guidance on low-level sanctions in ADM Chapter K5 will apply.

Note 2: Only if the claimant attends the interview as required but refuses or fails to accept the new commitments can the DM consider terminating the award of UC after a cooling off period."

This guidance has been hardened up from the previous version (see the 2022/23 edition of this volume), but in what is submitted is the wrong direction. It can be accepted that as at the point that a claimant fails to attend or properly participate in a "commitments review interview" that failure does not in itself justify terminating the award of universal credit for failing to satisfy the basic condition in s.4(1)(e) of the WRA 2012. There could be a sanction under s.27(2), as explained above, although note that neither s.15, with reg.93, nor s.23(1) allow participation in an interview to be required for the sole purpose of reviewing or discussing the claimant commitment. Under s.15 and reg.93 the purpose must be related to wider matters relating to work prospects, opportunities or activities and under s.23(1) must be related to the imposition or compliance with a work-related requirement. However, for similar reasons as discussed above, it would be wrong to allow a claimant to stymie the process of review by refusing to participate in interviews, even though the first sanction might continue until the claimant met the compliance condition of participating in an interview. The claimant's loss of benefit might not be total, especially if there was concurrent entitlement to new style JSA, so that under reg.5 of the JSA Regulations 2013 (discussed in the notes to reg.111) payment of that benefit could not be affected by the sanction, only the universal credit element topping up the amount of new style JSA. It is submitted that a point would come where a revised claimant commitment could be put formally to a claimant for acceptance within a reasonable time, despite there having been no interview, so that a failure to accept that most up-to-date version would constitute a failure to satisfy s.4(1)(e).

The confusion that can result from a misunderstanding of the ADM guidance is well illustrated in *FO v SSWP (UC)* [2022] UKUT 56 (AAC). There, according to the DWP, the appellant claimant's partner (therefore also a claimant) had been set an online "To-do" on her universal credit account on March 23, 2020 to accept her claimant commitments (sic) by March 29, 2020 (later extended to April 14, 2020). In the absence of such acceptance, the couple's "claim" was "closed" on April 14, 2020. The appeal against that decision was disallowed by the First-tier Tribunal. Judge Wikeley had no difficulty in allowing the further appeal because the documentary evidence submitted to the First-tier Tribunal was hopelessly inadequate and substituting a decision that the universal credit award should not have been terminated on April 14, 2020. There was no copy of the claimant commitment document said not have been accepted or of the "To-do", let alone of any existing document or evidence of prior discussions, so that the DWP's submission relied almost entirely on mere assertion about what had happened. Even before the Upper Tribunal, the Secretary of State's representative was unable to provide any of that material or explain why, given the suspension of work search and availability requirements from March 30, 2020 due to the coronavirus pandemic, the matter was pursued after that date.

However, in the course of the Upper Tribunal proceedings, the Secretary of State's representative made a submission that the First-tier Tribunal erred in law in finding that entitlement would automatically end where a claimant failed to accept a claimant commitment in circumstances where there was an award already in place, repeating the substance of the guidance in ADM J1034. The difficulty with that submission is that it would seem that if a "To-do" of the form described above has been placed on a claimant's account a revised claimant commitment must have been prepared that has become the most up-to-date version. Although the condition, through the combination of ss.4(1)(e) and 14(5) of the WRA 2012, of having accepted the most up-to-date version of the claimant commitment could not be said to have ceased to be satisfied until after the expiry of the time given for acceptance, after that point the existence of the previous claimant commitment would not seem to be an obstacle to the termination of the couple's award. The submission also noted that the representative had been unable to find any documentary evidence of any discussion (or, it seems, any appointment for one) about the contents of the revised claimant commitment before the "To-do" of March 23, 2020. Such a breach of the duty of fairness or the "prior information duty" (see the notes to s.14 of the WRA 2012) could undermine the validity of a revised claimant commitment on appeal against the termination of an award, if the claimant or the subsisting evidence raised an issue as to a lack of a fair opportunity to make meaningful representations about the contents of the revised claimant commitment. The judge's substituted decision in *FO* that the award of universal credit should not have been terminated on April 14, 2020 might be better supported on that basis (or on the judge's alternative reasoning that by April 14, 2020 there were exceptional circumstances absolving the partner under what is now reg.16(1)(b) from the condition of having accepted a claimant commitment), rather than on the apparent basis of the Secretary of State's submission. But if in other cases the lack of opportunity was created by a claimant's own unreasonable failure to participate in an interview there can hardly be said to have been any unfairness.

FO also illustrates that where there are joint claimants a failure by one to satisfy the basic conditions in s.4(1) of the WRA 2012 means, subject to some exceptions in reg.3, that neither has any entitlement to universal credit (s.3(2)(a)).

Paragraph (1)

On a new claim, if the claimant commitment is accepted within the time specified by the Secretary of State (as extended under para.(3) if applicable), and by a method prescribed in para.(4), the basic condition is deemed to be satisfied from the first day of the period claimed for. Otherwise, the condition would only be met from the date on which the acceptance by a prescribed method actually took place. Paragraph (1) must therefore be made under s.4(7) of the WRA 2012. Under s.14(2) of the WRA 2012, the Secretary of State may review and up-date a claimant commitment as he thinks fit and under s.14(5) a claimant has to accept the most-up-date version. Such circumstances do not seem to fall within either paras (1) or (2), although para.(3) refers to a period within which a claimant is required to accept an up-dated claimant commitment and its possible extension. There is doubt whether an acceptance under such circumstances strictly takes effect only from its actual date or from the date of the preparation of the up-dated version, but the point may not arise in practice because prior to the expiry of the period given for acceptance of the most up-to-date version the condition in s.4(1)(e) would be satisfied by the acceptance of the existing version (see the discussion of *FO* above). 2.56

Paragraph (2)

Where no claim is required to be made (see reg.6 of the Claims and Payments Regulations 2013), effectively the same rule is applied as in para.(1) with effect from the first day of the award. 2.57

Paragraph (3)

This paragraph allows the Secretary of State, in defined circumstances, to extend the period within which a person is required (which is only in the sense of required in order to take advantage of giving a retrospective effect to the acceptance) to accept a claimant commitment or an up-dated version. It is arguable that no such authorisation is needed to allow the Secretary of State to extend any period as first specified under paras (1) or (2), so that the form of the restrictions in sub-paras (a) and (b) may not matter too much. Those provisions purport to apply when a claimant has requested that the Secretary of State review any action proposed as a work search or work availability requirement (see ss.17(1)(b) and 18 of the WRA 2012) or whether any limitation should apply to those requirements (see reg.97 below). The main difficulty with them, apart from the fact that s.18 contains no 2.58

power for the Secretary of State to specify particular action in relation to a work availability requirement, is that the legislation contains no formal process of review of the "proposals" mentioned. The reference must presumably be to the power under s.24(3) of the WRA 2012 for the Secretary of State to revoke or change any requirement imposed under the Act or any specification of action to be taken and to a request to exercise that power in relation to action specified under ss.17 or 18. Those difficulties perhaps reinforce the argument for the Secretary of State being able to extend the period for acceptance of the claimant whenever it appears reasonable to do so, although that would involve giving no effective force to para. (3). See the notes to s.14 of the WRA 2012 for the administrative guidance on "cooling-off periods".

Paragraph (4)

2.59   This paragraph, as allowed by s.14(5) of the WRA 2012, requires that any acceptance of a claimant commitment that can count for the purposes of s.4(1)(e) be done electronically, by telephone or in writing, with the Secretary of State able to specify which in any particular case. "Electronically" will no doubt cover a range of methods, but in practice the method specified is via a "To Do" action placed on the claimant's electronic journal where a button must be clicked to indicate acceptance. It seems bizarre that acceptance orally or otherwise face-to-face is not allowed, although the telephone is covered. Both methods are capable of being recorded in some permanent form. But the standard method is in keeping with the imperative towards on-line administration, even though claimants who think that everything was agreed in the meeting with their work coach may easily get confused. In so far as no account is taken of the circumstances of claimants with disabilities and the problem cannot be taken care of under reg.16 this provision must be vulnerable to a challenge under the Human Rights Act 1998 for discrimination contrary to art.14 of the European Convention on Human Rights.

Claimant commitment—exceptions

2.60   **16.**—[¹(1)] A person does not have to meet the basic condition to have accepted a claimant commitment if the Secretary of State considers that—

    (a) the person cannot accept a claimant commitment because they lack the capacity to do so; or

    (b) there are exceptional circumstances in which it would be unreasonable to expect the person to accept a claimant commitment.

[¹(2) A person does not have to meet the basic condition to have accepted a claimant commitment if the person is terminally ill.]

DEFINITIONS

    "claimant commitment"—see WRA 2012 s.14(1)
    "terminally ill" —see reg.2.

AMENDMENT

    1. Universal Credit and Employment and Support Allowance (Claimant Commitment Exceptions) (Amendment) Regulations 2022 (SI 2022/60) reg.2 (February 15, 2022).

GENERAL NOTE

2.61   As authorised by s.4(2), the basic condition in s.4(1)(e) of the WRA 2012 does not have to be met where the claimant either lacks the capacity to accept a claimant commitment (para.(1)(a)) or there are exceptional circumstances in which it would be unreasonable to expect the claimant to accept a claimant commitment (para.(1)(b)), plus now, from February 15, 2022, where the claimant is terminally ill (para.(2)). Both parts of para.(1), but especially sub-para.(b), contain elements of judgment. If "accepting" a claimant commitment has the restricted meaning suggested in the notes to s.14 of the WRA 2012, that will affect when it might be unreasonable to expect a claimant to do so. If a claimant would be unable or experience undue difficulty in accepting a claimant commitment by one of the methods required by reg.15(4), that would suggest that it would be unreasonable to expect the claimant to take those steps to accept the claimant commitment. See Williams, Lack of commitment?, *Welfare Rights Bulletin 274* (February 2020) p.4 for some suggestions of arguments that might possibly be made relying on what is now reg.16(1)(b), e.g. where a claimant genuinely believed that there was no need to do more to accept a commitment after agreement at an interview with the work coach or where the claimant commitment contained unlawful conditions (but note the corrections on some technical matters in the online version of this article).

The introduction with effect from February 15, 2022 of the specific rule in para.(2) that a person who is terminally ill is not required to accept a claimant commitment was intended to avoid the risk that for some terminally ill claimants it might have been found under para.(1)(b) that the circumstances were not exceptional or did not make it unreasonable to accept a commitment (Explanatory Memorandum to SI 2022/60 para.7.2). A claimant who is terminally ill must be treated as having limited capability for work and work-related activity (Sch.9, para.1), so if properly identified as such cannot have any work-related requirements imposed (WRA 2012, s.19(2)(a)). Any claimant commitment sought to be put to a claimant for acceptance in such circumstances could therefore have only very limited content, but the existence of para.(2) may make the avoidance of that process more straightforward. At the time of the amendment, the definition of "terminally ill" in reg.2 was in terms of death in consequence of a progressive disease being reasonably expected within six months, as referred to in the Explanatory Note and the Explanatory Memorandum to SI 2022/60. Since then the definition has been amended by SI 2022/260 with effect from April 4, 2022 to substitute 12 months for six months.

The effect of para.(2) is somewhat limited by the restriction of the definition of "terminally ill" to those who are suffering from a progressive disease. There will be others with an equal claim that having to accept a claimant commitment is unreasonable, such as those who have suffered some severe personal injury which they are unlikely to survive for long, who fall outside para.(2).

The rule in what was then reg.16(b) may have been of particular importance during the 2020 coronavirus outbreak, when "conditionality" was suspended for three months from March 30, 2020 and was applied in that context in *FO v SSWP (UC)* [2022] UKUT 56 (AAC) (see the notes to reg.15). Since there was no new legislation to lift the operation of s.4(1)(e) during that period, in contrast to the position on the work search and work availability requirements (see the notes to ss 17 and 18), allowing entitlement on new claims without s.4(1)(e) being met appears to have been the key to not imposing those requirements. The terms of reg.16(b) on exceptional circumstances and unreasonableness would plainly have been met. So an award of universal credit could then have been made without needing to consider what work-related requirements might be imposed and need to be included in the claimant commitment. That would then have allowed the condition in reg.6(1) of the Social Security (Coronavirus) (Further Measures) Regulations 2020 (SI 2020/371) that a new claimant has an award of universal credit to be met, so that sub-paras (a) and (c) could be applied to lift the work search requirement and suspend the work availability requirement. Although para.11 of Memo ADM 04/20, purporting to explain the effect of reg.6, gave no clue that those provisions were linked (presumably because the Further Measures Regulations did not need to amend reg.16 at all), it is submitted that such a mechanism must have been envisaged. For existing claimants as at March 30, 2020, who had already accepted a commitment, the work search and work availability requirements were expressly lifted by reg.6(1)(b). For other requirements, there were to be no sanctions for failing to comply and/or a flexibility in reviewing requirements over the telephone.

The period of application of reg.6 of the Further Measures Regulations expired at the end of June 30, 2020, the power to extend the three-month period not having been exercised. On July 1, 2020 it was announced in Parliament (Under-Secretary of State, Mims Davies, WQ 62431) that from that date the requirement for universal credit claimants (among others) to accept a claimant commitment was being reintroduced. The commitments of existing claimants would be reviewed and up-dated as capacity allowed. It appears that the reintroduction for new claimants was also to be phased in.

It is unclear whether, in a case in which a claimant is entitled to both universal credit and new style JSA (so that in accordance with reg.5 of the JSA Regulations 2013 no work-related or connected requirements can be imposed in relation to JSA), the claimant would still be required to accept a claimant commitment to retain entitlement to JSA. Even if the claimant is so required, the effect of reg.5 would be that it was the universal credit claimant commitment that was the controlling document.

Financial conditions

Minimum amount

2.62   **17.** For the purposes of section 5(1)(b) and (2)(b) of the Act (financial conditions: amount payable not less than any prescribed minimum) the minimum is one penny.

DEFINITION

"the Act"—see reg.2.

Capital limit

2.63   **18.**—(1) For the purposes of section 5(1)(a) and (2)(a) of the Act (financial conditions: capital limit)—
  (a) the prescribed amount for a single claimant is £16,000; and
  (b) the prescribed amount for joint claimants is £16,000.
  (2) In a case where the claimant is a member of a couple, but makes a claim as a single person, the claimant's capital is to be treated as including the capital of the other member of the couple.

DEFINITIONS

  "claimant"—see WRA 2012 s.40.
  "couple"—see WRA 2012 ss.39 and 40.
  "joint claimants"—see WRA 2012 s. 40.
  "prescribed"—*ibid.*
  "single claimant"—*ibid.*
  "single person"—see WRA 2012 ss.40 and 1(2)(a).

GENERAL NOTE

2.64   This provides that the capital limit for universal credit for both a single claimant and joint claimants is £16,000. Thus the capital limit for universal credit is the same as for income support, income-based JSA, income-related ESA and housing benefit (there is no capital limit for working tax credit and child tax credit). The £16,000 limit has not altered since 2006. In the Institute for Government and the SSAC's 2021 joint report *Jobs and benefits: The Covid-19 challenge* it was noted that if the limit had risen in line with prices since 2006 it would be close to £23,500 (or £25,000: different figures are given) and recommended that the limit should be increased to £25,000 and subsequently automatically indexed to maintain its real value (pp.22 and 31). That recommendation was summarily rejected in the Government's response of March 22, 2022.

See the notes to s.5 of the WRA 2012, the provision actually imposing the limit, for why the burden of showing that the value of capital does not exceed £16,000 falls on the claimant.

Under para.(2), where a claimant who is a member of a couple makes a claim as a single person (see reg.3(3) for the circumstances in which this may occur) the capital of the other member of the couple counts as the claimant's.

For the rules on calculating capital, including important disregards, see regs 45–50 and 75–77 and Sch.10.

With effect from July 24, 2019, reg.51 of the Transitional Provisions Regulations 2014, as inserted by reg.3 of the Universal Credit (Managed Migration Pilot and Miscellaneous Amendments) Regulations 2019 (SI 2019/1152), supplies a transitional capital disregard to claimants who (i) were previously entitled to a tax credit and had capital exceeding £16,000; (ii) are given a migration notice that existing benefits are to terminate; and (iii) claim universal credit within the deadline. The disregard is of any capital exceeding £16,000. The disregard can apply only for 12 assessment periods and ceases (without the possibility of revival) following any assessment period in which the amount of capital the claimant has falls below £16,000. See regs 56 and 57 of the Transitional Provisions Regulations for further provisions on termination of the protection. The £16,000 non-disregarded capital that the claimant by definition possesses will produce an assumed yield as income of £174 per month under reg.72. Paragraph 7 of Sch.2 to the Transitional Provisions Regulations, inserted by the same Regulations, contains a disregard as capital of any amount paid as a lump sum by way of a "transitional SDP amount" under that Schedule.

Restrictions on entitlement

Restrictions on entitlement—prisoners etc.

19.—(1) Entitlement to universal credit does not arise where a person is—   2.65
  (a) a member of a religious order who is fully maintained by their order;
  (b) a prisoner; or
  (c) serving a sentence of imprisonment detained in hospital.

(2) Paragraph (1)(b) does not apply during the first 6 months when the person is a prisoner where—
  (a) the person was entitled to universal credit immediately before becoming a prisoner, and the calculation of their award included an amount for the housing costs element; and
  (b) the person has not been sentenced to a term in custody that is expected to extend beyond that 6 months.

(3) In the case of a prisoner to whom paragraph (2) applies, an award of universal credit is not to include any element other than the housing costs element.

(4) In paragraph (1)(c) a person serving a sentence of imprisonment detained in hospital is a person who is—
  (a) being detained—
    (i) under section 45A or 47 of the Mental Health Act 1983 (power of higher courts to direct hospital admission; removal to hospital of persons serving sentence of imprisonment etc), and

(ii) before the day which the Secretary of State certifies to be that person's release date within the meaning of section 50(3) of that Act (in any case where there is such a release date); or

(b) being detained under—

(i) section 59A of the Criminal Procedure (Scotland) Act 1995 (hospital direction), or

(ii) section 136 of the Mental Health (Care and Treatment) (Scotland) Act 2003 (transfer of prisoners for treatment of mental disorder).

DEFINITIONS

"housing costs element"—see regs 2 and 25.
"prisoner"—see reg.2 as modified by SI 2020/409.

GENERAL NOTE

2.66   WRA 2012, s.6(1)(a) provides that "entitlement to universal credit does not arise . . . in prescribed circumstances even though the requirements of section 3 [i.e., the requirements to satisfy the basic conditions and the financial conditions] are met". Regulation 19 is made under that power. Its effect is that, where a person's circumstances fall within para.(1), entitlement to universal credit "does not arise" even though that person otherwise meets all the conditions of entitlement. Those circumstances as that the claimant is a fully maintained member of a religious order, a prisoner (subject to para.(2)), or serving a sentence of imprisonment in a hospital (as defined in para.(4)).

The wording "entitlement . . . does not arise" in both s.6 and reg.19 creates problems. It would have been more natural to say that a person whose circumstances fall within para.(1) "is not entitled to Universal Credit" even if he or she satisfies s.3.

One possibility is that the wording may have been chosen to forestall any suggestion that the rules in reg.19 amount to conditions of disentitlement or disqualification (in which case, subject to the principles enunciated by the House of Lords in *Kerr v Department of Social Development*, [2004] UKHL 23 (also reported as *R 1/04 (SF)*), the burden would be on the Secretary of State to show that affected claimants were not entitled to universal credit, rather than for the claimants to prove that they were). However, this seems unlikely. Whether or not a person is a fully maintained member of a religious order, a prisoner, or serving a sentence of imprisonment in a hospital are not questions that would normally raise difficult issues of proof. And if this was the intention, it is not entirely clear that s.6 and reg.19 achieve it.

2.67   Whatever the reason for the wording, the problem it creates is that (to use prisoners as an example) although departmental policy is that prisoners should generally have no entitlement to universal credit other than under reg.19(2) (see ADM E3030 and E3040), that is not what s.6 and reg.19 say. They only say that entitlement does not arise where a person is a prisoner. But that does not cover the position in which entitlement has already arisen but the claimant subsequently becomes a prisoner. If s.6 and reg.19 contained a clear statement that a person who is a prisoner "is not entitled" to universal credit (except where reg.19(2) applies), then imprisonment would be a relevant change of circumstances and a ground for superseding the decision awarding universal credit. As it is, the effect of reg.19 appears to be limited to cases in which a new claim is made by a person who is already a prisoner because it is only in such cases that there is any issue about whether entitlement has "arisen". This view is reinforced by s.6(1)(b) and (c) and (2) which provide that entitlement to universal credit does not arise if the basic conditions or the financial conditions are met for a period shorter than a prescribed period or for up to seven days at the beginning of a period during which those conditions are met. In those provisions the "entitlement ... does not arise" wording is being applied to circumstances where there is no existing entitlement, as is apt.

Paragraphs (2) and (3)
The above analysis, creates some difficulties in the interpretation of para.(2).   **2.68**
This says that para.(1)(b) "does not apply" during the first six months when the person is a prisoner where that person was entitled to universal credit immediately before becoming a prisoner, and certain other circumstances exist. If what is said above is correct, then para.(1)(b) does not apply at all in such a case, irrespective of the other circumstances. (That is not an objection to the analysis. The "entitlement ... does not arise" wording is in primary legislation and the way in which the Secretary of State has interpreted that wording when making secondary legislation is not a guide to what it actually means).
The policy which para.(2) seeks to implement is that where someone with an existing award of universal credit that includes the housing costs element is sentenced to a term in custody that is not expected to extend beyond that 6 months, entitlement to universal credit is retained but the award may not include any element other than the housing costs element.
See also the commentary under the headings *Members of religious orders* and *Person serving a sentence of imprisonment in hospital* in the General Note to reg.21 of the IS Regulations in Vol.V.

[¹ **Waiting Days**

19A. [⁴ ...]]   **2.69**

AMENDMENTS

1. Universal Credit (Waiting Days) (Amendment) Regulations 2015 (SI 2015/1362) reg.2(1)(a) (August 3, 2015).
2. Universal Credit and Miscellaneous Amendments Regulations 2015 (SI 2015/1754) reg.2(3) (Assessment periods beginning on or after November 4, 2015).
3. Universal Credit and Miscellaneous Amendments Regulations 2015 (SI 2015/1754) reg.5 (Assessment periods beginning on or after November 4, 2015).
4. Universal Credit (Miscellaneous Amendments, Saving and Transitional Provision) Regulations 2018 (SI 2018/65) reg.3(3) (February 14, 2018).

DEFINITIONS

"terminally ill"—*ibid.*
"weekly earnings"—*ibid.*
"work-related requirements"—see WRA 2012 s.13.

GENERAL NOTE

WRA 2012 s.6(1)(c) provides that "entitlement to universal credit does not arise   **2.70**
... for a prescribed period at the beginning of a period during which" the claimant satisfies the basic and financial conditions for universal credit (i.e., as required by WRA 2012 s.3). By s.6(2), the period for which there is no entitlement may not exceed seven days.
Regulation 19A was made under the power conferred by s.6(1)(c) and provided that with effect from August 3, 2015, entitlement to universal credit was normally deferred for seven "waiting days". The regulation was revoked with effect from February 4, 2018. See the commentary on p.161 of the 2017/18 edition Vol. V for details of how the regulation operated when it was in force.

PART 3

AWARDS

Introduction

2.71   **20.** This Part contains provisions for the purposes of sections 7 and 8 of the Act about assessment periods and about the calculation of the amount of an award of universal credit.

DEFINITIONS

"the Act"—see reg.2.
"assessment period"—see WRA 2012 ss.40 and 7(2).

GENERAL NOTE

2.72   Part 3 is made under powers conferred by ss.7 to 12 WRA 2012 and is concerned with the calculation of an award of universal credit. There are two underlying principles. The first is that an award is made by reference to an "assessment period" (s.7 and reg.21). The second is that the amount of the award is calculated by ascertaining the claimant's (or claimants') "maximum amount" and then deducting "the amounts to be deducted", namely all unearned income and some earned income (s.8 and reg.22).

[¹ Awards

2.73   **20A.** [² . . .]]

AMENDMENTS

1. Universal Credit (Waiting Days) (Amendment) Regulations 2015 (SI 2015/1362) reg.2(1)(b) (August 3, 2015).
2. Universal Credit (Miscellaneous Amendments, Saving and Transitional Provision) Regulations 2018 (SI 2018/65) reg.3(4) (February 14, 2018).

GENERAL NOTE

2.74   When it was in force between August 3, 2015 and February 14, 2018, reg.20A clarified that where entitlement to another benefit is conditional on a person "having an award of universal credit" a person does not have such an award on any day when they are not entitled to universal credit (e.g., on waiting days). The intention was to prevent the reasoning of the Upper Tribunal in *SSWP v SJ (IS)* [2015] UKUT 0127 (AAC) (see the commentary to reg.7(3) and (4) of the Social Fund Maternity and Funeral Expenses (General) Regulations 2005) from being extended to universal credit. Following the abolition of waiting days by the revocation of reg.19A with effect from February 14, 2018, reg.20A would no longer have served any purpose and it has therefore been revoked too.

Assessment periods

2.75   **21.**—(1) An assessment period is [⁴ . . .] a period of one month beginning with the first date of entitlement and each subsequent period of one month during which entitlement subsists.
[²(1A) [³ . . .]]
(2) Each assessment period begins on the same day of each month except as follows—

(a) if the first date of entitlement falls on the 31st day of a month, each assessment period begins on the last day of the month; and

(b) if the first date of entitlement falls on the 29th or 30th day of a month, each assessment period begins on the 29th or 30th day of the month (as above) except in February when it begins on the 27th day or, in a leap year, the 28th day.

[⁴ (2A) But paragraphs (1) and (2) are subject to regulation 21A (assessment period cycle to remain the same following change in the first date of entitlement).]

[¹ (3) Where a new award is made to a single person without a claim by virtue of regulation 9(6)(a) or (10) of the Claims and Payments Regulations (old award has ended when the claimant ceased to be a member of a couple) each assessment period for the new award begins on the same day of each month as the assessment period for the old award.

(3A) Where a new award is made to members of a couple jointly without claim by virtue of regulation 9(6)(b) or (7) of the Claims and Payments Regulations (two previous awards have ended when the claimants formed a couple) each assessment period for the new award begins on the same day of each month as the assessment period for whichever of the old awards ended earlier.

(3B) Where a claim is treated as made by virtue of regulation 9(8) of the Claims and Payments Regulations (old award ended when a claimant formed a couple with a person not entitled to universal credit), each assessment period in relation to the new award begins on the same day of each month as the assessment period for the old award.

(3C) Where a claim is made by a single person or members of a couple jointly and the claimant (or either joint claimant) meets the following conditions—

(a) the claimant was previously entitled to an award of universal credit the last day of which fell within the 6 months preceding the date on which the claim is made; and

(b) during that 6 months—

(i) the claimant has continued to meet the basic conditions in section 4 of the Act (disregarding the requirement to have accepted a claimant commitment and any temporary period of absence from Great Britain that would be disregarded during a period of entitlement to universal credit); and

(ii) the claimant was not excluded from entitlement by regulation 19 (restrictions on entitlement – prisoners etc.),

each assessment period for the new award begins on the same day of each month as the assessment period for the old award or, if there was an old award in respect of each joint claimant, the assessment period that ends earlier in relation to the date on which the claim is made.

(3D) For the purposes of this regulation it does not matter if, at the beginning of the first assessment period of the new award, the following persons do not meet the basic conditions in section 4(1)(a) and (c) of the Act (at least 18 years old and in Great Britain) or if they are excluded from entitlement under regulation 19 (restrictions on entitlement – prisoners etc.) provided they meet those conditions (and are not so excluded) at the end of that assessment period—

(a) in a case to which paragraph (3B) applies, the member of the couple who was not entitled to universal credit; or

(b) in a case to which paragraph (3C) applies, the member of the couple who does not meet the conditions mentioned in that paragraph.

(3E) In this regulation "the Claims and Payments Regulations" means the Universal Credit, Personal Independence Payment, Jobseeker's Allowance and Employment and Support Allowance (Claims and Payments) Regulations 2013.]

(5) [¹ ...]

(6) [¹ ...]

AMENDMENTS

1. Universal Credit (Digital Service) Amendment Regulations 2014 (SI 2014/2887) reg.3(1) (November 26, 2014). The amendment is subject to the saving provision in reg.5 of SI 2014/2887 (see pp.799–800 of the 2020/21 edition of Vol.V of this series).

2. Universal Credit (Waiting Days) (Amendment) Regulations 2015 (SI 2015/1362) reg.2(1)(c) (August 3, 2015).

3. Universal Credit (Miscellaneous Amendments, Saving and Transitional Provision) Regulations 2018 (SI 2018/65) reg.3(5) (February 14, 2018).

4. Universal Credit (Miscellaneous Amendments, Saving and Transitional Provision) Regulations 2018 (SI 2018/65) reg.3(5) (April 11, 2018).

DEFINITIONS

"assessment period"—see WRA 2012 ss.40 and 7(2).
"claim"—see WRA 2012 s.40.
"couple"—see WRA 2012 ss.39 and 40.
"jobseeker's allowance"—see reg.2.
"personal independence payment"—*ibid.*

GENERAL NOTE

2.76   WRA 2012, s.7(1) provides that universal credit "is payable in respect of each complete assessment period within a period of entitlement". "Assessment period" is defined by s.7(2) as a "period of prescribed duration" and "period of entitlement" is defined by s.7(4) as a "period during which entitlement to universal credit subsists". Section 7(3) empowers the Secretary of State to make regulations about when an assessment period is to start, for universal credit to be payable in respect of a period shorter than an assessment period and for the amount payable in respect of a period shorter than an assessment period. Regulation 21 is made under the powers conferred by s.7(2) and (3).

2.77   *Paragraph (1)* provides that an assessment period is a period of one month beginning with the first date of entitlement and each subsequent period of one month during which entitlement subsists.

2.78   *Paragraph (1A)* clarifies that where the waiting days rule applies (see the General Note to reg.19A), the first day of entitlement (and therefore the first day of the assessment period) is the day after the expiry of the seven waiting days.

2.79   *Paragraph (2)* makes provision to avoid the administrative problems that would otherwise occur in shorter months. The general rule is that each assessment period begins on the same day of each month. But that is not always possible when the first assessment period began on the 29th, 30th or 31st of a month because not all months have more than 28 days. Therefore:

- if the first date of entitlement falls on the 31st day of a month, each subsequent assessment period begins on the last day of the month (para.(2)(a)); or

254

- if the first date of entitlement falls on the 29th or 30th day of a month, each subsequent assessment period begins on the 29th or 30th day of the month except in February when it begins on the 27th day or, in a leap year, the 28th day.

Paragraphs (3)–(3B): Reg.9(6)–(8) and (10) of the Claims and Payments Regulations 2.80
2013 (see the definition in para.(3E)) specify circumstances in which it is possible to become entitled to universal credit without making a claim for it. All of those circumstances involve there having been a previous award of universal credit. Paras (3)–(3B) govern the day on which the first assessment period begins under the new award:

- *Paragraph (3)* applies where an award is made to a single person who had previously been awarded universal credit as one of two joint claimants, but who has ceased to be a member of a couple, either through relationship breakdown (reg.9(6)(a) of the Claims and Payments Regulations 2013) or through death (reg.9(10)). In such circumstances, each assessment period for the new award begins on the same period of each month as the assessment period for the old award.

- *Paragraph (3A)* applies either (1) where a joint award of universal credit ends because one former joint claimant has formed a new couple with a third person who is already entitled to universal credit (reg.9(6)(b)) or (2) where two single claimants who are already entitled to universal credit form a couple. In those cases, the dates on which the assessment periods began under the previous awards will not necessarily be the same, so para.(3A) provides that the assessment periods for the new award will begin on the same day of each month as the assessment period for whichever of the two old awards ended earlier.

- *Paragraph (3B)* applies if a joint award of universal credit ends because one former joint claimant has formed a new couple with a third person who was not previously entitled to universal credit (reg.9(8)), and provides that each assessment period for the new award begins on the same period of each month as the assessment period for the old award. This rule applies even if—at the beginning of the first assessment period under the new award—one member of the new couple was under 18, or was not in Great Britain, or was excluded from entitlement under reg.19,as long as they were 18 or over, in Great Brittan, and not excluded from entitlement at the end of that assessment period (para.(3D)).

Paragraph (3C) is not—or, at any rate, not necessarily—concerned with relationship 2.81
formation or breakdown, but rather with repeat claims. It applies if a new claim for universal credit is made and the claimant (or either or both joint claimants) was (or were) entitled to universal credit within the previous six months and, during the period between the old award and the new claim, the claimant (or both claimants):

- were at least 18 years old, below state pension credit age, in Great Britain (other than for periods of temporary absence that would have been disregarded under reg.11 if there had been an award of universal credit at the time) and were not receiving education; and

- were not excluded from entitlement to universal credit by reg.19 as a member of a religious order, as a prisoner, or as a person serving a sentence of imprisonment detained in hospital.

If the new claim is made by a couple, and—at the beginning of the first assessment period under the new award—one member was under 18, or was not in Great Britain, or was excluded from entitlement under reg.19, the conditions in the two bullet points above are treated as having been met provided was 18 or over, in Great Britain and not excluded from entitlement at the end of that assessment period (para.(3D)).

Where para.(3C) applies, each assessment period for the new award begins on the same day of the month as each assessment period of the old award or, if there were two old assessment periods (*i.e.,* because two people who were previously single claimants have formed a couple between the end of the old award and the new claim), on the same day of the month as whichever assessment period of the old award ended earlier.

Under reg.26(5) of the Claims and Payments Regulations 2013, a claim must be made before the end of the assessment period in respect of which it is made in order to benefit from para.(3C).

This will normally be more favourable to claimants that the rules for initial claims. The claims process for repeat claimants is intended to be simpler. In addition, the fact that the first assessment period of the new award will normally begin before the date of the new claim (*i.e.,* unless that date happens to coincide with the start of an assessment period) means that the claimant(s) will be entitled to universal credit before that date (although any income earned during the assessment period from a previous employment will be brought into account). However, where any claimant is not in work at the date of the new claim and has ceased being in paid work since the old award ended, the amount of universal credit paid for the first assessment period is reduced (technically, "apportioned") unless the new claim is made within seven days of the date on which work ceased: see reg.22A, below.

[¹Assessment period cycle to remain the same following change in the first date of entitlement

2.82

21A.—(1) This regulation applies where—

(a) the first date of entitlement has been determined;

(b) it is subsequently determined that the first date of entitlement falls on a different date (the "start date"); and

(c) applying regulation 21(1) and (2) following that subsequent determination (and thereby changing the beginning of each assessment period) would, in the opinion of the Secretary of State, cause unnecessary disruption to the administration of the claim.

(2) Where this regulation applies—

(a) the first assessment period is to be a period of a length determined by the Secretary of State beginning with the start date;

(b) the amount payable in respect of that first assessment period is to be calculated as follows—

$$N \times \left(\frac{A \times 12}{365} \right)$$

where—

N is the number of days in the period; and

A is the amount calculated in relation to that period as if it were an assessment period of one month; and

(c) regulation 21(1) and (2) apply to the second and subsequent assessment periods as if the day after the end of the first assessment period were the first date of entitlement.]

AMENDMENT

1. Universal Credit (Miscellaneous Amendments, Saving and Transitional Provision) Regulations 2018 (SI 2018/65) reg.3(6) (April 11, 2018).

Deduction of income and work allowance

2.83

22.—(1) The amounts to be deducted from the maximum amount in accordance with section 8(3) of the Act to determine the amount of an award of universal credit are—

(a) all of the claimant's unearned income (or in the case of joint claimants all of their combined unearned income) in respect of the assessment period; and

[¹ (b) the following amount of the claimant's earned income (or, in the case of joint claimants, their combined earned income) in respect of the assessment period—

(i) in a case where no work allowance is specified in the table below (that is where a single claimant does not have, or neither of joint claimants has, responsibility for a child or qualifying young person or limited capability for work), [² 55%] of that earned income; or

(ii) in any other case, [² 55%] of the amount by which that earned income exceeds the work allowance specified in the table.]

(2) The amount of the work allowance is—

(a) if the award contains no amount for the housing costs element, the applicable amount of the higher work allowance specified in the table below; and

(b) if the award does contain an amount for the housing costs element, the applicable amount of the lower work allowance specified in that table.

[¹ (3) In the case of an award where the claimant is a member of a couple, but makes a claim as a single person, the amount to be deducted from the maximum amount in accordance with section 8(3) of the Act is the same as the amount that would be deducted in accordance with paragraph (1) if the couple were joint claimants.]

[¹ Higher work allowance	
Single claimant—	
responsible for one or more children or qualifying young persons and/or has limited capability for work	[³ £631]
Joint claimants	
responsible for one or more children or qualifying young persons and/or where one or both have limited capability for work	[³ £631]
Lower work allowance	
Single claimant—	
responsible for one or more children or qualifying young persons and/or has limited capability for work	[³ £379]
Joint claimants—	
responsible for one or more children or qualifying young persons and/or where one or both have limited capability for work]	[³ £379]

AMENDMENTS

1. Universal Credit (Work Allowance) Amendment Regulations 2015 (SI 2015/1649) reg.2 (Assessment periods beginning on or after April 11, 2016).

2. Universal Credit (Work Allowance and Taper) (Amendment) Regulations 2021 (SI 2021/1283) reg.2(1) (Assessment periods beginning on or November 24, 2021).

3. Social Security Benefits Up-rating Order 2023 (SI 2023/316) art.33 (Assessment periods beginning on or after April 10, 2023).

DEFINITIONS

"the Act"—see reg.2.
"assessment period"—see WRA 2012, ss.40 and 7(2).
"child"—see WRA 2012, s.40.
"claimant"—*ibid*.
"couple"—see WRA 2012, ss.39 and 40.
"earned income"—see reg.2.
"housing costs element"—see regs 2 and 25.
"joint claimants"—see WRA 2012, s.40.
"limited capability for work"—see WRA 2012, ss.40 and 37(1).
"qualifying young person"—see WRA 2012, ss.40 and 10(5) and regs 2 and 5.
"responsible for a child or qualifying young person"—see regs 2, 4 and 4A.
"single claimant"—see WRA 2012, s.40.
"unearned income"—see reg.2.
"work"—see WRA 2012, s.40.

GENERAL NOTE

2.84   Under s.8(1) WRA 2012, the amount of an award of universal credit is the balance of the maximum amount less the amounts to be deducted which, by s.8(3), are to be two prescribed amounts, one in respect of earned income and the other in respect of unearned income. Regulation 22 is made under s.8(3) and specifies how those prescribed amounts are to be determined.

2.85   *Paragraph (1)* contains the three general principles. First, the claimant's (or the claimants' combined) *unearned* income (i.e., as calculated in accordance with regs 65-74) is deducted in full (para.(1)(a)). Second, where no claimant has either responsibility for a child or qualifying young person or limited capability for work, 55% of *earned* income (i.e., as calculated in accordance with regs 51-64) is deducted. Third, where any claimant has responsibility for a child or qualifying young person or limited capability for work, the deduction is 55% of the amount by which the claimant's (or the claimant's combined) earned income exceeds the "work allowance" specified in the table to the regulation (para.(1)(b)(ii)).

2.86   *Paragraph (3)* modifies those principles where a member of a couple is claiming as a single claimant under reg.3(3): the couple's combined income is take into account when calculation earned and unearned income, even though the circumstances of the other member of the couple will be excluded when calculating his or her maximum amount (see reg.36(3)).

Paragraph (1)(b) is—or, at any rate, was until April 11, 2016 see below—the main mechanism by which the policy that, under universal credit, claimants will always be better off in work is achieved. The "work allowance" is what would previously have been described as an earnings disregard: an amount deducted from a claimant's earnings before any means-test is carried out. But, even at the lowest rate, it is a more generous disregard than applied for the purposes of IS, income-based JSA and income-related ESA. Even where there is no responsibility for a child or qualifying young person—and therefore no work allowance—the 55% "taper" means that the claimant keeps 45 pence in every additional pound he or she earns, whereas under IS, income-based JSA and income-related ESA, benefit was reduced pound for pound so that, once a claimant's earnings exceeded the earnings disregard (and ignoring any potential entitlement to WTC), there was no financial incentive to work unless he or she could earn enough to come off income-related benefits altogether.

Before April 11, 2016, the work allowances specified in most cases were higher than those that now appear above. In addition, work allowances were also specified for claimants who were not responsible for a child or qualifying young person, For a more detailed discussion of the effects of the reduction and removal of work allowances in those cases, see *Universal Credit—An Introduction* above.

Paragraph (2)
The amount of the work allowance to be deducted from earned income in cases **2.87** where a claimant has responsibility for a child or qualifying young person is specified in para.(2) and the table at the end of the regulation. The higher work allowance is applicable when the award of universal credit does not contain the housing costs element and the lower work allowance when it does. Very few universal credit claimants will not have to pay anything towards housing costs. The most likely recipients of the higher work allowance are, those living as non-dependants in another person's household, owner-occupiers whose earnings exclude them from entitlement to housing costs under Sch.5, para.4 and those renters treated as not liable to make payments under Sch.2, paras 5 to 10.

[¹ Apportionment where re-claim delayed after loss of employment

22A.—(1) This regulation applies where— **2.88**
  (a) a new award is made in a case to which regulation 21(3C) (new claim within 6 months of a previous award) applies; and
  (b) the claimant (or either joint claimant) is not in paid work and has ceased being in paid work since the previous award ended, other than in the 7 days ending with the date on which the claim is made.
(2) In calculating the amount of the award for the first assessment period in accordance with section 8 of the Act—
  (a) the amount of each element that is to be included in the maximum amount; and
  (b) the amount of earned and unearned income that is to be deducted from the maximum amount,
are each to be reduced to an amount produced by the following formula—

$$N \times \left(\frac{A \times 12}{365} \right)$$

Where—
N is the number of days in the period beginning with the date on which the claim is made and ending with the last day of the assessment period; and
A is the amount of the element that would otherwise be payable for that assessment period or, as the case may be, the amount of earned and unearned income that would otherwise be deducted for that assessment period.
(3) The period of 7 days in paragraph (1)(b) may be extended if the Secretary of State considers there is good reason for the delay in making the claim.

AMENDMENT

1. Universal Credit (Digital Service) Amendment Regulations 2014 (SI 2014/2887) reg.3(1)(d) (November 26, 2014). The amendment is subject to the saving provision in reg.5 of SI 2014/2887 (see pp.799–800 of the 2020/21 edition of Vol.V of this series).

DEFINITIONS

"assessment period"—see WRA 2012 ss.40 and 7(2) and reg.21.
"claim"—see WRA 2012 s.40.

"claimant"—*ibid.*
"earned income"—see reg.2 and regs 51-64.
"joint claimants"—see WRA 2012 s.40.
"maximum amount"—see WRA 2012 s.8(2).
"unearned income"—see reg.2 and regs 65-74.

GENERAL NOTE

2.89   The effect of the saving provision in reg.5 of SI 2014/2887 is that the new reg.22A only applies in "Full Service" (or "Digital Service") areas (see *Universal Credit—An Introduction*, above). It does not affect claims that are subject to the "Live Service" rules (as to which see the commentary to reg.6 of the Claims and Payments Regulations 2013 (below) and pp.432-3 of the 2013/14 edition).

Until November 25, 2014, it was unnecessary in some circumstances to re-claim universal credit if there had been a gap in entitlement of no more than six months. However, in Full Service cases only, and from November 26, 2014, a claim is now necessary but such repeat claims are subject to more favourable rules (see reg.21(3C) above). In particular, the assessment period from the old award of universal credit is adopted, with the effect that the claimant will normally become entitled to universal credit before the date of his or her claim.

However, in cases where the new claim is made more than seven days after any claimant ceased paid work, reg.22A removes the benefit of that more favourable rule. The monthly amounts of each element included in the maximum amount for the assessment period and of the earned and unearned income received in the assessment period are apportioned by multiplying by 12 and dividing by 365 to give a daily rate and then multiplying by the number of days between the date of claim and the end of the assessment period. Note that the apportioned result is likely to less favourable to the claimant than simply starting a new assessment period on the date of claim would have been. Under the apportionment, income earned during the assessment period in the claimant's former employment is taken into account, albeit at a reduced rate. If the assessment period had started at the date of claim, that income would have been received before it started and would not be taken into account.

According to the explanatory memorandum to SI 2014/2887 reg.22A was introduced ". . . to encourage claimants to re-claim universal credit as quickly as possible. Evidence has shown that where claimants enter a conditionality regime within two weeks of losing a job it significantly decreases their time between periods of employment".

Under para.(3), the seven day time limit for re-claiming may be extended if the Secretary of State (and, on appeal, the First-tier Tribunal or Upper Tribunal) considers there is good reason for the delay in making the claim.

PART 4

ELEMENTS OF AN AWARD

Introduction

2.90   **23.**—(1) This Part contains provisions about the amounts ("the elements") under—

(a) section 9 (the standard allowance);
(b) section 10 (responsibility for children and young persons);
(c) section 11 (housing costs); and
(d) section 12 (particular needs and circumstances),

of the Act that make up the maximum amount of an award of universal credit, as provided in section 8(2) of the Act.

(2) The elements to be included in an award under section 12 of the Act in respect of particular needs or circumstances are—
  (a) [¹ . . .] the LCWRA element
  (b) the carer element (see regulations 29 and 30); and
  (c) the childcare costs element (see regulations 31 to 35).

AMENDMENT

1. Employment and Support Allowance and Universal Credit (Miscellaneous Amendments and Transitional and Savings Provisions) Regulations 2017 (SI 2017/204) reg. 4(1) and (3) (April 3, 2017).

DEFINITION

"the Act"—see reg.2.

GENERAL NOTE

The maximum amount for the purposes of s.8 WRA is the total of: 2.91

• the standard allowance: WRA 2012, s.9 and reg.36;

• an amount for each child or young person for whom a claimant is responsible ("the child element") WRA 2012, s.10 and reg.24;

• any amount included in respect of any liability of the claimant to make payments in respect of the accommodation they occupy as their home ("the housing costs element"): WRA 2012, s.11 and regs 25 and 26; or

• any amount included in respect of "other particular needs and circumstances": WRA 2012, s.12 and regs.27 to 35.

The amounts to be included in respect of other particular needs and circumstances are the LCWRA element (regs 27 and 28), the carer element (see regs 29 and 30) and the childcare costs element (regs 31–35). The former LCW element was abolished with effect from April 3, 2017 by the Employment and Support Allowance and Universal Credit (Miscellaneous Amendments and Transitional and Savings Provisions) Regulations 2017 (SI 2017/204) subject to the transitional and savings provisions in Sch.2, Pt 2 to those Regulations (see below).

Responsibility for children or young persons

The child element

24.—(1) The amount to be included in an award of universal credit for 2.92
each child or qualifying young person for whom a claimant is responsible [² and in respect of whom an amount may be included under section 10] ("the child element") is given in the table in regulation 36.
  (2) An additional amount as shown in that table is to be included in respect of each child or qualifying young person who is disabled and that amount is—
  (a) the lower rate, where the child or qualifying young person is entitled to disability living allowance [³, child disability payment] [⁴, adult disability payment] or personal independence payment (unless sub-paragraph (b) applies); or
  (b) the higher rate where the child or qualifying young person is—
      (i) entitled to the care component of disability living allowance at the highest rate [³, the care component of child disability

payment at the highest rate in accordance with regulation 11(5) of the DACYP Regulations][⁴, the daily living component of adult disability payment at the enhanced rate in accordance with regulation 5(3) of the Disability Assistance for Working Age People (Scotland) Regulations 2022] or the daily living component of personal independence payment at the enhanced rate, or

(ii) [¹ . . .] blind.

AMENDMENTS

1. Universal Credit and Miscellaneous Amendments (No.2) Regulations 2014 (SI 2014/2888) reg.3(1)(b) (Assessment periods beginning on or after November 26, 2014).
2. Welfare Reform and Work Act 2016 (c.7) s.14(5)(a) (April 6, 2017).
3. Social Security (Scotland) Act 2018 (Disability Assistance for Children and Young People) (Consequential Modifications) Order 2021 (SI 2021/786) Sch.11 para.4 (July 26, 2021).
4. Social Security (Disability Assistance for Working Age People) (Consequential Amendments) Order 2022 (SI 2022/177) reg.13(4) (March 21, 2022).

DEFINITIONS

"adult disability payment"—see reg.2.
"blind"—*ibid.*
"child"—see WRA 2012, s.40.
"child disability payment"—see reg.2.
"child element"—*ibid.*
"the DACYP Regulations"—*ibid.*
"disability living allowance"—*ibid.*
"disabled"—see WRA 2012, s.40.
"personal independence payment"—see reg.2.
"responsible for a child or qualifying young person"—see regs 2, 4 and 4A.
"qualifying young person"—see WRA 2012, s.40 and 10(5) and regs 2 and 5.

GENERAL NOTE

2.93   The child element includes two amounts, which are specified in reg.36. The first, which is included for each child or qualifying young person for whom a claimant is responsible, is £269.58 per assessment period subject to a maximum of two children: see regs 24A and 24B and Sch.12.

Before April 6, 2017 the rate of the child element was higher for the first child or qualifying young person for whom the claimant was responsible. Under reg.43 of the Transitional Provisions Regulations 2014, the higher rate continues to apply where the claimant is responsible for a child or qualifying young person born before April 6, 2017. The transitionally protected higher rate was £277.08 from 2017/18–2019/20, £281.20 in 2020/21, £282.50 in 2021/2022, £290.00 in 2022/23, and is £315.00 in 2023/24: see art.33(2) of, and Sch.13, to SI 2023/316.

An additional amount is included for each child or qualifying young person who is entitled to disability living allowance or personal independence payment or a Scottish equivalent or is registered as blind. The higher amount of £456.89 per assessment period is included where the child or qualifying young person is blind or entitled to the highest rate of the care component of disability living allowance or the enhanced rate of personal independence payment or a Scottish equivalent; the lower amount of £146.31 is included in any other case.

In *R. (SC, CB and 8 children) v Secretary of State for Work and Pensions,* two mothers and their children challenged the two-child limit on two grounds. The first was that the limit was incompatible with their Convention Rights to respect for their private and family lives (i.e. under art.8 ECHR) and to marry and to found a family (art.12). The second was that the limit discriminated against them unlawfully contrary to art.14 taken together with art.8 and art.1 of the First Protocol. However, that challenge was rejected by the High Court (Ouseley J) [2018] EWHC 864 (Admin); [2018] 1 W.L.R. 5425; the Court of Appeal (Patten, Leggatt and Nicola Davies LJJ) [2019] EWCA Civ 615; [2019] 1 W.L.R. 5687; and the Supreme Court (Lords Reed and Hodge, Lady Black, and Lords Lloyd-Jones, Kitchin, Sales and Stephens) [2021] UKSC 26; [2022] A.C. 223. The challenge in *SC* was to the two-child limit as it applied to CTC, but the reasoning of the Supreme Court applies equally to the other benefits to which the limit applies, including universal credit.

An application has subsequently been made (by different claimants) to the ECtHR, on the grounds which failed in *SC*.

In *SSWP v MS (UC)* [2023] UKUT 44 (AAC) (February 15, 2023) the Upper Tribunal decides that the child element of universal credit is not a social security family benefit under Regulation (EC) 883/2004. In this respect the UC child element is therefore differently classified from child tax credit. So the UC child element is not payable in respect of a child who: is living abroad and therefore deemed not to be a child for whom the claimant is "responsible" within the meaning of reg.4 of the Universal Credit Regulations, even if the child is a member of the claimant's family within the meaning of arts 1 and 67 of Regulations (EC) 883/2004. The UT holds that the UC child element is not severable from the other parts of UC, and that even if it were severable, it would remain social assistance, outside the scope of art.67.

[¹ Availability of the child element where maximum exceeded

24A.—(1) Where a claimant is responsible for more than two children or qualifying young persons, the amount mentioned in section 10(1) of the Act is to be available in respect of—

    [² (za) any child or qualifying young person in relation to whom an exception applies in the circumstances set out in—

        (i) paragraph 3 (adoptions) or paragraph 4 (non-parental caring arrangements) of Schedule 12; or

        (ii) paragraph 6 of Schedule 12 by virtue of an exception under paragraph 3 of that Schedule having applied in relation to a previous award;]

    (a) the first and second children or qualifying young persons in the claimant's household; and

    (b) the third and any subsequent child or qualifying young person in the claimant's household if—

        (i) the child or qualifying young person is transitionally protected; or

        (ii) an exception applies in relation to that child or qualifying young person [² in the circumstances set out in paragraph 2 (multiple births), paragraph 5 (non-consensual conception) or, except where sub-paragraph (za)(ii) applies, paragraph 6 (continuation of existing exception in a subsequent award) of Schedule 12].

(2) A reference in paragraph (1) to a child or qualifying young person being the first, second, third or subsequent child or qualifying young person in the claimant's household is a reference to the position of that child or qualifying young person in the order determined in accordance with regulation 24B.

2.94

(3) A child or qualifying young person is transitionally protected [³ if the child or qualifying young person was born before 6th April 2017.]

(4) [² ...]]

AMENDMENT

1. Social Security (Restrictions on Amounts for Children and Qualifying Young Persons) Amendment Regulations 2017 (SI 2017/376) reg.2(1) and (3) (April 6, 2017).

2. Universal Credit and Jobseeker's Allowance (Miscellaneous Amendments) Regulations 2018 (SI 2018/1129) reg.3(1) and (3) (November 28, 2018).

3. Universal Credit (Restriction on Amounts for Children and Qualifying Young Persons) (Transitional Provisions) Amendment Regulations 2019 (SI 2019/27) reg.3 (February 1, 2019).

GENERAL NOTE

2.95 From April 6, 2017 until October 31, 2018, the rules described in this Note applied to existing universal credit claimants only (including those who claimed after April 6, 2017 and subsequently became responsible for two or more children or qualifying young persons). During that interim period, a person who was responsible for two or more children or qualifying young persons could not make a new claim for universal credit—and therefore needed to claim IS/JSA/ESA and CTC (and, where relevant, HB) instead—unless the claim was made within six months of a previous award terminating under reg.21(3C) or was made by a single person within one month of an award of universal credit terminating because that person ceased to be a member of a couple. See generally, reg.39 of the Transitional Provisions Regulations 2014.

From April 6, 2017 s.10(1A) of the WRA 2012 (as inserted by WR&WA 2016, s.14(1)-(4)) provides that the child element of universal credit established by s.10(1) "is to be available in respect of a maximum of two persons who are either children or qualifying young persons for whom a claimant is responsible." However, s.10(4) provides that "[r]egulations may provide for exceptions to subsection (1) or (1A). Regulations 24A and 24B are made under that power. Reg.24A and Sch.12 create exceptions to the "two-child limit".

In the interests of brevity, the rest of this note will refer to "child" and "children" as if those words included qualifying young persons.

2.96 *Paragraph (1)* provides that where a claimant is responsible for two or more children, the child element is to be available in respect of:

- any child to whom the exceptions (see below) for adoptions or non-parental caring arrangements in paras 3 and 4 of Sched 12 (including any extension of an adoption exception under para. 6 of Sch.12) apply: see subpara.(za).

  Children into whom these exceptions apply are excluded when determining the order of children under reg.24B: see reg.24B(2A);

- the first and second children (as determined in accordance with reg.24B): see subpara.(a) and para.(2); and

- any additional child:

  – who was born before 6 April 2017 and is therefore transitionally protected: see subpara.(b)(i) and para.(3); or

  – to whom the exceptions for multiple births or non-consensual conception in paras 2 and 5 of Sch.12: see subpara (b)(ii); or

  – who have the benefit of any continuing exception under para.6 of Sch.12 except for a continuing exception for adoption (which is already covered by subpara.(za)(ii)): see, again, subpara.(b)(ii).

264

Children to whom these exceptions apply are not excluded when determin-   **2.97**
ing the order of children under reg.24B. The exceptions therefore only apply
to third and subsequent children because if a first or second child fell within
the exception s/he would be eligible for a child element in any event under
sub-para.(a).

Exceptions

These are set out in Sch.12. They apply in certain cases where there has been: **2.98**

- a multiple birth (para.2);

- an adoption (para.3);

- a "non-parental caring arrangement" (para.4);

- non-consensual conception (para.5); or

- a previous exception where the claimant is a step-parent of the child.

In *R. (SC, CB and 8 children) v Secretary of State for Work and Pensions* [2018]
EWHC 864 (Admin); [2018] 1 W.L.R. 5425, as well as the main, unsuccessful,
challenge to the two-child limit, a successful challenge was made to the rationality
of restricting the two-child limit exemptions to children born in a particular order,
such that where a third child was born to a family which already had an adoptive
child or a "non-parental caring arrangement" child, the third child would not be
eligible for benefit. The Secretary of State did not seek to appeal against Ouseley J's
finding that this was irrational, and remedied the position with reg.3 of the Universal
Credit and Jobseeker's Allowance (Miscellaneous Amendments) Regulations 2018
(SI 2018/1129). However, that litigation, and the amending regulations, did not
address the situation of households whose first or second child is the result of non-
consensual conception or multiple birth. Those households benefit from exceptions
only where the relevant child is the third or subsequent child, a situation which is
capable of generating striking results. For example, a childless woman who was
raped and consequently gave birth to twins would not receive benefit for any voluntarily conceived children she might subsequently bear.

Multiple births

The child element is available for the third or subsequent child in a household   **2.99**
where that child was one of two or more children born as the result of the same
pregnancy, the claimant is the child's (non-adoptive) parent and is responsible for at
least two of the children born as a result of that pregnancy and the child is not the
first in order (*i.e.*, under reg.24B) of the children born as a result of that pregnancy
(see Sch.12, para.2).

In plain English what this means is that the childcare element is included for all
children born as a result of a multiple birth as long as the household did not already
include two or more older children.

Adoption

The child element is available for an adoptive child (irrespective of how many   **2.100**
other children the household already includes) except where, the claimant (or their
partner) was the child's step parent immediately before the adoption or is the child's
(non-adoptive) parent (see Sch.12, para.3). There are also exceptions in certain
cases where the child has been adopted in or from another country.

Non-parental caring arrangements

The child element is available for the third or subsequent child in a household   **2.101**
where the child's parent is herself (or himself) a child (not, in this case, a qualifying

young person) and the claimant (or either joint claimant) is responsible for the child's parent: see para.4(1)(b).

There is a further exception where the claimant (or either joint claimant) is a "friend or family carer" as defined in para.4(2): see para.4(1)(a). That definition covers people who are responsible for a child but who are not (and whose partner, if any, is not) a parent or step parent of the child and have care of the child under a variety of different statutes, or who are entitled to guardian's allowance for the child or who have undertaken the care of the child in circumstances where it is likely that the child would otherwise be looked after by a local authority.

Non-consensual conception

2.102   This exception applies where the claimant is the child's parent and the Secretary of State (or, on appeal, a Tribunal) accepts that the child "is likely to have been conceived as a result of sexual intercourse to which the claimant did not agree by choice or did not have the freedom and capacity to agree by choice": see para.5(1) (a) and (b). It is also a condition that the claimant "is not living at the same address as the other party to the intercourse". The use of the present tense ("is not living") suggests that the exception can apply if the claimant lived with the other party at the time of the non-consensual conception but no longer does so. That is implicitly confirmed by para.5(5)(b) (see below).

There is a partial definition of the circumstances in which the claimant is to be treated as not having the freedom or capacity to agree by choice to sexual inter-course in para.5(2). They include (but are not limited to) circumstances in which (at the time of conception) the two parties were "personally connected", the other party was "repeatedly or continuously engaging in behaviour towards [the claimant] that was controlling or coercive" and that behaviour had a "serious effect" on the claimant.

Under para.5(5), the claimant and other party are "personally connected" if, at or around the time of the conception, the were in an intimate personal relationship with each other, or were living together as members of the same family having previously been in an intimate personal relationship with each other.

Under para.5(6), behaviour is to be regarded as having a "serious effect" on the claimant if it caused her to fear, on at least two occasions, that violence would be used against her or caused her serious alarm or distress which had a substantial adverse effect on her day-to-day activities.

The Secretary of State may accept the claimant's unsupported word that she is not living at the same address as the other party (para.5(4)). However, under para.5(3), he may only determine that the child is likely to have been conceived as a result of sexual intercourse to which the claimant did not agree by choice or did not have the freedom and capacity to agree by choice in two sets of circumstances.

The first set of circumstances apply if:

- there has been a conviction for rape or controlling or coercive behaviour in an intimate family relationship, or an analogous offence under the law of a country outside Great Britain; or

- an award of compensation has been made has been made under the Criminal Injuries Compensation Scheme in respect of a "relevant criminal injury" (as defined in para.5(7)); and

where the offence was committed, or the criminal injury caused, by the other party and resulted in the conception or diminished the claimant's freedom or capacity to agree by choice to the sexual intercourse that resulted in the conception (see para5(3)(b)).

The second set of circumstances apply if the claimant provides evidence from an "approved person" which demonstrates that the claimant has had contact with that, or another, approved person and her circumstances "are consistent with those of a person to whom" paras 5(1)(a) and (1)(b)(i) apply. "Approved person" is defined by para.5(7) as "a person of a description specified on a list approved by the Secretary of State ... and acting in their capacity as such". That list can be found in Form NCC1, *Support for a child conceived without your consent (England, Scotland and Wales)*, which those claiming to have conceived a child non-consensually must complete. The list reads:

- a healthcare professional in a Sexual Assault Referral Centre, or

- other healthcare professionals, such as a doctor, midwife, nurse or health visitor

- a registered social worker

- a specialist support worker from an approved organisation as listed on http://www.gov.uk/government/publications/support-for-a-child-conceived-without-your-consent

At the time of going to press, that website lists:

- members of The Survivors Trust;

- members of Rape Crisis England and Wales;

- Refuge;

- certain member organisations of Women's Aid Federation Northern Ireland and Women's Aid Federation of England.

Note that there is no restriction on when the claimant must have had contact with the approved person.

Under reg. 42 of the Transitional Provisions Regulations 2013, the Secretary of State may treat the requirement for evidence from an approved person as satisfied where the claimant has previously provided such evidence to HMRC for the purposes of the corresponding exception in relation to CTC.

Continuation of an existing exception for step-parents

Para.5 of Sch.12 applies where the claimant is the step-parent of a child ("A"); has previously had the benefit of an exception in a joint award of universal credit with one of A's parents; in that award the claimant was also responsible for one or more children born as a result of the same pregnancy as A; A is not the first in order (*i.e.*, under reg.24B) of the children born as a result of that pregnancy; and that award ended because the step-parent and parent ceased to be a couple, or in any other circumstances in which the assessment periods for a later award begin and end on the same day of each month as an earlier award under reg.21.   **2.103**

In those circumstances, if the step-parent continues to be responsible for A, under the new award, the childcare element continues to be available for A, even if they are the third or subsequent child in a household.

Finally, under reg.41 of the Transitional Provisions Regulations 2014, a similar exception applies where, within 6 months before the step-parent became entitled to universal credit, they had an award of CTC, IS or old style JSA in which an exception corresponding with one of those set out above applied in respect of A.

[¹ Order of children and qualifying young persons

24B.—(1) Subject to to [² paragraphs (2) and (2A)], the order of children or qualifying young persons in a claimant's household is to be determined by reference to [² the date of birth of each child or qualifying young person for whom the claimant is responsible, taking the earliest date first.]   **2.104**

(2) In a case where—

(a) the date in relation to two or more children or qualifying young persons for whom the claimant is responsible (as determined under paragraph (1)) is the same date; [² . . .]

(b) [² . . .]

the order of those children or qualifying young persons (as between themselves only) in the claimant's household is the order determined by the Secretary of State that ensures that the amount mentioned in section 10(1) of the Act is available in respect of the greatest number of children or qualifying young persons.

[² (2A) Any child or qualifying young person to whom regulation 24A(1) (za) applies is to be disregarded when determining the order of children and qualifying young persons under this regulation.]

(3) In this regulation and Schedule 12, "claimant" means a single claimant or either of joint claimants.]

AMENDMENTS

1. Social Security (Restrictions on Amounts for Children and Qualifying Young Persons) Amendment Regulations 2017 (SI 2017/376) reg.2(1) and (3) (April 6, 2017).

2. Universal Credit and Jobseeker's Allowance (Miscellaneous Amendments) Regulations 2018 (SI 2018/1129) reg.3(1) and (4) (November 28, 2018).

GENERAL NOTE

2.105   This regulation establishes the rules for determining the order of children and qualifying young persons ("children" as in the General Note to reg.24A) in a household for the purposes of the "two-child limit" in s.10(1A) WRA 2012 (see the General Note to reg.24A above) by allocating a date to each child for whom the claimant is responsible. The child with the earliest date is first in the order and so on.

    The general rule in *para. (1)* is that where the claimant (or either joint claimant) is the child's parent or step-parent (other than by adoption) the date is the child's date of birth. Otherwise, the date is the date on which the claimant became responsible for the child or, if two joint claimants became responsible on different dates, the earlier of those dates.

2.106   *Paragraph (2)* establishes a qualification and an exception to that general rule. The qualification applies where the para.(1) rule determines the same date for two or more children. The exception applies where a claimant gives birth to a child less than 10 months after becoming responsible for another child as a result of a "non-parental caring arrangement" (see Sch.12, para.4). In either case, the Secretary of State must determine the order of those children so as to maximise the number of children for whom the child element is available.

    Paragraph (2A) provides that children and young persons who fall within reg.24A(1)(za)—*i.e.*, those to whom the exceptions for adoptions or non-parental caring arrangements in paras 3 and 4 of Sched 12 (including any extension of an adoption exception under para.6 of Sch.12) apply.

Housing costs

The housing costs element

2.107   **25.**—(1) Paragraphs (2) to (4) specify for the purposes of section 11 of the Act (award of universal credit to include an amount in respect of any liability of a claimant to make payments in respect of the accommodation they occupy as their home)—

(a) what is meant by payments in respect of accommodation (see paragraph (2));

(b) the circumstances in which a claimant is to be treated as liable or not liable to make such payments (see paragraph (3));

(c) the circumstances in which a claimant is to be treated as occupying or not occupying accommodation and in which land used for the purposes of any accommodation is to be treated as included in the accommodation (see paragraph (4)).

(2) The payments in respect of accommodation must be—

(a) payments within the meaning of paragraph 2 of Schedule 1 ("rent payments");

(b) [¹ . . .];

(c) payments within the meaning of paragraph 7 of that Schedule ("service charge payments").

(3) The circumstances of the liability to make the payments must be such that—

(a) the claimant (or either joint claimant)—

　　(i) has a liability to make the payments which is on a commercial basis, or

　　(ii) is treated under Part 1 of Schedule 2 as having a liability to make the payments; and

(b) none of the provisions in Part 2 of that Schedule applies to treat the claimant (or either joint claimant) as not being liable to make the payments.

(4) The circumstances in which the accommodation is occupied must be such that—

(a) the claimant is treated under Part 1 of Schedule 3 as occupying the accommodation as their home (including any land used for the purposes of the accommodation which is treated under that Part as included in the accommodation); and

(b) none of the provisions in Part 2 of that Schedule applies to treat the claimant as not occupying that accommodation.

(5) References in these Regulations—

(a) to the housing costs element are to the amount to be included in a claimant's award under section 11 of the Act;

(b) to a claimant who meets the payment condition, the liability condition or the occupation condition are, respectively, to any claimant in whose case the requirements of paragraph (2), (3) or (4) are met (and any reference to a claimant who meets all of the conditions specified in this regulation is to be read accordingly).

AMENDMENT

1. Loans for Mortgage Interest Regulations 2017 (SI 2017/725) reg. 18 and Sch. 5 para. 5(a) (April 6, 2018).

DEFINITIONS

"the Act"—see reg. 2.
"claimant"—see WRA 2012, s. 40.

GENERAL NOTE

2.108   Section 11 of the WRA 2012 allows for universal credit to include "an amount in respect of any liability of a claimant to make payments in respect of the accommodation they occupy as their home". It also provides that the accommodation must be residential accommodation and must be in Great Britain, and that the accommodation can be the whole or part of a building and need not comprise separate and self-contained premises. All the other detailed rules relating to the housing costs element are in this regulation and reg.26 and in Schs 1–5 to these Regulations (made under the powers in s.11).

Paragraphs (2) to (4) contain the three basic conditions for the payment of a housing costs element: the payment condition (para.(2)), the liability condition (para.(3)) and the occupation condition (para.(4)).

Under para.(2) and Sch.1 the payments in respect of the accommodation must be "rent payments", or "service charges" (referred to hereafter as "eligible payments"). See the notes to Sch.1 for further discussion. Owner-occupier payments are not eligible, pursuant to the Loans for Mortgage Interest Regulations 2017 (SI 2017/725), but note that those Regulations make provision for such persons to claim loans instead.

Under para.(3) and Sch.2 the claimant (or either joint claimant) must be liable to make the eligible payments on a commercial basis, or be treated as liable to make them, and must not be treated as not liable to make them. See the notes to Sch.2.

Under para.(4) and Sch.3 the claimant (or each claimant in the case of joint claimants: s.40 of the WRA 2012) must be treated as occupying the accommodation as their home, and not be treated as not occupying it. See the notes to Sch.3.

Note:

- Paragraph 4 of Sch.4 which excludes any 16 or 17 year old who is a care leaver (defined in reg.8(4)) from entitlement to a housing costs element.

- The lower work allowance applies if an award includes a housing costs element (reg.22(2)(b)).

- People who live in "specified accommodation" (see Sch.1, paras 3(h) and 3A, together with the definition of "exempt accommodation" in para.1 of Sch.1) do not receive help with housing costs through universal credit but for the time being at least this will continue to be provided by way of housing benefit.

Amount of the housing costs element—renters and owner-occupiers

2.109   **26.**—(1) This regulation provides for the amount to be included in an award in respect of an assessment period in which the claimant meets all the conditions specified in regulation 25.

(2) Schedule 4 has effect in relation to any claimant where—
(a) the claimant meets all of those conditions; and
(b) the payments for which the claimant is liable are rent payments (whether or not service charge payments are also payable).

(3) Schedule 5 has effect in relation to any claimant where—
(a) the claimant meets all of those conditions; and
(b) the payments for which the claimant is liable are—
  (i) [¹ . . .]
  (ii) service charge payments [¹ . . .].

(4) Where both paragraphs (2) and (3) apply in relation to a claimant who occupies accommodation under a shared ownership tenancy—

(a) an amount is to be calculated under each of Schedules 4 and 5; and
(b) the amount of the claimant's housing cost element is the aggregate of those amounts.

(5) But where, in a case to which paragraph (4) applies, there is a liability for service charge payments, the amount in respect of those payments is to be calculated under Schedule 4.

(6) "Shared ownership tenancy" means—
(a) in England and Wales, a lease granted on payment of a premium calculated by reference to a percentage of the value of accommodation or the cost of providing it;
(b) in Scotland, an agreement by virtue of which the tenant of accommodation of which the tenant and landlord are joint owners is the tenant in respect of the landlord's interest in the accommodation or by virtue of which the tenant has the right to purchase the accommodation or the whole or part of the landlord's interest in it.

AMENDMENT

1. Loans for Mortgage Interest Regulations 2017 (SI 2017/725) reg.18 and Sch.5, para.5(b) and (c) (April 6, 2018).

DEFINITION

"claimant"—see WRA 2012 s.40.

GENERAL NOTE

This provides that the amount of the housing costs element for renters (whether or not service charges are also payable) is to be calculated in accordance with Sch.4 (para.(2)). The amount for owner-occupiers (whether or not service charges are also payable) is calculated in accordance with Sch.5 (para.(3)(a) and (b)(i)). Schedule 5 also applies if only service charges are payable (para.(3)(b)(ii)). If the claimant occupies the accommodation under a shared ownership tenancy (defined in para.(6)), the amount of the claimant's (or claimants') housing costs element is the aggregate of the amount calculated under Schs 4 and 5 (para.(4)); in the case of shared ownership any amount for service charges is calculated under Sch.4 (para.(5)).

Note reg.39(4) of the Decisions and Appeals Regulations 2013 which provides that if the Secretary of State considers that he does not have all the relevant information or evidence to decide what housing costs element to award, the decision will be made on the basis of the housing costs element that can immediately be awarded.

Particular needs or circumstances—capability for work

Award to include [¹ LCWRA element]

27.—[¹ (1) An award of universal credit is to include an amount in respect of the fact that a claimant has limited capability for work and work-related activity ("the LCWRA element").]

(2) The [¹ amount of that element is] given in the table in regulation 36.

(3) Whether a claimant has limited capability for [¹ ...] work and work-related activity is determined in accordance with Part 5.

2.110

2.111

[¹ (4) In the case of joint claimants, where each of them has limited capability for work and work-related activity, the award is only to include one LCWRA element.]

AMENDMENT

1. Employment and Support Allowance and Universal Credit (Miscellaneous Amendments and Transitional and Savings Provisions) Regulations 2017 (SI 2017/204) reg.4(1) and (4) (April 3, 2017).

DEFINITIONS

"claimant"—see WRA 2012 s.40.
"limited capability for work"—see WRA 2012 ss.40 and 37(1).
"limited capability for work-related activity"—see WRA 2012 ss.40 and 37(2).
"work-related activity"— see WRA 2012 s.40.

GENERAL NOTE

2.112   Section 12(2)(a) and (b) WRA 2012 allows for an award of universal credit to include an additional element if the claimant (or each claimant in the case of joint claimants: s.40 WRA 2012) has limited capability for work and work-related activity ("LCWRA"). Paras (1) and (2) establish that element at a rate (in 2023/24) of £390.06. See reg.29(4) where the claimant also qualifies for the carer element (note if it is the other member of the couple that qualifies for the carer element reg.29(4) will not apply).

If both joint claimants have LCWRA, only one additional element will be included (para.(4)).

See reg.36 for the amount of the LCWRA element and reg.28 for when it will be included.

The former LCW element was abolished with effect from April 3, 2017 by the Employment and Support Allowance and Universal Credit (Miscellaneous Amendments and Transitional and Savings Provisions) Regulations 2017 (SI 2017/204) subject to the transitional and savings provisions in Sch.2, Pt 2 to those Regulations (see below). In 2023/24, the transitional rate of the LCW element is £146.31: see art.32(2) of, and Sch.13 to, SI 2023/316. See pp.166-167 of the 2016/17 edition of Vol.V for the rules that apply if Sch.2. Pt 2 applies and both joint claimants are entitled to the LCW or LCWRA elements or one is entitled to the LCW element and the other is entitled to the LCWRA element.

LCW and LCWRA are assessed in accordance with Part 5 of these Regulations. Under reg.39(1) a claimant will have LCW if it has been decided on the basis of an assessment under these Regulations or Part 4 of the ESA Regulations 2013 that they have LCW, or if they are treated as having LCW because any of the circumstances in Sch.8 apply (see reg.39(6)). Similarly, under reg.40(1), a claimant will have LCWRA if it has been decided on the basis of an assessment under these Regulations that they have LCW and LCWRA or under Part 5 of the ESA Regulations 2013 that they have LCWRA, or if they are treated as having LCW and LCWRA because any of the circumstances in Sch.9 apply (see reg.40(5)).

See reg.41 as to when an assessment may be carried out.

Note regs 19 to 27 of the Universal Credit (Transitional Provisions) Regulations 2014 (see Pt IV of this Volume) which concern the transition from old style ESA, income support on the ground of incapacity for work or disability and other incapacity benefits to universal credit.

In relation to the effect of a determination of LCW (or not), see reg.40(1) and (2) of the Decisions and Appeals Regulations 2013 which is the equivalent of reg.10 of the Social Security and Child Support (Decisions and Appeals) Regulations 1999. See the notes to reg.10 in Vol.III of this series.

Period for which the [² . . .] LCWRA element is not to be included

28.—(1) An award of universal credit is not to include the [² . . .] LCWRA element until the beginning of the assessment period that follows the assessment period in which the relevant period ends.

2.113

(2) The relevant period is the period of three months beginning with—

(a) if regulation 41(2) applies (claimant with [¹ monthly] earnings equal to or above the relevant threshold) the date on which the award of universal credit commences or, if later, the date on which the claimant applies for the [² . . .] LCWRA element to be included in the award; or

(b) in any other case, the first day on which the claimant provides evidence of their having limited capability for work in accordance with the Medical Evidence Regulations.

(3) But where, in the circumstances referred to in paragraph (4), there has been a previous award of universal credit—

(a) if the previous award included the [² . . .] LCWRA element, paragraph (1) does not apply; and

(b) if the relevant period in relation to that award has begun but not ended, the relevant period ends on the date it would have ended in relation to the previous award.

(4) The circumstances are where—

(a) immediately before the award commences, the previous award has ceased because the claimant ceased to be a member of a couple or became a member of a couple; or

(b) within the six months before the award commences, the previous award has ceased because the financial condition in section 5(1)(b) (or, if it was a joint claim, section 5(2)(b)) of the Act was not met.

(5) Paragraph (1) also does not apply if—

(a) the claimant is terminally ill; or

(b) the claimant—

(i) is entitled to an employment and support allowance that includes the support component [² . . .], or

(ii) was so entitled on the day before the award of universal credit commenced and has ceased to be so entitled by virtue of section 1A of the Welfare Reform Act 2007 (duration of contributory allowance).

(6) [² . . .]

(7) Where, by virtue of this regulation, the condition in section 5(1)(b) or 5(2)(b) of the Act is not met, the amount of the claimant's income (or, in the case of joint claimants, their combined income) is to be treated during the relevant period as such that the amount payable is the prescribed minimum (see regulation 17).

AMENDMENTS

1. Universal Credit and Miscellaneous Amendments Regulations 2015 (SI 2015/1754), reg.2(3) (November 4, 2015, or in the case of existing awards, the first assessment period beginning on or after November 4, 2015).

2. Employment and Support Allowance and Universal Credit (Miscellaneous Amendments and Transitional and Savings Provisions) Regulations 2017 (SI 2017/204) reg.4(1) and (5) (April 3, 2017).

"the Act"—see reg.2.
"assessment period"—see WRA 2012 ss.40 and 7(2) and reg.21.
"claim"—see WRA 2012 s.40.
"claimant"—*ibid.*
"couple"—see WRA 2012 ss.39 and 40.
"employment and support allowance"—see reg.2.
"joint claimants"—see WRA 2012 s.40.
"LCW element"—see regs.2 and 27.
"LCWRA element"—*ibid.*
"limited capability for work"—see WRA 2012 ss.40 and 37(1).
"limited capability for work-related activity"—see WRA 2012 ss.40 and 37(2).
"Medical Evidence Regulations"—see reg.2.
"monthly earnings"—see regs 2 and 90(6).
"work-related activity"—see WRA 2012 s.40.

GENERAL NOTE

2.114   The LCWRA element will not normally be included until the beginning of the assessment period following the assessment period in which the "relevant period" ends (para.(1)), but see the exceptions below.

The "relevant period" is a three months waiting period, starting on the first day on which the claimant submits a medical certificate, or if reg.41(2) applies because the claimant has monthly earnings equal to or above the "relevant threshold" (16 × the national minimum national wage, which is £10.42 per hour from April 1, 2023, converted to a monthly amount by multiplying by 52 and dividing by 12), the date on which the claimant's universal credit award starts, or the date the claimant applies for the LCWRA element to be included, if later (para.(2)).

A claimant does not have to serve the three months waiting period if they:

- were previously entitled to universal credit including the LCWRA element, or the three months waiting period for the LCWRA element in relation to the previous award had started but not ended, and the previous award ended immediately before the current award started because the claimant had stopped being or become a couple, or ended in the six months before the current award started because the income condition was not met (and note para.(7)). If the three month waiting period in the previous award had not been completed, the claimant will have to serve the remainder of it (paras.(3) and (4));

- are terminally ill (para.(5)(a)); or

- are entitled to ESA that includes the support component, or was so entitled on the day before the universal credit award started but the ESA ended because of the 52 week limit on entitlement to contributory ESA (para.(5)(b)).

In *JW v SSWP (UC)* [2022] UKUT 117 (AAC), the Upper Tribunal decides that a claimant who had been entitled to an award of ESA including the support component, and then claims UC, can avoid the three month waiting period even if there is a gap between receipt of the two benefits, provided the ending of ESA entitlement was not due to the claimant ceasing to meet the support component criteria:

"[14] ... the various exceptional circumstances set out in regulation 28(3)–(5) do not represent a complete code of exemptions from the normal three-month rule. Indeed, there is a common thread between the apparently disparate exceptions provided for by paragraphs (3)–(5) inclusive. None of these exceptions deals with the situation in which a claimant was previously entitled to a legacy benefit (i.e. one of those means-tested social security benefits that is in the process of being phased out by the introduction of Universal Credit). The situation of claimants entitled to legacy benefits (and to national insurance credits in default of such entitlement) is governed by the Universal Credit (Transitional Provisions) Regulations 2014."

With effect from June 29, 2023 reg.4 of the Social Security and Universal Credit (Miscellaneous Amendments) Regulations 2023 (SI 2023/543) inserts a new para.6:

"(6) Paragraph (1) does not apply where a claimant has limited capability for work and it is subsequently determined that they have limited capability for work and work-related activity."

Particular needs or circumstances–carers

Award to include the carer element

29.—(1) An award of universal credit is to include an amount ("the carer element") specified in the table in regulation 36 where a claimant has regular and substantial caring responsibilities for a severely disabled person, but subject to paragraphs (2) to (4).

(2) In the case of joint claimants, an award is to include the carer element for both joint claimants if they both qualify for it, but only if they are not caring for the same severely disabled person.

(3) Where two or more persons have regular and substantial caring responsibilities for the same severely disabled person, an award of universal credit may only include the carer element in respect of one them and that is the one they jointly elect or, in default of election, the one the Secretary of State determines.

[¹ (4) Where an amount would, apart from this paragraph, be included in an award in relation to a claimant by virtue of paragraphs (1) to (3), and the claimant has limited capability for work and work-related activity (and, in the case of joint claimants, the LCWRA element has not been included in respect of the other claimant), only the LCWRA element may be included in respect of the claimant.]

2.115

AMENDMENT

1. Employment and Support Allowance and Universal Credit (Miscellaneous Amendments and Transitional and Savings Provisions) Regulations 2017 (SI 2017/204) reg.4(1) and (6) (April 3, 2017).

DEFINITIONS

"carer element"—see reg.2.
"claimant"—see WRA 2012 s.40.
"disabled"—*ibid.*
"joint claimants"—see WRA 2012 s.40.
"LCW element"—see regs 2 and 27.
"LCWRA element"—*ibid.*
"limited capability for work"—see WRA 2012 ss.40 and 37(1).
"limited capability for work-related activity"—see WRA 2012 ss.40 and 37(2).
"regular and substantial caring responsibilities for a severely disabled person"—
    see regs 2 and 30.
"severely disabled"—*ibid.*
"work"—*ibid.*
"work-related activity"—*ibid.*

2.116   The carer element (£185.86 per assessment period: see reg.36) is included in the maximum amount if a claimant has "regular and substantial caring responsibilities for a severely disabled person" (as defined in reg.30): para.(1). Where there is a joint claim, and both parties have regular and substantial caring responsibilities for a severely disabled person, the amount is included twice, as long as they are caring for different severely disabled people: para.(2). However, if awards would also include the LCWRA element (see regs 27 and 28) as well as the carer element, then only the LCWRA element is included, unless (in the case of a joint claim), the LCWRA element has been included in respect of the other member of the couple (see reg.27(4)). This reflects the fact that, at £185.86 per assessment period, the carer element is not as high as the LCWRA element at £390.06.

Paragraph (3) governs the situation where two or more people have regular and substantial caring responsibilities for the same person. Only one of those carers can have the carer element included in an award of universal credit. They can agree between them which it is to be but, if they do not do so, the Secretary of State will decide. Under reg.50(2) and Sch.3, para.4 of the Decisions and Appeals Regulations 2013, there is no right of appeal against the Secretary of State's decision on that point.

Meaning of "regular and substantial caring responsibilities for a severely disabled person"

2.117   **30.**—(1) For the purposes of Part 1 of the Act and these Regulations, a person has regular and substantial caring responsibilities for a severely disabled person if they satisfy the conditions for entitlement to a carer's allowance or would do so but for the fact that their earnings have exceeded the limit prescribed for the purposes of that allowance.

(2) Paragraph (1) applies whether or not the person has made a claim for a carer's allowance.

(3) But a person does not have regular and substantial caring responsibilities for a severely disabled person if the person derives earned income from those caring responsibilities.

DEFINITIONS

"carer's allowance"—see reg.2.
"disabled"—see WRA 2012 s.40.
"prescribed"—see WRA 2012 s.40.
"severely disabled"—see WRA 2012 s.40.

GENERAL NOTE

2.118   A claimant has regular and substantial caring responsibilities for a severely disabled person if he or she satisfies the conditions of entitlement to carer's allowance apart from the general earnings limit (see Vol.I) as long as he or she does not have earned income from those responsibilities. It is not necessary for the claimant to have claimed carer's allowance (para.(2)): it is enough that they would meet the conditions of entitlement if they did.

Particular needs or circumstances—childcare costs

Award to include childcare costs element

2.119   **31.** An award of universal credit is to include an amount in respect of childcare costs ("the childcare costs element") in respect of an assessment period in which the claimant meets both—

(a) the work condition (see regulation 32); and
(b) the childcare costs condition (see regulation 33).

DEFINITION

"childcare costs element"—see reg.2.

GENERAL NOTE

The childcare costs element is included in the maximum amount if a claimant   2.120
satisfies both the work condition (reg.32) and the childcare costs condition (reg.33).
By reg.34, the amount of the element is 85 per cent of the charges incurred by the
claimant for "relevant childcare" up to a maximum of £646.35 per assessment
period for a single child (£951 from June 28, 2023) or £1,108.04 for two or more
children (£1,630 from June 28, 2023) (reg.36). The childcare costs element is not
reduced under the benefit cap: see reg.81(1) and (2).

The work condition

32.—(1) The work condition is met in respect of an assessment period   2.121
if—
  (a) the claimant is in paid work or has an offer of paid work that is due
     to start before the end of the next assessment period; and
  (b) if the claimant is a member of a couple (whether claiming jointly
     or as a single person), the other member is either in paid work or is
     unable to provide childcare because that person—
     (i) has limited capability for work,
     (ii) has regular and substantial caring responsibilities for a severely
       disabled person, or
     (iii) is temporarily absent from the claimant's household.
(2) For the purposes of meeting the work condition in relation to an
assessment period a claimant is to be treated as being in paid work if—
  (a) the claimant has ceased paid work—
     (i) in that assessment period,
     (ii) in the previous assessment period, or
     (iii) if the assessment period in question is the first or second assess-
       ment period in relation to an award, in that assessment period
       or in the month immediately preceding the commencement of
       the award; or
  (b) the claimant is receiving statutory sick pay, statutory maternity pay,
     [2 . . .] statutory paternity pay, [2 . . .] statutory adoption pay [1, statu-
     tory shared parental pay] [3, statutory parental bereavement pay] or
     a maternity allowance.

AMENDMENTS

1. Shared Parental Leave and Statutory Shared Parental Pay (Consequential
Amendments to Subordinate Legislation) Order 2014 (SI 2014/3255) art.28(1)
and (3)(c) (December 31, 2014).
2. Shared Parental Leave and Statutory Shared Parental Pay (Consequential
Amendments to Subordinate Legislation) Order 2014 (SI 2014/3255) art.28(1)
and (3)(a) and (b) (April 5, 2015). The amendments are subject to the transitional
provision in art.35 (see below).
3. Parental Bereavement Leave and Pay (Consequential Amendments to
Subordinate Legislation) Regulations 2020 (SI 2020/354) reg.28(1) and (3) (April
6, 2020).

Definitions

"assessment period"—see WRA 2012, ss.40 and 7(2).
"claimant"—see WRA 2012, s.40.
"maternity allowance"—see reg.2.
"paid work"—ibid.
"single person"—see WRA 2012, ss.40 and 1(2)(a).
"statutory adoption pay"—see reg.2.
"statutory maternity pay"—*ibid.*
"statutory paternity pay"—*ibid.*
"statutory shared parental pay"—*ibid.*
"statutory sick pay"—*ibid.*
"work"—see WRA 2012, s.40.

General Note

2.122   A claimant satisfies the work condition if she or he is in paid work or has an offer of paid work that is due to start before the end of the next assessment period: para. (1)(a). For joint claims (or in cases where by a member of a couple claims as a single person under reg.3(3)) there is an additional condition that the other member is either in paid work or is unable to provide childcare for one of the reasons set out in heads (i)–(iii). Claimants are treated as if they were still in paid work if they have stopped work within the periods set out in para.(2)(a) or if they are receiving statutory sick pay, statutory maternity pay, statutory paternity pay, statutory shared parental pay, statutory adoption pay (see Vol.IV) or a maternity allowance (see Vol.I).

The childcare costs condition

2.123   **33.**—(1) The childcare costs condition is met in respect of an assessment period if—
[¹ (za) the claimant has paid charges for relevant childcare that are attributable to that assessment period (see regulation 34A) and those charges have been reported to the Secretary of State [² before the end of the assessment period that follows the assessment period in which they were paid];]
    (a) [¹ the charges are in respect of]—
        (i) a child, or
        (ii) a qualifying young person who has not reached the 1st September following their 16th birthday,
    for whom the claimant is responsible; and
    (b) the charges are for childcare arrangements—
        (i) that are to enable the claimant to take up paid work or to continue in paid work, or
        (ii) where the claimant is treated as being in paid work by virtue of regulation 32(2), that are to enable the claimant to maintain childcare arrangements that were in place when the claimant ceased paid work or began to receive those benefits.
[¹ (2) The late reporting of charges for relevant childcare may be accepted in the same circumstances as late notification of a change of circumstances may be accepted under regulation 36 of the Universal Credit, Personal Independence Payment, Jobseeker's Allowance and Employment and Support Allowance (Decisions and Appeals) Regulations 2013 and, in such cases, subject to regulation 34A below, all or part of any such charges may be taken into account in any assessment period to which they relate.]

[² (3) For the purposes of paragraph (2), "the relevant notification period" in regulation 36 of the Universal Credit, Personal Independence Payment, Jobseeker's Allowance and Employment and Support Allowance (Decisions and Appeals) Regulations 2013 means a period of time ending on the last day of the assessment period that follows the assessment period in which the charges for relevant childcare were paid.]

AMENDMENT

1. Universal Credit (Digital Service) Amendment Regulations 2014 (SI 2014/2887) reg.2(1) and (2) (November 26, 2014). The amendment is subject to the saving provision in reg.5 of SI 2014/2887 (see pp.799–800 of the 2020/21 edition of Vol.V of this series).
2. Universal Credit (Childcare Costs and Minimum Income Floor) (Amendment) Regulations 2019 (SI 2019/1249) reg.2 (October 3, 2019).

DEFINITIONS

"assessment period"—see WRA 2012, ss.40 and 7(2).
"claimant"—see WRA 2012, s.40.
"paid work"—see reg.2.
"relevant childcare"—see reg.35.
"responsible for a child or qualifying young person"—see regs 2, 4 and 4A.

GENERAL NOTE

A claimant satisfies the childcare costs condition in the circumstances set out in para.(1)(za), (a) and (b). Those paragraphs are cumulative. All three must apply before the childcare costs condition is satisfied.

2.124

Paragraph (1)(za) applies if a claimant has paid charges for relevant childcare (as defined in reg.35) that are attributable to the assessment period under consideration and, subject to para.(2), have been reported to the Secretary of State before the end of that period. Reg.34A governs the assessment period to which charges are attributable.

In *Secretary of State for Work and Pensions v Salvato* [2021] EWCA Civ 1482; [2022] P.T.S.R. 366, the Court of Appeal allowed an appeal from a decision of the High Court ([2021] EWHC 102 (Admin); [2021] P.T.S.R. 1067 (Chamberlain J)) that the reg.33(1)(za) "Proof of Payment rule" (i.e. the requirement that the claimant should actually have paid childcare costs, as opposed to merely incurring a liability to do so, before the childcare costs element can be paid) was irrational and unlawfully discriminatory contrary to art.14, taken together with art.8 of, and with art.1 of the First Protocol to, the European Convention on Human Rights. The Court of Appeal decided that the "Proof of Payment rule" was rational and justified.

Paragraph (1)(a) applies if the charges are in respect of a child or a qualifying young person for whom she the claimant is responsible. A qualifying young person ceases to count for these purposes on September 1st following his or her 16th birthday.

2.125

Paragraph (1)(b) applies if the charges are for childcare arrangements to enable the claimant to work or to maintain childcare arrangements that were in place before a period when she or he is not in paid work but is treated by reg.32(2) as if she or he were.

2.126

Under para.(2) the Secretary of State may accept childcare charges that are reported after the end of the assessment period after the end of the assessment period to which they are attributable, in the same circumstances as any late notification of a change of circumstances may be accepted under reg.36 of the Decisions and Appeals Regulations 2013 (see Vol.III of this series).

Amount of childcare costs element

2.127   **34.**—(1) The amount of the childcare costs element for an assessment period is the lesser of—

[¹ (a) [² 85%] of the charges paid for relevant childcare that are attributable to that assessment period; or]

(b) the maximum amount specified in the table in regulation 36.

(2) In determining the amount of charges paid for relevant childcare, there is to be left out of account any amount—

(a) that the Secretary of State considers excessive having regard to the extent to which the claimant (or, if the claimant is a member of a couple, the other member) is engaged in paid work; or

(b) that is met or reimbursed by an employer or some other person or is covered by other relevant support.

(3) "Other relevant support" means payments out of funds provided by the Secretary of State or by Scottish or Welsh Ministers in connection with the claimant's participation in work-related activity or training.

AMENDMENT

1. Universal Credit (Digital Service) Amendment Regulations 2014 (SI 2014/2887) reg.2(1) and (3) (November 26, 2014). The amendment is subject to the saving provision in reg.5 of SI 2014/2887 (see pp.799–800 of the 2020/21 edition of Vol.V of this series).

2. Universal Credit and Miscellaneous Amendments Regulations 2015 (SI 2015/1754) reg.6 (Assessment periods beginning on or after April 11, 2016).

DEFINITIONS

"childcare costs element"—see reg.2.
"claimant"—see WRA 2012, s.40.
"couple"—see WRA 2012, ss.39 and 40.
"relevant childcare"—see reg.2 and reg.35.
"work"—see WRA 2012, s.40.

GENERAL NOTE

2.128   *Paragraph (1)*: See the note to reg.31.

The effect of the saving provision in reg.5 of SI 2014/2887 is that the amendment to para.(1) with effect from November 26, 2014 (but not the increase in the rate at which childcare costs are met from 70% to 85% with effect from April 11, 2016) only applies in "Full Service" (or "Digital Service") cases (see *Universal Credit—An Introduction* above). For the text of para.(1) as it continues to apply in "Live Service" cases (except for the change from 70% to 85%), see p.150 of the 2013/14 edition.

2.129   *Paragraphs (2) and (3)*: Charges for relevant childcare are not taken into account to the extent that the Secretary of State considers them excessive; if they are reimbursed by the claimant's employer or some other person; or if they are covered by "other relevant support" (as defined in para.(3)) paid to claimants participating in work-related activity or training.

[¹ Charges attributable to an assessment period

2.130   **34A.**—(1) Charges paid for relevant childcare are attributable to an assessment period where—

(a) those charges are paid in that assessment period for relevant childcare in respect of that assessment period; or

(b) those charges are paid in that assessment period for relevant child-care in respect of a previous assessment period; or

(c) those charges were paid in either of the two previous assessment periods for relevant childcare in respect of that assessment period.

(2) For the purposes of paragraph (1)(c), where a claimant pays charges for relevant childcare in advance, the amount which they have paid in respect of any assessment period is to be calculated as follows:

Step 1

Take the total amount of the advance payment (leaving out of account any amount referred to in regulation 34(2)).

Step 2

Apply the formula—

$$\left(\frac{PA}{D}\right) \times AP$$

Where—

PA is the amount resulting from step 1;

D is the total number of days covered by the payment referred to in step 1, and

AP is the number of days covered by the payment which also fall within the assessment period in question.

(3) In this regulation, a reference to an assessment period in which charges are paid, or in respect of which charges are paid, includes any month preceding the commencement of the award that begins on the same day as each assessment period in relation to a claimant's current award.

AMENDMENT

1. Universal Credit (Digital Service) Amendment Regulations 2014 (SI 2014/2887) reg.2(1) and (4) (November 26, 2014). The amendment is subject to the saving provision in reg.5 of SI 2014/2887 (see pp.799–800 of the 2020/21 edition of Vol.V of this series).

DEFINITIONS

"assessment period"—see WRA 2012 ss.40 and 7(2) and reg.21.
"claimant"—see WRA 2012 s.40.
"relevant childcare"—see reg.2 and reg.35.

GENERAL NOTE

Reg.34A governs when childcare charges are attributable to an assessment period   **2.131** for the purposes of reg.33(1)(za).

Para.(1) provides that charges are attributable either:

- to the assessment period in which they are paid if they are for relevant childcare in that period or (in arrears) for relevant childcare in a previous assessment period (sub-paras (a) and (b)) including, in the latter case, periods before the start of the award of universal credit (para.(3)); or

- to the assessment period in which the relevant childcare is provided if they were paid in advance in one of the two previous assessment periods (sub-para.(1)(c)). In practice, this means that childcare charges can be paid at least two months, and sometimes up to three months, in advance. Again, the previous periods can be before the start of the award of universal credit (para.(3)).

Para. (2) sets out the formula for deciding the amount of childcare charges paid in advance under para.(1)(c) that is to be attributed to an assessment period. The full amount of the advance payment (other than sums that are to be left out of account under reg.34(2) because they are excessive or are met or reimbursed by another person) is divided it by the number of days to which it relates, to produce a daily rate, and then multiplied by the number of days in the assessment period.

Meaning of "relevant childcare"

2.132

35.—(1) "Relevant childcare" means any of the care described in paragraphs (2) to (5) other than care excluded by paragraph (7) or (8).

(2) Care provided in England for a child—
(a) by a person registered under Part 3 of the Childcare Act 2006; or
[¹(b) by or under the direction of the proprietor of a school as part of the school's activities—
    (i) out of school hours, where a child has reached compulsory school age, or
    (ii) at any time, where a child has not yet reached compulsory school age; or]
[¹(c) by a domiciliary care provider registered with the Care Quality Commission in accordance with the requirements of the Health and Social Care Act 2008.]

(3) Care provided in Scotland for a child—
(a) by a person in circumstances in which the care service provided by the person consists of child minding or of day care of children within the meaning of [¹ schedule 12 to the Public Services Reform (Scotland) Act 2010 and is registered under Part 5 of that Act; or]
(b) by a childcare agency where the care service consists of or includes supplying, or introducing to persons who use the service, childcarers within the meaning of [¹ paragraph 5 of schedule 12 to the Public Services Reform (Scotland) Act 2010; or]
(c) by a local authority in circumstances in which the care service provided by the local authority consists of child minding or of day care of children within the meaning of [¹ schedule 12 to the Public Services Reform (Scotland) Act 2010 and is registered under Part 5 of that Act].

(4) Care provided in Wales for a child—
(a) by a person registered under Part 2 of the Children and Families (Wales) Measure 2010;
(b) in circumstances in which, but for articles 11, 12 or 14 of the Child Minding and Day Care Exceptions (Wales) Order 2010, the care would be day care for the purposes of Part 2 of the Children and Families (Wales) Measure 2010;
(c) by a childcare provider approved in accordance with a scheme made by the National Assembly for Wales under section 12(5) of the Tax Act 2002 [³ or made by the Welsh Ministers under section 60 (promotion etc. of well-being) of the Government of Wales Act 2006];
[¹(d) out of school hours, by a school on school premises or by a local authority;]
[¹ (e) by a person who is employed, or engaged under a contract for services, to provide care and support by the provider of a domiciliary support service within the meaning of Part 1 of the Regulation and Inspection of Social Care (Wales) Act 2016; or]

(f) by a foster parent in relation to the child (other than one whom the foster parent is fostering) in circumstances in which the care would be child minding or day care for the purposes of Part 2 of the Children and Families (Wales) Measure 2010 but for the fact that the child is over the age of the children to whom that Measure applies.

(5) Care provided anywhere outside Great Britain by a childcare provider approved by an organisation accredited by the Secretary of State.

[¹ (5A) In paragraph (2)(b), "school" means a school that Her Majesty's Chief Inspector of Education, Children's Services and Skills is, or may be, required to inspect.]

(6) In paragraphs (2)(b) and (4)(d)—

(a) "proprietor", in relation to a school, means—
   (i) the governing body incorporated under section 19 of the Education Act 2002, or
   (ii) if there is no such governing body, the person or body of persons responsible for the management of the school; and

(b) "school premises" means premises that may be inspected as part of an inspection of the school.

(7) The following are not relevant childcare—

(a) care provided for a child by a close relative of the child, wholly or mainly in the child's home; and

(b) care provided by a person who is a foster parent of the child.

(8) Care is not within paragraph (2)(a) if it is provided in breach of a requirement to register under Part 3 of the Childcare Act 2006.

(9) In this regulation "child" includes a qualifying young person mentioned in regulation 33(1)(a)(ii).

AMENDMENT

1. Social Security (Miscellaneous Amendments) (No.2) Regulations 2013 (SI 2013/1508) reg.3(1) and (6) (July 29, 2013).

2. Social Security and Child Support (Regulation and Inspection of Social Care (Wales) Act 2016) (Consequential Provision) Regulations 2018 (SI 2018/228) reg.14 (April 2, 2018).

3. Universal Credit (Childcare in Wales) (Amendment) Regulations 2021 (SI 2021/228) reg.2 (March 25, 2021).

DEFINITIONS

"child"—see WRA 2012 s.40 and para.(9).
"foster parent"—see reg.2.
"local authority"—ibid.
"qualifying young person"—see WRA 2012 s.40 and 10(5) and regs 2 and 5.

GENERAL NOTE

Under reg.33(1)(a), charges only count for the purposes of the childcare costs condition if they are paid for "relevant childcare". Regulation 35 defines that phrase. By para.(1) care is "relevant childcare" if it falls within paras (2) to (5) unless it is excluded by paras (7) or (8).   2.133

Paragraphs (2)–(5): The details differ as between England, Scotland and Wales but the rule may be summarised as being that to qualify as relevant childcare, the care must be provided by a person authorised or approved by an organ of the state to do so. In England and Wales, it can also be provided by the "proprietor"   2.134

of a "school" on "school premises". The words and phrase in quotation marks are defined in paras (5A) and (6).

2.135 *Paragraphs (7) and (8)*: Care is not relevant childcare if it is provided by an unregistered childminder (para.(8)), by a foster parent (para.(7)(b)) or by a close relative of the child (or qualifying young person: see para.(9)) wholly or mainly in the child's own home (para.(7)(a)).

General

Table showing amounts of elements

2.136   **36.**—(1) The amounts of the standard allowance, the child element, the [³ LCWRA element] and the carer element (which are all fixed amounts) and the maximum amounts of the childcare costs element are given in the following table.

(2) The amount of the housing costs element is dealt with in regulation 26.

(3) In the case of an award where the claimant is a member of a couple, but claims as a single person, the amounts are those shown in the table for a single claimant.

Element	Amount for each assessment period
Standard allowance—	
single claimant aged under 25	[⁵ £292.11]
single claimant aged 25 or over	[⁵ £368.74]
joint claimants both aged under 25	[⁵ £458.51]
joint claimants where either is aged 25 or over	[⁵ £578.82]
Child element—	
[⁵ ...]	[⁵ ...]
[⁵ each] child or qualifying young person	[⁵ £269.58]
Additional amount for disabled child or qualifying young person—	
lower rate	[⁵ £146.31]
higher rate	[⁵ £456.89]
[³ LCWRA element]—	
[³ ...]	[³ ...]
limited capability for work and work-related activity	[⁵ £390.06]
Carer element	[⁵ £185.86]
Childcare costs element—	
maximum amount for one child	[⁵ £646.35]
maximum amount for two or more children	[⁵ £1,108.04]

AMENDMENTS

1. Welfare Benefits Up-rating Order 2015 (SI 2015/30) art.13 and Sch. 5 (Assessment periods beginning on or after April 6, 2015).
2. Universal Credit and Miscellaneous Amendments Regulations 2015 (SI 2015/1754) reg.6 (Assessment periods beginning on or after April 11, 2016).
3. Employment and Support Allowance and Universal Credit (Miscellaneous Amendments and Transitional and Savings Provisions) Regulations 2017 (SI 2017/204) reg.4(1) and (7) (April 3, 2017).
4. Welfare Reform and Work Act 2016 s.14(5)(b) (April 6, 2017).
5. Social Security Benefits Up-rating Order 2023 (SI 2023/316) art 33(2) and Sch.13 (assessment periods beginning on or after April 10, 2023).

DEFINITIONS

"assessment period"—see WRA 2012, ss.40 and 7(2).
"carer element"—see reg.2.
"child element"—*ibid.*
"childcare costs element"—see reg.2.
"claimant"—see WRA 2012, s.40.
"disabled"—*ibid.*
"housing costs element"—see regs 2 and 25.
"joint claimants"—see WRA 2012, s.40.
"LCWRA element"—see regs 2 and 27.
"limited capability for work"—see WRA 2012, ss.40 and 37(1).
"limited capability for work-related activity"—see WRA 2012, ss.40 and 37(2).
"qualifying young person"—see WRA 2012, s.40 and 10(5) and regs 2 and 5.
"single claimant"—see WRA 2012, s.40.

GENERAL NOTE

The amount of each element in the universal credit calculation is prescribed by   2.137
the table (other than the housing costs element, the amount of which is prescribed
by reg.26(2)). Para.(3) provides that where a member of a couple claims as a single
person (i.e., under reg.3(3)), it is the amounts for a single person that apply.

For the rules about entitlement to each of the elements, see the notes to the earlier
regulations in Pt 4.

The amounts in the table have been up-rated six times since the first edition of
this volume. The current amounts are as set out above and, with two exceptions,
apply from April 10, 2023.

The two exceptions referred to above are the two amounts for the childcare
costs element. The original 2013/14 rates of £532.29 and £912.50 were continued through 2014/2015 and 2015/2016 but were increased from the first assessment period beginning on or after April 11, 2016, and then from April 9, 2018 to
the level still current from April 2023.

The other current amounts would normally also have been up-rated in April
2016. However, on March 16, 2016, s.11 and Sch.1 of the Welfare Reform and Work
Act 2016 came into force. As a result the following amounts were frozen at their
2015/16 levels for four tax years and were not up-rated again until April 6, 2020:

- all the rates of the standard allowance (para.1(j) of Sch.1 to the 2016 Act);
- the lower rate of the additional amount for a disabled child or qualifying
  young person (para.1(k)); and
- the LCW element (para.1(l)).

The amounts for the child element, the higher rate of the additional amount for a
disabled child or qualifying young person, the LCWRA element, the carer element,
the childcare costs element, and the housing costs element were not subject to the

four-year freeze. However, they were not up-rated for 2016/17 as the Secretary of State decided that those amounts had maintained their value in relation to prices as measured by the Consumer Prices Index over the 12 month period ending September 2015 (which had showed negative inflation of 0.1%): see para.4.2 of the Explanatory Memorandum to SI 2016/230.

Before April 6, 2017 the rate of the child element was higher for the first child or qualifying young person for whom the claimant was responsible. Under reg.43 of the Transitional Provisions Regulations 2014, the higher rate continues to apply where the claimant is responsible for a child or qualifying young person born before April 6, 2017. In 2023/24, the transitionally protected higher rate is £315.00.

With effect from June 28, 2023, the universal credit childcare cost maximum amounts increase to £951 for one child and £1,630 for two children: see the Universal Credit (Childcare) (Amendment) Regulations 2023 (SI 593/2023), reg.2. Those regulations post-date the cut-off point for this edition so are not incorporated in the main text.

Run-on after a death

2.138   **37.** In calculating the maximum amount of an award where any of the following persons has died—

    (a) in the case of a joint award, one member of the couple;

    (b) a child or qualifying young person for whom a claimant was responsible; [1 ...]

    (c) in the case of a claimant who had regular and substantial caring responsibilities for a severely disabled person, that person [1; or

    (d) a person who was a non-dependant within the meaning of paragraph 9(2) of Schedule 4,]

the award is to continue to be calculated as if the person had not died for the assessment period in which the death occurs and the following two assessment periods.

AMENDMENT

1. Universal Credit and Miscellaneous Amendments Regulations 2014 (SI 2014/597) reg.2(1) and (3) (April 28, 2014).

DEFINITIONS

"assessment period"—see WRA 2012, ss.40 and 7(2).
"claimant"—see WRA 2012, s.40.
"couple"—see WRA 2012, ss.39 and 40.
"regular and substantial caring responsibilities for a severely disabled person"—
    see regs 2 and 30.
"responsible for a child or qualifying young person"—see regs 2, 4 and 4A.
"severely disabled"—see WRA 2012, s.40.

GENERAL NOTE

2.139   Where a joint claimant, a child or qualifying young person for whom a claimant is responsible, a severely disabled person for whom a claimant had regular and substantial caring responsibilities or, from April 28, 2014, a non-dependant dies, the award of universal credit runs-on (i.e., it continues as if that person had not died) for the assessment period in which the death occurred and the following two assessment periods.

PART 5

CAPABILITY FOR WORK OR WORK-RELATED ACTIVITY

Introduction

38. The question whether a claimant has limited capability for work, or for work and work-related activity, is to be determined for the purposes of the Act and these Regulations in accordance with this Part.

2.140

DEFINITIONS

"the Act"—see reg.2.
"work-related activity"—see WRA 2012, s.40.

GENERAL NOTE

The question of whether a person has limited capability for work ("LCW") or limited capability for work and work-related activity ("LCWRA") is relevant for three reasons. Firstly, if a person has LCW or LCWRA, it affects the work requirements that can or cannot be imposed on him/her (see ss.19(2)(a) and 21(1)(a) WRA 2012). Secondly, it will entitle him/her to an additional element as part of their universal credit (see regs 27–28), although note reg.29(4) where the claimant is also eligible for the carer element. Thirdly, it determines which level of the lower or higher work allowance (if applicable) applies (see reg. 22).

2.141

Note also that the minimum age for claiming universal credit is 16 (not 18) if a person has LCW or is waiting for a work capability assessment and has submitted a medical certificate stating that they are not fit for work (see reg.8(1)(a) and (b)). In addition, if a claimant's universal credit award includes the LCWRA element, or the claimant (or either or both joint claimants) is receiving new style ESA that includes the support component, the benefit cap does not apply (see reg.83(1)(a)).

Limited capability for work

39.—(1) A claimant has limited capability for work if—

2.142

(a) it has been determined that the claimant has limited capability for work on the basis of an assessment under this Part or under Part 4 of the ESA Regulations; or

(b) the claimant is to be treated as having limited capability for work (see paragraph (6)).

(2) An assessment under this Part is an assessment as to the extent to which a claimant who has some specific disease or bodily or mental disablement is capable of performing the activities prescribed in Schedule 6 or is incapable by reason of such disease or bodily or mental disablement of performing those activities.

(3) A claimant has limited capability for work on the basis of an assessment under this Part if, by adding the points listed in column (3) of Schedule 6 against each descriptor listed in column (2) of that Schedule that applies in the claimant's case, the claimant obtains a total score of at least—

(a) 15 points whether singly or by a combination of descriptors specified in Part 1 of that Schedule;

(b) 15 points whether singly or by a combination of descriptors specified in Part 2 of that Schedule; or

(c) 15 points by a combination of descriptors specified in Parts 1 and 2 of that Schedule.

(4) In assessing the extent of a claimant's capability to perform any activity listed in Schedule 6, it is a condition that the claimant's incapability to perform the activity arises—

(a) in respect of any descriptor listed in Part 1 of Schedule 6, from a specific bodily disease or disablement;

(b) in respect of any descriptor listed in Part 2 of Schedule 6, from a specific mental illness or disablement; or

(c) in respect of any descriptor or descriptors listed in—

(i) Part 1 of Schedule 6, as a direct result of treatment provided by a registered medical practitioner for a specific physical disease or disablement, or

(ii) Part 2 of Schedule 6, as a direct result of treatment provided by a registered medical practitioner for a specific mental illness or disablement.

(5) Where more than one descriptor specified for an activity applies to a claimant, only the descriptor with the highest score in respect of each activity which applies is to be counted.

(6) [¹ Subject to paragraph (7),] A claimant is to be treated as having limited capability for work if any of the circumstances set out in Schedule 8 applies.

[¹ (7) Where the circumstances set out in paragraph 4 or 5 of Schedule 8 apply, a claimant may only be treated as having limited capability for work if the claimant does not have limited capability for work as determined in accordance with an assessment under this Part.]

AMENDMENT

1. Universal Credit and Miscellaneous Amendments Regulations 2014 (SI 2014/597) reg. 2(4) (April 28, 2014).

DEFINITIONS

"the Act"—see reg.2.
"claimant"—see WRA 2012 s.40.
"ESA Regulations"—see reg.2.
"limited capability for work"—see WRA 2012 ss.40 and 37(1).

GENERAL NOTE

2.143   A claimant will have LCW if it has been decided on the basis of an assessment under these Regulations or Part 4 of the ESA Regulations 2013 that they have LCW, or if they are treated as having LCW because any of the circumstances in Sch.8 apply (paras (1) and (6)). The effect of para.(7) is that a claimant can only be treated as having LCW under para.4 of Sch.8 (substantial risk to their health or that of someone else) or para.5 of Sch.8 (life threatening disease) once a work capability assessment has been carried out and they have been assessed as not having LCW.

Note that if a claimant has reached the qualifying age for state pension credit (the qualifying age for state pension credit for both men and women is the pensionable age for women (s.4(4) WRA 2012 and s.1(6) State Pension Credit Act 2012)—since April 2010 this has been increasing from 60 and will reach 65 in November 2018) and is entitled to disability living allowance or personal independence payment, they are treated as having LCW (para.6 of Sch.8).

See Sch.6 for the activities and descriptors for assessing LCW. They are the same as the activities and descriptors in Sch.2 to the ESA Regulations 2008 and Sch.2 to the ESA Regulations 2013 for assessing LCW.

Limited capability for work and work-related activity

40.—(1) A claimant has limited capability for work and work-related activity if—

   (a) it has been determined that—
      (i) the claimant has limited capability for work and work-related activity on the basis of an assessment under this Part, or
      (ii) the claimant has limited capability for work related activity on the basis of an assessment under Part 5 of ESA Regulations; or
   (b) the claimant is to be treated as having limited capability for work and work-related activity (see paragraph (5)).

2.144

(2) A claimant has limited capability for work and work-related activity on the basis of an assessment under this Part if, by reason of the claimant's physical or mental condition—

   (a) at least one of the descriptors set out in Schedule 7 applies to the claimant;
   (b) the claimant's capability for work and work-related activity is limited; and
   (c) the limitation is such that it is not reasonable to require that claimant to undertake such activity.

(3) In assessing the extent of a claimant's capability to perform any activity listed in Schedule 7, it is a condition that the claimant's incapability to perform the activity arises—

   (a) in respect of descriptors 1 to 8, 15(a), 15(b), 16(a) and 16(b)—
      (i) from a specific bodily disease or disablement; or
      (ii) as a direct result of treatment provided by a registered medical practitioner for a specific physical disease or disablement; or
   (b) in respect of descriptors 9 to 14, 15(c), 15(d), 16(c) and 16(d)—
      (i) from a specific mental illness or disablement; or
      (ii) as a direct result of treatment provided by a registered medical practitioner for a specific mental illness or disablement.

(4) A descriptor applies to a claimant if that descriptor applies to the claimant for the majority of the time or, as the case may be, on the majority of the occasions on which the claimant undertakes or attempts to undertake the activity described by that descriptor.

(5) [¹ Subject to paragraph (6),] A claimant is to be treated as having limited capability for work and work-related activity if any of the circumstances set out in Schedule 9 applies.

[¹ (6) Where the circumstances set out in paragraph 4 of Schedule 9 apply, a claimant may only be treated as having limited capability for work and work-related activity if the claimant does not have limited capability for work and work-related activity as determined in accordance with an assessment under this Part.]

AMENDMENT

1. Universal Credit and Miscellaneous Amendments Regulations 2014 (SI 2014/597) reg.2(5) (April 28, 2014).

DEFINITIONS

   "the Act"—see reg.2.
   "claimant"—see WRA 2012 s.40.
   "ESA Regulations"—see reg.2.

"limited capability for work"—see WRA 2012 ss.40 and 37(1).
"limited capability for work-related activity"—see WRA 2012 ss.40 and 37(2).

GENERAL NOTE

2.145   A claimant will have LCW and LCWRA if it has been decided on the basis of an assessment under these Regulations that they have LCW and LCWRA or under Part 5 of the ESA Regulations 2013 that they have LCWRA, or if they are treated as having LCW and LCWRA because any of the circumstances in Sch.9 apply (see paras (1) and (5)). The effect of para.(6) is that a claimant can only be treated as having LCW and LCWRA under para.4 of Sch.9 (substantial risk to their health or that of someone else) once a work capability assessment has been carried out and they have been assessed as not having LCW and LCWRA.

Note that if a claimant has reached the qualifying age for state pension credit (the qualifying age for state pension credit for both men and women is the pensionable age for women (s.4(4) WRA 2012 and s.1(6) State Pension Credit Act 2012)—since April 2010 this has been increasing from 60 and will reach 65 in November 2018) and is entitled to the highest rate of the care component of disability living allowance, the enhanced rate of the daily living component of personal independence payment, attendance allowance or armed forces independence payment (see the definition of "attendance allowance" in reg.2 which includes armed forces independence payment) they are treated as having LCW and LCWRA (para.5 of Sch.9).

See Sch.7 for the activities and descriptors for assessing LCW and LCWRA. They are the same as the activities and descriptors in Sch.3 to the ESA Regulations 2008 and in Sch.3 to the ESA Regulations 2013.

Work Capability Assessment

When an assessment may be carried out

2.146   **41.**—(1) The Secretary of State may carry out an assessment under this Part where—

(a) it falls to be determined for the first time whether a claimant has limited capability for work or for work and work-related activity; or

(b) there has been a previous determination and the Secretary of State wishes to determine whether there has been a relevant change of circumstances in relation to the claimant's physical or mental condition or whether that determination was made in ignorance of, or was based on a mistake as to, some material fact,

but subject to paragraphs (2) to (4).

(2) If the claimant has [¹ monthly] earnings that are equal to or exceed the relevant threshold, the Secretary of State may not carry out an assessment under this Part unless—

(a) the claimant is entitled to attendance allowance, disability living allowance [³, child disability payment] [⁴, adult disability payment] or personal independence payment; or

(b) the assessment is for the purposes of reviewing a previous determination that a claimant has limited capability for work or for work and work-related activity that was made on the basis of an assessment under this Part or under Part 4 or 5 of the ESA Regulations,

and, in a case where no assessment may be carried out by virtue of this paragraph, the claimant is to be treated as not having limited capability for work unless they are treated as having limited capability for work or for work and work-related activity by virtue of regulation 39(6) or 40(5).

(3) The relevant threshold for the purposes of paragraph (2) is the amount that a person would be paid at the hourly rate set out in [² regulation 4 of the National Minimum Wage Regulations] for 16 hours a week [¹, converted to a monthly amount by multiplying by 52 and dividing by 12].

(4) If it has previously been determined on the basis of an assessment under this Part or under Part 4 or 5 of the ESA Regulations that the claimant does not have limited capability for work, no further assessment is to be carried out unless there is evidence to suggest that—

    (a) the determination was made in ignorance of, or was based on a mistake as to, some material fact; or

    (b) there has been a relevant change of circumstances in relation to the claimant's physical or mental condition.

AMENDMENTS

1. Universal Credit and Miscellaneous Amendments Regulations 2015 (SI 2015/1754), reg.2(4) (November 4, 2015, or in the case of existing awards, the first assessment period beginning on or after November 4, 2015).

2. Social Security (Jobseeker's Allowance, Employment and Support Allowance and Universal Credit) (Amendment) Regulations 2016 (SI 2016/678), reg.5(3) (July 25, 2016).

3. Social Security (Scotland) Act 2018 (Disability Assistance for Children and Young People) (Consequential Modifications) Order 2021 (SI 2021/786) Sch.11 para.5 (July 26, 2021).

4. Social Security (Disability Assistance for Working Age People) (Consequential Amendments) Order 2022 (SI 2022/177) art.13(5) (March 21, 2022).

DEFINITIONS

"adult disability payment"—see reg.2.
"attendance allowance"—*ibid.*
"child disability payment"—*ibid.*
"claimant"—see WRA 2012 s.40.
"disability living allowance"—see reg.2.
"ESA Regulations"—*ibid.*
"limited capability for work"—see WRA 2012 ss.40 and 37(1).
"limited capability for work-related activity"—see WRA 2012 ss.40 and 37(2).
"monthly earnings"—see regs 2 and 90(6).
"National Minimum Wage Regulations" – see reg. 2.
"personal independence payment"—*ibid.*
"work-related activity"—see WRA 2012 s.40.

GENERAL NOTE

Paragraph (1)   2.147
This provides when a work capability assessment can be carried out but it is subject to paras (2)–(4).

Paragraphs (2) and (3)   2.148
The effect of these two paragraphs is that a claimant who has monthly earnings that are equal to or above the "relevant threshold" (16 × the national minimum national wage, which is £10.42 per hour from April 1, 2023, converted to a monthly amount by multiplying by 52 and dividing by 12) is treated as not having LCW (unless they are deemed to have LCW under reg.39(6) and Sch.8 or LCW and LCWRA under reg.40(5) and Sch.9) and no assessment may be carried out. But this rule does not apply if the claimant:

- is entitled to disability living allowance, personal independence payment, attendance allowance, Scottish child or adult disability payment or armed forces independence payment (see the definition of "attendance allowance" in reg.2 which includes armed forces independence payment); or

- has already been assessed as having LCW or LCW and LCWRA under these Regulations or Pt 4 or 5 of the ESA Regulations 2013 and the purpose of the assessment is to review that determination.

Paragraphs (2) and (3) thus contain what could be viewed as a rump of a "permitted work rule" (somewhat oddly placed in a regulation that is also concerned with when an assessment may be carried out). But the effect of para.(2)(b) is that a claimant will only be treated as not having LCW under para.(2) if their weekly earnings are equal to or above the relevant threshold (see para.(3)) *and* they have not yet been assessed under the work capability assessment. If the claimant has already been assessed as having LCW or LCW and LCWRA, para.(2) will not apply, although the work capability assessment may well be re-applied in these circumstances. Until it is determined that the claimant does not have LCW or LCW and LCWRA, the claimant's universal credit award will continue to include the LCW or LCWRA element (as appropriate) (confirmed in para.G1035 ADM).

Note reg.40(1) and (2) of the Decisions and Appeals Regulations 2013 which provides that a determination that a person has, or does not have, LCW, or is to be treated as having, or not having, LCW, that has been made for the purposes of new style ESA or universal credit is conclusive for the purpose of any further decision relating to that benefit.

2.149   *Paragraph (4)*

If it has been decided that the claimant does not have LCW either under these Regulations or the ESA Regulations 2013, no further assessment will be carried out for the purposes of universal credit unless the evidence suggests that the decision was made in ignorance of or mistake as to a material fact or that there has been a relevant change in the claimant's physical or mental condition (para.(4)). Note that this provision applies without time limit.

Assessment—supplementary

2.150   **42.**—(1) The following provisions apply to an assessment under this Part.

(2) The claimant is to be assessed as if the claimant were fitted with or wearing any prosthesis with which the claimant is normally fitted or normally wears or, as the case may be, wearing or using any aid or appliance which is normally, or could reasonably be expected to be, worn or used.

(3) If a descriptor applies in the case of the claimant as a direct result of treatment provided by a registered medical practitioner for a specific disease, illness or disablement, it is to be treated as applying by reason of the disease, illness or disablement.

DEFINITION

"claimant"—see WRA 2012 s.40.

Information requirement

2.151   **43.**—(1) The information required to determine whether a claimant has limited capability for work or for work and work-related activity is—

(a) any information relating to the descriptors specified in Schedule 6 or 7 requested by the Secretary of State in the form of a questionnaire; and

(b) any additional information that may be requested by the Secretary of State.

(2) But where the Secretary of State is satisfied that there is enough information to make the determination without the information mentioned in paragraph (1)(a), that information is not required.

(3) Where a claimant fails without a good reason to comply with a request under paragraph (1), the claimant is to be treated as not having limited capability for work or, as the case may be, for work and work- related activity.

(4) But paragraph (3) does not apply unless the claimant was sent a further request to provide the information at least 3 weeks after the date of the first request and at least 1 week has passed since the further request was sent.

DEFINITIONS

"claimant"—see WRA 2012 s.40.
"limited capability for work"—see WRA 2012 ss.40 and 37(1).
"limited capability for work-related activity"—see WRA 2012 ss.40 and 37(2).
"work-related activity"—see WRA 2012 s.40.

GENERAL NOTE

On paras (3) and (4), see regs 22 and 37 of the ESA Regulations 2008 and the notes to those regulations in Vol.V of this series. **2.152**

Medical examinations

44.—(1) Where it falls to be determined whether a claimant has limited capability for work or for work and work-related activity, the claimant may be called by or on behalf of a health care professional approved by the Secretary of State to attend a medical examination. **2.153**

(2) Where a claimant who is called by or on behalf of such a health care professional to attend a medical examination fails without a good reason to attend or submit to the examination, the claimant is to be treated as not having limited capability for work or, as the case may be, for work and work-related activity.

(3) But paragraph (2) does not apply unless—
(a) notice of the date, time and place of the examination was given to the claimant at least 7 days in advance; or
(b) notice was given less than 7 days in advance and the claimant agreed to accept it.

DEFINITIONS

"claimant"—see WRA 2012 s.40.
"health care professional"—see reg.2.
"limited capability for work"—see WRA 2012 ss.40 and 37(1).
"limited capability for work-related activity"—see WRA 2012 ss.40 and 37(2).
"work-related activity"—see WRA 2012 s.40.

GENERAL NOTE

See regs 23 and 38 of the ESA Regulations 2008 and the notes to those regulations in Vol.V of this series. But note that unlike regs 23 and 38, the notice under reg.44 does not have to be in writing (see para.(3)). **2.154**

PART 6

CALCULATION OF CAPITAL AND INCOME

CHAPTER 1

CAPITAL

Introduction

2.155   **45.** This Chapter provides for the calculation of a person's capital for the purpose of section 5 of the Act (financial conditions) and section 8 of the Act (calculation of awards).

DEFINITION

"the Act"—see reg.2.

GENERAL NOTE

2.156   It has been said for many years in the predecessors to this volume that "resources are to be either capital or income. There is nothing in between". That statement was cited with approval in *R(IS) 3/93* and without disapproval in *R(IS) 9/08*. On the distinction between capital and income, see the notes to reg.66(1) (unearned income), where there is some limited discussion of the general principles. Those general principles are not explored here, because the approach to income other than earnings to be taken into account in universal credit is different from that in income support, earnings have their own special definitions and deemings and, as noted below, there is a simpler approach to capital. There are particularly important disregards and deemings of capital to be income in reg.46. There will be reference back to the general principles at the appropriate places.

Compared with income support, income-based JSA, income-related ESA and housing benefit, the rules for the treatment of capital under universal credit are refreshingly concise. For example, there are only 19 paragraphs in Sch.10 (capital to be disregarded), whereas Sch.10 to the Income Support Regulations has over 70 (although a few have been omitted over the years).

The capital limit for universal credit for both a single claimant and joint claimants is £16,000 (see reg.18(1)). Note that where a claimant who is a member of a couple makes a claim as a single person (see reg.3(3) for the circumstances in which this may occur) the capital of the other member of the couple counts as the claimant's (reg.18(2)).

With effect from July 24, 2019, reg.51 of the Transitional Provisions Regulations 2014, as inserted by reg.3 of the Universal Credit (Managed Migration Pilot and Miscellaneous Amendments) Regulations 2019 (SI 2019/1152), supplies a transitional capital disregard to claimants who (i) were previously entitled to a tax credit and had capital exceeding £16,000; (ii) are given a migration notice that existing benefits are to terminate; and (iii) claim universal credit within the deadline. The disregard is of any capital exceeding £16,000. The disregard can apply only for 12 assessment periods and ceases (without the possibility of revival) following any assessment period in which the amount of capital the claimant has falls below £16,000. See regs 56 and 57 of the Transitional Provisions Regulations for further provisions on termination of the protection. The £16,000 non-disregarded capital that the claimant by definition possesses will produce an assumed yield as income of £174 per month under reg.72. Paragraph 7 of Sch.2 to the Transitional Provisions Regulations, inserted by the same Regulations, contains a disregard as capital of any amount paid as a lump sum by way of a "transitional SDP amount" under that Schedule.

What is included in capital?

46.—(1) The whole of a person's capital is to be taken into account   2.157
unless—
  (a) it is to be treated as income (see paragraphs (3) and (4)); or
  (b) it is to be disregarded (see regulation 48).
(2) A person's personal possessions are not to be treated as capital.
(3) Subject to paragraph (4), any sums that are paid regularly and by
reference to a period, for example payments under an annuity, are to be
treated as income even if they would, apart from this provision, be regarded
as capital or as having a capital element.
(4) Where capital is payable by instalments, each payment of an instalment is to be treated as income if the amount outstanding, combined with
any other capital of the person (and, if the person is a member of a couple,
the other member), exceeds £16,000, but otherwise such payments are to
be treated as capital.

GENERAL NOTE

  The whole of a claimant's capital, both actual and notional (see reg.50), counts   2.158
towards the £16,000 limit under reg.18(1), except if it is treated as income under
paras (3) and (4), or is ignored under Sch.10 or regs 75 and 76 (para.(1)). There
is also the important provision in para.(2) that personal possessions, however
acquired, are not to be treated as capital and so cannot count towards the capital
limits (see the detailed notes below). In the case of joint claimants, it is their combined capital that counts towards the £16,000 limit (s.5(2)(a) WRA 2012). A child's
capital is not taken into account.
  See the notes to s.5 of the WRA 2012 for why the burden of proving that capital
does not exceed £16,000 lies on the claimant.
  Note reg.49 which maintains the rule that applies for income support, old style
JSA, old style ESA and housing benefit that it is only if a debt is secured on a capital
asset that it can be deducted.
  There is a great deal of case law, both in the context of other social security benefits and more generally, that will be equally applicable in the context of universal
credit. See also the notes to reg.66(1) (unearned income) on the distinction between
income and capital.
  Although there is no definition of capital in the legislation, the general principle
would appear, by necessary implication especially from the rules on calculation and
valuation in reg.49, to be that anything that is not in its nature income and is not
expressly to be treated as not being capital or to be disregarded is to count if it is
capable of being sold or being converted into value in the claimant's hands (e.g. by
withdrawing money from an account, surrendering an insurance policy or raising
money by borrowing on the strength of possession of an asset or interest). The
discussion in the rest of this note (see in particular the section on *Choses in action*)
illustrates the range of things that can fall within that principle. That range will
change as social and economic developments happen. For instance, at some point,
the valuation of digital assets, such as non-fungible tokens, cryptocurrency etc.,
may have to be addressed, including how they fit into the notions of capital and of
personal possessions. There is extensive discussion of the existing legal framework
in the Law Commission's *Digital Assets: Consultation Paper* (Law Com No.256, July
28, 2022). Now see *Digital Assets: Final report* (Law Com. No.412, June 27, 2023).
  Note the discussion in the notes to reg.49 of the question of the date within an
assessment period as at which the value of capital is to be taken for the purposes of
the various limits and the calculation of "tariff" income. The unstated underlying
principle, by analogy with rules on when a supersession on the ground of change of
circumstances takes effect, appears to be that it is the position as at the end of each
assessment period that matters, including the possible attribution of notional capital

consequent on disposals during the assessment period. That position then applies for the whole of that assessment period.

Distinguishing between actual and notional capital

2.159   *AB v SSWP and Canterbury CC (IS and HB)* [2014] UKUT 212 (AAC) emphasises the importance of decision-makers and tribunals making a clear distinction in their findings of fact as to whether the claimant has actual or notional capital. If it is found that the claimant has actual capital over £16,000, there will usually be no entitlement to universal credit. If the claimant shows that they possess capital of less than £16,000, because some of it has been spent or otherwise disposed of, it is usually necessary to consider whether they should be treated as possessing notional capital (see reg.50(1) and the notes to that regulation). In this case the claimant's wife had received an inheritance. On the DWP's discovery of this, supersession of the claimant's income support and housing benefit was sought. The burden therefore shifted to the claimant to show that his wife no longer possessed that capital. See *R(SB) 38/85* where Commissioner Hallett held at para.18:

> "The claimant says that he expended this sum of £18,700 in repaying loans. It is for him to prove that this is so. Failing a satisfactory account of the way in which the money has been disposed of, it will be open to the tribunal, and a natural conclusion, to find that the claimant still has, in some form or other, that resource and consequently to conclude that his actual resources are above the prescribed limit."

The tribunal's statement of reasons in *AB* concluded that the claimant "should be deemed to still have, through his partner, capital in excess of £16,000". Judge Wikeley held that the ambiguity inherent in the use of the word "deemed" (or "treated") meant that it was not sufficiently clear whether the tribunal had found that the claimant, through his wife, still had the capital from the inheritance in some form or whether he had deprived himself of it for the purpose of obtaining benefit such as to be fixed with notional capital. In addition, the tribunal had failed to adequately explain why it did not accept the claimant's wife's explanation. In relation to this issue Judge Wikeley emphasises the importance of having a sound evidential basis for an adverse credibility finding against a claimant.

MS v DfC (JSA) [2020] NICom 42 holds that where a tribunal is not satisfied by a claimant's assertion that they have disposed of money, so that the amount remains part of their actual capital, it is not necessary for the tribunal to make a positive finding of fact about where the money was actually held. Submissions to the contrary were based on a misreading of remarks in *DMcC v DSD (IS)* [2012] NICom 326. That is different from a situation like that in *WR v SSWP (IS)* [2012] UKUT 127 (AAC), where the tribunal was not satisfied by the claimant's explanation of why she had made payments to each of her parents. That dissatisfaction did not justify a conclusion that the money involved remained part of her actual capital.

Actual capital

2.160   There is a good deal of law on actual capital.

The first condition is of course that the capital resource is the claimant's or their partner's. This is not as simple as it sounds.

In *CIS/634/1992* the claimant was made bankrupt on November 29, 1990. However, his trustee in bankruptcy was not appointed until April 1991. Between November 29 and December 28, 1990, when he claimed income support, the claimant divested himself of most of his capital. Under the Insolvency Act 1986 (subject to certain exceptions) a bankrupt's property does not vest in their trustee in bankruptcy on the making of a bankruptcy order, but only when the trustee is appointed. The appointment does not have retrospective effect. It is held that since he had failed to give a satisfactory account of how he had disposed of his capital he was to be treated as still possessing it (*R(SB) 38/85* referred to in the notes to reg.50). Thus the claimant was not entitled to income support prior to the appointment of the trustee in bankruptcy because until then he possessed actual capital over the income support limit.

KS v SSWP (JSA) [2009] UKUT 122 (AAC), reported as [2010] AACR 3, however, disagrees with *CIS/634/1992*. Judge Mark points out that a person cannot realise or use any part of their capital after a bankruptcy order has been made and that, subject to any order of the court, it will vest in his trustee in due course. Whether the capital remained the claimant's with a nil value or whether it ceased to be his capital at all (on which Judge Mark did not reach any firm conclusion), the result was that the claimant had no capital, or no capital of any value, after the bankruptcy order had been made.

In *SH v SSWP* [2008] UKUT 21 (AAC) Judge Turnbull also does not reach a final conclusion as to whether money in a bank account or other property that is subject to a restraint order under s.77 of the Criminal Justice Act 1988 (now the Proceeds of Crime Act 2002) or a freezing order ceases to be the claimant's capital. He was inclined to think that such assets remained the claimant's capital. However, their market value would be nil since the claimant was prohibited by court order from disposing of them. *CS v Chelmsford BC (HB)* [2014] UKUT 518 (AAC) takes the same view as *SH* but again without reaching a final conclusion on the point. In *CS*, which concerned assets subject to a restraint order under the Proceeds of Crime Act 2002, Judge Markus points out that not only is a restraint order under the Proceeds of Crime Act 2002 not expressed to deprive people of their interest in the property but also the terminology of the Act consistently presupposes that they retain their interest in property that is subject to a restraint order. Its market value, however, would be nil.

R(IS) 9/04 confirms that assets being administered on a patient's behalf either at the Court of Protection or by their receiver remain the patient's assets which have to be valued at their current market value (see reg.49) (following *CIS/7127/1995*). Such assets are held under a "bare trust" with the entire beneficial ownership remaining with the patient. The fact that the Court had discretionary powers of control over the management of the patient's property for their benefit did not mean that the patient's beneficial ownership had ceased.

However, capital that a claimant is under a "certain and immediate liability" to repay at the moment of its receipt by, or attribution to, the claimant, will not count as their capital (*CIS/2287/2008*). In *CIS/2287/2008* the Commissioner decides that the principle in *Chief Adjudication Officer v Leeves*, reported as *R(IS) 5/99*, does apply to capital as well as income. However, it only applies at the moment of receipt or attribution and is relevant only to the issue of whether money or an asset should be classified as the claimant's capital. *Leeves* does not apply if the liability to repay arises after something has become capital in the claimant's hands. That issue continues to be governed by the principle in *R(SB) 2/83* that, in calculating capital, liabilities are not to be deducted, except those expressly provided for in the legislation. *SSWP v GF (ESA)* [2017] UKUT 333 (AAC), discussed later in this note under the heading *Deduction of liabilities*, is a recent application of the principle of *R(SB) 2/83*. See also *JH v SSWP* [2009] UKUT 1 (AAC) which explains that *Leeves* only operates where, outside trust relationships, there is a certain obligation of immediate repayment or return of the asset to the transferor. It does not bite where the claimant is under some liability to a third party.

Interests under a will or intestacy when someone has died

The ADM (paras H1169–1178) contains guidance adopting in para.H1174 the general principle that a beneficiary under a will or intestacy has no legal or equitable interest in any specific property while the estate remains unadministered. The personal representative in those circumstances has full ownership of the assets of the estate. That principle was applied by the Tribunal of Commissioners in *R(SB) 5/85*, relying on the foundational Privy Council decision in *Commissioner of Stamp Duties (Queensland) v Livingston* [1965] A.C. 694.

2.161

However, there are two important qualifications. The first is that, even where the *Livingston* principle applies, the beneficiary has a right to have the deceased's estate properly administered. That is a chose in action that has a market value. It can be transferred and can be borrowed against. Depending on the particular circumstances, the market value can be considerable and not far off the value that would be put on the asset(s) in question if owned outright. That point was made clearly by Commissioner Howell in para.28 of his decision in *R(IS) 1/01* and nothing to the contrary was said in the Court of Appeal in *Wilkinson v Chief Adjudication Officer*, reported as part of *R(IS) 1/01*, in upholding the Commissioner's decision. Nor is *R(SB) 5/85* to the contrary: the Commissioners there expressly noted that the claimant had a chose in action (para.7). It is submitted that that is the basis on which the later decision of Commissioner Howell in *CIS/1189/2003* is to be supported. The claimant there was the sole residuary beneficiary under her mother's will and the estate, whose main asset was a property that the claimant did not live in, remained unadministered for several years, so that the property had not actually vested in the claimant. In para.11, the Commissioner said that the claimant was beneficially entitled to the property from the date of her mother's death subject only to the formalities needed to perfect her title, so that for all practical purposes she had an entitlement equivalent to full beneficial ownership. That proposition can easily be misinterpreted, but in para.12 the Commissioner noted that as the claimant was the sole *residuary* beneficiary, it was para.28 of *R(IS) 1/01* that was applicable. So the valuation was of the claimant's chose in action, but in the circumstances the difference in value from that of full beneficial ownership was negligible.

The second qualification is that the position may be different where there has been a specific gift of some asset, as was the case in *R(IS) 1/01*, where the will of the claimant's mother gave the claimant and her brother equal shares in some income bonds and other money in a bank account and in a property. The matter was put very strongly by Commissioner Howell in para.27 of his decision, where he said that the *Livingston* principle had:

"never had any application to property specifically devised or bequeathed by a will. Such property becomes in equity the property of the legatee as soon as the testator dies, subject only to the right of the personal representative to resort to it for payment of debts if the remainder of the estate is insufficient for this purpose [citations omitted]."

No specific comment on that proposition was made in the judgments of the Court of Appeal in *Wilkinson*, but Mummery LJ did note generally that the evidence did not suggest that there was any question of the executors needing to have recourse to the property for payment of debts or that there was any other legal obstacle to the immediate completion of the administration of the estate and to an assent by the executors vesting the property in the names of the claimant and her brother as joint owners. That strongly suggests that what was being considered was a valuation of the claimant's chose in action, rather than of some equitable interest. It is submitted that that is the proper approach. The valuation would therefore be sensitive to the possibilities mentioned by Mummery LJ in the particular case, as well as to the value of the underlying asset. That approach would hold also for personal property or money, although there it should be noted that the process of the personal representative giving an assent, i.e. an indication that a certain asset is not required for administration purposes and may pass under the will or (possibly) an intestacy into the ownership of the beneficiary, does not need to be in writing and may be implied from conduct.

Beneficial ownership

2.162   The mere fact that an asset or a bank or building society account is in the claimant's sole name does not mean that it belongs to the claimant. It is the "beneficial ownership" which matters. It is only such an interest that has a market value. The claimant may hold the asset under a trust which means that they cannot simply treat the asset as theirs, but must treat it as if it belonged to the beneficiary or beneficiaries under the trust. It is they who are "beneficially entitled." A trustee may also be a beneficiary, in which case the rule in reg.47 may come into play, or may have no beneficial interest at all (see further below under *Claimant holding as trustee*).

The basic principle was confirmed, as might have been thought unnecessary, by Judge Poynter in *SSWP v LB of Tower Hamlets and CT* (IS & HB) [2018] UKUT 25 (AAC) (see the notes under *Claimant holding as a trustee* for the details). However, it appeared that local authorities had routinely been submitting in housing benefit cases, wrongly taking a single sentence from the same judge's earlier decision in *CH/715/2006* out of context, that only legal interests were relevant.

These issues often arise in the context of attributing the beneficial ownership of former matrimonial assets. One example is *R(IS) 2/93*. The claimant had a building society account in her sole name, which she had had since before her marriage. Her husband deposited the bulk of the money in it, including his salary. On their separation, the AO and the SSAT treated the entire amount in the account as part of the claimant's capital. The Commissioner holds that she was not solely beneficially entitled to the money so that the equivalent of reg.47 on jointly held capital had to operate (although that operation would not now be accepted as following in such circumstances: see the notes to reg.47). There is helpful guidance on the limited circumstances in which the "presumption of advancement" (i.e. that when a husband puts an asset into his wife's name he intends to make an outright gift of it) will operate in modern circumstances. (Note that the presumption of advancement was due to be abolished by s.199 of the Equality Act 2010 but this section has not yet been brought into force.) And see *CIS/982/2002* on the valuation of a share in a frozen joint bank account. Note also *R(IS) 10/99* below. In *CIS/553/1991*, where a house was in the husband's sole name, it was held that its valuation should take into account the wife's statutory right of occupation under the Matrimonial Homes Act 1967. See also *R(IS) 1/97*, where the claimant, who separated from his wife, agreed that she could live in the former matrimonial home, which was in his sole name, for her lifetime, which the Commissioner considered created a constructive trust.

In most cases of spouses or civil partners, in whoever's name the asset is, there will be some degree of joint ownership. But if an asset is in the sole name of one, the other should not be treated as having a half share as a beneficial tenant in common under reg.47 until it has been established that they do own at least part of it. On this, see *R(IS) 1/03*, which holds that a person's right to seek a lump sum payment or property transfer order under the Matrimonial Causes Act 1973 is not a capital asset. Moreover, *CIS/984/2002* should also be noted in this context. This holds that money held by the claimant's solicitor pending quantification of the statutory charge to the Legal Services Commission under s.10(7) of the Access to Justice Act 1999 was not part of the claimant's capital. Until that quantification had been carried out, it was not possible to identify any particular amount as the claimant's capital. Another way of looking at it was to treat the statutory charge as an incumbrance for the purpose of the equivalent of reg.49(1)(b) (see *CIS/368/1993*). Nor was any part of the money available to the claimant on application for the purposes of reg.51(2) of the Income Support Regulations. See also *CIS/7097/1995*, discussed in the notes to reg.47.

In *LC v Bournemouth Borough Council (HB)* [2016] UKUT 175 (AAC), the proceeds of sale of a former matrimonial home were being held in a solicitors' client account until the claimant's partner and his ex-wife agreed how the sum was to be split or the issue was resolved by a court order after a Financial Dispute Resolution hearing. In the judge's view the value of the capital prior to agreement or an order of the court would be minimal. The local authority had jumped the gun by treating the claimant as having capital in excess of £16,000 from the date the proceeds were placed in the client account.

Claimant holding as trustee

It would take many whole books to explore all the circumstances in which a trust relationship arises such that a person who holds the legal ownership of assets is

2.163

subject to trust duties towards other people and so is a trustee and either has no beneficial interest in the assets or only a partial interest. The notes that follow concentrate on the social security case law, but only the barest outline of the general law can be given. In novel or complex cases there may need to be reference to specialist trust books. Sometimes the social security cases refer helpfully to the more general authorities. See, for recent examples, *SSWP v LB of Tower Hamlets and CT (IS & HB)* [2018] UKUT 25 (AAC) on resulting trusts and *VMcC v SSWP (IS)* [2018] UKUT 63 (AAC) on the *Quistclose* principle, both discussed further below.

The following notes first deal briefly with express trusts, where the existence and terms of the trust are stated or accepted, then with circumstances in which trusts arise by some form of implication, i.e implied, resulting or constructive trusts.

A trust can be created by declaration when assets are acquired (e.g. the familiar transfer of a house to a couple as beneficial joint tenants or tenants in common) or over assets already owned. In relation to assets other than land, no particular formality is required, although there must be certainty as to the assets covered by the trust and the beneficiaries as well as on the intention to create a trust. There may therefore be difficult questions in particular cases over whether there is sufficient persuasive evidence of the existence of a trust (as exemplified in several cases discussed below). It is in general for a claimant who has been shown to be the legal owner of an asset to show that they are not a beneficial owner (*MB v Royal Borough of Kensington and Chelsea (HB)* [2011] UKUT 321 (AAC) and *CT*, above).

In relation to trusts of land, *SB v SSWP (IS)* [2012] UKUT 252 (AAC) is a useful reminder that s.53(1)(b) of the Law of Property Act 1925 only requires a trust relating to land to be evidenced in writing. Absence of writing makes the trust unenforceable but not void. The tribunal had found that there was no trust of the property in question because there was no trust deed. That error of law had led the tribunal to fail to investigate and make findings on whether there had been a declaration of trust, whether the scope of the trust was certain, the subject matter of the trust, the objects/persons intended to benefit from any such trust and (in the absence of any documentation) whether the surrounding circumstances were consistent with the existence of a trust. It follows from the principle that the trust is merely unenforceable that the existence of later evidence in writing satisfies s.53(1) from the date of the original declaration. It is also said that the statute cannot be used as an instrument of fraud, so that a person who has taken the property knowing of the trust cannot be heard to deny the trust, despite there being no evidence in writing. Note also that s.53(1) does not apply to implied, resulting or constructive trusts.

In *R(IS) 1/90*, the claimant established a building society account in his own name which was to be used solely to finance his son's medical education. He executed no documents about the account. It was argued that there was sufficient evidence of a declaration of trust over the account, but the Commissioner held that the claimant had not unequivocally renounced his beneficial interest in the sum in the account. Although he had earmarked the money for the son's education, the situation was like an uncompleted gift and there was insufficient evidence of a declaration of trust.

For the position under Scots law see *R(IS) 10/99*. The claimant agreed that he would pay his former wife (from whom he was separated) £22,250, representing a share of his pension. When he claimed income support, the claimant had £15,500 in his bank account that he said he was holding for his wife. The Commissioner decides that the £15,500 was not subject to a trust. That was because there had been no delivery of the subject of the trust, nor any satisfactory equivalent to delivery, "so as to achieve irrevocable divestiture of the truster [the equivalent of the settlor in English law] and investiture of the trustee in the trust estate", as required by Scots law (see *Clark Taylor & Co Ltd v Quality Site Development (Edinburgh) Ltd* 1981 S.C. 11). There was no separate bank account and there had been no clear indication to the claimant's wife that the money was held on trust for her. In addition, as the truster would have been the sole trustee, the Requirements of Writing

(Scotland) Act 1995 required the trust to be proved in writing. That had not been done. Nor was there an "incumbrance" within the meaning of the equivalent of reg.49(1)(b) preventing the claimant disposing of the money. The consequence was that the £15,500 counted as the claimant's capital. No doubt the result would have been the same if the principles of trust law in England and Wales had been applied. Mere mental earmarking of an asset for a particular purpose is not enough to show the existence of a trust.

For a further case which considered whether a trust had been validly constituted for the purposes of Scots law, see *CSIS/639/2006*.

One particular instance of a resulting trust is where a person gives or loans some amount to another to be used for a particular purpose. In *R(SB) 53/83* the claimant's son had paid him £2,850 to be used for a holiday in India. The claimant died without taking the holiday or declaring the existence of the money to the DHSS. The Commissioner, applying the principle of *Barclays Bank Ltd v Quistclose Investments Ltd* [1970] A.C. 567, held that there was a trust to return the money to the son if the primary purpose of the loan was not carried out. Since the Commissioner held that there had been no overpayment while the claimant was alive, this must mean that the claimant held the money on trust to use it for the specified purpose or to return it (a result most recently confirmed by the decision of the Privy Council in the *Prickly Bay* case: see further below). It was not part of the claimant's resources. This is an important decision, which overtakes some of the reasoning of *R(SB) 14/81* (see the notes to reg.49). The actual decision in *R(SB) 53/83* was reversed (by consent) by the Court of Appeal, because the Commissioner had differed from the appeal tribunal on a point of pure fact. *R(SB) 1/85* holds that this does not affect its authority on the issue of principle. In *R(SB) 1/85*, the claimant's mother-in-law had some years previously provided the money for the purchase of the lease of a holiday chalet for the use of the claimant's mentally handicapped son, Keith. The lease was in the claimant's name and its current value was probably about £5,000. The AO's initial statement of the facts was that the mother-in-law had bought the chalet in the claimant's name. The Commissioner held that this would give rise to a presumption of a resulting trust in her favour, so that the claimant would have no beneficial interest in the chalet—nothing he could sell. The presumption could be rebutted if in fact the mother-in-law had made an outright gift to the claimant, or to Keith. In the second case the claimant again would have no beneficial interest. In the first, he would be caught, for even if he had said that he intended to use the chalet purely for Keith, there was not the necessary written evidence of the trust (Law of Property Act 1925 s.53). Another possibility was that the mother-in-law had made a gift to the claimant subject to an express (but unwritten) trust in favour of Keith, when again the claimant clearly would not be the beneficial owner, as that would be a fraud. This is a very instructive decision, which will give valuable guidance in sorting out many family-type arrangements.

The dangers and difficulties of *Quistclose* were pointed out in *CSB/1137/1985*, particularly where family transactions are concerned. There, the claimant had received loans of £1,000 and £500, to fund a trip to India, from friends originally from the same village, who both later provided letters to say that, as the trip had not been taken, they had asked for, and received, their money back. Commissioner Rice held that the tribunal had gone wrong in law in concluding, following *R(SB) 53/83*, that the claimant did not have any beneficial interest in the funds, because the relationship between the lenders and the claimant indicated that nothing as sophisticated as the imposition of a trust had been intended. Rather, it had not been shown that there was any restriction on the claimant's use of the money.

Judge Wikeley in *VMcC v SSWP (IS)* [2018] UKUT 63 (AAC) has recently helpfully summarised the test required for the imposition of a *Quistclose* trust as set out in recent authority (in particular *Twinsectra Ltd v Yardley* [2002] 2 A.C. 164 and *Bellis v Challenor* [2015] EWCA Civ 59) and also discussed the distinction between *R(SB) 53/83* and *CSB/1137/1985*. The summary in para.42 is this:

"The funds must be transferred on terms, typically for a stated purpose, which do not leave them at the free disposal of the transferee;
There must be an intention to create what is, viewed objectively, a trust;
A person creates a trust by their words or conduct, not their innermost thoughts;
If such a trust is created, then the beneficial interest in the property remains in the transferor unless and until the purposes for which it has been transferred have been fulfilled;
If such a trust is not created, then the ordinary consequence is that the money becomes the property of the transferee, who is free to apply it as they choose."

In addition, *Twinsectra* established that if there is a lack of clarity in identifying the stated purpose such that the funds cannot be applied the transferor's beneficial interest continues. Judge Wikeley acknowledged that there appeared to be a very thin line between the circumstances in *R(SB) 53/83* and *CSB/1137/1985*, but suggested in para.48 that, as well as the purpose being more specific, it might have been significant that the funds in *R(SB) 53/83* had been transferred, while the transaction in *CSB/1137/1985* was described in terms of a loan. With respect, it is hard to see why the transaction being a loan should point towards the claimant in *CSB/1137/1985* being subject to no trust obligations. It might be thought that the distinction, fine though it may be, was more in there not having been the necessary words or conduct, rather than innermost thoughts.

The Privy Council in *Prickly Bay Waterside Ltd v British American Insurance Co Ltd* [2022] UKPC 8; [2022] 1 W.L.R. 2087, while accepting the value of summaries of principles, in particular of those established by the judgment of Lord Millett in *Twinsectra*, warned against not going back to the "core analysis" in that judgment. It was emphasised again that it is not enough that money is provided for a particular purpose. The question is whether the parties intended that the money should be at the free disposition of the recipient. An intention that it should not be need not be mutual, in the sense of being shared or reciprocated, but could be imposed by one party and acquiesced in by the other. A *Quistclose* trust is a default trust, so can be excluded or moulded by the terms of the parties' express agreements. In the particular case, involving complex commercial transactions in which a sum was loaned to a bank that contracted to guarantee payment of the purchase price of a property on future completion, it was significant to the outcome that a *Quistclose* trust had not been established that there had been no requirement that the sum be segregated by the bank from its other funds. It is submitted that in other contexts, such as family or other relatively informal arrangements more likely to be encountered in the social security context, a lack of segregation, say into a separate account, would not carry nearly such weight.

Cases in which *Quistclose* has been applied include the following. In *R(SB) 12/86*, £2,000 was lent to the claimant on condition that she did not touch the capital amount, but only took the interest, and repaid the £2,000 on demand. The £2,000 was not part of her capital, never having been at her disposal. The Commissioner in *CSB/975/1985* was prepared to apply the principle to a loan on mortgage from a Building Society for property renovation. But it would have to be found that the loan was made for no other purpose and was to be recoverable by the Building Society if for any reason the renovations could not be carried out. The furthest extension so far of the *Quistclose* principle is in *CFC/21/1989*. The claimant's father paid her each month an amount to meet her mortgage obligation to a building society. The Commissioner accepts that the money was impressed with a trust that it should be used only for that purpose and did not form part of her capital. The extension is that the purpose was to meet expenditure on an item that could be covered by income support.

The facts in *VMcC* were very unusual. The claimant, who was a member of the Traveller community, had two accounts with TSB and Nationwide opened in her own name when she was a child (probably when she was about seven) for members of her family to put money in for her future education. When she became pregnant at the age of 19 she was disowned by her family and claimed income support in April 2015, disclosing two bank accounts, but not the TSB and Nationwide accounts. She said she only became aware of those accounts at a compliance interview in July 2015 and in August produced evidence that both accounts had been closed. She said that all the amounts in the accounts (some £13,000) had been returned to the family members by her mother, save for £2,000 that she was allowed to keep for her baby. The decision-maker treated all the amounts as the claimant's, generating a tariff income, and that was upheld on appeal. The tribunal found that as the claimant had opened the accounts she would have known of them and concluded that she could have used the money as she pleased. If her mother or the family had wanted to set aside money for her education they could have opened a trustee account. Judge Wikeley set the tribunal's decision aside because there was not evidence to support the finding that the claimant had opened the TSB and Nationwide accounts and gave some guidance to a new tribunal on rehearing. In para.44 he cited what had been said in the commentary in Vol.II of this series, that there may well be evidential difficulties in establishing the components of a *Quistclose* trust in the context of family arrangements, not least because there is often no contemporary documentation, but stressed that the absence of a paper trail is not necessarily determinative. In principle a *Quistclose* trust can be created informally and by word of mouth, although very careful fact-finding is necessary. After comparing the outcomes of *R(SB) 53/83* and *CSB/1137/1995* (see above), he mentioned in para.47 two particular factors to be considered in family-type cases:

"The first is that in practice it is unusual for informal family arrangements to be contemporaneously evidenced in writing (whether within the Traveller community or elsewhere). The second is that if the Appellant's account about being cast out by the community is accepted, that in itself may explain the failure of witnesses to attend an oral hearing to support her."

The question was not what was objectively reasonable (or what a High Street solicitor would have advised) but whether the claimant's account could be accepted in the light of what was customary in the particular community (para.61). It should also be noted that the Secretary of State accepted that an account may contain funds subject to a trust mixed with funds that are not so subject (para.51).

Cases in which *Quistclose* has not been applied include the following, many of which illustrate the thinness of the line between an outright gift or loan and one subject to an implied trust. *R(IS) 5/98* reached a similar outcome without any mention of *Quistclose*. The claimant had transferred her flat to her daughter partly on the condition that her daughter looked after her. It was held that the gift failed when this condition was not fulfilled and the daughter held the flat on trust for her mother. An appeal against this decision was dismissed by the Court of Appeal (*Ellis v Chief Adjudication Officer*, reported as part of *R(IS) 5/98*). The claimant had argued that the condition was void for uncertainty but this was rejected by the Court (and in accordance with the principles summarised in *VMcC* that would have led to the beneficial interest remaining with the mother from the outset).

In *YH v SSWP (IS)* [2015] UKUT 85 (AAC) the claimant raised a loan on his property and gave the money to his sons to establish a business. The sons used the money to set up the business and made the repayments on the loan. The *Quistclose* principle did not apply because there was no evidence to suggest that the lender had advanced the money on the condition that it was only to be used to establish the sons' business. A borrower does not create a trust in favour of the lender simply by having their own clear intention as to the application of the money. There was no separation between legal and beneficial interest so far as the sons were concerned, so that there was a question of whether the claimant had notional capital on the deprivation under the equivalent of reg.50(1).

A further example occurred in *CIS/5185/1995*, which held that *Quistclose* did not apply to a student grant which the claimant became liable to repay to the education authority when he left his course early. The grant could not be disregarded under the *Quistclose* principle because the education authority retained no beneficial interest in the grant. The authority merely reserved the right to demand repayment of a sum calculated according to the unexpired balance of the relevant term when the person ceased to be a student. In *Chief Adjudication Officer v Leeves*, reported as *R(IS) 5/99*, it was conceded on behalf of the claimant that there was no constructive trust in these circumstances, since no proprietary right had been retained by the education authority, nor had any fiduciary obligation been created.

In *MW v SSWP (JSA)* [2016] UKUT 469 (AAC), reported as [2017] AACR 15, a Scottish case, it was held that circumstances which would in England and Wales have given rise to a *Quistclose* trust did not do so as a matter of Scots law, because Scots law did not recognise a trust where the sole beneficiary was a trustee. The claimant had been lent money by his mother in order to buy his house. If it was not used for that purpose it was to be returned. Judge Gamble held that nevertheless the claimant was subject to a personal obligation to his mother to use the money only for the specified purpose, which in Scots law had a similar effect to a *Quistclose* trust, so that for the period in question the money lent did not form part of his capital. It is perhaps unclear to a non-Scots lawyer just why a trust could not be recognised (would not the mother also be a beneficiary?), but that appears not to matter as the essence of the decision is in the effect of the personal obligation identified by the judge.

So far as resulting trusts in general are concerned, the most authoritative statement is that of Lord Browne-Wilkinson, speaking for the majority of the House of Lords, in *Westdeutsche Landesbank Girozentrale v Islington LBC* [1996] A.C. 669 at 708:

"Under existing law a resulting trust arises in two sets of circumstances: (A) where A makes a voluntary payment to B or pays (wholly or in part) for the purchase of property which is vested either in B alone or in the joint names of A and B, there is a presumption that A did not intend to make a gift to B: the money or property is held on trust for A (if he is the sole provider of the money) or in the case of a joint purchase by A and B in shares proportionate to their contributions. It is important to stress that this is only a presumption, which presumption is easily rebutted either by the counter-presumption of advancement or by direct evidence of A's intention to make an outright transfer .... (B) [*Quistclose* cases]."

That statement was cited in para.48 of *SSWP v LB of Tower Hamlets and CT (IS & HB)* [2018] UKUT 25 (AAC), where it was also noted that in *R(SB) 49/83* Commissioner Hallett stated that "the principle that purchase of land in the name of another gives rise to a resulting trust for the true purchaser has been settled for centuries". The principle rests on giving effect to the common intention of the parties.

In *R(SB) 49/83* the claimant had bought a house, but said that this was on behalf of his son, who had not been able to obtain a loan in his own name but was paying off the loan. The Commissioner held that if this could be established, the claimant would hold the house on a resulting trust for his son. However, he stressed that the credibility of the claimant's evidence, in the light of any further documents that came forward, needed to be carefully tested. For instance why did the house have to be transferred into the claimant's name, rather than him guaranteeing a loan to his son?

In *CT* the claimant bought a house in her sole name with a buy-to-let mortgage, intending that the mortgage interest would be met by the rental income. The purchase price and expenses came to £377,728.09. The mortgage loan was for £310,215. The claimant only had £250 capital to contribute, so agreed with a friend, Mr G, for him to contribute the remaining £67,263.09. They could reach no agreement at the time about what interest that gave him in the property. On claims for income support and housing benefit the claimant was initially treated as having capital of the value of the house less the amount of the incumbrance of the mortgage and 10% for expenses of sale. A tribunal held that she held the property on a resulting trust for Mr G. That decision was upheld by the Upper Tribunal on the basis that the claimant's beneficial interest was only 0.04% of the value (£250 as against £67,362.09). That result would follow from the plain application of the general resulting trust principles, in that the payments of mortgage had no effect on the beneficial interests, as while the house was let they came out of the rent (to which the two would have been entitled in proportion to their beneficial interests). That was not affected by a period in which the claimant was forced to live in the house while her own home was uninhabitable and she paid the mortgage interest. That was equivalent to her paying an occupation rent.

The main submission made by the Secretary of State on the appeal to the Upper Tribunal was that the tribunal's approach was incompatible with that of the Supreme Court in *Jones v Kernott* [2011] UKSC 53; [2012] 1 A.C. 776, under which what was fair in the light of the whole course of dealings between the parties was determinative. Judge Poynter provides a helpful analysis of the effect of the decisions in *Stack v Dowden* [2007] UKHL 17; [2007] 2 A.C. 432 and *Jones v Kernott* in "family home" type cases. The principles applicable in such cases were summarised as follows in para.51 of the joint judgment of Lady Hale and Lord Walker in *Jones v Kernott* (the words in square brackets in sub-para.(1) were added by Judge Poynter when citing this passage in *CT*):

"*Conclusion*
51. In summary, therefore, the following are the principles applicable in a case such as this, where a family home is bought in the joint names of a cohabiting couple who are both responsible for any mortgage, but without any express declaration of their beneficial interests.
(1) The starting point is that equity follows the law and they are joint tenants both in law and in equity. [As this decision will be read by people who are not legally qualified, I should explain that the phrase "joint tenants" in this context has a technical legal meaning and is not a generic reference to any co-owner. To summarise, the distinction being drawn by the Supreme Court is between "joint tenants", who always own a property equally, and "tenants in common" who may own a property in equal shares but do not necessarily do so.]
(2) That presumption can be displaced by showing (a) that the parties had a different common intention at the time when they acquired the home, or (b) that they later formed the common intention that their respective shares would change.
(3) Their common intention is to be deduced objectively from their conduct:

"the relevant intention of each party is the intention which was reasonably understood by the other party to be manifested by that party's words and conduct notwithstanding that he did not consciously formulate that intention in his own mind or even acted with some different intention which he did not communicate to the other party" (Lord Diplock in *Gissing v Gissing* [1971] A.C. 886, 906).

Examples of the sort of evidence which might be relevant to drawing such inferences are given in *Stack v Dowden*, at para 69.
(4) In those cases where it is clear either (a) that the parties did not intend joint tenancy at the outset, or (b) had changed their original intention, but it is not possible to ascertain by direct evidence or by inference what their actual intention was as to the shares in which they would own the property, "the answer is that each is entitled to that share which the court considers fair having regard to the whole course of dealing between them in relation to the property": Chadwick LJ in *Oxley v Hiscock* [2005] Fam 211, para.69. In our judgment, "the whole course of dealing ... in relation to the property" should be given a broad meaning, enabling a similar range of factors to be taken into account as may be relevant to ascertaining the parties' actual intentions.
(5) Each case will turn on its own facts. Financial contributions are relevant but there are many other factors which may enable the court to decide what shares were either intended (as in case (3)) or fair (as in case (4))."

Judge Poynter took the view that, while the "family home" category has been expanded to some extent beyond the confines of cohabiting couples, it could not apply in *CT*, where the purchase of the house was intended as an investment, with no intention of the claimant and Mr G living together there or anywhere else. Therefore the traditional resulting trust approach was correct.

However, the important, but somewhat inconclusive, Privy Council case of *Marr v Collie* [2017] UKPC 17, [2018] A.C. 631 shows that things are not as simple as that, while not throwing doubt on the actual result in *CT*.

Mr Marr, a banker, and Mr Collie, a building contractor, were in a personal relationship in the Bahamas from 1991 to 2008. During that time a number of properties were acquired, not for them to live in, that were conveyed into their joint names. Mr Marr provided the purchase price and paid the mortgage instalments. According to Mr Marr, Mr Collie repeatedly assured him that he would make an equal contribution to the costs, but never did. According to Mr Collie, he was to carry out renovations and works on the properties, some of which he did. There were also purchases of a truck and a boat that were registered in joint names. After the relationship broke down Mr Marr brought proceedings claiming that he was entitled to full beneficial ownership of those properties and the truck and boat. At first instance, the judge, relying on *Laskar v Laskar* [2008] EWCA Civ 347, [2008] 1 W.L.R. 2695, held that the *Stack v Dowden* presumption that a conveyance into joint names indicated a legal and beneficial joint tenancy unless the contrary was proved applied only in the "domestic consumer context". So, as the properties were intended primarily as investments, that presumption did not apply even though there was a personal relationship between the parties and there was a presumption that there was a resulting trust in favour of Mr Marr unless Mr Collie could demonstrate that a gift to him had been intended, which the judge concluded he had failed to do. On appeal, the Court of Appeal of the Bahamas found that there was cogent evidence of Mr Marr having intended that the beneficial interest in the properties be shared equally, so that the presumption of a resulting trust was rebutted. However, that was in large part in reliance on a 2005 email from Mr Marr that he had not been given the opportunity to comment on. For that reason and because the Court of Appeal's conclusions on the common intention of the parties failed to address a number of factual findings by the first instance judge, the Privy Council allowed Mr Marr's appeal, but was unable to substitute a decision in view of the absence of a proper examination of the parties' intentions. Thus the discussion of the general principles noted below was not anchored in a concrete application to specific findings of fact.

Lord Kerr, giving the judgment of a Board that included both Lady Hale and Lord Neuberger, opined in para.40 that by stating in para.58 of *Stack v Dowden* that the starting point, at least in the domestic consumer context, was that conveyance into joint names indicates both legal and beneficial joint tenancy, unless and until the contrary is proved, Lady Hale did not intend that the principle be confined to the purely domestic setting. Nor was *Laskar,* a case of the purchase of the claimant's council house, for letting out, effectively funded by the claimant's daughter, to be regarded as an authority to the contrary. Thus where a property was bought in the joint names of a cohabiting couple, even if that was as an investment, the "resulting trust solution" did not provide the inevitable answer on beneficial ownership (para.49). However, "save perhaps where there is no evidence from which the parties' intentions can be identified", the answer was not to be provided by the triumph of one presumption over another (Lady Hale's starting point as against the resulting trust solution). Rather, the context of the parties' common intention, or lack of it, was crucial (para.54) and apparently (it is not entirely clear) it was accepted that that common intention could alter after the initial acquisition of the property (para.55).

Applying those principles to the facts of *CT*, it would seem that there was a lack of any common intention both at the time of acquisition of the property and subsequently about what beneficial interest the claimant and Mr G should have.

Accordingly, either the case was one where the resulting trust solution should apply for that reason (most probable) or it was one where the lack of common intention in the context of an investment property was sufficient to displace the starting point of the beneficial interests following the legal ownership.

The main lesson to be taken from *Marr v Collie* is perhaps that great care needs to be taken in making findings of fact about the parties' intentions, common or otherwise, both at the time of acquisition of the property in question and subsequently. In addition it is noteworthy that the Privy Council apparently accepted that the same approach applied to the acquisition of chattels, in the form of the truck and boat, as to the acquisition of real property. What in particular is left unclear, even though the notion of a clash of presumptions was rejected, is on which party does the burden fall of showing that the common intention works in their favour. Or is the common intention to be identified on an objective analysis of the evidence, including the evaluation of credibility, without resort to propositions about burden of proof?

The same principle can apply to cases where a claimant has an account into which someone else's money is put either solely or mixed with the claimant's own money. In *R(IS) 9/08* payments of a boarding-out allowance which the foster parent had saved up over the years were not held on trust for the children in her care. However, *MC v SSWP (IS)* [2015] UKUT 600 (AAC) reaches the opposite conclusion where the claimant had saved up her daughters' disability living allowance in an account in the claimant's name. A tribunal accepted that in relation to an earlier period the claimant was holding the money on trust for her daughters. However, when she used a substantial part of the money to meet rent arrears, the tribunal considered that this suggested that what was previously held on trust had been subsequently "converted" into the claimant's capital by her actions. Judge Wikeley holds, however, that this was wrong in law. First, as the claimant had been made an appointee by DWP to act on behalf of her daughters in benefit matters, she was acting as a de facto trustee. Second, this was an obvious example of an informal trust over money, created without any legal formalities. Third, paying off rent arrears helped to keep a roof over the daughters' heads and was a perfectly reasonable use of their savings, consistent with the purposes of the trust. See also *DL v Southampton CC (CTB)* [2010] UKUT 453 (AAC) for a case where the tribunal failed to make adequate findings of fact about the circumstances in which the claimant's daughter had transferred funds into the claimant's savings account, so as to be able to decide whether there was a resulting trust or not.

JK v SSWP (JSA) [2010] UKUT 437 (AAC), reported as [2011] AACR 26, holds that by asking whether there was a trust the tribunal had posed the wrong question in relation to Scots law. It should have considered whether the presumption of ownership had been rebutted under Scots law. The claimant had contended that some of the money in his and his wife's joint account belonged to his mother-in-law. Applying the principle in *Cairns v Davidson* 1913 S.C. 1053, the tribunal should have considered, by way of such written or oral evidence available to it that it accepted, whether the presumption in favour of all the money in the joint account belonging to the claimant and his wife had been rebutted, so as to establish whether or not some of it belonged to his mother-in law.

It will sometimes be the case that the claimant's explanation as to why they are holding capital for someone else may involve some unlawful purpose, e.g. in order to conceal assets from the HMRC. In *MC v SSWP* [2010] UKUT 29 (AAC) the claimant had purchased a house for £26,000 in her own name. The money had come from her bank account. She asserted that £14,000 of the £26,000 had been paid into her account by her husband by way of a gift for their son and that the remaining £12,000 was her son's money which had been paid into her bank account because he had no bank account of his own. The tribunal found that the only explanation for her son providing the £12,000 was to "deny monies obtained illicitly to the revenue or that the sums were obtained from some illegal sources" and that as a consequence her son was estopped from denying that the capital belonged to the claimant. Judge Turnbull points out, however, that this was wrong in law. As the

House of Lords held in *Tinsley v Milligan* [1994] 1 A.C. 340, the principle that prevents a person putting forward evidence of his own wrongdoing in order to establish a resulting trust in his favour only applies where the person needs to put forward that evidence in order to rebut the presumption of advancement or of resulting trust. It does not apply where the person does not need to assert the illegality and only needs to show that he paid or contributed to the purchase price. In this case the claimant's son would be able to rely on the presumption of resulting trust without asserting any illegality. The question therefore was, in so far as it was accepted that the money was provided by her son, whether there was a resulting trust in his favour or whether he had intended to make a gift to the claimant.

DF v SSWP (ESA) [2015] UKUT 611 (AAC) concerns the question of whether the claimant could argue that he was not the beneficial owner of the funds in an Individual Savings Account (ISA) that was in his name. One of the conditions for an ISA account is that money invested in the account is in the beneficial ownership of the account holder (see reg.4(6) of the Individual Savings Account Regulations 1998 (SI 1998/1870) (ISA Regulations 1998)). The claimant maintained that the money in his ISA account really belonged to his daughter. His daughter confirmed this, stating that the ISA was designed to keep her money away from an unreliable partner. The Secretary of State argued that a person in whose name an ISA is held has to be regarded as the beneficial owner of the money in the account, relying on the decision in *CIS/2836/2006*. While that decision concerned the Personal Equity Plan Regulations 1989 (SI 1989/469), the ISA Regulations 1998 were said to be identical.

Judge Mitchell, however, concludes that *CIS/2836/2006* is restricted to "presumption of advancement" cases, i.e. cases in which the money is given by someone standing in loco parentis to a child, or by a husband to a wife, where there is a presumption that a gift was intended (note that the presumption of advancement was due to be abolished by s.199 of the Equality Act 2010 but this section has not yet been brought into force). To the extent that *CIS/2836/2006* could be read as going further, in his view it was not consistent with the decision in *Tinsley v Milligan* (above). He also holds that *CIS/2836/2006* did not decide that ISA-type legislation operates to extinguish beneficial interests of third parties in ISA deposits. Neither the ISA Regulations 1998 nor the enabling power under which they were made (Income and Corporation Taxes Act 1988 s.333(2)) had the effect of altering existing rights in relation to property. The legislation was only concerned with creating a special account with special tax advantages.

Judge Mitchell then goes on to reject the Secretary of State's argument that the law of illegality meant that, as a matter of public policy, the claimant could not rely on a beneficial interest that he had previously denied. This was inconsistent with the Supreme Court's decision in *Hounga v Allen* [2014] UKSC 47; [2014] 1 W.L.R. 2889 and the Court of Appeal's decision in *R. (Best) v Secretary of State for Justice (Rev 1)* [2015] EWCA Civ 17. In his view it was better for a First-tier Tribunal in an ISA case to ignore the role that may or may not be played by the law of illegality and simply focus on whether it accepted that the beneficial interest in the funds lay elsewhere. He does, however, point out the risks that a claimant runs in arguing that a third party has a beneficial interest in the sums deposited in an ISA, namely conceding that any ISA tax reliefs were improperly awarded and the possibility of criminal proceedings for a tax offence under s.106A of the Taxes Management Act 1970 (see para.17 of the decision).

An illustration of a constructive trust, which does not operate on the basis of a common intention but on it being unconscionable for the person with the legal interest to deny the beneficial interest of another, is *R(SB) 23/85*. The claimant's wife in a home-made and legally ineffective deed of gift purported to give an uninhabitable property to her son. He, as intended, carried out the works to make it habitable. The Commissioner held that, although a court will not normally "complete" such an "uncompleted gift" in favour of someone who has not given valuable consideration, one of the situations in which a transfer of the property will be ordered is where the intended recipient is induced to believe that he has or will have an interest in the property and acts on that belief to his detriment. Thus in the meantime the claimant's wife held the property merely as a "bare trustee" and could not lawfully transfer it to anyone but the son. There is discussion of what kind of action might give rise to the right to complete the gift in *R(SB) 7/87*, where there was evidence of the claimant's intention to give a flat to her two sons, but all that one son had done in reliance was to redecorate the flat prior to its sale. See also *CIS/807/1991* on proprietary estoppel.

However, similar circumstances should probably now be approached from the standpoint of the principles adopted in the decision of the Supreme Court in *Guest v Guest* [2022] UKSC 27, [2022] 3 W.L.R. 911 on proprietary estoppel and the nature of the remedies available in equity. Lord Briggs, giving the majority judgment (two justices dissented), conducted an exhaustive survey of the English and Australian case law, as well as academic debate, and rejected the theory that the aim of the remedy was to compensate the person given a promise or assurance about the acquisition of property for the detriment suffered in reliance on the promise or assurance, rather than primarily to hold the person who had given the promise or assurance to the promise or assurance, which would usually prevent the unconscionability inherent in the repudiation of the promise or assurance that had been detrimentally relied on (paras 71 and 61). However, the remedy was a flexible one dependent on the circumstances. Lord Briggs summarised the principles as follows:

> "74. I consider that, in principle, the court's normal approach should be as follows. The first stage (which is not in issue in this case) is to determine whether the promisor's repudiation of his promise is, in the light of the promisee's detrimental reliance upon it, unconscionable at all. It usually will be, but there may be circumstances (such as the promisor falling on hard times and needing to sell the property to pay his creditors, or to pay for expensive medical treatment or social care for himself or his wife) when it may not be. Or the promisor may have announced or carried out only a partial repudiation of the promise, which may or may not have been unconscionable, depending on the circumstances.
>
> 75. The second (remedy) stage will normally start with the assumption (not presumption) that the simplest way to remedy the unconscionability constituted by the repudiation is to hold the promisor to the promise. The promisee cannot (and probably would not) complain, for example, that his detrimental reliance had cost him more than the value of the promise, were it to be fully performed. But the court may have to listen to many other reasons from the promisor (or his executors) why something less than full performance will negate the unconscionability and therefore satisfy the equity. They may be based on one or more of the real-life problems already outlined. The court may be invited by the promisor to consider one or more proxies for performance of the promise, such as the transfer of less property than promised or the provision of a monetary equivalent in place of it, or a combination of the two.
>
> 76. If the promisor asserts and proves, the burden being on him for this purpose, that specific enforcement of the full promise, or monetary equivalent, would be out of all proportion to the cost of the detriment to the promisee, then the court may be constrained to limit the extent of the remedy. This does not mean that the court will be seeking precisely to compensate for the detriment as its primary task, but simply to put right a disproportionality which is so large as to stand in the way of a full specific enforcement doing justice between the parties. It will be a very rare case where the detriment is equivalent in value to the expectation, and there is nothing in principle unjust in a full enforcement of the promise being worth more than the cost of the detriment, any more than there is in giving specific performance of a contract for the sale of land merely because it is worth more than the price paid for it. An example of a remedy out of all proportion to the detriment would be the full enforcement of a promise by an elderly lady to leave her carer a particular piece of jewellery if she stayed on at very low wages,

which turned out on valuation by her executors to be a Faberge worth millions. Another would be a promise to leave a generous inheritance if the promisee cared for the promisor for the rest of her life, but where she unexpectedly died two months later."

Thus, in circumstances where proprietary estoppel might be in play (as would probably now be the case on similar facts to *R(SB) 23/85* and *R(SB) 7/87*), great care would be needed in establishing the primary facts and, outside the clearest cases, in a deeper investigation of the principles of law governing the nature of any remedy available. And would a repudiation of a promise when the promisor would otherwise be forced to rely on a means-tested benefit be unconscionable? However, even if it were to be concluded that the claimant did not hold the property in question on trust for someone else, the possibility of a claim in equity, e.g. for some monetary compensation, might well affect the valuation of the property.

Note also the doctrine of secret trusts, under which a person who receives property under an intestacy when the deceased refrained from making a will in reliance on that person's promise to carry out their expressed intentions, holds the property on trust to carry out those intentions *(CSB/989/1985)*. The doctrine also applies to property left by will where on the face of the will the property has been left to A but this is on the understanding that A is merely a trustee of it in favour of B.

For an example of where there may have been a secret trust, see *GK v SSWP (JSA)* [2012] UKUT 115 (AAC). In that case the claimant had inherited money from her aunt which she understood from conversations with her aunt was to be shared between her five children and herself. She used the money to purchase some land, which, although in her sole name, she regarded as belonging to all six of them. Judge Mark held that the tribunal had erred in not considering whether there was a secret trust.

CIS/213/2004 and *CIS/214/2004* concerned the applicability of French law. A property in France had been purchased in the name of the claimant but the purchase price and renovation costs had been met by Ms V. Ms V was not the claimant's partner but they had a son and the purpose of putting the property in the claimant's name was so that their son and not Ms V's other children would inherit it (under French law all five of Ms V's children would otherwise have been entitled to an interest in the property). On the same day that the property was purchased the claimant executed a holograph will bequeathing a "usufruct" (the French equivalent of a life interest) in the property to Ms V. Applying the Recognition of Trusts Act 1987, which implements the Hague Convention of 1986 on the law applicable to trusts and their recognition, the Commissioner concludes that French law was the applicable law. But since French law does not recognise the concept of a trust, it followed that there was no resulting or constructive trust in favour of Ms V (although in the Commissioner's view if English law had been applicable the facts would have given rise to such a trust). The Commissioner directed the Secretary of State to obtain a further opinion as to the remedies available under French law to Ms V if the claimant decided to treat the property as his own, but after receiving this concluded that there was no reason under French law or otherwise why the value of the property should not be included in the claimant's capital. The claimant appealed against this decision to the Court of Appeal but the appeal was dismissed *(Martin v Secretary of State for Work and Pensions* [2009] EWCA Civ 1289; [2010] AACR 9).

It will be an error of law if a tribunal fails to consider the question of the applicable law in relation to property abroad *(MB v Royal Borough of Kensington & Chelsea (HB)* [2011] UKUT 321 (AAC)). The claimant in *MB* was an Irish national, who had, while domiciled and resident in Ireland, bought a property in Ireland with the assistance of a mortgage from an Irish bank. In those circumstances it was difficult to see how the applicable law could be other than Irish law, but the tribunal had not referred to this issue at all, nor had it sought any evidence as to the nature and content of Irish law and the Irish law of trusts (foreign law is a question of fact (see *R(G) 2/00*, at para.20)).

Choses in action

There is also a remarkable range of interests in property which do have a present 2.164
market value and so are actual capital resources. These are usually things in action
(or choses in action), rights to sue for something. See the earlier section of this
note on *Interests under a will or intestacy when someone has died* for specific discussion of the importance of considering the existence of choses in action. Debts,
even where they are not due to be paid for some time, are things in action which
can be sold. A good example is *R(SB) 31/83* where the claimant in selling a house
allowed the purchaser a mortgage of £4,000, to be redeemed in six months. The
debt conferred a right to sue and had to be valued at what could be obtained on
the open market. In *CJSA/204/2002* the claimant had lent her son £8,500 for the
deposit on a flat. The Commissioner holds that the legal debt owed by the son to
the claimant had to be valued in order to decide whether the claimant had actual
capital in excess of £8,000 (which was then the prescribed limit). The terms of
the loan, including the rate of any interest and whether there was any security for
the loan, as well as the terms of repayment, were clearly relevant to this valuation.
Once the value of the loan had been determined, the question of deprivation of
capital then had to be considered. To the extent that the value of the loan was less
than £8,500, to that extent the claimant had deprived herself of capital. However,
on the facts the Commissioner found that the claimant had not deprived herself
of the capital for the purpose of securing entitlement to, or increasing the amount
of, jobseeker's allowance (see further the note to reg.50(1)). See also *JC v SSWP*
[2009] UKUT 22 (AAC) which points out that the value of the loan will depend
on whether it is likely to be recoverable. If the claimant had lent the money with
no expectation of getting it back, he had in effect reduced the value of the chose in
action to nil. The issue of deprivation of capital then arose. *R 2/09(IS)*, a Northern
Ireland decision, gives further guidance on the approach to choses in action and
their value.

In *GS v DSD (IS)* [2012] NI Com 284 (another Northern Ireland decision)
the claimant agreed in June 2004 to buy a house (not yet built) from Mr McK in
return for the transfer of ownership of the claimant's present house, plus £33,000.
The £33,000 was paid by cheque in August 2006. However, the building work was
delayed due to the illness of Mr McK's brother and the house was only eventually
built during 2009. But by March 2010 (the date of the decision under appeal) the
agreement still had not been fulfilled due to difficulties with Mr McK's title to the
land. Mr McK accepted that the £33,000 deposit would be returned if these difficulties could not be resolved. Commissioner Stockman points out that a chose in
action can only arise upon breach of contract, or possibly frustration of contract;
the mere existence of the contract did not give rise to the right to sue for return of
the deposit. The difficulty was determining whether there had been a breach of contract and in identifying when that occurred. In the circumstances of this case, where
there was no date for the completion of the contract and the delay in completing the
building work had been waived by the claimant because of the personal friendship
between Mr McK and himself, the claimant would not have had a strong case for
breach of contract for unreasonable delay. This would have a resultant effect on the
value of the chose in action, for which there was unlikely to be a ready market. The
Commissioner decides that the value of the chose in action was nil from August
2006 and £3,000 from November 2008 up to March 2010.

An action for breach of fiduciary duty against an attorney appointed under the
Enduring Powers of Attorney Act 1985 who had used the claimant's capital to repay
her own debts also constitutes actual capital; so too would a claim against the attorney for misapplication of capital on the ground that she had made gifts outside the
circumstances sanctioned by s.3(5) of the 1985 Act (this allows an attorney to make
gifts (to herself or others) "provided that the value of each such gift is not unreasonable having regard to all the circumstances and in particular the size of the donor's
estate") (*R(IS) 17/98*).

Bank or building society accounts

2.165   A more direct way of holding capital is in a bank or building society account. In *CSB/296/1985* the claimant's solicitor received £12,000 damages on behalf of the claimant and placed the money on deposit, presumably in the solicitor's client account. The Commissioner held that the £12,000 was an actual resource of the claimant, on the basis that there was no difference in principle between monies being held by a solicitor on behalf of a client and monies held by a bank or building society on behalf of a customer. This decision was upheld by the Court of Appeal in *Thomas v Chief Adjudication Officer*, reported as *R(SB) 17/87*. Russell LJ says "the possession of this money by the solicitors as the agent for the claimant was, in every sense of the term, possession by the claimant."

         However, note *CIS/984/2002* which holds that money held by the claimant's solicitor pending quantification of the statutory charge to the Legal Services Commission under s.10(7) of the Access to Justice Act 1999 was not part of the claimant's capital. Until that quantification had been carried out, it was not possible to identify any particular amount as the claimant's capital. Another way of looking at it was to treat the statutory charge as an incumbrance for the purpose of the equivalent of reg.49(1) (b) (see *CIS/368/1993*).

         See also *LC v Bournemouth Borough Council (HB)* [2016] UKUT 175 (AAC), where the proceeds of sale of a former matrimonial home were being held in a solicitors' client account until the claimant's partner and his ex-wife could agree how the sum was to be split or the issue was resolved by a court order after a Financial Dispute Resolution hearing. In Judge White's view the value of the capital prior to agreement or an order of the court would be minimal.

         The approach taken in *Thomas* seems to involve valuing the amount of money directly, not as a technical chose in action. However, the importance of the legal relationship between a bank and a customer being one of debtor and creditor was revealed in *CSB/598/1987*. A large cheque was paid into the claimant's wife's bank account on October 9, 1987. The amount was credited to her account on that date, but the cheque was not cleared until October 15. The bank's paying-in slips reserved the bank's right to "postpone payment of cheques drawn against uncleared effects which may have been credited to the account." The effect was that the bank did not accept the relationship of debtor and creditor on the mere paying in of a cheque. Thus the amount did not become part of the claimant's actual resources until October 15. A person who deliberately refrains from paying in a cheque may be fixed with notional capital under reg.50(1).

         CIS/255/2005 concerned the effect on capital of the issue of a cheque. The Commissioner holds that the claimant's capital was reduced from the date that the cheque was issued (this would not apply if the cheque was postdated). After that time she could not honestly withdraw money from her bank account so as to leave insufficient funds to meet the cheque.

         In *R(IS) 15/96* the Commissioner confirms that money in a building society or bank (or solicitor's client) account is an actual resource in the form of a chose in action. It is not, as the SSAT had decided, held in trust. If the money is in an account from which it can be withdrawn at any time, its value is the credit balance (less any penalties for early withdrawal, etc.). But if the money cannot be withdrawn for a specified term the value will be less (although the notional capital rules may come into play in respect of the difference in value: *CIS/494/1990*; see also *R(IS) 8/04*.

Interests in trusts

2.166   The nature of interests in capital under trusts gives rise to several problems. It is clear that a person may have an absolute vested interest under a trust, although payment is deferred, e.g. until the age of 21. This was the case in *R(SB) 26/86*, where the resource was held to be the person's share of the fund. However, an interest may be contingent on reaching a particular age. This appears to have been one of the assumptions on which the Court of Appeal decided the unsatisfactory case of

Peters v Chief Adjudication Officer, reported as *R(SB) 3/89*. It was conceded that sums were held on trust to be paid over to each of three sisters on attaining the age of 18, with the power to advance up to 50 per cent of the capital before then. In the end, the Court of Appeal accepted the valuation of half of the full value for each sister under 18. The precise finding may depend on the supplementary benefit rule on discretionary trusts, which was not translated into the income support or universal credit legislation. But some statements about the general market value of such interests are made. May LJ says "in an appropriate market a discretionary entitlement of up to 50 per cent now and at least 50 per cent in, say, six months in a given case, or three to four years in another, could well be said to have a value greater than 50 per cent of the capital value of the trust." This clearly supports the view that a contingent interest has a market value and so is actual capital. See also *CTC 4713/2002* which concerned a similar trust in favour of the claimant's son to that in *Peters* (although in this case the trustees had power to advance the whole of the fund). The Commissioner notes that in *Peters* the Court of Appeal had accepted the valuation agreed by the parties without argument. He acknowledged that each case must turn on its facts and that valuation of different interests would differ depending on such factors as the nature of the underlying investments (there was evidence in this case that due to lack of investor confidence the market value of the fund was much diminished); in addition in this case, unlike *Peters*, the whole of the fund could be advanced. However, he concluded that the Court of Appeal's approach in *Peters* led to a valuation of the claimant's son's equitable interest as being more or less equal to the whole net value of the trust fund (less 10 per cent for the expenses of sale).

A life interest in a trust fund or the right to receive income under a liferent in Scots law is a present asset which can be sold and has a market value (*R(SB) 2/84*, *R(SB) 43/84*, *R(SB) 15/86* and *R(SB) 13/87*). The practical effect is reversed for income support by para.13 of Sch.10 to the Income Support Regulations, but no such disregard is included in Sch.10 to the present Regulations.

All interests which can be sold or borrowed against will need to be considered. However, in the case of an interest under a discretionary trust, the DWP will normally only take payments of capital (or income) into account when they are actually made.

In *R(IS) 9/04* it was argued that funds held by the Court of Protection were analogous to those held by a discretionary trustee. Since neither the claimant nor her receiver could insist on the Court releasing any part of the funds it was contended that the market value of the claimant's actual interest was so small as to be negligible. However, the Commissioner followed *CIS/7127/1995* in holding that the entire beneficial interest in the funds administered by the Court remained with the claimant to whom alone they belonged. The fact the Court had discretionary powers of control over the management of a patient's property for his or her benefit did not mean that the patient's beneficial ownership had ceased. The funds therefore had to be valued at their current market value, less any appropriate allowance for sale expenses, in the normal way (see reg.49).

Realisation of assets

2.167

R (SB) 18/83 stresses that there are more ways of realising assets than sale. In particular, assets can be charged to secure a loan which can be used to meet requirements. In that case the asset was a minority shareholding in a family company. The Commissioner says that only a person prepared to lend money without security would do so in such circumstances. The articles of association of the company provided that if a shareholder wanted to sell shares they were to be offered to the existing shareholders at the fair value fixed by the auditors. The Commissioner holds that the regulations do not require assets to be valued at a figure higher than anything the person would realise on them, i.e. the auditor's fair value. This is in line with the purpose of the capital cut-off that a claimant can draw on resources until they fall below the limit.

This approach to valuation can usefully deal with unrealisable assets. See the notes to reg.49. However, it is no part of the definition of capital that it should be immediately realisable, although its market value may be affected by such factors. It remains possible for claimants to be fixed with large amounts of actual capital that are not immediately available to them by everyday means, but may have a value in some specialised market.

Deduction of liabilities

2.168   The general rule is that the whole of a capital resource is to be taken into account. Liabilities are not to be deducted from the value (*R(SB) 2/83*). In general, the "remedy" if the capital limits are in issue, is for the claimant to discharge the liability, the amount of which cannot, by virtue of reg.50(2) constitute notional capital under the deprivation rule.

SSWP v GF (ESA) [2017] UKUT 333 (AAC) is an illustration of the application of the principle. For one part of the period in issue the claimant's brother-in-law had paid a costs order of some £48,000 made against the claimant in the expectation at least that he would be repaid once the 120-day notice period for withdrawal of funds in the claimant's building society bond with a balance of £75,000 had expired. On the evidence available the judge rightly concluded that there was no implied, resulting or constructive trust and that the claimant's debt did not change the beneficial ownership of the funds in the bond. However, there could in other similar cases be evidence of discussions or arrangements before the brother-in-law made his payment that could lead to a conclusion either that the debt had been secured on the claimant's rights in the bond or that the claimant had made a declaration of trust. In *GF* itself no such argument could have helped the claimant because even if he had not been the beneficial owner of £48,000 of the balance in the bond, the value of the remainder (even subject to the 120-day notice provision) would no doubt have exceeded £16,000.

Otherwise, it is only if a debt is secured on the capital asset that it can be deducted, at the stage specifically required by reg.49 (*R(IS) 21/93*). See the notes to reg.49 and note *JRL v SSWP (JSA)* [2011] UKUT 63 (AAC), reported as [2011] AACR 30. There, the claimant had three accounts with the same bank, of which one was in credit, one was overdrawn, and one had a nil balance. The three-judge panel pointed out that this meant that the claimant was both a creditor and a debtor of the same body. Under the bank's terms and conditions, the bank had a contractual right to debit at any time any of a customer's accounts which were in credit with sums sufficient to clear the customer's indebtedness to the bank. This created what was effectively a charge on the customer's credit balance(s). The market value of the account that was in credit was therefore its net value after deduction of the amount of the claimant's overdraft on his other account.

Personal possessions

2.169   Note that personal possessions are not treated as capital (para.(2)). There is no equivalent to the rule for income support, old style JSA, old style ESA and housing benefit that personal possessions are taken into account if they have been acquired with the intention of reducing capital in order to secure, or increase, entitlement to benefit (see, e.g., para.10 of Sch.10 to the Income Support Regulations in Vol.V of this series). However, in such circumstances claimants may be found to have notional capital under reg.50(1) and (2), by reason of having deprived themselves of capital through the mechanism of acquisition of personal possessions. For reg.50(1) to operate, the deprivation must have been for the purpose of securing entitlement to or increasing the amount of universal credit (rather than any other benefit), which may significantly limit its effect in relation to acquisitions some way in the past. In addition, reg.50(2), in a provision not replicated in relation to any other benefits (except state pension credit), prevents claimants being treated as having deprived themselves of capital if they have purchased goods or services and the expenditure was reasonable in the circumstances (see further in the notes to that provision).

R(H) 7/08 was a case about whether a moveable but static caravan, attached to mains services on a non-residential site, was a "personal possession" for the purposes of the disregard in the housing benefit legislation. A tribunal had decided that it was not, so that its value counted as capital. The Commissioner held that it erred in law in doing so. After a discursive discussion of the legislative background and the scant authority, he said this in para.53:

> "My conclusion is that 'personal possessions' mean any physical assets other than land and assets used for business purposes. . . . [This] avoids uncertainty of scope and difficulties of application. It is consistent with the legislative history of the disregard and the more humane approach to resource-related benefits that has increasingly been shown over the period of the welfare state. It recognises the increased emphasis that has been given over recent decades to ways of assisting claimants off welfare by not requiring particular categories of possessions to be disposed of for what may be a relatively short period on benefit."

That approach would seem to require that the actual value of items acquired mainly, or even solely, as investments be disregarded, but there will sometimes be very difficult lines to be drawn in particular circumstances even if that basis were accepted. At what point might coins, say, or gold bars cease to be regarded as personal possessions and be regarded as a way of holding capital in the same way as everyday cash?

Might it still be argued that, as Commissioner Jacobs was not directly concerned in *R(H) 7/08* with any line between personal possessions and investments, the decision does not exclude a conclusion that the adjective "personal" is an indication that something has to be used at least partly for personal or domestic or household purposes, not solely for investment? Prior to its amendment in October 2014 by s.3(1) of the Inheritance and Trustees' Powers Act 2014, the definition of "personal chattels" in s.55(1)(x) of the Administration of Estates Act 1925 (for the purposes of identifying how an estate is to be distributed on intestacy), as well as setting out a long list of specific items, included "articles of household or personal use or ornament". The courts, bearing in mind the test in terms of the use made of the article at the time of death, took quite a generous approach to when that use had a personal element. In one case, *Re Reynolds' Will Trusts* [1966] 1 W.L.R. 19, the aptly named Stamp J, having held the intestate's valuable stamp collection, built up since childhood as his main hobby, to be part of his personal chattels, suggested that if he had gone into a shop and bought a similar collection that he then installed in his flat it could hardly be said that that was an article of personal use. Regulation 46(2) makes no express reference to the use made of any possession, but it may be arguable that the word "personal" entails the exclusion of items with no element of personal enjoyment or cherishing (such as collections of jewellery, art work, stamps etc locked away in a safe or bank vault and never inspected). However, such an approach would again involve the drawing of difficult lines after careful investigation that it may be thought that the legislation was intended to avoid. It would have been helpful if matters had been made plainer on the face of the legislation.

No doubt, whatever the general answer, the more evidence there is that an item was acquired by a person for investment, the stronger the argument would be for its cost having been a deprivation of capital under reg.50(1), subject to the working out of the scope of the exception in reg.50(2)(b) for purchasing goods and services where the expenditure was reasonable.

Capital treated as income

2.170

Under paras (3) and (4), certain payments that might otherwise be capital are treated as income (and therefore do not count as capital).

Paragraph (4) deals with capital payable by instalments. If the amount outstanding plus the claimant's (including, in the case of couples, the other member of the couple's) other capital is more than £16,000, each instalment when paid is treated as income. Otherwise the payment counts as capital. That position follows inevitably from the nature of capital payable by instalments, but was confirmed to operate in the circumstances of the purchase price of a house being paid in monthly instalments over ten years in *Lillystone v Supplementary Benefits Commission* [1982] 3 F.L.R. 52. If para.(4) applies to treat the instalment as income, then reg.66(1)(l) includes the income as unearned income that is to be taken into account in full. See the notes to reg.66(1) for difficulties about how such income is to be attributed to particular assessment periods.

There may be some conundrums in working out the application of para.(4) in particular cases. Presumably the value of the claimant's other capital is tested as at the date that each instalment is received. Then in taking the value of "other capital", presumably the capital value of the right to continue receiving the instalments must be excluded, otherwise there would be unfair double counting with the amount outstanding (even though the market value would no doubt be less than the amount outstanding). That capital value is not disregarded for universal credit purposes, as it is for income support and other benefits (Income Support Regulations Sch.10 para.16: Vol.V of this series). Thus, it is theoretically possible for the £16,000 limit under para.(4) to be breached while the value of the claimant's capital in accordance with reg.49, including the value of the right to continue receiving the instalments, does not exceed £16,000, so that entitlement to universal credit would not be removed entirely under the capital rule.

Weekly sums that the claimant was allowed to withdraw for living expenses from his bank account which was subject to a restraint order under s.77 of the Criminal Justice Act 1988 did not constitute capital payable by instalments (*SH v SSWP* [2008] UKUT 21 (AAC)). The old style JSA equivalent of para.(4) only applied if there was a contractual or other obligation on the part of some other person to pay a capital sum to the claimant by instalments.

Paragraph (3) applies to sums (other than capital payable by instalments) that are paid regularly and by reference to a period, such as payments under an annuity. They are treated as income, even if they would otherwise be regarded as capital or as having a capital element. This is wider than the previous rule in, e.g., reg.41(2) of the Income Support Regulations (which only applies to payments under an annuity) and would seem to be an attempt to draw more of a line between capital and income. Although para.(3) thus has an important effect in drawing that line for the purposes of the Regulations as a whole, it is submitted that its operation must be limited to treating the payments concerned as income in the general sense or to circumstances where they would otherwise constitute capital. That is because capital treated as income under para.(3) or (4) counts as unearned income under reg.66(1)(l), to be taken into account as full. If reg.66(1)(l) were to be taken to apply to every sum paid regularly and by reference to a period, that would subvert the express limitation imposed by the other parts of reg.66(1). For instance, the great majority of social security benefits, both within the UK and abroad, are paid regularly and by reference to a period. If they then fell within reg.66(1)(l), that would render nugatory the careful specification in reg.66(1)(a), (b), (c) and (da) of the benefits that are to be taken into account (with the necessary result that any not specified are not to be taken into account). That cannot possibly have been intended. See the notes to reg.66(1)(l) for how it is suggested that provision must be interpreted.

Note the "assumed yield from capital" rule in reg.72(1) (the equivalent to the "tariff income rule" for income support, old style JSA, old style ESA and housing benefit). That rule does not apply to capital that is disregarded or produces income that is taken into account under reg.66(1)(i) (annuities) or (j) (trusts) (reg.72(2)). If the rule produces any assumed income, actual income from capital is treated as capital from the day that it is due to be paid (reg.72(3)).

Jointly held capital

2.171   **47.** Where a person and one or more other persons have a beneficial interest in a capital asset, those persons are to be treated, in the absence of evidence to the contrary, as if they were each entitled to an equal share of the whole of that beneficial interest.

GENERAL NOTE

This provision is much the same in structure as the income support and income-based JSA equivalents (reg.52 of the Income Support Regulations and reg.115 of the JSA Regulations 1996), with the addition of the apparently significant words "in the absence of evidence to the contrary". However, close analysis suggests that those words are ineffective for the vast majority of practical purposes and that reg.47, like its equivalents, achieves only limited results of substance.

That conclusion follows from the decision of the Court of Appeal in *Hourigan v Secretary of State for Work and Pensions* [2002] EWCA Civ 1890, reported as *R(IS) 4/03*. There the claimant bought her council house with a contribution of five-sixths of the purchase price from her son. The legal estate was transferred to her in her sole name, but it was accepted that in those circumstances she held the legal estate on trust for herself and her son as tenants in common in the proportions of their contributions to the purchase price. The Secretary of State argued that reg.52 of the Income Support Regulations applied because the claimant and her son were beneficially entitled to the capital asset of the equitable interest in the house and that as a result she had to be treated as having a half share in the equitable interest, although her actual share was one-sixth. It was argued that it was that deemed half share that had to be valued as capital, in which case the claimant was not entitled to income support because the capital limit was breached. Brooke LJ held that it would be a misuse of language to say that the claimant and her son were both beneficially entitled to a capital asset in the form of the house because the beneficial interest of each as a tenant in common was a separately disposable asset. To interpret reg.52 in the way contended for by the Secretary of State would require very much clearer words. Not only was it unfair to the claimant to treat her as possessing more capital than she could actually realise, but the Secretary of State's argument could also work unfairly in favour of claimants (e.g. if it had been a claimant who had a five-sixths share who was deemed to have only a half-share). Thus it was only the claimant's actual one-sixth share as tenant in common that fell to be valued as capital.

Brooke LJ accepted that the language of reg.52 could apply to circumstances in which the claimant and one or more persons were jointly entitled to the equitable interest in the same capital asset. In that situation the effect of reg.52 was to treat the joint tenancy as severed and to deem the claimant to have an equal share (with the other joint tenants), with there being a tenancy in common as between the claimant and the other joint tenant(s).

That appears correct, but the limit of the effect of reg.47 (just as for reg.52 of the Income Support Regulations) would appear to be in deeming that there has been a severance of the joint tenancy of the beneficial interest (as can be carried out by a joint tenant at any time or by selling or otherwise alienating or attempting to alienate the interest as a joint tenant). The limit is because there is no need for any regulation to deem that the claimant's share on severance is proportionate to the number of former joint tenants (i.e. a half share if there were previously two, a third share if there were previously three etc). That consequence follows from the nature of a joint tenancy, where there is only one interest (the so-called unity of interest), so that the interest of each tenant must be the same in extent, nature and duration. *Goodman v Gallant* [1985] EWCA Civ 15, [1986] Fam. 106 establishes that the sole exception could be where the terms of the trust establishing the joint tenancy expressly provided that on any severance the shares were not to be equal (which would be a vanishingly rare circumstance). There is no room at the stage of severance (or deemed severance) for going back to, say, the amount of contribution to the purchase price, to justify anything other than an equal share. (But do not forget that tenancies in common created in other ways can, and often do, have unequal shares). Thus, if the claimant in *Hourigan* had expressly had the council house conveyed to her to hold in trust for herself and her son as joint tenants, there could have been no escape, regardless of any regulations, from the consequence on a severance (actual or deemed) of the joint tenancy in the beneficial interest that her share as tenant

2.172

in common was one-half. It could make no difference that the son had contributed five-sixths of the purchase price. It is a common elementary student error to think otherwise, one into which it appears that Auld LJ fell in *Hourigan*.

The upshot is that, once it is determined that reg.47 is restricted to joint tenancies, the reference to the absence of evidence to the contrary becomes redundant. The purported relevance of the phrase "in the absence of evidence to the contrary" to the deeming in reg.47 can only be to the shares in which the beneficial interest is to be held under the tenancy in common (the phrase "in equal shares" having long been accepted as indicating a tenancy in common). Evidence to the contrary cannot prevent the deeming of a tenancy in common because in all circumstances where there was still actually a joint tenancy there would be evidence to the contrary, i.e. whatever the evidence was that produced that actual result, and the regulation could then never apply at all. However, no evidence to the contrary could influence the shares under the deemed tenancy in common, because the equal shares follow from the nature of a joint tenancy, subject to the rare exception where the express terms of a trust indicate a different share on severance (see above).

In cases, like the above, involving real property, there will usually be no difficulty in identifying the property subject to a joint tenancy. It may not be so easy when the joint interest is in some other asset or in a bank or building society account. That is shown by *CIS/7097/1995*. There, the claimant's husband went to live permanently in a nursing home. To help finance the cost of that accommodation, £7,000 of the husband's National Savings certificates were cashed in and the proceeds paid into the couple's joint bank account, so that the nursing home could be paid regularly by direct debit. There was evidence that the intention had not been that the sum should form part of the joint money in the account. The £7,000 had been declared as the husband's own money in an application to the local authority for financial assistance with the fees and a separate tally was kept of the use of that money. The AO treated the claimant's capital as including half of the balance in the joint account, including the proceeds of the husband's National Savings certificates, which took her over the limit, so that she was not entitled to income support. The Commissioner reversed that decision. There was clear evidence that the normal presumption of joint beneficial ownership between a husband and wife operating a joint bank account did not apply in relation to the £7,000. It was obviously intended that the proceeds of the husband's National Savings certificates were to remain his sole property and had been paid into the joint account merely for convenience. They did not form part of the claimant's capital. The Commissioner also analysed the nature of joint beneficial ownership and ownership in equal shares in a way consistent with what is said above.

A similar approach was taken in the Scottish case of *JK v SSWP (JSA)* [2010] UKUT 437 (AAC), reported as [2011] AACR 26. The claimant contended that some of the money in his and his wife's joint bank account belonged to his mother-in-law. It was held that the First-tier Tribunal, instead of asking whether there was a trust in favour of the mother-in-law, should have considered, by reference to such oral or written evidence available to it that it accepted, whether under Scots law (see *Cairns v Davidson* 1913 S.C. 1053) the presumption in favour of all the money in the joint account belonging to the claimant and his wife had been rebutted, so as to establish whether or not some of it belonged to the mother-in-law.

Valuation under regulation 47

2.173   It is the deemed equal share that has to be valued, not the proportionate share of the overall value (see the Court of Appeal's decision in *Chief Adjudication Officer v Palfrey*, reported as part of *R(IS) 26/95*, which had upheld the Tribunal of Commissioners' decisions in *CIS/391/1992* and *CIS/417/1992* (reported as part of *R(IS) 26/95*. The Tribunal of Commissioners gave detailed guidance as to the basis of a proper valuation of such a share (*CIS 391/1992*, paras 53 and 54), which is still relevant as a foundation for later decisions. In both *CIS/391/1992* and *CIS/417/1992* ownership was shared with relatives who were unable or unwilling to sell the property or buy the claimant's interest. The Commissioners recognised, as did the Court of Appeal, that the market value in such cases may well be nil, although as discussed below all will depend on the circumstances of particular cases.

In *Palfrey* the Tribunal of Commissioners state that the SSAT should have exercised its inquisitorial jurisdiction to call for the documents under which the property was acquired in order to sort out the beneficial ownership, but that may not be necessary where there is no dispute about the actual conveyancing history (*CIS/127/1993*).

The current guidance to decision makers in Ch.H1 of the ADM (in particular paras H1638 – H1642) suggests that they should obtain an expert opinion on the market value of a deemed share in land/premises. It gives quite rigorous and detailed guidance, in the main firmly based on the case law discussed below fleshing out what is entailed by the principle laid down in *Palfrey*, on the criteria for a valuation to be acceptable. For instance, the guidance states that where the other owners will not buy the share or agree to a sale of the asset as a whole, the expert should not simply assume that a court would order a sale but must consider the particular circumstances and take into account legal costs, length of time to obtain possession, etc. The guidance also says that the expert would need to explain whether on the facts of the case there was any market for the deemed share, explain what assumptions, if any, have been made, whether and, if so what, comparables have been considered and indicate how the value of the deemed share had been calculated. The expert should also indicate their experience and/or knowledge of the market for shared interests in real property. Slightly oddly, it is said in para.H1641 that in working out the reg.49(1) value of the premises, only 10 per cent for expenses of sale should be deducted and not anything for encumbrances, because they will already have been taken into account in the expert's valuation. That may work out if the expert has had full information about the nature and amount of the encumbrances, but that may need to be checked before the process as set out in reg.49(1) is short-circuited.

If that guidance was carefully followed, there would little problem in the production of acceptable evidence on behalf of the Secretary of State, although of course there would always be room for differences of opinion as a matter of judgment. However, experience over the years shows continuing difficulties in the production of valuations that properly adopt the principles of *Palfrey*. There have also been some differences of expression in the cases that have created some uncertainties, although it is submitted below that the basic principles have not been subverted.

R(IS) 3/96 contains a useful discussion as to whether the District Valuer's opinion supplied in that case met the requirements of *CIS/391/1992*. *R(JSA) 1/02* was concerned with valuing the claimant's interest in his former matrimonial home. His wife, from whom he was separated and who was in ill-health, continued to live there with their daughter, who had learning difficulties. The valuation obtained by the Jobcentre on a standard form (A64A/LA1) gave the open market value as £30,000 and the claimant's deemed undivided share as £9,200. No reasons were given for that conclusion. The property was leasehold but there was no evidence as to the remaining term of the lease, or as to the condition of the property. There was also no evidence as to the age of the daughter and no consideration as to whether a court would order a sale (which seemed very unlikely, given the purpose for which the property had been acquired and the purpose for which it was being used). The Commissioner, referring to *CIS/191/1994*, holds that there was no evidence that the claimant's capital exceeded the then prescribed limit of £8,000. He stated that everything depended on the facts and the evidence before the tribunal. In this case the valuation evidence was so unsatisfactory as to be worthless. He set out the following guidance on valuation:

"13. Proper valuation evidence should include details of the valuer's expertise, the basis on which he or she holds him or herself out as able to give expert evidence in relation to the property in question. Where it is the sale of a share in a property which is in issue, the evidence should deal with the valuer's experience in relation to such shares, and their sale. The property, and any leasehold interest, should be described in sufficient detail, including details of the length of any lease, of any special terms in it, and of the location, size and condition of the property, to show that the factors relevant to its value have been taken into account, and the reasons for the conclusion as to the value should be given. A similar approach should be applied to a share of a property, and an explanation should be given of the factors identified as relevant to the valuation, and how they affect it. The expert should also give evidence of any comparables identified, or of other reasons why it is concluded that the share could be sold at any particular price. If there is no evidence of actual sales of such interests, an acceptable explanation of the absence of such evidence should be given.

14. I appreciate that, in cases of this kind, this will on occasions be a counsel of perfection which cannot be realised. Where a valuer does not have relevant information, and proceeds upon assumptions, the report should state what is missing, and should also state the assumptions upon which it is based. This will normally give the claimant the opportunity to correct any mistaken assumptions or other errors of fact in the report."

See also *JC-W v Wirral Metropolitan BC (HB)* [2011] UKUT 501 (AAC), paras 13–18, for Judge Mark's critical comments in relation to the District Valuer's valuation in that case, and *MN v LB Hillingdon (HB)* [2014] UKUT 427 (AAC) and *PE v SSWP (SPC)* [2014] UKUT 387 (AAC) noted below.

It will not always be the case that a deemed equal share in a property will be of minimal value, even if the other co-owners are unwilling to sell. As *Wilkinson v Chief Adjudication Officer*, CA, March 24, 2000, reported as *R(IS) 1/01*, illustrates, the purposes for which the joint ownership was established will need to be scrutinised in order to assess whether a court would order a sale. In *Wilkinson* the claimant's mother had died, leaving her home to the claimant and her brother jointly "to do with as they wish". It was accepted that the mother had expressed the hope that the claimant's brother would live in the house with his son when his divorce proceedings in Australia were resolved (although there was nothing in the will to that effect). The claimant contended that the capital value of her half-share in the property was of a nominal value only, because her brother was unwilling to leave the property and unwilling to sell his share in it. She maintained that a court would not order a sale under s.30 of the Law of Property Act 1925 (repealed with effect from January 1, 1998 and replaced by ss.14 and 15 of the Trusts of Land and Appointment of Trustees Act 1996). But the Court of Appeal, by a majority (Mummery and Potter LJJ), disagreed. This was not a case like *Palfrey* where property had been acquired by joint owners for a collateral purpose (e.g. for them to live in as long as they wished) and that purpose would be defeated by ordering a sale. On the contrary, this was a case where an order for sale would enable the claimant's mother's wishes, as expressed in her will, to be carried out. Her brother's unwillingness to sell or pay the claimant for the value of her share was in fact having the effect of defeating that testamentary purpose. Potter LJ said that the proper starting point for valuation of the claimant's half-share was half the market value of the house with vacant possession, with a discount for any factors materially affecting her ability to market the house on that basis. The tribunal's conclusion that in the circumstances the value of her half-share was half of the market value of the house less 10% for expenses of sale and a charge to the testatrix's former husband was upheld. Evans LJ, however, took the opposite view. He considered that the claimant's share should be valued on the basis that a sale would not be ordered because this would defeat the mother's wish that her son and grandson be allowed to live in the property. As this case illustrates, much will depend on the circumstances in a particular case (and the view that is taken of those circumstances).

On very similar facts (a mother leaving a property to the claimant and his two sisters in equal shares, with no restriction or superadded purpose expressed in the will) the approach in *Wilkinson* was applied to the same effect in *JM v Eastleigh Borough Council (HB)* [2016] UKUT 464 (AAC).

Those cases were ones where there was no obstacle to the sale of the property with vacant possession, even though there might have been some normal delay in the process during which the disregard in para.6 of Sch.10 could come into play. The approach of starting with the market value of the property as a whole and then dividing by the number of joint owners, but not ignoring other factors, does not undermine the fundamental principle that under reg.47 it is the claimant's deemed severed share (i.e. as a deemed tenant in common) that must be valued. The following decisions illustrate some of problems of valuation in the more complicated cases where there is real doubt whether a court would order a sale if other joint owners were unwilling to agree.

In *CIS/3197/2003* the claimant owned a house with her daughter, who had a two-thirds share. (As we now know as a result of *Hourigan*, such circumstances do not fall within reg.47, but the approach to valuation is still relevant). The claimant went into a nursing home, leaving the house in the occupation of her daughter and the daughter's disabled child. The daughter would not agree to a sale of the house nor was she willing to buy out the claimant's share. It seemed unlikely that a court would order a sale. In view of the Secretary of State's failure to provide proper evidence of the value of the claimant's share the Commissioner found that the value of the claimant's interest was nil. However, he added that tribunals should not approach the matter in this way. If the evidence was incomplete, they should adjourn with directions as to the ways in which the evidence should be supplemented and should not decide the case on the burden of proof. Clearly where there has been no attempt to obtain any valuation evidence this should apply. However, if such attempts have been made and the evidence remains inadequate, it is suggested that the burden of proof may need to come into play (and indeed this was the approach taken in both *R(IS) 3/96* and, in effect, *R(JSA) 1/02*). For example, in *R(IS) 3/96* it was held that grounds for revising the claimant's award had not been shown in the light of the deficiencies in the District Valuer's report and in *R(JSA) 1/02* the Commissioner substituted his own decision on the existing evidence despite such deficiencies.

Despite the above case law, examples have continued to crop up of a claimant's share in a property being wrongly valued simply as a proportion of the whole, rather than the claimant's actual or deemed share being properly valued, taking into account all the relevant circumstances. See, for instance, *R(IS) 5/07* and *AM v SSWP (SPC)* [2010] UKUT 134 (AAC).

Examples of inadequate valuation evidence from the District Valuer, where a tribunal erred in law by relying on it, also continue to arise, such as *MN v London Borough of Hillingdon (HB)* [2014] UKUT 427 (AAC). The claimant there had been living in the jointly-owned matrimonial home with his wife, who had serious mental health problems, and their severely disabled son. However, it became necessary for the claimant and his son to leave, due to deterioration in his wife's health. Judge Ovey, after noting that the District Valuer appeared to have arrived at her valuation by halving the total value of the property and deducting just under 1 per cent, despite having been given details of the circumstances of the case, stated:

"32. . . . As a matter of common sense, it seems unlikely in the extreme that a purchaser would pay just under half the vacant possession value of a property for a half interest which would not enable him to occupy the property without first obtaining some form of court order against a defendant suffering from paranoid schizophrenia who was in occupation of a former matrimonial home, bought for the purpose of being a home, and who might be entitled to a property adjustment order. . . ."

See also *PE v SSWP (SPC)* [2014] UKUT 387 (AAC) which concerned the value of the claimant's interest in his former home, which remained occupied by his wife, son and step-son (the step-son had mental health problems). The District Valuer's valuation was based on an assumption that there had been a hypothetical application under the Trusts of Land and Appointment of Trustees Act 1996. The

Secretary of State argued that in the circumstances of the case the District Valuer's assumption was unrealistic. Although no divorce proceedings were in place at the time, any application under the 1996 Act would be likely to generate such proceedings by the other party who was likely to obtain a more favourable outcome under the Matrimonial Causes Act 1973. Judge Jacobs accepted that the evidence relied on by the tribunal as to valuation was therefore flawed and decided, with the consent of the Secretary of State, that there were no grounds to supersede the decision awarding state pension credit.

There is a difficult balance between what might be a counsel of perfection (as in *R(JSA) 1/02*) and a realistic approach to what assumptions are acceptable in the inevitably imprecise exercise of valuing hypothetical interests. *Reigate and Banstead BC v GB (HB)* [2018] UKUT 225 (AAC) shows that tribunals should not go overboard in picking holes in a District Valuer's report. On the assumption (quite possibly inaccurate) that the claimant and his daughter were beneficial joint tenants and that there had not already been a severance, the tribunal went wrong in the reasons it relied on to find that the District Valuer had not properly valued the claimant's deemed equal share as a tenant in common and had not taken into account the possible need for an application to the court, as the property was occupied by the daughter and her son. In particular, the District Valuer did not need to provide evidence of a local market for an interest of the kind the claimant was deemed to have. There is undoubtedly a market for actual interests of the kind deemed to exist by reg.47 (see the many cases discussed above), often in specialist auctions, although that is no doubt not well-known to claimants. But there remains a question how much detail a District Valuer needs to give of the existence of such a market and of the prices fetched for comparable interests to validly underpin the valuation.

Capital disregarded

2.174 **48.**—(1) Any capital specified in Schedule 10 is to be disregarded from the calculation of a person's capital (see also regulations 75 to 77).

(2) Where a period of 6 months is specified in that Schedule, that period may be extended by the Secretary of State where it is reasonable to do so in the circumstances of the case.

GENERAL NOTE

2.175 The number of disregards in Sch.10 is considerably reduced from those that apply for income support, old style JSA, old style ESA and housing benefit but they cover many of the same items, such as premises, business assets, rights in pension schemes, earmarked assets, etc. But note that some of the disregards that are in Schedules for the purposes of those benefits are to be found elsewhere in these Regulations, e.g., in regs 46(2), 49(3), 75 and 76. See also reg.77 in relation to companies in which the person is like a sole trader or partner. And note that with effect from May 21, 2020 there is a disregard as capital (for 12 months from the date of receipt) for the self-employed of any payment in respect of a furloughed employee under the Coronavirus Job Retention Scheme or "by way of a grant or loan to meet the expenses or losses of the trade, profession or vocation in relation to the outbreak of coronavirus disease" (Universal Credit (Coronavirus) (Self-employed Claimants and Reclaims) (Amendment) Regulations 2020 (SI 2020/522) reg.2(2)) (see discussion in the note to para.7 of Sch.10 and the general note for other disregards stemming from provisions outside the Universal Credit Regulations).

Note the general extension on the grounds of reasonableness that can be applied to the six months' period in any of the provisions in Sch.10 (para.(2)).

With effect from July 24, 2019, reg.51 of the Transitional Provisions Regulations 2014, as inserted by reg.3 of the Universal Credit (Managed Migration Pilot and Miscellaneous Amendments) Regulations 2019 (SI 2019/1152), supplies a transitional capital disregard to claimants who (i) were previously entitled to a tax credit and had capital exceeding £16,000; (ii) are given a migration notice that existing benefits are to terminate; and (iii) claim universal credit within the deadline. The disregard is of any capital exceeding £16,000. The disregard can apply only for 12 assessment periods and ceases (without the possibility of revival) following any assessment period in which the amount of capital the claimant has falls below £16,000. See regs 56 and 57 of the Transitional Provisions Regulations for further provisions on termination of the protection. The £16,000 non-disregarded capital that the claimant by definition possesses will produce an assumed yield as income of £174 per month under reg.72. Paragraph 7 of Sch.2 to the Transitional Provisions Regulations, inserted by the same Regulations, contains a disregard as capital of any amount paid as a lump sum by way of a "transitional SDP amount" under that Schedule.

Valuation of capital

49.—(1) Capital is to be calculated at its current market value or sur-   2.176
render value less—
  (a) where there would be expenses attributable to sale, 10 per cent; and
  (b) the amount of any encumbrances secured on it.
(2) The market value of a capital asset possessed by a person in a country outside the United Kingdom is—
  (a) if there is no prohibition in that country against the transfer of an amount equal to the value of that asset to the United Kingdom, the market value in that country; or
  (b) if there is such a prohibition, the amount it would raise if sold in the United Kingdom to a willing buyer.
(3) Where capital is held in currency other than sterling, it is to be calculated after the deduction of any banking charge or commission payable in converting that capital into sterling.

GENERAL NOTE

The rules for the valuation of capital are the same as for income support, old style   2.177
ESA and JSA and housing benefit. Paragraph (1) is the equivalent of reg.49 of the Income Support Regulations. Paragraph (2) on assets outside the UK is the equivalent of reg.50. Paragraph (3) on capital held in foreign currency previously took the form of a disregard (para.21 of Sch.10 to the Income Support Regulations).
The general rule under para.(1) is that the market value of the asset is to be taken. The surrender value will be taken if appropriate (the disregard in para.9 of Sch.10 of the value of life insurance policies must refer to whichever value has been chosen). The value at this stage does not take account of any encumbrances (always spelt with an "i" in the former legislation) secured on the assets, since those come in under sub-para.(b) (*R(IS) 21/93*). There is no definitive requirement that there be a local market (*Reigate and Banstead BC v GB (HB)* [2018] UKUT 225 (AAC)), but the way in which markets work in practice in whatever asset is in question must be taken into account.
In *R(SB) 57/83* and *R(SB) 6/84* the test taken is the price that would be commanded between a willing buyer and a willing seller at a particular date. In *R(SB) 6/84* it is stressed that in the case of a house it is vital to know the nature and extent of the interest being valued. Also, since what is required is a current market value, the Commissioner holds that an estate agent's figure for a quick sale was closer to the proper approach than the District Valuer's figure for a sale within three months. All the circumstances must be taken into account in making the valuation. Arguments have been raised that during the 2020 coronavirus outbreak, in the period when estate agents' offices were closed and most viewings impossible, there was no market in existence for domestic properties. In *CIS/553/1991* it is held that in valuing a former matrimonial home the wife's statutory right of occupation under the Matrimonial Homes Act 1967 has to be taken into account. See further the decisions discussed under *Valuation under reg.47* in the notes to reg.47.

Reigate and Banstead BC v GB (above, and in detail in the notes to reg.47) is a helpful example of valuation of an interest as a tenant in common, in that case a deemed such interest, and of an acceptable District Valuer's report.

RM v Sefton Council (HB) [2016] UKUT 357 (AAC), reported as [2017] AACR 5, provides a good practical example of the valuation of a property with sitting shorthold tenants.

Similarly, if chattels are being valued, it is what they could be sold for that counts, not simply what was paid for them (*CIS/494/1990, CIS/2208/2003*). See also *JJ v SSWP (IS)* [2012] UKUT 253 (AAC) which points out that where a sale of a chattel is by auction there are buyer's premiums added as well as seller's commission and that this could result in the seller being treated as having much more capital than he would realise on a sale. In the judge's view this was not the object of the regulations and the valuation had to be based on the standard test of what the claimant could expect to realise on a transaction between a willing seller and a willing buyer. Despite the disregard in universal credit of the value of personal possessions (reg.46(2)) and of business assets (paras 7 and 8 of Sch.10), it may occasionally be necessary to take the value of chattels, e.g. if a claimant retains former business assets beyond the limits of para.8 of Sch.10 or if investment assets are found to fall outside the meaning of "personal possessions" (see the notes to re.46(2)).

Sometimes a detailed valuation is not necessary, such as where the value of an asset is on any basis clearly over the prescribed limit of £16,000) (*CIS/40/1989*). That, however, has the undesirable result that no baseline has been established for assessing the effects of future disposals of the assets.

Shares

2.178   It is accepted that the test of the willing buyer and the willing seller is the starting point for the valuation of shares (*R(SB) 57/83, R(SB) 12/89* and *R(IS) 2/90*). The latter case emphasises that in the income support context, as would also be the case for universal credit, the value must be determined on the basis of a very quick sale, so that the hypothetical willing seller would be at a corresponding disadvantage. In the case of private companies there is often a provision in the articles of association that a shareholder wishing to sell must first offer the shares to other shareholders at a "fair value" fixed by the auditors (this was the case in *R(SB) 18/83* and *R(IS) 2/90*). Then the value of the shares ought not to be higher than the fair value, but for benefit purposes may well be less. The possible complications are set out in *CSB/488/1982* (quoted with approval in *R(SB) 12/89* and *R(IS) 2/90*). In *R(IS) 8/92* it is suggested that the market value is what a purchaser would pay for the shares subject to the same restriction. Whether the shareholding gives a minority, equal or controlling interest is particularly significant. All the circumstances of the share structure of the company must be considered. For instance, in *R(SB) 12/89* shares could only be sold with the consent of the directors, which it was indicated would not be forthcoming. It seems to be agreed that valuation according to Revenue methods is not appropriate (*R(SB) 18/83* and *R(IS) 2/90*), although it is suggested in *R(SB) 12/89* that the Revenue Shares Valuation Division might be able to assist tribunals. It is not known if this is so. What is absolutely clear is that the total value of the company's shareholding cannot simply be divided in proportion to the claimant's holding (*R(SB) 18/83*).

However, in para.14 of *P v SSWP and P (CSM)* [2018] UKUT 60 (AAC) it was said, in a passage not necessary to the decision, that the tribunal in that child support case:

> "was correct in basing the value of the shares on the book value of the company's net assets, without making any discount to reflect the difficulty in selling part of the shareholding in a private company. In *Ebrahimi v Westbourne Galleries Limited* [1973] A.C. 360 it was held that in some circumstances a limited company could co-exist with a 'quasi-partnership' between those involved in the company, for example, if the shareholders were bound by personal relationships involving

mutual confidence, if the shareholders were in practice involved in the conduct of the business, and if the transfer of the shares was restricted. In *re Bird Precision Bellows Ltd.* [1986] Ch. 658 Oliver LJ held [674A] that in a 'quasi-partnership' case it was appropriate that: 'the shares of the company should be valued as a whole and that the petitioners should then simply be paid the proportionate part of that value which was represented by their shareholding, without there being made a discount for the fact that this was a minority shareholding'."

It is not though clear how far that approach should be translated to means-tested benefits and how far it turns on the particular context of the child support variation provisions with their stress on a parent's control in practice over a company (see para.15 of *P*). But the application of reg.77 (company analogous to a partnership or one-person business) would have to be considered in such circumstances. If that provision applies, reg.77(2) expressly requires that the actual value of the claimant's shareholding be disregarded and the claimant be treated as owning the capital of the company, or the appropriate proportion of it (see the notes to reg.77 for further discussion).

In the case of shares in companies quoted on the London Stock Exchange the Revenue method of valuation should be used (*R(IS) 18/95*). This involves looking at all the transactions relating to the relevant share during the previous day, taking the lowest figure and adding to this a quarter of the difference between the lowest and the highest figure. The Commissioner considered that decision-makers could use the valuation quoted in newspapers (which is the mean between the best bid and best offer price at the close of business the previous day) to obtain approximate valuations. However, where a completely accurate valuation was essential, the Revenue method would need to be adopted. See also *DW v SSWP (JSA)* [2012] UKUT 478 (AAC).

Valuation affected by difficulties in realisation

2.179

The proper approach to valuation can usefully deal with unrealisable assets. Sometimes their market value will be nil (e.g. a potential interest under a discretionary trust: *R(SB) 25/83*; assets that are subject to a restraint or freezing order: *SH v SSWP* [2008] UKUT 21 (AAC); *CS v Chelmsford BC (HB)* [2014] UKUT 518 (AAC)); sometimes it will be very heavily discounted. However, if the asset will be realisable after a time, it may have a current value. The claimant may be able to sell an option to purchase the asset in the future (see *R(IS) 8/92*) or borrow, using the asset as security. But the valuation must reflect the fact that the asset is not immediately realisable. In *R(IS) 4/96* the claimant had on his divorce transferred his interest in the former matrimonial home to his wife in return for a charge on the property which could only be enforced if she died, remarried or cohabited for more than six months. The claimant's former wife was 46 and in good health. A discount had to be applied to the present day value of the charge to reflect the fact that it might not be realisable for as long as 40 years or more; consequently it was unlikely to be worth more than £3,000. See also *CIS/982/2002* in which the Commissioner sets out a number of detailed questions that had to be considered when valuing the claimant's share (if any) in a joint bank account that had been frozen following the claimant's separation from her husband. And note *LC v Bournemouth Borough Council (HB)* [2016] UKUT 175 (AAC), discussed in the notes to reg.46.

In *JC-W v Wirral MBC (HB)* [2011] UKUT 501 (AAC) Judge Mark concluded that nobody would be willing to purchase (for more than a nominal amount) the claimant's beneficial interest pending divorce in two heavily mortgaged properties, one of which was only partly built, in respect of which the claimant's parents-in-law claimed an interest in the proceeds of sale, and which the claimant's husband was unwilling to sell.

As the Tribunal of Commissioners in *R(SB) 45/83* point out, the market value (in that case of an interest in an entire trust fund) must reflect the outlay the purchaser would expect to incur in obtaining transfer of the assets and the profit they would expect as an inducement to purchase. If there might be some legal difficulty in obtaining the underlying asset (as there might have been in *R(SB) 21/83* and in *R(IS) 13/95*, where shares were held in the names of the claimant's children) this must be taken into account.

See also *MB v Wychavon DC (HB)* [2013] UKUT 67 (AAC) which concerned the valuation of the claimant's beneficial interest under a declaration of trust made by his mother in relation to a property held in the mother's name. The claimant had contributed 10 per cent towards the purchase price. In the absence of a family member willing to purchase the claimant's share, Judge Mark finds that the market value of the claimant's interest was substantially less than the amount of his contribution to the purchase price (he decided it was less than half that amount). However, it was possible that there would be no market at all for the claimant's share, in which case its value would be nil.

Where the property is jointly owned, see the decisions discussed under *Valuation under reg.47* in the notes to reg.47.

Deductions from market value

2.180   The general rule is that the whole of a capital resource is to be taken into account. Liabilities are not to be deducted from the value (*R(SB) 2/83* and *SSWP v GF (ESA)* [2017] UKUT 333 (AAC)). The "remedy" in such a case is for the claimant to discharge the liability, which does not give rise to notional capital under the deprivation rule (see reg.50(2)(a)). It is only where a debt is secured on the capital asset that it is deducted under reg.49(1)(b).

In this connection, note *JRL v SSWP (JSA)* [2011] UKUT 63 (AAC), reported as [2011] AACR 30. The claimant had three accounts with the same bank, of which one was in credit, one was overdrawn and one had a nil balance. The Three-Judge Panel pointed out that this meant that the claimant was both a creditor and a debtor of the same body. Under the bank's terms and conditions, the bank had a contractual right to debit at any time any of a customer's accounts which were in credit with sums sufficient to clear the customer's indebtedness to the bank. This created what was effectively a charge on the customer's credit balance(s). The market value of the account that was in credit was therefore its net value after deduction of the amount of the claimant's overdraft on his other account.

The first deduction to be made is a standard 10 per cent if there would be any expenses attributable to sale, as there almost always will be. The second is the amount of any encumbrance secured on the asset. There is particularly full and helpful guidance on the nature of incumbrances on real property and the evidence which should be examined in *R(IS) 21/93*, and see below. In *R(IS) 10/99* the Commissioner points out that the word "encumbrance" is unknown to the law of Scotland, but goes on to interpret the equivalent of sub-para.(b) as meaning that there must be something attached to the capital in question that prevents the claimant from disposing of it.

The standard case of a debt being secured on a capital asset is a house that is mortgaged. The amount of capital outstanding will be deducted from the market value of the house. In *R(SB) 14/81* the claimant had been lent £5,000 for work on his bungalow, which was mortgaged to secure the debt. He had £3,430 left. Although he was obliged to make monthly repayments this liability could not be deducted from the £3,430, for the debt was not secured on the money. However, the principle of *R(SB) 53/83* (see the notes to reg.46) would make the money not part of the claimant's resources. In *JH v SSWP* [2009] UKUT 1 (AAC) the site owner's commission payable on the sale of a beach hut was not "an incumbrance secured on" the hut but a personal contractual obligation on the seller which could not be enforced against the asset itself.

In *R(SB) 18/83* the Commissioner says that personal property such as shares (or money) can be charged by a contract for valuable consideration (e.g. a loan) without any writing or the handing over of any title documents. But this is not the case in Scots law (*R(SB) 5/88*). In *R(IS) 18/95* the claimant's brokers had a lien on his shares for the cost of acquisition and their commission which fell to be offset against the value of the shares. *CIS/368/1993* concerned money held under a solicitor's undertaking. £40,000 of the proceeds of sale of the claimant's house was retained by his solicitors in pursuance of an undertaking to his bank given because of a previous charge on the property. The Commissioner decides that the undertaking was an incumbrance within the equivalent of sub-para.(b). It was the equivalent of a pledge or lien and was secured on the proceeds of sale. Thus the £40,000 did not count as part of the claimant's resources. See also *CIS/984/2002* which concerned money held by the claimant's solicitor pending quantification of the statutory charge to the Legal Services Commission under s.10(7) of the Access to Justice Act 1999. The Commissioner holds that this was not part of the claimant's capital until the charge had been quantified, as until then it was not possible to identify any particular amount as the claimant's capital. He added that another way of looking at it was to treat the statutory charge as an incumbrance for the purpose of the equivalent of sub-para.(b).

In *R(IS) 5/98* the claimant transferred her flat to her daughter on the understanding that the daughter would care for her in the flat and pay off the mortgage. The daughter complied with the second condition, but evicted her mother from the flat. The Commissioner decides that the gift of the flat to the daughter had been subject to the condition that she looked after her mother. As that condition had not been fulfilled, the gift failed and the daughter held the property on trust for the claimant. In valuing the claimant's interest, the mortgage was to be deducted because the daughter was to be treated as subrogated to the rights of the mortgagee. In addition, the costs of the litigation to recover the property from the daughter also fell to be deducted. The claimant appealed against this decision to the Court of Appeal but her appeal was dismissed (*Ellis v Chief Adjudication Officer*, reported as part of *R(IS) 5/98*).

Notional capital

50.—(1) A person is to be treated as possessing capital of which the person has deprived themselves for the purpose of securing entitlement to universal credit or to an increased amount of universal credit.

(2) A person is not to be treated as depriving themselves of capital if the person disposes of it for the purposes of—

(a) reducing or paying a debt owed by the person; or

(b) purchasing goods or services if the expenditure was reasonable in the circumstances of the person's case.

(3) Where a person is treated as possessing capital in accordance with this regulation, then for each subsequent assessment period (or, in a case where the award has terminated, each subsequent month) the amount of capital the person is treated as possessing ("the notional capital") reduces—

(a) in a case where the notional capital exceeds £16,000, by the amount which the Secretary of State considers would be the amount of an award of universal credit that would be made to the person (assuming they met the conditions in section 4 and 5 of the Act) if it were not for the notional capital; or

(b) in a case where the notional capital exceeds £6,000 but not £16,000 (including where the notional capital has reduced to an amount equal to or less than £16,000 in accordance with sub-paragraph (a)) by the amount of unearned income that the notional capital is treated as yielding under regulation 72.

DEFINITION

"unearned income"—see reg.2.

2.181

GENERAL NOTE

Paragraph (1)

2.182
Under universal credit the only circumstance in which someone will be treated as having notional capital is where they have deprived themselves of it for the purpose of securing, or increasing, entitlement to universal credit (although note also reg.77(2) in relation to companies in which the person is like a sole trader or partner).

Deprivation

There is a considerable amount of case law on the "deprivation rule"—see the extensive notes to reg.51(1) of the Income Support Regulations in Vol.V of this series. That will be referred to below, but note that some of the case law will need to be read in the light of para.(2). The very important exceptions there for reducing or paying a debt or purchasing reasonable goods and services take a lot of formerly contentious areas out of consideration for universal credit.

In particular, the principle laid down in *R(SB) 38/85* will no doubt be relevant, that once it is shown that a person did possess, or received, a capital asset, the burden shifts to that person to show that it has ceased to be part of their actual capital, apparently whether on an initial claim or on revision or supersession by the Secretary of State (*LP v SSWP (ESA)* [2018] UKUT 389 (AAC), at para.13). If the person fails to show that, the proper conclusion is then that the asset remains part of their actual capital, rather than to invoke any notional capital rule (see *R(SB) 40/85*). Tribunals should therefore in such circumstances avoid vague formulations such as 'the claimant is treated as having capital of £x' and make it clear whether the conclusion is that the person has actual or notional capital of that amount (see *AB v SSWP and Canterbury CC (IS and HB)* [2014] UKUT 212 (AAC)). One consequence of the difference is that, if a person is found to have actual capital as a consequence of not having shown that some asset or assets have been disposed of, there is no statutory diminishing capital rule to be applied. Normally where a claimant is not entitled to benefit because the amount of capital exceeds the £16,000 limit (or the amount of assumed tariff income from capital over £6,000 precludes entitlement) the 'remedy' is to dip into the capital to meet living and/or other reasonable expenses or pay off some debt and to claim again when the amount of capital has reduced to the level that allows entitlement. However, a claimant may be in difficulty in making such an argument while maintaining that the assets in question had been disposed of.

MS v DfC (JSA) [2020] NICom 42 holds that where a tribunal is not satisfied by a claimant's assertion that they have disposed of money, so that the amount remains part of their actual capital, it is not necessary for the tribunal to make a positive finding of fact about where the money was actually held. Submissions to the contrary were based on a misreading of remarks in *DMcC v DSD (IS)* [2012] NICom 326. That is different from a situation like that in *WR v SSWP (IS)* [2012] UKUT 127 (AAC), where the tribunal was not satisfied by the claimant's explanation of why she had made payments to each of her parents. That dissatisfaction did not justify a conclusion that the money involved remained part of her actual capital.

In *CIS 634/1992* the claimant was made bankrupt on November 29, 1990. Between November 29 and December 28, 1990, when he claimed income support, he divested himself of most of his capital. His trustee in bankruptcy was not appointed until April 1991. Under s.284 of the Insolvency Act 1986 any disposal of property or payment by a bankrupt between the presentation of a bankruptcy petition and the vesting of their estate in their trustee is void (except with the consent or later ratification of the court). The claimant could not therefore in law deprive himself of any resources from November 29, onwards and the equivalent of para.(1) could not apply. However, since the claimant had failed to give a satisfactory account of how he had disposed of his capital, the Commissioner held he was to be treated as still possessing it in accordance with *R(SB) 38/85*. Thus he was held not to be entitled to income support prior to the appointment of the trustee in bank-ruptcy because until then he possessed actual capital over the income support limit. However, in *KS v SSWP (JSA)* [2009] UKUT 122 (AAC), reported as [2010] AACR 3, Judge Mark agreed that the effect of s.284 of the Insolvency Act was that the deprivation rule could not apply, but disagreed that a bankrupt's capital remains their capital until the appointment of the trustee in bankruptcy. He pointed out that a bankrupt cannot realise or use any part of their capital after a bankruptcy order has been made and that, subject to any order of the court, it will vest in their trustee in due course. Whether the capital remains their capital with a nil value or whether it ceases to be their capital at all (on which the judge did not reach any firm conclu-sion), the result was that the claimant in that case had no capital, or no capital of any value, after the bankruptcy order had been made. As a reported decision, *KS* is to be given more weight on this issue.

It is suggested that *R(SB) 38/85* should not be taken as sanctifying the Department's common practice of requiring claimants to produce receipts to substantiate their expenditure and of automatically treating them as still having the balance of their capital not covered by receipts. As the Commissioner in *CIS/515/2006* pointed out, it is inherently improbable that a claimant will be able to produce receipts for day to day expenditure, particularly in relation to a period sometimes several years in the past. Claimants should be asked to produce what records they do have and can be asked to explain any large or unusual payments. But to demand actual receipts for all expenditure, however small, particularly over a lengthy period is not reasonable. General conclusions should be drawn on the basis of the claimant's oral evidence and the documentary evidence that is available. See also *KW v SSWP (IS)* [2012] UKUT 350 (AAC) in which lack of receipts for the claimant's alleged expenditure on sexual services was understandable, given the nature of that expenditure. The question as to whether this expenditure took place, and if so, how much, therefore came down to a question of credibility.

It is arguable that someone cannot deprive themselves of something which they have never possessed, but it may be that a deliberate failure to acquire an asset is also a deprivation. In *CSB/598/1987* it was suggested that a deliberate failure to pay a cheque into a bank account could be a deprivation. See also *CIS/1586/1997* which stated that a sale at a known undervalue and the release of a debtor from a debt were capable of amounting to deprivation. However, someone does not deprive themselves of an asset by failing to seek a lump sum payment or property transfer order under the Matrimonial Causes Act 1973, since the right to make an applica-tion under the Act is not a capital asset (*R(IS) 1/03*). Moreover, even if this had constituted deprivation, the claimant's reasons for not bringing proceedings (which included, inter alia, fear of her abusive husband) clearly indicated that her purpose had not been to secure entitlement to income support.

R(IS) 7/07 decides that the rule can apply to deprivations made by someone who only later becomes the claimant's partner. About a year before she became the claim-ant's partner, Ms H, who was unemployed and who had been in receipt of JSA, sold her house. She used the proceeds of sale to, among other things, repay her daugh-ter's debts of £30,000 and to take her family on holiday. The tribunal found that in disposing of her capital Ms H had acted with the purpose of securing entitlement to income support. Commissioner Jacobs considered that this conclusion was one that was open to the tribunal to make on the evidence before it. He then went on to decide that the claimant was caught by the rule in para.(1) even though Ms H was not his partner at the time of the deprivation. In his view the combined effect of s.134(1) of the SSCBA 1992 and the enabling provision in s.136(5)(a) was to treat a partner's deprivation of capital as a deprivation by the claimant, even though they were not a couple at the time. The focus of the deprivation rule was on the purpose of a past disposal but it operated at the time when entitlement was in issue, so that the reference to the claimant (which by virtue of reg.23(1) of the Income Support Regulations included a reference to the claimant's partner) related to the person's status at that time. The Commissioner stated:

"Both in aggregating the capital of the members of a family and in taking account of notional capital, the legislation fulfils an anti-avoidance function. If notional capital were not aggregated, a future partner could dispose of capital before coming to live with the claimant or couples could separate in order to dispose of capital before reuniting ... The notional capital rule will only apply to a future partner where there has been conduct that is related to future entitlement to benefit either for the person alone or as a member of a family. That will limit the circumstances in which the rule applies and restrict it to those cases in which a course of conduct has been directed at future benefit entitlement."

In relation to universal credit s.5(1)(a) of the WRA 2012 is the equivalent of s.134(1) of the SSCBA 1992, but s.5(2)(a) expressly provides in the case of joint claimants for the £16,000 capital limit to be applied to their combined capital (and see para.4(5) of Sch.1 to the WRA 2012). Paragraph 4(2)(e) of Sch.1 is more explicit than s.136(5)(a) of the SSCBA 1992, but would only be needed in cases where a claimant who is a member of a couple claims as a single claimant (reg.3), when reg.18(2) provides for the capital of the other member of the couple to be included in the claimant's, apparently for all purposes under the Regulations. Thus there seems no obstacle to applying the reasoning in *R(IS) 7/07* to universal credit.

Although it is not made absolutely explicit in *R(IS) 7/07*, it would seem that the Commissioner (and the tribunal) must have taken the view that Ms H was at least contemplating becoming the claimant's partner at the time of the disposals because otherwise there was no basis for the finding that Ms H had deprived herself of capital for the purpose of securing entitlement to income support (there is no indication that as a single person she would qualify for income support since before she received the proceeds of sale of her house she had been in receipt of JSA). Under reg.50(1) the deprivation has to be for the purpose of securing entitlement to universal credit or an increased amount of it (see further below). It is suggested that the decision should therefore be limited to such circumstances, that is where the parties may become a couple in the future. Moreover, this would seem to be in line with the Commissioner's view of when the rule will apply to a future partner (see above).

The decision in *R(IS) 7/07* was a refusal of leave to appeal by the Commissioner. The claimant applied for judicial review of the Commissioner's decision but his application was dismissed (*R. (on the application of Hook) v Social Security Commissioner and Secretary of State for Work and Pensions* [2007] EWHC 1705 (Admin), reported as part of *R(IS) 7/07*).

If the claimant's attorney appointed under the Enduring Powers of Attorney Act 1985 repays a loan or makes gifts of the claimant's capital this may amount to deprivation by the claimant, since the attorney is the agent of the claimant (*CIS/12403/1991*). In that case there was a question as to whether the loan was the responsibility of the claimant or the attorney and whether the gifts were allowable under s.3(5) of the 1985 Act, which permitted the making of gifts "provided that the value of each such gift is not unreasonable having regard to all the circumstances and in particular the size of the donor's estate". The Commissioner states that the new tribunal would have to consider whether the payments were properly made; if not, there would be a claim against the attorney which would constitute actual capital; if they were properly made, the question of deprivation would have to be considered. Under the Mental Capacity Act 2005, enduring powers of attorney have from October 1, 2007 been replaced by lasting powers of attorney, but existing powers continue in effect. Section 12(2) of the 2005 Act is in similar terms to s.3(5) of the 1985 Act.

It should also be remembered that another result of *R(SB) 38/85* and *R(SB) 40/85* is that there is a deprivation of capital whenever a person ceases by their own act to possess some asset, even though some other asset is received in return. Otherwise it would be possible to convert capital that counts towards the limits into a form in which it is disregarded without falling foul of the notional capital rule. However, para.(2) of the present regulation sets out important limitations on the effect of that principle, which are not present in the income support or old style ESA or JSA legislation (see below).

There is no equivalent in reg.50 (or in reg.75) to reg.51(1)(a) of the Income Support Regulations (reg.115(1)(a) of the ESA Regulations 2008 and reg.113(1)(a) of the JSA Regulations 1996) excluding the operation of the deprivation rule where the capital disposed of is derived from a payment made in consequence of a personal injury and is placed on trust. If the sum was initially paid without restriction and that action, or the purchase of an annuity, was not taken, then after the expiry of the 12 months allowed for a reg.75 disregard by reg.75(6) there would be no applicable disregard. Therefore, depending on the amounts involved and the other circumstances, it could appear on the face of it that such a transfer of the capital either before or after the expiry of the 12 months was for the purpose of securing entitlement to universal credit or increasing its amount. The person would then have to be treated (as there is no discretion) as still possessing the amount disposed of. However, it is suggested that the policy behind reg.75 is so clear that where funds deriving from a personal injury are held in the ways specified in paras.(2) – (5) of reg.75 there should be no effect on universal credit entitlement, that the notional capital rule should not be applied in these circumstances.

Purpose

There is a great deal of case law on when there has been a deprivation of capital for the purpose of securing entitlement to or increasing the amount of benefit. See the very full discussion in the notes to reg.51(1) of the Income Support Regulations in Vol.V of this series. The issues are simplified to quite an extent for universal credit by the exclusions from the application of the notional capital rule in para.(2): where the disposal is for the purposes of reducing or paying a debt and where it is for the purposes of purchasing good or services if the expenditure was reasonable in the circumstances. That has removed some of the most difficult questions, although there are still problems (see the notes to para.(2) below). The main remaining potential ways of disposing of capital are transferring it to other people and converting it into a source of income or a different form of capital which is either disregarded or would have a lesser value for universal credit purposes. The general principles established through the cases remain relevant to universal credit, though.

(i) Knowledge of the capital limit

CIS/124/1990 held that it must be proved that the person actually knew of the capital limit rule, otherwise the necessary deliberate intention to obtain benefit could not have been present. It is not enough that the person ought to have known of the rule. The crunch comes, and the resolution with the approach in *R(SB) 40/85* (where it was suggested that the existence of some limit might be said to be common knowledge), in the assessment of the evidence about the person's knowledge. The Commissioner stressed that the person's whole background must be considered, including experience of the social security system and advice which is likely to have been received from the family and elsewhere. The burden of proof is on the Secretary of State, but in some circumstances a person's assertion that they did not know of the rule will not be credible. In *CIS/124/1990* itself the claimant was illiterate and spoke and understood only Gujerati. The Commissioner said that this should put her in no better or worse situation than a literate claimant whose mother tongue was English, but that the possibility of misunderstandings in interpretation should be considered. *CIS/124/1990* was followed in *R(SB) 12/91*, where the necessity of a positive finding of fact, based on sufficient evidence, that the person knew of the capital limit was stressed. Evidence that the person had been in receipt of supplementary benefit or income support for some years was not in itself enough. But information that the person has received, together with their educational standing and other factors, will be material in deciding whether actual knowledge exists or not. *CIS/30/1993* similarly held that it is not possible to infer actual knowledge of the capital limit simply from the claimant signing a claim form which contained that

2.183

2.184

information. The claimant there was partially sighted and had not completed the claim form herself but merely signed it. It was necessary for the tribunal to indicate what evidence satisfied it that the claimant did know of the capital limit.

Where a claimant had not previously claimed a means-tested benefit, nor made any inquiry about the conditions of entitlement, nor had any dealings with benefits, a specific finding that they knew of the capital limit was required (*Waltham Forest LBC v TM* [2009] UKUT 96 (AAC)).

However, in *RB v SSWP (ESA)* [2016] UKUT 384, Judge Markus, while accepting that normally a precise finding has to be made, said that there are some cases where there is no potentially credible alternative explanation for the payments made by the claimant and where the facts speak for themselves on both purpose and knowledge. So in the particular case the tribunal's statement that, after rejecting the claimant's explanations, it was left with only one conclusion that he had deprived himself of capital to continue to obtain old style ESA encompassed his knowledge of the effect of having the capital. It was also relevant that the claimant had never suggested at any stage of the case that he did not know of the capital limit. It is submitted, though, that when what is in issue is not whether the notional capital is above the £16,000 limit, but whether it would give rise to an assumed yield of income by exceeding £6,000, be necessary to consider whether the claimant knew of that rule, which is not as well-known as the £16,000 limit. That point was unfortunately not explored in *RB*, although it potentially arose on the facts found by the tribunal (see the discussion in para.2.185 below).

See also the discussion below of the effect of advice having been given by an officer of the DWP

(ii) The test for "purpose"

2.185
The decision-maker has to show that the person's purpose is one of those mentioned in para.(1). That approach was applied in *LP v SSWP (ESA)* [2018] UKUT 389 (AAC) at para.13, but see the discussion of *RB v SSWP (ESA)* [2016] UKUT 384 (AAC) below. There is unlikely to be direct contemporaneous evidence of purpose (although there might be letters or documents), so that primary facts must be found from which an inference as to purpose can be drawn (*CSB/200/1985*, *R(SB) 40/85*). And of course what the claimant says or writes to a tribunal is evidence that must be properly assessed. See further discussion below.

Although in *R(SB) 38/85*, where a "predominant purpose" test was rejected, there was a faint suggestion that it was enough that a subsidiary purpose was to obtain the benefit in question, the test in *R(SB) 40/85* has been accepted. There, Commissioner Monroe said that obtaining the benefit or an increased amount must be a "significant operative purpose". If the obtaining of benefit was a foreseeable consequence of the transaction then, in the absence of other evidence, it could be concluded that that was the person's purpose. That would exclude some cases caught by the width of the approach to deprivation, e.g. where a resource is converted into another form in which it is still taken into account. For then there would be no effect on eligibility for benefit. But beyond that situation there remain great difficulties. The Commissioners mention a number of relevant factors, e.g. whether the deprivation was a gift or in return for a service, the personal circumstances of the person (e.g. age, state of health, employment prospects, needs), whether a creditor was pressing for repayment of a loan. It must be an issue of fact when these other factors indicate that the reasonably foreseeable consequence of obtaining benefit was not a significant operative factor. A tribunal is not entitled to infer that the claimant had the relevant purpose simply from rash and excessive expenditure with some knowledge of some sort of capital limit—it has to go further and consider whether on its assessment of the claimant's character and thinking that is what happened (*CH/264/2006*, a case on the equivalent housing benefit provision). As *R(H) 1/06* (another case on the equivalent housing benefit provision) confirms, the test is a subjective one, which depends upon the evidence about the particular claimant in question (the claimant in that case was a schizophrenic whose mental state was such that he was unlikely to fully appreciate the implications of his behaviour and had limited capacity to plan for the future). See also *KW v SSWP (IS)* [2012] UKUT 350 (AAC) in which the claimant spent £40 to £100 a day of his inheritance on "one or two females out of four doing some fetish things for me". The claimant had a personality disorder and may not have appreciated the potential implications of his behaviour.

R(H) 1/06 was followed in *CIS/218/2005*, where the claimant had made large gifts to her children from the proceeds of the sale of her former matrimonial home. The Commissioner stated that whether a gift is reasonable or prudent, although relevant, does not answer the question of whether it was made for the purpose of securing or increasing entitlement to income support. The test is not one of reasonableness or prudence but what has to be considered is the claimant's purpose. On the other hand, in *CJSA/1425/2004* the fact that it was reasonable for the claimant to pay his credit card debts in order to avoid further liability for interest led to the conclusion that this had not been done for the purpose of obtaining or increasing entitlement to income-based JSA. The payment of debts, reasonably or not is now taken out of consideration for universal credit purposes by para.(2)(a), but reasonableness will have to be considered under para.(2)(b) if assets have been spent on goods or services. The length of time between the disposal of the capital and the claiming of benefit may also be relevant (*CIS/264/1989*).

A number of decisions have firmed up the general principles and given helpful examples, sometimes using different language to express the same essentials. The Commissioner in *R(SB) 9/91* stressed that a positive intention to obtain benefit must be shown to be a significant operative purpose. It was not enough for the adjudication officer merely to prove that the obtaining of benefit was a natural consequence of the transaction in question. The claimant had transferred her former home to her two daughters. Evidence was given that her sole intention was to make a gift to her daughters, as she intended to leave the property to them in her will and it was no longer of any use to her (she being permanently in need of residential nursing care). Commissioner Rice noted that that did not explain why the transfer was made when it was, why the proceeds of sale of the property would not have been of use to the claimant and what she thought she would live on if she gave the property away. She had been in receipt of supplementary benefit for several years. On the evidence the obtaining of benefit was a significant operative purpose. The decision thus endorsed the attribution of a purpose to a claimant by implication from all the circumstances, but the conclusion must be in terms of the claimant's purpose, not in terms of the natural consequences of the transaction in question. *R(H) 1/06*, referred to above, reiterated that it is necessary for a tribunal to determine the claimant's actual (i.e. subjective) intention. In effect, the question whether the person would have carried out the transaction at the same time if there had been no effect on eligibility for benefit is a useful one.

In some circumstances the principles of *Kerr v Department for Social Development* [2004] UKHL 23; [2004] 1 W.L.R. 1372; *R 1/04 (SF)* may be relevant, even though the burden of showing a prohibited purpose lies on the Secretary of State, in that a failure by a claimant to come forward with evidence within their knowledge to support their explanations for the making of payments may support an inference that the purpose was to obtain benefit. That was the case in *RB v SSWP (ESA)* [2016] UKUT 384 (AAC). The claimant, who had been in receipt of income-related ESA since January 2013, received some £26,000 from a divorce settlement on March 7, 2014. On March 26, 2014, he made two payments of £6,000 each to his parents, which he said was to repay loans. On April 9, 2014, he paid £5,760 to his landlord by way of a year's rent in advance. The claimant supplied bank statements showing a number of cash withdrawals from his mother's account totalling £8,980 between June 2012 and April 2014, but no statements for his father's bank account. The tribunal confirmed the initial decision that all three payments had been made to reduce his capital below £16,000 and secure entitlement to ESA, so that the equivalent of reg.50(1) applied and entitlement to ESA ceased. It stated that it could not be "sure to the required standard" that the withdrawals from the mother's account, in the light of the pattern of amounts, were not merely to meet her own living expenses and that, with the absence of any contemporaneous evidence of the loans and of bank statements from the father's account, the claimant had not established that he had borrowed £12,000 from his parents. The advance payment of rent was said to be ridiculous in the absence of evidence that it was required by his tenancy agreement, so that it had to be concluded that it had been made to deprive himself of capital. Judge Markus held that the tribunal had not erred in law in its approach to the burden and standard of proof. She took perhaps a generous view in reading the tribunal's statement of reasons as a whole, which in parts had given the appearance of requiring the claimant to disprove, to a level of sureness, that the payments were not made for the purpose of securing entitlement to ESA. Applying the *Kerr* principle that the claimant should supply as much information as he reasonably could, the state of the evidence was such that, the tribunal having rejected the claimant's credibility in general, there could have been no doubt that the finding as to the purpose of the payments was properly established.

It is unfortunate that the following conundrum was not addressed in *RB*. There was no mention of the claimant having other capital assets. On that basis, by the time that he paid the year's rent in advance his actual capital had been reduced below £16,000 by the two payments to his parents. Could it then be said that his purpose was to secure entitlement to ESA? If he had sufficient knowledge of the capital rules for the regulation to apply in the first place, it is plainly arguable that it could not. It would be odd to draw a line between claimants who knew that there was a capital rule, but not of the amount of the limit, and claimants who knew of the significance of the amount of £16,000. However, the question would then have to be asked whether the advance payment of rent was made for the purpose of increasing the amount of ESA, by reducing the amount of tariff income treated as produced by capital exceeding £6,000. In those circumstances, it might then be argued that a specific finding needed to be made as to the claimant's knowledge of the rules on tariff income from capital below £16,000.

In *CIS/242/1993*, another case where the claimant had gone into residential care, the Commissioner reached the opposite conclusion on the facts to that in *R(SB) 9/91*. The claimant's son had cared for his mother for 15 years. When she went into a residential care home, she gave her share of the proceeds of sale of their jointly owned home to her son to be used towards the purchase of his flat. The Commissioner accepted that she had relinquished her share in gratitude to her son and not to secure income support.

2.186   In *R(IS) 13/94* the claimant's capital was in excess of the statutory limit when he purchased his council house. The deposit used up enough of his capital to bring him below the limit. It was necessary to consider whether para.(1) applied to this use of the capital since the claimant was apparently dependent on income support to meet the mortgage interest. But in *R(IS) 15/96* using a criminal injuries compensation award to pay off part of a mortgage was not caught by para.(1) (now see para.(2)(a)). The SSAT had found that the claimant's purpose had been to secure his future and to reduce the burden on the DSS for his mortgage payments. That was a matter for the judgment of the tribunal.

A further example is *CJSA/204/2002*. The claimant had agreed to provide the deposit for a flat that she and her son would buy. In the event the claimant did not move into the new flat with her son and his girlfriend because of a disagreement but she still lent her son the deposit. The claimant did correspond with her solicitor about obtaining security for the loan but no formal agreement or legal charge was entered into. The Commissioner held that the claimant clearly had reasons for keeping her promise to lend the deposit (for example, so as not to let her son down or sour relations further) and in his view there had been no deprivation within the rule. See also *R(IS) 1/03* above, under *Deprivation*. It may often be pertinent in similar cases to pose the *R(SB) 9/91* question of what the claimant thought they would live on if the asset in question was disposed of.

In *CIS/109/1994* and *CIS/112/1994* the claimants had used their capital to purchase an annuity and a life insurance policy respectively. In *CIS/109/1994* the claimant was both physically and mentally frail and lived in a nursing home. The tribunal found that at the material time she had no knowledge of the income support capital and deprivation of capital rules, and entered into the transaction on her son's advice, who considered that this was the best use of her capital to enable her to stay in the nursing home. The Commissioner held that the tribunal had not erred in concluding that she had not purchased the annuity in order to obtain income support. In *CIS/112/1994* the Commissioner decided that para.(1) did apply, but that para.15 of Sch.10 to the Income Support Regulations applied to disregard the value of the life policy. Thus what the Commissioner considered would have been an unfair "double counting" of notional and actual capital was avoided. See also *R(IS) 7/98* where capital had been used to purchase an "investment bond". The Commissioner decided that the bond fell within the definition of "policy of life insurance" in reg.2(1) and so could be disregarded under para.15 of Sch.10. But the claimant's intention at the time of the investment had to be considered to see whether para.(1) applied. The value of any policy of life insurance is disregarded as capital by para.9 of Sch.10 to the Universal Credit Regulations, but the value of an annuity is not. There may therefore be "double counting" issues resulting from the lack of any discretion in the application of reg.50(1), which may not be resolved through the diminishing notional capital rule in para.(3) (see below).

Where a transaction has no effect on the claimant's entitlement, as in *CJSA/3937/2002* where the property transferred was the house in which the claimant was living (which was therefore disregarded under para.1 of Sch.8 to the JSA Regulations 1996), an intention to secure entitlement to income-based JSA was not shown.

In many cases of alleged deprivation of capital there will have been a course of spending, often on various items, and sometimes over a considerable period of time. In *R(H) 1/06*, the Commissioner emphasised the need to go through all the various items of expenditure, taking account of any explanations put forward by the claimant, and to reach a specific determination as to: (i) what amounts (if any) represent deprivation of capital in excess of a reasonable level of general expenditure in the claimant's circumstances; and (ii) what had been the claimant's purpose at the time and whether this included an intention to obtain benefit. The tribunal had erred in simply expressing its decision in generalised terms without attempting to analyse the movements on the claimant's account during the relevant period. *CIS/1775/2007* makes the same point. The tribunal had been wrong to treat all payments as having been made with the same motivation but should have considered each type of expenditure separately when applying the significant operative purpose test.

It has been held that where the claimant had been accurately warned about the consequences of a transaction by the local DSS office (i.e. that the equivalent of reg.50(1) would be applied) and still went ahead, this showed that he could not have had as any part of his purpose securing of entitlement, or continued entitlement, to income support (*CIS 621/1991*). But there must be limits to generalising from this decision. Can claimants, in cases not involving specific Departmental advice, be heard to say that because of their existing knowledge of the capital limits and the notional capital rules they anticipated that depriving themselves of some capital asset would not affect entitlement to benefit because they would be treated as having notional capital as a result, and thereby secure the very opposite result on the basis that their purpose could not have been to secure or increase entitlement? To admit the validity of such an argument would seem to involve internal contradictions in identifying claimants' purposes, not to mention ludicrous outcomes. That argument cannot be right.

An even more misguided suggestion, extraordinarily made on behalf of the Secretary of State, was rejected in *LP v SSWP (ESA)* [2018] UKUT 389 (AAC) at paras 8–11. This was that, since at the time of the deprivation (of amounts received as lump sums from a personal pension scheme) the claimant was in receipt of the maximum amount of income-related ESA she could aspire to, she could not have thought that spending the money could increase the amount of that benefit and securing or increasing benefit could not have been an operative purpose. The fundamental mistake in that suggestion was to ignore the potential purpose of securing entitlement for the weeks following the receipt of the capital if the DWP were informed or found out about the receipt. That could have been in her thoughts.

The effect of DWP advice on the claimant's intention was further considered in *LH v SSWP (IS)* [2014] UKUT 60 (AAC), although somewhat inconclusively because in the end the judge decided on the evidence that the operative purpose of the deprivation was the paying off of debts, regardless of the advice given. The claimant received £54,000 from an endowment policy. She did not inform the DWP at the time because she thought that since the policy had been set up to pay a mortgage the proceeds did not count as capital, but should not be used for ordinary living expenses. However, she did not need to use the money to pay off her mortgage and used part of it to pay other debts that charged a higher rate of interest. When she was later visited by a DWP officer, she sought advice from him about the impact on her income support entitlement of using the proceeds from the policy to pay off her debts before meeting her mortgage liability. He informed her that it was reasonable and acceptable to pay off outstanding loans and debts before using the remainder to pay off part of the mortgage, as long as she did not spend the money on, for example, exotic holidays. The officer did not advise the claimant that she would be able to secure entitlement to income support if she used the remaining excess capital in the way she was doing, nor was this the advice sought by the claimant. After the visit she continued to use the proceeds of the policy to pay her debts before paying off part of the mortgage.

Judge Wright rightly emphasised that the effect of the advice depends on precisely what advice is sought, and given, and its context. He disagreed with the obiter remarks made in *CIS/307/1992* that advice given that a proposed disposal would in no way affect entitlement would of itself nullify any finding of adverse intention under para.(1) and thus insulate a claimant from being caught by para.(1). In his view (again obiter), if a claimant sought advice from the DWP in relation to disposal of capital, e.g. an inheritance, and was wrongly advised that that would not affect their entitlement, arguably securing or retaining entitlement to income support would still have been the significant operative purpose behind the disposal of the capital. That was the object desired. On the other hand, if the claimant was being taken to court over debts, the advice given would not change the position that staying on benefit was not a "significant operative purpose", the main motivation being to pay the debts.

It is submitted that the first view mentioned in the previous paragraph is of dubious validity. Surely, if a claimant is advised in the particular terms mentioned, even though the consequence of the disposal might be that the claimant's entitlement continues (not being excluded by the capital rule) or can quickly be re-established, it can be argued that their operative purpose is to do whatever the disposal achieves and that consequence on entitlement is not operative. But the precise terms of any advice will be crucial.

Effect of bankruptcy on the notional capital rule

2.187   In *Waltham Forest LBC v TM* [2009] UKUT 96 (AAC) the claimant used the proceeds of sale of a property to repay loans to three family members three months before he was made bankrupt. The issue was whether any resulting notional capital that the claimant was found to have for the purposes of his housing benefit claim was part of his estate as a bankrupt. It was held that since by definition the claimant does not possess the capital but is only deemed to do so for the purposes of entitlement to benefit, notional capital is not part of a bankrupt's estate as defined in the Insolvency Act 1986. Thus the application of the notional capital rule was not affected by the claimant's bankruptcy. *KS v SSWP (JSA)* [2009] UKUT 122

(AAC), reported as [2010] AACR 3, agreed with *TM* where the deprivation occurs before a bankruptcy order is made. After the making of the order, however, claimants cannot deprive themselves of capital for the purposes of para.(1) (see under *Deprivation* at the beginning of this note). Judge Mark went on to suggest that if a claimant presents a petition, or possibly fails to resist a petition presented by a creditor, and is declared bankrupt as a result, they may be found to have deprived themselves of capital if they have taken this step (or not opposed the petition) for the purpose of securing entitlement to benefit. The capital they would have deprived themselves of would be the capital they were entitled to after taking into account what they would have to pay to avoid bankruptcy. This is unlikely to be much in most circumstances.

The operation of para.(1) is restricted to circumstances where the person's purpose is related to entitlement to universal credit. That is in contrast to the terms of reg.113(1) of the JSA Regulations 1996 (which covers purposes related to both old style JSA and income support) and of reg.115(1) of the ESA Regulations 2008 (which covers purposes related to all of old style ESA and JSA and income support), but not to the terms of reg.51(1) of the Income Support Regulations (which is restricted to income support). *R(IS) 14/93* was concerned with a similar problem on the transfer to income support from the corresponding supplementary benefit provisions in 1988. That was whether claimants who deprived themselves of capital under the supplementary benefit regime, before income support existed, could be said to have done so for the purpose of securing entitlement to income support so as to be caught by reg.51(1) once the income support legislation had come into force. The decisions on the point do not now need to be examined in detail. *R(IS) 14/93* held that the words "income support" in reg.51(1) could not be taken to refer to means-tested benefits that previously went under the name of supplementary benefit. Thus, if a deprivation of capital occurs while a person is receiving, or contemplating a claim for, income support or old style JSA or ESA, it may be arguable, depending on the exact circumstances, that if there is later a claim for universal credit the purpose of the deprivation was not to secure entitlement to universal credit. It may also be slightly more onerous to establish the person's knowledge of the capital rules in universal credit, as a new and not yet familiar benefit, especially if previous entitlement had been to tax credits, where the amount of capital did not affect entitlement.

The reasoning behind that outcome is supported by the decision of the Northern Ireland Commissioner in *DB v DfC (JSA)* [2021] NICom 43 on the scope of the Northern Ireland equivalent (in identical terms) of reg.113(1) of the JSA Regulations 1996. The claimant had been entitled to old style ESA. On November 25, 2016, the decision was given that she was not entitled from August 2015, apparently on the basis that, although she asserted that she had disposed of some £40,000 of capital that she said did not belong to her, it was her capital and she had not shown that she had disposed of it. She claimed old style JSA on September 14, 2017. On October 16, 2017, it was decided that she was not entitled, on the basis that her actual capital exceeded £16,000, despite her further assertions of having depleted bank accounts. A revision of that decision and submissions made on appeal were hopelessly confused as between actual and notional capital, but the decision of October 16, 2017, was never formally changed. The appeal tribunal found that the claimant had deprived herself of more than £40,000 in 2016 for the principal purpose of bringing her capital below the limits to obtain benefits including JSA, so that she was treated as having notional income over £16,000 after the application of the diminishing notional capital rule (reg.114). The Chief Commissioner held, as had been submitted by the DfC, that because reg.113(1) could only bite when the claimant's purpose was securing entitlement to or increasing the amount of old style JSA or income support, the appeal tribunal had failed to make the necessary findings of fact or show that it had applied the legally correct approach. It was inherently improbable that when depriving herself of capital while in receipt of ESA, more than a year before she claimed JSA, the claimant had possible entitlement to JSA in mind.

The decision also illustrates that on a new claim neither the decision-maker nor a tribunal on appeal is bound by the findings of fact on capital that have underpinned a decision of non-entitlement on capital grounds. The basis of the ESA decision, that the claimant as at that date still had actual capital of more than £40,000, did not have to be adopted on the JSA claim.

Paragraph (2)

2.188   Paragraph (2)(a) provides that someone will not be treated as having deprived themselves of capital if they have used it to repay or reduce a debt. This provision avoids a lot of difficult issues under the notional capital rules for other benefits about the exact circumstances in which paying off debts in whole or part might indicate that securing entitlement to or increasing the amount of benefit was not a significant operative purpose of the deprivation. It appears to have a very wide application. There is no requirement that the debt is legally enforceable, or even that it is due to be repaid, or any restriction as to the type of debt involved. It should therefore apply to the repayment of loans from family or friends (subject to possible issues about when there is sufficient evidence to establish the existence of the debt on the balance of probabilities) and to the repayment of overdrafts or credit card balances as well as mortgages, personal loans etc. Although para.(2)(a) expressly refers to debts owed by the person who carries out the deprivation, it is submitted that where the person is a member of a couple (whose capital would be aggregated under reg.18(2) or s.5(2) of the WRA 2012) payment of a debt owed by the other member of the couple would be covered.

Under para.(2)(b) the deprivation rule is not to apply if the deprivation takes the form of purchase of goods or services and the expenditure was reasonable in the circumstances of the person concerned. It is not at all clear what might be covered by the word "goods". Regulation 46(2) provides that personal possessions are not to be treated as capital. In the notes to that provision the approach in *R(H) 7/08* is mentioned, that personal possessions mean any physical assets other than land and assets used for business purposes, with no distinctions to be drawn, say to exclude assets acquired for investment. However, a question is raised there whether the use of the adjective "personal" could be taken to exclude items used solely as investments. It could be argued here that "goods" should not have any narrower meaning than whatever is the correct meaning of personal possessions in reg.46(2). Indeed, it would seem that in the absence of the adjective "personal" the meaning should include things used for business purposes. On the other hand, it could be argued that the word "goods" suggests items used in the course of daily living, even though they might be regarded as capital purchases, so that it would not cover items acquired for investment or something like a classic car. The practical importance of such uncertainties may be lessened by the condition of reasonableness. That test must depend on reasonableness as at the date of the potential deprivation, rather than as assessed later with the benefit of hindsight. Although the relevant circumstances will include the person's financial situation and prospects at the time, including the likelihood of having to claim a means-tested benefit and how much the person actually knew about the capital limits for such benefits, it is submitted that the assessment of benefit must balance the principle that in general people are free to spend their own money on whatever they like against what is reasonable in relation to the community of taxpayers who fund universal credit.

If the deprivation is by way of buying goods and the expenditure is found not to have been reasonable, the claimant on the face of it would be fixed with the amount of the expenditure as notional capital and also actual capital in the form of the market value of the goods bought. Under reg.51(1) of the Income Support Regulations and equivalents there had to be a process of treating the deprivation of capital as restricted to the difference between the former and the latter. There will be no such problem in relation to universal credit if the meaning of "personal possessions" (which are not to be treated as capital under reg.46(2)) encompasses everything that could be classified as goods under para.(2)(b).

Note that if neither of the two situations in para.(2) apply, it remains necessary to consider whether the person did deprive themselves of the capital for the purpose of securing, or increasing, entitlement to universal credit. That will have to be considered, for instance, where a claimant buys some interest in property, e.g. in the home.

Paragraph (3)

This paragraph contains the diminishing notional capital rule for universal credit. If the notional capital is more than £16,000, it is reduced in each subsequent assessment period, or each subsequent month if the universal credit award has ceased, by the amount of universal credit that the person would have received but for the notional capital. In the case of a person who has notional capital of between £6,000 and £16,000, the notional capital reduces by the amount of income deemed to be generated by that amount of capital under the "assumed yield from capital" rule in reg.72(1).

2.189

This diminishing notional capital rule is different from that in income support (reg.51A of the Income Support Regulations), old style ESA (reg.116 of the ESA Regulations 2008) or old style JSA (reg.114 of the JSA Regulations 2006). Those provisions apply whenever taking the notional capital into account has either taken the claimant out of entitlement or resulted in a reduction in the amount of benefit received. Then the amount of notional capital is reduced week by week by the amount of benefit in question that would otherwise have been paid for that week. Thus the rule can apply regardless of the initial amount of the notional capital. What matters is whether the combination of actual capital (if any) and notional capital takes the claimant over a relevant limit.

By contrast, para.(3) on its face applies only where the amount of notional capital alone exceeds either £16,000 or £6,000. If a claimant has actual capital of £15,000 and is then fixed with £2,000 of notional capital, so that there can no longer be entitlement to universal credit, the terms of para.(3) are not met and there apparently can be no reduction in the £2,000 of notional capital. If the claimant had no actual capital and was fixed with £17,000 of notional capital para.(3) could apply. That difference in treatment within universal credit and between different means-tested benefits seems inequitable. However, it may be that there is unjustified double counting in the other benefits in favour of claimants who have actual capital. In the example quoted of £15,000 actual capital and £2,000 notional capital, the claimant would need to dip into actual capital to meet essential living expenses in the absence of the previous benefit payments, and that expenditure on goods and services would no doubt be accepted as reasonable under para.(2)(b). So once the actual capital had reduced below £14,000, there could be entitlement again. The difference is that a universal credit claimant cannot take advantage of a reduction in the amount of notional capital in addition to that reduction in actual capital, whereas it appears that income support, old style ESA and old style JSA claimants can. There are similar problems where it is a combination of actual and notional capital that takes the claimant over the £6,000 limit for an assumed yield under reg.72(1). It may be that the problems and inequities are so great that the references to notional capital exceeding £6,000 or £16,000 must be interpreted as references to the amount of notional capital taking the claimant over one or other of those limits, whether on its own or in combination with actual capital.

There may, despite the application of para.(3), be difficult issues of apparently unfair double counting. Say that a universal credit recipient receives some lump sum of over £16,000 and with the plain purposes of retaining entitlement uses it to buy an annuity. Not only will the claimant be fixed under para.(1) with the amount disposed of as notional capital, but the capital value of annuity is not disregarded under Sch.10 and the payments of income under the annuity count in full as unearned income under reg.66(1)(i). It is not obvious that reducing the amount of notional capital assessment period by period by the amount of universal credit that would have been paid if the claimant did not have the notional capital is adequate compensation.

Presumably a person's notional capital will be calculated in the same way as if it were actual capital, that is, by applying any relevant disregard, although neither reg.50 nor reg.48 specifically states this. This is assumed in para.H1885 ADM.

CHAPTER 2

EARNED INCOME

Introduction

2.190   **51.** This Chapter provides for the calculation or estimation of a person's earned income for the purposes of section 8 of the Act (calculation of awards).

DEFINITIONS

> "the Act"—see reg.2.
> "earned income"—see reg.52.

GENERAL NOTE

2.191   In the case of joint claimants their income is aggregated (see s.8(4)(b) of the WRA 2012). If a member of a couple is claiming as a single person (see reg.3(3) for the circumstances in which this can happen) the income of the other member of the couple is taken into account when calculating the universal credit award (see reg.22(3)).

Any income of a child is ignored.

In calculating universal credit, 55 per cent of the claimant's, or the claimants' combined earned income, or, where a work allowance is applicable, 55 per cent of the excess over the amount of the allowance is taken into account (see s.8(3) WRA 2012 and reg.22). Immediately prior to November 24, 2021 the taper rate was 63 per cent.

Regulations 52–64 deal with the calculation of earned income and regs 65–74 with unearned income. Regulations 75–77 contain a number of additional rules in relation to treatment of a person's capital and income.

Meaning of "earned income"

2.192   **52.** "Earned income" means—

(a) the remuneration or profits derived from—
  (i) employment under a contract of service or in an office, including elective office,
  (ii) a trade, profession or vocation, or
  (iii) any other paid work; or
(b) any income treated as earned income in accordance with this Chapter.

DEFINITION

> "paid work"—see reg.2.

GENERAL NOTE

2.193   Paragraph (a) spells out what counts as earned income. It comprises earnings as an employee, as an office-holder, including a holder of elective office, such as a local councillor, self-employed earnings, and remuneration or profits from any other paid work (for the definition of "paid work" see reg.2).

Note first that sub-para.(ii) uses the term "trade, profession or vocation", which is then labelled as "self-employed earnings" in reg.57. The term is that used in the

Income Tax (Trading and Other Income) Act 2005 (ITTOIA) in the Part to do with the taxation of trading income, but there is no direct adoption of the tax rules as there is for employed earnings in reg.55. Thus, the term would, in principle, be given its own meaning, especially as the meaning of "self-employed earner" in s.2(1)(b) of the SSCBA 1992 has not been incorporated either, but the recent approach of the courts has been that the definitions should be applied uniformly across the tax and benefits systems. That was the line strongly taken by the Court of Appeal in the child support context in *Hakki v Secretary of State for Work and Pensions* [2014] EWCA Civ 530 and *French v Secretary of State for Work and Pensions* [2018] EWCA Civ 470; [2018] AACR 25 in cases of "professional" poker players, even though there was a coherent case to be made that the policy arguments against treating the profits of gambling as taxable (that that would enable gambling losses to be set off against all profits from any self-employment) did not apply in the light of specific child support legislation preventing that. It was held that gambling winnings are only earnings from self-employment where they are an adjunct to a trade or profession (e.g. where someone was paid fees for appearing on TV programmes advising the public how to play poker and had incidental winnings from other participants).

One particular potential consequence of the restriction of the category of self-employed earnings to remuneration or profit derived from a trade etc., as opposed to the approach in s.2(1) of SSCBA of covering any gainful employment that is not employed earner's employment, is in the treatment of income derived from property. See the notes to reg.77(1) (2.299) for discussion of the tax case law suggesting that "trade" is a narrower concept than "business" and that there is a difference between the exploitation of an interest in property (as by letting it out) and trading (as in running a hotel or bed and breakfast establishment). Thus, in the present context, decisions on whether and when the duties involved in the letting out of a single tenanted property could constitute a business or self-employment in the s.2(1) of SSCBA sense (e.g. *R(FC) 2/92* and *RM v Sefton Council (HB)* [2016] UKUT 357 (AAC), reported as [2017] AACR 5) may not be on point, although *RM* contains extensive helpful citations from the general case law. But could the duties involved in, say, maintaining and cleaning the common parts of a house of rooms let out to students be "paid work" within para.(a)(iii)? It is suggested that the answer is no, because the work cannot be regarded as done for payment or in expectation of payment, as required by the definition in reg.2, because the rent is paid fundamentally for the occupation of the property or part of it and only tangentially for any specific work done in support of the letting. Rent or other payments for the occupation of premises are not unearned income as they are not listed in reg.66(1) (see in particular the note to reg.66(1)(m)). If the capital value of the premises is not disregarded (e.g. as the claimant's home or as an asset used for the purposes of a trade etc.) and is not high enough to exclude entitlement altogether, it would give rise to an assumed yield as income under reg.72(1) and any actual income derived from that capital, specifically including rent is treated as capital from the day it is due to be paid (reg.72(2)).

The DWP regards shared lives carers (who receive fees from the NHS or local authorities for looking after adults with care needs) as self-employed, whereas foster-carers are regarded as not self-employed and not even engaged in work, because what they provide is a service, not work. The result for the latter would be that none of their income as foster-carers counts for universal credit purposes, because it is not listed in reg.66. That distinction in treatment seems hard to justify (see further below). If, as seems to be the case, shared lives carers are properly treated as self-employed, why should that conclusion not also apply to foster-carers, who not uncommonly make an organised "career" of fostering. In either case, there might then be difficult questions whether rent or contributions to accommodation costs and household expenses paid out of benefits received by the looked-after person could be regarded as income other than earnings, and so not to count as not listed in reg.66, or as part of the actual receipts of the trade, profession or vocation being carried on. If there is a self-employment being carried on, such a separation out of expenses and receipts seems artificial.

What might fall within sub-para.(iii) as paid work that does not already fall within sub-para.(i) (contract of employment or office) or (ii) (self-employment) and how income derived from it should be treated is left inexcusably obscure in the Regulations, despite the nature of the modern labour market and economy having rendered the category more important since 2013. Indeed, especially when full consideration is given to the terms of reg.66(1)(m) on unearned income, the whole question is deeply problematic. No clues are given in the chapters of the ADM (H3 and H4) on earned income—employed earnings and earned income—self-employed earnings.

Some exclusions are established by the definition of "paid work" in reg.2. The general meaning is work done for payment or in expectation of payment. Thus, activity carried out for recreation or mainly as a hobby does not count even if products are occasionally sold (e.g. a hobby painter or art collector or allotment holder who occasionally sells paintings or produce). That would not be "work" or done "for" payment. Nor would activities done in the course of being trained (in the absence of a contract of employment), although that conclusion might also be based on any payment made not being in return for the carrying out of the activities (see *R(FIS) 1/83* and *Smith v Chief Adjudication Officer*, reported as *R(IS) 21/95*, on the enterprise allowance). No doubt, some activities done within a family setting, out of natural love and affection, would also not be regarded as work, even if the beneficiary of the service agreed to make some payment going beyond expenses and the activity would be regarded as work if done by some unconnected person (though then query the attribution of notional earned income under reg.60(3) where services are provided at less than the going rate). However, the boundaries are very hard to establish. There is some old case law from family credit (where claimants wanted to be classified as in remunerative work to qualify). In *R(FC) 2/90*, the claimants were full-time officers of the Salvation Army, whose relationship with the organisation was expressly agreed to be spiritual and not contractual, but received free accommodation and living allowances. Commissioner Goodman held that the onerous duties of a Salvation Army officer were work and that the payments were in return for that work, so that the claimants were engaged in remunerative work.

The work must then be done for payment or in expectation (not mere hope) of payment. That seems to entail that payment must have been arranged in advance of the work or been reasonably expected from a course of dealing or was a motive for undertaking some preparatory activity. Thus a gift received after the carrying out of some task for which no payment had been arranged or expected would not be derived from paid work. There is a somewhat wider exclusion in the definition where the person is a volunteer (not further defined) or engaged by a charitable or voluntary organisation (also not further defined) and the payment received is for expenses. That seems to entail, if no charitable or voluntary organisation is involved, asking whether the person would be regarded as a volunteer if the payments for expenses were ignored. Thus, the unemployed painter and decorator who agrees to paint a elderly neighbour's house in return for being reimbursed for the cost of the paint would appear not to be engaged in paid work within sub-para.(iii). Regulation 60(3) on notional earned income would not automatically be excluded from application, because reg.60(4)(a) only supplies an exemption from its operation where a person is engaged to provide services by a charitable or voluntary organisation. But the neighbour's means to pay would be relevant under reg.60(3).

There nonetheless remains quite a wide category of people carrying out activities for or in expectation of payment who do not become employees each time that they are engaged and do not operate with sufficient regularity or organisation to be said to trading. So the unemployed painter and decorator who agrees as a one-off to paint the elderly neighbour's house for so much a day, not related to the cost of materials, would be engaged in paid work when doing so. Readers can no doubt envisage many other examples of other sorts of activities, like babysitting or occasional buying and selling of items on websites. An increasingly important category would be those working in the gig economy, in the sense of using an online platform to offer services like giving rides, making deliveries, running errands etc, but whose activity is not sufficiently regular or organised to amount to a trade.

The difficulty then is to work out how the payments for the service in question are to be taken into account. Regulations 54 and 54A apply to all forms of earned income, so that the calculation in any assessment period would be based on the actual amount received in that period, with the possibility of the surplus earnings rule applying. However, regs.55 (including the deduction of income tax etc paid) and 56 only apply to "employed earnings" (i.e. within reg.52(a)(i)) and regs 57 to 59 and 62 to 64 only apply to "self-employed earnings" (i.e. within reg.52(a)(ii)). Regulation 60 on notional earned income applies to all forms. So does reg.61, but the only part that is not restricted to employed earnings is the obligation in para.(1) to provide such information as the Secretary of State requires. Thus there is nothing in the legislation to say how much of any reg.52(a)(iii) payment is to be taken into account as earned income in any assessment period. In that circumstance, the principle of *Parsons v Hogg* [1985] 2 All E.R. 897, appendix to *R(FIS) 4/85*, can be invoked, so that the income to be taken into account is not the gross amount received, but the receipts after the payment of expenses wholly and necessarily incurred in the course of winning those receipts. That principle would not, though, allow the deduction of any income tax, social security contributions or pension contributions paid in the assessment period in question. In the great majority of cases within the scope of universal credit there will probably be no liability to income tax or social security contributions (bearing in mind that the income tax £1,000 trading allowance applies to miscellaneous income, including casual earnings, as well as to trading income). However, it is possible that someone could receive substantial amounts through a portfolio of activities on which income tax would be payable under s.687 of ITTOIA.

That point exposes a more serious internal contradiction within the 2013 Regulations. Regulation 66(1)(m) lists income that is taxable under Part 5 of ITTOIA as a category of unearned income, that is therefore to be taken into account for universal credit purposes. Part 5 of ITTOIA includes s.687, which charges income tax on income from any source that is not charged to income tax under any other provision of ITTOIA or any other Act, and is the provision under which casual earnings, not derived from employment or self-employment, are taxed. Although this has not previously been noted by your commentator in past editions, and is not mentioned in the part of the ADM dealing with reg.66(1)(m), that appears to produce the result that income derived from paid work within reg.52(a) (iii) is simultaneously earned income and unearned income. Such a result cannot of course be allowed. The counting twice of the same amount as income cannot be allowed, but the way out is not clear. It is submitted in the more detailed notes to reg.66(1)(m) that payments that fall within the meaning of earned income in reg.52 cannot be made subject to the operation of reg.66(1).

It appears that para.(a) establishes an overarching condition that payments that would fall to be calculated as employed earnings or self-employed earnings be remuneration or profit derived from the sources specified. That would cover the provisions in reg.55 for adopting income tax principles as a matter of calculation and in regs 57–59 on self-employed earnings. See the notes to reg.55 for some of the income tax case law on the "from the employment" test.

On para.(b), see regs 55(4) and (4A), 62 (minimum income floor) and 77(3) (person standing in a position analogous to that of a sole owner or partner in relation to a company carrying on a trade). Note also reg.60 on notional earned income.

Meaning of other terms relating to earned income

53.—(1) In this Chapter—

"car" has the meaning in section 268A of the Capital Allowances Act 2001;   2.194

"employed earnings" has the meaning in regulation 55;

"gainful self-employment" has the meaning in regulation 64;

"HMRC" means Her Majesty's Revenue and Customs;

"motor cycle" has the meaning in section 268A of the Capital Allowances Act 2001;

"PAYE Regulations" means the Income Tax (Pay As You Earn) Regulations 2003;

"relievable pension contributions" has the meaning in section 188 of the Finance Act 2004;

"self-employed earnings" has the meaning in regulation 57; and

"start-up period" has the meaning in regulation 63.

(2) References in this Chapter to a person participating as a service user are to—

    (a) a person who is being consulted by or on behalf of—

        (i) a body which has a statutory duty to provide services in the field of health, social care or social housing; or

        (ii) a body which conducts research or undertakes monitoring for the purpose of planning or improving such services,

    in their capacity as a user, potential user, carer of a user or person otherwise affected by the provision of those services; or

[¹ (ab) a person who is being consulted by or on behalf of—

        (i) the Secretary of State in relation to any of the Secretary of State's functions in the field of social security or child support or under section 2 of the Employment and Training Act 1973; or

        (ii) a body which conducts research or undertakes monitoring for the purpose of planning or improving such functions,

    in their capacity as a person affected or potentially affected by the exercise of those functions or the carer of such a person;]

    (b) the carer of a person consulted under [¹ sub-paragraphs (a) or (ab)].

AMENDMENT

1. Social Security (Miscellaneous Amendments) Regulations 2015 (SI 2015/67) reg.2(1)(g) and (2) (February 23, 2015).

DEFINITION

"Her Majesty's Revenue and Customs"—see Interpretation Act 1978 Sch.1.

Calculation of earned income—general principles

2.195

54.—(1) The calculation of a person's earned income in respect of an assessment period is, unless otherwise provided in this Chapter, to be based on the actual amounts received in that period.

(2) Where the Secretary of State—

    (a) makes a determination as to whether the financial conditions in section 5 of the Act are met before the expiry of the first assessment period in relation to a claim for universal credit; or

    (b) makes a determination as to the amount of a person's earned income in relation to an assessment period where a person has failed to report information in relation to that earned income,

that determination may be based on an estimate of the amounts received or expected to be received in that assessment period.

DEFINITIONS

"the Act"—see reg.2.

"assessment period"—see WRA 2012 ss.40 and 7(2) and reg.21.

"claim"—see WRA 2012 s.40.
"earned income"—see reg.52.

GENERAL NOTE

Under para.(1), the normal rule is that a person's earned income (as defined in   2.196
reg.52 and so covering both employed earnings and self-employed earnings as well
as remuneration or profit derived from other paid work, whatever that is) is to be
based on the actual amount received during an assessment period.

In *PT v SSWP (UC)* [2015] UKUT 696 (AAC) the claimant claimed universal
credit on January 6, 2015 and received his final wages from his previous job on
January 16, 2015. These were taken into account in calculating his entitlement to
universal credit in the first assessment period. The claimant contended that they
should not have been taken into account as his job had ended. Judge Jacobs raises
the question of how there can be an assessment period before a decision has been
made that the claimant is entitled to universal credit. He accepts the Secretary of
State's explanation that the answer lies in s.5(1)(b) of the WRA 2012. The assessment period is fixed by reference to the first date of entitlement (reg.21(1)). Until
the decision is made on entitlement, s.5(1)(b) provides for income to be calculated
on the assumption that an award will be made. The earnings were received during
the first assessment period and so fell to be taken into account under para.(1). It
did not matter that the employment had ceased to exist by the time the wages were
paid. Nor can it matter that the wages were earned in respect of weeks prior to the
first assessment period. It is the time of receipt that is crucial.

However, para.(2) allows an estimate to be made (i) where the calculation is made
before the expiry of the first assessment period or (ii) where there has been a failure
to report information about earned income in an assessment period.

The principle exemplified in *PT* has been affirmed many times since, although
many cases in the end turn on the application of reg.61 on employed earnings
reported to HMRC and then to the DWP through Real Time Information (RTI).
A new and significantly changed reg.61 was introduced with effect from November
16, 2020. See the notes to reg.61 for detailed discussion of the interpretation of
those new provisions. It is though necessary to explore the authorities developed
on the validity or otherwise of the terms of the regulations before that amendment,
both because some cases from before November 16, 2020 are still working their way
through the system and to help understand the structure of the current provisions.

Johnson, Pantellerisco and the pre-November 16, 2020 law
A judicial review challenge to the inflexibility of the structure of assessment   2.197
periods and the attribution of earned income actually received in each period (or
information received from HMRC under the real time information provisions of
reg.61), which, as operated by the DWP, could easily lead to two regular monthly
payments being counted in one assessment period and none in another, was first
heard in November 2018. However, the Divisional Court (*R. (Johnson) v Secretary
of State for Work and Pensions* [2019] EWHC 23 (Admin), Singh LJ and Lewis J)
decided that it did not need to address the issues of irrationality, breach of art.14
(discrimination) of the ECHR and breach of the Equality Act 2010 that had been
raised originally. That was because it concluded that the DWP had been interpreting
regs 54 and 61 wrongly and that the correct interpretation removed the claimants'
problems. That conclusion was overturned by the Court of Appeal on the Secretary
of State's appeal in *Secretary of State for Work and Pensions v Johnson* [2020] EWCA
Civ 778; [2020] P.T.S.R. 1872. The regulations were to be interpreted in the way
put forward by the DWP, but the court rejected the Secretary of State's appeal
because the claimants' case succeeded on the ground that there was irrationality
in the failure, when the regulations were drafted and subsequently, to make an
express adjustment to avoid the adverse consequences for those in the claimants'
circumstances of applying the basic reg.54 rule of using the date of receipt of earned

income to decide in which assessment period it counted. There was then no need to consider the alternative ground of discrimination.

The court did not in either of the judgments suggest that any part of reg.54 or 61 was invalid or say what the consequences of its conclusions on irrationality were on the entitlement decisions challenged by the four claimants. However, as discussed below, the declaration contained in the order dated June 30, 2020, presumably accepted on behalf of the Secretary of State as consistent with the judgments, appears to go further. On June 25, 2020, the Under-Secretary of State, Will Quince, confirmed in Parliament that the DWP did not intend to appeal against the judgment (HC Hansard, Vol.677, col.1456).

The four *Johnson* claimants were all single claimants of youngish children, so qualifying for the work allowance, and in monthly paid employment. All of their employers were Real Time Information (RTI) employers. Ms Johnson was paid on the last working day of each month, unless (according to Rose LJ) that was a non-banking day, in which case she was paid earlier. Ms Barrett was paid on the 28th of each month, unless that was a non-banking day, in which case she was paid on the last working day before the 28th. Ms Woods was paid on the last working day of each month (presumably with a similar dispensation if that was a non-banking day). Ms Stewart was paid on the 28th of each month (again presumably with a similar dispensation) Ms Johnson's assessment period ran from the last day of each month to the penultimate day of the following month. Ms Barrett's and Ms Stewart's assessment periods ran from the 28th of each month to the 27th of the following month. Ms Woods' assessment period ran from the 30th of each month to the 29th of the following month. The problems arose when the attribution of payments to a particular assessment period was affected by what Rose LJ called "the non-banking day salary shift".

To take the facts of Ms Johnson's case as an example, she was paid her salary for November 2017 on November 30, 2017 and her salary for December 2017 on December 29, 2017, since December 30 and 31, 2017 were a Saturday and Sunday. (Note that it is accordingly not entirely clear whether that represented payment on the contractual pay-day, Saturday and Sunday not being working days, rather than being a precise example of non-banking day salary shift, but that term might have been intended not to exclude situations where there was in fact no shift from the contractual pay-day). It appears that her employer reported the payments through the RTI system to HMRC on the dates of payment and the information transmitted to the DWP on the same date. A decision-maker took the view that, since the information about both payments was received within the assessment period running from November 30, 2017 to December 30, 2017, reg.61 required them both to be taken into account in that assessment period. The result was that 63% of the excess of the amount of the two payments (after the deductions required by reg.55(5)) over her work allowance of £192 was deducted from the maximum amount of universal credit for that period. It was the decision to that effect on January 6, 2018 that Ms Johnson challenged in her judicial review application. It was accepted that, on that basis, her earnings in the assessment period running from December 31, 2017 to January 30, 2018 would be nil (payment of the January 2018 salary being due on Wednesday January 31, 2018). There would then be no deduction at all for earnings from the maximum amount of universal credit for that assessment period, resulting in a much higher amount of universal credit than in a one-payment assessment period, but Ms Johnson would have been "deprived" of the ability to use £192 worth of work allowance against each separate payment of salary (see further below for discussion of the amount of net losses involved). Ms Woods' challenge was in essence the same, to a decision on January 3, 2018 taking both November and December salary payments into account in the assessment period running from November 30, 2017 to December 29, 2017.

Ms Barrett and Ms Stewart were more definite examples of non-banking day salary shift. If their pay-day of the 28th of the month was a Saturday or Sunday or a bank holiday, they would be paid at least a day earlier, the payment apparently to be taken into account in the assessment period ending on the 27th of that month (see below for why the employers' RTI returns should in accordance with HMRC guidance/instructions nevertheless have designated payment as made on the 28th).

The Divisional Court concluded that in both reg.54(1) and 61, but with the emphasis on the former, the use of the formula that the amount of earned income "in respect of" an assessment period is to be "based on" the actual amounts received in that period, or the HMRC information received by the Secretary of State in that period, meant that there was "intended to be some other factor, not the mere mechanical addition of monies received in a particular period, which the calculation has to address" (para.51). That other factor was said to be the period in respect of which the earned income was earned, so that there might need to be an adjustment where it was clear that the amounts received in an assessment period did not, in fact, reflect the amounts received in respect of the period of time included within that assessment period. There was a direction that claimants' earned income was to be calculated in accordance with that principle. It is not now necessary to go into more detail on the Divisional Court's reasoning or into the criticisms made of it in the 2019/20 edition of this volume (at 2.164), because its conclusion has been shortly rejected by the Court of Appeal as a matter of construction.

Rose LJ, giving the lead judgment, held that the terms "to be based on" and "in respect of" did not have to be given the meaning given by the Divisional Court to have some substantial content. Looking at the use of different phrases throughout the legislation, "in respect of" meant no more than "in" or "for". The formula of "to be based on" made sense in support of the DWP's approach because of the need to take account of provisions like reg.55(3) on the disregard of certain categories of receipts, which entailed not using the full amount of actual receipts. The Divisional Court's approach also left open many questions about other circumstances in which an adjustment might be made, that reg.54 was intended to avoid, in particular because the universal credit system was designed to be automated, so that decisions could be made by computer without the need for a manual intervention. Another important factor was that "earned income" as defined in reg.52 covered a very wide range of payments, including many where the pattern of payment might well be genuinely irregular. The general principle in reg.54 had to apply to all such payments and in general it made sense for the amount actually received in the assessment period to be not only the starting point but also the finishing point. It was then not possible to give the phrase "is to be based on" in reg.61(2)(a) any different meaning from that in reg.54.

The Secretary of State's challenge to the Divisional Court's reasoning was thus found to be soundly based, but her appeal was nonetheless dismissed because the claimants' arguments on irrationality were accepted. Despite the challenge to specific decisions, Rose LJ described the irrationality arguments, on the basis of her acceptance of the general good sense of the reg.54 rule, as directed at "the initial and ongoing failure of the SSWP to include in the Regulations a further express adjustment to avoid the consequence of the combination of the non-banking day salary shift and the application of regulation 54 for claimants in the position of the Respondents" (para.47).

Counsel for the Secretary of State had accepted that the result of reg.54 for the claimants was arbitrary and that there was no policy reason why they should be faced with the difficulties involved, but submitted that no solution to their difficulties had been found that was not outweighed by other factors. Rose LJ agreed with the Divisional Court that the way that reg.54, as construed in the way she accepted, applied to the claimants was "odd in the extreme". She accepted that there was a wide and frequent oscillation in the amounts of universal credit payable and the total income available to the claimants assessment period to assessment period, leading to budgeting difficulties, the expense of taking out loans or going into overdraft, the effect on entitlement to other advantages (e.g. council tax reduction) and associated stress and anxiety. She also accepted that, through the loss of the benefit of the work allowance in assessment periods when no earned income was received, the claimants suffered an overall loss of income compared with a claimant whose assessment period was dated in a way that required each regular payment of monthly salary to be taken into account in its own assessment period. (Despite that acceptance, it appears in fact very difficult to work out whether any individual claimant would be worse or better off by sometimes having two monthly salaries counted in one assessment period and sometimes none: the calculations are too complicated to explore here). There could also possibly be an effect on other aspects of the universal credit scheme, such as the earnings exemption from the benefit cap, but that did not affect any of the claimants involved.

Rose LJ rejected the Secretary of State's submission that the oscillation was a reflection of a central feature of the scheme in responding immediately to changes in claimants' circumstances as they move in and out of work. Rather, there was no change here in the claimants' circumstances or irregularity in the pattern of their receipt of monthly payments. The oscillation was a response only to whether the regular monthly pay date coincided with the end date of the assessment period. There was no practical way for the claimants to alter the dates of their assessment periods once they were set at the date of claim (having received no warning of the potential consequences) or to alter their contractual pay-day, but there was evidence that the consequences cut across the overall policy of the scheme by creating perverse employment incentives for the claimants to change or turn down employment on the basis of payment patterns.

The Secretary of State had put forward three reasons for not resolving the problems of non-banking day salary shift either initially or once the scheme was in operation, linked it seems by the argument that to do so would undermine the coherence of the universal credit scheme as a whole. The first was that the suggested irrationality was based on the misconception of aligning an assessment period with a calendar month or that the problem arose from the irregularity of payment set against the intended regular and fixed pattern of assessment periods. Rose LJ rejected that characterisation of the origin of the difficulty. The second reason was the need for "bright lines" in the rules for the attribution of receipts of earned income, that would inevitably lead to some hard cases falling just on the wrong side. Rose LJ accepted the need for bright lines in many circumstances, but noted that the regulations contained several exceptions to such lines where the policy imperative overrode the need for simplicity and that, as the claimants submitted, flexibility was allowed when it was in the Secretary of State's interests. Careful and detailed drafting had been adopted to address specific issues. It could not be impossible to draft an exception to cover the particular problem highlighted in *Johnson*, which involved significant and predictable, but arbitrary, effects, and it was not a valid argument against doing so that there might be other groups of claimants for whom such a solution could not be found. The third reason was the need for a rule that would allow the calculation of the amount of a universal credit award to take place in an automated way without the need for manual intervention. Such automation was said to have many advantages for claimants and the cost of rebuilding the calculator in the computer system was said to be substantial. Rose LJ could not accept that the computer programme could not be altered to recognise cases where the end of a claimant's assessment period coincided with the salary pay date, so that action might be needed to prevent two payments counting in one assessment period when there was a non-banking day salary shift.

Rose LJ also took into account the potential size of the cohort affected, suggesting (without adjudicating between the competing figures put forward by the parties) that many tens of thousand were likely to be involved. That was because 75% of working people are paid monthly, the most common pay-day being the last working day of the month followed by the 28th, and many claims are made towards the end of the month when jobs come to an end. She also considered it significant that there was no practical way for the claimants to get themselves out of the situation, that the problem was arbitrary in nature and without prior warning to the claimant (increasing stress) and in particular involved inconsistency with the policy of incentivising work. Thus there were serious personal consequences for those affected and results that ran counter to some fundamental features of the universal credit scheme.

Although the threshold for establishing irrationality was very high, here the refusal to put in place a solution to the very specific problem was an outcome that no reasonable Secretary of State would have adopted. There was to be a direction (to be agreed by counsel) focusing on that specific problem, that would leave it to the Secretary of State to consider the best way to solve the problem (para.110). Underhill LJ agreed, saying that there was nothing to justify a conclusion that no solution could be devised without causing unacceptable cost or problems elsewhere in the system, but also that the case turned on its own particular circumstances. He added, at para.116, that the case turned on its own very particular circumstances and had no impact on the lawfulness of the universal credit system more generally.

The court's discussion of the construction of reg.54 was rather limited and it is arguable that a proper basis had not been established for regarding the need for automated calculation (not mentioned anywhere in the legislation) as a significant factor in identifying the purpose that the provision was intended to achieve. However, since the closer textual analysis, especially in the relationship with reg.61(2)(b), set out in para.2.164 of the 2019/20 edition of what was then Vol.V of this series, supports the same construction, that may not matter. As there was no further appeal to the Supreme Court, the issue appears settled unless it is raised again in some other case that reaches the Court of Appeal at least.

It is also arguable that the Court of Appeal here, perhaps because of the way that the court below had approached the issues, gave insufficient attention in general to reg.61 as in force at the relevant time and the various specific provisions within it, since all the employers concerned were RTI employers. Those specific provisions could possibly have qualified the general principle in reg.54 and it was accepted that reg.61(2) applied. Rose LJ said two interesting things, possibly inconsistent, about reg.61. In para.44 she rejected the submission for the claimants that they could rely on reg.61(3), on the ground that there was nothing inaccurate or untimely in the information the employers were providing to HMRC and the DWP, so that there was nothing incorrect in a way specified in reg.61(3). In para.86 she referred to HMRC guidance/instructions that employers should report payment on the contracted pay date in the RTI feed even if payment was made earlier. She cited guidance dealing with Easter 2019 and information on behalf of the claimants that such general guidance had been in place since at least 2018. The guidance may, therefore, not have been in place at the time of the particular decisions challenged by the four claimants, but surely should have played a much more prominent part in the discussion of the ongoing rationality. If an employer in a non-banking day salary shift case where payment is made early enters the date of actual payment in the relevant field (43) of the Full Payment Submission instead of the contractual date, surely it is arguable on the pre-November 16, 2020 form of reg.61 that the information received from HMRC is incorrect in a material respect within s.61(3)(b)(ii), so that the general rule in reg.61(2) need not apply. Regulation 54 would then apply, but with the power to treat a payment of employed earnings received in one assessment period as received in a later period (reg.61(5)(a)). As Rose LJ notes, the following of the HMRC guidance would have obviated the problems for claimants paid on the last day of the month (and, it would seem, for most of those paid on a fixed day of the month, such as the 28th), but not for those paid on the last working day of the month (like Ms Johnson and Ms Woods). That would be because the "early" date of actual payment would still be the contractual or usual pay date. The following of the HMRC guidance/instruction by employers and the use of reg.61(3)(b)(ii) when it was not followed would greatly decrease the size of the cohort subject to extremely odd outcomes. See the notes to reg.61 for further details of the HMRC guidance/instructions.

It is not at all clear how the Court of Appeal's decision on irrationality left the four claimants concerned in practical terms or affected other monthly-paid claimants whose usual pay day is close to the end of their assessment period. The nature of the irrationality accepted and para.110 of Rose LJ's judgment seems to envisage that the terms of the applicable provisions would only be changed through amendment once the Secretary of State, as directed, had come up with a solution to the specific problem. That would have raised difficult questions about whether the Secretary of State would have been required to make any such amendment retrospective, so as to affect the amount of universal credit that should have been awarded (under the terms of the amendment) in the decisions specifically challenged by the four claimants in *Johnson* and in the cases of other claimants. However, the declaration made in the order of June 30, 2020 is as follows:

> "It is declared that the earned income calculation method in Chapter 2 of Part 6 of the Universal Credit Regulations 2013 is irrational and unlawful as employees paid monthly salary, whose universal credit claim began on or around their normal pay date, are treated as having variable earned income in different assessment periods when pay dates for two (consecutive) months fall in the same assessment period in the way described in the judgment."

Thus, rather than a focus on the process of legislating a solution to the specific problem in *Johnson*, the declaration appears to bite on the substance of the legislation and to declare the outcome of the application of regs 54 and 61 for claimants affected by that problem to be "irrational and unlawful". That would in principle be so from the date that those provisions first came into effect. While such a declaration does not directly invalidate any part of those provisions, the inevitable effect must be that the four *Johnson* claimants cannot now, in relation to the decisions challenged, have an irrational and unlawful outcome applied.

That is consistent with the approach of Rose LJ in para.108 of *Johnson*, where she said that the claimants' argument of discrimination under the ECHR did not arise for consideration because of the success of their case on irrationality. It is submitted that the judge, and thus the Court, could only have taken that view if she thought that the four *Johnson* claimants had, by that success, achieved all that they could have achieved by success in the discrimination argument. Since the judicial reviews were directed against the decisions made in particular assessment periods in 2017 or 2018, the Court must by necessary implication from that part of the judgment have accepted that those decisions had to be re-made without applying the method of calculation found to be unlawful, even though the apparent mismatch between the nature of irrationality accepted and that result was unaddressed in the judgments. A mere redrafting of the regulations with effect from a subsequent date would not achieve that result. There is thus strong support, not just in the terms of the declaration, but also in Rose LJ's judgment, that *Johnson* means that the earned income calculation method in the pre-November 16, 2020 form of the regulations has been unlawful from the outset.

The above argument was referred to by Judge Wright in his much more detailed decision in *JN v SSWP (UC)* [2023] UKUT 49 (AAC). The claimant was an employee paid on the last Wednesday of each month. It was accepted by the Secretary of State that her circumstances were on all fours with those in *Johnson*. She appealed against four decisions that she was not entitled to universal credit in assessment periods in which two monthly payments were reported. (Incidentally, the last decision under appeal was dated November 28, 2020 and might therefore have related to the assessment period ending on November 27, 2020, but it was rightly agreed that the new reg.61 did not take effect in her case until the next assessment period: Decisions and Appeals Regulations 2013 Sch.1 para.32). The First-tier Tribunal dismissed the appeal on the basis that it had to apply the regulations in force at the relevant times. On the further appeal, the Secretary of State submitted that that had been right and that the declaration in *Johnson* had no effect until the unlawfulness exposed in that decision was removed by the November 16, 2020 amendment, which was not retrospective. The judge comprehensively demolishes that submission. First, he shows with copious authority that a declaration is a binding statement by the court upon the existence of a legal state of affairs and that the Secretary of State, as a Minister of HM Government, was required by a core principle of the rule of law to act in conformity with it (para.33). Thus, the declaration in *Johnson* was a binding statement that the earned income calculation method in the regulations was irrational and unlawful. The crucial question of when that binding effect bit then turned on the terms of the declaration, which had no express temporal qualification. There were conflicting indications in the judgments in *Johnson*, but Judge Wright concludes (para.56) that the Court of Appeal intended it to bite at least from the date of the decisions under appeal in that case in 2017 or 2018, well before the assessment periods in issue in *JN*. He therefore did not need to consider any argument that the effect should extend back to the start of the universal credit scheme.

In substituting a decision on the claimant's appeals, the judge, while clear that the Secretary of State's initial decisions had to be set aside as they applied legislation that was irrational and unlawful, could find no obvious basis on which he could lawfully re-make those decisions. Accordingly, he left it to the Secretary of State to redecide on a lawful basis the claimant's entitlement to universal credit in the assessment periods in question, while noting that a way had apparently been found to make payments to the *Johnson* claimants by manual adjustments to the system. In past editions, suggestions have been made about what approaches could be taken in providing a remedy in similar cases, but it may well be that in cases before tribunals there is no alternative to requiring the Secretary of State to redecide the matter of entitlement. There would no doubt be a right of appeal against whatever was decided, if the claimant was dissatisfied. An "automated fix" for *Johnson* lookalike cases was said to have been put in place from August 2021.

The same questions apply to other claimants in the same situation who either have appeals or mandatory reconsideration applications already lodged or are awaiting decisions that had been deferred under the Secretary of State's powers in s.25 of the SSA 1998 and reg.53 of the Decisions and Appeals Regulations 2013. For claimants who now wish to challenge past decisions there are the hurdles of being in time for a valid challenge and of decisions made before *Johnson* not having arisen for "official error" because the error was only revealed by the Court of Appeal's decision. They may, though, wish to try the discrimination argument on which the court expressed no opinion to argue for invalidity of the regulations in so far as they have the outcome found irrational by the Court of Appeal.

But note again the suggestion made above that the problems for those paid on the last day of the month or on a fixed day of the month could be obviated by employers properly following HMRC instructions, where payment is made earlier because the contractual or usual pay day is a non-banking day, to report payment as made on the contractual or usual day. Then, if an employer fails to follow that instruction and reports the actual payment date, which circumstance is drawn to the DWP's attention, it is suggested that payment can be treated as made in another assessment period because the information received from HMRC is incorrect in a material respect (reg.61(3)(b)(ii), (4) and (5)(a) in their pre-November 16, 2020 form: see the notes to reg.61 for the significant differences in the new form and *DfC v OS (UC)* [2022] NICom 29).

Similar problems can arise for claimants who are paid four-weekly, bi-weekly or weekly, regardless of whether the normal pay day is a non-banking day or not. For instance, the pattern of four-weekly payment, being out of sync with the pattern of monthly assessment periods, will inevitably lead to two payments being counted in one assessment period in a year, causing a severe fluctuation in income (and potentially more severe problems in the other assessment periods in relation to the benefit cap: see below). The Secretary of State appears to have taken the view, based in particular on Underhill LJ's statements in *Johnson* and Rose LJ's acceptance at para.47 that in the great majority of circumstances the use of actual receipts was sensible and right, that the decision meant that the effect of the regulations could not be found irrational for any pay patterns other than monthly and that to do so would reintroduce the uncertainty for which the Court of Appeal had criticised the Divisional Court's approach. That seems to have been the central submission to the Administrative Court in *R. (Pantellerisco) v Secretary of State for Work and Pensions* [2020] EWHC 1944 (Admin); [2020] P.T.S.R. 2289, a case of four-weekly earnings, decided shortly after *Johnson* with the parties given the opportunity of comment on that decision and the direction given. Garnham J rightly rejected that submission. The only reasonable inference that could be drawn from the Court of Appeal's necessary restriction of its reasoning to the facts and evidence before it and from its observations that its conclusions did not undermine the whole structure of universal credit, or even the general structure of earnings calculation, is that there was no intention to exclude the possible application of a similar logic to other specific categories of case.

The context of *Pantellerisco* was the earnings exemption from the benefit cap under reg.82(1) (see further in the notes to reg.82) where a claimant's earnings in an assessment period equal or exceed the amount of the national minimum wage per hour times 16, converted to a monthly figure. The claimant was employed for 16 hours a week at the national minimum wage and was paid four-weekly. Because in 11 assessment periods out of 12 only one four-weekly payment was received and the monthly conversion then came out below the crucial level she had the benefit cap applied to her in those 11 assessment periods. If she had been paid at the same rate on a monthly basis, she would not have had the benefit cap applied at all and would have received perhaps £400 per month more. The judge carefully went through the same factors as identified in *Johnson* and came to the same conclusion that, the outcome of the balance being obvious and irresistible, no reasonable Secretary of State could have struck the balance in the way done in the regulations.

However, on the Secretary of State's appeal the Court of Appeal in *Pantellerisco v Secretary of State for Work and Pensions* [2021] EWCA Civ 1454; [2021] P.T.S.R. 1922 overturned the decision of Garnham J. Since the claimant's judicial review challenge was directed specifically against the operation of the earnings-related exception to the operation of the benefit cap for claimants paid four-weekly and working for 16 hours a work at national minimum wage level, see the general notes to Pt 7 on the benefit cap for a full discussion of that issue. In the closely reasoned judgment of Underhill LJ, the Court concluded that it was not irrational for the Secretary of State not to have introduced some solution to the problem that, compared with a claimant in identical circumstances who was paid monthly, Ms Pantellerisco was some £500 a year worse off because she was excepted from the benefit cap in only one assessment period in the year, not all 12. Any suggested solution would involve deeming (at least for benefit cap purposes) some earnings accrued in an assessment period, but not actually received, as having been received. That, in the judges' view, would do unacceptable damage to the system of calculating earnings by reference to receipts in assessment periods of calendar months and seriously undermine the reliability and workability of the assessment of entitlement, because all elements of the system had to fit together. The confirmation by Lord Reed in para.146 of *R. (SC) v Secretary of State for Work and Pensions* [2021] UKSC 26; [2022] A.C. 223 that in the context of social and economic policy, covering social security benefits, the test of unreasonableness should be applied with considerable care and caution, especially where a statutory instrument had been reviewed by Parliament, also appears to have been influential.

Thus, Ms Pantellerisco's application to the Supreme Court for permission to appeal having been refused, so far as the ordinary operation of regs 54 and 61, without the complication of the benefit cap exception, to claimants paid four-weekly or at any other weekly interval is concerned, there now appears no possibility of any conclusion of irrationality or unreasonableness. The effect of a downward fluctuation in universal credit entitlement in the one assessment period in a year (for the four-weekly paid) in which two payments are received is vastly less than that of the benefit cap rule, and might not arise, depending on the accident of how long a claimant was in receipt of universal credit and whether that period included a two-payment assessment period.

That approach was applied to a claimant paid fortnightly in *SSWP v LM (UC)* [2023] UKUT 73 (AAC). It had also been presaged to some extent in *LG v SSWP (UC)* [2021] UKUT 121 (AAC). There, the claimant was paid four-weekly and was not subject to the benefit cap. In the assessment period running from July 11, 2019 to August 10, 2019, she received two sets of four weeks' pay, on July 12 and August

9. As a result, the amount of universal credit to which she was entitled in that period was considerably reduced, if not completely wiped out (it is not clear which) by comparison with a period in which only one payment was received. The First-tier Tribunal disallowed the claimant's appeal, that had explicitly relied on *Johnson* and on Garnham J's decision in *Pantellerisco*, pointing out that she was advantaged in 11 months of the year by having only four weeks' pay taken into account against a month's universal credit allowance and disadvantaged only in one month. Judge May QC dismissed the further appeal, making clear his view that that level of disadvantage fell a very long way short of showing irrationality in the application of reg.54. Indeed, his view was that taking one of the payments out of attribution to the assessment period in question would unfairly advantage the claimant, if it resulted in only 12 payments, rather than 13, being taken into account over a year. Her representatives had not made any suggestion about how, if one payment were to be taken out of an assessment period in which two payments were actually received, it could be attributed across any other assessment periods.

One thing that did emerge from the evidence discussed by the Court of Appeal in *Pantellerisco* was that, following the report of March 12, 2019 by the House of Commons Work and Pensions Committee, the DWP was apparently considering whether some reform should be made to the rules on pay cycles, although nothing has yet emerged into the public domain.

An assessment period is normally a period of one month beginning with the first day of entitlement to universal credit and each subsequent month while entitlement continues (see reg.21(1)). See regs 57–59 below (with the addition of the new reg.54A on surplus earnings and reg.57A on unused losses, plus reg.62 on the minimum income floor) for the provisions on the calculation of self-employed earnings, including some inroads into the focus on actual receipts and expenditure in a particular assessment period. See regs.54A–56 and 61 for the provisions on the calculation of employed earnings involving slightly fewer inroads. The notes to reg.55 discuss the question of identifying the amount to be regarded as received. See the discussion of *SSWP v RW (rule 17) (UC)* [2017] UKUT 347 (AAC) and of *Johnson* in the notes to reg.61 below for circumstances in which the rules in that provision for taking account of real time information reported by an employer to HMRC and received by the Secretary of State in a particular assessment period must give way to the ordinary rule in reg.54 depending on date of receipt by the claimant.

Also see the notes to reg.61 for discussion of whether any alterations of existing awards resulting from increases or reductions in the amount of earned income are appealable.

[¹Surplus earnings

2.198

54A.—(1) This regulation applies in relation to a claim for universal credit where—

(a) the claimant, or either of joint claimants, had an award of universal credit (the "old award") that terminated within the 6 months ending on the first day in respect of which the claim is made;

(b) the claimant has not, or neither of joint claimants has, been entitled to universal credit since the old award terminated; and

(c) the total earned income in the month that would have been the final assessment period for the old award, had it not terminated, exceeded the relevant threshold.

(2) Where this regulation applies in relation to a claim, any surplus earnings determined in accordance with paragraph (3) are to be treated as earned income for the purposes of determining whether there is entitlement to a new award and, if there is entitlement, calculating the amount of the award.

(3) Surplus earnings are—

(a) if the claim in question is the first since the termination of the old award, the amount of the excess referred to in paragraph (1)(c) ("the original surplus");

(b) if the claim in question is the second since the termination of the old award, the amount, if any, by which—
  (i) the original surplus, plus
  (ii) the total earned income in the month that would have been the first assessment period in relation to the first claim,
exceeded the relevant threshold ("the adjusted surplus");

(c) if the claim in question is the third since the termination of the old award, the amount, if any, by which—
  (i) the adjusted surplus from the second claim, plus
  (ii) the total earned income in the month that would have been the first assessment period in relation to the second claim,
exceeded the relevant threshold;

(d) if the claim in question is the fourth or fifth since the termination of the old award, an amount calculated in the same manner as for the third claim (that is by taking the adjusted surplus from the previous claim).

(4) For the purposes of paragraph (3)—

(a) if the claim in question is the first joint claim by members of a couple, each of whom had an old award (because each was previously entitled to universal credit as a single person or as a member of a different couple), the amounts of any surplus earnings from the old award or from a previous claim that would have been treated as earned income if they had each claimed as a single person are to be aggregated; and

(b) if the claim in question is—
  (i) a single claim where the claimant had an old award, or made a subsequent claim, as a joint claimant, or
  (ii) a joint claim where either claimant had an old award, or made a subsequent claim, as a member of a different couple,
the original surplus, or any adjusted surplus, in relation to the old award is to be apportioned in the manner determined by the Secretary of State.

(5) No amount of surplus earnings is to be taken into account in respect of a claimant who has, or had at the time the old award terminated, recently been a victim of domestic violence (within the meaning given by regulation 98).

(6) In this regulation—

"total earned income" is the earned income of the claimant or, if the claimant is a member of a couple, the couple's combined earned income, but does not include any amount a claimant would be treated as having by virtue of regulation 62 (the minimum income floor);

"the nil UC threshold" is the amount of total earned income above which there would be no entitlement to universal credit, expressed by the following formula—

$$[^3(M - U) / 55 \times 100 + WA]$$

where—
M is the maximum amount of an award of universal credit;
U is unearned income;
WA is the work allowance; and
"the relevant threshold" is the nil UC threshold plus £300 [²£2,500].]

AMENDMENTS

1. Universal Credit (Surpluses and Self-employed Losses) (Digital Service) Amendment Regulations 2015 (SI 2015/345) reg.2(2), as amended by Universal Credit (Miscellaneous Amendments, Saving and Transitional Provision) Regulations 2018 (SI 2018/65) reg.7(3) (April 11, 2018).

2. Universal Credit (Surpluses and Self-employed Losses) (Digital Service) Amendment Regulations 2015 (SI 2015/345) reg.5, as inserted by Universal Credit (Miscellaneous Amendments, Saving and Transitional Provision) Regulations 2018 (SI 2018/65) reg.7(6) (modification effective from April 11, 2018 to March 31, 2019 as extended by the Secretary of State to March 31, 2023).

3. Universal Credit (Work Allowance and Taper) (Amendment) Regulations 2021 (SI 2021/1283) reg.2(2) (November 24, 2021, or, for existing claimants, any assessment period ending on or after November 24, 2021).

DEFINITIONS

"assessment period"—see WRA 2012 ss.40 and 7(2) and reg.21.
"claim"—see WRA 2012 s.40.
"claimant"—*ibid*.
"couple"—see WRA 2012 ss.40 and 39.
"earned income"—see reg.52.
"joint claimants"—see WRA 2012 s.40.
"maximum amount of an award of universal credit"—see WRA s.8(2).
"unearned income"—see regs 2 and 65 - 74.
"victim of domestic violence"—see WRA 2012 s.24(6)(b).
"work allowance"—see reg.22.

GENERAL NOTE

The general purpose of reg.54A is described as follows in the Explanatory Memorandum attached to SI 2018/65:

2.199

"7.7 This instrument makes a number of changes to the Universal Credit (Surpluses and Self-employed Losses) (Digital Service) Amendment Regulations 2015 which make provision to smooth the peaks and troughs of losses and earnings so that a fairer assessment as to Universal Credit entitlement is made over a period of time, longer than one month. This has, however, proved difficult to operate and simplification is required.

7.8 The current provision provides that the carrying forward of surplus earnings will apply to both employed and self-employed claimants. Where there is an increase in earnings that means Universal Credit is lost, the amount of that increase over the "relevant threshold" (which includes a de minimis of £300, but see below) will be taken into account and applied to future Universal Credit awards, for a maximum of 6 assessment periods. This ensures that those with fluctuating earning patterns are not unduly penalised or unfairly rewarded by receiving less or more Universal Credit than they would if they earned the same amount but were paid monthly. It also reduces the risk of claimants manipulating payment patterns to receive bigger payments of Universal Credit.

7.9 This instrument will also change the way that surplus earnings are applied when people reclaim Universal Credit within 6 months. Instead of taking account of earnings over the whole period of Universal Credit, only the earnings in the month where people make a claim will be counted. Where couples separate there will be more scope for flexibility in the way the surplus is apportioned. These changes will also increase the de minimis from £300 to £2500 for one year (which may be extended by the Secretary of State). This will assist the smooth implementation by the reducing the numbers affected in the early stages."

It seems odd to refer to sums like £2,500 or £300 as "de minimis" and that term is not used in the regulation itself. It could more accurately be described as an effective disregard of those amounts in determining whether the claimant has surplus earnings in any months. The initial use of the sum of £2,500 has restricted the effect of the regulation in the first six years from April 2018 (see the extensions noted below, with the possibility of further extensions) to fairly extreme upward variations in earned income and exclude the more routine fluctuations that might be covered by the unmodified form. Potential problems may therefore be to some extent masked during this period, although on the other hand there may also be the opportunity for further amendment before the provision begins to bite more routinely. The modification of the definition of "relevant threshold" in para.(6) and the identification of the "temporary de minimis period" for which it has effect is to be found in reg.5 of the Universal Credit (Surpluses and Self-employed Losses) (Digital Service) Amendment Regulations 2015 (SI 2015/345), as set out at the end of this Part. That provision first applied the modification to £2,500 for one year down to March 31, 2019, but on February 5, 2019 it was announced that the Secretary of State had made a determination to extend the period to March 31, 2020, as allowed by reg.5(2). There have been further annual extensions (by virtue of determinations dated March 5, 2020, March 23, 2021, March 3, 2022 and March 20, 2023) taking the operation of the modification down to March 31, 2024. The latest extension is included in the DWP's Guidance on regulations under the Welfare Reform Act 2012 on *gov.uk*.

The Social Security Advisory Committee (SSAC) expressed a number of serious misgivings about the proposals as amended by SI 2018/65 (set out in the letter of January 19, 2018 from the Chairman to the Secretary of State in their Report of January 2018 and response by the Secretary of State). They will be mentioned at appropriate points below.

Regulation 54A appears to be validly made in terms of the powers in para.4(1) and (3)(a) of Sch.1 to the WRA 2012 in the light of the decision of the Court of Appeal in *Owen v Chief Adjudication Officer*, April 29, 1999, dismissing an argument that shifting income from the period in which it was received to a different period was neither "calculation" nor "estimation" (see the notes to reg.35(2) of the Income Support Regulations in Vol.V of this series). But see the note to para.(2) below for an argument on irrationality. The provision initially applied only in digital service (full service) cases (see the saving provision in reg.4(1) of SI 2015/345), but is now of general application.

See the notes to reg.61 for discussion of whether any alterations of existing awards resulting from increases or reductions in the amount of earned income to be taken into account are appealable.

Regulation 54A entails the attribution of surplus earnings to assessment periods subsequent to the period in which the amount over the threshold was received. Since, by definition that receipt will have precluded entitlement in that period on income grounds, there is no need to enquire about the immediate effect on the claimant's capital. However, in relation to subsequent assessment periods for which a claim is made or treated as made, there is a question whether any funds actually still possessed by the claimant constitute capital if surplus earnings are to be treated under reg.54A as existing in that period (for instance through the receipt of a grant from the Coronavirus Self-Employed Income Support Scheme (SEISS)). On general principle (see *R(IS) 3/93* and *R(IS) 9/08*) income, and in particular earnings, does not metamorphose into capital until after the end of the period to which it is attributed under the relevant legislation. Although matters are not so clear in universal credit as in income support and similar benefits, that principle would seem to hold because of the irrationality of treating the same amount as both income and capital at the same time.

The principle could arguably extend to assessment periods in which surplus earnings are treated as possessed, so that any actual funds retained from the initial receipt are treated as earnings and not capital to the extent of the amount of surplus earnings taken into account in the period in question. Another way of looking at the situation might be to invoke the further principle in *R(SB) 2/83* that income does not metamorphose into capital until relevant liabilities, including tax liabilities, have been deducted. It could be argued that the operation of the surplus earnings rule on later claims is a relevant liability that should therefore lead to a corresponding reduction in the amount of capital to be taken into account. In income support and similar benefits the metamorphosis principle cannot apply to self-employed earnings, because of the method of calculating such earnings (*CIS/2467/2003*). However, since for universal credit both self-employed and employed earnings are calculated by reference to receipts and expenditure in particular assessment periods, the metamorphosis principle can be applied just as much to one as the other. One difference, though, is that in so far as the self-employed have capital in the form of sums deriving from payments that have caused surplus earnings, the disregards of business assets in paras 7 and 8 of Sch.10 can apply. And note that with effect from May 21, 2020 there is a disregard as capital (for 12 months from the date of receipt) for the self-employed of any payment in respect of a furloughed employee under the Coronavirus Job Retention Scheme or "by way of a grant or loan to meet the expenses or losses of the trade, profession or vocation in relation to the outbreak of coronavirus disease" (Universal Credit (Coronavirus) (Self-employed Claimants and Reclaims) (Amendment) Regulations 2020 (SI 2020/522) reg.2(2)).

Paragraph (1) sets out the basic conditions for the application of the regulation, which are subject to the exclusion in para.(5) of claimants who have recently been the victims of domestic violence. Paragraph (2) sets out the rule as to treating surplus earnings in one assessment period as earned income in certain later assessment periods. Paragraph (3) says what surplus earnings are and how they may be reduced or extinguished. Paragraph (4) deals with circumstances where surplus earnings were received when a couple had a joint claim, but later claim as single or as part of a different couple. Paragraph (6) supplies important definitions.

Paragraph (1)

The issue of surplus earnings arises on a claim for universal credit when the claimant or either of joint claimants had previously had an award of universal credit ("the old award") that had terminated within the six months before the first day of the period claimed for (sub-para.(a)). It does not matter by what method the award terminated, by virtue of a decision of the Secretary of State on revision or supersession or by the claimant withdrawing the claim. But the six months establishes the outer limit of how far back surplus earnings can be relevant on a new claim. The claimant or either joint claimant must not have been entitled to universal credit since that termination (remembering that there can be entitlement while nothing is payable) (sub-para.(b)). Then the final condition is that in the month that would have been the final assessment period for the old award if it had not terminated, total earned income in that month exceeded the "relevant threshold" (sub-para.(c)). It is that excess that is the starting point for calculating surplus earnings under para.(3). The relevant threshold is defined by way of a complicated formula in para.(6). The starting point is basically the amount of earned income that, after taking account of any unearned income (which counts in full), the appropriate work allowance, if any, and the 55% taper applied to earned income, would lead to there being no entitlement to universal credit. That is the "nil UC threshold". Immediately prior to November 24, 2021, the taper rate was 63%, that had been applicable since April 2017.

In the simplest case of a single claimant of 25 or over with no work allowance, no unearned income and no housing costs (so that the "maximum amount of an award of universal credit" would be limited to the standard allowance), that threshold would on April 2023 rates be £669.95 (the amount of which the standard allowance under reg,36(3) of £368.47 is 55%). Then the amount of £2,500 (currently, to decrease to £300 after March 31, 2024 unless there are further extensions to the substitution of the higher amount) is added to make the "relevant threshold". See pp.126–7 of CPAG's *Welfare Benefits and Tax Credits Handbook 2023/2024* for further examples.

Paragraph (1) thus applies to any form of earned income (defined in reg.52): employed earnings; self-employed earnings; and remuneration from any other paid work (for which see the discussion in the notes to reg.52), as well as notional earned

2.200

income. The latter category will cover amounts treated as possessed under regs 60 and 77(3), but any amount the claimant is treated as possessing under reg.62 (minimum income floor) is expressly excluded from the definition of "total earned income" in para.(6). The existence of surplus earnings need not have been the reason for the termination of the old award. That could have been, for instance, failing to accept a new claimant commitment or the withdrawal of the claim by the claimant. All that is necessary under sub-para.(c) is that in what would have been the final assessment period of the old award there were surplus earnings. Thus, claimants cannot avoid the operation of reg.54A by, once they know that the earned income received or to be received in a current assessment period will exceed the relevant threshold, quickly withdrawing their claim for that assessment period. That assessment period would seem still to be caught by sub-para.(c). The use of the words "final ... had it not terminated" is not problem-free. They cannot mean that the termination is to be ignored completely, because then the award might have continued into the future and it cannot be said what might have been the final assessment period. To make any sense, the words must be taken as referring to the month following the last actual assessment period under the old award, that would have been an assessment period if entitlement had not ceased after the last day of the last actual assessment period. However, that does seem to mean that if a claimant can predict in advance that a particularly large one-off receipt of earnings is to arrive at a particular time it might be worth withdrawing the universal credit claim for the assessment period immediately preceding the period in which the receipt is expected. That period would not then be caught by sub-para.(c) and a new claim for universal credit after the end of that period would not attract any surplus earnings, so that entitlement would be assessed on actual earned income receipts in the new assessment period. However, it would require very careful calculation whether the loss of two months' universal credit would outweigh the benefit of future freedom from the surplus earnings rule.

See the notes to reg.57 for the distinction between income receipts and capital receipts for the self-employed. Only income receipts go into the calculation of what is to be taken into account as self-employed earnings in any assessment period and is therefore capable of contributing to surplus earnings. Regulation 2(1)(a) of the Universal Credit (Coronavirus) (Self-employed Claimants and Reclaims) (Amendment) Regulations 2020 (SI 2020/522) requires receipts of Coronavirus SEISS payments to be treated as income receipts in the assessment period of receipt. Other kinds of coronavirus-related payments may plainly be capital receipts. But there may well be some such payments that are difficult to classify.

Paragraph (2)

2.201   Paragraph (2) provides that, where the conditions in para.(1) are met, surplus earnings as worked out under para.(3) are to be treated as earned income in determining entitlement under the new claim and calculating the amount of any award. Paragraph (3) deals with the consequences on the erosion of the amount of surplus earnings where the taking into account of the surplus earnings results in there not being entitlement on the first claim after the termination of the old claim and so on for further unsuccessful claims (see below for the details).

This process marks the clearest difference from the original 2015 form of the amending regulations, which spread the surplus earnings and thus their erosion over the six months following the assessment period in which the surplus earnings were received, regardless of whether a claim for universal credit was made in those months or not. The rule that the amount of surplus earnings will only be eroded, before the expiry of the six-month limit, for any month in which a claim is made, was one of the main causes of disquiet in the SSAC.

However, para.(3) says nothing about the consequences if the taking into account of surplus earnings on that first or a subsequent claim results in an award of universal credit, but of a lower amount than would have been calculated if they were not taken into account. That works in relation to the first assessment period under the new claim and award, but there is nothing in reg.54A to prevent the same amount of surplus earnings being taken into account for future assessment periods within the same period of entitlement under the award. Paragraph (2) is expressly in terms of an award and the amount of the award, not a particular assessment period. Paragraph (3) only provides for the erosion of the surplus earnings on a new or subsequent *claim*. Once a claim has been successful and an award has been made there can be no further claim during the period of entitlement and no scope for the mechanism of para.(3) to apply. Nor could even the six-month limit apply to stop that continuing effect, because under para.(1)(a) that applies by reference to the first day of the period for which the new claim is made, not each successive assessment period. The result on the face of it is that in such circumstances the claimant is fixed for ever (or at least within the same continuing period of entitlement) with the remaining amount of surplus earnings taken into account in the first assessment period under the new award. Indeed, that seemed to be the assumption in some of the examples given in Memo ADM 11/18 (although several of the original examples contained misleading or incomplete calculations). The examples now given in para. H3311 of the ADM and in Appendix 2 to chap.H3 include claimants who start off with a level of entitlement based on regular earnings and end up after the para.(3) process with a lower level of entitlement when an award is eventually made and the advice says that "surplus earnings have been eroded and no longer apply". But there is no explanation of how in the terms of reg.54A the surplus earnings that have been taken into account in the first assessment period under the new award cease to be taken into account in subsequent assessment periods.

It may well have been thought that para.(1)(b) (claimant has not been entitled to universal credit since the old award terminated) has the effect of preventing the attribution of surplus earnings beyond the first assessment period of some entitlement to universal credit. However, that does not work, because para.(1) contains the conditions for application of the surplus earnings rule in relation to a *claim*, not to an award. In the circumstances described above (and worked through in the example in the notes to para.(3) below), once some entitlement has been awarded for one assessment period there can be no new claim for the following assessment period. The award made for the first assessment period of entitlement continues into the next and subsequent assessment periods on the basis of the claim made for the first assessment period of entitlement. In relation to that claim, the condition in para. (1)(b) was satisfied because *at the date of that claim* the claimant will not have been entitled to universal credit since the old award terminated. It might in some circumstances be possible, in order to produce an equitable result, to interpret the word "claim" as extending to an award and a continuing award. However, that does not seem possible in the context of reg.54A, which so carefully distinguishes between claims and awards throughout.

That result is so obviously unfair, both in fixing claimants with deemed earnings that total more than the surplus earnings involved and in treating different claimants differently by the pure chance of the amount of surplus earnings, large or small, that is left at the end of the last para.(3) calculation that allows an award to be made (see the end of the example worked through in the note to para.(3) below), that it cannot be allowed to stand. However, it is difficult, if not impossible, to identify a technical means of interpretation by which the result can be avoided. Is the unfairness so intractable that the amending provisions can be regarded as irrational and ultra vires on that ground?

This problem would not have arisen on the original 2015 form of the amending regulations, where the erosion of surplus earnings would simply have followed month by month until eroded completely or six months was reached.

Paragraph (3)
Once an old award has terminated when there is an excess of total earned income over the relevant threshold, as identified in para.(1)(c), that "original surplus" (see para.(3)(a)) sits there waiting potentially to come into play once a new claim is made. But the amount of the original surplus remains the same if no claim is made until the six months in para.(1)(a) expires. The only way in the terms of reg.54A that

2.202

the amount of the original surplus can reduce is by the making of new claims. That may involve a claimant in making multiple new claims that will be bound not to lead to entitlement in order to reduce the amount of surplus earnings to a level that will allow satisfaction of the financial condition in s.5(1)(b) or 5(2)(b) of the WRA 2012.

Regulation 3 of the Universal Credit (Coronavirus) (Self-employed Claimants and Reclaims) (Amendment) Regulations 2020 (SI 2020/522) introduced with effect from May 21, 2020 a new reg.32A of the Claims and Payments Regulations 2013 allowing the Secretary of State, subject to any appropriate conditions, to treat a claimant as making a new universal credit claim on the first day of each of five subsequent potential assessment periods after non-entitlement because income is too high. That provision is quite general (as expressed in the guidance in Memo ADM 10/20), but the primary intention expressed in para.7.10 of the Explanatory Memorandum to the Regulations is to use the power where it is earnings received by a furloughed employee supported through the Coronavirus Job Retention Scheme or a grant from the Self-Employed Income Support Scheme (SEISS) that prevents the claimant from satisfying the financial conditions in s.5 of the WRA 2012. That is said to be to make it easier to bring claimants back into universal credit entitlement if actual earnings reduce in those subsequent periods and the surplus earnings are exhausted. There can be circumstances in which a claimant is, depending on the pattern of actual earnings and household circumstances, better off by not making a new universal credit claim for a particular period. It is not clear how the administrative arrangements for deemed claims in cases affected by coronavirus schemes might be able to take that into account or whether claimants might be able to assert that they should not be treated as making a claim. The problem of surplus earnings in this context is most likely to arise for actual (or deemed under reg.77) self-employed claimants. It is not known whether the Secretary of State is still exercising the discretion under reg.32A on the same basis. A condition normally applied is that the DWP has sufficient information to determine the deemed claim.

One of the most serious misgivings of the SSAC was whether claimants would sufficiently understand the need to make multiple unsuccessful claims so as to take the most beneficial action, especially as there are some circumstances (e.g. where a claimant's earnings do not immediately return to the regular level after a peak assessment period, but continue at a higher than regular, but not as high as the peak, level) when it will be more beneficial not to make new claims. As it was put in the chairman's letter of January 19, 2018:

> "One of our main concerns about these proposals is the assumption that claimants will have a detailed understanding of this complex policy, when in reality it seems likely most will not. Many may be disadvantaged simply due to that lack of detailed understanding of the complex rules underpinning this policy.
>
> For example, the only way that claimants can successfully erode surplus earnings that have taken them off Universal Credit is to make repeated monthly claims. But these are destined to fail until the surplus is eroded and entitlement resumes. Requiring claims to be made where it is known that they will be unsuccessful is, at best, counterintuitive and risks damaging the credibility of both this policy and Universal Credit more widely.
>
> ...
>
> There is also an assumption that it will be obvious to claimants making a repeat claim whether or not their circumstances have changed in a way that is likely to affect their Universal Credit entitlement. This may be the case where the only change is an increase or decrease in the claimant's earnings. But some changes of circumstances have less predictable outcomes, and multiple changes within a single assessment period are likely to create uncertainty. This might arise, for example, in situations where both members of a couple are in some form of paid work, one member's earnings can go up whilst the other member's goes down, or there may be changes in the household composition."

The Secretary of State's response to that concern was this:

"The re-claim process in Universal Credit is a simplified one, intentionally designed as a simple and swift process for claimants. For claimants whose only change is the level of earnings, the average time to complete a re-claim could be just eight minutes. The need for affected claimants to re-claim each month does not differ significantly from the current situation. Currently, where the level of earnings causes the UC entitlement to reduce to NIL and the claim to close, claimants need to re-claim if there is a change to their circumstances or level of earnings.

This is also the case with surplus earnings, the claimant has the same need to re-claim as there are no re-awards in Full Service. Notification from DWP on claim closure would advise the claimant of the need to re-claim if their circumstances change.

In addition, the Department will ensure that messaging and guidance, both for those claimants impacted by surplus earnings and for work coaches helping claimants, reinforces this message so that the claimant's responsibilities are clear and they are kept well-informed."

That response, apart from the objectionable nature of much of the terminology (e.g. "claim closure" etc), might be thought almost wilfully to ignore the difference between realising the need to make a claim when the circumstances suggest that entitlement is a real possibility and realising a need when the circumstances point against such a possibility. There was also no answer to the point that had been raised by the SSAC, about circumstances in which claiming would not be beneficial. Overall it is very hard to have any confidence in the ability of the information given at the time of the termination of the old award or in assistance to be given by work coaches to guide claimants through the labyrinth when the experienced experts drafting the DWP's advice to decision-makers could not get even simple examples of the operation of the rules right. And will claimants whose earnings have returned to what they regard as normal appreciate that there has been a change of circumstances?

The technical operation of para.(3) is this. On the first claim (within six months) since the termination of the old award the amount of the original surplus (paras (1) (c) and (3)(a)) is simply added into the calculation for the first assessment period under the claim along with the actual earned and unearned income in that period. If that, after applying the 55% taper to the earned income, leaves the claimant's income below the appropriate maximum amount of universal credit there is entitlement at that reduced level for that assessment period, with the uncertain consequences for future assessment periods under the award as discussed in the note to para.(2) above. If that leaves the claimant's income above the maximum amount there is no entitlement for the month that would have been an assessment period if there had been entitlement. On the next (second) claim, which cannot be made for any period starting earlier than the month for which no entitlement has been determined, surplus earnings will have to be considered under para.(3)(b). For that purpose one has to consider how far in the calculation on the first claim the original surplus plus any actual earned income in that month exceeded the relevant threshold. If there is no excess (i.e. the sum exactly equalled the relevant amount in the previous month), there are no longer any surplus earnings to be carried forward to the second claim. If there is an excess, that is the "adjusted surplus" to be taken into account in determining the second claim. The process then continues under sub-paras (c) and (d), but on these claims taking forward the adjusted surplus from the previous period rather than the original surplus, until there is no longer a surplus to be carried forward or entitlement arises or the six months expires.

That is all fairly impenetrable as an abstract explanation. Trying to work through an example may help the explanation (with caution in view of the criticisms above of the initial official guidance).

Imagine a single universal credit claimant with no children who is also a contributor as a self-employed earner to an annual book of social security legislation and has no other source of income. The claimant is paid an annual fee of £10,500 on May 10, 2023, in the middle of the assessment period running from May 1 to May 30, and no income tax or national insurance contribution is paid in that period. Entitlement will therefore terminate after the end of the previous assessment period as 55% of the self-employed earnings exceeds the maximum amount of universal credit at that date (£368.47 standard allowance with no work allowance as at May 2023).

On an immediate claim for the period from June 1, 2023, in which there will be no actual earned income, surplus earnings from the previous month must be considered under para.(3)(a). The nil UC threshold is £669.95 (the amount of which £368.47 is 55%) and the relevant threshold is £3,169.95 (£669.95 + £2,500). The claimant's earned income of £10,500 exceeded that relevant threshold, so the excess (£7,330.05) is surplus earnings (the original surplus) to be taken into account on this first new claim. The result is that there is no entitlement on that claim, as 55% of that amount (£4,031.53) exceeds the maximum amount of universal credit.

On the second new claim for the period from July 1, 2023, surplus earnings from the previous month must be considered under sub-para.(b). There is no actual earned income. The original surplus is £7,330.05 and the relevant threshold is £3,169.95, so that the excess is £4,160.10. That again is clearly enough to prevent entitlement after the 55% taper. But £4,160.10 then becomes the adjusted surplus to be carried forward to the next claim.

On the third new claim for the period from August 1, 2023, surplus earnings must be considered under sub-para.(c). The adjusted surplus of £4,160.10 from the previous month still exceeds the relevant threshold of £3,169.95, so that the excess of £990.15 is to be taken into account as surplus earnings. The amount after the 55% taper (£544.58) exceeds the maximum amount of universal credit, so there is no entitlement. But £990.15 becomes the adjusted surplus to be carried forward to the next claim.

On the fourth new claim for the period from September 1, 2023, surplus earnings must be considered under sub-para.(d). The adjusted surplus of £990.15 from the previous month does not exceed the relevant threshold of £3,169.95, so that no surplus earnings can be taken into account and the claimant becomes entitled to universal credit of the maximum amount (ignoring for the moment any possible issues under the minimum income floor (reg.62)).

If the fee had been £9,000 the claimant would have become entitled to the maximum amount on the third new claim (calculations as above but reducing the original surplus by £1,500).

If the fee had been £10,000, the claimant would have become entitled to universal credit, but at less than the maximum amount, on the third new claim, because the excess of the adjusted surplus from the second claim (£3,660.05) over the relevant threshold would have been £490.10, 55% of which is £273.95, less than the maximum amount of £368.47. So the award would have been £94.52 for the assessment period beginning on August 1, 2023. There would then be no surplus earnings to carry forward to a new claim, but no new claim would be possible as the claimant already had an award. Common sense and fairness dictate that in such circumstances the claimant should not be treated as having earned income of £490.10 (before the taper) for the assessment period beginning on September 1, 2023 and subsequent assessment periods, but as discussed in the notes to para.(2), the plain words of subs.(2) seem to require that result.

Remember always that surplus earnings cannot be applied on any *claim* more than six months after the termination of the old award (para.(1)(a)).

Paragraph (4)

2.203   Since the effect of a significant increase in the amount of earned income can under reg.54A affect claims up to six months in the future, claimants may well move in to and out of partnerships with others in that period. Paragraph (4) deals with those circumstances.

Sub-paragraph (a) covers new claims following the termination that are the first joint claim by a couple, both of whom have surplus earnings from an old award or claim when they were either single or members of a different couple that would have been taken into account if they had each claimed as a single person. In those circumstances the surplus earnings that would have counted if they had claimed as single persons are aggregated. That is straightforward if the previous awards or claims were as single persons. If they were as joint claimants, then that seems to bring in the rule in sub-para.(b) about apportionment.

Sub-paragraph (b) covers two alternatives. One is where the relevant claim is as a single person and the claimant had an old award or made a subsequent claim as a joint claimant. The other is where one or other member of a couple (or both) making a joint claim has an old award or made a subsequent claim as a member of a different couple. In both those cases the surplus, original or adjusted, is to be apportioned in the manner determined by the Secretary of State. There is thus a completely open-ended discretion, that of course must be exercised by reference to all the relevant circumstances and the aims of the legislation, as to the share of the surplus to be attributed to the claimant in question, a discretion that on any appeal is to be exercised by the tribunal on its own judgment of the circumstances. However, the guidance in para.H3313 of the ADM is that the proportion between the joint claimants is to be 50% unless there are any exceptional circumstances. Such guidance is inconsistent with the terms of para.(4)(b), under which to adopt any starting point (in effect a default position) that could be differed from only in exceptional circumstances would be placing an unlawful fetter on the discretion given.

The letter of January 19, 2018 from the chairman of the SSAC to the Secretary of State contained the following under the heading "Equality impact":

"The Committee noted that an equality impact had shown that there were no adverse effects on anyone with a protected characteristic. However it is clear that having, by default, a simple 50/50 apportionment of surplus earnings in the event that a couple separate would adversely affect any non-working partner, or the partner earning a lower amount relative to the current situation of allocating the surplus in proportion to the earnings of each individual of a couple. Some of the non-working partners, or partners on lower wages, are likely to have a protected characteristic (for example gender or those with a mental health condition), therefore we were surprised by the Department's assertion. Although, as was made clear to us, the legislation would give discretion for a different apportionment to be applied, the default position would be 50/50 and it would fall to individual claimants to make a request for it to be changed. Some individuals adversely affected might lack the understanding to request a revision of that decision; others may be put under some pressure from their former partner to accept the Department's decision."

The Secretary of State's response was as follows:

"The Department has changed the apportionment rules to provide greater clarity to claimants in understanding how a surplus is recovered. The apportionment rules would only come into force in the event a couple separating at the same time a surplus is outstanding also re-claimed within 6 months of the original surplus being created.

It is reasonable that a couple and their household would equally benefit from household income such as a one off bonus. As such, the surplus should be equally apportioned unless there are grounds that this is unreasonable.

Additionally, the regulations allow for a decision maker acting on behalf of the Secretary of State to consider the reasonableness of an individual's circumstances when looking at a decision on apportionment, allowing discretion to ensure claimants are adequately protected.

[Reference to the recent domestic violence exception to remove any financial disincentive from leaving an abusive relationship]."

Apart from it being laughable to suggest that greater clarity had been provided for claimants, either that response demonstrates a complete misunderstanding of the effect of para.(4)(b) or a change was made in its terms before SI 2018/65 was made. As it is, the guidance in the ADM appears to reflect the view set out in that response rather than the requirements of the legislation.

2.204   *Paragraph (5)*

This exclusion of the effect of reg.54A for recent victims of domestic violence can operate if the claimant has that status either at the time the old award terminated or at the time of the new claim being considered. Paragraph (5) refers on to reg.98, which contains the very wide definition of "domestic violence", what counts as recent and some conditions about having reported the domestic violence and notified the Secretary of State. Section 24(6)(b) of the WRA 2012 says when a person is to be regarded as a "victim" of domestic violence.

Employed earnings

2.205   **55.**—(1) This regulation applies for the purposes of calculating earned income from employment under a contract of service or in an office, including elective office ("employed earnings").

(2) Employed earnings comprise any amounts that are general earnings, as defined in section 7(3) of ITEPA, but excluding—

(a) amounts that are treated as earnings under Chapters 2 to 11 of Part 3 of ITEPA (the benefits code); and

(b) amounts that are exempt from income tax under Part 4 of ITEPA.

(3) In the calculation of employed earnings the following are to be disregarded—

(a) expenses that are allowed to be deducted under Chapter 2 of Part 5 of ITEPA; and

(b) expenses arising from participation as a service user (see regulation 53(2)).

(4) The following benefits are to be treated as employed earnings—

(a) statutory sick pay;

(b) statutory maternity pay;

(c) [³ . . .] statutory paternity pay;

(d) [³ . . .]

(e) statutory adoption pay [²; and]

[² (f) statutory shared parental pay.]

[¹ (4A) A repayment of income tax or national insurance contributions received by a person from HMRC in respect of a tax year in which the person was in paid work is to be treated as employed earnings unless it is taken into account as self-employed earnings under regulation 57(4).]

(5) In calculating the amount of a person's employed earnings in respect of an assessment period, there are to be deducted from the amount of general earnings or benefits specified in paragraphs (2) to (4)—

(a) any relievable pension contributions made by the person in that period;

(b) any amounts paid by the person in that period in respect of the employment by way of income tax or primary Class 1 contributions under section 6(1) of the Contributions and Benefits Act; and

(c) any sums withheld as donations to an approved scheme under Part 12 of ITEPA (payroll giving) by a person required to make deductions or repayments of income tax under the PAYE Regulations.

AMENDMENTS

1. Universal Credit and Miscellaneous Amendments (No.2) Regulations 2014 (SI 2014/2888) reg.4(2) (November 26, 2014, or in the case of existing awards, the first assessment period beginning on or after November 26, 2014).

2. Shared Parental Leave and Statutory Shared Parental Pay (Consequential Amendments to Subordinate Legislation) Order 2014 (SI 2014/3255) art.28(4)(c) and (d) (December 31, 2014).

3. Shared Parental Leave and Statutory Shared Parental Pay (Consequential Amendments to Subordinate Legislation) Order 2014 (SI 2014/3255) art.28(4)(a) and (b) (April 5, 2015). The amendments are subject to the transitional provision in art.35 (see Pt IV of this book).

DEFINITIONS

"Contributions and Benefits Act"—see reg.2.
"earned income"—see reg.52.
"ITEPA"—see reg.2.
"relievable pension contributions" —see reg.53(1).
"PAYE Regulations" —*ibid.*
"statutory adoption pay"—see reg.2.
"statutory maternity pay"—*ibid.*
"statutory shared parental pay"—*ibid.*
"statutory sick pay"—*ibid.*

GENERAL NOTE

This regulation applies to employed earnings (i.e., under a contract of service or as an office holder) (para.(1)). By reason of the overarching definition of "earned income" in reg.52, payments must be derived from such employment. See regs 57-59 for the calculation of self-employed earnings.

Unlike income support, old style JSA, old style ESA and housing benefit, what counts as employed earnings for the purposes of universal credit is in general defined in terms of the income tax rules (paras (2) and (3)(a)). However, not all amounts that HMRC treats as earnings count for universal credit purposes (see para.(2)(a)). Under para.(2))(a) benefits in kind, for example living accommodation provided by reason of the employment, are excluded. See paras (4) and (4A) for categories of payments deemed to be employed earnings.

The meaning of "general earnings" in s.7(3) of ITEPA (the Income Tax (Earnings and Pensions) Act 2003), which the beginning of para.(2) makes the starting point for calculating earned income, is earnings within Chap.1 of Part 3 of ITEPA or any amount treated as earnings, excluding exempt earnings. Section 62 of ITEPA, which constitutes Chap.1 of Part 3, provides in subs.(2) that earnings means:

"(a)   any salary, wages or fee;
 (b)   any gratuity or other profit or incidental benefit of any kind obtained by the employee if it is money or money's worth; and
 (c)   anything else that constitutes an emolument of the employment."

That meaning is thus very broad, and there are many categories deemed to be general earnings (see s.7(5) of ITEPA), but the meaning is immediately narrowed for universal credit purposes by para.(2)(a) of reg.55 in the exclusion of amounts treated as earnings in Chaps 2–11 of Pt 3 of ITEPA. Those items covers matters like expenses, vouchers, provision of living accommodation, cars, vans and related benefits and loans. The exclusion by para.(2)(b) of amounts exempt from income tax under Pt 4 of ITEPA would have followed in any event under the terms of ss.7(3) and 8 of ITEPA. The exemptions in Pt 4 of ITEPA, as specifically referred to in s.8, include mileage or transport allowances, travel and subsistence allowances, benefits for training and learning, recreational benefits

2.206

and a variety of other amounts, including in particular statutory redundancy payments (s.309). Section 8 also refers to exemptions elsewhere in ITEPA. There is some discussion of this in para.36 of *RMcE v DfC (UC)* [2021] NICom 59. The Northern Ireland Commissioner, though not having had submissions on the issue, must have been right in his tentative conclusion that the reference in reg.55(2) to general earnings as defined in s.7(3) of ITEPA must be read in the light of s.8 and the meaning given there to "exempt income". That follows from the specific exclusion in s.7(3) of exempt income. Thus, although reg.55(2)(b) refers only to amounts exempt from income tax under Pt 4 of ITEPA, the incorporation of the s.7(3) definition brings in other ITEPA exemptions. See the further discussion in the separate section below on payments on cessation of employment, including the effect of the amendments to ITEPA with effect from April 6, 2018 by virtue of the Finance (No.2) Act 2017.

As a matter of general principle, any payment, whether of an income or capital nature, can be a profit or emolument within s.62(2) of ITEPA, providing that it is a reward for past services or an incentive to enter into employment and provide future services. See *AH v HMRC (TC)* [2019] UKUT 5 (AAC), where Judge Wikeley discusses the relevant income tax case law, and *Minter v Kingston upon Hull CC* and *Potter v Secretary of State for Work and Pensions* [2011] EWCA Civ 1155; [2012] AACR 21, where Thomas LJ in para.29 emphasised the width of the phrase "any remuneration or profit derived from employment" in reg.35(1) of the Income Support Regulations, such that the essential issue was whether any payment was made in consideration of the employee's services, so as to be derived from the employment, whether it was on general principle to be regarded as capital or income. It would appear that if it is necessary for that effect of reg.55 to be authorised by para.4(3)(b) of Sch.1 to the WRA 2012 (regulations may specify circumstances in which income is to be treated as capital or capital is to be treated as income) the words are clear enough to come within that power.

DfC v RM (UC) [2021] NICom 36 confirms that basic principle in the context of a gross sum of £5,228.42 received in December 2018 by the claimant in settlement, after conciliation, of Industrial Tribunal proceedings against his employer for non-payment of wages or of holiday pay entitlement. The employer described the payment as a gesture of goodwill rather than in fulfilment of a contractual liability, but the payment was apparently calculated to cover 1.5 hours of work a week over a period from 2005 to 2012. The DfC treated the net payment, after deduction of income tax and national insurance, and including regular monthly salary, of £5,221.45 notified by HMRC in the particular assessment period through the real time information system (see reg.61) as employed earnings in respect of that period. The appeal tribunal allowed the claimant's appeal, finding under the equivalent of reg.61(3)(b)(ii) as in force at the time that the information received from HMRC did not reflect the definition of employed earnings in reg.55, so that the amount attributable to the settlement was not to be taken into account in the assessment period in question. On further appeal by the DfC, the Northern Ireland Commissioner rightly rejected its argument that the tribunal must have regarded the payment as capital, contrary to the principles set out in *Minter* and *Potter* (for full details of those decisions see the 2021/22 edition of Vol.V of this series at 2.204–06). Those decisions were not in point because the essential question under reg.55 is how the payment would be treated under s.62(2) of ITEPA, not a general categorisation as income or capital. The Commissioner then declined to hold the tribunal in error of law for failing to deal with the question of what the outcome would be under s.62(2). See the further discussion in the separate section below on compensation payments.

It is a necessary consequence of the centrality of determining what the outcome would be under s.62(2) of ITEPA that in any appeals on these issues the Secretary of State must provide explanatory material, legislation and case law relating to income tax if tribunals are to be able to perform their role properly (stressed in para.34 of *RMcE v DfC (UC)* [2021] NICom 59).

Note the decision of the Court of Appeal in *Commissioners for HMRC v Murphy* [2022] EWCA Civ 1112; [2023] 1 W.L.R. 51 on the meaning of "profit" in s.62(2)(b) of ITEPA. In a complex settlement of police officers' group claims for compensation for underpayment of overtime and certain allowances, the principal sum agreed to be paid by the Metropolitan Police Service ("the Met") covered only some of the claimants' costs. It did not include the amount of their solicitors' and counsel's "success fee" under a "damages-based agreement" or the amount of the premium paid on a policy insuring them against the risk of having to pay the Met's costs. But those amounts were deducted from the principal sum to be paid and only the balance was paid to the individual claimants. Mr Murphy had succeeded before the Upper Tribunal (Tax and Chancery Chamber) ("UTTCC") in an argument that his proportionate share of those amounts should be deducted from his share of the whole principal sum in calculating the "profit" within s.62(2)(b), as they were necessarily incurred in order to obtain the sum derived from his employment. The Court of Appeal held that to have been an error of law. In the context of the statutory scheme, all earnings from employment are taxable, subject only to the deductions allowed under the legislation. In s.62(2)(b) "profit" is used in the sense of "a material benefit derived from a property, position etc; income, revenue", one of the definitions in the *Oxford English Dictionary*. The expenditure not being allowable deductions nor having been incurred in the performance of Mr Murphy's duties, the sole question was whether the profit was "from" employment as a reward for services, as it clearly was, since the principal settlement sum related to amounts alleged to be due under the claimants' contracts of employment. It did not matter that they were left to meet some of their own costs.

E.ON UK Plc v Commissioners for HMRC [2022] UKUT 196 (TCC) also concerned the "from" test in s.9(2) of ITEPA, for universal credit purposes applied by reg.52(a). E.ON made a one-off payment, called a facilitation payment, to employees who were members of its final salary pension scheme, in which prospective changes adverse to members were being made. The UTTCC overturned the FtT's decision upholding HMRC's view that the payment was taxable. After a very full analysis of the complex package of which the facilitation payment was a part, the UTTCC concluded that the particular payment was not an inducement to provide future services on different terms, but in return for employees' consent to the adverse changes in the pension scheme and thus was not taxable. It was not even a case within the principle of *Kuehne and Nagel Drinks Logistics Ltd v Commissioners for HMRC* [2012] EWCA Civ 34; [2012] S.T.C. 840 (see the section below on *Payments of compensation*) where there are two reasons for a payment and it is enough that one related to employment was sufficiently substantial. There was extensive discussion of tax cases relating to pensions that might possibly have to be consulted if similar circumstances arise.

It is difficult to say how the principle adopted in *R(TC) 2/03* (a case on the meaning of "earnings" in reg.19(1) of the Family Credit Regulations) might apply to the identification of the "amount" that is to be taken into account under reg.55, and regarded as "received" under reg.54. In *R(TC) 2/03* the claimant's partner's employer made deductions from his current salary in order to recover an earlier overpayment of salary. His payslips showed the "gross for tax" figure as £76 less than his usual salary. The Commissioner held that his gross salary for the relevant months was the reduced figure, most probably on the basis that there had been a consensual variation of the contract of employment, so that the lower figure was the remuneration or profit derived from employment in the relevant months. In *MH v SSWP and Rotherham MBC (HB)* [2017] UKUT 401 (AAC) Judge Wikeley adopted and applied the analysis in *R(TC) 2/03*. The claimant received a redundancy payment of nearly £15,000 in March 2016, which was used to pay off debts and make home improvements. In May 2016 he was offered his old job back on condition that he repaid the employer the amount of the redundancy payment by monthly deductions from salary within the 2016/17 tax year. The claimant accepted those terms. On his monthly payslips his basic salary was stated as £2,719.04 before overtime with deductions including income tax and national insurance and the sum of £1,222,22 described as "BS loan". On his claim for housing benefit the local authority (and the First-tier Tribunal) decided that under the equivalent of regs 35 and 36 of the Income Support Regulations the gross earnings had to be taken into account and there was nothing to allow the deduction or disregard of the £1,222.22 repayment. The judge held that the proper analysis was that the claimant's contract of employment had been varied by agreement so that he was only entitled to receive a salary reduced by the amount of the repayment and that that amount was his gross earnings. In fact, the case appears stronger than that of *R(TC) 2/03* because the initial terms on which the claimant was re-engaged incorporated the repayments of the redundancy payment.

It is not clear in *MH* what amount was regarded as subject to PAYE income tax. If it was the reduced figure, as in *R(TC) 2/03*, then that would appear to be the amount to taken into account under reg.55 and regarded as received under reg.54. The receipt would presumably also be reflected in the real time information provided by HMRC to the DWP under reg.61. If the employer had regarded the higher figure as subject to PAYE income tax then it seems arguable that the amount to be treated as remuneration or profit derived from the employment (reg.52) and received under reg.54 is the lower figure. If the real time information reflected the higher figure, then it would have to be argued that reg.61(2) did not apply because the information was incorrect or failed to reflect the definition in reg.55 in some material respect (reg.61(3)(b)(ii)).

Under para.(3)(a) expenses that are deductible under ITEPA, Pt 5, Ch.2, are disregarded in calculating employed earnings—this includes, for example, expenses that are "wholly, exclusively and necessarily" incurred in the course of the claimant's employment (see s.336(1) of ITEPA). In addition, expenses from participation as a service user (defined in reg.53(2)) are ignored (para.(3)(b)), although payments for attendance at meetings, etc., will count as earnings.

Note that employed earnings are to be treated as also including statutory sick pay, statutory maternity pay, statutory paternity pay, statutory adoption pay and statutory shared parental pay (para.(4)).

Paragraph (4A), inserted with effect from November 26, 2014, treats a repayment of income tax or NI contributions received from HMRC in respect of a tax year in which the person was in paid work as employed earnings, unless it is taken into account as self-employed earnings. According to DWP (see ADM H3022), this can include repayments of income tax that relate to other sources, such as unearned income, as long as the claimant was in paid work in the tax year to which the repayment relates. ADM H3022 gives as an example a case in which a claimant receives a cheque for £200 from HMRC, which relates to an overpayment of £600 income tax in the tax year 2011/12 in which the claimant was in paid work and an underpayment of £400 in the following year. The amount that counts as employed earnings is £200, which is the repayment that the claimant received.

The proper, restricted, operation of para.(4A) has been very helpfully elucidated in *SK and DK v SSWP (UC)* [2023] UKUT 21 (AAC). There the claimant, who was on unpaid sick leave from his employer, received a bonus of £20,000 on May 20, 2020, within the assessment period running from April 29, 2020 to May 28, 2020 (AP 1). Under the PAYE system the employer deducted the amount of £6,893.60 for income tax before making the payment, which was reported to HMRC through the Real Time Information scheme. That was on the basis of a code issued by HMRC that was appropriate to a person regularly earning £20,000 a month over the whole tax year. Since that was not the case, on the claimant not receiving any further remuneration from his employer in subsequent months, under the PAYE system he received from the employer a "refund" of overpaid income tax of £2.144.60 in the assessment period running from May 29, 2020 to June 28, 2020 (AP 2) and further refunds in subsequent months. There was no dispute that the receipt of the net amount of the bonus in AP 1 resulted in a nil entitlement to universal credit, but the claimant appealed against the nil entitlement in AP 2 resulting from the taking into account of the £2,144.60. Among his arguments was that a repayment of income tax could only be treated as employed earnings under the conditions of para.(4A), which were not met as he was not in paid work in the tax year 2020/21. The First-tier Tribunal disallowed the appeal. On the further appeal Judge Ovey rejected the tribunal's reasoning but substituted her own decision to the same effect.

The judge's central point was that para.(4A) is restricted to cases where the repayment of income tax or national insurance contributions is received from HMRC, whereas in *SK*, if there could be said to have been a repayment on May 20, 2020 (see paras 47 and 48, set out in the notes to reg.61(2)), it was received from the employer, not HMRC. She shows convincingly from an analysis of the PAYE system that HMRC does not itself make any in-year repayments of overpaid income tax. Instead, they are either sorted out by in-year amendments of the PAYE code governing the amounts to be deducted by the employer or by a direct payment from HMRC after the end of the tax year in question. Similarly, repayments of other sorts of income tax are not made in-year, but by HMRC after the end of the tax year. Paragraph (4A) was concerned with such repayments made after the end of the tax year, as was confirmed by the terms of the Explanatory Memorandum to SI 2014/2888 and of the DWP's description of the amendment to the Social Security Advisory Committee (Annex B to the minutes of the meeting of September 3, 2014).

The judge went on to make suggestions, not necessary to the decision, about how para.(4A) might have been interpreted if it had been relevant, for example about how to work out the tax year in respect of which a bonus was paid, when the entitlement to a bonus arose and whether the claimant was "in paid work" in a tax year while on sick leave. While the claimant was in employment it did not matter that, by agreement with the employer, he did not do any work in that tax year.

In calculating a person's employed earnings in an assessment period the following are deducted: any income tax and Class 1 contributions paid in that assessment period, together with any contributions to a registered pension scheme and any charity payments under a payroll giving scheme made in that period (para.(5)). Since the definition of "relievable pension contributions" in reg.53(1) is by reference only to s.188 of the Finance Act 2004 it is arguable that the annual and lifetime limits imposed in other sections of that Act are not incorporated for universal credit purposes.

Information on a person's employed earnings and deductions made will normally be taken from what is recorded on PAYE records. See further the note to reg.61.

Payments on cessation of employment

There are no special provisions for the treatment of final earnings under universal credit. A claimant's final earnings will be taken into account in the assessment period in which they are paid under the general rule in reg.54(1), subject to the operation of reg.61 on real time information. See in particular *PT v SSWP (UC)* [2015] UKUT 696 (AAC), discussed in the notes to reg.54 and *SSWO v RW (rule 17) (UC)* [2017] UKUT 347 (AAC), discussed in the notes to reg.61. In *Secretary of State for Work and Pensions v Johnson* [2020] EWCA Civ 778; [2020] P.T.S.R. 1872 the Court of Appeal rejected the approach of the Divisional Court below to the interpretation of regs 54 and 61 and its reliance on the phrase "in respect of" in those provisions to introduce other factors than date of receipt into the identification of the assessment period to which a payment is attributed. In para.41 Rose LJ says that the phrase usually means nothing different from "for" or "in". That seems to have put paid to any argument that, say, final payments of earnings should be attributed to the relevant period of employment rather than to the assessment period in which the payment is received. The same would apply to items like week-in-hand payments, bonuses due for past work or holiday pay accrued under contractual or statutory entitlements for past periods.

Some payments made on termination of employment and not linked to past periods are "general earnings" under ss.7(3)(a) and 62 of ITEPA, in particular payments that are made by virtue of a contractual obligation (though see the post-April

2.207

2018 provisions discussed below), but some fall outside that meaning and so are liable to income tax only under the regime in ss.401–16 and do not come within reg.55. There is general guidance in HMRC's *Employment Income Manual* from para.12850 onwards. The dividing line in principle between payments that are general earnings and payments that fall within s.401 of ITEPA as made in connection with the termination of employment, and so not within s.62, is this. If the payment (including a part of a payment) is in satisfaction of a right to remuneration under the contract of employment it falls within s.62. If it is compensation for a breach of the contract of employment it falls within s.401. So, employment tribunal awards for unfair dismissal, damages for breach of contract and redundancy payments (statutory and contractual) will not count as they are only taxable under s.401 of ITEPA and so do not come within s.7(3) (see *Employment Income Manual*, paras 12960, 12970, 12978, 13005 and 13750). For other employment tribunal awards which do count as earnings see para.02550 of the *Employment Income Manual* and the section below on payments of compensation.

There have been amendments to s.7 of ITEPA and new ss.402A-402E added by the Finance (No.2) Act 2017, that apply to certain payments made on or after April 6, 2018 on the termination of employment that would otherwise fall within s.401. To be a "relevant" termination award the payment must not be a redundancy payment (statutory or contractual). Then so much of the payment as counts as post-employment notice pay (PENP) is taxable as general earnings. That is secured by the addition of new para.(ca) to s.7(5), which lists amounts that are to be treated as earnings under s.7(3)(b). PENP is in essence the amount of basic pay to which the employee would have been entitled after the date of termination of the contract if full statutory notice had been given, less the amount of any contractual payment in lieu of notice that was made. That appears to mean that if an employer makes some sort of global payment on termination, without it being broken down into particular elements, the PENP is to be taken into account as employed earnings for universal credit purposes.

The Northern Ireland Commissioner was therefore right to say in para.36 of *RMcE v DfC (UC)* [2021] NICom 59 that a payment that constituted PENP would count as employed earnings under the equivalent of reg.55. However, that was not relevant to the circumstances of the case, where the payment in issue was received before the amendments to ITEPA creating the new regime came into force.

The policy and legislative background to the amendments has been comprehensively described in House of Commons Library Briefing Paper No.8084 (May 8, 2018), *Taxation of termination payments*. That paper reproduces as an appendix a helpful statement of the legal background produced in 2013 by the amusingly named Office of Tax Simplification. There was on the existing law a distinction between a payment in lieu of notice on termination of the contract on less than the contractual notice that was provided for in the contract of employment (within s.62) and a payment made where there was no such provision or where the employer chose to terminate the contract without making a contractual payment in lieu of notice but made a payment for breach of the contract of employment instead (not within s.62). That distinction was considered not only to be very difficult to draw in particular cases but also to be unjustified.

Payments of compensation

2.208   This section is concerned with payments that are not clearly linked to the termination of employment, but contain an element that is linked to making up some shortfall in what was paid to the employee in the past. Such awards or payments in settlement may be made during the course of the employment or after it has ended. Because they come as a lump sum, their classification as capital or income has caused difficulties in other contexts, as mentioned above. In the present context, of course, the proper question is rather whether the award contains any amount that is "general earnings" as defined in s.7(3) of ITEPA.

As mentioned above, Commissioner Stockman in Northern Ireland has most recently confirmed that basic principle in *DfC v RM (UC)* [2021] NICom 36. The claimant received a gross sum of £5,228.42 received in December 2018 in settlement, after conciliation, of Industrial Tribunal proceedings against his employer for non-payment of wages or of holiday pay entitlement. The employer described the payment as a gesture of goodwill rather than in fulfilment of a contractual liability, but the payment was apparently calculated to cover 1.5 hours of work a week over a period from 2005 to 2012. The DfC treated the net payment, after deduction of income tax and national insurance, and including regular monthly salary, of £5,221.45 notified by HMRC in the particular assessment period through the real time information system (see reg.61) as employed earnings in respect of that period. The appeal tribunal allowed the claimant's appeal, finding under the equivalent of reg.61(3)(b)(ii) as in force at the time that the information received from HMRC did not reflect the definition of employed earnings in reg.55, so that the amount attributable to the settlement was not to be taken into account in the assessment period in question. The Commissioner rejected the DfC's misguided challenge on the ground that the tribunal must, wrongly, have considered that the payment was capital as asking the wrong question. However, he then considered that the inquisitorial duty of the tribunal, and the Commissioner, could not extend to the exploration of income tax law, rather than the familiar social security issues, in the absence of structured submissions (and apparently his view that there was at least a good argument that the payment was made in consideration of the abandonment of the proceedings, rather than in return for the claimant's service in the period from 2005 to 2012). The onus was thus firmly on the DfC to establish its case to the tribunal and the Commissioner. It had not done so, because it had not referred the tribunal or the Commissioner to any case law relevant to the taxation of compensation settlement payments.

It is submitted that that decision is based on too limited a view of the scope of the proper inquisitorial approach of appeal tribunals, and in particular of the Commissioner and, in Great Britain, the Upper Tribunal. It is not as if direct reference to ITEPA was a new feature for universal credit. That is the technique used for working tax credit (see the definition of "earnings" in reg.2 of the Tax Credits (Definition and Calculation of Income) Regulations 2002 in Vol.IV of this series, which also sets out most of the relevant provisions of ITEPA). And there is the instructive decision in *AH v HMRC (TC)* [2019] UKUT 5 (AAC) on that definition, mentioned briefly above (and dealt with in detail in Vol.IV at 2.222), where Judge Wikeley discussed and applied the income tax cases on the meaning of "emolument of employment" in s.62(2) of ITEPA. In those circumstances and when the adoption of the ITEPA test is an express part of the legislation to be applied, it appears wrong for the Commissioner not to have addressed the issue, possibly after obtaining further submissions. As it is, the decision in *RM* gives no guidance as to how future cases should be decided in substance (although of course it would as a Northern Ireland decision technically have had only persuasive authority in Great Britain).

In *AH*, the claimant had reached a draft settlement agreement on his claim against his NHS employer that it had made unlawful deductions from salary, in the sum of £16,000. However, because the parties wanted to avoid HM Treasury restrictions on compensation payments of more than £10,000, payment was made in two lump sums of £3,000 in August 2016 and March 2017 and by way of giving the claimant a 20-month fixed term contract of employment at £500 per month. In the event, before end of the fixed term the employer offered to pay the claimant the balance of his salary entitlement in a lump sum and the contract was terminated by mutual consent. HMRC took all the payments into account as employment income on the WTC claim. In the Upper Tribunal Judge Wikeley agreed. His analysis of the income tax authorities included that older cases decided when the formula of "emolument from employment" was in effect were still instructive although s.62(2) refers to "emolument of the employment". In addition, *Kuehne and Nagel Drinks Logistics Ltd v Commissioner for HMRC* [2012] EWCA Civ 34; [2012] S.T.C. 840 showed that where a payment was made for a reason other than being or becoming an employee (there to compensate for loss of future pension rights on the transfer of a business) and for a reason that was so related (there to encourage the heading off of strike action), it was enough to make the payment "from the employment" that the latter reason was sufficiently substantial, despite the existence of some other substantial reason. The claimant could only escape the conclusion that the payments made to reimburse him for non-payment of salary were emoluments of his employment if the arrangements, especially the fixed-term contract, were a sham, which the judge rejected.

The current HMRC guidance in its *Employment Income Manual* (EIM 12965, updated in respect of that paragraph on January 27, 2020) applies the principle that compensation should derive its character from the nature of the payment it replaces. That principle is of course familiar in the related, but different, social security context of income or capital (see *Minter* and *Potter above*). The guidance relies specifically on the decision in *Pettigrew v Commissioners for HMRC* [2018] UKFTT 240 (TC). Although as a First-tier decision it can have no precedential authority, it is based on an exhaustive survey of the case-law and a detailed analysis of the application of the principles to the facts.

Mr Pettigrew was a part-time fee-paid chairman of Industrial Tribunals and then an Employment Judge from 1996 to 2016. He lodged a claim against the Ministry of Justice (MoJ) for underpayments of fees for training, sitting and other days of service on the basis of discrimination by comparison with salaried office-holders. The MoJ offered him £55,045.42, including interest, in full and final settlement of his claim, which he accepted. When the payment was made, some £22,000 was deducted under PAYE. When submitting his 2014–15 self-assessment tax return Mr Pettigrew challenged that deduction on the basis that the payment was not arrears of wages or salary, but compensation for breach of the Part-Time Workers Regulations. That challenge was rejected by HMRC and by the FtT on appeal. After a comprehensive review of the authorities (which incidentally confirmed the relevance of the pre-ITEPA authority, as had been accepted by Lord Hodge in *RFC 2012 Plc (in liquidation) (formerly the Rangers Football Club Plc) v Advocate General for Scotland* [2017] UKSC 45; [2017] 1 W.L.R. 2767 at para.35), the judge distilled five principles (paras 75–79). Three in particular were (1) that a payment of compensation for loss of rights directly connected with an employment will generally be an emolument of that employment (para.76); (2) that the character for tax purposes of a payment of compensation for failure to make a payment due should be the same as that of the payment if it had been paid (para.78); and (3) that where there is more than one reason for the payment then the employment must be a sufficiently substantial reason for the payment to characterise it as an emolument of the employment (para.79). Applying those principles to the facts found, the lump sum payment, apart from the interest element, plainly constituted an emolument of Mr Pettigrew's employment, particularly as a result of principle (2). Although, as he had submitted, the prompt for the making of the payment was the settlement of the litigation of which he was part, the methodology and quantification of the payment was to remedy the underpayments under the contract of employment, so that the test in *Kuehne and Nagel* (principle (3)) was met.

Applying those principles to the facts of *RM* would seem to lead equally inevitably to the conclusion that the settlement payment constituted general earnings within s.62(2) of ITEPA and so employed earnings within reg.55.

Dividends

2.209 The overriding principle set out in reg.52(a) that earned income from employment under a contract of service or in an office must be remuneration or profit derived from that employment or office suggests that payments of dividends on shares cannot be earned income. They are derived from the ownership of the shares. However, sometimes payments that are described as dividends are not properly to be treated as such. The formal company law and accounting processes for declaring a dividend may not have been gone through or the whole transaction may be a sham. There may be other situations in which, although the payments are properly to be regarded as dividends they are derived from employment or an office, so are taxable as general earnings. See the discussion in *H v SSWP and C (CSM)* [2015] UKUT 621 (AAC), citing extensively from the decision in *CCS 2533/2014* (not currently on the AAC website), which itself relied on the decision (described as instructive) of the Court of Appeal in the tax case of *HMRC v PA Holdings Ltd* [2011] EWCA Civ 1414. The overall approach adopted by the Court of Appeal is to look at the substance, or reality, not the form. There, contractual bonuses were structured so as to be paid out as dividends from a company separate from the employing personal service company and were held to be taxable as general earnings. Such highly artificial arrangements are perhaps unlikely to be encountered in universal credit. In more routine cases, there may be little reason to dispute a division between the taking of earnings as an employee or director and taking of dividends as a shareholder.

Dividends are chargeable to income tax under Part 4 of the Income Tax (Trading and Other Income) Act 2005 (ITTOIA), so cannot as such fall within the definition of general earnings in s.7(3) of ITEPA. Nor are they unearned income, since they do not feature in the list in reg.66(1). They do not fall within reg.66(1)(m) because they are not taxable under Pt 5 of ITTOIA. However, if in substance the payments constitute remuneration derived from employment or an office they do fall within that definition. As a matter of principle, a decision-maker or tribunal would not be bound by HMRC having accepted payments as in substance of dividends taxable only under ITTOIA, but would have to come to an independent judgment on all the evidence available about whether payments were general earnings. However, how HMRC treated the payments would of course be a relevant factor to be considered., with the weight to be given to that treatment depending on how far it was based on a mere acceptance of statements on a tax return or on any further consideration of the particular circumstances.

See reg.77 for deemed capital and self-employed earnings where the claimant is like a sole trader or partner in relation to a company carrying on a trade. Dividends cannot be treated as part of self-employed earnings under that provision, because the calculation is in terms of the *company's* income, i.e. receipts less allowable expenses as under reg.57.

Employee involved in trade dispute

56. A person who has had employed earnings and has withdrawn their labour in furtherance of a trade dispute is, unless their contract of service has been terminated, to be assumed to have employed earnings at the same level as they would have had were it not for the trade dispute.

2.210

DEFINITIONS

"employed earnings"—see regs 53(1) and 55.
"trade dispute"—see reg.2.

GENERAL NOTE

There is no general disentitlement of claimants involved in a trade dispute for the purposes of universal credit, as there is for new style JSA (see s.14 of the new style Jobseekers Act 1995 in Vol.I of this series) and as there was for old style JSA, for both contributory and income-based JSA (see ss.14 and 15 of the old style Jobseekers Act 1995 in Vol.V of this series). Instead, reg.56 operates by deeming affected claimants to have employed earnings of the amount they would have had but for the trade dispute and applying that rule only in considerably more restricted circumstances than for the purposes of JSA, in essence in circumstances covered by s.14(2), but not those covered by s.14(1) of both forms of the Jobseekers Act 1995. Thus a person who becomes entitled to both universal credit and new style JSA on being without employment when affected by a stoppage of work due to a

2.211

trade dispute at their place of work, without having withdrawn their labour, could be disentitled to new style JSA under s.14(1) of the new style Jobseekers Act 1995, yet not be affected by reg.56. The JSA could then no longer be taken into account as unearned income in the calculation of the universal credit.

The universal credit rule applies in roughly the same circumstances as s.14(2) of both forms of the Jobseekers Act 1995, but since the equivalent of that provision only entered the preceding unemployment benefit legislation in 1986 no case law authority has built up on the interpretation of its terms. There has to be some speculation about that.

To be caught by the rule a universal credit claimant must have had employed earnings, i.e. earned income derived from employment under a contract of service or in an office (reg.55(1)), thus excluding the self-employed from the scope of the rule. It is not clear how far in the past the employed earnings could have been received, but the reference to the withdrawing of labour would suggest that whatever the occupation was from which the labour had been withdrawn would have to be one from the claimant had, immediately before the withdrawal, derived employed earnings.

Then, the rule can only be applied to claimants who have withdrawn their labour. That would cover straightforward strikes or refusals to carry out some significant part of contractual duties, even if the latter led to the employer sending the employees home completely. On the other hand, refusals to work voluntary overtime or works-to-rule would not be covered. And if an employer has initiated a lock-out before the occurrence of anything that would otherwise count as a withdrawal of labour it would seem that the employees could not be regarded as a having withdrawn their labour. A withdrawal must involve a voluntary choice not to work. Much more troublesome would be cases where employees decline to cross picket lines. Being physically prevented from entering work premises or being subjected to threats of violence against self or others would no doubt negate the necessary element of voluntary choice. At the other end of the spectrum, agreeing to polite and reasoned requests not to cross a picket line would also no doubt be regarded as a withdrawal of labour. But there will be many circumstances in the middle where the question will be very difficult to answer. If there are many pickets, with shouted insults and imprecations or more, when do spirited attempts at persuasion turn into intimidation?

The rule also requires that the individual's withdrawal of labour is in furtherance of a trade dispute. Regulation 2 incorporates the definition of "trade dispute" in s.244 of the Trade Union and Labour Relations (Consolidation) Act 1992, which is set out in full in the notes to reg.113. That definition is different from that in the new style Jobseekers Act 1995. It covers only disputes between workers and their employer, not disputes between employees and employees or, for that matter, employers and employers, but the subject-matter of the dispute is widely defined. There is no requirement that the dispute has led to any stoppages of work or similar, nor that the claimant potentially caught by reg.56 has any material interest in the outcome of the dispute. Presumably a trade dispute has to be in existence before a withdrawal of labour can be in furtherance of it. In para.6 of *R(U) 21/59* the Commissioner indicated that a dispute between an employer and an employee must have reached "a certain stage of contention before it may properly be termed a [trade] dispute". He was clearly satisfied that evidence that the workforce had met to consider their response to their employer's rejection of their claims concerning their terms of employment amounted to a trade dispute and suggested that one may well have existed some time before the meeting took place. However, in the unemployment benefit and JSA context such problems have tended to be short-circuited by the question of whether there had been a stoppage of work as a result of any trade dispute. That question does not arise in the universal credit context.

"Furtherance" presumably points towards whatever subjective intention behind the withdrawal of labour can properly be attributed to the claimant, rather than whether the withdrawal is likely to have any practical influence on the outcome of the trade dispute. That would be consistent with the inherent principle that a solo withdrawal of labour can trigger the application of reg.56. It is not necessary for the claimant to have acted in concert with others, provided that the withdrawal of labour was in furtherance of a trade dispute.

Note that the rule in reg.56 cannot apply, or continue to apply, if the claimant's contract of employment (presumably that relevant to the labour that has been withdrawn) has been terminated. It does not matter, in contrast to the position under s.14 of the new style Jobseekers Act 1995, that the termination of the contract is or was a move in the trade dispute. Nor does it appear to matter who terminates the contract.

Perhaps the most problematic part of reg.56, though, is the way that its effect is described if all the conditions for its application are met. It does not, as might have been expected, provide that claimants be assumed to have the employed earnings they would have received were it not for the withdrawal of their labour. It provides that they be assumed to have the employed earnings they would have received were it not for the trade dispute. Even if the trade dispute is between the claimant's own employer and workers, it is hard to see how the dispute as such, rather than actions taken in furtherance of the dispute, could have any effect on the claimant's earnings. If the meaning is to be taken as simply assuming that usual earnings continue unless the contract of employment is terminated, there will still be difficulties in identifying what is usual. For instance, if fluctuating hours of overtime are worked or fluctuating hours worked under a zero-hours contract, what hours are assumed to have been worked?

An argument might be raised, though, that other provisions render much of the above discussion academic. Claimants who withdraw their labour, either before claiming universal credit or during an award would prima facie be subject to a higher-level sanction under s.26(2)(d) or (4)(b). That withdrawal would not only be a ceasing of paid work and a losing of pay, but would be a breach of the contract of employment, even if there was no intention of permanently severing relations. Thus, it is arguable that the ceasing/losing was by reason of misconduct or, if not, was voluntarily and for no good reason. For the purposes of new style JSA there has not needed to be any debate of the difficult question whether decision-makers and tribunals could adjudicate on such issues without reaching a judgment on the merits of the trade dispute, something that the legislation has traditionally tried to avoid. That is first because the effect of s.14(2) of the new style Jobseekers Act 1995 would be to remove entitlement, so that while it applied there would be nothing for a sanction to bite on. In addition, reg.28(1)(d) of the JSA Regulations 2013 prohibits a reduction of benefit being applied where the sanctionable failure is that a claimant voluntarily ceases work or loses pay because of a strike (a "concerted stoppage of work") arising from a trade dispute. However, for universal credit there is no automatic disentitlement if the conditions of reg.56 are met, merely the deeming of usual earnings. But reg.113(1)(c) of the UC Regulations provides protection in the same terms as reg.28(1)(d) of the JSA Regulations 2013, but without the definition of "strike". In relation to both provisions there is a question whether they refer only to the particular sanction for ceasing paid work or losing pay voluntarily and for no good reason or whether they also cover the sanction for doing so by reason of misconduct, constituted by such voluntary action. The second alternative, on a purposive view and taking into account the policy of state neutrality in trade disputes, is more attractive. If so, then reg.56 does play the central role in trade dispute cases and the problems of its interpretation will need to be addressed sooner or later.

Self-employed earnings

57.—(1) This regulation applies for the purpose of calculating earned income that is not employed earnings and is derived from carrying on a trade, profession or vocation ("self-employed earnings").

[²(2) A person's self-employed earnings in respect of an assessment period are to be calculated as follows.

2.212

Step 1

Calculate the amount of the person's profit or loss in respect of each trade, profession or vocation carried on by the person by—
  (a) taking the actual receipts in that assessment period; and
  (b) deducting any amounts allowed as expenses under regulation 58 or 59.
Where a trade, profession or vocation is carried on in a partnership, take the amount of the profit or loss attributable to the person's share in the partnership.

Step 2

If the person has carried on more than one trade, profession or vocation in the assessment period, add together the amounts resulting from step 1 in respect of each trade, profession or vocation.

Step 3

Deduct from the amount resulting from step 1 or (if applicable) step 2 any payment made by the person to HMRC in the assessment period [³by way of national insurance contributions or income tax in respect of any trade, profession or vocation carried on by the person.]
If the amount resulting from steps 1 to 3 is nil or a negative amount, the amount of the person's self-employed earnings in respect of the assessment period is nil (and ignore the following steps).

Step 4

If the amount resulting from step 3 is greater than nil, deduct from that amount any relievable pension contributions made by the person in the assessment period (unless a deduction has been made in respect of those contributions in calculating the person's employed earnings).
If the amount resulting from this step is nil or a negative amount, the person's self-employed earnings in respect of the assessment period are nil (and ignore the following step).

Step 5

If the amount resulting from step 4 is greater than nil, deduct from that amount any unused losses (see regulation 57A), taking the oldest first.
If the amount resulting from this step is greater than nil, that is the amount of the person's self-employed earnings for the assessment period.
If the amount resulting from this step is nil or a negative amount, the amount of the person's self-employed earnings in respect of the assessment period is nil.]

  (3) [²...]
  (4) The receipts referred to in [³paragraph (2)] include receipts in kind and any refund or repayment of income tax, value added tax or national insurance contributions relating to the trade, profession or vocation.
  [¹(5) Where the purchase of an asset has been deducted as an expense in any assessment period and, in a subsequent assessment period, the asset is sold or ceases to be used for the purposes of a trade, profession or vocation carried on by the person, the proceeds of sale (or, as the case may be, the

amount that would be received for the asset if it were sold at its current market value) are to be treated as a receipt in that subsequent assessment period].

AMENDMENTS

1. Universal Credit and Miscellaneous Amendments (No.2) Regulations 2014 (SI 2014/2888) reg.4(3) (November 26, 2014, or in the case of existing awards, the first assessment period beginning on or after November 26, 2014).
2. Universal Credit (Surpluses and Self-employed Losses) (Digital Service) Amendment Regulations 2015 (SI 2015/345) reg.3(2) (April 11, 2018).
3. Universal Credit (Surpluses and Self-employed Losses) (Digital Service) Amendment Regulations 2015 (SI 2015/345) reg.3(3) (April 11, 2018).
4. Universal Credit (Miscellaneous Amendments, Saving and Transitional Provision) Regulations 2018 (SI 2018/65) reg.7(4)(a), (April 11, 2018, text to be inserted by SI 2015/345 amended with effect from February 14, 2018).

DEFINITIONS

"assessment period"—see WRA 2012, ss.40 and 7(2) and reg.21.
"Contributions and Benefits Act"—see reg.2.
"earned income"—see reg.52.
"employed earnings"—see regs 53(1) and 55.
"HMRC"—see reg.53(1).
"relievable pension contributions"—see reg.53(1).

GENERAL NOTE

2.213

This regulation, now from April 2018 supplemented by reg.57A on unused losses, applies for the purpose of calculating self-employed earnings. As with employed earnings, it is the actual amount received during the assessment period that is taken into account. Thus those who are self-employed will need to report their earnings every month.

Self-employed earnings are earnings that are not employed earnings and are derived from carrying on a trade, profession or vocation (para.(1)). On the tests for deciding whether a person is an employed earner or in self-employment, see, for example, *CJSA/4721/2001*. Guidance on what amounts to a trade can also be taken from the cases on what is a business for the purposes of the disregard of the assets of a business (Sch.10 para.7), such as *R(FC) 2/92* and *RM v Sefton Council (HB)* [2016] UKUT 357 (AAC), reported as [2017] AACR 5, on the question of when the ownership of a tenanted house is a business. But note that for universal credit the test is in terms of trade, a narrower concept than business (see the discussion, particularly in the context of rented property, in the notes to regs 52 and 77(1) (2.299)). Whether particular earnings are self-employed earnings for the purposes of universal credit is not determined by how they have been treated for other purposes, e.g. contribution purposes (see *CIS/14409/1996* and para.H4017 ADM).

Thus the first question is whether the person is engaged in self-employment. The issue will have to be determined according to the facts. Paragraph H4013 ADM quotes as examples someone who sells their two classic cars after losing their job because they can no longer afford their upkeep (who is not engaged in a trade) and someone who buys 10,000 toilet rolls from a wholesaler with the intention of selling them for a profit (who is so engaged). If it is decided that the person is engaged in self-employment, the question of whether they are in "gainful self-employment" will also need to be considered for the purpose of applying the minimum income floor rule (see the note to reg.62). If the person is not in gainful self-employment, no minimum income floor will apply and the person's actual self-employed earnings will be taken into account for the purposes of calculating their universal credit award.

This is not the place for any extensive discussion of how to distinguish between employed earners (i.e. those employed under a contract of service (employees) or office-holders) and self-employed earners. In most cases there will be no difficulty in identifying a claimant who falls within reg.57 as opposed to reg.55. There is a still helpful, although now dated, summary of the traditional factors in pp.98–103 of Wikeley, Ogus & Barendt, *The Law of Social Security* (5th edn). See also *CJSA/4721/2001*. There is perhaps a recent tendency to give particular significance to who takes the financial risk of operations as between the person doing the work and the employer/customer. Someone who sets up a limited company of which they are the sole or main employee and who controls the company through being the sole or majority shareholder is an employee, but reg.77 supplies a special regime in which they are treated as self-employed and the income of the company is to be calculated under reg.57.

There may be circumstances that fall outside both categories, in which case the category of "other paid work" in reg.52(a)(iii) would have to be considered. See the decision of the Court of Appeal in the child support case *Hakki v Secretary of State for Work and Pensions* [2014] EWCA Civ 530 in which a "professional" poker player was held not to be a self-employed earner on the ground that his activities lacked the necessary degree of organisation to amount to a trade, profession or vocation. The reasoning has been somewhat uncritically endorsed in the further child support case of *French v SSWP and another* [2018] EWCA Civ 470; [2018] AACR 25.

There are no specific rules excluding certain payments from being self-employed earnings (contrast, for example, reg.37(2) of the Income Support Regulations in Vol.V of this series).

The April 2018 re-casting of paras (2) and (3) into para.(2) does not change the basic substance of the method of calculation of self-employed earnings, apart from new rules on the treatment of losses including the incorporation of the operation of reg.57A on unused losses, but now expressly specifies a series of steps. The whole provision is directed to the calculation for a particular assessment period. The amendment operated only in relation to digital service (full service) cases by a detailed prescription of categories of claimant (see reg.4(1) of the Universal Credit (Surpluses and Self-employed Losses) (Digital Service) Amendment Regulations 2015 (SI 2015/345), as amended), but is now of general application. See previous editions for the previous form of reg.57(2) and (3), which has been subject to slight amendment in its application in live service cases (now extinct).

Note that the guidance on the *gov.uk* website entitled *Report business income and expenses to Universal Credit if you are self-employed*, as updated on May 23, 2023, initially contained a number of very significant errors that displayed a basic misunderstanding of the method of calculation under reg.57, as well as of the process when that method is applied by virtue of reg.77 (company analogous to a partnership or one person business). Corrections were made in an update on June 21, 2023.

Step 1

2.214   Now the starting point in step 1 is the actual receipts in the particular assessment period, regardless of when the work to earn those receipts was done, with the deduction of any allowable expenses under reg.58 or 59 (which apply to amounts paid in a particular assessment period, by necessary implication the same assessment period as for the actual receipts). Thus, it is not necessary that a claimant be engaged in self-employment in the assessment period in question, merely that there are actual receipts or allowable expenses incurred in that period that are derived from self-employment.

It is important that step 1 requires the calculation not just of a profit but also of a loss for each self-employment. Where the trade etc is carried on by a partnership, the claimant's share, which will depend on the terms of the partnership agreement, is taken. Note that drawings from a partnership or from a trade carried on as a self-employed person are not earnings from self-employment (*AR v Bradford Metropolitan DC* [2008] UKUT 30 (AAC), reported as *R(H) 6/09*), nor can they be regarded as unearned income. They are irrelevant to the method of calculation under reg.57 and, even if they did not fall outside the categories of unearned income in reg.66, to regard them as unearned income would entail an unfair double counting. Under para.(4)

receipts include receipts in kind and any refund or repayment of income tax, VAT or national insurance contributions for the self-employed. See the notes on para.(5) below for sale of stock and other assets. This method of calculating self-employed earnings is based on HMRC's "cash basis and simplified expenses accounting system" (the cash basis model, or "cash in/cash out"). According to para.H4141 of ADM, self-employed claimants will be asked to report monthly between seven days before and 14 days after the end date of each assessment period details of actual income receipts and actual expenditure on allowable expenses during the assessment period that has just come to an end. The work of compiling the necessary information and getting through to report it will be quite burdensome. If there is a failure to report on time, an estimate can be made under reg.54(2)(b).

There is a rather difficult issue about what might be called "start-up" costs, expenditure that would fall within the meaning of reg.58 but is incurred before the claimant starts offering or making available the services in question. Can the expenditure be regarded as wholly and exclusively incurred for the purposes of a trade, profession or vocation if it is incurred to enable the trade etc. to start operating in the future? In the absence of reg.57A, the answer would in a sense not matter, because unless the claimant had some receipts to go into step 1 of the calculation there would be no profit, so that expenditure could not reduce the level of earned income below nil. However, reg.57A requires the carrying forward into future assessment periods of "unused losses". Although quite substantial expenses might reasonably be incurred in such circumstances, it seems that they probably cannot be regarded as giving rise to unused losses under reg.57A. That is partly by analogy with the income tax rules, which do not allow the deduction of expenses incurred before the taxpayer starts trading in the sense above. Perhaps more pertinently, reg.57(1) refers to its purpose being the calculation of earned income derived from "carrying on" a trade, profession or vocation. The reference back to the reg.57 calculation in reg.57A in identifying an unused loss seems therefore by implication to impose a similar restriction, that only expenses incurred in the carrying on of a trade etc. can be taken into account, not expenses incurred merely in preparing to carry on the trade etc.

It must be the case that, as accepted in para.H4190 of ADM, capital receipts do not form part of actual receipts for the purposes of reg.57. Examples would be loans, grants, capital introduced into the business by the claimant or others or the proceeds of the sale of capital assets (where such a sale is not part of the business itself). The basic reasoning in *R(FC) 1/97* (and see the other cases mentioned in the notes to reg.37(1) of the Income Support Regulations in Vol.V of this series) would seem to apply, although there are some differences between the family credit legislation considered there and the provisions in these Regulations. However, it is plain that the object of reg.57 is to calculate the amount of earned *income* as defined in reg.52, as was important in *R(FC) 1/97*, in addition to the principle that the power to treat capital as earned income (in the terms of para.4(3)(b) of Sch.1 to the WRA 2012) can only be exercised by the use of express words in the regulation.

Coronavirus payments

It appeared that that principle might be tested in 2020 and 2021 in relation to grants under the Coronavirus Self-Employed Income Support Scheme (SEISS), but amending regulations have short-circuited the problem. These grants, for those who meet the conditions, were described in the March 26, 2020 HMRC guidance as taxable grants of 80% of taxable profits (as calculated by reference to an average over the previous three tax years, or fewer if that is all the evidence available) up to £2,500 per month. Two of the conditions for the grant are that the person's business has been adversely affected due to the coronavirus outbreak and that they intend to continue to trade in the tax year 2020/21. The amount of the grant does not, as confirmed in the Treasury Direction authorising the expenditure on the scheme (Coronavirus Act 2020 Functions of Her Majesty's Revenue and Customs (Self-Employment Income Support Scheme) Direction, signed on April 30, 2020), vary according to the degree of loss of current trading profits. Everyone who qualifies

2.215

and applies gets the 80% subject to the upper limit. The initial payment in late May or June 2020 (notionally to cover the months of May to July 2020) provided one quarter of the annual figure. The second grant (notionally to cover the months of August to October 2020) met only 70% of qualifying trading profits capped at £6,750 (see the Self-employed Income Support Scheme Extension Direction signed on July 1, 2020). The third and fourth tranches (notionally to cover the months of November 2020 to January 2021 and February to April 2021) went back to the original percentage and cap (see the Self-employed Income Support Scheme Grant Extension 3 Direction signed on November 21, 2020 and the Extension 4 Direction signed on April 6 and 7, 2021).

There is extensive discussion in the notes to reg.37 of the Income Support Regulations (which have not been amended) in Vol.V of this series of whether the grants are on general principle income or capital receipts. That discussion is not relevant to universal credit because, with effect from May 21, 2020, before any SEISS grants were to be made, reg.2(1)(a) of the Universal Credit (Coronavirus) (Self-employed Claimants and Reclaims) (Amendment) Regulations 2020 (SI 2020/522) requires SEISS grants to be treated as a receipt at step 1 of reg.57 in the assessment period in which they are received. If the 2020 amending regulations needed to be in exercise of the power to treat capital as earned income (WRA 2012, Sch.1, para.4(3)(b)) the words used seem clear enough to have that effect and in any case the general power in para.4(1)(c) is very wide. The definition of the SEISS in reg.2(3) of the amending regulations, although in terms of the Direction signed on April 30, 2020, encompasses all the various extensions to the scheme, because the later Directions take effect by way of modification of that signed on April 30, 2020. See the notes to reg.54A and to Sch.10 for the resulting operation of the surplus earnings rule, the possible attribution as capital and the disregards of capital in subsequent assessment periods.

Payments from the Small Business Grant Fund or the Retail, Hospitality and Leisure Fund are undifferentiated, in the sense that their purpose is not expressed any more specifically than that of general support for the businesses covered. The conditions for payment are rather different from those for SEISS and the March 2020 Department for Business, Energy & Industrial Strategy guidance says nothing about taxability. The grants can be made to business ratepayers who get certain forms of rate relief (one grant per property) and are to be paid at two rates: £10,000 if the rateable value of the property is up to £15,000 and £25,000 if the rateable value is over £15,000 up to £51,000. There is no condition that there has been any loss of trading income. It therefore seems probable that the nature of the grant is sufficiently far from that of compensation for loss of what would have been revenue receipts to be properly a capital receipt, akin to an injection of capital into the business, and thus not to be included as a receipt at step 1. The same reasoning would apply to receipts from any of the Local Restrictions Support Grant or Additional Restrictions Grant schemes, administered through local authorities and available from autumn 2020 onwards (see Ch.10 of the House of Commons Library Briefing Paper No.8847, *Coronavirus: Support for Businesses*, March 12, 2021), or from a coronavirus Restart Grant.

Loans under the Business Interruption Loan Schemes or the Bounce Back Loan Scheme (all replaced with effect from April 1, 2021 by the Recovery Loan Scheme) appear even more likely to be capital receipts, although the terms of particular agreements may need to be considered. That appears to be the assumption of the drafters of the Self-employed Claimants and Reclaims Regulations because reg.2(2) merely provides for a disregard as capital of grants or loans to claimants carrying on a trade etc. "to meet the expenses or losses of the trade, profession or vocation in relation to the outbreak of coronavirus disease" and the Regulations say nothing about treatment under step 1. See the notes to Sch.10 for whether the disregard succeeds in covering the grants and loans just mentioned or SEISS payments.

Self-employed claimants who have employees and a PAYE scheme may also receive payments under the Coronavirus Job Retention Scheme (CJRS) if they have one or more employees who have been "furloughed" under that scheme. Claimants trading through companies as if they are sole owners or partners who are deemed by reg.77 to be self-employed, so that the income of the company is to be treated as self-employed earnings calculated under reg.57, may also be treated as having the CJRS payments as a consequence of furloughing themselves. Paragraph 2.1 of the Schedule to the Coronavirus Act 2020 Functions of Her Majesty's Revenue and Customs (Coronavirus Job Retention Scheme) Direction signed on May 20, 2020 (modifying the scheme in the direction signed on April 15, 2020) describes the purpose of the scheme as to provide for payments to be made to employers "incurring costs of employment in respect of furloughed employees arising from the health, social and economic emergency in the United Kingdom resulting from coronavirus and coronavirus disease" and para.2.2 says that it is integral that payments are only made in reimbursement of qualifying expenditure incurred or to be incurred by the employer. Any payment must be returned if the employer becomes unwilling or unable to use it for the specified purpose (para.2.4(b)). Those strict conditions showing the purpose of replacing (up to the initial limits of 80% of qualifying expenditure and £2,500 per month, more limited assistance being available from August to the end of October 2020) what would otherwise have been revenue expenditure indicates that CJRS payments should be regarded as income receipts.

That again is the assumption of the drafters of the Self-employed Claimants and Reclaims Regulations. Paragraph 7.7 of the Explanatory Memorandum to the Regulations says that CJRS payments will "not be taken into account in the self-employed claimants UC as earnings (and the claimant will not be able to treat the wages covered by CJRS as expenses in the calculation of their earnings)". However, the actual terms of the Regulations appear to achieve the very opposite of that primary aim. They contain nothing to say that the payments are not to be treated as actual receipts under para.(a) of step 1, but reg.2(1)(b) provides that no deduction is to be made at para.(b) of step 1 for "expenses comprising the salary or wages paid to an employee in so far as those expenses are covered by a payment under the [CJRS]". That seems to have the effect that the CJRS payment counts towards the person's profit in the assessment period of receipt, but in so far as the payment is used for its proper purpose that expenditure cannot be deducted. Regulation 2(2)(a) provides that a CJRS payment is to be disregarded as capital for 12 months, but that cannot affect the inevitable conclusion, accepted in the Explanatory Memorandum, that the payment to the self-employed person is an income receipt. Perhaps decision-makers will apply the policy rather than the words of the Regulations. The word "covered" presumably allows the no-deduction rule to be imposed in the particular assessment period to which a CJRS payment relates, even if the payment was not actually received in that period.

If the analysis above is correct, the intention stated in para.7.8 of the Explanatory Memorandum has been implemented, that where "self-employed UC claimants who are trading through a limited company which "employs" them [and are] supported as a furloughed employee under CJRS ... payments will be treated as earnings and applied to the UC award". See the notes to reg.77 for further explanation. What remains mysterious is how the Regulations achieve any differential treatment between such claimants and ordinary self-employed claimants.

The CJRS was subject to a complicated series of extensions, taking the scheme down to September 30, 2021, the details of which do not need to be set out here (see the House of Commons Library Briefing Paper No.8847, above, for these and other schemes). There have been varying levels of reimbursement of salary costs (reimbursement of employer's national insurance and pension contributions not having been available beyond July 21, 2020). As at April 1, 2021 the level of reimbursement of salary for full furlough was 80%. In the extensions announced in the March 2021 budget that level was to reduce to 70% in July 2021 and to 60% in August and September 2021. From July 1, 2020 "flexible furlough" has been available.

Step 2

Step 2 applies only where the person carries on more than one trade, profession or vocation in the assessment period in question and requires the adding together of the respective results under step 1. Thus a loss in one trade etc goes to offset a profit in another.

Step 3

Step 3 requires the deduction from the figure produced by step 1 (and 2, if applied) of any payment actually made in the assessment period in question to HMRC by way of self-employed national insurance contributions or income tax. Many self-employed people do not pay national insurance contributions and income tax regularly, but they can arrange with HMRC to make such payments monthly. It will obviously be to their advantage for universal credit purposes (to minimise fluctuations in the amounts of earned income to be taken into account) to do so. The process of calculation may stop at the end of step 3. If the resulting figure is nil or a negative amount, then the self-employed earnings for the assessment period are nil. If there is a negative amount there will then be an "unused loss" as defined in reg.57A(1) that can be taken into account in subsequent assessment periods if the process then gets to step 5.

Step 4

Step 4 applies if step 3 results in a positive amount. Then the amount of any relievable pension contributions made in the assessment period in question is deducted, unless already deducted in calculating employed earnings (under reg.55(5)—presumably if not all of the amount was needed to reduce employed earnings to nil, the remainder can be deducted under step 4). See the notes to reg.55 for discussion of "relievable pension contributions". If the resulting figure is nil or a negative amount, then the self-employed earnings for the assessment period are nil. If there is a negative amount at this stage there is not an "unused loss" under reg.57A(1).

Step 5

Step 5 applies if step 4 results in a positive amount. Then at that final stage any unused losses from past assessment periods that have not been extinguished under reg.57A are to be deducted. If the resulting figure is positive, that is the amount of self-employed earnings for the assessment period in question. If the resulting figure is nil or a negative amount, the self-employed earnings are nil. The oldest unused losses are to be looked at first. Although it would have been better if the process had been spelled out, for the structure of regs 57 and 57A to be workable it must be assumed that once deducting a particular unused loss produces a nil result or a negative figure, no more recent unused losses are to be deducted. See the notes to reg.57A for how that affects the amount of unused losses available in subsequent assessment periods.

Note in particular the effect of the saving provision in reg.4(4) of the Universal Credit (Surpluses and Self-employed Losses) (Digital Service) Amendment Regulations 2015, as amended, which provides that there is to be no unused loss under reg.57A from any assessment period that began before April 11, 2018.

Under para.(5), where the purchase of an asset has been deducted as an expense in any assessment period, and in a subsequent assessment period the asset is sold, or ceases to be used for the purpose of the claimant's self-employment, the proceeds of sale, or the amount that would have been received if the asset had been sold at its current market value, will be treated as a receipt in that subsequent period. Paragraph H4181 of the ADM advises decision makers that the full amount of the proceeds of sale (or deemed proceeds of sale) is to be taken into account, even if only a proportion of the purchase price was deducted as a expense in the assessment period in which the asset was purchased because the claimant's self-employed earnings in that assessment period were less than the price of the asset. This provision would seem to embody a somewhat rigid approach which does not take into account the realities of self-employment which usually needs to be viewed over a much longer period than an assessment period (i.e., a month). To quote an example given in the ADM, if a claimant pays £400 for display material in an assessment period in which their earnings are only £100, so that only £100 of the expense is taken into account as this reduces their earnings to nil, it does not seem fair that the whole of the sale price (or deemed sale price) should count as a receipt in a subsequent assessment period, rather than the equivalent of the expenses reduction they were allowed. But now the unused loss in the assessment period in which the display material was purchased can be taken into account under step 5 and reg.57A in subsequent assessment periods, so that the unfairness is diminished. The guidance accepts that if an asset was only to be used partially for business purposes, only that proportion of the proceeds of sale is to be taken into account as a receipt.

This method of calculation, even on the assumption that claimants will be able to supply accurate information month by month, might be expected in many cases to produce considerable fluctuations between assessment periods depending on the chance of when receipts come in and when expenses are incurred. In the case of fluctuations downwards, reg.62 on the minimum income floor may come into play. If a self-employed person is in gainful self-employment as defined in reg.64, would apart from the operation of reg.62 or 90 be subject to all work-related requirements and their actual earned income in an assessment period is below the minimum income floor (usually the hourly national minimum wage times 35), their earned income is deemed to be equal to that threshold. However, the test for gainful self-employment is quite strict. The person must be carrying on a trade, profession or vocation as their main employment and derive self-employed earnings from that. In addition, the trade, profession or vocation must be "organised, developed, regular and carried on in the expectation of profit". Those last conditions, and also the exclusion of the 12-month start-up period under reg.63, will exclude many claimants with fluctuating or more casual operations. See the notes to reg.64 for further discussion. If reg.62 does not apply, the actual level of self-employed earnings as calculated under the present regulation must be taken. Even if reg.62 does apply to some assessment periods, it supplies no mechanism for evening out fluctuations to a higher level for other assessment periods. If earned income exceeds the minimum income floor in any assessment period, the actual level must be taken.

The April 2018 provisions on taking account of losses will give some mitigation in evening out fluctuations in the level of self-employed earnings, but may also lead to an increased application of the minimum income floor. In addition, the new provisions on surplus earnings in reg.54A will add to the unpredictability of outcomes when, as is likely to be the case for any self-employed person, there are continual fluctuations month by month in actual receipts and in expenditure. There are still likely to be differences in total annual income between those universal credit claimants whose earnings are of a regular monthly amount and those (many of whom will be self-employed) who earn the same amount over the year but subject to fluctuations. See the House of Commons Work and Pensions Committee's May 2018 report *Universal Credit: supporting self-employment* (HC 997).

See also reg.77 for the special rules that apply to those whose control of a company is such that they are like a sole trader or a partner. In those circumstances, amongst other things, the company's income or the person's share of it is to be treated as the person's income and calculated under reg.57 as if it were self-employed earnings. It is, though, far from clear how that notional conversion is to take place. Under reg.57, in the case of actual self-employed earnings, the calculation is based on actual receipts in any assessment period less permitted deductions for expenses under regs 58 and 59. Presumably therefore, "the income of the company" does not mean the net income of the company as might be calculated for corporation tax purposes or under ordinary accounting principles. Presumably it means the actual receipts of the company in the assessment period in question less the deductions for expenses under regs 58 and 59, looking at expenditure on behalf of the company rather than by the person in question. It is difficult to say whether in practice information will be available as to such receipts and expenditure in a current assessment period of a month. A further problem is how to calculate the deductions from gross profits under step 3 of para. (2) for national insurance contributions and income tax paid to HMRC in the assessment period and relievable pension contributions made in that period, when the person's actual tax and national insurance status will not have been as a self-employed earner. But some difficulties may be avoided by the provision in reg.77(3)(c) that if the person's activities in the course of the company's trade are their main employment reg.62 (minimum income floor) is to be applied.

See the notes to reg.61 for discussion of whether any alterations of existing awards resulting from increases or reductions in the amount of earned income, including self-employed earnings, are appealable.

[¹Unused losses

2.216   **57A.**—(1) For the purposes of regulation 57(2), a person has an unused loss if—

(a) in calculating the person's self-employed earnings for any of the previous [²...] assessment periods, the amount resulting from steps 1 to 3 in regulation 57(2) was a negative amount (a "loss"); and

(b) the loss has not been extinguished in a subsequent assessment period.

(2) For the purposes of paragraph (1)(b) a loss is extinguished if no amount of that loss remains after it has been deducted at step 5 in regulation 57(2).

(3) Where a person was entitled to a previous award of universal credit and the last day of entitlement in respect of that award fell within the 6 months preceding the first day of entitlement in respect of the new award, the Secretary of State may, for the purposes of this regulation (provided the person provides such information as the Secretary of State requires), [²treat—

(a) the assessment periods under the previous award; and

(b) any months between that award and the current award in respect of which a claim has been made,

as assessment periods under the current award.]]

AMENDMENTS

1. Universal Credit (Surpluses and Self-employed Losses) (Digital Service) Amendment Regulations 2015 (SI 2015/345) reg.3(4) (April 11, 2018).

2. Universal Credit (Miscellaneous Amendments, Saving and Transitional Provision) Regulations 2018 (SI 2018/65) reg.7(4)(b) (text to be inserted by SI 2015/345 amended with effect from February 14, 2018) (April 11, 2018).

DEFINITIONS

"assessment period"—see WRA 2012 ss.40 and 7(2) and reg.21.
"self-employed earnings"—see regs 53(1) and 57.

GENERAL NOTE

2.217   Although reg.57A came into force on April 11, 2018, the saving provision in reg.4(4) of the Universal Credit (Surpluses and Self-employed Losses) (Digital Service) Amendment Regulations 2015 (SI 2015/345), as amended, secures that no unused loss is to be produced from any assessment period that began before that date. It will therefore take some months at least for practical consequences to build up.

An "unused loss" arises in any previous assessment period under reg.57A(1) when the result after step 3 of the calculation of self-employed earnings in reg.57(2) produces a negative figure. That requires calculating profit or loss (i.e. actual receipts in the assessment period less allowable expenses incurred in the same period) for each trade, profession or vocation, combining the figures if more than one trade etc is carried on, and deducting income tax and national insurance payments made to HMRC in that period. Note that the reg.57A test is applied without taking any account of the deduction of the amount of relievable pension contributions under step 4 in reg.57(2). The loss in the form of the negative amount is then "unused" in the sense that the amount of self-employed earnings taken into account in the assessment period in question can never be less than nil.

On the face of it, when such an unused loss is to be taken into account in a subsequent assessment period under reg.57(2), where it comes in at step 5, there is no time limit on how far in the past the relevant assessment period was (subject to the saving that only assessment periods beginning on or after April 11, 2018 can count). The limit to 11 previous assessment periods that existed in previous forms of the amending regulation was removed in the final form. However, the DWP's view is that the rule only operates for assessment periods within the same continuous period of entitlement to universal credit as under the current award, subject to the linking rule in para.(3) of reg.57A, so that a break in entitlement prevents the taking into account of unused losses in pre-break assessment periods. That view must be based on the definition of assessment period in reg.21(1) as "a period of one month beginning with the first date of entitlement and each subsequent period of one month *during which entitlement subsists*" (emphasis added), as well as on the perceived need for para.(3). There may be some doubt about the validity of the emphasised part of reg.21(1) under the powers given in s.7(2) of the WRA 2012 and elsewhere. But leaving that aside and assuming that a month only amounts to an "assessment period" when within a period of universal credit entitlement, that seems to supply no reason why what were undoubtedly assessment periods during the pre-break period of entitlement are not "previous assessment periods" under para.(1)(a). It is suggested that some specific words would have been needed in reg.57A to produce the result that only assessment periods in the current period of entitlement could count and that the existence of para.(3) is insufficient to produce a necessary implication that the plain words of para.(1)(a) do not mean what they say. Thus it is arguable that a break in entitlement does not break the ability to go back to previous assessment periods for unused losses.

If that argument does not work, then para.(3) allows the Secretary of State, where the break in entitlement is of less than six months, to treat the assessment periods in the pre-break period of entitlement and the months in the break as assessment periods under the current award. If that is done, the unused losses in the pre-break period of entitlement and in the deemed assessment periods during the break can then be taken into account if necessary under reg.57(2). There is a discretion ("may") as to whether the deeming should be done, subject to the condition that the claimant provides any required information (presumably mainly as to receipts and expenses in months in the break which were not actually assessment periods). It is not clear what sort of factors might indicate that the basic rule should not be applied. On any appeal a tribunal can make its own judgment as to the exercise of the discretion.

Unused losses are only to be taken into account in step 5 in reg.57(2) if they have not been extinguished (reg.57A(1)(b)). Paragraph (2) links that matter to such use in step 5, but in slightly peculiar terms. It is clear enough that, if the process suggested in the notes to reg.57(2) is followed and only the unused losses, starting with the oldest, that are needed to reduce the final figure to nil or a negative amount are deducted under step 5, the losses that have not needed to be deducted at all are not extinguished. The peculiarity is in relation to the final or sole loss used. Say, for instance, that the figure remaining at the end of step 4 is £300 and the oldest or sole unextinguished unused loss is £500. That produces a negative amount of £200 in step 5 and the amount of self-employed earnings to be taken into account is nil. But to what extent is the unused loss of £500 extinguished by that operation? One would expect it to have been extinguished to the extent of £300. However, para. (2) seems to assume that a loss is either extinguished in its entirety or not extinguished in its entirety and states that a loss is extinguished if "no amount of that loss remains" after it has been deducted in step 5. That test is not clear. In one sense the whole of the £500 unused loss in the example was deducted, producing a negative figure and an amount of self-employed earnings of nil. What does it mean to ask if no amount of the loss "remains"? It seems that, to make any sense, it must mean that in the example £200 remained, because that amount was not needed to reduce the final figure to nil. That then is hard to reconcile with the apparent effect of the plain words of para.(2) that the whole of the £500 unused loss remains unextinguished, because it cannot be said that no amount of that loss remains. That is not the approach taken in the examples given in para.H4503 of the ADM, which are consistent with the carrying forward in the example above of only £200 of unused loss. That would involve interpreting "loss" in para.(2) as meaning something like the whole or part of the original unused loss as identified in para.(1), in so far as not already used up in step 5 of a reg.57 calculation.

Remember of course that if the result of bringing in unused losses results in a low or nil amount of self-employed earnings, the minimum income floor under reg.62 may well come into play.

Permitted expenses

2.218

58.—(1) The deductions allowed in the calculation of self-employed earnings are amounts paid in the assessment period in respect of—
   (a) expenses that have been wholly and exclusively incurred for purposes of the trade, profession or vocation; or
   (b) in the case of expenses that have been incurred for more than one purpose, an identifiable part or proportion that has been wholly and exclusively incurred for the purposes of the trade, profession or vocation,
excluding any expenses that were incurred unreasonably.

(2) Payments deducted under paragraph (1) may include value added tax.

(3) No deduction may be made for payments in respect of—
   (a) expenditure on non-depreciating assets (including property, shares or other assets held for investment purposes);
   (b) [² . . .]
   (c) repayment of capital [¹ . . .] in relation to a loan taken out for the purposes of the trade, profession or vocation;
   (d) expenses for business entertainment.

[¹(3A) A deduction for a payment of interest in relation to a loan taken out for the purposes of the trade, profession or vocation may not exceed £41.]

(4) This regulation is subject to regulation 59.

AMENDMENTS

1. Social Security (Miscellaneous Amendments) (No.2) Regulations 2013 (SI 2013/1508) reg.3(7) (July 29, 2013).

2. Universal Credit (Surpluses and Self-employed Losses) (Digital Service) Amendment Regulations 2015 (SI 2015/345) reg.3(5) (April 11, 2018).

DEFINITIONS

"assessment period"—see WRA 2012, ss.40 and 7(2) and reg.21.
"self-employed earnings"—see reg 53(1) and 57.

GENERAL NOTE

This regulation, and reg.59, provide for the deductions that can be made from self-employed earnings. Only these deductions can be made in addition to those under steps 3 and 4 of reg.57(2) for national insurance contributions and income tax paid to HMRC and relievable pension contributions.

2.219

The amount of the deduction will normally be the actual amount of the permitted expenses paid in the assessment period, but note para.(4). The effect of para.(4) is that the alternative deductions under reg.59 in respect of the expenses referred to in paras (2)–(4) of that regulation may be made instead. However, note that in the case of a car, the actual costs involved in acquiring or using it are not allowable and the only deduction that can be made is a flat rate deduction for mileage under reg.59(2). Regulation 53(1) gives "car' the same meaning as in s.268A(1) of the Capital Allowances Act 2001. That provision excludes motorcycles, vehicles of a construction primarily suited for the conveyance of goods or some other burden and vehicles of a type not commonly used as a private vehicle and unsuitable for such use. The ADM (paras H4231 and H4234) accepts that black cabs or hackney carriages are not cars, because they are specially adapted for business use, in contrast to minicabs or taxis of that kind.

To be deductible, the expenses must have been paid in the assessment period, be reasonable and have been "wholly and exclusively" incurred for the purposes of the self-employment (para.(1)), but note para.(1)(b). See para.H4214 ADM for examples of allowable expenses. Permitted expenses include value added tax (para.(2)).

Paragraph (1)(b) specifically provides for the apportionment of expenses that have been incurred for more than one purpose (e.g., for business and private purposes). In such a case, a deduction will be made for the proportion of the expenses that can be identified as wholly and exclusively incurred for the purposes of the self-employment. See *R(FC) 1/91* and *R(IS) 13/91* which hold that any apportionment already agreed by HMRC should normally be accepted. But note the alternative flat-rate deductions for expenses if someone uses their home for business purposes in reg.59(3). See also reg.59(4) which provides for flat-rate deductions from expenses if business premises are also used for personal use.

No deduction can be made for the payments listed in para.(3). The limitation of sub-para.(a) to non-depreciating assets confirms that reasonable capital expenditure on depreciating assets or stock-in-trade is to be deducted. Sub-paragraph (b) formerly excluded the deduction of losses from previous assessment periods, but has now been overtaken by the new form of reg.57(2) and reg.57A.

Repayments of capital on a loan taken out for the purposes of the self-employment are not deductible (para.(3)(c)) but deductions can be made for interest paid on such a loan up to a limit of £41 per assessment period (para.(3A)). Paragraph (3A) was introduced to bring universal credit into line with the tax rules which now allow a deduction of up to £500 annually for interest payments made on loans taken out for the purposes of a business. This will include interest on credit cards and overdraft charges if the original expense related to the business. According to para.H4217 ADM only £41 can be deducted in any assessment period, regardless of the number of relevant loans a person has and for what purposes. It might just be arguable that the terms of para.(3A) are sufficient to rebut the normal presumption under s.6(c) of the Interpretation Act 1978 that the singular includes the plural, especially if the person carries on more than one trade etc.

Flat rate deductions for mileage and use of home and adjustment for personal use of business premises

59.—(1) This regulation provides for alternatives to the deductions that would otherwise be allowed under regulation 58.

2.220

(2) Instead of a deduction in respect of the actual expenses incurred in relation to the acquisition or use of a motor vehicle, the following deductions

are allowed according to the mileage covered on journeys undertaken in the assessment period for the purposes of the trade, profession or vocation—

(a) in a car, van or other motor vehicle (apart from a motorcycle), 45 pence per mile for the first 833 miles and 25 pence per mile thereafter; and

(b) on a motorcycle, 24 pence per mile,

and, if the motor vehicle is a car [¹ . . .], the only deduction allowed for the acquisition or use of that vehicle is a deduction under this paragraph.

(3) Where a person carrying on a trade, profession or vocation incurs expenses in relation to the use of accommodation occupied as their home, instead of a deduction in respect of the actual expenses, a deduction is allowed according to the number of hours spent in the assessment period on income generating activities related to the trade, profession or vocation as follows—

(a) at least 25 hours but no more than 50 hours, £10;

(b) more than 50 hours but no more than 100 hours, £18;

(c) more than 100 hours, £26.

(4) Where premises which are used by a person mainly for the purposes of a trade, profession or vocation are also occupied by that person for their personal use, whether alone or with other persons, the deduction allowed for expenses in relation to those premises is the amount that would be allowed under regulation 58(1) if the premises were used wholly and exclusively for purposes of the trade, profession or vocation, but reduced by the following amount according to the number of persons occupying the premises for their personal use—

(a) £350 for one person;

(b) £500 for two persons;

(c) £650 for three or more persons.

AMENDMENT

1. Social Security (Miscellaneous Amendments) (No.2) Regulations 2013 (SI 2013/1508) reg.3(8) (July 29, 2013).

DEFINITIONS

"the Act"—see reg.2.
"assessment period"—see WRA 2012 ss.40 and 7(2) and reg.21.
"car"—see reg.53(1).
"motor cycle"—*ibid.*

GENERAL NOTE

2.221   This regulation provides for alternative deductions to those that would otherwise be permitted under reg.58 to be chosen (para.(1)). However, note that in the case of a car, there is no choice: only a flat rate deduction for mileage is allowed and no deduction can be made for the actual cost of buying or using the car (para.(2)). This does not apply to other motor vehicles. See the notes to reg.58 for the meaning of "car".

Under para.(2), a deduction for mileage on journeys undertaken for the purposes of the business in the assessment period:

● on a motorcycle, of 24 pence per mile; or

● in a car, van or other motor vehicle (other than a motorcycle), of 45 pence per mile for the first 833 miles and 25 pence per mile after that,

can be made instead of the actual cost of buying or using the motor vehicle (in the case of a car this is the only permitted deduction).

If someone uses their own home for the purposes of their self-employment, a flat-rate deduction of:

- £10 for at least 25 hours but no more than 50 hours;

- £18 for more than 50 hours but no more than 100 hours; or

- £26 for more than 100 hours,

of "income generating activities" related to the self-employment in an assessment period can be made instead of the actual expenses incurred in the use of the home (para.(3)). The guidance in paras H4241–H4242 ADM suggests that "income generating activities" include providing services to customers, general administration of the business (e.g. filing and record-keeping) and action to secure business (e.g. sales and marketing) but do not include being on call (e.g. a taxi driver waiting for customers to ring), the use of the home for storage or time spent on completing tax returns (presumably on this basis DWP would also discount any time spent collating evidence of actual receipts and expenses for the purposes of the person's universal credit claim).

For the alternative provision for apportionment of expenses, see reg.58(1)(b).

Paragraph (4) provides that if the person lives in premises that are mainly used for business purposes, the expenses that would be allowed if the premises were used wholly and exclusively for the purposes of the person's self-employment are to be reduced by a set amount depending on the number of people living in the premises. The reduction is £350 for one person, £500 for two and £650 for three or more people in each assessment period. It is not entirely clear but the reduction under this paragraph appears to be a set rule, rather than an alternative to an apportionment under reg.58(1)(b).

Notional earned income

60.—(1) A person who has deprived themselves of earned income, or whose employer has arranged for them to be so deprived, for the purpose of securing entitlement to universal credit or to an increased amount of universal credit is to be treated as possessing that earned income. 2.222

(2) Such a purpose is to be treated as existing if, in fact, entitlement or higher entitlement to universal credit did result and, in the opinion of the Secretary of State, this was a foreseeable and intended consequence of the deprivation.

(3) If a person provides services for another person and—
(a) the other person makes no payment for those services or pays less than would be paid for comparable services in the same location; and
(b) the means of the other person were sufficient to pay for, or pay more for, those services,
the person who provides the services is to be treated as having received the remuneration that would be reasonable for the provision of those services.

(4) Paragraph (3) does not apply where—
(a) the person is engaged to provide the services by a charitable or voluntary organisation and the Secretary of State is satisfied that it is reasonable to provide the services free of charge or at less than the rate that would be paid for comparable services in the same location;
(b) the services are provided by a person who is participating as a service user (see regulation 53(2)); or
(c) the services are provided under or in connection with a person's participation in an employment or training programme approved by the Secretary of State.

DEFINITIONS

> "earned income"—see reg.52.
> "a person who is participating as a service user"—see reg.53(2).

GENERAL NOTE

2.223   This regulation treats a person as having employed or self-employed earnings or earned income from other paid work in two situations. For the rules relating to notional unearned income, see reg.74.

Paragraphs (1)–(2)

2.224   This contains the deprivation of earnings rule for universal credit. It applies if someone has deprived themselves of earned income, for the purpose of securing entitlement to, or increasing the amount of, universal credit. It also applies if the person's employer has "arranged for" the deprivation. Presumably this will only apply if the person's purpose was to secure, or increase, entitlement to universal credit by way of the arrangement and the employer's purpose is not relevant.

See the notes to reg.50(1) on deprivation of capital for discussion of the general notion of deprivation and, in particular, when the purpose is to be said to be to secure entitlement to universal credit or to an increased amount. No doubt, as for capital, the basic test is whether that was a significant operative purpose. See below for discussion of whether the deeming of the existence of a prohibited purpose in para.(2), where the result was a foreseeable and intended result of the deprivation, makes any real difference. There is some authority from the child support jurisdiction that a refusal to take up an offer of employment would not be a deprivation of income (*CCS/7967/1995*), although leaving a job may be depending on the circumstances (*CCS/4056/2004*). In the latter circumstance, note the existence of higher-level sanctions under s.26(2)(d) and (4)(b) for voluntarily and for no good reason ceasing paid work or losing pay. Ceasing paid work for the purpose of securing universal credit or an increased amount would certainly not be a good reason. Cutting back on availability as a self-employed person and reducing hours or days of availability under a zero hours contract or a part-time arrangement could presumably also count as deprivations.

The operation of para.(1) is restricted to circumstances where the person's purpose is related to entitlement to universal credit. That is in contrast to the terms of reg.105(1) of the JSA Regulations 1996 (which covers purposes relating to both old style JSA and income support) and of reg.106(1) of the ESA Regulations 2008 and reg.42(1) of the Income Support Regulations (which both cover purposes relating to all of old style ESA and JSA and income support). *R(IS) 14/93* was concerned with a similar problem on the transfer to income support from the corresponding supplementary benefit provisions in 1988 in relation to the notional capital. That was whether claimants who deprived themselves of capital under the supplementary benefit regime, before income support existed, could be said to have done so for the purpose of securing entitlement to income support so as to be caught by reg.51(1) of the Income Support Regulations once the income support legislation had come into force. The Commissioner holds that the words "income support" in reg.51(1) cannot be taken to refer to means-tested benefits that previously went under the name of supplementary benefit. Thus, if a deprivation of earned income occurs while a person is receiving, or contemplating a claim for, income support or old style JSA or ESA, it may be arguable, depending on the exact circumstances, that if there is later a claim for universal credit the purpose of the deprivation was not to secure entitlement to universal credit. But there might in such circumstances be a continuing deprivation for that purpose if there was not an earlier permanent deprivation.

Note, however, para.(2). The effect of para.(2) is that the person will be deemed to have the necessary purpose if they did obtain universal credit, or more universal credit, and in the opinion of the Secretary of State, this was "a foreseeable and intended consequence" of the deprivation. To some extent para.(2) represents a codification of the case law on the "purpose" part of the traditional deprivation rule. However, it seems likely that much will continue to depend on the view taken by the Secretary of State (and on appeal a tribunal) of the person's intention. It is far from clear what difference there is meant to be between *an* "intended consequence" in para.(2) and "purpose" (interpreted as meaning significant operative purpose) in para.(1). If there is no difference there would be no point in including the deeming in para.(2). It may have been thought that the conditions in para.(2) are easier to determine one way or the other, but it is submitted that a consequence is not intended as well as foreseeable just because a person realises that it will result from the deprivation.

There is a rather difficult question for how long following the deprivation the notional earned income is to be attributed. Presumably, the prima facie answer is for as long as the earned income could reasonably have been expected to continue if the deprivation had not taken place. But if the act of deprivation or something else has the effect that the source of the earned income cannot be reconnected (e.g. because a former employer would not take the claimant back or change arrangements again), can there be any justification for applying the rule in para.(1)?

Regulation 52(b) includes notional earned income as within the meaning of "earned income", but none of regs 54 (on earned income), 55 (on employed earnings) or 57 (on self-employed earnings) say anything about how notional earned income is to be integrated into their calculations. Presumably, at the least the definitions and deductions included in and under those provisions must be applied as if the notional earned income had actually been received.

Paragraphs (3)–(4)

If the two conditions in para.(3)(a) and (b) are met (of the claimant having provided a service for which no payment or less than the going rate is made and the person who received the service having the means to pay or pay more) there is no discretion whether or not to apply the rule, unless the claimant comes within one of the exceptions in para.(4). However, the application of both the rule and the exception in para.(4)(a) involve a number of value judgments (e.g. in relation to "comparable services", what remuneration (if any) it is "reasonable" to treat the claimant as having received and whether it is "reasonable" for the claimant to provide the service free of charge or at less than the going rate if they are working for a charitable or voluntary organisation).

The first overriding condition is that the claimant provides services for another person. In the previous income support and equivalent provision (reg.42(6) of the Income Support Regulations: Vol.V of this series) the condition was of performing "a service". It is suggested that no difference of substance can have been intended, so that the authority on those provisions is still relevant.

In *CIS/2916/1997* the claimant was spending time in her mother's shop to keep her mother company following recent bereavements. The Commissioner said that whether this amounted to a "service" was a question of fact and degree, having regard, inter alia, to the effort and time put in (see *Clear v Smith* [1981] 1 W.L.R. 399 on whether there could be "work" without remuneration) but in particular to the advantage derived by the mother. If the help given was substantial, the claimant was providing a service.

In *R(SB) 3/92* the Commissioner held that the rule applied where a mother provided services to her disabled adult son out of love and affection. On appeal in *Sharrock v Chief Adjudication Officer* (March 26, 1991; Appendix to *R(SB) 3/92*) the Court of Appeal agreed that such relationships came within the supplementary benefit provision, providing that the service provided was of a character for which an employer would be prepared to pay. In *CIS/93/1991* the Commissioner held that the principle of *Sharrock* applies to reg.42(6) of the Income Support Regulations, which thus covered services provided within informal family relationships without any contract. In *CIS/422/1992* (which again concerned Mrs Sharrock), the Commissioner held that she was a volunteer and that it was reasonable for her to provide her services free (which provided an exception under reg.42(6A)). The evidence was that

2.225

her son made a substantial contribution to the household expenses. If she were to charge for her services the whole basis of the arrangement between them would have to change, which could have a deleterious effect on their relationship. However, note that there is no exception for a mere volunteer in para.(4)(a), only for someone engaged by a voluntary or charitable organisation.

Under para.(3)(a) the "employer" must either make no payment or pay less than is paid for comparable services in the same location. Since the amount of notional earned income is set according to what is reasonable for comparable services, it seems that provision of some comparable services on a remunerated basis must be shown to exist in all cases. It is not clear how restricted "the same location" is. Regulation 42(6) of the Income Support Regulations refers to "the area".

Some of the points made in *R(SB) 13/86* on the previous supplementary benefit provision seem also to apply to para.(3). It is necessary to identify the "employer" for whom the services were provided. "Person" includes a company or other corporate employer (Interpretation Act 1978 Sch.1). Thus in *R(IS) 5/95* where the claimant, who was an employee and director of a small company, was working unpaid because of the company's financial difficulties, and *CSJSA/23/2006* which concerned the sole director and majority shareholder of an unlimited company who was not paid for his part-time work for the company, it was necessary to consider whether the notional income rule applied. See also *CCS/4912/1998* which held that a similar child support rule applied where a person provided his services through a personal service company that he had set up himself and which was paying him a very low hourly rate and *R(CS) 9/08* where it was held that application of that rule had to be considered in the case of a salary sacrifice arrangement whereby an employer made contributions to an occupational pension scheme of the amount contractually agreed to be foregone by the employee.

Particulars of the services provided and any payments made must be ascertained. See *CIS/701/1994* on the factors to consider when assessing comparable employment (the claimant in that case was again a carer) and the amount of notional earnings. In *CSJSA/23/2006* the tribunal had erred in simply adopting the decision-maker's use of the national minimum wage as the appropriate comparator for deciding the amount of the claimant's notional earnings. The test was what was paid for a comparable employment in the area and so relevant findings of fact needed to be made to establish local comparable earnings. In addition, in a case where there was no actual or implied contract, the period over which the earnings were payable and when they were due to be paid also had to be established in accordance with what were the likely terms of employment in a similar job in the area.

CIS/11482/1995 decided that a suggestion that, although earnings in kind did not count as income in calculating entitlement to income support (see reg.55(2)(a) for the same result for universal credit), they should be taken into account in deciding whether a payment of earnings had been made under reg.42(6) of the Income Support Regulations was incorrect. The claimant's wife worked as a shop assistant for 12 hours a week for which she was paid £5 in cash and took goods to the value of £36 from the shelves. The Commissioner held that since earnings in kind were ignored when considering whether any payment at all of earnings had been made, that had also to be the case when deciding whether a person was paid less than the rate for comparable employment. Thus in considering whether the claimant's wife was paid less than the rate for comparable employment, the £36 that she received in goods was to be left out of account. But to avoid unfair double counting it was necessary to deduct any cash payments in the calculation of her notional earnings under reg.42(6). That was permissible because reg.42(6) allowed the amount of earnings which would be paid for comparable employment to be adjusted where circumstances made it reasonable. However, it would not be "reasonable" to deduct the earnings in kind because that did not involve a double counting as the actual value of the earnings in kind was disregarded. The same would seem to apply for para.(3).

Under para.(3)(b) the Secretary of State must show that the person to whom the services were provided had sufficient means to pay, or pay more, for the services.

For income support and equivalents it is for the claimant to show the "employer's" means were insufficient. That is something could well cause difficulties for claimants reluctant to make embarrassing enquiries or if the "employer" is reluctant to provide information. So the change in the burden is welcome, but there the public interest in preventing employers from economising at the expense of the social security budget means that intrusive enquiries may have to be made on behalf of the Secretary of State. The Court of Appeal in *Sharrock v Chief Adjudication Officer* suggests that "means" refers simply to monetary resources and is a matter of broad judgment. No automatic test of ignoring certain benefits or regarding an income above income support (or now universal credit) level as available should be adopted. In *CIS/93/1991*, the claimant looked after his elderly and severely disabled father, but declined to give any information about the father's means. The Commissioner confirms that in such circumstances the basic rule of para.(6) must be applied, but subject to the exception for volunteers. Now the consequence if information could not be obtained from the father would be that para.(3) could not be applied.

Paragraph (4) specifies three situations in which the rule in para.(3) will not apply. First, under sub-para.(a) those engaged by charities or voluntary organisations are not to have any notional earned income if it is reasonable for them to provide their services free of charge or at less than the going rate. The Commissioner in *CIS/93/1991* held that the means of the "employer" is a factor in assessing reasonableness here, but other factors are relevant too. In *CIS/701/1994* the Commissioner expressed the view that if a person had substantial resources that were genuinely surplus to requirements, that would be different from the situation, for example, of a person saving towards the costs of future residential care. It should be noted that the test is whether it is reasonable to provide the services free of charge or at less than the going rate, rather than whether it is reasonable for payment not to be made for the service, although this is a factor (*CIS/147/1993*). If the claimant was receiving training while, or by doing, the work, that may be relevant (*R(IS) 12/92*).

In *CIS/93/1991* the Commissioner pointed out that the aim of the rule is clearly to prevent an employer who has the means to pay the going rate profiting at the expense of the public purse. If, therefore, an organisation arranges to undertake painting work (as in *CIS147/1993*, although it was an individual claimant volunteer), which otherwise would have remained undone, there is no element of financial profit to the employer in the claimant doing the work. If, however, the employer would have paid if the organisation had not offered to have it done for nothing or a small amount, it may be concluded that it was not reasonable for the services to be provided free of charge or at less than the going rate.

The absence of an individual volunteer from this exception removes a number of difficult issues for determination, as compared with the income support and equivalent rules. But that means that when services are being provided without charge within family settings or to one-person companies or similar by an employee or director it is much more likely that notional earned income will have to be attributed. Perhaps it can be regarded as something of a quid pro quo that it is for the Secretary of State to show under para.(3)(b) that the means of the "employer" are sufficient to pay, or pay more.

Secondly, para.(4)(b) covers services provided by someone participating as a service user, as defined in reg.53(2). There is no further condition as to whether it is reasonable to provide the services free of charge or at less than the going rate.

Thirdly, para.(4)(c) covers the situation where a person is on an approved employment programme or training scheme (not further defined), with no further condition.

[¹Information for calculating earned income – real time information etc.

61.—(1) Unless paragraph (2) applies, a person must provide such information for the purposes of calculating their earned income at such times as the Secretary of State may require.

2.226

Real time information

(2) Where a person is, or has been, engaged in an employment in respect of which their employer is a Real Time Information employer—

    (a) the amount of the person's employed earnings from that employment for each assessment period is to be based on the information reported to HMRC under the PAYE Regulations and received by the Secretary of State from HMRC in that assessment period; and

    (b) for an assessment period in which no information is received from HMRC, the amount of employed earnings in relation to that employment is to be taken to be nil.

Exceptions to use of Real Time Information

(3) Paragraph (2) does not apply where—

    (a) in relation to a particular employment the Secretary of State considers that the employer is unlikely to report information to HMRC in a sufficiently accurate or timely manner;

    (b) it appears to the Secretary of State that the amount of a payment reported to HMRC is incorrect, or fails to reflect the definition of employed earnings in regulation 55 (employed earnings), in some material respect; or

    (c) no information is received from HMRC in an assessment period and the Secretary of State considers that this is likely to be because of a failure to report information (which includes the failure of a computer system operated by HMRC, the employer or any other person).

(4) Where paragraph (2) does not apply by virtue of any of the exceptions in paragraph (3) the [Secretary] of State must determine the amount of employed earnings for the assessment period in question (or, where the exception in paragraph (3)(a) applies, for each assessment period in which the person is engaged in that employment) in accordance with regulation 55 (employed earnings) using such information or evidence as the Secretary of State thinks fit.

Reallocation of reported payments

(5) Where it appears to the Secretary of State that a payment of employed earnings has been reported late, or otherwise reported in the wrong assessment period, the Secretary of State may determine that the payment is to be treated as employed earnings in the assessment period in which it was received.

(6) Where a person is engaged in an employment where they are paid on a regular monthly basis and more than one payment in relation to that employment is reported in the same assessment period, the Secretary of State may, for the purposes of maintaining a regular pattern, determine that one of those payments is to be treated as employed earnings in respect of a different assessment period.

Consequential adjustments

(7) Where the Secretary of State makes a determination under any of paragraphs (4) to (6), the Secretary of State may make such other adjustment to the calculation of the person's employed earnings as may be necessary to avoid duplication or to maintain a regular payment pattern.

(8) In this regulation "Real Time Information Employer" has the meaning in regulation 2A(1) of the PAYE Regulations.]

AMENDMENT

1. Universal Credit (Earned Income) Amendment Regulations 2020 (SI 2020/1138) reg.2 (November 16, 2020).

DEFINITIONS

"assessment period"—see WRA 2012, ss.40 and 7(2) and reg.21.
"earned income"—see reg.52.
"employed earnings"—see regs 53(1) and 55.
"HMRC"—see reg.53(1).
"PAYE Regulations"—*ibid.*

GENERAL NOTE

The form of reg.61 set out above is that substituted by the amending regulations with effect from November 16, 2020. For the form in force immediately before that date, and some of the earlier history, readers must consult the 2020/21 edition of what was then Vol.V of this series, *Universal Credit.* The pre-November 2020 form of reg.61 will be discussed below in noting the changes made. To understand those changes, and also because there will still be appeals coming through to do with period before November 16, 2020, it is still necessary to consider the effects of the decision of the Court of Appeal in *Secretary of State for Work and Pensions v Johnson* [2020] EWCA Civ 778; [2020] P.T.S.R. 1872. See the notes to reg.54 for a full description of that decision.

2.227

The explanatory memorandum to the amending regulations (SI 2020/1138) recited that in *Johnson* the Court of Appeal decided that the lack of adjustment in the drafting of regs 54 and 61 for those who have two calendar monthly salary payments taken into account in one assessment period due to a "non-banking day salary shift" was not rational and continued:

"7.4 These regulations therefore provide a solution to that Judgment. The policy intent is to ensure that ordinarily no more than one set of calendar monthly salary payments from a single employer are taken into account in each assessment period. This will also enable certain claimants to benefit from any applicable work allowance in each assessment period. This change in regulations will allow DWP to reallocate a payment reported via real time information (RTI) to a different assessment period, either because it was reported in the wrong assessment period, or (in the case of monthly paid employee) it is necessary to maintain a regular payment cycle. This issue applies to less than 1% of the people who are working and receiving Universal Credit."

The new reg.61 was thus presented as if it were not just "a solution", but the complete solution to the irrationality identified by the Court of Appeal, as explained in the notes to reg.54, and necessarily operative only prospectively from that date. That assumption also seems to have underlaid the DWP's presentation to the Social Security Advisory Committee on October 7, 2020 (SSAC Minutes October 2020), following which the SSAC agreed not to take the proposed regulations on formal reference. Such an assumption fails to grapple with the consequences of the terms of the declaration agreed by the parties (set out in the notes to reg.54 and exhaustively explored in *JN v SSWP (UC)* [2023] UKUT 49 (AAC)), which declares the earned income calculation method in the regulations to be irrational and unlawful as applied to the monthly paid employees identified. An important consequence appears to be that neither the four *Johnson* claimants nor any others who are able to bring an effective challenge to any past decisions can have that unlawful method applied to them in relation to periods before November 16, 2020. That is supported by the approach of

Rose LJ in para.108 of *Johnson*, where she said that the claimants' argument of discrimination under the ECHR did not arise for consideration because of the success of their case on irrationality. It is submitted that the judge, and thus the Court, could only have taken that view if she thought that the four *Johnson* claimants had, by that success, achieved all that they could have achieved by success in the discrimination argument. Since the judicial reviews were directed against the decisions made in particular assessment periods in 2017 or 2018, the Court must by necessary implication from that part of its judgment have accepted that those decisions had to be re-made without applying the method of calculation found to be unlawful, even though the apparent mismatch between the nature of irrationality accepted and that result was unaddressed in the judgments. A mere redrafting of the regulations with effect from a subsequent date does not achieve that result.

It is still submitted that *Johnson* means that the earned income calculation method in the pre-November 16, 2020 form of the regulations has been unlawful from the outset. Although in *JN v SSWP (UC)* [2023] UKUT 49 (AAC) Judge Wright analysed the effect of the declaration in *Johnson*, which had no express temporal qualification, by reference to somewhat inconsistent statements in the judgments as biting from the date of the Secretary of State's decisions that were under appeal in *Johnson* (i.e. some dates in 2017 and 2018), he did not need to consider any argument that the effect should go back to the start of the scheme. See the notes to reg.54 for the details of *JN*, including the judge's conclusion in remaking the decisions on the claimant's appeals against the Secretary of State's decisions relating to four assessment periods, having set aside those decisions as applying legislation that was irrational and unlawful, that he had no basis on which he could substitute a lawful decision. He therefore left the decisions to be remade on a lawful basis by the Secretary of State, noting that a way had apparently been found to do that for the *Johnson* claimants by manual adjustments to the system. An "automated fix" was said to have been put into operation from August 2021.

However, as from November 16, 2020 (probably in relation to assessment periods beginning on or after that date: see para.32 of Sch.1 to the Decisions and Appeals Regulations 2013 for the rule on supersessions where there is an existing award) the new form of reg.61 must be applied (subject to arguments that other categories of claimant might succeed in irrationality or discrimination arguments, although such arguments seem ruled out of success by the Court of Appeal's decision in *Pantellerisco v Secretary of State for Work and Pensions* [2021] EWCA Civ 1454; [2021] P.T.S.R. 1922, at least for those paid four-weekly or at similar intervals, as discussed in the notes to reg.54). The main difference from the previous form of reg.61 is in the substitution of the new paras (5) to (7), giving various discretionary powers, for the previous para.(5) and in the omission of the previous para.(6) (see detailed discussion below). There have also been several changes to the drafting of paras (1) to (4), some of which are merely cosmetic or clarificatory, such as the helpful introduction of some sub-headings, but some of which potentially introduce changes of substance. The integration of the changes into the structure of reg.61 has not been entirely coherent. The administrative guidance in Memo ADM 27/20 did little more than paraphrase the terms of the regulation and does not seem to have been incorporated into the text of Ch.H3 of the ADM.

The SSAC, despite considering the new regulation to be sufficiently helpful to claimants that a formal reference of the proposal was not necessary, remained "concerned that the new arrangements will be overly reliant on claimants to notify the Department when they have received two monthly payments in a single assessment period and that as a result a significant number could still fail to benefit from a work allowance every month as they should" (letter of October 23, 2020 from the Chair to the Secretary of State). Therefore, they recommended that the Department should closely monitor the impact of the change. The DWP had accepted that their manual process would depend on claimants coming forward with information, but said that it intended to ask employed claimants about the interval at which they are paid at the start of the claim, so as to flag up cases that might encounter problems in the future.

Note that the new powers in reg.61 are not restricted to cases where the work allowance is in play, as it was for the four *Johnson* claimants. The discretions may thus sometimes be very difficult to exercise, especially where claimants would be better off overall (apart from difficulties caused by fluctuations in total income) by having two monthly payments taken into account in the same assessment period and none in another period. That may be problematic if the DWP develops changes to its computer systems to attempt to apply the terms of the new reg.61 automatically without having to rely on claimants coming forward with information.

The regulation as a whole is concerned with the provision of information on earned income. It is one of the most distinctive features of universal credit that it was designed so that normally PAYE information would be used in a way that could be dealt with by an automated computer system to calculate a person's employed earnings and that direct reporting of employed earnings by a claimant ("self-reporting") would only be a fall-back position. That was a significant factor in universal credit assessment being on a monthly basis, with payment made in arrears after the end of each assessment period.

Paragraph (1)

Paragraph (1), unchanged from the old form, contains a general rule that a claimant must provide the information that the Secretary of State requires for the purposes of calculating their earned income (note that earned income includes not only employed earnings, including earnings as an office-holder, but also self-employed earnings, remuneration from any other paid work and income treated as earned income: see reg.52). Thus, self-employed claimants come within this self-reporting rule. However, para.(1) is subject to para.(2), which applies only to those with employed earnings.

2.228

Paragraph (2)

The new para.(2) is in substance the same as the previous para.(2), except that the rules are said to be "in respect of" particular assessment periods rather than "for" them. There has thus been no change to the unequivocal rule in para.(2)(b) that the amount of employed earnings "is to be taken to be nil" for any assessment period in which no information is received from HMRC. However, it would appear that, as discussed further below, in order to allow the new provisions to bite on the mischief identified in the explanatory memorandum, para.(2) must be read as subject to paras (5) to (7) as well as to the exceptions expressly made in para.(3). Otherwise the reallocation of a payment to an assessment period in which no information was received from HMRC, necessary to those provisions, would be impossible.

2.229

Under para.(2), if the claimant's employer is a "Real Time Information employer" (defined in para.(7)), the calculation of the claimant's employed earnings in respect of each assessment period is to be based on the information that is reported to HMRC through the PAYE system and received by the Secretary of State from HMRC in that period (sub-para.(a)). If no information is received from HMRC in an assessment period, the claimant's earnings from that employment are to be taken to be nil (sub-para.(b)). It should especially be noted that the language of sub-para.(b) is different from that of sub-para.(a) ("is to be taken" as opposed to "is to be based on").

Since October 6, 2013 most employers have been Real Time Information employers (see reg.2A(1)(d) of the Income Tax (Pay As You Earn) Regulations 2003 (SI 2003/2682) ("the PAYE Regulations")). Under reg.67B of the PAYE Regulations a Real Time Information employer is required to deliver specified information to HMRC before or at the time of making payments to an employee. The instructions to employers on reporting are to record amounts on the normal payment date. HMRC's October 2019 (Issue 80) Employer Bulletin contains a clarification of the rules about the date on which pay should be reported in a Real Time Information Full Payment Submission as having been made when the normal payment date falls on a non-banking day. Whether the payment is made before or after the normal payment date it should be reported as having been made on the normal date. The Bulletin also contains guidance relating to early payments around Christmas 2019, applying the same rule. What was described as a temporary "easement" for Christmas 2018 has been made permanent. The same should apply when a payment is not made on the normal payment date for any other reason. Those instructions have been repeated with general application in s.1.8 of HMRC *Guidance 2020 to 2021: Employer further guide to PAYE and National Insurance contributions* (CWG2, as updated on May 14, 2020 and available on the internet). What perhaps started as mere guidance has been firmed up into what are now very precise instructions.

Initially, it was considered that para.(2) established a rigid rule of attribution to the assessment period in which the HMRC information was received, that could only be displaced under the conditions in para.(3). That certainly was the assumption in *SSWP v RW (rule 17) (UC)* [2017] UKUT 347 (AAC), discussed below in relation to para.(3). The decision of the Divisional Court in *R. (Johnson and others) v Secretary of State for Work and Pensions* [2019] EWHC 23 (Admin) cast doubt on that assumption by rejecting the Secretary of State's interpretation of regs 54 and 61, relying on a mistaken interpretation of the phrase "on the basis of" (see the notes to reg.54). That doubt was removed by the Court of Appeal's decision to the contrary on appeal. However, the Secretary of State's appeal was not allowed, because the court found that it had been irrational for her not to have included some provision in the legislation to avoid the problems arising for the four monthly-paid claimants from the extremely odd results of applying the accepted interpretation to them. See the notes to reg.54 for a full discussion of the Court of Appeal's decision and the unanswered questions arising about its effect.

Thus, in the new para.(2), sub-para.(a) has the same meaning as above and the meaning of sub-para.(b) is plain and apparently absolute: if no information is received from HMRC in an assessment period the claimant's employed earnings are to be nil. However, although para.(2) is not expressly made subject to the rest of reg.61, in order to give the rest of the provision some practical operation, it must be regarded as subject not only to the exceptions in paras (3) and (4), but also to the discretionary powers in paras (5) to (7). Those powers must be able to treat a claimant as having employed earnings in an assessment period in which no information was received from HMRC.

NM v SSWP (UC) [2021] UKUT 46 (AAC) supplies a practical example of the operation of the basic rule in para.(2), on the pre-November 16, 2020 form of reg.61. The claimant ceased employment in September 2017 and claimed universal credit. In two assessment periods following the first under his award he received, after negotiation and conciliation, payments representing unpaid wages and holiday pay (the return of a deposit on his uniform did not count as earned income: see the notes to para.(3)(b) below). The employer reported the payments through the RTI system, apparently at the correct time. Judge Jacobs confirmed that there was no basis in any arguments of fairness to disapply the basic rule to the wages and holiday pay. Paragraph (3)(a) as it stood at the time could not apply because there was nothing to indicate that information from the employer was unlikely to be sufficiently accurate or timely. Paragraph (3)(b)(ii) as it then stood could not apply because the information received from HMRC was not incorrect. The information was correct as to the payments made, even though they should have been made earlier. The judge's statement in para.14 that "matters relating to the timing of the payment" were irrelevant to para.(3)(b)(ii) must not be taken out of context. It does not detract from the argument (see the notes to that provision in the 2020/21 edition of what was then Vol.V of this series, *Universal Credit* and to para.(3)(b) below) that if an employer reports a payment as having been made on a date that is not in accordance with HMRC guidance/instructions that renders the information received from HMRC incorrect (but contrast the words of the new para.(3)(b)).

The most recent example is *SK and DK v SSWP (UC)* [2023] UKUT 21 (AAC) (see the notes to reg.55(4A) for the full details). There the claimant, who was on unpaid sick leave from his employer, received a bonus of £20,000 on May 20, 2020, within the assessment period running from April 29, 2020 to May 28, 2020 (AP 1). Under the PAYE system the employer deducted the amount of £6,893.60 for income tax before making the payment, which was reported to HMRC through the Real Time Information scheme. That was on the basis of a code issued by HMRC that was appropriate to a person regularly earning £20,000 a month over the whole tax year. Since that was not the case, on the claimant not receiving any further remuneration from his employer in subsequent months, under the PAYE system he received from the employer a "refund" of overpaid income tax of £2.144.60 in the assessment period running from May 29, 2020 to June 28, 2020 (AP 2) and further refunds in subsequent months. There was no dispute that the receipt of the net amount of the bonus in AP 1 resulted in a nil entitlement to universal credit, but the claimant appealed against the nil entitlement in AP 2 resulting from the taking into account of the £2,144.60. Among his arguments was that a repayment of income tax could only be treated as employed earnings under the conditions of reg.55(4A), which were not met as he was not in paid work in the tax year 2020/21. The First-tier Tribunal disallowed the appeal. On the further appeal Judge Ovey rejected the tribunal's reasoning but substituted her own decision to the same effect.

Having shown that reg.55(4) only applies to repayments of income tax made directly by HMRC to the taxpayer, not to in-year adjustments to tax to be deducted under PAYE, the judge convincingly shows that there was no alternative to taking the two payments into account as employed earnings under reg.61(2) in the assessment periods in which they were reported, giving this explanation:

"47. For completeness, I add also that although it is convenient to speak in terms of a tax repayment or refund under the PAYE Regulations, there is a sense in which that is not strictly what happens. In broad terms, the mechanism of the PAYE Regulations involves the payment by the employer to HMRC each month (or each quarter, in some cases) of the global amount payable for income tax by all its employees determined in accordance with their various tax codes. Tax codes may, however, be adjusted from time to time, with the result that the deduction made in respect of some employees may have been too high and the deduction made in respect of other employees may have been too low. The amount payable to HMRC in any month may reflect any adjustments which may be required to give effect to past over-deductions or under-deductions. Any repayment or refund is therefore likely to be achieved not by any payment by HMRC but by a set-off against the next month's liability.

48. It follows that when a claimant receives a tax refund through PAYE it may fairly be said that what is being received is a part of the remuneration earned which was held back for the purpose of meeting a tax liability but which is now being released. It is clearly entirely appropriate to treat such a payment as employed earnings…"

Paragraphs (3) and (4)

The new para.(3), establishing three exceptions from the para.(2) rules, is made non-discretionary. Then the first exception in the new sub-para.(a) is in substance the same as in the previous sub-para.(a) with some rejigging of language. The second exception in the new sub-para.(b) is the replacement of the previous sub-para.(b)(ii), but with significant changes. The exception now only applies if the amount of a payment reported to HMRC is incorrect or fails to reflect the definition of employed earnings in reg.55. Previously, the reference was to the information received from HMRC. The new sub-para.(c) is in substance the same as the previous sub-para.(b)(i), again with some slight rejigging of language.

Where one of the conditions in para.(3) is met the Secretary of State must determine the amount of employed earnings in accordance with reg.55 (on what count as employed earnings) and such information or evidence as the Secretary of State

2.230

thinks fit (para.(4). The same must apply to a tribunal on appeal. The power granted by para.(4), although restricted to circumstances where one of the para.(3) exceptions applies and to the particular assessment period(s) affected by the exception, appears very open. It attracts the power in para.(7) to make such other adjustments as may be necessary to avoid duplication or to maintain a regular payment pattern. That would seem to entail a power to reallocate employed earnings to assessment periods other than those affected by the exception. But it is not clear whether such a power of reallocation was intended only to arise under paras (5) and (6), or whether the restrictions in those paragraphs can be sidestepped by the use of paras (3) and (4).

Sub-paragraph (a) applies where, in relation to a particular employment, the Secretary of State considers that the employer is unlikely to report information to HMRC in a sufficiently accurate or timely manner. The effect may thus operate over more than one assessment period. *NM* (above) confirms that the fact that the employer was making payments later than it should did not trigger the form of this exception then in force. It was the reporting of the information about payments that had to be unlikely to be inaccurate or timely. That point is made even clearer by the wording of the new form in sub-para.(a).

The conditions of the Northern Ireland equivalent of sub-para.(a) were found to be satisfied in *AF v DfC (UC)* [2023] NICom 18. The claimant was paid monthly, the due date apparently being the 24th of the month. Her assessment period ran from the 28th of one month to the 27th of the next. She was paid on July 24, 2020, but there was a delay in issuing a payslip until July 31, 2020 and that was the date on which the RTI report was made to HMRC and on to the DfC. Her August salary was paid on August 24, 2020 and reported on that date. The DfC, having apparently calculated the claimant's entitlement to UC for the assessment period ending on July 27, 2020 on the basis that no earned income was to be taken into account, calculated her entitlement for the assessment period ending on August 27, 2020 on the basis that the two payments were to be taken into account as earned income. The claimant's appeal against the decision on that assessment period was disallowed by the appeal tribunal without any reference in its statement of reasons to the equivalent of reg.61. Commissioner Stockman found that plainly to be an error of law, especially as there was evidence before the tribunal of the claimant having informed the DfC that the issue with a delayed payslip had occurred previously. On that evidence he substituted a decision applying the equivalent of sub-para.(a), finding that the information from the employer was manifestly not accurate or timely, and recalculating the claimant's entitlement for the assessment period ending on August 27, 2020 on the basis of actual receipt in that period only of the payment made on August 24, 2020. He did though note there would need to be an adjustment of entitlement for the assessment period ending on July 27, 2020, but the claimant would have the benefit of the work allowance in that period, that she would otherwise have lost. The Commissioner did not identify the power under which that adjustment could be made, but it would apparently lie in the power to revise for official error (GB Decisions and Appeals Regulations 2013, reg.9).

It is submitted that it was crucial to this decision that the issue had occurred before, so that a judgment could be made about the particular employment, not merely the particular assessment period. If the issue had arisen for the first time in relation to the payment due on July 24, 2020, it is submitted that there would have had to be consideration of para.(3)(b) in its pre-November 16, 2020 form. Your commentator's view is that that provision could have applied, but Commissioner Stockman has in other cases rejected that outcome (see below).

Sub-paragraph (b) applies where it appears to the Secretary of State that the amount of a payment reported to HMRC (by the employer) is incorrect or fails to reflect the definition of employed earnings in reg.55 in some material respect. By contrast, the old para.(3)(b)(ii) applied where the information received from HMRC was incorrect, or failed to reflect the definition of employed earnings, in some material respect. That appears to be a significant change.

It was argued in the notes to reg.61 in the 2020/21 edition of what was then Vol.V of this series, *Universal Credit*, that if an employer reported a payment was made on the actual date it was made instead of the date specified in HMRC guidance/instructions (i.e. the usual pay day) the information received from HMRC was incorrect in a material effect, so that a departure from the para.(2) rules was authorised. That argument seems no longer to hold, because the new sub-para.(b) only operates if the *amount* of the payment reported to HMRC is incorrect etc, not if the date reported is incorrect (but see new para.(5) below on reporting in the "wrong" assessment period).

It is still submitted that that argument has considerable force in relation to the pre-November 16, 2020 regulation, but it should be noted that it has attracted no judicial support. It was not mentioned in *SSWP v RW (rule 17) (UC)* [2017] UKUT 347 (AAC) (discussed below in relation to sub-para.(c)), where it could have been relevant, as suggested in the 2020/21 edition. Moreover, in *Johnson* in the Court of Appeal at para.44, Rose LJ rejected the claimants' argument that they could rely on reg.61(3), apparently in the form of sub-para.(b)(ii) as then in force.

Further, the argument was explicitly rejected by Commissioner Stockman in the Northern Ireland case of *DfC v OS (UC)* [2022] NICom 29. There, the claimant's last day of work was November 9, 2018. He claimed universal credit on November 19, 2018. In the assessment period ending on December 18, 2018 he received payments relating to his work down to November 9. Although the DfC appeared not to have identified the amounts accurately in its initial decision, it was agreed before the Commissioner that the relevant payments were a payment of £404.34 in final wages on November 23 and a payment of £225.52 in accrued holiday pay on November 30. Those amounts were apparently reported by the employer through RTI on those dates. The appeal tribunal erroneously applied the post-November 16, 2020 form of the equivalent of reg.61 (which of course was not in force at the relevant time) in holding that no payments fell to be attributed to the assessment period ending on December 18, because the payments were not *for* that assessment period. It was agreed on the DfC's appeal that the tribunal's decision should be set aside for applying the wrong legislation and that the Commissioner should substitute a decision on the underlying appeal. The argument made for the claimant was that he had been entitled to be made the two payments on November 16 (presumably as the next normal or contractual pay-day) and that in accordance with the PAYE legislation and HMRC guidance pay should be recorded on the date on which the employee is entitled to be paid. Therefore, the information provided by HMRC (presumably) on November 23 and/or 30 was incorrect in a material respect because the payment date should have been November 16.

The Commissioner rejected that argument, though finding some force in it. He considered that the key word in issue was "incorrect" and continued in para.35:

"The term 'incorrect', when applied to information, it appears to me, has the meaning of being inaccurate or being wrong. I can find no authority for construing the expression 'the information received from HMRC is incorrect … in some material respect' to encompass the situation where otherwise accurate information is not recorded on the correct date. There may well be a legitimate expectation that information should be provided on a particular date under legislation and guidance. A failure to do so may well be an incorrect application of the relevant PAYE rules. However, in the absence of persuasive authority, I cannot hold that this procedural failing renders the information 'incorrect' when it amounts to accurate information being provided at the wrong date."

It is submitted that "incorrect" was not the sole key word, but that the word "information" was of equal significance and that the payment date included in the RTI information received from HMRC could be regarded as inaccurate or wrong if the identification of the date did not follow HMRC instructions. Nor is it clear how the absence of existing persuasive authority was relevant to construing the meaning of the relevant provision. In other cases, even under the current form of reg.61, there may be difficult issues following the ending of employment about when particular payments are due to be made and how that fits in with PAYE and RTI reporting obligations.

In *Johnson*, Ms Barrett and Ms Stewart were usually paid on the 28th of each month). Their assessment periods ran from the 28th of one month to the 27th of the next. When the 28th was a non-banking day (Saturday, Sunday or bank holiday) they were paid on last working day before the 28th and their employers reported the date of actual payment on their Full Payment Submission. Rose LJ said that there was nothing inaccurate or untimely in the information provided by the employers to HMRC and the DWP. However, as she noted at para.86, HMRC guidance/instructions (or what was called an "easement" in relation to Easter 2019) had been from at least 2018 to report payment on the usual pay day. There is therefore some doubt whether those instructions were in effect at the date of the decisions challenged in *Johnson* and, if so, how strong the instructions/guidance was. However, the court was considering a continuing failure to make legislative provision for the specific problem of monthly-paid claimants with assessment periods ending near the end of the month and it was clear from the limited evidence it had that HMRC were from 2018 or 2019 telling employers that that was how they were to report payment dates. Rose LJ then failed to connect up that evidence with her conclusion in para.44 in a way that must undermine the force of that conclusion. Surely, doing no more than applying the everyday meaning of "incorrect", it must be arguable that where the employer has failed to follow HMRC instructions the information passed on to the DWP is incorrect in a material respect under old sub-para.(b)(ii). That would, as explained in more detail below, have allowed the Secretary of State or a tribunal on appeal to treat earnings actually received on one date as received on the usual pay day, if that resulted in it counting in a later assessment period (para.(5) of the old reg.61). A practical problem would have been whether the DWP was able to identify that information was incorrect in the sense above from what was sent to it from HMRC or whether claimants would need to alert the DWP to the occurrence of a shift.

Note that the argument above would appear not to have been of assistance to claimants who, like Ms Johnson and Ms Woods, are usually paid on the last working day of the month. That is because, if the "non-banking day salary shift" occurs, it would merely identify what is the last working day of the month and the date of actual payment would be correctly reported by the employer as the usual pay day. It could possibly help some claimants like those in *Pantellerisco v Secretary of State for Work and Pensions* [2021] EWCA Civ 1454; [2021] P.T.S.R. 1922 (see the notes to reg.54 for the details) who are paid four-weekly, but only in very occasional circumstances (say where payment on a Thursday instead of a bank holiday Friday would take a payment into a different assessment period).

NM v SSWP (UC) [2021] UKUT 46 (AAC) supplies an example of information not reflecting the definition of employed earnings in reg.55. The employer's report to HMRC included the amount of a deposit paid by the claimant for his uniform as a security guard that was returned to him after his employment ended. That was not employed earnings within s.62 of ITEPA, so not within reg.55. Therefore, the information did not reflect the definition and the amount was not to be included under reg.61.

Sub-paragraph (c) applies where no information is received from HMRC in an assessment period and it is likely that that is because of a failure to report information (to HMRC), including failures of computer systems, including those of HMRC. This is a rather specialised provision. Presumably, the "failure" refers mainly to an employer's non-fulfilment of the duty under reg.67B of the PAYE Regulations, mentioned above, and does not require any fault, merely an absence of that duty having been carried out. Thus the inclusion of a failure of HMRC's own computer systems seems to be an extension.

In *SSWP v RW (rule 17) (UC)* [2017] UKUT 347 (AAC), the Secretary of State's submission to the Upper Tribunal supported the application of the equivalent of sub-para.(c) (para.(3)(b)(i) of the old reg.61) in a way that appears wrong.

HMRC's real time earnings feed showed notification on two dates in February 2016 (February 1, 2016 and February 29, 2016) of the claimant having received earnings. Her assessment period ran from the first of each calendar month to the last day of that month. Both receipts were taken into account in relation to February 2016, resulting in a much reduced universal credit entitlement. The claimant's case on appeal was that her January 2016 earnings were received on Sunday January 31, 2016, but not reported by her employer until the next day (as apparently confirmed in HMRC documents). She had no control over when the earnings information was reported. The First-tier Tribunal, in allowing the appeal and altering the assessment of entitlement for the February 2016 assessment period by removing the payment actually made on January 31, rejected the Secretary of State's argument at that stage that para.(3) did not justify any departure from the basic rule in para.(2)(a). The tribunal relied on two alternative reasons that the Secretary of State challenged on appeal to the Upper Tribunal. On receipt of detailed directions from Judge Wright, the Secretary of State applied to withdraw the appeal, saying that it had been concluded that the case could be brought within para.(3)(b)(i) of the old reg.61 on the basis that reporting a payment by an employer after the date on which it was actually made can be considered a failure by the employer. In the light of that explanation, Judge Wright consented to the withdrawal of the appeal. He directed that his decision recording that withdrawal, although it determined none of the issues involved, go onto the AAC website as the Secretary of State's reasoning might be relevant in other cases.

However, the reliance on para.(3)(b)(i) of the old reg.61 in relation to the January 2016 assessment period, even if justified, appears to have been a red herring. Paragraph (3)(b) applied in respect of a particular assessment period. If no information was received from HMRC because of a failure by the employer that could only have affected entitlement in the January 2016 assessment period and not entitlement in the February 2016 assessment period. It appears that the tribunal altered the amount of entitlement for the February 2016 assessment period and it is not clear what, if any, adjustment was made in relation to the January 2016 assessment period. Further, it appears a more natural reading of para.(3)(b)(i) that it applied only where no information had been received from HMRC by the date on which a decision is made about a particular assessment period, not where information has been received by that date but it involved some late recording of receipts. Thus the reason for the Secretary of State's support of the tribunal's decision in relation to the February 2016 assessment period appears flawed.

The result might possibly have been different under the new form of reg.61. Sub-paragraph (c) now makes it clearer that it applies when no information has been received from HMRC "in an assessment period", making the crucial time the end of each assessment period. So, "in" the January 2016 assessment period, no information was received from HMRC. That would release the power in para.(4) to adjust the amount of employed earnings to be attributed to that assessment period by adding the payment made on January 31, 2016, despite the existence of para.(2) (b) (see the notes to paras (2) and (5)). But crucially, the new power in para.(7) to make consequential adjustments would allow the removal of that payment from the assessment for the February 2016 assessment period. That would "avoid duplication". And even if sub-para.(c) did not apply, the situation in *RW* would appear to fall within the new para.(5), the January 31, 2016 payment having been reported to HMRC late, or possibly in the wrong assessment period (see below). That would specifically allow that payment to be treated as employed earnings in the assessment period in which it was received.

Paragraph (5)

The new para.(5) is the first major departure from the previous structure, although it seems to have limited effect. It gives the Secretary of State (and thus a tribunal on appeal) discretion, where a payment has been reported late or in the wrong assessment period, to treat the payment as employed earnings in the

2.231

assessment period in which it was received. In the context, "reported" must mean reported to HMRC under the RTI system. Paragraph (5) applies whatever the usual pay interval; it is not restricted to those, like the *Johnson* claimants, who are paid monthly. However, it cannot solve the systemic problem identified in *Pantellerisco* (above) for those paid four-weekly of there inevitably being one assessment period each year containing two usual pay-days, which was left unadjusted by that litigation.

The power given by para.(5) is limited to treating a payment as part of employed earnings in the assessment period in which it was received. That would assist in equivalent circumstances to those *RW* (see immediately above). Paragraph (5) does not in itself authorise any more extensive reallocation. For instance, take a claimant with an assessment period running from the 28th of one month to the 27th of the next, who is usually paid on the 28th of the month and is paid their December salary on December 23. If the employer, say because office systems were down over the period, did not report the payment through the RTI system until January 3, that would appear to fall within the "late report" category. But para.(5) would only allow the payment to be allocated to the assessment period including December 23, i.e. the same assessment period to which the payment received as usual on November 28 would have been allocated. For the payment to be allocated to the assessment period beginning on December 28, to avoid the *Johnson* irrationality, there would apparently have to be recourse to para.(6), with its limitation to those paid on a regular monthly basis. But the operation of para.(5) brings in the general power to make any "other adjustments" in new para.(7), which might open up the possibility of reallocation to an assessment period other than that of receipt and of application to claimants paid otherwise than monthly. But what then would have been the point of the restriction in effect in para.(5)?

Presumably, para.(5) is not made expressly subject to para.(6) because both provisions are discretionary, thus allowing the Secretary of State and tribunals to apply whichever is more appropriate, as the justice of the case requires. But para.(6) only applies to claimants who are paid on a regular monthly basis, not to claimants paid at any other intervals. Although para.(2)(b), requiring the taking of employed earnings to be nil in respect of any assessment period in which no information is received by the DWP from HMRC, has not been made expressly subject to paras (5) to (7), that result must presumably follow in order to allow those provisions to operate (see the notes to para.(2) above).

It is no doubt easy enough to identify when a report to HMRC is made late, but what is meant by a report being made "in the wrong assessment period" remains obscure. Presumably, it covers only an assessment period other than that in which the report ought to have been made in accordance with HMRC guidance/instructions, rather than wrongness in any wider sense. But if the report is made after the "right" assessment period, the case would appear already to be covered by the lateness provision. Possibly, there could be some independent operation if the report was made before the "right" assessment period, but there would still be the limitation as to the date to which the payment can be allocated, subject to the possible application of para.(7). There is no guidance as to the meaning of "the wrong assessment period" or example of the application of the rule in Memo ADM 27/20.

Paragraph (6)

2.232   The new para.(6) is the main provision designed to deal with the problem identified by the Court of Appeal in *Johnson*. It is restricted to employees paid on a regular monthly (calendar monthly: Interpretation Act 1978 Sch.1) basis. That formula, including the word "basis", must entail that the scope is not restricted to those usually paid on the same day each month, so long as their pay is calculated per month and they are paid a month at a time. Then, if more than one payment is reported (to HMRC) in any one assessment period, the Secretary of State and a tribunal on appeal may, for the purposes of maintaining a regular pattern, allocate one (but only one) of those payments to a different assessment period, either earlier or later. The discretion, particularly in conjunction with the general power in new para.(7) to make any other adjustments, is fairly open, so long as a purpose (main purpose?) is to maintain a regular pattern (of allocation of monthly payments). Although para.(2)(b), requiring the taking of employed earnings to be nil in respect of any assessment period in which no information is received by the DWP from HMRC, has not been made expressly subject to paras (5) and (6), that result must presumably follow in order to allow those provisions to operate (see the notes to para.(2) above).

See the note to para.(5) above for an example of how para.(6) might be applied. Note that it is not necessary for a report to have been made to HMRC on any wrong date or that there has been a "non-banking day salary shift" in the strictest sense. All that is necessary is that more than one payment has been reported for a monthly-paid claimant in the same assessment period. If the pattern of usual payment on the last working day of the month produces that result, reporting on the two usual pay-days will have been in accordance with HMRC guidance/instructions and there will not have been a "shift" in the sense of a departure from the usual pay-day, but para.(6) can be applied. It might just be that payments other than monthly salary could trigger the potential application of para.(6), for instance if a claimant received a bonus or a reimbursement of non-allowable expenses on a different date from the usual monthly pay-day. But in such a case, there would be no need to exercise the discretion to reallocate such a payment.

Paragraph (7)

The effect of the power in the new para.(7) to make other adjustments in the calculation of employed earnings has been discussed in the notes to paras (4)–(6) above.

2.233

Right of appeal

The previous para.(6), apparently giving a power to make adjustments where decisions are made under reg.41(3) of the Decisions and Appeals Regulations 2013, arguably unnecessarily, has not been reproduced in the new form of reg.61, but a footnote to the preamble to SI 2020/1138 does refer to reg.41(1) and to s.159D(1)(b)(vi) of the SSAA 1992 (effect of alterations affecting universal credit). Under the latter provision (for which see Vol.III of this series) an alteration (i.e., an increase or decrease) in the amount of a claimant's employed earnings as a result of information provided to the Secretary of State by HMRC takes effect without any further decision by the Secretary of State. However, if the claimant disputes the figure used in accordance with reg.55 to calculate their employed earnings in any assessment period, they can ask the Secretary of State to give a decision in relation to that assessment period (which must be given within 14 days of the request, or as soon as practicable thereafter).

2.234

The point of that provision might appear to be to give the claimant a right of appeal, but there are obstacles to such a conclusion in the unnecessary obscurities in the chain of legislation involved. Paragraph 6(b)(v) of Sch.2 to the SSA 1998 (Pt I of this volume) provides that no appeal lies against a decision as to the amount of benefit to which a person is entitled where the amount is determined by an alteration of a kind referred to in s.159D(1)(b) of the SSAA. Thus, even though the alteration is given effect through a Secretary of State's decision, rather than without such a decision as in the general application of s.159D, at first sight there can be no appeal against the decision. It would appear that para.6(b)(v) applies as much to a decision removing entitlement entirely as well as to one reducing the amount of entitlement. The claimant would then be restricted to applying for revision on the "any time" ground in reg.10(a) of the Decisions and Appeals Regulations 2013 (with consequently no right of appeal if unsuccessful) or to an application for judicial review.

However, that effect would arguably be inconsistent with art.6 of the ECHR (fair trial) under the Human Rights Act 1998, on the basis that revision or judicial review would not be adequate alternatives to a right to appeal. There would then be an obligation under s.3 to interpret legislation in a way compatible with ECHR rights. It is possible to interpret the phrase "an alteration of a kind referred to" in s.159D(1)(b) of the SSAA 1992 as used in para.6(b) of Sch.2 to the SSA 1998 as only applying to an alteration that is not merely referred to in s.159D(1)(b) but is not subject to any exception or condition that requires a decision to be given by the Secretary of State. Subsection (1) of s.159D makes its effect subject to such exceptions and conditions as may be prescribed. Regulation 41(3) of the Decisions and Appeals Regulations 2013 may legitimately be regarded as such an exception or condition. Thus, if the process under reg.41(3) leads to the giving of a decision by the Secretary of State, para.6(b) can be interpreted as not standing in the way of there being a right of appeal in the normal way.

That interpretation of para.6(b) of Sch.2 to the SSA 1998 could also lessen, but not completely remove, the adverse consequences of the wider effect of s.159D(1)(b) of the SSAA 1992. Section 159D(1)(b) on alterations to existing awards of universal credit applies to a much wider range of circumstances than the equivalent provisions for other benefits. In addition to alterations in the statutory rates of universal credit or of new style ESA or JSA or other benefit income, head (iii) applies to an alteration in any amount to be deducted in respect of earned income under s.8(3)(a) of the WRA 2012. "Earned income", in accordance with reg.52, covers not just employed earnings, but also remuneration or profit derived from a trade, profit or vocation (i.e. self-employed earnings) or from any other paid work. Thus the prohibition in para.6(b)(v) of Sch.2 would appear to have applied to the circumstances covered by reg.41 even if those circumstances had not been prescribed for the purposes of s.159D(1)(b)(vi). Further, and more seriously, the prohibition on its face extends to any decision on an existing award turning on an alteration for any reason in the amount of any kind of earned income (all of which fall to be deducted from the maximum amount of universal credit under s.8(3)(a)). There is some doubt whether reg.41(3) of the Decisions and Appeals Regulations, establishing the exception from or condition relating to s.159D(1)(b) applies only in relation to cases where there is a dispute under reg.61(6) about the information provided by HMRC and not to other disputes about the amount of employed earnings. Does reg.41(3) only operate as a qualification to reg.41(1) on s.159D(b)(vi) cases or does it have a stand-alone operation on its own terms, which could then apply to any dispute about the amount of employed earnings? The obligation under s.3 of the Human Rights Act 1998 to interpret legislation so as to be compatible with ECHR rights would probably lead to the second alternative being adopted, protecting the right of appeal in those cases. However, can the terms of reg.41(3), with the express reference to reg.55 of the Universal Credit Regulations and employed earnings, possibly be interpreted as also applying to the other forms of earned income that count under s.8(3)(a) of the WRA 2012, i.e. self-employed earnings, other paid work and, it appears, notional earned income (see reg.52)? That would arguably entail the addition or substitution of too many words changing the substance of the provision to be considered part of any legitimate process of interpretation. If reg.41(3) is thus restricted to employed earnings, there is nothing to prevent the operation of s.159D(1)(b)(iii) and para.6(b) in requiring alterations in amounts of self-employed earnings, other paid work and notional earned incomes to take effect without any Secretary of State decision and therefore without anything to appeal against. If that outcome would be considered to entail an inconsistency with art.6 (fair trial) of the ECHR, then the argument at the level of the First-tier or Upper Tribunal would probably have to be that the terms of the secondary legislation cannot be allowed to stand in the way of the provision of a fair trial in any individual case, without seeking to say how the defect in the legislation should be remedied generally.

See also para.22 of Sch.1 to the Decisions and Appeals Regulations 2013 which provides that a supersession decision made where a claimant's employed earnings have reduced and they have provided the information for the purpose of calculating those earnings at the times required by the Secretary of State takes effect from the first day of the assessment period in which that change occurred.

Gainful self-employment

[¹Minimum income floor

62.—(1) This regulation applies to a claimant who—

(a) is in gainful self-employment (see regulation 64); and

(b) would, apart from this regulation [⁴or regulation 90], fall within section 22 of the Act (claimants subject to all work-related requirements).

(2) Where this regulation applies to a single claimant, for any assessment period in respect of which the claimant's earned income is less than their individual threshold, the claimant is to be treated as having earned income equal to that threshold.

(3) Where this regulation applies to a claimant who is a member of a couple, for any assessment period in respect of which—

(a) the claimant's earned income is less than their individual threshold; and

(b) the couple's combined earned income is less than the couple threshold,

the claimant is to be treated as having earned income equal to their individual threshold minus any amount by which that amount of earned income combined with their partner's earned income would exceed the couple threshold.

(4) In this regulation, references to the claimant's individual threshold and to the couple threshold are to the amounts set out in regulation 90(2) and 90(3) respectively, converted to net [² . . .] amounts by—

(a) [² . . .]

(b) deducting such amount for income tax and national insurance contributions as the Secretary of State considers appropriate.

[³(4A) Where this regulation applies in respect of an assessment period in which surplus earnings are treated as an amount of earned income under regulation 54A (surplus earnings), that amount is to be added to the claimant's earned income before this regulation is applied and, in the case of joint claimants, it is to be added to the earned income of either member of the couple so as to produce the lowest possible amount of combined earned income after this regulation is applied.]

(5) An assessment period referred to in this regulation does not include an assessment period which falls wholly within a start-up period or begins or ends in a start-up period.]

2.235

AMENDMENTS

1. Universal Credit and Miscellaneous Amendments (No.2) Regulations 2014 (SI 2014/2888) reg.4(5) (November 26, 2014, or in the case of existing awards, the first assessment period beginning on or after November 26, 2014).

2. Universal Credit and Miscellaneous Amendments Regulations 2015 (SI 2015/1754) reg.2(5) (November 4, 2015, or in the case of existing awards, the first assessment period beginning on or after November 4, 2015).

3. Universal Credit (Surpluses and Self-employed Losses) (Digital Service) Amendment Regulations 2015 (SI 2015/345) reg.2(3) (April 11, 2018).

4. Universal Credit (Childcare Costs and Minimum Income Floor) (Amendment) Regulations 2019 (SI 2019/1249) reg.3 (October 3, 2019).

DEFINITIONS

"assessment period"—see WRA 2012, ss.40 and 7(2) and reg.21.
"claimant"—see WRA 2012, s.40.
"couple"—see WRA 2012, ss.39 and 40.
"earned income"—see reg.52.
"gainful self-employment"—see regs 53(1) and 64.
"individual threshold"—see regs 2 and 90(2).
"joint claimants"—see WRA 2012 s.40.
"national insurance contribution"—see reg.2.
"start-up period"—see regs 53(1) and 63.
"work-related requirement"—see WRA 2012, ss.40 and 13(2).

GENERAL NOTE

Temporary coronavirus provisions

2.236   The last of the temporary coronavirus provisions relevant to the minimum income floor expired on July 31, 2022. See previous editions of this volume for the details.

2.237   This regulation, authorised by para.4(1), (3)(a) and (4) of Sch.1 to the WRA 2012, provides for the "minimum income floor" which applies to certain self-employed claimants and deems them to be receiving that level of income although their actual earnings from self-employment, plus other earned income, if any, are lower. It is an anti-abuse provision which was presumably introduced partly because of the difficulties of checking the hours of work and takings of the self-employed and partly to provide an incentive against sitting back in unproductive self-employment while relying on universal credit to make up income. The operation of the rule has been considerably affected from April 2018 by the operation of the provisions in reg.54A for spreading surplus earnings and in regs 57(2) and 57A on unused losses in self-employment.

A judicial review challenge to the general operation of reg.62, based on alleged differences in treatment of the self-employed and employed earners was rejected by the Administrative Court (Laing J) in *R. (on the application of Parkin) v Secretary of State for Work and Pensions* [2019] EWHC 2356 (Admin).

Ms Parkin had worked in the theatre as a self-employed person for some years before she claimed universal credit in 2017. Her profits in the 2017/18 tax year were £2,306 and in 2018/19 £2,842.24. She also had some earnings as an employee. A minimum income floor (MIF) of £861.11 per month was applied to her on the basis that she was in gainful self-employment within the meaning of reg.64. Her appeal against that on the ground that she was not in gainful self-employment was refused by a First-tier Tribunal in May 2019. Over the 20 months of her universal credit award down to June 2019 she received £5,318.65 less in universal credit for herself and the one child included in the award than if she had been employed with equivalent earnings and £610.86 less than if she had not been employed at all.

The first ground of Ms Parkin's judicial review challenge to the effect of reg.62 was that there was a breach of art.14 of the ECHR. Laing J accepted that art.8 (respect for family life) and probably art.1 of Protocol 1 (protection of property) was engaged and that there was a difference in treatment between self-employed and employed earners. However, she held that the self-employed and employed earners were not in relevantly analogous circumstances and that, even if that was wrong, the difference in treatment was not manifestly without reasonable foundation and so was justified. The essence of her reasoning appears in paras 103, 107 and 108 of the judgment:

"103. It is clear that one of the intentions of the statutory scheme is to make work pay, and to encourage claimants to do more productive activities in order to encourage them, over time, to reduce their reliance on benefits. The practical effects of the legal distinctions between the two groups mean that a work requirement imposed on an employee has an immediate, predictable and measurable effect. There is no directly effective practical equivalent in the case of a self-employed claimant. If Parliament and the executive wanted to achieve the aims I have described in the case of self-employed claimants, a different mechanism had to be designed in order to influence their behaviour. I therefore consider that employed and self-employed claimants are not in relevantly analogous situations for the purposes of this scheme. I also consider, for that reason, that I can, and should, conclude at this stage of the analysis that this part of the claim fails.

107. The question then is whether the MIF, in particular, because it applies to [gainfully self-employed] claimants and not to employed or unemployed claimants, is [manifestly without reasonable foundation]. As I have said in paragraph 103, above, a work requirement and an [individual threshold] amount to a practical and objective tool for influencing the behaviour of employed claimants. Their combined effects are visible and can be measured. The differences between claimants which flow from their decisions to be employed or self-employed mean that a work requirement and an [individual threshold] cannot produce the same effects for self-employed claimants. The imposition of a work requirement on a self-employed claimant would not necessarily make his business more profitable, which is what is at issue.

108. The MIF, however, is such a mechanism. Its effect coheres with the aims I have described, because it encourages self-employed claimants who are in [gainful self-employment] and who wish to claim UC, but whose enterprises consistently generate low profits, to think carefully about whether they should continue to be in [gainful self-employment]. The MIF encourages such thought because its effect is to treat a self-employed claimant as generating profits equivalent to what he would earn from employment at the [national minimum wage], whether or not he in fact generates such profits. It encourages a rational claimant in that position to ask whether continuing in [gainful self-employment] is in his own best interests, and whether he should take up employment instead, or change the balance of his activities between self-employment and employment so that, while continuing to be self-employed, self-employment is no longer his main employment, with the result that he would cease to be in [gainful self-employment] for the purposes of the scheme, and be subject to work requirements instead."

The same reasoning supported the rejection of the argument that the MIF regulations were irrational at common law. There had also been compliance with s.149 of the Equality Act 2010 by reference to the impact of the universal credit scheme as a whole.

It may be arguable that the judge's suggestions about how a claimant could alter the balance between employment and self-employment, so that self-employment would no longer be the main employment and therefore fall outside the meaning of gainful self-employment (see further in the notes to reg.64) and the reach of the MIF, are not entirely realistic. However, that would probably not be enough to undermine the reasoning completely. Note that self-employment falls outside the meaning of gainful self-employment if there is not an expectation of profit.

A new form of reg.62 was introduced on November 26, 2014 in order to make "clearer provision about the calculation of the MIF [minimum income floor] when a self-employed person is a member of a couple (or when both members of a couple are self-employed)" (see the Explanatory Memorandum which accompanies SI 2014/2888). It is a distinct improvement on the previous form of reg.62. However, some confusion still remains, partly because the phrase "individual threshold" as used in reg.62 does not have quite the same meaning as that phrase in reg.90, even though reg.62(4) cross-refers to reg.90. This is because under para.(4)(b) of this regulation "appropriate" deductions for income tax and NI contributions may be made when calculating a claimant's individual threshold, which is not the case under reg.90 (see below).

There was a further amendment, said to implement the original policy intention, with effect from October 3, 2019. In the condition in para.(1)(b) for the application of the MIF that the claimant would be subject to all work-related requirements, not only is the effect of reg.62 itself to be ignored but also the effect of reg.90 on earnings thresholds. See the notes below on *Would be subject to all work-related requirements*.

Regulation 62 will only apply if in any assessment period a claimant

- is in "gainful self-employment" (as defined in reg.64) (para.(1)(a)); *and*

- is not in a "start-up period" (see reg.63) (para. (5)); *and*

- would, apart from this regulation, fall within s.22 WRA 2012 (claimant subject to all work-related requirements) (para.(1)(b)); *and*

- in the case of a single claimant, their self-employed earnings, together with any other earned income (as defined in reg.52), are below their individual threshold (para.(2)); *or*

  in the case of a couple, their self-employed earnings, together with any other earned income, are below their individual threshold, and the couple's combined earned income is below the couple threshold (para.(3)).

If all four of those conditions are met (subject to the temporary coronavirus provisions) then claimants are deemed to have earned income equal to the threshold even though their actual earned income is lower.

Gainful self-employment

2.238   For what might or might not count as gainful self-employment and for the effect of reg.2(1)(b) and (c) of the Coronavirus Further Measures Regulations, see the notes to reg.64. The conditions in reg.64 go a good way beyond the simple issue of whether the activity is carried on in the expectation of gain and must be carefully considered. In particular, the trade, profession or vocation must be the claimant's main employment and must be organised, developed and regular.

Not in start-up period

2.239   See the notes to reg.63 for what is a start-up period and how long it can last. In brief, following the September 26, 2020 amendment to reg.63, it can start where a claimant who is in gainful self-employment has not previously been subject to the MIF in relation to the trade, profession or vocation that is now the main employment and is taking active steps to increase the earnings from that self-employment to the level of the individual threshold. Then the period lasts for 12 months starting with that assessment period unless the claimant ceases to be in gainful self-employment or ceases to take the active steps to increase earnings. Note that with effect from March 30, 2020 down to at least July 31, 2021, the Secretary of State had a discretion (intended for use where expedient as a consequence of the coronavirus outbreak) to extend a start-up period as appropriate (reg.2(1)(d) of the Coronavirus Further Measures Regulations).

Would be subject to all work-related requirements

2.240   The requirement that the claimant would, apart from the operation of the MIF or reg.90, fall within s.22 of the WRA 2012 and thus not be exempted from the imposition of any work-related requirement adds an important limitation, that must not be overlooked in a focus on the level of earned income in the particular assessment period (see further below). The final condition is that the claimant or claimants' earned income is below the reg.62 individual or couple threshold as appropriate.

410

It must, because of the third condition (in para.(1)(b)), be asked in all cases whether some provision in or under ss.19—22 exempts the claimant from one or more work-related requirements. In particular, prior to October 3, 2019 the operation of reg.90 needed to be considered. As discussed below, this provision exempts claimants from all work-related requirements if their monthly earnings before any deduction for income tax, national insurance contributions or relievable pension contributions (reg.90(6)(a)) at least equal their individual threshold under reg.90(2), called the conditionality earnings threshold. In the great majority of cases anyone with earnings at that level would not fall within the scope of reg.62, but it should be noted that reg.90(6)(b) requires, in cases where earned income fluctuates or is likely to fluctuate, a monthly averaging over any identifiable cycle or otherwise over three months or such other period as may enable the average to be determined more accurately. That can apply to earnings from employment or other paid work as well as to earnings from self-employment. However, it is in the nature of self-employment in particular that earned income (i.e. actual receipts less allowable expenses in each assessment period) will fluctuate month by month, even in businesses that are well established and large scale. Thus if in a particular assessment period the amount of a claimant's earned income fell below the reg.62 individual threshold it could not immediately be assumed that the MIF would apply. The monthly average could at least equal the reg.90 individual threshold (the conditionality earnings threshold) so that the claimant remained exempted from all work-related requirements.

The position changed with the October 2019 amendment so that if a claimant is only exempted from work-related requirements through the operation of reg.90 that does not prevent the application of the MIF. The change was said by the DWP to restore the original policy intention and was explained in the Explanatory Memorandum as follows:

"7.9 [The amendment is] to make clear that a reference to a claimant in the All Work Related Requirements conditionality group includes those who are exempt from the requirement to look for work only because their earnings exceed the Conditionality Earnings Threshold.
7.10 The Conditionality Earnings Threshold is only relevant to employed claimants and, as such, has no role in the application of the Minimum Income Floor. For example, a claimant could meet the Conditionality Earnings Threshold as a result of average earnings over a period of time if they are an employed earner. However, self-employed universal credit claimants are expected to plan for fluctuations in income in the same way as all other self-employed people must do and which is part of running a sustainable business. Gainfully self-employed claimants are expected to earn at or above the set assumed level in each assessment period and, where earnings fall short of this, the Minimum Income Floor is applied."

If the Explanatory Memorandum intended to suggest that reg.90 only applies to employed earners, that is incorrect. "Earned income" is plainly defined in reg.52 to cover both earnings derived from a contract of service or office and earnings derived from self-employment. So the suggestion must have been more that the mechanism of reg.90 was inadequate in itself to apply the appropriate pressure to self-employed claimants either to abandon unproductive self-employment or to make it more productive. That may be debateable, but what is clear is that the amendment has from October 2019 onwards rendered redundant the discussion above of whether the averaging provision in reg.90(6) might prevent the application of the MIF in an assessment period in which earnings fell below the MIF.

The reference in para.(1)(b) to "apart from this regulation" is necessary because of reg.90(5), which exempts any claimant who is treated by reg.62 as having earned income from all work-related requirements (by putting them within s.19 of the WRA 2012). If it were not for that qualification there would be an endless loop by which application of the MIF led to the conditions for its application not being met. The effect of reg.90(5) should not, though, be forgotten while the MIF is in operation.

Actual earned income below individual or couple's threshold

2.241   Although "earned income" is defined in reg.52(a) merely in terms of the remuneration or profits derived from employment, self-employment or other paid work, it would seem that paras (2) and (3) must be taken as referring to the amount of earned income to be taken into account for universal credit purposes, thus requiring the deduction of income tax, national insurance contributions and relievable pension contributions (employed earnings: reg.55(5) (plus payroll giving); self-employed earnings: reg.57(2)). But note that under para.(4)(b) there is no power to deduct relievable pension contributions or payroll giving from the individual or couple threshold. Claimants who made large pension contributions might therefore have particular need of the possibility that the MIF does not apply because they are exempted from all work-related requirement under reg.90. Although the MIF cannot apply unless the self-employment is the claimant's main employment, employed earnings or income from other paid work may come into the calculation, especially in the case of joint claimants.

The new (April 2018) para.(4A) confirms that where surplus earnings calculated under reg.54A are to be applied in any assessment period they are to be taken into account as part of claimants' earned income for reg.62 purposes. If the surplus earnings are sufficient on their own to wipe out entitlement to universal credit that consequence does not matter. If the surplus earnings on their own do not have that effect, then they may, depending on their level, help lift earned income up to the individual or couple threshold, so that MIF does not apply and actual earnings plus surplus earnings are taken against the maximum amount of universal credit. Income deemed to exist by reg.62 does not count in the calculation of surplus earnings under reg.54A (reg.54A(5)). The new (April 2018) provision on unused losses for the self-employed (reg.57A) may work in the opposite direction. Unused losses (unused in the sense that a claimant's self-employed earnings to be counted against the maximum amount in the assessment period in which received cannot be less than nil) from any past assessment period can now operate to reduce the amount of self-employed earnings as calculated under reg.57(2). That could have the effect of taking the amount of earned income in the current assessment period below the individual or couple threshold and triggering the application of the MIF when it would not be triggered on the current earnings. The fairness entailed in the operation of reg.57A on its own would be impaired by that. Fluctuations in earnings, and in particular the new taking into account of fluctuations in terms of past losses by the self-employed, are likely to have unpredictable, and sometimes harsh effects, on the application of the MIF.

Some claimants might think of forming limited companies of which they are the sole or main employee and director in order to pursue the business that would otherwise have been the trade, profession or vocation followed as a self-employed person, aiming not to be self-employed at all and so free of the MIF rules. In most cases, that does not work because of the effect of reg.77(3)(b) and (c). Where a person stands in a position analogous to that of a sole trader or partner in relation to a company carrying on a trade or a property business the company's income or the claimant's share of it is to be treated as the claimant's income and calculated under reg.57 as if it were self-employed earnings and, if the claimant's activities in the course of the trade are their main employment, reg.62 is to apply. See the notes to regs 57 and 77 for some complications and the limited exceptions in reg.77(5).

For a claimant's individual threshold for the purposes of reg.62, the starting point is reg.90(2). This provides that a claimant's individual threshold is the hourly rate of the national minimum wage for a claimant of that age multiplied by, in the case of a claimant who would otherwise be subject to all work-related requirements under s.22 of the WRA 2012, the expected number of hours per week (usually 35, see reg.88). In the case of a claimant who would otherwise fall within ss.20 or 21, the multiplier is 16. That can be relevant when one of joint claimants is subject to all work-related requirements, but their partner is not (see below for couples). This amount is then multiplied by 52 and divided by 12 (to make it monthly), from which is deducted "such amount for income tax and national insurance contributions as the Secretary of State considers appropriate" (para.(4)). Presumably this will normally be the amount for income tax and NI contributions that would be payable if the claimant's actual earned income was at this level but para.(4)(b) does not actually say that.

If the claimant's earned income is less than this figure (the minimum income floor) they will be treated as having earned income equal to this figure (para.(2)). If it equals or exceeds this figure reg.62 does not apply and the claimant's actual earnings will be taken into account in the normal way.

Example 1

Michael is single, aged 25 and a self-employed plumber. He declares earnings of £580 (£700 less permitted expenses of £120) for the current assessment period. He also has employed earnings of £200 a month as he works in a hardware store on Saturday mornings. His minimum income floor is £1,410.00 a month (35 hours a week x £10.42 x 52 ÷ 12, rounded down, less £170.00 for notional income tax and NI contributions). As his self-employed earnings and employed earnings added together amount to £780, this is less than his minimum income floor and so he is treated as having earnings of £1,410.00 and his universal credit is assessed on that basis.

2.242

In the case of a couple, the position is more complicated. Under para.(3), in addition to the condition that the claimant's earned income is less than their individual threshold (as calculated under para.(4)), the couple's combined earned income must also be less than the couple threshold (as calculated under para.(4)) for reg.62 to apply. The starting point for calculating the couple threshold under para.(4) is reg.90(3). This provides that in the case of joint claimants their individual thresholds are added together (see reg.90(3)(b) for how the threshold is calculated in the case of a person who is a member of a couple but claims as a single person by virtue of reg.3(3)). This amount is then multiplied by 52 and divided by 12 (to make it monthly), from which is deducted "such amount for income tax and national insurance contributions as the Secretary of State considers appropriate" (para.(4)(b)).

If these two conditions are met, the claimant will be treated as having earned income equal to their individual threshold, less any amount by which that deemed earned income combined with their partner's earned income exceeds the couple threshold (para.(3)).

Example 2

Rafiq and Maggie are a couple (both over 25) and they have one child, Charlie, who is aged 2. Rafiq has a photography business and Maggie works in a pub in the evenings. Maggie's earnings are £800 and Rafiq's are £500 in the current assessment period.

Maggie has been accepted as the "responsible carer" for Charlie and so falls within s.21(1)(aa) of the WRA 2012. Her individual threshold is therefore £722.00 (16 hours a week x £10.42 x 52 ÷ 12, rounded down, = £722.00), with no income tax or NI contribution deductions at this level of earnings).

Rafiq's individual threshold is £1,410.00 a month (35 hours a week x £10.42 x 52 ÷ 12, rounded down, less £170.00 for notional income tax and NI contributions).

Rafiq and Maggie's actual combined earnings are £1,300 (£500 + £800). This is below their joint earnings threshold of £2,132.00 (£1,410.00 for Rafiq + £722.00 for Maggie).

However, adding Rafiq's minimum income floor to Maggie's actual earnings gives £2,210.00 (£1,410.00 + £800). That is £78.00 above their joint earnings threshold of £2,132.00, so Rafiq is treated as having earnings of £1,332.00

(£1,410.00 less £78.00). Their universal credit is assessed on the basis of earned income of £2,132.00 (Rafiq's deemed earnings of £1,332.00 plus Maggie's actual earnings of £800).

Note that if reg.62 does apply in an assessment period, a claimant will not be subject to work-related requirements in that assessment period (see reg.90(1) and (5)).

Note also that income a claimant is deemed to have by virtue of reg.62 does not count as earned income for the purpose of the benefit cap (see reg.82(4)).

See the notes to reg.61 for discussion of whether any alterations of existing awards resulting from increases or reductions in the amount of earned income apart from employed earnings, which could include such changes resulting from the application of the MIF, are appealable.

Start-up period

2.243   **63.**—(1) A "start-up period" is a period of 12 months and applies from the beginning of the assessment period in which the Secretary of State determines that a claimant is in gainful self-employment where—

[¹(a) regulation 62 (minimum income floor) has not previously applied to the claimant in relation to the trade, profession or vocation which is currently the claimant's main employment (whether in relation to the current award or a previous award); and]

(b) the claimant is taking active steps to increase their earnings from that employment to the level of the claimant's individual threshold (see regulation 90).

(2) But no start-up period may apply in relation to a claimant where a start-up period has previously applied in relation to that claimant, whether in relation to the current award or any previous award of universal credit, unless that previous start-up period—

(a) began more than 5 years before the beginning of assessment period referred to in paragraph (1); and

(b) applied in relation to a different trade, profession or vocation which the claimant has ceased to carry on.

(3) The Secretary of State may terminate a start-up period at any time if the person is no longer in gainful self-employment or is no longer taking the steps referred to in paragraph (1)(b).

AMENDMENT

1. Universal Credit (Managed Migration Pilot and Miscellaneous Amendments) Regulations 2019 (SI 2019/1152) reg.6(1) (September 26, 2020).

DEFINITIONS

"assessment period"—see WRA 2012 ss.40 and 7(2) and reg.21.
"claimant"—see WRA 2012 s.40.
"gainful self-employment"—see regs 53(1) and 64.
"individual threshold"—see regs 2 and 90(2).

GENERAL NOTE

Temporary coronavirus provisions

2.244   The last of the temporary coronavirus provisions relevant to the minimum income floor expired on July 31, 2022. See previous editions of this volume for the details.

If the claimant is in a "start-up period", the minimum income floor does not apply even if they are in gainful self-employment (as defined in reg.64) (see reg.62(5)).   2.245

A start-up period is a period of 12 months starting from the beginning of the assessment period in which the Secretary of State decides that the claimant is in gainful self-employment, provided that the claimant (i) had not previously been subject to the MIF in relation to the trade, profession or vocation that is now their main employment (on which see the notes to reg.64 on gainful self-employment); and (ii) is taking active steps to increase their earnings from that self-employment to the level of their individual threshold under reg.90, i.e., the level at which they will no longer have to meet work-related requirements (para.(1)).

See the notes in the 2020/21 edition of what was then Vol.V of this series for the position before the introduction of the present form of para.(1)(a) on September 26, 2020. It was then a condition that the relevant trade, profession or vocation had been begun in the previous 12 months, thus excluding from the protection of the start-up period claimants whose self-employment was long-standing, even though they had not claimed universal credit in the past. The amendment appears to dilute the encouragement not to continue with self-employment in some disorganised or irregular way, so avoiding the application of the MIF by not being in "gainful self-employment", that the old rule had supplied. That encouragement now resides in the condition of taking active steps to increase earnings under para.(1)(b) and the power in para.(3) to terminate a start-up period if that condition is no longer met (see the further discussion below). The new form of para.(1)(a) has also rendered redundant the special rule applied in "managed migration" cases by reg.59 of the Transitional Provisions Regulations 2014 and that provision has been revoked from the same date.

The new form of para.(1)(a) has also affected the practical scope of application of para.(2) by directly excluding from the protection of the start-up period anyone who has ever previously been subject to the MIF in relation to the current trade, profession or vocation. Para.(2) provides that there cannot be a start-up period if a start-up period has previously applied to the claimant unless that previous period *both* began more than five years before the assessment period of the Secretary of State's determination of gainful self-employment *and* applied in relation to a different trade, profession or vocation from the current one. If any previous start-up period in relation to the same trade, profession or vocation was followed by an application of the MIF, no matter how far in the past, the condition in para.(1)(a) would already have been failed. So para.(2) can only bite in relation to the same trade, profession or vocation if for some reason (such as ceasing to claim or ceasing to being gainfully employed) there was no application of the MIF, but a start-up period had begun to run. If the current main employment is different from the previous trade, profession or vocation (a test that might be very difficult to apply in practice if there have been changes in some, but not all, elements of the business in question), then the condition in para.(1)(a) is met, but para.(2) would still prevent the initiation of a current start-up period if a previous start-up period began within the five years before the assessment period of the Secretary of State's current determination of gainful self-employment.

But it must always be remembered that if a claimant is making a first claim for universal credit para.(2) cannot have any operation and the new para.(1)(a) must by definition also be satisfied.

Although it is often said that the start-up period only protects the first 12 months of self-employment from the operation of the MIF, in fact the combination of the conditions in para.(1) can extend much longer from the start of the particular self-employment in issue. First, any period of self-employment before the start of entitlement to universal credit is irrelevant. Then, the forward 12 months only starts to run with the assessment period in which the Secretary of State recognises that the claimant is in gainful self-employment as defined in reg.64. Before that date the claimant needs no protection from the MIF because regulation 62 will not apply (reg.62(1)(a)), although of course any profits from the self-employment will count as earned income.

If the claimant is no longer in gainful self-employment, or is not taking active steps to increase their earnings as required by para.(1)(b), the Secretary of State can end the start-up period (para.(3)).

In the first case, the MIF could no longer be applied, as would also be so if the claimant ceased to be subject to all work-related requirements. It is not quite clear what consequences should follow if the Secretary of State chooses not to exercise the discretion to terminate the start-up period. Presumably, the period, being defined in para.(1) simply as the period of 12 months from the beginning of the relevant assessment period, continues to run despite the non-application of the MIF or even the ending of entitlement to universal credit (see ADM para.H4102, example 2). That position is supported by the perceived need for the power in para.(3) to terminate a start-up period if the claimant is no longer taking active steps to increase earnings in accordance with para.(1)(b). Then, if the other conditions for the application of the MIF became satisfied again within that 12 months, the claimant would be able to benefit from the protection of the start-up period rule for the remainder of the 12 months. If the Secretary of State chooses to terminate the start-up period, which power is restricted to circumstances where the claimant is no longer in gainful employment, not extending to ceasing to be subject to all work-related requirements or to be entitled to universal credit at all, then on a successful reclaim within a year, the protection of the start-up period rule would be excluded by para.(2)(a). Any specific challenge to any such choice by the Secretary of State to terminate a start-up period on that ground would probably, because the determination would not affect the claimant's entitlement to universal credit or its amount, have to be by way of judicial review.

In the second case, providing that the circumstances do not point to a ceasing to be in gainful self-employment (which would lead to the non-application of the whole MIF rule and the choices discussed above), the power to terminate the start-up period would appear to be the only sanction to enforce the condition in para.(1)(b) of taking active steps to increase earnings up to the level of the individual threshold in reg.90, known as the conditionality earnings threshold (see the notes to reg.90). The ADM gives no guidance as to what might or might not be regarded as "active steps". The steps must be rationally directed to moving the level of earnings to that level at least, in general that of the national minimum wage for the weekly numbers of hours expected of the claimant under reg.88. Presumably, for the para.(3) power to be exercised the claimant must no longer be taking any active steps to that end, rather than merely taking less than the work coach considers reasonable.

Meaning of "gainful self-employment"

2.246
64. A claimant is in gainful self-employment for the purposes of regulations 62 and 63 where the Secretary of State has determined that—

(a) the claimant is carrying on a trade, profession or vocation as their main employment;

(b) their earnings from that trade, profession or vocation are self-employed earnings; and

(c) the trade, profession or vocation is organised, developed, regular and carried on in expectation of profit.

DEFINITIONS

"claimant"—see WRA 2012, s.40.
"self-employed earnings"—see regs 53(1) and 57.

GENERAL NOTE

Temporary coronavirus provisions
2.247
The last of the temporary coronavirus provisions relevant to the minimum income floor expired on July 31, 2022. See previous editions of this volume for the details.

This defines when a claimant is in "gainful self-employment". This is important **2.248** because it determines whether the "minimum income floor" (see reg.62) applies to the claimant's earned income. Although the regulation does not expressly say that a claimant is *only* in gainful self-employment when its conditions are met, it appears to be a necessary implication that a claimant is not in gainful self-employment when the conditions are not met.

Claimants are in gainful self-employment if they are carrying on a trade, profession or vocation as their main employment, the earnings from which are self-employed earnings, and the trade, profession or vocation is "organised, developed, regular and carried on in expectation of profit". The mere hope of profit is not enough. There must be a realistic expectation not just of bringing money in, but of profit. If any of these conditions are not met, the claimant will not be in gainful self-employment. It appears that if the claimant's earnings are from "other paid work" (reg.52(a)(iii)) reg.64 cannot apply, but it is not at all clear what sort of work can fall into that category.

In order to decide whether claimants are in gainful self-employment, they will be asked to attend a Gateway interview soon after making a claim for universal credit or after declaring that they are in self-employment.

There is lengthy guidance on the gainful self-employment test at paras H4020–4058 ADM.

Carrying on a trade etc.

The guidance gives little attention to the question of whether and when a claim-   **2.249** ant is carrying on a trade etc under para.(b), treating that as mainly subsumed in the issue of regularity under para.(c). However, it appears that there is a prior condition that the claimant is both carrying on a trade etc and doing so as their main employment. There may be difficult questions whether a claimant is currently carrying on a trade etc, for instance where there are seasonal periods of non-activity or some circumstances intervene to interrupt activity and in which the future of the trade cannot be predicted. In *KD v SSWP (UC)* [2020] UKUT 18 (AAC), a case where there was apparently just a slackening off in gardening work in the winter rather than a period of complete inactivity, the judge did not think that authorities on the rules for other benefits were of any help in deciding how the minimum income floor (MIF) rules were to apply. But there may be some guidance in the cases on whether a person is engaged in remunerative work under reg.5 of the Income Support Regulations (and equivalents) or has ceased to be employed as a self-employed earner for the purposes of para.3 of Sch.8 (disregard of earnings). See the notes to those provisions in Vol.V of this series for full discussion.

In *R(JSA) 1/09* Judge Rowland took the view that there is a distinction between whether a person is employed as a self-employed earner, which he took to mean trading, and whether the person, if so employed, is engaged in remunerative work or part-time work as a self-employed earner (in particular for the purposes of the condition of entitlement of not being engaged in remunerative work). That distinction has sometimes been summarised as the difference between being in work and being at work (see para.18 of *R(JSA) 1/07*, in the context of employed earners). He also took the view that a person ceased to be so employed on no longer being employed in the former sense. Although some of the reasoning in that case has been doubted in subsequent decisions, it is submitted that the basic distinction remains. The notion of carrying on a trade etc in reg.64 appears to be equivalent to the question of whether a person is employed, in the above sense of trading, rather than to being engaged in self-employment.

Paragraph 27020 of the DMG (repeated in substance in para.H4055 of ADM) suggests nine factors potentially relevant to whether a person is no longer trading, rather than there merely being an interruption in the person's activities in a continuing employment. The substance of that approach (although then directed to whether the claimant was in gainful employment within the definition of self-employment) was approved in *CIS/166/1994*, although in some other cases reservations have been expressed. The nine factors overlap somewhat and it is recognised that not all will be relevant in a particular case, but represent a sensible approach. In summary, they are whether the person has reasonable prospects of work in the near future; whether the business is a going concern and regarded as such by others; whether the person is genuinely available for and seeking alternative work; whether the person hopes or intends to resume work when conditions improve; whether the person is undertaking any activities in connection with the self-employment; whether there is any work in the pipeline; whether the person is regarded as self-employed by HMRC; whether the person is making it known that the business can take on work; and whether the interruption is part of the normal pattern of the business.

It has though been made clear in some recent decisions that neither an intention to resume self-employment in the future nor the existence of a past seasonal pattern of activity and non-activity in itself requires a conclusion for income support and equivalent purposes that the person is still trading and is still employed in self-employment. The old style JSA claimant in *Saunderson v Secretary of State for Work and Pensions* [2012] CSIH 102; [2013] AACR 16 had worked as a self-employed golf caddie in St Andrews in the spring and summer months for several years. The claim was after the end of the summer season, when his authorisation to act as a caddie had been withdrawn and there was no commitment that he would be able to work in the next or subsequent years. The question was whether entitlement was excluded by reason of the claimant being treated as engaged in remunerative work in periods in which he carried out no activities. The Inner House of the Court of Session held that such a deeming could only operate when the claimant was "in work" in the ordinary meaning of the word. That seems to involve essentially the same factors as the question of whether the person is carrying on trade. The court remitted the question to a new tribunal for decision but said this in para.20 (the language being coloured by arguments that the self-employed had to be treated differently from employees):

> "Plainly there may be many self-employed trading or professional activities in which it is not difficult to say that the professional or trading activity continues notwithstanding an idle period. An example might be the arable farmer who, having ploughed and sowed the winter wheat in the autumn, has relatively little to do until the arrival of the spring. In some respects, one might draw an analogy with a schoolteacher whom one would readily say was in work albeit that his teaching duties are punctuated by school holidays in which he has little by way of professional activity to perform. But conversely, there will be seasonally pursued activities which, while treated in their exercise for contractual or fiscal reasons as a 'self-employed' activity, are in their substance little different from employment. Typically (but not exclusively), such *quasi* employed activities might be those in which the individual has no significant commercial capital invested and the temporal limit on his exercise of that technically self-employed activity is dictated by seasonal factors affecting demand for the person's services."

A Northern Ireland Commissioner followed *Saunderson* in *TC v DSD (JSA)* [2013] NI Com 65. He held that the claimant had ceased self-employment as an eel-fisherman when he made his claim in September 2011 although he hoped to resume fishing in May 2012. For the months of January to April statutory rules prohibited fishing and it was not economically worthwhile to fish from October to December. In the particular year the gearbox of his engine broke in early August and he could not afford a repair or source a replacement in time to resume fishing that season. Some further discussion of the weighing-up of the factors considered relevant would have been helpful. In particular, the steps that the claimant was taking and intended to take in the months before May 2012, to get his boat in a condition to resume fishing, and possibly to recruit helpers, could have been said to point to his continuing to be in work. But the uncertainty of the outcome of such steps as at the date of decision perhaps outweighed that factor in the context of the length of the break and the test not requiring a permanent cessation of employment. What was clear was that the mere fact that the claimant had fished during the restricted season for several years did not automatically lead to a conclusion that the self-employment had not ceased in August 2011.

Main employment

The ADM guidance suggests that the question of whether the self-employment is the claimant's main employment will depend on a number of factors, such as the hours spent undertaking it each week, whether this is a significant proportion of the claimant's expected hours per week, how many hours (if any) the claimant spends on employed activity, the amount of income received, whether the claimant receives a greater proportion of their income from self-employed or employed activity, and whether self-employment is the claimant's main aim. The ordinary use of language would suggest that if the self-employed activity in question, however slight or unprofitable, beyond a de minimis level, is all that the claimant does by way of employment, then that has to be their main employment. However, that is not the view taken in para.H4023 of the ADM, where it is said that in such circumstances, if the activity is for only a few hours a week or is on a low-paid basis, it should not be regarded as the main employment. There are various elaborate examples given where either of those factors on their own are said to have that effect, so as to avoid the need to examine the criteria laid down in para.(c).

2.250

Organised, developed, regular and expectation of profit

In order to decide whether the self-employment is "organised, developed, regular and carried on in expectation of profit", the guidance suggests that factors such as whether the work is undertaken for financial gain, the number of hours worked each week, whether there is a business plan, the steps being taken to increase the income from the work, whether the business is being actively marketed or advertised, how much work is in the pipeline and whether HMRC regard the activity as self-employment may be relevant. None of those factors seem related specifically to regularity, which will have to be determined in accordance with the overall pattern of activity. Difficult questions may arise where the nature of the trade etc carried on creates seasonal fluctuations or even seasonal periods of non-activity.

JF v HMRC (TC) [2017] UKUT 334 (AAC) concerned the definition of "self-employed" in reg.2(1) of the Working Tax Credit (Entitlement and Maximum Rate) Regulations 2002 as in force with effect from April 6, 2015 (see Vol.IV of this series), which includes a condition that the trade, profession or vocation be "organised and regular". Judge Wikeley gave guidance that, in assessing organisation and regularity for the purposes of WTC, HMRC should "get real" and adjust expectations about the documentary support to be expected for the modest enterprises often involved. Nor should the facts that a claimant did not have an accountant or a business plan necessarily mean that the condition was not met. However, by contrast with the position in WTC, self-employed universal credit claimants will no doubt often be arguing that their business is not organised, developed and regular, so as to avoid the operation of the minimum income floor under reg.62, rather than the other way round, to qualify for WTC.

In *KD v SSWP (UC)* [2020] UKUT 18 (AAC), the gardener's case mentioned above, the judge did not wish, having not had argument on both sides, to express a definitive conclusion on whether regular meant having a constant frequency or merely according to a standard pattern over some period, so that the trade would continue to be regular through a predictable shortage of work. However, he considered that it would be going too far to say that almost constant frequency was required and was not prepared to overturn the tribunal's conclusion that the claimant was in gainful self-employment although the level of his work and income fell off in the winter months. Again, there may be a testing of the matter in the context of the 2020/21 coronavirus outbreak, especially once the person starts to undertake some activities, such as preparation in adapting premises or procedures for being able to start earning money again. Could such activity be said to be "regular" in that special context?

2.251

Clearly if the claimant's business is an established one that has been operating for some time and is still receiving income, it may be relatively straightforward to decide that the claimant is in gainful self-employment. If, however, the business is receiving little or no income, it may be that the self-employment is no longer "organised", "regular" or "carried on in expectation of profit". All the circumstances will need to be considered, including future prospects and whether this is part of the normal pattern of the claimant's work. A claimant may still be in gainful employment while unable to work through illness but in that situation should consider submitting medical certificates with a view to no longer being subject to all work-related requirements and thus the minimum income floor not applying. And at some point it would be said that the claimant had ceased to carry on the business.

If the claimant is not in gainful self-employment, the minimum income floor will not apply and the claimant's actual self-employed earnings will be taken into account.

CHAPTER 3

UNEARNED INCOME

Introduction

2.252   **65.** This Chapter provides for the calculation of a person's unearned income for the purposes of section 8 of the Act (calculation of awards).

DEFINITION

"the Act"—see reg.2.

What is included in unearned income?

2.253   **66.**—(1) A person's unearned income is any of their income, including income the person is treated as having by virtue of regulation 74 (notional unearned income), falling within the following descriptions—
  (a) retirement pension income (see regulation 67) [² to which the person is entitled, subject to any adjustment to the amount payable in accordance with regulations under section 73 of the Social Security Administration Act 1992 (overlapping benefits)];
  (b) any of the following benefits to which the person is entitled, subject to any adjustment to the amount payable in accordance with regulations under section 73 of the Social Security Administration Act 1992 (overlapping benefits)—
    (i) jobseeker's allowance,
    (ii) employment and support allowance,
    (iii) carer's allowance,
    (iv) [¹ . . .],
    (v) widowed mother's allowance,
    (vi) widowed parent's allowance,
    (vii) widow's pension,
    (viii) maternity allowance, or
    (ix) industrial injuries benefit, excluding any increase in that benefit under section 104 or 105 of the Contributions and Benefits Act (increases where constant attendance needed and for exceptionally severe disablement);
  (c) any benefit, allowance, or other payment which is paid under the law of a country outside the United Kingdom and is analogous to a benefit mentioned in sub-paragraph (b);

   (d) payments made towards the maintenance of the person by their spouse, civil partner, former spouse or former civil partner under a court order or an agreement for maintenance;

[²(da) foreign state retirement pension;]

   (e) student income (see regulation 68);

   (f) a payment made under section 2 of the Employment and Training Act 1973 or section 2 of the Enterprise and New Towns (Scotland) Act 1990 which is a substitute for universal credit or is for a person's living expenses;

   (g) a payment made by one of the Sports Councils named in section 23(2) of the National Lottery etc. Act 1993 out of sums allocated to it for distribution where the payment is for the person's living expenses;

   (h) a payment received under an insurance policy to insure against—

      (i) the risk of losing income due to illness, accident or redundancy, or

     (ii) the risk of being unable to maintain payments on a loan, but only to the extent that the payment is in respect of owner-occupier payments within the meaning of paragraph 4 of Schedule 1 in respect of which an amount is included in an award for the housing costs element;

   (i) income from an annuity (other than retirement pension income), unless disregarded under regulation 75 (compensation for personal injury);

   (j) income from a trust, unless disregarded under regulation 75 (compensation for personal injury) or 76 (special schemes for compensation);

   (k) income that is treated as the yield from a person's capital by virtue of regulation 72;

   (l) capital that is treated as income by virtue of regulation 46(3) or (4);

[²(la) PPF periodic payments;]

   (m) income that does not fall within sub-paragraphs [²(a) to (la)] and is taxable under Part 5 of the Income Tax (Trading and Other Income) Act 2005 (miscellaneous income).

[²(2) In this regulation—

   (a) in paragraph (1)(da) "foreign state retirement pension" means any pension which is paid under the law of a country outside the United Kingdom and is in the nature of social security;

   (b) in paragraph (1)(f) and (g) a person's "living expenses" are the cost of—

      (i) food;

     (ii) ordinary clothing or footwear;

    (iii) household fuel, rent or other housing costs (including council tax),

for the person, their partner and any child or qualifying young person for whom the person is responsible;

   (c) in paragraph (1)(la) "PPF periodic payments" has the meaning given in section 17(1) of the State Pension Credit Act 2002.]

AMENDMENTS

1. Pensions Act 2014 (Consequential, Supplementary and Incidental Amendments) Order 2017 (SI 2017/422) art.43(3) (April 6, 2017, subject to arts 2 and 3).

2. Universal Credit (Miscellaneous Amendments, Saving and Transitional Provision) Regulations 2018 (SI 2018/65) reg.3(9) (April 11, 2018).

DEFINITIONS

"bereavement allowance"—see reg.2.
"carer's allowance" —*ibid.*
"child" —see WRA 2012 s.40
"employment and support allowance" —see reg.2.
"industrial injuries benefit" —*ibid.*
"jobseeker's allowance" —*ibid.*
"maternity allowance" —*ibid.*
"partner"—*ibid.*
"qualifying young person" —see WRA 2012 ss.40 and 10(5) and regs 2 and 5.
"retirement pension income"—see reg.67.
"widowed mother's allowance" —see reg.2.
"widowed parent's allowance" —*ibid.*
"widow's pension"—*ibid.*

MODIFICATION

With effect from June 16, 2014, reg.66 is modified by reg.25 of the Universal Credit (Transitional Provisions) Regulations 2014 (SI 2014/1230) (see Pt IV of this Volume). The modification applies where an award of universal credit is made to a claimant who is entitled to incapacity benefit or severe disablement allowance, in which case reg.66 applies as if incapacity benefit or, as the case may be, severe disablement allowance were added to the list of benefits in reg.66(1)(b).

2.254 GENERAL NOTE

Paragraph (1)

Universal credit adopts the general approach taken in state pension credit of specifying what is to be included as unearned income. If a type of income is not listed as included, it is ignored and does not affect the claimant's (or claimants') award. Accordingly, there is no need for any general provisions disregarding specified kinds of unearned income (but see regs 75 and 76, expressly mentioned in para. (1)(i) and (j)). However, note that rather than, as for state pension credit, providing in regulations that all social security benefits count as unearned income except those specified as excluded, reg.66 lists the benefits that do count. That leaves occasional difficulty in deciding whether certain payments count as within the wide meaning given to "retirement pension income".

It follows from that approach that reg.26(1)(a) of the Victims' Payments Regulations 2020 (SI 2020/103) was unnecessary in relation to universal credit in providing that a victims' payment or a lump sum under those Regulations was to be disregarded as income in addition to as capital (on which see the notes to reg.76 and Sch.10). It is enough that such payments of compensation are not listed in reg.66(1). Similarly, it was merely necessary to do nothing to amend reg.66(1) to secure that various coronavirus payments were not to be taken into account as unearned income. The main example is the taxable £500 payment, administered by local authorities, made to those in England entitled to a qualifying income-related benefit (including universal credit) who were required by NHS Test and Trace on or after September 28, 2020 (down to at least summer 2021) to self-isolate for 14 (or ten) days, were unable to work from home and would lose income from employment or self-employment as a result. Nor was the discretionary payment available to those not entitled to a qualifying benefit listed in reg.66(1). Nor were payments under the very similar, but not identical, schemes available in Wales, Scotland and Northern Ireland. See the notes to reg.54A for discussion of the question whether any amount left out of the £500 after the end of the isolation period, or possibly after the assessment period of receipt, is to be taken into account as capital. Another example would be payments by local authorities to assist vulnerable households and families with children with essential needs under the 2020 Covid Winter Grants scheme, continued under the name Covid Local Support Grants until September 30, 2021 and then under the name of the Household Support Fund. By the same token, the £350 per month "thank you" payments under the Homes for Ukraine scheme will not count as unearned income.

Similarly, the one-off non-taxable £500 payment made to working tax credit ("WTC") recipients in April 2021, to provide extra support when the temporary coronavirus uplift to WTC ended on April 5, 2021, would not have constituted unearned income if the claimant had claimed universal credit by the time of receipt even if it had been a payment of WTC (which the HMRC guidance on the scheme stresses it is not), as WTC is not listed in reg.66(1)(b). But the payment appears to be of a capital nature, for which there is no disregard in Sch.10, and, even if it were income, it is arguable that an unspent amount of the £500 constitutes capital. See the notes to reg.45 and Sch.10. The HMRC guidance says that benefits will not be affected by receipt of the payment.

There cannot be a definitive list of kinds of income that cannot be taken into account as unearned income, but a few categories can be mentioned. Payments of dividends do not count, but see the notes to regs 55 (employed earnings) and 77(4) on when they may be treated as earned income in substance. Interest on bank or building society accounts and other investments does not count, nor does rental income or payments from people occupying the claimant's home (see the note below on income taxable under Pt 5 of ITTOIA for why), although if the letting is part of a trade or business it will go towards the calculation of earnings from self-employment: see the notes to reg.57. All of those propositions are subject to the rule in reg.72(3) that if the claimant's capital is assumed to yield monthly "tariff" income under reg.72(1), where the value of the capital exceeds £6,000, any actual income derived from capital ("for example rental, interest or dividends") is to be treated as part of the claimant's capital. In addition, the amount of the income, if not spent by the claimant, will become part of their capital, probably after the end of the assessment period in which the income was received.

Thus payments from relatives (except those caught by para.(1)(d)) or friends or charities (see the view expressed in para.13 of *AMS v SSWP (PC) (final decision)* [2017] UKUT 381 (AAC), [2018] AACR 27 on the comparable state pension credit structure) or local authorities fall outside the scope of unearned income, as do drawings from a partnership or a self-employed business or from, say, a director's loan account within a company structure (though see reg.57 on self-employed earnings and reg.77 on companies analogous to a partnership or a one-person business).

See the notes to para.(1)(b) below for some of the social security benefits that are not taken into account.

In calculating universal credit, all of the claimant's, or the claimants' combined, unearned income that counts is taken into account in full (see s.8(3) of the WRA 2012 and reg.22). There are also some circumstances in which income not listed in reg.66 will affect the application of particular provisions, e.g. the amount of charges allowed in the childcare costs element under reg.34 is reduced to the extent that they are met or reimbursed by some other person or by other relevant support (i.e. in connection with participation in work-related activity or training).

What is income

The first requirement for unearned income to be taken into account, before examining the list in para.(1), is that the amount concerned is income rather than capital. That is covered in the present section. It is also a requirement, it is suggested, that the amount is income that the claimant "has". That is covered in the following section.

It has been said for many years in the predecessors to this volume that "resources are to be either capital or income. There is nothing in between". That statement was

2.255

cited with approval in *R(IS) 3/93* and without disapproval in *R(IS) 9/08*. The distinction between income and capital has given rise to many problems in the context of means-tested benefits, as well as in other legal contexts. There is very extensive discussion of the general principles in the notes to reg.23 of the Income Support Regulations in Vol.V of this series. Not all of that discussion needs to be repeated here. That is mainly because of the important deemings in reg.46(3) and (4) and the fact that the structure of reg.66 means that even if something is income it may fall outside the exhaustive list of categories in para.(1).

Regulation 46(3) provides that, subject to reg.46(4), any sums paid regularly and by reference to a period are to be treated as income even if they would otherwise be regarded as capital. Regulation 46(4) deals with capital payable by instalments, deeming such instalments sometimes to be income, depending on the level of overall capital. Then reg.66(1)(l) lists capital treated as income by virtue of reg.46(3) or (4) as unearned income. Although reg.46(3) builds on the traditional approach that the "essential feature of receipts by way of income is that they display an element of periodic recurrence. Income cannot include ad hoc receipts" (Bridge J in *R. v Supplementary Benefits Commission Ex p. Singer* [1973] 1 W.L.R. 713), it makes the rule more positive. Ad hoc receipts, like the one-off £15 loan to a striking miner by a local authority to meet hire purchase arrears in *R(SB) 29/85*, would still be excluded. But any arguments that loans could never constitute income (already in substance disposed of by *Chief Adjudication Officer v Leeves* (CA), reported as *R(IS) 5/99*, and *Morrell v Secretary of State for Work and Pensions* [2003] EWCA Civ 536, reported as *R(IS) 6/03*)) cannot stand. If the sums are paid regularly and by reference to a period they must be treated as income, subject to reg.46(4) and to the potential argument, based on *Leeves*, that sums have not become income in the claimant's hands (on which, see the following section).

But there is then a problem with the inclusion of capital treated as income by virtue of reg.46(3) or (4) in para.(1)(l). As suggested in the notes to reg.46, that could not possibly have been intended to have the effect that any payment made regularly and by reference to a period must be taken into account as unearned income. That would include, for example, many social security benefits carefully not listed in para. (1)(b), rental payments, regular payments from relatives or friends (whether gifts or loans) and other categories mentioned above as excluded, all of which are plainly acknowledged as intended not to be taken into account. However, it is submitted that it is significant that para.(1)(l) does not apply to every payment treated as income by virtue of reg.46(3) or (4), but only to *capital* treated as income by virtue of those provisions. Thus, it appears that payments that are in their nature income cannot fall within para.(1)(l) and only count for universal credit purposes if listed in some other part of para.(1). On that basis, para.(1)(l) covers only capital payments that are paid either regularly and by reference to a period (reg.46(3)) or by instalments (reg.46(4)).

There is no deeming for payments that are not paid regularly (and the test in reg.46(3) seems to be of the pattern of actual payment, rather than due dates) or have no relation to a period (e.g. they are to help with sporadically arising needs). There might therefore be difficult questions arising in theory about whether the payments were income, rather than capital. Then the other traditional criterion of "the true characteristic of the payment in the hands of the recipient" (see *R. v National Insurance Commissioner Ex p. Stratton* [1979] I.C.R. 209, Appendix II to *R(U) 1/79*, and *Minter v Kingston upon Hull CC* and *Potter v Secretary of State for Work and Pensions* [2011] EWCA Civ 1155; [2012] AACR 21) might come into play. See *R(H) 8/08* for a case where the tribunal gave inadequate consideration to whether the payment by the claimant's accountant of his rent on 20–25 occasions over 33 months constituted income. But in practice, the questions would not have to be answered if the payment would fall outside the para.(1) list anyway. There could of course be an impact on the capital limit rules if the payment was regarded as capital and the value of the claimant's other capital was close to a significant level, but the difference would be slight in reality, because unspent income would relatively quickly metamorphose into capital.

Payments of capital by instalments will usually be easily identified, such as the payment of the purchase price of a house by monthly instalments in *Lillystone v Supplementary Benefits Commission* [1982] 3 F.L.R. 52, where each instalment was on the common law test capital. Now, for universal credit, that would still be the case if the claimant's other capital and the amount of the instalments outstanding did not exceed £16,000. If those amounts did exceed £16,000, reg.46(4) deems each instalment to be income, to be taken into account under para.(1)(l).

A particular area that has given rise to difficulty is where a claimant receives a lump sum, such as of compensation for personal injury or for unfair dismissal or for breach of equal pay or similar legislation. Other examples would be payments of lump sums of arrears of some entitlement or advance payments. The area of personal injury and payments from compensation funds is dealt with by regs 75 and 76. The other compensation cases, on which *Minter* and *Potter* make clear that the central question is whether the compensation was for loss of income or for loss of a capital asset, are to do with earnings. So far as unearned income is concerned, the area of concern is with lump sum payments of arrears or possibly advance payments in commutation of income, exemplified by payments of arrears of social security benefits.

In principle, payments of benefits that would have had the character of income if paid on their due date retain that character when paid in arrears as a lump sum (*R(SB) 4/89* and *CH/1561/2005*). That is entirely consistent with the principle behind the Court of Appeal's decision in *Minter* and *Potter* (above) on lump sum payments of compensation in settlement of equal pay claims. So the same should apply to payments that were not benefit as such, but compensation for the non-payment of benefit over some past period. There seems no reason why that principle should not apply for universal credit purposes, if the income falls within a para.(1) category. In *R(SB) 4/89*, the Commissioner, relying on the principle in *McCorquodale v Chief Adjudication Officer*, reported as *R(SB) 1/88*, held that the income should be taken into account in the periods for which it would have been taken into account if paid on the due dates. There is no equivalent clear rule on due dates for unearned income in the universal credit scheme. There are thus particularly difficult issues about how to take such lump sum payments of unearned income into account, discussed below under the heading *Attribution of unearned income to assessment periods.*

When is income the claimant's
    Regulation 66(1) starts with the assumption that it is concerned with income that   2.256
is a person's. Paragraph 4(3)(a) of Sch.1 to the WRA 2012 authorises the making of regulations specifying the circumstances in which a person is to be treated as "having or not having capital or earned or unearned income". Thus, it appears necessary, before the list of categories in para.(1) is reached, to be satisfied that the claimant "has" the income concerned. That must entail, except in the category of notional income in reg.74 and assumed yield from capital in regs 66(1)(k) and 72, that the income has actually been received by the claimant or become at their disposal. See the section below on *Attribution of unearned income to assessment periods* for discussion of how those provisions affect that issue.

    One founding proposition was established by the Court of Appeal in *Chief Adjudication Officer v Leeves*, reported as *R(IS) 5/99*. The claimant there had been a full-time student in receipt of a local authority grant, the instalment for each term being paid in advance. He abandoned his course shortly after receiving an instalment and having spent all the money on paying off mortgage arrears and other debts. About a month later the local authority wrote to him formally terminating his grant from the date of abandonment, informing him that he had been overpaid by a specified amount and requesting that repayment be made as soon as possible. The adjudication officer decided that the amount of the grant had to be taken into account in calculating the claimant's income support until the end of the term. The grant was income and had been received and under the ordinary non-student provisions was to be taken into account from the due date of payment for the period in respect of which it was payable. It did not matter that the money had all been spent. Potter LJ, with whom the other judges agreed, took the view that "income" was to be given its natural and ordinary meaning. He accepted that the decision would have been right for grants that were not repayable, but that moneys received, or required to be treated as received, "under a certain obligation of immediate repayment" did not have the character of income. Prior to his receipt of the letter from the local authority, the claimant was not in that position, because there was no "certain and immediate" obligation to repay, his undertaking on accepting the grant having merely been to repay such sum as might be determined if he abandoned the course. His liability had not yet crystalised. However, on receipt of the demand from the local authority he came under an immediate obligation in relation to an ascertained sum and from that date the remainder of the grant was not income.

That principle was affirmed in *Morrell* (above). There the regular payments by way of loan from the claimant's mother were income despite there being a repayment obligation. But the basis of the arrangement was that the claimant would repay when her problems decreased or she found work, so that there was no certain obligation of immediate repayment. In *R(JSA) 4/04* there was no such obligation in relation to a student loan at the dates in question, because under the legislation in force repayment could only start in the April following the academic year for which the loan was made. Nor did it matter that the loan might have been made wrongly unless and until the Secretary of State took action to determine that there had been an overpayment. By contrast, in *R(H) 5/05* the Commissioner held that drawing on an agreed overdraft facility is borrowing, as is the honouring of a cheque taking an overdraft over an agreed limit. Those loans could be capable of constituting income, were it not for the fact that the standard terms of bank overdrafts were that they were repayable on demand, although a demand might not be made while the overdraft stayed within agreed limits. The Commissioner considered that there was a certain obligation of immediate repayment, because the amount overdrawn could be identified day by day, and the obligation was immediate even though the bank chose not to enforce it. That brought the *Leeves* principle into operation. The Commissioner considered that that was also in accord with the ordinary and natural meaning of "income", as one would not naturally speak of someone having income by incurring expenditure and running up an overdraft. *R(H) 5/05* did not refer to the decision of the Court of Appeal in *R. v West Dorset DC Ex p. Poupard* (1998) 20 H.L.R. 295 that borrowings by way of a bank overdraft secured on capital and used for living expenses was income for the purposes of the housing benefit scheme as it was at the time. However, *R(H) 8/08*, at para.26, and *AR v Bradford MDC* [2008] UKUT 30 (AAC), reported as *R(H) 6/09*, at paras 16–21, plainly indicate that that decision is no longer relevant in the light of changes in the nature of the governing legislation and of *Leeves*.

The Commissioner in *R(H) 5/05* did not have to decide whether the use of a credit card with no immediate liability to repay beyond the minimum amount each month created a funding facility for regularly recurring expenses to be taken into account as income. He cast some doubt on *CH/3393/2003*, in which it was held that it did. That decision was more strongly disapproved in *R(H) 8/08*, at para.27, and *AR* (above), at para.22.

There is also a line of cases where the circumstances seem to be stronger than in *Leeves*, in that there is not merely a certain obligation of immediate repayment, but a legal mechanism has been applied to effect repayment.

In *R(IS) 4/01* the Commissioner decided, applying *Leeves* on the natural and ordinary meaning of "income", that the part of the claimant's occupational pension that was being paid to his former wife under an attachment of earnings order did not count as his income for the purposes of income support. He concluded that, in the absence of a statutory definition, income meant "money paid regularly to the recipient or to his order but not money which is being paid and which he cannot prevent from being paid directly to a third party instead of him". In *CH/1672/2007* the half of the claimant's pension that he was required to pay to his wife under the terms of a court order following a judicial separation did not count as his income. However, income subject to a direction that could be revoked at any time (in that case a pension signed over by a nun to a religious order under a deed of trust) remained the claimant's income (*C10/06–07(IS)*, a Northern Ireland decision). So did the half of his annuities that the claimant in *CH/1076/2008* voluntarily paid to his wife from whom he was separated. In that case the Commissioner drew attention to the "further problem" that would need to be considered if the annuities were retirement annuity pensions in connection with a former employment, namely the conditions in s.91 of the Pension Schemes Act 1995 for assignment of such an annuity.

In addition, see *CIS/5479/1997* in which an overpayment of an occupational pension was being recovered by the Italian authorities by withholding the complete amount of the monthly payments of the pension. Only the net amount actually received by the claimant was his income. The same result would follow for a UK benefit where there has been not only a decision that past benefit has been overpaid and is legally recoverable, but also a decision that deductions are to be made from current benefit to effect repayment. Then, in the absence of any express provision to the contrary, the gross amount of the current benefit would be subject to the legally imposed deduction and only the net amount would be the claimant's income. The Commissioner may well, though, have gone too far in referring to *Leeves* as confirming his own view that in the general context of the income support scheme income to be taken into account was income that was actually paid to a claimant. He stated that if a claimant who had not actually received income was to be treated as having that income, that had to be achieved by a specific provision in the legislation, but *BL v SSWP (SPC)* [2018] UKUT 4 (AAC) (below) shows that that is an overgeneralisation, while not doubting the outcome of *CIS/5479/1997*.

In *R(IS) 4/02* the same Commissioner applied that approach to conclude, contrary to the view taken in *CIS/212/1989*, para.9 (and followed with some hesitation in *CIS/295/1994*), that payments of the claimant's husband's annuity which had vested in his trustee in bankruptcy under s.306 of the Insolvency Act 1986 were not part of his income (and thus not part of the claimant's income) for the purposes of income support. See also *R(IS) 2/03*, which agreed with *R(IS) 4/02* (on the basis of the principle in *Re Landau* [1998] Ch. 223, affirmed in *Krasner v Dennison* [2001] Ch. 76) that *CIS/212/1989* should no longer be followed. Thus the payments under the claimant's self-employed pension annuity that were being applied entirely for the benefit of his creditors were not his actual income (see the note to reg.74 for the position in relation to notional income). Note that the law has now changed so as to exclude pension rights from a bankrupt's estate (Welfare Reform and Pensions Act 1999 s.11 and 12), but only for bankruptcy orders made on or after May 29, 2000. The general principle of the meaning of "income", however, will remain of significance.

BL v SSWP (SPC) [2018] UKUT 4 (AAC) provides a very helpful illustration of the general principles (see the extract set out at para.1.64 of this volume). Payments of the claimant's personal pension to his ex-wife were his income because they were made at his order and he retained practical control over the money. Under a deed of separation he had undertaken to make maintenance payments of a specified amount. Once he started to draw the personal pension he directed the provider to pay those amounts to his ex-wife. It did not matter that the claimant never actually received those amounts from the pension provider. He was still free to deal with that money as he wished and retained not just legal, but also practical, control over it. The statement in *CIS/5479/1997* noted above about claimants who have not actually received income was distinguished as based on different facts. It is submitted that that statement should not be taken out of its context of a withholding of social security payments to recover a debt owed to the social security institution making the payments.

SH v SSWP [2008] UKUT 21 (AAC) concerned the weekly sums which the claimant was allowed to withdraw for living expenses from his bank account which was subject to a restraint order under s.77 of the Criminal Justice Act 1988. It was held that these sums were not income at the time of withdrawal but remained capital. Furthermore there was nothing in the JSA Regulations 1996 which treated those payments of capital as income. They were not capital payable by instalments within the meaning of reg.104(1) of the JSA Regulations 1996 (the equivalent of reg.46(4)) as that provision only applied if there was a contractual or other obligation on the part of some other person to pay a capital sum to the claimant by instalments.

Drawings from a partnership (or a business) are not income other than earnings, nor are they earnings from self-employment (*AR v Bradford MDC* [2008] UKUT 30 (AAC), reported as *R(H) 6/09*). Nor are drawing from a director's loan account within a company structure. They are movements of the claimant's capital from one place to another, as in *SH* (above).

CIS/25/1989 held that, applying the principle of *Parsons v Hogg* [1985] 2 All E.R. 897, Appendix to *R(FIS) 4/85*, from the context of earnings, expenditure necessary to produce income is to be deducted to produce a figure of gross income, as was the term in the relevant legislation. The claimant was entitled to £21.60 per month sickness benefit from the Ideal Benefit Society only while he continued to make a £60 annual payment to the Society. The monthly equivalent (£5) was to be deducted from the £21.60. There have since been conflicting views about the correctness of that decision in the context of the income support legislation on income other than earnings. It was rejected in *CIS 563/1991*. In *R(IS) 13/01* the Commissioner thought that arguably the principle in *Parsons v Hogg* should apply to income other than earnings, but decided that he ought to follow *CIS/563/1991* rather than *CIS/25/1989* on the basis that the former decision had fully considered and rejected the reasoning in *CIS/25/1989*. However, that approach to the issue of precedent where there are two conflicting decisions of equal status has now been overtaken, so that the merits of the decisions should be considered (see *R(IS) 9/08*). More important, the context of the universal credit legislation is significantly different. First, the relevant phrase is not "gross income", but "income" and it was the use of the word "gross" that led to the Commissioner's view in *CIS/563/1991*. Secondly, there is nothing in the universal credit legislation, apart from the provisions on student income, to say how much of any payment of income is to be taken into account or positively providing any deductions or disregards. The perceived need to provide in para.(1)(a) and (b) for taking account of any adjustment in the amount of a benefit under the Overlapping Benefits Regulations suggests that the gross amount would otherwise have been used in s.8(3) of the WRA 2012, but it is arguable that too much should not be inferred from that rule outside sub-paras (a) and (b). In those circumstances, it is submitted that the elementary considerations of fairness behind the approach in *CIS/25/1989* should be applied and that where expenditure has to be incurred in order to produce any unearned income, the amount of that expenditure should be deducted before the income is taken into account. It is the case, though, that it is hard to envisage the practical application of that approach to most of the categories listed in para.(1) (possibly under sub-para.(h) if there was an obligation to continue paying premiums to receive benefits under the insurance policy or under sub-para.(m) for some types of income taxable under Pt 5 of ITTOIA).

Similar questions can be raised about whether, where the type of unearned income concerned is subject to income tax, the amount of income tax due should be deducted in calculating the amount of income to be taken into account. That would apply to most kinds of retirement pension income, including state retirement pension (para.(1)(a) and (1a)), some social benefits (British and non-UK—para.(1) (b) and (c)), some income from trusts (para.(1)(j)) and income taxable under Pt 5 of ITTOIA (para.(1)(m)). One starting point of principle must be that, in general, the ordinary and natural meaning of "income" entails that the existence of liabilities that the claimant has or incurs to persons other than the payer of the income does not affect the amount of income to be taken into account. That is consistent with *BL v SSWP (SPC)*, discussed above, and with *Leeves* (where crucially it was a certain obligation of immediate repayment, i.e. to the payer of the grant, that took the sum subject to repayment out of the meaning of income). So a mere liability to account to HMRC for the income tax due on a receipt of unearned income would not prevent the gross amount of the receipt being taken into account, in the absence of any express provision in the regulations requiring a deduction. But what if income tax has been deducted by the payer as required by legislation and HMRC practice, to be remitted to HMRC, before paying the net amount to the claimant? Surely then an argument can be made by analogy with the cases discussed above where the claimant cannot prevent an amount being paid to some third party by virtue of a legal process, so that only the amount actually received by the claimant should be taken into account. The alternative would require the amount of universal credit to be reduced by income that was never available to the claimant as the result of a legal process, a result that is to be avoided if at all possible.

Retirement pension income

On para.(1)(a) (retirement pension income), see the note to reg.67, in particular   **2.257**
on the meanings of occupational pension. In so far as retirement pension income consists of elements of the state retirement pension (all of which are covered in reg.67), the April 2018 amendment confirms that the amount to be taken into account is the figure after any adjustment under the Overlapping Benefits Regulations. The new para.(1)(da) includes a foreign state retirement pension (defined in para.(2)(a)). That definition appears very wide ("pension … in the nature of social security") when the term "pension" is often used to refer to any periodical social security payments. However, it must be arguable that this is a case where the definition takes on meaning from the nature of term defined, so that para. (1)(d) is restricted to benefits paid on retirement.

Note that the notional unearned income rule in reg.74 has a particular application to retirement pension income. A person who has reached the qualifying age for state pension credit is to be treated as possessing any such income they might expect to be entitled to if a claim were made, even if no application has been made (reg.74(3) and (4)). So a person who defers taking their UK retirement pension or an occupational or personal pension beyond state retirement age will be treated as if they had taken the pension at that age. See the notes to reg.74 for more detail and discussion about how far reg.74(4) qualifies reg.74(3). Regulation 74(3) applies only to retirement pension, so not to a foreign state retirement pension under para. (1)(da), but that would apparently fall under reg.74(1).

Note also that there is a particular issue about the treatment of payments of retirement income when a claimant reaches the qualifying age for state pension credit, now that (from November 25, 2020) entitlement to universal credit does not end until the first day of the assessment period following that in which that age is reached (para.26 of Sch.1 to the Decisions and Appeals Regulations 2013). A further issue has emerged where decisions on claims for retirement pension or the putting of entitlement into payment has been delayed. See below under the heading of *Attribution of unearned income to assessment periods*.

Benefits

Not all benefit income is taken into account—see para.(1)(b) for the benefits that   **2.258**
do count in addition to those within the meaning of retirement pension income (note that this will also include incapacity benefit or severe disablement allowance if the claimant is entitled to either of these benefits: see the modification made to para. (1)(b) by reg.25 of SI 2014/1230 referred to above). Thus, for example, child benefit is ignored, as is disability living allowance, attendance allowance and personal independence payment. War disablement pension and war widows', widowers' or surviving civil partners' pensions are also ignored (for income support, old style JSA, old style ESA and housing benefit there is only a £10 disregard). Bereavement allowance, which has been abolished prospectively for deaths on or after April 6, 2017 has been taken out of the list of benefits in para.(1)(b), but remains in the list in relation to awards of the allowance made before April 6, 2017 or to awards made in relation

to deaths before that date (see arts 2 and 3 of the amending Order, SI 2017/422). The monthly payments of the new bereavement support payment have not been put into the list, so will not count as income for universal credit purposes, whether paid on time or in arrears. In so far as any payment of arrears is to be treated as capital it is disregarded as such under para.18(1)(c) of Sch.10 (plus, in the case of arrears under the Bereavement Payments (Remedial) Order 2013, para.20(2)). The initial one-off lump sum payment appears to have the character of capital and is disregarded as such under para.20(2) of Sch.10.

Note that the benefits listed are all defined in reg.2 specifically by reference to British legislation. Thus the equivalent benefits under Northern Ireland legislation are not covered. Because sub-para.(c) on analogous benefits is restricted to those paid under the law of a country outside the UK, which includes Northern Ireland, it appears that Northern Ireland equivalent benefits cannot count as unearned income. Similarly, benefits payable under Scottish legislation that might look as though they fall within sub-para.(b), like carer's allowance supplement (see Vol.IV of this series), do not do so and cannot fall within sub-para.(c) as analogous.

The definitions of JSA and ESA (listed in heads (i) and (ii)) in reg.2 are in terms restricting the meaning to new style JSA and new style ESA. Thus when a claimant previously entitled to a legacy benefit is entitled to the two-week run-on of housing benefit, extended to income support, IBJSA and IRESA from July 22, 2020, none of those receipts count as unearned income under reg.66(1). None of those benefits is listed in sub-para.(b). However, the effect of reg.8B(b) of the Transitional Provisions Regulations 2014, as inserted with effect from July 22, 2020 by reg.4(4) of the Universal Credit (Managed Migration Pilot and Miscellaneous Amendments) Regulations 2019 (SI 2019/1152), is that, where a claimant has become entitled to new style JSA or ESA on the termination of an award of IBJSA or IRESA, unearned income is to be calculated as if the claimant had been entitled to the new style award from the first day of their universal credit award.

By virtue of reg.10 of the Universal Credit (Transitional Provisions) Regulations 2014 (see the notes to that provision in Pt IIIA), any payment of an "existing benefit" (IBJSA, IRESA, income support or housing benefit, but excluding for these purposes joint claim JSA and any tax credits) made to a claimant who is not entitled to it in respect of a period that falls within a universal credit assessment period is to fall within reg.66(1)(b) as unearned income. The overpayment involved is not then recoverable in the ordinary way. It will in effect be recovered through the deduction in the calculation of universal credit.

In *R. (on the application of Moore) v Secretary of State for Work and Pensions* [2020] EWHC 2827 (Admin); [2021] P.T.S.R. 495, Swift J, while finding two of the grounds of judicial review arguable (discrimination under art.14 of the ECHR read with art.8 and/or art.1 of Protocol 1 and common law irrationality), rejected the case for the claimants against the inclusion of maternity allowance in the list of social security benefits to count in full as unearned income, although statutory maternity pay (SMP) counts as earned income with the advantage of the 55% taper and the work allowance. The claimant did not qualify for SMP because she had not worked for her employer for long enough when she started her maternity pay, so had to claim maternity allowance. Permission to apply for judicial review on the ground of breach of the public sector equality duty (s.149 of the Equality Act 2010) was refused. The Court of Appeal refused the claimant permission to appeal in a reasoned judgment following a short hearing (*Moore v Secretary of State for Work and Pensions* [2021] EWCA Civ 970).

The decision in *Moore* has been followed and applied after detailed consideration by the Northern Ireland High Court in *In the Matter of an Application by 'RK' for Judicial Review* [2022] NIQB 29.

Special provision is made in the annual social security benefit up-rating orders for the assessment period in which the up-rated amount is to be taken into account. Thus art.1(4) of the Social Security Benefits Up-rating Order 2023 (SI 2023/316), in conjunction with art.1(3)(p), ensures that in the case of a beneficiary who has an award of universal credit the provision up-rating the social security benefit comes into force for the purpose of calculating entitlement to universal credit on the first day of the first assessment period to commence on or after April 10, 2023.

Non-UK benefits

Under sub-para.(c) payments of benefit under the law of a country outside the UK that is analogous to a benefit listed in sub-para.(b) count as unearned income. Because the UK includes Northern Ireland and the benefits in sub-para.(b) are carefully defined in reg.2 by reference to the specific Great Britain legislation, this seems to have the anomalous effect that benefits paid under Northern Ireland social security legislation do not count as unearned income for universal credit purposes. See below for the opposite outcome in relation to benefits that are included within retirement pension income. 2.259

Benefits payable under Scottish legislation that are in the nature of income (e.g. carer's allowance supplement) likewise cannot fall within sub-para.(b) or (c).

See *LR v SSWP (UC)* [2022] UKUT 65 (AAC) on the question of analogy. The claimant came into receipt of an Irish widow's contributory pension following the death of her husband in 2018. Entitlement to that pension depended on a claimant's spouse or civil partner having died and having made sufficient qualifying contributions and on the claimant being under pensionable age for state pension and not having remarried or otherwise become part of a couple. It was payable indefinitely, although on reaching the age of 66 it would be necessary to reapply because, if the claimant qualified for state pension there could be a transfer. Judge West accepted in para.64 that to be "analogous" the foreign benefit must be similar or comparable in relevant respects, but does not have to be identical. The essential question was whether the two benefits are similar in terms of their nature and purpose. In *LR*, the Irish pension was on that test analogous to widow's pension under sub-para.(b)(vii), i.e. a pension under s.38 of the SSCBA 1992 (reg.2, on the assumption that the reference there to s.39 is a correctable mistake). The pensions produced a weekly income for life and the conditions for entitlement were very similar, except that widow's pension did not extend to widowers or civil partners and was payable only to widows aged at least 45 when their husband died, which differences did not undermine the analogy. It did not matter, despite the reference in sub-para.(b) to benefits to which a person was entitled, that the claimant could not have been entitled to British widow's pension, because that was restricted to deaths before April 8, 2001, and was entitled to bereavement support payment, which is not in the sub-para.(b) list.

Under sub-para.(da), with the definition in para.(2)(a), foreign state retirement pension is listed. The definition appears very wide ("pension ... in the nature of social security") when the term "pension" is often used to refer to any periodical social security payments. But perhaps this is a case where the definition takes on meaning from the nature of the term defined, so that sub-para.(da) is restricted to benefits paid on retirement or at least linked to old age. The definition is restricted to pensions paid under the law of a country outside the UK, so that pensions paid under Northern Ireland legislation are not covered. However, the meaning of retirement pension income in sub-para.(a) is, through the reference on to the state pension credit legislation in reg.67, extended to the Northern Ireland legislation corresponding to the British legislation listed.

Payments towards maintenance

Under para.(1)(d) payments "towards the maintenance of a person" from their spouse, or former spouse, or civil partner, or former civil partner, under a court order or maintenance agreement count. Thus maintenance payments that are not made pursuant to an agreement (e.g., ad hoc voluntary payments) will be ignored. There is also no provision for treating such payments as unearned income if they are made directly to a third party. Maintenance for a child is ignored. Note first that para.(1)(d) only applies to current or ex-spouses or civil partners, not to someone who had been living with the claimant as if married or a civil partner. Note also that 2.260

payments from any other member of the family apart from spouses/civil partners, e.g. parents, for maintenance are not included.

The list in reg.66 does not include charitable or voluntary payments and so these will be ignored. On the meaning of charitable and voluntary payments, see the notes to para.15 of Sch.9 to the Income Support Regulations in Vol.V of this series.

Student income

2.261   Here "student income" does not mean any income that someone who is a student has, but the particular forms of income that a person undertaking a course of education, study or training is to be treated as having under reg.68. Any other forms of income, apart from earnings, can only be taken into account in so far as they fall within some other category in para.(1), e.g. training allowances (para. (1)(f) and reg.68(6)). The forms of income covered by reg.68 are student loans, i.e. loans towards maintenance under specified legislation, including loans that have not been taken out but could be acquired by reasonable steps, and grants to under-21s for non-advanced education. See the notes to regs.68 and 69–71 for further details and for how the amounts are to be attributed to particular assessment periods. Although it is a condition of entitlement to universal credit not to be receiving education (s.4(1)(d) of the WRA 2012) there are exceptions to that condition in reg.14 and a claimant with a partner who receives education may be entitled.

Training allowances

2.262   Payments from employment and training programmes under s.2 of the Employment and Training Act 1973 or s.2 of the Enterprise and New Towns (Scotland) Act 1990 are only taken into account in so far as they are a substitute for universal credit (e.g., a training allowance) or for a person's living expenses (para. (1)(f)). See para.(2)(b) for what counts as "living expenses".

Income protection insurance

2.263   Under para.(1)(h) payments under an insurance policy count but only if the policy was to insure against the contingencies in heads (i) and (ii). Under head (ii) payments under a mortgage (or other loan) protection policy will only be taken into account if the payment is to pay interest on a mortgage or loan secured on the person's home or to meet "alternative finance payments" (see the notes to paras 4–6 of Sch.1) *and* if the person's universal credit award includes a housing costs element under para.4 of Sch.1. Thus insurance policy payments to meet, e.g., capital repayments or policy premiums, will be ignored.

It is arguable that if, for instance, a claimant is obliged to continue paying premiums under the insurance policy to receive the payments, the amount of the premium payable in each assessment period should be deducted applying the principle of *Parsons v Hogg* [1985] 2 All E.R. 897, appendix to *R(FIS) 4/85* (see the end of the section *When is income the claimant's* above).

Annuities

2.264   Income from an annuity (other than retirement pension income) counts unless it was purchased with personal injury compensation (reg.75) as does income from a trust (unless it is disregarded under regs 75 or 76) (para.(1)(i) and (j)).

Note that if income is being taken into account under this provision, there can be no assumed yield under reg.72 from any capital exceeding £6,000 in value associated with the annuity (reg.72(2)). In most cases such capital could only consist of the right to continue to receive the annuity for the remainder of its term, which could have a market value, on the principle explained in *R(SB) 43/84*.

Income from trusts

2.265   The general rule is that any payment from a trust that is income, rather than capital, counts as unearned income. Exceptions are payments from sums of personal injury compensation held on trust (reg.76(4)) and payments from certain compensation schemes (reg.77). It may sometimes be difficult to say as a matter of general principle whether a payment from a trust is of capital or income, but reg.46(3) deems any sums paid regularly and by reference to a period to be income. Further, reg.46(4) deems each instalment of capital payable by instalments to be income if the amount of capital outstanding (aggregated with any other capital that the claimant has or is treated as having) exceeds £16,000. If the amount of aggregated capital does not exceed £16,000, the payment is to be treated as capital. Note that interests under trusts may well have a capital value (see the notes to reg.46 under the heading *Interests in trusts*) and that there is nothing in Sch.10 to disregard such capital (but see regs 76 and 77)

It was pointed out in *Q v SSWP (JSA)* [2020] UKUT 49 (AAC) that many everyday forms of holding assets jointly involve trusts, such as, in that case, funds belonging to the claimant held in a building society account in joint names. The same would apply where the beneficial interest in the funds, whoever put them in, is expressly or by implication to be held under a joint tenancy. The legal interest in the debt owed by the building society or bank would still be held jointly by those named on the account in trust for themselves as joint tenants. The same would also apply to other assets, including real property, held jointly (see the extensive discussion in the notes to reg.46). Thus, if the trust assets yield income, e.g. in the form of interest, dividends or rental payments, that would appear to be income from a trust under para.(1)(j), to be taken into account in full as unearned income. However, it is rather difficult to see why such a result would have been intended when such income, if received without the intervention of a trust, would not count as unearned income at all under reg.66(1), except through the mechanism of reg.72 and para.(1)(k) if the value of capital including that producing the income exceeded £6,000. But maybe the exclusion of the operation of reg.72 in trust and annuity cases (reg.72(2)) is regarded as establishing a balance.

Assumed income from capital

On para.(1)(k), "assumed yield from capital" (the equivalent to the "tariff income   **2.266** rule" for income support, old style JSA, old style ESA and housing benefit), see the note to reg.72. That applies where the claimant has capital (thus excluding any disregarded capital) in excess of £6,000, when an income of £4.35 per month for each £250 of excess is assumed. If any such income is assumed, reg.72(3) provides that any actual income derived from that capital ("for example rental, interest or dividends") is to be treated as part of the person's capital from the day it is due to be paid. That produces some strange consequences where a claimant is in receipt of rent or some payment for occupation of premises, where not trading in lettings as a self-employed person (see the notes to reg.57). The plain assumption in reg.72(3) is that such income is to be treated as derived from capital in the sense of the value of whatever interest the claimant has in the premises. But neither actual income derived from capital nor rental payments, nor contributions towards household expenses is included in the list of what counts as unearned income. There can only be the assumed income where the value of capital is over £6,000, with the consequence of adding the actual income to the amount of capital, which will go towards keeping it over the £6,000. Regulation 72 can never apply where the income is from letting out some part of the claimant's home, because the capital value of the home is disregarded, so that no yield can be assumed from it.

Capital treated as income

Paragraph (1)(l) includes as income capital that is treated as income under   **2.267** reg.46(3) (regular payments by reference to a period) or (4) (capital payable by instalments in certain circumstances)—see the note to reg.46. See also the notes above under the heading *What is income* for the proposition that para.(1)(l) does not apply to every payment treated as income by virtue of reg.46(3) or (4), but only to *capital* treated as income by virtue of those provisions. That is in particular because of the use of the word "capital" in para.(1)(l). Thus, it appears that payments that are in their nature income cannot fall within para.(1)(l) and only count for universal credit purposes if listed in some other part of para.(1). On that basis, para.(1)(l) covers only payments that are in their nature capital that are paid either regularly and by reference to a period (reg.46(3)) or by instalments (reg.46(4)). If that is correct, it is unfortunate that the relationship of para.(1)(l) with reg.46(3) and (4) was not made more explicit.

PPF periodic payments

2.268   By virtue of para.(7) the definition in s.17(1) of the State Pension Credit Act 2002 (Pt I of this volume) is incorporated. The Pension Protection Fund ("PPF") was set up under the Pensions Act 2004 in order to provide protection for members of defined benefit (i.e. normally final salary) occupational pension schemes and in relation to the defined elements of hybrid pension schemes that were wound up from April 6, 2005 onwards because of the employer's insolvency. For the complex provisions see Pt 2 of the Pensions Act 2004 and the equivalent Northern Ireland provisions. PPF periodic payments do not fall within the meaning of "retirement pension income" in para.(1)(a). By contrast, payments under the Financial Assistance Scheme Regulations 2005, intended to cover defined benefit occupational pension schemes that wound up between January 1997 and April 2005 because of employer insolvency, are included in the meaning of retirement pension income (s.16(1)(n) of the State Pension Credit Act 2002) and so fall within para.(1)(a).

Other income taxable under Pt 5 of ITTOIA

2.269   Paragraph (1)(m) covers other income that does not fall within sub-paras (a)–(la) and is taxable under Pt 5 of the Income Tax (Trading and Other Income) Act 2005 (ITTOIA). The types of income liable to income tax under Pt 5 include receipts from intellectual property, like royalty payments, income from films and sound recordings, income received as a settlor of a trust and income from estates in administration. Those are the categories mentioned in para.H5111 of the ADM and might therefore not be expected to crop up commonly (except perhaps income from estates in administration).

However, what the ADM does not mention, and your commentator has overlooked in previous editions, is that Pt 5 of ITTOIA also contains s.687 (see Vol.IV of this series) making taxable any income not charged to income tax under any provision in ITTOIA or any other Act. In particular, that is the provision under which casual earnings, not derived from employment under a contract of employment or office or from a trade, profession or vocation are taxed. That appears to produce the result that income derived from other paid work within reg.52(a)(iii) is simultaneously earned income and unearned income within sub-para.(m) (see the extensive discussion in the notes to reg.52 for the wide range of activities that in the present-day labour market might give rise to such earnings). Such a result cannot of course be allowed. The counting twice of the same amount as income cannot be allowed, but the way out is not clear. It is submitted that, although the introductory words of reg.66(1) state that a person's unearned income is any of their income falling within the descriptions that follow or reg.74, thus appearing to apply to any income listed whether it would otherwise be regarded as earned income or not, the application of sub-paras (a)–(m) must be coloured by the overall restriction of the scope of Ch.3 of the Regulations to the calculation of unearned income. It is true that para.4(3)(c) of Sch.1 to the WRA 2012 gives the power to make regulations specifying circumstances in which earned income is to be treated as unearned, but that does not authorise such treatment unless the income ceases to be treated as earned. Thus, it is submitted that the words of sub-para.(m) (and probably the whole of para.(1)) must be interpreted as not applying to any income that has already been specifically included as earned income by some other provision of the Regulations.

The question might well be asked whether income from letting property, not as part of a trade, is taxable under s.687 of ITTOIA and so within sub-para.(m).

The answer seems to be that it is not, because the profits of a property business are taxable under Pt 4 of ITTOIA. The notion of a business would on the face of it exclude activities like letting out a room in the home or letting out a single property, but the definitions of a person's "property business" in ss.264 and 265 of ITTOIA cover not only businesses carried on for generating income from land, but also every transaction that a person enters into for that purpose otherwise than in the course of such a business (ss.264(b) and 265(b)). Thus, such income, not being listed in reg.66(1) and not being earned income does not count for universal credit purposes unless and until it metamorphoses into capital.

See the end of the separate section *When is income the claimant's* above for how liability to income tax on the income received is or is not taken into account. It is suggested there that if income tax has been deducted by the payer for remission to HMRC it is only the net amount actually received by the claimant that is to be taken into account. It might also be arguable that expenditure necessary to produce the income is to be deducted applying the principle of *Parsons v Hogg* [1985] 2 All E.R. 897, appendix to *R(FIS) 4/85*, also discussed in that section.

Attribution of unearned income to assessment periods

Unearned income is calculated monthly in accordance with reg.73, except in the case of student income which is calculated in accordance with reg.71. Regulations 68 and 71 in combination also contain the rules for what amount of student income is to be attributed to what assessment period.   **2.270**

What neither reg.66 nor any other provision on unearned income does is to provide any general rule at to how to decide to which assessment periods particular receipts are to be attributed. Regulation 68 does provide a rule for student income, but otherwise the Regulations are silent, as is Chapter H5 of the ADM. There is no equivalent of reg.31 of the Income Support Regulations (Vol.V of this series) with a general rule that income other than earnings is to be treated as paid on the date it is due to be paid. Nor is there any equivalent of the final part of reg.29(2), that the period to which income other than earnings is attributed begins with the date on which the payment is treated as made under reg.31.

In most cases, where a regular amount of income is received monthly or more frequently, there will be no practical problem. However, a couple of examples can be taken to indicate the problem. First, (A) suppose that a claimant receives income from a trust (para.(1)(j)) or instalments of capital that are treated as income (para. (1)(l)) on a quarterly basis in arrears, that the most recent receipt was on April 1 and that the first assessment period in the universal credit claim begins on May 1. Is the monthly equivalent to be taken into account immediately and, if not, how is the next payment on July 1 to be treated? Secondly, (B) suppose that either before or during an existing universal credit award the claimant receives a lump sum payment (less than £5,000) of arrears of a social security benefit falling within para.(1)(a) or (b) that relates to a period before the beginning of entitlement to universal credit. Although such a payment would not be disregarded as capital under para.18 of Sch.10 or reg.10A of the Universal Credit (Transitional Provisions) Regulations 2014, the better view (see above under *What is income*) is that benefit that would have been income if paid on the due date retains its character as income even though paid as a lump sum as arrears (see also the notes to para.18 of Sch.10). Is the lump sum to be taken into account forward from the date of receipt or ignored as unearned income as not relating to an assessment period within the award period?

It is submitted that the principle to be applied is that the monthly equivalent of such payments is to be attributed to the assessment period to which it relates. However, that conclusion unfortunately does not rest on clear statements in the legislation, but on inferences from scattered provisions and its overall structure.

First, it appears clear that the general rule for earnings, of taking each payment into account in the assessment period in which it is received, does not apply to unearned income. That rule only applies to earnings by virtue of the specific provisions in regs 54, 57 and 61. There are no such specific provisions for unearned income. And the requirement in reg.73(1) for unearned income to be calculated as a monthly amount is inconsistent with a rule like the earnings rule.

Second, para.4(3)(a) of Sch.1 to the WRA 2012 authorises the making of regulations specifying circumstances in which a person is to be treated as "having or not having" unearned income, which perhaps points towards a test of having such income, as do the terms of the deeming of having such income in regs 68 (student income) and 74(1) (notional income). But that in itself does not tell us in what assessment period any amount of unearned income is to be taken into account. Paragraph 4(3)(a) would seem to authorise regulations like reg.66(1) defining what sort of income is to be treated as the claimant's and thus that the claimant has, but go no further.

Third, although s.8(3)(b), providing in relation to each assessment period for the deduction of an amount "in respect of unearned income calculated in the pre-scribed manner" in calculating entitlement, does not in itself take matters further forward, the authorisation in para.4(1)(c) of Sch.1 of regulations providing for the calculation or estimation of unearned income in respect of an assessment period begins to suggest the way forward. That is taken on by reg.22(1)(a), providing that the amounts to be deducted include all of the claimant's unearned income (or com-bined unearned income for joint claimants) "in respect of the assessment period" in question. That suggests that the test is of what unearned income is to be regarded as "in respect of" of each assessment period. But is that merely a reflection of the terms of s.8(3)(b) or a rule requiring the finding of a connection of substance between an amount and the assessment period?

Fourth, other regulations are consistent with the second of those alternatives. In particular, reg.73(2A) operates on the assumption that it is the period in respect of which the payment was made that matters, not the period for which the payment is available to be used as income. It applies when the period in respect of which income is paid begins or ends during an assessment period and then supplies a method of calculation of the amount to be taken into account in that period to reflect the number of days in respect of which the unearned income was paid that fall within that period. That provision can only make sense on the basis that "in respect of" identifies the days that the payment of income was for, or in other words the days to which the payment of income relates.

If that is correct, how do the two examples above work out? On example (A), regular quarterly payments in arrears from a trust or in instalments of capital treated as income, reg.73(2)(c) tells us that the monthly equivalent is to be calculated by mul-tiplying by four and dividing by 12. The monthly equivalent of the payment received on April 1 could not be treated as unearned income in the assessment periods begin-ning on May 1 and June 1, because it related entirely to, was "in respect of" the three months prior to April 1. It would not, on that basis, matter that the income was available for the claimant to use in the three months forward from April 1. The amount received would, though, so far as not spent or legitimately disposed of, prob-ably count as part of the claimant's capital. But what should be taken into account in the assessment period beginning on May 1 and June 1 in respect of the payment due on July 1? That payment would be in respect of the previous three months, but could that be used as the basis for taking the monthly equivalent into account for those two assessment periods before the payment had actually been made. Even assuming that full information had been given by the claimant, there might possibly be a change in the amount that the claimant would not know about in advance (such as an increase for inflation or as the result of an alteration in exchange rates). Possibly the answer is that if the amount does not fluctuate, the amount of the April 1 payment can be used to calculate the monthly equivalent for the May and June assessment periods, but that if there is fluctuation then, in the absence of an identifiable cycle, an average can be taken over three months or some other period, presumably prior to the assess-ment period in question (reg.73(3)). However, that is somewhat speculative unless and until there is some authoritative elucidation.

On example (B), a lump sum payment of arrears of a benefit listed in para.(1)(a) or (b) for a period before the start of universal credit entitlement, the answer is clear on the approach suggested above. The payment is to be treated as income and was paid in respect of a period entirely prior to any assessment period and so could not be taken into account as unearned income, even though the money would be available to spend during the period of entitlement. It would therefore presumably metamorphose into capital immediately on receipt and would, so far as not spent or legitimately disposed of, not be disregarded (Sch.10 para.18). Any continuing award of the benefit concerned would of course count as unearned income. If the period covered by the arrears included the date of the start of universal credit entitlement, the awarding decision would fall to be revised under reg.12 of the Decisions and Appeals Regulations 2013.

It is very unfortunate that there should have to be such speculation about matters that would have been expected to be settled clearly by straightforward regulations.

There is a further problem of attribution that arises when a claimant (or the younger of joint claimants) reaches the qualifying age for state pension credit (i.e. state retirement age), so that the condition of entitlement in s.4(1)(b) of the WRA 2012 is no longer met. With effect from November 25, 2020 the new form of para.26 of Sch.1 to the Decisions and Appeals Regulations 2013 provides that any consequential universal credit supersession takes effect from the beginning of the assessment period following the assessment period in which the person reaches the crucial age. That raises the possibility that the claimant might become entitled to retirement pension or state pension or state pension credit relating to the period from the crucial birthday, which period could begin during the last assessment period of entitlement. So far as state pension credit is concerned, that does not matter as that benefit is not listed in reg.66(1). For retirement pension or state pension, there would be a calculation under reg.73(2A) of the appropriate proportion of the monthly amount of the income to cover the days in respect of which the pension was paid. That will work smoothly if the pension is paid on time, so that the calculation can be done shortly after the end of the last assessment period of universal credit entitlement. What is not entirely clear is what should happen if for some reason the first pension payment is delayed beyond the end of that assessment period (except where no claim for pension has been made, when notional income will be deemed under reg.74(3)). There have been reports of the DWP ignoring such a payment and reports to the contrary. As it has been submitted above that the test for attribution is whether the income is related to ("in respect of") any days in the assessment period in question, that later payment of income would be relevant. But how long could a decision-maker legitimately wait to make a decision on the final assessment period? Just possibly, universal credit could be awarded without taking into account any pension as unearned income, followed immediately by a supersession on the ground that it is expected that a relevant change of circumstances (the award of retirement pension or state pension) will occur (reg.23(1)(b) of the Decisions and Appeals Regulations 2013).

Those speculative problems became concrete following the delays in 2021 in making decisions on claims for retirement pension and putting payment into place. Until payment is put into place no actual unearned income (for an under-pension-age claimant's partner) from that source exists to be taken into account as retirement pension income for universal credit purposes under reg.66(1)(a) and there can be no notional unearned income under reg.74 because an "application" has been made for retirement pension. Universal credit awards were then apparently made taking no retirement income from that source into account. When payment of retirement pension is put into place there may be a large payment of arrears due. Following the principles put forward above, that payment constitutes unearned income and is to be attributed to the assessment periods covered by the weeks to which the arrears relate. That circumstance will, depending on the date from which universal credit had been awarded, constitute a ground of revision of the original award of universal credit from the outset, under reg.12 of the Decisions and Appeals Regulations 1999 and s.9(3) of the SSA 1998, or of supersession on the ground of relevant change of circumstances from the first day of the assessment period in which the entitlement to retirement pension arose, under reg.23(1) of the Decisions and Appeals Regulations 1999 and para.31(2)(a)(i) of Sch.1 to the SSA 1998. That will give rise to an overpayment of universal credit that is recoverable under s.71ZB of the SSAA 1992, possibly by deduction from the arrears of retirement pension otherwise payable. Whether there has been such a deduction or not, the amount of arrears actually remaining in the claimant's possession after the end of the assessment periods to which it has been attributed can then metamorphose into capital, whose value would not fall to be disregarded under para.18 of Sch.10 to the Universal Credit Regulations (see para.18(1)(c)). However, if a universal credit overpayment recoverability decision has been made, but there has been no direct deduction from the arrears and repayment has not yet occurred, it is arguable that to the extent of the amount determined to be recoverable the arrears have not metamorphosed into capital because that amount constitutes a "relevant liability" to be taken into account *(R(SB) 2/83* and see the discussion at para.3.197 in relation to the surplus earnings rule in reg.54A) even though different benefits are involved.

Note that special provision is made in the annual social security benefit up-rating orders for the assessment period in which the up-rated amount of a benefit that counts as unearned income is to be taken into account. Thus art.1(4) of the Social Security Benefits Up-rating Order 2023 (SI 2023/316), in conjunction with art.1(3)(p), ensures that in the case of a beneficiary who has an award of universal credit the provision up-rating the social security benefit comes into force for the purpose of calculating entitlement to universal credit on the first day of the first assessment period to commence on or after April 10, 2023.

Meaning of "retirement pension income"

2.271
67.—(1) Subject to paragraph (2), in regulation 66(1)(a) "retirement pension income" has the same meaning as in section 16 of the State Pension Credit Act 2002 as extended by regulation 16 of the State Pension Credit Regulations 2002.

(2) Retirement pension income includes any increase in a Category A or Category B retirement pension mentioned in section 16(1)(a) of the State Pension Credit Act 2002 which is payable under Part 4 of the Contributions and Benefits Act in respect of a person's partner.

DEFINITIONS

"Contributions and Benefits Act"—see reg.2.
"partner"—*ibid.*

GENERAL NOTE

2.272
"Retirement pension income" has the same meaning for the purposes of universal credit as it does for state pension credit. See the notes to s.16 of the State Pension Credit Act 2002 and reg.16 of the State Pension Credit Regulations 2002 in Pts I and III of this volume. The definition covers most kinds of UK state retirement pension provision, thus including the equivalent Northern Ireland provisions to British provisions and occupational or personal pension payments, including from overseas arrangements. Presumably para.(2) is felt to be necessary because s.16(1) (a) of the 2002 Act does not refer to such increases (although in the case of a couple it is their combined income that counts (s.8(4)(b) of the WRA 2012)).

In relation to occupational and personal pension schemes it is necessary to follow a longer chain of references, through s.17(1) of the 2002 Act to s.1 of the Pension Schemes Act 1993. Personal pension schemes are relatively easily identified, but there are sometimes difficulties in differentiating occupational pension schemes, income from which does count in universal credit, and other sorts of schemes income from which does not. The definition in s.1 of the 1993 Act has been amended over the years. The reference for purposes of the Universal Credit Regulations is presumably to the current form, rather than the form in force at the time when the 2002 Regulations were laid. In summary, s.1(1) gives the meaning as "a pension scheme" established for the purpose of providing benefits to, or in respect of, people with service in employment, or to, or in respect of, other people by an employer, employee or some representative body. That on its face seems rather circular, but s.1(5) provides that "pension scheme" means a scheme or other arrangement comprised in one or more instruments or arrangements, having or capable of having effect so as to provide benefits to or in respect of people (a) on retirement; (b) on having reached a particular age; or (c) on termination of employment. That can cover schemes that include death in service benefits to partners, children or dependants of employees and benefits on early retirement or termination of employment for medical reasons. It can then be difficult to work out whether employers' schemes for benefits payable on disablement or death come within that definition. For instance, although various Armed Forces Pension Schemes are clearly within the definition, what about the various pre-2005 War Pensions Schemes and similar and the Armed Forces Compensation Scheme? It is submitted that the latter are not occupational pension schemes. A possible test (no more than that) might be that if a scheme does not provide any benefits on retirement, reaching a particular age or termination of employment independent of incapacity, disablement or death of the employee, it is not an occupational pension scheme. A note to ADM para.H5010 advises that a non-taxable attributable Service Invalidity Pension (SIP) or a Service Attributable Pension (SAP) is a pension awarded to members of the armed forces who are discharged on medical grounds as a result of illness or injury attributed to service. SAPs and non-taxable attributable SIPs are not occupational pensions and are not taken into account.

There is not the space here to mention most of the further categories listed in s.16 of the 2002 Act as extended by reg.16 of the 2002 Regulations. Income from retirement annuity contracts and from annuities bought with the proceeds of personal pension schemes are covered, as are regular payments under an equity release scheme. Payments from a former employer, i.e. not from an occupational scheme as such, on early retirement for ill-health or disability are also covered.

Note the category of notional unearned income in reg.74(3) and (4), where a person has failed to apply for retirement pension income that is available or has deferred taking an annuity or income drawdown that is available from a scheme.

Person treated as having student income

68.—(1) A person who is undertaking a course [1of education, study or training] (see regulation 13) and has a student loan[2, a postgraduate [3 ...] loan] or a grant in respect of that course, is to be treated as having student income in respect of—

(a) an assessment period in which the course begins;

(b) in the case of a course which lasts for two or more years, an assessment period in which the second or subsequent year begins;

(c) any other assessment period in which, or in any part of which, the person is undertaking the course, excluding—

    (i) an assessment period in which the long vacation begins or which falls within the long vacation, or

    (ii) an assessment period in which the course ends.

(2) Where a person has a student loan [2 or a postgraduate [3 ...] loan], their student income for any assessment period referred to in paragraph (1) is to be based on the amount of that loan.

(3) Where paragraph (2) applies, any grant in relation to the period to which the loan applies is to be disregarded except for—

2.273

(a) any specific amount included in the grant to cover payments which are rent payments in respect of which an amount is included in an award of universal credit for the housing costs element;

(b) any amount intended for the maintenance of another person in respect of whom an amount is included in the award.

(4) Where paragraph (2) does not apply, the person's student income for any assessment period in which they are treated as having that income is to be based on the amount of their grant.

(5) A person is to be treated as having a student loan [² or a postgraduate [³...] loan] where the person could acquire [² a student loan or a postgraduate [³...] loan] by taking reasonable steps to do so.

(6) Student income does not include any payment referred to in regulation 66(1)(f) (training allowances).

(7) In this regulation and regulations 69 to 71—

"grant" means any kind of educational grant or award, excluding a student loan or a payment made under a scheme to enable persons under the age of 21 to complete courses of education or training that are not advanced education;

"the long vacation" is a period of no less than one month which, in the opinion of the Secretary of State, is the longest vacation during a course which is intended to last for two or more years;

[³ "postgraduate loan" means a loan to a student undertaking a postgraduate master's degree course or a postgraduate doctoral degree course pursuant to regulations made under section 22 of the Teaching and Higher Education Act 1998;]

"student loan" means a loan towards a student's maintenance pursuant to any regulations made under section 22 of the Teaching and Higher Education Act 1998, section 73 of the Education (Scotland) Act 1980 or Article 3 of the Education (Student Support) (Northern Ireland) Order 1998 and includes, in Scotland, a young student's bursary paid under regulation 4(1)(c) of the Students' Allowances (Scotland) Regulation 2007.

AMENDMENTS

1. Universal Credit (Consequential, Supplementary, Incidental and Miscellaneous Provisions) Regulations 2013 (SI 2013/630) reg. 38(5) (April 29, 2013).

2. Social Security (Treatment of Postgraduate Master's Degree Loans and Special Support Loans) (Amendment) Regulations 2016 (SI 2016/743) reg. 6(2) (August 4, 2016).

3. Social Security (Income and Capital) (Miscellaneous Amendments) Regulations 2020 (SI 2020/618) reg.8(2) (July 15, 2020).

DEFINITIONS

"assessment period"—see WRA 2012, ss.40 and 7(2) and reg.21.
"housing costs element"—see regs 2 and 25.

GENERAL NOTE

2.274   See the notes to reg.13 for when a person is regarded as undertaking a course of education, study or training. If someone who is exempt from the requirement not to be receiving education under reg.14 has student income that is taken into account in calculating their universal credit award, they will not have any work requirements (see reg.89(1)(e)(ii) and reg.89(1)(da) for couples where only one partner is a student). If the person leaves their course, student income is taken into account up to the end of the assessment period before the one in which they leave the course. That is because the person is no longer undertaking the course and so para.(1) of this regulation does not apply (the change of circumstance will take effect from the first day of the assessment period in which it occurs—para.20 of Sch.1 to the Decisions and Appeals Regulations 2013). In addition, the terms of reg.68(1)(c)(ii) prevent a person being treated as having student income in the assessment period in which the course ends. As any student income that is left over at the end of a course or when a person finally abandons or is dismissed from it does not fall within any other paragraph in reg.66(1), it will be ignored.

Paragraph (1)

2.275
This provides for the assessment periods (i.e. months) in which student income will be taken into account. These are any assessment periods during which, or during part of which, the person is undertaking the course of education, study or training, including the assessment period in which the course begins, or any subsequent year of the course begins. But student income will be ignored in the assessment period in which the course ends, in the assessment period in which the long vacation (defined in para.(7)) starts and in any assessment periods that fall wholly within the long vacation.

Paragraphs (2)–(7)

2.276
These paragraphs define what counts as student income. It does not include training allowances and payment for living expenses taken into account under reg.66(1)(f) (para.(6)).

If a person has a student loan or a postgraduate loan (both defined in para.(7)), or is treated as having a student loan or a postgraduate loan under para.(5), the amount of that loan counts as income and any grant (defined in para.(7)) paid for the same period as the loan is ignored. But any specific amount included in the grant for rent payments which are being met by universal credit, or any amount intended for the maintenance of another person included in the person's universal credit award, will count as income (paras (2) and (3)).

With effect from July 2020 postgraduate doctoral degree loans have been brought within the general definition of "postgraduate loan", so that they are subject to the same rules as previously applied only to master's degree loans. Doctoral degree loans were introduced in 2018, at the same annual rate as for master's degree loans (i.e. £11,836 for courses starting on or after August 1, 2022 and £12,167 for courses starting on or after August 1, 2023, with an overall cap of, for 2022/23, £27,892 and, for 2023/24, £28,673. It would seem that prior to July 2020 postgraduate doctoral degree loans would have fallen within the definition of "student loan", since the relevant English regulations were made under s.22 of the Teaching and Higher Education Act 1998, meaning that the 30% rule in reg.69(1A) would not have applied, but only a loan going towards maintenance would have counted. It is not known if the 30% rule was applied in practice before the July 2020 amendments.

If the person does not have, and is not treated under para.(5) as having, a student loan or a postgraduate loan, grant income is taken into account (para.4)).

Note the exclusion from the definition of "grant" of payments made to enable people under 21 to complete courses of non-advanced education or training. This means that payments from the 16–19 Bursary Fund and educational maintenance allowances (in so far as they still exist) do not count as student income (they are fully disregarded for the purposes of income support, old style JSA, old style ESA and housing benefit). Paragraph H6008 ADM also states that grant income does not include any payment derived from Access Funds (although the basis for this is not clear).

"Student loan" for the purposes of regs 68–71 only includes a loan towards the student's maintenance (see para.(7)). So, for instance, the special support element (intended to contribute to the costs of books, childcare, travel and equipment) of any special support maintenance loan is not included. In Scotland, a student loan also includes a young student's bursary. Any loan for tuition fees will be ignored.

See regs 69–71 for the calculation of student income. There is a disregard for student income of £110 per assessment period (reg.71).

Calculation of student income—student loans [¹ and postgraduate [²...] loans]

2.277   **69.**—(1) Where, in accordance with regulation 68(2), a person's student income is to be based on the amount of a student loan for a year, the amount to be taken into account is the maximum student loan (including any increases for additional weeks) that the person would be able to acquire in respect of that year by taking reasonable steps to do so.

[¹ (1A) Where, in accordance with regulation 68(2), a person's student income is to be based on the amount of a postgraduate [²...] loan for a year, the amount to be taken into account is 30 per cent. of the maximum postgraduate [²...] loan that the person would be able to acquire by taking reasonable steps to do so.]

(2) For the purposes of calculating the maximum student loan in paragraph (1) [¹ or the maximum postgraduate [²...] loan in paragraph (1A)] it is to be assumed no reduction has been made on account of—

(a) the person's means or the means of their partner, parent or any other person; or

(b) any grant made to the person.

AMENDMENTS

1. Social Security (Treatment of Postgraduate Master's Degree Loans and Special Support Loans) (Amendment) Regulations 2016 (SI 2016/743) reg. 6(3) (August 4, 2016).

2. Social Security (Income and Capital) (Miscellaneous Amendments) Regulations 2020 (SI 2020/618) reg.8(3) (July 15, 2020).

DEFINITIONS

"grant"—see reg.68(7).
"partner"—see reg.2.
"postgraduate loan—see reg.68(7).
"student loan"—see regs 2 and 68(7).

GENERAL NOTE

2.278   The amount of a student loan that is taken into account is the maximum amount (including any increases for additional weeks) that the person could obtain for that year if they took reasonable steps to do so (para.(1)), bearing in mind the amounts, not being towards the student's maintenance, that are excluded from the definition in reg.68(7). In the case of a postgraduate loan, it is 30 per cent of the maximum postgraduate loan that the person could obtain for that year if they took reasonable steps to do so (para.(1A)). No reduction is made for any assessed contribution from a parent or partner (or any other person) or for any grant which may have reduced the loan.

In *CH/4429/2006* the claimant's partner had a religious objection to taking out a loan and it was argued that that made it unreasonable for him to do so. The Commissioner rejected that argument on the basis that "reasonable" only qualified the steps that could be taken to acquire a student loan. It is understood that that decision is under challenge in an appeal currently before the Upper Tribunal.

See reg.71 for how the amount of student income to be taken into account in an assessment period is calculated (note the disregard of £110).

Calculation of student income—grants

2.279

70. Where, in accordance with regulation 68(4), a person's student income is to be based on the amount of a grant, the amount to be taken into account is the whole of the grant excluding any payment—

(a) intended to meet tuition fees or examination fees;

(b) in respect of the person's disability;

(c) intended to meet additional expenditure connected with term time residential study away from the person's educational establishment;

(d) intended to meet the cost of the person maintaining a home at a place other than that at which they reside during their course, except where an award of universal credit includes an amount for the housing costs element in respect of those costs;

(e) intended for the maintenance of another person, but only if an award of universal credit does not include any amount in respect of that person;

(f) intended to meet the cost of books and equipment;

(g) intended to meet travel expenses incurred as a result of the person's attendance on the course; or

(h) intended to meet childcare costs.

DEFINITION

"grant"—see regs 2 and 68(7).

GENERAL NOTE

2.280

If a grant counts as student income (on which see reg.68 and the note to that regulation), the whole of the grant is taken into account, subject to the disregards in paras (a)–(h). The disregards in paras (d) and (e) do not apply if the person's universal credit award includes an amount in respect of housing costs (para.(d)) or for the maintenance of another person (para.(e)) (see also reg.68(3)).

See reg.71 for how the amount of student income to be taken into account in an assessment period is calculated (note the disregard of £110).

Calculation of student income—amount for an assessment period

2.281

71. The amount of a person's student income in relation to each assessment period in which the person is to be treated as having student income in accordance with regulation 68(1) is calculated as follows.

Step 1

Determine whichever of the following amounts is applicable—

(a) [[1] in so far as regulation 68(2) applies to a person with a student loan,] the amount of the loan (and, if applicable, the amount of any grant) in relation to the year of the course in which the assessment period falls; [[1] . . .]

[[1] (aa) in so far as regulation 68(2) applies to a person with a postgraduate [[2] ...] loan, 30 per cent. of the amount of the loan in relation to the year of the course in which the assessment period falls; or]

(b) if regulation 68(4) applies (person with a grant but no student loan [[1] or postgraduate [[2] ...] loan]) the amount of the grant in relation to the year of the course in which the assessment period falls.

But if the period of the course is less than a year determine the amount of the grant or loan in relation to the course.

Step 2

Determine in relation to—
(a) the year of the course in which the assessment period falls; or
(b) if the period of the course is less than a year, the period of the course,
the number of assessment periods for which the person is to be treated as
having student income under regulation 68(1).

Step 3

Divide the amount produced by step 1 by the number of assessment
periods produced by step 2.

Step 4

Deduct £110.

AMENDMENTS

1. Social Security (Treatment of Postgraduate Master's Degree Loans and Special
Support Loans) (Amendment) Regulations 2016 (SI 2016/743) reg. 6(4) (August
4, 2016).
2. Social Security (Income and Capital) (Miscellaneous Amendments) Regulations
2020 (SI 2020/618) reg.8(4) (July 15, 2020).

DEFINITIONS

"grant"—see regs 2 and 68(7).
"postgraduate loan"—see reg.68(7).
"student loan"—see regs 2 and 68(7).

GENERAL NOTE

2.282 The amount of a person's student income that is to be taken into account in each
assessment period (i.e. month) is worked out as follows:

Step 1:
(a) if the person has, or is treated as having, a student loan, calculate the annual
amount of the loan, plus, if applicable, the annual amount of any grant that is
to be taken into account (see regs 68 and 70), for that year of the course; or
(b) if the person has, or is treated as having, a postgraduate loan, calculate 30
per cent. of the loan for that year of the course; or
(c) if the person has a grant but does not have, and is not treated as having, a
student loan, or a postgraduate loan, calculate the amount of the grant for
that year of the course; or
(d) if the course lasts for less than a year, calculate the amount of the loan and/
or grant for the course.

Step 2: calculate the number of assessment periods for which the person is to be
treated as having student income in that year of the course, or if the course lasts
for less than a year, during the course, in accordance with reg.68(1). Note that
this will include assessment periods during which the person was undertaking the
course and which count under reg.68(1), even if the person had not made a claim
for universal credit at that time. See H6140-6144 ADM (example 2).

Step 3: divide the amount in Step 1 by the number of assessments periods in Step 2.

Step 4: deduct £110, as £110 of student income is ignored in each assessment
period.

General

Assumed yield from capital

72.—(1) A person's capital is to be treated as yielding a monthly income   2.283
of £4.35 for each £250 in excess of £6,000 and £4.35 for any excess which
is not a complete £250.

(2) Paragraph (1) does not apply where the capital is disregarded or
the actual income from that capital is taken into account under regulation
66(1)(i) (income from an annuity) or (j) (income from a trust).

(3) Where a person's capital is treated as yielding income, any actual
income derived from that capital, for example rental, interest or dividends,
is to be treated as part of the person's capital from the day it is due to be
paid to the person.

GENERAL NOTE

This contains the universal credit equivalent of the tariff income rule that applies   2.284
for income support, old style JSA, old style ESA and housing benefit. Under universal credit it is referred to as "assumed yield from capital", which is then taken into
account in full under reg.66(1)(k).

If a person has capital above £6,000 but below £16,000, it is treated as producing £4.35 per month for each complete £250 above £6,000 and £4.35 per month
for any odd amount left over (para.(1)). But this does not apply if the capital is
disregarded (see Sch.10 and regs 75 and 76), or if the actual income is taken into
account under reg.66(1)(i) (income from an annuity) or (j) (income from a trust)
(para.(2)). And remember the deductions that must be made under reg.49 in reaching the value of capital.

If the assumed yield from capital rule does apply, actual income from the
capital counts as part of the person's capital from the day it is due to be paid (para.
(3)). This rule could produce some tricky conundrums if the amount of the claimant's capital is very close to the £6,000 boundary or to a boundary between different
amounts of assumed yield. Say that a claimant with an assessment period from the
first to last day of the calendar month and with no other capital owns a heavily mortgaged second property whose capital value for universal credit purposes is £5,900 and
which is rented out for £500 a month, payable on the 21st. Prima facie, when the rent
is received it does not count as actual unearned income as it is not listed in reg.66(1),
nor is it to be added to the claimant's capital because the capital is not treated under
para.(1) as yielding an income. If the claimant retained the amount of the rent into
the next assessment period, their capital would increase to £6,400, but if the £500
had immediately been spent on mortgage interest, that would not happen. However, if
the capital value of the property was £6,100, what would happen? Would the £500 be
treated as capital because at the date it was due to be paid income was being assumed
and, if so, would the assumed income for that assessment period be based on £6,100
or £6,600? Or should the calculation not be made until the end of the assessment
period? If by that date the claimant had used the £500 for the mortgage interest and
so no longer had that capital, should the assumed yield be based on £6,100? Readers
can no doubt think up more complicated scenarios.

Unearned income calculated monthly

73.—(1) A person's unearned income is to be calculated as a monthly   2.285
amount.

(2) Where the period in respect of which a payment of income is made is
not a month, an amount is to be calculated as the monthly equivalent, so
for example—

(a) weekly payments are multiplied by 52 and divided by 12;
(b) four weekly payments are multiplied by 13 and divided 12;
(c) three monthly payments are multiplied by 4 and divided by 12; and
(d) annual payments are divided by 12.

[¹(2A) Where the period in respect of which unearned income is paid begins or ends during an assessment period the amount of unearned income for that assessment period is to be calculated as follows—

$$N \times \left(\frac{M \times 12}{365} \right)$$

where N is the number of days in respect of which unearned income is paid that fall within the assessment period and M is the monthly amount referred to in paragraph (1) or, as the case may be, the monthly equivalent referred to in paragraph (2).]

(3) Where the amount of a person's unearned income fluctuates, the monthly equivalent is to be calculated—

(a) where there is an identifiable cycle, over the duration of one such cycle; or
(b) where there is no identifiable cycle, over three months or such other period as may, in the particular case, enable the monthly equivalent of the person's income to be determined more accurately.

(4) This regulation does not apply to student income.

AMENDMENT

1. Universal Credit (Digital Service) Amendment Regulations 2014 (SI 2014/2887) reg.4 (November 26, 2014). The amendment is subject to the saving provision in reg.5 of SI 2014/2887 (see 2020/21 edition of Vol.V of this series).

DEFINITIONS

"assessment period"—see WRA 2012 ss.40 and 7(2) and reg.21.
"student income"—see reg.68.

GENERAL NOTE

Paragraphs (1) and (2)

2.286 Unearned income is calculated as a monthly amount (paras (1) and (2)). But unlike earned income the amount taken into account in an assessment period (i.e. month) is not necessarily the amount actually received in that month. If the amount of the unearned income varies, the monthly equivalent is calculated in accordance with para.(3)).

See the notes to reg.66 under the heading *Attribution of unearned income to assessment periods* for discussion of how payments of unearned income are to be attributed to particular assessment periods in the absence of specific provisions providing a general rule.

Paragraph (2A)

2.287 This paragraph provides an exception to the general rule that unearned income is calculated as a monthly amount. For assessment periods (i.e. months) during which unearned income starts and/or finishes, only an amount based on the actual days in respect of which the income is paid will be taken into account. That is likely mainly to affect benefit payments and pensions.

Note that the amendment which inserted para.(2A) is subject to a saving provision–see reg. 5 of the Universal Credit (Digital Service) Amendment Regulations

2014. The effect is that para.(2A) only applies to awards in relation to claims from people living in areas where the "digital service" (also referred to by DWP as the "full service") is in operation or from such persons who subsequently form a new couple or who separate after being part of a couple. Its operation is now general.

Paragraph (3)

This provides that if there is an identifiable cycle, the amount of unearned income received during that cycle is converted into a monthly amount (para.(3)(a)). If there is no cycle, the amount taken into account is averaged over three months, or over another period if this produces a more accurate monthly equivalent (para.(3)(b)). See the notes to reg.5(2)–(3A) of the Income Support Regulations in Vol.V of this series for discussion of when there is a recognisable cycle, making the necessary allowances for the present regulation applying only to unearned income. There is no equivalent here to paras (3)–(3A) of reg.5. "Identifiable" cannot mean anything different from "recognisable".

2.288

Paragraph (4)

This regulation does not apply to the calculation of student income. See reg.71 for the amount of a person's student income that is to be taken into account in each assessment period.

2.289

Notional unearned income

74.—(1) If unearned income would be available to a person upon the making of an application for it, the person is to be treated as having that unearned income.

2.290

(2) Paragraph (1) does not apply to the benefits listed in regulation 66(1)(b).

(3) A person who has reached the qualifying age for state pension credit is to be treated as possessing the amount of any retirement pension income for which no application has been made and to which the person might expect to be entitled if a claim were made.

(4) The circumstances in which a person is to be treated as possessing retirement pension income for the purposes of universal credit are the same as the circumstances set out in regulation 18 of the State Pension Credit Regulations 2002 in which a person is treated as receiving retirement pension income for the purposes of state pension credit.

DEFINITION

"retirement pension income"—see reg.67.

GENERAL NOTE

Paragraphs (1) and (2)

A person is treated as having unearned income if "it would be available to [them] upon the making of an application for it". But that does not apply to the benefits listed in reg.66(1)(b).

2.291

A person should only be treated as having unearned income under para.(1) if it is clear that it would be paid if an application for it was made. Thus, for example, para. (1) would not apply to payments from a trust that are within the discretion of the trustees. A decision-making process by the trustees would have to be followed before a payment could be made, so that the income could not be said to be available upon making an application for it.

It is commonly said that no rule similar to those applied under paras (3) and (4) below can be applied to a person who has not attained the qualifying age for state pension credit. However, it is not clear why para.(1) should not apply to retirement pension income that a claimant could access before reaching that age. Members of both occupational and personal pension schemes can usually choose to take some or all of their entitlements under the scheme from the age of 55 and that may create income by the buying of an annuity or by drawdown from the funds in the scheme. Since those are options that are freely available and that the scheme administrators are bound to implement, the terms of para.(1) would seem to apply. "Retirement pension income" is defined in s.16 of the State Pension Credit Act 2002, to which reg.67 refers, simply in terms including income from an occupational pension scheme or a personal pension scheme (subs.(1)(f)) with no condition about the age at which the income is taken. The contrary argument would presumably be that the specific provisions in paras (3) and (4) linked to qualifying age for state pension credit are sufficient to indicate that they constitute the complete rules for retirement pension income, to the exclusion of para.(1). But para.(1) is not made subject to paras (3) and (4).

Paragraphs (3) and (4)

2.292   A person who has reached the qualifying age for state pension credit will be treated as having retirement pension income (defined in reg.67), first, under para.(3), of income that the person might expect to be entitled to if a claim were made for it, where no application has been made. Second, under para.(4), a person who has reached that age is to be treated as possessing retirement pension income in the same circumstances as set out in reg.18 of the State Pension Credit Regulations 2002 (Pt III of this volume). Only paras (1)–(1CB) of reg.18 specifically refer to retirement pension income, but presumably paras (1D)–(5), which refer to income from occupational pension schemes and money purchase benefits, which are within the meaning of retirement pension income in s.16 of the State Pension Credit Act 2002, are also intended to be incorporated. If so, paras (3) and (4) of reg.74 appear to cover much of the same ground. Paragraph (3) is in very general terms, but para.(4) may cover some circumstances that do not fall within the notion of not applying for income to which a person might expect to be entitled. See the notes to reg.18 of the SPC Regulations in Pt III of this volume and in particular to reg.42(2ZA) – (2C) of the Income Support Regulations in Vol.V of this series for more detailed consideration. A summary of the effect is given below.

Very much in general, the following are covered. A person who defers taking their state pension is treated as having the amount applicable if the pension had been taken at the qualifying age. A person who defers taking benefits from an occupational pension scheme beyond the scheme's retirement age, where the scheme allows that, is treated as having the amount of pension that would have been received if benefits had started at the normal age. A person in a defined contribution occupational pension scheme who does not buy an annuity or take advantage of income drawdown after state pensionable age is treated as having the amount of the annuity that could have been bought with the fund. The qualifying age for state pension credit was 60 but since April 2010 it has gradually risen in line with the staged increase in pensionable age for women and reached 65 in November 2018; thereafter state pension age for both men and women started to rise from 65 in December 2018, to reach 66 by October 2020. Although it is a condition of entitlement to universal credit that a person is below the qualifying age for state pension credit (see s.4(1)(b) of the WRA 2012), a couple may still be entitled if one member of the couple is under that age (see reg.3(2)) and the other is not.

If a person below the qualifying age for state pension credit chooses not to apply for retirement pension income, he or she will not be caught by paras (3) and (4), but see the notes to paras (1) and (2) for the possible application of those provisions.

For the rules relating to notional earned income, see reg.60.

CHAPTER 4

MISCELLANEOUS

Compensation for personal injury

75.—(1) This regulation applies where a sum has been awarded to a   2.293
person, or has been agreed by or behalf of a person, in consequence of a
personal injury to that person.

(2) If, in accordance with an order of the court or an agreement, the person
receives all or part of that sum by way of regular payments, those payments
are to be disregarded in the calculation of the person's unearned income.

(3) If the sum has been used to purchase an annuity, payments under the
annuity are to be disregarded in the calculation of the person's unearned income.

(4) If the sum is held in trust, any capital of the trust derived from that
sum is to be disregarded in the calculation of the person's capital and any
income from the trust is to be disregarded in the calculation of the person's
unearned income.

(5) If the sum is administered by the court on behalf of the person or can
only be disposed of by direction of the court, it is to be disregarded in the calculation of the person's capital and any regular payments from that amount
are to be disregarded in the calculation of the person's unearned income.

(6) If the sum is not held in trust or has not been used to purchase an
annuity or otherwise disposed of, but has been paid to the person within
the past 12 months, that sum is to be disregarded in the calculation of the
person's capital.

GENERAL NOTE

This regulation provides for an extensive disregard of compensation for personal   2.294
injury, both as capital and income.

Firstly, the compensation is ignored for 12 months from the date it is paid to the
person (para.(6)). Thus if it is spent during that 12 months or reduces to £6,000 or
less, it will not have any effect on universal credit.

Secondly, if the compensation is held in trust, it will be disregarded as capital
indefinitely and any income from the trust will be disregarded in the calculation of
the person's unearned income (para.(4) and reg.66(1)(j)). It is often assumed if the
amount is held in trust that will guarantee that the funds are at the least in some
account separate from the claimant's other assets, if not held in some specifically
created personal injury or other form of trust. However, that does not take into
account the decision in *Q v SSWP (JSA)* [2020] UKUT 49 (AAC) that funds held
in a joint bank or building society account with someone else are subject to a trust.
There, funds derived a payment to the claimant of personal injury compensation
were paid into joint accounts with one or other of her parents. Judge Poynter held
that since there was no suggestion of any intention to make a gift of any of the funds
to her parents, there would be a resulting trust under which the claimant and the
parent held the chose in action (the right to payment of the moneys in the account)
jointly on trust for the benefit of the claimant. For the purposes of the disregard as
capital of the value of the trust fund where the funds of the trust are derived from
a payment in consequence of a personal injury to the claimant in para.17 of Sch.8
to the JSA Regulations 1996, the form of the trust did not matter, so that para.17
applied. Although the wording of the disregard in para.(4) is different from that being
considered in *Q*, the words "in trust" are not a term of art that has some special or
technical meaning. Giving them their ordinary and natural meaning would mean that
para.(4) should apply whenever the sum derived from personal injury compensation

is subject to a trust, so that, as in *Q*, the form of the trust should not matter. Similarly, if the compensation payment is administered by a court, or can only be disposed of by direction of a court, its capital value is ignored and any regular payments from it are ignored in the calculation of the person's unearned income (para.(5)).

Thirdly, if the compensation is used to purchase an annuity, payments under the annuity are disregarded as unearned income (para.(3) and reg.66(1)(i)).

Fourthly, if, in accordance with a court order or agreement, the person receives all or part of the compensation by way of regular payments, these are ignored as unearned income (see para.(2)).

Although paras (3)–(5) refer to "the sum" awarded or agreed, in contrast to para. (2), which refers to all or part of that sum, it is submitted that in the overall context, "the sum" in paras (3)–(5) must be interpreted to include part of that sum and amounts derived from the original award or agreement.

The discussion at a meeting of the Social Security Advisory Committee (SSAC) on December 8, 2021 in relation to the Social Security (Income and Capital Disregards) (Amendment) Regulations 2021 (SI 2021/1405) (see the notes to reg.76) revealed some conceptual problems in the relationship of capital disregards to the calculation of the amount of capital possessed at a particular date. The essence of the problem put to DWP officials was what would happen if a claimant received a compensation payment within the disregard introduced by those regulations, acquired further non-disregarded capital and then spent a substantial amount of capital: how would it be known what pot of capital the expenditure came out of (SSAC minutes December 8, 2021, para.2.2(f))? The answer given in the letter dated January 12, 2022 from the Minister for Welfare Delivery, David Rutley, (Annex C to the minutes) was that:

> "the Department does not attempt to distinguish the capital derived from a compensation payment from other capital (with the exception of personal injury compensation that has been placed in trust). Wherever a claimant has received a payment of capital which is disregarded, whether indefinitely or for a prescribed period, their capital threshold is effectively increased by the amount of the original payment for the duration of that period. This is regardless of whether it was simply paid into a bank account with other funds or held or invested elsewhere."

That reply leaves it rather unclear what view is taken where a sum derived from compensation for personal injury to the claimant is held in trust, apparently being based on the mistaken view (see above) that that necessarily involves the sum being held in a segregated account. If the sum is so held, whether in a specially created trust or in a joint account of the kind in issue in *Q v SSWP (JSA)* [2020] UKUT 49 if it is used only for money from that source, there should be little difficulty in identifying when payments have been made out of that account, so that the payments out will not serve to reduce the amount of any other capital held by the claimant. The difficulty arises if the sum is held for the benefit of the claimant in a joint account which also contains funds of the claimant from other sources (or is not held in trust at all). The Minister's reply would then suggest that a payment out of the fund would leave the amount disregarded under reg.75(4) or (6) unaffected. That outcome might be justifiable in general (see the notes to Sch.10), but it is far from clear how that approach should hold if, say, the payment out is for a purpose specifically covered by the compensation payment, e.g. providing disability adaptations to a home.

There appears to be no problem with the relationship with reg.50(1) on notional capital (deprivation for the purpose of securing entitlement to or increasing the amount of universal credit) if the court order or agreement directly requires the making of regular payments (para.(2)) or the holding of the compensation payment on trust (para.(4)) or control by a court (para.(5)). However, an apparent problem could arise in cases in which the payment has initially been paid to the person concerned and later some or all of the amount is placed into a trust or is used to purchase an annuity. If that action had not been taken, the disregard under para.

(6) could not have lasted for longer than 12 months. Therefore, depending on the amounts involved and other circumstances, it could appear on the face of it that the transfer of the capital was for the purpose of securing entitlement to universal credit or increasing its amount after the running out of that 12 months, so that the person would be treated as still possessing the amount disposed of. There is no equivalent in reg.50 to reg.51(1)(a) of the Income Support Regulations (reg.113(1)(a) of the JSA Regulations 1996 and reg.115(1)(a) of the ESA Regulations 2008) excluding its operation where the capital disposed of is derived from a payment made in consequence of a personal injury and is placed on trust. However, as suggested in the notes to reg.50(1) above, the intention of reg.75 is so clearly that the holding of funds in the ways set out in paras (3)–(5) should not affect entitlement to universal credit that it is submitted that the notional capital rule cannot be applied in those circumstances. The only penalty for continuing to hold funds as capital with no restrictions after the expiry of 12 months from the date of initial payment should be the loss of the para.(6) disregard for so long as the funds remain held in that way.

"Personal injury" is not given any definition in the WRA 2012 or these Regulations. The phrase must therefore be given its ordinary meaning, which in *R(SB) 2/89* was held to include a disease and any injuries suffered as a result of a disease (e.g. amputation of both legs following meningitis and septicaemia), as well as any accidental or criminal injury.

Compensation for personal injury includes all heads of an award for personal injury (*Peters v East Midlands Strategic Health Authority* [2009] EWCA Civ 145; [2010] Q.B. 48, a decision on the meaning of "an award of damages for a personal injury" in para.44(2)(a) of Sch.10 to the Income Support Regulations (see Vol.V of this series) but the same reasoning will apply). In particular, it is not restricted to general damages for pain, suffering and loss of amenity, but can include other heads of loss, such as loss of earnings and any sum awarded by a court in respect of the cost of providing accommodation and care. See also *R(IS) 15/96* (para.18), applying that approach to criminal injuries compensation.

KQ v SSWP (IS) [2011] UKUT 102 (AAC), reported as [2011] AACR 43, holds that a compensation payment received from negligent solicitors, which purely related to what should have been claimed from a negligent surgeon responsible for damage to the claimant, was in consequence of the personal injury to the claimant. Judge Levenson accepts that the chain of causation does not go on for ever and so damages for the stress caused by the negligent solicitors or an element of punitive damages might not come within the disregards in para.12 or 12A of Sch.10. But there was no such element in the compensation in this case.

The disregards in reg.75 are in terms of compensation paid to a "person" in consequence of personal injury "to that person". Thus, where both members of a couple are claimants under s.2(1)(b) of the WRA 2012 it does not matter which of them is the recipient of the compensation, providing that it was in consequence of a personal injury to that person. However, they do not apply where the personal injury is to someone else, such as where an award is made under the Fatal Accidents Act 1976 (*CP v SSWP (IS)* [2011] UKUT 157 (AAC)). There, the claimant, who had Down's syndrome, received substantial compensation under the 1976 Act after her mother (and primary carer) was killed in a road traffic accident. Paragraph 12 of Sch.10 did not bite on such an award where the personal injury (or rather the fatality) was suffered by the claimant's mother, not the claimant. Nor would reg.75.

Special schemes for compensation etc.

76.—(1) This regulation applies where a person receives a payment from   2.295
a scheme established or approved by the Secretary of State or from a trust
established with funds provided by the Secretary of State for the purpose of—
    (a) providing compensation [¹or support] in respect of [³any of the following]—

    (i) a person having been diagnosed with variant Creutzfeldt-Jacob disease or infected from contaminated blood products,

   (ii) the bombings in London on 7th July 2005,

  (iii) persons who have been interned or suffered forced labour, injury, property loss or loss of a child during the Second World War; [¹...]

  [¹(iv) the terrorist attacks in London on 22nd March 2017 or 3rd June 2017,

   (v) the bombing in Manchester on 22nd May 2017], [² ...]

  [²(vi) the fire at Grenfell Tower on 14th June 2017; [³...]]

  [³(vii) historic institutional child abuse in the United Kingdom;]

(b) supporting persons with a disability to live independently in their accommodation.

[²(1A) This regulation also applies where a person receives a payment from—

(a) the National Emergencies Trust, registered charity number 1182809;

(b) the Child Migrants Trust, registered charity number 1171479, under the scheme for former British child migrants; or

(c) the Royal Borough of Kensington and Chelsea or a registered charity where the payment is made because that person was affected by the fire at Grenfell Tower on 14th June 2017 or is the personal representative of such a person.]

[³(d) the scheme established by the Windrush Compensation Scheme (Expenditure) Act 2020.]

(2) Any such payment, if it is capital, is to be disregarded in the calculation of the person's capital and, if it is income, is to be disregarded in the calculation of the person's income.

(3) In relation to a claim for universal credit made by the partner, parent, son or daughter of a diagnosed or infected person referred to in paragraph (1)(a)(i) a payment received from the scheme or trust, or from the diagnosed or infected person or from their estate is to be disregarded if it would be disregarded in relation to an award of state pension credit by virtue of paragraph 13 or 15 of Schedule 5 to the State Pension Credit Regulations 2002.

AMENDMENTS

1. Social Security (Emergency Funds) (Amendment) Regulations 2017 (SI 2017/689) reg.9 (June 19, 2017).

2. Social Security (Income and Capital) (Miscellaneous Amendments) Regulations 2020 (SI 2020/618) reg.8(5) (July 15, 2020).

3. Social Security (Income and Capital Disregards) (Amendment) Regulations 2021 (SI 2021/1405) reg.8 (January 1, 2022).

DEFINITIONS

"claim"—see WRA 2012 s.40.
"partner"—see reg.2.

GENERAL NOTE

2.296   This regulation disregards payments from various compensation and support schemes and schemes to support people with a disability to live independently set up or approved by the Government. Any payment from these schemes or trusts is ignored as capital if it is capital, and as income if it is income (para.(2) and reg.66(1)(j)). Payments of capital under para.(3) that are made to a parent of a person diagnosed with variant Creutzfeldt-Jacob disease are disregarded for two years; in the case of a payment to a parent of a person infected from contaminated blood products they are ignored until two years after the date of the person's death.

There are some technical problems with the addition with effect from January 1, 2022 of the disregards of payments from approved schemes providing compensation in respect of historic institutional child abuse in the UK (para.(1)(a)(vii)) and from the Windrush Compensation Scheme (para.(1A)(d)). All the schemes so far in existence provide payments in the nature of capital, so that a disregarding as income does not in practice arise. But in any event, for universal credit purposes, the fact that the payments, even if in the nature of income, would not fall within any category of unearned income in reg.66(1) would mean that they could not be taken into account.

The Explanatory Memorandum to the amending regulations reveals that four child abuse compensation schemes had been approved by the Secretary of State as at January 1, 2022: under the Historical Institutional Abuse (Northern Ireland) Act 2019; the Redress for Survivors (Historical Child Abuse in Care) (Scotland) Act 2021; the London Borough of Lambeth Redress Scheme and the London Borough of Islington's proposed support payment scheme. All provide one-off capital payments. The Memorandum also reveals that payments under the Northern Ireland and Lambeth schemes could have been made prior to January 1, 2022. The application of the disregards provided under SI 2021/1405 to such pre-January 2022 payments has been authorised by a ministerial direction from the Secretary of State, acting under "common law powers" (see the letters of December 3, 2021 between the Permanent Secretary and the Secretary of State, published on the internet). The Windrush Compensation Scheme has also been making payments for some time. The correspondence above states that extra-statutory arrangements agreed with HM Treasury provided for the disregard in practice of such payments in means-tested benefits from the outset. It might be thought that the delay in putting that outcome on a proper statutory basis is symptomatic of the way in which the victims of that scandal have been treated.

Those arrangements raise questions as to what a tribunal on appeal should do if it has evidence of receipt prior to January 1, 2022 of a payment that would have been disregarded under the amendments if it had been received on or after that date. The legislation that a tribunal is bound to apply would not allow a disregard of such a payment unless it fell within the existing "personal injury" disregard in reg.75 (possible for some historic institutional child abuse payments, though not for payments to next of kin or those who had merely been in "harm's way" or for Windrush Compensation Scheme payments). However, if an express submission from the DWP recorded the practical result of the application of the disregard either on the basis of a ministerial direction or an extra-statutory arrangement, it would appear that the issue of the treatment of the payment would not arise on the appeal (see s.12(8)(a) of SSA 1998) and it is submitted that it would then be irrational for the tribunal to exercise its discretion to consider the issue nonetheless. If evidence of a payment that had not been taken into account as capital emerged in the course of an appeal, but there was no express DWP submission to explain that outcome, it is submitted that a tribunal with knowledge of the matters mentioned above could still legitimately conclude that the issue did not arise on the appeal and decline to exercise its discretion under s.12(8)(a). Memo ADM 21/21 on the effect of the amendment to reg.76 says nothing about these questions, although it does name the currently approved historic institutional child abuse schemes and give the date of approval (December 10, 2021).

The discussion at a meeting of the Social Security Advisory Committee (SSAC) on December 8, 2021 in relation to SI 2021/1405 revealed some conceptual problems in the relationship of capital disregards to the calculation of the amount of capital possessed at a particular date (see further discussion in the notes to Sch.10).

The essence of the problem put to DWP officials was what would happen if a claimant received a compensation payment within the disregard introduced by those regulations, acquired further non-disregarded capital and then spent a substantial amount of capital: how would it be known what pot of capital the expenditure came out of (SSAC minutes December 8, 2021, para.2.2(f))? The answer given in the letter dated January 12, 2022 from the Minister for Welfare Delivery, David Rutley, (Annex C to the minutes) was that:

> "the Department does not attempt to distinguish the capital derived from a compensation payment from other capital (with the exception of personal injury compensation that has been placed in trust). Wherever a claimant has received a payment of capital which is disregarded, whether indefinitely or for a prescribed period, their capital threshold is effectively increased by the amount of the original payment for the duration of that period. This is regardless of whether it was simply paid into a bank account with other funds or held or invested elsewhere."

There must be a question whether that approach is justified if the compensation covers certain specific purposes and the expenditure was for one of those purposes.

Company analogous to a partnership or one person business

2.297
77.—(1) Where a person stands in a position analogous to that of a sole owner or partner in relation to a company which is carrying on a trade or a property business, the person is to be treated, for the purposes of this Part, as the sole owner or partner.

(2) Where paragraph (1) applies, the person is to be treated, subject to paragraph (3)(a), as possessing an amount of capital equal to the value, or the person's share of the value, of the capital of the company and the value of the person's holding in the company is to be disregarded.

(3) Where paragraph (1) applies in relation to a company which is carrying on a trade—

  (a) any assets of the company that are used wholly and exclusively for the purposes of the trade are to be disregarded from the person's capital while they are engaged in activities in the course of that trade;

  (b) the income of the company or the person's share of that income is to be treated as the person's income and calculated in the manner set out in regulation 57 as if it were self-employed earnings; and

  (c) where the person's activities in the course of the trade are their main employment, the person is to be treated as if they were in gainful self-employment and, accordingly, regulation 62 (minimum income floor) applies [1 . . .].

(4) Any self-employed earnings which the person is treated as having by virtue of paragraph (3)(b) are in addition to any employed earnings the person receives as a director or employee of the company.

(5) This regulation does not apply where the person derives income from the company that is employed earnings by virtue of Chapter 8 (workers under arrangements made by intermediaries)[2, Chapter 9 (managed service companies) or Chapter 10 (workers' services provided through intermediaries) of Part 2 of ITEPA and that income is derived from activities that are the person's main employment].

(6) In paragraph (1) "property business" has the meaning in section 204 of the Corporation Tax Act 2009.

AMENDMENTS

1. Universal Credit and Miscellaneous Amendments (No.2) Regulations 2014 (SI 2014/2888) reg.4(6) (November 26, 2014, or in the case of existing awards, the first assessment period beginning on or after November 26, 2014).

2. Universal Credit and Jobseeker's Allowance (Miscellaneous Amendments) Regulations 2018 (SI 2018/1129) reg.3(5) (November 5, 2018).

DEFINITIONS

"employed earnings"—see regs 53(1) and 55.
"ITEPA"—see reg.2.
"self-employed earnings"—see regs 53(1) and 57.

GENERAL NOTE

If a person's control of a company, which is carrying on a trade or a property business (defined in para.(6)), is such that they are like a sole trader or a partner, the value of the person's shareholding is disregarded and they are treated as having a proportionate share of the capital of the company (para.(2)) and a proportionate share of the company's income as if that was self-employed earnings (para.(3)(b)). However, the general rule in para.(3)(a) in cases where the company is carrying on a trade is that so long as the person is engaged in activities in the course of the company's trade the company's assets are disregarded as capital. Those rules are similar to those in reg.51(4) and (5) of the Income Support Regulations, reg.115(6) and (7) of the ESA Regulations 2008 and reg.113(4) and (5) of the JSA Regulations 1996 (Vol.V of this series), but by no means identical, in particular in the provision for the special category of property businesses. The rules are easily overlooked, as they were in relation to the discretionary housing benefit rule in *CA v Hastings BC (HB)* [2022] UKUT 57 (AAC), especially if the claimant has initially been vague about the exact nature of the legal relationships. Some unpacking and identification of potential problems is necessary.

2.298

Note that the heading to reg.77, with its reference to one-person businesses, can easily mislead, as can the tendency in social security case law and discussion to regard trades and businesses as more or less the same. That may have infected the commentary in past editions. The precise terms of the regulation must be considered. Thus, as developed further in the notes to para.(1) below, that provision only applies where a company is carrying on a either a trade, not merely a business, or a property business, the definition of which includes any transaction entered into for the purpose of generating income from land whether the operation would ordinarily be regarded as a business or not. Outside of those categories, the general principles of company law apply, as summarised below.

The basic legal position is that if there is a company, the shareholders' assets are the value of the shares, not the value of the company's assets *(R(SB) 57/83)*. But under para.(1), if claimants are in a position analogous to a sole owner or partner in the business of the company (on which, see *R(IS) 8/92* for helpful guidance in paras 8 and 9), the value of their shareholding is disregarded, and they are treated as possessing a proportionate share of the value of the capital of the company, as specified in para.(2). There is usually little difficulty if the analogy is with a sole owner. If it is with a partner, the line between such a person and someone who is merely a shareholder or investor in the company is whether the person is in a position to exercise significant influence over the way the business is conducted *(R(IS) 8/92*, applied in *CA*, above). The value is the net worth of the company's total assets taken together *(R(IS) 13/93)*. The value of one particular asset within the total is not relevant in itself. However, as long as the claimant undertakes activities in the course of the the company's trade (but not where there is merely a property business), the amount produced by para.(2) is disregarded (para.(3)(a)). Temporary interruptions in activity (e.g. holidays, short-term sickness) ought not to prevent para.(3)(a) from applying. It was accepted in *R(IS) 13/93* that any activities which are more than de minimis satisfy para.(3)(a). See also *R(IS) 14/98* discussed in the note to para.(3). In addition, under para.(3)(b), if para.(1) applies, the claimant's share of the income of the company is to be treated as their earnings from self-employment under reg.57.

First, note that under para.(5) the regulation as a whole does not apply where the person concerned receives employed earnings from the company that are chargeable to income tax under Chapter 8 (workers under arrangements made by intermediaries), 9 (managed service companies) or, from November 5, 2018, 10 (workers' services provided through intermediaries) of Part 2 of the Income Tax (Earnings and Pensions) Act 2003 (ITEPA). The November 2018 amendment also introduced the important condition for the application of the exception in para. (5) that the activities producing those earnings are the person's main employment. There is no such exclusion in the income support and old style ESA and JSA rules. Chapter 8 of Part 2 of ITEPA is concerned with what are known as IR35 or "off-payroll" arrangements, under which a person provides services to a client who would be an employer except that the arrangements are made by a third party to whom the client makes the payments in return for the services. Then, subject to conditions, the payments to the third party are treated as employed earnings of the person concerned and chargeable to income tax. Chapter 9 applies to similar effect where the intermediary is a managed service company, i.e. one under the control of the service provider(s). Chapter 10 has, from April 6, 2017, applied special rules to cases where the client is a public authority.

Paragraph (1)

2.299   The general operation of para.(1) is described above. Before it can operate it must be established that the company that actually owns the capital in question is carrying on either a trade or a property business. "Trade" is given no special definition and there are many disputed and grey areas in the meaning given in other legal contexts. Given the overall approach of the Regulations in adopting tax law concepts and the express adoption of a tax meaning of "property business" in para.(6), that context may supply some pointers. It is clear in that context that "trade" is a narrower concept than "business" (see *American Leaf Blending Co Sdn. Bhd v Director-General of Inland Revenue* [1979] A.C. 676 (PC) and *Griffiths v Jackson* (1982) T.C. 583, both referred to in many other cases including *Ramsay v HMRC* [2013] UKUT 226 (TC), long extracts from which are set out in *RM v Sefton Council (HB)* [2016] UKUT 357 (AAC) reported as [2017] AACR 5). Distinctions are drawn between investing in some asset that yields a return and the trading in such assets and between the exploitation of an interest in property (as by letting it out) and trading. Thus in *Griffiths*, Vinelott J held that the letting out of specially converted student flats was the exploitation of interests in property, not a trade. But by contrast, a person or company running a hotel or a bed and breakfast establishment would be carrying on a trade.

Some companies not carrying on a trade may be carrying on a "property business", also within para.(1), but not within the para.(3) rules. But remember that some companies carrying on a property business may get within the meaning of carrying on a trade. The definition in s.204 of the Corporation Tax Act 2009, as incorporated by para.(6), does not in itself take matters forward, merely saying that the term includes both UK and overseas property businesses. One has to go on to ss.205–207 to find provisions that a property business consists of (a) every business that the company carries on for generating income from land in the UK and outside, as the case may be, and (b) every transaction that the company enters into for that purpose otherwise than in the course of such a business. It is also provided that generating income from land means exploiting it as a source of rents or other receipts. Schedule 1 to the Interpretation Act 1978 defines "land" to include "building and other structures, land covered with water, and any estate, interest, easement, servitude or right in or over land". Thus, the definition appears to cover, not just companies that are carrying on a business, in the ordinary meaning of the word, for the purposes of generating income from land, but also any transaction entered into by a company for that purpose, whether that is part of the company's business or not or whether the company is carrying on any business at all, in the ordinary meaning of the word, or not. Paragraph H4365 of the ADM refers to the paying of tax on the profits of the business as a condition, but it is not at all clear that the provision in s.204(2) of the 2009 Act that references in that Act to a property business are to such a business in so far as any profits of the business are chargeable to tax under Ch.3 of the Part of the Act containing s.204, affects the "meaning" of property business in s.204. Such uncertainty is another penalty of the highly unhelpful method of legislation by reference, instead of setting out directly the kinds of company intended to be covered by reg.77.

If the definition of property business is in issue in an appeal, the comments of Commissioner Stockman in para.34 of *RMcE v DfC (UC)* [2021] NICom 59 in relation to reg.55 would be equally pertinent. For appeal tribunals to be able to perform their role properly the Secretary of State must provide explanatory material, legislation and case law relating to the relevant tax provisions.

Questions have been raised about the position where a claimant has put their own money into the company, so that that amount is owed to them, possibly through a director's loan account, by a separate legal person (the company). That debt would be a chose in action with a capital value. While the claimant is engaged in the company's trade there is no problem with the amount of the money held by the company being disregarded as capital under para.(3)(a). But what is the status of the claimant's personal chose in action in the right to repayment of the debt? Does that still count as the claimant's capital, since there is no specific disregard of its value? It is (tentatively) suggested that giving effect to para.(1) requires one to translate the claimant's relationship with the company into the relationship that would obtain if the claimant was carrying on the trade as a sole owner or partner. In such a case the money would have been regarded as moved from the claimant's personal assets into funds employed risked in the trade. As a sole trader is able freely to transfer funds between personal and trade assets (see *R(SB) 4/85* and the notes to para.7 of Sch.10), there would be no question of the creation of a chose in action in the form of a debt from one person to another. If that is correct, the deeming under para.(1) extends to deeming the actual chose in action not to exist. Although things might be more complicated in the case of deemed partners, it would be anomalous if the same result did not follow.

Paragraph (2)

The approach adopted in *R(IS) 13/93* to the income support rule must also apply to para.(2) in that the value of the company's capital (by reference to which the amount of the person's notional capital is assumed) means the net total value after liabilities have been taken into account. The fact that the company owns some particularly valuable asset or assets does not on its own mean that the claimant's notional capital must be over the limit. The net worth must be identified, no doubt by looking at accounts and using standard accounting practices. It would seem that liabilities could include the amount of any debt owed to the deemed owner. Where the person's position is not analogous to that of a sole owner, but to a partner, the identification of the proportionate share may raise difficult issues of judgment. In *R(IS) 13/93* the Commissioner seemed prepared to adopt the proportionate shareholding as the criterion. There should then be no difficulty in the disregarding under para.(2) of the actual value of the person's shareholding in the company.

2.300

Paragraph (3)

There are further departures from the income support and old style ESA and JSA position in para.(3), in deeming the person's proportionate share of the company's income to be self-employed earnings (sub-para.(b)) and in applying the minimum income floor where the person's activities in the trade are their main employment (sub-para.(c)), as well as the disregard of assets in sub-para.(a). It is important to note that the whole of para.(3) applies only to companies carrying on a trade and not to companies merely carrying on a property business. That distinction has been queried in past editions, but it is now submitted that in view of the particular meanings to be

2.301

given to "trade" and "property business" (see above) it makes sense. A person who has property that is rented out, the income from which is not unearned income under reg.66(1), should not be able to escape having its value taken into account as capital by acquiring the property through a company that they control, or by transferring it to such a company, unless the company is genuinely carrying on a trade.

Under para.(3)(b) the income of the company or a proportionate share is to be treated as income of the person concerned and calculated under reg.57 as if it were self-employed earnings. That appears to be so even if the person concerned undertakes no activities in the course of the business. It is far from clear how the notional conversion is to take place. Under reg.57, in the case of actual self-employed earnings, the calculation is based on actual receipts in any assessment period less permitted deductions for expenses under regs 58 and 59. Presumably, therefore "the income of the company" does not mean the net income of the company as might be calculated for corporation tax purposes or under ordinary accounting principles. Presumably it means the actual receipts of the company in the assessment period in question less the deductions for expenses under regs 58 and 59, looking at expenditure on behalf of the company rather than by the person in question. It is difficult to say whether in practice information will be available as to such receipts and expenditure in a current assessment period of a month. Even if that is so, there might well be large fluctuations month by month. A further problem is how to calculate the deductions from gross profits under steps 3 and 4 of reg.57(2) for national insurance contributions and income tax paid to HMRC in the assessment period and relievable pension contributions made in that period, when the person's actual tax and national insurance status will not have been as a self-employed earner.

See para.(4) for the effect of the person having employed earnings. Note that normally any remuneration paid by the company to the claimant as a director or an employee will be deducted as an expense at step 1(b) of the reg.57 calculation. Any dividends received by the claimant will simply not figure in the reg.77 operation because they are not either a receipt of the company or an allowable expense under regs 57 and 58. Nor will they normally count as employed earnings and they do not constitute unearned income.

See the notes to reg.57 for payments made under the Coronavirus Job Retention Scheme (CJRS) to claimants caught by reg.77 who had furloughed themselves as employees in law and the effect of the Universal Credit (Coronavirus) (Self-employed Claimants and Reclaims) (Amendment) Regulations 2020 (SI 2020/522), in force from May 21, 2020. As explained in those notes, such payments must be treated as income receipts of the company, that then are to be taken into account as an actual receipt at step 1 of reg.57(2), by virtue of reg.77(3)(b). There is nothing in the Self-employed Claimants Regulations to prevent that effect and no specific reference to reg.77. But reg.2(1)(b) provides that no deduction is to be made under step 1 of reg.57(2) for salary or wages paid to an employee in so far as that payment is covered by a payment under the CJRS. Thus the income of the company with which the self-employed person is fixed by the operation of reg.77 includes the CJRS payment, with a deduction for the furloughed employee's salary only in so far as the company paid the employee more than the initial 80% (or the later lower amounts covered by the CJRS) of qualifying salary. In order for the CJRS payment to have been properly received a corresponding payment out must have been made by the employer, that the scheme then reimbursed. That appears to be fair when reg.77(4) is considered. If the deemed self-employed person also has employed earnings from the company (as the person must have done to get the CJRS payment) those earnings are to be taken into account as earned income as well as the deemed self-employed earnings. Normally, although those employed earnings would count, the expense of the salary paid to the deemed self-employed person would be deducted at step 1 of reg.57(2).

In the light of the difficulties with para.(3)(b), the effect of para.(3)(c) may be particularly important. Where the person's activities in the course of the company's trade are their main employment they are deemed to be in gainful self-employment, so that reg.62 on the minimum income floor applies. For any assessment period in which reg.62 applies (see the notes to that provision) and the claimant's earned income is less than their individual threshold, the earned income is deemed to be equal to that amount. The weekly amount is effectively the hourly national minimum wage multiplied by the expected number of hours under reg.88. That level of income exempts the claimant from all work-related requirements (reg.90(1) and (5) and s.19 of the WRA 2012), but the deemed amount would be taken into account in calculating the amount of benefit payable.

The other element of para.(3) is the disregard of assets of the company that would otherwise be deemed to be part of the claimant's capital by reason of the person's deemed status as sole owner or partner in the business (sub-para.(a)). There are two conditions. The person must be engaged in activities in the course of the company's trade. In reg.51(4) and (5) of the Income Support Regulations, reg.115(6) and (7) of the ESA Regulations 2008 and reg.113(4) and (5) of the JSA Regulations 1996 the condition is that the person undertakes activities in the course of the business of the company. On that form of words the Commissioner in *R(IS) 13/93* was satisfied that the claimant's wife, who took telephone messages and received mail for the company, as well as being a director, was taking part in the company's business. He also said that although the activities were low key, he was far from certain that they were de minimis. It is not entirely clear that he was intending to lay down a rule that any activity beyond something that was de minimis (i.e. so trivial as to be equivalent to nothing) would do, rather than merely describing the circumstances of the particular case, but a principle that anything of substance would do appears right. Does a test in the terms of being engaged in activities in the course of the company's trade require a different approach? In *Chief Adjudication Officer v Knight*, reported as part of *R(IS) 14/98*, the Court of Appeal was concerned with the disregard of the assets of a business in which a person was engaged as a self-employed earner. The claimant was described as a sleeping partner in a farming business with her son and his wife. The court held that that the risking of her assets in the business and her right to a share of profits did not constitute a sufficient positive involvement to conclude that she was engaged in the business. But it was recognised that each case would have to be decided individually. That does not suggest any plain difference in approach, and it is submitted that the word "engaged" does not in its ordinary meaning require anything more extensive than "undertaking activities".

It should be noted that para.(3)(a) applies only while the person is actually engaged in activities. No doubt short breaks, such as for weekends or longer holidays, are to be ignored. But there is no provision in it, as there is in para.6 of Sch.10 to the Income Support Regulations and in para.8 of Sch.10 to the present Regulations (business assets) for an extension where the person has ceased to carry on a trade, business or vocation within the previous six months (extendable) in certain circumstances such as incapacity being thought not to be permanent. It may be arguable that the disregard in para.8 of Sch.10 can apply to the notional capital to be possessed under para.(2) if its conditions would have applied if the person had actually previously been carrying on the business as a self-employed person.

The second condition for the disregard under para.(3)(a) is that the assets are used wholly and exclusively for the purposes of the company's trade. That is not a condition in reg.51(5) of the Income Support Regulations, reg.115(7) of the ESA Regulations 2008 or reg.113(5) of the JSA Regulations 1996, under which the whole of the person's deemed capital under the equivalent of para.(2) is disregarded. Does the phrase "wholly and exclusively" exclude the disregarding of the value of assets that have a dual use? An obvious example would be a vehicle used for both business and personal purposes. In relation to the deduction of expenses in the calculation of the net profits of self-employed earners under reg.38(3)(a) of the Income Support Regulations (reg.98(3)(a) of the ESA Regulations 2008 and reg.101(4)(a) of the JSA Regulations 1996), where it is a condition that the expenses were wholly and exclusively defrayed for the purposes of the employment, it has been held that apportionment can extend not only to items where specific different uses can be identified (e.g. telephone calls or petrol costs) but also to items where there can be an apportionment on a time basis (e.g. vehicle insurance): *R(FC) 1/91, CFC/26/1989* and *R(IS) 13/91*. However, there are still some expenses that are not capable of apportionment, such as the cost of clothing or lunches. Where the use of an asset is in issue, there will be less room for apportionment. To take the example of a vehicle to be used equally for business and for personal purposes, for example, although the expenditure on vehicle tax, insurance and maintenance costs could be apportioned just as much as fuel costs, when looked at as a single asset to be valued it is hard to see how it could be said to be wholly and exclusively used for the purposes of the company's trade if it was used for any non-trivial non-trade purpose. Nonetheless, there might possibly be some things, like money in a bank account or a stock of stationery that could be regarded as made up of some assets used wholly and exclusively for the purposes of the company's trade and some not so used. Nor is it necessarily fatal to a conclusion that the asset is used wholly and exclusively for the purposes of the company's trade that a person derives some private advantage from it (e.g. a particularly comfortable office chair or one adapted to a person's disability or physiology).

The second condition seems unfairly restrictive compared to the position in income support and old style ESA and JSA and also compared to the treatment under universal credit of those actually in self-employment. There, para.7 of Sch.10 requires the disregard of assets used "wholly or mainly" for the purposes of the trade, business or vocation being carried on. In view of the express condition in para.(3)(a), it appears that a person could not rely on the wider disregard in para.7 of Sch.10 in relation to their deemed notional capital, on the same basis as suggested above in relation to para.8 of Sch.10. Indeed, that may cast doubt on the validity of the argument about para.8.

Paragraph (4)

2.302   If someone treated as having self-employed earnings under para.(3)(b) also has employed earnings from the company, either as an employee or in the office of director, the two sources of income are both to be taken into account. Dividends are not normally employed earnings, being derived from the ownership of the shares on which they are paid. But sometimes the label of dividend cannot properly be applied to the payments made or dividends properly so called can constitute remuneration derived from a contract of employment or in an office. Dividends cannot constitute unearned income because they do not appear in the exhaustive list in reg.66(1). They are not remuneration or profit derived from employment under a contract of employment or in an office (reg.52(a)(i)). Nor are they general earnings as defined in s.7(3) of ITEPA, being chargeable to income tax under Chapters 3–5 of Part 4 of the Income Tax (Trading and Other Income) 2005 (ITTOIA). It is different if the labelling as dividends is a sham or, taking the broader approach of recent authority, the payments are in substance or reality earnings. See the further discussion in the notes to reg.55 under the heading *Dividends*.

Do not forget that although the claimant's employed earnings from the company count as part of their income, the expense of paying those earnings will be deducted from the receipts of the company under the deemed application of reg.57.

PART 7

THE BENEFIT CAP

GENERAL NOTE

Introduction

2.303   Regulations 78–83 are made under ss.96–97 of the WRA 2012. They establish a "benefit cap" under which affected claimants can receive no more in social security benefits than £25,323 pa or £16,967 pa in Greater London and £22,020 pa or £14,753 pa elsewhere. In both cases, the higher of those limits applies to joint claimants or those responsible for a child or qualifying young person and the lower to single claimants who are not responsible a child or a qualifying young person. The higher rates apply irrespective of how many people are in the benefit unit: families consisting of a couple with six children are capped at the same rate as a single parent with one.

How the benefit cap works   **2.304**
    Under reg.79, the benefit cap applies where the total amount of the "welfare benefits" (as defined in WRA 2012 s.96(10)) exceed whichever "relevant amount" applies: see reg.80A. The amount of universal credit that the claimant would otherwise be awarded for the assessment period is reduced by the amount of the excess: reg.81.

Calculation of entitlement to welfare benefits   **2.305**
    Regulation 80 deals with how the amount of the claimant's (or claimants') entitlement to "welfare benefits" is calculated. The rule is that the total entitlement to all specified benefits during the assessment period is taken into account except where that entitlement is not payable because of the overlapping benefit rules: reg.80(1). Under reg.66, many of the benefits listed in WRA 2012 s.96(10) are taken into account as unearned income when calculating entitlement to universal credit. Regulation 80(4) provides that they are to be taken into account for benefit cap purposes at the same rate as they are taken into account under reg.66. Universal credit itself is (obviously) taken into account at the rate to which the claimant(s) would be entitled if the benefit cap did not apply: reg.80(2). Regulation 80(3) provides (presumably for the avoidance of doubt) that where a claimant is disqualified from receiving (new-style) ESA by virtue of reg.93 ESA Regulations 2013, that benefit is not taken into account. Finally, reg.80(5) provides that where a "welfare benefit" is awarded in respect of a period other than a month (which will always be the case, except for universal credit itself) the monthly equivalent is to be calculated in the same way as for other unearned income under reg.73.

Exceptions   **2.306**
    There are a number of exceptions, where the benefit cap does not apply, or the reduction is less than the full amount of the excess. The benefit cap does not apply in any assessment period:

- where the award of universal credit includes the LCWRA element, or the carer element, or a claimant (including one or more joint claimants) is receiving "new-style" ESA at a rate that includes the support component: reg.83(1)(a) and (j);

- during which a claimant or a qualifying young person for whom they are responsible is receiving carer's allowance or a claimant is receiving industrial injuries benefit, attendance allowance, disability living allowance or personal independence payment, or guardian's allowance: reg.83(1)(b), (c), (f), (g), (i) and (k) and note that—for obvious reasons—those benefits are not "welfare benefits" as defined in WRA 2012 s.96(10);

- a child or qualifying young person for whom a claimant is responsible is receiving disability living allowance or personal independence payment: reg.83(1)(f) and (g); and

- a claimant is receiving a war pension (as defined in reg.83(2)) or certain payments under the Armed Forces and Reserve Forces Compensation Scheme: reg.83(1)(d) and (c).

Where a claimant (or a child or qualifying young person) is entitled to attendance allowance, disability living allowance, personal independence payment—or a war pension or a relevant payment under the Armed Forces Compensation Scheme—but is not receiving it because he or she is in a hospital or a care home, the benefit cap does not apply by virtue of reg.83(1)(h).

Under reg.82(1), the benefit cap does not apply if the claimant's earned income (or the claimants' combined earned income) in the assessment exceeds "the amount of earnings that a person would be paid at the hourly rate set out in regulation 4 of the National Minimum Wage Regulations for 16 hours per week, converted to a monthly amount by multiplying by 52 and dividing by 12" or during the nine month "grace period" as defined in reg.82(2). The rules on the "minimum income floor" in reg.62 (which, in this instance, would be advantageous for the claimant(s)) do not apply to the calculation of earned income in this context.

Finally, where the award of universal credit includes the childcare costs element, the amount of that element is deducted from the amount of the reduction under reg.81. If that amount exceeds the excess of the total entitlement to welfare benefits over the relevant amount, then no reduction is made: reg.81(1) and (2).

Legal challenges

2.307   On March 18, 2015, in *R (SG and others (previously JS and others) v Secretary of State for Work and Pensions* [2015] UKSC 16; [2015] 1 W.L.R. 1449, the Supreme Court (Lords Reed, Carnwath and Hughes, Lady Hale and Lord Kerr dissenting) rejected a legal challenge to the benefit cap on the grounds that it unlawfully discriminated against women in breach of art.14 of, read with art.1 of the First Protocol to, ECHR; and infringed art.3(1) of the United Nations Convention on the Rights of the Child.

On November 26, 2015, in *Hurley v Secretary of State for Work And Pensions* [2015] EWHC 3382 (Admin); [2016] P.T.S.R. 636, Collins J held that the failure to exempt individual family carers caring for adult family members from the benefit cap constituted unlawful discrimination contrary to contrary to Art.14 of—taken together with Art.1 of the First Protocol to, or Art.8 of—the ECHR. The government responded to the judgment by removing carer's allowance from the list of "welfare benefits" in WRA 2012 s.96(10) (see WR&WA 2016 s.8(4)) and by adding exceptions to reg.83 where the claimant (or a qualifying young person for whom they are responsible) is entitled to carer's allowance; or where the carer element is included in the ward of universal credit; or where the claimant is entitled to guardian's allowance.

On June 22, 2017 in *R (DA and Others) v Secretary of State for Work and Pensions* [2017] EWHC 1446 (Admin); [2017] P.T.S.R. 1266, Collins J ruled that the application of the benefit cap (under the equivalent provisions of the Housing Benefit Regulations 2006) to lone parents of children under two infringed their Convention Rights under arts 8 and 14 ECHR taken together. In particular, the applicants were unable to work for 16 hours a week (i.e., so as to take advantage of the earnings exception: see reg.82) because of their caring responsibilities and the cost of childcare. However, on March 15, 2018, the Court of Appeal (Leveson P and Sir Patrick Elias, McCombe LJ dissenting) allowed the Secretary of State's appeal against Collins J's decision ([2018] EWCA Civ 504); [2018] P.T.S.R. 1606, and on May 15, 2019, the Supreme Court (Lords Reed, Wilson, Carnwath, Hughes and Hodge, Lady Hale and Lord Kerr dissenting) dismissed a further appeal together with another appeal backed by CPAG: see further, *R (DA and others and DS and others) v Secretary of State for Work and Pensions* [2019] UKSC 21; [2019] 1 W.L.R. 3289.

On July 20, 2020, the High Court (Garnham J) allowed a challenge to the benefit cap as it affects UC claimants who are paid four-weekly: see *R (Pantellerisco) v Secretary of State for Work and Pensions* [2020] EWHC 1944 (Admin); [2020] P.T.S.R. 2289. As there are 13 four-week periods in each year and only 12 assessment periods, the Regulations treated the claimant as earning 1/13 of her annual salary in 11 of those assessment periods and 2/13 in one of them. By regulation 82(1)(a) the benefits cap does not apply to assessment periods in which the claimant's earned income is equal to or exceeds the amount of earnings that a person would be paid for 16 hours work at the national minimum wage, converted to a monthly amount by multiplying by 52 and dividing by 12. As the claimant actually did work 16 hours a week at the national minimum wage, she would have been exempt from the benefit cap for the whole year if she had been treated as earning 1/12 of her annual salary in each assessment period. However, in 11 out of 12 assessment periods, the universal credit earned income calculation treated her as if she had only worked for 28 days with the result that she was not exempt from the cap. In the claimant's case, that left her approximately £463 worse off in each of the 11 assessment periods in respect of which her benefit was capped. The judge described this issue as the "lunar month problem". It is similar to the "non-banking day salary shift" problem: see the discussion of *Secretary of State for Work and Pensions v Johnson and others* [2020] EWCA Civ 778; [2020] P.T.S.R. 1872 in the General Note to reg.54. Following the Court of Appeal's reasoning in *Johnson*, the judge allowed the application for judicial review and declared that "the calculation required by regulation 82(1)(a) read together with regulation 54 of the Universal Credit Regulations 2013 is irrational and unlawful in so far as employees who are paid on a four weekly basis (as opposed to a calendar monthly basis) are treated as having earned income of only 28 days' earnings in 11 out of 12 assessment periods a year." However, the Court of Appeal allowed an appeal from that decision by the Secretary of State and dismissed the claim ([2021] EWCA Civ 1454; [2021] P.T.S.R. 1922).

Introduction

78.—(1) This Part makes provision for a benefit cap under section 96 of the Act which, if applicable, reduces the amount of an award of universal credit.

(2) In this Part "couple" means—

(a) joint claimants; or

(b) a single claimant who is a member of a couple within the meaning of section 39 of the Act and the other member of that couple,

and references to a couple include each member of that couple individually.

2.308

DEFINITION

"the Act"—see reg.2.

Circumstances where the benefit cap applies

79.—(1) Unless regulation 82 or 83 applies, the benefit cap applies where the welfare benefits to which a single person or couple is entitled during the reference period exceed the relevant amount [¹ determined under regulation 80A (relevant amount)].

(2) The reference period for the purposes of the benefit cap is the assessment period for an award of universal credit.

(3) [¹. . .]

(4) [¹. . .]

2.309

AMENDMENT

1. Benefit Cap (Housing Benefit and Universal Credit) (Amendment) Regulations 2016 (SI 2016/909) reg.3(1) and (2) (assessment periods beginning on or after November 7, 2016).

DEFINITIONS

"assessment period"—see WRA 2012 ss.40 and 7(2).
"bereavement allowance"—see reg.2.

"carer's allowance"—*ibid.*
"child"—see WRA 2012 s.40.
"claimant"—*ibid.*
"Contributions and Benefits Act"—see reg.2.
"couple"—see reg.78(2).
"employment and support allowance"—see reg.2.
"jobseeker's allowance"—*ibid.*
"joint claimants"—see WRA 2012 s.40.
"maternity allowance"—see reg.2.
"qualifying young person"—see WRA 2012 s.40 and 10(5) and regs 2 and 5.
"responsible for a child or qualifying young person"—see regs 2, 4 and 4A.
"single claimant"—see WRA 2012 s.40.
"single person"—see WRA 2012 ss.40 and 1(2)(a).
"welfare benefit"—see WRA 2012 s.96(10).
"widowed mother's allowance"—see reg.2.
"widowed parent's allowance"—*ibid.*
"widow's pension"—*ibid.*

GENERAL NOTE

2.310   Although "couple" is defined by reg.78(2) as including a member of a couple who is permitted to claim as a single person under reg.3(3), the higher "relevant amount" in reg.79(3)(a) is only available to "joint claimants" and those responsible for a child or a qualifying young person. A member of a couple claiming as a single person who is not responsible for a child or a qualifying young person, will therefore be capped at the lower rate.

The welfare benefits to which reg.79 applies are defined by WRA 2012 s.96(10) as bereavement allowance, child benefit, child tax credit, ESA, housing benefit, incapacity benefit, IS, JSA, maternity allowance, severe disablement allowance, universal credit, widow's pension, widowed mother's allowance and widowed parent's allowance.

Manner of determining total entitlement to welfare benefits

2.311   **80.**—(1) Subject to the following provisions of this regulation, the amount of a welfare benefit to be used when determining total entitlement to welfare benefits is the amount to which the single person or couple is entitled during the reference period subject to any adjustment to the amount payable in accordance with regulations under section 73 of the Social Security Administration Act 1992 (overlapping benefits).

(2) Where the welfare benefit is universal credit, the amount to be used is the amount to which the claimant is entitled before any reduction under regulation 81 or under section 26 or 27 of the Act.

[¹ (2A) Where the welfare benefit is housing benefit under section 130 of the Contributions and Benefits Act, the amount to be used is nil.]

(3) Where a person is disqualified for receiving an employment and support allowance by virtue of section 18 of the Welfare Reform Act 2007, it is disregarded as a welfare benefit.

(4) Where an amount of a welfare benefit is taken into account in assessing a single person's or a couple's unearned income for the purposes of an award of universal credit the amount to be used is the amount taken into account as unearned income in accordance with regulation 66.

(5) Where a welfare benefit is awarded in respect of a period that is not a month, the amount is to be calculated as the monthly equivalent as set out in regulation 73 (unearned income calculated monthly).

AMENDMENT

1. Benefit Cap (Housing Benefit and Universal Credit) (Amendment) Regulations 2016 (SI 2016/909) reg.3(1) and (3) (assessment periods beginning on or after November 7, 2016).

DEFINITIONS

"couple"—see reg.78(2).
"earned income"—see reg.2.
"single person"—see WRA 2012 ss.40 and 1(2)(a).
"unearned income"—see reg.2.

[¹ Relevant amount

80A.—(1) The relevant amount is determined by dividing the applicable annual limit by 12.
    2.312

(2) The applicable annual limit is—

(a) [² £16,967] for a single claimant resident in Greater London who is not responsible for a child or qualifying young person;

(b) [² £25,323] for—
    (i) joint claimants where either joint claimant is resident in Greater London;
    (ii) a single claimant resident in Greater London who is responsible for a child or qualifying young person;

(c) [² £14,753] for a single claimant not resident in Greater London who is not responsible for a child or qualifying young person;

(d) [² £22,020] for—
    (i) joint claimants not resident in Greater London;
    (ii) a single claimant not resident in Greater London who is responsible for a child or qualifying young person.

(3) For the purposes of section 96 of the Act (benefit cap) and this regulation a claimant is resident in Greater London if—

(a) where the housing costs element is included in the claimant's award of universal credit—
    (i) accommodation in respect of which the claimant meets the occupation condition is in Greater London; or
    (ii) the claimant is in receipt of housing benefit in respect of a dwelling (which has the meaning given in section 137 of the Contributions and Benefits Act) in Greater London;

(b) where the housing costs element is not included in the claimant's award of universal credit—
    (i) accommodation that the claimant normally occupies as their home is in Greater London; or
    (ii) where there is no accommodation that the claimant normally occupies as their home, the Jobcentre Plus office to which the Secretary of State has allocated their claim is in Greater London.]

AMENDMENTS

1. Benefit Cap (Housing Benefit and Universal Credit) (Amendment) Regulations 2016 (SI 2016/909) reg.3(1) and (4) (assessment periods beginning on or after November 7, 2016).
2. Benefit Cap (Annual Limit) (Amendment) Regulations 2023 (SI 2023/335) reg.3 (assessment periods beginning on or after April 10, 2023).

Reduction of universal credit

2.313   **81.**—(1) Where the benefit cap applies in relation to an assessment period for an award of universal credit, the amount of the award for that period is to be reduced by—

  (a) the excess; minus
  (b) any amount included in the award for the childcare costs element in relation to that assessment period.

(2) But no reduction is to be applied where the amount of the childcare costs element is greater than the excess.

(3) The excess is the total amount of welfare benefits that the single person or the couple are entitled to in the reference period, minus the relevant amount [¹ determined under regulation 80A].

AMENDMENT

1. Benefit Cap (Housing Benefit and Universal Credit) (Amendment) Regulations 2016 (SI 2016/909) reg.3(1) and (5) (assessment periods beginning on or after November 7, 2016).

DEFINITIONS

"childcare costs element"—see reg.2.
"assessment period"—see WRA 2012 ss.40 and 7(2).

Exceptions—earnings

2.314   **82.**—(1) The benefit cap does not apply to an award of universal credit in relation to an assessment period where—

  (a) the claimant's earned income or, if the claimant is a member of a couple, the couple's combined earned income, is equal to or exceeds [¹ the amount of earnings that a person would be paid at the hourly rate set out in regulation 4 of the National Minimum Wage Regulations for 16 hours per week, converted to a monthly amount by multiplying by 52 and dividing by 12]; or
  (b) the assessment period falls within a grace period or is an assessment period in which a grace period begins or ends.

(2) A grace period is a period of 9 consecutive months that begins on the most recent of the following days in respect of which the condition in paragraph (3) is met—

  (a) a day falling within the current period of entitlement to universal credit which is the first day of an assessment period in which the claimant's earned income (or, if the claimant is a member of a couple, the couple's combined earned income is [¹ less than—
    (i) where the assessment period began before 1st April 2017, £430; or
    (ii) in any other case, the amount calculated in accordance with paragraph (1)(a)];
  (b) a day falling before the current period of entitlement to universal credit which is the day after a day on which the claimant has ceased paid work.

(3) The condition is that, in each of the 12 months immediately preceding that day, the claimant's earned income or, if the claimant was a member of a couple, the couple's combined earned income was equal to or [¹ exceeded—

(a) in any month beginning before 1st April 2017, £430; and

(b) in any other case, the amount calculated in accordance with paragraph (1)(a)].

(4) "Earned income" for the purposes of this regulation does not include income a person is treated as having by virtue of regulation 62 (minimum income floor).

AMENDMENT

1. Universal Credit (Benefit Cap Earnings Exception) Amendment Regulations 2017 (SI 2017/138) reg.2(1) and (3) (Assessment periods beginning on or after April 1, 2017).

DEFINITIONS

"assessment period"—see WRA 2012 ss.40 and 7(2).
"claimant"—see WRA 2012 s.40.
"couple"—see reg.78(2).
"earned income"—see reg.2 and para.(4).

GENERAL NOTE

See the discussion of *R (Pantellerisco) v Secretary of State for Work and Pensions* [2021] EWCA Civ 1454 in the General Note to Part 7 (above).

Exceptions—entitlement or receipt of certain benefits

83.—(1) The benefit cap does not apply in relation to any assessment period where— 2.315

(a) the LCWRA element is included in the award of universal credit or the claimant is receiving an employment and support allowance that includes the support component;

(b) a claimant is receiving industrial injuries benefit;

(c) a claimant is receiving attendance allowance;

(d) a claimant is receiving a war pension;

(e) a claimant is receiving a payment under article 15(1)(c) or article 29(1)(a) of the Armed Forces and Reserve Forces (Compensation Scheme) Order 2011;

(f) a claimant, or a child or qualifying young person for whom a claimant is responsible, is receiving disability living allowance;

(g) a claimant, or a qualifying young person for whom a claimant is responsible, is receiving personal independence payment;

(h) a claimant, or a child or qualifying young person for whom a claimant is responsible, is entitled to a payment listed in [¹ sub-paragraphs (b) to (g)] [⁴, (ha) or (hb)] but—

(i) is not receiving it by virtue of regulation 6 (hospitalisation) or regulation 7 (persons in care homes) of the Social Security (Attendance Allowance) Regulations 1991,

(ii) it is being withheld by virtue of article 53 of the Naval, Military and Air Forces etc (Disablement and Death) Service Pensions Order 2006 (maintenance in hospital or an institution),

(iii) is not receiving it by virtue of regulation 8 (hospitalisation) or regulation 9 (persons in care homes) of the Social Security (Disability Living Allowance) Regulations 1991, [⁴ . . .]

(iv) in the case of personal independence payment, is not receiving it by virtue of regulations under section 85 (care home residents) or 86 (hospital in-patients) of the Act.

[⁴ (iva) in the case of adult disability payment, is not receiving it by virtue of regulation 27 (effect of admission to a care home on ongoing entitlement to daily living component) or 28 (effect of admission to hospital on ongoing entitlement to Adult Disability Payment) of the Disability Assistance for Working Age People (Scotland) Regulations 2022, or]

[³ (v) is not receiving it by virtue of regulation 17 (effect of admission to a care home on ongoing entitlement to care component) of the DACYP Regulations;]

[² (ha) a claimant, or a child or qualifying young person for whom a claimant is responsible, is receiving child disability payment;]

[⁴ (hb) a claimant, or qualifying young person for whom a claimant is responsible, is receiving adult disability payment;]

[¹ (i) a claimant, or a qualifying young person for whom a claimant is responsible, is entitled to carer's allowance;

(j) the carer element is included in the award of universal credit;

(k) a claimant is entitled to guardian's allowance under section 77 of the Contributions and Benefits Act.]

(2) For the purposes of this regulation, "war pension" means—

(a) any pension or allowance payable under any of the instruments listed in section 639(2) of ITEPA—

(i) to a widow, widower or a surviving civil partner, or

(ii) in respect of disablement;

(b) a pension payable to a person as a widow, widower or surviving civil partner under any power of Her Majesty otherwise than under an enactment to make provision about pensions for or in respect of persons who have been disabled or have died in consequence of service as members of the armed forces of the Crown;

(c) a payment which is made under any of—

(i) the Order in Council of 19th December 1881,

(ii) the Royal Warrant of 27th October 1884, or

(iii) the Order by His Majesty of 14th January 1922,

to a widow, widower or surviving civil partner of a person whose death was attributable to service in a capacity analogous to service as a member of the armed forces of the Crown and whose service in such capacity terminated before 31st March 1973;

(d) a pension paid by the government of a country outside the United Kingdom which is analogous to any of the pensions, allowances or payments mentioned in paragraphs (a) to (c).

AMENDMENT

1. Benefit Cap (Housing Benefit and Universal Credit) (Amendment) Regulations 2016 (SI 2016/909) reg.3(1) and (6) (assessment periods beginning on or after November 7, 2016).

2. Social Security (Scotland) Act 2018 (Disability Assistance for Children and Young People) (Consequential Modifications) Order 2021 (SI 2021/786) Sch.11 para.6 (July 26, 2021).

3. Social Security (Scotland) Act 2018 (Information-Sharing and Disability Assistance) (Consequential Provision and Modifications) Order 2021 (SI 2021/1188) art.12(2) (November 22, 2021).

4. Social Security (Disability Assistance for Working Age People) (Consequential Amendments) Order 2022 (SI 2022/177) art.13(6) (March 21, 2022).

Definitions

"the Act"—see reg.2.
"adult disability payment"—*ibid.*
"attendance allowance"—*ibid.*
"child"—see WRA 2012, s.40.
"child disability payment"—see reg.2.
"claimant"—see WRA 2012 s.40.
"the DACYP Regulations"—see reg.2.
"disability living allowance"—*ibid.*
"employment and support allowance"—*ibid.*
"industrial injuries benefit"—*ibid.*
"ITEPA"—*ibid.*
"partner"—*ibid.*
"personal independence payment"—*ibid.*
"responsible for a child or qualifying young person"—see regs 2, 4 and 4A.
"qualifying young person"—see WRA 2012, s.40 and 10(5) and regs 2 and 5.

PART 8

Claimant Responsibilities

Chapter 1

Work-Related Requirements

Introductory

Introduction

84. This Chapter contains provisions about the work-related require-   2.316
ments under sections 15 to 25 of the Act, including the persons to whom
they are to be applied, the limitations on those requirements and other
related matters.

Definition

"work-related requirement"—see WRA 2012 ss.40 and 13(2)

Meaning of terms relating to carers

85. In this Chapter—   2.317
"relevant carer" means—
(a) a parent of a child who is not the responsible carer, but has caring
responsibilities for the child; or
(b) a person who has caring responsibilities for a person who has a physical or mental impairment; and
"responsible foster parent" in relation to a child means a person who is
the only foster parent in relation to that child or, in the case of a couple
both members of which are foster parents in relation to that child,

the member who is nominated by them in accordance with regulation 86.

DEFINITIONS

"child"—see WRA 2012 s.40
"couple"—see WRA 2012 ss.40 and 39
"foster parent"—see reg.2
"responsible carer"—see WRA 2012 ss.40 and 19(6)

GENERAL NOTE

2.318   The definitions of "relevant carer" and "responsible foster parent" are relevant for the purposes of regs 86, 88, 89(1)(f), 91(2), 96(3) and 97(2). A child is a person under the age of 16. Responsibility for a child is to be determined in accordance with the rules in regs 4 and 4A, under which the basic test is whether the child normally lives with the person in question. The definition of "relevant carer" allows the inclusion into that category of people who do not count as responsible under the reg.4 rules but nevertheless have caring responsibilities (not further defined) for the child in question or have caring responsibilities for a person of any age who has a physical or mental impairment (not further defined). If a child has only one foster parent, that person is the "responsible foster parent". If both members of a couple are foster parents of the child, there must be a nomination of one of them under reg.86.

Nomination of responsible carer and responsible foster parent

2.319   **86.**—(1) This regulation makes provision for the nomination of the responsible carer or the responsible foster parent in relation to a child.

(2) Only one of joint claimants may be nominated as a responsible carer or a responsible foster parent.

(3) The nomination applies to all the children, where there is more than one, for whom either of the joint claimants is responsible.

(4) Joint claimants may change which member is nominated—

(a) once in a 12 month period, starting from the date of the previous nomination; or

(b) on any occasion where the Secretary of State considers that there has been a change of circumstances which is relevant to the nomination.

DEFINITIONS

"child"—see WRA 2012 s.40
"joint claimant"—*ibid.*
"responsible carer"—see WRA 2012 ss.40 and 19(6)
"responsible foster parent"—see reg.85

GENERAL NOTE

2.320   This regulation provides, for the purposes of s.19(6) of the WRA 2012 and reg.85, for the nomination by a couple of which one of them is to be the "responsible carer" or "responsible foster parent". Under s.19(6) the nomination has to be made jointly. Presumably that is implied where the nomination is of the responsible foster parent under reg.85. Where more than one child is involved, the same nomination must cover all of them. The nomination can be changed once within 12 months from the date of the previous nomination or when there has been a relevant change of circumstances

References to paid work

87. References in this Chapter to obtaining paid work include obtaining more paid work or [¹better-paid work].

2.321

AMENDMENT

1. Social Security (Qualifying Young Persons Participating in Relevant Training Schemes) (Amendment) Regulations 2017 (SI 2017/987) reg.4(5) (November 6, 2017, in full service areas only).

DEFINITION

"paid work"—see reg.2

GENERAL NOTE

References to obtaining paid work, which appears to include self-employment as well as employment, includes obtaining more or better-paid work. This provision does not appear to add anything to the conditions of most of the provisions to which obtaining paid work is relevant. The amendment adding the hyphen between "better" and "paid" applied only for digital service (full service) cases. Its application is now general.

2.322

Expected hours

88.—(1) The "expected number of hours per week" in relation to a claimant for the purposes of determining their individual threshold in regulation 90 or for the purposes of regulation 95 or 97 is 35 unless some lesser number of hours applies under paragraph (2).

2.323

(2) The lesser number of hours is—
  (a) where—
       (i) the claimant is a relevant carer, a responsible carer [¹(subject to the following sub-paragraphs)] or a responsible foster parent, and
       (ii) the Secretary of State is satisfied that the claimant has reasonable prospects of obtaining paid work,
       the number of hours that the Secretary of State considers is compatible with those caring responsibilities;
[¹(aa) where the claimant is a responsible carer of a child who has not yet reached compulsory school age, the number of hours that the Secretary of State considers is compatible with those caring responsibilities;]
  (b) where the claimant is a responsible carer for a child [¹who has reached compulsory school age but who is] under the age of 13, the number of hours that the Secretary of State considers is compatible with the child's normal school hours (including the normal time it takes the child to travel to and from school); or
  (c) where the claimant has a physical or mental impairment, the number of hours that the Secretary of State considers is reasonable in light of the impairment.

AMENDMENT

1. Employment and Support Allowance and Universal Credit (Miscellaneous and Transitional and Savings Provisions) Regulations 2017 (SI 2017/204) reg.6 (April 3, 2017).

DEFINITIONS

"child"—see WRA 2012 s.40.
"claimant"—*ibid.*
"relevant carer"—see reg.85.
"responsible carer"—see WRA 2012 ss.40 and 19(6).
"responsible foster parent"—see reg.85.

GENERAL NOTE

2.324   Regulation 90 calculates the amount of earnings that will take a claimant out of being subject to all work-related requirements under s.22 of the WRA 2012 by reference to the "expected number of hours per week" and the national minimum wage. Regulation 95 uses the same number as one of the tests for the time that a claimant has to spend in action aimed at obtaining paid work to avoid being deemed not to have complied with the work search requirement under s.17 of the WRA 2012. Regulation 97(2) allows certain claimants to limit the work for which they must be available and for which they must search to work for the expected number of hours per week. Regulation 88 defines the expected number of hours for all these purposes.

The number under para.(1) is 35, unless some lesser number is applicable under para.(2). Can the number be reduced to zero? Why not? Zero is a number and it is less than 35. There are four alternative categories in para.(2).

Sub-paragraph (a) applies where the claimant is a relevant carer, a responsible carer (for a child (under 16) or anyone else, unless already covered by one of sub-paras (aa)-(c)) or a responsible foster parent (see s.19(6) of the WRA 2012 and reg.85 above), and so has some substantial caring responsibility. Then, if the claimant nonetheless has reasonable prospects of obtaining paid work (including obtaining more or better-paid work), the expected hours are what is compatible with those caring responsibilities.

Sub-paragraph (aa) applies where the claimant is the responsible carer (as defined in s.19(6) of the WRA 2012 simply in terms of responsibility for the child, on which see reg.4) of a child under compulsory school age, where the number of hours is to be reduced to what is compatible with those caring responsibilities, without any condition of having reasonable prospects of obtaining paid work. Compulsory school age is reached at the beginning of the school terms following 1 January, 1 April or 1 September, according to which date first follows the child's fifth birthday.

Sub-paragraph (b) applies where the claimant is a responsible carer (as defined in s.19(6) of the WRA 2012) for a child under the age of 13, when the expected hours are those compatible with the child's normal school and travel hours. How should this apply in home-schooling cases?

Sub-paragraph (c) applies where the claimant has a physical or mental impairment (not further defined), when the expected hours are those reasonable in the light of the impairment. This is an important rule in the structure of the application of work-related requirements in a benefit not restricted to jobseekers, and one where the argument that the expected hours under reg.88 can be zero is particularly relevant.

Note that the application of the deeming of non-compliance with the work search requirement under reg.95(1) if the expected hours of action are not taken is subject to deductions of hours under reg.95(2), including for temporary circumstances. Also note regs 96–99 on circumstances in which the work availability and work search requirements cannot be imposed or are moderated, particularly reg.96(4) (voluntary work), reg.96(5) (existing employment), reg.97(2) (physical or mental impairment) and reg.99(4) and (5)(c) (unfitness for work for short periods).

Work-related groups

Claimants subject to no work-related requirements

89.—(1) A claimant falls within section 19 of the Act (claimants subject   2.325
to no work-related requirements) if—
  (a) the claimant has reached the qualifying age for state pension credit;
  (b) the claimant has caring responsibilities for one or more severely
       disabled persons for at least 35 hours a week but does not meet the
       conditions for entitlement to a carer's allowance and the Secretary of
       State is satisfied that it would be unreasonable to require the claim-
       ant to comply with a work search requirement and a work availability
       requirement, including if such a requirement were limited in accord-
       ance with section 17(4) or 18(3) of the Act;
  (c) the claimant is pregnant and it is 11 weeks or less before her expected
       week of confinement, or was pregnant and it is 15 weeks or less since
       the date of her confinement;
  (d) the claimant is an adopter and it is 12 months or less since—
        (i) the date that the child was placed with the claimant, or
       (ii) if the claimant requested that the 12 months should run from a
             date within 14 days before the child was expected to be placed,
             that date;
[²(da) the claimant is a member of a couple entitled to universal credit by
       virtue of regulation 3(2)(b) and has student income in relation to
       the course they are undertaking which is taken into account in the
       calculation of the award;]
  (e) the claimant does not have to meet the condition in section 4(1)(d)
       of the Act (not receiving education) by virtue of regulation 14 and—
        (i) is a person referred to in paragraph (a) of that regulation (under
             21, in non-advanced education and without parental support),
             or
       (ii) has student income in relation to the course they are undertak-
             ing which is taken into account in the calculation of the award;
             or
  (f) the claimant is the responsible foster parent of a child under the age
       of 1.
  (2) In paragraph (1)(b) "severely disabled" has the meaning in section 70
of the Contributions and Benefits Act.
  (3) In paragraph (1)(d)—
  (a) "adopter" means a person who has been matched with a child for
       adoption and who is, or is intended to be, the responsible carer for
       the child, but excluding a person who is a foster parent or close rela-
       tive of the child; and
  (b) a person is matched with a child for adoption when it is decided by
       an adoption agency that the person would be a suitable adoptive
       parent for the child.
  [¹(4) For the purposes of paragraph (1)(e)(ii), a claimant is not to be
treated as having student income where—
  (a) that income is a postgraduate [³ ...] loan; and
  (b) the course in respect of which the loan is paid is not a full-time course.
  (5) In paragraph (4), "postgraduate [³ ...] loan" has the meaning given
in regulation 68(7).]

AMENDMENTS

1. Social Security (Treatment of Postgraduate Master's Degree Loans and Special Support Loans) (Amendment) Regulations 2016 (SI 2016/743) reg.6(5) (August 4, 2016).

2. Universal Credit (Miscellaneous Amendments, Saving and Transitional Provision) Regulations 2018 (SI 2018/65) reg.3(10) (April 11, 2018).

3. Social Security (Income and Capital) (Miscellaneous Amendments) Regulations 2020 (SI 2020/618) reg.8(6) (July 15, 2020).

DEFINITIONS

"child"—see WRA 2012 s.40.
"claimant"—*ibid.*
"close relative"—see reg.2.
"Contributions and Benefits Act"—*ibid.*
"postgraduate loan"—see para.(5) and reg.68(7).
"responsible carer"—see WRA 2012 ss.40 and 19(6).
"responsible foster parent"—see reg.85.

GENERAL NOTE

Temporary Coronavirus Provisions

2.326   The last of the temporary coronavirus provisions relevant to the imposition of work-related requirements expired on November 12, 2020. See previous editions of this volume for the details.

2.327   Section 19(2) of the WRA 2012 sets out in paras (a), (b) and (c) three categories of claimants who can be subject to no work-related requirements: (a) those who have limited capability for work and work-related activity; (b) those who meet the definition of having regular and substantial caring responsibilities for a severely disabled person (i.e. satisfy the conditions, apart from level of earnings and claiming, for carer's allowance, but gain no earned income from the caring: reg.30); and (c) those who are the responsible carer for a child under the age of one. Paragraph (d) of s.19(2) includes claimants of a description prescribed in regulations. Regulation 89(1) sets out categories prescribed for this purpose, as noted below. Regulation 90 prescribes another category, dependent on earnings. See also reg.98 on recent victims of domestic violence.

The categories prescribed for the purpose of s.19(2)(d) are as follows:

(a) Claimants who have reached the qualifying age for state pension credit. The qualifying age for men is the same as for a woman born on the same day and for women depends on the date of birth in accordance with a complicated formula. See p.776 of and Appendix 11 to CPAG's *Welfare benefits and tax credits handbook* (2019/2020 edition) for the details. For anyone born before April 6, 1950 the age is 60. For those born on or after that date there is a sliding scale that rose to 65 in November 2018, reaching 66 by October 2020 and 67 by some date from 2026. Although single claimants who have reached the qualifying age for state pension credit cannot be entitled to universal credit (WRA 2012 s.4(1)(b)), someone of that age can be a joint claimant with a partner under that age (a "mixed age couple").

(b) Claimants who do not meet the conditions of entitlement for carer's allowance, but have caring responsibilities for at least 35 hours per week for a severely disabled person (defined in the same way as for carer's allowance: para.(2)), where it would be unreasonable to expect the claimant to comply with a work search and a work availability requirement, even with limitations. Some claimants who fall within this category will already be covered by s.19(2)(b) and it is not easy to work out who could benefit from the extension. Perhaps the main category would be those who are paid for the caring, who are expressly excluded from the scope of s.19(2)(b) by the definition in reg.30 above.

(c) Claimants who are pregnant in the period from 11 weeks before the expected date of confinement and 15 weeks after the date of confinement.

(d) Claimants who are "adopters" (i.e. who have been matched with a particular child for adoption under the complicated conditions in para.(3)) within 12 months or so of placement. It does not matter how old the child is, so long as below the age of 16. Any person who is actually the responsible carer of a child under the age of one is already covered by s.19(2)(c). It appears that para.(d) can continue to apply after the child has actually been adopted, for the 12 months following placement. See para.(f) for foster parents.

(da) Claimants who are part of a joint claim couple where one claimant fails to meet the basic condition in s.4(1)(d) of the WRA 2012 not to be receiving education, but the other meets that condition or is excepted from it, but only where student income for the course being attended has been taken into account in the calculation of the award of universal credit. Regulation 3(2)(b) allows such a couple to be entitled to universal credit. See regs 68-71 for student income and how it is taken into account. The aim of this addition in April 2018 was to provide uniformity for couples with the treatment of single claimants in education under sub-para.(e).

(e) Claimants who, by virtue of reg.14(1)(a), do not have to meet the basic condition in s.4(1)(d) of the WRA 2012 of not receiving education or who have student income (see regs 68–71) that is taken into account in the award of universal credit.

(f) Claimants who are the responsible foster parent (there can only be one under reg.85) of a child under the age of one. It appears that such a person cannot get within s.19(2)(c) because reg.4(6)(a) prevents their being treated as responsible for the child while the child is "looked after" by a local authority under s.22 of the Children Act 1989 or s.17(6) of the Children (Scotland) Act 1995.

Claimants subject to no work-related requirements—the earnings thresholds

90.—(1) A claimant falls within section 19 of the Act (claimants subject to no work-related requirements) if the claimant's [²monthly] earnings are equal to or exceed the claimant's individual threshold.   2.328

(2) A claimant's individual threshold is the amount that a person of the same age as the claimant would be paid at the hourly rate applicable under [³regulation 4 or regulation 4A(1)(a) to (c)] of the National Minimum Wage Regulations for—

(a) 16 hours per week, in the case of a claimant who would otherwise fall within section 20 (claimants subject to work-focused interview requirement only) or section 21 (claimants subject to work-preparation requirement) of the Act; or

(b) the expected number of hours per week in the case of a claimant who would otherwise fall within section 22 of the Act (claimants subject to all work-related requirements)[²,

converted to a monthly amount by multiplying by 52 and dividing by 12].

(3) A claimant who is a member of a couple falls within section 19 of the Act if the couple's combined [²monthly] earnings are equal to or exceed whichever of the following amounts is applicable—

(a) in the case of joint claimants, the sum of their individual thresholds; or

(b) in the case of a claimant who claims universal credit as a single person by virtue of regulation 3(3), the sum of—

(i) the claimant's individual threshold, and
(ii) the amount a person would be paid for 35 hours per week at the hourly rate specified in [³regulation 4] of the National Minimum Wage Regulations[²,

converted to a monthly amount by multiplying by 52 and dividing by 12].

(4) A claimant falls within section 19 of the Act if the claimant is employed under a contract of apprenticeship and has [²monthly] earnings that are equal to or exceed the amount they would be paid for—

(a) 30 hours a week; or
(b) if less, the expected number of hours per week for that claimant,

at the rate specified in [³ regulation 4A(1)(d)] of the National Minimum Wage Regulations[², converted to a monthly amount by multiplying by 52 and dividing by 12].

[¹(5) A claimant falls within section 19 of the Act if they are treated as having earned income in accordance with regulation 62 (minimum income floor).]

(6) [² A person's monthly earnings are]—

(a) [² the person's] earned income calculated or estimated in relation to the current assessment period before any deduction for income tax, national insurance contributions or relievable pension contributions; or

(b) in a case where the person's earned income fluctuates (or is likely to fluctuate) the amount of that income[², calculated or estimated before any deduction for income tax, national insurance contributions or relievable pension contributions, taken as a monthly average]—

(i) where there is an identifiable cycle, over the duration of one such cycle, or
(ii) where there is no identifiable cycle, over three months or such other period as may, in the particular case, enable the [²monthly] average to be determined more accurately,

[²and the Secretary of State may, in order to enable monthly earnings to be determined more accurately, disregard earned income received in respect of an employment which has ceased.]

(7) [³...]

AMENDMENTS

1. Universal Credit and Miscellaneous Amendments (No.2) Regulations 2014 (SI 2014/2888) reg.4(7) (November 16, 2014).
2. Universal Credit and Miscellaneous Amendments Regulations 2015 (SI 2015/1754) reg.2(6) (November 4, 2015).
3. Social Security (Jobseeker's Allowance, Employment and Support Allowance and Universal Credit) (Amendment) Regulations 2016 (SI 2016/678) reg.5(4) (July 25, 2016).

DEFINITIONS

"the Act"—see reg.2.
"assessment period"—see WRA 2012 ss.40 and 7(2), and reg.21.
"claimant"—see WRA 2012 s.40(1).
"couple"—see WRA 2012 ss.40 and 39.
"earned income"—see regs 2 and 52.
"joint claimants"—see WRA 2012 s.40.

"National Minimum Wage Regulations"—see reg.2.
"single person"—see WRA 2012 ss.40 and 1(2)(a).

GENERAL NOTE

Regulation 90 prescribes additional circumstances, beyond those prescribed by reg.89, in which a claimant falls within s.19(2)(d) of the WRA 2012 and therefore can be subject to no work-related requirements. Thus, if a single claimant or a couple falls within reg.90 no requirement can be imposed under s.20 (work-focused interview) or 21 (work preparation) although the conditions in s.20(1) or 21(1)(a)–(b) are met (see the notes to those provisions for why their express words forbid such an exercise, that has apparently sometimes been operated in practice). That prohibition is even clearer if s.22 (all work-related requirements) appears to be in play, e.g. where a claimant is "merely" the responsible carer of a child aged three or over. The basic test under para.(1) is that the claimant's monthly earnings are at least equal to their "individual threshold", known administratively as the conditionality earnings threshold. This provision is necessary because universal credit, in contrast to the terms of pre-existing benefits, can be payable while a claimant is in work. The policy is that if a claimant is already earning above a minimum level there is no need to require them to do anything to seek further paid work. Entitlement then depends on the income calculation under s.8 of the WRA 2012. See further the notes to reg.99.

Note that reg.6(1A)(a) requires the rounding down to the nearest pound of any amounts produced by reg.90 calculations.

Paragraph (3) applies the para.(1) test to couples. For joint claimants their individual thresholds are added together, as are their monthly earnings. The threshold is calculated under para.(2) by multiplying the hourly rate of national minimum wage by, in the case of a claimant who would otherwise be subject to all work-related requirements under s.22 of the WRA 2012, the expected number of hours per week (see reg.88, starting point 35). In the case of a claimant who would otherwise fall within s.20 or 21, the multiplier is 16.

Under para.(6) monthly earnings are earned income as calculated under Chapter 2 of Part 6 of the Universal Credit Regulations (i.e. regs 51–64) in each monthly assessment period but without deductions for income tax, national insurance contributions or pension contributions, subject to an averaging provision in sub-para. (b) where earned income fluctuates or is likely to fluctuate. The ordinary calculation in regs 51–64 involves the use of "real time" information. In the case of both employment and self-employment the calculation of earned income in respect of any assessment period (i.e. month) is to be based on amounts received in that assessment period (regs 54, 55, 57 and 57A), as now confirmed as a matter of construction by the Court of Appeal in *Secretary of State for Work and Pensions v Johnson* [2020] EWCA Civ 778; [2020] P.T.S.R. 1872 and *Pantellerisco v Secretary of State for Work and Pensions* [2021] EWCA Civ 1454; [2021] P.T.S.R. 1922 discussed in detail in the notes to regs 54 and 61. *Johnson* found that the outcome, especially the fluctuations in the amounts of earnings taken into account in different assessment periods when the general pattern of earnings was regular, was irrational and unlawful for claimants in the very particular categories involved. It is yet to be seen what method of calculation might be accepted as rational prior to the substitution of the November 2021 for of reg.61, but for most claimants the general rule in regs 54 and 61 is to be applied. In those cases, it may be proper for the amount of universal credit to fluctuate month by month or for the claimant to fall in and out of entitlement on the means test. However, if entitlement continues there are plainly arguments against a claimant drifting in and out of exemption from all work-related requirements on the basis of the amount of earned income. That is presumably the thinking behind para.(6)(b). The reference to fluctuation of earned income must be to fluctuation over more than one assessment period, because fluctuation within each assessment period does not affect the total for that month. Under sub-para.(i) it is not clear whether the identifiable cycle refers merely to the pattern of receipts or to

2.329

the pattern of the employment or self-employment or other paid work that produces the income. There is no reference to a cycle "of work", as there is in reg.42(2)(b) of the JSA Regulations 2013, so that the stricture in *KN v DfC (JSA)* [2022] NICom 21 against conflating a cycle of payment with a cycle of work does not apply. In the overall context of universal credit, with the emphasis in regs 54 and 61 on receipts in a particular assessment period, it may be that it is a cycle of payment that is more important. It would appear that there cannot be an identifiable cycle until it has started and come to an end, which is by definition the start of the next cycle, at least once. Given the difficulties that the notion of a recognisable cycle has given in other contexts it may be that most cases will be dealt with by sub-para.(ii), which requires the taking of an average over the previous three months or such other period as in the particular case enables the weekly average to be determined more accurately. That gives a very wide discretion.

Note also the important power at the end of para.(6) to disregard earned income from an employment that has ceased.

In relation to self-employment some of the problems mentioned above will be avoided by the application of the reg.62 minimum income floor (para.(5)). Providing that a person meets the quite stringent conditions in reg.64 for being in gainful self-employment and is not in a 12-month start-up period (reg.63), earned income below the individual threshold is deemed to be at that level. In those circumstances the claimant is exempted from all work-related requirements by para.(5). If as result of the application of the Secretary of State's discretion in reg.2(1) of the Social Security (Coronavirus) (Further Measures) Regulations 2020 (SI 2020/371, in effect from March 30, 2020) a claimant is not treated as having earned income under the MIF when they normally would be, so that para.(5) does not apply, reg.2(1)(e) allows the Secretary of State to exempt the claimant from any work search or work availability requirement.

Prior to October 3, 2019, in the converse situation where a person was exempted from all work-related requirements through the operation of reg.90 apart from para.(5), the provisions of reg.62 on the MIF could not apply (reg.62(1)(b) in its original form). See the notes to reg.62 for how that, and in particular the averaging process under reg.90(6), could then affect the MIF. According to the Explanatory Memorandum to the Universal Credit (Childcare Costs and Minimum Income Floor) (Amendment) Regulations 2019 (SI 2019/1249), that did not reflect the policy intention. Regulation 3 of those Regulations inserts into reg.62(1)(b), with effect from October 3, 2019, the rule that for the MIF to apply the claimant must be subject to all work-related requirements not only apart from the effect of reg.62, but also apart from the effect of reg.90. It remains the case that, if a claimant in exempted from any work-related requirement under any provision apart from reg.62 or 90, the MIF cannot apply.

Claimants subject to work-focused interview requirement only

2.330

91.—(1) [¹ . . .].

(2) A claimant falls within section 20 of the Act if—

(a) the claimant is the responsible foster parent in relation to a child aged at least 1;

(b) the claimant is the responsible foster parent in relation to a qualifying young person, and the Secretary of State is satisfied that the qualifying young person has care needs which would make it unreasonable to require the claimant to comply with a work search requirement or a work availability requirement, including if such a requirement were limited in accordance with section 17(4) or 18(3) of the Act;

(c) the claimant is a foster parent, but not the responsible foster parent, in relation to a child or qualifying young person, and the Secretary of State is satisfied that the child or qualifying young person has care needs which would make it unreasonable to require the claimant to comply with a work search requirement or a work availability requirement, including if such a requirement were limited in accordance with section 17(4) or 18(3) of the Act;

(d) the claimant has fallen within paragraph (a), (b) or (c) within the past 8 weeks and has no child or qualifying young person currently placed with them, but expects to resume being a foster parent; or

(e) the claimant has become a friend or family carer in relation to a child within the past 12 months and is also the responsible carer in relation to that child.

(3) In paragraph (2)(e) "friend or family carer" means a person who is responsible for a child, but is not the child's parent or step-parent, and has undertaken the care of the child in the following circumstances—

(a) the child has no parent or has parents who are unable to care for the child; or

(b) it is likely that the child would otherwise be looked after by a local authority because of concerns in relation to the child's welfare.

AMENDMENT

1. Welfare Reform and Work Act 2016 s.17(2)(a) (April 3, 2017).

DEFINITIONS

"the Act"—see reg.2.
"child"—see WRA 2012 s.40.
"claimant"—*ibid.*
"foster parent"—see reg.2.
"qualifying young person"—see regs 2 and 5.
"responsible carer"—see WRA 2012 ss.40 and 19(6).
"responsible foster parent"—see reg.85.
"work availability requirement"—see WRA 2012 ss.40 and 18(1).
"work search requirement"—see WRA 2012 ss.40 and 17(1).

GENERAL NOTE

Paragraph (1)

Paragraph (1) had formerly prescribed the relevant maximum age of a child for the purposes of s.20(1)(a) of the WRA 2012 to enable a responsible carer to be exempted from all work-related requirements except the work-focused interview requirement (initially five and then, from April 2014, three). From April 3, 2017 the operation of s.20(1)(a) has by its terms been restricted to responsible carers of a child aged one (responsible carers of a child under one being exempted from all work-related requirements under s.19(1)(c)). There is no longer any power to prescribe an age in regulations.   **2.331**

Paragraph (2)

This provision prescribes the categories of claimant who are subject only to the work-focused interview requirement under s.20(1)(b) and any connected requirements under s.23. They cover mainly foster parents.   **2.332**

Under sub-para.(a) responsible foster parents of children of any age from one to 15 are covered. Responsible foster parents of children under one are exempted from all work-related requirements under reg.89(1)(f).

That is extended to young persons in education up to the age of 19 if it would be unreasonable to subject the claimant to other work-related requirements (sub-para.(b)).

Sub-paragraph (c) extends the scope of sub-paras (a) and (b) to foster parents who do not meet the condition of being "responsible" if the child or qualifying young person has care needs that make it unreasonable to subject the claimant to other work-related requirements.

Sub-paragraph (d) allows the effect of sub-paras (a)–(c) to continue for eight weeks after the claimant ceases to have any child or qualifying young person placed with them, if a new placement is expected.

Sub-paragraph (e) applies to claimants who are responsible carers of a child of any age up to 15 if they fall within the meaning of "friend or family carer" in para.(3).

[¹Claimants subject to work preparation requirement

2.333 **91A.** [² . . .].]

AMENDMENTS

1. Income Support (Work-Related Activity) Miscellaneous Amendments Regulations 2014 (SI 2014/1097) reg.16(3) (April 28, 2014).
2. Welfare Reform and Work Act 2016 s.17(2)(b) (April 3, 2017).

GENERAL NOTE

2.334 See the notes to s.21 of the WRA 2012. The operation of that section in so far as it exempts responsible carers of a child from all work-related requirements except the work-focused interview and work preparation requirement has from April 3, 2017 been directly controlled by the terms of s.21 (the child must be aged two and no less or more). There is thus no need for a prescription of conditions including an age in regulations and the former duty in s.21(5) so to do has also been removed.

Claimants subject to all work-related requirements—EEA jobseekers

2.335 **92.** [¹ . . .]

AMENDMENT

1. Universal Credit (EEA Jobseekers) Amendment Regulations 2015 (SI 2015/546) reg.3 (June 10, 2015).

GENERAL NOTE

2.336 For the discriminatory effect of this provision on the entitlement of certain EEA claimants with a right to reside before its revocation in June 2015 see the notes to the 2013/14 edition of what was then Vol.V of this series. Now see reg.9 above, as extensively amended.

The work-related requirements

Purposes of a work-focused interview

2.337 **93.** The purposes of a work-focused interview are any or all of the following—

   (a) assessing the claimant's prospects for remaining in or obtaining paid work;

(b) assisting or encouraging the claimant to remain in or obtain paid work;

(c) identifying activities that the claimant may undertake that will make remaining in or obtaining paid work more likely;

(d) identifying training, educational or rehabilitation opportunities for the claimant which may make it more likely that the claimant will remain in or obtain paid work or be able to do so;

(e) identifying current or future work opportunities for the claimant that are relevant to the claimant's needs and abilities;

(f) ascertaining whether a claimant is in gainful self-employment or meets the conditions in regulation 63 (start-up period).

DEFINITIONS

"claimant"—see WRA 2012 s.40.
"obtaining paid work"—see reg.87.
"paid work"—see reg.2.

GENERAL NOTE

This provision prescribes the purposes of a work-focused interview under the definition in s.15(2) of the WRA 2012. The purposes could probably not be set out more widely, especially given that obtaining paid work includes obtaining more or better paid work and that s.15 covers work preparation as well as work. Arguably, even if there is no realistic prospect of a claimant obtaining any kind of paid work, the purpose of assessing those prospects or lack of prospects in an interview could still be fulfilled.

Note that the prescribed purposes do not include the discussion of the drawing up or revision of a claimant commitment as such, but the matters prescribed may be relevant to what requirements are to be included in a claimant commitment.

Work search requirement—interviews

94. A claimant is to be treated as not having complied with a work search requirement to apply for a particular vacancy for paid work where the claimant fails to participate in an interview offered to the claimant in connection with the vacancy.

DEFINITIONS

"claimant"—see WRA 2012, s.40.
"paid work"—see reg.2.
"work search requirement"—see WRA 2012 ss.40 and 17(1).

GENERAL NOTE

This provision, made under s.25(a) of the WRA 2012, applies when the Secretary of State has required under s.17(1)(b) that the claimant take the particular action of applying for a specified vacancy for paid work. If the claimant fails to participate in an interview offered in connection with the vacancy the work search requirement is deemed not to have been complied with. See the notes to s.17, and the notes to ss.15 and 27 for "participation" in an interview.

Work search requirement—all reasonable action

95.—(1) A claimant is to be treated as not having complied with a work search requirement to take all reasonable action for the purpose of obtaining paid work in any week unless—

(a) either—

    (i) the time which the claimant spends taking action for the purpose of obtaining paid work is at least the claimant's expected number of hours per week minus any relevant deductions, or

2.338

2.339

2.340

2.341

(ii) the Secretary of State is satisfied that the claimant has taken all reasonable action for the purpose of obtaining paid work despite the number of hours that the claimant spends taking such action being lower than the expected number of hours per week; and

(b) that action gives the claimant the best prospects of obtaining work.

(2) In this regulation "relevant deductions" means the total of any time agreed by the Secretary of State—

(a) for the claimant to carry out paid work, voluntary work, a work preparation requirement, or voluntary work preparation in that week; or

(b) for the claimant to deal with temporary childcare responsibilities, a domestic emergency, funeral arrangements or other temporary circumstances.

(3) For the purpose of paragraph (2)(a) the time agreed by the Secretary of State for the claimant to carry out voluntary work must not exceed 50% of the claimant's expected number of hours per week.

(4) "Voluntary work preparation" means particular action taken by a claimant and agreed by the Secretary of State for the purpose of making it more likely that the claimant will obtain paid work, but which is not specified by the Secretary of State as a work preparation requirement under section 16 of the Act.

DEFINITIONS

"claimant"—see WRA 2012 s.40.
"expected number of hours"—see regs 2 and 88.
"obtaining paid work"—see reg.87.
"paid work"—see reg.2.
"work preparation requirement"—see WRA 2012 ss.40 and 16(1).
"work search requirement"—see WRA 2012 ss.40 and 17(1).

GENERAL NOTE

Temporary Coronavirus Provisions
2.342　The last of the temporary coronavirus provisions relevant to the work search requirement expired on November 12, 2020. See previous editions of this volume for the details.

2.343　This regulation, made under s.25(a) of the WRA 2012, deems certain claimants not to have complied with a work search requirement under s.17(1)(a) of the WRA 2012 to take all reasonable action for the purpose of obtaining paid work (including more or better paid work). Although in form meeting the conditions in reg.95 merely lifts the deeming of non-compliance if its conditions are met, there would seem to be little point in making such detailed provision if claimants were not to be positively treated as having complied if the conditions are met. See the notes to s.17 and see reg.97 for limitations on the kind of work that needs to be searched for. A failure for no good reason to comply with the requirement under s.17(1)(a) can lead to a medium-level sanction under s.27(2)(a) of the WRA 2012 and reg.103(1)(a).

To avoid the deeming a claimant must get within *both* sub-paras.(a) *and* (b) of para.(1).

There are two alternative routes to getting within sub-para.(a). Although the route in head (i), relating to spending the "expected hours" (starting point under reg.88, 35), has been described as the "primary" rule in some previous editions, it is now submitted that that is misleading. Although head (ii), with the route of having taken all reasonable action in the week in question, applies only if the claimant spent less than the expected hours, logically the two routes are of equal status. One of the routes had to appear before the other in sub-para.(a) and the two routes could with the same effect have been put in the opposite order. The effect of reading the two provisions together is that there is no rigid rule that claimants be held to spending the expected hours in work search week after week, even though that may be the easiest point to start the enquiry. The ultimate test is what is reasonable. The sentence in the middle of para.32 of *S v SSWP (UC)* [2017] UKUT 477 (AAC) (see the notes to s.14 of the WRA 2012 for the details) saying that if "a claimant spends less than 35 hours, or the quality of the work search is disputed, he will need to rely on section 27(2) [i.e. the "for no good reason" rule] if he seeks to avoid a sanction" is not to be taken to indicate the contrary. That sentence is immediately followed by an acknowledgement of the effect of head (ii).

The para.(1)(a)(i) route requires that the claimant must spend at least the "expected number of hours per week" (reg.88), less deductions for work, voluntary work or work preparation or various emergency, urgent or other temporary difficulties (para.(2), subject to the further rules in paras (3) and (4)), in taking action for the purpose of obtaining paid work. Note that the starting point of expected hours under reg.88 may be reduced from 35 (arguably to nil, if appropriate) to take account of responsibility for certain categories of young children, of certain other regular caring responsibilities and physical or mental impairments. The time to count as a deduction under para.(2) must be agreed by the Secretary of State. The words might suggest that the agreement must come in advance of the activity that might qualify. However, it would seem unrealistic for claimants to predict, say, the future occurrence of domestic emergencies so as to seek the Secretary of State's agreement in advance. Thus, it would seem, and would be in line with the normal pattern of claimants making a declaration that they have been seeking work in the assessment period that is ending, that a subsequent agreement will do (although no doubt it would be sensible for claimants to raise potential issues in advance where possible). It must be the case that, while the Secretary of State appears to have an open-ended discretion whether or not to agree to any particular hours being deducted under para.(2), on appeal against any sanction for failure to comply with the work search requirement under s.17(1)(a) of the WRA 2012 a tribunal is allowed to substitute its own judgment about what should have been agreed. Even if it were to be held that whatever had or had not been agreed by the Secretary of State has to control whether there had been a sanctionable failure, the reasonableness or otherwise of the Secretary of State's view would be relevant to whether a failure to comply was "for no good reason". The deductions for hours spent in paid work and voluntary work are important, as is that for work preparation requirements in securing a rational co-ordination among the various work-related requirements. Would para.(2)(b) allow the Secretary of State to allow short "holidays" from work search responsibilities, under the heading of temporary circumstances or temporary child care responsibilities (cf. reg.19(1)(p) and (2) of the JSA Regulations 1996)? Or would such an allowance fall more naturally under reg.99(5)(b) (work search requirement not to be imposed where it would be unreasonable to do so because of temporary child care responsibilities or temporary circumstances)?

If the claimant does not meet the expected hours condition, which for the majority of claimants will be 35 hours per week, sub-para.(a) can nevertheless be satisfied through head (ii) if the claimant has taken all reasonable action in the week in question for the purpose of obtaining paid work. This is an important provision which, if properly applied, would go a good way to meeting the commonly expressed criticism that in the real world it is impossible for many claimants to fill 35 hours week after week with meaningful work search action.

In *RR v SSWP (UC)* [2017] UKUT 459 (AAC), the First-tier Tribunal, in upholding two medium-level sanctions on the basis that the claimant had not taken work-search action for the 35 expected hours in two weeks, failed to consider whether there should be deductions from 35 hours under reg.95(2)(b) when there was evidence of circumstances (having to deal with the fall-out from divorce or other family proceedings) that could have amounted to a domestic emergency or other temporary circumstances. The tribunal appeared to think that the 35 hours were immutable, which was plainly an error of law. Alternatively, the claimant could have been taken to satisfy the condition in s.17(1)(a) through reg.95(1)(a)(ii), which applies even though the expected hours, less deductions, are not met. The decision-maker and the tribunal put some emphasis on the claimant having agreed in her claimant commitment to prepare and look for work for 35 hours a week. Judge Wikeley pointed out that the claimant commitment was only in terms of "normally" spending 35 hours a week, but in fact the number of hours specified in a claimant commitment cannot be directly relevant unless they establish a lesser number of hours under reg.88(2) or an agreement to a deduction of hours under reg.95(2). The test is in terms of the expected hours less deductions, which the claimant commitment merely records, or "all reasonable action" under reg.95(1)(a)(ii). It is worth noting that the claimant commitment in *RR* (following what appears to be a standard form) specified 35 hours normally for a combination of work preparation (s.16(1) of the WRA 2012) *and* work search, so did incorporate an unquantified deduction under reg.95(2)(a).

The judge, in re-making the decision in the claimant's favour, did not expressly consider the condition that a deduction under para.(2) be agreed by the Secretary of State. He must either have regarded that condition as one on which a First-tier Tribunal was entitled to substitute its own agreement or have regarded the Secretary of State's support of the appeal in the Upper Tribunal and of the substitution of a decision as necessarily involving agreement to a deduction. He also suggested that an alternative way of looking at the case could have been to consider whether reg.99(5)(b) applied (domestic emergency or temporary circumstances), so that no work search requirement could be imposed for the weeks in question. See the notes to reg.99.

Under (b), the action under (a) must give the claimant the best prospects of obtaining work. Taken at face value that condition imposes an almost impossibly high standard, because there will nearly always be something extra that the claimant could do to improve prospects of obtaining work. The condition must therefore be interpreted in a way that leaves some work for condition (a) to do and with some degree of common sense, taking account of all the circumstances, especially any factors that have led to a reduction in the expected hours below 35 or a deduction under para.(1)(a)(i) and (2), as well as matters such as the state of the local labour market, what the claimant has done in previous weeks and how successful or otherwise those actions were (compare reg.18(3) of the JSA Regulations 1996). The work search requirement in s.17(1)(a) of the WRA 2012 is only to take all reasonable action. The reference here in secondary legislation to the best prospects of obtaining work cannot be allowed to make the test as set out in the primary legislation stricter than that. There will of course be considerable difficulty in checking on the precise number of hours spent in taking relevant action, depending on what might count as action (see the notes to s.17), and in what might be required from claimants in the way of record keeping. It may be that it will be much easier to define non-compliance with the requirement in s.17(1)(b) to take particular action specified by the Secretary of State, although such a failure will only attract a low-level sanction under s.27(2)(a) and reg.104(1)(b)(iii).

In the Upper Tribunal's substituted decision in *RR* (above) there was no express consideration of the overriding condition in sub-para.(b). That must be regarded as having been satisfied in the absence of it having been raised on behalf of the Secretary of State in the support of the appeal to the Upper Tribunal.

In *S v SSWP (UC)* [2017] UKUT 477 (AAC) (see the notes to s.14 of the WRA 2012 for the details), the basis on which the First-tier Tribunal seemed to have accepted that the claimant had failed to take all reasonable action for the purpose of obtaining paid work in the various weeks in question was that he had failed to apply for vacancies outside the healthcare sector that the DWP said were suitable. The claimant's evidence was somewhat inconsistent and unconvincing, but he appears to have said that, although he did not apply for any vacancies, he had spent 35 hours in each week checking jobs websites and local newspapers. If that had been accepted, it could have been argued (see the beginning of this note) that, subject to the operation of para.(2)(b), the claimant not only escaped the deeming of non-compliance in para.(1) but fell to be treated as having complied with the s.17(1)(a) requirement. That point was not addressed in the Upper Tribunal's substituted decision dismissing the claimant's appeal (on the issue of "no good reason"). There was certainly evidence on which it could have been concluded that the action taken by the claimant, even if taking up 35 hours each week, had not given him the best prospects of obtaining work. It would have been better if it had been spelled out just where the inadequacy of the claimant's job search fitted into the legislative structure. Did the claimant fail the expected hours test in para.(2)(a)(i) without being rescued by para.(2)(a)(ii) or did he get within para.(2)(a)(i), but fail the para.(2)(b) test?

Work availability requirement—able and willing immediately to take up paid work

96.—(1) Subject to paragraph (2) a claimant is to be treated as not having complied with a work availability requirement if the claimant is not able and willing immediately to attend an interview offered to the claimant in connection with obtaining paid work.

2.344

(2) But a claimant is to be treated as having complied with a work availability requirement despite not being able immediately to take up paid work, if paragraph (3), (4) or (5) applies.

(3) This paragraph applies where—

(a) a claimant is a responsible carer or a relevant carer;

(b) the Secretary of State is satisfied that, as a consequence the claimant needs a longer period of up to 1 month to take up paid work, or up to 48 hours to attend an interview in connection with obtaining work, taking into account alternative care arrangements; and

(c) the claimant is able and willing to take up paid work, or attend an interview, on being given notice for that period.

(4) This paragraph applies where—

(a) a claimant is carrying out voluntary work;

(b) the Secretary of State is satisfied that, as a consequence, the claimant needs a longer period of up to 1 week to take up paid work, or up to 48 hours to attend an interview in connection with obtaining work; and

(c) the claimant is able and willing to take up paid work, or attend an interview, on being given notice for that period.

(5) This paragraph applies where a claimant—

(a) is employed under a contract of service;

(b) is required by section 86 of the Employment Rights Act 1996, or by the contract of service, to give notice to terminate the contract;

(c) is able and willing to take up paid work once the notice period has expired; and

(d) is able and willing to attend an interview on being given 48 hours notice.

DEFINITIONS

"claimant"—see WRA 2012 s.40.
"obtaining paid work"—see reg.87.

"paid work"—see reg.2.
"relevant carer"—see reg.85.
"responsible carer"—see WRA 2012 ss.40 and 19(6).
"work availability requirement"—see WRA 2012 ss.40 and 18(1).

GENERAL NOTE

Temporary Coronavirus Provisions

2.345   The last of the temporary coronavirus provisions relevant to the work availability requirement expired on November 12, 2020. See previous editions of this volume for the details.

2.346   This regulation is made under s.25 of the WRA 2012 and relates to the work availability requirement under s.18(1) and (2) of being able and willing immediately to take up paid work or more or better paid work. See reg.97 for limitations on the kind of work for which a claimant must be available and reg.99, and in particular para. (5), for other situations in which the ordinary test of being able and willing immediately to take up work or attend an interview is modified.

Paragraph (1)

2.347   Paragraph (1) simply confirms that the requirement of being able and willing immediately to take up paid work extends to being able and willing immediately to attend an interview in connection with obtaining paid work, subject to the exemptions in paras (3)-(5), through the operation of para.(2).

Paragraphs (2) to (5)

2.348   A claimant who falls within paras (3), (4) or (5) is to be treated as complying with the work availability requirement, including as extended by para.(1). Paragraph (3) applies to those with child-care or other caring responsibilities who would need to take up to one month to take up paid work or up to 48 hours to attend an interview and are able and willing to do so if given that length of notice. Can para.(3)(b) allow claimants with caring responsibilities (noting that such claimants do not need to have sole or main responsibility) to have a holiday without needing to arrange some means of taking up work offers or interviews immediately? Or would such an allowance fall more naturally under reg.99(5A) or (5B) with (5)(b) (no need to be available immediately where work search requirement not to be imposed because it would be unreasonable to do so because of temporary child care responsibilities or temporary circumstances)? Paragraph (4) applies to claimants doing voluntary work (not further defined), subject to the same conditions. Paragraph (5) applies to claimants in employment who are required to give notice to terminate their contract of employment and who are able and willing to take up paid work once that notice has expired and to attend an interview on 48 hours' notice.

Work search requirement and work availability requirement—limitations

2.349   97.—(1) Paragraphs (2) to (5) set out the limitations on a work search requirement and a work availability requirement.

(2) In the case of a claimant who is a relevant carer or a responsible carer or who has a physical or mental impairment, a work search and work availability requirement must be limited to the number of hours that is determined to be the claimant's expected number of hours per week in accordance with regulation 88.

(3) A work search and work availability requirement must be limited to work that is in a location which would normally take the claimant—

(a) a maximum of 90 minutes to travel from home to the location; and

(b) a maximum of 90 minutes to travel from the location to home.

(4) Where a claimant has previously carried out work of a particular nature, or at a particular level of remuneration, a work search requirement and a work availability requirement must be limited to work of a similar nature, or level of remuneration, for such period as the Secretary of State considers appropriate, but only if the Secretary of State is satisfied that the claimant will have reasonable prospects of obtaining paid work in spite of such limitation.

(5) The limitation in paragraph (4) is to apply for no more than [¹4 weeks] beginning with—

(a) the date of claim; or

(b) if later, the date on which the claimant ceases paid work after falling within section 19 of the Act by virtue of regulation 90 (claimants subject to no work-related requirements- the earnings thresholds).

(6) Where a claimant has a physical or mental impairment that has a substantial adverse effect on the claimant's ability to carry out work of a particular nature, or in particular locations, a work search or work availability requirement must not relate to work of such a nature or in such locations.

AMENDMENT

1. Universal Credit and Jobseeker's Allowance (Work Search and Work Availability Requirements—limitations) (Amendment) Regulations 2022 (SI 2022/108) reg.2 (February 8, 2022).

DEFINITIONS

"claimant"—see WRA 2012 s.40.
"expected number of hours per week"—see regs 2 and 88.
"relevant carer"—see reg.85.
"responsible carer"—see WRA 2012 ss.40 and 19(6).
"work availability requirement"—see WRA 2012 ss.40 and 18(1).
"work search requirement"—see WRA 2012 ss.40 and 17(1).

GENERAL NOTE

2.350

This regulation is made under ss.17(4) and (5) (work search requirement) and 18(3) and (4) (work availability requirement) of the WRA 2012. It sets out limitations on the kind of work that a claimant can be required to search for or be able and willing immediately to take up. See reg.99 for other situations in which the ordinary tests for those requirements are modified.

Paragraph (2)

2.351

This paragraph establishes an important limitation on the kind of work that can be considered, but only for the particular categories of claimant identified: those with child care responsibilities and the disabled (anyone with a physical or mental impairment). Those categories of claimant can only be required to search for or be able and willing to take up work for no more than the number of hours per week compatible with those circumstances, as worked out under reg.88 (which could, it is suggested in the notes to reg.88, be zero). So, as far as the work search requirement is concerned, this limitation appears to apply as much to the sort of work in relation to which the Secretary of State may specify particular action under s.17(1)(b) of the WRA 2012 as to the requirement under s.17(1)(a) to take all reasonable action for the purpose of obtaining paid work or more or better paid work. Although the drafting of para. (2) appears to limit the hours for which either requirement is applicable, it can only, in view of the terms of the regulation-making powers in ss.17(4) and 18(3), relate to the hours of work to which the relevant requirement can be attached. See para.(6) for permissible limitations relating to the location and nature of employment for those with a physical or mental impairment.

Note that under s.19(1) and (2)(a) no work-related requirements can imposed on a claimant who has limited capability for work and work-related activity, nor can any be imposed on a claimant with regular and substantial caring responsibilities for a severely disabled person (s.19(2)(b)) or who is the responsible carer for a child under the age of one (s.19(2)(c)). Note the other categories prescribed in reg.89. Other groups of claimants with caring responsibilities are free of the work search and work availability requirements under ss.20 and 21 of the WRA 2012. Claimants with limited capability for work fall into that category by reason of s.21(1)(a).

Paragraph (3)

2.352   A work search or availability requirement cannot relate to work in a location where the claimant's normal travel time either from home to work or from work to home would exceed 90 minutes, subject to a possible further limitation in para.(6) for some disabled claimants. Travel times below that limit could be relevant in relation to a sanction for non-compliance with a requirement, on the question of whether the claimant had no good reason for the failure to comply. On that question all circumstances could be considered, including the effect of any physical or mental impairment not serious enough to count under para.(6), whereas under this provision time is the conclusive factor unless the location is completely excluded under para.(6).

Paragraphs (4) and (5)

2.353   A claimant who has previously carried out work of a particular nature or at a particular level of remuneration is to have the kind of work to be considered limited to similar conditions for so long as considered appropriate up to four weeks from the date of claim or ceasing to fall within s.19 of the WRA 2012 by virtue of the level of earnings (para.(5)). Presumably in the case of level of remuneration the similarity must be in real terms, taking account of inflation. But the rule only applies if and so long as the claimant will have reasonable prospects of work subject to that limitation.

The February 2022 amendment to para.(5) purportedly to reduce the maximum period for which para.(4) can apply from three months to four weeks, subject to the transitional provision in reg.4 of the amending regulations, is of very doubtful validity. Even if valid, it has attracted serious criticism from various sources for a failure to follow proper Parliamentary procedures. To understand that and the doubt as to validity it is necessary to unpack in some detail what had hitherto been a relatively inoffensive and uncontroversial provision, promoting a limited protection of job skills and avoiding a need to make difficult decisions about the proper scope of work search when the period out of work might be short.

Note first that the central part of the provision in para.(4), building on similar rules that applied to old style JSA and in the past to unemployment benefit, contains considerable flexibility. Although, once its conditions are met, the limitations as to work search and availability must be applied, there are quite complicated hurdles to be jumped before that stage is reached. The claimant must first have previously carried out work of a particular nature or at a particular level of remuneration. That work could have been self-employment. There is no limit as to how far in the past the work could have been carried out, but the further in the past the more likely it is that one of the following two conditions might not be met. The second condition in para.(4) is that the claimant has reasonable prospects of obtaining paid work subject to the limitations about nature of work and/or level of remuneration. There could be many circumstances, such as the claimant having moved to a different area or suffered some significant deterioration in physical or mental capacity or the lapse of time having rendered the claimant's previous experience redundant, where no such reasonable prospects exist. The third condition is that the compulsory application of the limitations is to last only for such period as is considered appropriate (subject to the time-limit in para.(5)). Similar factors to those relevant to the second condition might also be relevant here, avoiding difficult judgments about when prospects of obtaining work are reasonable or not. But the nature of the job skills up for protection, as well as other wider considerations, such as the state of the national and local job market and economy, might also be relevant. The length of the appropriate period could be less than the maximum or possibly no period could be appropriate. Thus, although in practice many claimants with recent work experience might, prior to February 2022, have been allowed three months with limited work search and availability without too much investigation, that was by no means inevitable.

It should also be noted that after the expiry of the maximum period under para. (5) the protection of job skills does not become completely irrelevant. Outside the special circumstances catered for in regs 95, 96, 98 and 99, the general work search requirement is only to take all reasonable action for the purpose of obtaining paid work (WRA 2012, s.17(1)(a)) and particular actions specified by the Secretary of State under s.17(1)(b) must as a matter of principle also be reasonable. Although s.18 on the work availability requirement makes no explicit reference to the nature of the work for which the claimant has to be available, it is suggested that by necessary implication, especially considering the power in s.18(3) for the Secretary of State to specify limitations on the work availability requirement beyond those in regulations, that requirement must be in line with the proper work search requirement. It is plainly arguable that it is reasonable for claimants with specific and recent job skills and who have reasonable prospects of obtaining paid work of that kind and/ or level of remuneration to limit their work search for a period beyond the para. (5) maximum, at least until a point where the reasonableness of the prospects is undermined. Such an approach might also produce more enduring beneficial results for the economy as a whole. As it was well put by the Institute for Government and the Social Security Advisory Committee (SSAC) at p.33 of their 2021 joint report *Jobs and benefits: The Covid-19 challenge*, a "constructive relationship between work coaches and claimants in finding not just any job but suitable jobs is likely to yield better enduring results for both individuals and the economy than merely enforcing work search conditions".

The impetus for the 2022 amendments, as set out in the Explanatory Memorandum to SI 2022/108, was the adoption of the "Way to Work" campaign, to enable 500,000 people currently out of work into jobs by the end of June 2022. However, that Memorandum gave no other information about the nature of that campaign except that it was launched on January 26, 2022. The thinking behind the campaign was perhaps revealed in paras 7.3 and 7.4:

"7.3 Claimants with skills and experience for a specific type of role will be permitted up to four weeks to secure employment in that sector from their date of claim. After this period, they will be expected to widen their job search into other suitable sectors where they may find employment that can support them whilst they consider their longer-term career options. This will be part of their work-related requirements for receiving their benefit payment.
7.4 This change will enable jobcentres to promote wider employment opportunities for claimants, working with employers to fill local vacancies, supporting people back into work more quickly. This could reduce the time claimants spend out of work, thus preventing them from moving further away from the labour market—a factor that makes it increasingly difficult to get a job."

The Secretary of State had written to the SSAC on February 3, 2022 informing it that she was not going to refer the proposal to make the regulations to it in advance, by reason of urgency, and was also dispensing with the "21-day rule" (i.e. that in general there should be at least a 21-day gap between the making of regulations and their coming into force, to allow Parliamentary scrutiny and to give those affected a chance to react to the provisions). Paragraph 3.2 of the Explanatory Memorandum says that "the regulations could not have been made and laid sooner as the policy was only formulated very recently, and they had to come into effect as quickly as possible in order to achieve the target of getting 500,000 people into work by the end of June". Some more information was given at a scrutiny session of the House of Lords Secondary Legislation Scrutiny Committee on March 8, 2022 and in later correspondence, including that there were currently 1.2 million job vacancies nationally (although higher figures were given at some points). According to para.19 of the Committee's highly critical report (33rd Report):

"At the oral evidence session, we were told that the *Way to Work* campaign also included a national team and local employer teams that were focused on producing more vacancies. We also discovered that during the pandemic period DWP had doubled its number of work coaches and opened 200 new jobcentres around the country, and, in consequence, is now in a position to devote 50 minutes a week to each claimant's needs so as to encourage them back into work. Given the current high number of vacancies, DWP takes the view that claimants should broaden their job search at a much earlier stage than previously: the change made by these Regulations provides the ability to enforce that where necessary."

The Committee considered that the 500,000 June 2022 target, and the resulting urgency, was self-imposed and arbitrary and did not justify the avoidance of normal procedures. The Explanatory Memorandum was misleading in several ways, especially in not explaining how the specific amendment would contribute to achieving that target, as opposed to all the other elements of the campaign. The Committee therefore drew the regulations specially to the attention of Parliament.

The Joint Committee on Statutory Instruments, in its 30th Report for the session 2021–22 (HL 189, HC 56-xxx), also drew the special attention of both Houses to the regulations on the ground of failure to comply with proper legislative practice in respect of the 21-day rule. There was apparently a debate in the House of Commons Delegated Legislation Committee on April 20, 2022, but a motion to prevent the instrument becoming law lapsed on the ending of the Parliamentary session on April 28, 2002. Following further scrutiny at its meeting of March 28, 2022, the SSAC decided on a fine balance not to take the regulations on formal reference.

On June 23, 2022 (published on the internet on July 6, 2022), the Chair of the SSAC wrote to the Secretary of State to say that after careful consideration the Committee had decided not to take the regulations shortening the "permitted period" on formal reference, but wished to record a number of concerns and make some advisory recommendations. It is worth quoting the statement of concerns relating to the role of the regulatory changes in enhancing the overall policy intent verbatim (footnotes have been omitted):

"Scale of the challenge

In order to assess whether the regulation change could deliver and was proportionate to the policy intent, we were keen to understand the relative size of the role of the regulatory change in combination with the other measures as part of the Way to Work scheme, and the scale of the increase in off-flow into work that would be expected to be required to achieve the 500k target. Officials were unable to provide an estimate of the overall scale of the change from the combined programme or of the expected contribution of the regulatory change. We appreciate that this is difficult to do, but whether this goal involves an increase in off-flow rates of 10%, 50% or 100% compared to an expected counterfactual has a material impact on the proportionality of the policy response.

Given that the off-flow from benefits into employment for the month of February (which would be unlikely to have yet been significantly affected by the programme's components) had been estimated at around 114K – so that on average only 96.5K per month needed to be achieved over the remaining four months to meet the target – it seems as if the required impact could be at the lower end of the scale, and more aligned to avoiding a drop in off-flow rates rather than appreciably boosting them.

We also sought to understand the number of jobseekers whose search expectations would be changed by these regulations for the duration of the scheme. Unfortunately, officials were not in a position to provide an estimate of the scale of the change.

Evidence base

We were informed that the rationale for the reduction in the duration of the permitted period was that there was a unique moment in the labour market as, post-COVID, there were significantly higher than normal levels of sectoral shift and high levels of vacancies – which meant there would be greater benefit from jobseekers expanding their search into new sectors at an earlier point.

We have sought access to evidence that could underpin the basis of the decision to shorten the permitted period. We understand that the choice of four weeks as the new duration was a judgment informed by feedback from work coaches. However, no data or explanation has been made available to indicate what the impact would be of making the change. In fact, the evidence offered indicated that there was no noticeable increase in the historic off-flow rate after the 13-week point, suggesting that the extant pattern of broadening of the work-search expectations, at least at this point, did not have a discernible impact.

Our concerns are compounded by the lack of a clear positive outcome expected as a result of the reduction in the permitted period. We are told that no estimate is available of what a positive outcome would be either in terms of the number claiming the benefits, or the fiscal impact though presumably these have been incorporated in the latest forecasts produced by the Office for Budget Responsibility and adopted by the Government in the Spring Statement.

We asked your officials for an assessment of the baseline (historic) patterns of off-flow, and how these might have been expected to evolve in coming months absent these change in these regulations, alongside any early indication of patterns in the early months of the programme (see Appendix for details). Unfortunately, this information has not been shared with the Committee.

Potential negative impact

At the time of our scrutiny, no assessment had been made of the risk of individuals entering roles that were inconsistent with their qualifications/experience, or simply wrong for them in terms of their career path and ambitions, nor of the risk that increased competition from more highly qualified people would make it more difficult for longer-term unemployed people to find work. Similarly, no consideration had been made of the impact on those with part-time, or other flexible, job-search expectations for whom the four-week cut-off could be disproportionate and one that will certainly vary by protected characteristics, most obviously sex and disability.

There was some acknowledgement that there may be negative consequences from these changes, for example increased cycling on and off benefits, and job mismatches leading to more churn for employers and to claimants potentially having career paths hindered. However, there was no analysis of how to mitigate against negative effects, particularly where those with protected characteristics might be disproportionately impacted.

Evaluating the effectiveness of the permitted period change

These regulations were brought in to deal with a unique moment in the economy as it reopened from COVID restrictions, resulting in a very high number of labour market vacancies. However, the regulations do not have a sunset clause and the Committee would be concerned that, without a proper review of the impact of these regulations, they may be left on the statute book, despite the labour market situation having substantially changed. Therefore, the Committee very much welcomes that in your letter to me of 3 February, you committed to undertake such an evaluation of the regulations at the end of June to assess their effectiveness and whether they should be retained.

The way in which the regulations would be reviewed in terms of (a) by what criteria they would be deemed a success, and (b) how such criteria would be evaluated is in need of detailed thought. It will also be important to differentiate the criteria on which the regulations are evaluated with respect to the current unique point in time and the assessment whether they should be retained for what should then be much more normal times ahead. However, when we asked officials how they plan to undertake this, it was clear that such thinking had not yet matured.

Urgency

The regulations had been laid under the urgency provision before being presented to this Committee for scrutiny. I have previously written to you seeking a better understanding of the nature of the urgency in this instance. As you know, this Committee is supportive of the use of "urgency" where legislation is being brought forward as a direct consequence of either an external factor or a fiscal event. Indeed we welcomed the use of urgency, and expedited our own statutory scrutiny process, to ensure that essential support could be introduced quickly in response to recent crises in Afghanistan and Ukraine. However, a compelling argument for urgency in this specific case remains unclear to us.

We were informed that the regulations had to bypass the scrutiny of the Committee before coming into force, as "every day" was essential in ensuring that the Government can meet its own target. However, there was no explanation of what impact there might be in waiting a few weeks for the Committee to complete its statutory scrutiny – either on the specific issue of the target or in terms of the broader proposals.

Similarly, it is not clear why the target could not simply have been put back a short period, or why the rest of the Way to Work programme could not proceed whilst the permitted period proposals were considered by the Committee."

Despite that politely devastating analysis, success of the Way to Work campaign was declared on June 30, 2022 by way of a tweet and a press release asserting that over half a million people had been helped into work thanks to the campaign in five months (later quoted in the House of Commons by the then Prime Minister on July 6, 2022). That declaration was apparently based on an answer to a Parliamentary Question on June 30, 2022 revealing an estimate using management information that as of June 29, 2022 at least 505,400 unemployed universal credit and JSA claimants had moved into work during the campaign. That use of the figures was castigated by the Director General for Regulation in the Office for Statistics Regulation in his letter of July 29, 2022 to the Permanent Secretary of the DWP. He concluded that it was difficult to attribute and quantify the impact of the campaign in the absence of a clearly defined and published target and details of how it would be measured and reported, so that the way that the DWP had communicated information did not uphold the principles of being trustworthy, of high quality and offering public value. A more targeted point might have been to note the speciousness of using evidence of the numbers who moved into work *during* the campaign to support the assertion that all those claimants had been helped into work *by* the campaign. A further written answer to a Parliamentary Question on September 5, 2022 revealed that no estimate had been made of the number of unemployed universal credit and JSA claimants who would have moved into work between January and June 2022 in the absence of the Way to Work campaign.

Overall, it is hard to avoid the conclusion that this whole shabby episode was little more than a small-scale exercise in grandiose posturing with every appearance of having been foisted on the DWP with no time for thought or preparation. However, the episode is not over. There has been no public sign of the promised evaluation of the effectiveness of the amending regulations and of whether they should be retained (the September 2022 written answer suggests that there has been no attempt at any real evaluation or at meeting the concerns of the SSAC or the Office for Statistics Regulations). But the amendments are unlikely to be reversed while a high level of job vacancies continues, even though that state of affairs is likely to produce a high level of off-flow from benefit independently of the amendments' effect. A letter of May 23, 2023 from the Minister for Employment, Guy Opperman, to the Chair of the House of Commons Work and Pensions Select Committee gives the appearance of attempting to rewrite history by saying that the DWP had achieved its ambition to see at least 500,000 people move into work from universal credit and JSA *during* the campaign (emphasis added by commentator). The letter did say that assurances had been given to the Office for Statistics Regulation about future adherence to its principles.

A close examination of the way in which reg.14(3) of the JSA Regulations 2013 and reg.97(4) and (5) work, as set out above (but not carried out by the Parliamentary committees), would also have fatally undermined any case for urgency. Given the existing power to set an appropriate period for the operation of the provisions at less than 13 weeks, even where a claimant might have reasonable prospects of obtaining paid work subject to the limitations, there was no reason why work coaches should not, immediately on the implementation of the campaign, have taken into account the number of job vacancies nationally and locally, the state of the national and local economy and other measures being undertaken as part of the Way to Work campaign in determining that the "permitted" period should be something less than 13 weeks, say four weeks. What they could not have properly done, in the absence of the February 2022 amendment, would have been to adopt a rigid or blanket view that the permitted period should be no more than four weeks in all cases. The particular circumstances of individual claimants would have had to be considered. But that is what work coaches are supposed to do in producing a personally tailored set of work requirements to be recorded in the claimant commitment, especially with the additional time made available, and would anyway be necessary outside the permitted period (see further below). The substance of the campaign could have been started immediately without the need for any urgent amendment.

That is important, not merely as a criticism of the processes adopted, but because it raises serious doubts about the validity of the amendments. *Howker v Secretary of State for Work and Pensions* [2002] EWCA Civ 1623; [2003] I.C.R. 405, also reported as *R(IB) 3/03* (see Vol.III of this series at para.1.250), established that a failure to follow the mandatory provisions in s.172 of SSAA 1992 for reference to the SSAC of proposals to make regulations led to the invalidity of the regulations and that the then Social Security Commissioners had jurisdiction to decide that that was so. That no doubt now applies to the Upper Tribunal and presumably to the First-tier Tribunal. *Howker* was a case where the SSAC was misled by incorrect information from DWP officials into agreeing under s.173(1)(b) to there being no reference to it. *IC v Glasgow City Council and SSWP (HB)* [2016] UKUT 321 (AAC), reported as [2017] AACR 1, was specifically concerned with the exemption for urgency in s.173(1)(a). Although the three-judge panel of the Upper Tribunal rejected the argument that the Secretary of State had failed to show a need for urgency on the facts of the case, its decision operated on the basis that if that argument had been accepted it would mean that the regulations in question were invalid. In the case of SI 2022/108 it appears that on any objective analysis urgency could not be shown.

Note also that the Explanatory Memorandum to SI 2022/108, in para.2.2 as well as in para.7.2 quoted above, contains misleading statements about the effect of the amendments. The former says that the amendment will require claimants to search more widely for available jobs beyond those of a similar nature or level of remuneration to that of previous work following the fourth week of their claim. The suggestion that that will be an automatic expectation is repeated in para.7.2. That is misleading because, as explained above, where para.(4) has ceased to apply the reasonableness of restricting job search and availability to a similarly limited scope must be considered in the individual circumstances of each particular claimant in asking what is all reasonable action to obtain paid work under s.17(1).

There is a transitional provision in reg.4 of the amending regulations (see para.2.735 below). If on February 8, 2022, a claimant had a work search or availability requirement limited under para.(4), the limitation is to extend for the length of the existing permitted period or until March 7, 2022 if earlier.

Note that there was no equivalent amendment to regs 16 and 20 of the JSA Regulations 1996 on old style JSA.

Paragraph (6)

2.354   A claimant who has a physical or mental impairment which has a substantial adverse effect on their ability to carry out work of a particular nature or in particular locations (a significant additional condition over and above that of impairment on its own) is to have the kind of work to be considered under the work search and work availability requirements limited to avoid such work.

Victims of domestic violence

2.355   **98.**—(1) Where a claimant has recently been a victim of domestic violence, and the circumstances set out in paragraph (3) apply—

   (a)   a work-related requirement imposed on that claimant ceases to have effect for a period of 13 consecutive weeks starting on the date of the notification referred to in paragraph (3)(a); and

   (b)   the Secretary of State must not impose any other work-related requirement on that claimant during that period.

[²(1A) Where a claimant referred to in paragraph (1) is a person who falls within section 22 of the Act (claimants subject to all work-related requirements) and is the responsible carer of a child, the Secretary of State must not impose a work search requirement or a work availability requirement on that claimant for a further period of 13 consecutive weeks beginning on the day after the period in paragraph (1)(a) expires.]

   (2) A person has recently been a victim of domestic violence if a period of 6 months has not expired since the violence was inflicted or threatened.

   (3) The circumstances are that—

   (a)   the claimant notifies the Secretary of State, in such manner as the Secretary of State specifies, that domestic violence has been inflicted on or threatened against the claimant by the claimant's partner or former partner or by a family member during the period of 6 months ending on the date of the notification;

   (b)   this regulation has not applied to the claimant for a period of 12 months before the date of the notification;

   (c)   on the date of the notification the claimant is not living at the same address as the person who inflicted or threatened the domestic violence; and

   (d)   as soon as possible, and no later than 1 month, after the date of the notification the claimant provides evidence from a person acting in an official capacity which demonstrates that—

         (i)   the claimant's circumstances are consistent with those of a person who has had domestic violence inflicted or threatened against them during the period of 6 months ending on the date of the notification, and

        (ii) the claimant has made contact with the person acting in an official capacity in relation to such an incident, which occurred during that period.

(4) In this regulation—

[¹"coercive behaviour" means an act of assault, humiliation or intimidation or other abuse that is used to harm, punish or frighten the victim;

"controlling behaviour" means an act designed to make a person subordinate or dependent by isolating them from sources of support, exploiting their resources and capacities for personal gain, depriving them of the means needed for independence, resistance or escape or regulating their everyday behaviour;

"domestic violence" means any incident, or pattern of incidents, of controlling behaviour, coercive behaviour, violence or abuse, including but not limited to—

    (a) psychological abuse;

    (b) physical abuse;

    (c) sexual abuse;

    (d) emotional abuse;

    (e) financial abuse,

regardless of the gender or sexuality of the victim;]

"family member", in relation to a claimant, means the claimant's grandparent, grandchild, parent, step-parent, parent-in-law, son, step-son, son-in-law, daughter, step-daughter, daughter-in-law, brother, step-brother, brother-in-law, sister, step-sister, sister-in law and, if any of those persons is member of a couple, the other member of the couple;

"health care professional" means a person who is a member of a profession regulated by a body mentioned in section 25(3) of the National Health Service Reform and Health Care Professions Act 2002;

"person acting in an official capacity" means a health care professional, a police officer, a registered social worker, the claimant's employer, a representative of the claimant's trade union, or any public, voluntary or charitable body which has had direct contact with the claimant in connection with domestic violence;

"registered social worker" means a person registered as a social worker in a register maintained by—

    [⁴(a) Social Work England;]

    [³(b) Social Care Wales;]

    (c) The Scottish Social Services Council; or

    (d) The Northern Ireland Social Care Council.

AMENDMENTS

1. Social Security (Miscellaneous Amendments) (No.2) Regulations 2013 (SI 2013/1508) reg.3(1) (October 29, 2013).

2. Universal Credit and Miscellaneous Amendments (No.2) Regulations 2014 (SI 2014/2888) reg.8(2) (November 26, 2014).

3. Social Security (Social Care Wales) (Amendment) Regulations 2017 (SI 2017/291) reg.2 (April 1, 2017).

4. Children and Social Work Act 2017 (Consequential Amendments) (Social Workers) Regulations 2019 (SI 2019/1094) reg.2(c) and Sch.3 para.30 (July 9, 2019).

DEFINITIONS

"claimant"—see WRA 2012 s.40.

"partner"—see reg.2.

"victim of domestic violence"—see WRA 2012 s.24(6)(b).
"work-related requirement"—see WRA 2012 ss.40 and 13(2).

GENERAL NOTE

2.356   This regulation, made as required by s.24(5) and (6) of the WRA 2012, exempts recent victims of domestic violence from the imposition of any work-related requirements for a period of 13 weeks from the date of notification to the Secretary of State under para.(3)(a) and lifts the effect of any existing imposition for the same period. The regulation appears to be defective to the extent that it makes no provision for exemption from the imposition of a connected requirement under s.23 of the WRA 2012, which is not a "work-related requirement" as defined in s.13(2). Thus the duty in s.24(5) to exempt recent victims of domestic violence from any requirement under Part 1 of the Act has not been fully carried out, but that would not seem to affect the validity of what has been provided in reg.98.

Paragraph (1A), in effect from November 26, 2014, requires the extension of the normal 13-week suspension under para.(1) for a further 13 weeks where the claimant is the responsible carer (see ss.19(6) and 40 of the WRA 2012 and reg.4) of a child.

For these purposes, para.(4) now provides a comprehensive definition of "domestic violence", instead of the former reference to a particular page of a difficult to find Department of Health document. It uses the terms of the government's official approach to the meaning of domestic violence across departments, which had not previously been used as a statutory definition. Note that the new criminal offence of controlling or coercive behaviour in intimate or familial relationships under s.76 of the Serious Crime Act 2015, while using the terms of controlling and coercive behaviour (the meaning of which is discussed in Home Office Statutory Guidance of December 2015) contains conditions that are different from those in reg.98. While the definition here expressly includes coercive behaviour and controlling behaviour (both given their own definition in para.(4)), any other incident of abuse of any kind can come within the ambit of domestic violence. Thus, although the specific definition of "coercive behaviour" requires the act or abuse to be used to harm, punish or frighten the victim and the specific definition of "controlling behaviour" is restricted to acts designed to make the victim subordinate or dependant by particular means (as taken to extremes by the vile Rob Titchener in *The Archers*), abuse of similar kinds where that specific form of intention or purpose is not present or is difficult to prove can nonetheless be domestic violence. The width of that makes the specific conditions in para.(3) for the application of reg.98 particularly important.

Section 24(6)(b) of the WRA 2012 defines a victim of domestic violence as a person on or against whom domestic violence (as defined above) is inflicted or threatened. Under s.24(6)(c) and para.(2) a person is to be treated as having recently been a victim of domestic violence if no more than six months has expired since the infliction or threat.

Paragraph (3)

2.357   This paragraph lays down four quite restrictive conditions that must all be satisfied for reg.98 to apply. Under sub-para.(a) the claimant must have notified the Secretary of State of the infliction or threatening of domestic violence by a partner, former partner or family member (as defined in para.(4)) within the previous six months. Under sub-para.(b), reg.98 must not have applied within the 12 months before the notification. Under sub-para.(c), the claimant must not on the date of the notification have been living at the same address as the person named as the assailant. Under sub-para.(d), the claimant must also provide, as soon as possible and no more than one month after the notification, evidence from a person acting in an official capacity (defined quite widely in para.(4)) both that the claimant's circumstances are consistent with having had domestic violence inflicted or threatened in the six months before notification and that the claimant had made contact (apparently not necessarily within the six months) with the person in relation to an incident of infliction or threat of domestic violence that occurred during the six months before notification.

Circumstances in which requirements must not be imposed

99.—(1) Where paragraph (3), (4)[², (4A)] [¹ . . .] or (6) applies—

2.358

(a) the Secretary of State must not impose a work search requirement on a claimant; and

(b) "able and willing immediately to take up work" under a work availability requirement means able and willing to take up paid work, or attend an interview, immediately once the circumstances set out in paragraph (3), (4)[², (4A)] [¹ . . .] or (6) no longer apply.

(2) A work search requirement previously applying to the claimant ceases to have effect from the date on which the circumstances set out in paragraph (3), (4)[², (4A)] [¹ . . .] or (6) begin to apply.

[¹(2A) Where paragraph (5) applies—

(a) the Secretary of State must not impose a work search requirement on a claimant; and

(b) a work search requirement previously applying to the claimant ceases to have effect from the date on which the circumstances set out in paragraph (5) begin to apply.

(2B) Where paragraph (5A) applies "able and willing to take up work" under a work availability requirement means able and willing to take up paid work, or to attend an interview, immediately once the circumstances set out in paragraph (5A) no longer apply.

(2C) Where paragraph (5B) applies, "able and willing to take up work" under a work availability requirement means—

(a) able and willing to take up paid work immediately once the circumstances set out in paragraph (5B) no longer apply; and

(b) able and willing to attend an interview before those circumstances no longer apply.]

(3) This paragraph applies where—

(a) the claimant is attending a court or tribunal as a party to any proceedings or as a witness;

(b) the claimant is a prisoner;

(c) regulation 11(3) (temporary absence from Great Britain for treatment or convalescence) applies to the claimant;

(d) any of the following persons has died within the past 6 months—

(i) where the claimant was a member of a couple, the other member,

(ii) a child or qualifying young person for whom the claimant or, where the claimant is a member of a couple, the other member, was responsible, or

(iii) a child, where the claimant was the child's parent;

(e) the claimant is, and has been for no more than 6 months, receiving and participating in a structured recovery-orientated course of alcohol or drug dependency treatment;

(f) the claimant is, and has been for no more than 3 months, a person for whom arrangements have been made by a protection provider under section 82 of the Serious Organised Crime and Police Act 2005; or

(g) the claimant is engaged in an activity of a kind approved by the Secretary of State as being in the nature of a public duty.

(4) [⁴Subject to paragraph (4ZA), this paragraph] applies where the claimant—

    (a) is unfit for work—

        (i) for a period of no more than 14 consecutive days after the date that the evidence referred to in sub-paragraph (b) is provided, and

        (ii) for no more than 2 such periods in any period of 12 months; and

    (b) provides to the Secretary of State the following evidence—

        (i) for the first 7 days when they are unfit for work, a declaration made by the claimant in such manner and form as the Secretary of State approves that the claimant is unfit for work, and

        (ii) for any further days when they are unfit for work, if requested by the Secretary of State, a statement given [⁵ . . .] in accordance with the rules set out in Part 1 of Schedule 1 to the Medical Evidence Regulations which provides that the person is not fit for work.

[⁴(4ZA) Where paragraph (4ZB) applies, paragraph (4) will only apply to a claimant if the Secretary of State makes a decision to carry out an assessment under regulation 41(1)(b).

(4ZB) This paragraph applies where—

    (a) (i) it has previously been determined on the basis of an assessment under Part 5 of these Regulations or under Part 4 or 5 of the ESA Regulations that the claimant does not have limited capability for work; or

        (ii) the claimant has previously been treated as not having limited capability for work or, as the case may be, for work and work-related activity under regulation 43(3) or 44(2); and

    (b) the condition specified in the evidence provided by the claimant in accordance with paragraph (4)(b) is in the opinion of the Secretary of State the same, or substantially the same, as the condition specified in the evidence provided by the claimant before the date—

        (i) of the determination that the claimant does not have limited capability for work; or

        (ii) that the claimant was treated as not having limited capability for work or, as the case may be, for work and work-related activity.]

[²(4A) This paragraph applies for one or more periods of one month, as provided for in paragraphs (4B) and (4C), where the claimant is the responsible carer of a child and an event referred to in sub-paragraph (a) or (b) has taken place in the last 24 months and has resulted in significant disruption to the claimant's normal childcare responsibilities—

    (a) any of the following persons has died—

        (i) a person who was previously the responsible carer of that child;

        (ii) a parent of that child;

        (iii) a brother or sister of that child; or

        (iv) any other person who, at the time of their death, normally lived in the same accommodation as that child and was not a person who was liable to make payments on a commercial basis in respect that accommodation; or

    (b) the child has been the victim of, or witness to, an incident of violence or abuse and the claimant is not the perpetrator of that violence or abuse.

(4B) Paragraph (4A) is not to apply for more than one period of one month in each of the 4 consecutive periods of 6 months following the event (and, if regulation 98 or paragraph (3)(d) of this regulation applies in respect of the same event, that month is to run concurrently with any period for which that regulation or paragraph applies).

(4C) Each period of one month begins on the date specified by the Secretary of State after the claimant has notified the Secretary of State of the circumstances in paragraph (4A) provided that the Secretary of State is satisfied that the circumstances apply.]

(5) This paragraph applies where the Secretary of State is satisfied that it would be unreasonable to require the claimant to comply with a work search requirement [¹ . . .], including if such a requirement were limited in accordance with section 17(4) [¹ . . .] of the Act, because [⁴ . . .]

    (a) [⁴the claimant] is carrying out a work preparation requirement or voluntary work preparation (as defined in regulation 95(4));

    (b) [⁴the claimant] has temporary child care responsibilities or is dealing with a domestic emergency, funeral arrangements or other temporary circumstances; [⁴ . . .]

    (c) [⁴the claimant] has been unfit for work for longer than the period of 14 days specified in paragraph (4)(a) or for more than 2 such periods in any period of 12 months and, where requested by the Secretary of State, provides the evidence mentioned in paragraph (4)(b)(ii). [⁴; or

    (d) paragraph (4) would apply to the claimant but for paragraph (4ZA).]

[¹(5A) This paragraph applies where the Secretary of State is satisfied that it would be unreasonable to require the claimant to comply with a work availability requirement to be able and willing to—

    (a) take up paid work; and

    (b) attend an interview,

(including if such a requirement were limited in accordance with section 18(3) of the Act) because the claimant falls within [⁵sub-paragraph (a), (b), (c) or (d)] of paragraph (5).

(5B) This paragraph applies where the Secretary of State is satisfied that it would be—

    (a) unreasonable to require the claimant to comply with a work availability requirement to be able and willing to take up paid work because the claimant falls within [⁴ sub-paragraph (a), (b), (c) or (d)] of paragraph (5); and

    (b) reasonable to require the claimant to comply with a work availability requirement to attend an interview,

including if such a requirement were limited in accordance with section 18(3) of the Act.]

[³[⁶(6) This paragraph applies where—

    (a) the claimant has monthly earnings (excluding any that are not employed earnings) that are equal to, or more than, the amount that a person would be paid at the hourly rate set out in regulation 4 of the National Minimum Wage Regulations for [⁷15] hours per week, converted to a monthly amount by multiplying by 52 and dividing by 12; or

    (b) the claimant is a member of a couple whose combined monthly earnings (excluding any that are not employed earnings) are equal to, or more than, the amount that a person would be paid at the hourly rate set out in regulation 4 of the National Minimum Wage Regulations for [7 24] hours per week, converted to a monthly amount by multiplying by 52 and dividing by 12.]

(6A) In paragraph (6) "employed earnings" has the meaning in regulation 55.]

(7) In this regulation "tribunal" means any tribunal listed in Schedule 1 to the Tribunals and Inquiries Act 1992.

AMENDMENTS

1. Universal Credit and Miscellaneous Amendments Regulations 2014 (SI 2014/597) reg.2(7) (April 28, 2014).

2. Universal Credit and Miscellaneous Amendments) (No. 2) Regulations 2014 (SI 2014/2888) reg.8(3) (November 26, 2014).

3. Universal Credit (Work-Related Requirements) In Work Pilot Scheme and Amendment Regulations 2015 (SI 2015/89) reg.3 (February 19, 2015).

4. Universal Credit (Miscellaneous Amendments, Saving and Transitional Provision) Regulations 2018 (SI 2018/65) reg.3(11) (April 11, 2018).

5. Social Security (Medical Evidence) and Statutory Sick Pay (Medical Evidence) (Amendment) (No.2) Regulations 2022 (SI 2022/630) reg.4(3)(b) (July 1, 2022).

6. Universal Credit (Administrative Earnings Threshold) (Amendment) Regulations 2022 (SI 2022/886) reg.2 (September 26, 2022).

7. Universal Credit (Administrative Earnings Threshold) (Amendment) Regulations 2023 (SI 2023/7) reg.2 (January 30, 2023).

DEFINITIONS

"child"—see WRA 2012 s.40.
"claimant"—*ibid.*
"couple"—see WRA 2012, ss.40 and 39.
"ESA Regulations"—see reg.2.
"Medical Evidence Regulations"—*ibid.*
"monthly earnings"—*ibid.*
"National Minimum Wage Regulations"—*ibid.*
"paid work"—*ibid.*
"prisoner"—*ibid.*
"qualifying young person"—see WRA 2012 ss.40 and 10(5).
"responsible carer"—see WRA 2012 ss.40 and 19(6).
"voluntary work preparation"—see reg.95(4).
"work availability requirement"—see WRA 2012 ss.40 and 18(1).
"work preparation requirement"—see WRA 2012 ss.40 and 16(1).
"work search requirement"—see WRA 2012 ss.40 and 17(1).

GENERAL NOTE

Temporary Coronavirus Provisions

2.359   The last of the temporary coronavirus provisions relevant to reg.99 expired on August 31, 2021. See previous editions of this volume for the details.

2.360   This regulation is made under ss.22(2) and 24(1)(a) of the WRA 2012 in respect of the work search and availability requirements and under s.18(5) in respect of the work availability requirement. Its structure was revised in 2014 to make its operation somewhat clearer, although at the cost of a more complicated interaction of various paragraphs. Some requirements were tightened and some relaxed, also.

The central rule is under paras (1) and (2) and operates where any of paras (3), (4), (4A) (incorporating (4B) and (4C)) or (6) applies. Under para.(1)(a) no work search requirement can be imposed in those circumstances (and any already imposed requirement lapses: para.(2)) and under para.(1)(b) the work availability requirement is adjusted to require only that the claimant be willing and able to take up paid work or attend an interview immediately once the circumstances in question cease to apply. Paragraphs (3), (4), (4A) and (6) cover fairly specifically defined circumstances, dealt with separately below.

Paragraph (2A) operates where para.(5) applies, to the same effect as under paras (1)(a) and (2) on the work search requirement in relation to the circumstances in para.(5). Paragraph (5) also covers fairly specifically defined circumstances, but with the additional condition that it be unreasonable to require compliance with the work search requirement, and is dealt with separately below.

Paragraph (2B) operates where para.(5A) applies, to the same effect as under para.(1)(b) in relation to the circumstances in para.(5A). Paragraph (5A) involves a judgment that it would be unreasonable to require the claimant to be able and willing to take up paid work <u>and</u> attend an interview (see further below).

Paragraph (2C) operates where para.(5B) applies, but only so as to lift the requirement to be willing and able to take up an offer of paid work, not to lift the requirement to be willing and able to attend an interview. The judgment required under para.(5B) is thus that it would be unreasonable to require the claimant to be able and willing to take up paid work, but reasonable to require willingness and ability to attend an interview (see further below).

Paragraph (3)
Paragraph (3) lists a number of categories of claimant where the circumstances mean that the claimant could not be expected to look for or take up work or attend an interview, generally of a temporary nature: 2.361

(a) Attending a court or tribunal (defined in para.(7)) as a party to proceedings or as a witness, apparently so long as the hearing continues for a party and so long as attendance is required for a witness.
(b) A prisoner, under the reg.2 definition covering those detained in custody pending trial or sentence on conviction or under sentence or on temporary release, but excluding anyone detained in hospital under mental health legislation. Under the temporary coronavirus modification mentioned above, prisoners on temporary release are excluded from this provision for the period from April 8, 2020 to November 12, 2020 (see the notes to reg.15(2) of the JSA Regulations 1996 in Vol.V of this series for further details).
(c) Temporary absence from Great Britain in connection with medical treatment for illness etc or convalescence, or accompanying a partner or child or qualifying young person undergoing such treatment or convalescence, under the conditions in reg.11(3). See the notes to that provision.
(d) The claimant's then partner, a child or qualifying young person for whom the claimant or partner was responsible or a child of the claimant has died within the previous six months. See para.(4A)(a) for circumstances in which the operation of paras (1) and (2) can be triggered by the death within the previous 24 months of various people connected with a child.
(e) Attending a structured recovery-oriented course of alcohol or drug dependency treatment, for no more than six months.
(f) Having protection arrangements made under s.82 of the Serious Organised Crime and Police Act 2005 (protection of persons involved in investigations or proceedings whose safety is considered to be at risk), for no more than three months. Arrangements for protection are made by protection providers (e.g. Chief Constables and any of the Commissioners for HMRC).
(g) Any other activity of a kind approved by the Secretary of State as being in the nature of a public duty, apparently for as long as the activity and approval lasts. It is therefore unclear whether on any appeal against a sanction where the application of this paragraph is in issue a First-tier Tribunal is required to accept non-approval of an activity by the Secretary of State or can substitute its own judgment.

Paragraphs (4)–(4ZB)

2.362   A claimant who is unfit for work (not further defined) and provides a self-certificate for the first seven days and, if requested, a statement under the Medical Evidence Regulations (see Vol.I of this series) for any further days falls within the basic rules in para.(1) on both the work search and the work availability requirement. But the benefit of para.(4) is limited to a period of no more than 14 days after the evidence is provided and to no more than two such periods in any 12 months. There is a possible extension of those restrictions under para.(5)(c) in relation to the work search requirement or under para.(5A) or (5B) in relation to the work availability requirement.

There appears on the original form of para.(4) no reason why a claimant should not take the benefit of its provisions from the first day of entitlement to universal credit. But from April 2018 an additional limitation on the operation of para.(4) has been created by the new paras (4ZA) and (4ZB), designed to deal with the common circumstances where a claimant's entitlement to new style ESA has been terminated by reason of a determination following an assessment that they do not have limited capability for work or such a determination has been made under the universal credit provisions, so that the claimant no longer has an automatic exemption from the work search and work availability requirements under s.21(1)(a), or the claimant has previously been deemed not to have limited capability for work or work-related activity for failing to comply with an information requirement or failing to attend or submit to a medical examination (regs 43(3) and 44(2)). Such a universal credit determination would result in a decision removing the limited capability for work or limited capability for work and work-related activity element which would be appealable, but there is no provision for deeming capability and qualification for the appropriate element while the appeal is pending. If the claimant has appealed against the new style ESA decision after the mandatory reconsideration process, the circumstances in which limited capability for work will be deemed for those purposes has been severely restricted. If that deeming does operate, it appears not to translate into universal credit. The effect under regs 39(1)(a) and 40(1)(a)(ii) only follows a new style ESA determination that a claimant does have limited capability for work or for work-related activity.

In the circumstances described above, as prescribed in para.(4ZB)(a), a claimant can only take unrestricted advantage of para.(4) if the condition specified in the medical evidence provided under para.(4)(b) is not the same or substantially the same as the condition specified in the evidence provided by the claimant before the determination of not having limited capability for work (para.(4ZB)(b)). Paragraph (4ZA), which applies the conditions in para.(4ZB), then restricts a claimant who cannot satisfy that test from taking advantage of para.(4) except where the Secretary of State decides to carry out an assessment under reg.41(1)(b) (see the discussion below for the limited circumstances covered). Thus, the claimant is not in general permitted for these purposes to undermine the judgment on capability for work embodied in the adverse new style ESA or universal credit determination. However, paras (5)(d) and (5A) and (5B) allow the application of para.(4) where it would be unreasonable to require a claimant who would otherwise be caught by para.(4ZA) to comply with a work search or availability requirement.

The Explanatory Memorandum for SI 2018/65 describes the effect of these amendments as follows in paras 7.14 and 7.15:

"7.14 This instrument amends regulation 99 of the Universal Credit Regulations (and makes equivalent amendments to regulation 16 of the Jobseeker's Allowance Regulations 2013) to prevent work search and work availability requirements being automatically switched off for illness in certain circumstances. The amendments apply to claimants who have undergone a work capability assessment and been found not to have limited capability for work, and to claimants who have failed to attend a medical examination or comply with a request for information and are treated as not having limited capability for work. In other words, claimants who are, or are treated as being, fit for work. Where such claimants produce evidence that they are unfit for work and the condition mentioned in the evidence is the same, or substantially the same, as the condition for which they were assessed in the work capability assessment, work search and work availability requirements will only be switched off if they have been referred for another assessment as to their capability for work.

7.15 If such a claimant has not been referred for another assessment, regulations will continue to allow for work search and work availability requirements to be switched off if it would be unreasonable for a claimant to comply with such requirements."

That seems accurate so far as universal credit is concerned, but not for new style JSA (see the notes to reg.16 of the JSA Regulations 2013 in Vol.I of this series).

A number of points need brief mention. Note first that paras (4ZA) and (4ZB) only apply where the previous assessment and determination of no limited capability for work or deeming was for the purposes of new style ESA or universal credit. It does not apply if it was for the purposes of old style ESA. Then on its face it applies whenever in the past the adverse determination was made. It may need to be decided whether in order to operate in a rational and fair way the provisions should be limited to the most recent determination of no limited capability for work under new style ESA or universal credit. Third, the comparison to be made in para.(4ZB)(b) is between the condition(s) specified in the evidence provided by the claimant before the previous adverse determination or deeming and the condition(s) specified in the evidence put forward by the claimant in support of the application of para.(4). The evidence provided by the claimant before the adverse determination will presumably cover primarily a medical certificate, but also any questionnaire completed by the claimant and any other evidence, from medical professionals or otherwise, put forward (and, it would seem, the claimant's oral evidence to any tribunal and any further evidence put forward there). It will not cover the opinions of any approved health care professional who has carried out a medical examination, even though it is usually on the basis of those opinions that adverse determinations are made, because that evidence was not provided by the claimant. The evidence to be provided under para.(4)(b) is a self-certificate for the first week and then a medical certificate. Difficulties can be anticipated in making a comparison between what may be a fairly informal and short specification in a self-certificate and the previous evidence. And is it enough to trigger para.(4ZB)(b) that, say, the sole condition specified in the new self-certificate or medical certificate is substantially the same as one, but only one, out of several that were specified before the adverse determination? The reference to "the condition specified" seems to require that a mere worsening in the condition(s) previously specified, even a substantial worsening, does not result in a condition that is not the same. But what if, say, a condition affecting one part of the body starts to affect another part? Is that the same condition?

The rule in para.(4ZA) allowing the lifting of the work search and work availability requirements on the ordinary para.(4) basis, despite the previous determination or deeming, only where the Secretary of State makes a decision to carry out an assessment under reg.41(1)(b) has much more limited scope than first appears. An assessment is not the medical examination (if any) under reg.44, but the assessment by a decision-maker on behalf of the Secretary of State of the extent to which a claimant is or is not capable of carrying out the activities prescribed in Sch.6 (i.e. the points-scoring exercise) (reg.39(2)). There may well be doubt about the exact point when the Secretary of State makes a decision to carry out an assessment, but no doubt it can be accepted that one has been made if the Secretary of State starts the evidence-gathering process by sending a questionnaire to the claimant and/or referring the case to the organisation running medical examinations by health care professionals. However, the Secretary of State's powers to carry out an assessment are circumscribed. Paragraph (4ZA) operates only where the power under reg.41(1)(a) is used, which is limited to cases where the Secretary of State wishes to determine whether since a previous limited capability for work determination there has been a relevant change of circumstances in relation to the claimant's physical or mental condition or whether the previous determination was made in ignorance of or was based on a mistake as to some material fact. Those are terms that relate primarily to the exercise of powers of supersession or revision. It might be thought that if the Secretary of State is merely considering what determination to make under paras (4)–(4ZB) as the result of a claimant's producing medical evidence under para. (4)(b) she does not need to determine any of the things mentioned. However, the further restriction in reg.41(4), to which reg.41(1) is expressly subject, prohibits the carrying out of a further assessment where there has been a previous new style ESA or universal credit determination adverse to the claimant unless there is evidence to suggest ignorance or mistake of material fact or a relevant change of circumstances. Thus, a mere assertion by the claimant that the previous determination was wrong will probably not do, but otherwise the regulations appear to leave a great deal of discretion to the Secretary of State as to when to carry out an assessment following a previous adverse determination.

Remember the provision in paras (2A) and (5)(d), in effect disapplying the effect of paras (4ZA) and (4ZB) when it is unreasonable to require the claimant to comply with any work search requirement and that in paras (2B) and (2C) and (5A) - (5C) modifying the work availability requirement on similar conditions. See the notes to para.(5)(c) below for the suggestion that it allows, where reasonable, the lifting of the requirements from those unfit for work for longer periods than allowed under para.(4) regardless of the existence of any previous determination or deeming.

Paragraphs (4A)–(4C)

2.363   Paragraph (4A) supplies a number of further circumstances, all related to children, in which paras (1) and (2) operate to lift the work search requirement and modify the work availability requirement. The claimant must be the responsible carer of a child (as defined in s.19(6) of the WRA 2012 and see regs 4 and 4A for how responsibility is determined) and reg.26 on nomination by joint claimants. Then one of the events specified in sub-paras (a) and (b) must have occurred in the 24 months prior to the week in question and have resulted in significant disruption to the claimant's normal childcare responsibilities. Although it is not entirely clear, it seems to be necessary that the event is continuing to result in significant disruption in the week in question, not just at or shortly after the time of the event. "Normal childcare responsibilities" should be given its ordinary everyday meaning.

Sub-paragraph (a) applies when one of the persons listed (i.e. a parent or responsible carer or brother or sister of the child or someone else who lived in the same accommodation other than a commercial lodger) has died. Sub-paragraph (b) applies where the child has been the victim of or has witnessed an incident of violence or abuse not perpetrated by the claimant.

Paragraphs (4B) and (4C) limit each application of para.(4A) to a period of one month and to no more than one such application in each of the four periods of six months following the incident in question. Note the possibility of the application of para.(5)(b) without those limits in some circumstances that could have fallen within para.(4A).

Note also that under s.19(2)(c) of the WRA 2012 no work-related requirements may be imposed on the responsible carer of a child under the age of one, that under s.20(1)(a) only the work-focused interview requirement may be imposed on a claimant who is the responsible carer of a child aged one and that under s.21(1)(b) only the work-focused interview and work preparation requirements may be imposed on a claimant who is the responsible carer of a child aged two.

Paragraph (5)

2.364   The direct operation of para.(5) has since April 28, 2014 been limited to the work search requirement. See paras (5A) and (5B) for the effect on the work availability requirement where one of the conditions in para.(5)(a)–(d) is satisfied.

In four sorts of circumstances the imposition of a work search requirement, even as limited under reg.97, is prohibited where it would be unreasonable for the claimant to comply.

Sub-paragraph (a) applies if the claimant is carrying out a work preparation requirement (s.16(1) of the WRA 2012) or voluntary work preparation (reg.95(4)). It appears that voluntary work preparation could include the doing of voluntary work if agreed by the Secretary of State (see the definition in reg.95(4)).

Sub-paragraph (b) applies if the claimant has temporary child care responsibilities (for any child) or is dealing with a domestic emergency, funeral arrangements (for a claimant who is already covered by para.(3)(d)) or with other temporary circumstances. In *RR v SSWP (UC)* [2017] UKUT 459 (AAC) (see the notes to reg.95), Judge Wikeley suggested that another way of looking at the case, rather than exploring deductions from 35 as the expected number of hours under reg.95(2), was to consider whether a work search requirement could not be imposed for the weeks in question on the basis that the claimant was dealing with a domestic emergency or other temporary circumstances (reg.99(5)(b)). His suggestion that reg.99(2A) and (5) apply only when the circumstances are such that it is unreasonable to require the claimant to comply with any work search requirement at all, rather than merely to undertake more than reduced hours of work search action under reg.95, appears right. The evidence in *RR* probably did not support such a conclusion.

Sub-paragraph (c) applies where the claimant is unfit for work and produces a medical certificate if required and the restrictions in para.(4) have been exceeded. This is an important extension to the provision in para.(4) but subject to the overriding condition that it is unreasonable to require the claimant to undertake any work search activities. It must surely be the case, especially in view of the insertion of sub-para.(d) in April 2018, that sub-para.(c) applies regardless of the existence of any previous determination or deeming that the claimant does not have limited capability for work or work-related activity. It is enough, subject to the reasonableness and evidence conditions, that the claimant has been unfit for work for more than 14 days or has exceeded the two periods limit.

Sub-paragraph (d) mitigates the rigour of the paras (4ZA) and (4ZB) rules by in effect disapplying them when it would be unreasonable to require the claimant to comply with any work search requirement.

Would para.(5)(b) allow the Secretary of State to allow short "holidays" from work search responsibilities (and a modification of work availability requirements under para.(5A) or (5B)), under the heading of temporary circumstances or temporary child care responsibilities if satisfied that it would be reasonable to do so (cf. reg.19(1)(p) and (2) of the JSA Regulations 1996)? It is a feature of the universal credit scheme that it will apply to claimants in substantial work, who will have statutory holiday entitlements, as will family members of claimants not themselves in work. If so allowed, there would then be no need to consider the possible application of reg.95(2)(b) or 96(3)(b).

Paragraphs (5A) and (5B)
2.365

Where it would be unreasonable, because of the satisfaction of any of the conditions in para.(5)(a)–(d), for the claimant to be required to be able and willing immediately either to take up paid work or attend an interview, the work availability requirement is adjusted to require the claimant to be willing and able to do so immediately the condition ceases to be satisfied (paras (5A) and (1)(b)). Paragraph (5B) produces the equivalent effect where it would be unreasonable to require the claimant to be willing and able immediately to take up paid work, but reasonable to require willingness and ability to attend an interview.

Paragraphs (6) and (6A)
2.366

Where a claimant or joint claimants are not already free of all work-related requirements by reason of having earnings of at least the individual earnings threshold or the combined thresholds, the "conditionality earnings threshold" (reg.90), the work search and availability requirements are not to be imposed if the monthly amount of employed earnings, as defined in reg.55, converted to a weekly equivalent, at least equals the level set by para.(6). That level is called by the DWP the administrative earnings threshold (AET) and the level of conditionality to be applied when those modifications operate is called the "light touch regime", by contrast with the "intensive work search regime" where all work-related requirements are imposed. Para.(6) has used a number of different formulae over the years, for details of which see the previous editions of this volume. This section of the note concentrates on the formula in force from September 23, 2022 onwards, when a new form of para.(6) was substituted. There has also, from February 2015 to the present been provision for pilot schemes to operate by which qualifying claimants are randomly selected to be treated as though para.(6) was not in existence. See the separate section of this note below.

Regulation 4 of the National Minimum Wage Regulations 2015 (see the definition in reg.2), as amended, sets the hourly rate (£9.50 as from April 2022; £10.42 as from April 2023) for employees aged at least 23, what the government calls the national living wage. Thus, as confirmed in the Explanatory Memorandum to SI 2022/886, the monthly rates prescribed under the new para.(6) with effect from September 26, 2022 were £494 (sub-para.(a) for individual claimants) and £782 (sub-para.(b) for couples). That was the result of multiplying £9.50 by 12 for a single claimant or 19 for a couple, performing the translation to a monthly figure and applying the rounding rule under reg.6(1A)((b). The figures under the previous form of para.(6) were £355 and £567 respectively. If employed earnings (n.b. not self-employed earnings or income from other paid work under reg.52(a)(iii)) equal or exceed the relevant figure, work search and work availability requirements may not be imposed so long as the employed earnings do not fall below the AET, unless the claimant falls within one of the pilot schemes and is to be treated as if para.(6) does not exist.

The rationale for the September 2022 increase in the threshold, exposing more claimants to the more rigorous parts of the conditionality and sanctions regime, was set out as follows in the revised Explanatory Memorandum (the original version was found to be inadequate by the House of Lords Secondary Legislation Scrutiny Committee: *13th Report of Session 2022/23*, HL Paper 68, October 13, 2022):

"7.1 The current AET is equivalent to an individual claimant working 8.62 hours per week earning the National Living Wage (NLW). The current AET for couples is equivalent to them working 13.77 hrs per week between them earning the National Living Wage (NLW).

7.2 When Universal Credit (UC) claimants earn more than their Conditionality Earnings Threshold (CET) they move into the Working Enough conditionality group, where no conditionality requirements are applied, and the claimants do not regularly interact with a work coach. The CET is a flexible threshold which is calculated based on the number of hours an individual claimant can reasonably be expected to undertake work or work-related activities based on their circumstances. In most cases, it is set at the rate equivalent to working 35 hours at the NLW, but this can be adjusted to take account of health conditions or caring responsibilities.

7.3 Where a UC claimant is subject to all work-related requirements, the Administrative Earnings Threshold (AET) is used to determine which conditionality regime the claimant is allocated to. UC claimants are placed in the Intensive Work Search (IWS) regime if they are earning less than their AET, or placed in the Light Touch regime if they are earning at or above their AET but below their CET. Those in the IWS regime are required to accept a Claimant Commitment agreeing work search requirements and work availability requirements as well as work preparation and work-focused interview requirements. Whereas those in Light Touch are not required to comply with work search requirements or work availability requirements.

7.4 This instrument will support UC claimants to progress in work by extending work coach support to more UC claimants on low incomes. Work coaches provide regular on-going tailored support, and claimants will be able to access a comprehensive range of training and skills provision based on their needs.

7.5 Departmental analysts have estimated that this change to the AET will bring in an estimated additional 114,000 claimants into the IWS regime from the Light Touch regime (16.5% of Light Touch claimants). This change will require impacted claimants to review and agree a new Claimant Commitment with a work coach, agreeing appropriate work search requirements which will be revised and updated regularly.

7.6 The policy intent is to support those who find themselves in low income to help them access opportunities to increase their earnings. This might be by increasing their hours, progressing in their current role/sector, or switching careers."

Paragraph 7.4 might be thought somewhat disingenuous in that there seems nothing to have prevented more extensive work coach support being provided to claimants in the light touch regime through the operation of the work-focused interview and work preparation requirements. Nor did the Memorandum explain what was wrong with the previous method of calculating the AET. That was done more explicitly in the DWP's presentation to the SSAC. Paragraph 3.3 of the revised minutes of the SSAC meeting of January 26, 2022 (publication of the minutes of this item having been delayed until SI 2022/886 was laid) contained the explanation that the effect was to return the AET to the real level set in 2015, which had been eroded since because wages had risen faster than benefit levels, which had featured in the previous method of calculation.

With effect from January 30, 2023, the threshold was increased by making the multiple of hours 15 for a single claimant and 24 for a couple, on the 2022/23 level of the NMW resulting in a significant increase in the threshold to £617 and £988 per month respectively. From April 2023 those figures are £677 and £1,053. It was estimated that about 130,000 additional claimants would be moved into the intensive work search regime (para.7.4 of the Explanatory Memorandum to SI 2023/7), which it was said would enable regular contact with a work coach that had not in practice happened previously. It appears that in practice those in the light touch regime, and thus potentially subject to the work-focused interview and work preparation requirements, were only required to attend interviews in the first and eighth weeks on the regime, although they could volunteer for meetings with a work coach. The *Spring Budget 2023* (para.4.146) promised a future change in the abandonment of the higher threshold for couples, with each joint claimant to be subject to the individual AET, which would be raised to 18 times the hourly national minimum wage. There is at the time of going to press no date set for those changes, but it has been suggested that there might be a rise in the couple's AET to 29 hours when the individual AET increases to 18, prior to the abandonment of the couple's AET.

There are number of obscurities in the practical application of the AET rules. First, it may have been the case that under the pre-September 2022 form on para. (6) the couple's AET only applied if both joint claimants had employed earnings. The new form of para.(6) no longer contains the condition that "the couple has combined earnings". Instead, para.(6)(b) talks of a claimant who is a member of a couple whose combined monthly earnings exceed the relevant figure. The natural meaning could arguably extend to a couple where one couple is in employment and one is not. Their combined earnings could be said to be whatever the first claimant earns plus nil from the second claimant.

The identification of the "monthly earnings" to be set against the AET in any particular assessment period is also not free from difficulty. The definition of that phrase in reg.2 gives it the meaning in reg.90(6), part of the regulation dealing with the conditionality earnings threshold. See the notes to reg.99(6), subject to the point that while that provision applies to all forms of earned income under reg.52, reg.99(6) expressly excludes anything that is not employed earnings. The main elements of the general definition are that it applies to the earnings calculated or estimated in relation to a particular assessment period, but without any deduction for income tax, national insurance contributions or pension contributions (reg.90(6)(a)) and that where the earnings fluctuate or are likely to fluctuate there can be an averaging process (reg.90(6)(b)). There is also a discretion to disregard earnings in respect of an employment that has ceased. The starting point, in the light of regs.54 and 61, must be on the gross amounts received in a particular assessment period, but the averaging provision must not be forgotten in cases where there is a gap in regular receipts, perhaps because of the way a pattern of payment falls or because of a pattern involving periods of non-working or reduced working, e.g. outside school terms or due to seasonal factors. There is a lot of judgment involved in determining whether there is an identifiable cycle (probably of payment, rather than merely work), which could in some cases extend over a year or, if there is no identifiable cycle, choosing a period over which to determine the amount of monthly earnings accurately. There is also an overall practical problem that the actual receipts in an assessment period cannot be finally calculated until after the end of that period, yet are meant to control what work requirements are to be imposed on the claimant, and what the claimant should have been doing, during that past period. It may be that that is only a real problem where a claimant starts work or extra work and that during a period of employment either the use of an estimate under reg.90(6)(a) or averaging under reg.90(6)(b) can avoid an unprofitable churning into and out of work requirements.

The Pilot Scheme exceptions

According to para.7.14 of the Explanatory Memorandum to the Universal Credit (Work-Related Requirements) In Work Pilot Scheme and Amendment Regulations 2015, reg.99(6) was initially put in a discretionary form because it had not then been worked out what form of intervention in the way of conditionality would be most effective where the claimant was in work. But it was envisaged that para.(6) would later be revoked when it was known how the work availability and work search requirements could be operated in an appropriate way for all those in work. The 2015 Regulations therefore represent an interim position, which has endured for some considerable time during the slow development of policy.

The Pilot Scheme Regulations (see later in this volume) allow the Secretary of State to select on a random basis certain "qualifying claimants" who would otherwise benefit from para.(6), i.e. who would otherwise be subject to light touch conditionality, to be treated on the basis that para.(6) does not exist. The other conditions under reg.7 of those Regulations for being a "qualifying claimant" are falling within s.22 of the WRA 2012 (subject to all work-related requirements), not falling within reg.98 (victims of domestic violence) and not falling within reg.99(3) (except sub-para.(a) or (g)) or (5)(c). The effect of the Regulations was to expire after three years from February 19, 2015, but that period has been extended, as allowed by s.41(5) of the WRA 2012, for a further six years so far (Universal Credit (Work-Related Requirements) In Work Pilot Scheme (Extension) Order 2018 (SI 2018/168), as supplemented by the 2019, 2020, 2021, 2022 and 2023 Universal Credit (Work-Related Requirements) In Work Pilot Scheme (Extension) Orders (SIs 2019/249, 2020/152, 2021/147, 2022/139 and 2023/157) and may well, in view of the slow development of policy described below, be extended further.

This is a very important provision, allowing experiments ("test and learn") to take place on how to apply the principle of conditionality to those in more than merely subsidiary work, a question apparently not worked out when the scheme to which in-work conditionality was central was legislated for or in the several years since. The claimants selected for the experiments will bear the brunt of any unfairness or rough justice or impracticability revealed in the experiments. Although the large trial described below has finished, so that the terms of para.(6) will apply unaffected in most cases, smaller-scale research and testing will continue.

See the House of Commons Work and Pensions Committee's report on *In-work progression in Universal Credit* (Tenth Report of Session 2010-16, May 2016, HC 549) for a critical but supportive description of the pilot scheme. The government's response to the report was published as HC 585 on July 21, 2016, in which it was anticipated that the necessary 15,000 participants would have been identified by early autumn 2016, to be randomly allocated into groups receiving either frequent, moderate or minimal support. This was known as the randomised controlled trial (RCT). The DWP's evidence to the Committee was that sanctions would be applied for failures to meet in-work requirements without good reason "as a last resort" (para.47 of HC 549), a phrase repeated in para.27 of HC 585. It is not clear how this can operate in practice, as a decision-maker has no discretion not to impose a sanction or to modify its effects if the statutory conditions for imposition are met. Presumably, the intention is that work coaches or other officers will only refer cases to a decision-maker for a sanction as a last resort. On March 23, 2017 the DWP published *In-Work Progression Trial Progress Update: April 2015 to October 2016.* This revealed that 15,455 people had been on the trial and that during the update period 319 sanctions had been imposed, mainly at the low level for failing to participate in meetings or telephone calls.

The Social Security Advisory Committee published an interesting paper, *In-work progression and Universal Credit* (Occasional Paper No.19) in November 2017. The paper welcomed the DWP's adoption of a cautious test and learn approach and the current RCT, but recommended that the DWP should test a wider range of interventions and quickly develop a wider understanding of the variety of circumstances of working claimants who will fall within the ambit of universal credit. It also recommended tackling operational complexities that can be an obstacle to in-work progression and clarifying policy in a number of areas, such as where claimants are working part-time in order to study, re-train or pursue other interests. The government's response in the policy paper *DWP response to SSAC report on In-work progression and Universal Credit: government response* (March 6, 2018) was to welcome the report, but to stress that the DWP considered itself as still at a relatively early stage in understanding what works and that developments would be informed by a "multi-faceted suite of tests and trials" over the following four years. Clarification of policy and the appropriate guidance to and training of work coaches would emerge from that process.

The Work and Pensions Committee returned to the topic in its report of November 6, 2018 on *Benefit Sanctions* (HC 995 2017-19). The DWP's September 2018 report on the completion of the RCT had found a positive impact on behaviours and increased earnings 52 weeks on (an effect subsequently confirmed at 78 weeks: DWP Ad hoc Report 75, October 2019) for those in the more supported groups. However, the important thing was the tailoring of the support to individual needs rather than frequency. Experience of being sanctioned had no apparent effect on outcomes. The Committee recommended that conditionality and sanctions should not be applied to in-work claimants until universal credit had been fully rolled out and then only on the basis of robust evidence of effectiveness. The DWP (House of Commons Work and Pensions Committee, *Benefit Sanctions: Government Response* (HC 1949 2017-19, February 11, 2019), partially accepted that recommendation, but only to the extent of agreeing that the development of policy should be evidence-based and committing to a cautious approach, involving further research and testing of a range of interventions and a better understanding of structural barriers to progression for in-work claimants.

CHAPTER 2

SANCTIONS

Introduction

100.—(1) This Chapter contains provisions about the reduction in the amount of an award of universal credit in the event of a failure by a claimant

2.367

which is sanctionable under section 26 or 27 of the Act ("a sanctionable failure").

[¹(1A) In this Chapter references to a "current sanctionable failure" are to a sanctionable failure in relation to which the Secretary of State has not yet determined whether the amount of an award of universal credit is to be reduced under section 26 or 27 of the Act.]

(2) How the period of the reduction for each sanctionable failure is to be determined is dealt with in regulations 101 to 105.

(3) When the reduction begins or ceases to have effect is dealt with in regulations 106 to 109.

(4) How the amount of a reduction is calculated for an assessment period in which the reduction has effect is set out in regulations 110 and 111.

(5) Regulations 112 to 114 provide for some miscellaneous matters (movement of sanctions from a jobseeker's allowance or an employment and support allowance, cases in which no reduction is made for a sanctionable failure and prescription of work placement scheme for the purposes of section 26(2)(a) of the Act).

AMENDMENT

1. Social Security (Jobseeker's Allowance, Employment and Support Allowance and Universal Credit) (Amendment) Regulations 2016 (SI 2016/678) reg.5(5) (July 25, 2016).

DEFINITIONS

"the Act"—see reg.2.
"assessment period"—see WRA 2012 ss.40 and 7(2) and reg.21.
"claimant"—see WRA 2012 s.40.
"employment and support allowance"—see reg.2.
"jobseeker's allowance"—*ibid.*

Reduction periods

General principles for calculating reduction periods

2.368

101.—(1) The number of days for which a reduction in the amount of an award is to have effect ("the reduction period") is to be determined in relation to each sanctionable failure in accordance with regulations 102 to 105, but subject to paragraphs (3) and (4).

(2) Reduction periods are to run consecutively.

(3) If the reduction period calculated in relation to a sanctionable failure in accordance with regulations 102 to 105 would result in the total outstanding reduction period exceeding 1095 days, the reduction period in relation to that failure is to be adjusted so that the total outstanding reduction period does not exceed 1095 days.

(4) [¹...]

(5) In paragraph (3) "the total outstanding reduction period" is the total number of days for which no reduction in an award under section 26 or 27 of the Act has yet been applied.

AMENDMENT

1. Social Security (Jobseeker's Allowance, Employment and Support Allowance and Universal Credit) (Amendment) Regulations 2016 (SI 2016/678) reg.5(6) (July 25, 2016).

DEFINITIONS

"the Act"—see reg.2.
"sanctionable failure"—see reg.100(1).

GENERAL NOTE

Under reg.100 and this provision the way in which a sanction bites is through **2.369** a reduction in the amount of an award of universal credit for a period determined under regs 101–105 (the "reduction period": para.(1)) for each sanctionable failure. A sanctionable failure is a failure which is sanctionable under s.26 or 27 of the WRA 2012. This regulation contains some general rules on sanctions.

Under para.(2) reduction periods for separate sanctionable failures run consecutively. That is subject to the general overall three-year limit in paras (3) and (5). The drafting is fairly impenetrable, but the upshot seems to be that if adding a new reduction period to the end of an existing period or, more likely, chain of reduction periods would take the total days in the periods over 1095 days the new reduction period is to be adjusted to make the total 1095 days exactly. Now that the rule previously in para.(4), about previous sanctionable failures in the 13 days before another sanctionable failure not counting, has been incorporated into the specific provisions in regs 102 – 104 and tidied up, there can be no question of that rule qualifying the effect of para.(3) to allow a total outstanding reduction period to exceed 1095 days, as had been suggested in the 2013/14 edition of this Volume.

Note also the circumstances prescribed in reg.109 (earnings over the individual threshold for 26 weeks) in which a reduction is to be terminated and the circumstances prescribed in reg.113 where there is to be no reduction despite the existence of a sanctionable failure. Under reg.111(3) the amount of the reduction is nil in an assessment period at the end of which the claimant is subject to no work-related requirements because of having limited capability for work and work-related activity under s.19 of the WRA 2012.

On May 9, 2019, following a report of November 6, 2018 by the House of Commons Work and Pensions Committee on *Benefit Sanctions* (HC 995 2017-19), the Secretary of State (Amber Rudd) made a written statement to Parliament (HCWS1545) including the following:

"I have reviewed my Department's internal data, which shows that a six-month sanction already provides a significant incentive for claimants to engage with the labour market regime. I agree with the Work and Pensions Select Committee that a three-year sanction is unnecessarily long and I feel that the additional incentive provided by a three-year sanction can be outweighed by the unintended impacts to the claimant due to the additional duration. For these reasons, I have now decided to remove three year sanctions and reduce the maximum sanction length to six months by the end of the year."

That decision was implemented (perhaps not fully in spirit) in the November 2019 amendment to reg.102. Note in particular that there was no amendment to reg.101(3), so that in combination with the rule in para.(2) on reduction periods running consecutively it is still possible for a claimant subject to multiple reduction periods to have a total outstanding reduction period of 1095 days.

Higher-level sanction

102.—(1) This regulation specifies the reduction period for a sanction- **2.370** able failure under section 26 of the Act ("higher level sanction").

[¹(2) Where the sanctionable failure is not a pre-claim failure, the reduction in the circumstances described in the first column of the following table is the period set out in—

511

(a) the second column, where the claimant is aged 18 or over on the date of the sanctionable failure;
(b) the third column, where the claimant is aged 16 or 17 on the date of the sanctionable failure.

Circumstances in which reduction period applies	Reduction period where claimant aged 18 or over	Reduction period where claimant aged 16 or 17
Where there has been no previous sanctionable failure by the claimant giving rise to a higher-level sanction	91 days	14 days
Where there have been one or more previous sanctionable failures by the claimant giving rise to a higher-level sanction and the date of the most recent previous sanctionable failure is not within 365 days beginning with the date of the current sanctionable failure	91 days	14 days
Where there have been one or more previous sanctionable failures by the claimant giving rise to a higher-level sanction and the date of the most recent previous sanctionable failure is within 365 days, but not within 14 days, beginning with the date of the current sanctionable failure and the reduction period applicable to the most recent previous sanctionable failure is— (a) 14 days (b) 28 days (c) 91 days (d) 182 days [²...]	– / – / 182 days / [²182 days]	28 days / 28 days / – / –
Where there have been one or more previous sanctionable failures by the claimant giving rise to a higher-level sanction and the date of the most recent previous sanctionable failure is within 14 days beginning with the date of the current sanctionable failure and the reduction period applicable to the most recent previous sanctionable failure is— (a) 14 days (b) 28 days (c) 91 days (d) 182 days [²...]	– / – / 91 days / 182 days	14 days / 28 days / – / –.]

(3) But where the other sanctionable failure referred to in paragraph (2) was a pre-claim failure it is disregarded in determining the reduction period in accordance with that paragraph.

(4) Where the sanctionable failure for which a reduction period is to be determined is a pre-claim failure, the period is the lesser of—

    (a) the period that would be applicable to the claimant under paragraph (2) if it were not a pre-claim failure; or

    (b) where the sanctionable failure relates to paid work that was due to last for a limited period, the period beginning with the day after the date of the sanctionable failure and ending with the date on which the limited period would have ended,

minus the number of days beginning with the day after the date of the sanctionable failure and ending on the day before the date of claim.

[¹(5) In this regulation—

"higher-level sanction" means a sanction under section 26 of the Act;

"pre-claim failure" means a failure sanctionable under section 26(4) of the Act.]

AMENDMENTS

1. Social Security (Jobseeker's Allowance, Employment and Support Allowance and Universal Credit) (Amendment) Regulations 2016 (SI 2016/678) reg.5(7) (July 25, 2016).

2. Jobseeker's Allowance and Universal Credit (Higher-Level Sanctions) (Amendment) Regulations 2019 (SI 2019/1357) reg.3 (November 27, 2019).

DEFINITIONS

"the Act"—see reg.2.
"claimant"—see WRA 2012 s.40.
"current sanctionable failure"—see reg.100(1A).
"reduction period"—see reg.101(1).
"sanctionable failure"—see reg.100(1).

GENERAL NOTE

2.371

Higher-level sanctions are applicable to failures under s.26 of the WRA 2012. Such failures fall outside the scope of regs 103–105 and no failures under s.27 can come within the present regulation. Note the effect of reg.113 in specifying circumstances in which no reduction is to be applied although there has been a sanctionable failure. There is a distinction between "pre-claim failures", i.e. a failure under s.26(4) (before the relevant claim failing for no good reason to take up an offer of paid work or ceasing paid work or losing pay by reason of misconduct or voluntarily and for no good reason), and other failures.

The form of para.(2), specifying the length of sanctions reduction periods for non-pre-claim failures, was re-cast with effect from July 25, 2016 to spell out more precisely much the same effect as previously. It is unhelpful that the individual entries in the table are not numbered. Boxes have been added by the publishers to aid clarity. The rules for 16 and 17-year-olds are no longer separated out from those for claimants aged at least 18, but now appear in column 3 of the table. None of the rules set out below may take the overall length of a total outstanding reduction period (reduction periods run consecutively) over 1095 days (reg.101(2) and (3)).

The general rule for adults in the first entry in column 2 is that the reduction period is 91 days if there have been no other higher-level UC sanctionable failures (or equivalent new style ESA or JSA failures if the claimant moved to universal credit with some days of an ESA or JSA reduction period outstanding: reg.112 and Sch.11 para.3) within the previous 365 days (counting the day of the current sanctionable failure). Contrary to what was said in the note to reg.113 in the 2013/14 edition of what was then Vol.V of this series, it appears that if no reduction of benefit was imposed in relation to a previous sanctionable failure, by reason of reg.113, that failure has not "given rise to" a higher-level sanction so as to count for the purposes of the table. However, if a reduction has been terminated under reg.109, the failure would appear to count because it has given rise to a sanction, even though the period of the reduction has not lasted as long as originally set. It might be argued, for the purposes of the later parts of the table, that the relevant period of reduction was no longer applicable, but the definition of "reduction period" in reg.101(1) is in terms of the initial fixing of the period, with no reference to the effect of reg.109. However, para.(3) secures that pre-claim sanctionable failures (only failures under s.26(4) of the WRA 2012: para.(5)) do not count in this process.

Matters become more complicated when there has been a previous relevant failure within the 365 days. But the amendment with effect from November 27, 2019 has led to a considerable simplification through the removal of the category requiring a reduction period of 1095 days. To start at the end of the table, if the sole or most recent previous sanctionable failure was within the 13 days immediately preceding the date of the current failure, the period of reduction for the current failure is of equal length (either 91 or 182 days) to that for the previous failure. But note that the result of reg.101(2) and (3) is that the new period is to be added on to the end of the previous period, subject to the overall 1095-day limit. If the most recent previous sanctionable failure falls outside that 13-day period but within the 364 days immediately preceding the date of the current failure, the period of reduction for the current failure is 182 days. But note again the effect of reg.101(2) and (3).

The November 2019 amendment is in strict fulfilment of the decision announced by the then Secretary of State, Amber Rudd (written statement to Parliament, HCWS1545, May 9, 2019), set out in the notes to reg.101, to remove three-year sanctions for third or subsequent failures and to reduce the maximum sanction length to six months by the end of the year. However, as explained above and in the notes to reg.101, in universal credit and new style JSA, by contrast with the position for old style JSA (see reg.70(2) of the JSA Regulations 1996), the effect of the rules that reduction periods run consecutively, which has not been amended, is that if there have been multiple sanctionable failures within a year a claimant may have a total outstanding reduction period of up to 1095 days imposed. Thus, the precise terms of the decision have been carried out, but it may be said that the spirit of the reasoning behind it has not been adopted for universal credit and new style JSA.

Regulation 5(3) of the amending regulation made the transitional provision that, where an award of universal credit was subject to a 1095-day reduction under s.26 (or such a reduction was treated as falling under s.26) as at November 27, 2019, that reduction was to be terminated where the award had been reduced for at least 182 days. That appears to apply whether the 182 days expired before, on or after November 27, 2019, provided that the award was subject to the 1095-day reduction on that date. It then appears that, once the 1095-day reduction had been terminated the reduction period "applicable" to the previous sanctionable failure became 182 days, so that the case would fall within the new form of para.(d) of the third part of the table.

There is a similar structure for 16 and 17-year-olds, with only two levels of reduction period, at 14 and 28 days.

For pre-claim sanctionable failures, under para.(4) the number of days between the date of the failure and the date of the relevant claim is deducted from the number of days in the reduction period calculated as under para.(2). That is subject to the further rule that if the sanctionable failure relates to paid work that was due to last only for a limited period, the period down to the date when the work was due to end is substituted for the para.(2) period in the calculation. Presumably that is to give an incentive to people to take such work. See also reg.113(1)(e).

Medium-level sanction

103.—(1) This regulation specifies the reduction period for a sanction-able failure under section 27 of the Act (other sanctions) where it is a failure by the claimant to comply with—

    (a) a work search requirement under section 17(1)(a) (to take all reason-able action to obtain paid work etc.); or

    (b) a work availability requirement under section 18(1).

    [[1](2) The reduction in the circumstances described in the first column of the following table is the period set out in—

    (a) the second column, where the claimant is aged 18 or over on the date of the sanctionable failure;

    (b) the third column, where the claimant is aged 16 or 17 on the date of the sanctionable failure.

Circumstances in which reduction period applies	*Reduction period where claimant aged 18 or over*	*Reduction period where claimant aged 16 or 17*
Where there has been no previous sanctionable failure by the claimant that falls within paragraph (1)	28 days	7 days
Where there have been one or more previous sanctionable failures by the claimant that fall within paragraph (1) and the date of the most recent previous sanctionable failure is not within 365 days beginning with the date of the current sanctionable failure	28 days	7 days
Where there have been one or more previous sanctionable failures by the claimant that fall within paragraph (1) and the date of the most recent previous sanctionable failure is within 365 days, but not within 14 days, beginning with the date of the current sanctionable failure and the reduction period applicable to the most recent previous sanctionable failure is— (a) 7 days (b) 14 days (c) 28 days (d) 91 days	 – – 91 days 91 days	 14 days 14 days – –
Where there have been one or more previous sanctionable failures by the claimant that fall within paragraph (1) and the date of the most recent previous sanctionable failure is within 14 days beginning with the date of the current sanctionable failure and the reduction period applicable to the most recent previous sanctionable failure is—		

Circumstances in which reduction period applies	Reduction period where claimant aged 18 or over	Reduction period where claimant aged 16 or 17
(a) 7 days	–	7 days
(b) 14 days	–	14 days
(c) 28 days	28 days	–
(d) 91 days	91 days	–.]

AMENDMENT

1. Social Security (Jobseeker's Allowance, Employment and Support Allowance and Universal Credit) (Amendment) Regulations 2016 (SI 2016/678) reg.5(8) (July 25, 2016).

DEFINITIONS

"the Act"—see reg.2.
"claimant"—see WRA 2012 s.40.
"current sanctionable failure"—see reg.100(1A).
"reduction period"—see reg.101(1).
"sanctionable failure"—see reg.100(1).

GENERAL NOTE

2.373   This regulation applies to failures for no good reason to comply with two particular work-related requirements to which the claimant in question is subject: the requirement under s.17(1)(a) of the WRA 2012 to take all reasonable action to obtain paid work (but note, not the requirement under s.17(1)(b) to take particular action specified by the Secretary of State, where only some failures to comply fall under s.26 and the higher-level sanctions regime) and the work availability requirement in s.18(1). Note that none of the circumstances specified in reg.113 (no reduction to be applied though sanctionable failure) are relevant to medium-level sanctions under s.27.

The form of para.(2), specifying the length of the sanction reduction period, has been re-cast with effect from July 25, 2016 to spell out more precisely much the same effect as previously. It is unhelpful that the individual entries in the table are not numbered. Boxes have been added by the publishers to aid clarity. The rules for 16 and 17-year-olds are no longer separated out from those for claimants aged at least 18, but now appear in column 3 of the table. None of the rules set out below may take the overall length of a total outstanding reduction period (reduction periods run consecutively) over 1095 days (reg.101(2) and (3)).

The general rule for adults in the first entry in column 2 is that the reduction period is 28 days if there have been no other medium-level UC sanctionable failures (or equivalent new style ESA or JSA failures if the claimant moved to universal credit with some days of an ESA or JSA reduction period outstanding: reg.112 and Sch.11 para.3) within the previous 365 days (counting the day of the current sanctionable failure). Arguably, the effect there having been no reduction of benefit in relation to a previous sanctionable failure, by reason of reg.113, is not quite the same as under reg.102, because here there is no reference to the previous failure having "given rise to" a medium-level sanction. If reg.113 applies there is still a sanctionable failure, although no reduction of benefit is to be applied. However, for the purposes of the later parts of the table, a reduction period applicable to the previous sanctionable failure must be identified. If reg.113 has been applied to that failure there can be no reduction period applicable. Consequently it must be arguable that for the purposes of the table as a whole

516

previous sanctionable failures to which reg.113 has been applied do not count. See the notes to reg.102 for the opposite effect where a reduction period has been terminated under reg.109.

The reduction period under para.(1) as from July 25, 2016 is 28 days if there have been no other medium-level sanctionable failures (or equivalent new style ESA or JSA sanctionable failures) at all or only outside the past period of 365 days including the date of the current sanctionable failure. If the most recent relevant sanctionable failure was in the past period of 14 days including the date of the current sanctionable failure, the length of the reduction period is equal to that for the most recent failure. Where the most recent relevant failure was further in the past but still within the 365 days, the length of the reduction period is 91 days. That is in substance the same result as under the previous form of reg.20 and reg.101(4).

There is a similar structure for 16 and 17-year-olds, with only two levels of reduction period, at seven and 14 days.

Low-level sanction

104.—(1) This regulation specifies the reduction period for a sanctionable failure under section 27 of the Act (other sanctions) where—   2.374
- (a) the claimant falls within section 21 (claimants subject to work preparation requirement) or 22 (claimants subject to all work-related requirements) of the Act on the date of that failure; and
- (b) it is a failure to comply with—
  - (i) a work-focused interview requirement under section 15(1),
  - (ii) a work preparation requirement under section 16(1),
  - (iii) a work search requirement under section 17(1)(b) (to take any particular action specified by the Secretary of State to obtain work etc.), or
  - (iv) a requirement under section 23(1), (3) or (4) (connected requirements: interviews and verification of compliance).

(2) Where the claimant is aged 18 or over on the date of the sanctionable failure, the reduction period is the total of—
- (a) the number of days beginning with the date of the sanctionable failure and ending with—
  - (i) the day before the date on which the claimant meets a compliance condition specified by the Secretary of State,
  - (ii) the day before the date on which the claimant falls within section 19 of the Act (claimant subject to no work-related requirements),
  - (iii) the day before the date on which the claimant is no longer required to take a particular action specified as a work preparation requirement by the Secretary of State under section 16, or
  - (iv) the date on which the award terminates (other than by reason of the claimant ceasing to be, or becoming, a member of a couple),

  whichever is soonest; and
- [¹(b) in the circumstances described in the first column of the following table, the number of days in the second column.

Circumstances applicable to claimant's case	Number of days
Where there has been no previous sanctionable failure by the claimant that falls within paragraph (1)	7 days
Where there have been one or more previous sanctionable failures by the claimant that fall within paragraph (1) and the date of the most recent previous sanctionable failure is not within 365 days beginning with the date of the current sanctionable failure	7 days
Where there have been one or more previous sanctionable failures by the claimant that fall within paragraph (1) and the date of the most recent previous sanctionable failure is within 365 days, but not within 14 days, beginning with the date of the current sanctionable failure and the reduction period applicable to the most recent previous sanctionable failure is—	
(a) 7 days (b) 14 days (c) 28 days	14 days 28 days 28 days
Where there have been one or more previous sanctionable failures by the claimant that fall within paragraph (1) and the date of the most recent previous sanctionable failure is within 14 days beginning with the date of the current sanctionable failure and the reduction period applicable to the most recent previous sanctionable failure is— (a) 7 days (b) 14 days (c) 28 days	 7 days 14 days 28 days]

(3) Where the claimant is aged 16 or 17 years on the date of the sanctionable failure, the reduction period is—
   (a) the number of days beginning with the date of the sanctionable failure and ending with—
      (i) the day before the date on which the claimant meets a compliance condition specified by the Secretary of State,
      (ii) the day before the date on which the claimant falls within section 19 of the Act (claimant subject to no work-related requirements),
      (iii) the day before the date on which the claimant is no longer required to take a particular action specified as a work preparation requirement by the Secretary of State under section 16, or
      (iv) date on which the award terminates (other than by reason of the claimant ceasing to be, or becoming, a member of a couple),
   whichever is soonest; and
[¹(b) if there was another sanctionable failure of a kind mentioned in paragraph (1) within 365 days, but not within 14 days, beginning with the date of the current sanctionable failure, 7 days.]

AMENDMENT

1. Social Security (Jobseeker's Allowance, Employment and Support Allowance and Universal Credit) (Amendment) Regulations 2016 (SI 2016/678) reg.5(9) (July 25, 2016).

DEFINITIONS

"the Act"—see reg.2.
"claimant"—see WRA 2012 s.40.
"compliance condition"—see WRA 2012 s.27(6).
"current sanctionable failure"—see reg.100(1A).
"reduction period"—see reg.101(1).
"sanctionable failure"—see reg.100(1).

GENERAL NOTE

This regulation applies only to claimants who are subject to all work-related requirements under s.22 of the WRA 2012 or to the work preparation requirement under s.21 at the time of the sanctionable failure. Then a low-level sanction is attracted by a failure for no good reason to comply with a work-focused interview requirement under s.15(1), a work preparation requirement under s.16(1), a work search requirement under s.17(1)(b) to take particular action specified by the Secretary of State (see reg.103—medium-level sanction—for failures to comply with the requirement to take all reasonable action to obtain paid work under s.17(1)(a)) or one of the extensive connected requirements under s.23.

2.375

The calculation of the reduction period under para.(2) is more complicated than that for higher and medium-level sanctions. It is made up of a period of flexible length depending on the ongoing circumstances under sub-para.(a) plus a fixed period of days under sub-para.(b) to be added to the sub-para.(a) period. Note that none of the circumstances specified in reg.113 (no reduction to be applied though sanctionable failure) are relevant to low-level sanctions under s.27.

The basic rule in sub-para.(a) is that the period runs until any compliance condition specified by the Secretary of State is met. See the notes to s.27(5) of the WRA 2012 for the authorisation for this provision. A compliance condition is either that the failure to comply ceases to exist (e.g. the claimant attends a work-focused interview) or a condition as to future compliance. The condition must in accordance with s.27(5)(a) and sub-para.(a)(i) be specified by the Secretary of State. Although s.27(7) allows the Secretary of State to notify a claimant of a compliance condition in such manner as he determines, the approach of the Supreme Court in *R (on the application of Reilly and Wilson) v Secretary of State for Work and Pensions* [2013] UKSC 68; [2014] 1 A.C. 453 and of the Court of Appeal in *SSWP v Reilly and Hewstone* and *SSWP v Jeffrey and Bevan* [2016] EWCA Civ 413; [2017] 3 Q.B. 657; [2017] AACR 14 to the "prior information duty" and the requirements of fairness might possibly be relevant to the substance of what must be specified (and see the further discussion in the notes to s.27(5)). The sub-para.(a) period will also end if the claimant becomes subject to no work-related requirements for any reason under s.19 of the WRA 2012, is no longer required to take a specific action as a work preparation requirement or the award of universal credit terminates.

It is understood that during the 2020 coronavirus outbreak any contact by the claimant with the DWP was treated as meeting a compliance condition.

Under sub-para.(b) the additional number of days is seven if there have been no other low-level sanctionable failures (or equivalent new style ESA or JSA failures if the claimant moved to universal credit with some days of an ESA or JSA reduction period outstanding: reg.112 and Sch.11 para.3) in the previous 365 days (counting the day of the current sanctionable failure). Arguably, the effect of there having been no reduction of benefit in relation to a previous sanctionable failure, by reason of reg.113, is not quite the same as under reg.102, because here there is no reference to the previous failure having "given rise to" a low-level sanction. If reg.113 applies there is still a sanctionable failure, although no reduction of benefit is to be applied. However, for the purposes of the later parts of the table, a reduction period applicable to the previous sanctionable failure must be identified. If reg.113 has been applied to that failure there can be no reduction period applicable. Consequently it must be arguable that for the purposes of the table as a whole previous sanctionable failures to which reg.113 has been applied do not count. See the notes to reg.102 for the opposite effect where a reduction period has been terminated under reg.109.

The second general rule, where there has been at least one previous low-level sanctionable failure in the 365 day period, is that the para.(b) reduction period is 14 days, where the reduction period for the most recent sanctionable failure was seven days and 28 days in all other cases (subject to the possible application of reg.101(3)). The exception to that general rule is where the most recent sanctionable failure occurred within 14 days before the current sanctionable failure, including the day of that failure. In that case, the reduction period is to be of the same length as that applicable to the previous sanctionable failure.

Under para.(3) for claimants aged under 18, the same rules as in para.(2)(a) apply, plus an additional seven days if there has been one or more low-level sanctionable failures in the previous 365 days (excluding the most recent 14 days).

Lowest-level sanction

2.376   **105.**—(1) This regulation specifies the reduction period for a sanctionable failure under section 27 of the Act (other sanctions) where it is a failure by a claimant who falls within section 20 of the Act (claimants subject to work-focused interview requirement only) to comply with a requirement under that section.

(2) The reduction period is the number of days beginning with the date of the sanctionable failure and ending with—

(a) the day before the date on which the claimant meets a compliance condition specified by the Secretary of State;

(b) the day before the date on which the claimant falls within section 19 of the Act (claimant subject to no work-related requirements); or

(c) the day on which the award terminates (other than by reason of the claimant ceasing to be, or becoming, a member of a couple),

whichever is soonest.

DEFINITIONS

"the Act"—see reg.2.
"claimant"—see WRA 2012 s.40.
"compliance condition"—see WRA 2012 s.27(6).
"reduction period"—see reg.101(1).
"sanctionable failure"—see reg.100(1).

GENERAL NOTE

2.377   This regulation applies only to claimants who are subject only to the work-focused interview requirement under s.20 of the WRA 2012. The reduction period for a sanctionable failure to comply with that requirement runs until the claimant meets a compliance condition specified by the Secretary of State (see notes to reg.104), becomes subject to no work-related requirements for any reason under s.19 or the award of universal credit terminates.

520

When reduction to have effect

Start of the reduction

106. A reduction period determined in relation to a sanctionable failure   2.378
takes effect from—

(a) the first day of the assessment period in which the Secretary of State determines that the amount of the award is to be reduced under section 26 or 27 of the Act (but see also regulation 107(2));

(b) if the amount of the award of universal credit for the assessment period referred to in paragraph (a) is not reduced in that period, the first day of the next assessment period; or

(c) if the amount of the award for the assessment period referred to in paragraph (a) or (b) is already subject to a reduction because of a previous sanctionable failure, the first day in respect of which the amount of the award is no longer subject to that reduction.

DEFINITIONS

"the Act"—see reg.2.
"assessment period"—see WRA 2012 ss.40 and 7(2) and reg.21.
"claimant"—see WRA 2012 s.40.
"reduction period"—see reg.101(1).
"sanctionable failure"—see reg.100(1).

GENERAL NOTE

These rules for the start of the reduction period follow fairly logically from the   2.379
structure of the sanctions regime. Where no other reduction period is running
the reduction period starts either in the assessment period (month) in which the
decision to make the reduction is made or in the following assessment period (paras.
(a) and (b)). If there is already a reduction applied in that assessment period, then,
unless affected by the overall limit in reg.101(3) and (5), the new period starts on
the expiry of the existing one.

Reduction period to continue where award terminates

107.—(1) If an award of universal credit terminates while there is an   2.380
outstanding reduction period, the period continues to run as if a daily
reduction were being applied and if the claimant becomes entitled to a new
award (whether as single or joint claimant) before that period expires, that
award is subject to a reduction for the remainder of the total outstanding
reduction period.

(2) If an award of universal credit terminates before the Secretary of State
determines that the amount of the award is to be reduced under section 26
or 27 of the Act in relation to a sanctionable failure and that determination
is made after the claimant becomes entitled to a new award the reduction
period in relation to that failure is to have effect for the purposes of paragraph (1) as if that determination had been made on the day before the
previous award terminated.

DEFINITIONS

"the Act"—see reg.2.
"claimant"—see WRA 2012 s.40.

"joint claimants"—*ibid.*
"reduction period"—see reg.101(1).
"sanctionable failure"—see reg.100(1).
"single claimant"—see WRA 2012 s.40.

GENERAL NOTE

2.381   If an award of universal credit terminates while there is an outstanding reduction period, subsequent days count as if an actual reduction of benefit were being
applied, so that on any further claim for universal credit the claimant is subject to
the reduction only for the remainder of the period (para.(1)). If an award of universal credit terminates before the Secretary of State has made a decision about
a reduction for a sanctionable failure, but a new award is in place by the time the
decision is made (so that under reg.106 the reduction period would otherwise
take effect in the current assessment period), the reduction period starts as if the
decision had been made on the day before the previous award terminated.

Note that if on or after the termination of entitlement to universal credit the
claimant is entitled to new style JSA, the reduction of benefit under the universal credit sanction for its unexpired period transfers to the award of JSA (JSA
Regulations 2013 reg.30)

Suspension of a reduction where fraud penalty applies

2.382   **108.**—(1) A reduction in the amount of an award under section 26 or 27
of the Act is to be suspended for any period during which the provisions of
section 6B, 7 or 9 of the Social Security Fraud Act 2001 apply to the award.

(2) The reduction ceases to have effect on the day on which that period
begins and begins again on the day after that period ends.

DEFINITION

"the Act"—see reg.2.

When a reduction is to be terminated

2.383   **109.**—(1) A reduction in the amount of an award under section 26 or 27
of the Act is to be terminated where—
(a) since the date of the most recent sanctionable failure which gave rise
     to a reduction, the claimant has been in paid work for a period of, or
     for periods amounting in total to, at least [¹six months]; and
(b) the claimant's [¹monthly] earnings during that period or those
     periods were equal to or exceeded—
     (i)   the claimant's individual threshold, [²...]
     [²(ia) where the claimant has no individual threshold, the amount that
            a person would be paid at the hourly rate specified in regulation
            4 or regulation 4A(1)(a) to (c) of the National Minimum Wage
            Regulations for 16 hours per week, converted to a monthly
            amount by multiplying by 52 and dividing by 12, or]
     (ii) if paragraph (4) of regulation 90 applies (threshold for an
            apprentice) the amount applicable under that paragraph.
(2) The termination of the reduction has effect—
(a) where the date on which paragraph (1) is satisfied falls within a
     period of entitlement to universal credit, from the beginning of the
     assessment period in which that date falls; or
(b) where that date falls outside a period of entitlement to universal
     credit, from the beginning of the first assessment period in relation
     to any subsequent award.

(3) A claimant who is treated as having earned income in accordance with regulation 62 (minimum income floor) in respect of an assessment period is to be taken to have [¹ monthly] earnings equal to their individual threshold in respect of [¹ . . .] that assessment period.

AMENDMENTS

1. Universal Credit and Miscellaneous Amendments Regulations 2015 (SI 2015/1754) reg.2(8) (November 4, 2015).
2. Social Security (Jobseeker's Allowance, Employment and Support Allowance and Universal Credit) (Amendment) Regulations 2016 (SI 2016/678) reg.5(10) (July 25, 2016).

DEFINITIONS

"the Act"—see reg.2.
"assessment period"—see WRA 2012, ss.40 and 7(2) and reg.21.
"claimant"—see WRA 2012, s.40.
"individual threshold"—see regs 2 and 90(2).
"sanctionable failure"—see reg.100(1).
"National Minimum Wage Regulations"—see reg.2.

GENERAL NOTE

Any reduction for any level of sanction or sanctions terminates where since the date of the most recent sanctionable failure the claimant has been in paid work with earnings at least equal to the appropriate individual threshold for at least six months, not necessarily consecutive. It does not matter what the total outstanding reduction period is. The claimant could have had a reduction period of 1095 days imposed, yet after six months' work at minimum wage level (which will have reduced the outstanding period accordingly) the basis for the entire reduction disappears, just as much as if the outstanding period was much shorter. Paragraph (2) confirms that the termination takes effect immediately if the condition in para.(1) is met while the claimant is entitled to universal credit. If the claimant is not then entitled to universal credit the termination takes effect from the beginning of the first assessment period under any new award. Note that this regulation does not take away the status of any sanctionable failure(s) on which the terminated reduction period was based. Thus for the purpose of asking in the future whether there have been other sanctionable failures within 364 days of a new sanctionable failure all such sanctionable failures must be counted.

2.384

See also reg.119(3) below, under which any hardship payments made under the conditions in reg.116 cease to be recoverable where the claimant has had earnings of the same level as specified in reg.109 for six months after the last day on which a reduction was applied.

There was a technical difficulty in the operation of reg.109(1)(b) in that under the definition of "individual threshold" in reg.90(2) only claimants who would otherwise (if it were not for the effect of reg.90(1) and s.19 of the WRA 2012) be subject to some work-related requirement could have an individual threshold and so take advantage of the provision in para.(1). That gap has been filled by the new para.(1)(b)(ia), specifying an amount of earnings in terms of the national minimum wage hourly rate and 16 hours per week for claimants without an individual threshold as such.

Amount of reduction

Amount of reduction for each assessment period

110. Where it has been determined that an award of universal credit is to be reduced under section 26 or 27 of the Act, the amount of the reduction

2.385

for each assessment period in respect of which a reduction has effect is to be calculated as follows.

Step 1

Take the number of days—
 (a) in the assessment period; or
 (b) if lower, the total outstanding reduction period,
and deduct any days in that assessment period for which the reduction is suspended in accordance with regulation 108.

Step 2

Multiply the number of days produced by step 1 by the daily reduction rate (see regulation 111).

Step 3

If necessary, adjust the amount produced by step 2 so that it does not exceed—
 (a) the amount of the standard allowance applicable to the award; or
 (b) in the case of a joint claim where a determination under section 26 or 27 of the Act applies only in relation to one claimant, half the amount of that standard allowance.

Step 4

Deduct the amount produced by steps 2 and 3 from the amount of the award for the assessment period after any deduction has been made in accordance with Part 7 (the benefit cap).

DEFINITIONS

 "the Act"—see reg.2.
 "assessment period"—see WRA 2012 ss.40 and 7(2) and reg.21.
 "claimant"—see WRA 2012, s.40.
 "standard allowance"—see WRA 2012, s.9.

GENERAL NOTE

2.386   This apparently complex calculation will work out easily enough in practice. Its main point is to translate the daily rate of reduction under reg.111 into the appropriate amount for an assessment period, depending on the number of days in the period affected by a reduction. There is a rule of substance concealed in step 3, in that the reduction can never exceed the amount of the claimant's standard allowance, or half of a couple's standard allowance.

 However, see the notes to reg.111 below for discussion of the capricious results that can follow from the way in which the daily reduction rate is calculated under reg.111 and from the principle that in accordance with ss.26 and 27 of the WRA 2012 the reduction is to be applied to the overall award of universal credit, however that is made up.

 See those notes and the notes to reg.5 of the JSA Regulations 2013 in Vol.I of this series and to paras 1 and 2 of Sch.11 to the present Regulations for further discussion of the anomalous results where a universal credit recipient is also entitled to another social security benefit (in particular new style ESA or JSA) and for the non-use of regulation-making powers that could have avoided them.

Daily reduction rate

111.—(1) The daily reduction rate for the purposes of regulation 110 is,   2.387
unless paragraph (2), or (3) applies, an amount equal to the amount of the
standard allowance that is applicable to the award multiplied by 12 and
divided by 365.

(2) The daily reduction rate is 40 per cent of the rate set out in paragraph
(1) if, at the end of the assessment period—

  (a) the claimant is aged 16 or 17;

  (b) the claimant falls within section 19 of the Act (claimant subject to no
     work-related requirements) by virtue of—

     (i) subsection (2)(c) of that section (responsible carer for a child
       under the age of 1), or

     (ii) regulation 89(1)(c),(d) or (f) (adopter, claimant within 11
       weeks before or 15 weeks after confinement or responsible
       foster parent of a child under the age of 1); or

  (c) the claimant falls within section 20 (claimant subject to work-
     focused interview only).

(3) The daily reduction rate is nil if, at the end of the assessment period,
the claimant falls within section 19 of the Act by virtue of having limited
capability for work and work-related activity.

(4) The amount of the rate in [¹paragraphs (1) and (2)] is to be rounded
down to the nearest 10 pence.

(5) In the case of joint claimants—

  (a) each joint claimant is considered individually for the purpose of
     determining the rate applicable under paragraphs (1) to (3); and

  (b) half of any applicable rate is applied to each joint claimant
     accordingly.

Amendment

1. Universal Credit (Consequential, Supplementary, Incidental and
Miscellaneous Provisions) Regulations 2013 (SI 2013/630) reg.38(7) (April 29,
2013).

Definitions

    "the Act"—see reg.2.
    "assessment period"—see WRA 2012 ss.40 and 7(2) and reg.21.
    "claimant"—see WRA 2012, s.40.
    "joint claimants"—*ibid.*
    "limited capability for work and work-related activity"—see WRA 2012, ss.40
      and 37(1) and (2).
    "single claimant"—see WRA 2012, s.40.
    "standard allowance"—see WRA 2012, s.9.

General Note

    The basic rule under para.(1) is that the reduction for the purposes of the calcu-   2.388
lation in reg.110 is by the whole amount equal to that of the claimant's standard
allowance under s.9 of the WRA 2012. There is on the face of it no reduction to the
elements that can make up the maximum amount of universal credit for responsibility for children and young persons (s.10), housing costs (s.11) or particular
needs and circumstances (s.12). In the case of joint claimants, under para.(5) each

claimant is considered separately for the purposes of calculating the reduction and treated as having half of the standard allowance applicable to them as joint claimants.

Under para.(2) the reduction is by 40 per cent of the standard allowance, rather than 100 per cent, for claimants under 18, claimants subject to no work-related requirements under s.19 of the WRA 2012 by virtue of s.19(2)(c) (responsible carer of a child under one) or reg.89(1)(c), (d) or (f) and claimants subject to the work-focused interview requirement only under s.20.

Despite the apparent simplicity of these rules, there are a number of complicating elements that create a degree of uncertainty. First, the effect of the rounding down under para.(4) to the nearest 10p in producing the daily rate of reduction from the amount of the standard allowance, which is expressed in reg.36 as a monthly amount, i.e. for each assessment period, is fairly clear. When the daily rate is multiplied by the number of days affected by the sanction in each assessment period in step 2 of reg.110 the result will often be less than the exactly proportionate share of the actual standard allowance. If a claimant's universal credit award was made up only of the standard allowance, then even a 100% reduction could leave some small amount still payable.

Second, the specification of the reduction rate in terms of the amount of the standard allowance, rather than the amount of the claimant's award of universal credit, creates problems in certain circumstances. In particular, this is so where the claimant has income to be deducted from the "maximum amount" (the appropriate standard allowance plus any additional elements for children, childcare costs, housing costs etc). Take a simple example of a single universal credit claimant of 25 doing no work who is also entitled to new style JSA of, from April 2023, £84.80 per week through satisfaction of the contribution conditions. The standard allowance is as at April 2023, £368.74 per month, which is also the maximum amount. That would appear to produce a universal credit award of £0.27 per month. If the claimant were then made subject to a 100% sanction for a 30-day assessment period, multiplying the daily reduction rate of £12.00 by 30 would produce a figure of £360. But the concept of a reduction cannot allow the amount of universal credit otherwise payable to go below zero, so that the actual reduction could be no more than £0.27 per month. It must not then be forgotten that reg.5 of the JSA Regulations 2013 prevents any reduction being applied to the claimant's new style JSA entitlement when there is also entitlement to universal credit, even though there may have been a sanctionable failure under the new style JSA legislation. Regulation 42 of the ESA Regulations 2013 does the same in relation to new style ESA. See the notes to reg.5 of the JSA Regulations 2013 in Vol.I of this series for the history of a proposal to alter the effect of reg.5 and of reg.42 of the ESA Regulations 2013 that currently appears unlikely to be implemented in the near future.

However, things would become much more complicated if the claimant had a housing costs and/or a children element included in the universal credit maximum amount, so that the amount payable was higher. The basic calculation of the amount of the reduction under reg.110 by reference to the standard allowance would stay the same. But, since ss.26 and 27 of the WRA 2012 and reg.110 provide simply for the reduction of the amount of an award of universal credit by the amount calculated under reg.110, there appears to be nothing to prevent the reduction in this second case biting into potentially the whole of universal credit award, subject only to the limit under step 3 of reg.110 of the amount of the standard allowance. These results appear arbitrary and unrelated to the merits of cases, but equally appear to follow inexorably from the structure of the universal credit legislation. In the example used, the claimant will still have the £84.80 per week of new style JSA intact (or some other source of income in other cases), which can be used to meet essential expenses.

Those simple examples do no more than scratch the surface of other complexities that may arise. They make the existence of the provision for hardship payments, now restricted to 100% reduction cases, in regs 115-119 even more important, although the conditions for payment are extremely restrictive.

Under para.(3) a nil reduction is to be applied, apparently for a whole assessment period, if at the end of that period the claimant is subject to no work-related requirements under s.19 by virtue of having limited capability for work and work-related activity (see s.19(2)(a)). The effect of applying a daily reduction, but making the rate nil, appears to be that any assessment periods falling within para. (3) count as part of the period of reduction under the sanction in question.

See reg.113 for circumstances in which no reduction is to be applied despite the existence of a sanctionable failure that would otherwise trigger a reduction and reg.109 for the termination of all outstanding reductions if a claimant has earnings equal to the individual threshold (see reg.90(2)) for 26 weeks.

Miscellaneous

Application of ESA or JSA sanctions to universal credit

112. Schedule 11 has effect in relation to persons who are, or have been, entitled to an employment and support allowance or a jobseeker's allowance and who are, or become, entitled to universal credit.

2.389

DEFINITIONS

"employment and support allowance"—see reg.2.
"jobseeker's allowance"—*ibid.*

GENERAL NOTE

The general effect of Sch.11 is that if a claimant moves from new style ESA or JSA to universal credit with some days of an ESA or JSA reduction period outstanding, the reduction for those days translates to the universal credit awards. The failures giving rise to those reductions count as previous sanctionable failures at the equivalent level for the purpose of calculating the length of the reduction period for higher, medium and low-level sanctions under regs 102–104.

2.390

Failures for which no reduction is applied

113.—(1) No reduction is to be made under section 26 or 27 of the Act for a sanctionable failure where—

2.391

(a) the sanctionable failure is listed in section 26(2)(b) or (c) (failure to apply for a particular vacancy for paid work, or failure to take up an offer of paid work) and the vacancy is because of a strike arising from a trade dispute;

(b) the sanctionable failure is listed in section 26(2)(d) (claimant ceases paid work or loses pay), and the following circumstances apply—

(i) the claimant's work search and work availability requirements are subject to limitations imposed under section 17(4) and 18(3) in respect of work available for a certain number of hours,

(ii) the claimant takes up paid work, or is in paid work and takes up more paid work that is for a greater number of hours, and

(iii) the claimant voluntarily ceases that paid work, or more paid work, or loses pay,

within a trial period;

(c) the sanctionable failure is that the claimant voluntarily ceases paid work, or loses pay, because of a strike arising from a trade dispute;

(d) the sanctionable failure is that the claimant voluntarily ceases paid work as a member of the regular or reserve forces, or loses pay in that capacity;

(e) the sanctionable failure is listed in section 26(4) (failure to take up an offer of paid work, or to cease paid work or lose pay before making a claim), and the period of the reduction that would otherwise apply under regulation 102(4) is the same as, or shorter than, the number of days beginning with the day after the date of the sanctionable failure and ending with the date of claim;

(f) the sanctionable failure is that the claimant voluntarily ceases paid work in one of the following circumstances—

   (i) the claimant has been dismissed because of redundancy after volunteering or agreeing to be dismissed,

   (ii) the claimant has ceased work on an agreed date without being dismissed in pursuance of an agreement relating to voluntary redundancy, or

   (iii) the claimant has been laid-off or kept on short-time to the extent specified in section 148 of the Employment Rights Act 1996, and has complied with the requirements of that section; or

(g) the sanctionable failure is that the claimant by reason of misconduct, or voluntarily and for no good reason, ceases paid work or loses pay, but the claimant's [¹ monthly] earnings (or, if the claimant is a member of a couple, their joint [¹ monthly] earnings) have not fallen below [¹the amount specified in] regulation 99(6) (circumstances in which requirements must not be imposed).

(2) In this regulation "regular or reserve forces" has the same meaning as in section 374 of the Armed Forces Act 2006.

AMENDMENT

1. Universal Credit and Miscellaneous Amendments Regulations 2015 (SI 2015/1754) reg.2(9) (November 4, 2015).

DEFINITIONS

"the Act"—see reg.2.
"claimant"—see WRA 2012 s.40.
"couple"—see WRA 2012 ss.40 and 39.
"paid work"—see reg.2.
"redundancy"—*ibid.*
"sanctionable failure"—see reg.100(1).
"trade dispute"—see reg.2.
"work availability requirement"—see WRA 2012 ss.40 and 18(1).
"work search requirement"—see WRA 2012 ss.40 and 17(1).

GENERAL NOTE

2.392   This is an important provision in prescribing, under ss.26(8)(a) and 27(9)(a) of the WRA 2012, cases of sanctionable failure for which no reduction of benefit can be imposed. However, none of the circumstances specified are relevant to medium, low or lowest-level sanctions arising under s.27. Note that if a case comes within this regulation that does not affect the status of the sanctionable failure in question. It can still count if in relation to a future sanctionable failure it has to be asked whether there have been any sanctionable failures at the equivalent level in the previous 365 days. See the notes to regs 103 and 104 for further discussion. It will be different if, as under reg.102, the question to be asked is whether there has been a previous sanctionable failure giving rise to a sanction. If reg.113 has applied, the failure would appear not have given rise to a sanction. There remains scope for argument that in some of the circumstances listed there is a good reason for the particular claimant's failure to comply with the requirement in question, so that there is not in fact a sanctionable failure.

The cases are as follows:

(a) Where the sanctionable failure is failing for no good reason to apply for a particular vacancy for paid work or to take up an offer of paid work (WRA 2012, s.26(2)(b) or (c)), no reduction is to be imposed if the vacancy arose because of a strike arising from a trade dispute. "Trade dispute" is defined in reg.2 by adopting the rather long definition in s.244 of the Trade Union and Labour Relations (Consolidation) Act 1992:

"(1) In this Part a "trade dispute" means a dispute between workers and their employer which relates wholly or mainly to one or more of the following—

(a) terms and conditions of employment, or the physical conditions in which any workers are required to work;

(b) engagement or non-engagement, or termination or suspension of employment or the duties of employment, of one or more workers;

(c) allocation of work or the duties of employment between workers or groups of workers;

(d) matters of discipline;

(e) a worker's membership or non-membership of a trade union;

(f) facilities for officials of trade unions; and

(g) machinery for negotiation or consultation, and other procedures, relating to any of the above matters, including the recognition by employers or employers' associations of the right of a trade union to represent workers in such negotiation or consultation or in the carrying out of such procedures.

(2) A dispute between a Minister of the Crown and any workers shall, notwithstanding that he is not the employer of those workers, be treated as a dispute between those workers and their employer if the dispute relates to matters which—

(a) have been referred for consideration by a joint body on which, by virtue of provision made by or under any enactment, he is represented, or

(b) cannot be settled without him exercising a power conferred on him by or under an enactment.

(3) There is a trade dispute even though it relates to matters occurring outside the United Kingdom, so long as the person or persons whose actions in the United Kingdom are said to be in contemplation or furtherance of a trade dispute relating to matters occurring outside the United Kingdom are likely to be affected in respect of one or more of the matters specified in subsection (1) by the outcome of the dispute.

(4) An act, threat or demand done or made by one person or organisation against another which, if resisted, would have led to a trade dispute with that other, shall be treated as being done or made in contemplation of a trade dispute with that other, notwithstanding that because that other submits to the act or threat or accedes to the demand no dispute arises.

(5) In this section—

"employment" includes any relationship whereby one person personally does work or performs services for another; and

"worker", in relation to a dispute with an employer, means—

(a) a worker employed by that employer; or

(b) a person who has ceased to be so employed if his employment was terminated in connection with the dispute or if the termination of his employment was one of the circumstances giving rise to the dispute."

That is a fairly comprehensive definition, although as compared with s.35(1) of the Jobseekers Act 1995 it does not cover disputes between employees and employees. "Strike" is not defined. It is possible that vacancies could arise because of industrial action short of a strike. There seems no good reason why claimants who on principle are not prepared to apply for such vacancies or accept offers should not also be protected. Perhaps it is arguable that in any event they have a good reason for failing to comply with the requirement in question, so that there is no sanctionable failure.

(b) This provision protects claimants who take up work for a trial period, but only current universal credit claimants who are required only to search for and be available for work subject to limitations as to hours of work under reg.97, made under ss.17(4) and 18(3) of the WRA 2012. Then if such a claimant takes up work, or more work, for more than the hours of limitation for a trial period, but then voluntarily gives up that work or extra work or loses pay within the trial period, there is to be no reduction. As above, it would be arguable there was good reason for such action, so no sanctionable failure.

(c) This provision provides the same protection as under sub-para.(a) for voluntarily ceasing paid work or losing pay because of a strike arising from a trade dispute.

(d) Members of the armed forces, both regular and reserve forces, who voluntarily cease paid work as such or lose pay, cannot suffer a reduction on that ground, whatever the circumstances.

(e) Where there is a pre-claim sanctionable failure and the reduction period normally applicable would expire on or before the date of the relevant universal credit claim, there is to be no reduction. It may be that the same result is achieved by reg.102(4).

(f) This provides protection in the same circumstances as prescribed in reg.71 of the JSA Regulations 1996 (Vol.V of this series) and reg.28(1)(f) of the JSA Regulations 2013 (Vol.I of this series), except that there the claimant is deemed not to have left employment voluntarily and so not subject to any sanction. Here the claimant is merely protected from having a reduction of benefit imposed, subject to any argument that there was a good reason under general principles for voluntarily ceasing work, so no sanctionable failure.

Sub-paragraph (f) provides protection in the context of a sanctionable failure in the form of voluntarily ceasing paid work in three situations. First, it protects claimants who have been dismissed by their employer because of redundancy after volunteering or agreeing to be dismissed. The reference to "dismissal" might be thought unfortunate if it were to perpetuate or risk reopening old controversies on its precise meaning. Were it the sole protective limb, *R(U) 3/91* ought probably to be followed to give it a wide meaning. But taking a narrower meaning might not now matter much, since head (ii) protects claimants who have left their employment on a date agreed with their employer without being dismissed, in pursuance of an agreement relating to voluntary redundancy. "Redundancy", rather than dismissal, is thus the key limiting factor. It presumably means one of the facts set out in s.139(1) of the Employment Rights Act 1996, i.e. (a) the fact that the employer has ceased, or intends to cease, to carry on the business in the place where the employee [the UC claimant] was employed; and (b) the fact that the requirements of that business for employees to carry out work of a particular kind, or for employees to carry out work of a particular kind in the place where [the claimant] was employed, have ceased or diminished or are expected to cease or diminish. The third situation of protection covers claimants who have been laid off or kept on short-time to the extent specified in s.148 of the Employment Rights Act 1996 and have complied with the requirements of that section, thus protecting claimants like the one in *CU/71/1994*. Section 148 of the 1996 Act enables those laid off or kept on short time to claim a redundancy payment if they serve on their employer written notice of their intention to do so. They must have been laid off or kept on short time either for four or more consecutive weeks or for a series of six or more weeks within a period of 13 weeks prior to service of the notice. To get the s.148 payment, the employee must terminate the contract of employment and not be dismissed by the employer.

(g) Under reg.99(6) it may be determined that a claimant's or joint claimants' earnings are at a level where a work search or work availability requirement is not to be imposed, although the earnings are below the individual threshold or combined individual thresholds that has to be reached to make the claimant(s) subject to no work-related requirements under s.19 of the WRA 2012 and reg.90. If that decision is made after a claimant by reason of misconduct or voluntarily and for no good reasons ceases paid work or loses pay, no reduction of benefit is to be imposed.

Sanctionable failures under section 26—work placements

[¹114.—(1) A placement on the Mandatory Work Activity Scheme is a prescribed placement for the purpose of section 26(2)(a) of the Act (sanctionable failure not to comply with a work placement).

(2) In paragraph (1) "the Mandatory Work Activity Scheme" means a scheme provided pursuant to arrangements made by the Secretary of State and known by that name that is designed to provide work or work-related activity for up to 30 hours per week over a period of 4 consecutive weeks with a view to assisting claimants to improve their prospects of obtaining employment.]

2.393

AMENDMENT

1. Universal Credit (Consequential, Supplementary, Incidental and Miscellaneous Provisions) Regulations 2013 (SI 2013/630) reg.38(8) (April 29, 2013).

DEFINITIONS

"the Act"—see reg.2.
"claimant"—see WRA 2012 s.40.
"paid work"—see reg.2.
"work-related activity"—see WRA 2012 s.40.

GENERAL NOTE

See the notes to s.26(2)(a) of the WRA 2012 for the validity of this provision in giving sufficient detail of the nature of the Mandatory Work Activity Scheme to constitute a description of the scheme, as required by s.26(2)(a), not just a label, and for the circumstances in which failure to comply with a requirement to undertake a placement could give rise to a sanction. Note that the scheme need not be designed to provide work that is paid and that prospects of employment (not further defined) can in their ordinary meaning include prospects of self-employment. The scheme has ceased to operate after April 2016.

2.394

Chapter 3

HARDSHIP

Introduction

2.395   **115.** This Chapter contains provisions under section 28 of the Act for the making of hardship payments where the amount of an award is reduced under section 26 or 27 of the Act.

DEFINITION

"the Act"—see reg.2.

Conditions for hardship payments

2.396   **116.**—(1) The Secretary of State must make a hardship payment to a single claimant or to joint claimants only where—

(a) the claimant in respect of whose sanctionable failure the award has been reduced under section 26 or 27 of the Act is aged 18 or over;

(b) the single claimant or each joint claimant has met any compliance condition specified by the Secretary of State under regulation 104(2)(a)(i);

(c) the single claimant or either joint claimant completes and submits an application—

   (i) approved for the purpose by the Secretary of State, or in such other form as the Secretary of State accepts as sufficient, and

   (ii) in such manner as the Secretary of State determines;

(d) the single claimant or either joint claimant furnishes such information or evidence as the Secretary of State may require, in such manner as the Secretary of State determines:

(e) the single claimant or each joint claimant accepts that any hardship payments that are paid are recoverable;

(f) the Secretary of State is satisfied that the single claimant or each joint claimant has complied with all the work-related requirements that they were required to comply with in the 7 days proceeding the day on which the claimant or joint claimants submitted an application in accordance with sub-paragraph (c); [¹ . . .]

(g) the Secretary of State is satisfied that the single claimant or each joint claimant is in hardship; [¹and

(h) the daily reduction rate in regulation 111(1) applies for the purposes of the reduction in respect of the claimant under section 26 or 27 of the Act.]

(2) For the purposes of paragraph (1)(g) a single claimant or joint claimants must be considered as being in hardship only where—

(a) they cannot meet their immediate and most basic and essential needs, specified in paragraph (3), or the immediate and most basic and essential needs of a child or qualifying young person for whom the single claimant or either of joint claimants is responsible, only because the amount of their award has been reduced—

   (i) under section 26 or 27 of the Act, by the daily reduction rate set out in [¹regulation 111(1)], or

532

     (ii) by the daily reduction rate prescribed in regulations made under section 6B(5A), 7(2A) or 9(2A) of the Social Security Fraud Act 2001 which is equivalent to the rate referred to in paragraph (i);

  (b) they have made every effort to access alternative sources of support to meet, or partially meet, such needs; and

  (c) they have made every effort to cease to incur any expenditure which does not relate to such needs.

(3) The needs referred to in paragraph (2) are—

  (a) accommodation;

  (b) heating;

  (c) food;

  (d) hygiene.

AMENDMENT

1. Universal Credit and Miscellaneous Amendments Regulations 2014 (SI 2014/597) reg.2(12) (April 28, 2014).

DEFINITIONS

    "the Act"—see reg.2.
    "claimant"—see WRA 2012 s.40.
    "joint claimants"—*ibid.*
    "sanctionable failure"—see reg.100(1).
    "single claimant"—see WRA 2012 s.40.
    "work-related requirement"—see WRA 2012 ss.40 and 13(2).

GENERAL NOTE

This regulation is made under s.28 of the WRA 2012 and sets out the very   **2.397**
stringent conditions for the making of hardship payments to claimants to whom a sanction has been applied under s.26 or 27, that limitation being imposed by reg.115 and s.28(1)(a). The amount and period of any payment is dealt with in regs 117 and 118. Paragraph (1) of reg.116 lays down seven conditions, all of which must be satisfied. Paragraphs (2) and (3) provide a further exhaustive definition of when claimants can be considered to be in hardship for the purpose of condition (g) in para.(1). No payment can be made under reg.117 for any period prior to the date on which all the conditions in para.(1) are met.

The opening words of para.(1), by providing that the Secretary of State *must* make a hardship payment only where all its conditions are met, appear to open the door to the Secretary of State making payments on a discretionary basis where the conditions are not met. However, that is not the case, because s.28 only allows additional payments of universal credit to be made in hardship cases when regulations so provide. It must remain open to the Secretary of State to make payments, not of universal credit, on an extra-statutory basis, but no doubt the circumstances would have to be truly exceptional to persuade them to do so.

Paragraph (1)

The seven conditions are as follows: **2.398**

  (a) The claimant to whom the sanction has been applied must be aged at least 18. Under-18s can be sanctioned, but will not have the amount of benefit reduced to nil, as for most over-18s (see reg.111(1) and (2)).

  (b) Under reg.104(2)(a) reduction periods for low-level sanctions last unless and until the claimant satisfies a compliance condition specified by the Secretary of State, i.e. the failure to comply with the work-related requirement in question has come to an end or a condition about future compliance is met (WRA 2012, s.27(6)), plus a fixed period on top. If such a compliance condition has been specified, a hardship payment can only be made after it has been met. The result is that in these cases a hardship payment can only be made during the final fixed period.

(c)   The claimant or one of joint claimants must make an application for a hardship payment. The Secretary of State may accept an application in any sufficient form, but it is not clear what could also be required by the additional condition of the submission of the application being in such manner as determined by the Secretary of State. Condition (f) below can make the timing of an application important, but there seems nothing to stop multiple applications being made day by day.

(d)   The claimant must have supplied any information or evidence required by the Secretary of State.

(e)   The claimant or both joint claimants must accept that any hardship payments are recoverable. Since the recoverability is imposed by reg.119 and s.71ZH of the Administration Act, independent of any advance agreement by the claimant, it is not clear quite what level or manner of acceptance will satisfy this condition. The claimant in a sense has no option but to submit to what the law requires, no matter how vehemently dislike of the result is expressed.

(f)   The claimant or both joint claimants must have complied with all work-related requirements imposed in the seven days preceding, presumably immediately preceding, the day of submission of the application under condition (c).

(g)   The most fundamental condition is that the claimant or both joint claimants are in hardship, presumably as at the date of making the payment or possibly as at the date of the application in question. Because of the use of the present tense, it is arguable that it is not a necessary condition that the claimant or claimants are expected to be in hardship for the duration of the period covered by the payment. Paragraphs (2) and (3) define when a claimant can be accepted as in hardship.

(h)   The effect of this provision, operative from April 2014, is to prevent any entitlement to a hardship payment arising for a claimant whose reduction in benefit under the sanction is only by 40% under reg.111(2), rather than by 100% under reg.111(1).

Paragraphs (2) and (3)

2.399   The use of the word "only" means that claimants can only be accepted as in hardship if they meet all three of the following conditions:

(a)   The claimant or both joint claimants must be unable to meet their most immediate and basic and essential needs, or those of children or young person for whom they are responsible, only by reason of the reduction in benefit due to a sanction or of a reduction for a benefit offence under the Social Security Fraud Act 2001. The only needs to be considered are accommodation, heating, food and hygiene (para.(3)) and then this condition limits consideration to immediate, basic and essential needs of those kinds. That plainly involves a large element of judgment, but the highly restrictive intention is made clear. There is no specific category of need relating to children no matter how young, e.g. for bedding, clothing or education.

(b)   The claimant or both joint claimants must have made every effort to access alternative sources of support to at least go towards meeting needs within condition (a). Some limitations must necessarily be implied either in terms of what efforts can be required or in terms of what alternative sources of support can be considered. The alternative source must at least be lawful. But presumably claimants are not to be required to beg on the streets. Are they to be required to go to back street or payday lenders? How far are they required to explore sources from which there is no practical possibility of support?

(c)   The claimant or both joint claimants must have made every effort to cease to incur expenditure not related to condition (a) needs. Given the restrictive scope of those needs, the range of expenditure to be considered is wide. But again some notions of reasonableness and practicability must necessarily be implied, especially if avoiding immediate expenditure in the short term might lead to disproportionate financial penalties or burdens in the longer term.

The period of hardship payments

[¹**117.**—(1) A hardship payment is to be made in respect of a period which—

(a) begins with the date on which all the conditions in regulation 116(1) are met; and

(b) unless paragraph (2) applies, ends with the day before the normal payment date for the assessment period in which those conditions are met.

(2) If the period calculated in accordance with paragraph (1) would be 7 days or less, it does not end on the date referred to in paragraph (1)(b) but instead ends on the normal payment date for the following assessment period or, if earlier, the last day on which the award is to be reduced under section 26 or 27 of the Act or under section 6B(5A), 7(2A) or 9(3A) of the Social Security Fraud Act 2001.

(3) In this regulation "the normal payment date" for an assessment period is the date on which the Secretary of State would normally expect to make a regular payment of universal credit in respect of an assessment period in a case where payments of universal credit are made monthly in arrears.]

2.400

AMENDMENT

1. Universal Credit (Consequential, Supplementary, Incidental and Miscellaneous Provisions) Regulations 2013 (SI 2013/630) reg.38(9) (April 29, 2013).

DEFINITIONS

"assessment period"—see WRA 2012 ss.40 and 7(2) and reg.21.
"joint claimants"—see WRA 2012 s.40.
"single claimant"—*ibid.*

GENERAL NOTE

2.401

The substituted form of reg.117 (in operation from the outset of the universal credit scheme) represents a simplification and clarification of the original form. Each hardship payment is made for a limited period. Once each period expires a new application must be made. Under para.(1)(a) the period of a payment starts when all the conditions in reg.116(1) are met. For that to be so the claimant must, amongst other things, have completed and submitted an application either on the approved form or in some other manner accepted by the Secretary of State (reg.116(1)(c)). The period ends under the general rule in para.(1)(b) on the day before the normal payment day for the assessment period in which the application was made, following which a new application has to be made for the next period. Under para.(2), if the application of para.(1)(b) would result in a period of hardship payment of less than eight days the period extends to the day before the normal payment day for the next assessment period.

The amount of hardship payments

2.402

118. The amount of a hardship payment for each day in respect of which such a payment is to be made is to be determined in accordance with the formula—

$$60\% \text{ of } \left(\frac{(A \times 12)}{365} \right)$$

where A is equal to the amount of the reduction in the single claimant's or joint claimants' award calculated under regulation 110 for the assessment period preceding the assessment period in which an application is submitted under regulation 116(1)(c).

DEFINITIONS

"assessment period"—see WRA 2012, ss.40 and 7(2), and reg.21.
"joint claimants"—see WRA 2012, s.40.
"single claimant"—*ibid.*

GENERAL NOTE

2.403   The amount of any hardship payment payable per day is effectively 60 per cent of the reduction in the amount of benefit in the assessment period before that in which the application is made. See reg.111 for the daily reduction rate for different categories of claimant.

Recoverability of hardship payments

2.404   **119.**—(1) Subject to paragraphs (2) and (3), hardship payments are recoverable in accordance with section 71ZH of the Social Security Administration Act 1992.

[¹(2) Paragraph (1) does not apply in relation to any assessment period in which—

(a) the single claimant, or each joint claimant, falls within section 19 of the Act by virtue of regulation 90 (claimants subject to no work-related requirements – the earnings threshold);

(b) where regulation 90 applies to one of the joint claimants only, the joint claimants' combined monthly earnings are equal to or exceed the amount of the individual threshold; or

(c) where regulation 90 does not apply to the single claimant or to either of the joint claimants, that claimant or the joint claimants' combined monthly earnings are equal to or exceed the amount that a person of the same age as the claimant, or the youngest of the joint claimants, would be paid at the hourly rate specified in regulation 4 or regulation 4A(1)(a) to (c) of the National Minimum Wage Regulations for 16 hours per week, converted to a monthly amount by multiplying by 52 and dividing by 12,

(3) Paragraph (1) ceases to apply where, since the last day on which the claimant's or the joint claimants' award was subject to a reduction under section 26 or 27 of the Act—

(a) the single claimant, or each joint claimant, has fallen within section 19 of the Act by virtue of regulation 90 (claimants subject to no work-related requirements – the earnings threshold);

(b) where regulation 90 applied to one of the joint claimants only, the joint claimants' have had combined monthly earnings that are equal to or exceed the amount of the individual threshold; or

(c) where regulation 90 did not apply to the single claimant or to either of the joint claimants, that claimant or the joint claimants' have had combined monthly earnings that are equal to or exceed the amount that a person of the same age as the claimant, or the youngest of the joint claimants, would be paid at the hourly rate specified in

regulation 4 or regulation 4A(1)(a) to (c) of the National Minimum Wage Regulations for 16 hours per week, converted to a monthly amount by multiplying by 52 and dividing by 12,
for a period of, or more than one period where the total of those periods amounts to, at least 6 months.]

AMENDMENT

1. Social Security (Jobseeker's Allowance, Employment and Support Allowance and Universal Credit) (Amendment) Regulations 2016 (SI 2016/678) reg.5(11) (July 25, 2016).

DEFINITIONS

"the Act"—see reg.2.
"claimant"—see WRA 2012 s.40.
"individual threshold"—see regs 2 and 90(2).
"joint claimants"—see WRA 2012 s.40.
"National Minimum Wage Regulations"—see reg.2
"single claimant"—see WRA 2012 s.40.

GENERAL NOTE

The basic rule is that any hardship payment is recoverable from the person to whom it was paid (Administration Act, s.71ZH(2)(a)), by the means provided in ss.71ZC to 71ZF. A payment made to one of joint claimants is treated as also paid to the other (s.71ZH(4)). The amount is not recoverable during any assessment period in which the claimant or both joint claimants are subject to no work-related requirements by reason of having earnings of at least the individual threshold(s) under reg.90 (para.(2)(a) and (b)). The same applies under the new provision in para.(2)(c) to claimants who do not have an individual threshold as defined in reg.90(2) because they would not otherwise have been subject to any work-related requirement who meet the test of earnings at the rate of 16 times the national minimum wage hourly rate. It appears from the contrast with the terms of para. (3) that once the reason for freedom from any work-related requirements ceases, the payment becomes recoverable again. Under para.(3) recoverability ceases if since the end of the sanction period the claimant or both joint claimants have had earnings of at least the para.(2) level for a period or periods amounting to six months.

2.405

The maximum rate of recovery from payments of universal credit is 40% of the standard allowance (Social Security (Overpayments and Recovery) Regulations 2013 (Vol.III of this series) reg.11(2)(a) and (3)(b)). The report of November 6, 2018 by the House of Commons Work and Pensions Committee on *Benefit Sanctions* (HC 995 2017-19), para.132, recommended that the rate should be no higher than what was affordable by the claimant, with a default rate of 5% of the standard allowance. The DWP (House of Commons Work and Pensions Committee, *Benefit Sanctions: Government Response* (HC 1949 2017-19, February 11, 2019, paras 90-93) rejected the 5% suggestion as unacceptably diluting the effect of sanctions. It stated that it had announced in November 2018 that to assist those in debt it had reduced the normal maximum rate of deduction to 30% of the standard allowance. Where other higher priority deductions are in place there is a corresponding adjustment to the rate of recovery of hardship payments.

Schedule 1

Meaning of Payments in Respect of Accommodation

General

Interpretation

2.406 1. In this Schedule—

"approved premises" means premises approved by the Secretary of State under section 13 of the Offender Management Act 2007 (which contains provision for the approval etc. of premises providing accommodation for persons granted bail in criminal proceedings or for or in connection with the supervision or rehabilitation of persons convicted of offences);

"care home"—

(a) in England [4 ...], means a care home within the meaning of section 3 of the Care Standards Act 2000;

[(aa) in Wales, means a place at which a care home service within the meaning of Part 1 of the Regulation and Inspection of Social Care (Wales) Act 2016 is provided wholly or mainly to persons aged 18 or over;]

(b) in Scotland, means a care home service within the meaning of paragraph 2 of Schedule 12 to the Public Services Reform (Scotland) Act 2010; and

(c) in [4 any of the above cases], includes an independent hospital;

[1 "exempt accommodation" has the meaning given in paragraph 4(10) of Schedule 3 to the Housing Benefit and Council Tax Benefit (Consequential Provisions) Regulations 2006;]

"housing association" has the meaning given by section 1(1) of the Housing Associations Act 1985;

"independent hospital"—

(a) in England, means a hospital as defined by section 275 of the National Health Service Act 2006 that is not a health service hospital as defined by that section;

(b) in Wales, has the meaning assigned to it by section 2 of the Care Standards Act 2000;

(c) in Scotland, means an independent health care service as defined in section 10F(1)(a) and (b) of the National Health Service (Scotland) Act 1978;

"registered charity" means a charity entered in the register of charities maintained under Part 4 of the Charities Act 2011 or a body entered on the register of charities maintained under the Charities and Trustee Investment (Scotland) Act 2005;

"shared ownership tenancy" has the meaning given in regulation 26(6);

"tent" means a moveable structure that is designed or adapted (solely or mainly) for the purpose of sleeping in a place for any period and that is not a caravan, a mobile home or a houseboat;

[1 ...]

"voluntary organisation" means a body (other than a public or local authority) whose activities are carried on otherwise than for profit.

Rent payments

Rent payments

2.407 2. "Rent payments" are such of the following as are not excluded by paragraph 3—

(a) payments of rent;

(b) payments for a licence or other permission to occupy accommodation;

(c) mooring charges payable for a houseboat;

(d) in relation to accommodation which is a caravan or mobile home, payments in respect of the site on which the accommodation stands;

(e) contributions by residents towards maintaining almshouses (and essential services in them) provided by a housing association which is—

(i) a registered charity, or

(ii) an exempt charity within Schedule 3 to the Charities Act 2011.

Payments excluded from being rent payments

2.408 3. The following are excluded from being "rent payments"—

(a) payments of ground rent;

(b) payments in respect of a tent or the site on which a tent stands;

    (c)   payments in respect of approved premises;

    (d)   payments in respect of a care home;

    (e)   [¹ . . .]

    (f)   payments which are owner-occupier payments [² within the meaning of Schedule 1 of the Loans for Mortgage Regulations 2017];

    (g)   payments which are service charge payments within the meaning of paragraph 7.

[¹ (h)   payments in respect of accommodation specified in paragraph 3A] [³;

    (i)   payments in respect of accommodation specified in paragraph 3B.]

[¹ Specified accommodation

3A.—(1) The accommodation referred to in paragraph 3(h) is accommodation to which one   **2.409**
or more of the following sub-paragraphs applies.

(2) This sub-paragraph applies to accommodation which is exempt accommodation.

(3) This sub-paragraph applies to accommodation—

    (a)   which is provided by a relevant body;

    (b)   into which the claimant has been admitted in order to meet a need for care, support or supervision; and

    (c)   where the claimant receives care, support or supervision.

(4) This sub-paragraph applies to accommodation which—

    (a)   is provided by a local authority or a relevant body to the claimant because the claimant has left the home as a result of domestic violence; and

    (b)   consists of a building, or part of a building, which is used wholly or mainly for the non-permanent accommodation of persons who have left their homes as a result of domestic violence.

(5) This sub-paragraph applies to accommodation—

    (a)   which would be a hostel within the meaning of paragraph 29(10) (renters excepted form shared accommodation) of Schedule 4 (housing costs element for renters) but for it being owned or managed by a local authority; and

    (b)   where the claimant receives care, support or supervision.

(6) In this paragraph—

"domestic violence" has the meaning given in regulation 98 (victims of domestic violence);

"relevant body" means a—

    (a)   council for a county in England for each part of which there is a district council;

    (b)   housing association;

    (c)   registered charity; or

    (d)   voluntary organisation].

[¹ Temporary Accommodation

3B.—(1) The accommodation referred to in paragraph (3)(i) is accommodation which falls   **2.410**
within Case 1 or Case 2.

(2) Case 1 is where—

    (a)   rent payments are payable to a local authority;

    (b)   the local authority makes the accommodation available to the renter—

        (i)   to discharge any of the local authority's functions under Part II of the Housing (Scotland) Act 1987, Part VII of the Housing Act 1996 or Part 2 of the Housing (Wales) Act 2014, or

        (ii)   to prevent the person being or becoming homeless within the meaning of Part II of the Housing (Scotland) Act 1987, Part VII of the Housing Act 1996 or Part 2 of the Housing (Wales) Act 2014; and

    (c)   the accommodation is not exempt accommodation.

(3) Case 2 is where—

    (a)   rent payments are payable to a provider of social housing other than a local authority;

    (b)   that provider makes the accommodation available to the renter in pursuance of arrangements made with it by a local authority—

        (i)   to discharge any of the local authority's functions under Part II of the Housing (Scotland) Act 1987, Part VII of the Housing Act 1996 or Part 2 of the Housing (Wales) Act 2014, or

        (ii)   to prevent the person being or becoming homeless within the meaning of Part II of the Housing (Scotland) Act 1987, Part VII of the Housing Act 1996 or Part 2 of the Housing (Wales) Act 2014; and

    (c)   the accommodation is not exempt accommodation.

(4) Sub-paragraph (1) applies irrespective of whether the renter is also liable to make service charge payments.

(5) In sub-paragraph (3), "provider of social housing" has the meaning given in paragraph 2 of Schedule 4.]

Owner-occupier payments

Owner-occupier payments

2.411   4.—[² . . .]

Meaning of "loan interest payments"

2.412   5. [² . . .]

Meaning of "alternative finance payments"

2.413   6.—[² . . .]

Service charge payments

Service charge payments

2.414   7.—(1) "Service charge payments" are payments which—
   (a) fall within sub-paragraph (2);
   (b) are not excluded by sub-paragraph (3); and
   (c) in any case to which paragraph 8 applies, meet all of the conditions set out in that paragraph.
   (2) The payments falling within this sub-paragraph are payments of amounts which are, in whole or in part—
   (a) payments of, or towards, the costs of or charges for providing services or facilities for the use or benefit of persons occupying accommodation; or
   (b) fairly attributable to the costs of or charges for providing such services or facilities connected with accommodation as are available for the use or benefit of persons occupying accommodation.
   (3) Payments are excluded by this sub-paragraph where—
   (a) [² a qualifying loan within the meaning of regulation 2 of the Loans for Mortgage Interest Regulations 2017] was taken out for the purposes of making the payments; or
   (b) the services or facilities to which the payments relate are provided for the use or benefit of any person occupying—
       (i) a tent,
       (ii) approved premises,
       (iii) a care home, or
       (iv) exempt accommodation.
   (4) It is irrelevant for the purposes of sub-paragraph (2)—
   (a) whether or not the payments are separately identified as relating to the costs or charges referred to in sub-paragraph (2);
   (b) whether they are made in addition to or as part of any other payment (including a payment that would otherwise be regarded as a rent payment within the meaning of paragraph 2);
   (c) whether they are made under the same or a different agreement as that under which the accommodation is occupied.

Additional conditions: social rented sector renters and owner-occupiers

2.415   8.—(1) This paragraph applies for the purposes of calculating the amount of housing costs element to be included in a claimant's award of universal credit but only as regards calculations made under—
   (a) Part 5 of Schedule 4 (social rented sector [³ ...]); or
   (b) Schedule 5 (housing costs element for owner-occupiers).
   (2) The following are the conditions referred to in paragraph 7(1)(c).
   (3) The first condition is that making the payments is a condition on which the right to occupy the accommodation depends.
   (4) The second condition is that the payments fall within one or more of the following categories:

Category A—Payments to maintain the general standard of the accommodation

Payments within this category are for—
   (a) the external cleaning of windows, but only in relation to upper floors of a multi-storey building;

(b) other internal or external maintenance or repair of the accommodation, but only where the payments are separately identifiable as relating to such maintenance or repair and payable by—
    (i) a claimant who occupies accommodation under a shared ownership tenancy, or
    (ii) a claimant in whose case any amount of housing costs element to be included in their award in respect of those payments would fall to be calculated under Schedule 5.

Category B—Payments for the general upkeep of areas of communal use

Payments within this category are for ongoing maintenance or cleaning of, and the supply of water, fuel or any other commodity relating to the common use of, internal or external areas, including areas for reasonable facilities (such as laundry rooms or children's play areas).

Category C—Payments in respect of basic communal services

Payments within this category are for provision, ongoing maintenance, cleaning or repair in connection with basic services generally available to all persons living in the accommodation (such as refuse collection, communal lifts, secure building access or wireless or television aerials to receive a service free of charge).

Category D—Accommodation-specific charges

Payments within this category are specific to the particular accommodation occupied by a claimant but are limited to payments for the use of essential items contained in it (such as furniture or domestic appliances).

(5) The third condition is that the costs and charges to which the payments relate are of a reasonable amount and relate to services or facilities of such description as it is reasonable to provide.

(6) The fourth condition is that the payments are none of the following—
(a) payments to the extent that they relate to the costs of or charges for providing services or facilities in respect of which payments out of public funds might otherwise be made (irrespective of whether the claimant has any entitlement to payments so made);
(b) payments in connection with the use of an asset which result in the transfer of the asset or any interest in it;
(c) payments to the extent that they relate to the costs of or charges for providing food, medical services or personal services (including personal care) of any description.

(7) Payments that are not service charge payments within the meaning of paragraph 7 by reason only that they fail to meet any of the conditions set out in sub-paragraphs (3) to (6) are nevertheless to be treated as if they were such service charge payments for the purposes of paragraphs 3(g) and 4(2).

AMENDMENTS

1. Housing Benefit and Universal Credit (Supported Accommodation) (Amendment) Regulations 2014 (SI 2014/771) reg.2(2) (November 3, 2014).

2. Loans for Mortgage Interest Regulations 2017 (SI 2017/725) reg.18 and Sch.5, para.5(e) (April 6, 2018).

3. Universal Credit (Miscellaneous Amendments, Saving and Transitional Provision) Regulations 2018 (SI 2018/65) reg.3(12) (April 11, 2018).

4. Social Security and Child Support (Regulation and Inspection of Social Care (Wales) Act 2016) (Consequential Provision) Regulations 2018 (SI 2018/228) reg.14(1) and (2) (April 2, 2018).

DEFINITION

"claimant"—see WRA 2012 s.40.

GENERAL NOTE

2.416   In order to be eligible for a housing costs element, the claimant (or claimants) must meet the three basic conditions in reg.25(2) to (4): the payment condition, the liability condition, and the occupation condition. This Schedule is concerned with the payment condition.

    Under reg.25(2) there are two types of payments that can be met: rent payments and service charge payments.

Paragraphs 2, 3 and 3A

2.417   Paragraph 2 lists the payments that are eligible as rent payments and para.3 the payments that are not eligible. Note that the amount of the housing costs element may be restricted under Sch.4 if the rent is higher than allowed (private tenants and temporary accommodation) or the accommodation is larger than allowed (social rented sector).

    The payments listed in para.2 include most of the payments that can be met by housing benefit but not all, e.g. payments by way of mesne profits (or, in Scotland, violent profits) are not included.

    Under para.3 payments in respect of ground rent and in respect of a tent and the site on which it stands are excluded (para.3(a) and (b)). These qualify as "other housing costs" for income support, old style JSA and old style ESA but there seems to be no provision for such payments under universal credit.

    Payments by Crown tenants no longer seem to be excluded (as they are for housing benefit).

    Paragraph 3(h), together with para.3A, inserted with effect from November 3, 2014, excludes payments in respect of "specified accommodation". There are four categories of "specified accommodation", the first of which, exempt accommodation, was previously excluded under para. 3(e) (now omitted).

    The four categories are: (i) "exempt accommodation" (as defined in para.1–this is accommodation which is a "resettlement place" or accommodation provided by a non-metropolitan county council, a housing association, a registered charity or a voluntary organisation, where care, support or supervision is provided to the claimant by that body or a person acting on its behalf); (ii) accommodation provided by a "relevant body" (as defined in para. 3A(6)) into which the claimant has been admitted because of a need for care, support or supervision, which they receive; (iii) temporary accommodation provided by a local authority or a relevant body for people who have left home because of domestic violence, e.g., a women's refuge (note the definition of "domestic violence" in reg. 98(4), which is quite wide); and (iv) hostels owned or managed by a local authority where the claimant receives care, support or supervision. Note that in the case of categories (ii) and (iv) the care, support or supervision does not have to be provided by the relevant body or on its behalf, or by the local authority or on its behalf, as it does in the case of exempt accommodation.

    Claimants living in specified accommodation are eligible for housing benefit. Corresponding amendments have been made to the Housing Benefit Regulations 2006 (SI 2006/213), the effect of which is to exclude housing benefit paid to claimants living in specified accommodation from the HB benefit cap for housing benefit purposes (see regs 75C(2)(a) and 75H of those Regulations–the exemption previously only applied to claimants living in exempt accommodation). Housing benefit is not included in the list of welfare benefits in reg. 79(4) to which the universal credit benefit cap applies.

Paragraphs 7 and 8

2.418   Service charge payments are eligible payments if they fall within para.7(2) and are not excluded under para.7(3). They do not have to be separately identified, nor does it matter if they are paid in addition to, or as part of, any other payment (including a rent payment within the meaning of para.2), or if they are paid under the same or a different agreement than that under which the accommodation is occupied (para.7(4)).

Note the additional conditions in para.8 that have to be met in the case of service charge payments by social sector renters (other those in temporary accommodation). This does not apply to private renters.

According to para.F2074 ADM, where service charges are for the provision of an eligible service, the relevant proportion of staffing costs of a person (e.g. a concierge, groundskeeper or caretaker) employed to provide the eligible service can be included, as can the relevant proportion of the costs of managing and administering eligible services, if the claimant is liable for these costs.

Regulation 25(3)

SCHEDULE 2

CLAIMANT TREATED AS LIABLE OR NOT LIABLE TO MAKE PAYMENTS

PART I

TREATED AS LIABLE TO MAKE PAYMENTS

Certain other persons liable to make payments

1.—(1) A claimant is to be treated as liable to make payments where the person who is liable to make the payments is— 2.419

(a) any child or qualifying young person for whom the claimant (or if the claimant is a member of a couple, either member) is responsible; or

(b) in the case of a claimant who is a member of a couple claiming as a single person, the other member of the couple.

(2) Sub-paragraph (1)(b) does not apply to a person who is claiming as a single person by virtue of regulation 3(4).

Failure to pay by the person who is liable

2.—(1) A claimant is to be treated as liable to make payments where all of the conditions specified in sub-paragraph (2) are met. 2.420

(2) These are the conditions—

(a) the person who is liable to make the payments is not doing so;

(b) the claimant has to make the payments in order to continue occupation of the accommodation;

(c) the claimant's circumstances are such that it would be unreasonable to expect them to make other arrangements;

(d) it is otherwise reasonable in all the circumstances to treat the claimant as liable to make the payments.

(3) In determining what is reasonable for the purposes of sub-paragraph (2)(d) in the case of owner-occupier payments, regard may be had to the fact that continuing to make the payments may benefit the person with the liability to make the payments.

Payments waived in return for repair work

3. A claimant is to be treated as liable to make payments where— 2.421

(a) the liability to make payments is waived by the person ("P") to whom the liability is owed; and

(b) the waiver of that liability is by way of reasonable compensation for reasonable repair or re-decoration works carried out by the claimant to the accommodation which P would otherwise have carried out or been required to carry out.

Rent free periods

4.—(1) Where the arrangements under which the claimant occupies the accommodation provide for rent free periods, the claimant is to be treated as liable to make rent payments and service charge payments in respect of accommodation for the whole of any rent free period. 2.422

(2) In paragraph (1), "rent free period" has the meaning given in paragraph 7(4) of Schedule 4.

PART 2

TREATED AS NOT LIABLE TO MAKE PAYMENTS

Liability to make rent and other payments to close relative

2.423   **5.**—(1) A claimant is to be treated as not liable to make rent payments where the liability to make them is owed to a person who lives in the accommodation and who is—

    (a) if the claimant is a member of a couple, the other member; or

    (b) a child or qualifying young person for whom—

        (i) the claimant is responsible, or

        (ii) if the claimant is a member of a couple, the other member is responsible; or

    (c) a close relative of—

        (i) the claimant, or

        (ii) if the claimant is a member of a couple, the other member, or

        (iii) any child or qualifying young person who falls within paragraph (b).

(2) A claimant who is treated under sub-paragraph (1) as not liable to make rent payments to any person is also to be treated as not liable to make service charge payments where the liability to make the service charge payments is to the same person.

Liability to make rent and other payments to company

2.424   **6.**—(1) A claimant is to be treated as not liable to make rent payments where the liability to make them is owed to a company and the owners or directors of the company include—

    (a) the claimant;

    (b) if the claimant is a member of a couple, the other member;

    (c) a qualifying young person for whom a person who falls within paragraph (a) or (b) is responsible; or

    (d) a close relative of any of the above who lives in the accommodation with the claimant.

(2) A claimant who is treated under sub-paragraph (1) as not liable to make rent payments to the company is also to be treated as not liable to make service charge payments where the liability to make the service charge payments is to—

    (a) the same company; or

    (b) another company of which the owners or directors include any of the persons listed in sub-paragraph (1)(a) to (d).

(3) In this paragraph, "owner", in relation to a company ("C"), means a person ("A") who has a material interest in C.

(4) For the purposes of sub-paragraph (3), A has a material interest in C if A—

    (a) holds at least 10% of the shares in C; or

    (b) is able to exercise a significant influence over the management of C by virtue of A's shareholding in C; or

    (c) holds at least 10% of the shares in a parent undertaking ("P") of C; or

    (d) is able to exercise a significant influence over the management of P by virtue of A's shareholding in P; or

    (e) is entitled to exercise, or control the exercise of, voting power in C which, if it consists of voting rights, constitutes at least 10% of the voting rights in C; or

    (f) is able to exercise a significant influence over the management of C by virtue of A's entitlement to exercise, or control the exercise of, voting rights in C; or

    (g) is entitled to exercise, or control the exercise of, voting power in P which, if it consists of voting rights, constitutes at least 10% of the voting rights in P; or

    (h) is able to exercise a significant influence over the management of P by virtue of A's entitlement to exercise, or control the exercise of, voting rights in P.

(5) For the purposes of sub-paragraph (4), references to "A" are to—

    (a) the person; or

    (b) any of the person's associates; or

    (c) the person and any of the person's associates taken together.

(6) For the purposes of sub-paragraph (5), "associate", in relation to a person ("A") holding shares in an undertaking ("X") or entitled to exercise or control the exercise of voting power in relation to another undertaking ("Y"), means—

    (a) the spouse or civil partner of A;

    (b) a child or step-child of A (if under 18);

    (c) the trustee of any settlement under which A has a life interest in possession (in Scotland a life interest);

    (d) an undertaking of which A is a director;

    (e) a person who is an employee or partner of A;

(f) if A has with any other person an agreement or arrangement with respect to the acquisition, holding or disposal of shares or other interests in X or Y, that other person;

(g) if A has with any other person an agreement or arrangement under which they undertake to act together in exercising their voting power in relation to X or Y, that other person.

(7) In sub-paragraph (6)(c), "settlement" means any disposition or arrangement under which property is held on trust (or subject to comparable obligations).

(8) For the purposes of this paragraph—

"parent undertaking" has the same meaning as in the Financial Services and Markets Act 2000 (see section 420 of that Act);

"shares" means—

(a) in relation to an undertaking with shares, allotted shares (within the meaning of Part 17 of the Companies Act 2006);

(b) in relation to an undertaking with capital but no share capital, rights to share in the capital of the body;

(c) in relation to an undertaking without capital, interests—

    (i) conferring any right to share in the profits, or liability to contribute to the losses, of the body, or

    (ii) giving rise to an obligation to contribute to the debts or expenses of the undertaking in the event of a winding up;

"voting power", in relation to an undertaking which does not have general meetings at which matters are decided by the exercise of voting rights, means the rights under the constitution of the undertaking to direct the overall policy of the undertaking or alter the terms of its constitution.

Liability to make rent and other payments to a trust

2.425

7.—(1) A claimant is to be treated as not liable to make rent payments where the liability to make them is owed to a trustee of a trust and the trustees or beneficiaries of the trust include—

(a) the claimant;

(b) if the claimant is a member of a couple, the other member;

(c) a child or qualifying young person for whom a person who falls within paragraph (a) or (b) is responsible; or

(d) a close relative of any of the above who lives in the accommodation with the claimant.

(2) A claimant who is treated under sub-paragraph (1) as not liable to make rent payments to the trustee of a trust is also to be treated as not liable to make service charge payments where the liability to make the service charge payments is to—

(a) a trustee of the same trust; or

(b) a trustee of another trust of which the trustees or beneficiaries include any of the persons listed in sub-paragraph (1)(a) to (d).

Liability to make owner-occupier and other payments to member of same household

2.426

8.—(1) A claimant is to be treated as not liable to make owner-occupier payments where the liability to make the payments is owed to a person who lives in the claimant's household.

(2) A claimant who is treated under sub-paragraph (1) as not liable to make owner-occupier payments to any person is also to be treated as not liable to make service charge payments where the liability to make the service charge payments is to the same person.

(3) A claimant is to be treated as not liable to make service charge payments where—

(a) there is no liability to make rent payments or owner-occupier payments; but

(b) the liability to make service charge payments is to a person who lives in the claimant's household.

Arrears of payments

2.427

9.—(1) A claimant is to be treated as not liable to make payments in respect of any amount which—

(a) represents an increase in the sum that would be otherwise payable; and

(b) is the result of—

    (i) outstanding arrears of any payment or charge in respect of the accommodation,

    (ii) outstanding arrears of any payment or charge in respect of other accommodation, previously occupied by the claimant, or

    (iii) any other unpaid liability to make a payment or charge.

(2) Sub-paragraph (1) does not apply if the claimant is treated as not liable to make the payments under any of the preceding provisions of this Part of this Schedule.

Contrived liability

2.428   **10.**—(1) A claimant is to be treated as not liable to make payments where the Secretary of State is satisfied that the liability to make the payments was contrived in order to secure the inclusion of the housing costs element in an award of universal credit or to increase the amount of that element.

(2) Sub-paragraph (1) does not apply if the claimant is treated as not liable to make the payments under any of the preceding provisions of this Part of this Schedule.

DEFINITIONS

"child"—see WRA 2012 s.40.
"claimant"—*ibid.*
"close relative"—see reg.2.
"couple"—see WRA 2012 ss.39 and 40.
"partner"—see reg.2.
"qualifying young person"—see WRA 2012 ss.40 and 10(5) and regs 2 and 5.
"rent free period"—see Sch.4, para.7(4).
"single person"—see WRA 2012 ss.40 and 1(2)(a).

GENERAL NOTE

2.429   In order to be eligible for a housing costs element, the claimant (or claimants) must meet the three basic conditions in reg.25(2) to (4): the payment condition, the liability condition, and the occupation condition. This Schedule is concerned with the liability condition.

Note that the Loans for Mortgage Interest Regulations 2017 (SI 2017/725) mean that from April 6, 2018, UC no longer enables a claimant to meet the liability condition through liability for "owner-occupier payments". However, Sch.2 has not yet been amended to remove references to that category.

Under reg.25(3) the claimant (or either joint claimant) must be liable to make rent payments or service charge payments on a commercial basis, or be treated as liable to make them, and must not be treated as not liable to make them. "Liable" is not defined but presumably requires a legal (as opposed to a moral) liability (see *R v Rugby BC HBRB ex parte Harrison* [1996] 28 HLR 36 and the discussion on the meaning of "liability" in the notes to reg. 8 of the Housing Benefit Regulations in *CPAG's Housing Benefit and Council Tax Reduction Legislation*; it is also the view taken in para.F2081 ADM).

For the meaning of "on a commercial basis", see the notes to "*Board and lodging accommodation*" in reg.2 of the Income Support Regulations in Vol.V of this series and the notes to reg.9(1)(a) of the Housing Benefit Regulations in *CPAG's Housing Benefit and Council Tax Reduction Legislation*.

Paragraphs 1–4

2.430   Under para.1 a claimant is treated as liable to make payments if the person who is liable is (i) a child or qualifying young person for whom the claimant (or the other member of the couple in the case of a couple) is responsible (sub-para.(1)(a)); or (ii) the other member of the couple, if the claimant is a member of a couple but claiming as a single person (see reg.3(3) for the circumstances in which this can apply) (sub-para.(1)(b)); note that sub-para.(1)(b) does not apply in the case of polygamous marriages (sub-para.(2)).

A claimant is also treated as liable to make payments if the payments have been waived by the person to whom they were due (e.g. a landlord) as reasonable compensation for the claimant carrying out reasonable repair or redecoration works which the person would otherwise have had to carry out (para.3), or, in the case of rent and service charge payments, during rent free periods (para.4).

Paragraph 2 applies where the person who is liable to make the payments is not doing so. The claimant will be treated as liable if the claimant has to make the payments in order to continue to occupy the accommodation, it would be unreasonable to expect the claimant to make other arrangements and it is reasonable to treat the claimant as liable. These conditions are similar to those in, e.g., reg.8(1)(c) of the Housing Benefit Regulations and para.2(1)(b) of Sch.3 to the Income Support Regulations (see the notes to para.2 of Sch.3 in Vol.V of this series), except for the added condition that it would be unreasonable to expect the claimant to make other arrangements.

Paragraphs 5–10   2.431

These paragraphs deal with when the claimant will be treated as not liable to make payments in respect of their home. Note that some of the exclusions only apply to some types of eligible payments. The situations in which this rule applies to rent payments are reduced compared with housing benefit (see reg.9 of the Housing Benefit Regulations). Note that the "on a commercial basis" requirement applies to any liability to make payments in respect of accommodation under universal credit (see reg.25(3)(a)(i)).

Paragraphs 5–7   2.432

A claimant is treated as not liable to make rent payments and service charges payments if the liability is to the following:

- Someone who also lives in the accommodation, and who is (i) the other member of the couple if the claimant is a member of a couple; (ii) a child or qualifying young person for whom the claimant or other member of the couple is responsible (see reg.4); or (iii) a close relative (defined in reg.2) of the claimant, the other member of the couple or the child or qualifying person (para.5).

  "Lives in the accommodation" probably means the same as "resides in the dwelling" in reg.9(1)(b) of the Housing Benefit Regulations (see the notes to reg.9(1)(b) in *CPAG's Housing Benefit and Council Tax Reduction Legislation*).

- A company, and the owners or directors of the company include (i) the claimant; (ii) the other member of the couple if the claimant is a member of a couple; (iii) a qualifying young person for whom the claimant or other member of the couple is responsible; or (iv) a close relative of the claimant, other member of the couple or qualifying young person (in the case of a close relative, they must live in the accommodation with the claimant) (para.6(1) and (2)).

  Note that the claimant will also be treated as not liable to pay the service charges if the liability for them is to another company whose owners or directors include any of the people listed in para.6(1) (para.6(2)(b)).

  An owner of a company for the purposes of para.6 is a person who has a "material interest" in it (para.6(3)). See para.6(4)–(8) for the detail.

- A trustee of a trust, and the trustees or beneficiaries of the trust include (i) the claimant; (ii) the other member of the couple if the claimant is a member of a couple; (iii) a child or qualifying young person for whom the claimant or other member of the couple is responsible; or (iv) a close relative of the claimant, other member of the couple or child or qualifying young person (in the case of a close relative, they must live in the accommodation with the claimant) (para.7(1) and (2)).

  Note that the claimant will also be treated as not liable to pay the service charges if the liability for them is to a trustee of another trust whose trustees or beneficiaries include any of the people listed in para.7(1) (para.7(2)(b)).

  See the notes to reg.9(1)(e) and (f) of the Housing Benefit Regulations in *CPAG's Housing Benefit and Council Tax Reduction Legislation.*

Paragraph 8

2.433   Paragraph 8(1) and (2) are concerned with owner-occupier payments and service charges payments. They treat a claimant as not liable to make owner-occupier payments and service charges payments if the liability is to a person who is lives in the claimant's household. Clearly this is different from "lives in the accommodation" under paras 5 to 8. On the meaning of "household", see the notes to *"couple"* (under the heading *"Spouses and civil partners"*) in reg.2 of the Income Support Regulations in Vol.V of this series.

Under para.8(3) a claimant is treated as not liable to make service charges payments if they are not liable for rent payments or owner-occupier payments and the liability for the service charges is to someone who is a member of the claimant's household.

Paragraph 9

2.434   This paragraph only applies if paras 5–8 do not apply (sub-para.(2)). It applies to all types of eligible payments.

It treats a claimant as not liable to pay any increase in the amount that they would otherwise be liable to pay, if that increase is the result of outstanding arrears of any payment or charge in respect of their current or previous accommodation. This also applies in respect of "any other unpaid liability to make a payment or charge" (see sub-para.(1)(b)(iii)) but only if that results in an increase in the amount the claimant is liable to pay.

An example of a payment that would come within para.9 is where a tenant has agreed to pay off arrears of rent by paying an increased amount of rent each month. They will be treated under para.9 as not liable to pay the extra amount above the rent that was originally agreed.

Paragraph 10

2.435   This paragraph only applies if paras 5–8 do not apply (sub-para.(2)). It applies to all types of eligible payments.

It contains a similar rule to the contrived tenancy provision in housing benefit (see reg.9(1)(l) of the Housing Benefit Regulations). See the notes to reg.9(1)(l) in *CPAG's Housing Benefit and Council Tax Reduction Legislation*. But note that reg.9(1) (l) refers to the liability being "created to take advantage of the housing benefit scheme", whereas the test under para.10 is that the liability "was contrived in order to secure the inclusion of the housing costs element". There may be a distinction between "created" and "contrived".

Regulation 25(4)

Schedule 3

Claimant Treated as Occupying or not Occupying Accommodation

Part I

Treated as Occupying Accommodation

The occupation condition: the general rule

2.436   1.—(1) The general rule is that a claimant is to be treated as occupying as their home the accommodation which the claimant normally occupies as their home.

(2) Subject to the following provisions of this Part, no claimant is to be treated as occupying accommodation which comprises more than one dwelling.

(3) Where none of those provisions applies and the claimant occupies more than one dwelling, regard is to be had to all the circumstances in determining which dwelling the claimant normally occupies as their home, including (among other things) any persons with whom the claimant occupies each dwelling.

(4) "Dwelling"—
    (a) in England and Wales, means a dwelling within the meaning of Part 1 of the Local Government Finance Act 1992;
    (b) in Scotland, means a dwelling within the meaning of Part 2 of that Act.

Croft land included in accommodation

2.—(1) Where accommodation which a claimant normally occupies as their home is situated on or pertains to a croft, croft land used for the purposes of the accommodation is to be treated as included in the accommodation.
    (2) "Croft" means a croft within the meaning of section 3(1) of the Crofters (Scotland) Act 1993.

2.437

Claimant living in other accommodation during essential repairs

3.—(1) Where a claimant—
    (a) is required to move into accommodation ("the other accommodation") on account of essential repairs being carried out to the accommodation the claimant normally occupies as their home;
    (b) intends to return to the accommodation which is under repair; and
    (c) meets the payment condition and the liability condition in respect of either the other accommodation or the accommodation which they normally occupy as their home (but not both),
the claimant is to be treated as normally occupying as their home the accommodation in respect of which those conditions are met.
    (2) A claimant is subject to the general rule in paragraph 1 where—
    (a) sub-paragraph (1)(a) and (b) apply to the claimant; but
    (b) the claimant meets the payment condition and the liability condition in respect of both the other accommodation and the accommodation which they normally occupy as their home.

2.438

Claimant housed in two dwellings by provider of social housing

4.—(1) In sub-paragraph (2), "relevant claimant" means a claimant who meets all of the following conditions—
    (a) the first condition is that the claimant has been housed in two dwellings ("accommodation A" and "accommodation B") by a provider of social housing on account of the number of children and qualifying young persons living with the claimant;
    (b) the second condition is that the claimant normally occupies both accommodation A and accommodation B with children or qualifying young persons for whom the claimant is responsible;
    (c) the third condition is that the claimant meets the payment condition and the liability condition in respect of both accommodation A and accommodation B (and for these purposes it is irrelevant whether the claimant's liability is to the same or a different person).
    (2) In the case of a relevant claimant, both accommodation A and accommodation B are to be treated as the single accommodation which the relevant claimant normally occupies as their home.
    (3) In sub-paragraph (1), "provider of social housing" has the meaning given in paragraph 2 of Schedule 4.

2.439

Moving home: adaptations to new home for disabled person

5.—(1) Sub-paragraph (2) applies where—
    (a) the claimant has moved into accommodation ("the new accommodation") and, immediately before the move, met the payment condition and liability condition in respect of the new accommodation; and
    (b) there was a delay in moving in that was necessary to enable the new accommodation to be adapted to meet the disablement needs of a person specified in sub-paragraph (3).
    (2) The claimant is to be treated as occupying both the new accommodation and the accommodation from which the move was made ("the old accommodation") if—
    (a) immediately before the move, the claimant was entitled to the inclusion of the housing costs element in an award of universal credit in respect of the old accommodation; and
    (b) the delay in moving into the new accommodation was reasonable.
    (3) A person is specified in this sub-paragraph if the person is—
    (a) a claimant or any child or qualifying young person for whom a claimant is responsible; and
    (b) in receipt of—

2.440

(i) the care component of disability living allowance at the middle or highest rate,
[¹ (ia) the care component of child disability payment at the middle or highest rate in accordance with regulation 11(5) of the DACYP Regulations,]

(ii) attendance allowance, [² . . .]

(iii) the daily living component of personal independence payment [², or]

[² (iv) the daily living component of adult disability payment at the standard or enhanced rate.]

(4) No claimant may be treated as occupying both the old accommodation and the new accommodation under this paragraph for more than one month.

Claimant living in other accommodation because of reasonable fear of violence

2.441

6.—(1) This paragraph applies where—

(a) a claimant is occupying accommodation ("the other accommodation") other than the accommodation which they normally occupy as their home ("the home accommodation"); and

(b) it is unreasonable to expect the claimant to return to the home accommodation on account of the claimant's reasonable fear of violence in the home, or by a former partner, against the claimant or any child or qualifying young person for whom the claimant is responsible; but

(c) the claimant intends to return to the home accommodation.

(2) The claimant is to be treated as normally occupying both the home accommodation and the other accommodation as their home if—

(a) the claimant meets the payment condition and the liability condition in respect of both the home accommodation and other accommodation; and

(b) it is reasonable to include an amount in the housing costs element for the payments in respect of both the home accommodation and the other accommodation.

(3) Where the claimant meets the payment condition and the liability condition in respect of one accommodation only, the claimant is to be treated as normally occupying that accommodation as their home but only if it is reasonable to include an amount in the housing costs element for the payments in respect of that accommodation.

(4) No claimant may be treated as occupying both the home accommodation and the other accommodation under sub-paragraph (2) for more than 12 months.

Moving in delayed by adaptations to accommodation to meet disablement needs

2.442

7.—(1) The claimant is to be treated as having occupied accommodation before they moved into it where—

(a) the claimant has since moved in and, immediately before the move, met the payment condition and the liability condition in respect of the accommodation;

(b) there was a delay in moving in that was necessary to enable the accommodation to be adapted to meet the disablement needs of a relevant person; and

(c) it was reasonable to delay moving in.

(2) "Relevant person" means a person specified in paragraph 5(3).

(3) No claimant may be treated as occupying accommodation under this paragraph for more than one month.

Moving into accommodation following stay in hospital or care home

2.443

8.—(1) The claimant is to be treated as having occupied accommodation before they moved into it where—

(a) the claimant has since moved in and, immediately before the move, met the payment condition and the liability condition in respect of that accommodation; and

(b) the liability to make the payments arose while the claimant was a patient or accommodated in a care home (or, in the case of a joint claim, while both joint claimants were patients or were accommodated in a care home).

(2) No claimant may be treated as occupying the accommodation under this paragraph for more than one month.

(3) In this paragraph—

"care home" has the meaning given in paragraph 1 of Schedule 1;

"patient" means a person who is undergoing medical or other treatment as an in-patient in any hospital or similar institution.

PART 2

TREATED AS NOT OCCUPYING ACCOMMODATION

Periods of temporary absence exceeding 6 months

9.—(1) Subject to sub-paragraphs (2) and (3), a claimant is to be treated as no longer occupying accommodation from which they are temporarily absent where the absence exceeds, or is expected to exceed, 6 months.

(2) Sub-paragraph (1) does not apply to a claimant who falls within paragraph 3.

(3) Where a claimant who falls within paragraph 6 is temporarily absent from the accommodation which they normally occupy as their home, the claimant is to be treated as no longer occupying that accommodation where the absence exceeds, or is expected to exceed, 12 months.

2.444

AMENDMENTS

1. Social Security (Scotland) Act 2018 (Disability Assistance for Children and Young People) (Consequential Modifications) Order 2021 (SI 2021/786) Sch.11 para.7 (July 26, 2021).

2. Social Security (Disability Assistance for Working Age People) (Consequential Amendments) Order 2022 (SI 2022/177) art.13(7) (March 21, 2022).

DEFINITIONS

"adult disability payment"—see reg.2.
"attendance allowance"—*ibid.*
"care home"—see Sch.1, para.1.
"child"—see WRA 2012 s.40.
"child disability payment"—see reg.2.
"claimant"—see WRA 2012 s.40.
"the DACYP Regulations"—see reg.2.
"disability living allowance"—*ibid.*
"partner"—*ibid.*
"personal independence payment"—*ibid.*
"provider of social housing"—see Sch.4, para.2.
"qualifying young person"—see WRA 2012 ss.40 and 10(5) and regs 2 and 5.

GENERAL NOTE

In order to be eligible for a housing costs element, the claimant (or claimants) must meet the three basic conditions in reg.25(2) to (4): the payment condition, the liability condition, and the occupation condition. This Schedule is concerned with the occupation condition.

2.445

Under reg.25(4) the claimant (or each claimant in the case of joint claimants: s.40 WRA 2012) must be treated as occupying the accommodation as his/her home and not be treated as not occupying it. Croft land is included (see para.2).

Paragraph 1

This contains the general rule that the claimant must be normally occupying the accommodation as their home (sub-para(1)). On the meaning of "normally occupying", see the notes to "dwelling occupied as the home" in reg.2 of the Income Support Regulations in Vol.V of this series.

2.446

In addition, the claimant cannot usually be treated as occupying accommodation which comprises more than one dwelling (sub-para.(2)). However, there are exceptions to these rules (see below). Where these exceptions do not apply, and the claimant (or claimants: s.40 WRA 2012) occupies more than one dwelling, to decide which is the dwelling normally occupied as the home, all the circumstances, including the people who live with the claimant (or claimants) in each dwelling, are to be taken into account (sub-para.(3)).

On the question of whether in certain circumstances two physically separate buildings can constitute one "dwelling", see the notes to reg.2 of the Income Support Regulations in Vol.V of this series. Where a claimant is housed in two dwellings by a "provider of social housing" (defined in Sch.4, para.2), see para.4 below.

Paragraph 3

2.447   If the claimant has to move into temporary accommodation because essential repairs (see *R(SB) 10/81*) are being carried out to their normal home, intends to return to that home, and satisfies the payment and liability conditions for either the temporary accommodation or their normal home (but not both), they are treated as occupying as their home the accommodation in respect of which the payment and liability conditions are met (sub-para.(1)). If the claimant satisfies the payment and liability conditions for both the temporary accommodation and their normal home, they are treated as occupying the accommodation that they normally occupy as their home (sub-para.(2)). This may not necessarily be the accommodation that was their normal home.

There is no time limit in para.3 itself as to how long it can apply.

Paragraph 4

2.448   This allows a housing costs element to be paid for two dwellings in the following circumstances. If the claimant (or claimants: s.40 WRA 2012) has been housed in two dwellings by a "provider of social housing" (defined in para.2 of Sch.4) due to the number of children and qualifying young persons living with them, the claimant normally occupies both dwellings with children or qualifying young persons (see reg.5) for whom they are responsible (see reg.4) and the claimant meets the payment and liability conditions in respect of both dwellings, the claimant will be treated as normally occupying both dwellings as their home.

This paragraph can apply without time limit.

See para.17 of Sch.4 as to how the housing costs element is calculated under para.4. A single calculation is made for both dwellings together. This will be carried out under Pt 5 of Sch.4 if the rent is paid to a social sector landlord for both dwellings and neither is temporary accommodation (see para.21 of Sch.4 for the meaning of "temporary accommodation"). Otherwise, the calculation is made under Pt 4 of Sch.4, including applying the four bedroom limit. Note that under para.25(3)–(4) of Sch.4, if the cap rent for the two dwellings is different (e.g. because they are in different areas), the cap rent that is lower at the time the housing costs element is first calculated is the cap rent that applies. The calculation of the renter's housing costs element will continue to be based on that cap rent for as long as the renter is housed in those two homes.

Paragraphs 5 and 7

2.449   Under para.5 a claimant (or claimants) can be treated as occupying two homes for up to one month if the claimant:
  (i)   has moved into their new home;
  (ii)   met the payment and liability conditions for that home immediately before they moved in,
  (iii)   was entitled to a housing costs element in respect of their old home immediately before the move; and
  (iv)   the delay in moving in was reasonable and was necessary to enable the new home to be adapted to the disablement needs (not defined) of the claimant (or claimants: s.40 WRA 2012) or any child or qualifying young person for whom the claimant (or claimants) is responsible. The person with the disablement needs must be in receipt of the middle or highest rate of the care component of disability living allowance, the daily living component of personal independence payment (either rate), attendance allowance or armed forces independence payment (note that the

definition of "attendance allowance" in reg.2 includes armed forces independence payment).

If the above circumstances apply but the claimant was not receiving a housing costs element in respect of their old home immediately before they moved in, para.7 will apply to treat the claimant as occupying their home for up to one month before they move in.

On the meaning of "moving in" see *R(H) 9/05* and on "adapting the accommodation to meet disablement needs" see the notes to para.3(7)(c)(i) of Sch.3 to the Income Support Regulations in Vol.V of this series.

See para.18 of Sch.4 as to how the housing costs element is calculated under para.5. Note that any housing cost contributions for non-dependants are only deducted from the housing costs element for the old home.

Paragraph 6

If the claimant is living in accommodation other than the accommodation they normally occupy as their home because of a reasonable fear of violence in the home, or from a former partner against them or any child or qualifying young person (see reg.5) for whom they are responsible (see reg.4), and they intend to return to the accommodation they normally occupy as their home, they can be treated as occupying both for up to 12 months. This applies if they meet the payment and liability conditions in respect of both the accommodation they normally occupy as their home and the other accommodation, provided that it is reasonable to pay a housing costs element for both. If the claimant only satisfies the payment and liability conditions in respect of one accommodation, they will be treated as occupying that accommodation as their home but only if it is reasonable to pay a housing costs element for that accommodation.

If a claimant in these circumstances is living in a refuge, it is unlikely that they will meet the payment condition for that accommodation (see para.3(h), together with para.3A, of Sch.1, under which payments in respect of "specified accommodation" do not count as rent payments. "Specified accommodation" includes temporary accommodation provided by a local authority or a "relevant body" (defined in para.3A(6)) for people who have left home because of domestic violence (defined in reg.98(4)) (para.3A(4))). However, if they are living in "specified accommodation", they can claim housing benefit for that accommodation.

Note para.9(3) which provides that such a claimant can no longer be treated as temporarily absent from the accommodation which they normally occupy as their home if the absence lasts, or is expected to last, more than 12 months.

See para.19 of Sch.4 as to how the housing costs element is calculated under para.6 where the claimant is entitled to a housing costs element for both homes. This will be calculated for each home under Pt 4 of Sch.4 or under Pt 5 of Sch.4, as the case may be. Note that any housing cost contributions for non-dependants are only deducted from the housing costs element for the home that the claimant is normally occupying.

2.450

Paragraph 8

Under this paragraph a claimant can be treated as occupying their home for up to one month before they move in if they met the payment and liability conditions immediately before moving in and they became liable to make the payments while they were a patient (defined in sub-para.(3)) or in a care home (defined in para.1 of Sch.1), or in the case of joint claimants, while both of them were patients or in a care home.

2.451

Paragraph 9

Unless the absence is due to essential repairs (see para.3) or a fear of violence (see para.6), if a claimant is temporarily absent from the accommodation, they will

2.452

be treated as no longer occupying it if the absence has lasted, or is expected to last, more than six months.

This is a considerably simplified provision compared with the rules for temporary absence that apply for the purposes of housing benefit and income support, old style JSA and old style ESA housing costs.

If at any time during the six months it becomes clear that the absence is likely to exceed six months, the claimant will be treated as no longer occupying the accommodation from that point (this could apply from the start if the absence was expected to last more than six months from the beginning). However, if the claimant returns to the accommodation for a period, even a very short period, the six months should restart. See *R v Penrith DC Housing Benefit Review Board ex p. Burt* (1990) 22 H.L.R. 292, where Simon Brown J. accepted (dealing with the equivalent provisions relating to housing benefit) that "any period of return, however short, within the...period is sufficient of itself to end the period of temporary absence", and that absence would be unbroken only if it was "literally continuous". As pointed out in *Burt,* the relevance of a return being very brief is that it may make it easier for a decision maker to conclude that in all the circumstances the property is no longer accommodation which, as a matter of fact, the claimant "normally occupies as their home". But that is a separate question, arising under para.1 not para.9. See further the notes to paras 3(8)–(12) of Sch.3 to the Income Support Regulations in Vol.V of this series.

Note that if a person was entitled to universal credit which included a housing costs element immediately before becoming a prisoner (defined in reg.2 as modified by SI 2020/409), and they have not been sentenced to a term in custody which is expected to last more than six months, they will be entitled to universal credit consisting of a housing costs element only during their first six months' absence as a prisoner (see reg.19(2) and (3)).

Regulation 26(2)

SCHEDULE 4

HOUSING COSTS ELEMENT FOR RENTERS

PART I

GENERAL

Introduction

2.453   1.—(1) This Schedule contains provisions about claimants to whom regulation 26(2) applies.

(2) Claimants who fall within sub-paragraph (1) are referred to in this Schedule as "renters" (and references to "joint renters" are to joint claimants to whom regulation 26(2) applies).

(3) Part 2 of this Schedule sets out [¹² [¹⁶ an exception]] to section 11(1) of the Act for certain renters in whose case an award of universal credit is not to include an amount of housing costs element calculated under this Schedule.

(4) The following Parts of this Schedule provide for the calculation of the amount of housing costs element to be included under regulation 26(2) in a renter's award of universal credit—

(a) Part 3 contains general provisions that apply to all calculations, whether under Part 4 or Part 5;

(b) Part 4 applies in relation to renters who occupy accommodation in the private rented sector [¹⁴ ...]; and

(c) Part 5 applies in relation to renters who occupy accommodation in the social rented sector [¹⁴ ...].

Interpretation

2.454   2. In this Schedule—

[²² "domestic violence" has the meaning given by regulation 98(4);]

[⁸ "exempt accommodation" has the meaning given in paragraph 4(10) of Schedule 3 to the Housing Benefit and Council Tax Benefit (Consequential Provisions) Regulations 2006;]

"extended benefit unit" has the meaning given in paragraph 9;

"Housing Act functions" means functions under section 122 of the Housing Act 1996 (functions of rent officers in connection with universal credit, housing benefit and rent allowance subsidy and housing credit);

"housing cost contribution" has the meaning given in paragraph 13;

"joint renter" has the meaning given in paragraph 1(2);

"listed persons", in relation to a renter, means—
  (a) the renter;
  (b) where the renter is a member of a couple, the other member of the couple; and
  (c) any child or qualifying young person for whom the renter (or either joint renter) is responsible;

[¹ "member of the armed forces" means a member of the regular forces or the reserve forces within the meaning of section 374 of the Armed Forces Act 2006;]

"non-dependant" has the meaning given in paragraph 9(2);

"provider of social housing" means—
  (a) a local authority;
  (b) a non-profit registered provider of social housing;
  (c) in relation to accommodation which is social housing, a profit-making registered provider of social housing;
  (d) a registered social landlord;

"registered social landlord" means—
  (a) a body which is registered in the register maintained by the Welsh Ministers under Chapter 1 of Part 1 of the Housing Act 1996;
  (b) a body which is registered in the register maintained by the Scottish Housing Regulator under section 20(1) of the Housing (Scotland) Act 2010;

[²² "relative" has the meaning given by section 63(1) of the Family Law Act 1996;]

"relevant payments" has the meaning given in paragraph 3;

"the Rent Officers Order 2013" means the Rent Officers (Universal Credit Functions) Order 2013;

"renter" means a single renter within the meaning of paragraph 1(2) or each of joint renters;

"renter who requires overnight care" is to be understood in accordance with paragraph 12(3) to (5);

"shared accommodation" has the meaning given in paragraph 27;

"social housing" has the meaning given in sections 68 to 77 of the Housing and Regeneration Act 2008.

"Relevant payments" for purposes of this Schedule

3.—(1) "Relevant payments" means one or more payments of any of the following descriptions—   2.455
  (a) rent payments;
  (b) service charge payments.

(2) "Rent payments", in relation to any calculation under Part 4 or 5 of this Schedule, has the meaning given in paragraph 2 of Schedule 1.

(3) "Service charge payments"—
  (a) for the purposes of calculations under Part 4 of this Schedule, has the meaning given in paragraph 7 of Schedule 1;
  (b) for the purposes of calculations under Part 5 of this Schedule, is to be understood in accordance with paragraphs 7 and 8 of Schedule 1.

PART 2

[¹² [¹⁶ EXCEPTION]] TO INCLUSION OF HOUSING COSTS ELEMENT

No housing costs element for 16 or 17 year old care leavers

4. Section 11(1) of the Act (housing costs) does not apply to any renter who is 16 or 17 years   2.456
old and is a care leaver.

[¹² No housing costs element for certain renters aged at least 18 but under 22

4A. [¹⁶ ...]   2.457

Persons to whom paragraph 4A does not apply – general

2.458   **4B.** [¹⁶ ...]

Persons to whom paragraph 4A does not apply – periods of work

2.459   **4C.** [¹⁶ ...]]

PART 3

GENERAL PROVISIONS ABOUT CALCULATION OF AMOUNT OF
HOUSING COSTS ELEMENT FOR RENTERS

Application of Part 3

2.460   **5.** This Part contains provisions of general application in calculating the amount of a renter's housing costs element under Part 4 or 5 of this Schedule.

Payments taken into account

Relevant payments to be taken into account

2.461   **6.**—(1) Where a renter meets the payment condition, liability condition and occupation condition in respect of one or more descriptions of relevant payment, each such description is to be taken into account for the purposes of the calculation under Part 4 or 5 of this Schedule.

(2) No account is to be taken of any amount of a relevant payment to the extent that all of the conditions referred to in sub-paragraph (1) are not met in respect of that amount.

(3) Any particular payment for which a renter is liable is not to be brought into account more than once, whether in relation to the same or a different renter (but this does not prevent different payments of the same description being brought into account in respect of an assessment period).

Relevant payments calculated monthly

2.462   **7.**—(1) Where any relevant payment is to be taken into account under paragraph 6, the amount of that payment is to be calculated as a monthly amount.

(2) Where the period in respect of which a renter is liable to make a relevant payment is not a month, an amount is to be calculated as the monthly equivalent, so for example—

(a) weekly payments are multiplied by 52 and divided by 12;

[⁷ (aa) two-weekly payments are multiplied by 26 and divided by 12;]

(b) four-weekly payments are multiplied by 13 and divided by 12;

(c) three-monthly payments are multiplied by 4 and divided by 12; and

(d) annual payments are divided by 12.

(3) Where a renter is liable for relevant payments under arrangements that provide for one or more rent free periods, [⁷ subject to sub-paragraph (3A),] the monthly equivalent is to be calculated over 12 months by reference to the total number of relevant payments which the renter is liable to make in that 12 month period.

[⁷ (3A) Where sub-paragraph (3) applies and the relevant payments in question are—

(a) weekly payments, the total number of weekly payments which the renter is liable to make in any 12 month period shall be calculated by reference to the formula—

$$52 - RFP;$$

(b) two-weekly payments, the total number of two-weekly payments which the renter is liable to make in any 12 month period shall be calculated by reference to the formula—

$$26 - RFP;$$

(c) four-weekly payments, the total number of four-weekly payments which the renter is liable to make in any 12 month period shall be calculated by reference to the formula—

$$13 - RFP;$$

where "RFP" is the number of rent free periods in the 12 month period in question.].

(4) "Rent free period" means any period in respect of which the renter has no liability to make one or more of the relevant payments which are to be taken into account under paragraph 6.

Room allocation

Size criteria applicable to the extended benefit unit of all renters

    8.—(1) In calculating the amount of the renter's housing costs element under Part 4 or 5 of this Schedule, a determination is to be made in accordance with the provisions referred to in sub-paragraph (2) as to the category of accommodation which it is reasonable for the renter to occupy, having regard to the number of persons who are members of the renter's extended benefit unit (see paragraph 9).

    (2) The provisions referred to in this sub-paragraph are the following provisions of this Schedule—

    (a) in respect of a calculation under Part 4, paragraphs 9 to 12 and 26 to 29;

    (b) in respect of a calculation under Part 5, paragraphs 9 to 12.

2.463

Extended benefit unit of a renter for purposes of this Schedule

    9.—(1) For the purposes of this Schedule, the members of a renter's extended benefit unit are—

    (a) the renter (or joint renters);

    (b) any child or qualifying young person for whom the renter or either joint renter is responsible; and

    (c) any person who is a non-dependant.

    (2) A person is a non-dependant if the person [⁶ normally] lives in the accommodation with the renter (or joint renters) and is none of the following—

    (a) a person within sub-paragraph (1)(a) or (b);

    (b) where the renter is a member of a couple claiming as a single person, the other member of the couple;

    (c) a foster child;

    (d) a person who is liable to make payments on a commercial basis in respect of the person's occupation of the accommodation (whether to the renter, joint renters or another person);

    (e) a person to whom the liability to make relevant payments is owed or a member of their household;

    (f) a person who has already been treated as a non-dependant in relation to a claim for universal credit by another person liable to make relevant payments in respect of the accommodation occupied by the renter.

[⁶ (g) a child or qualifying young person for whom no-one in the renter's extended benefit unit is responsible.]

    (3) "Foster child" means a child in relation to whom the renter (or either joint renter) is a foster parent.

2.464

Number of bedrooms to which a renter is entitled

    10.—(1) A renter is entitled to one bedroom for each of the following categories of persons in their extended benefit unit—

    (a) the renter (or joint renters);

    (b) a qualifying young person for whom the renter or either joint renter is responsible;

    (c) a non-dependant who is not a child;

    (d) two children who are under 10 years old;

    (e) two children of the same sex;

    (f) any other child.

    (2) A member of the extended benefit unit to whom two or more of the descriptions in sub-paragraph (1) apply is to be allotted to whichever description results in the renter being entitled to the fewest bedrooms.

    (3) In determining the number of bedrooms to which a renter is entitled, the following must also be taken into account—

    (a) the provisions of paragraph 11 as to treatment of periods of temporary absence of members of the renter's extended benefit unit;

    (b) any entitlement to an additional bedroom in accordance with paragraph 12;

    (c) for the purpose of any calculation under Part 4 of this Schedule, the additional requirements in paragraphs 26 to 29.

2.465

Temporary absence of member of renter's extended benefit unit

    11.—(1) A member of the renter's extended benefit unit who is temporarily absent from the accommodation occupied by the renter is to be included in a determination of the number of bedrooms to which the renter is entitled ("relevant determination") in the circumstances specified in sub-paragraphs (2) to (4).

2.466

(2) In the case of a child or qualifying young person, the circumstances specified in this sub-paragraph are that the relevant determination relates to any time—

(a) during the first 6 months of the absence of a child or qualifying young person for whom the renter is treated as not being responsible in accordance with regulation 4(6)(a) (child or qualifying young person looked after by local authority) where, immediately before the local authority started looking after them, the child or qualifying young person was included in the renter's extended benefit unit and the renter's award included the housing costs element;

(b) during the first 6 months of the absence of a child or qualifying young person for whom the renter is treated as not being responsible in accordance with regulation 4(6)(b) (child or qualifying young person is a prisoner) where—

　(i) immediately before becoming a prisoner, the child or qualifying young person was included in the renter's extended benefit unit and the renter's award included the housing costs element, and

　(ii) the child or qualifying young person has not been sentenced to a term in custody that is expected to extend beyond that 6 months; or

(c) before the renter or joint renter ceases to be responsible for a temporarily absent child or qualifying young person in accordance with regulation 4(7) (absence exceeding specified duration).

(3) In the case of a renter, the circumstances specified in this sub-paragraph are that the relevant determination relates to any time when—

(a) the temporary absence from Great Britain of the renter is disregarded in accordance with regulation 11(1) or (2); or

(b) the renter is a prisoner to whom regulation 19(2) (existing award includes housing costs when person becomes a prisoner) applies.

(4) In the case of a non-dependant, the circumstances specified in this sub-paragraph are that—

(a) the relevant determination relates to any time during a period specified in sub-paragraph (5); and

(b) immediately before the start of that period, the non-dependant was included in the renter's extended benefit unit and [², in the circumstances specified in sub-paragraph (5)(a) to (c),] the renter's award included the housing costs element.

(5) The specified periods are—

(a) the first month of the non-dependant's temporary absence from Great Britain and, if the circumstances of the non-dependant are such as would be disregarded for the purposes of regulation 11(2) (death of a close relative), a further one month;

(b) the first 6 months of the non-dependant's temporary absence from Great Britain in the circumstances described in regulation 11(3)(a) (absence solely in connection with treatment for illness or physical or mental impairment);

(c) the first 6 months that the non-dependant is a prisoner where the non-dependant has not been sentenced to a term in custody that is expected to extend beyond that 6 months.

[³ (d) any period during which a non-dependant who is the son, daughter, step-son or step-daughter of a renter or joint renters is a member of the armed forces away on operations.]

(6) Any non-dependant who is temporarily absent from the accommodation occupied by the renter in circumstances other than those specified in sub-paragraphs (4) and (5) is not to be treated as being a member of the renter's extended benefit unit if that absence exceeds, or is expected to exceed, 6 months.

[⁶ **Additional room**

2.467　　　12.—[¹¹ (A1) A renter is entitled to an additional bedroom if one or more of the following persons satisfies the overnight care condition (see sub-paragraph (3))—

(a) the renter;

(b) a person in the renter's extended benefit unit;

(c) a child in respect of whom the renter satisfies the foster parent condition (see sub-paragraphs (4) and (5)).]

(1) A renter is entitled to an additional bedroom if they satisfy any of the following conditions—

(a) [¹¹ . . .]

(b) the foster parent condition [¹¹ . . .]; or

(c) the disabled child condition (see sub-paragraph (6)) [¹¹;

(d) the disabled person condition (see sub-paragraph (6A))].

[¹¹ (2) Sub-paragraphs (A1) and (1) apply subject to sub-paragraphs (8) and (9).]

(3) [[11] A person satisfies] the overnight care condition if—
  (a) they are in receipt of—
        (i) the care component of disability living allowance at the middle or highest rate;
  [[18] (ia) the care component of child disability payment at the middle or highest rate in accordance with regulation 11(5) of the DACYP Regulations;]
       (ii) attendance allowance; [[20] ...]
      (iii) the daily living component of personal independence payment; [[20] or]
  [[20] (iv) the daily living component of adult disability payment at the standard or enhanced rate;]
  (b) one or more persons who do not live in the renter's accommodation are engaged to provide overnight [[11] care for the person] and to stay overnight in the accommodation on a regular basis; and
  (c) overnight care is provided under arrangements entered into for that purpose.
(4) A renter satisfies the foster parent condition if the renter is—
  (a) a foster parent; or
  (b) an adopter with whom a child has been placed for adoption.
(5) For the purposes of sub-paragraph (4) "foster parent" includes a person who would be a foster parent, but for the fact that they do not currently have any child placed with them, provided that any period since the date when their last placement ended (or, if they have not yet had a child placed with them, since the date when they were approved to be a foster parent) does not exceed 12 months.
(6) A renter satisfies the disabled child condition if they or another member of their extended benefit unit are responsible for a child who would (but for the provisions of this paragraph) be expected to share a bedroom and that child is—
  (a) in receipt of the care component of disability living allowance at the middle or highest rate; and
  [[18] (aa) in receipt of the care component of child disability payment at the middle or highest rate in accordance with regulation 11(5) of the DACYP Regulations;]
  (b) by virtue of their disability, not reasonably able to share a room with another child.
[[11] (6A) A renter satisfies the disabled person condition if they would (but for the provisions of this paragraph) be expected to share a bedroom with a joint renter and—
  (a) the renter is in receipt of—
        (i) the care component of disability living allowance at the middle or highest rate;
  [[18] (ia) the care component of child disability payment at the middle or highest rate in accordance with regulation 11(5) of the DACYP Regulations;]
       (ii) attendance allowance at the higher rate;
      (iii) the daily living component of personal independence payment; [[20] ...]
  [[20] (iv) the daily living component of adult disability payment at the standard or enhanced rate; and]
  (b) the renter is, by virtue of their disability, not reasonably able to share a bedroom with the joint renter.]
(7) [[11] ...]
(8) Where a renter, or one or both of joint renters, satisfy the disabled child condition in relation to one or more children, they are entitled to as many additional bedrooms as are necessary to ensure that each such child has their own bedroom.
[[11] (9) The renter is, or joint renters are, entitled to one additional bedroom for each of the following that apply—
  (a) one or more persons satisfy the overnight care condition;
  (b) the renter, or one or both of joint renters, satisfies the foster parent condition;
  (c) the renter, or one or both of joint renters, satisfies the disabled child condition; or
  (d) the renter, or one or both of joint renters, satisfies the disabled person condition.]]

Housing cost contributions

Housing cost contributions
13.—(1) In calculating the amount of the housing costs element under Part 4 or 5 of this Schedule, a deduction is to be made in respect of each non-dependant who is a member of the renter's extended benefit unit.
  (2) Paragraph (1) is subject to paragraphs 15 and 16.
  (3) Any amount to be deducted under sub-paragraph (1) is referred to in this Schedule as a "housing cost contribution".

2.468

Amount of housing cost contributions

2.469　　**14.**—(1) The amount of each housing cost contribution to be deducted under paragraph 13 is [²¹ £85.73].

(2) Deductions are not to be made until the amount has been determined which results from all other steps in the calculation required in relation to the renter under Parts 4 and 5 of this Schedule.

(3) Where the sum of all the housing cost contributions to be deducted in the renter's case exceeds the amount referred to in sub-paragraph (2)—

　　(a) the amount determined under this Schedule is to be reduced to nil; but
　　(b) no further reduction in respect of housing cost contributions is to be made from the renter's award.

Exempt renters

2.470　　**15.**—(1) No deduction is to be made under paragraph 13 in the case of—

　　(a) any renter who is a single person to whom sub-paragraph (2) applies; or
　　(b) any joint renter where at least one joint renter is a person to whom sub-paragraph (2) applies.

(2) This sub-paragraph applies to—

　　(a) a person who is [⁹ . . .] blind;
　　(b) a person in receipt of the care component of disability living allowance at the middle or highest rate;
[¹⁸ (ba) a person in receipt of the care component of child disability payment at the middle or highest rate in accordance with regulation 11(5) of the DACYP Regulations;]
　　(c) a person in receipt of attendance allowance;
　　(d) a person in receipt of the daily living component of personal independence payment;
[²⁰ (da) a person in receipt of the daily living component of adult disability payment at the standard or enhanced rate;]
　　(e) a person who is entitled to a payment within paragraph (b), (c) [²⁰, (d) or (da)] but is not receiving it under, as the case may be—
　　　　(i) regulation 8 of the Social Security (Disability Living Allowance) Regulations 1991,
　　　　(ii) regulation 6 of the Social Security (Attendance Allowance) Regulations 1991,
　　　　(iii) regulation 21 of the Social Security (General Benefit) Regulations 1982 [²⁰ . . .]
　　　　(iv) regulations under section 86 of the Act (payment of personal independence payment while a person is a hospital in-patient) [²⁰; or]
　　[²⁰ (v) regulation 28 (effect of admission to hospital on ongoing entitlement to Adult Disability Payment) of the Disability Assistance for Working Age People (Scotland) Regulations 2022].

No deduction for housing cost contributions in respect of certain non-dependants

2.471　　**16.**—(1) No deduction is to be made under paragraph 13 in respect of any non-dependant who is a member of the renter's extended benefit unit to whom sub-paragraph (2) applies.

(2) This sub-paragraph applies to—

　　(a) a person who is under 21 years old;
　　(b) a person in receipt of state pension credit;
　　(c) a person in receipt of the care component of disability living allowance at the middle or highest rate;
　　(d) a person in receipt of attendance allowance;
　　(e) a person in receipt of the daily living component of personal independence payment;
[²⁰ (ea) a person in receipt of the daily living component of adult disability payment at the standard or enhanced rate;]
　　(f) a person who is entitled to a payment within paragraph (c), (d) [²⁰, (e) or (ea)] but is not receiving it under, as the case may be—
　　　　(i) regulation 8 of the Social Security (Disability Living Allowance) Regulations 1991,
　　　　(ii) regulation 6 of the Social Security (Attendance Allowance) Regulations 1991,
　　　　(iii) regulation 21 of the Social Security (General Benefit) Regulations 1982 [²⁰ . . .]
　　　　(iv) regulations under section 86 of the Act (payment of personal independence payment while a person is a hospital in-patient) [²⁰; or]
　　[²⁰ (v) regulation 28 (effect of admission to hospital on ongoing entitlement to Adult Disability Payment) of the Disability Assistance for Working Age People (Scotland) Regulations 2022].

    (g)   a person in receipt of carer's allowance;

    (h)   a person who is a prisoner;

    (i)   a person who is responsible for a child under 5 years old.

[⁴ (j)   a person who is a member of the armed forces away on operations who—

        (i)   is the son, daughter, step-son or step-daughter of a renter or joint renters, and

       (ii)   resided with the renter or joint renters immediately before leaving to go on operations and intends to return to reside with the renter or joint renters at the end of the operations.]

Calculations involving more than one accommodation

Single calculation for renter treated as occupying single accommodation

17.—(1) This paragraph applies to any renter where, under paragraph 4 of Schedule 3 (claimant housed in two dwellings by provider of social housing), two dwellings ("accommodation A" and "accommodation B") occupied by a renter are treated as the single accommodation in respect of which the renter meets the occupation condition.   **2.472**

(2) The amount of the renter's housing costs element is to be determined by a single calculation in respect of accommodation A and accommodation B as if they were one, taking account of—

    (a)   all relevant payments in respect of accommodation A and all relevant payments in respect of accommodation B; and

    (b)   the total number of bedrooms in accommodation A and accommodation B taken together.

[¹⁴ (3) The single calculation is to be made under Part 5 of this Schedule in any case where the renter's liability to make rent payments in respect of accommodation A and accommodation B is to a provider of social housing.]

(4) In any other case, the single calculation is to be made under Part 4 of this Schedule.

Calculation where move to new accommodation delayed for adaptations for disabled person

18.—(1) Sub-paragraph (2) applies to any renter where, under paragraph 5 of Schedule 3 (moving home: adaptations to new home for disabled person), the renter meets the occupation condition in respect of both the new accommodation and the old accommodation.   **2.473**

(2) The amount of the renter's housing costs element under this Schedule is to be calculated as follows.

Step 1

Calculate an amount in accordance with Part 4 or Part 5 of this Schedule (as the case may be) in respect of both—

    (a)   the new accommodation; and

    (b)   the old accommodation.

Step 2

Add together the amounts determined in step 1.

Step 3

If a deduction was made for housing cost contributions in respect of both the new accommodation and the old accommodation, take the amount of the housing costs contributions deducted in respect of the new accommodation and add that to the amount resulting from step 2.

(3) In this paragraph, references to "the new accommodation" and "the old accommodation" are to be understood in accordance with paragraph 5 of Schedule 3.

Calculation where renter moves out because of reasonable fear of violence

19.—(1) Sub-paragraph (2) applies to any renter where, under paragraph 6(2) of Schedule 3 (claimant living in other accommodation because of reasonable fear of violence), the renter meets the occupation condition in respect of both the home accommodation and the other accommodation.   **2.474**

(2) The amount of the renter's housing costs element under this Schedule is to be calculated as follows:

Step 1

Calculate an amount in accordance with Part 4 or Part 5 of this Schedule (as the case may be) in respect of—
(a) the home accommodation; and
(b) the other accommodation.

Step 2

Add together the amounts determined in step 1.

Step 3

If a deduction was made for housing cost contributions in respect of both the home accommodation and the other accommodation—
(c) determine which accommodation the renter normally occupies as their home; and
(d) take the amount of the housing costs contributions deducted in respect of the accommodation not so occupied and add that to the amount resulting from step 2.
(3) In this paragraph, references to "the home accommodation" and "the other accommodation" are to be understood in accordance with paragraph 6 of Schedule 3.

PART 4
PRIVATE RENTED SECTOR [14 ...]

Application of Part 4
2.475
20.—[14 (1) This Part applies to renters who are liable to make rent payments to a person other than a provider of social housing.]
(2) Sub-paragraph (1) applies irrespective of whether renters are also liable to make service charge payments.

Meaning of "temporary accommodation"
2.476
21. [14 . . .]

The calculation of the housing costs element under this Part

The amount of housing costs element under this Part
2.477
22. The amount of the renter's housing costs element under this Part is to be calculated as follows:

Step 1

Determine—
(a) the amount of the renter's core rent; and
(b) the amount of the renter's cap rent,
and identify which is the lower amount (if both amounts are the same, that is the identified amount).

Step 2

Deduct the sum of the housing cost contributions (if any) under paragraph 13 from the amount identified in step 1.
The result is the amount of the renter's housing costs element calculated under this Part.

Core rent
2.478
23. Except where paragraph 24 applies, the renter's core rent is to be determined as follows:

Step 1

Determine the amount of each relevant payment to be taken into account under paragraph 6.

Step 2

Determine the period in respect of which each relevant payment is payable and, in accordance with paragraph 7, determine the amount of the payment in respect of a month.

Step 3

If there is more than one relevant payment, add together the amounts determined in step 2 in relation to all relevant payments.
The result is the renter's core rent.

Core rent for joint tenants

2.479

   24.—(1) This paragraph applies where, in respect of the accommodation occupied by the renter, one or more persons other than the renter are liable to make relevant payments which are of the same description as those for which the renter is liable and which are to be taken into account under paragraph 6.

   (2) The following steps are to be taken in order to determine the renter's core rent.

Step 1

   Determine the total of all relevant payments referred to in sub-paragraph (1) for which the renter and others are liable in respect of the accommodation taken as a whole.

Step 2

   Determine the period in respect of which each relevant payment is payable and, in accordance with paragraph 7, determine the amount of the payment in respect of a month.

Step 3

   Add together all of the amounts determined in step 2 in relation to all relevant payments.

Step 4

   Find the allocated amount in accordance with whichever of sub-paragraphs (3) to (5) applies in the renter's case.

   The result is the renter's core rent.

   (3) Where the only persons liable to make relevant payments are listed persons, the allocated amount is the amount resulting from step 3 in sub-paragraph (2).

   (4) Where the persons liable for the relevant payments are one or more listed persons and one or more other persons, the allocated amount is to be found by the applying the formula—

$$\left(\frac{A}{B}\right) \times C$$

   where—

   "A" is the amount resulting from step 3 in sub-paragraph (2),

   "B" is the total number of all persons (including listed persons) liable to make the relevant payments, and

   "C" is the number of listed persons [5 liable to make relevant payments].

   (5) If the Secretary of State is satisfied that it would be unreasonable to allocate the amount resulting from step 3 in sub-paragraph (2) in accordance with sub-paragraph (4), that amount is to be allocated in such manner as the Secretary of State considers appropriate in all the circumstances, having regard (among other things) to the number of persons liable and the proportion of the relevant payments for which each of them is liable.

Cap rent

2.480

   25.—(1) The renter's cap rent is to be determined as follows.

Step 1

   Determine the category of accommodation to which the renter is entitled under paragraphs 8 to 12 and 26 to 29.

Step 2

   Having regard to the determination at step 1, determine the maximum allowable amount for the renter under sub-paragraph (2) or (4) (as the case may be).

   The result is the renter's cap rent.

   (2) The maximum allowable amount to be used in relation to the renter is the local housing allowance which applies at the relevant time to—

     (a) the broad rental market area in which the renter's accommodation is situated; and

     (b) the category of accommodation determined at step 1 as that to which the renter is entitled.

   (3) But the maximum allowable amount in relation to the renter is to be determined under sub-paragraph (4) in any case where—

    (a) paragraph 4 of Schedule 3 (claimant housed in two dwellings by provider of social housing) applies to the renter; and

    (b) the maximum allowable amount determined under sub-paragraph (2) for the renter in relation to accommodation A and the amount so determined in relation to accommodation B are different (references to accommodation A and accommodation B are to be understood in accordance with paragraph 4 of Schedule 3); and

    (c) a single calculation is to be made in relation to the renter under paragraph 17 (renter treated as occupying single accommodation).

(4) In any such case, the maximum allowable amount to be used in making the single calculation required by paragraph 17—

    (a) is to be determined by reference to the accommodation for which the amount referred to in sub-paragraph (3)(b) is lower when the calculation is first made; and

    (b) is to continue to be determined by reference to that accommodation for so long as paragraph 4 of Schedule 3 applies to the renter in respect of the same accommodation A and the same accommodation B; and

    (c) is to be re-determined in accordance with paragraphs (a) and (b) on each occasion when the renter is re-housed in any other accommodation, provided that paragraph 4 of Schedule 3 continues to apply to the renter.

(5) In this paragraph—

"broad rental market area" means the broad rental market area determined under article 3 of the Rent Officers Order 2013;

"local housing allowance", in relation to a broad rental market area, means the amount determined by a rent officer for that area under article 4 of the Rent Officers Order 2013;

"relevant time" means the time at which the amount of the renter's housing costs element is calculated under paragraph 22.

Further provisions about size criteria for cases to which this Part applies

Four bedroom limit

2.481   **26.** In calculating the amount of a renter's housing costs element under paragraph 22, no renter is entitled to more than 4 bedrooms.

Specified renters entitled to shared accommodation only

2.482   **27.**—(1) In calculating the amount of a renter's housing costs element under paragraph 22, any specified renter (within the meaning of paragraph 28) is entitled to shared accommodation only.

(2) "Shared accommodation" means the category of accommodation specified in paragraph 1(a) of Schedule 1 to the Rent Officers Order 2013.

Meaning of "specified renters"

2.483   **28.**—(1) For the purposes of paragraph 27, "specified renter" means a renter in respect of whom all of the following conditions are met.

(2) The first condition is that the renter is a single person (or a member of a couple claiming as a single person) who—

    (a) is under 35 years old; and

    (b) is not an excepted person under paragraph 29.

(3) The second condition is that the renter is not responsible for any children or qualifying young persons.

(4) The third condition is that no person is a non-dependant in relation to the renter.

Renters excepted from shared accommodation

2.484   **29.**—(1) "Excepted person" means any renter ("E") who falls within any of sub-paragraphs (2) to [²² (9C)].

[¹⁰ (2) E is at least 18 but under [¹⁷ 25] years old and was a care leaver (within the meaning of regulation 8) before reaching the age of 18.]

(3) [¹⁰ . . .]

(4) E is at least [¹⁷ 16] but under 35 years old and—

    (a) has, for a total of at least 3 months (whether or not continuously), lived in one or more hostels for homeless people; and

    (b) whilst E was living in such a hostel, was offered and has accepted services which the Secretary of State considers are intended to assist E to be rehabilitated or resettled within the community.

(5) E is under 35 years old and is in receipt of—

    (a) the care component of disability living allowance at the middle or highest rate;

[^{18} (aa) the care component of child disability payment at the middle or highest rate in accordance with regulation 11(5) of the DACYP Regulations;]

   (b) attendance allowance; [^{20} . . .]

   (c) the daily living component of personal independence payment[^{20}; or]

[^{20} (d) the daily living component of adult disability payment at the standard or enhanced rate].

(6) In relation to England and Wales, E is under 35 years old and is the subject of active multi-agency management pursuant to arrangements established by a responsible authority under section 325(2) of the Criminal Justice Act 2003 (arrangements for assessing etc. risks posed by certain offenders).

(7) In relation to Scotland, E is under 35 years old and is the subject of active multi-agency risk management pursuant to arrangements established by the responsible authorities under section 10(1) of the 2005 Act (arrangements for assessing and managing risks posed by certain offenders).

(8) In relation to Scotland, E is under 35 years old and—

   (a) section 10(1) of the 2005 Act does not apply to E by reason only of the fact that section 10(1)(b) or (d) has not been brought fully into force; and

   (b) E is considered by the Secretary of State to be a person who may cause serious harm to the public at large.

(9) In relation to Scotland, E is under 35 years old and—

   (a) section 10(1) of the 2005 Act does not apply to E by reason only of the fact that section 10(1)(e) has not been brought fully into force; and

   (b) by reason of an offence of which E has been convicted, E is considered by the Secretary of State to be a person who may cause serious harm to the public at large.

[^{15} (9A) E is under 35 years old and satisfies the foster parent condition (within the meaning of paragraph 12(4)).]

[^{22} (9B) E is under 35 years old and—

   (a) after attaining the age of 16 had domestic violence inflicted upon or threatened against them ("the victim") by their partner or former partner, or by a relative; and

   (b) provides evidence from a person acting in an official capacity which demonstrates that—

      (i) the victim's circumstances are consistent with their having had domestic violence inflicted upon or threatened against them; and

      (ii) the victim has contacted a person acting in an official capacity in relation to such an incident.

(9C) E is under 35 years old and has been the subject of a positive conclusive grounds determination relating to modern slavery.]

(10) In this paragraph—

"the 2005 Act" means the Management of Offenders etc. (Scotland) Act 2005;

"care home", "registered charity" and "voluntary organisation" have the meaning given in Schedule 1;

[^{22} "competent authority" means a person who is a competent authority within the meaning of the Trafficking Convention;

"compulsory labour", "forced labour", "servitude" and "slavery" have the same meaning as in Article 4 of the Convention for the Protection of Human Rights and Fundamental Freedoms, agreed by the Council of Europe at Rome on 4th November 1950 as it has effect for the time being in relation to the United Kingdom;]

"hostel" means a building—

   (a) in which there is provided, for persons generally or for a class of persons, domestic accommodation, otherwise than in separate and self-contained premises, and either board or facilities for the preparation of food adequate to the needs of those persons, or both; and

   (b) which—

      (i) is managed or owned by a provider of social housing other than a local authority, or

      (ii) is operated other than on a commercial basis and in respect of which funds are provided wholly or in part by a government department or agency or a local authority, or

      (iii) is managed by a voluntary organisation or a registered charity and provides care, support or supervision with a view to assisting those persons to be rehabilitated or resettled within the community; and

   (c) which is not a care home;

"hostel for homeless people" means a hostel the main purpose of which is to provide accommodation together with care, support or supervision for homeless people with a view to assisting such persons to be rehabilitated or resettled within the community.

[²² "person acting in an official capacity" means a health care professional (within the meaning given by regulation 98(4)), a police officer, a registered social worker (within the meaning given by regulation 98(4)), the victim's employer, or any public, voluntary, or charitable body which has had direct contact with the victim in connection with domestic violence;

"positive conclusive grounds determination relating to modern slavery" means a determination made by a competent authority that an individual is a victim of trafficking in human beings, slavery, servitude or forced or compulsory labour;

"the Trafficking Convention" means the Council of Europe Convention on Action against Trafficking in Human Beings (done at Warsaw on 16th May 2005);

"trafficking in human beings" has the same meaning as in the Trafficking Convention.]

PART 5

SOCIAL RENTED SECTOR [¹⁴ ...]

Application of Part 5

2.485   30.—[¹⁴ (1) This Part applies to renters who are liable to make rent payments to a provider of social housing.]

(2) Sub-paragraph (1) applies irrespective of whether renters are also liable to make service charge payments.

[¹³ Amount taken into account as the relevant payment]

Deduction from relevant payments of amounts relating to use of particular accommodation

2.486   31. In determining the amount of any relevant payment to be taken into account under paragraph 6, a deduction is to be made for any amount which the Secretary of State is satisfied—

(a) is included in the relevant payment; but

(b) relates to the supply to the accommodation of a commodity (such as water or fuel) for use by any member of the renter's extended benefit unit.

Power to apply to rent officer if relevant payments excessive

2.487   32.—(1) Sub-paragraph (2) applies where it appears to the Secretary of State that the amount of any relevant payment for which the renter is liable in respect of accommodation occupied by the renter is greater than it is reasonable to meet by way of the housing costs element under this Part.

(2) The Secretary of State may apply to a rent officer for a determination to be made as to the amount of the relevant payment by the officer in exercise of the officer's Housing Act functions.

(3) Sub-paragraph (4) applies in any case where a rent officer determines that a landlord might, at the time of the application under sub-paragraph (2), reasonably have expected to obtain a lower amount of the description of relevant payment referred to the rent officer.

(4) The lower amount determined by the rent officer is to be used in making the calculation under this Part, instead of the amount of the relevant payment for which the renter is liable, unless the Secretary of State is satisfied that it is not appropriate to use that lower amount.

2.488   **[¹³ Reduction under tenant incentive scheme**

32A.—(1) Where a reduction in the rent or service charge payments for which a renter would otherwise have been liable is applied by a provider of social housing under an approved tenant incentive scheme, the amount of any relevant payment to be taken into account under paragraph 6 is to be determined as if no such reduction had been applied.

(2) In paragraph (1) "approved tenant incentive scheme" means a scheme which is—

(a) operated by a provider of social housing and designed to avoid rent arrears by allowing reductions in rent or service charges or other advantages in return for meeting specified conditions; and

(b) approved by the Secretary of State.]

The calculation of the housing costs element under this Part

The amount of housing costs element

2.489   33. The amount of the renter's housing costs element under this Part is to be calculated by reference to the formula—

$$S - HCC$$

where—

"S" is the amount resulting from whichever of paragraph 34 or 35 applies in the renter's case, and

"HCC" is the sum of the housing cost contributions (if any) under paragraph 13.

Determining the amount from which HCC deductions are to be made

34. Except where paragraph 35 applies, amount S referred to in paragraph 33 is to be found as follows: **2.490**

Step 1

Determine which relevant payments are to be taken into account under paragraph 6 and determine the amount of each of them (applying paragraphs 31 and 32(3) and (4) as necessary).

Step 2

Determine the period in respect of which each relevant payment is payable and, in accordance with paragraph 7, determine the amount of the payment in respect of a month.

Step 3

If there is more than one relevant payment, add together the amounts determined in step 2 in relation to all relevant payments.

Step 4

Determine under paragraph 36(1) whether an under-occupation deduction is to be made and, if one is to be made, determine the amount of the deduction under paragraph 36(2) and deduct it from the amount resulting from step 2 or 3 (as the case may be).

The result is amount S from which the sum of the housing costs contributions are to be deducted under paragraph 33.

Determining the amount from which HCC deductions are to be made: joint tenants

35.—(1) This paragraph applies where, in respect of the accommodation occupied by the renter, one or more persons other than the renter is liable to make relevant payments which are of the same description as those for which the renter is liable and which are to be taken into account under paragraph 6.   **2.491**

(2) Amount S referred to in paragraph 33 is to be found as follows:

Step 1

Determine the total of all relevant payments referred to in sub-paragraph (1) for which the renter and others are liable in respect of the accommodation taken as a whole (applying paragraphs 31 and 32(3) and (4) as necessary).

Step 2

Determine the period in respect of which each relevant payment is payable and, in accordance with paragraph 7, determine the amount of the payment in respect of a month.

Step 3

Add together all of the amounts determined in step 2 in relation to all relevant payments.

Step 4

Find amount S in accordance with whichever of sub-paragraphs (3) to (5) applies in the renter's case.

The result is amount S from which the sum of the housing costs contributions are to be deducted under paragraph 33.

(3) Where the only persons liable to make relevant payments are listed persons, amount S is the amount resulting from step 3 in sub-paragraph (2) less the amount of the under-occupation deduction (if any) required by paragraph 36.

(4) Where the persons liable for the relevant payments are one or more listed persons and one or more other persons, amount S is to be found by the applying the formula—

$$\left(\frac{A}{B}\right) \times C$$

where—
"A" is the amount resulting from step 3 in sub-paragraph (2),
"B" is the total number of all persons (including listed persons) liable to make the relevant payments, and
"C" is the number of listed persons [⁵ liable to make relevant payments].

(5) If the Secretary of State is satisfied that it would be unreasonable to determine amount S in accordance with sub-paragraph (4), amount S is to be determined in such manner as the Secretary of State considers appropriate in all the circumstances, having regard (among other things) to the number of persons liable and the proportion of the relevant payments for which each of them is liable.

Under-occupancy deduction

2.492

36.—(1) A deduction for under-occupancy is to be made under this paragraph where the number of bedrooms in the accommodation exceeds the number of bedrooms to which the renter is entitled under paragraphs 8 to 12.

(2) Where a deduction is to be made, the amount of the deduction is to be determined by the formula—

$$A \times B$$

where—
"A"—
  (a) in relation to any deduction under paragraph 34, is the amount resulting from step 2 or 3 in that paragraph (as the case may be), or
  (b) in relation to any deduction under paragraph 35(3), is the amount resulting from step 3 in paragraph 35(2);
"B" is the relevant percentage.

(3) The relevant percentage is 14% in the case of one excess bedroom.
(4) The relevant percentage is 25% in the case of two or more excess bedrooms.
(5) No deduction for under-occupation is to be made in calculating the amount of the renter's housing costs element under this Part in any case to which regulation 26(4) to (6) (shared ownership) applies.

[¹⁹ (6) No deduction for under occupation is to be made in calculating the amount of a renter's housing cost element under this part where—
  (i) domestic violence has been inflicted upon or threatened against the claimant or a member of the claimant's extended benefit unit ("the victim") by that person's partner or former partner, or by a relative;
  (ii) the victim is not living at the same address as the person who inflicted or threatened the domestic violence, except where that person is a qualifying young person and is a dependant of a member of the claimant's extended benefit unit; and
  (iii) the claimant provides evidence from a person acting in an official capacity which demonstrates that the claimant is living in a property adapted under a sanctuary scheme and—
    (aa) the victim's circumstances are consistent with those of a person who has had domestic violence inflicted upon or threatened against them; and
    (bb) the victim has made contact with the person acting in an official capacity in relation to such an incident;
  (b) in this paragraph—
    [²² "person acting in an official capacity" has the meaning given to it in regulation 98(4) of these Regulations;]
    [²² ...]
    "sanctuary scheme" means a scheme operated by a provider of social housing enabling victims of domestic violence to remain in their homes through the installation of additional security to the property or the perimeter of the property at which the victim resides.]

AMENDMENTS

1. Universal Credit (Miscellaneous Amendments) Regulations 2013 (SI 2013/803), reg.2(3)(a) (April 29, 2013).
2. Universal Credit (Miscellaneous Amendments) Regulations 2013 (SI 2013/803), reg.2(3)(b)(i) (April 29, 2013).
3. Universal Credit (Miscellaneous Amendments) Regulations 2013 (SI 2013/803), reg.2(3)(b)(ii) (April 29, 2013).
4. Universal Credit (Miscellaneous Amendments) Regulations 2013 (SI 2013/803), reg.2(3)(e) (April 29, 2013).
5. Social Security (Miscellaneous Amendments) (No.2) Regulations 2013 (SI 2013/1508), reg.3(10) (July 29, 2013).
6. Housing Benefit and Universal Credit (Size Criteria) (Miscellaneous Amendments) Regulations 2013 (SI 2013/2828), reg.4 (December 4, 2013).
7. Universal Credit and Miscellaneous Amendments Regulations 2014 (SI 2014/597) reg.2(13) (April 28, 2014).
8. Housing Benefit and Universal Credit (Supported Accommodation) (Amendment) Regulations 2014 (SI 2014/771) reg.2(3) (November 3, 2014).
9. Universal Credit and Miscellaneous Amendments (No.2) Regulations 2014 (SI 2014/2888) reg.3(1)(c) (November 26, 2014, or in the case of existing awards, the first assessment period beginning on or after November 26, 2014).
10. Universal Credit (Care Leavers and Looked After Children) Amendment Regulations 2016 (SI 2016/543) reg.3 (May 26, 2016).
11. Housing Benefit and Universal Credit (Size Criteria) (Miscellaneous Amendments) Regulations 2017 (SI 2017/213) reg.6 (Assessment periods beginning on or after April 1, 2017).
12. Universal Credit (Housing Costs Element for claimants aged 18 to 21) (Amendment) Regulations 2017 (SI 2017/652) reg.2(1) and (3) (April 1, 2017).
13. Universal Credit (Tenant Incentive Scheme) Amendment Regulations 2017 (SI 2017/427) reg.2 (April 30, 2017).
14. Universal Credit (Miscellaneous Amendments, Saving and Transitional Provision) Regulations 2018 (SI 2018/65) reg.3(13) (April 11, 2018).
15. Universal Credit and Jobseeker's Allowance (Miscellaneous Amendments) Regulations 2018 (SI 2018/1129) reg.3(1) and (6)(d) (November 28, 2018).
16. Universal Credit and Jobseeker's Allowance (Miscellaneous Amendments) Regulations 2018 (SI 2018/1129) reg.3(1) and (6)(a)-(c) (December 31, 2018).
17. Social Security Benefits Up-rating Order 2021 (SI 2021/162) art.33(3) (assessment periods beginning on or after April 12, 2021.
18. Housing Benefit and Universal Credit (Care Leavers and Homeless) (Amendment) Regulations 2021 (SI 2021/546) reg.3 (May 31, 2021).
19. Social Security (Scotland) Act 2018 (Disability Assistance for Children and Young People) (Consequential Modifications) Order 2021 (SI 2021/786) Sch.11 para.8 (July 26, 2021).
20. Domestic Abuse Support (Relevant Accommodation and Housing Benefit and Universal Credit Sanctuary Schemes) (Amendment) Regulations 2021 (SI 2021/991) reg.4 (Assessment periods beginning on or after October 1, 2021).
21. Social Security (Disability Assistance for Working Age People) (Consequential Amendments) Order 2022 (SI 2022/177) art.13(8) (March 21, 2022).
22. Housing Benefit and Universal Credit (Victims of Domestic Abuse and Victims of Modern Slavery) (Amendment) Regulations 2022 (SI 2022/942) reg.3 (October 1, 2022).
23. Social Security Benefits Up-rating Order 2023 (SI 2022/316) art.33(3) (Assessment periods beginning on or after April 10, 2023).

DEFINITIONS

"the Act"—see reg.2.
"adult disability payment"—*ibid.*

"assessment period"—see WRA 2012 ss.40 and 7(2) and reg.21.
"attendance allowance"—see reg.2.
"blind"—*ibid.*
"care leaver"—see regs 2 and 8.
"carer's allowance"—see reg.2.
"child"—see WRA 2012 s.40.
"child disability payment"—see reg.2.
"claim"—see WRA 2012 s.40.
"claimant"—*ibid.*
"couple"—see WRA 2012 ss.39 and 40.
"the DACYP Regulations"—see reg.2.
"disability living allowance"—*ibid.*
"disabled"—see WRA 2012 s.40.
"foster parent"—see reg.2.
"joint claimants"—see WRA 2012 s.40.
"local authority"—see reg.2.
"personal independence payment"—*ibid.*
"prisoner"—see reg.2 as modified by SI 2020/409.
"qualifying young person"—see WRA 2012 ss.40 and 10(5) and regs 2 and 5.
"registered as blind"—see reg.2.
"single person"—see WRA 2012 ss.40 and 1(2)(a).

GENERAL NOTE

2.493   *Paragraphs 1–7*
This Schedule concerns the calculation of the housing costs element for "renters" (see para.1(2)). For the definition of "renter" see para.2. References to "joint renters" are to joint claimants who are renters (para.1(2)).

For a renter (or joint renters) to be entitled to a housing costs element under this Schedule, they must meet the payment, liability and occupation conditions in respect of one or more "relevant payments" (para.6(1) and (2)).

"Relevant payments" for the purpose of Sch.4 mean rent payments (for the meaning of rent payments see para.2 of Sch.1 and note the exclusions in para.3) and service charges (on which see para. 7 of Sch.1 in relation to service charge payments calculated under Pt 4 of this Schedule and paras 7 and 8 of Sch.1 in relation to service charge payments calculated under Pt 5 of this Schedule (para.3)). Relevant payments are calculated as a monthly amount (see para.7). Where a renter has the benefit of rent and/or service charge free periods (see the definition of "rent free period" in para.7(4)), the conversion to a monthly figure is based on a standard 52 week year (see para. 7(3) and the formula in para.7(3A)). In *R. (Caine) v Secretary of State for Work and Pensions* [2020] EWHC 2482 (Admin), the High Court (Julian Knowles J) rejected a challenge to the formulae for converting weekly to monthly amounts.

Para 4 establishes an exception: no housing costs element is to be included in the universal credit award of any 16 or 17 year old renter who is a care leaver as defined in reg.8(4)). The former exclusion of certain 18-21 year olds from entitlement to hosuing costs (as to which see pp.359-360 and 388-389 of the 2018-19 edition of this volume) was revoked with effect from December 31, 2018 by SI 2018/1129.

Part 3 of this Schedule contains general provisions, which apply to all calculations under the Schedule. The rules in Pt 4 apply to renters in the private sector or who occupy temporary accommodation. Part 5 applies to renters in the social rented sector.

A housing costs element for renters is normally paid to the claimant as part of their universal credit award. However, it can be paid to another person (e.g. the claimant's landlord) if this appears to the Secretary of State to be necessary to protect the interest of the claimant, their partner, a child or qualifying young person for whom the claimant or their partner is responsible or a severely disabled person in respect of whom the claimant receives a carer element (see reg.58(1) of the Claims and Payments Regulations 2013).

Note also reg.39(4) of the Decisions and Appeals Regulations 2013 which provides that if the Secretary of State considers that he does not have all the relevant information or evidence to decide what housing costs element to award, the decision will be made on the basis of the housing costs element that can immediately be awarded.

Paragraphs 8–12 and 26–29

In order to calculate the amount of a renter's housing costs element, it is first necessary to decide the number of "bedrooms"—a word that is not defined—that they are allowed under "the size criteria" (para.8). This depends on who counts as a member of the renter's "extended benefit unit". **2.494**

The extended benefit unit comprises the renter, or joint renters, any child or qualifying young person (see reg.5) for whom the renter or either joint renter is responsible (see reg.4), and any non-dependant (para.9(1)).

A non-dependant is a person who normally lives in the renter's (or joint renters') accommodation and who is not excluded under para.9(2). There is no definition of "normally lives in the accommodation" but see the notes to reg.3(1) of the Income Support Regulations in Vol.V of this series on the general meaning of "residing with".

See paras 10–12 for the number of bedrooms allowed. Para.12 has been amended with effect from April 1, 2017 by SI 2017/213 to reflect the judgment of the Supreme Court in *R (Carmichael and Rourke) (formerly known as MA and Others) v Secretary of State for Work and Pensions* [2016] UKSC 58; [2016] 1 W.L.R. 4550 that the previous law discriminated unlawfully against adult couples who cannot share a bedroom because of the disabilities of at least one member of the couple and renters who need an extra room to accommodate an overnight carer for a disabled child.

The effect of the *Carmichael* decision was that, as they related to those groups, the restrictions in paras 10–12 had been unlawful since they came into force (and that the equivalent restrictions in the housing benefit schemes had been unlawful since April 1, 2013, when they came into force). As the legislation was only amended to remove the discrimination with effect from April 1, 2017, the question arose what the First-tier Tribunal and Upper Tribunal should do in appeals relating to the intervening period. In *Secretary of State for Work and Pensions v Carmichael and Sefton Council* [2018] EWCA Civ 548; [2018] 1 W.L.R. 3429, the Court of Appeal decided by a majority—and contrary to the previously orthodox view of the law—that courts and tribunals have no power to disapply either primary or secondary legislation that infringes Convention Rights. However, in *RR v Secretary of State for Work and Pensions* [2019] UKSC 52; [2019] 1 W.L.R. 6430, the Supreme Court allowed the claimant's appeal: see further the discussion in Vol.III.

Note that in the case of renters in the private sector or who occupy temporary accommodation (see para.21 for the meaning of "temporary accommodation") the maximum number of bedrooms allowed is four (see para.26). There is no limit for renters in the social rented sector. In addition, in the case of private sector renters and those in temporary accommodation, the housing costs element for single claimants (including a member of a couple who is claiming as a single person: see reg.3(3)) aged under 35, with no children or qualifying young persons for whom they are responsible and no non-dependants, is restricted to the local housing allowance rate for one bedroom shared accommodation, unless they are exempt from this restriction (see paras 27–29).

Under para.10, a renter is allowed one bedroom for each of the categories of people in they extended benefit unit listed in sub-para.(1). If a person falls into more than one category, they are treated as in the category that results in the renter being allowed the lowest number of bedrooms (see sub-para.(2)). Paragraph F3112 ADM gives the following example of when sub-para.(2) might apply. A couple have four children, two boys aged 15 and 6 and two girls aged 12 and 8. The two boys could be allocated one room and the two girls one room under sub-para.(1)(e). Alternatively, having allocated the two girls one room under sub-para.(1)(e), the boys could be allocated one room each under sub-para.(1)(f). But as the first alternative results in a fewer number of bedrooms, that will be the number of bedrooms (two) that is allocated.

Note that joint renters (i.e. joint claimants: see para.1(2)) are allowed one bedroom but a non-dependant couple will be allocated one bedroom each (although a housing cost contribution (see paras 13–16) may be made in respect of each of them).

Under para.12, a renter is allowed additional bedrooms for each of the following conditions that they meet: (i) the overnight care condition (for the test for this see sub-para.(3)); (ii) the foster parent condition (see sub-paras (4) and (5) for the test); or (iii) the disabled child condition (see sub-para.(6) for the test). If the renter satisfies two or more of the conditions, the number of additional bedrooms allowed will be the total for both or all conditions (sub-para.(9)).

If both joint renters (i.e. joint claimants: see para.1(2)) satisfy the overnight care condition, they will only be allowed one additional bedroom (sub-para.(7)). (Note that the overnight care condition does not apply in the case of a disabled child who needs overnight care, but see the Court of Appeal's judgment in *Rutherford* below.) Similarly, only one additional bedroom will be allowed if both joint renters meet the foster parent condition (sub-para.(7)). However, if one or both of them satisfies both these conditions, one additional bedroom will be allowed in respect of each condition.

Example

2.495   Amy and Nick are foster parents to two children. Nick also meets the overnight care condition. They are allowed two additional bedrooms. One for satisfying the overnight care condition and one for satisfying the foster parent condition.

If the disabled child condition is met, one additional bedroom will be allowed for each disabled child (see sub-para.(8)).

Note that the disabled child condition applies if it is the renter (or joint renters) *or* a member of the renter's extended benefit unit (i.e. including a non-dependant) who is responsible for the disabled child. The requirement under sub-para.(6)(b) that the child is "not reasonably able to share a room with another child" will be a matter of judgment, depending on the circumstances.

See para.11 for the circumstances in which a renter, a child or qualifying young person or a non-dependant will continue to count for the purpose of deciding the number of bedrooms allowed, despite being temporarily absent. Note also the temporary absence rule for a claimant (or claimants) in para.9 of Sch.3.

See also reg.37 (run-on after a death). Under this provision if a joint claimant, a child or qualifying young person (see reg.5) for whom a claimant was responsible (see reg.4), a severely disabled person for whom a claimant had regular and substantial caring responsibilities (see reg.30) or a non-dependant who was a member of the claimant's extended benefit unit (para.9(1)(c) and (2)) dies the claimant's universal credit award continues to be calculated as if the person had not died for the assessment period in which the death occurred and the following two assessment periods. Thus if such a death affects the number of bedrooms a renter is allowed, it will not do so for that run-on period.

Paragraphs 13–16

2.496   After the calculation of the renter's (or joint renters') housing costs element has been carried out under Pt 4 or 5 of this Schedule, a deduction (referred to as a "housing cost contribution") is made for non-dependants, unless they, or the renter, or joint renters, are exempt. The deduction has been £73.89 since April 8, 2019 for each non-dependant who is a member of the renter's extended benefit unit.

Paragraphs 17–19

2.497   See the notes to paras 4, 5 and 6 of Sch.3.

Paragraphs 20–25

2.498

The housing costs element for private sector renters and those in temporary accommodation (as defined in para.21) is calculated by taking the lower of the renter's core rent and their cap rent and deducting from that amount any housing cost contributions (para.22).

Core rent

2.499

If the renter is solely liable to make the relevant payments, their core rent is the total of the monthly equivalents of the rent payments (as defined in para.2 of Sch.1) and service charges (see para.7 of Sch.1) that they are liable (or treated as liable) to pay (para.23).

If the renter is jointly liable with another person or persons to make the relevant payments, their core rent is worked out by taking the total of the monthly equivalents of the rent payments and service charges for which they and the other person(s) are liable for the whole accommodation and applying the following rules.

If the only people who are jointly liable are "listed persons" (as defined in para.2) (i.e. the renter, their partner and any child or qualifying young person for whom either of them is responsible), the renter's core rent is that total amount (para.24(3)). If the liability is with one or more people who are not listed persons, the total amount is divided by the number of people who are liable and multiplied by the number of listed persons who are liable to make the relevant payments (para.24(4)). This is the renter's core rent. If, however, the Secretary of State (and on appeal a tribunal) is satisfied that it would be unreasonable to apportion the liability in this way, it is to be apportioned in a way that is appropriate in the circumstances (para.24(5)). Paragraph F3197 ADM gives the following example of where such an adjustment might be appropriate. Two brothers are joint tenants of a three bedroom property. One brother has his daughter living with him and pays two thirds of the rent. The decision maker considers that this is reasonable and that the appropriate core rent for that brother is two thirds (not half) of the rent payable.

Cap rent

2.500

A renter's cap rent depends on the category of dwelling, i.e. how many bedrooms they are allowed under the size criteria, subject to the four bedroom limit (see paras 8–12 and 26–29). Their cap rent is the local housing allowance that applies at the time their housing costs element is calculated for that category of dwelling in the area in which they live (para.25(1) and (2)). For how the cap rent is calculated if para.4 of Sch.3 (claimant housed in two dwellings by provider of social housing) applies, see the note to para.4 of Sch.3.

Paragraphs 30–36

2.501

The housing costs element for social sector renters (other than those in temporary accommodation, as defined in para.21) is calculated as follows. First, a deduction is made from any relevant payments (as defined in para.6) of any amount that is for the supply of a commodity (e.g. water or fuel) to the accommodation for use by the renter or any member of their extended benefit unit (para.31). Secondly, if, on the application of the Secretary of State, a rent officer has determined that a landlord might reasonably expect to get a lower amount than the amount of the relevant payment the renter pays, that lower figure will be used in the calculation of the renter's housing costs element, unless the Secretary of State (or on appeal a tribunal) considers that it is not appropriate to use that lower amount (para.32). An example might be where the rent is higher because it includes payment for modifications made to enable a disabled person to live in the property (see para.F3253 ADM) but the wording of para.32(4) is quite wide and is not restricted to this type of situation. Note, however, that (like housing benefit) there is no right of appeal against "so much of a decision as adopts a decision of a rent officer . . ." (para.6 of Sch.3 to the Decisions and Appeals Regulations 2013).

Thirdly, if the number of bedrooms in the accommodation is more than the number the renter is allowed under paras 8–12, an "under-occupation deduction" will be made. The reduction is 14 per cent in the case of one excess bedroom and 25 per cent in the case of two or more excess bedrooms (see para.36).

If a renter is solely liable to make the relevant payments, this deduction will be made from the monthly equivalent of the total of the rent payments and service charges that they are liable (or treated as liable) to pay, as reduced in accordance with paras 31 and 32(3) and (4), if applicable (para.34, step 4).

If the renter is jointly liable with another person or persons to make the relevant payments, an under-occupancy deduction will only be made if the only people who are jointly liable are "listed persons" (as defined in para.2) (i.e. the renter, their partner and any child or qualifying young person for whom either of them is responsible) (para.35(3)). If the joint liability is with one or more people who are not listed persons, no under-occupancy deduction will be made (there is no reference to such a deduction in para.35(4)).

Note also that no under-occupancy deduction is made in the case of a shared ownership tenancy (see para.36(5)).

Under para.35(3)-(5) the rules for working out the amount of the renter's housing costs element if they are jointly liable with another person or persons to make the relevant payments are the same that apply for the purpose of working out a renter's core rent under Part 4 of this Schedule (see above).

A deduction will be made for any housing cost contribution (para.33).

The new para.36(6) is made to remedy the legislative incompatibility with Convention rights identified by the First Section of the ECtHR in *JD & A v United Kingdom* (Apps 32949/17 and 34614/17) [2019] ECHR 753. A victim of domestic violence living in "sanctuary scheme" accommodation was discriminated against, contrary to art.14 of the ECHR read with art.1 of Protocol 1, by having an under-occupation deduction made from her benefit. The effect on her was disproportionately prejudicial (see [91] and [103]–[105]): a major aim of the under-occupation deduction policy was encouraging tenants to move to smaller accommodation, but sanctuary schemes existed to allow tenants to stay where they were, and the UK provided no weighty reasons to justify prioritising the former aim over the latter.

The decision of the ECtHR conflicts directly with the decision of the Supreme Court in *R. (Carmichael) v Secretary of State for Work and Pensions* [2016] UKSC 58; [2016] 1 W.L.R. 4550, where the same argument from the same litigant (*A*) was rejected by a majority of the Court (Hale DPSC and Carnwath JSC dissenting). The UK's request for the case to be referred to the Grand Chamber was rejected, so the ECtHR decision is final.

Regulation 26(3)

SCHEDULE 5

HOUSING COSTS ELEMENT FOR OWNER-OCCUPIERS

PART I

GENERAL

Introduction

2.502

1.—(1) This Schedule contains provisions about claimants to whom regulation 26(3) applies.

(2) Claimants who fall within sub-paragraph (1) are referred to in this Schedule as "owner-occupiers" (and references to "joint owner-occupiers" are to joint claimants to whom regulation 26(3) applies).

(3) Part 2 of this Schedule sets out an exception to section 11(1) of the Act for certain owner-occupiers in whose case an award of universal credit is not to include an amount of housing costs element calculated under this Schedule.

(4) Part 3 of this Schedule provides for a qualifying period that is to elapse before an amount of housing costs element calculated under this Schedule may be included in an owner-occupier's award of universal credit.

(5) Part 4 provides for the calculation of the amount of housing costs element to be included under this Schedule in an owner-occupier's award of universal credit.

Interpretation

2. In this Schedule—   2.503

[¹[⁷ . . .]]

[⁷. . .]

"joint owner-occupier" has the meaning given in paragraph 1;

[⁷ ...]

"owner-occupier" means a single owner-occupier within the meaning of paragraph 1(2) or each of joint owner-occupiers;

"qualifying period" has the meaning given in paragraph 5;

[¹ "relevant date" means, in relation to an owner-occupier, the date on which an amount of housing costs element calculated under this Schedule is first included in the owner-occupier's award;]

"relevant payments" has the meaning given in paragraph 3;

[⁷. . .]

"Relevant payments" for purposes of this Schedule

3.—[⁷ (1) "Relevant payments" means one or more payments which are service charge pay-   2.504
ments.]

(2) [⁷ ...]

(3) "Service charge payments" is to be understood in accordance with paragraphs 7 and 8 of that Schedule.

PART 2

EXCEPTION TO INCLUSION OF HOUSING COSTS ELEMENT

No housing costs element where owner-occupier has any earned income

4.—(1) Section 11(1) of the Act (housing costs) does not apply to any owner-occupier in   2.505
relation to an assessment period where—

  (a) the owner-occupier has any earned income; or

  (b) if the owner-occupier is a member of a couple, either member of the couple has any earned income.

(2) Sub-paragraph (1) applies irrespective of the nature of the work engaged in, its duration or the amount of the earned income.

(3) Nothing in this paragraph prevents an amount calculated under Schedule 4 from being included in the award of any claimant who falls within regulation 26(4) to (6) (shared ownership).

PART 3

NO HOUSING COSTS ELEMENT FOR QUALIFYING PERIOD

No housing costs element under this Schedule for qualifying period

5.—(1) An owner-occupier's award of universal credit is not to include any amount of   2.506
housing costs element calculated under this Schedule until the beginning of the assessment period that follows the assessment period in which the qualifying period ends.

(2) "Qualifying period" means a period of—

  (a) in the case of a new award, [⁶ 9] consecutive assessment periods in relation to which—

(i) the owner-occupier has been receiving universal credit, and

(ii) would otherwise qualify for the inclusion of an amount calculated under this Schedule in their award;

(b) in any case where an amount calculated under this Schedule has for any reason ceased to be included in the award, [6 9] consecutive assessment periods in relation to which the owner-occupier would otherwise qualify for the inclusion of an amount calculated under this Schedule in their award.

(3) Where, before the end of a qualifying period, an owner-occupier for any reason ceases to qualify for the inclusion of an amount calculated under this Schedule—

(a) that qualifying period stops running; and

(b) a new qualifying period starts only when the owner-occupier again meets the requirements of sub-paragraph (2)(a) or (b).

Application of paragraph 5: receipt of JSA and ESA

2.507

6.—(1) This paragraph applies to any owner-occupier who immediately before the commencement of an award of universal credit is entitled to—

(a) a jobseeker's allowance; or

(b) an employment and support allowance.

(2) In determining when the qualifying period in paragraph 5 ends in relation to the owner-occupier, any period that comprises only days on which the owner-occupier was receiving a benefit referred to in sub-paragraph (1) may be treated as if it were the whole or part of one or more assessment periods, as determined by the number of days on which any such benefit was received.

Application of paragraph 5: joint owner-occupiers ceasing to be a couple

2.508

7.—(1) This paragraph applies where—

(a) an award of universal credit to joint owner-occupiers is terminated because they cease to be a couple;

(b) a further award is made to one of them (or to each of them); and

(c) in relation to the further award (or in relation to each further award), the occupation condition is met in respect of the same accommodation as that occupied by the joint owner-occupiers as their home.

(2) In determining when the qualifying period in paragraph 5 ends in relation to the further award (or each further award), the whole or part of any assessment period which would have counted in relation to the award that is terminated is to be carried forward and taken into account in relation to the further award (or each further award).

(3) But where, immediately before the joint owner-occupiers' award was terminated, an amount of housing costs element calculated under this Schedule was already included in the award, no qualifying period under paragraph 5 applies to the owner-occupier in relation to the commencement of the further award (or each further award).

(4) For the purposes of sub-paragraph (1)(b), it is irrelevant whether the further award—

(a) is made on a claim; or

(b) by virtue of regulation 9(6) of the Universal Credit, Personal Independence Payment, Jobseeker's Allowance and Employment and Support Allowance (Claims and Payments) Regulations 2013 is made without a claim.

PART 4

CALCULATION OF AMOUNT OF HOUSING COSTS ELEMENT FOR OWNER-OCCUPIERS

Payments to be taken into account

2.509

8.—(1) Where an owner-occupier meets the payment condition, liability condition and occupation condition in respect of one or more relevant payments and the qualifying period has ended, each of the relevant payments is to be taken into account for the purposes of the calculation under this Part.

(2) No account is to be taken of any amount of a relevant payment to the extent that the conditions referred to in sub-paragraph (1) are not met in respect of that amount.

(3) Any particular payment for which an owner-occupier is liable is not to be brought into account more than once, whether in relation to the same or a different owner-occupier (but this does not prevent different payments of the same description being brought into account in respect of an assessment period).

The amount of housing costs element

    9. The amount of the owner-occupier's housing costs element under this Schedule is [⁷ the amount resulting from paragraph 13] in respect of all relevant payments which are to be taken into account under paragraph 8.   **2.510**

Amount in respect of interest on loans

    10. [⁷. . .]   **2.511**

Amount in respect of alternative finance arrangements

    11.—[⁷. . .]   **2.512**

Standard rate to be applied under paragraphs 10 and 11

    12.—[⁷. . .]   **2.513**

Amount in respect of service charge payments

    13.—(1) This paragraph provides for the calculation of the amount to be included in the owner-occupier's housing costs element under this Schedule in respect of relevant payments which are service charge payments.   **2.514**

    (2) The amount in respect of the service charge payments is to be calculated as follows.

Step 1

    Determine the amount of each service charge payment.

Step 2

    Determine the period in respect of which each service charge payment is payable and determine the amount of the payment in respect of a month (see sub-paragraphs (3) and (4)).

Step 3

    If there is more than one service charge payment, add together the amounts determined in step 2.

    The result is the amount to be included under this Schedule in respect of service charge payments.

    (3) Where the period in respect of which an owner-occupier is liable to make a service charge payment is not a month, an amount is to be calculated as the monthly equivalent, so for example—

        (a) weekly payments are multiplied by 52 and divided by 12;

  [⁵ (aa) two-weekly payments are multiplied by 26 and divided by 12;]

        (b) four-weekly payments are multiplied by 13 and divided by 12;

        (c) three-monthly payments are multiplied by 4 and divided by 12; and

        (d) annual payments are divided by 12.

    (4) Where an owner-occupier is liable for service charge payments under arrangements that provide for one or more service charge free periods, [⁵ subject to sub-paragraph (4A),] the monthly equivalent is to be calculated over 12 months by reference to the total number of service charge payments which the owner-occupier is liable to make in that 12 month period.

    [⁵ (4A) Where sub-paragraph (4) applies and the service charge payments in question are—

        (a) weekly payments, the total number of weekly service charge payments which the owner-occupier is liable to make in any 12 month period shall be calculated by reference to the formula—

$$52 - SCFP;$$

        (b) two-weekly payments, the total number of two-weekly service charge payments which the owner-occupier is liable to make in any 12 month period shall be calculated by reference to the formula—

$$26 - SCFP;$$

        (c) four weekly payments, the total number of four-weekly service charge payments which the owner-occupier is liable to make in any 12 month period shall be calculated by reference to the formula—

$$13 - SCFP;$$

where "SCFP" is the number of service charge free periods in the 12 month period in question.]

    (5) "Service charge free period" means any period in respect of which the owner-occupier has no liability to make one or more of the service charge payments which are to be taken into account under paragraph 8.

AMENDMENTS

1. Universal Credit and Miscellaneous Amendments Regulations 2014 (SI 2014/597) reg.2(14)(a) (April 28, 2014).
2. Universal Credit and Miscellaneous Amendments Regulations 2014 (SI 2014/597) reg.2(14)(b) (April 28, 2014).
3. Universal Credit and Miscellaneous Amendments Regulations 2014 (SI 2014/597) reg.2(14)(c) (April 28, 2014).
4. Universal Credit and Miscellaneous Amendments Regulations 2014 (SI 2014/597) reg.2(14)(d) (April 28, 2014).
5. Universal Credit and Miscellaneous Amendments Regulations 2014 (SI 2014/597) reg.2(14)(e) (April 28, 2014).
6. Social Security (Housing Costs Amendments) Regulations 2015 (SI 2015/1647) reg.5(2) (April 1, 2016). The amendment is subject to the saving provision in reg.8 of SI 2015/1647 (see Pt IV).
7. Loans for Mortgage Interest Regulations 2017 (SI 2017/725) reg.18 and Sch.5 para.5(f) (April 6, 2018).

DEFINITIONS

"the Act"—see reg.2.
"assessment period"—see WRA 2012, ss.40 and 7(2) and reg.21.
"claim"—see WRA 2012, s.40.
"claimant"—*ibid*.
"couple"—see WRA 2012, ss.39 and 40.
"earned income"—see reg.2.
"employment and support allowance"—*ibid*.
"jobseeker's allowance"—*ibid*.
"personal independence payment"—*ibid*.

GENERAL NOTE

2.515   *Paragraphs 1–4*
This Schedule concerns the calculation of the housing costs element for "owner-occupiers" (see para.1(2)). For the definition of "owner-occupier" see para.2. References to "joint owner-occupiers" are to joint claimants who are owner-occupiers (para.1(2)).

For an owner-occupier (or joint owner-occupier) to be entitled to a housing costs element under this Schedule, they must meet the payment, liability and occupation conditions in respect of one or more "relevant payments" (as defined in para.3) and the qualifying period (see paras 5–7) must have ended.

"Relevant payments" for the purposes of Sch.5 are service charges (on which see paras 7 and 8 of Sch.1). If the claimant (or claimants) is only liable for service charges payments, these will be calculated under this Schedule (see reg.26(3)). But if the claimant has a shared ownership tenancy, any service charges are calculated in accordance with Sch.4 (reg.26(5)).

Note the significant exclusion in para.4 from entitlement to a housing costs element under Sch.5. If an owner-occupier, or if they are a member of a couple, either member of the couple, has *any* earned income in an assessment period (i.e. month), they will not be entitled to a housing costs element in that assessment period. However, in the case of a shared ownership tenancy, rent payments and service charges can still be met (para.4(3)).

Paragraphs 5–7
2.516   There is a waiting period (referred to as "a qualifying period") for owner-occupier and service charges payments. In the case of a new award of universal credit, a housing costs element cannot be included until there have been nine consecutive

assessment periods (i.e. months) during which the owner-occupier has been receiving universal credit *and* would otherwise have qualified for a housing costs element under Sch.5 (para.5(2)(a)). A housing costs element is included from the start of the next assessment period. If, once awarded, there is a break in entitlement to a housing costs element under Sch.5 (e.g. because of earnings), the owner-occupier has to serve a further nine consecutive months during which they would otherwise qualify for a housing costs element before they can be awarded a housing costs element under Sch.5 again (para.5(2)(b)). This applies even if the owner-occupier continues to be entitled to universal credit during the break in entitlement to a housing costs element under Sch.5. If during a waiting period an owner-occupier ceases to qualify for a housing costs element under Sch.5, that waiting period ends and a new waiting period will have to be served (para.5(3)).

Note that before April 1, 2016 the waiting period under para.5(2)(a) and (b) was only three consecutive assessment periods. The amendment which increased the waiting period to nine months is subject to a saving provision (see reg.8 of the Social Security (Housing Costs Amendments) Regulations 2015 in Pt IV of this Volume). The effect of the saving provision in relation to universal credit is that for those claimants who are entitled, or treated as entitled, to one or more relevant benefits (i.e., income support, old style JSA, old style ESA or universal credit) for a continuous period which includes March 31, 2016, the form of reg.5(2)(a) and (b) and of reg. 29 of the Universal Credit (Transitional) Regulations 2014 that were in force before the April 1, 2016 amendments continues to have effect. So for claimants who are in a waiting period on March 31, 2016 the waiting period for a housing costs element remains three consecutive assessment periods.

Paragraphs 6 and 7 contain exceptions to the rule in para.5.

If immediately before the owner-occupier's award of universal credit began, s/he was entitled to new style JSA or new style ESA, the days that s/he was only receiving one of these benefits can count towards the waiting period (para.6).

Under para.7, if a universal credit award made to joint owner-occupiers comes to an end because they have ceased to be a couple, and a further award is made to one of them who continues to occupy the same accommodation as they did when they were a couple, the further award will include a housing costs element under Sch.5 without a waiting period if a housing costs element was included in the joint award. If a housing costs element was not yet included in the joint award, any assessment period, or part of an assessment period, which counted towards the waiting period under the joint award counts towards the waiting period for the new award. If both members of the former couple remain in the same accommodation and both claim and are awarded universal credit again, this provision will apply to both of them.

The waiting period may also be extinguished or reduced under reg.29 of the Transitional Provisions Regulations 2014, which applies where in the one month before the claim for universal credit was made, or treated as made, the owner occupier, or his/her partner or former partner, was entitled to income support, old style JSA or old style ESA that included help with housing costs or did not yet do so only because a waiting period was being served.

Paras 8, 9 and 13

The amount for service charges that can be included in an owner-occupier's housing costs element is the monthly equivalent of the actual service charge payment or payments (see para.13). Where the owner-occupier has the benefit of service charge free periods (defined in para.13(5)), the conversion to a monthly figure is based on a standard 52 week year (see para. 13(4) and the formula in para.13(4A)).

Note:

- No "housing cost contribution" for a non-dependant is made in the case of amounts awarded under Sch.5 (this is to be contrasted with the position under income support, old style JSA and old style ESA).

2.517

- Under reg.39(4) of the Decisions and Appeals Regulations 2013, if the Secretary of State considers that he does not have all the relevant information or evidence to decide what housing costs element to award, the decision will be made on the basis of the housing costs element that can immediately be awarded.

Regulation 39(2) and(3)

SCHEDULE 6

ASSESSMENT OF WHETHER A CLAIMANT HAS LIMITED CAPABILITY FOR WORK

PART I

2.518

PHYSICAL DISABILITIES

(1)	(2)		(3)
Activity	Descriptors		Points
1. Mobilising unaided by another person with or without a walking stick, manual wheelchair or other aid if such aid is normally or could reasonably be worn or used.	1	(a) Cannot, unaided by another person, either: (i) mobilise more than 50 metres on level ground without stopping in order to avoid significant discomfort or exhaustion; or (ii) repeatedly mobilise 50 metres within a reasonable timescale because of significant discomfort or exhaustion.	15
		(b) Cannot, unaided by another person, mount or descend two steps even with the support of a handrail.	9
		(c) Cannot, unaided by another person, either: (i) mobilise more than 100 metres on level ground without stopping in order to avoid significant discomfort or exhaustion; or (ii) repeatedly mobilise 100 metres within a reasonable timescale because of significant discomfort or exhaustion.	9
		(d) Cannot, unaided by another person, either: (i) mobilise more than 200 metres on level ground without stopping in order to avoid significant discomfort or exhaustion; or (ii) repeatedly mobilise 200 metres within a reasonable timescale because of significant discomfort or exhaustion.	6
		(e) None of the above applies.	0
2. Standing and sitting.	2	(a) Cannot move between one seated position and another seated position which are located next to one another without receiving physical assistance from another person.	15
		(b) Cannot, for the majority of the time, remain at a work station: (i) standing unassisted by another person (even if free to move around); (ii) sitting (even in an adjustable chair); or (iii) a combination of paragraphs (i) and (ii),	9

(1)	(2)			(3)
Activity	Descriptors			Points
			for more than 30 minutes, before needing to move away in order to avoid significant discomfort or exhaustion.	
		(c)	Cannot, for the majority of the time, remain at a work station:	6
		(i)	standing unassisted by another person (even if free to move around);	
		(ii)	sitting (even in an adjustable chair); or	
		(iii)	a combination of paragraphs (i) and (ii),	
			for more than an hour before needing to move away in order to avoid significant discomfort or exhaustion.	
		(d)	None of the above applies.	
3. Reaching.	3	(a)	Cannot raise either arm as if to put something in the top pocket of a coat or jacket.	15
		(b)	Cannot raise either arm to top of head as if to put on a hat.	9
		(c)	Cannot raise either arm above head height as if to reach for something.	6
		(d)	None of the above applies.	0
4. Picking up and moving or transferring by the use of the upper body and arms.	4	(a)	Cannot pick up and move a 0.5 litre carton full of liquid.	15
		(b)	Cannot pick up and move a one litre carton full of liquid.	9
		(c)	Cannot transfer a light but bulky object such as an empty cardboard box.	6
		(d)	None of the above applies.	0
5. Manual dexterity.	5	(a)	Cannot press a button (such as a telephone keypad) with either hand or cannot turn the pages of a book with either hand.	15
		(b)	Cannot pick up a £1 coin or equivalent with either hand.	15
		(c)	Cannot use a pen or pencil to make a meaningful mark with either hand.	9
		(d)	Cannot single-handedly use a suitable keyboard or mouse.	9
		(e)	None of the above applies.	0
6. Making self understood through speaking, writing, typing, or other means which are normally or could reasonably be used, unaided by another person.	6	(a)	Cannot convey a simple message, such as the presence of a hazard.	15
		(b)	Has significant difficulty conveying a simple message to strangers.	15
		(c)	Has some difficulty conveying a simple message to strangers.	6
		(d)	None of the above applies.	0
7. Understanding communication by: (i) verbal means (such as hearing or lip reading) alone; (ii) non-verbal means (such as reading 16 point	7	(a)	Cannot understand a simple message, such as the location of a fire escape, due to sensory impairment.	15
		(b)	Has significant difficulty understanding a simple message from a stranger due to sensory impairment.	15

(1)	(2)	(3)
Activity	Descriptors	Points
print or Braille) alone; or print or Braille) alone; or (iii) a combination of sub-paragraphs (i) and (ii), using any aid that is normally or could reasonably be used, unaided by another person.	(c) Has some difficulty understanding a simple message from a stranger due to sensory impairment.	6
	(d) None of the above applies.	0
8. Navigation and maintaining safety using a guide dog or other aid if either or both are normally used or could reasonably be used.	8 (a) Unable to navigate around familiar surroundings, without being accompanied by another person, due to sensory impairment.	15
	(b) Cannot safely complete a potentially hazardous task such as crossing the road, without being accompanied by another person, due to sensory impairment.	15
	(c) Unable to navigate around unfamiliar surroundings, without being accompanied by another person, due to sensory impairment.	9
	(d) None of the above applies.	0
9. Absence or loss of control whilst conscious leading to extensive evacuation of the bowel and/or bladder, other than enuresis (bed-wetting), despite the wearing or use of any aids or adaptations which are normally or could reasonably be worn or used.	9 (a) At least once a month experiences: (i) loss of control leading to extensive evacuation of the bowel and/or voiding of the bladder; or (ii) substantial leakage of the contents of a collecting device, sufficient to require cleaning and a change in clothing.	15
	(b) The majority of the time is at risk of loss of control leading to extensive evacuation of the bowel and/or voiding of the bladder, sufficient to require cleaning and a change in clothing, if not able to reach a toilet quickly.	6
	(c) Neither of the above applies.	0
10. Consciousness during waking moments.	10 (a) At least once a week, has an involuntary episode of lost or altered consciousness resulting in significantly disrupted awareness or concentration.	15
	(b) At least once a month, has an involuntary episode of lost or altered consciousness resulting in significantly disrupted awareness or concentration.	6
	(c) Neither of the above applies.	0
11. Learning tasks.	11 (a) Cannot learn how to complete a simple task, such as setting an alarm clock.	15
	(b) Cannot learn anything beyond a simple task, such as setting an alarm clock.	9
	(c) Cannot learn anything beyond a moderately complex task, such as the steps involved in operating a washing machine to clean clothes.	6
	(d) None of the above applies.	0

(1)	(2)	(3)
Activity	Descriptors	Points
12. Awareness of everyday hazards (such as boiling water or sharp objects).	12 (a) Reduced awareness of everyday hazards leads to a significant risk of: (i) injury to self or others; or (ii) damage to property or possessions, such that the claimant requires supervision for the majority of the time to maintain safety.	15
	(b) Reduced awareness of everyday hazards leads to a significant risk of: (i) injury to self or others; or (ii) damage to property or possessions, such that the claimant frequently requires supervision to maintain safety.	9
	(c) Reduced awareness of everyday hazards leads to a significant risk of: (i) injury to self or others; or (ii) damage to property or possessions, such that the claimant occasionally requires supervision to maintain safety.	6
	(d) None of the above applies.	0
13. Initiating and completing personal action (which means planning, organisation, problem solving, prioritising or switching tasks).	13 (a) Cannot, due to impaired mental function, reliably initiate or complete at least two sequential personal actions.	15
	(b) Cannot, due to impaired mental function, reliably initiate or complete at least two sequential personal actions for the majority of the time.	9
	(c) Frequently cannot, due to impaired mental function, reliably initiate or complete at least two sequential personal actions.	6
	(d) None of the above applies.	0
14. Coping with change.	14 (a) Cannot cope with any change to the extent that day to day life cannot be managed.	15
	(b) Cannot cope with minor planned change (such as a pre-arranged change to the routine time scheduled for a lunch break), to the extent that, overall, day to day life is made significantly more difficult.	9
	(c) Cannot cope with minor unplanned change (such as the timing of an appointment on the day it is due to occur), to the extent that, overall, day to day life is made significantly more difficult.	6
	(d) None of the above applies.	0
15. Getting about.	15 (a) Cannot get to any place outside the claimant's home with which the claimant is familiar.	15
	(b) Is unable to get to a specified place with which the claimant is familiar, without being accompanied by another person.	9
	(c) Is unable to get to a specified place with which the claimant is unfamiliar without being accompanied by another person.	6
	(d) None of the above applies.	0

(1)	(2)	(3)
Activity	Descriptors	Points
16. Coping with social engagement due to cognitive impairment or mental disorder.	16 (a) Engagement in social contact is always precluded due to difficulty relating to others or significant distress experienced by the claimant.	15
	(b) Engagement in social contact with someone unfamiliar to the claimant is always precluded due to difficulty relating to others or significant distress experienced by the claimant.	9
	(c) Engagement in social contact with someone unfamiliar to the claimant is not possible for the majority of the time due to difficulty relating to others or significant distress experienced by the claimant.	6
		0
	(d) None of the above applies.	
17. Appropriateness of behaviour with other people, due to cognitive impairment or mental disorder.	17 (a) Has, on a daily basis, uncontrollable episodes of aggressive or disinhibited behaviour that would be unreasonable in any workplace.	15
	(b) Frequently has uncontrollable episodes of aggressive or disinhibited behaviour that would be unreasonable in any workplace.	15
	(c) Occasionally has uncontrollable episodes of aggressive or disinhibited behaviour that would be unreasonable in any workplace.	9
	(d) None of the above applies.	0

Part II

2.519   Mental, Cognitive and Intellectual Function Assessment

Definitions

"claimant"—see WRA 2012 s.40.
"limited capability for work"—see WRA 2012 ss.40 and 37(1).

General Note

2.520   The activities and descriptors for assessing whether a claimant has LCW are the same as the activities and descriptors in Sch.2 to the ESA Regulations 2008. See the notes to Sch.2 to the 2008 Regulations in Vol.I of this series. They are also the same as the activities and descriptors in Sch.2 to the ESA Regulations 2013.

SCHEDULE 7   **2.521**

ASSESSMENT OF WHETHER A CLAIMANT HAS LIMITED CAPABILITY FOR
WORK AND WORK-RELATED ACTIVITY

Activity	Descriptors
1. Mobilising unaided by another person with or without a walking stick, manual wheelchair or other aid if such aid is normally or could reasonably be worn or used.	1. Cannot either: (a) mobilise more than 50 metres on level ground without stopping in order to avoid significant discomfort or exhaustion; or (b) repeatedly mobilise 50 metres within a reasonable timescale because of significant discomfort or exhaustion.
2. Transferring from one seated position to another.	2. Cannot move between one seated position and another seated position located next to one another without receiving physical assistance from another person.
3. Reaching.	3. Cannot raise either arm as if to put something in the top pocket of a coat or jacket.
4. Picking up and moving or transferring by the use of the upper body and arms (excluding standing, sitting, bending or kneeling and all other activities specified in this Schedule).	4. Cannot pick up and move a 0.5 litre carton full of liquid.
5. Manual dexterity.	5. Cannot press a button (such as a telephone keypad) with either hand or cannot turn the pages of a book with either hand.
6. Making self understood through speaking, writing, typing, or other means which are normally, or could reasonably be, used unaided by another person.	6. Cannot convey a simple message, such as the presence of a hazard.
7. Understanding communication by: (i) verbal means (such as hearing or lip reading) alone; (ii) non-verbal means (such as reading 16 point print or Braille) alone; or (iii) a combination of sub-paragraphs (i) and (ii), using any aid that is normally, or could reasonably, be used unaided by another person.	7. Cannot understand a simple message, such as the location of a fire escape, due to sensory impairment.
8. Absence or loss of control whilst conscious leading to extensive evacuation of the bowel and/or voiding of the bladder, other than enuresis (bed-wetting), despite the wearing or use of any aids or adaptations which are normally or could reasonably be worn or used.	8. At least once a week experiences: (a) loss of control leading to extensive evacuation of the bowel and/or voiding of the bladder; or (b) substantial leakage of the contents of a collecting device sufficient to require the individual to clean themselves and change clothing.

9. Learning tasks.	9 Cannot learn how to complete a simple task, such as setting an alarm clock, due to cognitive impairment or mental disorder.
10. Awareness of hazard.	10 Reduced awareness of everyday hazards, due to cognitive impairment or mental disorder, leads to a significant risk of: (a) injury to self or others; or (b) damage to property or possessions, such that the claimant requires supervision for the majority of the time to maintain safety.
11. Initiating and completing personal action (which means planning, organisation, problem solving, prioritising or switching tasks).	11 Cannot, due to impaired mental function, reliably initiate or complete at least two sequential personal actions.
12. Coping with change.	12 Cannot cope with any change, due to cognitive impairment or mental disorder, to the extent that day to day life cannot be managed.
13. Coping with social engagement, due to cognitive impairment or mental disorder.	13 Engagement in social contact is always precluded due to difficulty relating to others or significant distress experienced by the claimant.
14. Appropriateness of behaviour with other people, due to cognitive impairment or mental disorder.	14 Has, on a daily basis, uncontrollable episodes of aggressive or disinhibited behaviour that would be unreasonable in any workplace.
15. Conveying food or drink to the mouth.	15 (a) Cannot convey food or drink to the claimant's own mouth without receiving physical assistance from someone else; (b) Cannot convey food or drink to the claimant's own mouth without repeatedly stopping or experiencing breathlessness or severe discomfort; (c) Cannot convey food or drink to the claimant's own mouth without receiving regular prompting given by someone else in the claimant's presence; or (d) Owing to a severe disorder of mood or behaviour, fails to convey food or drink to the claimant's own mouth without receiving: (i) physical assistance from someone else; or (ii) regular prompting given by someone else in the claimant's presence.
16. Chewing or swallowing food or drink.	16 (a) Cannot chew or swallow food or drink; (b) Cannot chew or swallow food or drink without repeatedly stopping or experiencing breathlessness or severe discomfort; (c) Cannot chew or swallow food or drink without repeatedly receiving regular prompting given by someone else in the claimant's presence; or (d) Owing to a severe disorder of mood or behaviour, fails to: (i) chew or swallow food or drink; or (ii) chew or swallow food or drink without regular prompting given by someone else in the claimant's presence.

586

(SI 2013/376 Sch. 7)

DEFINITIONS

"claimant"—see WRA 2012 s.40.
"limited capability for work"—see WRA 2012 ss.40 and 37(1).
"limited capability for work-related activity"—see WRA 2012 ss.40 and 37(2).

GENERAL NOTE

2.522

The activities and descriptors for assessing whether a claimant has LCW and LCWRA are the same as the activities and descriptors in Sch.3 to the ESA Regulations 2008 for assessing whether a claimant has LCWRA. See the notes to Sch.3 to the 2008 Regulations in Vol.I of this series. They are also the same as the activities and descriptors in Sch.3 to the ESA Regulations 2013.

Regulation 39(6)

SCHEDULE 8

CIRCUMSTANCES IN WHICH A CLAIMANT IS TO BE TREATED AS HAVING
LIMITED CAPABILITY FOR WORK

Receiving certain treatments

2.523

1. The claimant is receiving—
   (a) regular weekly treatment by way of haemodialysis for chronic renal failure;
   (b) treatment by way of plasmapheresis; or
   (c) regular weekly treatment by way of total parenteral nutrition for gross impairment of enteric function,

or is recovering from any of those forms of treatment in circumstances in which the Secretary of State is satisfied that the claimant should be treated as having limited capability for work.

In hospital

2.524

2.—(1) The claimant is—
   (a) undergoing medical or other treatment as [¹ a patient] in a hospital or similar institution; or
   (b) recovering from such treatment in circumstances in which the Secretary of State is satisfied that the claimant should be treated as having limited capability for work.

(2) The circumstances in which a claimant is to be regarded as undergoing treatment falling within sub-paragraph (1)(a) include where the claimant is attending a residential programme of rehabilitation for the treatment of drug or alcohol dependency.

(3) For the purposes of this paragraph, a claimant is to be regarded as undergoing treatment as a patient in a hospital or similar institution only if that claimant has been advised by a health care professional to stay [² for a period of 24 hours or longer] following medical or other treatment.

Prevented from working by law

2.525

3.—(1) The claimant—
   (a) is excluded or abstains from work pursuant to a request or notice in writing lawfully made or given under an enactment; or
   (b) is otherwise prevented from working pursuant to an enactment,

by reason of it being known or reasonably suspected that the claimant is infected or contaminated by, or has been in contact with a case of, a relevant infection or contamination.

(2) In sub-paragraph (1) "relevant infection or contamination" means—
   (a) in England and Wales—
      (i) any incidence or spread of infection or contamination, within the meaning of section 45A(3) of the Public Health (Control of Disease) Act 1984 in respect of which regulations are made under Part 2A of that Act (public health protection) for the purpose of preventing, protecting against, controlling or providing a public health response to, such incidence or spread, or
      (ii) tuberculosis or any infectious disease to which regulation 9 of the Public Health (Aircraft) Regulations 1979 (powers in respect of persons leaving aircraft) applies or to which regulation 10 of the Public Health (Ships) Regulations 1979 (powers in respect of certain persons on ships) applies; and

587

(b)　in Scotland any—
   (i)　infectious disease within the meaning of section 1(5) of the Public Health etc (Scotland) Act 2008, or exposure to an organism causing that disease; or
   (ii)　contamination within the meaning of section 1(5) of that Act, or exposure to a contaminant,
to which sections 56 to 58 of that Act (compensation) apply.

Risk to self or others

2.526　　4.—(1) The claimant is suffering from a specific illness, disease or disablement by reason of which there would be a substantial risk to the physical or mental health of any person were the claimant found not to have limited capability for work.

(2) This paragraph does not apply where the risk could be reduced by a significant amount by—
   (a)　reasonable adjustments being made in the claimant's workplace; or
   (b)　the claimant taking medication to manage their condition where such medication has been prescribed for the claimant by a registered medical practitioner treating the claimant.

Life threatening disease

2.527　　5. The claimant is suffering from a life threatening disease in relation to which—
   (a)　there is medical evidence that the disease is uncontrollable, or uncontrolled, by a recognised therapeutic procedure; and
   (b)　in the case of a disease that is uncontrolled, there is a reasonable cause for it not to be controlled by a recognised therapeutic procedure.

Disabled and over the age for state pension credit

2.528　　6. The claimant has reached the qualifying age for state pension credit and is entitled to disability living allowance [3, personal independence payment or adult disability payment].

AMENDMENTS

1. Universal Credit (Consequential, Supplementary, Incidental and Miscellaneous Provisions) Regulations 2013 (SI 2013/630), reg.38(10) (April 29, 2013).
2. Social Security (Miscellaneous Amendments) (No.2) Regulations 2013 (SI 2013/1508), reg.3(11) (July 29, 2013).
3. Social Security (Disability Assistance for Working Age People) (Consequential Amendments) Order 2022 (SI 2022/177) art.13(9) (March 21, 2022).

DEFINITIONS

"adult disability payment"—see reg.2.
"claimant"—see WRA 2012 s.40.
"disability living allowance"—see reg.2.
"health care professional"–*ibid*.
"limited capability for work"—see WRA 2012 ss.40 and 37(1).
"personal independence payment"—see reg.2.

GENERAL NOTE

2.529　　Paragraph 1 is similar, though not identical, to reg.26 of the ESA Regulations 2008; para. 2 is similar, though not identical, to reg.25 of those Regulations; and para. 3 is the same as reg.20(1)(c) and (2) of the 2008 Regulations. See the notes to regs 20, 25 and 26 of the 2008 Regulations in Vol.I of this series.

Note that Sch.8 does not contain provisions for treating a claimant who is (i) terminally ill; (ii) a pregnant woman whose health, or whose unborn child's health, is at serious risk of damage: or (iii) receiving treatment for cancer as having limited capability for work. Such a claimant will be treated as having LCW and LCWRA under paras 1 to 3 respectively of Sch.9 (see below).

There is no equivalent of para.6 in the ESA Regulations 2008.

Paragraphs 4 and 5 together contain very similar provisions to those in reg. 29 of the 2008 Regulations (see the notes to reg.29 in Vol.1 of this series). Note the amendment to reg. 39 made on April 28, 2014, the effect of which is that a claimant can only be treated as having LCW under paras 4 or 5 if they have been assessed as not having LCW. Regulation 29 of the 2008 Regulations already contains such a provision.

Regulation 40(5)

SCHEDULE 9

CIRCUMSTANCES IN WHICH A CLAIMANT IS TO BE TREATED AS HAVING LIMITED CAPABILITY FOR WORK AND WORK-RELATED ACTIVITY

Terminal illness
1. The claimant is terminally ill.

2.530

Pregnancy
2. The claimant is a pregnant woman and there is a serious risk of damage to her health or to the health of her unborn child if she does not refrain from work and work-related activity.

2.531

Receiving treatment for cancer
3. The claimant is—
   (a) receiving treatment for cancer by way of chemotherapy or radiotherapy;
   (b) likely to receive such treatment within 6 months after the date of the determination of capability for work and work-related activity; or
   (c) recovering from such treatment,
and the Secretary of State is satisfied that the claimant should be treated as having limited capability for work and work-related activity.

2.532

Risk to self or others
4. The claimant is suffering from a specific illness, disease or disablement by reason of which there would be a substantial risk to the physical or mental health of any person were the claimant found not to have limited capability for work and work-related activity.

2.533

Disabled and over the age for state pension credit
5. The claimant has reached the qualifying age for state pension credit and is entitled to attendance allowance, the care component of disability living allowance at the highest rate or the daily living component of personal independence payment at the enhanced rate [¹ or the daily living component of adult disability payment at the enhanced rate in accordance with regulation 5(3) of the Disability Assistance for Working Age People (Scotland) Regulations 2022].

2.534

AMENDMENT

1. Social Security (Disability Assistance for Working Age People) (Consequential Amendments) Order 2022 (SI 2022/177) art.13(10) (March 21, 2022).

DEFINITIONS

"adult disability payment"—see reg.2.
"attendance allowance"—*ibid.*
"child"—see WRA 2012, s.40.
"claimant"—*ibid.*
"limited capability for work"—see WRA 2012, ss.40 and 37(1).
"limited capability for work-related activity"—see WRA 2012, ss.40 and 37(2).
"personal independence payment"—see reg.2.

GENERAL NOTE

For the equivalent of (i) para.1, see regs 20(1)(a) and 35(1)(a) of the ESA Regulations 2008; (ii) para.2, see regs 20(1)(d) and 35(1)(c) of those Regulations; and (iii) para.3, see regs 20(1)(b) and 35(1)(b) of the 2008 Regulations. See the notes to regs 20 and 35 of the 2008 Regulations in Vol.I of this series.

2.535

589

There is no equivalent of para.5 in the ESA Regulations 2008.

Paragraph 4 contains very similar provisions to those in regs 29(2)(b) and 35(2) of the 2008 Regulations (see the notes to regs 29 and 35 in Vol.1 of this series). Note the amendment to reg. 40 made on April 28, 2014, the effect of which is that a claimant can only be treated as having LCW and LCWRA under para.4 if they have been assessed as not having LCW and LCWRA. Regulations 29 and 35 of the 2008 Regulations already contain such a provision.

Regulation 48

SCHEDULE 10

CAPITAL TO BE DISREGARDED

Premises

2.536   1.—(1) Premises occupied by a person as their home.

(2) For the purposes of this paragraph and paragraphs 2 to 5, only one set of premises may be treated as a person's home.

2. Premises occupied by a close relative of a person as their home where that close relative has limited capability for work or has reached the qualifying age for state pension credit.

3. Premises occupied by a person's former partner as their home where the person and their former partner are not estranged, but living apart by force of circumstances, for example where the person is in residential care.

4.—(1) Premises that a person intends to occupy as their home where—

(a) the person has acquired the premises within the past 6 months but not yet taken up occupation;

(b) the person is taking steps to obtain possession and has commenced those steps within the past 6 months; or

(c) the person is carrying out essential repairs or alterations required to render the premises fit for occupation and these have been commenced within the past 6 months.

(2) A person is to be taken to have commenced steps to obtain possession of premises on the date that legal advice is first sought or proceedings are commenced, whichever is earlier.

5. Premises that a person has ceased to occupy as their home following an estrangement from their former partner where—

(a) the person has ceased to occupy the premises within the past 6 months; or

(b) the person's former partner is a lone parent and occupies the premises as their home.

6. Premises that a person is taking reasonable steps to dispose of where those steps have been commenced within the past 6 months.

Business assets

2.537   7. Assets which are used wholly or mainly for the purposes of a trade, profession or vocation which the person is carrying on.

8. Assets which were used wholly or mainly for a trade, profession or vocation that the person has ceased to carry on within the past 6 months if—

(a) the person is taking reasonable steps to dispose of those assets; or

(b) the person ceased to be engaged in carrying on the trade, profession or vocation because of incapacity and can reasonably expect to be reengaged on recovery.

Rights in pensions schemes etc.

9. The value of any policy of life insurance.

2.538   10.—(1) The value of any right to receive a pension under an occupational or personal pension scheme or any other pension scheme registered under section 153 of the Finance Act 2004.

(2) "Occupational pension scheme" and "personal pension scheme" have the meaning in section 1 of the Pension Schemes Act 1993.

11.—(1) The value of a funeral plan contract.

(2) "Funeral plan contract" means a contract under which the person makes payments to a person to secure the provision of a funeral and where the sole purpose of the plan is the provision of a funeral.

590

Amounts earmarked for special purposes

12. An amount deposited with a housing association as a condition of the person occupying premises as their home.

2.539

13. An amount received within the past 6 months which is to be used for the purchase of premises that the person intends to occupy as their home where that amount—

    (a) is attributable to the proceeds of the sale of premises formerly occupied by the person as their home;

    (b) has been deposited with a housing association as mentioned in paragraph 12; or

    (c) is a grant made to the person for the sole purpose of the purchase of a home.

14. An amount received under an insurance policy within the past 6 months in connection with the loss or damage to the premises occupied by the person as their home or to their personal possessions.

15. An amount received within the past 6 months that is to be used for making essential repairs or alterations to premises occupied or intended to be occupied as the person's home where that amount has been acquired by the person (whether by grant or loan or otherwise) on condition that it is used for that purpose.

Other payments

16. A payment made within the past 12 months under Part 8 of the Contributions and Benefits Act (the social fund).

2.540

17.—(1) A payment made within the past 12 months by or on behalf of a local authority—

    (a) under section 17, 23B, 23C or 24A of the Children Act 1989, section 12 of the Social Work (Scotland) Act 1968 [², or section 29 or 30 of the Children (Scotland) Act 1995 or section 37, 38, 109, 110, 114 or 115 of the Social Services and Well-being (Wales) Act 2014]; or

    (b) under any other enactment in order to meet a person's welfare needs related to old age or disability, other than living expenses.

(2) In sub-paragraph (1) "living expenses" has the meaning in regulation 66(2).

18.—(1) A payment received within the past 12 months by way of arrears of, or compensation for late payment of—

    (a) universal credit;

    (b) a benefit abolished by section 33 of the Act; or

    (c) a social security benefit which is not included as unearned income under regulation 66(1)(a) or (b).

(2) "Social security benefit" means a benefit under any enactment relating to social security in any part of the United Kingdom [⁵and includes armed forces independence payment under the Armed Forces and Reserve Forces (Compensation Scheme) Order 2011].

[⁹18ZA. Any payment within the past 12 months of widowed parent's allowance—

    (a) to the survivor of a cohabiting partnership (within the meaning in section 39A(7) of the Contributions and Benefits Act) who is entitled to a widowed parent's allowance for a period before the Bereavement Benefits (Remedial) Order 2023 comes into force, and

    (b) in respect of any period of time during the period ending with the day before the survivor makes the claim for a widowed parent's allowance.]

[⁸18A. A payment received within the past 12 months by way of local welfare provision including arrears and payments in lieu of local welfare provision.]

19. A payment to a person by virtue of being a holder of the Victoria Cross or George Cross.

[¹20.—[⁹(1)] A payment made within the past 12 months of bereavement support payment in respect of the rate set out in regulation 3(2) or (5) of the Bereavement Support Payment Regulations 2017 (rate of bereavement support payment).]

[⁹(2) Where bereavement support payment under section 30 of the Pensions Act 2014 (bereavement support payment) has been paid within the past 12 months to the survivor of a cohabiting partnership (within the meaning in section 30(6B) of the Pensions Act 2014) in respect of a death occurring before the day the Bereavement Benefits (Remedial) Order 2023 comes into force, any amount of that payment which is—

    (a) in respect of the rate set out in regulation 3(1) of the Bereavement Support Payment Regulations 2017, and

    (b) paid as a lump sum for more than one monthly recurrence of the day of the month on which their cohabiting partner died.]

[³21. Any early years assistance given within the past 12 months in accordance with section 32 of the Social Security (Scotland) Act 2018.]

[⁴22. Any funeral expense assistance given within the past 12 months in accordance with section 34 of the Social Security (Scotland) Act 2018.]

[⁶23. Any assistance given within the past 52 weeks in accordance with the Carer's Assistance (Young Carer Grants) (Scotland) Regulations 2019.]

[⁷24. Any winter heating assistance given within the past 52 weeks in accordance with regulations made under section 30 of the Social Security (Scotland) Act 2018.]

AMENDMENTS

1. Pensions Act 2014 (Consequential, Supplementary and Incidental Amendments) Order 2017 (SI 2017/422) art.43(4) (April 6, 2017).

2. Social Services and Well-being (Wales) Act 2014 and the Regulation and Inspection of Social Care (Wales) Act 2016 (Consequential Amendments) Order 2017 (SI 2017/901) art.15 (November 2, 2017).

3. Social Security (Scotland) Act 2018 (Best Start Grants) (Consequential Modifications and Saving) Order 2018 (SI 2018/1138) art.11 (December 10, 2018).

4. Social Security (Scotland) Act 2018 (Funeral Expense Assistance and Early Years Assistance) (Consequential Modifications and Savings) Order 2019 (SI 2019/1060) art.19(2) (September 16, 2019).

5. Social Security (Capital Disregards) (Amendment) Regulations 2019 (SI 2019/1314) reg.8(2) (October 31, 2019).

6. Social Security (Scotland) Act 2018 (Young Carer Grants, Short-Term Assistance and Winter Heating Assistance) (Consequential Provision and Modifications) Order 2020 (SI 2020/989) art.8 (November 9, 2020).

7. Social Security (Scotland) Act 2018 (Young Carer Grants, Short-Term Assistance and Winter Heating Assistance) (Consequential Provision and Modifications) Order 2020 (SI 2020/989) art.21 (November 9, 2020).

8. Universal Credit (Local Welfare Provision Disregard) (Amendment) Regulations 2022 (SI 2022/448) reg.2(3) (May 4, 2022).

9. Bereavement Benefits (Remedial) Order 2023 (SI 2023/134) art.13 (February 9, 2023).

DEFINITIONS

"close relative"—see reg.2.
"Contributions and Benefits Act"—*ibid.*
"grant"—see regs 2 and 68(7).
"local welfare provision"—see reg.2.
"partner"—*ibid.*
"widowed parent's allowance"—*ibid.*

GENERAL NOTE

2.541   The list of capital that is ignored for the purposes of universal credit is greatly reduced compared with that which applies for the purposes of income support, old style JSA, old style ESA and housing benefit. Many of the provisions in Sch.10 are similar to those that apply for those benefits but not all. Paragraph 11—the disregard of the value of a funeral plan—is new.

The opportunity has been taken to group the disregards in a more coherent and easy to follow structure. The notes below follow that structure and note the equivalences with and differences from the provisions in Sch.10 to the Income Support Regulations (see Vol.V of this series for detailed discussion). The disregards can apply to notional capital. By virtue of reg.48(2), where any period of six months is specified in Sch.10 it can be extended by the Secretary of State (and on any appeal by a tribunal) if it is reasonable to do so in the circumstances. Any specified period of 12 months is not extendable.

Note that, in addition to the categories specified in Sch.10, there are specific disregards of capital in reg.75(4), (5) and (6) (sums derived from compensation for

personal injury to claimant), reg.76 (special compensation schemes) and reg.77(3)
(a) (assets of company where claimant treated as sole owner or partner). Further,
reg.51 of the Universal Credit (Transitional Provisions) Regulations 2014, as inserted
by reg.3 of the Universal Credit (Managed Migration Pilot and Miscellaneous
Amendments) Regulations 2019 (SI 2019/1152) with effect from July 24, 2019, supplies a transitional capital disregard to claimants who (i) were previously entitled to
a tax credit and had capital exceeding £16,000; (ii) are given a migration notice that
existing benefits are to terminate; and (iii) claim universal credit within the deadline.
The disregard is of any capital exceeding £16,000. The disregard can apply only
for 12 assessment periods and ceases (without the possibility of revival) following
any assessment period in which the amount of capital the claimant has falls below
£16,000. See regs 56 and 57 of the Transitional Provisions Regulations for further
provisions on termination of the protection. The £16,000 non-disregarded capital
that the claimant by definition possesses will produce an assumed yield as income of
£174 per month under reg.72. There is no capital limit for tax credits. Paragraph 7 of
Sch.2 to the Transitional Provisions Regulations, inserted by the same Regulations,
contains a disregard as capital of any amount paid as a lump sum by way of a "transitional SDP amount" under that Schedule.

See the notes to para.18 below for the additional effect of regs 10A, 10B and 10C
(arrears of various benefits disregarded as capital) of the Transitional Provisions
Regulations 2014.

With effect from May 29, 2020, reg.26(1)(a) of the Victims' Payments Regulations
2020 (SI 2020/103) (see later in this Part) provides that a victims' payment or
a lump sum under those Regulations is to be disregarded as capital or income.
Under the Regulations payments are to be made to those injured in a "Troubles-
related incident", which is defined in s.10(11) of the Northern Ireland (Executive
Formation etc) Act 2019 as "an incident involving an act of violence or force carried
out in Ireland, the UK or anywhere in Europe for a reason related to the constitutional status of Northern Ireland or to political or sectarian hostility between people
there". In so far as any such payment constitutes income it is not listed in reg.66(1),
so is not to be taken into account as unearned income. In so far as it constitutes
capital, either initially or on metamorphosing into capital (see the notes to reg.45),
it is to be disregarded without any limit as to how long ago the payment was made.

With effect from April 1, 2022, reg.2(1) of the Universal Credit (Energy Rebate
Scheme Disregard) Regulations 2022 (SI 2022/257) (see later in this Part) provides
that any payment received under the Energy Rebate Scheme 2022 is to be disregarded as capital for 12 months from the date of receipt. That scheme is defined
in reg.2(2) of the 2022 Regulations as the scheme to provide financial support in
respect of energy bills that was announced in Parliament on February 3, 2022 and
any comparable scheme announced by the Welsh or Scottish Ministers. The disregard thus formally applies to all the elements of that scheme, but in practice it can
only apply to the £150 rebate to council tax payers in bands A–D or the discretionary payment to vulnerable people who do not pay council tax or whose property is
in bands E–H. Other elements of the scheme would not involve payments of capital.

"Cost of living payments" under the Social Security (Additional Payments) Act
2022 and the 2023 Act, both those to recipients of specified means-tested benefits
and "disability" payments, are not to be taken into account for any universal credit
purposes by virtue of s.8(b) of both Acts.

Finally, note that with effect from May 21, 2020, reg.2(2) of the Universal Credit
(Coronavirus) (Self-employed Claimants and Reclaims) (Amendment) Regulations
2020 (SI 2020/522) introduced a disregard as capital for 12 months of any payment
made to a self-employed claimant under the Coronavirus Job Retention Scheme or
by way of a grant or loan to meet the expenses or losses of the trade, profession or
vocation in relation to the outbreak of coronavirus disease. See further discussion
in the note to para.7.

However, there has not been any specific provision for some other coronavirus-related payments. See the notes to reg.66 for the taxable £500 payment,

administered by local authorities, made to those in England entitled to a qualifying income-related benefit (including universal credit) who were required by NHS Test and Trace on or after September 28, 2020 (down at least to summer 2021) to self-isolate for 14 (or ten) days, were unable to work from home and would lose income from employment or self-employment and the discretionary payments available to those not entitled to a qualifying benefit. The payments appear to be in the nature of income, in the form of compensation for the loss of earnings that would otherwise have been received. As such they were not to be taken into account as unearned income since they are not listed in reg.66(1). There is, though, the possibility that any amount remaining out of the £500 at the end of the required days of self-isolation, or more probably after the end of the assessment period of receipt, would then be treated as capital under the usual principles (see the notes to para.7 below and to reg.54A for discussion in the context of surplus earnings).

The intention was expressed in the guidance on scheme eligibility that the £500 payments were not to be taken into account as capital for benefit purposes. There has been no amendment to the universal credit legislation to secure that result. So far as "legacy benefits" are concerned, the payments, being made by local authorities, appear to constitute "local welfare provision" within the capital disregard in para.18A of Sch.10 to the Income Support Regulations (see Vol.V of this series) and the equivalent provisions for other benefits. The phrase is very widely defined in reg.2(1) of those Regulations. There is now, from May 4, 2022, an equivalent disregard in para.18A of the present Schedule, which thus was not in operation at the time the payments were made. The closest provision at the time was para.17 (see the notes below), but that applies only to payments from local authorities under specific legislation that would not cover the Test and Trace payments or under any legislation to meet welfare needs related to old age or disability, but excluding living expenses. The payments are not linked to old age or disability and, even if they were, would fall foul of the living expenses exclusion.

It was announced in the March 2021 budget that an automatic one-off £500 support payment would be made by HMRC to those in receipt of working tax credit (or child tax credit alone if eligible for WTC but income too high for payability), in view of the withdrawal after April 5, 2021 of the temporary uplift to WTC rates during the coronavirus pandemic. The payment was to be made in April 2021 without the need for any claim and under powers in the Coronavirus Act 2020. It was therefore not a payment of WTC and would appear to be in the nature of a capital receipt, rather than income. According to LA Welfare Direct 3/2021, the payment was to be disregarded for housing benefit and universal credit purposes, but there has been no amendment of the legislation for the purposes of universal credit (or legacy benefits). The payment does not fall within the disregard for local authority welfare payments in para.17, because it is not made under any of the legislation specified there (see the previous paragraph) or paid by a local authority. No other provision of Sch.10 appears to have applied. Even if the payment were regarded as income, as some kind of supplement to the regular WTC payments, it is not linked to any particular period, so that any unspent sum out of the £500 would appear to become capital under the principles discussed in the notes to reg.45.

The disregards can apply to capital that a claimant is treated as possessing under reg.48 (notional capital), providing that the terms of the particular paragraph of Sch.10 are satisfied (see discussion in the note to para.6). Although the references in Sch.10 are to a person, not to a claimant, that is merely in accord with 48(2) applying the Sch.10 disregards to the calculation of "a person's capital". Thus when a paragraph in Sch.10 refers to the circumstances of a person it means the person whose capital would otherwise count in the claimant's case, i.e. the claimant or either of joint claimants.

The discussion at a meeting of the Social Security Advisory Committee (SSAC) on December 8, 2021 in relation to the Social Security (Income and Capital Disregards) (Amendment) Regulations 2021 (SI 2021/1405) (see the notes to reg.76) revealed some conceptual problems in the relationship of capital disregards to the calculation of the amount of capital possessed at a particular date. The essence of the problem put to DWP officials was what would happen if a claimant received a compensation payment within the disregard introduced by those regulations, acquired further non-disregarded capital and then spent a substantial amount of capital: how would it be known what pot of capital the expenditure came out of (SSAC minutes December 8, 2021, para.2.2(f))? The answer given in the letter dated January 12, 2022 from the Minister for Welfare Delivery, David Rutley, (Annex C to the minutes) was that:

"the Department does not attempt to distinguish the capital derived from a compensation payment from other capital (with the exception of personal injury compensation that has been placed in trust). Wherever a claimant has received a payment of capital which is disregarded, whether indefinitely or for a prescribed period, their capital threshold is effectively increased by the amount of the original payment for the duration of that period. This is regardless of whether it was simply paid into a bank account with other funds or held or invested elsewhere."

That approach ought for consistency to apply to all capital disregards applying to payments rather than other assets, though probably if funds derived from any sort of compensation payment are held in a segregated account with no payments in from any other source (whether subject to a trust or not) a payment out of that fund would go to reduce the amount disregarded (see the notes to reg.75). No doubt it is right that for social security purposes no-one should have to get into all the difficulties that have arisen in other areas of the law in identifying whether specific funds that have paid into some mixed account have been depleted by subsequent payments out. However, it is far from clear how that approach should hold, say, if a payment out is made for a purpose for which the compensation was specifically paid. If part of personal injury compensation, not held in trust or in a segregated account, was specifically to cover disability adaptations to a home, would it be right, after expenditure for that purpose, to continue simply to regard the capital threshold as increased by the amount of the original disregard?

There appears to have been a misunderstanding in the discussion of this issue by the SSAC and the DWP in the assumption that an amount of compensation held in trust, e.g. qualifying for the indefinite disregard of personal injury compensation under reg.75(4), would be held in a separate account from a claimant's other assets, so that the conceptual problem would be avoided. However, that does not take into account the decision in *Q v SSWP (JSA)* [2020] UKUT 49 (AAC) that funds held in a joint bank or building society account with someone else are subject to a trust. It is argued in the notes to reg.75(4) that, although the wording of the disregard is different from that being considered in *Q*, the words "in trust" are not a term of art that has some special meaning and so should apply whenever the sum derived from personal injury compensation is subject to a trust. The question then would not be whether the compensation has been placed in trust, in the sense of being put into a specifically created trust, but simply whether the sum is held on trust.

The categories of disregards under Sch.10 are as follows:

Para. 1	Premises occupied as a person's home;
Para. 2	Premises occupied as home by close relative with LCW or over pension age;
Para. 3	Premises occupied as home by former partner living apart by force of circumstances;
Para. 4	Various premises that person intends to occupy as home;
Para. 5	Premises ceased to be occupied as home following estrangement;
Para. 6	Premises where taking reasonable steps to dispose;
Para. 7	Assets used for purposes of trade etc. being carried on;
Para. 8	Assets previously used for purposes of trade etc no longer carried on;
Para. 9	Life insurance policies;
Para. 10	Pension rights;
Para. 11	Funeral plan contracts;
Para. 12	Housing association deposits;

Para. 13	Amounts to be used to purchase new home;
Para. 14	Insurance payments for home or personal possessions;
Para. 15	Amounts received to be used for essential repairs or alterations;
Para. 16	Social fund payments in past 12 months;
Para. 17	Welfare payments in past 12 months;
Para. 18	Arrears or compensation for late payment of certain benefits in past 12 months;
Para. 18ZA	Arrears of widowed parent's allowance;
Para. 18A	Local welfare provision;
Para. 19	Victoria Cross and George Cross payments;
Para. 20	Lump sum bereavement support payments in past 12 months;
Para. 21	Scottish early years assistance in past 12 months;
Para. 22	Scottish funeral expense assistance in past 12 months;
Para. 23	Scottish young carer grants in past 52 weeks;
Para. 24	Scottish winter heating assistance in past 52 weeks.

Premises

2.542   *Paragraph 1* (premises occupied as the home) is equivalent to para.1 of the income support Sch.10 except that it is in terms of premises rather than a dwelling. Only one set of premises (whatever the precise meaning of that might be: see the notes to reg.2(1) of the Income Support Regulations for cases on when separate properties could constitute one dwelling) can be treated as the home. That rule is expressly extended to paras 2–5, as is not done in the income support Sch.10. Presumably the premises need not be residential accommodation providing that they are lived in as a home. Presumably also the reference to one set of premises allows account to be taken of the provisions in Sch.3 allowing claimants to be treated as occupying more than one accommodation in limited circumstances. It would be consistent then to disregard the value of any interest the claimant has in either accommodation or both.

Paragraph 2 (premises occupied by a close relative as their home) is the equivalent of para.4(a) of the income support Sch.10, except that it is restricted to close relatives of the claimant instead of any relative or a partner. The alternative test (to that of having attained state pension credit qualifying age) of the relative having limited capability for work may possibly be more restrictive than that of being incapacitated. Regulations 38–44 only apply to determining whether a *claimant* has limited capability for work, or for work and work-related activity. Thus it is arguable either that the words "limited capability for work" merely have their ordinary meaning or that it is not necessary that the relative be in receipt of any benefit or credit based on a determination as to limited capability for work.

Paragraph 3 (premises occupied by a former partner as their home) is the equivalent of para.4(b) of the income support Sch.10, but with slightly different conditions. The application of para.4(b) is excluded where there has been a divorce from the former partner or a dissolution of a civil partnership as well as where the claimant and the former partner are estranged. The application of para.3 is not automatically excluded by divorce or the dissolution of a civil partnership, but is where there is estrangement, which may or may not follow such procedures, especially after some lapse of time. More important is the positive condition, not present in para.4(b) of the income support Sch.10, that the two are living apart by force of circumstances. That will prevent the application of the disregard for many non-estranged former partners. But it will apply to claimants who are in a residential home and so no longer share a household with their former partner for that reason. See also the potential disregard in para.5 where the claimant has ceased within the previous 6 months (or longer where the former partner is a lone parent) to occupy premises following an estrangement from their former partner.

Estrangement is a slippery concept that has generated case law in other benefits from which it is difficult to take clear guidance, not least because it is hard to see just what policy objective is served by preventing the application of the disregard when the claimant is estranged from the former partner. In the absence of any definition in the legislation, estrangement must be given its ordinary meaning in context. Some difference in expression among decisions, none of which purport to give definitions, is therefore to be expected and too much attention should not be given to such differences that may simply stem from the circumstances of the particular case in which the question was addressed (*CIS/4096/2005* and *AC v SSWP (IS)* [2015] UKUT 49 (AAC)). The discussion below attempts to concentrate on principles on which there is general agreement without citing all the decisions mentioned in past editions.

First, it is well established that estrangement is not the same as separation (*CIS/4843/2002*, *R(IS) 5/07*) and that separation does not necessarily imply estrangement (*R(IS) 5/05*). Nor does divorce or dissolution of a civil partnership necessarily imply estrangement, but no doubt normally the initial circumstances would indicate estrangement as discussed below and there would have to be some real intention to resume living together to found a different conclusion. By definition, to be a former partner the person must at least no longer be a member of the same household as the claimant. It must be remembered that, as pointed out in *R(IS) 5/05*, a person may temporarily be living away from a claimant and yet still be a member of the household. That is so on the general meaning of the term and as the basis of the special rule in reg.3(6), which purports to limit that effect of a temporary absence to six months (the form of reg.3(6) appears to be somewhat circular, because it refers to temporary absence from the claimant's household when a temporary absence would mean that the household was still shared, so "household" may have to mean little more than accommodation). Examples might be where a spouse or partner is in a care or nursing home or hospital or caring for a sick relative or friend in another place for a time that is realistically hoped to be temporary. In such circumstances, the two remain a couple as defined in s.39 of the WRA 2012 and partners, so that the two must claim universal credit as joint claimants. But the value of the premises where the person is staying (if the other partner happened to have an interest in them) could not be disregarded under para.1 (because only one set of premises occupied as the home is covered) or para.2 (because a partner is not a close relative) or para.3 (because the person is not a *former* partner). If the separation has been permanent or open-ended from the outset (so as not to be merely temporary) or becomes non-temporary after a change of circumstances (including the time that it has continued), the person will be a former partner.

If there is separation such as to make the person a former partner, "estrangement" must entail something further in order to give some force to the condition of not being estranged. *R(IS) 5/05* agrees with *R(SB) 2/87* that estrangement has a "connotation of emotional disharmony". That has been accepted in subsequent decisions, but the important matter is the context in which such disharmony is to be assessed. There can be friendly relations between the claimant and former partner although they are estranged for the purposes of the disregard (*R(IS) 5/05*, para.12, *CPC/683/2007*, *CH/377/2007* and *Bristol CC v SJP (HB)* [2019] UKUT 360 (AAC), paras 34–37, where there is a helpful summary of the earlier decisions). The way that Commissioner Rowland put it in *R(IS) 5/05* was that the question was whether the parties had ceased to consider themselves a couple, as has been accepted and applied in later cases. That needs some unpacking because "couple" has a particular meaning within the legislation that by definition cannot be met where the person is a former partner. So the word must be used in a more general everyday sense.

In para.13 of *CPC/683/2007*, Commissioner Jacobs said this:

> "It seems to me that the proper analysis of the relationship between the claimant and his wife is this. They remain married and have no plans to divorce. He would like to resume living with her, but she is opposed to the idea. The reality is that they will never resume living as husband and wife; the claimant accepts that. However, they are not hostile to each other on a personal level and he feels

a continuing responsibility towards her. This leads him to help her when she cannot manage on account of her ill-health. In other words, there is no emotional disharmony between the claimant and his wife as adults, but there is emotional disharmony between them as partners. That is a key distinction, because the language used in the legislation is attempting to identify those cases in which the relationship between the parties is such that it is appropriate for their finances to be treated separately for the purposes of benefit entitlement. Once the facts of the case are set out, they seem to me to allow of only one interpretation, which is that the couple are estranged."

The distinction between disharmony as partners and disharmony as adults is a useful one. It is no doubt going too far to say, as the same judge did in *CH/117/2005*, that two people are not estranged if they retain all the indicia of partners apart from physical presence in the same household, at least if that were to be taken out of context to represent a test that separation equals estrangement unless that condition is met. That would not be compatible with a proper consideration of the circumstances of particular cases and an application of the ordinary meaning of estrangement. But it perhaps illustrates one end of the continuum, where although the person is a former partner, because the separation is non-temporary, they and the claimant would be members of the same household if it were not for the circumstances enforcing the separation. At the other end of the continuum are cases where a relationship has broken down such that there is no current prospect of a resumption of living together. Then, no matter how amicable and co-operative the parties might be about, say children, finances and other practical matters, there is estrangement. There is an emotional disharmony between them as partners.

In *CIS/4096/2005*, Commissioner Jupp, in a different context, indicated that estrangement does not require mutuality of feeling. Disharmony can arise from one person's attitude to another even though the other party may not wish the situation to be as it is. The form of para.3 does not ask whether one party is estranged from the other, as for other benefits, but whether the person and the former partner are not estranged. So the question is whether a state of estrangements exists between them. If the realistic position is that the attitude of one party prevents any resumption of a relationship as partners, the fact that the other party did not wish the situation to be as it was or hoped that the estrangement might not be permanent (*CH/377/2007*) does not on its own point against a conclusion that the other party is estranged from the first.

If estrangement is approached in the way suggested above there will be little work for the additional condition of living apart by force of circumstances to do. For the parties not to be estranged something very like that will have to be the case. Note that some people may be in residential care and yet estranged. And someone may be in residential care on a temporary basis, such that the parties remain a couple and the person is not a *former* partner.

Paragraph 4(1)(a) (premises acquired within past 6 months and intends to occupy as the home) is the equivalent of para.2 of the income support Sch.10, with a very slightly wider application. Paragraph 2 requires any extension to the period of 26 weeks from acquisition to be reasonable in the circumstances to enable the claimant to obtain possession and commence occupation. Under para.4(1)(a), provided as always that there is an intention to occupy the premises as the home, the extension to the period of six months under reg.48(2) can be made whenever it is reasonable in the circumstances.

Paragraph 4(1)(b) (commenced steps to obtain possession of premises within the past 6 months) is the equivalent of para.27 of the income support Sch.10. The provisions in sub-para.(2) about when a person is to be deemed to have commenced steps to obtain possession make the conditions the same as under para.27, except that any extension to the period of 6 months under reg.48(2) can be made whenever it is reasonable in the circumstances instead of being linked to enabling obtaining possession and commencing occupation.

Paragraph 4(1)(c) (essential repairs or alterations, commenced within the past 6 months, to render premises fit for occupation) is the equivalent of para.28 of the income support Sch.10, but with a narrower scope. The income support disregard starts from the date on which steps were first taken to effect the repairs, which can cover getting a grant or loan for the cost of the works, applying for permissions or consulting an architect or contractors. In para.4(1)(c) the person must be carrying out the essential repairs or alterations. It is not clear where in the preparatory process that might start. Nor is it entirely clear that alterations essential for occupation by the particular person (e.g. adaptations for someone who is disabled) are covered. The alterations might need to be required to render the premises fit for occupation by anyone. However, note that if the claimant has already taken up occupation as the home para.1 will apply and that if the premises were acquired within the previous six months (extendable) there is the more general disregard in para.4(1)(a). Regulation 48(2) allows the six months from commencement to be extended as reasonable.

Paragraph 5 (claimant ceased to occupy premises as home following estrangement from former partner) is the equivalent of para.25 of the income support Sch.10, except that it does not automatically apply on divorce or the dissolution of a civil partnership, only on estrangement. See the notes to para.3 for discussion of estrangement. The 6 months under sub-para.(b) can be extended where reasonable in the circumstances under reg.48(2).

The disregard applies in any circumstances for the first six months (extendable where reasonable: reg.48(2)) after the claimant ceases to occupy the previous home (sub-para.(a). Otherwise the premises must be occupied by the former partner as their home and the former partner must be a lone parent (sub-para.(b)). "Lone parent" is not defined in the Regulations or in the WRA 2012 (by contrast it is defined in the Income Support Regulations). It is therefore arguable that the phrase is to be given its ordinary everyday meaning, without any technical tests to do with responsibility or membership of the household or even the age of the children or young persons in question, accepting that it must be the case that the former partner does not have a current partner as defined in reg.2. However, it is also arguable that in the context of the Regulations as a whole the phrase must be taken to refer to someone who is responsible for a child or young person under reg.4. That makes the initial test whether the child normally lives with the person concerned, but where the child normally lives with two or more people, then only one can be taken as responsible and that is the person who has the main responsibility (reg.4(4)). The people concerned can make a joint declaration as to who has main responsibility, subject to decision by the Secretary of State in default of agreement or if the nomination does not reflect the actual arrangements. The issue could be problematic where the claimant and the former partner have children who move between their now separate households on a more or less equal basis. It appears that who has the child benefit is not only not determinative, but may be irrelevant to an assessment which is focused on responsibility in substance (see *MC v SSWP (UC)* [2018] UKUT 44 (AAC) in the notes to reg.4).

Paragraph 6 (commenced taking reasonable steps to dispose of premises within past 6 months) is the equivalent of para.26 of the income support Sch.10. The 6 months can be extended where reasonable in the circumstances under reg.48(2). In both provisions the disregard applies to any premises, not just premises occupied as the home. Thus it should cover land without any building on it (*R(IS) 4/97*).

Steps to dispose of premises can include many preparatory steps before actually putting them on the market. Things that have been accepted include obtaining a solicitor's quotation for sale charges and obtaining an estate agent's valuation (*JT v Leicester CC (CTB)* [2012] UKUT 445 (AAC)), making a genuine approach to another tenant in common to agree a sale (*JH v SSWP* [2009] UKUT 1 (AAC)), bringing ancillary relief proceedings within a divorce suit (*R(IS) 5/05*) or even the bringing of divorce proceedings (*CIS/195/2007*). That last decision suggests that if, once steps have first been taken, there is some temporary suspension of activity (e.g. because of family pressures, threats of violence or efforts at reconciliation), that does not necessarily mean that steps are no longer being taken, but it would all depend on the circumstances. What are "reasonable" steps is a question of fact with a margin of judgment involved, but according to *R(IS) 4/97* the test is an objective one. So if a property is put up for sale at a totally unrealistic price, the disregard would not apply. If the asking price was later lowered to something realistic, it could start to apply and it would be that date at which reasonable steps commenced and at which the primary six months started to run.

In some cases, where reasonable steps stop being taken (as opposed to there being a mere temporary suspension or diminution of activity) and are later resumed it will be right to regard the commencement of reasonable steps as taking place at the beginning, not at the date of the resumption. But that is not necessarily always the case (see *SP v SSWP* [2009] UKUT 255 (AAC)). If premises are genuinely taken off the market and later, in different circumstances, are put on the market again, it is arguable that the disregard can start to be applied afresh, with a new six months starting to run. A gap in the receipt of benefit would not automatically have that effect, but could be one of the relevant circumstances to be taken into account.

It was decided in *CIS/30/1993* that the income support disregard could not apply to premises that the claimant had already disposed of, but was treated as still possessing the value of under the notional capital rule. That was because the income support disregard only applied if the claimant was taking reasonable steps to dispose of the premises, which was impossible as only the new owner could take such steps. That reasoning would apply equally to para.6 as the person who has to be taking the reasonable steps must be the person whose capital would be relevant to the universal credit claim were it not for the effect of reg.48(2) in applying the Sch.10 disregards.

Business assets

2.543   *Paragraph 7* (assets of trade etc. being carried on) is the equivalent of the first part of para.6(1) of the income support Sch.10. Income support para.6 uses the terms of assets of a business owned in whole or in part by the claimant for the purposes of which he is engaged as a self-employed earner. In view of the meaning of self-employed earner, the use here of the terms "used wholly or mainly for the purposes of a trade, profession or vocation" comes to the same thing. Paragraph 7 applies while the claimant is carrying on that trade, profession or vocation. See the notes to reg.64 for when a person is carrying on a trade etc, from which it is clear that a person may be trading in that sense ("in work") while not currently engaged in activities ("at work"). In this respect, it is arguable that the scope of para.7 is broader than that of the income support para.6(1). For those purposes, it has been held that to be "engaged in" a business a claimant must be performing some business activities in some practical sense as an earner (see the discussion of *Chief Adjudication Officer v Knight*, reported as part of *R(IS) 14/98*, in the notes to para.6(1) of the income support Sch.10 in Vol.V of this series). That appears to make the test whether the self-employed person is "at work". But the concept of "carrying on" a trade etc. in para.7 is significantly different. See the notes to para.8 below for the apparent resulting mismatch between the two provisions.

Note that with effect from May 21, 2020, reg.2(2) of the Universal Credit (Coronavirus) (Self-employed Claimants and Reclaims) (Amendment) Regulations 2020 (SI 2020/522) introduced a 12-month disregard as capital of any payment made to a self-employed claimant under the Coronavirus Job Retention Scheme (CJRS) or by way of a grant or loan to meet the expenses or losses of the trade, profession or vocation in relation to the outbreak of coronavirus disease. For the CJRS disregard to apply, the claimant must have one or more employees who were furloughed (see further in the notes to reg.57) or be a person deemed to be self-employed under reg.77 (company analogous to partnership or one-person business) who has furloughed themselves or other employees. The second disregard would appear to be intended to cover grants under the Self-Employed Income Support Scheme (SEISS), the Small Business Grant Fund or the Retail, Hospitality and Leisure Grant Fund (or similar funds) and loans under the Business Interruption Loan Schemes or the Bounce Back Loan Scheme (all replaced after March 31, 2021 by the Recovery Loan Scheme) or similar. The wording is problematic, because it is not clear that the conditions and method of calculation of all those schemes show that the payments are "to meet" expenses or losses (see the discussion in the notes to reg.57), rather than being undifferentiated in nature. Paragraph 7.12 of the Explanatory Memorandum to the Regulations mentions several of the above schemes, but oddly not the SEISS, as being covered. There is no guidance on the issue in para.4 of Memo ADM 10/20. It would appear, however, that, whether or not any payment was to be treated as an income receipt (see again the notes to reg.57), the capital represented by funds retained in the business after the assessment period of receipt would have been disregarded anyway under the principles discussed below while the claimant was continuing to carry on the trade etc (or under para.8 if the claimant had ceased to do so). The funds would be used for the purposes of the business.

The income support disregard applies to the assets of a business partly or wholly owned by a claimant. Here, para.7 applies to assets wholly or mainly "used" for the purposes of the trade etc. The income support disregard therefore appears to apply to any asset used to any extent beyond the de minimis in the business. For instance, the value of a vehicle used for 10% of the time for self-employment and for 90% of the time for personal purposes would seem to be disregarded under that rule. It is accordingly arguable that the universal credit position would be different, so that the value of the vehicle would not be disregarded under para.7 unless the business use amounted to more than 50%. But, if that test is met, the whole value of the asset is disregarded. There is no scope for any apportionment. By contrast, it seems that the use of the word "used" involves no more restrictive condition than under the income support disregard. There, business assets are distinguished from personal assets by asking whether they are "part of the fund employed and risked in the business" *(R(SB) 4/85)*. The question whether assets are used for the purposes of a trade etc is substantially the same.

In answering those questions, the income tax and accounting position are factors to be taken into account, but are not conclusive *(CFC/10/1989)*. The Commissioner in *R(SB) 4/85* noted that, while people in a business partnership owe a duty to the other partner(s) to keep business assets severed from and not mixed with their own assets, the same does not apply to sole traders. They can mix their own and business assets together and can freely transfer items from business to personal assets and vice versa. Although so far as money is concerned it is much more straightforward if a self-employed person maintains a business account separate from any personal accounts and keeps receipts and expenditure to the appropriate account, many of those in small-scale self-employment will not maintain any separate bank or building society account. The account may even be a joint account with a person not involved in the business. That in itself is not fatal to the identification of some sums in the mixed account as employed and risked in the business. It becomes a matter of whether there is sufficient evidence (and no doubt it falls to the claimant to come forward with the evidence if there is no separate business account) to be able to identify such an asset. Thus, for instance, if claimants can show that they have a sum of money in a mixed account that is set aside to meet income tax due for payment in the future on their self-employed earnings, that would seem to fall within the scope of this disregard. By contrast, in *CIS/2467/2003* money put by an author into a Maxi ISA, designed for personal savings by medium or long term investment, was found not to have been employed in the business, but to be in the personal sphere as the proceeds of the business. The Commissioner stated that claimants who wished to benefit from the para.6 disregard in relation to money that was not in a separate business account would have to show a clear demarcation between the assets of the business and personal assets. However, it is submitted that that should be taken more as an explanation of why, on the circumstances of the particular case, the claimant had failed to show that he could benefit from the disregard than as a rule of thumb to be applied in place of the principle laid down in *R(SB) 4/85*. Everything depends on the assessment of the evidence in individual cases.

In the particular context of universal credit, the above principles may help to resolve a conundrum stemming from the method of calculating earnings, at least for the self-employed if not for employees. The rule for the self-employed in reg.57 is that income receipts are taken into account in the assessment period in which they are received. The principle that an amount cannot be income and capital at the same time (see *R(IS) 3/93* and *R(IS) 9/08*) would then probably entail that the receipt and funds derived from it could not be capital during that assessment period. But any proceeds left over in future assessment periods would be capital, it appears regardless of whether surplus earnings would be attributed to those periods under reg.54A as result of the amount of the particular receipt. But the proceeds would still be assets used for the purposes of the trade etc, so would be disregarded as capital under para.7. There is no such escape route for employees. But see the notes to reg.54A (at 2.196) for the argument that the amount of any retained earnings to be taken into account as surplus earnings in any assessment period does not count as capital because the application of reg.54A represents a liability that has to be deducted before the metamorphosis from earnings to capital takes place. That argument can work for the self-employed and employees. See also the special disregard for the self-employed of some coronavirus payments or loans with effect from May 21, 2020 in reg.2(2) of the Self-employed Claimants and Regulations as noted above.

R(FC) 2/92 holds that the ownership by an individual of a tenanted house is not in itself a business, although there may come a point, depending on the circumstances, at which the amount of administration and/or activity involved even in the letting out of a single property could amount to self-employment. See also *RM v Sefton Council (HB)* [2016] UKUT 357 (AAC), reported as [2017] AACR 5, where there was an exceptionally comprehensive survey of the existing authorities. It concluded that, apart from the mere carrying out of the duties of a landlord of one dwelling being insufficient, there are no hard and fast rules, merely factors that point one way or the other. But note carefully that for universal credit the test for the disregard is in terms of trade, profession or vocation and that trade is a narrower concept than business (see the discussion, particularly in the context of rented property, in the notes to regs 52 and 77(1) (See 2.299)).

Paragraph 8 (assets of trade etc. that ceased to carry on within the past 6 months) is the equivalent of the second part of para.6(1) and para.6(2) of the income support Sch.10. The disregard is arguably narrower in scope than the income support disregard because it applies only when the claimant has ceased to carry on the trade etc, which may, for the reasons given in the notes to para.7, entail a more definite cessation of trading as a whole, rather than a ceasing to be engaged in activities. Sub-para.(a), where the carrying on of trade ceased for any reason, is limited to circumstances where the claimant is taking reasonable steps to dispose of the assets. Presumably, that allows the value of only some assets, to which that applies, to be disregarded, leaving the value of the rest to count against the capital limits. Under sub-para.(b) the claimant must have ceased to be engaged in carrying on the trade etc because of incapacity (not further defined) and have a reasonable expectation of re-engaging on recovery. That is odd language, because if there has merely been a cessation of engagement in practical activities in the business, with the reasonable expectation of re-engagement once the incapacity is over, the conclusion in most cases would be that the claimant had not ceased to carry on the trade etc., so that the para.7 disregard would still apply. There would only be an easy fit with para.7 if that provision did not apply once a claimant had ceased to be engaged in activities. But on any basis a claimant should not be deprived of a disregard in the circumstances covered by para.8(b). Note that, by contrast with the income support position, incapacity has to be the reason for the cessation of engagement, not merely a reason for a continuation of a cessation started for another reason or a reason for not beginning to play a part in a business for the first time. The period of 6 months since ceasing to be engaged can be extended where reasonable in the circumstances under reg.48(2).

Note that where reg.77 applies (person in a position analogous to that of a sole trader or partner in relation to a company carrying on a trade treated as sole owner or partner and as possessing capital equal to the value of the company's capital, or a share), the value of that deemed capital is disregarded by reg.77(3)(a) while the person is engaged in activities in the course of that trade.

Rights in pensions schemes etc.

Note first that many provisions in the income support Sch.10 disregarding the capital value of the right to receive various forms of income are not replicated in the present Schedule (e.g. paras 11 (annuities, but see reg.46(3)), 12 (trust funds derived from personal injury compensation, but see reg.75(4)), 13 (life interests and liferents), 16 (capital payable by instalments, but see reg.46(4)), 24 (rent)).

2.544

Paragraph 9 (life insurance policies) is the equivalent of para.15 of the income support Sch.10. The latter refers to the surrender value. Paragraph 9 does not, but in the light of reg.49(1), the disregard must apply to whichever of the market value or surrender value has been applied to the policy.

Paragraph 10 (occupational or personal pension schemes) is the equivalent of para.23 of the income support Sch.10. The right to receive a pension from the schemes mentioned is not capable of being bought or sold and so would have no capital value anyway. There is no equivalent in the present Schedule to para.23A of the income support Sch.10 disregarding the value of any funds held under a personal pension scheme. It is no doubt considered that such funds do not form part of the capital of the member of the scheme, whose interests are only in the rights under the scheme rather than in the fund itself.

In the Institute for Government and the Social Security Advisory Committee's 2021 joint report *Jobs and benefits: The Covid-19 challenge* it was recommended that the value of Lifetime ISAs should be disregarded as capital because they are used by individuals, particularly the self-employed who have no access to occupational schemes, as a form of pension provision (pp.23 and 31). That recommendation was rejected in the Government's response of March 22, 2022, in particular on the ground that investments where the government had made a contribution to encourage saving should be taken into account.

Paragraph 11 (funeral plan contracts) has no equivalent in the income support Sch.10.

Amounts earmarked for special purposes

Paragraph 12 (housing association deposits as a condition of occupying the home) is the equivalent of para.9(a) of the income support Sch.10. The latter defines housing association.

2.545

Paragraph 13(a) (amounts received within the past 6 months attributable to proceeds of sale of previous home to be used for the purchase of premises to be occupied as the home) is the equivalent of para.3 of the income support Sch.10. Under the latter, the sum must be directly attributable to the proceeds of sale, rather than merely attributable. The emphasis of the 6-month condition is different. Under income support para.3 the intention must be to occupy new premises within 26 weeks of the sale of the previous home. Under para.13(a) there is simply a limit (extendable under reg.48(2)) of 6 months from the receipt of the proceeds of sale and no condition that the intention be to occupy the new home within any particular period. See *R(IS) 7/01* on the effect of the test of "is to be used". It was held there that there must not only be an intention to use the proceeds to buy a new home (which can include buying land to build a house on), but also "reasonable certainty" that it will be so used. A mere hope that the proceeds will be used at some future date for another home is not sufficient.

In *EAM v SSWP (UC)* [2020] UKUT 247 (AAC), Judge Poynter declined to follow *R(IS) 7/01* and the other decisions referred to there as being inconsistent with the principle conclusively confirmed in *In re B (Children)* [2008] UKHL 35, [2009] A.C. 11 that there is only one civil standard of proof and that is proof that the fact in issue more probably occurred than not. His view was that to apply a test in terms of any kind of certainty was to place a higher burden on the claimant than the balance of probabilities. Although he agreed with the proposition in *R(IS) 7/01* that a mere genuine intention to use the sum to purchase a new home is not enough, he continued in para.33 that the phrase "is to be used for the purchase of premises" is about "what in all the circumstances of the case (including the claimant's intentions) is likely to happen in practice". Then he said in para.34 that to the extent that the *R(IS) 7/01* test requires a claimant to prove any fact to any standard other than the balance of probabilities he declined to follow that decision.

There are at least two problems in applying *EAM*. One is that it was not necessary to the decision for the judge to reach a definite conclusion on the correctness of *R(IS) 7/01*. On the facts as found by the First-tier Tribunal, the remaining amount attributable to the proceeds of sale of the claimant's home (£37,000) was not enough to buy a new home for her and her partner, so that they would need a mortgage, which on the balance of probabilities they would be unable to secure because of the level of their indebtedness. Accordingly, although the tribunal had been inconsistent on the nature of the test and had seemed to apply a test of practical certainty in concluding that the sum was not to be disregarded, its decision was not set aside because the same result would have followed if Judge Poynter's suggested test had been used. That undermines the basis for not following a reported decision that might otherwise have existed if a First-tier Tribunal or the Secretary of State considered Judge Poynter's reasoning, especially as supported by House of Lords' authority, to be persuasive.

The second problem is that the judge's reasoning appears dubious. There is a slight uncertainty about whether the disagreement with *R(IS) 7/01* extended only to the burden of proving facts necessary to the application of the legislative test or whether it extended also to the burden of showing that that test is met in all the circumstances as established by findings of fact. On balance, the latter seems to be intended. But then the result in accordance with para.33 is that the test to be applied is whether it is more likely than not that the sum will be used for the purchase of premises. Such a test appears, as a matter of the ordinary use of language, to be significantly different from and less restrictive than the legislative test in terms of "is to be used". Arguably, Judge Poynter's approach conflates the nature of the burden of proving that the legislative test is met with the true meaning of that test.

Unless and until *EAM* is taken to the Court of Appeal or is given the status of a reported decision or there is some further decision clarifying the issue (which may well take some years), tribunals may wish to hedge their bets by applying both approaches in the alternative, but only if properly satisfied that the outcome would be the same whichever was applied. If not so satisfied, a choice will have to be made as to whether the reasoning in *EAM* is sufficiently persuasive to be preferred to the approach approved in *R(IS) 7/01*.

A claimant who has a sum attributable to the proceeds of sale of home A and is currently living in home B may claim the advantage of the disregard provided that there is the requisite intention and reasonable certainty of use in relation to home C (*CIS/4269/2003*). However, the change in the condition for universal credit as compared to income support, of having received the sum within the previous six months (extendable) rather than intending to occupy the new home within 26 weeks (extendable) makes such a scenario more difficult to get within the terms of the disregard. The disregard cannot apply if the claimant has already bought a new home prior to the sale of the former home and at the time of the purchase it was not intended that the former home would be sold (*WT v DSD (IS)* [2011] NI Com 203).

Paragraph 13(b) (amounts received within the past 6 months to be used for the purchase of premises to be occupied as the home that have been deposited with a housing association) is the equivalent of para.9(b) of the income support Sch.10. See the notes to para.13(a) for "is to be used". The six months can be extended where reasonable in the circumstances under reg.48(2).

Paragraph 13(c) (grant received in the past 6 months for sole purpose of purchase of a home) appears to be the equivalent of para.37(a) of the income support Sch.10, but without any limitation as to the source of the grant. The definition of "grant" in reg.68(7) (see reg.2) does not seem applicable in the context of para.13(c). See the notes to para.13(a) for "is to be used". The six months can be extended where reasonable in the circumstances under reg.48(2).

Paragraph 14 (amount received within the past 6 months under an insurance policy in connection with loss of or damage to the home or personal possessions) is the equivalent of para.8(a) of the income support Sch.10, but without the condition that the sum be intended for repair and replacement. The 6 months can be extended where reasonable in the circumstances under reg.48(2).

Paragraph 15 (amount received within the past 6 months to be used for essential repairs or alterations to premises occupied or to be occupied as the home, where condition that it be used for that purpose) is the equivalent of para.8(b) of the income support Sch.10. See the notes to para.13(a) on the effect of the test of "is to be used". The 6 months can be extended where reasonable in the circumstances under reg.48(2).

Other payments

Paragraph 16 (social fund payments made within the past 12 months) is the equivalent of para.18 of the income support Sch.10. The 12 months is not extendable.

2.546

Paragraph 17 (local authority welfare payments made within the past 12 months) appears to be the equivalent of paras 17(1) and (2) and 67 of the income support Sch.10 with some extension, but not so as to replicate the scope of para.18A of that Schedule on "local welfare provision". Under sub-para.(a) only payments by a local authority under the specified legislation, to do with the welfare of children, are disregarded. Under sub-para.(b) there is no restriction to any particular legislative provision as the source of the power to make the payment, but it must be to meet a person's welfare needs related to old age or disability, subject to the exception of payments for living expenses. That is a good deal narrower than the category of "local welfare provision" now, from May 4, 2022, covered by para.18A. See the notes near the beginning of this commentary for the possible consequences for the one-off support payment to be made to working tax credit recipients in April 2021. It must always be asked whether payments constitute income rather than capital. But even if a payment, such as possibly the WTC payment, is income, any unspent sum out of that income will metamorphise into capital under the principles discussed in the notes to reg.45 (and see *R(IS) 3/93* and *R(IS) 9/08*). See the notes to reg.66 for the question of how payments of unearned income should be attributed to assessment periods. The 12 months is not extendable.

Paragraph 18 (arrears or compensation for late payment received within the past 12 months of universal credit and certain social security benefits) is the equivalent of para.7 of the income support Sch.10, although the specification of the other benefits covered is through a different method. The 12 months is not extendable. There is no provision, as there is for income support and other legacy benefits, for a longer disregard for large payments of arrears or compensation where the late payment was the result of official error or an error of law (but see regs 10A, 10B and 10C of the Transitional Provisions Regulations, mentioned below). The benefits abolished by s.33 of the WRA 2012 are income-based JSA, income-related ESA, income support, housing benefit, council tax benefit (already abolished), child tax credit and working tax credit. Benefits falling outside reg.66(1)(a) and (b) and therefore covered by the disregard will include child benefit, attendance allowance, any care or mobility component of disability living allowance, any daily living component or mobility component of personal independence payment and the monthly payments of the new bereavement support payment, as well as Scottish child payments and adult and child disability payments. Thus payments of arrears (or compensation for late payment) of the benefits listed in reg.66(1)(a) or (b), including retirement pension income and new style ESA and JSA, do not attract the capital disregard.

In principle, payments of benefits that would have had the character of income if paid on their due date retain that character when paid in arrears as a lump sum (*R(SB) 4/89* and *CH/1561/2005*, and see *Minter v Kingston upon Hull CC* and *Potter v Secretary of State for Work and Pensions* [2011] EWCA Civ 1155, reported as [2012] AACR 21 on lump sum payments of compensation in settlement of equal pay claims, discussed in the notes to reg.66). In *R(SB) 4/89*, the Commissioner, relying on the principle in *McCorquodale v Chief Adjudication Officer*, reported as *R(SB) 1/88*, held that the income should be taken into account in the periods for which it would have been taken into account if paid on the due dates. In view of the absence of a clear rule in regs.66 and 73 on the assessment period in which payments of unearned income are to be taken into account (see the notes to reg.66), it is arguable that the same principle would apply to universal credit. But there is also a principle that if any amount of income is left over after the end of the period to which it is properly to be attributed that amount metamorphoses into capital (*R(SB) 2/83* and *R(IS) 3/93*). Looking at the date on which the payment of arrears or compensation is made, by definition all the periods to which the income would have been attributed if paid on the due dates would have passed, so that the lump sum would constitute capital from that point on. The disregard would therefore bite at that point, if applicable. If, however, the lump sum should be taken into account as unearned income for a forward period starting with the assessment period in which it is paid, it would not constitute capital in the assessment periods in which it was so attributed, except to the extent that there were amounts left over from that attributed to each succeeding assessment period.

See reg.10A of the Universal Credit (Transitional Provisions) Regulations 2014 (Pt IIB of this volume), inserted with effect from September 11, 2018. This allows a longer period of disregard as capital in cases where a payment of arrears of benefit, or of compensation for arrears due to the non-payment of benefit, amounts to £5,000 or more and the period of entitlement to which the payment relates began before legacy benefits are totally abolished (introductory part of reg.10A(1) and para.(1)(d)). All cases of arrears or compensation for non-payment of benefit are covered. Apparently any benefit can be involved, as there is no special definition of that word. Thus benefits not included in the scope of para.18 are included, as well as the disregard being able to extend beyond 12 months (see below). There is no restriction to cases of official error or error of law. There are then two alternatives. The first (para.(1)(a)(i)) is that the payment is received during a current award of universal credit, in which case the disregard applies for 12 months from the date of receipt if the payment would have been disregarded if the claimant had been entitled to a legacy benefit or SPC. The second (para.(1)(ii)) is that the payment was received during an award of a legacy benefit or SPC and no more than a month elapsed between the ending of that award and the start of entitlement to universal credit. In that case the disregard applies for the same period if the payment was disregarded under the rules of the earlier award.

Regulation 10B of the Transitional Provisions Regulations 2014, inserted with effect from October 31, 2019, applies a disregard as capital for 12 months from the date of receipt to payments of arrears (or compensation for arrears) of maternity allowance (excluded from para.18 because listed in reg.66(1)(b)) of less than £5,000, if the conditions in reg.10A(1)(a)-(d) are met.

Regulation 10C of the Transitional Provisions Regulations 2014, inserted with effect from July 15, 2020, applies a disregard as capital for 12 months from the date of receipt of certain compensatory payments for delay or failure to carry out an assessment for old style contributory ESA, with additional conditions and a potential extension for payments of £5,000 or more.

Note that all these payments would, in accordance with the principles explained above, retain their character as income. Whether that has an effect on universal credit entitlement depends first on how far the period to which the payments falls before the start of the period of any universal credit award. To the extent that it does fall before, there can be no effect. To the extent that it does not there can be a revision under reg.12 of the Decisions and Appeals Regulations 2013. But that depends on whether the benefit concerned is listed in reg.66(1)(b). If not, the payment cannot be taken into account as unearned income.

Paragraph 18ZA (arrears of widowed parent's allowance) and the February 2023 amendment to para.20 on bereavement support payment deal with the consequences of payments of arrears made under the Bereavement Benefits (Remedial) Order 2023.

The legislation on widowed parent's allowance (WPA), and bereavement support payment (BSP) that replaced it for deaths after April 5, 2017, was declared incompatible with the ECHR by discriminating against children whose parents were cohabiting but not married to each other or in a civil partnership (see *Re McLaughlin's Application for Judicial Review* [2018] UKSC 48, [2018] 1 W.L.R. 4250 and *R (Jackson and others) v Secretary of State for Work and Pensions* [2020] EWHC 183, [2020] 1 W.L.R. 1441 in Vol.I of this series). The Remedial Order allows retrospective claims to be made for those benefits from August 30, 2018 onwards and accordingly for arrears of benefit to be paid if the conditions of entitlement are met. The new para.18ZA, and the amended para.20 on BSP, deal with the consequences of such payments on universal credit entitlement, although with somewhat differing outcomes, stemming from WPA being included as unearned income in reg.66(1)(b)(vi), to be taken into account in full in calculating entitlement, and from BSP not being so included.

The Explanatory Memorandum misleadingly asserts in para.7.15 that the Remedial Order provides for payments of arrears under the Order to be treated as capital and disregarded for the purposes of income-related benefits, in line with assurances that had been given by the government to the Joint Committee on Human Rights and in its response to public consultation on a draft of the Order (see *Draft Bereavement Benefits (Remedial Order 2022: Second Report* (HC 834, HL Paper 108) (December 6, 2022), para.61). However, it is absolutely plain that the amendments made by the Order do nothing to deem any payment of arrears to be capital. The new provisions like para.18ZA merely provide for a disregard of the payment for 52 weeks in so far as it is properly to be regarded as capital. It has been firmly established at least since the decision in *R(SB) 4/89* that cumulative arrears of social security benefits that would have been income if paid on time retain their nature as income though paid as a lump sum (see the notes to para.18). Then, as argued in the notes to reg.66 (under the heading *Attribution of unearned income to assessment periods*, 2.270), the monthly amounts of the arrears would be taken into account in the past assessment periods to which they related. That would trigger the Secretary of State's power to revise the decision(s) awarding universal credit in reg.12 of the Decisions and Appeals) Regulations 2013 (Vol.III of this series) for any periods to which the arrears were attributable as income and a resulting overpayment would be recoverable certainly under s.71ZB of the SSAA 1992 (and see in particular subs. (5)), but also possibly under s.74(2) and (4).

That that is the legal position (apart from the s.74(2) point) was effectively conceded by Viscount Younger, the Minister for Work and Pensions in the House of Lords, in a letter of February 2, 2023 to Baroness Sherlock (deposited in the Library of the House of Lords), in which he said this:

"It is right that usual rules apply in these cases, to ensure that we don't treat cohabitee claimants differently to those claimants who were in a legal union with the deceased. WPA is taken into account as income when assessing entitlement to other means-tested benefits. Where a claimant was in receipt of a legacy income-related benefit during the period of entitlement for WPA, we will offset any overpayment of the relevant benefit from the retrospective lump sum of WPA and pay a net WPA award. Where a claimant was in receipt of Universal Credit during the period of WPA entitlement, the claimant may incur an overpayment of Universal Credit as a consequence of receiving a retrospective WPA award. We will make this clear to claimants, so that they are able to make an informed choice about making a claim."

The Explanatory Memorandum appears not so far to have been corrected, despite the error having been made plain to those responsible, and DMG Memo 2/23 makes no mention of this issue.

Lord Younger's letter states that for universal credit claimants arrears of WPA will be paid in full, with a universal credit overpayment to follow, with no process of abatement (what he calls an offset) of the amount of the arrears payable, as for legacy benefits, but does not explain why. It may be that the administrative and computer systems are not currently capable of carrying out that operation, but there also appears to be a suggestion that there is not a legal power to abate/offset. It might have been thought that, despite the amendment to s.74(2) of the SSAA 1992 in February 2013 allowing abatement where more universal credit has been paid than would have been if a prescribed payment had been made on time, that provision cannot apply because no payments have been prescribed for that purpose in the Social Security (Overpayments and Recovery) Regulations 2013. However, WPA is a prescribed payment under reg.8(1)(i) of the Social Security (Payments, Overpayments and Recovery) Regulations 2008, which thus allows the abatement of such payments. There then seems no reason why, given the specific amendment to the general effect of s.74(2), the abatement process should not be used where it is excess universal credit that had been paid.

A further obstacle has been thought to lie in the exceptionally obscure provisions of reg.16 of the Overpayments and Recovery Regulations 2013 (Vol.III of this series) on offsetting, and in particular para.(4). However, close analysis suggests that reg.16 simply cannot apply where the entitlement to the benefit that then counts as unearned income for the past arises from a new claim, as here. It only applies where an original decision has been revised, superseded or set aside on appeal (para.(1)).

If those arguments are wrong and s.74(2) abatement is not available, recoverability of the overpaid universal credit would undoubtably arise under s.71ZB of the SSAA 1992. It might then be asked why the overpayment of universal credit cannot be deducted from the WPA arrears under s.71ZC and reg.10 of the Overpayment and Recovery Regulations 2013 on recovery by deduction from benefits, which specifies any benefits under Pts 2 to 5 of the SSCBA 1992 that are payable as open to such recovery. But there would then be a problem of timing. There could not be a revision of the decisions awarding universal credit and identifying an overpayment until after there had been a decision on the retrospective WPA claim that specified what amounts the claimant was entitled to and for what periods. Regulation 16 of the Decisions and Appeals Regulations 1999 would not appear to allow suspension of payment of the WPA merely because that might give rise to an overpayment of a different benefit. Thus, if the abatement process under s.74(2) of the SSAA 1992 is not properly available, as it is for legacy benefits, it may be that there is no way of adopting an equivalent process and that the consequences of illicitly delaying payment of the WPA arrears until after the universal credit authorities have made the overpayment recovery decision are too messy to contemplate.

It is therefore to be hoped that the warning to claimants mentioned by Lord Younger will be sufficiently explicit to deter them from spending any of the money that would be needed to cover the universal credit overpayment. The payment of arrears will immediately, because the assessment periods to which it is to be attributed as income will all be in the past, metamorphose into capital on accepted principles (see *R(IS) 3/93* and *R(IS) 9/08* and the notes to reg.18). The new para.18ZA will of course operate to disregard that amount, including that for any periods when there was universal credit entitlement, as capital for 12 months from receipt.

Note that the outcome for BSP (see the amendment to para.20) is different because BSP is not included in the list of benefits in reg.66(1) that count as unearned income for universal credit purposes.

Paragraph 18A (local welfare provision) was introduced with effect from May 4, 2022 to provide a capital disregard for "local welfare provision", as newly defined in reg.2. The definition is in the same terms as for the corresponding disregard that has existed for some time for other means-tested benefits. It covers occasional financial or other assistance given by or on behalf of a local authority or the Scottish or Welsh Ministers to help to meet an immediate short-term need arising out of an exceptional event or circumstances that has to be met to avoid a risk to an individual's well-being or to enable individuals to establish or maintain a settled home. According to the Explanatory Memorandum to the amending regulations (SI 2022/448) that is to bring the universal credit provision into line with that for other means-tested benefits, there never having been any policy intention that such payments should be taken into account as capital, the problem having become particularly apparent in the light of the introduction of the £350 per month "thank you" payments under the Homes for Ukraine scheme and the extension of the Household Support Fund (the successor of the Covid Winter Grant Scheme and the Local Grant Scheme).

Paragraph 19 (Victoria Cross and George Cross) is the equivalent of para.46 of the income support Sch.10.

Paragraph 20 (bereavement support payments) now covers two different elements of these payments. In so far as payments have the nature of income they do not count as unearned income because they are not in the list in reg.66(1). In the first month of entitlement to bereavement support payment (BSP) there is entitlement to a one-off addition to the usual rate, under reg.3(2) or (5) of the Bereavement Support Payment Regulations 2017 (in Vol.I of this series). If that is to be regarded as capital, its amount is disregarded under sub-para.(1) and that disregard will continue to operate for 12 months from receipt if the amount is not spent or disposed of in that first month (see the introductory part of the note to Sch.10 at 2.541). Any payment of arrears of the ordinary monthly payments would be disregarded as capital under reg.18.

Sub-paragraph (2) was added with effect from February 9, 2023 to deal specifically with the consequences of receipt of a payment of arrears of BSP on a retrospective claim under the Bereavement Benefits (Remedial) Order 2023. See the note to para.18ZA for the general background to such payments. Although a payment of arrears of ordinary monthly payments would in its nature be income attributable to the past assessment periods to which it was attributed, it would on receipt and retention immediately metamorphose into capital, which is then disregarded for 12 months under sub-para.(2). Arguably, the amendment was unnecessary because arrears of BSP are already disregarded as capital for the same period under para.18(1)(c).

Paragraph 21 disregards as capital any Scottish early years assistance, but only where given within the 12 months before the date in question. The restriction of this disregard to receipts within the previous 12 months does not apply to other means-tested benefits (see, for instance, para.75 of Sch.10 to the Income Support Regulations). Early years assistance is not listed in reg.66 of the Universal Credit Regulations 2013, so cannot count as unearned income, although since it takes the form of lump sum payments it probably could not have constituted income in any event.

Paragraph 22 disregards as capital any Scottish funeral expense assistance, but only where given within the 12 months before the date in question. The benefit is implemented by the Funeral Expense Assistance (Scotland) Regulations 2019 (SSI 2019/292) (see Pt XIII of Vol.IV of this series). Funeral expense assistance is not listed in reg.66, so cannot count as unearned income, although since it takes the form of lump sum payments would probably not have constituted income in any event.

Paragraph 23 (Scottish young carer grants) disregards as capital, with effect from November 9, 2020, the annual grants under the specified regulations (SSI 2019/324: see Pt XIII of Vol.IV of this series) received in the previous 52 weeks. The grants of (from April 2023) £369.65, limited to one a year, are payable in Scotland to carers aged 16 to 18 who care for at least 16 hours a week over a 13-week period for a person who normally receives a disability benefit. The 52-week limitation is absent from the equivalent provisions for "legacy benefits". Since the 2019 Regulations came into operation on October 21, 2019, there appears to have been a gap during which the grants were not disregarded as capital for the purposes of universal credit or legacy benefits. Young carer grants are not listed as unearned income in reg.66(1), but appear plainly to be in the nature of capital.

Paragraph 24 (Scottish winter heating assistance) disregards as capital, with effect from November 9, 2020, grants under the Winter Heating Assistance for Children and Young People (Scotland) Regulations 2020 (SSI 2020/352, also in operation from November 9, 2020: see Pt XIII of Vol.IV of this series) received in the previous 52 weeks. There was initially an automatic annual grant in November 2020 to a family of £200 (£235.70 for 2023) for each child entitled to the highest rate of the care component of DLA in the week of September 21–27, 2020. A single annual payment of £55.05 is now available to claimants with awards of qualifying benefits. The 52-week limitation is absent from the equivalent provisions for "legacy benefits". Winter heating assistance is not listed as unearned income in reg.66(1), but appears plainly to be in the nature of capital.

Omissions

2.547 A number of categories disregarded for the purposes of income support and old style ESA and JSA are thus not included in the universal credit Sch.10 or regs 75–77. Some cover very specific circumstances, but all are apparently deserving. They include payments of expenses of attending various schemes relating to jobseeking, the value of the right to receive the outstanding amount of capital payable by instalments, payments under a council tax reduction scheme and educational maintenance allowances.

Regulation 112

SCHEDULE 11

APPLICATION OF ESA OR JSA SANCTIONS TO UNIVERSAL CREDIT

Moving an ESA sanction to UC

2.548 1. (1) This paragraph applies where—
 (a) a person is, or has ceased to be, entitled to an employment and support allowance;
 (b) there is a reduction relating to the award of the employment and support allowance under section 11J of the Welfare Reform Act 2007; and
 (c) the person becomes entitled to universal credit.
(2) Any reduction relating to the award of the employment and support allowance is to be applied to the award of universal credit.
(3) The period for which the reduction is to have effect is the number of days which apply to the person under regulations 52 and 53 of the ESA Regulations minus—
 (a) any days which have already resulted in a reduction to the amount of the employment and support allowance; and
 (b) if the award of the employment and support allowance has terminated, any days falling after the date of that termination and before the date on which the award of universal credits starts, and that period is to be added to the total outstanding reduction period.
(4) The amount of the reduction in the award of universal credit for any assessment period in which the reduction is applied is the amount calculated in accordance with regulation 110.

Moving a JSA sanction to UC

2.549 2. (1) This paragraph applies where—
 (a) a person is, or has ceased to be, entitled to a jobseeker's allowance;
 (b) there is a reduction relating to the person's award of a jobseeker's allowance under section 6J or 6K of the Jobseekers Act 1995; and
 (c) the person becomes entitled to universal credit.
(2) Any reduction relating to the award of the jobseeker's allowance is to be applied to the award of universal credit.

(3) The period for which the reduction is to have effect is the number of days which apply to the person under regulations 19 to 21 of the Jobseeker's Allowance Regulations 2013 minus—
  (a) any days which have already resulted in a reduction to the amount of the jobseeker's allowance; and
  (b) if the award of the jobseeker's allowance has terminated, any days falling after the date of that termination and before the date on which the award of universal credits starts, and that period is to be added to the total outstanding reduction period.

(4) The amount of the reduction in the award of universal credit for any assessment period in which the reduction is applied is the amount calculated in accordance with regulation 110.

Effect of ESA or JSA sanction on escalation of UC sanction　2.550
  3. Where—
  (a) a reduction in relation to an award of an employment and support allowance or an award of a jobseeker's allowance is applied to an award of universal credit by virtue of paragraph 1 or 2;
  (b) there is a subsequent sanctionable failure under section 26 or 27 of the Act; and
  (c) the failure giving rise to the reduction in relation to the award of an employment and support allowance or the award of a jobseeker's allowance ("the previous failure") and the reduction period determined for that failure correspond with a failure specified under section 26 or 27 of the Act to which the same reduction period would apply under Chapter 2 of Part 8 of these Regulations,
for the purposes of determining the reduction period for that subsequent failure, the previous failure is to be treated as if it were the corresponding failure under section 26 or 27 of the Act.

GENERAL NOTE

Paragraphs. 1 and 2
  Paragraphs 1 and 2 constitute an important element of the relationship between　2.551 new style ESA and JSA and universal credit. They provide that where a claimant is entitled to new style ESA or JSA and is subject to a sanction under s.11J of the WRA 2007 or s.6J or 6K of the WRA 2012 and then becomes entitled to universal credit, and also where the claimant ceases to be entitled to new style ESA or JSA, the ESA or JSA reduction is to be applied to the universal credit award. That works in practice if entitlement to ESA or JSA has ceased, but if that entitlement continues, it is the case that the unreduced (see reg.42 of the ESA Regulations 2013 and reg.5 of the JSA Regulations 2013 disapplying the sanctions regime for those benefits in the circumstances of dual entitlement) amount of ESA or JSA counts as income in the calculation of the amount of any universal credit award and so cuts into the amount available for reduction under the universal credit sanction. That sanction cannot as such reduce the amount of new style ESA or JSA payable. It is in the nature of a reduction in the amount of an award of benefit that the reduction cannot exceed the amount of that particular award. That has the anomalous results discussed in the notes to reg.5 of the JSA Regulations 2013 in Vol.I of this series.
  The WRA 2012 contains a regulation-making power that could have been used to avoid these anomalous results. This is in para.2 of Sch.5, which applies when a claimant is entitled to both universal credit and a "relevant benefit", i.e. new style ESA or JSA. Paragraph 2(2) allows regulations in particular to provide in such circumstances for no amount to be payable by way of the relevant benefit. A Departmental memorandum to the House of Lords Select Committee on Delegated Powers and Regulatory Reform (see para.1.273) indicated that among the intended uses of the powers in para.2 was to specify in cases of dual entitlement whether the claimant would be paid only universal credit or only the relevant benefit or both. It was also intended to set out, if sanctions were applicable, which benefit was to be reduced first and to provide, if appropriate, that the application of a sanction to one benefit did not increase the amount of another. However, no regulations have been made to carry out those intentions. The only use of para.2 appears to have been in making reg.42 of the ESA Regulations 2013 and reg.5 of the JSA Regulations 2013, under the power in para.2(3), para.2(2) not being mentioned in the list of statutory powers invoked in the preamble to the Regulations. If regulations had provided that when there was dual entitlement no amount of new style ESA or JSA was to be payable, then there would

have been no income from the benefit concerned to be taken into account in the calculation of the amount of universal credit payable and any reduction of benefit under a sanction would bite on the whole amount of the universal credit in the ordinary way. The non-application of the work-related and connected requirements for new style JSA and the sanctions regime under new style ESA and JSA would then have been part of a coherent structure. But that is not the actual state of the legislation.

It might be asked whether the provisions for reduction periods under the universal credit provisions to be applied to a new style ESA or JSA award and vice versa supply a way out of the anomalies. The answer is no. Regulation 61 of the ESA Regulations 2013 and reg.30 of the JSA Regulations 2013 only apply where a claimant ceases to be entitled to universal credit and is or becomes entitled to new style ESA or JSA. In those circumstances any universal credit sanction reduction period is applied to the ESA or JSA award. Regulations 61 and 30 do not apply during any period of dual entitlement. By contrast, when the opposite direction is considered, reg.43 of the ESA Regulations 2013 and reg.6 of the JSA Regulations 2013 apply only where the claimant is entitled to new style ESA or JSA subject to a sanction reduction period, becomes entitled to universal credit and *remains* entitled to new style ESA or JSA. But the result is that the reduction ceases to be applicable to the ESA or JSA award. That appears merely to reinforce the position under reg.42 of the ESA Regulations 2013 and reg.5 of the JSA Regulations 2013. The unreduced amount of ESA or JSA counts as income in the calculation of the amount of the universal credit award and only the "topping up" element of universal credit can be subject to reduction.

Paragraph 3

2.552   Under para.3, where a new style ESA or JSA sanction has been applied to universal credit under para.1 or 2, it can count as a "previous sanctionable failure" for the purposes of calculating the length of the reduction period for a subsequent universal credit sanction under s.26 or 27 of the WRA 2012 (see regs 102–104). Where there have been previous universal credit (and these equivalent) sanctionable failures within the previous 365 days including the date of the current sanctionable failure (but not within the previous 14 days), that affects the length of the reduction period. Note that it is not every previous new style ESA or JSA sanction that has that effect under para.3. It is only such a sanction that has been applied to universal credit. The position is thus not the same as under regs 19–21 of the JSA Regulations 2013 where there is express reference to previous universal credit sanctions as well as new style JSA sanctions (and new style ESA sanctions in the case of reg.21) as capable of being previous sanctionable failures. Regulation 19 of the ESA Regulations 2013 refers to previous new style JSA sanctionable failures and universal credit sanctionable failures at the appropriate level as well as to previous new style ESA low-level sanctionable failures. It also appears that an old style ESA or JSA sanctionable failure occurring within the 365 days cannot count as a previous sanctionable failure.

[¹ Regulation 24A(4)]

SCHEDULE 12

AVAILABILITY OF THE CHILD ELEMENT WHERE MAXIMUM EXCEEDED – EXCEPTIONS

Introduction

2.553   1. This Schedule provides for cases where, for the purposes of regulation 24A, an exception applies in relation to a child or qualifying young person for whom a claimant is responsible ("A").

Multiple births

2.554   2. An exception applies where—
(a) the claimant is a parent (other than an adoptive parent) of A;
(b) A was one of two or more children born as a result of the same pregnancy;

    (c) the claimant is responsible for at least two of the children or qualifying young persons born as a result of that pregnancy; and

    (d) A is not the first in the order of those children or qualifying young persons as determined under regulation 24B.

Adoptions

3. An exception applies where A has been placed for adoption with, or adopted by, the claimant in accordance with the Adoption and Children Act 2002 or the Adoption and Children (Scotland) Act 2007, but not where—

    (a) the claimant (or, if the claimant is a member of a couple, the other member)—

        (i) was a step-parent of A immediately prior to the adoption; or

        (ii) has been a parent of A (other than by adoption) at any time;

    (b) the adoption order made in respect of A was made as a Convention adoption order (as defined, in England and Wales, in section 144 of the Adoption and Children Act 2002 and in Scotland, in section 119(1) of the Adoption and Children Scotland Act 2007); or

    (c) prior to that adoption, A had been adopted by the claimant (or, if the claimant is a member of a couple, the other member) under the law of any country or territory outside the British Islands.

2.555

Non-parental caring arrangements

4.—(1) An exception applies where the claimant—

    (a) is a friend or family carer in relation to A; or

    (b) is responsible for a child who is a parent of A.

(2) In this paragraph, "friend or family carer" means a person who is responsible for A, but is not (or, if that person is a member of a couple, neither member is) A's parent or step-parent and—

    (a) is named in a child arrangements order under section 8 of the Children Act 1989, that is in force with respect to A, as a person with whom A is to live;

    (b) is a special guardian of A appointed under section 14A of that Act;

    (c) is entitled to a guardian's allowance under section 77 of the Contributions and Benefits Act in respect of A;

    (d) in whose favour a kinship care order, as defined in section 72(1) of the Children and Young People (Scotland) Act 2014, subsists in relation to A;

    (e) is a guardian of A appointed under section 5 of the Children Act 1989 or section 7 of the Children (Scotland) Act 1995;

    (f) in whom one or more of the parental responsibilities or parental rights respectively described in section 1 and 2 of the Children (Scotland) Act 1995 are vested by a permanence order made in respect of A under section 80 of the Adoption and Children (Scotland) Act 2007;

    (g) fell within any of paragraphs (a) to (f) immediately prior to A's 16th birthday and has since continued to be responsible for A; or

    (h) has undertaken the care of A in circumstances in which it is likely that A would otherwise be looked after by a local authority.

2.556

Non-consensual conception

5.—(1) An exception applies where—

    (a) the claimant ("C") is A's parent; and

    (b) the Secretary of State determines that—

        (i) A is likely to have been conceived as a result of sexual intercourse to which C did not agree by choice, or did not have the freedom and capacity to agree by choice; and

        (ii) C is not living at the same address as the other party to that intercourse ("B").

(2) The circumstances in which C is to be treated as not having the freedom or capacity to agree by choice to the sexual intercourse are to include (but are not limited to) circumstances in which, at or around the time A was conceived—

    (a) B was personally connected to C;

    (b) B was repeatedly or continuously engaging in behaviour towards C that was controlling or coercive; and

    (c) that behaviour had a serious effect on C.

(3) The Secretary of State may make the determination in sub-paragraph (1)(b)(i) only if—

    (a) C provides evidence from an approved person which demonstrates that—

        (i) C had contact with that approved person or another approved person; and

2.557

(ii) C's circumstances are consistent with those of a person to whom sub-paragraphs (1)(a) and (1)(b)(i) apply; or

  (b) there has been—

    (i) a conviction for—

      (aa) an offence of rape under section 1 of the Sexual Offences Act 2003 or section 1 of the Sexual Offences (Scotland) Act 2009;

      (bb) an offence of controlling or coercive behaviour in an intimate or family relationship under section 76 of the Serious Crime Act 2015; or

      (cc) an offence under the law of a country outside Great Britain that the Secretary of State considers to be analogous to the offence mentioned in sub-paragraph (aa) or (bb) above; or

    (ii) an award under the Criminal Injuries Compensation Scheme in respect of a relevant criminal injury sustained by C,

where it appears likely to the Secretary of State that the offence was committed, or the criminal injury was caused, by B and resulted in the conception of A or diminished C's freedom or capacity to agree by choice to the sexual intercourse which resulted in that conception.

(4) The Secretary of State may make the determination in sub-paragraph (1)(b)(ii) where the only available evidence is confirmation by C that that sub-paragraph applies.

(5) For the purposes of sub-paragraph (2)(a), B was personally connected to C if, at or around the time A was conceived—

  (a) they were in an intimate personal relationship with each other; or

  (b) they were living together and—

    (i) were members of the same family; or

    (ii) had previously been in an intimate personal relationship with each other.

(6) For the purposes of sub-paragraph (2)(c), B's behaviour had a serious effect on C if—

  (a) it caused C to fear, on at least two occasions, that violence would be used against C; or

  (b) it caused C serious alarm or distress which had a substantial adverse effect on C's day-to-day activities.

(7) In sub-paragraph (3)—

"approved person" means a person of a description specified on a list approved by the Secretary of State for the purposes of sub-paragraph (3)(a) and acting in their capacity as such;

"Criminal Injuries Compensation Scheme" means the Criminal Injuries Compensation Scheme under the Criminal Injuries Compensation Act 1995; and

"relevant criminal injury" means—

  (a) a sexual offence (including a pregnancy sustained as a direct result of being the victim of a sexual offence);

  (b) physical abuse of an adult, including domestic abuse; or

  (c) mental injury,

as described in the tariff of injuries in the Criminal Injuries Compensation Scheme.

(8) For the purposes of sub-paragraph (5)(b)(i), B and C were members of the same family if, at or around the time A was conceived—

  (a) they were, or had been, married to each other;

  (b) they were, or had been, civil partners of each other;

  (c) they were relatives (within the meaning given by section 63(1) of the Family Law Act 1996);

  (d) they had agreed to marry each other, whether or not the agreement had been terminated;

  (e) they had entered into a civil partnership agreement (within the meaning given by section 73 of the Civil Partnership Act 2004), whether or not the agreement had been terminated;

  (f) they were both parents of the same child; or

  (g) they had, or had had, parental responsibility (within the meaning given in regulation 4A(2)) for the same child.

Continuation of existing exception in a subsequent award

2.558

6. An exception applies where—

  (a) the claimant ("C") is A's step-parent;

  (b) none of the exceptions under paragraphs 2 to 5 above apply;

  (c) C has previously been entitled to an award of universal credit as a member of a couple jointly with a parent of A, in which an exception under paragraph 2, 3 or 5 above applied in relation to A;

614

(d) since that award terminated, each award of universal credit to which C has been entitled has been made—
  (i) as a consequence of a previous award having ended when C ceased to be a member of a couple or became a member of a couple; or
  (ii) in any other circumstances in which the assessment periods for that award begin on the same day of each month as the assessment periods for a previous award under regulation 21 (assessment periods); and
(e) where, in the award mentioned in sub-paragraph (c), an exception under paragraph 2 above applied in relation to A—
  (i) C is responsible for one or more other children or qualifying young persons born as a result of the same pregnancy as A; and
  (ii) A is not the first in the order of those children or qualifying young persons as determined under regulation 24B (order of children and qualifying young persons).

AMENDMENT

1. Social Security (Restrictions on Amounts for Children and Qualifying Young Persons) Amendment Regulations 2017 (SI 2017/376) reg.2(1) and (4) (April 6, 2017).

GENERAL NOTE

See the commentary to regs 24-24B.   2.559

The Rent Officers (Universal Credit Functions) Order 2013

(SI 2013/382) (AS AMENDED)

The Secretary of State for Work and Pensions makes the following Order in exercise of the powers conferred by section 122 of the Housing Act 1996.

[*In force April 29, 2013*]

ARRANGEMENT OF REGULATIONS

Citation and commencement

1.—This Order may be cited as the Rent Officers (Universal Credit Functions) Order 2013 and comes into force on 29th April 2013.   2.560

Interpretation

2.561   **2.**—In this Order—

"Welfare Reform Act" means the Welfare Reform Act 2012;

"the Universal Credit Regulations" means the Universal Credit Regulations 2013;

"accommodation" means any residential accommodation whether or not consisting of the whole or part of a building and whether or not comprising separate and self-contained premises;

[² "assessment period" has the same meaning as in section 40 of the Welfare Reform Act.]

[¹ . . .]

"assured tenancy"—

(a) in England [³ . . .], has the same meaning as in Part 1 of the Housing Act 1988, except that it includes—

     (i) a tenancy which would be an assured tenancy but for paragraph 2, 8 or 10 of Schedule 1 (tenancies which cannot be assured tenancies) to that Act; and

     (ii) a licence which would be an assured tenancy (within the extended meaning given in this definition) were it a tenancy; and

(b) in Scotland, has the same meaning as in Part 2 of the Housing (Scotland) Act 1988, except that it includes—

     (i) a tenancy which would be an assured tenancy but for paragraph 7 or 9 of Schedule 4 (tenancies which cannot be assured tenancies) to that Act; and

     (ii) any other form of occupancy which would be an assured tenancy (within the extended meaning given in this definition) were it a tenancy;

"broad rental market area" has the meaning given in article 3;

"housing payment" means a relevant payment within the meaning of paragraph 3 of Schedule 4 (housing costs element for renters) to the Universal Credit Regulations;

[³ "introductory standard contract" has the meaning given by the Renting Homes (Wales) Act 2016 (see section 16 of that Act);]

"local authority" means—

(a) in relation to England, the council of a district or London borough, the Common Council of the City of London or the Council of the Isles of Scilly;

(b) in relation to Wales, the council of a county or county borough; and

(c) in relation to Scotland, a council constituted under section 2 (constitution of councils) of the Local Government etc. (Scotland) Act 1994;

[³ "private landlord" has the meaning given by the Renting Homes (Wales) Act 2016 (see section 10 of that Act);]

[³ "private registered provider of social housing" has the meaning given by section 80(3) of the Housing and Regeneration Act 2008;]

"provider of social housing" has the meaning given in paragraph 2 of Schedule 4 to the Universal Credit Regulations;

[³ "registered social landlord" means a person registered in the register maintained under section 1 of the Housing Act 1996(61);]

"relevant time" means the time the request for the determination is made or, if earlier, the date the tenancy ends;

[³ "secure contract" has the meaning given by the Renting Homes (Wales) Act 2016 (see section 8 of that Act);]

"service charge payments" has the meaning given in paragraph 7 of Schedule 1 (meaning of payments in respect of accommodation) to the Universal Credit Regulations;

[³ "standard contract" has the meaning given by the Renting Homes (Wales) Act 2016 (see section 8 of that Act), but does not include—

(a) an introductory standard contract,

(b) a prohibited conduct standard contract within the meaning given by the Renting Homes (Wales) Act 2016 (see section 116 of that Act), or

(c) a supported standard contract within the meaning given by the Renting Homes (Wales) Act 2016 (see section 143 of that Act);]

"tenancy" includes—

(a) in England and Wales, a licence to occupy premises; and

(b) in Scotland, any other right of occupancy,

and references to rent, a tenant, a landlord or any other expression appropriate to a tenancy are to be construed accordingly;

"tenant" includes, where the tenant is a member of a couple within the meaning of section 39 of the Welfare Reform Act, the other member of the couple;

"working day" means any day other than—

(a) a Saturday or a Sunday;

(b) Christmas Day or Good Friday; or

(c) a day which is a bank holiday under the Banking and Financial Dealings Act 1971 in any part of Great Britain.

AMENDMENTS

1. Rent Officers (Housing Benefit and Universal Credit Functions) (Amendment) Order 2013 (SI 2013/1544) art.4(2) (September 1, 2013).

2. Rent Officers (Housing Benefit and Universal Credit Functions) (Local Housing Allowance Amendments) Order 2014 (SI 2014/3126) art.4(2) (January 8, 2015).

3. Renting Homes (Wales) Act 2016 (Consequential Amendments to Secondary Legislation) Regulations 2022 (SI 2022/907) Sch.1 para.28.

Broad rental market area determinations

3.—(1) Broad rental market area determinations taking effect on 29th April 2013 are determined in accordance with paragraph (7) and all other broad rental market area determinations are determined in accordance with paragraphs (2) to (6).

2.562

(2) A rent officer must, at such times as the rent officer considers appropriate and if the Secretary of State agrees—

(a) determine one or more broad rental market areas; and

(b) in respect of that broad rental market area, or those broad rental market areas, give to the Secretary of State a notice which identifies the local authority areas and the postcodes contained within the broad rental market area (or each of them).

[² (2A) The power in paragraph (2) is not limited by paragraph 2(2) of Schedule 1.]

(3) A broad rental market area is an area within which a person could reasonably be expected to live having regard to facilities and services for the

617

purposes of health, education, recreation, personal banking and shopping, taking account of the distance of travel, by public and private transport, to and from those facilities and services.

(4) A broad rental market area must contain—

(a) residential premises of a variety of types, including such premises held on a variety of tenures; and

(b) sufficient privately rented residential premises to ensure that, in the rent officer's opinion, the local housing allowance for the categories of accommodation in the area for which the rent officer is required to determine a local housing allowance is representative of the rents that a landlord might reasonably be expected to obtain in that area.

(5) Every part of Great Britain must fall within a broad rental market area and a broad rental market area must not overlap with another broad rental market area.

(6) Any broad rental market area determination made in accordance with paragraph (2) is to take effect—

(a) on the day the determination is made for the purpose of enabling a rent officer to determine a local housing allowance for that area; and

[4 (b) for all other purposes on the next relevant Monday following the day on which the determination is made.]

(7) For broad rental market area determinations that take effect on 29th April 2013, a rent officer must use the broad rental market area determinations determined in accordance with article 4B of, and Schedule 3B to, the Rent Officers (Housing Benefit Functions) Order 1997 or the Rent Officers (Housing Benefit Functions) (Scotland) Order 1997 that apply on 29th April 2013.

[3 (8) "Relevant Monday" has the same meaning as in article 4(4).]

AMENDMENTS

1. Rent Officers (Housing Benefit and Universal Credit Functions) (Local Housing Allowance Amendments) Order 2013 (SI 2013/2978) art.4(2) (January 13, 2014).

2. Rent Officers (Housing Benefit and Universal Credit Functions) (Local Housing Allowance Amendments) Order 2016 (SI 2016/1179) art.4(1) and (2) (January 23, 2017).

3. Rent Officers (Housing Benefit and Universal Credit Functions) (Amendment) Order 2017 (SI 2017/1323) art.4(1) and (2) (January 26, 2018).

4. Rent Officers (Housing Benefit and Universal Credit Functions) (Amendment and Modification) Order 2021 (SI 2021/1380) (January 31, 2022).

Local housing allowance determinations

2.563   **4.**—(1)[5 . . .]

[5 (1)] [1 In 2014 and in each subsequent year, on the date specified in paragraph [5 (2)],] a rent officer must—

(a) for each broad rental market area determine, in accordance with Schedule 1, a local housing allowance for each of the categories of accommodation set out in paragraph 1 of Schedule 1; and

(b) notify the Secretary of State of the local housing allowance determination made in accordance with sub-paragraph (a) for each broad rental market area.

[¹[³ [⁵ (2)] The date specified for the purposes of paragraph [⁵ (1)] is the last working day of January [⁶ and also the 31st March 2020].]]

[⁴ [⁵ (3) Any local housing allowance determination made in accordance with paragraph (1) is to take effect—
  (a) in the case of a person with an existing UC entitlement—
      (i) on the relevant Monday where that is the first day of an assessment period for the person in question; or
      (ii) where the relevant Monday is not the first day of an assessment period for that person, on the first day of the next assessment period following that; or
  (b) in any other case, on the relevant Monday.]]

[⁶ (3A) The determinations made in accordance with paragraph (1) on the 31st March 2020 shall take effect (under paragraph (3)) in place of the determinations made in accordance with paragraph (1) on the 31st January 2020.]

[⁵ (4) For the purposes of this article—
"a person with an existing UC entitlement" means a person who is entitled to universal credit on the relevant Monday;
"relevant Monday" means the first Monday in the first tax year that commences following the day on which the determination is made;
"tax year" means a period beginning with 6th April in one year and ending with 5th April in the next.]

AMENDMENTS

1. Rent Officers (Housing Benefit and Universal Credit Functions) (Amendment) Order 2013 (SI 2013/1544), art.4(3) (September 1, 2013).
2. Rent Officers (Housing Benefit and Universal Credit Functions) (Local Housing Allowance Amendments) Order 2013 (SI 2013/2978), art.4(2) (January 13, 2014).
3. Rent Officers (Housing Benefit and Universal Credit Functions) (Local Housing Allowance Amendments) Order 2014 (SI 2014/3126) art.4(3) (January 8, 2015).
4. Rent Officers (Housing Benefit and Universal Credit Functions) (Local Housing Allowance Amendments) Order 2014 (SI 2014/3126) art.4(4) (January 8, 2015).
5. Rent Officers (Housing Benefit and Universal Credit Functions) (Local Housing Allowance Amendments) Order 2015 (SI 2015/1753) art.4(2) (November 2, 2015).
6. Social Security (Coronavirus) (Further Measures) Regulations 2020 (SI 2020/371) reg.4(3)(a) (March 30, 2020).

DEFINITIONS

"accommodation"—see art.2.
"assessment period"—*ibid.*
"broad rental market area"—see arts 2 and 3.

Housing payment determination

5.—Where a rent officer receives a request from the Secretary of State for a determination in respect of housing payments for accommodation let by a provider of social housing, the rent officer must—
  (a) determine in accordance with Schedule 2 whether each of the housing payments specified by the Secretary of State in that request is reasonable for that accommodation; and

2.564

(b) where the rent officer determines that a housing payment is not reasonable, determine in accordance with Schedule 2 the amount that is reasonable for the accommodation and notify the Secretary of State of that amount.

DEFINITIONS

"accommodation"—see art.2.
"assessment period"--*ibid.*
"housing payment"—see art.2 and Universal Credit Regs, Sch.4, para.3.

Redeterminations

2.565   **6.**—(1) Where a rent officer has made a determination under article 3, 4 or 5 ("the determination") and paragraph (2) applies, a rent officer must make a further determination ("a redetermination") and notify the Secretary of State of the redetermination.

(2) This paragraph applies where—

(a) the determination was made under article 3 or 4 and the rent officer considers that there is an error in relation to that determination; or

(b) the determination was made under article 5 and—

  (i) the Secretary of State requests that the rent officer makes a redetermination;

  (ii) the Secretary of State informs the rent officer that the information supplied when requesting the determination was incorrect or incomplete; or

  (iii) the rent officer considers that there is an error in relation to the determination.

(3) Where a rent officer makes a redetermination the rent officer must do so in accordance with the provisions of this Order that applied to the determination and use the same information that was used for the determination except that, where the information used was incorrect or incomplete, the rent officer must use the correct or complete information.

(4) Where a rent officer makes a redetermination by virtue of paragraph (2)(b)(i), the rent officer must have regard to the advice of at least one other rent officer in relation to that redetermination.

Information

2.566   **7.**—Where a rent officer considers that the information supplied by the Secretary of State or a landlord under regulation 40 (information to be provided to rent officers) of the Universal Credit, Personal Independence Payment, Jobseeker's Allowance and Employment and Support Allowance (Claims and Payments) Regulations 2013 is incomplete or incorrect, the rent officer must—

(a) notify the Secretary of State or the landlord of that fact; and

(b) request that the Secretary of State or the landlord supplies the further information or to confirm whether, in their opinion, the information already supplied is correct and, if they agree that it is not, to supply the correct information.

Means of giving notice

8.—Any notice given by a rent officer under this Order may be given in writing or by electronic means unless the Secretary of State requests that notice is given in writing only.

2.567

Article 4

SCHEDULE 1

LOCAL HOUSING ALLOWANCE DETERMINATIONS

Categories of accommodation

1. The categories of accommodation for which a rent officer is required to determine a local housing allowance in accordance with article 4 are—

2.568

(a) accommodation where the tenant has the exclusive use of only one bedroom and where the tenancy provides for the tenant to share the use of one or more of—
    (i) a kitchen;
    (ii) a bathroom;
    (iii) a toilet; or
    (iv) a room suitable for living in;
(b) accommodation where the tenant has the exclusive use of only one bedroom and exclusive use of a kitchen, a bathroom, a toilet and a room suitable for living in;
(c) accommodation where the tenant has the use of only two bedrooms;
(d) accommodation where the tenant has the use of only three bedrooms;
(e) accommodation where the tenant has the use of only four bedrooms.

[¹ Local housing allowance for category of accommodation in paragraph 1

2.—(1) Subject to paragraph 5 (anomalous local housing allowances) the rent officer must determine a local housing allowance for each category of accommodation in paragraph 1 as follows.

2.569

[⁸ [⁹ (2) The local housing allowance for any category of accommodation is the lower of—

(a) the rent at the 30th percentile determined in accordance with paragraph 3; and
(b) for a category of accommodation listed in column 1 of the following table, the amount listed in column 2 of that table (maximum local housing allowance)—

1. Category of accommodation as specified in paragraph 1	2. Maximum local housing allowance for that category of accommodation
paragraph 1(a) (one bedroom, shared accommodation)	£ 1,283.96
Paragraph 1(b) (one bedroom, exclusive use)	£ 1,283.96
Paragraph 1(c) (two bedrooms)	£ 1,589.99
Paragraph 1(d) (three bedrooms)	£ 1,920.00
Paragraph 1(e) (four bedrooms)	£2,579.98]]

(2A) [⁸ ...]
(2B) [⁸ ...]
(3) [⁸ ...]
(3A) [⁸ ...]
(4) Where the local housing allowance would otherwise not be a whole number of pence, it must be rounded to the nearest whole penny by disregarding any amount less than half a penny and treating any amount of half a penny or more as a whole penny.]

Rent at the 30th percentile

2.570

3.—(1) The rent officer must determine the rent at the 30th percentile in accordance with the following sub-paragraphs.

(2) The rent officer must compile a list of rents.

[10 (3) The rent officer must compile a list of rents in ascending order of the rents which, in the rent officer's opinion, are payable—

    (a) for each category of dwelling specified in paragraph 1—

        (i) in England, let under an assured tenancy, or

        (ii) in Wales—

            (aa) before the day on which section 239 of the Renting Homes (Wales) Act 2016 comes into force, let under an assured tenancy, or

            (bb) on or after that day, let under a relevant occupation contract; and

    (b) in the 12 month period ending on the 30th day of the September preceding the date of the determination.]

(4) The list must include any rents which are of the same amount.

(5) The criteria for including an assured tenancy [10 or a relevant occupation contract, as the case may be,] on the list of rents in relation to each category of accommodation specified in paragraph 1 are that—

    (a) the accommodation let under the assured tenancy [10 or relevant occupation contract] is in the broad rental market area for which the local housing allowance for that category of accommodation is being determined;

    (b) the accommodation is in a reasonable state of repair; and

    (c) the assured tenancy [10 or relevant occupation contract] permits the tenant to use exclusively or share the use of, as the case may be, the same number and type of rooms as the category of accommodation in relation to which the list of rents is being compiled.

[1 (6) Sub-paragraph (7) applies where the rent officer is not satisfied that the list of rents in respect of any category of accommodation would contain sufficient rents, payable in the 12 month period ending on the 30th day of the September preceding the date of the determination for accommodation in the broad rental market area, to enable a local housing allowance to be determined which is representative of the rents that a landlord might reasonably be expected to obtain in that area.]

(7) In a case where this sub-paragraph applies, the rent officer may add to the list rents for accommodation in the same category in other areas in which a comparable market exists.

(8) Where rent is payable other than monthly the rent officer must use the figure which would be payable if the rent were to be payable monthly by calculating the rent for a year and dividing the total by 12.

(9) When compiling the list of rents for each category of accommodation, the rent officer must—

    (a) assume that no-one had sought or is seeking the tenancy who would have been entitled to housing benefit under Part 7 of the Social Security Contributions and Benefits Act 1992(12) or universal credit under Part 1 of the Welfare Reform Act; and

    (b) exclude the amount of any rent which, in the rent officer's opinion, is fairly attributable to the provision of services performed or facilities (including the use of furniture) provided for, or rights made available to, the tenant and which would not be classed as service charge payments.

(10) The rent at the 30th percentile in the list of rents ("R") is determined as follows—

    (a) where the number of rents on the list is a multiple of 10, the formula is—

$$R = \frac{\text{the amount of the rent at P} + \text{the amount of the rent at P1}}{2}$$

    where—

        (i) P is the position on the list found by multiplying the number of rents on the list by 3 and dividing by 10; and

        (ii) P1 is the following position on the list;

    (b) where the number of rents on the list is not a multiple of 10, the formula is—

$$R = \text{the amount of the rent at P2}$$

    where P2 is the position on the list found by multiplying the number of rents on the list by 3 and dividing by 10 and rounding the result upwards to the nearest whole number.

[10 (11) In this paragraph, "relevant occupation contract" means—

(a) a secure contract in relation to which the landlord is a registered social landlord, a private registered provider of social housing, or a private landlord,

(b) a standard contract, or

(c) an introductory standard contract in relation to which the landlord is a registered social landlord or a private registered provider of social housing.]

[¹ Maximum local housing allowance

4. [² [⁴ . . .]]]

2.571

Anomalous local housing allowances

5. Where—

2.572

(a) the rent officer has determined the local housing allowance for each of the categories of accommodation in paragraph 1 in accordance with the preceding paragraphs of this Schedule; and

(b) the local housing allowance for a category of accommodation in paragraph 1(b) to (e) is lower than the local housing allowance for any of the categories of accommodation which precede it,

that local housing allowance is to be the same as the highest local housing allowance which precedes it.

[⁵ 5A. [⁸ ...] [⁷ [⁸...]]]
6. [¹ [³ [⁴ . . .]]]

AMENDMENTS

1. Rent Officers (Housing Benefit and Universal Credit Functions) (Local Housing Allowance Amendments) Order 2013 (SI 2013/2978) art.4(3) (January 13, 2014).

2. Rent Officers (Housing Benefit and Universal Credit Functions) (Local Housing Allowance Amendments) Order 2014 (SI 2014/3126) art.4(5) (January 8, 2015).

3. Rent Officers (Housing Benefit and Universal Credit Functions) (Local Housing Allowance Amendments) Order 2014 (SI 2014/3126) art.4(6) and Sch.3 (January 8, 2015).

4. Rent Officers (Housing Benefit and Universal Credit Functions) (Local Housing Allowance Amendments) Order 2015 (SI 2015/1753) art.4(3) (November 2, 2015).

5. Rent Officers (Housing Benefit and Universal Credit Functions) (Local Housing Allowance Amendments) Order 2016 (SI 2016/1179) art.4(1) and (3) (January 23, 2017).

6. Rent Officers (Housing Benefit and Universal Credit Functions) (Amendment) Order 2017 (SI 2017/1323) art.4 (January 26, 2018).

7. Rent Officers (Housing Benefit and Universal Credit Functions) (Amendment) Order 2018 (SI 2018/1332) art.4 (January 25, 2019).

8. Rent Officers (Housing Benefit and Universal Credit Functions) (Amendment) Order 2020 (SI 2020/27) art.4(1) and (3) (January 30, 2020).

9. Social Security (Coronavirus) (Further Measures) Regulations 2020 (SI 2020/371) reg.4(3)(b) (March 30, 2020).

10. Renting Homes (Wales) Act 2016 (Consequential Amendments to Secondary Legislation) Regulations 2022 (SI 2022/907) Sch.1 para.28.

MODIFICATION

Article 4 of the Rent Officers (Housing Benefit and Universal Credit Functions) (Modification) Order 2023 (SI 2023/6) provides that, for the purposes of determining the local housing allowances in 2023, Sch.1 is to be read as if the following were substituted for para.2(2):

"(2) For all broad rental market areas the local housing allowance for any category of accommodation is the allowance determined for that category of accommodation on 31st March 2020."

623

Regulation 18 of the Renting Homes (Wales) Act 2016 (Saving and Transitional Provisions) Regulations 2022 (SI 2022/1172) makes transitional provision for the purpose of determining a local housing allowance under Sch.1. For so long as it is necessary to refer to rents payable before December 1, 2022 (the day on which s.239 of the Renting Homes (Wales) Act 2016 comes into force, abolishing assured tenancies in Wales), the value of rent which, in the rent officer's opinion, would have been payable for a category of dwelling, specified in para.1 of Sch.1 to the 2013 Order, in Wales let under an assured tenancy, is to be deemed to be the rent that would have been payable in relation to the relevant category of dwelling let under a relevant secure or standard contract. "Relevant secure or standard contract" means a secure or standard contract in relation to which the landlord does not meet the landlord condition in s.80(3) of the Housing Act 1985.

GENERAL NOTE

2.573   From January 30, 2020 to March 29, 2020, para.2(2) of Sch.1 read as follows:
"(2)   The local housing allowance for any category of accommodation is the lowest of—

(a) the rent at the 30th percentile determined in accordance with paragraph 3;

(b) the local housing allowance last determined for that category of accommodation (or, where the allowance is redetermined under article 6 (redeterminations), the allowance as so redetermined), increased by 1.7%; and

(c) for a category of accommodation listed in column 1 of the following table, the amount listed in column 2 of that table (maximum local housing allowance)—

1. Category of accommodation as in paragraph 1	2. Maximum local housing allowance for that accommodation
paragraph 1(a) (one bedroom, shared accommodation)	£1,218.57
paragraph 1(b) (one bedroom, exclusive use)	£1,218.57
paragraph 1(c) (two bedrooms)	£1,413.54
paragraph 1(d) (three bedrooms)	£1,657.25
paragraph 1(e) (four bedrooms)	£1,949.71".

Article 5

SCHEDULE 2

HOUSING PAYMENT DETERMINATION

2.574   1. The rent officer must determine whether, in the rent officer's opinion, each of the housing payments payable for the tenancy of the accommodation at the relevant time is reasonable.
2. If the rent officer determines under paragraph 1 that a housing payment is not reasonable, the rent officer must also determine the amount of the housing payment which is reasonable.
3. When making a determination under this Schedule, the rent officer must—
(a) have regard to the level of similar payments under tenancies for accommodation which—
(i) is let by the same type of landlord;
(ii) is in the same local authority area [[1] (but see paragraph 4)];

    (iii) has the same number of bedrooms; and

    (iv) is in the same reasonable state of repair,

as the accommodation in respect of which the determination is being made;

  (b) exclude—

    (i) the cost of any care, support or supervision provided to the tenant by the landlord or by someone on the landlord's behalf;

    (ii) any payments for services performed or facilities (including the use of furniture) provided for, or rights made available to, the tenant which are not service charge payments; and

  (c) where the accommodation is let at an Affordable Rent, assume that the rent is reasonable.

4. Where the rent officer is not satisfied that the local authority area contains sufficient accommodation to allow a determination of the housing payments which a landlord might reasonably have been expected to charge, the rent officer may have regard to the level of housing payments in one adjoining local authority area [¹ or one local authority area adjoining an adjoining local authority area or, if the rent officer considers it necessary, more than one such area].

5. For the purposes of this Schedule—

  (a) a housing payment is reasonable where it is not higher than the payment which the landlord might reasonably have been expected to obtain for the tenancy at the relevant time;

  (b) accommodation is let by the same type of landlord where—

    (i) in a case where the landlord of the accommodation in respect of which the determination is being made is a local authority, the landlord of the other accommodation is also a local authority; and

    (ii) in a case where the landlord of the accommodation in respect of which the determination is being made is a provider of social housing other than a local authority, the landlord of the other accommodation is also a provider of social housing other than a local authority;

  (c) accommodation is let at an Affordable Rent where—

    (i) the rent is regulated under a standard by the Regulator of Social Housing under section 194 of the Housing and Regeneration Act 2008(13) ("the 2008 Act") which requires the initial rent to be set at no more than 80% of the local market rent (including service charges); or

    (ii) the accommodation is let by a local authority and, under arrangements between the local authority and the Homes and Communities Agency (as established by section 1 of the 2008 Act), the Greater London Authority or the Secretary of State, the rent payable is set on the same basis as would be the case if the rent were regulated under a standard set by the Regulator of Social Housing under section 194 of the 2008 Act which requires the initial rent to be set at no more than 80% of the local market rent (including service charges).

AMENDMENT

1. Rent Officers (Housing Benefit and Universal Credit Functions) (Local Housing Allowance Amendments) Order 2016 (SI 2016/1179) art.4(1) and (4) (January 23, 2017).

DEFINITIONS

"accommodation"—see art.2.

"housing payment"—see art.2 and Universal Credit Regs, Sch.4, para.3.

"local authority"—see art.2.

"provider of social housing"—see art.2 and Universal Credit Regs, Sch.4, para.4.

"relevant time"—see art.2.

"service charge payments"—see art.2 and Universal Credit Regs, Sch.1 para.7.

"tenancy"—see art.2.

"tenant"—*ibid.*

The Universal Credit (Work-Related Requirements) In Work Pilot Scheme and Amendment Regulations 2015

(SI 2015/89)

Made on January 29, 2015 by the Secretary of State under sections 18(5), 22(2), 41(1)(a), (2)(b) and (4) and 42(2) and (3) of the Welfare Reform Act 2012, Part 3 being made with a view to ascertaining the extent to which the provision made by that Part is likely to promote people already in paid work remaining in work, or obtaining or being able to obtain, more work or better paid work, a draft having been laid before, and approved by resolution of, each House of Parliament in accordance with section 43(4) and (6)(b) of the Act, and the Social Security Advisory Committee having agreed in accordance with section 173(1) of the Social Security Administration Act 1992 that proposals in respect of these Regulations should not be referred to it.

2.575   *[In force February 19, 2015]*

REGULATIONS REPRODUCED

PART 1

INTRODUCTORY

PART 2

AMENDMENT OF THE UNIVERSAL CREDIT REGULATIONS

PART 3

THE IN WORK PILOT SCHEME

626

GENERAL NOTE

See the annotation to reg.99(6) and (6A), the provisions affected by the amend- 2.576
ment in reg.3 of the present Regulations, for the context in which the pilot schemes
will operate.

PART 1

INTRODUCTORY

Citation and commencement

1. These Regulations may be cited as the Universal Credit (Work-Related 2.577
Requirements) In Work Pilot Scheme and Amendment Regulations 2015,
and come into force at the end of the period of 21 days beginning with the
day on which they are made.

Interpretation

2. In these Regulations— 2.578
"the Act" means the Welfare Reform Act 2012;
[¹"monthly earnings" has the meaning in regulation 90(6) of the
Universal Credit Regulations;]
"qualifying claimant" has the meaning in regulation 7;
"the Universal Credit Regulations" means the Universal Credit
Regulations 2013; and
[¹ . . .].

AMENDMENT

1. Universal Credit and Miscellaneous Amendments Regulations 2015 (SI
2015/1754) reg.3(2) (November 4, 2015).

PART 2

AMENDMENT OF THE UNIVERSAL CREDIT REGULATIONS

New provision for suspension of mandatory work search and work availability requirements on account of earnings

3. – *The amendments effected by this regulation have been taken into account* 2.579
in the text of the Universal Credit Regulations 2013 elsewhere in this volume.

PART 3

THE IN WORK PILOT SCHEME

Provision made for piloting purposes

4.—(1) The following provision is made in accordance with section 41 of 2.580
the Act to test the extent to which the imposition of work-related requirements on persons already in paid work is likely to promote their remaining
in work, or obtaining or being able to obtain, more work or better-paid work.

(2) Regulation 99 of the Universal Credit Regulations (which provides for the suspension of work search requirements and work availability requirements where the claimant's [¹ monthly] earnings from employment or, if the claimant is a member of a couple, their combined [¹ monthly] earnings from employment, reach a specified amount) is to apply as if paragraph (6) were omitted.

(3) The provision made by paragraph (2) is to apply only in relation to qualifying claimants who have been selected by the Secretary of State in accordance with regulation 5 and notified of that selection in accordance with regulation 6.

(4) The provision made by paragraph (2) ceases to apply to a person who has been selected in accordance with regulation 5 where—

(a) that person ceases to be a qualifying claimant (but see paragraph (5)); or

(b) the Secretary of State has determined that that provision should cease to apply because—

(i) the person has moved to live in a different geographical area; or

(ii) the Secretary of State has determined that the testing of particular work-related requirements that have been imposed on that person has concluded.

(5) Where a person has been selected in accordance with regulation 5 and, by reason only of an increase or decrease in their [¹ monthly] earnings (or, if they are a member of a couple, the [¹ monthly] earnings of the other member) the person is no longer a qualifying claimant, paragraph (2) applies again if the person becomes a qualifying claimant again unless, in the intervening period—

(a) paragraph (2) has ceased to apply for another reason; or

(b) the person has ceased to be entitled to universal credit for a continuous period of 6 months or more.

AMENDMENT

1. Universal Credit and Miscellaneous Amendments Regulations 2015 (SI 2015/1754) reg.3(3) (November 4, 2015).

DEFINITIONS

"the Act"—see reg.2.

"claimant"—see WRA 2012 s.40.

"monthly earnings"—see reg.2 and the Universal Credit Regulations 2013 reg.90(6).

"qualifying claimant"—see regs 2 and 7.

"the Universal Credit Regulations"—see reg.2

"work"—see WRA 2012 s.40.

"work availability requirement"—see WRA 2012 ss.40 and 18(2).

"work search requirement"—see WRA 2012 ss.40 and 17(1).

"work-related requirement"—see WRA 2012 ss.40 and 13(2).

Selection of participants

2.581   5.—(1) A selection for the purpose of regulation 4 is to be made by the Secretary of State on a random sampling basis from persons who, at the time of the selection, are qualifying claimants.

(2) The Secretary of State may make a selection in accordance with paragraph (1) on more than one occasion and, on each occasion, the Secretary

of State may limit that selection to qualifying claimants living in a particular geographical area determined by the Secretary of State or to persons who have become qualifying claimants within a period determined by the Secretary of State.

DEFINITION

"qualifying claimant"—see regs 2 and 7.

Notification of participants

6.—(1) The Secretary of State must notify a claimant in writing when—

(a) the claimant is selected in accordance with regulation 5; and

(b) the provision made by regulation 4(3) ceases to apply to the claimant by virtue of regulation 4(4), unless it is because the claimant is no longer a qualifying claimant by reason only of a change in earnings.

(2) Where, for the purposes of this regulation, the Secretary of State sends a notice by post to the claimant's last known address, it is to be treated as having been given or sent on the day on which it was posted.

(3) Schedule 2 to the Universal Credit, Personal Independence Payments, Jobseeker's Allowance and Employment and Support Allowance (Claims and Payments) Regulations 2013 applies to the delivery of an electronic communication sent by the Secretary of State for the purposes of this regulation in the same manner as it applies to the delivery of electronic communications for the purposes of those Regulations.

2.582

DEFINITIONS

"claimant"—see WRA 2012 s.40.
"qualifying claimant"—see regs 2 and 7.

Meaning of "qualifying claimant"

7.—(1) A qualifying claimant is a person who—

(a) falls within section 22 of the Act (claimants subject to all work-related requirements);

(b) has [¹ monthly] earnings of such an amount (or, if the person is a member of a couple, the couple has combined [¹ monthly] earnings of such an amount) that, apart from regulation 4(2), regulation 99(6) of the Universal Credit Regulations would apply;

(c) is not a person on whom the Secretary of State must not impose work-related requirements by virtue of regulation 98 of the Universal Credit Regulations (victims of domestic violence); and

(d) is not a person to whom any of the following paragraphs of regulation 99 of the Universal Credit Regulations (circumstances in which requirements must not be imposed) applies—

(i) paragraph (3) (which provides for suspension of work search and work availability requirements for various reasons, including imprisonment and treatment for alcohol or drug dependency), except sub-paragraph (a) (claimant attending court as a witness etc.) and sub-paragraph (g) (claimant engaged in a public duty); or

(ii) paragraph (5)(c) (claimant unfit for work for longer than 14 days).

2.583

AMENDMENT

1. Universal Credit and Miscellaneous Amendments Regulations 2015 (SI 2015/1754) reg.3(3) (November 4, 2015).

DEFINITIONS

"the Act"—see reg.2.
"couple"—see WRA ss.40 and 39.
"monthly earnings"—see reg.2 and the Universal Credit Regulations 2013 reg.90(6).
"the Universal Credit Regulations"—see reg.2
"work availability requirement"—see WRA 2012 ss.40 and 18(2).
"work search requirement"—see WRA 2012 ss.40 and 17(1).

Expiry of the pilot scheme

2.584   8. This Part ceases to have effect at the end of the period of three years starting with the day on which these Regulations come into force, unless it continues in effect by order of the Secretary of State under section 41(5)(a) of the Act.

GENERAL NOTE

2.585   Part 3 of the Regulations (i.e. regs 4–8) would have expired in February 2018, but has been continued in effect ever since by the Secretary of State making annual orders as envisaged by reg.8. The most recent of those is the Universal Credit (Work-Related Requirements) In Work Pilot Scheme (Extension) Order 2023 (SI 2023/157), which keeps Pt 3 in effect throughout the 12 months beginning on February 19, 2023.

The Universal Credit (Surpluses and Self-employed Losses) (Digital Service) Amendment Regulations 2015

(SI 2015/345)

Made on February 23, 2015 by the Secretary of State in exercise of the powers conferred by s. 42(2) and (3) of, and para. 4(1), (3)(a) and (4) of Sch. 1 to, the Welfare Reform Act 2012, having been referred to the Social Security Advisory Committee in accordance with s. 172(1) of the Social Security Administration Act 1992.

[In force April 11, 2018]

Citation and commencement

2.586   1. These Regulations may be cited as the Universal Credit (Surpluses and Self-employed Losses) (Digital Service) Amendment Regulations 2015 and come into force on [¹11th April 2018].

AMENDMENT

1. Universal Credit (Miscellaneous Amendments, Saving and Transitional Provision) Regulations 2018 (SI 2018/65) reg.7(2) (February 14, 2018).

Carry forward of surplus earnings

2. *[Amendments incorporated into SI 2013/376]*

2.587

Self-employed earnings – treatment of losses

3. *[Amendments incorporated into SI 2013/376]*

2.588

[¹Saving

4. [(1)–(3) *Omitted*].

(4) In regulation 54A of the Universal Credit Regulations 2013 (as inserted [² ...]), "the old award" does not include an award the last day of which fell before [²11th April 2018] and, in regulation 57A (as inserted by regulation 3(4)), "unused loss" does not include the loss from an assessment period that [²began] before that date.]

2.589

AMENDMENTS

1. Universal Credit and Miscellaneous Amendments Regulations 2015 (SI 2015/1754) reg.21 (November 3, 2015).
2. Universal Credit (Miscellaneous Amendments, Saving and Transitional Provision) Regulations 2018 (SI 2018/65) reg.7(5) (February 14, 2018).

GENERAL NOTE

At one point during the introduction of UC, the benefit existed in two different forms depending on which computer system was operating in the area for the Jobcentre to which the claim was made: see further the General Note to the Welfare Reform Act 2012 (above). The amendments made by these Regulations applied in Digital (or "Full") Service areas. Regulation 4(1)–(3) preserved the unamended law for Live Service areas. As Live Service areas no longer exist, reg.4(1)–(3) has not been reproduced in this volume. Readers are referred instead to pp.575–576 of Vol.II of the 2021/22 edition.

2.590

[¹Transitional provision – temporary de minimis period

5.—(1) For the purposes of applying regulation 54A (surplus earnings) of the Universal Credit Regulations 2013 in relation to a claim for universal credit made in respect of a period that begins before the end of the temporary de minimis period, the meaning of "relevant threshold" in paragraph (6) of that regulation is modified by substituting "£2,500" for "£300".

(2) For the purposes of paragraph (1), the "temporary de minimis period" is the period beginning with the coming into force of regulation 54A and ending on 31st March 2019, but may be extended by the Secretary of State if the Secretary of State considers it necessary to do so to safeguard the efficient administration of universal credit.]

2.591

AMENDMENT

1. Universal Credit (Miscellaneous Amendments, Saving and Transitional Provision) Regulations 2018 (SI 2018/65) reg.7(6) (February 14, 2018).

GENERAL NOTE

2.592   See the notes to reg.54A of the Universal Credit Regulations 2013 for the effect of this important modification to the initial operation of the surplus earnings rules. Ever since the surplus earnings rules were brought into force, the Secretary of State has exercised her power annually to determine that the "temporary de minimis period" should be extended. The most recent Determination was dated March 20, 2023 and extends that position to April 2024 (see the DWP's Guidance on regulations under the WRA 2012 on *gov.uk*).

The Loans for Mortgage Interest Regulations 2017

(SI 2017/725)

Made on July 5, 2017 by the Secretary of State, in exercise of the powers conferred by sections 4(5), 35(1), 36(2) and (4) of the Jobseekers Act 1995, sections 2(3)(b) and sections 17(1) and 19(1) of the State Pension Credit Act 2002, sections 123(1)(a), 135(1), 137(1) and (2)(d) and 175(1), (3) and (4) of the Social Security Contributions and Benefits Act 1992, sections 4(2)(a), 24(1) and 25(2), (3) and (5)(a) of the Welfare Reform Act 2007, sections 11(3) and (4) and 42(1), (2) and (3)(a) of, and paragraph 1(1) of Schedule 6 to, the Welfare Reform Act 2012 and sections 18, 19 and 21 of the Welfare Reform and Work Act 2016.

This instrument contains only regulations made under, by virtue of, or consequential upon, sections 18, 19 and 21 of the Welfare Reform and Work Act 2016 and is made before the end of the period of 6 months beginning with the coming into force of those sections. Therefore, in accordance with section 173(5) of the Social Security Administration Act 1992, these Regulations are not required to be referred to the Social Security Advisory Committee.

[In force, see reg.1(2)]

Arrangement of Regulations

GENERAL NOTE

In the past, owner-occupiers who are entitled to IS, IBJSA, IRESA, SPC and uni-   2.594
versal credit could receive benefit to cover some of their housing costs. Such housing
costs were paid as part of the applicable amount (IS, IBJSA and IRESA): see
reg.17(1)(e) of, and Sch.3 to, the IS Regulations; reg.83(f) of, and Sch.2 to, the JSA
Regulations 1996; reg. 67(1)(c) of, and Sch.6 to, the ESA Regulations 2008; or of
the guarantee credit (SPC): see reg.6(6)(c) of, and Sch.2 to, the SPC Regulations;
or as the housing costs element of universal credit: see s.11 of the WRA 2012 and
regs 25 and 26 of, and Schs 1-3 and 5 to, the UC Regs 2013.

However, from April 6, 2018, these Regulations, which are made under ss.18, 19
and 21 WRWA 2016, provide for housing costs in respect of mortgage interest and
interest on home improvement loans, to be replaced by repayable, interest-bearing,
loans secured on the claimants' homes by way of a legal charge.

Owner-occupiers may still be eligible for some support under the legislation ref-
erenced in the first paragraph of this section; the principal (and in the case of UC,
only) category of eligible housing cost is service charge payments.

The bulk of the Regulations have been in force since July 27, 2017. It was therefore possible for the Secretary of State to make an offer of a loan for mortgage
interest before April 6, 2018. However, no amount was payable before that date:
see reg.8(1)(a). The new rules commenced for practical purposes on April 6, 2018,
when regs 18-21 and Sch.5, which repeal the Schedules referred to in the first
paragraph of this Note as they relate to mortgage interest payments and interest on
home improvement loans, came into force.

Also, on July 27, 2017, ss 20(2)-(7) and (10) of WRWA 2016 were brought into
force by reg.2 of the Welfare Reform and Work Act 2016 (Commencement No. 5)
Regulations 2017 (SI 2017/802). Among other things, these amend s.8 SSA 1998
to empower the Secretary of State to make decisions about loans under s.18 WRWA
2016. The consequence is that an appeal lies to the First-tier Tribunal against

such a decision under s.12 SSA 1998 and thence to the Upper Tribunal under s.11 TCEA 2007.

The remaining parts of s.20 WRWA 2016, which amend the substantive statute law relating to entitlement to housing costs as part of a means-tested benefit were brought into force on April 6, 2018.

It must be stressed that the changes brought about by these Regulations relate exclusively to owner-occupiers. Renters will continue to be entitled to either the housing costs element of universal credit under section 11 of the WRA 2012 and regs 25 and 26 of, and Schs 1-4 to, the UC Regs 2013, or to the Housing Benefit Regulations, or the Housing Benefit (Persons who have attained the qualifying age for state pension credit) Regulations 2006.

Citation and commencement

2.595   **1.**—(1) These Regulations may be cited as the Loans for Mortgage Interest Regulations 2017.

(2) These Regulations come into force—

(a) for the purposes of regulations 18 to 21, on 6th April 2018;

(b) for all other purposes, on 27th July 2017.

Interpretation

2.596   **2.**—(1) In these Regulations—

"the Act" means the Welfare Reform and Work Act 2016;

[[1] "alternative finance arrangements" has the meaning given in paragraph 5(4) of Schedule 1 to these Regulations;]

"alternative finance payments" has the meaning given in paragraph 5(3) of Schedule 1 to these Regulations;

"applicable amount" means—

(a) in the case of employment and support allowance, the claimant's weekly applicable amount under regulations 67 to 70 of the ESA Regulations;

(b) in the case of income support, the claimant's weekly applicable amount under regulations 17 to 21AA of the IS Regulations;

(c) in the case of jobseeker's allowance, the claimant's weekly applicable amount under regulations 83 to 86C of the JSA Regulations;

(d) in the case of an SPC claimant, the claimant's weekly appropriate minimum guarantee under section 2 of the State Pension Credit Act 2002;

(e) in the case of a UC claimant, the maximum amount of a claimant's award of universal credit under regulation 23(1) of the UC Regulations;

"assessment period" has the meaning given in regulation 21 of the UC Regulations;

"benefit unit" means a single claimant and his or her partner (if any) or joint claimants;

"benefit week" has the meaning given—

(a) in the case of employment and support allowance, in regulation 2 of the ESA Regulations;

(b) the case of income support, in paragraph 4 of Schedule 7 to the Claims and Payment Regulations;

(c) in the case of jobseeker's allowance, in regulation 1 of the JSA Regulations;

(d) in the case of state pension credit, in regulation 1 of the SPC Regulations;

"charge by way of legal mortgage" has the meaning given in section 132(1) of the Land Registration Act 2002;

"child" means a person under the age of 16;

"claimant" means a single claimant or each of joint claimants;

"Claims and Payment Regulations" means the Social Security (Claims and Payments) Regulations 1987;

"close relative" means a parent, parent-in-law, son, son-in-law, daughter, daughter-in-law, step-parent, step-son, step-daughter, brother, sister, or, if any of the preceding persons is one member of a couple, the other member of that couple;

[2 "conveyancer" means—

(a) in England and Wales, a conveyancer within the meaning of rule 217A of the Land Registration Rules 2003;

(b) in Scotland, a solicitor or advocate within the meaning of section 65 of the Solicitors (Scotland) Act 1980, or a conveyancing practitioner as defined in section 23 of the Law Reform (Miscellaneous Provisions) (Scotland) Act 1990;]

"couple" means—

(a) two people who are married to, or civil partners of, each other and are members of the same household;

(b) two people who are not married to, or civil partners of, each other but are living together as a married couple or civil partners;

"disabled person" has the meaning given—

(a) in the case of employment and support allowance, in paragraph 1(3) of Schedule 6 to the ESA Regulations,

(b) in the case of income support, in paragraph 1(3) of Schedule 3 to the IS Regulations;

(c) in the case of jobseeker's allowance, in paragraph 1(3) of Schedule 2 to the JSA Regulations;

(d) in the case of state pension credit, in paragraph 1(2)(a) of Schedule 2 to the SPC Regulations;

(e) in the case of universal credit, in paragraph 14(3) of Schedule 3 to these Regulations;

"dwelling"—

(a) in England and Wales, means a dwelling within the meaning of Part 1 of the Local Government Finance Act 1992;

(b) in Scotland, means a dwelling within the meaning of Part 2 of that Act;

"earned income" has the meaning given in Chapter 2 of Part 6 of the UC Regulations;

"ESA Regulations" means the Employment and Support Allowance Regulations 2008;

"existing claimant" means a claimant who is entitled to a qualifying benefit, including an amount for owner-occupier payments, on 5th April 2018;

"financial year" has the meaning given in section 25(2) of the Budget Responsibility and National Audit Act 2011;

"income" means any income which is, or which is treated as, an individual's, including payments which are treated as earnings, and which is not disregarded, under—

(a) in the case of employment and support allowance, Part 10 of the ESA Regulations;

(b) in the case of income support, Part 5 of the IS Regulations;

(c) in the case of jobseeker's allowance, Part 8 of the JSA Regulations;

(d) in the case of state pension credit, Part 3 of the SPC Regulations;

"IS Regulations" means the Income Support (General) Regulations 1987;

[1 "joint claimants"—

(a) in the case of jobseeker's allowance means—

    (i) members of a joint-claim couple who have jointly made a claim for, and are entitled to, income-based jobseeker's allowance; or

    (ii) members of a joint-claim couple who have made a claim for, but are not entitled to, such a benefit by reason only that they have income—

        (aa) equal to or exceeding the applicable amount, but

        (bb) less than the sum of that applicable amount and the amount of a loan payment applicable to the joint-claim couple;

(b) in the case of universal credit means members of a couple who have jointly made a claim for, and are entitled to, universal credit;]

"joint-claim couple" has the meaning in section 1(4) of the Jobseekers Act 1995;

"JSA Regulations" means the Jobseeker's Allowance Regulations 1996;

"legacy benefit" means income-related employment and support allowance, income support or income-based jobseeker's allowance;

"legacy benefit claimant" means a claimant who is entitled to [1, or is treated as entitled to,] a legacy benefit;

"legal estate" means any of the legal estates set out in section 1(1) of the Law of Property Act 1925;

"legal owner" means the owner, whether alone or with others, of a legal estate or, in Scotland, a heritable or registered interest, in the relevant accommodation;

"loan agreement" means an agreement entered into by a single claimant and his or her partner (if any), or each joint claimant, and the Secretary of State, which sets out the terms and conditions upon which the loan payments are made to the claimant;

"loan payments" means one or more payments, calculated under regulation 10, in respect of a claimant's liability to make owner-occupier payments in respect of the relevant accommodation;

"loan payments offer date" means the day on which the Secretary of State sends the loan agreement to a claimant;

"Modified Rules" means the Social Security (Housing Costs Special Arrangements) (Amendment and Modification) Regulations 2008;

"new claimant partner" has the meaning given in regulation 7 of the Transitional Provisions Regulations;

"non-dependant" has the meaning given—

(a) in the case of employment and support allowance, in regulation 71 of the ESA Regulations;

(b) in the case of income support, in regulation 3 of the IS Regulations;

(c) in the case of jobseeker's allowance, in regulation 2 of the JSA Regulations;

(d) in the case of state pension credit, in paragraph 1(4) of Schedule 2 to the SPC Regulations;

"owner-occupier payments" has the meaning given in regulation 3(2)(a);

"partner" means—

(a) where a claimant is a member of a couple, the other member of that couple;

(b) where a claimant is married polygamously to two or more members of the claimant's household, all such members;

"person who lacks capacity"—

(a) in England and Wales, has the meaning given in section 2 of the Mental Capacity Act 2005;

(b) in Scotland, means a person who is incapable under section 1(6) of the Adults with Incapacity (Scotland) Act 2000;

"polygamous marriage" means a marriage during which a party to it is married to more than one person and which took place under the laws of a country which permits polygamy;

"qualifying benefit" means income-related employment and support allowance, income support, income-based jobseeker's allowance, state pension credit or universal credit;

"qualifying lender" has the meaning given in section 19(7) of the Act;

"qualifying loan" means—

(a) in the case of a legacy benefit or state pension credit, a loan which qualifies under paragraph 2(2) or (4) of Schedule 1 to these Regulations;

(b) in the case of universal credit, a loan which qualifies under paragraph 5(2) of Schedule 1 to these Regulations;

"qualifying period" means a period of—

(a) [³ three] consecutive assessment periods in which a claimant has been entitled to universal credit;

(b) 39 consecutive weeks in which a claimant—

    (i) has been entitled to a legacy benefit; or

    (ii) is treated as having been entitled to such a benefit under—

        (aa) paragraph 14 of Schedule 3 to the IS Regulations;

        (bb) paragraph 13 of Schedule 2 to the JSA Regulations; or

        (cc) paragraph 15 of Schedule 6 to the ESA Regulations;

"qualifying young person" has the meaning given—

(a) in the case of a legacy benefit, in section 142 of the Social Security Contributions and Benefits Act 1992;

(b) in the case of state pension credit, in regulation 4A of the SPC Regulations;

(c) in the case of universal credit, in regulation 5 of the UC Regulations;

"relevant accommodation" means the accommodation which the claimant occupies, or is treated as occupying, as the claimant's home under Schedule 3;

"relevant date", apart from in regulation 21, means the first day with respect to which a claimant's liability to make owner-occupier payments is met by a loan payment;

[¹ "single claimant" means—

(a) an individual who has made a claim for, and is entitled to, a qualifying benefit;

(b) an individual who has made a claim for, but is not entitled to, a legacy benefit or state pension credit by reason only that the individual has, or, if the individual is a member of a couple, they have, income—

(i) equal to or exceeding the applicable amount, but

(ii) less than the sum of that applicable amount and the amount of a loan payment applicable to the individual;]

"single person" means an individual who is not a member of a couple;

"SPC claimant" means a claimant who is entitled to [¹, or is treated as entitled to,] state pension credit;

"SPC Regulations" means the State Pension Credit Regulations 2002;

"standard security" has the meaning in Part 2 of the Conveyancing and Feudal Reform (Scotland) Act 1970;

"transitional end day" has the meaning given in regulations 19(1) [¹, 19A(1) and (5)] and 20(2);

"Transitional Provisions Regulations" means the Universal Credit (Transitional Provisions) Regulations 2014;

"UC claimant" means a claimant who is entitled to universal credit;

"UC Regulations" means the Universal Credit Regulations 2013; and

"unearned income" has the meaning given in Chapter 3 of Part 6 of the UC Regulations.

(2) For the purposes of these Regulations, a reference to—

(a) entitlement to a qualifying benefit is to be read as a reference to entitlement as determined under the ESA Regulations, IS Regulations, JSA Regulations, SPC Regulations and UC Regulations;

[¹(aa) a person being treated as entitled to a qualifying benefit is to be read as a reference to a person who satisfies sub-paragraph (a) (ii) of the definition of "joint claimants" or sub-paragraph (b) of the definition of "single claimant", except in the definition of "qualifying period", regulation 21(5)(b) and paragraph 3 of Schedule 1;]

(b) the claimant's family or to being a member of the claimant's family means a reference to the claimant's partner and any child or qualifying young person who is the responsibility of the claimant or the claimant's partner, where that child or qualifying young person is a member of the claimant's household;

(c) a person being responsible for a child or qualifying young person is to be read as a reference to a person being treated as responsible for a child or qualifying young person in the circumstances specified in—

(i) in the case of employment and support allowance, regulation 156(10) of the ESA Regulations;

(ii) in the case of income support, regulation 15 of the IS Regulations;

(iii) in the case of jobseeker's allowance, regulation 77 of the JSA Regulations;

(iv) in the case of state pension credit and universal credit, regulation 4 of the UC Regulations;

(d) a person being a member of a household is to be read as a reference to a person being treated as a member of the household in the circumstances specified in—

(i) in the case of employment and support allowance, in regulation 156 of the ESA Regulations;

(ii) in the case of income support, in regulation 16 of the IS Regulations;

(iii) in the case of jobseeker's allowance, in regulation 78 of the JSA Regulations;

   (iv) in the case of state pension credit and universal credit, in regulation 5 of the SPC Regulations;

 (e) a person being engaged in remunerative work is to be read as a reference to a person being treated as engaged in remunerative work—

   (i) in the case of employment and support allowance, in regulations 41 to 43 of the ESA Regulations;

   (ii) in the case of income support, in regulations 5 and 6 of the IS Regulations;

   (iii) in the case of jobseeker's allowance, in regulations 51 to 53 of the JSA Regulations;

   (iv) in the case of state pension credit, in paragraph 2 of Schedule 2 to the SPC Regulations.

AMENDMENTS

1. Loans for Mortgage Interest and Social Fund Maternity Grant (Amendment) Regulations 2018 (SI 2018/307), reg.2(1) and (2) (April 6, 2018).

2. Loans for Mortgage Interest (Amendment) Regulations 2021 (SI 2021/131) reg.2(1) and (2) (March 15, 2021).

3. Loans for Mortgage Interest (Amendment) Regulations 2023 (SI 2023/226) reg.2(2) (April 3, 2023).

GENERAL NOTE

Most of the definitions listed above are self-explanatory. Where they are not, they are discussed in the commentary to the regulations in which the defined terms are used. **2.597**

The offer of loan payments

3.—(1) The Secretary of State may make an offer of loan payments to a claimant in respect of any owner-occupier payments the claimant is, or is to be treated as, being liable to make in respect of the accommodation which the claimant is, or is to be treated as, occupying as the claimant's home [¹ ...] **2.598**

(2) For the purposes of paragraph (1)—

 (a) owner-occupier payments are—

   (i) in the case of a legacy benefit claimant or SPC claimant, payments within the meaning of Part 1 of Schedule 1;

   (ii) in the case of a UC claimant, payments within the meaning of Part 2 of Schedule 1;

 (b) the circumstances in which a claimant is, or is to be treated as, being liable to make owner-occupier payments are—

   (i) in the case of a legacy benefit claimant or SPC claimant, the circumstances specified in Part 1 of Schedule 2;

   (ii) in the case of a UC claimant, the circumstances specified in Part 2 of Schedule 2;

 (c) the circumstances in which a claimant is, or is to be treated as, occupying accommodation as the claimant's home are—

   (i) in the case of a legacy benefit claimant or SPC claimant, the circumstances specified in Part 2 of Schedule 3;

   (ii) in the case of a UC claimant, the circumstances specified in Part 3 of Schedule 3.

(3) Where the liability for owner-occupier payments is shared with a person not in the benefit unit, the claimant shall be, or shall be treated as, liable to make owner-occupier payments by reference to the appropriate proportion of the payments for which the claimant is responsible.
[¹ ...]

AMENDMENT

1. Loans for Mortgage Interest (Amendment) Regulations 2023 (SI 2023/226) reg.2(3) (April 3, 2023).

DEFINITIONS

"benefit unit"—reg.2(1).
"claimant"—*ibid.*
"couple"—*ibid.*
"earned income"—*ibid.*
"legacy benefit claimant"—*ibid.*
"loan payments"—*ibid.*
"owner-occupier payments"—regs 2(1) and 3(2)(a).
"single person"—reg.2(1).
"SPC claimant"—*ibid.*
"UC claimant"—*ibid.*

GENERAL NOTE

2.599 *Paragraphs (1) and (2)*: Paragraph (1) empowers the Secretary of State to make "an offer of loan payments" in the following circumstances:

- first, the person to whom the offer is made must be a "claimant", defined in reg.2(1) as meaning "a single claimant or each of joint claimants";

- second, the offer can only be made in respect of "any owner-occupier payments".

    For "legacy benefit claimants" (i.e., those who are entitled to, or treated as entitled to, IRESA, IS or IBJSA: see reg.2(1)) and "SPC claimants" these are as defined in Sch.1, Pt 1. For "UC claimants", the definition is in Sch.1, Pt 2: see para.(2)(1)(a).

- third, the claimant must be liable, or treated as liable, to make those payments.

    The circumstances in which legacy benefit claimants and SPC claimants are, or are treated as, liable to make owner-occupier payments are set out in Sch.2, Pt 1. For UC claimants, those circumstances are set out in Sch.2, Pt 2: see para.(2)(1)(b). Where liability is shared, see also para.(2).

- fourth, the owner-occupier payments that the claimant is, or is treated as, liable to make must be in respect of accommodation which they are, or is treated as, occupying as his or her home.

    The circumstances in which legacy benefit claimants and SPC claimants are, or are treated as, occupying accommodation as their home, are set out in Sch.3, Pt 1. For UC claimants, those circumstances are set out in Sch.3, Pt 2: see para.(2)(1)(c).

The Secretary of State's offer will take the form of a draft loan agreement (as defined in reg.2(1)). The requirements for the offer to be accepted are set out in regs 4 and 5.

Paragraph (3) applies where the claimant is jointly liable for owner-occupier payments with someone who is not in the "benefit unit", which is defined by reg.2(1) as meaning "a single claimant and his or her partner (if any) or joint claimants".

In those circumstances, the claimant is only treated as liable for—and is therefore only eligible for a loan in respect of—"the appropriate proportion of the payments for which s/he is responsible". "Appropriate proportion" is not defined and its meaning in individual cases may give rise to disputes.

Acceptance of loan payments offer

4. The offer of loan payments is accepted where the Secretary of State has received the loan agreement signed by, in the case of a single claimant, the claimant and his or her partner (if any), or, in the case of joint claimants, each member of the couple, and the documents referred to in regulation 5(2).

2.600

DEFINITIONS

> "claimant"—reg.2(1).
> "couple"—*ibid.*
> "joint claimants"—*ibid.*
> "loan agreement"—*ibid.*
> "loan payments"—*ibid.*
> "partner"—*ibid.*
> "single claimant"—*ibid.*

GENERAL NOTE

Claimants do not have to accept the Secretary of State's offer. But if they do not do so, they will receive no help at all with owner-occupier payments because the legislation allowing such payments to be met by IS, IBJSA, SPC, IRESA or UC has been repealed.

2.601

To accept the Secretary of State's offer, the claimant—or both joint claimants—must sign the loan agreement and return it to the DWP with the documents set out in reg.5(2). The offer is not accepted until the Department has received the signed agreement ant those documents.

Conditions to meet before the loan payments can be made

5.—(1) The Secretary of State may make the loan payments if—
(a) the loan payments offer is accepted in accordance with regulation 4; and
(b) the conditions in paragraph (2) are met.
(2) The conditions are—
(a) in England and Wales—
  (i) where all of the legal owners are within the benefit unit, each legal owner has executed a charge by way of legal mortgage in favour of the Secretary of State in respect of the relevant accommodation;
  (ii) where one or more legal owners are not within the benefit unit, each legal owner within the benefit unit (if any) has executed an equitable charge in respect of their beneficial interest in the relevant accommodation;
(b) in Scotland, each legal owner within the benefit unit has executed a standard security in respect of his or her interest in the relevant accommodation;
(c) the Secretary of State has obtained the written consent referred to in paragraph (3); and

2.602

    (d) the information condition in regulation 6 is met within the period of 6 months ending with the day on which the loan payments offer is accepted.

(3) The consent required by paragraph (2)(c) is consent given in writing to the creation of the charge or, in Scotland, the standard security by any person in the benefit unit in occupation of the relevant accommodation, who is not a legal owner.

Definitions

"benefit unit"—reg.2(1).
"charge by way of legal mortgage"—*ibid.*
"legal owner"—*ibid.*
"loan payments"—*ibid.*
"relevant accommodation"—*ibid.*
"standard security"—*ibid.*

2.603   General Note

Paragraph (1): The drafting of paragraph (1) seems over-cautious. It states that the Secretary of State may make loan payments if the offer is accepted in accordance with reg.4 and the conditions in paragraph (2) are met. However, under reg.4, the offer is only accepted when the Secretary of State receives "the documents referred to in regulation 5(2)", so—at most—all that all that reg.5(1)(b) achieves is to prevent loan payments from being made where the information condition in reg.6 has not been satisfied during the preceding six months: see para.(2)(d).

Paragraphs (2) and (3) require three things. First, all the legal owners of the "relevant accommodation" (*i.e.,* the accommodation which the claimant occupies, or is treated as occupying, as his or her home under Sch.3: see reg.2(1)) must give the Secretary of State security for the repayment of the loan payments (paras (2)(a) and (b)). In other words, they have to create a second mortgage in favour of the Secretary of State. Second, everyone occupying the relevant accommodation who is not a legal owner must consent to the giving of that security (paras (2)(c) and (3)). Third, the information condition in reg.6 must have been satisfied within the period of six months ending on the day on which the loan offer is accepted (para.(2)(d)).

The type of security that must be given depends upon whether the relevant accommodation is in England and Wales or in Scotland and, in the former case, on whether the legal ownership of the relevant accommodation is held entirely by people in the benefit unit or shared with someone outside that unit.

If the relevant accommodation is in England or Wales and the legal ownership is held entirely by those within the benefit unit each legal owner must execute a charge by way of legal mortgage (defined by reg.2(1) as having the same meaning as in s.132(1) of the Land Registration Act 2002) over it. Where the legal ownership of the relevant accommodation is jointly held with someone who is not in the benefit unit, each legal owner must execute an equitable charge over his or her beneficial interest in the property. For the difference between legal and beneficial ownership, see the commentary to reg.46 of the Income Support Regulations in Vol.V and, e.g., *SSWP v LB Tower Hamlets and CT (IS & HB)* [2018] UKUT 25 (AAC) at paras 21-29.

If the relevant accommodation is in Scotland, then each legal owner within the benefit unit must execute a standard security in respect of her/his interest in the relevant accommodation. "Standard security" is defined by reg.2(1) as having "the meaning in Part 2 of the Conveyancing and Feudal Reform (Scotland) Act 1970".

Information condition

6.—(1) The information condition is that the Secretary of State has provided relevant information about the loan payments to a single claimant and his or her partner (if any) or each joint claimant.

(2) For the purposes of this regulation, "relevant information" is information about the loan payments which must include—

(a) a summary of the terms and conditions included within the loan agreement;

(b) where the circumstances in regulation 5(2)(a)(i) or (b) apply, an explanation that the Secretary of State will seek to obtain a charge or, in Scotland, a standard security in respect of the relevant accommodation;

(c) an explanation of the consent referred to in regulation 5(3); and

(d) information as to where a single claimant and his or her partner (if any) or each joint claimant can obtain further information and independent legal and financial advice regarding loan payments.

2.604

DEFINITIONS

"claimant"—reg.2(1).
"loan agreement"—*ibid.*
"loan payments"—*ibid.*
"partner"—*ibid.*
"relevant accommodation"—*ibid.*
"single claimant"—*ibid.*
"standard security"—*ibid.*

GENERAL NOTE

2.605

Taken together, reg.5(2)(d) and reg.6 require that the Secretary of State must have provided the claimant, and any partner, with the information specified in para. (2) at some point during the period of six months ending with the day on which the offer of loan payments is accepted. The regulations do not specify the consequences that are to follow if the information condition is not satisfied, or is not satisfied during that period.

Time of each loan payment

7. Each loan payment shall be made—

(a) in the case of a UC claimant, at monthly intervals in arrears; and

[1(b) in the case of a legacy benefit claimant or SPC claimant, at 4 weekly intervals in arrears.]

2.606

AMENDMENT

1. Loans for Mortgage Interest and Social Fund Maternity Grant (Amendment) Regulations 2018 (SI 2018/307), reg.2(1) and (3) (April 6, 2018).

DEFINITIONS

"claimant"—reg.2(1).
"legacy benefit claimant"—*ibid.*
"qualifying benefit"—*ibid.*
"qualifying lender"—*ibid.*
"SPC claimant"—*ibid.*
"UC claimant"—*ibid.*

2.607   Loan payments are always made in arrears. For UC claimants, they are made at monthly intervals, presumably to coincide with the claimant's assessment period. For those on other benefits, payment is 4-weekly in arrears.

Period covered by loan payments

2.608   **8.**—(1) The period in respect of which the loan payments shall be made shall begin on the later of—

(a) 6th April 2018;

(b) in the case of a UC claimant or legacy benefit claimant [2 , except where sub-paragraph (ba) or (bb) applies], the day after the day on which the qualifying period ends;

[2 (ba) in the case of a couple where one member is an SPC claimant receiving loan payments, the first day of entitlement to universal credit as a couple;

(bb) in the case of a couple where one member was formerly an SPC claimant receiving loan payments, the first day of entitlement to universal credit as a couple, if the first day of that entitlement is within the period of one month beginning with the day on which the entitlement to state pension credit ended;]

[1 (c) in the case of an [2 SPC claimant (who is not in a couple)], the first day of entitlement to state pension credit;]

(d) the transitional end day [1;

(e) a date requested by the claimant.]

[1 (2) If the day referred to in [2 sub-paragraphs (a), (b), (c) and (e) of paragraph (1)] is not the first day of the claimant's benefit week, in the case of a legacy benefit claimant or SPC claimant, or assessment period, in the case of a UC claimant, the day referred to shall be the first day of the first benefit week or first assessment period that begins after that date.]

[2 (3) In this regulation, "couple" means a couple entitled to universal credit as joint claimants under regulation 3(2)(a) of the UC Regulations.]

AMENDMENTS

1. Loans for Mortgage Interest and Social Fund Maternity Grant (Amendment) Regulations 2018 (SI 2018/307) reg.2(1) and (4) (April 6, 2018).

2. Loans for Mortgage Interest (Amendment) Regulations 2023 (SI 2023/226) reg.2(4) (April 3, 2023).

DEFINITIONS

"claimant"—reg.2(1).
"legacy benefit claimant"—*ibid.*
"loan payments"—*ibid.*
"qualifying period"—*ibid.*
"SPC claimant"—*ibid.*
"transitional end day"—*ibid.* and regs 19(1), 19A(1) and (5) and 20(2).
"UC claimant"—reg,2(1).

2.609   GENERAL NOTE

Subject to para.(2), entitlement to loan payments begins on—and any entitlement to housing costs therefore ends the day before—the latest of the five days specified in para.(1). Para.(2) modifies that rule by providing that if the day identified by para.(1) is not the first day of an assessment period (for UC claimants) or of a benefit week (for claimants of IS, IBJSA or IRESA), entitlement to loan payments instead begins on the first day of the next assessment period or benefit week.

"Qualifying period"

The phrase "qualifying period" is defined in reg.2(1). 2.610

For UC claimants, the effect of that definition, taken with sub-para.(1)(b) is that there is no entitlement to a loan payment unless they have first been entitled to universal credit for three consecutive assessment periods.

For claimants of IS, IBJSA, or IRESA the effect is that there is no entitlement to a loan payment unless they have been entitled to one of those benefits—or treated as so entitled by the provisions listed in head (1)(b)(ii) of the definition—for 39 consecutive weeks

Those provisions establish linking rules by which two or more periods of entitlement to one of those benefits are, in some circumstances treated as a single period of entitlement: see further Vol.V.

Where a claimant has moved from one of those benefits to another, see Sch.6, para.20(1)(c) to the ESA Regulations in Vol.V; and reg.32 of the Income Support (General) (Jobseeker's Allowance Consequential Amendments) Regulations 1996, and Sch.2, para.18(1)(c) to the JSA Regulations in Vol.V.

See the commentary to reg.9(7) below for the circumstances in which claimants of IS, IBJSA and IRESA who were previously in receipt of loan payments may receive them again without serving a further qualifying period.

Transitional end day

The transitional end day applies where a claimant was entitled to housing costs 2.611 before April 6, 2018 and benefits from the transitional provisions in regs 19, 19A and 20: see, further, the General Notes to those regulations.

Duration of loan payments

9.—(1) Subject to paragraph (2), loan payments shall continue to be 2.612 made indefinitely at the intervals specified in regulation 7.

(2) If one of the circumstances in paragraph (3) occurs, the Secretary of State shall terminate the loan payments immediately but subject to paragraph (4).

(3) The circumstances are that—

(a) the claimant ceases to be entitled [¹, or treated as entitled to,] to a qualifying benefit;

(b) the claimant ceases to be, or to be treated as, liable to make owner-occupier payments under Schedule 2;

(c) the claimant ceases to be, or to be treated as, occupying the relevant accommodation under Schedule 3;

(d) the loan agreement is terminated in accordance with its terms;

[² ...]

(4) The Secretary of State shall make the loan payments direct to the claimant for the period specified in paragraph (6) if—

(a) a claimant ceases to be entitled to a legacy benefit by reason that, in the case of a single claimant, the claimant or his or her partner (if any), or, in the case of joint claimants, either member of the couple, is engaged in remunerative work; and

(b) the conditions in paragraph (5) are met.

(5) The conditions are that, in the case of a single claimant, the claimant or his or her partner (if any), or, in the case of joint claimants, either member of the couple—

(a) is engaged in remunerative work which is expected to last for a period of no less than 5 weeks;

(b) is still liable or treated as liable to make owner-occupier payments under Schedule 2;

(c) has, for a continuous period of 26 weeks ending with the day on which he or she commences the work referred to in sub-paragraph (a), been entitled to a legacy benefit; and

(d) was, on the day before the day on which he or she commenced the work referred to in sub-paragraph (a), receiving loan payments under these Regulations.

(6) The period specified is the period of 4 weeks commencing with the day on which the relevant person is first engaged in remunerative work.

[² (7) If a legacy benefit claimant ceases to be entitled to, or treated as entitled to, a legacy benefit ("the old entitlement") but becomes entitled, or treated as entitled, again to the benefit ("the new entitlement") within the period of 52 weeks beginning with the day on which the claimant ceased to be entitled, or treated as entitled, to the old entitlement, and the claimant wishes to receive loan payments on the basis of the new entitlement, there is no requirement for the claimant to serve a new qualifying period.

(8) If a UC claimant ceases to be entitled to universal credit ("the old entitlement") but becomes entitled again to universal credit ("the new entitlement") within the period of 6 months beginning with the day on which the claimant ceased to be entitled to the old entitlement, and the claimant wishes to receive loan payments on the basis of the new entitlement, there is no requirement for the claimant to serve a new qualifying period.]

AMENDMENTS

1. Loans for Mortgage Interest and Social Fund Maternity Grant (Amendment) Regulations 2018 (SI 2018/307) reg.2(1) and (5) (April 6, 2018).

2. Loans for Mortgage Interest (Amendment) Regulations 2023 (SI 2023/226) reg.2(5) (April 3, 2023).

DEFINITIONS

"claimant"—reg.2(1).
"couple"—*ibid.*
"entitlement"—reg.2(2)(a).
"joint claimants"—reg.2(1).
"legacy benefit"—*ibid.*
"legacy benefit claimant"—*ibid.*
"loan agreement"—*ibid.*
"loan payments"—*ibid.*
"owner-occupier payments"—regs 2(1) and 3(2)(a).
"partner"—reg.2(1).
"qualifying benefit"—*ibid.*
"qualifying period"—*ibid.*
"relevant accommodation"—*ibid.*
"remunerative work"—reg.2(2)(e).

"single claimant"—reg.2(1).
"UC claimant"—*ibid.*

GENERAL NOTE

Paragraph (1). Once loan payments have started they continue indefinitely at monthly intervals for UC claimants, and four-weekly periods for other claimants, until one of the events in para.(2) occurs.

Paragraph (2). Loan payments come to an end if:

- the claimant ceases to be entitled, or treated as entitled, to a qualifying benefit (as defined in reg.2(1). However, where the benefit that has ended is IS, IBJSA or IRESA, and the reason that the benefit has come to an end is that the claimant or her/his partner has begun remunerative work, see paras (4)-(6);

- the claimant ceases to be liable, or to be treated as liable, to make owner occupier payments: see reg.3(2)(a) and (b) and Sch.1;

- the claimant ceases to occupy, or to be treated as occupying, the relevant accommodation: see reg.3(2)(c) and Sch.3;

- the loan agreement comes to an end; or

- for UC claimants, the claimant (or either joint claimant) begins to earn an income.

Paragraphs (4)-(6) create a four-week run-on for some claimants who are no longer eligible for loan payments because they have ceased to be entitled to IS, IBJSA or IRESA. The run-on applies if (1) the reason that entitlement to one of those benefits has ended is that the claimant or her/his partner (if any) have started remunerative work; (2) that work is expected to last for at least five weeks; (3) the claimant s still liable, or treated as liable to make owner-occupier payments; (4) on the day that the claimant or her/his partner commences remunerative work, the claimant has been entitled to one or more of those benefits for a continuous period of 26 weeks, and (5) on the previous day had been receiving loan payments.

Paragraph (7) is puzzling. What it appears to say is that where a claimant ceases to be entitled (or treated as entitled) to IS, IBJSA or IRESA but becomes entitled again within the following 52 weeks, it is not necessary for her/him to wait for a further qualifying period before loan payments can be made.

As the rule is about the circumstances in which the qualifying period does not apply, rather than about the circumstances in which loan payments come to an end, it might be thought to belong more naturally in reg.8 than reg.9.

More importantly, the rule has been drafted so narrowly that it seems likely that it will not be of practical benefit. The reference to the claimant becoming "entitled, or treated as entitled, *again* to the benefit" (emphasis added) suggests that the old entitlement and the new entitlement must be to the same benefit. However, the roll-out of universal credit means it is not in practice possible to make a fresh claim for IS, IBJSA or IRESA. Claimants who might otherwise have benefitted from this rule are likely to be required to claim universal credit, in which case, it will be necessary to serve a qualifying period of three consecutive assessment periods. (Note that while the current para.(7) is a version from 2023, it maintains unchanged the wording at issue here.)

Paragraph (8), while also more naturally belonging in reg.8, is more straightforward in its effect: gaps of no more than six months in UC entitlement do not require a claimant to serve a new qualifying period.

2.613

Calculation of each loan payment

2.614   **10.**—Subject to any deduction under regulation 14 [¹ or 14A], each loan payment shall be the aggregate of the amounts resulting from regulations 11 and 12.

AMENDMENT

1. Loans for Mortgage Interest and Social Fund Maternity Grant (Amendment) Regulations 2018 (SI 2018/307), reg.2(1) and (6) (April 6, 2018).

GENERAL NOTE

2.615   Regulation 10 is self-explanatory. The amount of each loan payment is calculated by adding together the amount for interest on qualifying loans (calculated under reg.11) and the amount for alternative finance arrangements (calculated under reg.12) and then subtracting any non-dependant deduction that falls to be made under reg.14 and any insurance payment deduction under reg.14A.

Calculation in respect of qualifying loans

2.616   **11.**—(1) Subject to paragraphs (3) and (4), the amount to be included in each loan payment for owner-occupier payments which are payments of interest on qualifying loans is determined as follows.

Step 1

Determine the amount of capital for the time being owing in connection with each qualifying loan to which the owner-occupier payments relate.

Step 2

If there is more than one qualifying loan, add together the amounts determined in step 1.

Step 3

Determine the identified amount which is the lower of—
(a) the amount resulting from step 1 or 2; and
(b) the capital limit specified in paragraph (2)(a) or (b).
If both amounts in (a) and (b) are the same, that is the identified amount.

Step 4

In respect of a legacy benefit claimant or SPC claimant, apply the following formula to achieve a weekly sum—

$$\frac{A \times SR}{52} - I$$

In respect of a UC claimant, apply the following formula to achieve a monthly sum—

$$\frac{A \times SR}{12} - I$$

In either case—

"A" is the identified amount in step 3,

"SR" is the standard rate that applies at the end of the calculation (see regulation 13), and

"I" is the amount of any income, in the case of a legacy benefit or SPC claimant, or unearned income, in the case of a UC claimant, above the claimant's applicable amount.

The result is the amount to be included in each loan payment for owner-occupier payments which are payments of interest on qualifying loans.

(2) The capital limit is—

(a) £200,000—

    (i) in the case of a legacy benefit claimant or SPC claimant where the Modified Rules apply;

    (ii) in the case of a UC claimant;

(b) £100,000 in all other cases.

(3) In the application of paragraph (2) to a qualifying loan (or any part of a qualifying loan) which was taken out for the purpose of making necessary adaptations to the accommodation to meet the needs of a disabled person—

(a) the qualifying loan (or the part of the qualifying loan) is to be disregarded for the purposes of steps 2 and 3; and

(b) "A" in step 4 is to be read as the amount resulting from step 1 in respect of the qualifying loan (or the sum of those amounts if there is more than one qualifying loan taken out for the purpose of making such adaptations) plus the amount (if any) resulting from step 3 in relation to any other qualifying loan or loans.

(4) Subject to paragraph (5), any variation in the amount of capital for the time being owing in connection with a qualifying loan is not to be taken into account after the relevant date until such time as the Secretary of State recalculates the amount which shall occur—

(a) on the first anniversary of the relevant date; and

(b) in respect of any variation after the first anniversary, on the next anniversary which follows the date of the variation.

(5) In respect of an existing claimant, the Secretary of State shall recalculate the amount of capital owing in connection with a qualifying loan on the anniversary of the date on which the claimant's qualifying benefit first included an amount for owner-occupier payments.

DEFINITIONS

"applicable amount"—reg.2(1).
"claimant"—*ibid.*
"disabled person"—*ibid.*
"existing claimant"—*ibid.*
"income"—*ibid.*
"legacy benefit claimant"—*ibid.*
"Modified Rules"—*ibid.*
"owner-occupier payments"—regs 2(1) and 3(2)(a).
"qualifying benefit"—*ibid.*
"qualifying loan"—*ibid.*
"relevant date"—*ibid.*
"SPC claimant"—*ibid.*
"UC claimant"—*ibid.*
"unearned income"—*ibid.*

GENERAL NOTE

2.617   Regulation 11 provides for the calculation of loan payments in respect of interest of qualifying loans. The calculation of loan payments in respect of alternative finance payments is governed by reg.12.

Under para.(1), there are four steps to that calculation. However, in order to follow those steps, it is first necessary to identify the capital limit applicable to the claimant, by applying the rules in para.(2) and also the "standard interest rate" (see reg.13, below).

Capital Limit

2.618   The general rule is that the capital limit is £100,000 for those claiming IS, IBJSA, IRESA or SPC and £200,000 for those claiming UC: see para.(2)(a)(ii) and (b). There is one exception, and one modification, to that rule.

The exception is in para.(2)(a)(i). Claimants of IS, IBJSA, IRESA and SPC also have a capital limit of £200,000 where the "Modified Rules" apply. That phrase is defined by reg.2(1) as meaning the Social Security (Housing Costs Special Arrangements) (Amendment and Modification) Regulations 2008 (SI 2008/3195): see further Vol.V.

The modification is in paras (3)-(4) and applies where the whole, or part of, a qualifying loan was taken out in order to make "necessary" adaptations to the accommodation to meet the needs of a disabled person (*i.e.*, as defined in reg.2(1)). To avoid circumlocution, this General Note will refer to that purpose as "the specified purpose" even though reg.11 does not itself use that term.

The legislative intention appears to be that any part of a loan taken out for the specified purpose is excluded when the capital limit applies so that if, for example, a claimant on IBJSA with a capital limit of £100,000 has a loan of £250,000, of which £25,000 was taken out for the specified purpose, the loan payment is calculated on capital of £125,000, £100,000 for the part of the loan that was not taken out for the specified purpose plus the £25,000 that was taken out for that purpose.

However, there must be doubt as to whether the modification is effective. Para. (3) states that it has effect in the application of "*paragraph (2)*" to a qualifying loan taken out for the specified purpose. But the modifications in para.(3) relate to Steps 2, 3 and 4 of the calculation (see below), which do not form part of para.(2) but rather para.(1). Para. (2) is about the amount of the capital limit, which is the same irrespective of the amount of the loan (or loans) and the purposes for which those loans were taken out. Indeed, the whole point of the capital limit is that it is a cap on the actual amount of the claimant's loan or loans. It therefore appears that the reference to "paragraph (2)" in the opening words of para.(3) should instead be to "paragraph (1)".

Moreover, even if it is possible to read para.(3) as referring to para.(1) (perhaps by the application of the rule in *Inco Europe Ltd v First Choice Distribution (a firm)* [2000] UKHL 15), the drafting of the modification is unnecessarily complex, and it is arguable that it has effects that are far more favourable to claimants than was intended: see below.

The calculation

2.619   Where the calculation relates to a loan (or loans), no part of which was taken out for the specified purpose, it is relatively straightforward.

Step 1

2.620   The first step is to determine the amount of capital owing on each qualifying loan "to which the owner-occupier payments relate".

650

For claimants of IS, IBJSA, IRESA and SPC, "owner-occupier payments" are defined by reg.3(2)(a) and para.2(1)(a), (2) and (4) of Sch.1 by reference to the purposes for which the loans were taken out. To the extent that a loan was taken out for any purpose not specified in para.2(2) of Sch.1, the capital will not be capital "to which the owner-occupier payments relate" and therefore will not be taken into account in the calculation.

By the same reasoning, for claimants of UC, reg.3(2)(a)(ii) and para.5(1)(a) and (2), the owner-occupier payments will relate to the capital if, but only if, it is secured on the relevant accommodation: the purpose for which the loan was taken out is irrelevant.

Step 2

If there is more than one qualifying loan, then the amounts determined separately in Step 1 are added together.

2.621

Step 3

The Step 1 or (if there is more than one qualifying loan) Step 2 figure is then compared with the claimant's capital limit (see above) and if it is higher than that limit, then the amount of the loan payment is calculated using the capital limit, not the amount of capital the claimant has actually borrowed.

2.622

Step 4

Step 4 is the last step in the calculation. The standard interest rate (see reg.13) is applied to the amount of capital identified in Step 3 and the product is then divided by either by 12 (to produce a monthly sum for UC claimants) or 52 (to produce a weekly sum for those on other qualifying benefits).

2.623

Then, finally, if UC claimants have *unearned* income—or those claiming other qualifying benefits have *any* income—in excess of their "applicable amount", the amount of the excess is deducted.

"Applicable amount" is defined in reg.2(1). For IS, IBJSA and IRESA it is the same as the applicable amount used in the calculation of those benefits. For SPC and universal credit, which do not use the concept of an "applicable amount" in the calculation of the award, the applicable amounts for the purpose of Step 4 are, respectively, the appropriate minimum guarantee (see s.2 SPCA 2002) and the maximum amount (see s.8(1) and (2) WRA 2012 and reg.23(1) of the UC Regulations).

Loans to adapt accommodation for disabled persons

How does that calculation differ, if the loan, or loans, or part of any loan is taken out for the specified purpose? As explained above, this depends upon the modifications made by para.(3) (and assumes that—contrary to what it actually says—para. (3) can be read as applying to para.(1), rather than para.(2)).

2.624

Step 1

At least at this stage, para.(3) does not modify Step 1.

2.625

Step 2

At Step 2, any part of the qualifying loan that was taken out to adapt the accommodation for the needs of a disabled person is disregarded: see para.(3)(a).

2.626

At this stage of the calculation the disregard of the capital disadvantages the claimant because it has the effect that capital borrowed to meet the needs of a disabled person does not count towards the total to which the standard rate of interest will be applied in Step 4.

As Step 2 only applies "[i]f there is more than one qualifying loan" and para.(3)(a) does not disregard the capital for the purposes of Step 1, the regulation creates the bizarre situation that—at this stage of the calculation—if a claimant has a single qualifying loan which includes amounts that were borrowed to adapt relevant accommodation to meet the needs of a disabled person, then no part of that capital is disregarded. However, if they have two or more such qualifying loans, all such capital is disregarded whichever loan it is part of.

Step 3

2.627   Where the loan includes capital that was borrowed for the specified purpose, it is difficult to work out what Step 3 requires. Para.(3)(a) says that such capital is to be disregarded for the purposes of that step. But from what amount or amounts is it to be disregarded?

Three amounts are mentioned in the unmodified Step 3, the capital limit, the Step 1 amount and the Step 2 amount.

It is not possible to disregard the amount of the loan taken out for the specified purpose from the capital limit because that figure is a notional amount. And, anyway, deducting the disregarded amount from that limit would reduce it and thereby work against the presumed policy intention that capital borrowed for this purpose should not be affected by the capital limit.

That leaves the Step 1 amount and the Step 2 amount. But capital borrowed to adapt accommodation for a disabled person has already been disregarded from the Step 2 amount. Should a second disregard now be made from that amount? And should such capital now be disregarded from the Step 1 amount as well? Given what is said below about the Step 4 calculation, the answers appear to be "no", and "the question is irrelevant".

Step 4

2.628   Where all or part of the qualifying loan (or loans) was taken out for the specified purpose, para.(3)(a) provides that the capital figure ("A" in the formula):

"... is to be read as the amount resulting from step 1 in respect of the qualifying loan (or the sum of those amounts if there is more than one qualifying loan taken out for the purpose of making such adaptations) plus the amount (if any) resulting from step three in relation to any other qualifying loan or loans."

Finally, the drafting of the modification for loans taken out to adapt accommodation for the needs of a disabled person begins to make some sense. The aggregate of the full amounts of such loans (i.e., the aggregate of the amounts identified in Step 1) is taken into account. Then, in addition, loans, no part of which were taken out for that purpose are taken into account at the Step 3 figure (i.e., to the extent that, cumulatively, they do not exceed the capital limit). That is why no capital was disregarded at Step 1: for specified purpose loans, Step 4 takes the Step 1 figure into account in full without, in effect, going through the Step 3 process (which is why it is irrelevant whether specified purpose capital is disregarded from the Step 1 figure at the Step 3 stage). It is also why capital borrowed for the specified purpose is disregarded from the Step 2 figure: if it were not, it would be double-counted at Step 4.

Discussion

2.629   Even though the drafting becomes clear at the Step 4 stage, it is unnecessarily complex. Moreover, the wording does not achieve the result that appears to have been intended. An example may assist:

652

Estelle has been awarded IBJSA and is an owner-occupier. Her capital limit is £100,000. However she has a mortgage of £250,000, of which £25,000 was taken out to adapt her home for the needs of her daughter, Brittney, who is a disabled person.

What was (presumably) intended was that the loan payment should be calculated on £125,000 (i.e., the capital limit of £100,000 plus the £25,000 needed to carry out adaptations for Britney) and that is what would have been achieved if the £25,000 had been taken out as a separate loan.

However, Estelle has only one loan and what, because para.(3)(b) does not distinguish between loans and part loans, it appears to have the effect that the whole of that loan is taken into account at the Step 1 figure, namely £250,000.

Moreover, suppose that (before she claimed JSA) Estelle took out a further loan of £75,000 for purposes that are eligible under para.2(4) of Sch.1 but did not include the specified purpose. Para.(3)(b) now appears to have the effect that the second loan is taken into account at the Step 3 figure, which is £75,000 because it is less than Estelle's capital limit. If so, Estelle's loan payments should be calculated on a loan of £325,000.

Revaluation of capital

Even though Step 1 of the calculation says that what is to be determined is the amount of capital *for the time being owing* in connection with each qualifying loan, the Step 1 figure is not in fact revalued every month (for UC claimants) or every week (for other claimants). Instead, except where the claimant is an "existing claimant", the amount is re-calculated annually on the anniversary of the relevant date and on each subsequent such anniversary: see para.(4). For existing claimants, the recalculation is performed on the anniversary of the date on which owner-occupier payments were included in the claimant's qualifying benefit.

2.630

Calculation in respect of alternative finance payments

12.—(1) The amount to be included in each loan payment for owner-occupier payments which are alternative finance payments is determined as follows.

2.631

Step 1

Determine the purchase price of the accommodation to which the alternative finance payments relate.

Step 2

Determine the identified amount which is the lower of—
(a) the amount resulting from step 1; and
(b) the capital limit specified in paragraph (2)(a) or (b).
If both amounts are the same, that is the identified amount.

Step 3

In respect of an SPC claimant, apply the following formula to achieve a weekly sum—

$$\frac{A \times SR}{52} - I$$

In respect of a UC claimant, apply the following formula to achieve a monthly sum—

$$\frac{A \times SR}{12} - I$$

In either case—

"A" is the identified amount in step 2,

"SR" is the standard rate that applies at the date of the calculation (see regulation 13), and

"I" is the amount of any income, in the case of an SPC claimant, or unearned income, in the case of a UC claimant, above the claimant's applicable amount.

The result is the amount to be included in each loan payment for owner-occupier payments which are alternative finance payments.

(2) The capital limit is—

(a) £200,000 in the case of an SPC claimant where the Modified Rules apply or a UC claimant;

(b) £100,000 in all other cases.

(3) For the purposes of paragraph (1), "purchase price" means the price paid by a party to the alternative finance arrangements other than the claimant in order to acquire the interest in the accommodation to which those arrangements relate less—

(a) the amount of any initial payment made by the claimant in connection with the acquisition of that interest; and

(b) the amount of any subsequent payments made by the claimant or any partner to another party to the alternative finance arrangements before—

(i) the relevant date; or

(ii) in the case of an existing claimant, the date on which the claimant's qualifying benefit first included an amount for owner-occupier payments,

which reduce the amount owed by the claimant under the alternative finance arrangements.

(4) Subject to paragraph (5), any variation in the amount for the time being owing in connection with alternative finance arrangements is not to be taken into account after the relevant date until such time as the Secretary of State recalculates the amount which shall occur—

(a) on the first anniversary of the relevant date; and

(b) in respect of any variation after the first anniversary, on the next anniversary which follows the date of the variation.

(5) In respect of an existing claimant, the Secretary of State shall recalculate the amount for the time being owing [¹ in connection with alternative finance arrangements] on the anniversary of the date on which the claimant's qualifying benefit first included an amount for owner-occupier payments.

AMENDMENT

1. Loans for Mortgage Interest and Social Fund Maternity Grant (Amendment) Regulations 2018 (SI 2018/307), reg.2(1) and (7) (April 6, 2018).

DEFINITIONS

"alternative finance payments"—reg.2(1).
"applicable amount"—*ibid.*
"claimant"—*ibid.*
"existing claimant"—*ibid.*
"income"—*ibid.*
"Modified Rules"—*ibid.*
"owner-occupier payments"—regs 2(1) and 3(2)(a).
"partner"—reg.2(1).
"qualifying benefit"—*ibid.*
"qualifying loan"—*ibid.*
"relevant date"—*ibid.*
"SPC claimant"—*ibid.*
"UC claimant"—*ibid.*
"unearned income"—*ibid.*

GENERAL NOTE

For the definition of "alternative finance payments" see Sch.1, para.5(3).   2.632
The calculation of loan payments made in respect of alternative finance payments is the same as that prescribed by reg.11 in respect of qualifying loans, except that:

- there is no modification where the alternative finance arrangements have been made in order to adapt the dwelling to meet the needs of a disabled person; and (more fundamentally)

- the Step 1 amount (*i.e.,* the capital element of the calculation) is the purchase price of the property (as set out in para.(3)), rather than the amount owing on a qualifying loan.

Standard rate to be applied under regulations 11 and 12

13.—(1) The standard rate is the average mortgage rate published by the   2.633
Bank of England which has effect on the 5th April 2018.

(2) The standard rate is to be varied each time that paragraph (3) applies.

(3) This paragraph applies when, on any reference day, the Bank of England publishes an average mortgage rate which differs by 0.5 percentage points or more from the standard rate that applies on that reference day (whether it applies by virtue of paragraph (1) or by virtue of a previous application of this paragraph).

(4) The average mortgage rate published on that reference day then becomes the new standard rate in accordance with paragraph (5).

(5) Any variation in the standard rate by virtue of paragraphs (2) to (4) shall come into effect at the end of the period of 6 weeks beginning with the day referred to in paragraph (3).

(6) At least 7 days before a variation of the standard rate comes into effect under paragraph (5), the Secretary of State must arrange for notice to be published on a publicly accessible website of—

(a) the new standard rate; and

(b) the day on which the new standard rate comes into effect under paragraph (5).

(7) For the purposes of this Regulation—

"average mortgage rate" means the effective interest rate (non-seasonally adjusted) of United Kingdom resident banks and building societies for loans to households secured on dwellings, published by the Bank of England in respect of the most recent period specified for that rate at the time of publication; and

"reference day" means any day falling on or after 6th April 2018.

DEFINITIONS

"dwelling"—reg.2(1).

GENERAL NOTE

2.634   The interest rate applied in Step 4 of the calculations under regs 11 and 12 is not the contractual rate due under the qualifying loan (or the rate inherent in the alternative finance arrangements) but, rather, the standard rate as determined in accordance with para.(1) and as subsequently varied under paras (2)-(6).

At the time of going to press, the standard rate is 2.61% per annum.

It is difficult to identify any publicly available website on which the notice required by para.(6) has been published.

Non-dependant deductions

2.635   **14.**—(1) In the case of a legacy benefit claimant or SPC claimant, a deduction from each loan payment shall be made in respect of any non-dependant in accordance with paragraph (2).

(2) The amount to be deducted is calculated as follows.

Step 1

Identify the amount which is the sum of the loan payment calculated under regulation 10 and the amount of housing costs (if any) paid to a claimant under—
  (a) paragraph 17 of Schedule 3 to the IS Regulations;
  (b) paragraph 16 of Schedule 2 to the JSA Regulations;
  (c) paragraph 18 of Schedule 6 to the ESA Regulations; or
  (d) paragraph 13 of Schedule 2 to the SPC Regulations.

Step 2

Identify the total amount of the non-dependant deductions applicable to the claimant under—
  (a) paragraph 18 of Schedule 3 to the IS Regulations;
  (b) paragraph 17 of Schedule 2 to the JSA Regulations;
  (c) paragraph 19 of Schedule 6 to the ESA Regulations; or
  (d) paragraph 14 of Schedule 2 to the SPC Regulations.

Step 3

Identify the proportion of the non-dependant deductions applicable to the loan payment and housing costs (if any) in Step 1 by applying the formula—

$$A \times (B \div C)$$

where—

"A" is the total amount of the non-dependant deductions identified in
    Step 2,
"B" is the amount of the loan payment calculated under regulation 10,
    and
"C" is the amount identified in Step 1.

The result is the amount of the non-dependant deduction to be made
from each loan payment in the case of a legacy benefit claimant or SPC
claimant.

DEFINITIONS

"claimant"—reg.2(1).
"ESA Regulations"—*ibid.*
"IS Regulations"—*ibid.*
"JSA Regulations"—*ibid.*
"legacy benefit claimant"—*ibid.*
"non-dependant"—*ibid.*
"SPC claimant"—*ibid.*
"SPC Regulations"—*ibid.*

GENERAL NOTE

For claimants of IB, IBJSA, IRESA and SPC, some housing costs are still available as part their benefit: see the commentary to Sch.3 to the Income Support Regulations in Vol.V. Reg.14 is designed to ensure that such claimants do not have a non-dependant deduction made twice, once as part of their benefits and once under these regulations. This is achieved by adjusting the non-dependant deduction made when calculating the amount of a loan payment in accordance with the formula set out in Step 3.   **2.636**

Non-dependant deductions are not applied to loan payments where the claimant is on universal credit.

[¹ **Insurance payment deduction**

14A.—(1) In the case of a legacy benefit claimant or UC claimant, where   **2.637**
the claimant or the claimant's partner is in receipt of a payment under a
policy of insurance taken out to insure against the risk of being unable to
maintain owner-occupier payments within the meaning of Schedule 1, a
deduction from the loan payment calculated under regulation 10 shall be
made equal to the amount received in respect of owner-occupier payments.

(2) Where the amount referred to in paragraph (1) is equal to or more
than the loan payment, the amount of the loan payment shall be zero.]

AMENDMENT

1. Loans for Mortgage Interest and Social Fund Maternity Grant (Amendment)
Regulations 2018 (SI 2018/307), reg.2(1) and (8) (April 6, 2018).

DEFINITIONS

"claimant"—reg.2(1).
"legacy benefit claimant"—*ibid.*
"loan payment"—*ibid.*
"owner-occupier payments"—*ibid.* and reg.3(2)(a) and Sch.1
"partner"—reg.2(1).
"UC claimant"—*ibid.*

GENERAL NOTE

2.638   This regulation is self-explanatory. No insurance payment deduction is made where the claimant's qualifying benefit is SPC.

Interest

2.639   **15.**—(1) The Secretary of State shall charge interest on the sum of the loan payments until the earlier of—

(a) the day on which the loan payments and accrued interest are repaid in full;

(b) the event referred to in regulation 16(1)(c) [¹;

(c) where the conditions in paragraph (1A) are met, the day on which the Secretary of State sends a completion statement to the claimant.]

[¹ (1A) The conditions are—

(a) the claimant requests a completion statement from the Secretary of State in order to repay all of the outstanding amount in accordance with regulation 16(8) and (9); and

(b) the outstanding amount is paid within 30 days beginning with the day on which the completion statement is sent by the Secretary of State to the claimant.

(1B) Where regulation 16(3) applies, the Secretary of State shall continue to charge interest on the outstanding amount until the day referred to in regulation 15(1).]

(2) Interest at the relevant rate shall accrue daily, with effect from the first day a loan payment is made to a qualifying lender or the claimant under regulation 17, and shall be added to the outstanding amount at the end of each month (or part month).

(3) The relevant rate is the interest rate for the relevant period.

(4) For the purposes of this regulation and [² regulations 16 and 16A], the outstanding amount is the sum of the loan payments and interest which has been charged under paragraph (1).

[¹ (4A) For the purposes of this regulation, a "completion statement" means a written statement setting out the outstanding amount owed by the claimant to the Secretary of State.]

(5) The interest rate referred to in paragraph (3) is the weighted average interest rate on conventional gilts specified in the most recent report published before the start of the relevant period by the Office for Budget Responsibility under section 4(3) of the Budget Responsibility and National Audit Act 2011.

(6) The relevant period is the period starting on—

(a) 1st January and ending on 30th June in any year; or

(b) 1st July and ending on 31st December in any year.

AMENDMENTS

1. Loans for Mortgage Interest and Social Fund Maternity Grant (Amendment) Regulations 2018 (SI 2018/307), reg.2(1) and (9) (April 6, 2018).

2. Loans for Mortgage Interest (Amendment) Regulations 2021 (SI 2021/131) reg.2(1) and (3) (March 15, 2021).

DEFINITIONS

"claimant"—reg.2(1).
"loan payments"—*ibid.*
"qualifying lender"—*ibid.*

GENERAL NOTE

In contrast with reg.13, this regulation is not about the rate of interest that is   2.640
applied to calculate the amount of loan payments. Rather, it is the rate that the
Secretary of State charges on the loan that she has made to the claimant (*i.e.*, by
making the loan payments) and which must be repaid in accordance with reg.16.

From January 1, 2022, the rate has been 0.8% (and is therefore less than the
standard rate). The derivation of that rate is complex. Section 4(3) of the Budget
Responsibility and National Audit Act 2011 requires the Office for Budget
Responsibility ("OBR") to prepare fiscal and economic forecasts "on at least two
occasions for each financial year". This is usually done to coincide with the Budget
and the Autumn Statement and the forecast, under the title, *Economic and Fiscal
Outlook*, is published on the OBR's website (http://obr.uk/publications/). The relevant figure is in a table in that document. The best way to discover it is to download
the document in PDF format and then search for "weighted average interest rate on
conventional gilts" which is the criterion specified in para.(5). That rate is reviewed,
twice yearly, with effect from January 1 and July 1: see para.(6).

Repayment

16.—(1) [² Subject to regulation 16A, the outstanding amount] shall   2.641
become immediately due and payable, together with any further interest
which accrues on that amount under regulation 15, where one of the following events occurs—

(a) the relevant accommodation is sold;
(b) legal or beneficial title in, or in Scotland, heritable or registered title
to, the relevant accommodation is transferred, assigned or otherwise
disposed of, unless paragraph (3) applies;
[¹ (c) in the case of—
   (i) a claimant who is the sole legal owner of the relevant accommodation or the legal owner of the accommodation with someone
other than a partner, the claimant's death;
   (ii) a claimant with a partner who is the sole legal owner of the relevant accommodation or the legal owner of the accommodation
with someone other than the claimant, the partner's death; or
   (iii) a claimant and partner who are both legal owners (whether or
not with anyone else) of the relevant accommodation, the death
of the last member of the couple.]

(2) Subject to paragraphs (4) to (7), repayment shall occur—
(a) in the event described in paragraph (1)(a) or (b), from the proceeds
of sale, transfer, assignment or disposition;
(b) in the event described in paragraph (1)(c), from the relevant person's
estate.

(3) This paragraph applies where legal or beneficial title is transferred
to—
(a) the claimant's partner, following the death of the claimant, where the
partner is in occupation of the relevant accommodation; or
[¹(aa) the claimant, following the death of the claimant's partner, where the
claimant is in occupation of the relevant accommodation; or]
(b) the claimant, from a former spouse or civil partner, under a court
order or an agreement for maintenance where the claimant is in
occupation of the relevant accommodation.

(4) Where, in England and Wales—
(a) the Secretary of State has a charge by way of legal mortgage over the
relevant accommodation; and

(b) there is insufficient equity available in the relevant accommodation to discharge the outstanding amount,

repayment shall be limited to the amount of available equity in the relevant accommodation after any prior ranking charges by way of legal mortgage have been repaid, and, in the event described in paragraph (1)(c), this shall be taken to be the amount of equity at the date of death of the relevant person.

(5) Where, in England and Wales—

(a) the Secretary of State has an equitable charge over one legal owner's equitable interest in the relevant accommodation, repayment shall be limited to the amount of that legal owner's equitable interest in the relevant accommodation and, in the event described in paragraph (1)(c), this shall be taken to be the value of that equitable interest at the date of death of the relevant person;

(b) the Secretary of State has an equitable charge over more than one legal owner's equitable interest in the relevant accommodation, repayment shall be limited to the sum of the equitable interests in the relevant accommodation of all legal owners within the benefit unit and, in the event described in paragraph (1)(c), this shall be taken to be the value of those equitable interests at the date of death of the relevant person.

(6) Where, in Scotland—

(a) the Secretary of State has a standard security over the whole or part of the relevant accommodation; and

(b) there is insufficient equity available in the whole or part of the relevant accommodation over which the standard security is held,

repayment shall be limited to the amount of available equity in the whole or part of the relevant accommodation over which the standard security is held after any prior ranking standard securities have been repaid, and, in the event described in paragraph (1)(c), this shall be taken to be the amount of equity at the date of death of the relevant person.

(7) In the event that the relevant accommodation is sold or legal or beneficial title in, or in Scotland, heritable or registered title to, the relevant accommodation is transferred, assigned or otherwise disposed of for less than market value, the disposal shall be treated as if it occurred at market value for the purposes of repayment.

(8) Subject to paragraph (9), a claimant shall be permitted to repay some or all of the outstanding amount before an event in paragraph (1) occurs if the amount of each repayment is equal to or more than £100.

(9) Where the outstanding amount is less than £100, a claimant shall be permitted to repay that sum in full in one repayment.

AMENDMENTS

1. Loans for Mortgage Interest and Social Fund Maternity Grant (Amendment) Regulations 2018 (SI 2018/307), reg.2(1) and (10) (April 6, 2018).

2. Loans for Mortgage Interest (Amendment) Regulations 2021 (SI 2021/131) reg.2(1) and (4) (March 15, 2021).

DEFINITIONS

"benefit unit"—reg.2(1).
"charge by way of legal mortgage"—*ibid.*
"claimant"—*ibid.*

"legal owner"—*ibid.*
"partner"—*ibid.*
"relevant accommodation"—*ibid.*
"standard security"—*ibid.*

GENERAL NOTE

The loan from the Secretary of State is repayable   **2.642**

- when the relevant accommodation is sold: see para.(1)(a);

- when the title to the relevant accommodation changes hands (para.1(b)) unless para.(3) applies;

- when the claimant dies unless

  — the claimant's partner is either the sole legal owner of the relevant accommodation (or the joint legal owner with someone other than the claimant), in which case the loan is repayable when the partner dies; or

  — the claimant and partner are both legal owners of the relevant accommodation, in which case the loan is repayable on the death of the surviving member of the couple.

In *R (Vincent and others) v Secretary of State for Work and Pensions* [2020] EWHC 1976 (Admin), the High Court (Andrews J) rejected submissions that para.16(1)(a) unlawfully discriminated against the claimants under art.14 ECHR taken together with A1P1 and/or art.8, as severely disabled people with a partner in receipt of Carer's Allowance and/or as dependent children of such persons. A challenge under the Public Sector Equality Duty was also dismissed.

Under para.(3) the loan is not repayable where the title is transferred (otherwise than by way of sale, in which case para.(1)(a) would apply) to the claimant or her/his partner on the death of the other member of the couple, where the person to whom title is transferred is in occupation of the relevant accommodation: see para.(3)(a) and (aa); or where the title is transferred to the claimant from a former spouse or civil partner either by court order or under a maintenance agreement and the claimant is occupying the relevant accommodation: see para.(3)(b).

The lack of any provision that deals with the reverse of the situation described in para.(3)(b) creates an apparent lacuna. What happens if the claimant deserts their spouse or civil partner and the accommodation is then transferred from the claimant to the civil partner? The answer seems to be that the loan, which is secured on the accommodation that has now been transferred to the former partner, becomes repayable under para.(1)(b). The practical answer may be that under para.(2)(a) repayment is to be made "from the proceeds of sale, transfer, assignment or disposition" and, depending upon the terms of the court order or maintenance agreement, there will often be no such proceeds.

Paragraphs (4)-(6) limit the amount repayable to the Secretary of State to the amount of the equity in the relevant accommodation after repayment of prior mortgages and charges.

Paragraph (7) prevents that rule from being abused by selling the relevant accommodation for less than its market value. In those circumstances the sale is treated as if it had been at market value for the purpose of repayment.

Paragraphs (8) and (9) allow the claimant to make voluntary repayments. Each repayment must be at least £100 unless the amount owing is less than £100 in which case the claimant may repay that amount in full in a single repayment.

[¹ Transferring the loan between properties

16A.—(1) Subject to paragraph (6), where the conditions in paragraphs (2) and (3) are met, regulation 16 (repayment) applies in relation to the new property referred to in paragraph (2) instead of in relation to the relevant accommodation ("Property 1").

(2) The first condition is that the claimant or the claimant's partner informs the Secretary of State that it is proposed to sell Property 1, and requests that the outstanding amount be transferred from Property 1 to a new property ("Property 2").

(3) The second condition is that prior to the completion of the sale of Property 1—

   (a) the conveyancer dealing with the sale of the property has provided a written undertaking to the Secretary of State to do the following—

      (i) to discharge the charge (in England and Wales), if any, or standard security (in Scotland), if any, in favour of the Secretary of State; and

      (ii) to transfer the outstanding amount to the conveyancer for the claimant or the claimant's partner, if not also acting on their behalf; and

   (b) the conveyancer for the claimant or the claimant's partner has provided a written undertaking to the Secretary of State to do the following—

      (i) to register a new charge (in England and Wales) or standard security (in Scotland) in favour of the Secretary of State for the outstanding amount in respect of Property 2; and

      (ii) if completion of the sale and completion of the purchase do not happen simultaneously to hold the outstanding amount to the order of the Secretary of State until completion of the purchase of Property 2.

(4) Where the Secretary of State meets the reasonable costs incurred by the conveyancer for the claimant or the claimant's partner for the purpose of transferring the loan from Property 1 to Property 2—

   (a) these costs may be added to the outstanding amount of the loan; and

   (b) any costs added to the outstanding amount are to be considered as a loan payment for the purpose of accruing interest under regulation 15.

(5) For the purposes of sub-paragraphs (a)(ii) and (b)(ii) of paragraph (3)—

   (a) in England and Wales, where the available equity in Property 1 as referred to in regulation 16(4), or, as the case may be, the amount of the equitable interest or interests, as referred to in regulation 16(5), is or are less than the outstanding amount, the reference in those sub-paragraphs to the outstanding amount is a reference to the available equity or to the amount of the equitable interest or interests, as the case may be; and

   (b) in Scotland, where the available equity in the whole or part of Property 1 over which the standard security is held, as referred to in regulation 16(6), is less than the outstanding amount, the reference in those sub-paragraphs to the outstanding amount is a reference to the available equity.

(6) If completion in respect of Property 2 does not take place within twelve weeks beginning with the date that completion of the sale of Property 1 occurs or by such later date as the Secretary of State may agree then paragraph (1) does not apply and the outstanding amount under regulation 16, together with any future interest which accrues on that amount under regulation 15, shall be immediately due and payable.

(7) For the purposes of this regulation references to a claimant includes a former claimant.

(8) Where, under paragraph (1), the provisions of regulation 16 apply in relation to Property 2, this regulation applies as if any reference to the relevant accommodation were a reference to Property 2 (with no limit to the number of times this regulation may be treated as applying in relation to a new property).]

AMENDMENT

1. Loans for Mortgage Interest (Amendment) Regulations 2021 (SI 2021/131) reg.2(1) and (5) (March 15, 2021).

DEFINITIONS

"claimant"—see reg.2(1).
"partner"—*ibid.*
"relevant accommodation"—*ibid.*
"standard security"—*ibid.*

GENERAL NOTE

Before March 15, 2021 the loan from the Secretary of State was immediately repayable in the circumstances set out in reg.16 with the effect that when the property subject to the Secretary of State's charge was sold, then, whatever the circumstances—even if, for example, the sale was part of a move to accommodation more suited to the needs of a disabled person—the proceeds of sale that might otherwise have been put towards the price of the new property were reduced by the amount that had to be repaid to the Secretary of State. **2.643**

From March 15, 2021, however, the introduction of reg.16A (and the linked amendment to reg.16) mean that, as long as the conditions in paras (2) and (3) are satisfied, the full equity (or the available equity (see para.(5)) in the existing property can be used towards the purchase of the new property. In those circumstances, the Secretary of State's charge over the existing property will be discharged and an equivalent charge registered against the new property on completion.

Those conditions are (a) that the claimant (or the claimant's partner) informs the Secretary of State that it is proposed to sell the existing property, and requests that the outstanding amount secured on that property be transferred to the new property (para.(2)); and (b) (in the normal case of a linked sale and purchase) that before completion of the sale of the existing property, the conveyancer dealing with that sale provides the Secretary of State with a written undertaking to discharge the charge on that property and to register a new charge against the new property (para.(3)). Para.(3) also makes provision for what happens if different conveyancers are acting on the sale and the purchase, or if the sale and purchase are not completed simultaneously. In the latter case the loan becomes immediately repayable if the sale and purchase are separated by more than 12 weeks (para.(6)).

Para.(4) provides for the reasonable legal costs of transferring the charge—but not *all* the legal costs of the sale and purchase—to be paid by the Secretary of State, and added to the amount of the loan, if the loan recipient so requests. Interest will be payable on any such costs on the same basis as on the original loan.

Para. (8) provides that there is no limit on the number of times that the security for the loan from the Secretary of State can be transferred to a new property.

Direct payments to qualifying lenders

2.644

17.—(1) Where the circumstances specified in paragraph (2) are met, the loan payments must be made by the Secretary of State direct to a claimant's lender.

(2) The circumstances referred to in paragraph (1) are that—

(a) money was lent to the claimant in respect of which owner-occupier payments in respect of the relevant accommodation are payable to a qualifying lender; and

(b) those owner-occupier payments are taken into account in calculating the amount of each loan payment under regulation 10.

(3) Where the circumstances in paragraph (2) are not met, the loan payments must be made to the claimant.

(4) Schedule 4 has effect in relation to payments made under paragraph (1).

DEFINITIONS

"claimant"—reg.2(1).
"loan payments"—*ibid.*
"owner-occupier payments"—regs 2(1) and 3(2)(a).
"qualifying lender"—*ibid.*
"relevant accommodation"—*ibid.*

GENERAL NOTE

2.645

In most cases, loan payments will be made to the lender rather than to the claimant. In fact, given the breadth of the circumstances specified in para.(2), loan payments will probably only ever be made to the claimant where the lender is not a "qualifying lender" as defined in reg.2(1) and s.19(7)-(9) WRWA 2016. Any financial institution or public authority is likely to come within that definition. All that remains seems to be private loans from one individual to another.

[[1] Consequential amendments

2.646

18.—(1) Subject to paragraph (2) and regulations 19, 19A and 20, the amendments in Schedule 5 have effect.

(2) The amendments made by Part 2 of Schedule 5 to the Social Security and Child Support (Decisions and Appeals) Regulations 1999 do not apply in relation to any decision or determination about an amount for owner-occupier payments under the substantive regulations as those regulations applied without the amendments made by Part 1 of Schedule 5.

(3) In this regulation, the "substantive regulations" means the ESA Regulations, IS Regulations, JSA Regulations, SPC Regulations and UC Regulations.]

AMENDMENT

1. Loans for Mortgage Interest and Social Fund Maternity Grant (Amendment) Regulations 2018 (SI 2018/307), reg.2(1) and (11) (April 6, 2018).

GENERAL NOTE

The consequential amendments made by Sch.5 have been taken in at the appropriate points in the text of the amended regulations. Those amendments are, however, subject to the transitional provisions made by regs 19, 19A and 20 below.

2.647

[¹ Transitional provision: loan offer made before 6th April 2018

19.—(1) Subject to regulation 20, in relation to an existing claimant in a case where the loan payments offer date occurs before 6th April 2018, the amendments made by Schedule 5 shall be treated as though they did not have effect until the earlier of the following days (where that day occurs after 6th April 2018) ("the transitional end day")—

2.648

(a) the day referred to in paragraph (2);

(b) the day after the day on which entitlement to a qualifying benefit ends.

(2) The day referred to is the later of—

(a) in the case of—

    (i) a legacy benefit claimant or SPC claimant, where 6th April 2018 is not the first day of the claimant's benefit week, the first day of the first benefit week that begins after 6th April 2018; or

    (ii) a UC claimant, where 6th April 2018 is not the first day of the claimant's assessment period, the first day of the first assessment period that begins after 6th April 2018;

(b) the relevant day in paragraph (3).

(3) The relevant day is the day after the day that is the earlier of—

(a) the day on which the Secretary of State receives notification from the claimant that the claimant does not wish to accept the offer of loan payments;

(b) the last day of the period of 4 weeks, beginning with the day after the day on which the Secretary of State has received both the loan agreement and the documents referred to in regulation 5(2), duly executed, where both the loan agreement and the documents are received within the period of 6 weeks beginning with the loan payments offer date; or

(c) the last day of the period of 6 weeks, beginning with the loan payments offer date, where the Secretary of State has not received both the loan agreement and the documents referred to in regulation 5(2), duly executed, within that period.

(4) Where in the case of—

(a) a legacy benefit claimant or SPC claimant, the relevant day referred to in paragraph (3) is not the first day of the claimant's benefit week, then the relevant day shall be the first day of the first benefit week that begins after the relevant day; or

(b) a UC claimant, the relevant day referred to in paragraph (3) is not the first day of the claimant's assessment period, then the relevant day shall be the first day of the first assessment period that begins after the relevant day.]

AMENDMENT

1. Loans for Mortgage Interest and Social Fund Maternity Grant (Amendment) Regulations 2018 (SI 2018/307), reg.2(1) and (12) (April 6, 2018).

DEFINITIONS

"assessment period"—reg.2(1) and reg.21 UC Regs 2013.
"benefit week"—reg.2(1).
"claimant"—*ibid.*
"entitlement"—reg.2(2)(a).
"existing claimant"—reg.2(1).
"legacy benefit claimant"—*ibid.*
"loan agreement"—*ibid.*
"loan payments"—*ibid.*
"loan payments offer date"—*ibid.*
"qualifying benefit"—*ibid.*
"SPC claimant"—*ibid.*
"transitional end day"—*ibid.* and para.(1).
"UC claimant"—reg.2(1).

GENERAL NOTE

2.649   Regs 19, 19A, 20 and 21 all establish transitional rules for "existing claimants" (*i.e.,* those entitled to a qualifying benefit including an amount for owner-occupier payments on April 5, 2018: see reg.2(1)). "Qualifying benefits" are IRESA, IS, IBJSA, SPC and universal credit. Reg.19 applies where the "loan payments offer date" (*i.e.,* the day on which the Secretary of State sent the loan agreement to the claimant under reg.3: see reg.2(1) (again)) was before April 6, 2018. In those circumstances:

- the consequential amendments made by Sch.5 do not come into effect until the "transitional end date": see also reg.8(1)(d); and

- section 11(1), (8), (9) and (11) of the Welfare Reform and Work Act 2016 (consequential amendments) are treated as though they are not in force in relation to the existing claimant: see reg.2(2) of SI 2018/438.

In the circumstances to which reg.19 applies, that date must be after April 6, 2018, and is either, the later of the days specified in para.(2), or (if earlier) the day after the day on which the claimant's entitlement to the qualifying benefit ends.

Ignoring, for the moment, the provisions about the "relevant day", the effect is that where April 6, 2018 is not the first day of the claimant's benefit week, or universal credit assessment period, the claimant continues to receive housing costs as part of his or her qualifying benefit until the first day of the benefit week or assessment period that begins after that date. This will mean that some universal credit claimants will get housing costs as part of their benefit for up to a month more than others purely because of the day of the month on which they first claimed universal credit.

For those claimants whose benefit weeks or assessment periods begin on April 6, 2018—and who are not affected by the rules in paras (3) and (4) about the relevant day—no transitional provision is required, and none has been made.

Paragraphs (3) and (4) deal with the position where the offer of loan payments was made before April 6, 2018 but is not accepted or rejected until after that date. In those circumstances, entitlement to payment of housing costs as part of a qualifying benefit ends and entitlement to a loan potentially begins on the "relevant day". Subject to the adjustment in para.(4), the rules are as follows:

- if the claimant does not execute and return the loan agreement and the other necessary documents so that the Secretary of State receives them by the last day of the period of six weeks beginning with the loan offer date, then the relevant day is the day after the last day of that six-week period;

- if the claimant does execute and return the loan agreement and the other necessary documents so that the Secretary of State receives them by the last day of that six-week period, the relevant day is the day after the last day of the period of four weeks beginning with the day on which the Secretary of State received those documents; and

- if the claimant notifies the Secretary of State that they do not wish to accept the offer of loan payments, the relevant day is the day after the Secretary of State receives that notification.

However, the need for the relevant day to be the first day of a benefit week or a universal credit assessment period means that the days identified by para.(3) are then adjusted by para.(4). If the relevant day is not the first day of a benefit week or assessment period, the first day of the following benefit week or assessment period becomes the new relevant day.

Reg.19 is subject to the rules about those who lack, or may lack, capacity in reg.20.

[¹ Transitional provision: loan offer made on or after 6th April 2018

19A.—(1) Subject to regulation 20 and paragraph (4), in relation to an existing claimant in a case where the loan payments offer date does not occur before 6th April 2018, the amendments made by Schedule 5 shall be treated as though they did not have effect until the earlier of the following days (where that day occurs after 6th April 2018) ("the transitional end day")—

2.650

(a) the relevant day in paragraph (2);
(b) the day after the day on which entitlement to a qualifying benefit ends;
(c) the day after the day on which the Secretary of State receives notification from the claimant that the claimant does not wish to receive loan payments.

(2) The relevant day is—
(a) 7th May 2018; or
(b) where the loan payments offer date occurs before 7th May 2018, the relevant day in regulation 19(3)(b) and (c) and (4).

(3) Where in the case of—
(a) a legacy benefit claimant or SPC claimant, the day referred to in paragraph (1)(c), or the relevant day as referred to in paragraph (2)(a), is not the first day of the claimant's benefit week, then that day or that relevant day is the first day of the first benefit week that begins after that day or that relevant day; or
(b) a UC claimant, the day referred to in paragraph (1)(c), or the relevant day as referred to in paragraph (2)(a), is not the first day of the claimant's assessment period, then that day or that relevant day is not the first day of the first assessment period that begins after that day or that relevant day.

(4) Paragraphs (1) to (3) do not apply in relation to an existing claimant where, as at the end of 5th April 2018—
(a) the Secretary of State, or a person authorised to exercise functions of the Secretary of State, has, before 19th March 2018 made a request to the claimant, whether orally or in writing, to provide information that is needed in order for the Secretary of State or that person to—
   (i) take steps to ascertain whether the claimant wishes to receive an offer of loan payments or not; or

      (ii) be able to send to the claimant the loan agreement and documents referred to in regulation 5(2); and

    (b) the claimant has not provided that information to the Secretary of State or that person.

(5) Subject to regulation 20, in the case of an existing claimant referred to in paragraph (4), where 6th April 2018 is not the first day of the claimant's benefit week, in the case of a legacy benefit or SPC claimant, or assessment period, in the case of a UC claimant, the amendments made by Schedule 5 shall be treated as though they did not have effect until the first day of the first benefit week or first assessment period that begins after that date ("the transitional end day").

AMENDMENT

1. Loans for Mortgage Interest and Social Fund Maternity Grant (Amendment) Regulations 2018 (SI 2018/307), reg.2(1) and (12) (April 6, 2018).

DEFINITIONS

"assessment period"—reg.2(1) and reg.21 UC Regs 2013.
"benefit week"—reg.2(1).
"claimant"—*ibid.*
"existing claimant"—*ibid.*
"legacy benefit claimant"—*ibid.*
"loan agreement"—*ibid.*
"loan payments"—*ibid.*
"loan payments offer date"—*ibid.*
"qualifying benefit"—*ibid.*
"SPC claimant"—*ibid.*
"transitional end day"—*ibid.* and paras (1) and (5).
"UC claimant"—reg.2(1).

GENERAL NOTE

2.651   For transitional provision generally, see the General Note to reg.19. Reg.19A governs the position where the "loan payments offer date" was *after* April 6, 2018.

Paragraph (1): In those circumstances, the transitional end day is the earliest of the day after the day on which entitlement to a qualifying benefit ends; the day after the day on which the Secretary of State is notified that the claimant does not wish to receive loan payments; and the relevant day as identified in para.(2). Where the transitional end day is determined in accordance with the first two of those alternatives, and is not the first day of the claimant's benefit week (for claimants of IS. IBJSA, IRESA and SPC) or assessment period (for claimants of universal credit), then the date is adjusted to the first day of the claimant's following benefit week or assessment period.

Paragraph (2): Where the loan payments offer date is on or after April 6, 2018 but before May 7, 2018, the relevant day is determined in accordance with reg.19(3) (b) and (c) and (4): see the commentary to those provisions in the General Note to reg.19.

The effect of para.(2)(a) is that where the loan payments offer date is made on or after May 7, 2018, no transitional provision applies. So, entitlement to housing costs will end on May 7, 2018 (or the last day of the benefit week or assessment period that includes May 7, 2018: see para.(3)) and eligibility for loan payments will begin on the date specified in reg.8.

668

Paragraphs (4) and (5): In some circumstances, the reason why the loan payments offer date is on or after April 6, 2018 is that the Secretary of State—or an authorised person on his behalf: see reg.22—has asked the claimant for information that is needed to establish that they are eligible for loan payments or to complete the loan agreement or other documents and the claimant has not replied. Where that request was made before March 19, 2018, paras (1)-(3) do not apply. The lack of the transitional protection established by those rules means entitlement to housing costs will end on April 6, 2018, subject to the usual adjustments to ensure that the changes come into force on the first day of a benefit period or assessment period: see para.(5).

Reg.19A is subject to the rules about those who lack, or may lack, capacity in reg.20.

[¹ Transitional provision: persons who lack capacity or may lack capacity identified before 6th April 2018

20.—(1) Paragraph (2) applies in relation to an existing claimant where, before 6th April 2018—   2.652

(a) the Secretary of State believes that the claimant is a person who lacks capacity to make some or all decisions about accepting an offer of loan payments; or

(b) on the basis of information received by the Secretary of State, the Secretary of State suspects that the claimant is a person who may lack such capacity,

(a "relevant claimant").

(2) In relation to a relevant claimant, the amendments made by Schedule 5 shall be treated as though they were not in force until the day that is the earlier of ("the transitional end day")—

(a) the relevant day in paragraph (3) or (8);

(b) the day after the day on which entitlement to a qualifying benefit ends.

(3) Subject to paragraph (8), the relevant day is the later of—

(a) 5th November 2018;

(b) where, in a case where paragraph (1)(b) applies, the Secretary of State believes before 5th November 2018 that the claimant is a person who lacks capacity as referred to in paragraph (1)(a), the day after the last day of the period of 6 weeks beginning with the day on which the Secretary of State forms that belief;

(c) where an application for a decision referred to in paragraph (7) is made before the later of 5th November 2018 and the relevant day under sub-paragraph (b), the day after the day specified in paragraph (4).

(4) The specified day is—

(a) the last day of the period of 6 weeks beginning with the day on which a person referred to in paragraph (7) ("relevant person") makes a decision referred to in paragraph (7); or

(b) the last day of the period of 6 weeks beginning with the day on which a relevant person receives notification that the application for such a decision is withdrawn.

(5) Where more than one application for a decision as referred to in paragraph (7) is made to a relevant person within the period referred to in paragraph (3)(c), then the periods in paragraph (4) do not start to run until the relevant person has made a decision with respect to the last of the applications to be dealt with, or the relevant person receives notification that all of the applications are withdrawn.

(6) Where an application for a decision as referred to in paragraph (7) is made to more than one relevant person within the period referred to in paragraph (3)(c), then, where the specified day under paragraph (4) would be different as between the applications made to the different relevant persons, the specified day is the later of the two days.

(7) The decisions referred to are—

(a) in England and Wales—

    (i) a decision by the Court of Protection whether or not to appoint a deputy under section 16(2) of the Mental Capacity Act 2005 with power to act on the claimant's behalf in respect of accepting an offer of loan payments;

    (ii) a decision by the Court of Protection whether or not, by making an order under section 16(2) of the Mental Capacity Act 2005, to decide on behalf of the claimant to accept an offer of loan payments; or

    (iii) a decision by the Public Guardian whether or not to register a lasting power of attorney under the Mental Capacity Act 2005 where the power includes power to act on the claimant's behalf with respect to accepting an offer of loan payments; or

(b) in Scotland—

    (i) a decision by the sheriff whether or not to make an order under section 58 of the Adults with Incapacity (Scotland) Act 2000 to appoint a guardian with power to act on the claimant's behalf with respect to accepting an offer of loan payments;

    (ii) a decision by the sheriff whether or not, by making an intervention order under section 53 of the Adults with Incapacity (Scotland) Act 2000, to decide on behalf of the claimant to accept an offer of loan payments; or

    (ii) a decision by the sheriff or the Court of Session whether or not to make an order under the Judicial Factors Act 1849 to appoint a judicial factor with power to act on the claimant's behalf with respect to accepting an offer of loan payments.

(8) Where, in a case where paragraph (1)(b) applies, the Secretary of State believes before 5th November 2018 that the claimant is not a person who lacks capacity as referred to in paragraph (1)(a), the relevant day is the day after the earlier of—

(a) the day specified in paragraph (9);

(b) the day on which the Secretary of State receives notification from the claimant that the claimant does not wish to receive loan payments.

(9) The specified day is—

(a) the last day of the period of 6 weeks beginning with the day on which the Secretary of State forms the belief in paragraph (8); or

(b) where the loan payments offer date occurs during the period in sub-paragraph (a), the day referred to in regulation 19(3)(b) and (c) and (4).

(10) Where in the case of—

(a) a legacy benefit claimant or SPC claimant, the relevant day referred to in paragraph (3) or (8) is not the first day of the claimant's benefit week, then the relevant day shall be the first day of the first benefit week that begins after the relevant day; or

(b) a UC claimant, the relevant day in paragraph (3) or (8) is not the first day of the claimant's assessment period, then the relevant day shall be the first day of the first assessment period that begins after the relevant day.]

AMENDMENT

1. Loans for Mortgage Interest and Social Fund Maternity Grant (Amendment) Regulations 2018 (SI 2018/307), reg.2(1) and (12) (April 6, 2018). The fact that sub-para.7(b) has two heads lettered "(ii)" is a requirement of the amending instrument and is not an editorial error.

DEFINITIONS

"assessment period"—reg.2(1) and reg.21 UC Regs 2013.
"benefit week"—reg.2(1).
"claimant"—*ibid.*
"entitlement"—reg.2(2)(a).
"existing claimant"—reg.2(1).
"legacy benefit claimant"—*ibid.*
"loan agreement"—*ibid.*
"loan payments"—*ibid.*
"loan payments offer date"—*ibid.*
"person who lacks capacity"—*ibid.*
"qualifying benefit"—*ibid.*
"SPC claimant"—*ibid.*
"transitional end day"—*ibid.* and para.(2).
"UC claimant"—*ibid.*

GENERAL NOTE

Regs 19 and 19A are subject to reg.20, which applies where the Secretary of State believes the claimant lacks capacity to make some or all decisions about accepting an offer of loan payments or, on the basis of information he has received, suspects that to be the case.

"Person who lacks capacity" is defined by reg.2(1) by reference to (in England and Wales) s.2 of the Mental Health Act 2005 or (in Scotland) as meaning a person who is incapable under s.1(2) of the Adults with Incapacity (Scotland) Act 2000. Under the former provision "a person lacks capacity in relation to a matter if at the material time he is unable to make a decision for himself in relation to the matter because of an impairment of, or a disturbance in the functioning of, the mind or brain". Under the latter, an "adult" is a person who aged 16 or more and "incapable" means incapable of acting, making decisions, communicating decisions, understanding decisions, or retaining the memory of decisions, by reason of mental disorder or of inability to communicate because of physical disability but not where the lack or deficiency in a faculty of communication can be made good by human or mechanical aid.

The capacity of the claimant is a matter of greater concern to the Secretary of State where what the claimant is being offered is a loan rather than a benefit payment. If the claimant lacks capacity to enter into the loan agreement or to execute the Secretary of State's charge or security over the property, the Secretary of State would be at risk that the agreement, and the charge or security, might be invalid.

The transitional provisions are complex but, in summary, have the effect that the new law does not come into force until any question about the claimant's capacity has been resolved.

2.653

Transition from legacy benefit to universal credit

2.654

21.—(1) Paragraph (3) applies where—

(a) an award of universal credit is made to a claimant who—

    (i) was entitled to [¹, or was treated as entitled to,] a legacy benefit (a "relevant award") at any time during the period of one month ending with the day on which the claim for universal credit was made or treated as made (or would have been so entitled were it not for termination of that award by virtue of an order made under section 150(3) of the Welfare Reform Act 2012 or the effect of the Transitional Provisions Regulations); or

    (ii) was at any time during the period of one month ending with the day on which the claim for universal credit was made or treated as made, the partner of a person ("P") who was at that time entitled to [¹, or was treated as entitled to,] a relevant award, where the award of universal credit is not a joint award to the claimant and P;

(b) on the relevant date—

    (i) the relevant award included an amount in respect of housing costs under—

      (aa) paragraphs 14 to 16 of Schedule 2 to the JSA Regulations;

      (bb) paragraphs 16 to 18 of Schedule 6 to the ESA Regulations; or

      (cc) paragraphs 15 to 17 of Schedule 3 to the IS Regulations; or

    (ii) the claimant was entitled to loan payments under these Regulations; and

(c) the amendments made by Schedule 5 apply in relation to the award of universal credit.

(2) In this regulation, the "relevant date" means—

(a) where paragraph (1)(a)(i) applies and the claimant was not entitled to [¹, or was treated as entitled to,] the relevant award on the date on which the claim for universal credit was made or treated as made, the date on which the relevant award terminated;

(b) where paragraph (1)(a)(i) applies, the claimant is not a new claimant partner and he or she was entitled to [¹, or was treated as entitled to,] the relevant award on the date on which the claim for universal credit was made, that date;

(c) where paragraph (1)(a)(i) applies, the claimant is a new claimant partner and he or she was entitled to [¹, or was treated as entitled to,] the relevant award on the date on which the claim for universal credit was treated as made, that date;

(d) where paragraph (1)(a)(ii) applies, the date on which the claimant ceased to be the partner of P or, if earlier, the date on which the relevant award terminated.

(3) Where this paragraph applies, regulation 8(1)(b) does not apply.

(4) Paragraph (5) applies where paragraph (1)(a) applies and the amendments made by Schedule 5 apply in relation to the award of universal credit, but—

(a) the relevant award did not include an amount in respect of housing costs because the claimant's entitlement (or, as the case may be, P's entitlement) was nil by virtue of—

    (i) paragraph 7(1)(b) of Schedule 2 to the JSA Regulations;

    (ii) paragraph 9(1)(b) of Schedule 6 to the ESA Regulations; or

    (iii) paragraph 8(1)(b) of Schedule 3 to the IS Regulations; or

(b) the amendments made by Schedule 5 applied in relation to the relevant award but the claimant was not entitled to loan payments by virtue of regulation 8(1)(b).

(5) Where this paragraph applies—

(a) the definition of "qualifying period" in regulation 2(1) does not apply; and

(b) "qualifying period" means the period of 273 days starting with the first day on which the claimant (or, as the case may be, P) was entitled to the relevant award, taking into account any period which was treated as a period of continuing entitlement under—

    (i) paragraph 13 of Schedule 2 to the JSA Regulations;

    (ii) paragraph 15 of Schedule 6 to the ESA Regulations; or

    (iii) paragraph 14 of Schedule 3 to the IS Regulations,

provided that, throughout that part of the qualifying period after the award of universal credit is made, receipt of universal credit is continuous and the claimant otherwise qualifies for loan payments under these Regulations.

(6) Paragraph (7) applies where—

(a) a claimant has an award of universal credit which becomes subject to the amendments made by Schedule 5; and

(b) regulation 29 of the Transitional Provisions Regulations applied in relation to the award.

(7) Where this paragraph applies—

(a) where paragraph (3) of regulation 29 of the Transitional Provisions Regulations applied in relation to the award, regulation 8(1)(b) does not apply; and

(b) where paragraph (5) of regulation 29 of the Transitional Provisions Regulations applied in relation to the award, paragraph (5) of this regulation applies in relation to the award.

AMENDMENT

1. Loans for Mortgage Interest and Social Fund Maternity Grant (Amendment) Regulations 2018 (SI 2018/307), reg.2(1) and (13) (April 6, 2018).

DEFINITIONS

"claimant"—reg.2(1).

"entitlement"—reg.2(2)(a).

"ESA Regulations"—reg.2(1).

"IS Regulations"—*ibid.*

"JSA Regulations"—*ibid.*

"legacy benefit"—*ibid.*

"loan payments"—*ibid.*

"new claimant partner"—*ibid.*

"partner"—*ibid.*

"qualifying period"—reg.2(1) as modified by para.(5).

"relevant date"—para.(2).

"Transitional Provisions Regulations"—reg.2(1).

GENERAL NOTE

This regulation makes transitional provision where a claimant transfers to universal credit from IS, IBJSA or IRESA.

2.655

Delegation

2.656   **22.** A function of the Secretary of State under these Regulations may be exercised by a person authorised for that purpose by the Secretary of State.

GENERAL NOTE

2.657   This regulation is made under s.19(5) of the WRWA 2016 which provides that the regulations "may provide for the Secretary of State to make arrangements with another person for the exercise of functions under the regulations".

Regulation 3(2)(a)

SCHEDULE 1

MEANING OF OWNER-OCCUPIER PAYMENTS

PART 1

LEGACY BENEFIT CLAIMANTS AND SPC CLAIMANTS

Application of Part 1
2.658   1. This Part applies to legacy benefit claimants and SPC claimants.

Payments of interest on qualifying loans and alternative finance payments
2.659   2.—(1) "Owner-occupier payments" means—
    (a) payments of interest on a loan which qualifies under sub-paragraph (2) or (4); and
    (b) in respect of an SPC claimant only, alternative finance payments within the meaning of paragraph 5(3).
(2) A loan qualifies under this sub-paragraph where the loan was taken out to defray monies applied for any of the following purposes—
    (a) acquiring an interest in the relevant accommodation; or
    (b) paying off another loan which would have qualified under paragraph (a) had it not been paid off.
(3) For the purposes of sub-paragraph (2), references to a loan also include a reference to money borrowed under a hire purchase agreement, as defined in section 189 of the Consumer Credit Act 1974, for any purpose specified in paragraph (a) or (b) of sub-paragraph (2).
(4) A loan qualifies under this sub-paragraph if it was taken out, with or without security, for the purpose of—
    (a) carrying out repairs and improvements to the relevant accommodation;
    (b) paying any service charge imposed to meet the cost of repairs and improvements to the relevant accommodation;
    (c) paying off another loan that would have qualified under paragraphs (a) and (b) had it not been paid off,
as long as the loan is used for that purpose within 6 months beginning with the date of receipt or as soon as reasonably practicable.
(5) In sub-paragraph (4), "repairs and improvements" means any of the following measures undertaken with a view to maintaining the fitness of the relevant accommodation, or any part of the building containing the relevant accommodation, for human habitation—
    (a) provision of a fixed bath, shower, wash basin, sink or lavatory, and necessary associated plumbing, including the provision of hot water not connected to a central heating system;
    (b) repairs to existing heating systems;
    (c) damp proof measures;
    (d) provision of ventilation and natural lighting;
    (e) provision of drainage facilities;
    (f) provision of facilities for preparing and cooking food;
    (g) provision of insulation;
    (h) provision of electric lighting and sockets;

    (i) provision of storage facilities for fuel or refuse;

    (j) repairs of unsafe structural defects;

    (k) adapting the accommodation for the special needs of a disabled person; or

    (l) provision of separate sleeping accommodation for persons of different sexes aged 10 or over but under the age of 20 who live with the claimant and for whom the claimant or the claimant's partner is responsible.

(6) Where a loan is applied only in part for the purposes specified in sub-paragraph (2) or (4), only that portion of the loan which is applied for that purpose shall qualify.

Loans incurred during relevant period

3.—(1) Subject to sub-paragraph (5), loans which, apart from this paragraph, qualify under paragraph 2(2) or (4) shall not so qualify where the loan was incurred during the relevant period.

    2.660

(2) The "relevant period" for the purposes of this paragraph is any period during which the person to whom the loan was made—

    (a) is entitled to, or is treated as entitled to, a legacy benefit or state pension credit; or

    (b) is living as a member of a family one of whom is entitled to, or is treated as entitled to, a legacy benefit or state pension credit,

together with any period falling between two such periods of entitlement separated by not more than 26 weeks.

(3) For the purposes of sub-paragraph (2), a person shall be treated as entitled to either a legacy benefit or state pension credit during any period when the person, the person's partner, or, where that person is a member of a joint-claim couple, the other member of that couple was not so entitled because—

    (a) that person, the person's partner or, where that person is a member of a joint-claim couple, the other member of that couple, was participating in an employment programme specified in regulation 75(1)(a) of the JSA Regulations; and

    (b) in consequence of such participation that person, the person's partner, or, where that person is a member of a joint-claim couple, the other member of that couple, was a person engaged in remunerative work and had income equal to or in excess of the applicable amount.

(4) Where a loan which qualifies under paragraph 2(2) was incurred during the relevant period—

    (a) for paying off an earlier loan, and that earlier loan qualified under paragraph 2(2) and was incurred during the relevant period; or

    (b) to finance the purchase of a property where an earlier loan, which qualified under paragraph 2(2) or (4) and was incurred during the relevant period in respect of another property, is paid off (in whole or in part) with monies received from the sale of that property,

then the amount of the loan to which sub-paragraph (1) applies is the amount (if any) by which the new loan exceeds the earlier loan.

(5) Loans taken out during the relevant period shall qualify as loans under paragraph 2(2) or (4), where a claimant satisfies any of the conditions specified in sub-paragraphs (6), (8) and (9), but—

    (a) where the claimant satisfies the condition in sub-paragraph (6), [¹ the amount of each loan payment calculated under regulation 10] shall be subject to the additional limitation imposed by sub-paragraph (7); and

    (b) where the claimant satisfies the conditions in more than one of these sub-paragraphs, only one sub-paragraph shall apply in the claimant's case, which shall be the one most favourable to the claimant.

(6) The first condition is that—

    (a) during the relevant period, the claimant or a member of the claimant's family acquires an interest ("the relevant interest") in the relevant accommodation; and

    (b) in the week preceding the week in which the relevant interest was acquired, the claimant or a member of the claimant's family was entitled to housing benefit.

(7) Where the condition in sub-paragraph (6) is satisfied, the amount of the loans which qualify shall initially not exceed the aggregate of—

    (a) the housing benefit entitlement referred to in sub-paragraph (6)(b); and

    (b) any amount included in the applicable amount of the claimant or a member of the claimant's family [¹ relating to housing costs] in that week,

and shall be increased subsequently only to the extent that it is necessary to take account of any increase in the standard rate under regulation 13 arising after the date of acquisition.

(8) The second condition is that the loan was taken out, or an existing loan increased, to acquire alternative accommodation more suited to the needs of a disabled person than the relevant accommodation which was occupied before the acquisition by the claimant.

(9) The third condition is that—

(a) the loan commitment increased in consequence of the disposal of the relevant accommodation and the acquisition of alternative accommodation; and

(b) the change of accommodation was made solely by reason of the need to provide separate sleeping accommodation for persons of different sexes aged 10 or over but under the age of 20 who live with the claimant and for whom the claimant or the claimant's partner is responsible.

PART 2

UC CLAIMANTS

Application of Part 2
2.661   4. This Part applies to UC claimants.

Payments of interest on loans and alternative finance payments
2.662   5.—(1) "Owner-occupier payments" means—

(a) payments of interest on a loan which qualifies under sub-paragraph (2);

(b) alternative finance payments within the meaning of sub-paragraph (3).

(2) A loan qualifies under this sub-paragraph if it is secured on the relevant accommodation.

(3) "Alternative finance payments" means payments that are made under alternative finance arrangements which were entered into to enable a person to acquire an interest in the relevant accommodation.

(4) "Alternative finance arrangements" has the meaning given in Part 10A of the Income Tax Act 2007.

AMENDMENT

1. Loans for Mortgage Interest and Social Fund Maternity Grant (Amendment) Regulations 2018 (SI 2018/307), reg.2(1) and (14) (April 6, 2018).

DEFINITIONS

"alternative finance payments"—reg.2(1) and para. 5(3).
"alternative finance arrangements"—para.5(4).
"applicable amount"—reg.2(1).
"couple"—*ibid.*
"disabled person"—*ibid.*
"entitlement"—reg.2(2)(a).
"family"—reg.2(2)(b).
"income"—reg.2(1).
"joint-claim couple"—*ibid.*
"JSA Regulations"—*ibid.*
"legacy benefit"—*ibid.*
"legacy benefit claimant"—*ibid.*
"owner-occupier payments"—regs 2(1) and 3(2)(a) and paras 2(1) and 5(1).
"partner"—reg.2(1).
"qualifying loan"—*ibid.*
"relevant accommodation"—*ibid.*
"relevant period"—para.3(2).
"repairs and improvements"—para.2(5).
"remunerative work"—reg.2(2)(e).
"SPC claimant"—reg.2(1).
"UC claimant"—*ibid.*

GENERAL NOTE

2.663

The phrase, "owner-occupier payments" is defined by reg.2(1) as having "the meaning given in regulation 3(2)(a)" which, in turn, gives effect to this Schedule.

The rules differ according to whether the claimant is on a "legacy benefit" or SPC, on the one hand, or on universal credit, on the other.

Paragraph 2: For the former group of claimants, owner-occupier payments are interest payments on:

- a loan to acquire an interest in the accommodation occupied, or treated as occupied as the claimant's home (see the definition of "relevant accommodation" in reg.2(1)) (or a loan to refinance such a loan): see para.2(2); or

- a loan to carry out repairs and improvements to the claimant's home, or to pay a service charge to meet the costs of such repairs or improvements (or a loan to refinance such a loan): see para.2(4).

For what counts as a repair or an improvement (para.2(5)), see the commentary to para.16 of Sch.3 to the IS Regulations in Vol.V.

Where a loan is only partly used to acquire an interest in the claimant's home or to carry out repairs and improvements, only that part qualifies for the purpose of para.2(1)(a) with the effect that a loan payment is only available to meet the interest on that part of the loan: see para.2(6).

For SPC claimants only, a payment in respect of "alternative finance arrangements" (see below) is also an owner occupier payment.

Paragraph 3 provides that, subject to the exceptions in sub-para.(5) loans that would otherwise qualify, do not qualify if they are taken out during the "relevant period" as defined in sub-para.(2). If a claimant refinances during the relevant period, then the amount that does not qualify is the amount by which the new loan exceeds the earlier loan: see sub-para.(4).

Paragraph 5: For UC claimants, the loan qualifies if it is secured on the relevant accommodation, irrespective of the purpose for which it was taken out: see sub-para.(1)(a). In addition, a payment in respect of "alternative finance arrangements" is also an owner occupier payment: see sub-para.(1)(b).

Alternative finance payments are defined by sub-para.(3) as payments that are made under "alternative finance arrangements" which were entered into to enable a person to acquire an interest in the relevant accommodation. Under sub-para.(4), "alternative finance arrangements" are defined by reference to Part 10A of the Income Tax Act 2007 and therefore "means ...(a) purchase and resale arrangements, (b) diminishing shared ownership arrangements, (c) deposit arrangements, (d) profit share agency arrangements, and (e) investment bond arrangements" (see section 564A(2) of that Act). All those types of arrangement are further defined by ss 564C–564G, and represent different types of what are known colloquially as an Islamic mortgage in which help from a financial institution to buy real property is structured in ways that do not involve the charging or payment of interest.

SCHEDULE 2

CIRCUMSTANCES IN WHICH A CLAIMANT IS, OR IS TO BE TREATED AS, LIABLE TO MAKE OWNER-OCCUPIER PAYMENTS

PART 1

LEGACY BENEFIT CLAIMANTS AND SPC CLAIMANTS

Application of Part 1

2.664
1. This Part applies to legacy benefit claimants and SPC claimants.

Liable or treated as liable to make payments

2.665
2.—(1) A claimant is liable to make owner-occupier payments where—

(a) in the case of a single claimant, the claimant or the claimant's partner (if any), or, in the case of joint claimants, either member of the couple, has a liability to make the payments;

(2) A claimant is to be treated as liable to make owner-occupier payments where—

(a) all of the following conditions are met—

(i) the person who is liable to make the payments is not doing so;

(ii) the claimant has to make the payments in order to continue occupation of the relevant accommodation; and

(iii) it is reasonable in all the circumstances to treat the claimant as liable to make the payments; or

(b) all of the following conditions are met—

(i) the claimant in practice shares the responsibility for the owner-occupier payments with other members of the household, none of whom are close relatives of, in the case of a single claimant, the claimant or the claimant's partner (if any), or, in the case of joint claimants, either member of the couple;

(ii) one or more of those members is liable to meet those payments; and

(iii) it is reasonable in all the circumstances to treat that member as sharing responsibility.

(3) Where any one or more, but not all, members of the claimant's family are affected by a trade dispute, the owner-occupier payments shall be treated as wholly the responsibility of those members of the family not so affected.

(4) For the purposes of sub-paragraph (2), "trade dispute" has the meaning given in section 244 of the Trade Union and Labour Relations (Consolidation) Act 1992.

Treated as not liable to make payments

2.666
3. A claimant is to be treated as not liable to make owner-occupier payments where the liability to make the payments is owed to a person who is a member of the claimant's household.

PART 2

UC CLAIMANTS

Application of Part 2

2.667
4. This Part applies to UC claimants.

Liable or treated as liable to make payments

2.668
5.—(1) A claimant is liable to make owner-occupier payments where—

(a) in the case of a single claimant, the claimant or the claimant's partner (if any), or, in the case of joint claimants, either member of the couple, has a liability to make the payments;

(2) A claimant is to be treated as liable to make owner-occupier payments where—

(a) the person who is liable to make the payments is a child or qualifying young person for whom the claimant is responsible;

(b) all of the following conditions are met—

(i) the person who is liable to make the payments is not doing so;

(ii) the claimant has to make the payments in order to continue occupation of the relevant accommodation;

    (iii) the claimant's circumstances are such that it would be unreasonable to expect them to make other arrangements; and

    (iv) it is otherwise reasonable in all the circumstances to treat the claimant as liable to make the payments; or

(c) the claimant—

    (i) has a liability to make the payments which is waived by the person ("P") to whom the liability is owed; and

    (ii) the waiver of that liability is by way of reasonable compensation for reasonable repair or re-decoration works carried out by the claimant to the relevant accommodation which P would otherwise have carried out or been required to carry out.

(3) [¹ Sub-paragraph (1)] does not apply to a person in a polygamous marriage who is a single claimant by virtue of regulation 3(4) of the UC Regulations.

Treated as not liable to make payments

6. A claimant is to be treated as not liable to make owner-occupier payments—   **2.669**

(a) where the liability to make the payments is owed to a person who is a member of the claimant's household;

(b) in respect of any amount which represents an increase in the sum that would otherwise be payable and is the result of—

    (i) outstanding arrears of any payment or charge in respect of the relevant accommodation;

    (ii) outstanding arrears of any payment or charge in respect of other accommodation previously occupied by the claimant; or

    (iii) any other unpaid liability to make a payment or charge; or

(c) where the Secretary of State is satisfied that the liability to make the owner-occupier payments was contrived in order to secure the offer of loan payments or increase the amount of each loan payment.

AMENDMENT

1. Loans for Mortgage Interest and Social Fund Maternity Grant (Amendment) Regulations 2018 (SI 2018/307), reg.2(1) and (15) (April 6, 2018).

DEFINITIONS

"child"—reg.2(1).
"couple"—*ibid.*
"family"—reg.2(2)(b).
"joint claimants"—reg.2(1).
"legacy benefit claimant"—*ibid.*
"loan payments"—*ibid.*
"owner-occupier payments"—regs 2(1) and 3(2)(a).
"member of a household"—reg.2(2)(b).
"partner"—reg.2(1).
"polygamous marriage"—*ibid.*
"qualifying young person"—*ibid.*
"relevant accommodation"—*ibid.*
"single claimant"—*ibid.*
"SPC claimant"—*ibid.*
"trade dispute"—para.2(4).
"UC claimant"—*ibid.*
"UC Regulations"—*ibid.*

GENERAL NOTE

See the commentary to Sch.2 to the UC Regulations, which is to similar effect, except that   **2.670**
the grounds on which a claimant is treated as not liable to make owner-occupier payments are more restricted under this Schedule.

The fact that sub-para.2(1) has a single head (a) with no head (b) or (c) etc. is not an editorial error.

SCHEDULE 3

CIRCUMSTANCES IN WHICH A CLAIMANT IS, OR IS TO BE, TREATED AS OCCUPYING
ACCOMMODATION

PART 1

GENERAL

Interpretation

2.671   1.—(1) In this Schedule—

"Abbeyfield Home" means an establishment run by the Abbeyfield Society including all bodies corporate or incorporate which are affiliated to that Society;

"care home"—

(a) in England and Wales, has the meaning given in section 3 of the Care Standards Act 2000;

(b) in Scotland, means a care home service within the meaning of paragraph 2 of Schedule 12 to the Public Services Reform (Scotland) Act 2010,

and in either case includes an independent hospital;

"croft" means a croft within the meaning of section 3(1) of the Crofters (Scotland) Act 1993;

"full-time student" has the meaning given—

(a) in the case of income support, in regulation 61(1) of the IS Regulations;

(b) in the case of jobseeker's allowance, in regulation 1(3) of the JSA Regulations;

(c) in the case of employment and support allowance, in regulation 131 of the ESA Regulations;

(d) in the case of state pension credit, in regulation 1(2) of the SPC Regulations;

"independent hospital"—

(a) in England, means a hospital as defined in section 275 of the National Health Service Act 2006 that is not a health service hospital as defined by that section;

(b) in Wales, has the meaning given in section 2 of the Care Standards Act 2000;

(c) in Scotland means an independent healthcare service as defined in section 10F(1)(a) and (b) of the National Health Service (Scotland) Act 1978;

"medically approved" means certified by a medical practitioner;

"patient" means a person who is undergoing medical or other treatment as an inpatient in a hospital or similar institution;

"period of study" has the meaning given—

(a) in the case of income support and state pension credit, in regulation 2(1) of the IS Regulations;

(b) in the case of jobseeker's allowance, in regulation 1(3) of the JSA Regulations;

(c) in the case of employment and support allowance, in regulation 2 of the ESA Regulations;

"residential accommodation" means accommodation which is a care home, Abbeyfield Home or independent hospital;

"training course" means a course of training or instruction provided wholly or partly by or on behalf of or in pursuance of arrangements made with, or approved by or on behalf of, Skills Development Scotland, Scottish Enterprise, Highlands and Islands Enterprise, a government department or the Secretary of State.

(2) In this Schedule, a reference to a claimant being liable to make owner-occupier payments is to be read as a reference to a person being treated as liable to make owner-occupier payments under Schedule 2.

PART 2

Legacy benefit claimants and SPC claimants

Application of Part 2

2.672   2. This Part applies to legacy benefit claimants and SPC claimants.

Occupying accommodation: general rule

2.673   3.—(1) Subject to the following paragraphs of this Part, the accommodation which the claimant occupies as the claimant's home or, if the claimant is a member of a family, the claimant and the claimant's family occupy as their home, is the accommodation which is normally occupied as the home.

(2) In determining whether accommodation is the accommodation normally occupied as the home for the purposes of sub-paragraph (1), regard shall be had to any other dwelling occupied by the claimant or, if the claimant is a member of a family, by the claimant and the claimant's family, whether or not that other dwelling is in Great Britain.

Full-time study

4.—(1) Subject to sub-paragraph (2), where a claimant is a full-time student or on a training course and is liable to make owner-occupier payments in respect of either (but not both)—

  (a) the accommodation which the claimant occupies for the purpose of attending the course of study or training course; or

  (b) the accommodation which the claimant occupies when not attending the course of study or training course,

the claimant shall be treated as occupying as the claimant's home the accommodation in respect of which the claimant is liable to make the owner-occupier payments.

(2) A claimant who is a full-time student shall not be treated as occupying accommodation as the claimant's home for any week of absence from it outside the period of study, other than an absence occasioned by the need to enter hospital for treatment.

2.674

Living in other accommodation during essential repairs

5. Where the claimant—

  (a) has been required to move into temporary accommodation by reason of essential repairs being carried out to the accommodation which the claimant occupies as the claimant's home ("the home accommodation"); and

  (b) is liable to make owner-occupier payments in respect of either (but not both) the home accommodation or the temporary accommodation,

the claimant shall be treated as occupying as the claimant's home the accommodation in respect of which the claimant is liable to make those payments.

2.675

Living in other accommodation due to fear of violence, where a claimant's partner is a full-time student or where moving into new accommodation

6. Where a claimant is liable to make owner-occupier payments in respect of two dwellings, the claimant shall be treated as occupying both dwellings as the claimant's home—

  (a) where—

    (i) the claimant has left and remains absent from the accommodation which the claimant occupies as the claimant's home ("the home accommodation") through fear of violence in the home or of violence by a close relative or former partner; and

    (ii) it is reasonable that owner-occupier payments should be met in respect of both the claimant's home accommodation and the claimant's present accommodation which the claimant occupies as the home;

  (b) in the case of a couple or a member of a polygamous marriage, where—

    (i) one partner is a full-time student or is on a training course and it is unavoidable that the members of the couple or polygamous marriage should occupy two separate dwellings; and

    (ii) it is reasonable that owner-occupier payments should be met in respect of both dwellings; or

  (c) where—

    (i) the claimant has moved into new accommodation occupied as the claimant's home, except where paragraph 5 applies, for a period not exceeding four benefit weeks from the first day of the benefit week in which the move occurs; and

    (ii) the claimant's liability to make owner-occupier payments in respect of both the new accommodation and the accommodation from which the move was made is unavoidable.

2.676

Moving in delayed for certain reasons

7.—(1) Where—

  (a) a claimant was delayed in moving into accommodation ("the new accommodation") and was liable to make owner-occupier payments in respect of that accommodation before moving in; and

  (b) the delay was reasonable and one of the conditions in sub-paragraphs (2) to (4) applies,

the claimant shall be treated as occupying the new accommodation as the claimant's home for the period of delay, not exceeding four weeks immediately prior to the date on which the claimant moved into the new accommodation.

2.677

(2) The first condition is that the delay occurred in order to adapt the accommodation to meet the needs of the claimant or a member of the claimant's family who is a disabled person.

(3) The second condition is that—

  (a) the move was delayed pending local welfare provision to meet a need arising out of the move or in connection with setting up the claimant's home in the new accommodation; and

  (b) in the case of a legacy benefit claimant only—

    (i) a member of the claimant's family is aged 5 or under;

    (ii) the claimant's applicable amount includes a pensioner premium or disability premium under Schedule 2 to the IS Regulations, Schedule 1 to the JSA Regulations or Schedule 4 to the ESA Regulations; or

    (iii) a child tax credit is paid for a member of the claimant's family who is disabled or severely disabled for the purposes of section 9(6) of the Tax Credits Act 2002;

(4) The third condition is that the claimant became liable to make owner-occupier payments in respect of the accommodation while the claimant was a patient or was in a residential home.

Temporary absence to try new accommodation of up to 13 weeks

2.678   8.—(1) This sub-paragraph applies to a claimant who enters residential accommodation—

  (a) for the purpose of ascertaining whether the accommodation suits the claimant's needs; and

  (b) with the intention of returning to the accommodation which the claimant occupies as the claimant's home ("the home accommodation") in the event that the residential accommodation proves not to suit the claimant's needs,

and while in the residential accommodation, the home accommodation is not let or sub-let to another person.

(2) A claimant to whom sub-paragraph (1) applies shall be treated as occupying the home accommodation during the period of absence, not exceeding 13 weeks in which the claimant is resident in the residential accommodation, but only where the total absence from the home accommodation does not exceed 52 consecutive weeks.

Temporary absence of up to 13 weeks

2.679   9. A claimant, except where paragraph 10 applies, shall be treated as occupying accommodation as the claimant's home throughout any period of absence not exceeding 13 weeks, where—

  (a) the claimant intends to return to occupy the accommodation as the claimant's home;

  (b) the part of the accommodation occupied by the claimant has not been let or sub-let to another person; and

(c) the period of absence is unlikely to exceed 13 weeks.

Absences for certain reasons up to 52 weeks

2.680   10.—(1) Where sub-paragraph (2) applies, a claimant is to be treated as occupying accommodation as the claimant's home ("the home accommodation") during any period of absence from it not exceeding 52 weeks beginning with the first day of that absence.

(2) This paragraph applies where a claimant's absence from the home accommodation is temporary and—

  (a) the claimant intends to return to occupy the home accommodation;

  (b) the home accommodation has not been let or sub-let;

  (c) the claimant is—

    (i) detained in custody on remand pending trial or, as a condition of bail, required to reside—

      (aa) in a dwelling, other than the home accommodation; or

      (bb) in premises approved under section 13 of the Offender Management Act 2007;

    (ii) detained pending sentence upon conviction;

    (iii) resident in a hospital or similar institution as a patient;

    (iv) undergoing or, the claimant's partner or child, or in the case of an SPC claimant, a person who has not attained the age of 20, is undergoing medical treatment, or medically approved convalescence, in accommodation other than residential accommodation;

    (v) undertaking a training course;

    (vi) undertaking medically approved care of another person;

    (vii) undertaking the care of a child or, in the case of an SPC claimant, a person under the age of 20 whose parent or guardian is temporarily absent from the dwelling occupied by that parent or guardian for the purpose of receiving medically approved care or medical treatment;

   (viii) a person who is receiving medically approved care provided in accommodation other than a residential home;

   (ix) a full-time student to whom paragraph 4(1) or 6(b) does not apply;

   (x) a person, other than a person to whom paragraph 8(1) applies, who is receiving care provided in residential accommodation; or

   (xi) a person to whom paragraph 6(a) does not apply and who has left the home accommodation through fear of violence in that accommodation, or by a person who was formerly his or her partner or is a close relative; and

  (d) the period of the claimant's absence is unlikely to exceed 52 weeks or, in exceptional circumstances, is unlikely substantially to exceed that period.

PART 3

UC CLAIMANTS

Application of Part 3

11. This Part applies to UC claimants.

2.681

Occupying accommodation: general rule

12.—(1) Subject to the following paragraphs of this Part, the accommodation which the claimant occupies as the claimant's home is the accommodation which the claimant normally occupies the home.

2.682

(2) Where the claimant occupies more than one dwelling, in determining whether accommodation is the accommodation normally occupied as the home for the purposes of sub-paragraph (1), regard is to be had to all the circumstances including (among other things) any persons with whom the claimant occupies each dwelling.

(3) Where accommodation which a claimant occupies as the claimant's home is situated on or pertains to a croft, croft land used for the purposes of the accommodation is to be treated as included in the accommodation.

Living in other accommodation due to essential repairs

13.—(1) Where a claimant—

2.683

  (a) is required to move into accommodation ("the other accommodation") on account of essential repairs being carried out to the accommodation the claimant occupies as the claimant's home ("the home accommodation");

  (b) intends to return to the home accommodation; and

  (c) is liable to make owner-occupier payments in respect of either the other accommodation or the home accommodation (but not both),

the claimant is to be treated as occupying as the claimant's home the accommodation in respect of which the owner-occupier payments are made.

Moving homes: adaptations to new home for disabled person

14.—(1) Sub-paragraph (2) applies where—

2.684

  (a) a claimant has moved into accommodation ("the new accommodation") and, immediately before the move, was liable to make owner-occupier payments in respect of the new accommodation; and

  (b) there was a delay in moving in to adapt the new accommodation in order to meet the needs of a disabled person.

(2) The claimant is to be treated as occupying both the new accommodation and the accommodation from which the move was made ("the old accommodation") if—

  (a) immediately before the move, the claimant was receiving loan payments or, in the case of an existing claimant, a qualifying benefit which includes an amount for owner-occupier payments, in respect of the old accommodation; and

  (b) the delay in moving into the new accommodation was reasonable.

(3) A person is disabled under this Part if the person is—

  (a) a claimant or any child or qualifying young person for whom the claimant is responsible; and

  (b) in receipt of—

     (i) the care component of disability living allowance at the middle or highest rate;

     (ii) attendance allowance; or

     (iii) the daily living component of personal independence payment.

(4) No claimant may be treated as occupying both the old accommodation and the new accommodation under this paragraph for more than one month.

Living in other accommodation due to fear of violence

2.685

15.—[² Sub-paragraphs (2) and (3) apply] where—

(a) a claimant is occupying accommodation ("the other accommodation") other than the accommodation which the claimant occupies as the claimant's home ("the home accommodation");

(b) it is unreasonable to expect the claimant to return to the home accommodation on account of the claimant's reasonable fear of violence in the home, or by a former partner, against the claimant or any child or qualifying young person for whom the claimant is responsible; and

(c) the claimant intends to return to the home accommodation.

(2) The claimant is to be treated as occupying both the home accommodation and the other accommodation as the claimant's home if—

(a) the claimant is liable to make payments in respect of both the other accommodation and the home accommodation; and

(b) it is reasonable to make loan payments in respect of both the home accommodation and the other accommodation.

(3) Where the claimant is liable to make [² owner-occupier] payments in respect of one accommodation only, the claimant is to be treated as occupying that accommodation as the claimant's home but only if it is reasonable to make loan payments in respect of that accommodation.

(4) No claimant may be treated as occupying both the home accommodation and the other accommodation under this paragraph for more than 12 months.

Moving in delayed by adaptations to accommodation to meet needs of disabled person

2.686

16.—(1) The claimant is to be treated as having occupied accommodation before the claimant moved into it where—

(a) the claimant has since moved in and, immediately before the move, the claimant is liable to make payments in respect of that accommodation;

(b) there was a delay in moving in that was necessary to enable the accommodation to be adapted to meet the needs of a disabled person; and

(c) it was reasonable to delay moving in.

(2) No claimant may be treated as occupying accommodation under this paragraph for more than one month.

Moving into accommodation following a stay in hospital or care home

2.687

17.—(1) The claimant is to be treated as having occupied accommodation before he or she moved into it where—

(a) the claimant has since moved in and, immediately before the move, the claimant was liable to make payments in respect of that accommodation; and

(b) the liability to make the payments arose while the claimant was a patient or accommodated in a care home (or, in the case of joint claimants, where both individuals were patients or were accommodated in a care home).

(2) No claimant may be treated as occupying the accommodation under this paragraph for more than one month.

Temporary absence exceeding 6 months

2.688

18.—(1) Subject to sub-paragraph (2), a claimant is to be treated as no longer occupying accommodation from which the claimant is temporarily absent where the absence exceeds, or is expected to exceed, 6 months.

(2) Where a claimant who falls within [¹ paragraph 15] is temporarily absent from the relevant accommodation, the claimant is to be treated as no longer occupying that accommodation where the absence exceeds, or is expected to exceed, 12 months.

AMENDMENTS

1. Loans for Mortgage Interest and Social Fund Maternity Grant (Amendment) Regulations 2018 (SI 2018/307), reg.2(1) and (16) (April 6, 2018).

2. Loans for Mortgage Interest (Amendment) Regulations 2021 (SI 2021/131) reg.2(1) and (6) (March 15, 2021).

DEFINITIONS

"applicable amount"—reg.2(1).
"benefit week"—*ibid.*
"care home"—para.1(1).
"child"—reg.2(1).
"close relative"—*ibid.*
"couple"—*ibid.*
"croft"—para.1(1).
"disabled person"—reg.2(1).
"dwelling"—*ibid.*
"ESA Regulations"—*ibid.*
"existing claimant"—*ibid.*
"family"—reg.2(2)(b).
"full-time student"—para.1(1).
"IS Regulations"—reg.2(1).
"joint claimants"—*ibid.*
"JSA Regulations"—*ibid.*
"legacy benefit claimant"—*ibid.*
"loan payments"—*ibid.*
"medically approved"—para.1(1).
"owner-occupier payments"—regs 2(1) and 3(2)(a).
"partner"—reg.2(1).
"patient"—para.1(1).
"period of study"—*ibid.*
"polygamous marriage"—reg.2(1).
"qualifying benefit"—*ibid.*
"qualifying young person"—*ibid.*
"relevant accommodation"—*ibid.*
"residential accommodation"—para.1(1).
"SPC claimant"—reg.2(1).
"SPC Regulations"—*ibid.*
"training course"—para.1(1).
"UC claimant"—reg.2(1).

GENERAL NOTE

See the commentary to Sch.3 to the UC Regulations (above), which is to similar effect.   2.689

Regulation 17

SCHEDULE 4

Direct payments to qualifying lenders

Direct payments
1. Each loan payment made to a qualifying lender directly under regulation 17(1) shall be the amount calculated under paragraph 2 [¹ ...] of this Schedule.   2.690

[¹ Determining the amount to be paid to a qualifying lender: one or more qualifying loans
2.—(1) Where one qualifying loan or alternative finance arrangement has been provided to a claimant by a qualifying lender, the amount that is to be paid direct to that lender is the amount of each loan payment.   2.691
(2) Where more than one qualifying loan or alternative finance arrangement has been provided to a claimant by a qualifying lender, the amount that is to be paid direct to that lender is the amount of each loan payment in respect of each of those loans or alternative finance arrangements added together.]

Determining the amount to be paid to a qualifying lender: more than one qualifying loan

2.692   3. [¹ ...]

Qualifying lenders to apply direct payments to discharge of claimant's liability

2.693   4. Where a direct payment is made under regulation 17(1) to a qualifying lender, the lender must apply the amount of the payment determined under either paragraph 2 or 3 of this Schedule towards discharging the claimant's liability to make owner-occupier payments in respect of which the direct payment was made.

Application by qualifying lenders of any amount which exceeds liability

2.694   5.—(1) Where—
- (a) a direct payment is made to a qualifying lender under regulation 17(1); and
- (b) the amount paid exceeds the claimant's liability to make owner-occupier payments to the qualifying lender,

the qualifying lender must apply the amount of excess in accordance with sub-paragraph (2).

(2) Subject to sub-paragraph (3), the qualifying lender must apply the amount of excess as follows—
- (a) first, towards discharging the amount of any liability of the claimant for arrears of owner-occupier payments in respect of the qualifying loan or alternative finance arrangement in question;
- (b) if any amount of the excess is then remaining, towards discharging any liability of the claimant to repay—
  - (i) the principal sum in respect of the qualifying loan or alternative finance arrangement; or
  - (ii) any other sum payable by the claimant to that lender in respect of that qualifying loan or alternative finance arrangement.

(3) Where owner-occupier payments on two or more qualifying loans or alternative finance arrangements are payable to the same qualifying lender, the lender must apply the amount of the excess as follows—
[¹ (a) first, towards discharging the amount of any liability of the claimant for arrears of owner-occupier payments in respect of the qualifying loan or alternative finance arrangement in respect of which the excess amount was paid;
- (b) if any amount of the excess is then remaining, towards discharging any liability of the claimant to repay—
  - (i) in respect of the loan or alternative finance arrangement referred to in paragraph (a), the principal sum or any other sum payable by the claimant to that lender; or
  - (ii) in respect of any other loan or alternative finance arrangement, any sum payable by the claimant to that lender where the liability to pay that sum is not already discharged.]

Fees payable by qualifying lenders

2.695   6.—[² ...]

Election not to be regarded as a qualifying lender

2.696   7.—(1) A body or person who would otherwise be within the definition of "qualifying lender" in the Act—
- (a) may elect not to be regarded as such for the purposes of these Regulations by giving notice to the Secretary of State in writing; and
- (b) may revoke any such notice by giving a further notice in writing.

(2) In respect of any financial year, a notice under sub-paragraph (1) which is given not later than 1st February before the start of the financial year, takes effect on 1st April following the giving of the notice.

(3) Where a body or person becomes a qualifying lender in the course of a financial year—
- (a) any notice of an election by the body or person under sub-paragraph (1)(a) must be given within 6 weeks ("the initial period") beginning with the date on which the body or person becomes a qualifying lender; and
- (b) no direct payments may be made under regulation 17(1) to the body or person before the expiry of the initial period.

(4) Sub-paragraph (3)(b) does not apply in any case where—
- (a) the person or body gives the Secretary of State notice in writing that that provision should not apply; and

686

(b) the notice is given before the start of the initial period or before that period expires.

(5) In relation to a notice under sub-paragraph (1)—

(a) where the notice is given by an electronic communication, it must be given in accordance with Schedule 2 of the Universal Credit, Personal Independence Payment, Jobseeker's Allowance and Employment and Support Allowance (Claims and Payments) Regulations 2013;

(b) where the notice is sent by post, it is to be treated as having been given on the day the notice was received.

Provision of information

8.—(1) A qualifying lender must, in respect of the claimant, provide the Secretary of State with information as to— **2.697**

(a) the owner-occupier payments payable by the claimant to the lender;

(b) the amount of the qualifying loan or alternative finance arrangement in respect of which owner-occupier payments are payable;

(c) the purpose for which the qualifying loan or alternative finance arrangement was made;

(d) the amount outstanding on the qualifying loan or alternative finance arrangement;

(e) the amount of arrears of owner-occupier payments due in respect of the qualifying loan or alternative finance payment;

(f) any change in the owner-occupier payments payable by the claimant to the lender; and

(g) the redemption of the qualifying loan or alternative finance arrangement, in the circumstances specified in paragraphs (2), (3) and (6).

(2) The information referred to in paragraph (1)(a) to (e) must be provided at the request of the Secretary of State where the claimant has made a claim for a qualifying benefit, provided that the Secretary of State may only make one request under this paragraph.

(3) The information referred to in paragraph (1)(d) and (f) must be provided where the Secretary of State makes a request for that information on or after the first day in respect of which loan payments are paid, or to be paid, to the qualifying lender on behalf of the claimant ("the first day"), provided that the Secretary of State may only make a request under this paragraph once in each period of 12 months referred to in paragraph (4).

(4) The period of 12 months is the period of 12 months beginning with the first day and each subsequent period of 12 months commencing on the anniversary of that day.

(5) A request may be made under paragraph (3) for the information referred to in paragraph (1)(d) even though that information has been requested in the same 12 month period (as referred to in paragraph (4)) under paragraph (2).

(6) The information referred to in sub-paragraph (1)(g) must be provided to the Secretary of State as soon as reasonably practicable once the qualifying lender has received notice that the qualifying loan or alternative finance arrangement is to be redeemed.

Recovery of sum wrongly paid

9.—(1) In the following circumstances, a qualifying lender must at the request of the Secretary of State repay any amount paid to the lender under regulation 17(1) which ought not to have been paid. **2.698**

(2) The circumstances are that, in respect of a claimant—

(a) the loan payments are terminated under regulation 9(2);

(b) the qualifying loan or alternative finance arrangement in respect of which owner-occupier payments are made has been redeemed; or

(c) both of the conditions in sub-paragraphs (3) and (4) are met.

(3) The first condition is that the amount of each loan payment determined under regulation 10 is reduced as a result of—

(a) the standard rate determined under regulation 13 having been reduced; or

(b) the amount outstanding on the qualifying loan or alternative finance arrangement having been reduced.

(4) The second condition is that no corresponding reduction was made to the amount calculated in respect of the qualifying lender under paragraph 2 or 3 of this Schedule.

(5) A qualifying lender is not required to make a repayment in the circumstances described in sub-paragraph (2)(a) unless the Secretary of State's request is made before the end of the period of two months starting with the date on which the loan payments are terminated.

AMENDMENTS

1. Loans for Mortgage Interest and Social Fund Maternity Grant (Amendment) Regulations 2018 (SI 2018/307), reg.2(1) and (17) (April 6, 2018).

2. Loans for Mortgage Interest (Transaction Fee) (Amendment) Regulations 2020 (SI 2020/666), reg.2 (August 2, 2020).

DEFINITIONS

"the Act"—reg.2(1)
"alternative finance payments"—reg.2(1).
"financial year"—*ibid.*
"loan payments"—*ibid.*
"owner-occupier payments"—regs 2(1) and 3(2)(a).
"qualifying benefit"—reg.2(1).
"qualifying lender"—*ibid.*
"qualifying loan"—*ibid.*

Regulation 18

SCHEDULE 5

CONSEQUENTIAL AMENDMENTS

2.699   *[Omitted]*

2.700   GENERAL NOTE

The consequential amendments made by Sch.5 have been incorporated at the appropriate places in the text of the amended regulations.

The Universal Credit (Managed Migration Pilot and Miscellaneous Amendments) Regulations 2019

(SI 2019/1152)

Made by the Secretary of State for Work and Pensions under the powers conferred by sections 4(2) and 42(1), (2) and (3) of, and paragraph 4(1), (3)(a) and (4) of Schedule 1 to, and paragraph 1(1), 3(1)(a), 4(1), (2)(a), (c) and (d) and (3) and 6(a) of Schedule 6 to, the Welfare Reform Act 2012.

In accordance with section 173(1)(b) of the Social Security Administration Act 1992 the Social Security Advisory Committee has agreed that the proposals in respect of regulations 2 and 7, and certain proposals in respect of regulation 3(8), should not be referred to it. In accordance with section 172(1) of that Act, the Secretary of State has referred all other proposals in respect of these Regulations to the Social Security Advisory Committee.

In accordance with section 176(1) of the 1992 Act, in so far as these Regulations relate to housing benefit, the Secretary of State has consulted with organisations appearing to her to be representative of the authorities concerned in respect of the proposals for these Regulations.

ARRANGEMENT OF REGULATIONS

Citation and commencement

1.—(1) These Regulations may be cited as the Universal Credit (Managed Migration Pilot and Miscellaneous Amendments) Regulations 2019.   2.701
(2) Regulations 2 and 3 and this regulation come into force on 24th July 2019.
(3) Regulations 4 and 5 come into force on 22nd July 2020.
(4) Regulation 6 comes into force on 23rd September 2020.
(5) Regulation 7 comes into force on 27th January 2021.

Managed migration pilot: limit on number of cases migrated

2. [¹ ...]   2.702

AMENDMENT

1. Universal Credit (Transitional Provisions) Amendment Regulations 2022 (SI 2022/752) reg.10 (July 25, 2022).

Amendment of the Universal Credit (Transitional Provisions) Regulations 2014: managed migration (including provision for persons previously entitled to a severe disability premium)

3.—(1) The Universal Credit (Transitional Provisions) Regulations 2014   2.703
are amended as follows.
(2)–(8) *(Amendments incorporated into the text of the Transitional Provisions Regulations in Part IIB of this volume)*

Two week run-on of income support, income-based jobseeker's allowance and income-related employment and support allowance: amendment of the Universal Credit (Transitional Provisions) Regulations 2014

4.—(1) The Universal Credit (Transitional Provisions) Regulations 2014   2.704
are amended as follows.
(2)–(7) *(Amendments incorporated into the Transitional Provisions Regulations in Part IIB of this volume)*

2.705 **Two week run-on of income-based jobseeker's allowance and income-related employment and support allowance: day appointed for abolition**

5.—(1) Subject to paragraph (2) where, in relation to any relevant claim for universal credit, an article ("the specified article") of any Order made under the powers in section 150(3) of the Welfare Reform Act 2012 provides for the coming into force of the amending provisions, the provision in that article for the day appointed is to be read as though the day appointed was the last day of the period of two weeks beginning with the day [¹ after the day] mentioned in that provision.

(2) For the purposes of paragraphs (6) and (7) of article 4 of the No.9 Order (conversion to employment and support allowance of awards of incapacity benefit and severe disablement allowance), including as they apply for the purposes of any other Order made under section 150(3) of the Welfare Reform Act 2012, the day appointed by the specified article for the coming into force of the amending provisions shall be treated as though it was the day that applies apart from this regulation.

(3) In this regulation—

"amending provisions" has the meaning given by article 2(1) of the No.9 Order;

"the No.9 Order" means the Welfare Reform Act 2012 (Commencement No.9 and Transitional and Transitory Provision and Commencement No.8 and Savings and Transitional Provisions (Amendment) Order 2013;

"relevant claim for universal credit" means a claim for universal credit made on or after 22nd July 2020 including a claim where, under the article in question, the amending provisions come into force despite incorrect information having been given by the claimant, but excluding any claim that is treated as made by a couple in the circumstances referred to in regulation 9(8) (claims for universal credit by members of a couple) of the Universal Credit, Personal Independence Payment, Jobseeker's Allowance and Employment and Support Allowance (Claims and Payments) Regulations 2013.

AMENDMENT

1. Universal Credit (Managed Migration Pilot and Miscellaneous Amendments) (Amendment) Regulations 2020 (SI 2020/826) reg.2(2) (August 4, 2020).

12 month exemption from the minimum income floor for new claimants

2.706   **6.**—(1) *(Amendment incorporated into the text of the UC Regulations)*
(2) *(Amendment incorporated into the text of the Transitional Provisions Regulations in Part IIB)*

Abolition of restriction on claims by persons entitled to a severe disability premium

2.707   **7.** *(Amendment incorporated into the text of the Transitional Provisions Regulations)*

(SI 2019/1357)

The Jobseeker's Allowance and Universal Credit (Higher-Level Sanctions) (Amendment) Regulations 2019

(SI 2019/1357)

Made by the Secretary of State for Work and Pensions under the powers conferred by sections 6J(5)(b) and (6), 19(4)(b) and (5), 35(1) and 36(4)(a) of the Jobseekers Act 1995 and sections 26(6)(b) and (7) and 42(1) and (3)(a) of the Welfare Reform Act 2012, the Social Security Advisory Committee having agreed that the proposals in respect of these Regulations should not be referred to it.

ARRANGEMENT OF REGULATIONS

Citation and commencement

1. These Regulations may be cited as the Jobseeker's Allowance and Universal Credit (Higher-Level Sanctions) (Amendment) Regulations 2019 and come into force on 27th November 2019.

2.708

Amendment of the Jobseeker's Allowance Regulations 1996

2. (*Amendment incorporated into the text of the JSA Regulations 1996 in Part III of Vol. V of this series*)

2.709

Amendment of the Universal Credit Regulations 2013

3. (*Amendment incorporated into the text of the Universal Credit Regulations 2013*)

2.710

Amendment of the Jobseeker's Allowance Regulations 2013

4. (*Amendment incorporated into the text of the JSA Regulations 2013 in Part VII of Vol. I of this series*)

2.711

Transitional provision

5.—(1) Where, on the date that these Regulations come into force, the amount of an award of jobseeker's allowance is subject to a reduction under section 19 of the Jobseekers Act 1995 for a period of 156 weeks, the reduction is to be terminated where, since the date that the reduction took effect, the award has been reduced for a period of at least 26 weeks.

2.712

(2) Where, on the date that these Regulations come into force, the amount of an award of jobseeker's allowance is subject to a reduction under section 6J of the Jobseekers Act 1995 for a period of 1095 days, the reduction is to be terminated where, since the date that the reduction took effect, the award has been reduced for a period of at least 182 days.

(3) Where, on the date that these Regulations come into force, the amount of an award of universal credit is subject to a reduction under section 26 of the Welfare Reform Act 2012, or which is treated as a reduction under section 26 of that Act by virtue of regulation 32(3) of the Universal Credit (Transitional Provisions) Regulations 2014(c), for a period of 1095 days, the reduction is to be terminated where, since the date that the reduction took effect, the award has been reduced for a period of at least 182 days.

The Victims' Payments Regulations 2020

SI 2020/103

[In force: February 24, 2020 and May 29, 2020]

The Secretary of State, Northern Ireland Office, makes these Regulations in exercise of the powers conferred by sections 10 and 11 of the Northern Ireland (Executive Formation etc) Act 2019.

The Secretary of State has had regard to advice given by the Commission for Victims and Survivors for Northern Ireland in accordance with section 10(10) of that Act.

PART 1

PRELIMINARY

Citation and commencement and extent

2.713

1.—(1) These Regulations may be cited as the Victims' Payments Regulations 2020.

(2) The following provisions come into force on the 24th February 2020—

(a) regulation 1;

(b) regulation 3;

(c) Schedule 1;

(d) paragraph 4(1) of Schedule 2, and regulation 15(8) so far as it relates to that paragraph;

(e) paragraphs 1, 4 and 5 of Schedule 3, and regulation 53 so far as it relates to that paragraph.

(3) The remaining provisions of these Regulations come into force on 29th May 2020.

(4) Except as provided by paragraphs (5) to (7), these Regulations extend to Northern Ireland only.

(5) Regulations 1, 2, 26, 28, 29 and 31 extend to England and Wales, Scotland and Northern Ireland.

(6) The amendments made by paragraph 2 of Schedule 3 extend to England and Wales only.

(7) Any other amendment made by these Regulations has the same extent as the provision it amends.

Disregard of payments and lump sums for certain purposes

26.—(1) A payment of victims' payments or a lump sum is to be disregarded—

2.714

  (a) from the calculation of a person's income or capital when determining entitlement to a relevant social security benefit;

  (b) for the purposes of an assessment of a person's ability to pay under regulations made under Article 36(6) or 99(5) (cost of providing residential accommodation) of the Health and Personal Social Services (Northern Ireland) Order 1972;

  (c) for the purposes of determining whether a person should repay (either fully or in part) an award of criminal injuries compensation where the application for that award was determined before these Regulations come into force.

(2) In paragraph (1)—

"criminal injuries compensation" means compensation under a scheme established under the Criminal Injuries Compensation Act 1995 or the Criminal Injuries Compensation (Northern Ireland) Order 2002;

"relevant social security benefit" means any of the following—

  (a) employment and support allowance under—

    (i) Part 1 of the Welfare Reform Act 2007 as it has effect apart from the amendments made by Schedule 3, and Part 1 of Schedule 14, to the Welfare Reform Act 2012 (to remove references to an income-related allowance);

    (ii) Part 1 of the Welfare Reform Act (Northern Ireland) 2007 as it has effect apart from the amendments made by Schedule 3, and Part 5 of Schedule 12, to the Welfare Reform Order (Northern Ireland) 2015 (to remove references to an income related allowance);

  (b) housing benefit under—

    (i) Part 7 of the Social Security Contributions and Benefits Act 1992, or

    (ii) Part 7 of the Social Security Contributions and Benefits (Northern Ireland) Act 1992;

  (c) income support under—

    (i) Part 7 of the Social Security Contributions and Benefits Act 1992, or

    (ii) Part 7 of the Social Security Contributions and Benefits (Northern Ireland) Act 1992;

  (d) jobseeker's allowance under—

    (i) the Jobseekers Act 1995 as it has effect apart from the amendments made by Part 1 of Schedule 14 to the Welfare Reform Act 2012 (to remove references to an income-based allowance);

    (ii) the Jobseekers (Northern Ireland) Order 1995 as it has effect apart from the amendments made by Part 1 of Schedule 12 to the Welfare Reform Order (Northern Ireland) 2015 (to remove references to an income-based allowance);

  (e) state pension credit under—

    (i) section 1 of the State Pension Credit Act 2002, or

    (ii) section 1 of the State Pension Credit Act (Northern Ireland) 2002;

  (f) universal credit under—

    (i) Part 1 of the Welfare Reform Act 2012, or

    (ii) Part 2 of the Welfare Reform (Northern Ireland) Order 2015.

GENERAL NOTE

2.715   The relevant provisions for universal credit purposes are reg.26(1)(a) and (2)(f). Under the Regulations payments are to be made to those injured in a "Troubles-related incident", which is defined in s.10(11) of the Northern Ireland (Executive Formation etc) Act 2019 as "an incident involving an act of violence or force carried out in Ireland, the United Kingdom or anywhere in Europe for a reason related to the constitutional status of Northern Ireland or to political or sectarian hostility between people there". In so far as any such payment constitutes income it is not listed in reg.66(1) of the Universal Credit Regulations, so would not be taken into account as unearned income for universal credit purposes even without the disregard in reg.26(1)(a). In so far as it constitutes capital, either initially or on metamorphosing into capital (see the notes to reg.54A of the Universal Credit Regulations), it is to be disregarded without any limit as to how long ago the payment was made.

The Employment and Support Allowance and Universal Credit (Coronavirus Disease) Regulations 2020

(SI 2020/289)

GENERAL NOTE

2.716   These Regulations came into force on March 30, 2020, and were subject to several extensions, but finally ceased to have effect from March 24, 2022, by virtue of reg.2 of the Employment and Support Allowance and Universal Credit (Coronavirus Disease) (Amendment) Regulations 2021 (SI 2021/1158). When in force they ensured that ESA claimants who met the eligibility conditions and were infected with Covid-19 (or self-isolating in line with government guidance, or looking after a child (or qualifying young person) who falls into either of these categories) could be treated as having limited capability for work without the requirement to provide any medical evidence or undergo a work capability assessment. They also removed the need for claimants to serve waiting days, enabling ESA to be paid from day one of any claim. For the text of the now repealed Regulations, see the 2021/22 edition of this work at paras 2.706–2.713 of Vol.II.

The Social Security (Coronavirus) (Further Measures) Regulations 2020

(SI 2020/371)

GENERAL NOTE

2.717   These regulations came into force on March 30, 2020 and were subject to several extensions, but finally ceased to have any effect in relation to universal credit on July 31, 2022. The main effect in relation to the imposition of work-related requirements expired on July 31, 2021, but the Universal Credit (Coronavirus) (Restoration of the Minimum Income Floor) Regulations 2021 (SI 2021/807) extended the effect of some parts of reg.2 for the longer period to allow a process of reintroduction of the minimum income floor rules. See the 2022/23 and earlier editions of this volume for the text of the regulations.

The Universal Credit (Coronavirus) (Self-employed Claimants and Reclaims) (Amendment) Regulations 2020

(SI 2020/522)

Made by the Secretary of State for Work and Pensions in exercise of powers conferred by sections 1(1) and 189(1), (4) and (6) of the Social Security Administration Act 1992 and section 42(1) to (3) of, and paragraph 4(1) and (6) of Schedule 1 to, the Welfare Reform Act 2012, it appearing inexpedient by reason of urgency to refer the proposals in respect of these Regulations to the Social Security Advisory Committee.

Citation and commencement

1. These Regulations may be cited as the Universal Credit (Coronavirus) (Self-employed Claimants and Reclaims) (Amendment) Regulations 2020 and come into force on 21st May 2020.

2.718

Treatment of payments to self-employed universal credit claimants

2.—(1) For the purposes of regulation 57 (self-employed earnings) of the Universal Credit Regulations 2013—

2.719

   (a) a payment under the Self-employment Income Support Scheme is to be treated as a receipt at step 1 of the calculation of self-employed earnings in the assessment period in which the claimant receives that payment; and

   (b) no deduction may be made at step 1 of that calculation in respect of expenses comprising the salary or wages paid to an employee in so far as those expenses are covered by a payment under the Coronavirus Job Retention Scheme.

(2) For the purposes of section 5 (financial conditions) and section 8 (calculation of awards) of the Welfare Reform Act 2012, any payment made to a claimant carrying on a trade, profession or vocation—

   (a) in relation to a furloughed employee under the Coronavirus Job Retention Scheme; or

   (b) by way of a grant or loan to meet the expenses or losses of the trade, profession or vocation in relation to the outbreak of coronavirus disease, is to be disregarded in the calculation of the claimant's capital for a period of 12 months from the date on which it is received.

(3) In this regulation—

"the Coronavirus Job Retention Scheme" means the scheme (as it has effect from time to time) that is the subject of the direction given by the Treasury on 15th April 2020 under section 76 of the Coronavirus Act 2020;

"the Self-employment Income Support Scheme" means the scheme (as it has effect from time to time) that is the subject of the direction given by the Treasury on 30th April 2020 under that section of that Act;

"coronavirus disease" has the meaning given in section 1 of the Coronavirus Act 2020.

2.720   The highly problematic effect of this provision, and of the new reg.32A of the Claims and Payments Regulations 2013 inserted by reg.3 (reclaims), is discussed in the notes to reg.57 of and para.7 of Sch.10 to the Universal Credit Regulations.

The definition of "the Coronavirus Job Retention Scheme" covers the later extensions to the scheme, because the later Treasury directions operate by way of modification of that signed on April 15, 2020. See the directions signed on June 25, 2020, November 12, 2020 and January 25, 2021 taking the operation of the scheme down to April 30, 2021. The same principle works for the definition of "the Self-employment Income Support Scheme (see the Treasury directions signed on July 1, 2020, November 21, 2020 and April 6 and 7, 2021, taking the operation of that scheme down to April 30, 2021 also).

Amendment of the UC etc. Claims and Payments Regulations

2.721   **3.** After regulation 32 (advance claim for and award of universal credit) of the Universal Credit, Personal Independence Payment, Jobseeker's Allowance and Employment and Support Allowance (Claims and Payments) Regulations 2013 insert—

"Reclaims of universal credit after nil award due to earnings

32A.—(1) This regulation applies where—

(a) a claim is made for universal credit, but no award is made because the condition in section 5(1)(b) or 5(2)(b) of the 2012 Act (condition that the claimant's income, or joint claimants' combined income is such that the amount payable would not be less than the prescribed minimum) is not met; or

(b) entitlement to an award of universal credit ceases because that condition is not met.

(2) The Secretary of State may, subject to any conditions the Secretary of State considers appropriate, treat the claimant (or joint claimants) as making a claim on the first day of each subsequent month, up to a maximum of 5, that would have been an assessment period if an award had been made or, as the case may be, if the award had continued".

The Universal Credit (Coronavirus) (Restoration of the Minimum Income Floor) Regulations 2021

(SI 2021/807)

2.722   These regulations came into force on July 31, 2021 and continued the effect of certain parts of reg.2 of the Social Security (Coronavirus) (Further Measures) Regulations 2020 (SI 2020/371), subject to various qualifications down to July 31, 2022. That was to allow a process of reintroduction of the minimum income floor rules. See the 2022/23 and earlier editions of this volume for the text of the regulations.

The Universal Credit and Jobseeker's Allowance (Work Search and Work Availability Requirements—limitations) (Amendment) Regulations 2022

(SI 2022/108)

Made by the Secretary of State at 10.35 a.m. on February 7, 2022 under sections 6D(4), 6E(3), 35 and 36(2) and (4) of the Jobseekers Act 1995 and sections 17(4), 18(3) and 42(1) to (3) of the Welfare Reform Act 2012 and laid before Parliament at 4.00 pm on February 7, 2002, it appearing to the Secretary of State that by reason of the urgency of the matter it was inexpedient to refer the proposals in respect of these Regulations to the Social Security Advisory Committee.

Citation, commencement and extent

1.—(1) These Regulations may be cited as the Universal Credit and Jobseeker's Allowance (Work Search and Work Availability Requirements—limitations) (Amendment) Regulations 2022 and come into force on 8th February 2022.

(2) Any amendment made by these Regulations has the same extent as the provision amended.

2.723

Amendment of the Universal Credit Regulations 2013

2. [*Amendment incorporated into the text of reg.97(5) of the Universal Credit Regulations 2013*]

2.724

Amendment of the Jobseeker's Allowance Regulations 2013

3. [*Amendment incorporated into the text of reg.14(3)(b) of the JSA Regulations 2013 in Vol.I of this series*]

2.725

Transitional provision

4. Where, on the date that these Regulations come into force, a work search requirement or work availability requirement is limited under regulation 97(4) of the Universal Credit Regulations 2013 or regulation 14(3) of the Jobseeker's Allowance Regulations 2013, the limitation is to end on—

(a) the day before the day on which the limitation no longer applies; or

(b) if earlier, 7th March 2022.

2.726

GENERAL NOTE

See the notes to reg.97(5) of the UC Regulations 2013 for the doubtful validity of the amendments made by regs 2 and 3 and their very limited practical effect.

2.727

The Universal Credit (Energy Rebate Scheme Disregard) Regulations 2022

(SI 2022/257)

Made by the Secretary of State under section 42(2) and (3) of, and paragraph 4(1) and (3) of Schedule 1 to, the Welfare Reform Act 2012, the Social Security Advisory Committee having agreed under section 173(1)(b) of the Social Security Administration Act 1992 that the proposals in respect of these Regulations should not be referred to it.

Citation, commencement and extent

2.728   **1.**—(1) These Regulations may be cited as the Universal Credit (Energy Rebate Scheme Disregard) Regulations 2022 and come into force on 1st April 2022.

(2) These Regulations extend to England and Wales and Scotland.

Capital disregard for Energy Rebate Scheme payments

2.729   **2.**—(1) Any payment a person receives under the Energy Rebate Scheme 2022 is to be disregarded for 12 months beginning with the date on which it is received in the calculation of the person's capital for the purpose of Part 1 of the Welfare Reform Act 2012 (Universal Credit).

(2) In this regulation—

"the Energy Rebate Scheme 2022" means the scheme to provide financial support in respect of energy bills which was announced in Parliament by the Chancellor of the Exchequer on 3rd February 2022 and any comparable scheme announced by Welsh Ministers or Scottish Ministers.

GENERAL NOTE

2.730   See the introductory note to Sch.10 to the Universal Credit Regulations 2013 for the effect of these Regulations.

PART IIB

TRANSITIONAL AND SAVINGS PROVISIONS

The Universal Credit (Transitional Provisions) Regulations 2014

2014/1230 (AS AMENDED)

The Secretary of State for Work and Pensions makes the following Regulations in exercise of the powers conferred by section 42(2) and (3) of and paragraphs 1(1) and (2)(b), 3(1)(a) to (c), 4(1)(a), 5(1), (2)(c) and (d) and (3)(a) and 6 of Schedule 6 to the Welfare Reform Act 2012.

In accordance with section 172(1) of the Social Security Administration Act 1992 ("the 1992 Act"), the Secretary of State has referred proposals in respect of these Regulations to the Social Security Advisory Committee.

In accordance with section 176(1) of the 1992 Act and, in so far as these Regulations relate to housing benefit, the Secretary of State has consulted with organisations appearing to him to be representative of the authorities concerned in respect of proposals for these Regulations.

[In force: June 16, 2014]

ARRANGEMENT OF REGULATIONS

PART 1

PART 2

CHAPTER 1

CHAPTER 2

CHAPTER 3

PART 1

Citation and commencement

1. (1) These Regulations may be cited as the Universal Credit (Transitional   2.733
Provisions) Regulations 2014.
(2) These Regulations come into force on 16th June 2014.

Interpretation

2. (1) In these Regulations—   2.734
"the 2002 Act" means the Tax Credits Act 2002;
[⁶"the 2006 (SPC) Regulations" means the Housing Benefit (Persons who
    have attained the qualifying age for state pension credit) Regulations
    2006;]
"the 2007 Act" means the Welfare Reform Act 2007;
"the Act" means the Welfare Reform Act 2012;
"assessment period" has the same meaning as in the Universal Credit
    Regulations;
[⁵"childcare costs element" has the meaning in the Universal Credit
    Regulations;]
"the Claims and Payments Regulations" means the Universal
    Credit, Personal Independence Payment, Jobseeker's Allowance
    and Employment and Support Allowance (Claims and Payments)
    Regulations 2013;
"contributory employment and support allowance" means a contribu-
    tory allowance under Part 1 of the 2007 Act as that Part has effect
    apart from the amendments made by Schedule 3, and Part 1 of
    Schedule 14, to the Act that remove references to an income-related
    allowance;
[¹ . . .]
[⁵ "deadline day" has the meaning in regulation 44;]
[⁶ "the Decisions and Appeals Regulations" means the Universal
    Credit, Personal Independence Payment, Jobseeker's Allowance
    and Employment and Support Allowance (Decisions and Appeals)
    Regulations 2013;]
[⁵ "earned income" has the meaning in Chapter 2 of Part 6 of the
    Universal Credit Regulations;]
"existing benefit" means income-based jobseeker's allowance, income-
    related employment and support allowance, income support, housing
    benefit and child tax credit and working tax credit under the 2002 Act,
    but see also [⁵paragraph (3) and] regulation 25(2);
[⁵ "final deadline" has the meaning in regulation 46;]
"First-tier Tribunal" has the same meaning as in the Social Security Act
    1998;
[⁵ "HMRC" means Her Majesty's Revenue and Customs;]
"housing benefit" means housing benefit under section 130 of the Social
    Security Contributions and Benefits Act 1992;
"income-based jobseeker's allowance" has the same meaning as in the
    Jobseekers Act 1995;
"income-related employment and support allowance" means an income-
    related allowance under Part 1 of the 2007 Act;

"income support" means income support under section 124 of the Social Security Contributions and Benefits Act 1992;

[⁵ "indicative UC amount" has the meaning in regulation 54;]

"joint-claim jobseeker's allowance" means old style JSA, entitlement to which arises by virtue of section 1(2B) of the Jobseekers Act 1995;

[⁵ "migration day" has the meaning in regulation 49;]

[⁵ "migration notice" has the meaning in regulation 44;]

"new claimant partner" has the meaning given in regulation 7;

"new style ESA" means an allowance under Part 1 of the 2007 Act as amended by the amendments made by Schedule 3, and Part 1 of Schedule 14, to the Act that remove references to an income-related allowance;

"new style JSA" means an allowance under the Jobseekers Act 1995 as amended by the amendments made by Part 1 of Schedule 14 to the Act that remove references to an income-based allowance;

[⁵ "notified person" has the meaning in regulation 44;]

"old style ESA" means an employment and support allowance under Part 1 of the 2007 Act as that Part has effect apart from the amendments made by Schedule 3, and Part 1 of Schedule 14, to the Act that remove references to an income-related allowance;

"old style JSA" means a jobseeker's allowance under the Jobseekers Act 1995 as that Act has effect apart from the amendments made by Part 1 of Schedule 14 to the Act that remove references to an income-based allowance;

"partner" in relation to a person ("A") means a person who forms part of a couple with A;

[⁶ "qualifying age for state pension credit" has the meaning given by section 1(6) of the State Pension Credit Act 2002;]

[⁵ "qualifying claim" has the meaning in regulation 48;]

[² "qualifying young person" has the same meaning as in the Universal Credit Regulations, but see also regulation 28;]

[⁴ "severe disability premium" means the premium in relation to an employment and support allowance under paragraph 6 of Schedule 4 to the Employment and Support Allowance Regulations 2008 or, as the case may be, the corresponding premium in relation to income support, old style JSA or housing benefit;]

[¹ "specified accommodation" means accommodation to which one or more of sub-paragraphs (2) to (5) of paragraph 3A of Schedule 1 to the Universal Credit Regulations applies;]

[⁶ "state pension credit" means state pension credit under the State Pension Credit Act 2002;]

[³ "temporary accommodation" means accommodation which falls within Case 1 or Case 2 under paragraph 3B of Schedule 1 to the Universal Credit Regulations;]

"tax credit" (including "child tax credit" and "working tax credit"), "tax credits" and "tax year" have the same meanings as in the 2002 Act;

"the Universal Credit Regulations" means the Universal Credit Regulations 2013;

[⁵ "total legacy amount" has the meaning in regulation 53;]

[⁵ "transitional capital disregard" has the meaning in regulation 51;]

[⁵ "transitional element" has the meaning in regulation 52;]

"Upper Tribunal" has the same meaning as in the Social Security Act 1998.

(2) For the purposes of these Regulations—

(a) the date on which a claim for universal credit is made is to be determined in accordance with the Claims and Payments Regulations;

(b) where a couple is treated, in accordance with regulation 9(8) of the Claims and Payments Regulations, as having made a claim for universal credit, references to the date on which the claim is treated as made are to the date of formation of the couple;

(c) where a regulation refers to entitlement to an existing benefit on the date on which a claim for universal credit is made or treated as made, such entitlement is to be taken into account notwithstanding the effect of regulations 5, 7 and 8 or termination of an award of the benefit before that date by virtue of an order made under section 150(3) of the Act.

[⁵(3) In these Regulations—

(a) references to an award of income-based jobseeker's allowance are to an award of old style JSA where the claimant is, or joint claimants are, entitled to the income-based allowance; and

(b) references to an award of income-related employment and support allowance are to an award of old style ESA where the claimant is entitled to the income-related allowance.

(4) In regulation 46 (termination of existing benefits if no claim before the deadline) [⁷ ...] "terminate" in relation to an award of income-based jobseeker's allowance or income-related employment and support allowance means treating that award as if the following provisions had come into force (including where a saving provision has ceased to apply) in relation to that award—

(a) section 33(1)(a) and (b) and (2) of the Act (abolition of benefits);

(b) paragraphs 22 to 26 of Schedule 3 to the Act (abolition of benefits: consequential amendments) and section 33(3) of the Act in so far as it relates to those paragraphs; and

(c) the repeals in Part 1 of Schedule 14 to the Act (abolition of benefits superseded by universal credit) that come into force if a claim is made for universal credit.]

AMENDMENTS

1. Universal Credit (Transitional Provisions) (Amendment) Regulations 2014 (SI 2014/1626) reg.3 (November 3, 2014).

2. Social Security (Restrictions on Amounts for Children and Qualifying Young Persons) Amendment Regulations 2017 (2017/376) reg.3(2) (April 6, 2017).

3. Universal Credit (Miscellaneous Amendments, Saving and Transitional Provision) Regulations 2018 (SI 2018/65) reg.6(3) (April 11, 2018).

4. Universal Credit (Transitional Provisions) (SDP Gateway) Amendment Regulations 2019 (SI 2019/10) reg.2(2) (January 16, 2019).

5. Universal Credit (Managed Migration Pilot and Miscellaneous Amendments) Regulations 2019 (SI 2019/1152) reg.3(2) (July 24, 2019).

6. Universal Credit (Persons who have attained state pension credit qualifying age) (Amendment) Regulations 2020 (SI 2020/655) reg.6(2) (November 25, 2020).

7. Universal Credit (Transitional Provisions) Amendment Regulations 2022 (SI 2022/752) reg.11 and Sch. para.1(2) (July 25, 2022).

DEFINITIONS

"the Act"—see reg.2(1).

GENERAL NOTE

Paragraph (1)

2.735 *"new claimant partner"*: where a single universal credit claimant becomes a member of a couple, and their award terminates, and the other member of the couple was not previously entitled to universal credit as a single person, but an award of universal credit is then made to the couple as joint claimants, then the other member of the couple is known as a "new claimant partner" (see also reg.7).

"new style ESA": in effect, this means (new variant) contribution-based ESA, shorn of its previous income-based element, and as defined in what were originally the Pathfinder areas as from April 29, 2013.

"new style JSA": similarly, this means (new variant) contribution-based JSA, again shorn of its income-related element, and as defined in those Pathfinder areas as from April 29, 2013.

Paragraph (2)(a)

2.736 The normal rule is that the date of a universal credit claim is the date the claim is received, whether electronically or by telephone or, if later, the first day for which the claim is made: see Claims and Payments Regulations 2013, reg.10.

Revocation and saving of the Universal Credit (Transitional Provisions) Regulations 2013

2.737 **3.** (1) The Universal Credit (Transitional Provisions) Regulations 2013 ("the 2013 Regulations") are revoked, subject to the savings in paragraphs (2) to (4).

(2) Chapters 2 and 3 of Part 2 (Pathfinder Group and treatment of invalid claims) of the 2013 Regulations continue to have effect in relation to a claim for universal credit—

(a) which was made before the date on which these Regulations come into force ("the commencement date"); and

(b) in respect of which no payment has been made to the claimant before the commencement date.

(3) Regulation 19 of the 2013 Regulations (advance payments of universal credit) continues to have effect in relation to an advance payment which was made in accordance with that regulation before the commencement date and regulation 17 of these Regulations does not apply to such a payment.

(4) Any other provision of the 2013 Regulations continues to have effect in so far as is necessary to give full effect to paragraphs (2) and (3).

DEFINITIONS

"the 2013 Regulations"–para.(1).
"the commencement date"–para.(2)(a).

GENERAL NOTE

This regulation provides for revocation of the Universal Credit (Transitional Provisions) Regulations 2013 (para.(1)), subject to certain savings (paras.(2)-(4)). These savings concern claimants who claimed universal credit before the date on which the 2014 Transitional Regulations came into force (June 16, 2014) and relate in particular to the treatment of invalid claims and recovery of advance payments of universal credit made under the 2013 Transitional Regulations. The intention is to ensure that the validity of a claim is judged in accordance with the provisions which were in force at the time the claim was made, and that advance payments made under the 2013 Transitional Regulations remain recoverable.

2.738

PART 2

CHAPTER 1

Secretary of State discretion to determine that claims for universal credit may not be made

4. [¹...]

2.739

AMENDMENT

1. Universal Credit (Transitional Provisions) Amendment Regulations 2022 (SI 2022/752) reg.2 (July 25, 2022).

[¹Restriction on claims for universal credit by persons entitled to a severe disability premium

4A.—[³[²...]]

2.740

AMENDMENTS

1. Universal Credit (Transitional Provisions) (SDP Gateway) Amendment Regulations 2019 (SI 2019/10) reg.2(3) (January 16, 2019).
2. Universal Credit (Managed Migration Pilot and Miscellaneous Amendments) Regulations 2019 (SI 2019/1152) reg.3(3) (July 24, 2019).
3. Universal Credit (Managed Migration Pilot and Miscellaneous Amendments) Regulations 2019 (SI 2019/1152) reg.7 (January 27, 2021).

GENERAL NOTE

There was a complex background to this provision originally inserted into the Regulations in January 2019. By way of context, universal credit, unlike the legacy means-tested benefits, does not include an equivalent component to severe disability premium (SDP). The Coalition Government maintained that universal credit would simplify means-tested support for disabled people, but disability organisations pointed out that the abolition of SDP could result in vulnerable claimants losing out financially. In response, the Government announced that transitional protection would be available to ensure that people moving onto universal credit did not lose out in cash terms at the point of transfer (i.e. if their universal credit entitlement was lower than their existing legacy benefits). However, it became apparent that transitional protection would only be available to claimants who were subject to "managed migration", i.e. having been required to transfer by the DWP. For claimants moving by "natural migration"—e.g. a change in their circumstances—there would be no such protection.

2.741

This differential treatment was challenged by way of judicial review in the High Court in R *(On the application of TP and AR) v Secretary of State for Work and Pensions* [2018] EWHC 1474 (Admin), in which two claimants previously in receipt of IR-ESA had to claim universal credit following a move to a full service area. In the absence of any equivalent to SDP they suffered a sudden and significant drop in their incomes. The judicial review claim was put on three grounds: (1) the absence of any additional payment in universal credit for those who previously qualified for SDP amounted to unlawful discrimination contrary to art.14 read with art.1 of the First Protocol to the ECHR; (2) the Universal Credit (Transitional Provisions) Regulations 2014 involved unlawful discrimination (on the same basis) because of the absence of any element of transitional protection; and (3) the Secretary of State had breached the Equality Act 2010 by failing to have due regard to the impact of removing the premiums for disabled people when making the Universal Credit Regulations 2013 and the Transitional Provisions Regulations.

In June 2018 Lewis J. dismissed the challenges on the first and third grounds of judicial review, but allowed the application on the second ground, holding that the Transitional Provisions Regulations did not strike a fair balance between the interests of the individual and the community respectively in bringing about a phased transition to universal credit. The impact on the individuals was apparent—their cash payments were now significantly lower than the amounts they had previously received. The Judge found there appeared to have been no consideration given to the justification for requiring the individual to assume the entirety of the difference between their previous benefits and universal credit; this was all the more striking given Government statements over the years that such persons could need assistance and there was a need to define precisely the circumstances in which persons would not receive assistance. In this case, the operation of the implementation arrangements was "manifestly without reasonable foundation" and failed to strike a fair balance (at [88]). The differential treatment was based on status and had not been objectively justified. Accordingly, Lewis J. held that the universal credit implementing arrangements gave rise to unlawful discrimination contrary to art.14 read with art.1 of the First Protocol to the ECHR. The High Court granted a declaration that there was unlawful discrimination, leaving the Secretary of State to determine how to rectify the unlawful discrimination (at [114]). Thus, Lewis J concluded as follows:

"[113] The 2013 Regulations establishing universal credit do not involve discrimination contrary to Article 14 ECHR in so far as they do not include any element which corresponds to the additional disability premiums payable under the previous regime. Any differential treatment between different groups is objectively justifiable.

[114] The implementing arrangements do at present give rise to unlawful discrimination contrary to Article 14 ECHR read with Article 1 of the First Protocol to the ECHR. There is differential treatment between the group of persons who were in receipt of additional disability premiums (the SDP and EDP) and who transferred to universal credit on moving to a different local housing authority area and so receive less money by way of income related support than they previously received and the group of persons in receipt of SDP and EDP and who move house within the same local housing authority area but are not required to transfer to universal credit and continue to receive the basic allowance and SDP and EDP and suffer no loss of income. That differential treatment is based on status. That differential treatment has not been objectively justified at present. A declaration will be granted that there is unlawful discrimination. The defendant will then be able to determine how to rectify the unlawful discrimination."

In R *(on the application of AR & SXC) v SSWP* [2020] EWCA Civ 37, the Court of Appeal dismissed the Secretary of State's appeal against the judgment of Lewis J. The Department advanced four grounds of appeal. The first was that the judge had been wrong to conclude that there was any appearance of discriminatory treatment against TP and AR. The Court of Appeal rejected this ground for appeal on the basis that "there can be no realistic dispute that there is a difference of treatment between TP and AR on the one hand and, on the other hand, people in an analogous situation, who do not have to apply for universal credit" (at [87]). The second ground of appeal was that the High Court had erred in holding that the difference of treatment in these cases was on the ground of an 'other status' for the purpose of art.14, namely a severely disabled person who moves to a different local authority area. The Court (Rose LJ dissenting) held that residence in a given local authority area could constitute a relevant status. The third ground of appeal was that Lewis J had been wrong to hold that the difference in treatment lacked an objective justification. This ground for appeal failed as, on the evidence that the DWP placed before Lewis J, there appeared to have been no consideration of the difference in treatment between the comparator groups. The final ground for appeal was that the High Court's declaration should have been limited to one that there had been a failure to 'consider' transitional payments, rather than that TP and AR had suffered unlawful discrimination by reason of the difference in payments. This ground was rejected as being based on a misunderstanding of Lewis J's reasoning. Moreover, the Court found that the DWP had failed in its duty of candour and co-operation by omitting to disclose to Lewis J that it had already made a policy decision both to stop moving more severely disabled people onto universal credit and to provide transitional payments for those who had already been transferred.

Following the High Court's decision in *R (on the application of TP and AR) v SSWP*, the DWP agreed to compensate the claimants in the case for the money they had lost as a result of moving onto universal credit, and to make ongoing payments of around £170 a month to reflect future loss which would be paid until changes to the regulations came into force.

The Government's immediate response, more broadly, was to issue a written statement explaining that "in order to support the transition for those individuals who live alone with substantial care needs and receive the Severe Disability Premium", the rules implementing universal credit would be changed. The Government announced that current claimants with an award including SDP who had a change of circumstances (normally meaning they would be subject to natural migration to universal credit) would not in fact move to the new benefit until they qualified for transitional protection—i.e. not until they were subject to "managed migration", i.e. as and when required to migrate by the DWP (written statement HCWS745, June 7, 2018, by the then Secretary of State, Esther McVey MP). The Secretary of State further stated that claimants who had already moved to universal credit and so lost their SDP would receive on-going compensation payments and an additional lump-sum payment to cover the period since they moved.

As a consequence there has been, in effect, a twin-track approach to further developments, namely first the relatively straightforward proposal to stop SDP claimants from transferring from legacy benefits to universal credit and, secondly, the more complex arrangements for providing transitional protection to those who have already transferred or will so transfer in due course.

As to the first track, the Universal Credit (Transitional Provisions) (SDP Gateway) Amendment Regulations 2019 (SI 2019/10), which came into force on January 16, inserted new reg.4A so as to prevent claimants of legacy benefits (IS, IR-ESA, IB-JSA or HB) with SDP from making a claim for universal credit. The exclusion also applies where an award of a legacy benefit has ended within the last month, so long as the claimant continued to satisfy the conditions for entitlement to the SDP. This exclusion is known as the "SDP gateway", although the "SDP roadblock" might be a more accurate description. DWP guidance to staff is available in Memo ADM 01/19 UC *Claimants entitled to Severe Disability Premium* (January 2019). As the Explanatory Memorandum to SI 2019/10 explains, "The regulations provide that these claimants will no longer naturally migrate to UC, but will remain on their existing benefits or be able to claim another existing benefit instead until such time as they are moved to Universal Credit as part of the Department's managed migration process." However, it should be noted that the SDP gateway has been prospectively repealed with effect from January 27, 2021 (see SI 2019/1152, reg.7), in response to the further High Court judgment in *R (on the application of TP, AR and SXC) v Secretary of State for Work and Pensions* [2019] EWHC 1116 (Admin). Swift J held there that the differential treatment between claimants with SDP who have already moved to universal credit and those who are prevented from doing so because of the SDP gateway was not justified (see further below).

As to the second track, it is fair to say that the DWP has had several attempts (to be precise, three goes as at the time of writing) at trying to develop a satisfactory solution for compensating those with financial losses.

First, transitional payment arrangements for claimants who had already moved to universal credit (and so had lost their SDP) were included in the draft Universal Credit (Managed Migration) Regulations laid before Parliament on November 5, 2018. An initial draft had been submitted to the SSAC, which undertook a public consultation on them over summer 2018. In the event, the DWP withdrew the draft regulations following wider concerns about its proposed approach to managed migration.

Secondly, the Department then included provisions on SDP transitional payments in the draft Universal Credit (Managed Migration Pilot and Miscellaneous Amendments) Regulations, laid before Parliament in January 2019. The regulations were subject to the affirmative procedure but no debate or vote took place in either House. In a case brought by the two claimants who had successfully challenged the DWP in the High Court in June 2018 (TP and AR), and a third claimant (SXC), the High Court (Swift J) ruled on May 3, 2019 that the Government's proposed scheme for SDP transitional payments was unlawful (*R (on the application of TP, AR and SXC) v Secretary of State for Work and Pensions* [2019] EWHC 1116 (Admin)). Under the proposed scheme set out in the second set of draft regulations, SDP recipients moving to universal credit on managed migration would receive top-ups of up to £180 a month, while those claimants who had already been subject to natural migration and lost their SDP would have received payments of £80 per months. Swift J. agreed that this difference in treatment could not be justified:

> "[59] …What needs to be justified extends to the difference in treatment between the SDP migrant group and the Regulation 4A group. The need for some form of explanation for the difference in treatment is all the more striking given the circumstances which, at the beginning of 2018, prompted the Secretary of State to consider the position of severely disabled benefits claimants. This was the point raised by the members of the House of Commons Select Committee on Work and Pensions on the effect that migration to Universal Credit was having on those who had previously been in receipt of SDP, and it was the point considered in the subsequent Departmental presentation (see above, at paragraphs 30 to 33).
>
> [60] No sufficient explanation for the difference in treatment has been provided. The Secretary of State's "bright line"/administrative efficiency submission explains the treatment of the SDP natural migrant group on its own terms, but does not explain why that group is treated differently to the Regulation 4A group. Both groups comprise severely disabled persons; all of whom meet the criteria for payment of SDP (or would continue to meet those criteria but for natural migration). The simple fact of natural migration is not a satisfactory ground of distinction because the trigger conditions for natural migration are not indicative of any material change in the needs of the Claimants (or the other members of the SDP natural migration group), as severely disabled persons. The same point is sufficient to dispose of the further suggestion in Miss Young's witness statement that the Secretary of State considered the SDP natural migrants as being in materially the same position as new welfare benefits claimants (i.e. severely disabled persons presenting themselves to the welfare benefits system for the first time, after the implementation of Universal Credit). There is no logical foundation for that view; if there were a logical foundation for it, it would negate the rationale for regulation 4A of the Transitional Provisions Regulations."

712

The High Court left it to the Government to decide what should happen next with regard to the regulations. The Court of Appeal subsequently dismissed the Secretary of State's appeal against Swift J's judgment (see *R (on the application of AR & SXC) v SSWP* [2020] EWCA Civ 37). A separate claim by SXC for compensation under the Human Rights Act 1988 was later dismissed by Swift J. (*SXC v Secretary of State for Work and Pensions* [2019] EWHC 2774 (Admin)). This takes us to the third attempt to deal with SDP transitional protection.

Thirdly, the final Universal Credit (Managed Migration Pilot and Miscellaneous Amendments) Regulations (SI 2019/1152) —which unlike the previous versions were subject to the negative procedure—were laid before Parliament on July 22, 2019 and (for present purposes) came into force two days later. They provide, among other things, for transitional payments for claimants who were in receipt of SDP who have already moved to universal credit, comprising ongoing monthly payments and an additional lump-sum covering the period since they moved.

Finally, the SDP gateway was repealed with effect from January 27, 2021 (see reg.7 of the Universal Credit (Managed Migration Pilot and Miscellaneous Amendments) Regulations 2019 (SI 2019/1152)). This was in response to the High Court's decision in *R. (on the application of TP, AR and SXC) v Secretary of State for Work and Pensions* [2019] EWHC 1116 (Admin). The consequence is that affected claimants will move to universal credit if a change of circumstances prompts them to make a claim for universal credit, in which event they may be eligible to be considered for transitional payments (see reg.63 and Sch.2, as substituted by reg.2 of the Universal Credit (Transitional Provisions) (Claimants previously entitled to a severe disability premium) Amendment Regulations 2021 (SI 2021/4)).

See further the judgment of Holgate J in *R. (on the application of TP and AR) v Secretary of State for Work and Pensions* [2022] EWHC 123 (Admin) (*TP and AR No.3*). This judgment includes a helpful analysis of *TP No.1* ([114]–[126]), *TP No.2* ([127]–[137] and the Court of Appeal's judgment in both appeals ([138]–[146]). *TP and AR No.3* is discussed in the commentary to reg.63 below. Note that the Court of Appeal refused (in forthright terms) the Secretary of State's application for permission to appeal against the decision of Holgate J. (CA-2022-000398; January 12, 2023).

CHAPTER 2

Exclusion of entitlement to certain benefits

5.—(1) Except as provided in paragraph (2), a claimant is not entitled to— 2.742
(a) income support;
(b) housing benefit;
(c) a tax credit; or
(d) state pension credit [² ...],
in respect of any period when the claimant is entitled to universal credit.
(2) Entitlement to universal credit does not preclude the claimant from entitlement—
[¹(a) to housing benefit in respect of specified accommodation or temporary accommodation;
(ab) to housing benefit or income support where regulation 8(2A) [³ or 46(1)] applies; [²...]
(b) during the first assessment period for universal credit, where the claimant is a new claimant partner, to—
  (i) income support, where an award to which the new claimant partner is entitled terminates, in accordance with regulation 7(4), after the first date of entitlement to universal credit;

   (ii) housing benefit, where regulation 7(5)(b) [² or (c)] applies and an award of housing benefit to which the new claimant partner is entitled terminates after the first date of entitlement to universal credit; [² ...]
   (iii) a tax credit, where an award to which the new claimant partner is entitled terminates, in accordance with the 2002 Act, after the first date of entitlement to universal credit [²; or
   (iv) state pension credit, where an award to which the new claimant partner is entitled terminates after the first date of entitlement to universal credit; or
 (c) during the last assessment period for universal credit, where the claimant reaches the qualifying age for state pension credit and paragraph 26 of Schedule 1 to the Decisions and Appeals Regulations applies, to housing benefit or state pension credit from the date the claimant reaches that age.]

AMENDMENTS

1. Universal Credit (Managed Migration Pilot and Miscellaneous Amendments) Regulations 2019 (SI 2019/1152) reg.4(2) (July 22, 2020).
2. Universal Credit (Persons who have attained state pension credit qualifying age) (Amendment) Regulations 2020 (SI 2020/655) reg.6(3) (November 25, 2020).
3. Universal Credit (Transitional Provisions) Amendment Regulations 2022 (SI 2022/752) reg.11 and Sch. para.1(3) (July 25, 2022).

DEFINITIONS

"the 2002 Act"—see reg.2(1).
"assessment period"—*ibid.*
"housing benefit"—*ibid.*
"income support"—*ibid.*
"new claimant partner"—*ibid.*
"specified accommodation"—*ibid.*
"tax credit"—*ibid.*

GENERAL NOTE

2.743   This regulation broadly performs the same function as reg.15(1)-(2A) of the 2013 Transitional Regulations. The basic rule is that entitlement to universal credit and entitlement to any of the benefits or tax credits in para.(1) are mutually exclusive. Provision is made to similar effect in relation to "old style JSA" and "old style ESA" by virtue of the various Commencement Orders made under s.150(3) of the Act, which bring into force repeals of the legislation relating to those benefits. References to "old style JSA" and "old style ESA" are to the versions of jobseeker's allowance and employment and support allowance which include an income-based, or income-related, allowance (see reg.2 above).

[¹ **Entitlement to universal credit and housing benefit: universal credit work allowance**

2.744   **5A.** Where a claimant has an award of universal credit and, in any assessment period, is also entitled to housing benefit for temporary accommodation and the award of universal credit does not include an amount for housing costs, regulation 22(2) of the Universal Credit

Regulations (amount of the work allowance) is to apply in relation to that assessment period as if the award did include an amount for housing costs.]

AMENDMENT

1. Universal Credit (Miscellaneous Amendments, Saving and Transitional Provision) Regulations 2018 (SI 2018/65) reg.6(4) (April 11, 2018).

DEFINITIONS

"assessment period"—see reg.2(1).
"housing benefit"—*ibid.*
"temporary accommodation"—*ibid.*
"Universal Credit Regulations"—*ibid.*

GENERAL NOTE

The new reg.5A provides that where in a universal credit assessment period a person is entitled to universal credit (without the housing costs element) and is also entitled to housing benefit for temporary accommodation, then that person is to be treated for the purposes of work allowances in universal credit as though they were entitled to universal credit with the housing costs element.

2.745

Exclusion of claims for certain existing benefits

6. [¹...]

AMENDMENT

1. Universal Credit (Transitional Provisions) Amendment Regulations 2022 (SI 2022/752) reg.3 (July 25, 2022).

2.746

[¹Restriction on claims for housing benefit, income support or a tax credit

6A.—(1) Except as provided by paragraphs (2) to (7) a person may not make a claim for housing benefit, income support, or a tax credit.

2.747

(2) Paragraph (1) does not apply to a claim for housing benefit in respect of specified accommodation or temporary accommodation.

(3) Paragraph (1) does not apply to a claim for housing benefit that is made during the last assessment period of an award of universal credit, where the claimant reaches the qualifying age for state pension credit and paragraph 26 of Schedule 1 to the Decisions and Appeals Regulations applies, in respect of entitlement arising from the date the claimant reaches that age.

(4) Paragraph (1) does not apply to a claim for housing benefit by a single person who has reached the qualifying age for state pension credit, or a member of a State Pension Credit Act couple where both members have reached that age or a member of a polygamous marriage where all members have reached that age.

(5) Paragraph (1) does not apply to a claim for housing benefit where—
(a) the claim is made by a member of a State Pension Credit Act couple who has reached the qualifying age for state pension credit and the other member has not reached that age; and

(b) one of the savings in the sub-paragraphs of article 4(1) of the Welfare Reform Act 2012 (Commencement No.31 and Savings and Transitional Provisions and Commencement No.21 and 23 and Transitional and Transitory Provisions (Amendment)) Order 2019 applies and the saving has not ceased to have effect under article 4(2) of that Order.

(6) Paragraph (1) does not apply to a claim for a tax credit where a person makes or persons make a claim for child tax credit or working tax credit and on the date on which he or she (or they) makes or make the claim he or she (or they) has or have an award of working tax credit or child tax credit respectively.

(7) Paragraph (1) does not apply to a claim for a tax credit where a person has or had, or persons have or had, an award of child tax credit or working tax credit in respect of a tax year and that person or those persons makes or make (or is or are treated as making) a claim for that tax credit for the next tax year.

(8) For the purposes of this regulation—

(a) "polygamous marriage" has the same meaning as in regulation 3(5) of the Universal Credit Regulations;

(b) "State Pension Credit Act couple" means a couple as defined in section 17(1) of the State Pension Credit Act 2002,

and a reference to the date on which a claim for a tax credit is made is a reference to the date on which such claim is made or treated as made as provided for in the Tax Credits (Claims and Notifications) Regulations 2002.]

AMENDMENT

1. Universal Credit (Transitional Provisions) Amendment Regulations 2022 (SI 2022/752) reg.4 (July 25, 2022).

Termination of awards of certain existing benefits: new claimant partners

2.748

7.—(1) This regulation applies where—

(a) a person ("A") who was previously entitled to universal credit [² . . .] ceases to be so entitled on becoming a member of a couple;

(b) the other member of the couple ("the new claimant partner") was not entitled to universal credit [² . . .] immediately before formation of the couple; [⁵ and]

(c) the couple is treated, in accordance with regulation 9(8) of the Claims and Payments Regulations, as having made a claim for universal credit. [⁵ ...]

(2) Subject to paragraphs (4) and (5), where this regulation applies, all awards of income support or housing benefit to which the new claimant partner would (were it not for the effect of these Regulations) have been entitled during the relevant period are to terminate, by virtue of this regulation—

(a) on the day before the first date on which the joint claimants are entitled to universal credit in connection with the claim; or

(b) if the joint claimants are not entitled to universal credit, on the day before the first date on which they would have been so entitled, if all of the basic and financial conditions applicable to them had been met; or

(c) if the new claimant partner became entitled to an award after the date on which it would otherwise terminate under sub-paragraph (a) or (b), at the beginning of the first day of entitlement to that award.

(3) For the purposes of this regulation, "the relevant period" is the period starting with the first day of the assessment period (in relation to A's award of universal credit) during which A and the new claimant partner formed a couple and ending with the date of formation of the couple.

(4) Where the new claimant partner was entitled during the relevant period to income support, he or she was at that time a member of a couple and the award included an amount in respect of the new claimant partner and their partner at that time ("P"), the award of income support terminates, by virtue of this regulation, on the date on which the new claimant partner and P ceased to be a couple for the purposes of the Income Support (General) Regulations 1987, unless it terminates on that date in accordance with other legislative provision, or terminated on an earlier date.

(5) An award of housing benefit to which the new claimant partner is entitled does not terminate by virtue of this regulation where—

(a) the award is in respect of [¹ specified accommodation] [³ or temporary accommodation]; [⁴...]

(b) the new claimant partner leaves the accommodation in respect of which housing benefit was paid, in order to live with A [⁴; or

(c) the new claimant partner has reached the qualifying age for state pension credit and the award is made in accordance with the 2006 (SPC) Regulations.]

(6) Where an award terminates by virtue of this regulation, any legislative provision under which the award terminates on a later date does not apply.

(7) Where the new claimant partner was, immediately before forming a couple with A, treated by regulation 11 as being entitled to a tax credit, the new claimant partner is to be treated, for the purposes of the 2002 Act, as having made a claim for the tax credit in question for the current tax year.

AMENDMENTS

1. Universal Credit (Transitional Provisions) (Amendment) Regulations 2014 (SI 2014/1626) reg.3 (November 3, 2014).

2. Universal Credit (Digital Service) Amendment Regulations 2014 (SI 2014/2887) reg.3(3) (November 26, 2014).

3. Universal Credit (Miscellaneous Amendments, Saving and Transitional Provision) Regulations 2018 (SI 2018/65) reg.6(6)(b) (April 11, 2018).

4. Universal Credit (Persons who have attained state pension credit qualifying age) (Amendment) Regulations 2020 (SI 2020/655) reg.6(5) (November 25, 2020).

5. Universal Credit (Transitional Provisions) Amendment Regulations 2022 (SI 2022/752) reg.5(2) (July 25, 2022).

DEFINITIONS

"the 2002 Act"—see reg.2(1).
"A"—para.7(1)(a).
"the Act"—see reg.2(1).
"assessment period"—*ibid.*
"the Claims and Payments Regulations"—*ibid.*
"housing benefit"—*ibid.*
"income support"—*ibid.*

"new claimant partner"—*ibid.*
"partner"—*ibid.*
"the relevant period"—para.(3).
"specified accommodation"—see reg.2(1).
"tax year"—*ibid.*

GENERAL NOTE

2.749   In broad terms this provision performs the same function as reg.16 of the 2013 Transitional Regulations, with various modifications. As a general rule, all existing benefit or tax credit awards will terminate when an award of universal credit is made to a newly formed couple, one of whom was previously entitled to universal credit and the other to an existing benefit (or tax credit). The mechanics of this process are different for existing benefit and tax credits awards respectively.

Thus where the conditions in para.(1) are met, the new claimant partner's award of income support or housing benefit will terminate as provided for in para.(2). Para.(4) deals with the timing of the termination of an earlier award of income support where the new claimant partner was receiving that benefit together with their own previous partner ("P"). Para.(5) provides for special cases where an award of housing benefit does not end, despite the general rule.

The process is rather more complicated with tax credits – where the new partner is treated as having an ongoing tax credit award by virtue of reg.11, then they are treated as having made a new claim for the current year, whether or not they actually have made such a claim (para.(7)), and any award made under such a deemed claim likewise terminates on the day before the start of the joint award of universal credit.

Paragraph (1)

2.750   The amendments to para.(1)(a) and (b) (the omission of the words "as a single parent") are each subject to the saving provision as set out in reg.5 of the Universal Credit (Digital Service) Amendment Regulations 2014 (SI 2014/2887).

Paragraph (7)

2.751   See further reg.11.

Termination of awards of certain existing benefits: other claimants

2.752   **8.**—(1) This regulation applies where—

(a) a claim for universal credit (other than a claim which is treated, in accordance with regulation 9(8) of the Claims and Payments Regulations, as having been made) is made[⁴, whether or not subsequently withdrawn].

(b) [⁴...]

(2) [²Where] this regulation applies, all awards of [³ [² . . .]] or a tax credit to which the claimant (or, in the case of joint claimants, either of them) is entitled on the date on which the claim is made are to terminate, by virtue of this regulation—

(a) on the day before the first date on which the claimant is entitled to universal credit in connection with the claim; or

(b) if the claimant is not entitled to universal credit, on the day before the first date on which he or she would have been so entitled, if all of the basic and financial conditions applicable to the claimant had been met.

[² (2A) Subject to paragraph (3), where this regulation applies, an award of [³ income support or] housing benefit to which the claimant is entitled on the day mentioned in paragraph (2)(a) or (b) terminates on the last day of the period of two weeks beginning with the day after that day (whether or not the person is also entitled to an award of [³ . . .] a tax credit).]

[⁴(2B) This regulation does not apply in the case of a single claimant who has reached the qualifying age for state pension credit or in the case of joint claimants who have both reached the qualifying age for state pension credit.]

(3) An award of housing benefit to which a claimant is entitled in respect of [¹ specified accommodation] [² or temporary accommodation] does not terminate by virtue of this regulation.

(4) Where this regulation applies and the claimant (or, in the case of joint claimants, either of them) is treated by regulation 11 as being entitled to a tax credit—

- (a) the claimant (or, as the case may be, the relevant claimant) is to be treated, for the purposes of the 2002 Act and this regulation, as having made a claim for the tax credit in question for the current tax year; and
- (b) if the claimant (or the relevant claimant) is entitled on the date on which the claim for universal credit was made to an award of a tax credit which is made in respect of a claim which is treated as having been made by virtue of sub-paragraph (a), that award is to terminate, by virtue of this regulation—
  - (i) on the day before the first date on which the claimant is entitled to universal credit; or
  - (ii) if the claimant is not entitled to universal credit, on the day before the first date on which he or she would have been so entitled, if all of the basic and financial conditions applicable to the claimant had been met.

(5) Where an award terminates by virtue of this regulation, any legislative provision under which the award terminates on a later date does not apply.

AMENDMENTS

1. Universal Credit (Transitional Provisions) (Amendment) Regulations 2014 (SI 2014/1626) reg.3 (November 3, 2014).
2. Universal Credit (Miscellaneous Amendments, Saving and Transitional Provision) Regulations 2018 (SI 2018/65) reg.6(7) (April 11, 2018).
3. Universal Credit (Managed Migration Pilot and Miscellaneous Amendments) Regulations 2019 (SI 2019/1152) reg.4(3) (July 22, 2020).
4. Universal Credit (Transitional Provisions) Amendment Regulations 2022 (SI 2022/752) reg.5(3) (July 25, 2022).

DEFINITIONS

"the 2002 Act"—see reg.2(1).
"the Act"—*ibid.*
"the Claims and Payments Regulations"—*ibid.*
"housing benefit"—*ibid.*
"income support"—*ibid.*
"specified accommodation"—*ibid.*
"tax credit"—*ibid.*
"tax year"—*ibid.*

GENERAL NOTE

2.753   As a general rule, all existing benefit or tax credit awards will terminate when an award of universal credit is made to a claimant. This regulation essentially performs the same function as reg.7 but for claimants who do not have a new claimant partner.

In *AD (A child, by her litigation friend TD) & PR v SSWP* [2019] EWHC 462 (Admin) the High Court had held that the failure to provide transitional protection for claimants who transferred to universal credit following an incorrect legacy benefit decision was not unlawful.

However, the High Court's decision was reversed by the Court of Appeal in *R (TD & Ors) v SSWP* [2020] EWCA Civ 618.

TD was a single parent entitled to IS, CTC (with a disabled child element) and carer's allowance. Her total entitlement (excluding HB) was £1,005.45 per month. She also received DLA, on behalf of her daughter, of £333.23 per month. In March 2017, the DWP stopped her IS award and her Job Centre advised her to claim universal credit, which was awarded in April 2017. TD's universal credit award was £872.90 a month, which was £136.99 a month less than she had been entitled under the legacy benefits. TD was unable to return to legacy benefits due to the application of regs 8 and 13. In August 2018, the DWP increased her daughter's DLA, meaning she was entitled to the highest rate of the disabled child element of CTC (up to April 2017) and, thereafter, the highest rate of the disabled child element of universal credit. As a result, the household's combined entitlement was now at the same level under universal credit as it would have been had TD continued to receive her legacy benefits. However, TD continued to seek a declaration and damages for the distress caused to them resulting from the drop in income at the time of transfer. She argued that the declaration sought would also benefit others in the same position who remained on a lower entitlement under universal credit.

PR was in receipt of ESA with the SDP and support component, and was also entitled to PIP when, in March 2017, the DWP stopped her ESA. She challenged that decision and claimed universal credit in April 2017. PR's legacy benefits entitled her to receive £814.67 per month, while her universal credit award was £636.58 per month, £178.09 less. The ESA decision was reversed in August 2017 but, as with TD, the 2014 Regulations precluded her from receiving or claiming any legacy benefits after her claim for universal credit.

TD (and her daughter) and PR were given permission for the judicial review challenge on three grounds: (1) that the treatment amounted to unlawful discrimination contrary to art.14 read with art.1 of the First Protocol to the ECHR (and in the case of TD and her daughter, it was said that their art.8 rights were also engaged); (2) that the decision of the Secretary of State to prevent those in the position of these claimants from returning to the legacy system, without providing for transitional protection, was irrational; and (3) that the SSWP had failed to comply with her Public Sector Equality Duty (PSED). In the High Court, May J. dismissed all three grounds.

However, the Court of Appeal accepted the Appellants' argument that, in their cases, the absence of transitional protection constituted discrimination contrary to art.14 of the ECHR. For art.14 purposes, the comparator group was, according to the Court of Appeal, "people who were entitled to legacy benefits and in whose cases no error was made by the Respondent". The High Court's analysis was flawed because, in considering whether the difference of treatment to which the Appellants had been subjected was justified, the judge failed to decide that matter for herself. Instead, the judge rejected the Appellants' case because she was persuaded that justification had been adequately considered by the Secretary of State. The Court of Appeal went on to decide that the difference of treatment was not justified and its effect was manifestly disproportionate for the Appellants, so that their rights under art.14 had been breached. The key consideration was identified in para.83 of the Court's judgment:

"83...these Appellants were treated as they were despite their successful reviews, for reasons to do with administrative cost and complexity, which have nothing to do with the merits of their cases; and that the only reason in reality why they moved from legacy benefits to UC was as a result of errors of law by the state itself."

The Court of Appeal gave a declaration that the Appellants' art.14 rights had been breached but added "it will be a matter for the Secretary of State to decide how to respond to a declaration". Whether or not the response will be to introduce transitional protection for all claimants, rather than limiting it to those undergoing "managed migration", remains to be seen. The Court's decision was not based on a finding that the absence of transitional protection was, in general, discrimination contrary to art.14. However, nor did the Court rule that its absence was, in general, justified. As explained above, the Court decided the case by reference to the, hopefully, infrequent circumstance of a misadvised claimant. Whether, in the absence of such circumstances, the UK Government's policy of granting transitional protection to universal credit "managed migrants", but not "natural migrants", falls foul of art.14 remains to be determined.

[¹Transitional housing payment

8A. Where an award of housing benefit terminates under regulation 8 [² [³or 46]]—

2.754

(a) the claimant is to be treated for the purposes of the Housing Benefit Regulations 2006 as entitled to universal credit during the period of two weeks mentioned in regulation 8(2A) [² [³or 46(1)]], even if no decision has been made on the claim; [²...]

(b) if a claim for universal credit is made because the claimant moves to new accommodation occupied as the claimant's home, then, notwithstanding anything in the Housing Benefit Regulations 2006, housing benefit is to be paid directly to the claimant during the period of two weeks mentioned in regulation 8(2A) [² [³or 46(1)]] [²; and

(c) if a claim for universal credit is made by a notified person then, notwithstanding anything in the Housing Benefit Regulations 2006, the weekly amount of housing benefit to which the person is entitled for that period of two weeks is the same as the weekly amount they were entitled to on the first day of that period.]

AMENDMENTS

1. Universal Credit (Miscellaneous Amendments, Saving and Transitional Provision) Regulations 2018 (SI 2018/65) reg.6(8) (April 11, 2018).

2. Universal Credit (Managed Migration Pilot and Miscellaneous Amendments) Regulations 2019 (SI 2019/1152) reg.3(5) (July 24, 2019).

3. Universal Credit (Transitional Provisions) Amendment Regulations 2022 (SI 2022/752) reg.11 and Sch. para.1(4) (July 25, 2022).

DEFINITION

"housing benefit"—see reg.2(1).

GENERAL NOTE

The amendments to reg.8 effective from April 11, 2018 provide for a transitional housing payment for claimants who migrate to universal credit when they are in receipt of housing benefit. In addition, the new reg.8(2A) allows a housing benefit award to continue for a period of two weeks beyond the day on which the person becomes entitled to universal credit. The new reg.8A in turn provides that, pending

2.755

the decision on the claim, the claimant is treated as entitled to universal credit for the purposes of the housing benefit award, and where the claimant makes a claim for universal credit because they have moved home, housing benefit will be paid directly to the claimant for the period of two weeks beginning with the day on which they become entitled to universal credit. The references to regs 46 and 47 provide for the amount of housing benefit to be frozen during the two-week run-on period in a case where the claimant is moved to universal credit.

[¹Effect on universal credit award of two week run-on of income support, income-based jobseeker's allowance and income-related employment and support allowance

2.756   **8B.** In a case where an award of income support, income-based job-seeker's allowance or income-related employment and support allowance is to continue for two weeks after the commencement of an award of universal credit by virtue of regulation 8(2A)[²or 46(1)] or by virtue of regulation 5 (two week run-on of income-based jobseeker's allowance and income-related employment and support allowance: day appointed for abolition) of the Universal Credit (Managed Migration Pilot and Miscellaneous Amendments) Regulations 2019—

(a)   regulation 79 of the Universal Credit Regulations applies as if the benefit in question was not included in the list of welfare benefits in section 96(10) of the Act (benefit cap); and

(b)   in a case where the claimant has become entitled to an award of new style JSA or new style ESA on the termination of an award of income-based jobseeker's allowance or income-related employment and support allowance, the claimant is to be treated, for the purposes of regulation 73 of the Universal Credit Regulations (unearned income calculated monthly), as if they had been entitled to that award of new style JSA or new style ESA from the first day of the award of universal credit.]

AMENDMENTS

1. Universal Credit (Managed Migration Pilot and Miscellaneous Amendments) Regulations 2019 (SI 2019/1152) reg.4(4) (July 22, 2020).

2. Universal Credit (Transitional Provisions) Amendment Regulations 2022 (SI 2022/752) reg.11 and Sch. para.1(5) (July 25, 2022).

GENERAL NOTE

2.757   This regulation provides for an award of income support, income-based jobseek-er's allowance or income-related employment and support allowance to continue for two weeks beyond the date on which it would otherwise have terminated as result of a claim for universal credit (or, in a managed migration case, a failure to make a claim by the deadline day). This reflects a recommendation by the SSAC, which was concerned that claimants who were reliant on (legacy) benefits paid fortnightly should not bear the risk from the Government's policy that universal credit is paid monthly. In the absence of such a run-on, claimants would otherwise be offered the choice between financial hardship (while waiting for the first universal credit payment) or getting into debt with the Department (by requesting an advance payment).

Treatment of ongoing entitlement to certain benefits: benefit cap

2.758   **9.** (1) This regulation applies where a claimant who is a new claimant partner, or who has (in accordance with regulation 26 of the Universal

Credit Regulations) been awarded universal credit in respect of a period preceding the date on which the claim for universal credit was made or treated as made—

(a) is entitled, in respect of the whole or part of the first assessment period for universal credit, to a welfare benefit (other than universal credit) mentioned in [¹section 96(10) of the Act (benefit cap)]; and

(b) is entitled to housing benefit at any time during the first assessment period for universal credit, or would be so entitled were it not for the effect of these Regulations.

(2) Where this regulation applies, regulation 79 of the Universal Credit Regulations applies, in relation to the claimant, as if the benefit in question was not included in the list of welfare benefits in [¹ section 96(10) of the Act].

AMENDMENT

1. Benefit Cap (Housing Benefit and Universal Credit) (Amendment) Regulations 2016 (SI 2016/909) reg.5(a) (November 7, 2016).

DEFINITIONS

"assessment period"—see reg.2(1).
"housing benefit"—*ibid.*
"new claimant partner"—*ibid.*
"the Universal Credit Regulations"—*ibid.*

GENERAL NOTE

This regulation provides for entitlement to some benefits (i.e. those listed in reg.79(4) of the Universal Credit Regulations 2013) to be disregarded for the purposes of the benefit cap during the claimant's first assessment period for universal credit. This applies where a claimant is entitled to universal credit from a date before the date on which they made a claim, or were treated as making a claim, and they were also previously entitled to housing benefit (which may already have been subject to the benefit cap). **7.759**

Treatment of overpayments

10.—(1) This regulation applies where— **2.760**

(a) an award of universal credit is made to a claimant who was previously entitled to an existing benefit other than a tax credit or a joint-claim jobseeker's allowance; and

(b) a payment of the existing benefit is made which includes payment ("the overpayment") in respect of a period—

    (i) during which the claimant is not entitled to that benefit (including non-entitlement which arises from termination of an award by virtue of an order made under section 150(3) of the Act or regulation 7, 8, or 14); and

    (ii) which falls within an assessment period for universal credit.

(2) Where this regulation applies, for the purposes of calculating the amount of an award of universal credit in respect of an assessment period—

(a) regulation 66 of the Universal Credit Regulations (what is included in unearned income?) applies as if the overpayment which was made in respect of that assessment period were added to the descriptions of unearned income in paragraph (1)(b) of that regulation; and

    (b)   regulation 73 of the Universal Credit Regulations (unearned income calculated monthly) does not apply to the overpayment.

(3) In so far as any overpayment is taken into account in calculating the amount of an award of universal credit in accordance with this regulation, that payment may not be recovered as an overpayment under—

    (a)   the Social Security (Payments on account, Overpayments and Recovery) Regulations 1988;

    (b)   the Housing Benefit Regulations 2006; or

    (c)   [¹ the 2006 (SPC) Regulations].

AMENDMENT

1. Universal Credit (Persons who have attained state pension credit qualifying age) (Amendment) Regulations 2020 (SI 2020/655) reg.6(6) (November 25, 2020).

DEFINITIONS

"the Act"—see reg.2(1).
"assessment period"—*ibid.*
"existing benefit"—*ibid.*
"joint-claim jobseeker's allowance"—*ibid.*
"overpayment"—para.(1)(b).
"tax credit"—see reg.2(1).
"the Universal Credit Regulations"—*ibid.*

GENERAL NOTE

2.761   This regulation provides that overpayments of existing benefits (other than joint-claim jobseeker's allowance or tax credits) that may arise on transition to universal credit are to be off-set against entitlement to universal credit (para.(1)). Thus, overpayments of existing benefits which may arise on transition to universal credit can be offset as unearned income against the claimant's entitlement to universal credit (para.(2)) and may not then be recovered under other legislation (para.(3)). This is because it will be recovered as unearned income from the universal credit award rather than as an excess payment under existing overpayments legislation.

[¹ Arrears of benefit disregarded as capital

2.762   **10A.**—(1) This regulation applies in relation to the calculation of an award of universal credit (the "current award") where the claimant has received a payment of arrears of benefit [²or armed forces independence payment], or a payment made to compensate for arrears due to the non-payment of benefit [²or armed forces independence payment], of £5,000 or more, and the following conditions are met—

    (a)   the payment—

        (i)   is received during the current award; or

        (ii)   was received during an award of an existing benefit or state pension credit (the "earlier award") and the claimant became entitled to the current award within one month of the date of termination of the earlier award;

    (b)   in the case of a payment falling within sub-paragraph (a)(i), it would be disregarded from the calculation of the claimant's capital if the claimant were entitled to an existing benefit or state pension credit;

(c) in the case of a payment falling within sub-paragraph (a)(ii), it was disregarded from the calculation of the claimant's capital for the purposes of the earlier award; and

(d) the period of entitlement to benefit [²or armed forces independence payment] to which the payment relates commences before the first date on which, by virtue of section 33 of the Act (abolition of benefits), no claimant is entitled to an existing benefit.

(2) Where this regulation applies, notwithstanding anything in the Universal Credit Regulations, the payment is to be disregarded from the calculation of the claimant's capital for 12 months from the date of receipt of the payment, or until the termination of the current award (if later).]

[²(3) "Armed forces independence payment" means armed forces independence payment under the Armed Forces and Reserve Forces (Compensation Scheme) Order 2011.]

AMENDMENTS

1. Social Security (Treatment of Arrears of Benefit) Regulations 2018 (SI 2018/932) reg.8 (September 11, 2018).
2. Social Security (Capital Disregards) (Amendment) Regulations 2019 (SI 2019/1314) reg.9(2) (October 31, 2019).

DEFINITIONS

"armed forces independence payment"—see para.(3).
"current award"—see para.(1).
"earlier award"—see para.(1)(a)(ii).
"existing benefit"—see reg.2(1).

GENERAL NOTE

The UC Regs 2013 provide for arrears of a means-tested benefit, or a payment to compensate for arrears, to be disregarded for a period of 12 months from the date the payment is received (see Sch.10 para.18). As originally enacted, there was no provision for such a payment to be disregarded for a longer period if it had been paid out because of official error. This regulation provides for the longer disregard to apply until the termination of the universal credit award where a payment of arrears of £5,000 or more has been received during an earlier award of an income-related benefit and the claimant becomes entitled to universal credit within one month of their earlier award terminating, or where it has been received during the universal credit award. Thus, the effect is that the arrears in question may be disregarded for the life of the benefit award rather than for the usual maximum of 52 weeks. This additional disregard only applies to a payment that relates to a period of entitlement to benefit which begins before migration of existing benefits to universal credit is completed.

2.763

[¹Arrears of maternity allowance disregarded as capital

10B.—(1) This regulation applies in relation to the calculation of an award of universal credit where—

2.764

(a) the conditions set out in regulation 10A(1)(a) to (d) are met; and
(b) the claimant has received a payment of arrears of maternity allowance, or a payment made to compensate for arrears due to the non-payment of maternity allowance, of under £5,000.

(2) Where this regulation applies, notwithstanding anything in the Universal Credit Regulations, the payment is to be disregarded from the calculation of the claimant's capital for 12 months from the date of receipt of the payment.

(3) "Maternity allowance" means a maternity allowance under section 35 of the Social Security Contributions and Benefits Act 1992 (state maternity allowance for employed or self-employed earner).]

<small>AMENDMENT</small>

1. Social Security (Capital Disregards) (Amendment) Regulations 2019 (SI 2019/1314) reg.9(3) (October 31, 2019).

<small>DEFINITIONS</small>

"maternity allowance" para.(3).
"Universal Credit Regulations" reg.2(1).

[¹Compensatory payment disregarded as capital

2.765   **10C.**—(1) This regulation applies in relation to the calculation of an award of universal credit where—

(a) the claimant has received a payment made to rectify, or to compensate for, an error made by an officer of the Department for Work and Pensions which was not caused or materially contributed to by any person outside the Department and which prevented or delayed an assessment of the claimant's entitlement to contributory employment and support allowance; and

(b) the payment is received before the first date on which, by virtue of section 33 of the Act (abolition of benefits), no claimant is entitled to an existing benefit.

(2) Where this regulation applies and the amount of the payment is less than £5,000, the payment is to be disregarded from the calculation of the claimant's capital for 12 months from the date of receipt of the payment.

(3) Where—

(a) this regulation applies;

(b) the amount of the payment is £5,000 or more; and

(c) the conditions set out in regulation 10A(1)(a) and (c) are met,

the payment is to be disregarded from the calculation of the claimant's capital for 12 months from the date of receipt of the payment, or until the termination of the current award (if later).]

<small>AMENDMENT</small>

1. Social Security (Income and Capital) (Miscellaneous Amendments) Regulations 2020 (SI 2020/618) reg.9 (July 15, 2020).

<small>GENERAL NOTE</small>

2.766   Universal credit replaces income-related ESA but not contribution-based ESA. Since, however, it is not possible to have entitlement to both universal credit and the original versions of ESA, the Government introduced new-style ESA in 2013 to provide a benefit which is wholly and exclusively based on National Insurance contributions, and so can be paid alongside universal credit. However, extra-statutory payments have had to be made to provide redress to people affected by initial errors in the way claims for new-style ESA were handled. These extra-statutory payments are intended to restore a claimant's award to as near as possible the amount that should have been payable, were it not for the incorrect advice. Where this payment would otherwise affect an individual's award of universal credit, it will be disregarded under this provision. HM Treasury has provided the DWP with the appropriate cover to disregard the extra-statutory payments for the interim period until the new regulation provided a firm statutory backing.

Ongoing awards of tax credits

11. (1) For the purposes of [²these Regulations]— 2.767
   (a) a person is to be treated as being entitled to working tax credit with effect from the start of the current tax year even though a decision has not been made under section 14 of the 2002 Act in respect of a claim for that tax credit for that tax year, if the person was entitled to working tax credit for the previous tax year and any of the cases specified in paragraph (2) applies; and
   (b) a person is to be treated as being entitled to child tax credit with effect from the start of the current tax year even though a decision has not been made under section 14 of the 2002 Act in respect of a claim for that tax credit for that tax year, if the person was entitled to child tax credit for the previous tax year and any of the cases specified in paragraph (2) applies[²;]
   [²and references to an award of a tax credit are to be read accordingly].
   (2) The cases are—
   (a) a final notice has not been given to the person under section 17 of the 2002 Act in respect of the previous tax year;
   (b) a final notice has been given, which includes provision by virtue of subsection (2) or (4) of section 17, or a combination of those subsections and subsection (6) and—
      (i) the date specified in the notice for the purposes of section 17(2) and (4) or, where different dates are specified, the later of them, has not yet passed and no claim for a tax credit for the current tax year has been made, or treated as made; or
      (ii) a claim for a tax credit has been made, or treated as made, on or before the date mentioned in paragraph (i), but no decision has been made in relation to that claim under section 14(1) of the 2002 Act;
   (c) a final notice has been given, no claim for a tax credit for the current year has been made, or treated as made, and no decision has been made under section 18(1) of the 2002 Act in respect of entitlement to a tax credit for the previous tax year; [¹. . .]
[¹(ca) a final notice has been given and the person made a declaration in response to a requirement included in that notice by virtue of section 17(2)(a), (4)(a) or (6)(a), or any combination of those provisions—
      (i) by the date specified on the final notice;
      (ii) if not in accordance with paragraph (i), within 30 days following the date on the notice to the person that payments of tax credit under section 24(4) of the 2002 Act have ceased due to the person's failure to make the declaration by the date specified in the final notice; or
      (iii) if not in accordance with paragraph (i) or (ii), before 31 January in the tax year following the period to which the final notice

relates and, in the opinion of Her Majesty's Revenue and Customs, the person had good reason for not making the declaration in accordance with paragraph (i) or (ii); or]

(d) a final notice has been given and—

    (i) the person did not make a declaration in response to provision included in that notice by virtue of section 17(2)(a), (4)(a) or (6)(a), or any combination of those provisions, by the date specified in the notice;

    (ii) the person was given due notice that payments of tax credit under section 24(4) of the 2002 Act had ceased due to his or her failure to make the declaration; and

    (iii) the person's claim for universal credit is made during the period of 30 days starting with the date on the notice referred to in paragraph (ii) or, where the person is a new claimant partner, notification of formation of a couple with a person entitled to universal credit is given to the Secretary of State during that period.

AMENDMENTS

1. Universal Credit (Miscellaneous Amendments, Saving and Transitional Provision) Regulations 2018 (SI 2018/65) reg.6(9) (February 14, 2018).

2. Universal Credit (Managed Migration Pilot and Miscellaneous Amendments) Regulations 2019 (SI 2019/1152) reg.3(6) (July 24, 2019).

DEFINITIONS

"the 2002 Act"—see reg.2(1).
"new claimant partner"—*ibid.*
"tax credit"—*ibid.*
"tax year"—*ibid.*

GENERAL NOTE

2.768   This regulation provides for a claimant to be treated as entitled to an award of a tax credit in certain cases, for the purposes of regs.7 and 8.

Modification of tax credits legislation: overpayments and penalties

2.769   **12.** (1) This regulation applies where—

(a) a claim for universal credit is made, or is treated as having been made; [³and]

(b) the claimant is, or was at any time during the tax year in which the claim is made or treated as made, entitled to a tax credit [³...];

(c) [³...].

(2) Where this regulation applies, the 2002 Act applies in relation to the claimant with the following modifications.

(3) In section 28—

(a) in subsection (1)—

    (i) after "tax year" in both places where it occurs, insert "or part tax year";

    [² (ii) in paragraph (b), for the words from "as if it were" to the end substitute "as an overpayment of universal credit"]

(b) [²...]

(c) omit subsection (5);

(d) in subsection (6) omit "(apart from subsection (5))".

[¹ (4) [². . .]]

(5) In section 48 after the definition of "overpayment" insert—

""part tax year" means a period of less than a year beginning with 6th April and ending with the date on which the award of a tax credit terminated,".

(6) In Schedule 2, in paragraph 6(1)(a) and (c) and (2)(a), after "for the tax year" insert "or part tax year".

AMENDMENTS

1. Universal Credit (Transitional Provisions) (Amendment) Regulations 2016 (SI 2016/232) reg.2 (April 1, 2016).
2. Tax Credits (Exercise of Functions in relation to Northern Ireland and Notices for Recovery of Tax Credit Overpayments) Order 2017 (2017/781) art.7 (September 25, 2017).
3. Universal Credit (Transitional Provisions) Amendment Regulations 2022 (SI 2022/752) reg.5(4) (July 25, 2022).

DEFINITIONS

"the 2002 Act"—see reg.2(1).
"the Act"—*ibid.*
"tax credit"—*ibid.*
"tax year"—*ibid.*

GENERAL NOTE

This regulation provides that, where a claim for universal credit is made by a claimant who was previously entitled to a tax credit, the Tax Credits Act 2002 is to apply to that claimant with certain modifications. For a full analysis of the impact of these modifications, see *HMRC v AS (TC)* [2023] UKUT 67 (AAC). The effect is that that any overpayments of tax credits may be treated as overpayments of universal credit and appropriate time limits apply in relation to the imposition of penalties. 2.770

[¹ Modification of tax credits legislation: finalisation of tax credits

12A. (1) This regulation applies where— 2.771

(a) a claim for universal credit is made, or is treated as having been made;

(b) the claimant is, or was at any time during the tax year in which the claim is made or treated as made, entitled to a tax credit [²...]

(c) [²...]

(2) Subject to paragraph (3), where this regulation applies, the amount of the tax credit to which the person is entitled is to be calculated in accordance with the 2002 Act and regulations made under that Act, as modified by the Schedule to these Regulations ("the modified legislation").

(3) Where, in the opinion of the Commissioners for Her Majesty's Revenue and Customs, it is not reasonably practicable to apply the modified legislation in relation to any case or category of cases, the 2002 Act and regulations made under that Act are to apply without modification in that case or category of cases.]

AMENDMENTS

1. Universal Credit (Transitional Provisions) (Amendment) Regulations 2014 (SI 2014/1626) reg.4 (October 13, 2014).

2. Universal Credit (Transitional Provisions) Amendment Regulations 2022 (SI 2022/752) reg.5(5) (July 25, 2022).

DEFINITIONS

"the 2002 Act"—see reg.2(1).
"the 2002 Act"—*ibid.*
"the modified legislation"—para.(2).
"tax credit"—see reg.2(1).
"tax year"—*ibid.*

GENERAL NOTE

2.772   This amendment is designed to smooth the transition from receipt of tax credits to an award of universal credit. It re-instates provision for in-year finalisation of tax credits for universal credit claimants (there was no equivalent to reg.17 of, and the Schedule to, the 2013 Transitional Regulations in the original version of the 2014 Transitional Regulations). By doing so, this provision allows tax credits awards to be finalised during the relevant tax year when a tax credit claimant makes the transition to universal credit (see paras.(1) and (2) and the Schedule), rather than after the end of the tax year. This is intended to reduce administrative complexity and confusion for the claimant by providing a clean break from tax credits, thus avoiding the claimant having to revert to providing HMRC with information about their circumstances and income after they have been receiving universal credit for some time. It also should thereby, in theory at least, ensure the claimant has a single interaction with HMRC so that HMRC only have to deal with their case once, as both the stopping of a tax credits award and the finalising of the award are dealt with upon transition to universal credit. In practice the modifications to the normal rules involve considerable complexity; for a full analysis see *HMRC v AS (TC)* [2023] UKUT 67 (AAC), which emphasises that the focus of the modified rules is on income *received in* the part-year period rather than income *attributable to* the part-year period.

    Although the intention is that in-year finalisation of tax credits awards is the default approach in the majority of cases, provision has been made (see para.(3)) to allow HMRC to continue to finalise tax credits awards after the end of the tax year, if they think that it is not practicable to apply the modified legislation to a particular case or class of case, e.g. where it proved difficult to verify income that is particularly complex, such as those cases including particular combinations of self-employed and other income. Para.(3) might also be invoked as a contingency to guard against unforeseen operational or IT difficulties.

Appeals etc relating to certain existing benefits

2.773   **13.**—(1) This regulation applies where, after an award of universal credit has been made to a claimant—

    (a) an appeal against a decision relating to the entitlement of the claimant to income support, housing benefit or a tax credit (a "relevant benefit") is finally determined;

    (b) a decision relating to the claimant's entitlement to income support is revised under section 9 of the Social Security Act 1998 ("the 1998 Act") or superseded under section 10 of that Act;

    (c) a decision relating to the claimant's entitlement to housing benefit is revised or superseded under Schedule 7 to the Child Support, Pensions and Social Security Act 2000; or

    (d) a decision relating to the claimant's entitlement to a tax credit is revised under section 19 or 20 of the 2002 Act, or regulations made under section 21 of that Act, or is varied or cancelled under section 21A of that Act.

(2) Where the claimant is a new claimant partner and, as a result of determination of the appeal or, as the case may be, revision or supersession of the decision the claimant would (were it not for the effect of these Regulations) be entitled to income support or housing benefit during the relevant period mentioned in regulation 7(3), awards of those benefits are to terminate in accordance with regulation 7.

(3) Where the claimant is not a new claimant partner and, as a result of determination of the appeal or, as the case may be, revision, supersession, variation or cancellation of the decision, the claimant would (were it not for the effect of these Regulations) be entitled to a relevant benefit on the date on which the claim for universal credit was made, awards of relevant benefits are to terminate in accordance with regulation 8 [¹ [² or 46]].

(4) The Secretary of State is to consider whether it is appropriate to revise under section 9 of the 1998 Act the decision in relation to entitlement to universal credit or, if that decision has been superseded under section 10 of that Act, the decision as so superseded (in either case, "the UC decision").

(5) Where it appears to the Secretary of State to be appropriate to revise the UC decision, it is to be revised in such manner as appears to the Secretary of State to be necessary to take account of—

(a) the decision of the First-tier Tribunal, Upper Tribunal or court, or, as the case may be, the decision relating to entitlement to a relevant benefit, as revised, superseded, varied or cancelled; and

(b) any finding of fact by the First-tier Tribunal, Upper Tribunal or court.

AMENDMENTS

1. Universal Credit (Managed Migration Pilot and Miscellaneous Amendments) Regulations 2019 (SI 2019/1152) reg.4(7) (July 22, 2020).
2. Universal Credit (Transitional Provisions) Amendment Regulations 2022 (SI 2022/752) reg.11 and Sch. para.1(6) (July 25, 2022).

DEFINITIONS

"the 1998 Act"—para.(1)(b).
"the 2002 Act"—see reg.2(1).
"First-tier Tribunal"—*ibid.*
"housing benefit"—*ibid.*
"income support"—*ibid.*
"new claimant partner"—*ibid.*
"relevant benefit"—para.(1)(a).
"tax credit"—see reg.2(1).
"the UC decision"—para.(4).
"Upper Tribunal"—see reg.2(1).

GENERAL NOTE

This regulation deals with appeals which are determined, and decisions about existing benefits which are revised or superseded, after the appellant has become entitled to universal credit (see para.(1)). Entitlement to income support, housing benefit or a tax credit arising from an appeal, revision or supersession will terminate in accordance with regulation 7 or 8 (paras.(2) and (3)) and a decision made about entitlement to universal credit may be revised to take account of any findings of fact by the relevant appeal body (paras.(4) and (5)). The equivalent provision in the 2013 Transitional Regulations (reg.18) applied only to new claimants partners; this provision applies to all claimants and not just new claimant partners. See further the note to reg.8 above.

2.774

Appeals etc relating to universal credit

2.775   **14.**—(1) This regulation applies where—

(a) a decision is made that a claimant is not entitled to universal credit ("the UC decision");

(b) the claimant becomes entitled to income support, housing benefit or a tax credit (a "relevant benefit");

(c) an appeal against the UC decision is finally determined, or the decision is revised under section 9 of the Social Security Act 1998;

(d) an award of universal credit is made to the claimant in consequence of entitlement arising from the appeal, or from the decision as revised; and

(e) the claimant would (were it not for the effect of regulation 5 and this regulation) be entitled to both universal credit and a relevant benefit in respect of the same period.

(2) Subject to paragraph (3), where this regulation applies—

(a) all awards of a relevant benefit to which the claimant would (were it not for the effect of these Regulations) be entitled are to terminate, by virtue of this regulation, at the beginning of the first day of entitlement to that award; and

(b) any legislative provision [² except regulation 8(2A)] under which an award would otherwise terminate on a later date does not apply.

(3) An award of housing benefit to which a claimant is entitled in respect of [¹ specified accommodation][² or temporary accommodation] does not terminate by virtue of this regulation.

AMENDMENTS

1. Universal Credit (Transitional Provisions) (Amendment) Regulations 2014 (SI 2014/1626) reg.3 (November 3, 2014).

2. Universal Credit (Miscellaneous Amendments, Saving and Transitional Provision) Regulations 2018 (SI 2018/65) reg.6(10) (April 11, 2018).

DEFINITIONS

"housing benefit"—see reg.2(1).
"income support"—*ibid.*
"relevant benefit"—para.(1)(b).
"specified accommodation"—see reg.2(1).
"tax credit"—*ibid.*
"the UC decision"—para.(1)(a).

GENERAL NOTE

2.776   This regulation concerns the situation where a claimant successfully appeals a decision that they are not entitled to universal credit, or such a decision is revised, but only after the claimant has become entitled to income support, housing benefit or a tax credit. In such a case, the award of the existing benefit terminates at the beginning of the first day of entitlement if there would otherwise be an overlap with the award of universal credit.

CHAPTER 3

Modification of Claims and Payments Regulations in relation to universal credit claimants

2.777   **15.**—(1) Where a claim for universal credit is made by a person who was previously entitled to an existing benefit, regulation 26 of the Claims and Payments

Regulations (time within which a claim for universal credit is to be made) applies in relation to that claim with the modification specified in paragraph (2).

(2) In paragraph (3) of regulation 26, after sub-paragraph (a) insert—

"(aa) the claimant was previously in receipt of an existing benefit (as defined in the Universal Credit (Transitional Provisions) Regulations 2014) and notification of expiry of entitlement to that benefit was not sent to the claimant before the date that the claimant's entitlement expired;".

DEFINITIONS

"the Claims and Payments Regulations"—see reg.2(1).
"existing benefit"—*ibid.*

GENERAL NOTE

Where a claim for universal credit is made by a claimant who was previously entitled to an existing benefit, this regulation modifies the application of reg.26(3) of the Claims and Payments Regulations 2013 in relation to the claimant. In practice it means that the time for claiming universal credit may be extended by up to one month, if the claimant was not given advance notice of termination of the award of existing benefit. The aim is to ensure that the same rule applies to claimants making the transition to universal credit from existing benefits as will apply in relation to universal credit and other benefits after the transitional period.
2.778

Persons unable to act

16. (1) Paragraph (2) applies where—
2.779

(a) a person ("P2") has been appointed, or treated as appointed, under regulation 33(1) of the Social Security (Claims and Payments) Regulations 1987 ("the 1987 Regulations") (persons unable to act) to exercise rights and to receive and deal with sums payable on behalf of a person who is unable to act ("P1"); or

(b) a person ("P2") has been appointed under regulation 18(3) of the Tax Credits (Claims and Notifications) Regulations 2002 ("the 2002 Regulations") (circumstances where one person may act for another in making a claim – other appointed persons) to act for a person who is unable to act ("P1") in making a claim for a tax credit.

(2) Where this paragraph applies and P1 is, or may be, entitled to universal credit, the Secretary of State may, if P2 agrees, treat the appointment of P2 as if it were made under regulation 57(1) of the Claims and Payments Regulations (persons unable to act) and P2 may carry out the functions set out in regulation 57(4) of those Regulations in relation to P1.

(3) Paragraph (4) applies where a person ("P2") was appointed, or treated as appointed, under regulation 57(1) of the Claims and Payments Regulations to carry out functions in relation to a person who is unable to act ("P1") and who was, or might have been, entitled to universal credit, but who has ceased to be so entitled, or was not in fact so entitled.

(4) Where this paragraph applies—

(a) the Secretary of State may, if P2 agrees, treat the appointment of P2 as if it were made under regulation 33(1) of the 1987 Regulations and P2 may exercise rights and receive and deal with sums payable in respect of existing benefits on behalf of P1; and

(b) the Board (within the meaning of the 2002 Regulations) may, if P2 agrees, treat the appointment of P2 as if it were made under regulation 18(3) of the 2002 Regulations and P2 may act for P1 in making a claim for a tax credit.

DEFINITIONS

"the 1987 Regulations"—para.(1)(a).
"the 2002 Regulations"—para.(1)(b).
"the Claims and Payments Regulations"—see reg.2(1).
"existing benefit"—*ibid.*
"tax credit"—*ibid.*

GENERAL NOTE

2.780   The effect of this regulation (which had no equivalent provision in the 2013 Transitional Regulations) is that a person who has been appointed to act on behalf of a claimant in relation to existing benefits and/or tax credits may be treated as having been appointed to act on their behalf in relation to universal credit and *vice versa.* This may be particularly relevant where claimants have mental health problems or where they suffer from other conditions that make communication with the Department very difficult or impossible. The aim of the provision is to make the process of transition between existing benefits and universal credit easier for claimants who are in this position.

[¹ **Waiting days**

2.781   **16A.** [² . . .]]

AMENDMENTS

1. Universal Credit (Waiting Days) (Amendment) Regulations 2015 (SI 2015/1362) reg.2(2) (August 3, 2015).
2. Universal Credit (Miscellaneous Amendments, Saving and Transitional Provision) Regulations 2018 (SI 2018/65) reg.6(11) (April 11, 2018).

Advance payments of universal credit

2.782   **17.** (1) This regulation applies where—
(a) the Secretary of State is deciding a claim for universal credit, other than a claim which is treated as having been made, in accordance with regulation 9(8) of the Claims and Payments Regulations;
(b) the claimant is, or was previously, entitled to an existing benefit ("the earlier award"); and
(c) if the earlier award terminated before the date on which the claim for universal credit was made, the claim for universal credit was made during the period of one month starting with the date of termination.
(2) Where this regulation applies—
(a) a single claimant may request an advance payment of universal credit;
(b) joint claimants may jointly request such a payment,
at any time during the first assessment period for universal credit.
(3) Where a request has been made in accordance with this regulation, the Secretary of State may make an advance payment to the claimant, or joint claimants, of such amount in respect of universal credit as the Secretary of State considers appropriate.
(4) After an advance payment has been made under this regulation, payments of any award of universal credit to the claimant or, in the case of joint claimants, to either or both of them, may be reduced until the amount of the advance payment is repaid.

734

(b) the claimant is to be treated as having limited capability for work and work-related activity for the purposes of regulation 27(1)(b) of those Regulations and section 19(2)(a) of [²the Act; and

(c) the claimant is to be treated as if the determination that they have limited capability for work and work-related activity, for the purposes of regulation 14(1)(b) of those Regulations, was made before the date on which the claimant started receiving education.]

(5) Unless the assessment phase applied and had not ended at the relevant date, in relation to a claimant who is treated as having limited capability for work and work-related activity under paragraph (4)(4)(b)—

(a) regulation 28 of the Universal Credit Regulations does not apply; and

(b) the LCWRA element is (subject to the provisions of Part 4 of the Universal Credit Regulations) to be included in the award of universal credit with effect from the beginning of the first assessment period.

(6) For the purposes of this regulation, a determination that the claimant [¹ had limited capability for work or, as the case may be, limited capability for work-related activity (within the meaning of Part 1 of the 2007 Act)], is to be taken into account even if the award of old style ESA subsequently terminated (in so far as it was an award of income-related employment and support allowance) before the date on which that determination was made, by virtue of an order made under section 150(3) of the Act.

(7) Where a claimant is treated, by virtue of this regulation, as having limited capability for work or, as the case may be, limited capability for work and work-related activity, the Secretary of State may at any time make a fresh determination as to these matters, in accordance with the Universal Credit Regulations.

(8) In this regulation and in regulations 20 to 27—

[¹ "assessment phase" has the same meaning as in the 2007 Act;]

"incapacity benefit" and "severe disablement allowance" have the same meanings as in Schedule 4 to that Act;

[¹ "LCWRA element" has the same meaning as in the Universal Credit Regulations.]

(9) For the purposes of this regulation and regulation 20, references to cases in which the assessment phase applied are references to cases in which sections 2(2)(a)[¹ and 4(4)(a)] of the 2007 Act applied and references to cases in which the assessment phase did not apply are references to cases in which those sections did not apply.

[¹ (10) For the purposes of this regulation, references to a determination that the claimant had limited capability for work do not include a determination made under regulation 30 of the Employment and Support Allowance Regulations 2008 (conditions for treating a claimant as having limited capability for work until a determination about limited capability for work has been made).]

AMENDMENT

1. Employment and Support Allowance and Universal Credit (Miscellaneous Amendments and Transitional and Savings Provisions) Regulations 2017 (SI 2017/204) reg.5(2) (April 3, 2017).

2. Universal Credit (Exceptions to the Requirement not to be receiving Education) (Amendment) Regulations 2021 (SI 2021/1224) reg.3 (December 15, 2021).

DEFINITIONS

"the Act"—see reg.2(1).
"assessment period"—*ibid.*
"assessment phase"—para.(8).
"incapacity benefit"—*ibid.*
"income-based jobseeker's allowance"—see reg.2(1).
"LCW element"—para.(8).
"LCWRA element"—*ibid.*
"old style ESA"—see reg.2(1).
"the relevant date"—para.(1)(a).
"severe disablement allowance"—para.(8).
"support component"—*ibid.*
"the Universal Credit Regulations"—see reg.2(1).
"work-related activity component"—para.(8).

GENERAL NOTE

2.787   The purpose of this apparently complex provision is relatively simple. It provides that a claimant may be treated as having limited capability for work, or limited capability for work and work-related activity, for the purposes of an award of universal credit, if they were previously so assessed for the purpose of old style ESA. If the claimant in question was in the process of assessment of their capability for work in connection with an award of employment and support allowance at the time the award terminated, the assessment period for universal credit will be adjusted accordingly, under reg.20.

Transition from old style ESA before the end of the assessment phase

2.788   **20.** (1) This regulation applies where—
(a) an award of universal credit is made to a claimant who was entitled to old style ESA on the date on which the claim for universal credit was made or treated as made ("the relevant date"); and
(b) on the relevant date, the assessment phase in relation to the claimant applied and had lasted for less than 13 weeks.
(2) Where this regulation applies—
(a) regulation 28(2) of the Universal Credit Regulations (period for which the [¹ . . .] LCWRA element is not to be included) does not apply; and
(b) for the purposes of regulation 28 of those Regulations, the relevant period is—
   (i) the period of 13 weeks starting with the first day of the assessment phase; or
   (ii) where regulation 5 of the Employment and Support Allowance Regulations 2008 (the assessment phase – previous claimants) applied to the claimant, the period which ends when the sum of the periods for which the claimant was previously entitled to old style ESA and the period for which the claimant is entitled to universal credit is 13 weeks.
(3) Where, on the relevant date, the assessment phase in relation to the claimant applied and had not ended and had lasted for more than 13 weeks—
(a) regulation 28 of the Universal Credit Regulations does not apply;
(b) [¹ . . .]

(c) if it is subsequently determined in accordance with Part 5 of the Universal Credit Regulations that the claimant has limited capability for work and work-related activity the LCWRA element is (subject to the provisions of Part 4 of those Regulations) to be included in the award of universal credit with effect from the beginning of the first assessment period.

(4) For the purposes of this regulation, the fact that an assessment phase applied in relation to a claimant on the relevant date is to be taken into account even if the award of old style ESA subsequently terminated (in so far as it was an award of income-related employment and support allowance) before that date by virtue of an order made under section 150(3) of the Act.

AMENDMENT

1. Employment and Support Allowance and Universal Credit (Miscellaneous Amendments and Transitional and Savings Provisions) Regulations 2017 (SI 2017/204) reg.5(3) (April 3, 2017).

DEFINITIONS

"the Act"—see reg.2(1).
"assessment period"—*ibid.*
"assessment phase"—see reg.19(8).
"income-based jobseeker's allowance"—*ibid.*
"LCW element"—see reg.19(8).
"LCWRA element"—*ibid.*
"old style ESA"—*ibid.*
"the relevant date"—para.(1)(a).
"the Universal Credit Regulations"—see reg.2(1).

GENERAL NOTE

This regulation provides that where a claimant was in the process of assessment of their capability for work in connection with an award of old style ESA at the time that award terminated, the assessment period for universal credit will be adjusted accordingly.

[¹ Transition from jobseeker's allowance following an extended period of sickness

20A.—(1) This regulation applies where—
 (a) the claimant's first day of entitlement to universal credit ("the relevant date"), immediately follows the claimant's last day of entitlement to a jobseeker's allowance; and
 (b) immediately before the relevant date, the claimant was treated as capable of work or as not having limited capability for work under regulation 55ZA of the Jobseeker's Allowance Regulations 1996 or regulation 46A of the Jobseeker's Allowance Regulations 2013 (extended period of sickness).
(2) Where this regulation applies—
 (a) regulation 28(2) of the Universal Credit Regulations (period for which [¹ . . .] LCWRA element is not to be included) does not apply; and
 (b) for the purposes of regulation 28 of those Regulations, the relevant period is the period starting with the first day of the period for which the claimant was treated as capable of work or as not having limited capability for work as specified in paragraph (1)(b).]

2.789

2.790

739

AMENDMENTS

1. Jobseeker's Allowance (Extended Period of Sickness) Amendment Regulations 2015 (SI 2015/339) reg.6 (March 30, 2015).
2. Employment and Support Allowance and Universal Credit (Miscellaneous Amendments and Transitional and Savings Provisions) Regulations 2017 (SI 2017/204) reg.5(4) (April 3, 2017).

DEFINITIONS

"the relevant date"—para.(1)(a).
"LCW element"—see reg.19(8).
"LCWRA element"—*ibid.*
"the Universal Credit Regulations"—see reg.2(1).

GENERAL NOTE

2.791 The Jobseeker's Allowance (Extended Period of Sickness) Amendment Regulations 2015 (SI 2015/339) enabled jobseeker's allowance claimants suffering from a short (or third) period of sickness to choose to remain on that benefit while on what is termed as an "extended period of sickness" (EPS) for a continuous period of up to 13 weeks in a 12 month period. The same regulations also made provision to enable the employment and support allowance assessment phase (before any additional ESA components become payable) and the universal credit relevant period (before any additional universal credit elements become payable) to be reduced by the time a claimant spends on an EPS. This regulation is accordingly designed to ensure that the calculation of the universal credit relevant period includes the EPS where jobseeker's allowance claimants make a claim for universal credit and move immediately into the universal credit relevant period.

Other claimants with limited capability for work: credits only cases

2.792 **21.** (1) This regulation applies where—
(a) an award of universal credit is made to a claimant who was entitled to be credited with earnings equal to the lower earnings limit then in force under regulation 8B(2)(iv), (iva) or (v) of the Social Security (Credits) Regulations 1975 ("the 1975 Regulations") on the date on which the claim for universal credit was made or treated as made (the "relevant date"); and
(b) neither regulation 19 nor regulation 20 applies to that claimant (whether or not, in the case of joint claimants, either of those regulations apply to the other claimant).
(2) Where, on or before the relevant date, it had been determined that the claimant would have limited capability for work (within the meaning of Part 1 of the 2007 Act) if he or she was entitled to old style ESA—
(a) [¹ . . .]
(b) the claimant is to be treated as having limited capability for work for the purposes of [¹ . . .] section 21(1)(a) of the Act.
(3) [¹ . . .]
(4) Where, on or before the relevant date, it had been determined that the claimant would have limited capability for work-related activity (within the meaning of Part 1 of the 2007 Act) if he or she was entitled to old style ESA—
(a) regulation 27(3) of the Universal Credit Regulations does not apply; and
(b) the claimant is to be treated as having limited capability for work and work-related activity for the purposes of regulation 27(1)(b) of those Regulations and section 19(2)(a) of the Act.

(5) Unless the notional assessment phase applied and had lasted for less than 13 weeks at the relevant date, in relation to a claimant who is treated as having limited capability for work and work-related activity under paragraph (4)—

    (a) regulation 28 of the Universal Credit Regulations does not apply; and

    (b) the LCWRA element is (subject to the provisions of Part 4 of the Universal Credit Regulations) to be included in the award of universal credit with effect from the beginning of the first assessment period.

(6) Where, on the relevant date, the notional assessment phase in relation to the claimant to whom the award was made applied and had lasted for less than 13 weeks—

    (a) regulation 28(2) of the Universal Credit Regulations does not apply; and

    (b) for the purposes of regulation 28 of those Regulations, the relevant period is the period of 13 weeks starting with the first day of the notional assessment phase.

(7) Where, on the relevant date, the notional assessment phase in relation to the claimant applied and had not ended and had lasted for more than 13 weeks—

    (a) regulation 28 of the Universal Credit Regulations does not apply;

    (b) [¹ . . .]

    (c) if it is subsequently determined in accordance with Part 5 of those Regulations that the claimant has limited capability for work and work-related activity, the LCWRA element is (subject to the provisions of Part 4 of those Regulations) to be included in the award of universal credit with effect from the beginning of the first assessment period.

(8) Where a claimant is treated, by virtue of this regulation, as having limited capability for work or, as the case may be, limited capability for work and work-related activity, the Secretary of State may at any time make a fresh determination as to these matters, in accordance with the Universal Credit Regulations.

(9) For the purposes of this regulation—

    (a) a determination that the claimant would have limited capability for work or, as the case may be, limited capability for work-related activity, if the claimant was entitled to old style ESA is to be taken into account even if the claimant subsequently ceased to be entitled as mentioned in paragraph (1)(a) before the date on which that determination was made because he or she became entitled to universal credit;

    (b) the fact that a notional assessment phase applied in relation to a claimant on the relevant date is to be taken into account even if the claimant subsequently ceased to be entitled as mentioned in paragraph (1)(a) before that date because the claimant became entitled to universal credit.

    (c) references to a determination that the claimant would have limited capability for work if the claimant was entitled to old style ESA do not include a determination made under regulation 30 of the Employment and Support Allowance Regulations 2008 (conditions for treating a claimant as having limited capability for work until a determination about limited capability for work has been made);

    (d) references to cases in which the notional assessment phase applied are references to cases in which sections 2(2)(a) [¹ and 4(4)(a)] of the 2007 Act would have applied to the claimant if he or she had been entitled to old style ESA in addition to the entitlement mentioned in paragraph (1)(a), but do not include cases in which the claimant is entitled as mentioned in paragraph (1)(a) under regulation 8B(2) (iva) of the 1975 Regulations;

(e) subject to sub-paragraph (f), the "notional assessment phase" is the period of 13 weeks starting on the day on which the assessment phase would have started in relation to the claimant, if he or she had been entitled to old style ESA and sections 2(2)(a) [¹ and 4(4)(a)] of the 2007 Act had applied;

(f) the notional assessment phase has not ended if, at the end of the 13 week period referred to in sub-paragraph (e), no determination has been made as to whether a claimant would have limited capability for work (within the meaning of Part 1 of the 2007 Act) if the claimant was entitled to old style ESA.

AMENDMENT

1. Employment and Support Allowance and Universal Credit (Miscellaneous Amendments and Transitional and Savings Provisions) Regulations 2017 (SI 2017/204) reg.5(4) (April 3, 2017).

DEFINITIONS

"the 1975 Regulations"—para.(1)(a).
"the 2007 Act"—see reg.2(1).
"the Act"—*ibid.*
"assessment period"—*ibid.*
"assessment phase"—see reg.19(8).
"LCW element"—*ibid.*
"LCWRA element"—*ibid.*
"old style ESA"—*ibid.*
"the relevant date"—para.(1)(a).
"the Universal Credit Regulations"—see reg.2(1).

GENERAL NOTE

2.793   This regulation makes similar provision to reg.20 but for claimants who were not entitled to old style ESA, but who were entitled to credits of contributions and earnings on the grounds of limited capability for work. In *JW v SSWP (UC)* [2022] UKUT 117 (AAC) the claimant had been entitled to income-related ESA at the support group rate but her claim ended when her partner took up full-time work. Six months later, the claimant applied for universal credit. The decision-maker and tribunal concluded, applying the general rule in reg.28 of the UC Regs 2013, that she had to wait for a further three months from the start of her universal credit claim before the limited capability for work-related activity (LCWRA) element became payable. However, Judge Wikeley observed that none of the exceptions to the general rule in reg.28 dealt with the situation in which a claimant had previously been entitled to a legacy benefit. Such cases required consideration of the UC (Transitional) Regulations 2014 and especially reg.21. Having concluded that the claimant fell within the terms of reg.8B(2)(a)(iv) of the Social Security (Credits) Regulations 1975 (see reg.21(1))—namely that a person can receive NI credits equivalent to the lower earnings limit for the relevant period if the only reason they are not entitled to ESA is that they did not satisfy the contribution conditions—Judge Wikeley held, allowing the claimant's appeal and re-making the decision under appeal, that reg.21(4) and (5) provided the mechanism for the payment of the LCWRA element from the start of the claimant's universal credit claim rather than after a further waiting period of three months.

Transition from income support payable on the grounds of incapacity for work or disability [¹ and other incapacity benefits]

22. (1) This regulation applies where an award of universal credit is made to a claimant [¹ (other than a claimant to whom regulation 23 or 24 applies)] who was entitled to income support on the grounds of incapacity for work or disability on the date on which the claim for universal credit was made or treated as made [¹ or is entitled to incapacity benefit or severe disablement allowance].

2.794

(2) Where this regulation applies—

(a) if it is determined in accordance with Part 5 of the Universal Credit Regulations that the claimant has limited capability for work—

    (i) the claimant is to be treated as having had limited capability for work for the purposes of regulation 27(1)(a) of the Universal Credit Regulations (award to include LCW and LCWRA elements) from the beginning of the first assessment period;

    (ii) regulation 28 of those Regulations (period for which the LCW or LCWRA element is not to be included) does not apply; and

    (iii) the LCW element is (subject to the provisions of Part 4 of the Universal Credit Regulations) to be included in the award with effect from the beginning of the first assessment period;

(b) if it is determined in accordance with Part 5 of the Universal Credit Regulations that the claimant has limited capability for work and work-related activity—

    (i) the claimant is to be treated as having had limited capability for work and work-related activity for the purposes of regulation 27(1)(b) of the Universal Credit Regulations from the beginning of the first assessment period;

    (ii) regulation 28 of those Regulations does not apply; and

    (iii) the LCWRA element is (subject to the provisions of Part 4 of the Universal Credit Regulations) to be included in the award of universal credit with effect from the beginning of the first assessment period.

(3) In this regulation—

"income support on the grounds of incapacity for work or disability" means an award of income support which is an "existing award" within the meaning of Schedule 4 to the 2007 Act.

AMENDMENT

1. Universal Credit (Transitional Provisions) (Amendment) Regulations 2014 (SI 2014/1626) reg.5(1) (October 13, 2014).

DEFINITIONS

"the 2007 Act"—see reg.2(1).
"assessment period"—*ibid.*
"incapacity benefit"—see reg.19(8).
"income support"—*ibid.*
"income support on the grounds of incapacity for work or disability"—para.(3).
"LCW element"—see reg.19(8).
"LCWRA element"—*ibid.*
"severe disablement allowance"—*ibid.*
"the Universal Credit Regulations"—see reg.2(1).

GENERAL NOTE

2.795   The process of transition from existing incapacity benefits to universal credit is dealt with in regs.22 to 25. Transition from income support awarded on the grounds of incapacity for work or disability is dealt with in reg. 22 and transition from incapacity benefit or severe disablement allowance is dealt with in regs.23 to 25. In both cases, the limited capability for work (LCW) or limited capability for work and work-related activity (LCWRA) elements may be included in an award of universal credit with effect from the start of the first assessment period, if the claimant is subsequently assessed as having limited capability for work or, in the case of a claimant approaching pensionable age, is entitled to certain other benefits. Regulations 26 and 27 make similar provision to regs.22-25 but in respect of claimants who although they were not entitled to an incapacity benefit were entitled to credits of earnings on the grounds of incapacity for work.

The various amendments to regs 22-26 which came into effect on October 13, 2014 were designed to ensure that incapacity benefit or severe disablement allowance claimants can have the LCW or LCWRA elements applied to their universal credit award, from the start of the first assessment period where they joined or made a universal credit claim, as quickly as possible. This is sought to be achieved by ensuring they either:

- remain in the employment and support allowance conversion process and undergo a work capability assessment to determine whether their existing incapacity award qualifies for conversion to new style ESA, inclusive of either the WRA or support component and where it does, allow this decision to be used to apply the LCW or LCWRA element to their universal credit award; or

- enter the universal credit assessment process and undergo a universal credit work capability assessment to ascertain whether the LCW or LCWRA element should be applied to their award.

Before the October 2014 amendments, claimants who have not commenced ESA conversion had the choice of either entering the universal credit assessment process or waiting until they undergo conversion to ascertain whether the LCW or LCWRA element should be applied to their universal credit award. The amendments are intended to ensure that where the claimant has not entered the ESA conversion process they now have to enter the universal credit process, if they want to be assessed and have the LCW or LCWRA element backdated. The significance of this change is that if they do not enter the universal credit assessment process they would have to wait until they are scheduled for ESA conversion to see if their existing incapacity award qualified for conversion to new style ESA, before the LCW or LCWRA element could be applied to their universal credit award. This is supposed to avoid any delay in these claimants accessing the additional financial support they will be entitled to if it is decided that they have LCW or LCWRA.

The amending regulations also ensure that where incapacity benefit claimants are in receipt of National Insurance credits only, and are not entitled to the appropriate level or component of a prescribed benefit to allow them to qualify for the LCW or LCWRA element in universal credit, that they will be treated in the same way as those incapacity benefit or severe disablement allowance claimants and will not have to serve the universal credit relevant period but can have the LCW or LCWRA element applied to their universal credit award, with retrospective effect, back to the start of the first assessment period, if it is subsequently determined by a universal credit work capability assessment that they have either LCW or LCWRA.

Transition from other incapacity benefits [[1]: assessment under the 2010 Regulations]

2.796   **23.** (1) This regulation applies where—

(a) an award of universal credit is made to a claimant who is entitled to incapacity benefit or severe disablement allowance [¹ ("the relevant award")]; and

[¹(b) on or before the date on which the claim for universal credit is made or treated as made, a notice has been issued to the claimant under regulation 4 of the Employment and Support Allowance (Transitional Provisions, Housing Benefit and Council Tax Benefit) (Existing Awards) (No.2) Regulations 2010 ("the 2010 Regulations") (notice commencing the conversion phase).]

[¹ (1A) Where this regulation applies, regulations 27(3) (award to include LCW and LCWRA elements) and 38 (determination of limited capability for work and work-related activity) of the Universal Credit Regulations do not apply and the question whether a claimant has limited capability for work, or for work and work-related activity, is to be determined, for the purposes of the Act and the Universal Credit Regulations, in accordance with this regulation.]

(2) [¹ Where it is determined in accordance with the 2010 Regulations that the relevant award qualifies for conversion into an award in accordance with regulation 7 of those Regulations (qualifying for conversion) and that award includes the work-related activity component]—

(a) [¹ ...];
(b) the claimant is to be treated as having had limited capability for work for the purposes of regulation 27(1)(a) of the Universal Credit Regulations from the beginning of the first assessment period;
(c) regulation 28(1) of those Regulations (period for which LCW or LCWRA element is not to be included) does not apply;
(d) the LCW element is (subject to the provisions of Part 4 of the Universal Credit Regulations) to be included in the award of universal credit with effect from the beginning of the first assessment period; and
(e) the claimant is to be treated as having limited capability for work for the purposes of section 21(1)(a) of the Act.

(3) [¹ Where it is determined in accordance with the 2010 Regulations that the relevant award qualifies for conversion into an award in accordance with regulation 7 of those Regulations and that award includes the support component]—

(a) [¹ ...];
(b) the claimant is to be treated as having had limited capability for work and work-related activity for the purposes of regulation 27(1)(b) of the Universal Credit Regulations from the beginning of the first assessment period;
(c) regulation 28(1) of those Regulations does not apply;
(d) the LCWRA element is (subject to the provisions of Part 4 of the Universal Credit Regulations) to be included in the award of universal credit with effect from the beginning of the first assessment period; and
(e) the claimant is to be treated as having limited capability for work and work-related activity for the purposes of section 19(2)(a) of the Act.

AMENDMENT

1. Universal Credit (Transitional Provisions) (Amendment) Regulations 2014 (SI 2014/1626) reg.5(2) (October 13, 2014).

DEFINITIONS

"the 2010 Regulations"—para.(1)(b).
"the Act"—see reg.2(1).
"assessment period"—*ibid.*
"incapacity benefit"—see reg.19(8).
"LCW element"—*ibid.*
"LCWRA element"—*ibid.*
"the relevant award"—para.(1)(a).
"severe disablement allowance"—see reg.19(8).
"support component"—*ibid.*
"the Universal Credit Regulations"—see reg.2(1).
"work-related activity component"—see reg.19(8).

GENERAL NOTE

2.797　　See General Note to reg.22.

Transition from other incapacity benefits: claimants approaching pensionable age

2.798　　**24.** (1) This paragraph applies where—

(a) an award of universal credit is made to a claimant who is entitled to incapacity benefit or severe disablement allowance;

(b) no notice has been issued to the claimant under regulation 4 (notice commencing the conversion phase) of the Employment and Support Allowance (Transitional Provisions, Housing Benefit and Council Tax Benefit) (Existing Awards) (No.2) Regulations 2010 ("the 2010 Regulations");

(c) the claimant will reach pensionable age (within the meaning of the 2010 Regulations) within the period of one year; and

(d) the claimant is also entitled to—

　(i) personal independence payment, where neither the daily living component nor the mobility component is payable at the enhanced rate;

　(ii) disability living allowance under section 71 of the Social Security Contributions and Benefits Act 1992 ("the 1992 Act"), where the care component is payable at the middle rate within the meaning of section 72(4) of that Act or the mobility component is payable at the lower rate within the meaning of section 73(11) of that Act (or both components are payable at those rates);

　(iii) attendance allowance under section 64 of the 1992 Act, where the allowance is payable at the lower rate in accordance with section 65 of that Act;

　(iv) an increase in the weekly rate of disablement pension under section 104 of the 1992 Act (increase where constant attendance needed), where the increase is of an amount which is equal to or less than the amount specified in paragraph 2(a) of Part V of Schedule 4 to that Act; or

　(v) any payment based on the need for attendance which is paid as an addition to a war disablement pension (which means any retired pay or pension or allowance payable in respect of disablement under an instrument specified in section 639(2) of the Income Tax (Earnings and Pensions) Act 2003), where the amount of that payment is equal to or less than the amount specified in paragraph 2(a) of Part V of Schedule 4 to the 1992 Act.

(2) Where paragraph (1) applies and paragraph (3) does not apply—

(a) regulation 27(3) of the Universal Credit Regulations (award to include LCW and LCWRA elements) does not apply;

(b) the claimant is to be treated as having limited capability for work for the purposes of regulation 27(1)(a) of those Regulations from the beginning of the first assessment period;

(c) regulation 28(1) of the Universal Credit Regulations (period for which LCW or LCWRA element is not to be included) does not apply;

(d) the LCW element is (subject to the provisions of Part 4 of the Universal Credit Regulations) to be included in the award of universal credit with effect from the beginning of the first assessment period; and

(e) the claimant is to be treated as having limited capability for work for the purposes of section 21(1)(a) of the Act.

(3) This paragraph applies where—

(a) an award of universal credit is made to a claimant who is entitled to incapacity benefit or severe disablement allowance;

(b) no notice has been issued to the claimant under regulation 4 of the 2010 Regulations;

(c) the claimant will reach pensionable age (within the meaning of the 2010 Regulations) within the period of one year; and

(d) the claimant is also entitled to—

    (i) personal independence payment, where either the daily living component or the mobility component is (or both components are) payable at the enhanced rate;

    (ii) disability living allowance under section 71 of the 1992 Act, where the care component is payable at the highest rate within the meaning of section 72(4) of that Act or the mobility component is payable at the higher rate within the meaning of section 73(11) of that Act (or both components are payable at those rates);

    (iii) attendance allowance under section 64 of the 1992 Act, where the allowance is payable at the higher rate in accordance with section 65 of that Act;

    (iv) armed forces independence payment under the Armed Forces and Reserve Forces (Compensation Scheme) Order 2011;

    (v) an increase in the weekly rate of disablement pension under section 104 of the 1992 Act, where the increase is of an amount which is greater than the amount specified in paragraph 2(a) of Part V of Schedule 4 to that Act; or

    (vi) any payment based on the need for attendance which is paid as an addition to a war disablement pension (which means any retired pay or pension or allowance payable in respect of disablement under an instrument specified in section 639(2) of the Income Tax (Earnings and Pensions) Act 2003), where the amount of that payment is greater than the amount specified in paragraph 2(a) of Part V of Schedule 4 to the 1992 Act.

(4) Where paragraph (3) applies (whether or not paragraph (1) also applies)—

(a) regulation 27(3) of the Universal Credit Regulations does not apply;

(b) the claimant is to be treated as having limited capability for work and work-related activity for the purposes of regulation 27(1)(b) of those Regulations from the beginning of the first assessment period;

(c) regulation 28(1) of the Universal Credit Regulations does not apply;

(d) the LCWRA element is (subject to the provisions of Part 4 of the Universal Credit Regulations) to be included in the award of universal credit with effect from the beginning of the first assessment period; and

(e) the claimant is to be treated as having limited capability for work and work-related activity for the purposes of section 19(2)(a) of the Act.

DEFINITIONS

"the 1992 Act"—para.(1)(d)(ii).
"the 2010 Regulations"—para.(1)(b).
"the Act"—see reg.2(1).
"assessment period"—*ibid.*
"incapacity benefit"—see reg.19(8).
"LCW element"—*ibid.*
"LCWRA element"—*ibid.*
"severe disablement allowance"—*ibid.*
"the Universal Credit Regulations"—see reg.2(1).
"work-related activity component"—see reg.19(8).

GENERAL NOTE

2.799   See General Note to reg.22.

Transition from other incapacity benefits: supplementary

2.800   **25.** (1) Where an award of universal credit is made to a claimant who is entitled to incapacity benefit or severe disablement allowance, regulation 66 of the Universal Credit Regulations (what is included in unearned income?) applies to the claimant as if incapacity benefit or, as the case may be, severe disablement allowance were added to the descriptions of unearned income in paragraph (1)(b) of that regulation.

(2) For the purposes of regulations [¹ 22,] 23 and 24 and this regulation only, incapacity benefit and severe disablement allowance are prescribed benefits under paragraph 1(2)(b) of Schedule 6 to the Act.

AMENDMENT

1. Universal Credit (Transitional Provisions) (Amendment) Regulations 2014 (SI 2014/1626) reg.5(3) (October 13, 2014).

DEFINITIONS

"the Act"—see reg.2(1).
"incapacity benefit"—see reg.19(8).
"severe disablement allowance"—*ibid.*
"the Universal Credit Regulations"—see reg.2(1).

GENERAL NOTE

See General Note to reg.22.   2.801

Other claimants with incapacity for work: credits only cases where claimant is approaching pensionable age

26. (1) This regulation applies where—   2.802

(a) an award of universal credit is made to a claimant who was entitled to be credited with earnings equal to the lower earnings limit then in force under regulation 8B(2)(a)(i), (ii) or (iii) of the Social Security (Credits) Regulations 1975 on the date on which the claim for universal credit was made or treated as made;

(b) the claimant will reach pensionable age within the meaning of the Employment and Support Allowance (Transitional Provisions, Housing Benefit and Council Tax Benefit) (Existing Awards) (No.2) Regulations 2010 within the period of one year; and

(c) [¹ none of regulations 22, 23 or 24 apply] to that claimant (whether or not, in the case of joint claimants, [¹ any] of those regulations apply to the other claimant).

(2) Where the claimant is entitled to a payment, allowance or increased rate of pension specified in regulation 24(1)(d) and is not entitled to a payment, allowance or increased rate of pension specified in regulation 24(3)(d)—

(a) regulation 27(3) of the Universal Credit Regulations (award to include LCW and LCWRA elements) does not apply;

(b) the claimant is to be treated as having limited capability for work for the purposes of regulation 27(1)(a) of those Regulations from the beginning of the first assessment period;

(c) regulation 28(1) of the Universal Credit Regulations (period for which the LCW or LCWRA element is not to be included) does not apply;

(d) the LCW element is (subject to the provisions of Part 4 of the Universal Credit Regulations) to be included in the award of universal credit with effect from the beginning of the first assessment period; and

(e) the claimant is to be treated as having limited capability for work for the purposes of section 21(1)(a) of the Act.

(3) Where the claimant is entitled to a payment, allowance or increased rate of pension specified in regulation 24(3)(d) (whether or not the claimant is also entitled to a payment, allowance or increased rate of pension specified in regulation 24(1)(d))—

(a) regulation 27(3) of the Universal Credit Regulations does not apply;

(b) the claimant is to be treated as having limited capability for work and work-related activity for the purposes of regulation 27(1)(b) of those Regulations from the beginning of the first assessment period;

(c) regulation 28(1) of the Universal Credit Regulations does not apply;

(d) the LCWRA element is (subject to the provisions of Part 4 of the Universal Credit Regulations) to be included in the award of universal credit with effect from the beginning of the first assessment period; and

(e) the claimant is to be treated as having limited capability for work and work-related activity for the purposes of section 19(2)(a) of the Act.

[¹ (4) Where the claimant is not entitled to a payment, allowance or increased rate of pension specified in either regulation 24(1)(d) or regulation 24(3)(d)—

    (a) if it is determined in accordance with Part 5 of the Universal Credit Regulations that the claimant has limited capability for work—

        (i) the claimant is to be treated as having had limited capability for work for the purposes of regulation 27(1)(a) of the Universal Credit Regulations from the beginning of the first assessment period;

        (ii) regulation 28 of the Universal Credit Regulations does not apply; and

        (iii) the LCW element is (subject to the provisions of Part 4 of the Universal Credit Regulations) to be included in the award with effect from the beginning of the first assessment period; and

    (b) if it is determined in accordance with Part 5 of the Universal Credit Regulations that the claimant has limited capability for work and work-related activity—

        (i) the claimant is to be treated as having had limited capability for work and work-related activity for the purposes of regulation 27(1)(b) of the Universal Credit Regulations from the beginning of the first assessment period;

        (ii) regulation 28 of the Universal Credit Regulations does not apply; and

        (iii) the LCWRA element is (subject to the provisions of Part 4 of the Universal Credit Regulations) to be included in the award of universal credit with effect from the beginning of the first assessment period.]

AMENDMENT

1. Universal Credit (Transitional Provisions) (Amendment) Regulations 2014 (SI 2014/1626) reg.5(4) (October 13, 2014).

DEFINITIONS

"the Act"—see reg.2(1).
"assessment period"—*ibid.*
"LCW element"—see reg.19(8).
"LCWRA element"—*ibid.*
"the Universal Credit Regulations"—see reg.2(1).
"the work-related activity component"—see reg.19(8).

GENERAL NOTE

2.803   Regulations 26 and 27 make similar provision to regs 22-25 but in respect of claimants who although they were not entitled to an incapacity benefit were entitled to credits of earnings under the Social Security (Credits) Regulations 1975 (SI 1975/556) on the grounds of incapacity for work.

Other claimants with incapacity for work: credits only cases

2.804   **27.** (1) This regulation applies where—

    (a) an award of universal credit is made to a claimant who was entitled to be credited with earnings equal to the lower earnings limit then in force under regulation 8B(2)(a)(i), (ii) or (iii) of the Social Security

(Credits) Regulations 1975 on the date on which the claim for universal credit was made or treated as made; and

(b) none of regulations 22, 23, 24 or 26 apply to that claimant (whether or not, in the case of joint claimants, any of those regulations apply to the other claimant).

(2) Where this regulation applies—

(a) if it is determined in accordance with Part 5 of the Universal Credit Regulations that the claimant has limited capability for work—

   (i) the claimant is to be treated as having had limited capability for work for the purposes of regulation 27(1)(a) of the Universal Credit Regulations (award to include LCW and LCWRA elements) from the beginning of the first assessment period;

   (ii) regulation 28 of the Universal Credit Regulations (period for which the LCW or LCWRA element is not to be included) does not apply; and

   (iii) the LCW element is (subject to the provisions of Part 4 of the Universal Credit Regulations) to be included in the award with effect from the beginning of the first assessment period;

(b) if it is determined in accordance with Part 5 of the Universal Credit Regulations that the claimant has limited capability for work and work-related activity—

   (i) the claimant is to be treated as having had limited capability for work and work-related activity for the purposes of regulation 27(1)(b) of the Universal Credit Regulations from the beginning of the first assessment period;

   (ii) regulation 28 of the Universal Credit Regulations does not apply; and

   (iii) the LCWRA element is (subject to the provisions of Part 4 of the Universal Credit Regulations) to be included in the award of universal credit with effect from the beginning of the first assessment period.

DEFINITIONS

"assessment period"—see reg.2(1).
"LCW element"—see reg.19(8).
"LCWRA element"—*ibid.*
"the Universal Credit Regulations"—see reg.2(1).

GENERAL NOTE

See General Notes to regs 22 and 26. 2.805

Meaning of "qualifying young person"

28. Where a person who would (apart from the provision made by this   2.806 regulation) be a "qualifying young person" within the meaning of regulation 5 of the Universal Credit Regulations is entitled to an existing benefit—

(a) that person is not a qualifying young person for the purposes of the Universal Credit Regulations; and

(b) regulation 5(5) of those Regulations applies as if, after "a person who is receiving" there were inserted "an existing benefit (within the meaning of the Universal Credit (Transitional Provisions) Regulations 2014),".

"existing benefit"—see reg.2(1).
"the Universal Credit Regulations"—*ibid.*

GENERAL NOTE

2.807   This regulation ensures that payments may not be made as part of an award of universal credit in respect of a young person who is entitled to existing benefits in their own right. Such persons cannot be claimed for by a parent or carer for the purposes of the Universal Credit Regulations 2013.

Support for housing costs

2.808   **29.** (1) Paragraph (3) applies where—
(a) an award of universal credit is made to a claimant who—
(i) was entitled to income-based jobseeker's allowance, income-related employment and support allowance or income support (a "relevant award") at any time during the period of one month ending with the day on which the claim for universal credit was made or treated as made (or would have been so entitled were it not for termination of that award by virtue of an order made under section 150(3) of the Act or the effect of these Regulations); or
(ii) was at any time during the period of one month ending with the day on which the claim for universal credit was made or treated as made, the partner of a person ("P") who was at that time entitled to a relevant award, where the award of universal credit is not a joint award to the claimant and P; and
(b) on the relevant date, the relevant award included an amount in respect of housing costs under—
(i) [² paragraph 16 of Schedule 2] to the Jobseeker's Allowance Regulations 1996 ("the 1996 Regulations");
(ii) [² paragraph 18 of Schedule 6] to the Employment and Support Allowance Regulations 2008 ("the 2008 Regulations"); or, as the case may be,
(iii) [² paragraph 17 of Schedule 3] to the Income Support (General) Regulations 1987 ("the 1987 Regulations").
(2) In this regulation, the "relevant date" means—
(a) where paragraph (1)(a)(i) applies and the claimant was not entitled to the relevant award on the date on which the claim for universal credit was made or treated as made, the date on which the relevant award terminated;
(b) where paragraph (1)(a)(i) applies, the claimant is not a new claimant partner and he or she was entitled to the relevant award on the date on which the claim for universal credit was made, that date;
(c) where paragraph (1)(a)(i) applies, the claimant is a new claimant partner and he or she was entitled to the relevant award on the date on which the claim for universal credit was treated as made, that date;
(d) where paragraph (1)(a)(ii) applies, the date on which the claimant ceased to be the partner of P or, if earlier, the date on which the relevant award terminated.
(3) Where this paragraph applies, paragraph 5 of Schedule 5 to the Universal Credit Regulations (no housing costs element under this Schedule for qualifying period) does not apply.

(4) Paragraph (5) applies where paragraph (1)(a) applies, but the relevant award did not include an amount in respect of housing costs because the claimant's entitlement (or, as the case may be, P's entitlement) was nil by virtue of—

(a) paragraph 6(1)(c) or 7(1)(b) of Schedule 2 to the 1996 Regulations;
(b) paragraph 8(1)(c) or 9(1)(b) of Schedule 6 to the 2008 Regulations; or, as the case may be,
(c) paragraph 6(1)(c) or 8(1)(b) of Schedule 3(4) to the 1987 Regulations.

(5) Where this paragraph applies—

(a) paragraph 5(2) of Schedule 5 to the Universal Credit Regulations does not apply; and
(b) the "qualifying period" referred to in paragraph 5 of that Schedule is the period of [1 273] days starting with the first day on which the claimant (or, as the case may be, P) was entitled to the relevant award, taking into account any period which was treated as a period of continuing entitlement under—
   (i) paragraph 13 of Schedule 2 to the 1996 Regulations;
   (ii) paragraph 15 of Schedule 6 to the 2008 Regulations; or, as the case may be,
   (iii) paragraph 14 of Schedule 3 to the 1987 Regulations,

provided that, throughout that part of the qualifying period after the award of universal credit is made, receipt of universal credit is continuous and the claimant otherwise qualifies for the inclusion of an amount calculated under Schedule 5 to the Universal Credit Regulations in their award.

(6) For the purposes of—

(a) paragraph (1)(b) of this regulation, inclusion of an amount in respect of housing costs in a relevant award is to be taken into account even if the relevant award subsequently terminated by virtue of an order made under section 150(3) of the Act, regulation 7 or, as the case may be, regulation 8, before the date on which that amount was included in the award;
(b) paragraph (5)(b) of this regulation, entitlement to a relevant award is to be treated as having continued until the relevant date even if the award subsequently terminated by virtue of an order made under section 150(3) of the Act, regulation 7 or, as the case may be, regulation 8, before that date.

AMENDMENTS

1. Social Security (Housing Costs Amendments) Regulations 2015 (SI 2015/1647) reg.6 (April 1, 2016).
2. Loans for Mortgage Interest Regulations 2017 (2017/725) Sch.5 para.6 (April 6, 2018).

DEFINITIONS

"the 1987 Regulations"—para.(1)(b)(iii).
"the 1996 Regulations"—para.(1)(b)(i).
"the 2008 Regulations"—para.(1)(b)(ii).
"the Act"—see reg.2(1).
"income-based jobseeker's allowance"—*ibid.*
"income-related employment and support allowance"—*ibid.*
"income support"—*ibid.*

"new claimant partner"—*ibid.*
"partner"—*ibid.*
"qualifying period"—para.(5)(b).
"relevant award"—para.(1)(a)(i).
"relevant date"—para.(2).
"the Universal Credit Regulations"—see reg.2(1).

GENERAL NOTE

2.809   This is a hideously opaque regulation. Where a universal credit claimant or their partner was previously entitled to old style JSA, old style ESA or income support, this regulation allows for any support for housing costs which was included in that award (paras.(1) and (2)), or time spent waiting to qualify for such support (paras. (4)–(6)), to be carried over to the award of universal credit (para.(3)), providing the claimant is entitled to the universal credit housing element. The amendment to para.(5)(b) is subject to the saving provision in reg.8 of the Social Security (Housing Costs Amendments) Regulations 2015 (SI 2015/1647).

Sanctions: transition from old style ESA

2.810   **30.**—(1) This regulation applies where—

(a) an award of universal credit is made to a claimant who was previously entitled to old style ESA ("the ESA award"); and

(b) on the relevant date, payments in respect of the ESA award were reduced under regulation 63 of the Employment and Support Allowance Regulations 2008 ("the 2008 Regulations").

(2) In this regulation, the "relevant date" means—

(a) where the claimant was not entitled to old style ESA on the date on which the claim for universal credit was made or treated as made, the date on which the ESA award terminated;

(b) where the claimant is not a new claimant partner and was entitled to old style ESA on the date on which the claim for universal credit was made, that date;

(c) where the claimant is a new claimant partner and was entitled to old style ESA on the date on which the claim for universal credit was treated as made, that date.

(3) Where this regulation applies—

(a) the failure which led to reduction of the ESA award ("the ESA failure") is to be treated, for the purposes of the Universal Credit Regulations, as a failure which is sanctionable under section 27 of the Act;

(b) the award of universal credit is to be reduced in relation to the ESA failure, in accordance with the provisions of this regulation and Chapter 2 of Part 8 of the Universal Credit Regulations (sanctions), as modified by this regulation; and

(c) the reduction is to be treated, for the purposes of the Universal Credit Regulations, as a reduction under section 27 of the Act.

(4) The reduction period for the purposes of the Universal Credit Regulations is a period of the number of days which is equivalent to the length of the fixed period applicable to the person under regulation 63(7) of the 2008 Regulations in relation to the ESA failure, minus—

(a) the number of days (if any) in that period in respect of which the amount of old style ESA was reduced; and

(b) if the ESA award terminated before the first date of entitlement to universal credit in connection with the current award, the number of days (if any) in the period after termination of that award, before the start of the universal credit award.

(5) Accordingly, regulation 101 of the Universal Credit Regulations (general principles for calculating reduction periods) applies in relation to the ESA failure as if, in paragraphs (1) and (3), for "in accordance with regulations 102 to 105", there were substituted "in accordance with regulation 30 of the Universal Credit (Transitional Provisions) Regulations 2014".

(6) For the purposes of this regulation, a determination that payments in respect of the ESA award are to be reduced under regulation 63 of the 2008 Regulations is to be taken into account even if the ESA award subsequently terminated (in so far as it was an award of income-related employment and support allowance) on a date before the date on which that determination was made, by virtue of an order made under section 150(3) of the Act.

DEFINITIONS

"the 2008 Regulations"—para.(1)(b).
"the Act"—see reg.2(1).
"the ESA award"—para.(1)(a).
"the ESA failure"—para.(3)(a).
"income-related employment and support allowance"—*ibid.*
"new claimant partner"—*ibid.*
"old style ESA"—*ibid.*
"relevant date"—para.(2).
"the Universal Credit Regulations"—see reg.2(1).

GENERAL NOTE

Regulations 30 to 34 deal with the treatment of any sanctions which have been imposed on awards of old style JSA and old style ESA, prior to a claimant's transition to universal credit. The underlying principle is one of equivalence of treatment. Such pre-existing sanctions will continue to have effect by way of deductions from the award of universal credit and past sanctions will also be taken into account for the purposes of determining the level of sanction applicable to any future sanctionable failure. However, where there is a period of entitlement to an existing benefit between two periods of entitlement to universal credit, any sanctions arising prior to that intervening period will not be taken into account.

So, for example, where a new universal credit claimant was previously entitled to ESA, and subject to an ESA sanction for failure to take part in a work-focussed interview or to undertake a work-related activity, the ESA failure is treated as a sanctionable failure for the purposes of universal credit (paras.(1) and (3)). The reduction period is adjusted accordingly (para.(4)).

2.811

Escalation of sanctions: transition from old style ESA

31. (1) This regulation applies where an award of universal credit is made to a claimant who was at any time previously entitled to old style ESA.

2.812

(2) Where this regulation applies, for the purposes of determining the reduction period under regulation 104 of the Universal Credit Regulations (low-level sanction) in relation to a sanctionable failure by the claimant, other than a failure which is treated as sanctionable by virtue of regulation 30—

(a) a reduction of universal credit in accordance with regulation 30; and

(b) any reduction of old style ESA under the Employment and Support Allowance Regulations 2008 ("the 2008 Regulations") which did not result in a reduction under regulation 30,

is, subject to paragraph (3), to be treated as arising from a sanctionable failure for which the reduction period which applies is the number of days which is equivalent to the length of the fixed period which applied under regulation 63 of the 2008 Regulations.

(3) In determining a reduction period under regulation 104 of the Universal Credit Regulations in accordance with paragraph (2), no account is to be taken of—

(a) a reduction of universal credit in accordance with regulation 30 if, at any time after that reduction, the claimant was entitled to an existing benefit;

(b) a reduction of old style ESA under the 2008 Regulations if, at any time after that reduction, the claimant was entitled to universal credit, new style ESA or new style JSA, and was subsequently entitled to an existing benefit.

DEFINITIONS

"the 2008 Regulations"—para.(2)(b).
"existing benefit"—see reg.2(1).
"new style ESA"—*ibid.*
"new style JSA"—*ibid.*
"old style ESA"—*ibid.*
"the Universal Credit Regulations"—*ibid.*

GENERAL NOTE

2.813   This provision ensures that any previous ESA fixed period reductions are taken into account when deciding the appropriate reduction period for the purposes of a universal credit sanction.

Sanctions: transition from old style JSA

2.814   32.—(1) This regulation applies where—

(a) an award of universal credit is made to a claimant who was previously entitled to old style JSA ("the JSA award");

(b) on the relevant date, payments in respect of the JSA award were reduced under section 19 (as it applied either before or after substitution by the Act) or section 19A of the Jobseekers Act 1995 ("the 1995 Act"), or under regulation 69B of the Jobseeker's Allowance Regulations 1996 ("the 1996 Regulations"); and

(c) if the JSA award was made to a joint-claim couple within the meaning of the 1995 Act and the reduction related to—

(i) in the case of a reduction under section 19 as it applied before substitution by the Act, circumstances relating to only one member of the couple; or,

(ii) in the case of a reduction under section 19 as it applied after substitution by the Act, a sanctionable failure by only one member of the couple,

the award of universal credit was made to that person.

(2) In this regulation, the "relevant date" means—

(a) where the claimant was not entitled to old style JSA on the date on which the claim for universal credit was made or treated as made, the date on which the JSA award terminated;

(b) where the claimant is not a new claimant partner and was entitled to old style JSA on the date on which the claim for universal credit was made, that date;

(c) where the claimant is a new claimant partner and was entitled to old style JSA on the date on which the claim for universal credit was treated as made, that date.

(3) Where this regulation applies—

(a) the circumstances or failure which led to reduction of the JSA award (in either case, "the JSA failure") is to be treated, for the purposes of the Universal Credit Regulations, as—

    (i) a failure which is sanctionable under section 26 of the Act, where the reduction was under section 19 of the 1995 Act; or

    (ii) a failure which is sanctionable under section 27 of the Act, where the reduction was under section 19A of the 1995 Act or regulation 69B of the 1996 Regulations;

(b) the award of universal credit is to be reduced in relation to the JSA failure, in accordance with the provisions of this regulation and Chapter 2 of Part 8 of the Universal Credit Regulations (sanctions), as modified by this regulation; and

(c) the reduction is to be treated, for the purposes of the Universal Credit Regulations, as a reduction under section 26 or, as the case may be, section 27 of the Act.

(4) The reduction period for the purposes of the Universal Credit Regulations is a period of the number of days which is equivalent to the length of the period of reduction which is applicable to the person under regulation 69, 69A or 69B of the 1996 Regulations, minus—

(a) the number of days (if any) in that period in respect of which the amount of old style JSA was reduced; and

(b) if the award of old style JSA terminated before the first date of entitlement to universal credit in connection with the current award, the number of days (if any) in the period after termination of that award, before the start of the universal credit award.

(5) Accordingly, regulation 101 of the Universal Credit Regulations applies in relation to the JSA failure as if, in paragraphs (1) and (3), for "in accordance with regulations 102 to 105", there were substituted "in accordance with regulation 32 of the Universal Credit (Transitional Provisions) Regulations 2014".

(6) Where the JSA award was made to a joint-claim couple within the meaning of the 1995 Act and the JSA failure related to only one member of the couple, the daily reduction rate for the purposes of the Universal Credit Regulations is the amount calculated in accordance with regulation 70(3) of the 1996 Regulations in respect of the JSA award, divided by seven and rounded down to the nearest 10 pence, unless regulation 111(2) or (3) of the Universal Credit Regulations (daily reduction rate) applies.

(7) Where the daily reduction rate is to be determined in accordance with paragraph (6), regulation 111(1) of the Universal Credit Regulations applies in relation to the JSA failure as if, for the words from "an amount equal to" to the end there were substituted the words "an amount determined in accordance with regulation 32 of the Universal Credit (Transitional Provisions) Regulations 2014".

(8) For the purposes of this regulation, a determination that payments in respect of the JSA award are to be reduced under regulation 69, 69A or 69B

of the 1996 Regulations is to be taken into account even if the JSA award subsequently terminated (in so far as it was an award of income-based job-seeker's allowance) on a date before the date on which that determination was made, by virtue of an order made under section 150(3) of the Act.

DEFINITIONS

"the 1995 Act"—para.(1)(b).
"the 1996 Regulations"—para.(1)(b).
"the 2002 Act"—see reg.2(1).
"income-based jobseeker's allowance"—*ibid.*
"the JSA award"—para.(1)(a).
"the JSA failure"—para.(3)(a).
"new claimant partner"—see reg.2(1).
"new style ESA"—*ibid.*
"new style JSA"—*ibid.*
"old style JSA"—*ibid.*
"relevant date"—para.(2).
"the Universal Credit Regulations"—see reg.2(1).

GENERAL NOTE

2.815   This has similar effect for JSA as reg.30 does for ESA. It is designed to ensure that current JSA sanctions carry forward into the universal credit scheme.

Escalation of sanctions: transition from old style JSA

2.816   **33.**—(1) This regulation applies where an award of universal credit is made to a claimant who was at any time previously entitled to old style JSA.

(2) Where this regulation applies, for the purposes of determining the applicable reduction period under regulation 102 (higher-level sanction), 103 (medium-level sanction) or 104 (low-level sanction) of the Universal Credit Regulations in relation to a sanctionable failure by the person, other than a failure which is treated as sanctionable by virtue of regulation 32—

(a) a reduction of universal credit in accordance with regulation 32; and

(b) any reduction of old style JSA under section 19 or 19A of the Jobseekers Act 1995 ("the 1995 Act"), or under regulation 69B of the 1996 Regulations which did not result in a reduction under regulation 32,

is, subject to paragraph (3), to be treated as arising from a sanctionable failure for which the reduction period is the number of days which is equivalent to the length of the period which applied under regulation 69, 69A or 69B of the 1996 Regulations.

(3) In determining a reduction period under regulation 102, 103 or 104 of the Universal Credit Regulations in accordance with paragraph (2), no account is to be taken of—

(a) a reduction of universal credit in accordance with regulation 32 if, at any time after that reduction, the claimant was entitled to an existing benefit;

(b) a reduction of old style JSA under section 19 or 19A of the 1995 Act, or under regulation 69B of the 1996 Regulations if, at any time after that reduction, the claimant was entitled to universal credit, new style ESA or new style JSA, and was subsequently entitled to an existing benefit.

"the 1995 Act"—para.(2)(b).
"the 1996 Regulations"—see reg.32(1)(b).
"existing benefit"—see reg.2(1).
"new style ESA"—*ibid.*
"new style JSA"—*ibid.*
"old style JSA"—*ibid.*
"the Universal Credit Regulations"—*ibid.*

GENERAL NOTE

This is the JSA equivalent of reg.31, which applies to ESA.   2.817

Sanctions: temporary return to certain existing benefits

34. If an award of universal credit terminates while there is an outstand-   2.818
ing reduction period (within the meaning of regulation 107 of the Universal
Credit Regulations) and the claimant becomes entitled to old style JSA,
old style ESA or income support ("the relevant benefit") during that
period—
  (a) regulation 107 of the Universal Credit Regulations (reduction period
      to continue where award terminates) ceases to apply; and
  (b) the reduction period is to terminate on the first date of entitlement
      to the relevant benefit.

DEFINITIONS

"income support"—see reg.2(1).
"old style ESA"—*ibid.*
"old style JSA"—*ibid.*
"relevant benefit"—see reg.34.
"the Universal Credit Regulations"—see reg.2(1).

GENERAL NOTE

This provision has the effect that where a claimant comes off universal credit and   2.819
claims one of the former benefits (e.g. JSA, because he is no longer in a relevant
area), then if he subsequently becomes entitled again to universal credit (e.g. by
forming a couple with a universal credit claimant) then the universal credit sanction does not bite, even if it had on the face of it not expired. This is because the
reduction period is deemed as having terminated on the first day of the award of the
existing benefit such as JSA.

Loss of benefit penalties: transition from existing benefits other than tax credits

35.—(1) Subject to paragraph (6), this regulation applies in the cases set   2.820
out in paragraphs (2) to (4).
  (2) The first case is where—
  (a) an award of universal credit is made to a claimant who is an offender;
  (b) the claimant was entitled to old style JSA, old style ESA, income
      support or housing benefit ("the earlier award") at any time during
      the period of one month ending with the date on which the claim for
      universal credit was made or treated as made (or would have been
      so entitled were it not for termination of that award by virtue of an
      order made under section 150(3) of the Act or, as the case may be,
      the effect of these Regulations); and

(c) payments in respect of the earlier award were, on the relevant date, subject to a restriction under section 6B (loss of benefit in case of conviction, penalty or caution for benefit offence), 7 (repeated benefit fraud) or 8 (effect of offence on joint-claim jobseeker's allowance) of the 2001 Act.

(3) The second case is where—

(a) an award of universal credit is made to a claimant who is an offender;

(b) another person who was the offender's family member (but is no longer their family member) was entitled to old style JSA, old style ESA, income support or housing benefit ("the earlier award") at any time during the period of one month ending with the date on which the claim for universal credit was made or treated as made; and

(c) payments in respect of the earlier award were, on the relevant date, subject to a restriction under section 9 (effect of offence on benefits for members of offender's family) of the 2001 Act.

(4) The third case is where—

(a) an award of universal credit is made to a claimant who is an offender's family member;

(b) the offender, or the claimant, was entitled to old style JSA, old style ESA, income support or housing benefit ("the earlier award") at any time during the period of one month ending with the date on which the claim for universal credit was made or treated as made; and

(c) payments in respect of the earlier award were, on the relevant date, subject to a restriction under section 6B, 7, 8 or, as the case may be, 9 of the 2001 Act.

(5) Where this regulation applies—

(a) any subsequent payment of universal credit to the claimant in respect of an assessment period which falls wholly or partly within the remainder of the disqualification period applicable to the offender is to be reduced in accordance with regulation 36; and

(b) regulation 3ZB of the 2001 Regulations does not apply.

(6) This regulation does not apply if the earlier award was a joint-claim jobseeker's allowance and—

(a) payments in respect of the award were, on the relevant date, subject to a restriction under section 8(2) of the 2001 Act; or

(b) the award of universal credit is not made to joint claimants who were, on the relevant date, both entitled to the joint-claim jobseeker's allowance.

(7) In this regulation and in regulation 36—

"the 2001 Act" means the Social Security Fraud Act 2001;

"the 2001 Regulations" means the Social Security (Loss of Benefit) Regulations 2001;

"disqualification period" has the meaning given in the 2001 Act, interpreted in accordance with the 2001 Regulations;

"earlier award" is to be interpreted in accordance with paragraph (2)(b), (3)(b) or, as the case may be, (4)(b) and, for the purposes of regulation 36, where there is more than one earlier award, the term refers to the award to which the claimant became entitled most recently;

"offender" means an offender within the meaning of the 2001 Act;

"offender's family member" has the same meaning as in the 2001 Act;

"the relevant date" means—

(a) in relation to the first case—

    (i) where the claimant was not entitled to the earlier award on the date on which the claim for universal credit was made or treated as made, the date on which the earlier award terminated;

    (ii) where the claimant is not a new claimant partner and was entitled to the earlier award on the date on which the claim for universal credit was made, that date;

    (iii) where the claimant is a new claimant partner and was entitled to the earlier award on the date on which the claim for universal credit was treated as made, that date;

  (b) in relation to the second case, the date on which the person entitled to the earlier award ceased to be the offender's family member or, if the award terminated before that date, the date on which the earlier award terminated;

  (c) in relation to the third case—

    (i) where the claimant was entitled to the earlier award but that entitlement terminated before the date on which the claim for universal credit was made or treated as made, the date on which the earlier award terminated;

    (ii) where the claimant is not a new claimant partner and was entitled to the earlier award on the date on which the claim for universal credit was made, that date;

    (iii) where the claimant is a new claimant partner and was entitled to the earlier award on the date on which the claim for universal credit was treated as made, that date;

    (iv) where the offender's family member was entitled to the earlier award, the date on which that person ceased to be the offender's family member or, if earlier, the date on which the earlier award terminated.

(8) For the purposes of this regulation, the fact that payments in respect of an earlier award were subject to a restriction is to be taken into account, even if the earlier award subsequently terminated before the date on which payments became subject to a restriction by virtue of an order made under section 150(3) of the Act (in so far as it was an award of income-based jobseeker's allowance or income-related employment and support allowance), regulation 7 or, as the case may be, regulation 8.

DEFINITIONS

"the 2001 Act"—para.(7).
"the 2001 Regulations"—*ibid.*
"the 2002 Act"—see reg.2(1).
"assessment period"—*ibid.*
"the disqualification period"—para.(7).
"earlier award"—*ibid.*
"housing benefit"—see reg.2(1).
"income support"—*ibid.*
"income-based jobseeker's allowance"—*ibid.*
"income-related employment and support allowance"—*ibid.*
"joint-claim jobseeker's allowance"—*ibid.*
"new claimant partner"—*ibid.*
"offender"—para.(7)
"offender's family member"—*ibid.*
"old style ESA"—see reg.2(1).
"old style JSA"—*ibid.*
"the relevant date"—para.(7).

2.821   This provision (taken with reg.36) has the effect that where a claimant moves to universal credit within one month of the end of an award of an existing benefit and is subject to a loss of benefit penalty, the penalty will in most cases continue on the basis of the rate applicable to the existing benefit for the remainder of the disqualification period. The usual rules relating to calculation of penalties within universal credit will not apply.

Loss of benefit penalties: reduction of universal credit

2.822   **36.** (1) Subject to paragraph (6) [¹ and to regulation 38], where regulation 35 applies, the amount of a reduction of universal credit in respect of an assessment period is to be calculated by multiplying the daily reduction rate by the number of days in the assessment period, unless paragraph (2) applies.

(2) Where the disqualification period ends during an assessment period, the amount of the reduction for that assessment period is (subject to paragraph (6)) to be calculated by multiplying the daily reduction rate by the number of days in the assessment period which are within the disqualification period.

(3) Subject to paragraphs (4) and (5), the daily reduction rate where regulation 35 applies is an amount which is equal to—

(a) the monetary amount by which payments in respect of the earlier award were reduced in accordance with section 6B or 7 of the 2001 Act or, as the case may be, regulation 3, 3ZA or 17 of the 2001 Regulations in respect of the last complete week before the relevant date (within the meaning of regulation 35);

(b) multiplied by 52;

(c) divided by 365; and

(d) rounded down to the nearest 10 pence.

(4) Where the monetary amount by which payments in respect of the earlier award would have been reduced would, if the claimant had remained entitled to the earlier award, have changed during the disqualification period because of an order made under section 150 of the Social Security Administration Act 1992 (annual up-rating of benefits)—

(a) the daily reduction rate is to be calculated in accordance with paragraph (3), but on the basis of the new amount by which payments would have been reduced; and

(b) any adjustment to the reduction of universal credit is to take effect from the first day of the first assessment period to start after the date of the change.

(5) Where the earlier award was a joint-claim jobseeker's allowance, the daily reduction rate is an amount which is equal to—

(a) the amount of the standard allowance applicable to the joint claimants under regulation 36 of the Universal Credit Regulations (table showing amounts of elements);

(b) multiplied by 12;

(c) divided by 365;

(d) reduced by 60%; and

(e) rounded down to the nearest 10 pence.

(6) The amount of the reduction under this regulation in respect of any assessment period is not to exceed the amount of the standard allowance which is applicable to the claimant in respect of that period.

AMENDMENTS

1. Universal Credit (Transitional Provisions) (Amendment) Regulations 2014 (SI 2014/1626) reg.6(1) (October 13, 2014).

DEFINITIONS

"the 2001 Act"—see reg.35(7).
"the 2001 Regulations"—*ibid.*
"assessment period"—see reg.2(1).
"the disqualification period"—see reg.35(7).
"earlier award"—*ibid.*
"joint-claim jobseeker's allowance"—see reg.2(1).
"the relevant date"—see reg.35(7).
"the Universal Credit Regulations"—see reg.2(1).

GENERAL NOTE

See General Note to reg.35. Note also that as compared with reg.35 of the 2013 Transitional Regulations provision for the transfer of loss of benefit penalties for fraudulent offences to a universal credit award has been amended in relation to the transfer of penalties from joint-claim JSA awards to an award of universal credit (para.(5)). In these cases the amount of the penalty applied to the universal credit award is reduced by 60%, if only one of the joint JSA claimants is subject to a penalty. This reflects the position in JSA where the member of the joint-claim couple who is not the benefit fraud offender can be paid JSA at the single person's rate.   **2.823**

[¹ Loss of benefit penalties: transition from working tax credit

37.—(1) This regulation applies where an award of universal credit is made   **2.824**
to a claimant who—
  (a) was previously entitled to working tax credit; and
  (b) is an offender, within the meaning of the 2002 Act.
(2) Where this regulation applies, the Social Security (Loss of Benefit) Regulations 2001 apply as if in regulation 3ZB of those Regulations—
  (a) in paragraph (1) at the beginning there were inserted "Subject to regulation 38 of the Universal Credit (Transitional Provisions) Regulations 2014,";
  (b) "disqualification period" includes a disqualification period within the meaning of the 2002 Act;
  (c) "offender" includes an offender within the meaning of the 2002 Act; and
  (d) "offender's family member" includes a person who is a member of the family (within the meaning of section 137(1) of the Social Security Contributions and Benefits Act 1992 of a person who is an offender within the meaning of the 2002 Act.]

AMENDMENTS

1. Universal Credit (Transitional Provisions) (Amendment) Regulations 2014 (SI 2014/1626) reg.6(2) (October 13, 2014).

DEFINITIONS

"the 2002 Act"—see reg.2(1).
"working tax credit"—*ibid.*

GENERAL NOTE

2.825   This regulation provides that where a working tax credit (WTC) claimant has a fraud penalty applied to their WTC award, the fraud penalty will be applied to the universal credit standard allowance, for the remaining period of that penalty. As a consequence, reg.38 below ensures that where a claimant has been in receipt of WTC and another existing benefit (e.g. housing benefit) and both awards have had a fraud penalty applied to them, the combination of these penalties will not exceed the universal credit standard allowance in any assessment period. This follows the approach taken with existing Department for Work and Pensions benefits where there is more than one fraud penalty applied to an existing benefit award upon the transition to universal credit.

[¹ Loss of benefit penalties: maximum total reduction

2.826   **38.** Where regulations 35 and 37 both apply to a claimant, the total amount of a reduction of universal credit in respect of any assessment period under—
   (a) regulation 36; and
   (b) regulation 3ZB of the Social Security (Loss of Benefit) Regulations 2001,
must not exceed the amount of the standard allowance which is applicable to the claimant in respect of that period.]

AMENDMENT

1. Universal Credit (Transitional Provisions) (Amendment) Regulations 2014 (SI 2014/1626) reg.6(2) (October 13, 2014).

DEFINITIONS

"assessment period"—see reg.2(1).

GENERAL NOTE

2.827   See General Note to reg.37.

[¹ PART 3

ARRANGEMENTS REGARDING CHANGES TO THE CHILD ELEMENT FROM APRIL 2017

Restriction on claims for universal credit during the interim period
2.828   **39.**—[² ...]]

AMENDMENTS

1. Social Security (Restrictions on Amounts for Children and Qualifying Young Persons) Amendment Regulations 2017 (2017/376) reg.3(3) (April 6, 2017).
2. Universal Credit (Restriction on Amounts for Children and Qualifying Young Persons) (Transitional Provisions) Amendment Regulations 2019 (SI 2019/27) reg.2 (February 1, 2019).

GENERAL NOTE

The repeal of this regulation is a consequence of the Government's decision to remove the retrospective application of the "two child rule" in universal credit. Under WRWA 2016, Government policy was to provide support in the CTC and universal credit regimes for a maximum of two children (with some exceptions). This rule applied to claims for children born on or after April 6, 2017 (the date that the legislation relating to the policy to provide support for a maximum of two children came into force). During an interim period following the introduction of the policy, new claims for families with three or more children were to be directed to tax credits and the child element in universal credit was to be paid for all children born before April 6, 2017. This interim period was due to come to an end on February 1, 2019. From that date, the policy was to apply to all new claims to universal credit regardless of the date of birth of the child. From that date, new claims for families with three or more children are no longer directed to tax credits and instead are made to universal credit. As a result of the Government announcement of January 11, 2019, families with three or more children will continue to receive an additional amount in universal credit for all children born before April 6, 2017.

[¹ Availability of the child element where maximum exceeded – transitionally protected children and qualifying young persons

40.—[² ...]]

2.829

AMENDMENTS

1. Social Security (Restrictions on Amounts for Children and Qualifying Young Persons) Amendment Regulations 2017 (2017/376) reg.3(3) (April 6, 2017).

2. Universal Credit (Restriction on Amounts for Children and Qualifying Young Persons) (Transitional Provisions) Amendment Regulations 2019 (SI 2019/27) reg.2 (February 1, 2019).

GENERAL NOTE

See General Note to reg.39.

[¹ Availability of the child element where maximum exceeded – continuation of exception from a previous award of child tax credit, income support or old style JSA

41.—(1) Where—

2.830

(a) the claimant ("C") is the step-parent of a child or qualifying young person ("A"); and

(b) within the 6 months immediately preceding the first day on which C became entitled to an award of universal credit, C had an award of child tax credit, income support or old style JSA in which an exception corresponding with an exception under paragraph 2, 3, 5 or 6 of Schedule 12 to the Universal Credit Regulations applied in respect of A,

paragraph 6 of that Schedule is to apply as if sub-paragraph (c) of that paragraph were satisfied, despite the fact that the previous award was not an award of universal credit.

(2) In this regulation, "step-parent" has the same meaning as in the Universal Credit Regulations.]

AMENDMENT

1. Social Security (Restrictions on Amounts for Children and Qualifying Young Persons) Amendment Regulations 2017 (2017/376) reg.3(3) (April 6, 2017).

[¹ Evidence for non-consensual conception where claimant previously had an award of child tax credit

42.—(1) This regulation applies for the purposes of paragraph 5 of Schedule 12(7) to the Universal Credit Regulations (exception for non-consensual conception).

2.831

(2) The Secretary of State may treat the condition in sub-paragraph (3) (a) of that paragraph 5 as met if the Secretary of State is satisfied that the claimant has previously provided the evidence referred to in that sub-paragraph to the Commissioners for her Majesty's Revenue and Customs for the purposes of the corresponding exception in relation to child tax credit.]

AMENDMENT

1. Social Security (Restrictions on Amounts for Children and Qualifying Young Persons) Amendment Regulations 2017 (2017/376) reg.3(3) (April 6, 2017).

[¹ Abolition of higher amount of the child element for first child or qualifying young person – saving where claimant responsible for a child or qualifying young person born before 6th April 2017

2.832   **43.** Section 14(5)(b) of the Welfare Reform and Work Act 2016(8) (which amends the Universal Credit Regulations by omitting the amount of the child element payable for the first child or qualifying young person) does not apply where the claimant is responsible for a child or qualifying young person born before 6th April 2017.]

AMENDMENT

1. Social Security (Restrictions on Amounts for Children and Qualifying Young Persons) Amendment Regulations 2017 (2017/376) reg.3(3) (April 6, 2017).

[¹PART 4

MANAGED MIGRATION TO UNIVERSAL CREDIT

The Migration Process

Migration notice

2.833   **44.**—(1) The Secretary of State may, at any time, issue a notice ("a migration notice") to a person who is entitled to an award of an existing benefit—

(a) informing the person that all awards of any existing benefits to which they are entitled are to terminate and that they will need to make a claim for universal credit; and

(b) specifying a day ("the deadline day") by which a claim for universal credit must be made.

(2) The migration notice may contain such other information as the Secretary of State considers appropriate.

(3) The deadline day must not be within the period of three months beginning with the day on which the migration notice is issued.

(4) If the person who is entitled to an award of an existing benefit is, for the purposes of that award, a member of a couple or a member of a polygamous marriage, the Secretary of State must also issue the migration notice to the other member (or members).

(5) The Secretary of State may cancel a migration notice issued to any person—

(a) if it has been issued in error; [² or]

(b) [²...]

(c) in any other circumstances where the Secretary State considers it necessary to do so in the interests of the person, or any class of person, or to safeguard the efficient administration of universal credit.

(6) A "notified person" is a person to whom a migration notice has been issued.]

AMENDMENTS

1. Universal Credit (Managed Migration Pilot and Miscellaneous Amendments) Regulations 2019 (SI 2019/1152) reg.3(7) (July 24, 2019).
2. Universal Credit (Transitional Provisions) Amendment Regulations 2022 (SI 2022/752) reg.11 and Sch. para.1(7) (July 25, 2022).

DEFINITIONS

"deadline day"—see para.(1)(b).
"existing benefit"—see reg.2(1).
"migration notice"—see para.(1).
"notified person"—see para.(6).

GENERAL NOTE

The background   2.834

Universal credit was first introduced on April 29, 2013. Initially claimants were required to satisfy the so-called "Pathfinder Group" and later the "gateway" conditions, in what were known as "live service" areas. As from November 26, 2014, it became possible to claim universal credit in "full service" or "digital service" areas without satisfying those criteria. Since December 12, 2018, all GB postcode districts and part-districts have been converted to digital service areas, in which universal credit must be claimed instead of one of the existing benefits (subject to certain exceptions where a legacy benefit may be claimed). Claimants of existing benefits who have had a change of circumstances have moved to universal credit by the process known as "natural migration".

The first managed migration pilot   2.835

The next phase in the roll-out of universal credit is "managed migration", whereby claimants of existing benefits are invited to make a claim for universal credit under the new Pt 4 of these Regulations. In the first instance this is being introduced on a pilot basis. This regulation provides for the issue of a migration notice, which in effect formally kick-starts the process of managed migration (although, according to official guidance, "before a migration notice is issued, claimants are informed about the migration process to ensure that they are ready to claim UC": see DMG Ch.M7: *Managed migration pilot and transitional protection* para.M7041). The migration notice informs a person that their existing benefits are to terminate and gives a deadline for claiming universal credit. Note that in the first instance at least this process is limited to a pilot, both geographically and numerically.

The first managed migration pilot, which was originally expected to last for up to 18 months, was confined to the Harrogate area and to a maximum of 10,000 awards of universal credit (see reg.2 (Managed migration pilot: limit on number of cases migrated) of the Universal Credit (Managed Migration Pilot and Miscellaneous Amendments) Regulations 2019 (SI 2019/1152), in force with effect from July 24, 2019). However, the Harrogate pilot was temporarily suspended on March 30, 2020, owing to the coronavirus crisis.

2.836   *The managed migration pilot resumed*

On April 25, 2022, the Secretary of State made the following statement to the House of Commons under the headline of "Completing the Move to Universal Credit by 2024" (HCWS780):

"In 2012, Parliament voted to end legacy benefits and replace them with a single modern benefit system, Universal Credit (UC). The UC system stood up to the challenges of the pandemic and ensured support was provided for a significant number of new claimants with varying needs across the country. As the rest of government and society returns to business as usual, it is appropriate to resume the process to complete the move to UC by 2024.

There are around 2.6 million households receiving legacy benefits and tax credits who need to move across to UC. The natural migration process, where claimants experience a change in circumstances and consequently move to UC, has largely continued throughout the last two years. The voluntary migration process has also been available throughout. We are taking steps to increase people's awareness of the fact that they could be better off financially if they were receiving Universal Credit, including through the publication of our document, *Completing the Move to Universal Credit*, today on GOV.UK. I will place copies in the libraries of both Houses.

In that document, we set out our analysis which estimates that 1.4 million (55%) of those on legacy benefits or tax credits would receive a higher entitlement on UC than on legacy benefits and would benefit from moving voluntarily, rather than waiting for a managed migration. This is particularly the case for tax credit claimants, with our analysis estimating around two-thirds of them would benefit. That is why we have included information on UC in this year's renewal forms for current tax credit recipients. It is important for current recipients to satisfy themselves that they would be better off on UC using independent benefit calculators before moving voluntarily, as once the claim is made, recipients cannot revert to tax credits or legacy benefits, nor receive any transitional protection payments. More information is included in the document.

For those claimants who do not choose to move and have not migrated naturally, we will manage their migration to UC. Parliament committed to providing transitional financial protection to those who are moved onto UC through the managed migration process. Whilst many households will be better off financially on UC, for those with a lower calculated award in UC than in their legacy benefits, transitional protection will be provided for eligible households. This means they will see no difference in their entitlement at the point they are moved to UC, provided there is no change in their circumstances during the migration process.

Before the pandemic, the department had started testing processes for managed migration in a pilot based in Harrogate. In 2020, the pilot was stopped to handle the significant increase in new claims for UC resulting from the pandemic. During this pilot there was proactive engagement with 80 people, 38 of these were moved to UC. 35 claimants were better off and only three people required transitional protection. The remainder of moves were not completed before the pilot was stopped. This pilot only involved claimants that the department had an existing relationship with. No claimants on Working Tax Credits were approached directly to commence a Move to UC.

The pilot provided valuable insights. First, while claimants will likely look for support from organisations they already know, such as a local authority, we are no longer assuming that all engagement needs to be managed by that organisation. Second, claimants can and will move autonomously, but some may need more support, particularly on digital access. The pandemic reinforced the importance of claimants being able to manage their own claims online and the strength of this system. Third, claimants can successfully choose a date for their claim, factoring in other income and expenditure points during the month. Finally, the pilot allowed the department to understand the processes and tools required to complete a managed move, such as those needed to calculate transitional protection.

As I have said to the House previously, we are not resuming the Harrogate pilot. We have learned from that experience and our wider experience over the last two years. As we complete the Move to UC, I am absolutely committed to making this a responsible and safe transition. Next month, we will be starting a multi-site approach across the country with a small number of claimants, approximately five hundred initially, being brought into the mandatory migration process. We will continue to develop our processes and systems to scale the migration process and complete by 2024.

We are resuming under existing regulations, though I intend to bring forward to Parliament amendments to the UC Transitional Provisions Regulations, following their consideration by the Social Security Advisory Committee.

Universal Credit is a dynamic welfare system fit for the 21st century. As part of our levelling up agenda to support the British public, we will continue to help people into work and progress in work, taking advantage of the recent reduction in the taper rate and boost to work allowances."

See also the DWP's accompanying press release (*https://www.gov.uk/government/news/managed-move-of-claimants-to-universal-credit-set-to-restart*). The new managed migration process commenced on May 9, 2022, but was confined to just two areas – Bolton and Medway. A coalition of charities has sent the Secretary of State an open letter calling for a halt to the managed migration process because of what they say is the risk to claimants' incomes: *https://www.mind.org.uk/news-campaigns/news/leading-charities-unite-to-tell-uk-government-to-halt-managed-migration/*.

Regulation 2 of the Universal Credit (Managed Migration Pilot and Miscellaneous Amendments) Regulations 2019 (SI 2019/1152), limiting the number of cases migrated to a maximum of 10,000 awards, was revoked with effect from July 25, 2022, by reg.10 of the Universal Credit (Transitional Provisions) Amendment Regulations 2022 (SI 2022/752).

On March 28, 2023 Mr G Opperman, Minister of State for Employment, made the following statement on the timetable for universal credit (*Move to Universal Credit Update*, Statement UIN HCWS678):

"Since its introduction in 2013, Universal Credit has protected the most vulnerable in society, supported households through periods of financial uncertainty, helped people progress in work and move into better paid jobs. A dynamic benefit that reflects people's needs from month to month, Universal Credit successfully supports millions of people, and ensures that individuals are provided with the support they need to increase their earnings and move into better paid quality jobs.

In April 2022, the Government set out its plan to complete the move to Universal Credit, and published Completing the move to Universal Credit, learning from the pilot that was paused in 2020.

In May 2022, we commenced our Discovery phase. Initially, we issued 500 Migration Notices to households in Bolton and Medway. This notification letter sets out the requirement to make a claim to Universal Credit, to continue to receive financial support from the Government. It advises that they have a minimum of three months to make their claim and provides details of the support available.

Following these initial notifications, we expanded the Discovery phase to Truro and Falmouth in July 2022, Harrow in August 2022, Northumberland in September 2022 and more recently all postcodes in Cornwall during February 2023.

In January 2023, we published our learning from the Earliest Testable Service, which set out our initial learnings from the Discovery phase. It also set out the Department's plans for Move to Universal Credit in 2023/24 and 2024/25.

We are now preparing to increase the numbers of Migration Notices issued and will expand into additional areas, bringing in the whole of Great Britain during 2023/24. Social security is a transferred matter in Northern Ireland.

Through 2023/24, our focus will be on notifying households that receive tax credits only, increasing volumes incrementally each month. As we move into 2024/25, all cases with tax credits (including those on both Employment Support Allowance and tax credits), all cases on Income Support and Jobseeker's Allowance (Income Based) and all Housing Benefit cases (including combinations of these benefits) will be required to move to Universal Credit.

At the point of moving over to Universal Credit (for those claimants moving through the managed migration process), legacy benefit claimants will be assessed for transitional protection and paid where appropriate. The aim of this temporary payment is to maintain benefit entitlement at the point of transition so that claimants will have time to adjust to the new benefit system.

In line with the 2022 Autumn statement, the Government is delaying the managed migration of claimants on income-related Employment Support Allowance (except for those receiving Child Tax Credit) to Universal Credit. Employment Support Allowance claimants are still however able to make a claim for Universal Credit if they believe that they will be better off.

This Government remains committed to making this a smooth and safe transition. As we move to the next phase of Move to Universal Credit, we will continue to build on our learning to ensure the service continues to meet the needs of those required to make the move to Universal Credit."

2.837   *Paragraphs (1)–(6)*

A person who receives a migration notice is a "notified person" (see para.(6)). A notice is only a migration notice if it contains two pieces of information (although other information may be included (para.(2)). First, the notice must inform "the person that all awards of any existing benefits to which they are entitled are to terminate and that they will need to make a claim for universal credit" (para.(1) (a))—thus transfer is not automatic, and a claim must be made. Second, the notice must also specify the day ("the deadline day") by which a claim for universal credit must be made (para.(1)(b)). Deadline day must not fall within three months of the date of issue of the migration notice (para.(3)) and may be extended (see reg.45). Where couples are concerned each member must be issued with a migration notice (para. (4)). Notices can be cancelled in the circumstances set out in para.(5)).

[¹Extension of the deadline day

2.838   **45.**—(1) The Secretary of State may determine that the deadline day should be changed to a later day either—

(a) on the Secretary of State's own initiative; or

(b) if a notified person requests such a change before the deadline day, where there is a good reason to do so.

(2) The Secretary of State must inform the notified person or persons of the new deadline day.]

AMENDMENT

1. Universal Credit (Managed Migration Pilot and Miscellaneous Amendments) Regulations 2019 (SI 2019/1152) reg.3(7) (July 24, 2019).

DEFINITIONS

"deadline day"—see reg.44(1)(b).
"notified person"—see reg.44(6).

General Note

This provides in very general terms for the circumstances in which the deadline   2.839
for making a universal credit claim following issue of a migration notice can be
extended. The deadline may be extended by the Secretary of State on her own
initiative or on receipt of a request from the notified person. All that is required (in
either instance) is "a good reason to do so". There is no statutory definition of "good
reason". The non-exhaustive list of examples in the official guidance refers to cases
where the claimant has difficulty completing the universal credit claim because
they have a physical or mental health condition, have learning difficulties, are in or
about to go in to hospital as an in-patient, have significant caring responsibilities, are
homeless or face a domestic emergency (*DMG Chapter M7: Managed migration pilot
and Transitional protection* para M7081). Providing the criteria are met, there is no
limit to the potential number of extensions that can be made (although cancellation
under reg.44(5) may be more appropriate) but in any case the notified person must
be advised of the new deadline (para.(2)). The official guidance also asserts that
there is no right to a mandatory reconsideration or appeal about being issued with
a migration notice, the deadline day or a refusal to extend a deadline or cancel the
notice. This guidance is presumably based on the premise that such actions are not
"made on a claim for, or on an award of, a relevant benefit" within s.12 SSA 1998
and, as they are not included within Sch.3 to that Act, do not carry a right of appeal.
It may, however, be possible to challenge such an action indirectly as a "building
block" to an "outcome decision" (e.g. no valid migration notice served so decision
to terminate existing award is incorrect). Such a challenge to extension notices may
raise issues analogous to those in *R(TC) 1/05*. Failing that, in theory at least, judicial
review must be available for a potential challenge.

[¹Termination of existing benefits if no claim before the deadline

46.—(1) Where a notified person has not made a claim for universal   2.840
credit on or before the deadline day, all awards of any existing benefits to
which the person is entitled terminate—

   (a) in the case of housing benefit, [² income support, income-based
       jobseeker's allowance or income-related employment and support
       allowance,] on the last day of the period of two weeks beginning with
       the deadline day; and
   (b) in the case of [²a tax credit], on the day before the deadline day.

(2) An award of housing benefit to which a claimant is entitled in respect
of specified accommodation or temporary accommodation does not terminate by virtue of this regulation.

(3) Where paragraph (1) applies and the notified person makes a claim
for universal credit—

   (a) after the deadline day; and
   (b) on or before the final deadline specified in paragraph (4),

then, notwithstanding anything in regulation 26 of the Claims and
Payments Regulations (time within which a claim for universal credit is to
be made) as modified by regulation 15 of these Regulations, the award is to
commence on the deadline day.

(4) The final deadline is the day that would be the last day of the first
assessment period in relation to an award commencing on the deadline day.

   (5) [³...]]

Amendments

1. Universal Credit (Managed Migration Pilot and Miscellaneous Amendments)
Regulations 2019 (SI 2019/1152) reg.3(7) (July 24, 2019).

2. Universal Credit (Managed Migration Pilot and Miscellaneous Amendments) Regulations 2019 (SI 2019/1152) reg.4(5) July 22, 2020).

3. Universal Credit (Transitional Provisions) Amendment Regulations 2022 (SI 2022/752) reg.11 and Sch. para.1(8) (July 25, 2022).

DEFINITIONS

"assessment period"—see reg.2(1).
"deadline day"—see reg.44(1)(b).
"existing benefit"—see reg.2(1).
"final deadline"—see para.(4).
"housing benefit"—see reg.2(1).
"migration notice"—see reg.44(1).
"notified person"—see reg.44(6).
"specified accommodation"—see reg.2(1).
"temporary accommodation—*ibid*.

GENERAL NOTE

2.841 This provides for termination of all awards of any existing benefits where a notified person does not claim universal credit by the deadline day (para.(1)). However, the DWP has indicated that it has no intention to use these powers during the pilot phase – rather action will be taken to encourage the claimant to make a claim for universal credit.

In the case of an income-based JSA or income-related ESA, "terminate" means treating the award in the same way as if WRA 2012 s.33(1)(a) or (b) (abolition of those benefits) and associated provisions had come into force. This means that any contribution-based or contributory allowance to which a claimant is entitled becomes an award of new style JSA or new style ESA (as defined in reg.2 of the 2014 Regulations). Where the person claims universal credit by the final deadline (which is the last day of the first assessment period of an award commencing on the deadline day) the award is backdated to the deadline day (paras.(3) and (4)). See also reg.47 (para.(5)).

[¹Notified persons who claim as a different benefit unit

2.842 **47.**—[² ...]

AMENDMENTS

1. Universal Credit (Managed Migration Pilot and Miscellaneous Amendments) Regulations 2019 (SI 2019/1152) reg.3(7) (July 24, 2019).
2. Universal Credit (Transitional Provisions) Amendment Regulations 2022 (SI 2022/752) reg.6(1) (July 25, 2022).

Transitional Protection

[¹Meaning of "qualifying claim"

2.843 **48.** A "qualifying claim" is a claim for universal credit by a single claimant who is a notified person or by joint claimants, both of whom are notified persons, where the claim is made on or before the final deadline (see regulation 46(4)).]

AMENDMENT

1. Universal Credit (Managed Migration Pilot and Miscellaneous Amendments) Regulations 2019 (SI 2019/1152) reg.3(7) (July 24, 2019).

DEFINITIONS

"final deadline"—see reg.46(4).
"notified person"—see reg.44(6).

GENERAL NOTE

The Secretary of State is required (see new regs 48 and 49) to determine whether   2.844
transitional protection applies where the person makes a "qualifying claim" as
defined by this provision. It follows these arrangements for transitional protection apply only to cases subject to *managed* migration, and not to cases affected
by *natural* migration (e.g. owing to a change of circumstances). The two types of
transitional protection are a "transitional capital disregard" (reg.51) and a "transitional element" (regs 52 to 55). The *transitional capital disregard* enables claimants
entitled to tax credits and with capital above £16,000 to be entitled to universal
credit for up to 12 months (technically 12 assessment periods). The *transitional
element* is an additional amount of universal credit based on the difference between
the total amount of existing benefits and the amount of universal credit entitlement. This is added to the award before income is deducted and erodes as other
elements increase.

But see also reg.58, enabling the Secretary of State to specify a later commencement date for an award on a qualifying claim.

[¹Meaning of "migration day"

49. "Migration day", in relation to a qualifying claim, means the day   2.845
before the first day on which the claimant is entitled to universal credit in
connection with that claim.]

AMENDMENT

1. Universal Credit (Managed Migration Pilot and Miscellaneous Amendments)
Regulations 2019 (SI 2019/1152) reg.3(7) (July 24, 2019).

DEFINITION

qualifying claim"—see reg.48.

GENERAL NOTE

Migration day, being the day before the start of a universal credit award, is used   2.846
as the marker to calculate any transitional protection due.

[¹Secretary of State to determine whether transitional protection applies

50.—(1) Before making a decision on a qualifying claim the Secretary of   2.847
State must first determine whether—
   (a) a transitional capital disregard is to apply; or
   (b) a transitional element is to be included,
(or both) in the calculation of the award.

(2) But the Secretary of State is not to determine whether a transitional
element is to be included in a case [² where—
   (a) notified persons who were a couple for the purposes of an award of
       an existing benefit when the migration notice was issued are single
       persons or members of a different couple for the purposes of a claim
       for universal credit; or

(b) notified persons who were single for the purposes of an award of an existing benefit when the migration notice was issued are a couple for the purposes of a claim for universal credit; or

(c) notified persons who were members of a polygamous marriage for the purposes of an award of an existing benefit when the migration notice was issued are a couple or single persons for the purposes of a claim for universal credit]].

AMENDMENTS

1. Universal Credit (Managed Migration Pilot and Miscellaneous Amendments) Regulations 2019 (SI 2019/1152) reg.3(7) (July 24, 2019).
2. Universal Credit (Transitional Provisions) Amendment Regulations 2022 (SI 2022/752) reg.6(2) (July 25, 2022).

DEFINITIONS

"notified person"—see reg.44(6).
"qualifying claim"—see reg.48.
"transitional capital disregard"—see reg.51.
"transitional element"—see reg.52.

GENERAL NOTE

2.848   Subject to the special cases in para.(2), the Secretary of State is under a duty to determine whether transitional protection applies on a qualifying claim. This must be done "*before* making a decision on a qualifying claim". The sequencing is important as otherwise the universal credit conditions of entitlement may not be satisfied or the amount of universal credit to which the claimant might be entitled might be less than any income taken into account. In addition, of course, transitional protection applies only to a qualifying claim (see reg.48), i.e. a claim made on or before the final deadline. Claimants who fail to claim under the managed migration rules will not be entitled to transitional protection even if they manage to make a successful claim at a later date. As the Explanatory Memorandum puts it:

"7.4 Provided that existing benefit claimants (and their partner, if they have one) make the UC claim by the deadline day specified in the notification, existing benefits will be paid up until the day before they made their UC claim and Transitional Protection will be considered. If they do not make a new UC claim by the deadline day, their existing benefits will end and will be paid up until the day before that day.

7.5 If claimants contact the Department after the deadline date but within one month of their existing benefits ending, their UC claim will automatically be backdated to the deadline date and Transitional Protection can be applied to the UC award. If a claimant does not contact the Department until after a month after the deadline date they were given, their claim will not be considered as a managed migration claim which means their claim will be assessed under the UC regulations5 without the consideration or award of Transitional Protection."

[¹The transitional capital disregard

2.849   **51.**—(1) A transitional capital disregard is to apply where, on the migration day, the claimant—

(a) is entitled to an award of a tax credit; and
(b) has capital exceeding £16,000.

(2) Where a transitional capital disregard applies, any capital exceeding £16,000 is to be disregarded for the purposes of—

(a) determining whether the financial condition in section 5(1)(a) or 5(2)(a) of the Act (capital limit) is met; and

(b) calculating the amount of an award of universal credit (including the indicative UC amount).

(3) Where a transitional capital disregard has been applied in the calculation of an award of universal credit but, in any assessment period, the claimant no longer has (or joint claimants no longer have) capital exceeding £16,000, the transitional capital disregard is not to apply in any subsequent assessment period.

(4) A transitional capital disregard is not to apply for more than 12 assessment periods.]

AMENDMENT

1. Universal Credit (Managed Migration Pilot and Miscellaneous Amendments) Regulations 2019 (SI 2019/1152) reg.3(7) (July 24, 2019).

DEFINITIONS

"assessment period"—see reg.2(1).
"migration day"—see reg.49.
"tax credit"—see reg.2(1).

GENERAL NOTE

Tax credit entitlement is not subject to any capital limit whereas universal credit claimants must not have capital over £16,000. The transitional capital disregard allows capital over £16,000 in the hands of former tax credit claimants to be disregarded for 12 months where the relevant conditions are satisfied (the 12 months need not be consecutive). The transitional capital disregard ceases to apply in the circumstances set out in para.(3) or those in reg.56.

2.850

[¹The transitional element

52.—(1) A transitional element is to be included in the calculation of an award if the total amount of any awards of existing benefits determined in accordance with regulation 53 ("the total legacy amount") is greater than the amount of an award of universal credit determined in accordance with regulation 54 ("the indicative UC amount").

2.851

(2) Where a transitional element is to be included in the calculation of an award, the amount of that element is to be treated, for the purposes of section 8 of the Act (calculation of awards), as if it were an additional amount to be included in the maximum amount under section 8(2) before the deduction of income under section 8(3).]

AMENDMENT

1. Universal Credit (Managed Migration Pilot and Miscellaneous Amendments) Regulations 2019 (SI 2019/1152) reg.3(7) (July 24, 2019).

DEFINITIONS

"existing benefit"—see reg.2(1).
"indicative UC amount"—see reg.54.
"total legacy amount"—see reg.53.

GENERAL NOTE

2.852 Transitional protection in the form of a "transitional element" applies (see para. (1)) if the "total legacy amount" (in effect the previous entitlement under existing benefits on the day before change-over—see reg.53) is more than the "indicative UC amount" (see reg.54). This method has been "designed to provide a balanced, like-for-like comparison of entitlement under the two regimes" (Explanatory Memorandum, para.7.15). Where transitional element applies, the difference is included in the universal credit award as a transitional element. It is treated as an additional amount to be included in the maximum amount of universal credit before the deduction of income (para.(2)). Rounding rules apply as under reg.61. The transitional element is no longer included in an award in the circumstances specified in reg.56. If the indicative UC amount is more than the total legacy amount, then obviously no such element is included.

[¹**The transitional element – total legacy amount**

2.853 **53.**—(1) The total legacy amount is the sum of the representative monthly rates of all awards of any existing benefits to which a claimant is, or joint claimants are, entitled on the migration day.

Tax credits

(2) To calculate the representative monthly rate of an award of working tax credit or child tax credit—

(a) take the figure for the daily rate of the award on the migration day provided by HMRC and calculated on the basis of the information as to the claimant's circumstances held by HMRC on that day; and

(b) convert to a monthly figure by multiplying by 365 and dividing by 12.

(3) For the purposes of paragraph (2)(a) "the daily rate" is—

(a) in a case where section 13(1) of the 2002 Act applies (relevant income does not exceed the income threshold or the claimant is entitled to a prescribed social security benefit), the maximum rate of each element to which the claimant is entitled on the migration day divided by 365; and

(b) in any other case, the rate that would be produced by applying regulations 6 to 9 of the Tax Credits (Income Thresholds and Determination of Rates) Regulations 2002(6) as if the migration day were a relevant period of one day.

IS, JSA(IB) and ESA(IR)

(4) To calculate the representative monthly rate of an award of income support, income-based jobseeker's allowance or income-related employment and support allowance—

(a) take the weekly rate on the migration day calculated in accordance with—

(i) in the case of income support, Part 7 of the Social Security Contributions and Benefits Act 1992 and the Income Support (General) Regulations 1987,

   (ii) in the case of income-based jobseeker's allowance, Part 1 of the Jobseekers Act 1995 and the Jobseeker's Allowance Regulations 1996, or

   (iii) in the case of income-related employment and support allowance, Part 1 of the 2007 Act, the Employment and Support Allowance Regulations 2008 and the Employment and Support Allowance (Transitional Provisions, Housing Benefit and Council Tax Benefit) (Existing Awards) (No.2) Regulations 2010,

on the basis of the information held by the Secretary of State on that day; and

  (b) convert to a monthly figure by multiplying by 52 and dividing by 12.

(5) The amount of an award of income-related employment and support allowance or income-based jobseeker's allowance is to be calculated before any reduction for a sanction.

(6) Where—

  (a) a claimant who is entitled to income-based jobseeker's allowance is also entitled to contribution-based jobseeker's allowance; or

  (b) a claimant who is entitled to income-related employment and support allowance is also entitled to a contributory allowance,

then, notwithstanding section 4(8) to (11) of the Jobseekers Act 1995 and section 6(3) to (7) of the 2007 Act (excess over the contributory allowance to be treated as attributable to the income-based, or income-related, allowance) the weekly rate in paragraph (4) is to be calculated as the applicable amount less the claimant's income (if any).

Housing benefit

(7) To calculate the representative monthly rate of an award of housing benefit—

  (a) take the weekly rate on the migration day calculated in accordance with Part 7 of the Social Security Contributions and Benefits Act 1992 and the Housing Benefit Regulations 2006, on the basis of the information held by the Secretary of State on that day, and convert to a monthly figure by multiplying by 52 and dividing by 12; or

  (b) in a case where the claimant has rent free periods, calculate the annual rate by multiplying the weekly rate (as above) by the number of weeks in the year in respect of which the claimant is liable to pay rent, and convert to a monthly figure by dividing by 12.

(8) For the purposes of paragraph (7), if the migration day falls in a rent free period, the weekly rate of housing benefit is to be calculated by reference to the amount of rent for the last complete week that was not a rent free period.

(9) In paragraphs (7) and (8) "rent free period" has the meaning in regulation 81 of the Housing Benefit Regulations 2006.

(10) In a case where regulation 8(3) (continuation of housing benefit in respect of specified accommodation or temporary accommodation) applies, no amount is to be included in the total legacy amount in respect of housing benefit.

The benefit cap

(11) Where—

(a) the existing benefits do not include an award of housing benefit, or they include an award of housing benefit that has been reduced to the minimum amount by virtue of Part 8A of the Housing Benefit Regulations 2006 (the benefit cap);

(b) Part 7 of the Universal Credit Regulations (the benefit cap) applies in the calculation of the indicative UC amount; and

(c) the claimant's total entitlement to welfare benefits (as defined in section 96(10) of the Act) on the migration day is greater than the relevant amount,

the total legacy amount is reduced by the excess (minus the amount for childcare costs referred to regulation 54(2)(b) where applicable) over the relevant amount.

(12) For the purposes of paragraph (11)—

(a) the amount of each welfare benefit is the monthly equivalent calculated in the manner set out in regulation 73 (unearned income calculated monthly) of the Universal Credit Regulations; and

(b) the "relevant amount" is the amount referred to in regulation 80A of those Regulations which is applicable to the claimant.]

AMENDMENT

1. Universal Credit (Managed Migration Pilot and Miscellaneous Amendments) Regulations 2019 (SI 2019/1152) reg.3(7) (July 24, 2019).

DEFINITIONS

"contributory employment and support allowance"—see reg.2(1).
"the daily rate"—see para.(3).
"existing benefit"—see reg.2(1).
"housing benefit"—*ibid.*
"income support"—*ibid.*
"income-based jobseeker's allowance"—*ibid.*
"income-related employment and support allowance"—*ibid.*
"migration day"—see reg.49.
"HMRC"—see reg.2(1).
"relevant amount"—see para.(11).
"rent free period"—see para.(9).
"tax credit"—see reg.2(1).
"total legacy amount"—see para.(1).

GENERAL NOTE

2.854   The total legacy amount is calculated by adding together the monthly rates of all awards of the existing benefits to which the claimant was entitled on migration day, i.e. the day before the universal credit award starts. That principle is established by para.(1). The remainder of the regulation deals with the necessary arithmetic with respect to tax credits (paras.(2) and (3)), income support, income-based JSA and income-related ESA (paras.(4)–(6)) and housing benefit (paras.(7)–(10)), subject to any benefit cap adjustment (paras.(11)–(12)).

[¹The transitional element – indicative UC amount

54.—(1) The indicative UC amount is the amount to which a claimant   2.855
would be entitled if an award of universal credit were calculated in accordance with section 8 of the Act by reference to the claimant's circumstances
on the migration day, applying the assumptions in paragraph (2).

(2) The assumptions are—

(a) if the claimant is entitled to an award of child tax credit, the claimant
is responsible for any child or qualifying young person in respect of
whom the individual element of child tax credit is payable;

(b) if the claimant is entitled to an award of working tax credit that
includes the childcare element, the indicative UC amount includes
the childcare costs element and, for the purposes of calculating the
amount of that element, the amount of the childcare costs is equal
to the relevant weekly childcare charges included in the calculation of the daily rate referred to in regulation 53(2), converted to a
monthly amount by multiplying by 52 and dividing by 12;

(c) the amount of the claimant's earned income is—

(i) if the claimant is entitled to an award of a tax credit, the annual
amount of any employment income or trading income, as
defined by regulation 4 or 6 respectively of the Tax Credits
(Definition and Calculation of Income) Regulations 2002, by
reference to which the representative monthly rate of that tax
credit is calculated for the purposes of regulation 53(2) converted to a net monthly amount by—

(aa) dividing by 12, and

(bb) deducting such amount for income tax and national insurance contributions as the Secretary of State considers
appropriate,

(ii) if paragraph (i) does not apply and the claimant is entitled to
an award of income support, income-based jobseeker's allowance or income-related employment and support allowance,
the amount of earnings by reference to which the representative
monthly rate of that benefit was calculated for the purposes of
regulation 53(4) to (6) (including nil if none were taken into
account) converted to a monthly amount by multiplying by 52
and dividing by 12, or

(iii) if paragraphs (i) and (ii) do not apply, but the claimant had
an award of housing benefit, the amount of earnings by
reference to which the representative monthly rate of that
benefit was calculated for the purposes of regulation 53(7)
to (10) (including nil if none were taken into account) converted to a monthly amount by multiplying by 52 and dividing
by 12.

(3) If the claimant would not meet the financial condition in section 5(1)
(b) of the Act (or, in the case of joint claimants, they would not meet the
condition in section 5(2)(b) of the Act) the claimant is to be treated, for the
purposes of calculating the indicative UC amount, as if they were entitled
to an award of universal credit of a nil amount.

(4) If a transitional capital disregard is to apply, the claimant is to be
treated as having met the financial condition in section 5(1)(a) or 5(2)(a)
of the Act (capital limit).

(5) The indicative UC amount is to be calculated after any reduction under Part 7 of the Universal Credit Regulations (the benefit cap) but before any reduction under section 26 (higher-level sanctions) or 27 (other sanctions) of the Act.

(6) But there is to be no reduction for the benefit cap under that Part where the amount of the claimant's earned income (or, in the case of a couple their combined earned income) on the migration day, calculated in accordance with paragraph (2)(c), is equal to or exceeds the amount specified in paragraph (1)(a) of regulation 82 (exceptions – earnings) of the Universal Credit Regulations.

(7) The calculation of the indicative UC amount is to be based on the information that is used for the purposes of calculating the total legacy amount, supplemented as necessary by such further information or evidence as the Secretary of State requires.]

AMENDMENT

1. Universal Credit (Managed Migration Pilot and Miscellaneous Amendments) Regulations 2019 (SI 2019/1152) reg.3(7) (July 24, 2019).

DEFINITIONS

"childcare costs element"—see reg.2(1).
"earned income"—*ibid.*
"housing benefit"—*ibid.*
"indicative UC amount"—see reg.54.
"migration day"—see reg.49.
"tax credit"—see reg.2(1).
"total legacy amount"—see reg.53.
"transitional capital disregard"—see reg.51.

GENERAL NOTE

2.856   The total legacy amount (reg.53) is a relatively straightforward concept to grasp. It is what the claimant was in fact entitled to under the existing benefit regime. The indicative UC amount is a less readily understandable concept. According to para. (1) it represents the hypothetical amount of universal credit to which the claimant would have been entitled to on migration day (i.e. the day before the universal credit award commenced) but subject to the various assumptions in para.(2). In addition, if the claimant would not meet the income financial condition of entitlement, they are treated for these purposes as being entitled to a nil award (para.(3)). Claimants are also treated as satisfying the capital financial condition where the transitional capital disregard applies (para.(4)). The indicative UC amount is worked out *after* any reduction due to the benefit cap (but see para.(6)) and *before* any reduction for a sanction (para.(5)).

[¹The transitional element – initial amount and adjustment where other elements increase

2.857   **55.**—(1) The initial amount of the transitional element is—

(a) if the indicative UC amount is greater than nil, the amount by which the total legacy amount exceeds the indicative UC amount; or

(b) if the indicative UC amount is nil, the total legacy amount plus any amount by which the income which fell to be deducted in accordance with section 8(3) of the Act exceeded the maximum amount.

(2) The amount of the transitional element to be included in the calculation of an award is—

   (a) for the first assessment period, the initial amount;

   (b) for the second assessment period, the initial amount reduced by the sum of any relevant increases in that assessment period;

   (c) for the third and each subsequent assessment period, the amount that was included for the previous assessment period reduced by the sum of any relevant increases (as in sub-paragraph (b)).

(3) If the amount of the transitional element is reduced to nil in any assessment period, a transitional element is not to apply in the calculation of the award for any subsequent assessment period.

(4) A "relevant increase" is [², subject to paragraph (5)] an increase in any of the amounts that are included in the maximum amount under sections 9 to 12 of the Act (including any of those amounts that is included for the first time), apart from the childcare costs element.]

[²(5) In cases where the LCW element is replaced by the LCWRA element, the "relevant increase" is to be treated as the difference between the amounts of those elements.

(6) In this regulation, "LCW element" and "LCWRA element" have the same meaning as in regulation 2 of the Universal Credit Regulations.]

AMENDMENTS

1. Universal Credit (Managed Migration Pilot and Miscellaneous Amendments) Regulations 2019 (SI 2019/1152) reg.3(7) (July 24, 2019).

2. Universal Credit (Transitional Provisions) Amendment Regulations 2022 (SI 2022/752) reg.7 (July 25, 2022).

DEFINITIONS

"assessment period"—see reg.2(1).
"childcare costs element"—*ibid.*
"relevant increase"—see para.(4).
"indicative UC amount"—see reg.54.
"total legacy amount"—see reg.53.
"transitional element"—see reg.52.

GENERAL NOTE

The amount of the transitional element to be included in the calculation of a   **2.858** universal credit award is, for the first assessment period (para.(2)(a)), the initial amount as defined by para.(1). The amount for subsequent periods is governed by para.(2)(b) and (c) as appropriate. In these later periods the amount can be reduced by relevant increases, as defined by para.(4).

[¹*Ending of transitional protection*

Circumstances in which transitional protection ceases

56.—(1) A transitional capital disregard or a transitional element does   **2.859** not apply in any assessment period to which paragraph (2) or (4) applies, or in any subsequent assessment period.

Cessation of employment or sustained drop in earnings

(2) This paragraph applies to an assessment period if the following condition is met—

    (a) in the case of a single claimant—

        (i) it is the assessment period after the third consecutive assessment period in which the claimant's earned income is less than the amount specified in regulation 99(6)(a) of the Universal Credit Regulations ("the single administrative threshold"), and

        (ii) in the first assessment period of the award, the claimant's earned income was equal to or more than that threshold; or

    (b) in the case of joint claimants—

        (i) it is the assessment period after the third consecutive assessment period in which their combined earned income is less than the amount specified in regulation 99(6)(b) of the Universal Credit Regulations ("the couple administrative threshold"), and

        (ii) in the first assessment period of the award, their combined earned income was equal to or more than that threshold.

[²(3) For the purposes of paragraph (2)—

(a) references to the amount specified in regulation 99(6)(a) and 99(6)(b) respectively of the Universal Credit Regulations are to the amount that was applicable on the first day of the award; and

(b) a claimant is to be treated as having earned income that is equal to or more than the single administrative threshold and the couple administrative threshold respectively in any assessment period in respect of which regulation 62 (minimum income floor) of the Universal Credit Regulations applies to that claimant or would apply but for regulation 62(5) of those Regulations (minimum income floor not to apply in a start-up period).]

Couple separating or forming

(4) This paragraph applies to an assessment period in which—

(a) joint claimants cease to be a couple or become members of a different couple; or

(b) a single claimant becomes a member of a couple, unless it is a case where the person may, by virtue of regulation 3(3) of the Universal Credit Regulations (claimant with an ineligible partner), claim as a single person.]

AMENDMENTS

    1. Universal Credit (Managed Migration Pilot and Miscellaneous Amendments) Regulations 2019 (SI 2019/1152) reg.3(7) (July 24, 2019).

    2. Universal Credit (Administrative Earnings Threshold) (Amendment) Regulations 2023 (SI 2023/7) reg.3 (January 30, 2023).

DEFINITIONS

    "assessment period"—see reg.2(1).
    "earned income"—*ibid.*
    "the couple administrative threshold"—see para.(2)(b)(i).

"the single administrative threshold"—see para.(2)(a)(i).
"transitional capital disregard"—see reg.51.
"transitional element"—see reg.52.

GENERAL NOTE

This provides for the circumstances in which transitional protection ceases. These   **2.860**
are where there is a reduction in earnings over a three-month period or where an award
ends (including where a couple separate or form—but note the exceptions turning on
reg.3(3) of the Universal Credit Regulations). Exceptionally, transitional protection
can be carried over to a subsequent award in certain circumstances under new reg.57.

[¹Application of transitional protection to a subsequent award

57.—(1) Where—   **2.861**
  (a) a transitional capital disregard is applied, or a transitional element is
      included, in the calculation of an award, and that award terminates;
      or
  (b) the Secretary State determines (in accordance with regulation 50) that
      a transitional capital disregard is to apply, or a transitional element is
      to be included in the calculation of an award, but the decision on the
      qualifying claim is that there is no entitlement to an award,
no transitional capital disregard is to apply and no transitional element is
to be included in the calculation of any subsequent award unless paragraph
(2) applies.
  (2) This paragraph applies if—
  (a) the reason for the previous award terminating or, as the case may
      be, there being no entitlement to an award, was that the claimant (or
      joint claimants) had earned income on account of which the finan-
      cial condition in section 5(1)(b) or 5(2)(b) of the Act (income is such
      that the amount payable is at least 1p) was not met; and
  (b) the claimant becomes entitled to an award within the period of three
      months beginning with—
      (i) where paragraph (1)(a) applies, the last day of the month that
          would have been the final assessment period of the previous
          award (had it not terminated), or
      (ii) where paragraph (1)(b) applies, the day that would have been
          the last day of the first assessment period had there been entitle-
          ment to an award.
  (3) Where paragraph (2) applies in a case where a previous award has
terminated, the new award is to be treated for the purposes of regulation 51
(transitional capital disregard), 55 (transitional element – initial amount and
adjustment where other elements increase) and 56 (circumstances in which
transitional protection ceases) as if it were a continuation of that award.]

AMENDMENT

1. Universal Credit (Managed Migration Pilot and Miscellaneous Amendments)
Regulations 2019 (SI 2019/1152) reg.3(7) (July 24, 2019).

DEFINITIONS

"assessment period"—see reg.2(1).
"earned income"—*ibid.*

"qualifying claim"—see reg.48.
"transitional capital disregard"—see reg.51.
"transitional element"—see reg.52.

GENERAL NOTE

2.862   The basic rule is that where transitional protection on a universal credit claim has
been lost (either because an award with transitional protection has ended or because
a qualifying claim with such protection has been disallowed) then it is lost forever
(para.(1)). However, there are exceptional cases in which transitional protection
once lost can be revived, as in the circumstances set out in para.(2).

[¹*Miscellaneous*

Qualifying claim – Secretary of State may set later commencement day

2.863   **58.** Where the Secretary of State decides a qualifying claim, and it is not
a case where the award is to commence before the date of claim by virtue
of regulation 46(3) [²...] (claim made by the final deadline) or regulation
26 of the Claims and Payments Regulations (time within which a claim
for universal credit is to be made) as modified by regulation 15 of these
Regulations, the Secretary of State may determine a day on which the
award of universal credit is to commence that is after, but no more than one
month after, the date of claim.]

AMENDMENTS

1. Universal Credit (Managed Migration Pilot and Miscellaneous Amendments)
Regulations 2019 (SI 2019/1152) reg.3(7) (July 24, 2019).
2. Universal Credit (Transitional Provisions) Amendment Regulations 2022 (SI
2022/752) reg.11 and Sch. para.1(9) (July 25, 2022).

DEFINITION

"qualifying claim"—see reg.48.

GENERAL NOTE

2.864   This enables the Secretary State to set a date for commencement of the award
of universal credit up to a month after the date of a qualifying claim (provided it
is not a case where the claim is to be backdated). According to the Explanatory
Memorandum, this provision "has been included to delay the start date of UC
claims if the number of claims that need to be assessed would put pressure on operational capacity to the point of threatening service delivery to claimants" (para.7.13).

[¹**Minimum income floor not to apply for first 12 months**

2.865   **59.** [²...]]

AMENDMENTS

1. Universal Credit (Managed Migration Pilot and Miscellaneous Amendments)
Regulations 2019 (SI 2019/1152) reg.3(7) (July 24, 2019).
2. Universal Credit (Managed Migration Pilot and Miscellaneous Amendments)
Regulations 2019 (SI 2019/1152) reg.6(2) (September 23, 2020).

As originally enacted, reg.59 provided for all notified persons who would other-   **2.866**
wise be subject to the minimum income floor (under which certain self-employed
claimants are to have an assumed level of earnings) to have the 12 month "start-
up" period without the requirement to have started their business within the past
12 months. However, reg.63 of the Universal Credit Regulations provides for a 12
month start-up period during which the minimum income floor does not apply.
That provision was amended so as to extend the start-up period to all claimants for
universal credit who are in gainful self-employment and have not previously been
subject to the minimum income floor (even if they have not started their business
within the past 12 months). As a result, reg.59 was revoked.

[¹Protection for full-time students until course completed

60.—[²(1)] Where a notified person does not meet the basic condition in   **2.867**
section 4(1)(d) of the Act (not receiving education) on the day on which all
awards of any existing benefit are to terminate as a consequence of a claim
for universal credit because the person is undertaking a full-time course
(see regulation 12(2) and 13 of the Universal Credit Regulations), that
condition is not to apply in relation to the notified person while they are
continuing to undertake that course.]

[²(2) Paragraph (1) does not apply to any assessment period in respect of
which a transitional element or transitional capital disregard would (if the
claimant had been entitled to that element or that disregard) have ceased
to apply by virtue of regulation 56 (circumstances in which transitional
protection ceases) or regulation 57 (application of transitional protection to
a subsequent award).]

AMENDMENTS

1. Universal Credit (Managed Migration Pilot and Miscellaneous Amendments)
Regulations 2019 (SI 2019/1152) reg.3(7) (July 24, 2019).
2. Universal Credit (Transitional Provisions) Amendment Regulations 2022 (SI
2022/752) reg.8 (July 25, 2022).

DEFINITIONS

"existing benefit"—reg.2(1).
"notified person"—see reg.44(6).

GENERAL NOTE

This provides for notified persons who are students, and entitled to existing ben-   **2.868**
efits, to be exempt from the exclusion of full-time students from universal credit
until they complete their course.

[¹Rounding

61. Regulation 6 of the Universal Credit Regulations (rounding) applies   **2.869**
for the purposes of calculating any amount under this Part.]

AMENDMENT

1. Universal Credit (Managed Migration Pilot and Miscellaneous Amendments)
Regulations 2019 (SI 2019/1152) reg.3(7) (July 24, 2019).

[¹Effect of revision, appeal etc. of an award of an existing benefit

2.870   **62.**—(1) Nothing in regulation 53 (total legacy amount) or 54 (indicative UC amount) requiring a calculation in relation to the transitional element to be made on the basis of information held on the migration day prevents the Secretary of State from revising or superseding a decision in relation to a claim for, or an award of, universal credit where—

(a) in the opinion of the Secretary of State, the information held on that day was inaccurate or incomplete in some material respect because of—
  (i) a misrepresentation by a claimant,
  (ii) a failure to report information that a claimant was required to report where that failure was advantageous to the claimant, or
  (iii) an official error; or
(b) a decision has been made on or after the migration day on—
  (i) an application made before migration day to revise or supersede a decision in relation to an award of an existing benefit (including the report of a change of circumstances), or
  (ii) an appeal in relation to such an application.

(2) In this regulation "official error" means an error that—

(a) was made by an officer of, or an employee of a body acting on behalf of, the Department for Work and Pensions, HMRC or a local authority that administers housing benefit; and
(b) was not caused, or materially contributed to, by any person outside that body or outside the Department, HMRC or local authority,

but excludes any error of law which is shown to have been such by a subsequent decision of the Upper Tribunal or of a court as defined in section 27(7) of the Social Security Act 1998.]

AMENDMENT

1. Universal Credit (Managed Migration Pilot and Miscellaneous Amendments) Regulations 2019 (SI 2019/1152) reg.3(7) (July 24, 2019).

DEFINITIONS

"HMRC"—see reg.2(1).
"migration day"—see reg.49.
"official error"—see para.(2).
"transitional element"—see reg.52.
"Upper Tribunal"—see reg.2(1).

GENERAL NOTE

2.871   This provision ensures that the requirement to apply the information held at the migration day when calculating transitional protection does not prevent the subsequent revision of the universal credit award in cases of misrepresentation or error or in order to give effect to an outstanding revision or appeal.

[¹Claimants previously entitled to a severe disability premium

2.872   **63.** Schedule 2 contains provision in respect of certain claimants who have been entitled to a benefit which included a severe disability premium.]

AMENDMENT

1. Universal Credit (Managed Migration Pilot and Miscellaneous Amendments) Regulations 2019 (SI 2019/1152) reg.3(7) (July 24, 2019).

DEFINITION

"severe disability premium"—see reg.2(1).

GENERAL NOTE

The original Sch.2 made provision for transitional payments to those claimants who had been entitled to a benefit that included a severe disability premium and moved to universal credit before the SDP gateway came into force (or, in some exceptional cases, while the SDP gateway was in force). Where such a case came to the attention of the Secretary of State, a flat rate payment was to be calculated and paid as a lump sum in respect of each month since the move to universal credit. The same amount was then to continue as a separate monthly payment until the Secretary of State was satisfied that it could be included in the calculation of the award (in the same way as if the claimant has moved to universal credit under the managed migration provisions). Now that the SDP gateway has been revoked, claimants who are entitled to a benefit that includes a severe disability premium will no longer be prevented from claiming universal credit and the new Sch.2 will take effect. When claimants are awarded universal credit, they will now be entitled to the flat rate payment as part of the calculation from the outset. See further the General Note to Sch.2 below.

2.873

The High Court has held that reg.63 and Sch.2, as originally enacted, discriminated against SDP natural migrants by failing to provide transitional relief for the loss of the enhanced disability premium (EDP), although some compensation was provided for the loss of the SDP: *R. (on the application of TP and AR) v Secretary of State for Work and Pensions* [2022] EWHC 123 (Admin) (*TP and AR No.3*). The claimants, TP and AR, had previously succeeded in the judicial reviews in *TP No.1* and *TP No.2*, which were both upheld in the Court of Appeal (see the commentary on reg.4A above). In *TP and AR No.3*, the claimants argued that the SDP transitional payment of £120 a month constituted unlawful discrimination under art.14 of the ECHR. This was because they had not been compensated for the loss of the EDP. As a result, they were still about £60 a month worse off than had they remained on legacy benefits. Thus, the judicial review challenge related solely to the lack of transitional protection in cases of natural migration to universal credit against the cliff-edge effect of suddenly experiencing the loss of the EDP element (para.74). It was accepted that the claim fell within the ambit of A1P1 of the ECHR for the purposes of art.14. Holgate J furthermore found that there was a difference in treatment (paras 148–151), which was on the ground of an "other status" (paras 152–157), and which could not be justified (paras 158–198). The Judge concluded (at para.196):

"I am not satisfied on the material before the Court that the broad aims of promoting phased transition, curtailing public expenditure or administrative efficiency required the denial of transitional relief against the loss of EDP for SDP natural migrants. Quite apart from that, I reach the firm conclusion that a fair balance has not been struck between the severity of the effects of the measure under challenge upon members of the SDP natural migrants group and the contribution that that measure makes to the achievement of the defendant's aims, *a fortiori* where there is no connection between the triggering event, the move to a home in a different local authority area, and any rational assessment of the disability needs of a severely disabled claimant."

The Court of Appeal subsequently refused (in forthright terms) the Secretary of State's application for permission to appeal against the decision of Holgate J. (CA-2022-000398, January 12, 2023).

[¹Discretionary hardship payments

2.874   **64.** [²...]

AMENDMENTS

1. Universal Credit (Managed Migration Pilot and Miscellaneous Amendments) Regulations 2019 (SI 2019/1152) reg.3(7) (July 24, 2019).
2. Universal Credit (Transitional Provisions) Amendment Regulations 2022 (SI 2022/752) reg.9 (July 25, 2022).

Regulation 12A

SCHEDULE [² 1]

MODIFICATION OF TAX CREDITS LEGISLATION (FINALISATION OF TAX CREDITS)

Modifications to the Tax Credits Act 2002

2.875   1. Paragraphs 2 to 10 prescribe modifications to the application of the 2002 Act where regulation 12A of these Regulations applies.

2. In section 7 (income test)—
   (a) in subsection (3), before "current year income" in each place where it occurs, insert "notional";
   (b) in subsection (4)—
      (i) for "current year" substitute "current part year";
      (ii) in paragraphs (a) and (b), before "tax year" insert "part";
   (c) after subsection (4), insert—

"(4A) In this section "the notional current year income" means—

   (a) in relation to persons by whom a joint claim for a tax credit is made, the aggregate income of the persons for the part tax year to which the claim relates, divided by the number of days in that part tax year, multiplied by the number of days in the tax year in which the part tax year is included and rounded down to the next whole number of pence; and
   (b) in relation to a person by whom a single claim for a tax credit is made, the income of the person for that part tax year, divided by the number of days in that part tax year, multiplied by the number of days in the tax year in which the part tax year is included and rounded down to the next whole number of pence.".

3. In section 17 (final notice)—
   (a) in subsection (1)—
      (i) omit "the whole or"; and
      (ii) in sub-paragraph (a), before "tax year" insert "part";
   (b) in subsection (3), before "tax year" insert "part";
   (c) in subsections (4)(a) and (4)(b), for "current year" in both places where it occurs, substitute "current part year";
   (d) in subsection (5)(a) for "current year" in both places where it occurs, substitute "current part year";
   (e) omit subsection (8).

4. In section 18 (decisions after final notice)—
   (a) in subsection (1), before "tax year" insert "part";
   (b) omit subsections (6) to (9);
   (c) in subsection (10), for "subsection (1), (5), (6) or (9)" substitute "subsection (1) or (5)";
   (d) in subsection (11)—
      (i) after "subsection (5)" omit "or (9)";
      (ii) omit paragraph (a);
      (iii) in paragraph (b) omit "in any other case,";
      (iv) before "tax year" in each place where it occurs, insert "part".

5. In section 19 (power to enquire)—
   (a) in subsection (1)(a) and (b), before "tax year" insert "part";

(b) in subsection (3), before "tax year" insert "part";
(c) for subsection (5) substitute—

"(5) "The relevant section 18 decision" means the decision under subsection (1) of section 18 in relation to the person or persons and the part tax year.";

(d) for subsection (6) substitute—

"(6) "The relevant section 17 date" means the date specified for the purposes of subsection (4) of section 17 in the notice given to a person or persons under that section in relation to the part tax year.";

(e) in subsection (11), before "tax year" insert "part";
(f) in subsection (12), before "tax year" in each place where it occurs, insert "part".
6. In section 20 (decisions on discovery)—
(a) in subsection (1), before "tax year" insert "part";
(b) in subsection (4)(a), before "tax year" insert "part";
(c) in subsection (5)(b), before "tax year" insert "part";
(d) in subsection (6)—
    (i) before "tax year" insert "part";
    (ii) in paragraph (a), for "section 18(1), (5), (6) or (9)" substitute "section 18(1) or (5)";
(e) in subsection (7), before "tax year" in each place where it occurs, insert "part".
7. In section 21 (decisions subject to official error), for "18(1), (5), (6) or (9)" substitute "18(1) or (5)".
8. In section 23 (notice of decisions)—
(a) in subsection (1), for "18(1), (5), (6) or (9)" substitute "18(1) or (5)";
(b) in subsection (3)—
    (i) after "18(1)" omit "or (6)";
    (ii) for paragraph (b) substitute—

        "(b) the notice of the decision under subsection (1) of section 18,".

9. In section 30(1) (underpayments), before "tax year" in each place where it occurs, insert "part".
10. In section 38 (appeals)—
(a) in subsection (1)(b), before "tax year" insert "part";
(b) for subsection (2), substitute—

"(2) "The relevant section 18 decision" means the decision under subsection (1) of section 18 in relation to the person or persons and the tax credit for the part tax year.".

Modifications to the Tax Credits (Definition and Calculation of Income) Regulations 2002

2.876

11. Paragraphs 12 to 23 prescribe modifications to the application of the Tax Credits (Definition and Calculation of Income) Regulations 2002 where regulation 12A of these Regulations applies.
12. In regulation 2(2) (interpretation), after the definition of "the Macfarlane Trusts" insert—
""part tax year" means a period of less than a year beginning with 6th April and ending with the date on which the award of a tax credit terminated;".
13. In regulation 3 (calculation of income of claimant)—
(a) in paragraph (1)—
    (i) before "tax year" insert "part";
    (ii) in Steps 1 and 2, after "of the claimant, or, in the case of a joint claim, of the claimants" insert "received in or relating to the part tax year";
    (iii) in the second and third sentences of Step 4, before "year" insert "part";
(b) in paragraph (6A), for the words from "ending on 31st March" to the end, substitute "ending on the last day of the month in which the claimant's award of a tax credit terminated";
(c) in paragraph (8)(b), before "year" insert "part".
14. In regulation 4 (employment income)—
(a) in paragraph (1)(a), before "tax year" insert "part";
(b) in paragraph (1)(b), (c), (d), (e), (g) and (k), before "year" insert "part";
(c) in paragraph (1)(f), after "ITEPA" insert "which is treated as received in the part tax year and in respect of which the charge arises in the part tax year";
(d) in paragraph (1)(h), after "week" insert "in the part tax year";

    (e) in paragraph (1)(i), for "that year" substitute "the tax year" and after "ITEPA" insert "which is treated as received in the part tax year";

    (f) in paragraph (1)(j), after "applies" insert "which is received in the part tax year";

    (g) in paragraph (1)(l), for "that year" substitute "the tax year" and after "ITEPA" insert "in respect of which the charge arises in the part tax year";

    (h) in paragraph (1)(m), after "paid" insert "in the part tax year";

    (i) in paragraph (4), in the first sentence and in the title of Table 1, after "employment income" insert "received in the part tax year";

    (j) in paragraph (5), after "calculating earnings" insert "received in the part tax year".

15. In regulation 5 (pension income)—

    (a) in paragraph (1), after ""pension income" means" insert "any of the following received in or relating to the part tax year";

    (b) in paragraph (2), in the first sentence and in the title of Table 2, after "pension income" insert "received in or relating to the part tax year";

    (c) in paragraph (3), after "income tax purposes", insert "in relation to the part tax year".

16. In regulation 6 (trading income)—

    (a) re-number the existing regulation as paragraph (1);

    (b) in paragraph (1) (as so re-numbered)—

        (i) in sub-paragraph (a), for "taxable profits for the tax year" substitute "actual or estimated taxable profits attributable to the part tax year";

        (ii) in sub-paragraph (b), for "taxable profit for the" substitute "actual or estimated taxable profit attributable to the part tax";

    (c) after paragraph (1) insert—

"(2) Actual or estimated taxable profits attributable to the part tax year ("the relevant trading income") is to be calculated by reference to the basis period (determined by reference to the rules in Chapter 15 of Part 2 of ITTOIA) ending during the tax year in which the claimant made, or was treated as making, a claim for universal credit.

(3) The relevant trading income is to be calculated by—

    (a) taking the figure for the actual or estimated taxable income earned in the basis period;

    (b) dividing that figure by the number of days in the basis period to give the daily figure; and

    (c) multiplying the daily figure by the number of days in the part tax year on which the trade, profession or vocation was carried on.".

17. In regulation 7 (social security income)—

    (a) in paragraph (1), after "social security income" insert "received in the part tax year";

    (b) in paragraph (3), in the opening words and in the title of Table 3, after "social security income" insert "received in the part tax year".

18. In regulation 8 (student income), after "in relation to a student" insert ", any of the following which is received in the part tax year".

19. In regulation 10 (investment income)—

    (a) in paragraph (1), after "gross amount" insert "received in the part tax year";

    (b) in paragraph (1)(e), before "year" insert "part tax";

    (c) in paragraph (2), in the opening words and in the title of Table 4, after "investment income" insert "received in the part tax year".

20. In regulation 11(1) (property income)—

    (a) omit "annual";

    (b) after "taxable profits" insert "for the part tax year".

21. In regulation 12(1) (foreign income), before "year" insert "part tax".

22. In regulation 13 (notional income), after "means income" insert "received in the part tax year".

23. In regulation 18 (miscellaneous income), after "means income" insert "received in the part tax year".

Modifications to the Tax Credits (Income Thresholds and Determination of Rates) Regulations 2002

2.877   24. Paragraphs 25 to 27 prescribe modifications to the application of the Tax Credits (Income Thresholds and Determination of Rates) Regulations 2002 where regulation 12A of these Regulations applies.

25. In regulation 2 (interpretation)—

(a) after the definition of "the income threshold" insert—

"part tax year" means a period of less than a year beginning with 6th April and ending with the date on which the award of a tax credit terminated;";

(b) in the definition of "the relevant income" insert "as modified by the Universal Credit (Transitional Provisions) Regulations 2014" at the end.

26. In regulation 7(3) (determination of rate of working tax credit)—
(a) in Step 1, in the definition of "MR", after "maximum rate" insert "(determined in the manner prescribed at the date on which the award of the tax credit terminated)";
(b) in Step 3—
  (i) in the definition of "I", before "tax year" insert "part";
  (ii) in the definition of "N1", before "tax year" insert "part".

27. In regulation 8(3) (determination of rate of child tax credit)—
(a) in Step 1, in the definition of "MR", after "maximum rate" insert "(determined in the manner prescribed at the date on which the award of the tax credit terminated)";
(b) in Step 3—
  (i) in the definition of "I", before "tax year" insert "part";
  (ii) in the definition of "N1", before "tax year" insert "part".

Modifications to the Tax Credits (Claims and Notifications) Regulations 2002

28. Paragraphs 29 to 34 prescribe modifications to the application of the Tax Credits (Claims and Notifications) Regulations 2002 where regulation 12A of these Regulations applies. **2.878**
29. In regulation 4 (interpretation), omit paragraph (b).
30. Omit regulation 11 (circumstances in which claims to be treated as made).
31. Omit regulation 12 (further circumstances in which claims to be treated as made).
32. In regulation 13 (circumstances in which claims made by one member of a couple to be treated as also made by the other)—
(a) in paragraph (1), after "prescribed by paragraph" omit "(2) or";
(b) omit paragraph (2).
33. In regulation 15(1)(c) (persons who die after making a claim)—
(a) omit "the whole or" and "after the end of that tax year but"; and
(b) for "section 18(1), (5), (6) or (9)" substitute "section 18(1) or (5)".
34. In regulation 33 (dates to be specified in notices)—
(a) in paragraph (a), for the words from "not later than 31st July" to "if later", substitute "not less than 30 days after the date on which the notice is given";
(b) omit paragraph (b) and the "and" which precedes it.

Modification to the Tax Credits (Payment by the Commissioners) Regulations 2002

35. Paragraph 36 prescribes a modification to the application of the Tax Credits (Payment by the Commissioners) Regulations 2002 where regulation 12A of these Regulations applies. **2.879**
36. Omit regulation 7 (prescribed circumstances for certain purposes).

Modification to the Tax Credits (Residence) Regulations 2003

37. Paragraph 38 prescribes a modification to the application of the Tax Credits (Residence) Regulations 2003 where regulation 12A of these Regulations applies. **2.880**
38. In regulation 3(5)(a) (circumstances in which a person is treated as not being in the United Kingdom)(26), omit "under regulation 11 or 12 of the Tax Credits (Claims and Notifications) Regulations 2002 or otherwise".]

AMENDMENTS

1. Universal Credit (Transitional Provisions) (Amendment) Regulations 2014 (SI 2014/1626) reg.4 (October 13, 2014).
2. Universal Credit (Managed Migration Pilot and Miscellaneous Amendments) Regulations 2019 (SI 2019/1152) reg.3(8) (July 24, 2019).

GENERAL NOTE

See General Note to reg.12A. **2.881**

Regulation 63

[¹[² SCHEDULE 2

Claimants previously entitled to a severe disability premium

2.882   **1.** This Schedule applies to an award of universal credit where the following conditions are met in respect of the claimant, or each of joint claimants.

2. The first condition is that the award was not made as a consequence of the claimant becoming a member of a couple where the other member was already entitled to an award of universal credit.

3. The second condition is that the claimant—

(a) was entitled (or was a member of a couple the other member of which was entitled) to an award of income support, income-based jobseeker's allowance or income-related employment and support allowance that included a severe disability premium within the month immediately preceding the first day of the award of universal credit; and

(b) continued to satisfy the conditions for eligibility for a severe disability premium up to and including the first day of that award.

4. Where this Schedule applies (subject to paragraphs 6 and 7), a transitional SDP element is to be included in the calculation of the award and the amount of that element is to be treated, for the purposes of section 8 of the Act, as if it were an additional amount to be included in the maximum amount under section 8(2) before the deduction of income under section 8(3).

5. The amount of the transitional SDP element in the first assessment period is—

(a) in the case of a single claimant—

(i) [³£132.12], if the LCWRA element is included in the award, or

(ii) [³£313.79], if the LCWRA element is not included in the award;

(b) in the case of joint claimants—

(i) [³£445.91], if the higher SDP rate was payable,

(ii) [³£132.12], if paragraph (i) does not apply and the LCWRA element is included in the award in respect of either of them, or

(iii) [³£313.79], if paragraph (i) does not apply and the LCWRA element is not included in the award in respect of either of them.

6. In respect of the second and each subsequent assessment period, regulation 55(2) (adjustment where other elements increase), regulation 56 (circumstances in which transitional protection ceases) and regulation 57 (application of transitional protection to a subsequent award) are to apply in relation to the transitional SDP element as if it were a transitional element in respect of which the amount calculated in accordance with paragraph 5 was the initial amount.

7. The award is not to include a transitional SDP element where the claim was a qualifying claim and the award is to include a transitional element.

8. In this Schedule—

"LCWRA element" has the meaning in the Universal Credit Regulations;

"the higher SDP rate" is the rate specified in sub-paragraph (ii) of paragraph 11(2)(b) of Schedule 4 to the Employment and Support Allowance Regulations 2008 or, as the case may be, the corresponding rate of a severe disability premium in relation to income support or income-based jobseeker's allowance.]]

AMENDMENTS

1. Universal Credit (Managed Migration Pilot and Miscellaneous Amendments) Regulations 2019 (SI 2019/1152) reg.3(8) (July 24, 2019).

2. Universal Credit (Transitional Provisions) (Claimants previously entitled to a severe disability premium) Amendment Regulations 2021 (SI 2021/4) reg.2 (January 27, 2021).

3. Social Security Benefits Up-rating Regulations 2023 (SI 2023/340) reg.7 (April 10, 2023).

GENERAL NOTE

2.883   There have been two operative versions of Sch.2 to these Regulations, introduced by reg.63. The first version of the Schedule was in force from July 24, 2019 while the second version was effective from January 27, 2021. In a case where the first day of an award of universal credit falls before the latter date then the original version of Sch.2 continues to apply (see Universal Credit (Transitional Provisions) (Claimants previously entitled to a severe disability premium) Amendment Regulations 2021 (SI 2021/4) reg.3).

The first version of Sch.2 in the 2014 Regulations provided for transitional payments in respect of certain claimants who were entitled to a severe disability premium (SDP) before claiming universal credit as a result of natural migration (e.g. a claim to universal credit prompted by a change in circumstances). Eligibility was governed by Sch.2 para.1 (all references in this paragraph are to the original version of the Schedule); there was no need for individuals to make a claim, as the DWP set up a specialist team to review universal credit claims and identify those claimants who might be eligible for a SDP transitional payment. The payments were based on a flat rate for each assessment period since the move to universal credit (see Sch.2 para.2). The flat rate was converted into a transitional element after a date determined by the Secretary of State; the effect was that a lump-sum payment was made to cover the period since the claimant moved to universal credit followed by an ongoing monthly payment thereafter (see Sch.2 para.3). Note that any such lump-sum payment was disregarded as capital for 12 months or for the duration of the universal credit award, whichever was longer (see Sch.2 para.7). This provision was necessary as some of the backdated payments were substantial (the average (in the sense of median) lump-sum payment is £2,280: see House of Commons Library, *Universal Credit and the Severe Disability Premium*, Briefing Paper 08494 November 5, 2019, p.7).

The second version of Sch.2, now in force, operates in circumstances where the SDP gateway has been revoked and so claimants who are entitled to a benefit that includes a severe disability premium will no longer be prevented from claiming universal credit. The new Sch.2 will accordingly take effect such that when claimants are awarded universal credit they will be entitled to the flat rate payment as part of the calculation from the outset. Paragraphs 1 to 3 set out the conditions for the application of the new Sch.2. The first condition is that the award must not have been made as consequence of claimant forming a couple with an existing universal credit claimant. The second condition is that the claimant must have been entitled, or the partner of a person entitled, to an award of income support, income-based JSA or income-related ESA that included a severe disability premium within the month before the start of the universal credit award. They must also have continued to meet the conditions for eligibility for a severe disability premium up to and including the first day of that award. Paragraphs 4 to 6 provide for the universal credit award to include a transitional SDP element. This is to be the amount specified in para.5 in the first assessment period and, in subsequent assessment periods, is to be treated as in the same way as if it were a transitional element awarded to a claimant who had moved to universal credit by managed migration. This means that after the first assessment period the amount may decrease if other elements increase or may cease if there is a change of circumstances.

Paragraph 7 prevents duplication by excluding a claimant from receiving a transitional SDP element if they are awarded a transitional element as a consequence of being moved to universal credit by managed migration.

The Universal Credit (Digital Service) Amendment Regulations 2014

(2014/2887)

GENERAL NOTE

At one point during the introduction of UC, the benefit existed in two different forms depending on which computer system was operating in the area for the Jobcentre to which the claim was made: see further the General Note to the Welfare Reform Act 2012 (above). The amendments made by these Regulations applied in Digital (or "Full") Service areas. Regulation 5 preserved the unamended law for

2.884

Live Service areas. As Live Service areas no longer exist, reg.5 has not been reproduced in this volume. Readers are referred instead to pp.799–800 of Vol.V of the 2020/21 edition.

The Employment and Support Allowance and Universal Credit (Miscellaneous Amendments and Transitional and Savings Provisions) Regulations 2017

(SI 2017/204)

In Force April 3, 2017

REGULATIONS REPRODUCED

2.885
1. Citation and commencement
2-6. *[Omitted]*
7. Consequential, transitional and savings provisions
Schedule 1 *[Omitted]*
Schedule 2
Part 1 [Reproduced in Vol.V]
Part 2 Universal Credit: transitional and savings provisions
  The Secretary of State for Work and Pensions makes the following Regulations in exercise of the powers conferred by sections 12(1), 17(4), 18(3), 19(2)(d), 25(a) and 42(3)(a) of the Welfare Reform Act 2012 and sections 15(4) and (5) and 34(1) of the Welfare Reform and Work Act 2016.
  In accordance with section 173(5)(b) of the Social Security Administration Act 1992, this instrument contains only regulations made by virtue of, or consequential upon, sections 15, 16, 17 and 34 of the Welfare Reform and Work Act 2016 and is made before the end of the period of 6 months beginning with the coming into force of those sections.
  In accordance with section 176(1) of the Social Security Administration Act 1992 the Secretary of State has consulted with organisations appearing to him to be representative of the authorities concerned.

GENERAL NOTE

2.886
Parts 1-3 of, and Sch.1 to, these Regulations, taken together and ss.15-17 of the Welfare Reform and Work Act 2016, abolish the LCW element of universal credit (and the work-related activity component of ESA) with effect from April 3, 2017 and make a number of consequential amendments. However, for universal credit, the abolition is subject to the transitional and savings provisions in Sch.2, Pt 2, to which effect is given by reg.2. Part 1 of the Schedule contains equivalent provisions for ESA and is reproduced in Vol.V.
  Under Pt.2 of Sch.2, claimants who are found to have—or are treated as having—limited capability for work, but not limited capability for work-related activity, continue to be entitled to the LCW component in the following circumstances:

- There was an award of universal credit immediately before April 3, 2017 and that award included the LCW element, or would have done so if that element were not excluded by the three-month waiting period in reg.28(1) of the Universal Credit Regulations (para.9).

- There was an award of universal credit immediately before April 3, 2017 and that award included the LCWRA element, and it is subsequently decided that the claimant only has limited capability for work (para.10). This only applies where the claimant has had both limited capability for work and limited capability for work-related activity throughout the period from April 3, 2017 to the date on which it is determined that they only have limited capability for work.

- There was a claim for universal credit before April 3, 2017 and—also before that date—the claimant provided medical evidence of having limited capability for work. In those circumstances, the claimant will be entitled to the LCW element even if the determination that they have limited capability for work is not made until after April 3, 2017 and even if that determination is made on revision by the Secretary of State or on appeal by the First-tier Tribunal or Upper Tribunal (para.11).

- Article 24 of the Welfare Reform Act 2012 (Commencement No 9 and Transitional and Transitory Provisions and Commencement No 8 and Savings and Transitional Provisions (Amendment)) Order 2013 (see Part IVB below) provides that, where an award of universal credit is made and subsequently a decision is made to revise or supersede and earlier decision about old style ESA (or old style JSA) (or there is a final decision on an appeal against such a decision) the Secretary of State must consider whether to revise (or, in some circumstances, supersede) the universal credit decision. Where the claim for old style ESA was made, or treated as made, before April 3, 2013 and a decision is made to revise the universal credit decision after that date, then, if the revising decision includes a determination that the claimant has limited capability for work, the LCW element is to be included in the universal credit award (para.12).

- The claimant was entitled to employment and support allowance immediately before April 3, 2017 and remains so entitled until the date on which a subsequent claim for universal credit is made or treated as made (para.13).

- The claimant does not fall within the previous paragraph but was entitled to incapacity credits immediately before April 3, 2017 and remains so entitled until the date on which a subsequent claim for universal credit is made or treated as made (para.14).

- The claimant is entitled to income support on the grounds of incapacity for work or disability, or incapacity benefit or severe disablement allowance immediately before April 3, 2017 and regs 22-24, 26 or 27 of the Universal Credit (Transitional Provisions) Regulations 2014 applies to him or her from then until the date on which a subsequent claim for universal credit is made or treated as made (para.15).

The LCW element continues to be payable under Sch,2, Pt.2 for as long as continues to be entitled to universal credit and to have limited capability for work (para.8(1)(b)). Continuity of entitlement is not broken (i) where the award of universal credit but a further award begins immediately because the claimant ceased to be a member of a couple or became a member of a couple (para.8(2)(a)); or (ii) the award ends because the claimant's income (or the joint claimants' combined income) was too high but a further award is made within six months (para.8(2)(b)).

Citation and commencement

1. These Regulations may be cited as the Employment and Support Allowance and Universal Credit (Miscellaneous Amendments and Transitional and Savings Provisions) Regulations 2017 and come into force on 3rd April 2017.

2.887

PART 4

CONSEQUENTIAL, TRANSITIONAL AND SAVINGS PROVISIONS

Consequential, transitional and savings provisions

2.888
    7.—(1) [Omitted]

(2) Schedule 2 contains transitional and savings provisions.

Regulation 7(2)

SCHEDULE 2

TRANSITIONAL AND SAVINGS PROVISIONS

PART 2

UNIVERSAL CREDIT: TRANSITIONAL AND SAVINGS PROVISIONS

Transitional and savings provisions: General

2.889
    8.—(1) The amendments made by regulations 4 and 5 and paragraphs 13, 16 and 17 of Schedule 1 do not apply—

(a) where a claimant has an award of universal credit in any of the circumstances in the following paragraphs; and

(b) for so long as the claimant continues to be entitled to universal credit and to have limited capability for work.

(2) For the purposes of sub-paragraph (1)(b), the reference to continuous entitlement to universal credit includes where an award has terminated and a further award is made and—

(a) immediately before the further award commences, the previous award has terminated because the claimant ceased to be a member of a couple or became a member of a couple; or

(b) within the six months beginning with the date that the further award commences, the previous award has terminated because the financial condition in section 5(1)(b) or, if it was a joint claim, section 5(2)(b), of the Welfare Reform Act 2012 was not met.

(3) In this Part—

"employment and support allowance" means an employment and support allowance under Part 1 of the Welfare Reform Act 2007;

"LCW element" and "LCWRA element" have the meanings in regulation 27 of the Universal Credit Regulations 2013 as it has effect apart from the amendments made by regulation 4(4) (which remove references to the LCW element);

"limited capability for work" has the meaning given in section 37(1) of the Welfare Reform Act 2012.

(4) The Universal Credit, Personal Independence Payment, Jobseeker's Allowance and Employment and Support Allowance (Claims and Payments) Regulations 2013 apply for the purpose of deciding the date on which a claim for universal credit is made or is to be treated as made.

Claimants entitled to the LCW element before 3rd April 2017

2.890
    9. The first circumstance is where immediately before 3rd April 2017 the award included the LCW element, or would have but for regulation 28(1) of the Universal Credit Regulations 2013, as it has effect apart from the amendments made by regulation 4(5)(a) (which removes the reference to the LCW element).

Claimants entitled to the LCWRA element before 3rd April 2017

2.891
    10. The second circumstance is where—

(a) immediately before 3rd April 2017 the award included the LCWRA element;

(b) on or after 3rd April 2017 a determination that the claimant has limited capability for work is made; and

(c) the claimant had limited capability for work and work-related activity throughout the period beginning immediately before 3rd April 2017 and ending with the date on which the determination that the claimant has limited capability for work is made.

Claimants who are providing evidence of having limited capability for work before 3rd April 2017

11. The third circumstance is where—
    (a) before 3rd April 2017—
        (i) it falls to be determined whether the claimant has limited capability for work; and
        (ii) the claimant has provided evidence of having limited capability for work in accordance with the Social Security (Medical Evidence) Regulations 1976; and
    (b) on or after 3rd April 2017 a determination that the claimant has limited capability for work is made on the basis of an assessment under Part 5 of the Universal Credit Regulations 2013, on revision under section 9 of the Social Security Act 1998 or on appeal.

          2.892

Claimants who appeal or seek revision of a decision relating to employment and support allowance

12. The fourth circumstance is where—
    (a) the claimant appeals or seeks revision under section 9 of the Social Security Act 1998 of a decision relating to the entitlement of the claimant to an employment and support allowance, where the claim for employment and support allowance was made or treated as made before 3rd April 2017; and
    (b) on or after 3rd April 2017, in accordance with article 24 of the Welfare Reform Act 2012 (Commencement No 9 and Transitional and Transitory Provisions and Commencement No 8 and Savings and Transitional Provisions (Amendment)) Order 2013, the Secretary of State considers it appropriate to revise under section 9 of the Social Security Act 1998 an award of universal credit so as to include the LCW element.

          2.893

Claimants entitled to employment and support allowance before 3rd April 2017

13. The fifth circumstance is where immediately before 3rd April 2017 the claimant was entitled to employment and support allowance and remains so entitled throughout the period beginning with 3rd April 2017 and ending with the date on which the claim for universal credit is made or treated as made.

          2.894

Claimants entitled to be credited with earnings under the Social Security (Credits) Regulations 1975 before 3rd April 2017

14. The sixth circumstance is where—
    (a) immediately before 3rd April 2017—
        (i) the claimant entitled to the award was entitled to be credited with earnings equal to the lower earnings limit then in force in respect of a week to which regulation 8B(2)(a)(iv), (iva) or (v) of the Social Security (Credits) Regulations 1975 applies; and
        (ii) paragraph 13 does not apply to that claimant; and
    (b) the claimant is so entitled in respect of each week that falls in the period beginning with 3rd April 2017 and ending with the date on which the claim for universal credit is made or treated as made.

          2.895

Claimants entitled to income support or other incapacity benefits before 3rd April 2017

15. The seventh circumstance is where regulation 22, 23, 24, 26 or 27 of the Universal Credit (Transitional Provisions) Regulations 2014 applies to the claimant throughout the period beginning immediately before 3rd April 2017 and ending with the date on which the claim for universal credit is made or treated as made.

          2.896

The Universal Credit (Housing Costs Element for claimants aged 18 to 21) (Amendment) Regulations 2017

(SI 2017/252)

2.897   *Made by the Secretary of State under sections 11(5)(a) and 42(2) and (3) of the Welfare Reform Act 2012.*

[In force April 1, 2017]

GENERAL NOTE

2.898   See the commentary to paras 4A-4C of Sch.4 to the Universal Credit Regulations at paras 2.386 – 2.388 of Vol.V of the 2018/19 edition.

These Regulations introduced the exclusions from entitlement to the housing costs element of universal credit contained in paras 4A-4C with effect from April 1, 2017. They were reproduced here because regs 3 and 4 contained transitional protection from those exclusion for, respectively, claimants not living in a digital service area and claimants who had been entitled to housing benefit or had an award of universal credit that included the housing costs element: see further paras 3.731-3.732 of Vol.V of the 2018/19 edition.

The Regulations were revoked with effect from December 31, 2018 by SI 2018/1129, which also revoked paras 4A-4C.

PART III

STATE PENSION CREDIT REGULATIONS

The State Pension Credit Regulations 2002

(SI 2002/1792) (AS AMENDED)

Made by the Secretary of State under s.175(3) to (5) of the Social Security Contributions and Benefits Act 1992, ss.7(4A), 9(4A) and 11(1) and (4) of the Social Security Fraud Act 2001 and ss.1(5), 2(3), (4) and (6), 3(4) to (8), 4(3), 5, 6(2), 7(4) and (7), 9(4) and (5), 12(2) and (3), 15, 16(2) and 17(1) and (2) of the State Pension Credit Act 2002

ARRANGEMENT OF REGULATIONS

PART I

General

PART II

Entitlement and amount

PART III

Income

PART I

General

Citation, commencement and interpretation

3.2   **1.**—(1) These Regulations may be cited as the State Pension Credit Regulations 2002 and shall come into force on 6th October 2003.

(2) In these Regulations—

"the Act" means the State Pension Credit Act 2002;

"the 1992 Act" means the Social Security Contributions and Benefits Act 1992;

[26 "the 2012 Act" means the Welfare Reform Act 2012;]

[3 "adoption leave" means a period of absence from work on ordinary or additional adoption leave in accordance with section 75A or 75B of the Employment Rights Act 1996;]

[⁴⁴ "adult disability payment" has the meaning given in regulation 2 of the Disability Assistance for Working Age People (Scotland) Regulations 2022;]

"the appointed day" means the day appointed under section 13(3) of the Act;

[³⁸ "approved blood scheme" means a scheme established or approved by the Secretary of State, or trust established with funds provided by the Secretary of State, for the purpose of providing compensation in respect of a person having been infected from contaminated blood products;]

[⁷ "the Armed Forces and Reserve Forces Compensation Scheme" means the scheme established under section 1(2) of the Armed Forces (Pensions and Compensation) Act 2004;]

[²⁷ "armed forces independence payment" means armed forces independence payment under the Armed Forces and Reserve Forces (Compensation Scheme) Order 2011;]

"attendance allowance" means—

    (a) an attendance allowance under section 64 of the 1992 Act;

    (b) an increase of disablement pension under section 104 or 105 of the 1992 Act;

    (c) [²⁹. . .]

    (d) [²⁹. . .]

    (e) a payment by virtue of article 14, 15, 16, 43 or 44 of the Personal Injuries (Civilians) Scheme 1983 or any analogous payment; or

[¹⁸ (f) any payment based on a need for attendance which is paid as part of a war disablement pension, or any other such payment granted in respect of disablement which falls within regulation 15(5)(ac);]

"benefit week" means the period of 7 days beginning on the day on which, in the claimant's case, state pension credit is payable;

[⁸ "board and lodging accommodation" means accommodation provided to a person or, if he is a member of a family, to him or any other member of his family, for a charge which is inclusive of—

    (i) the provision of that accommodation, and

    (ii) at least some cooked or prepared meals which both are cooked or prepared (by a person other than the person to whom the accommodation is provided or a member of his family) and are consumed in that accommodation or associated premises,

but not accommodation provided by a close relative of his or of his partner, or other than on a commercial basis;]

"care home" [³⁹ in England] has the meaning it has for the purposes of the Care Standards Act 2000 by virtue of section 3 of that Act [²and in [³⁹ Wales and] Scotland means a care home service];

[²² "care home service" [³⁹ in Wales means a care home service within the meaning of Part 1 of the Regulation and Inspection of Social Care (Wales) Act 2016 which is provided wholly or mainly to persons aged 18 or over and in Scotland] has the meaning assigned to it by paragraph 2 of Schedule 12 to the Public Services Reform (Scotland) Act 2010;]

[²³ "the Caxton Foundation" means the charitable trust of that name established on 28th March 2011 out of funds provided by the Secretary of State for the benefit of certain persons suffering from hepatitis C and other persons eligible for payment in accordance with its provisions;]

[43 "child abuse payment" means a payment from a scheme established or approved by the Secretary of State for the purpose of providing compensation in respect of historic institutional child abuse in the United Kingdom;]

"the Claims and Payments Regulations" means the Social Security (Claims and Payments) Regulations 1987;

"close relative" means a parent, parent-in-law, son, son-in-law, daughter, daughter-in-law, step-parent, step-son, step-daughter, brother, sister, [10 or if any of the preceding persons is one member of a couple, the other member of that couple]

[28 "contribution-based jobseeker's allowance" means an allowance under the Jobseekers Act 1995 as amended by the provisions of Part 1 of Schedule 14 to the 2012 Act that remove references to an income-based allowance, and a contribution-based allowance under the Jobseekers Act 1995 as that Act has effect apart from those provisions;]

[28 "contributory employment and support allowance" means an allowance under Part 1 of the Welfare Reform Act as amended by the provisions of Schedule 3, and Part 1 of Schedule 14, to the 2012 Act that remove references to an income-related allowance, and a contributory allowance under Part 1 of the Welfare Reform Act as that Part has effect apart from those provisions;]

[30 "couple" means—
   (a) two people who are married to, or civil partners of, each other and are members of the same household; or
   (b) two people who are not married to, or civil partners of, each other but are living together [40 as if they were a married couple or civil partners];]

[1 "the Computation of Earnings Regulations" means the Social Security Benefit (Computation of Earnings) Regulations 1996;

"dwelling occupied as the home" means the dwelling together with any garage, garden and outbuildings, normally occupied by the claimant as his home including any premises not so occupied which it is impracticable or unreasonable to sell separately, in particular, in Scotland, any croft land on which the dwelling is situated;]

"Eileen Trust" means the charitable trust of that name established on 29th March 1993 out of funds provided by the Secretary of State for the benefit of persons eligible for payment in accordance with its provisions;

[16 "the Employment and Support Allowance Regulations" means the Employment and Support Allowance Regulations 2008;]

[19 "enactment" includes an enactment comprised in, or in an instrument made under, an Act of the Scottish Parliament [29 or the National Assembly for Wales];]

[6 "equity release scheme" means a loan—
   (a) made between a person ("the lender") and the claimant;
   (b) by means of which a sum of money is advanced by the lender to the claimant by way of payments at regular intervals; and
   (c) which is secured on a dwelling in which the claimant owns an estate or interest and which he occupies as his home;]

[20 "foreign state retirement pension" means any pension which is paid under the law of a country outside the United Kingdom and is in the nature of social security;]

"the Fund" means moneys made available from time to time by the Secretary of State for the benefit of persons eligible for payment in accordance with the provisions of a scheme established by him on 24th April 1992 or, in Scotland, on 10th April 1992;

"full-time student" has the meaning prescribed in regulation 61(1) of the Income Support Regulations;

[¹² "the Graduated Retirement Benefit Regulations" means the Social Security (Graduated Retirement Benefit) Regulations 2005;]

[⁴² "Grenfell Tower payment" means a payment made to a person because that person was affected by the fire on 14th June 2017 at Grenfell Tower, or a payment to the personal representative of such a person—

(a) from the £5 million fund announced on 16th June 2017 for the benefit of certain persons affected by the fire on 14th June 2017 at Grenfell Tower and known as the Grenfell Tower Residents' Discretionary Fund;

(b) by the Royal Borough of Kensington and Chelsea; or

(c) by a registered charity;]

[⁷ "a guaranteed income payment" means a payment made under article 14(1)(b) or article 21(1)(a) of the Armed Forces and Reserve Forces (Compensation Scheme) Order 2005;]

[¹⁷ "the Health Service Act" means "the National Health Service Act 2006]; "the Health Service (Wales) Act" means "the National Health Service (Wales) Act 2006";]

[²⁸ "income-based jobseeker's allowance" means an income-based allowance under the Jobseekers Act 1995;]

[¹⁶ "income-related employment and support allowance" means an income-related allowance under Part 1 of the Welfare Reform Act (employment and support allowance);]

"the Income Support Regulations" means the Income Support (General) Regulations 1987;

[²¹ "independent hospital"—

(a) in England, means a hospital as defined by section 275 of the National Health Service Act 2006 that is not a health service hospital as defined by that section;

(b) in Wales, has the meaning assigned to it by section 2 of the Care Standards Act 2000; and

[²² (c) in Scotland, means an independent health care service as defined in section 10F(1)(a) and (b) of the National Health Service (Scotland) Act 1978;]]

[¹⁷ . . .]

[¹⁴ "the Independent Living Fund (2006)" means the Trust of that name established by a deed dated April 10, 2006 and made between the Secretary of State for Work and Pensions of the one part and Margaret Rosemary Cooper, Michael Beresford Boyall and Marie Theresa Martin of the other part;]

[¹⁷ . . .]

"the Jobseeker's Allowance Regulations" means the Jobseeker's Allowance Regulations 1996;

[²⁵ "local welfare provision" means occasional financial or other assistance given by a local authority, the Scottish Ministers or the Welsh Ministers, or a person authorised to exercise any function of, or provide a service to, them, to or in respect of individuals for the purpose of—

(a) meeting, or helping to meet, an immediate short term need—
  (i) arising out of an exceptional event, or exceptional circumstances; and
  (ii) that requires to be met in order to avoid a risk to the well-being of an individual; or
(b) enabling individuals to establish or maintain a settled home, where those individuals have been or, without the assistance, might otherwise be—
  (i) in prison, hospital, a residential care establishment or other institution; or
  (ii) homeless or otherwise living an unsettled way of life;]

[[11] "the London Bombings Relief Charitable Fund" means the company limited by guarantee (number 5505072) and registered charity of that name established on 11th July 2005 for the purpose of (amongst other things) relieving sickness, disability or financial need of victims (including families or dependants of victims) of the terrorist attacks carried out in London on 7th July 2005;]

[[37] "the London Emergencies Trust" means the company of that name (number 09928465) incorporated on 23rd December 2015 and the registered charity of that name (number 1172307) established on 28th March 2017;]

"the Macfarlane (Special Payments) Trust" means the trust of that name, established on 29th January 1990 partly out of funds provided by the Secretary of State, for the benefit of certain persons suffering from haemophilia;

"the Macfarlane (Special Payments) (No.2) Trust" means the trust of that name, established on 3rd May 1991 partly out of funds provided by the Secretary of State, for the benefit of certain persons suffering from haemophilia and other beneficiaries;

"the Macfarlane Trust" means the charitable trust, established partly out of funds provided by the Secretary of State to the Haemophilia Society, for the relief of poverty or distress among those suffering from haemophilia;

[[35] "member of the work-related activity group" means a claimant who has or is treated as having limited capability for work under either—
(a) Part 5 of the Employment and Support Allowance Regulations 2008 other than by virtue of regulation 30 of those Regulations; or
(b) Part 4 of the Employment and Support Allowance Regulations 2013 other than by virtue of regulation 26 of those Regulations;]

[[20] "MFET Limited" means the company limited by guarantee (number 7121661) of that name, established for the purpose in particular of making payments in accordance with arrangements made with the Secretary of State to persons who have acquired HIV as a result of treatment by the NHS with blood or blood products;]

[[42] "the National Emergencies Trust" means the registered charity of that name (number 1182809) established on 28th March 2019;]

[[41]"parental bereavement leave" means leave under section 80EA of the Employment Rights Act 1996;]

[[24] "paternity leave" means a period of absence from work on [[34] ...] paternity leave by virtue of section 80A or 80B of the Employment Rights Act 1996 [[34] ...];]

[[13] "patient", except in Schedule II, means a person (other than a prisoner) who is regarded as receiving free in-patient treatment within the meaning of regulation 2(4) and (5) of the Social Security (Hospital In-Patients) Regulations 2005;]

"pension fund holder" means with respect to [[15] an occupational pension scheme,] a personal pension scheme or retirement annuity contract, the trustees, managers or scheme administrators, as the case may be, of the scheme or contract concerned;

[[26] "personal independence payment" means personal independence payment under Part 4 of the 2012 Act;]

"policy of life insurance" means any instrument by which the payment of money is assured on death (except death by accident only) or the happening of any contingency dependent on human life, or any instrument evidencing a contract which is subject to payment of premiums for a term dependent on human life;

"prisoner" means a person who—

(a) is detained in custody pending trial or sentence upon conviction or under a sentence imposed by a court; or

(b) is on temporary release in accordance with the provisions of the Prison Act 1952 or the Prisons (Scotland) Act 1989,

other than a person detained in hospital under the provisions of the Mental Health Act 1983, or in Scotland, under the provisions of the [[9] Mental Health (Care and Treatment) (Scotland) Act 2003] or the Criminal Procedure (Scotland) Act 1995;

[[19] "public authority" includes any person certain of whose functions are functions of a public nature;]

"qualifying person" means a person in respect of whom [[42] a Grenfell Tower payment [[43], a child abuse payment or a Windrush payment] has been made or] payment has been made from the Fund [[4], the Eileen Trust [[20], MFET Limited] [[11], the Skipton Fund [[23], the Caxton Foundation] [[36], the Scottish Infected Blood Support Scheme][[37], [[38] an approved blood scheme], the London Emergencies Trust, the We Love Manchester Emergency Fund] [[42], the National Emergencies Trust] or the London Bombings Relief Charitable Fund]];

[[36] "Scottish Infected Blood Support Scheme" means the scheme of that name administered by the Common Services Agency (constituted by section 10 of the National Health Service (Scotland) Act 1978);]

[[31] . . .]

[[32] "shared parental leave" means leave under section 75E or 75G of the Employment Rights Act 1996;]

[[5] "the Skipton Fund" means the ex-gratia payment scheme administered by the Skipton Fund Limited, incorporated on 25th March 2004, for the benefit of certain persons suffering from hepatitis C and other persons eligible for payment in accordance with the scheme's provisions;]

[[28] "universal credit" means universal credit under Part 1 of the 2012 Act;]

[[2] "voluntary organisation" means a body, other than a public or local authority, the activities of which are carried on otherwise than for profit;]

"water charges" means—

(a) as respects England and Wales, any water and sewerage charges under Chapter 1 of Part V of the Water Industry Act 1991;

(b) as respects Scotland, any water and sewerage charges under Schedule 11 to the Local Government Finance Act 1992;

in so far as such charges are in respect of the dwelling which a person occupies as his home;

[[37] the We Love Manchester Emergency Fund" means the registered charity of that name (number 1173260) established on 30th May 2017;]

[[16] "the Welfare Reform Act" means the Welfare Reform Act 2007;]

[[43] "Windrush payment" means a payment made under the Windrush Compensation Scheme (Expenditure) Act 2020.]

(3) In these Regulations, unless the context otherwise requires, a member of [[11] a couple] is referred to as a partner and both members are referred to as partners.

[[31] (3A) References in these Regulations to a claimant participating as a service user are to—

(a) a person who is being consulted by or on behalf of—

  (i) a body which has a statutory duty to provide services in the field of health, social care or social housing; or

  (ii) a body which conducts research or undertakes monitoring for the purpose of planning or improving such services,

in their capacity as a user, potential user, carer of a user or person otherwise affected by the provision of those services; or

[[33] (ab) a person who is being consulted by or on behalf of—

  (i) the Secretary of State in relation to any of the Secretary of State's functions in the field of social security or child support or under section 2 of the Employment and Training Act 1973; or

  (ii) a body which conducts research or undertakes monitoring for the purpose of planning or improving such functions,

in their capacity as a person affected or potentially affected by the exercise of those functions or the carer of such a person;]

(b) the carer of a person consulted under [[33] sub-paragraphs (a) or (ab)].]

(4) In these Regulations, unless the context otherwise requires, a reference—

(a) to a numbered section is to the section of the Act bearing that number;

(b) to a numbered Part is to the Part of these Regulations bearing that number;

(c) to a numbered regulation or Schedule is to the regulation in, or Schedule to, these Regulations bearing that number;

(d) in a regulation or Schedule to a numbered paragraph is to the paragraph in that regulation or Schedule bearing that number;

(e) in a paragraph to a lettered or numbered sub-paragraph is to the sub-paragraph in that paragraph bearing that letter or number.

AMENDMENTS

1. State Pension Credit (Consequential, Transitional and Miscellaneous Provisions) Regulations 2002 (SI 2002/3019) reg.23(a) (October 6, 2003).

2. State Pension Credit (Consequential, Transitional and Miscellaneous Provisions) (No.2) Regulations 2002 (SI 2002/3197) reg.2 and Sch. para.1 (October 6, 2003).

3. State Pension Credit (Transitional and Miscellaneous Provisions) Amendment Regulations 2003 (SI 2003/2274) reg.2(2) (October 6, 2003).

4. Social Security (Miscellaneous Amendments) (No.2) Regulations 2004 (SI 2004/1141) reg.2(a) (May 12, 2004).

5. Social Security (Miscellaneous Amendments) (No.2) Regulations 2004 (SI 2004/1141) reg.2(b)(iv) (May 12, 2004).

6. Social Security (Housing Benefit, Council Tax Benefit, State Pension Credit and Miscellaneous Amendments) Regulations 2004 (SI 2004/2327) reg.7(2) (October 4, 2004).

7. Social Security (Miscellaneous Amendments) Regulations 2005 (SI 2005/574) reg.2(1) (April 4, 2005).

8. Social Security (Miscellaneous Amendments) (No.2) Regulations 2005 (SI 2005/2465) reg.6(2) (October 3, 2005).

9. Mental Health (Care and Treatment) (Scotland) Act 2003 (Modification of Subordinate Legislation) Order 2005 (SSI 2005/445) art.2 and Sch. para.35(1) (October 3, 2005).

10. Civil Partnership (Pensions, Social Security and Child Support) (Consequential, etc. Provisions) Order 2005 (SI 2005/2877) art.2(3) and Sch.3 para.35(2) (December 5, 2005).

11. Income-related Benefits (Amendment) (No.2) Regulations 2005 (SI 2005/3391) reg.7(2) (December 12, 2005).

12. Social Security (Deferral of Retirement Pensions, Shared Additional Pension and Graduated Retirement Benefit) (Miscellaneous Provisions) Regulations 2005 (SI 2005/2677) reg.13(2) (April 6, 2006).

13. Social Security (Hospital In-Patients) Regulations 2005 (SI 2005/3360) reg.8(2) (April 10, 2006).

14. Independent Living Fund (2006) Order 2007 (SI 2007/2538) art.6(2) (October 1, 2007).

15. Social Security (Miscellaneous Amendments) (No.5) Regulations 2007 (SI 2007/2618) reg.10(2) (October 1, 2007).

16. Employment and Support Allowance (Consequential Provisions) (No.2) Regulations 2008 (SI 2008/1554) reg.4(2) (October 27, 2008).

17. Social Security (Miscellaneous Amendments) (No.6) Regulations 2008 (SI 2008/2767) reg.5(2) (November 17, 2008).

18. Social Security (Miscellaneous Amendments) (No.7) Regulations 2008 (SI 2008/3157) reg.4(2) (January 5, 2009).

19. Social Security (Miscellaneous Amendments) (No.4) Regulations 2009 (SI 2009/2655) reg.5(2) (October 26, 2009).

20. Social Security (Miscellaneous Amendments) (No.2) Regulations 2010 (SI 2010/641) reg.6(3)(a) (April 6, 2010).

21. Health and Social Care Act 2008 (Miscellaneous Consequential Amendments) Order 2010 (SI 2010/1881) art.5 (October 1, 2010).

22. Public Services Reform (Scotland) Act 2010 (Consequential Modifications of Enactments) Order 2011 (SI 2011/2581) art.2 and Sch.2 para.35 (October 28, 2011).

23. Social Security (Miscellaneous Amendments) (No.3) Regulations 2011 (2011/2425) reg.15(2) (October 31, 2011).

24. Social Security (Miscellaneous Amendments) Regulations 2012 (2012/757) reg.5(2) (April 1, 2012).

25. Social Security (Miscellaneous Amendments) Regulations 2013 (SI 2013/443) reg.6(2) (April 2, 2013).

26. Personal Independence Payment (Supplementary Provisions and Consequential Amendments) Regulations 2013 (SI 2013/388) reg.8 and Sch. para.27(2) (April 8, 2013).

27. Armed Forces and Reserve Forces Compensation Scheme (Consequential Provisions: Subordinate Legislation) Order 2013 (SI 2013/591) art.7 and Sch. para.23(2) (April 8, 2013).

28. Universal Credit (Consequential, Supplementary, Incidental and Miscellaneous Provisions) Regulations 2013 (SI 2013/630) reg.33(2) (April 29, 2013).

29. Social Security (Miscellaneous Amendments) (No.3) Regulations 2013 (SI 2013/2536) reg.10(2) (October 29, 2013).

30. Marriage (Same Sex Couples) Act 2013 (Consequential Provisions) Order 2014 (SI 2014/107) art.2 and Sch.1 para.32 (March 13, 2014 for England & Wales only); Marriage and Civil Partnership (Scotland) Act 2014 and Civil Partnership

Act 2004 (Consequential Provisions and Modifications) Order 2014 (SI 2014/3229) art.29 and Sch.6 para.23 (December 16, 2014 for the United Kingdom).

31. Social Security (Miscellaneous Amendments) Regulations 2014 (SI 2014/591) reg.7(2) (April 28, 2014).

32. Shared Parental Leave and Statutory Shared Parental Pay (Consequential Amendments to Subordinate Legislation) Order 2014 (SI 2014/3255) art.10(2)(b) (December 31, 2014).

33. Social Security (Miscellaneous Amendments) Regulations 2015 (SI 2015/67) reg.2(2) (February 23, 2015).

34. Shared Parental Leave and Statutory Shared Parental Pay (Consequential Amendments to Subordinate Legislation) Order 2014 (SI 2014/3255) art.10(2)(a) (April 5, 2015).

35. Employment and Support Allowance and Universal Credit (Miscellaneous Amendments and Transitional and Savings Provisions) Regulations 2017 (SI 2017/204) reg.7(1) and Sch.1, para.5(2) (April 3, 2017).

36. Social Security (Scottish Infected Blood Support Scheme) Regulations 2017 (SI 2017/329) reg.5(2) (April 3, 2017).

37. Social Security (Emergency Funds) (Amendment) Regulations 2017 (SI 2017/689) reg.4(2) (June 19, 2017).

38. Social Security (Infected Blood and Thalidomide) Regulations 2017 (SI 2017/870) reg.5(2) (October 23, 2017).

39. Social Security and Child Support (Regulation and Inspection of Social Care (Wales) Act 2016) (Consequential Provision) Regulations 2018 (SI 2018/228) reg.8 (April 2, 2018).

40. Civil Partnership (Opposite-sex Couples) Regulations 2019 (SI 2019/1458) reg.41(b) and Sch.3 Part 2 para.61 (December 2, 2019).

41. Parental Bereavement Leave and Pay (Consequential Amendments to Subordinate Legislation) Regulations 2020 (SI 2020/354) reg.10(2) (April 6, 2020).

42. Social Security (Income and Capital) (Miscellaneous Amendments) Regulations 2020 (SI 2020/618) reg.4(2) (July 15, 2020).

43. Social Security (Income and Capital Disregards) (Amendment) Regulations 2021 (SI 2021/1405) reg.4(2) (January 1, 2022).

44. Social Security (Disability Assistance for Working Age People) (Consequential Amendments) Order 2022 (SI 2022/177) art.8(2) (March 21, 2022).

MODIFICATION

The definition of "prisoner" in regulation 1(2) is modified as from April 8, 2020 by reg.2 of the Social Security (Coronavirus) (Prisoners) Regulations 2020 (SI 2020/409). For details of the modification, see the General Note to this regulation.

DEFINITION

"claimant"—see SPCA 2002 s.17(1).

GENERAL NOTE

Paragraph (2)

3.3 *"Appointed day"*: This date was October 6, 2003: see State Pension Credit Act 2002 (Commencement No.5) and Appointed Day Order 2003 (SI 2003/1766) (C.75)).

"Board and lodging accommodation": On the importance of establishing, in this context, the precise status of someone staying with the claimant (e.g. as sub-tenant, lodger or non-dependant), see *KC v Secretary of State for Work and Pensions (SPC)* [2012] UKUT 114 (AAC).

"Care home": Section 3(1) of the Care Standards Act 2000 provides that "an establishment is a care home if it provides accommodation, together with nursing or personal care" for various categories of person (e.g. the ill, the disabled, those with mental disorders and those with alcohol or drug dependency). An establishment is not a care home if it is a hospital, independent clinic or children's home, or if it is excluded by regulations (see Care Standards Act 2000 s.3(3) and Care Homes Regulations 2001 (SI 2001/3965) reg.3)). For the (slightly differently phrased) Scottish definition of "care home", see Regulation of Care (Scotland) Act 2001 s.2. This defines a "care home" as an establishment in which a care home service is provided, i.e. accommodation together with nursing, personal care, or personal support for people by reason of their vulnerability or need. See further *SA v Secretary of State for Work and Pensions (IS)* [2010] UKUT 345 (AAC); [2011] AACR 16.

"Close relative": This definition is in identical terms to that used in reg.2(1) of the Income Support (General) Regulations 1987 (SI 1987/1967), and therefore will presumably be interpreted in the same way. Thus "brother" and "sister" include half-brothers and half-sisters, and persons who are adopted cease to have any legal relationship with their birth family (*R(SB) 22/87*). **3.4**

"Couple": This new streamlined definition is consequential upon the Marriage (Same Sex Couples) Act 2013—see further the Note at the start of this Volume. On the proper approach to the assessment of whether two persons are "living together as husband and wife" (now "living together as if they were a married couple or civil partners" in the statutory definition of couple), see *DK v SSWP* [2016] Scots CSIH 84.

"Dwelling occupied as the home": This also follows the income support definition: see para.2.25 above. See also *ED v Secretary of State for Work and Pensions* [2009] UKUT 161 (AAC), confirming that the basic meaning of this expression "does not extend to any land or other premises not occupied by the person in question, whatever the nature of the other premises" (at para.17). See further *PJ v Secretary of State for Work and Pensions (SPC)* [2014] UKUT 152 (AAC), holding that "a person who chooses for financial reasons not to live in his usual home for a period of three years cannot say that during that period he normally occupies the property as his home" (at para.16).

"Full-time student": For analysis of the complex case law on this term in the context of income support, see the commentary to Pt VIII of the Income Support (General) Regulations 1987 (SI 1987/1967) in Vol.V of this series. **3.5**

"Patient": This is the same definition as used for the purposes of income support (see reg.21(3) of the Income Support (General) Regulations 1987 (SI 1987/1967) in Vol.V of this series.

"Prisoner": This is also the same definition as used for the purposes of income support (see reg.21(3) of the Income Support (General) Regulations 1987 (SI 1987/1967). Note also that as from April 8, 2020, the definition of "prisoner" is to be read as if it did not include a person on temporary release in accordance with the provisions of the Prison Act 1952 (see Social Security (Coronavirus) (Prisoners) Regulations 2020 (SI 2020/409) reg.2). The purpose of this change was to make provision for those individuals on temporary release from a prison in England and Wales due to the outbreak of COVID-19 in Great Britain to access means-tested benefits during the period of that release. The regulations must be kept under review by the Secretary of State and "cease to have effect at the end of the period of eight months beginning on 13th March 2020" (SI 2020/409 reg.6). However, with effect from November 12, 2020, reg.2 of the Social Security (Coronavirus) (Prisoners) **3.6**

Amendment Regulations 2020 (SI 2020/1156) amended reg.6 of SI 2020/409 by substituting "14 months" for "eight months". Subsequently the end date for the regulations was revised to 31 August, 2021 (see the Social Security (Coronavirus) (Miscellaneous Amendments) Regulations 2021 (SI 2021/476), reg.4(6), further amending SI 2020/409, reg.6).

PART II

Entitlement and amount

[¹Disapplication of section 1(1A) of the Social Security Administration Act

3.7   **1A.**—Section 1(1A) of the Social Security Administration Act 1992 (requirement to state a national insurance number) shall not apply to a person who—

   (a) is a person in respect of whom a claim for state pension credit is made;

   (b) is subject to immigration control within the meaning of section 115(9)(a) of the Immigration and Asylum Act 1999;

   (c) does not satisfy the conditions of entitlement to state pension credit as specified in section 1(2); and

   (d) has not previously been allocated a national insurance number.]

AMENDMENT

1. Social Security (National Insurance Number Information: Exemption) Regulations 2009 (SI 2009/471) reg.8 (April 6, 2009).

GENERAL NOTE

3.8   This provision ensures that there is no requirement for a National Insurance number (NINo) to be allocated to an individual who has no leave to enter or remain in the United Kingdom where that person is a partner of a legitimate benefit claimant. See also the earlier Commissioner's decision *CH/3801/2004*.

[¹ Persons not in Great Britain

3.9   **2.** —(1) A person is to be treated as not in Great Britain if, subject to the following provisions of this regulation, he is not habitually resident in the United Kingdom, the Channel Islands, the Isle of Man or the Republic of Ireland.

   (2) No person shall be treated as habitually resident in the United Kingdom, the Channel Islands, the Isle of Man or the Republic of Ireland unless he has a right to reside in (as the case may be) the United Kingdom, the Channel Islands, the Isle of Man or the Republic of Ireland other than a right to reside which falls within paragraph (3) [⁹ or (3A)].

   (3) A right to reside falls within this paragraph if it is one which exists by virtue of, or in accordance with, one or more of the following—

   (a) regulation 13 of the [⁹ Immigration (European Economic Area) Regulations 2016];

   (b) regulation 14 of those Regulations, but only in a case where the right exists under that regulation because the person is—

(i) a jobseeker for the purpose of the definition of "qualified person" in regulation 6(1) of those Regulations, or

(ii) a family member (within the meaning of regulation 7 of those Regulations) of such a jobseeker; [¹¹or]

[⁵[⁹(bb) regulation 16 of those Regulations, but only in a case where the right exists under that regulation because the person satisfies the criteria in paragraph (5) of that regulation.]]

(c) [¹¹ . . .]

(d) [¹¹ . . .]

(e) [¹¹ . . .]

[⁹(3A) A right to reside falls within this paragraph if it exists by virtue of a person having been granted limited leave to enter, or remain in, the United Kingdom under the Immigration Act 1971 by virtue of—

(a) Appendix EU to the immigration rules made under section 3(2) of that Act; [¹² . . .]

(b) being a person with a Zambrano right to reside as defined in Annex 1 of Appendix EU to the immigration rules made under section 3(2) of that Act [¹²; or

(c) having arrived in the United Kingdom with an entry clearance that was granted under Appendix EU (Family Permit) to the immigration rules made under section 3(2) of that Act.]

[¹⁰(3B) Paragraph (3A)(a) does not apply to a person who—

(a) has a right to reside granted by virtue of being a family member of a relevant person of Northern Ireland; and

(b) would have a right to reside under the Immigration (European Economic Area) Regulations 2016 if the relevant person of Northern Ireland were an EEA national, provided that the right to reside does not fall within paragraph (3).]

(4) A person is not to be treated as not in Great Britain if he is—

[¹³(zza) a person granted leave in accordance with the immigration rules made under section 3(2) of the Immigration Act 1971, where such leave is granted by virtue of—

(i) the Afghan Relocations and Assistance Policy; or

(ii) the previous scheme for locally-employed staff in Afghanistan (sometimes referred to as the ex-gratia scheme);

(zzb) a person in Great Britain not coming within sub-paragraph (zza) or [¹⁴(h)] who left Afghanistan in connection with the collapse of the Afghan government that took place on 15th August 2021;]

[¹⁴(zzc) a person in Great Britain who was residing in Ukraine immediately before 1st January 2022, left Ukraine in connection with the Russian invasion which took place on 24th February 2022 and—

(i) has been granted leave in accordance with immigration rules made under section 3(2) of the Immigration Act 1971; [¹⁵ . . .]

(ii) has a right of abode in the United Kingdom within the meaning given in section 2 of that Act;] [¹⁵ . . .]

[¹⁵(iii) does not require leave to enter or remain in the United Kingdom in accordance with section 3ZA of that Act;]

[⁸ (za) a qualified person for the purposes of regulation 6 of the [⁹ Immigration (European Economic Area) Regulations 2016] as a worker or a self-employed person;

(zb) a family member of a person referred to in sub-paragraph (za) [¹⁰ . . .];

(zc) a person who has a right to reside permanently in the United Kingdom by virtue of regulation 15(1)(c), (d) or (e) of those Regulations;]

[¹⁰(zd) a family member of a relevant person of Northern Ireland, with a right to reside which falls within paragraph (3A)(a), provided that the relevant person of Northern Ireland falls within sub-paragraph (za), or would do so but for the fact that they are not an EEA national;]

[¹¹(ze) a frontier worker within the meaning of regulation 3 of the Citizens' Rights (Frontier Workers) (EU Exit) Regulations 2020;

(zf) a family member of a person referred to in sub-paragraph (ze), who has been granted limited leave to enter, or remain in, the United Kingdom by virtue of Appendix EU to the immigration rules made under section 3(2) of the Immigration Act 1971;]

(g) a refugee within the definition in Article 1 of the Convention relating to the Status of Refugees done at Geneva on 28th July 1951, as extended by Article 1(2) of the Protocol relating to the Status of Refugees done at New York on 31st January 1967;

[⁶ (h) a person who has been granted leave or who is deemed to have been granted leave outside the rules made under section 3(2) of the Immigration Act 1971 [¹⁴ . . .];

(hh) a person who has humanitarian protection granted under those rules;] [⁷ or]

(i) a person who is not a person subject to immigration control within the meaning of section 115(9) of the Immigration and Asylum Act 1999 and who is in the United Kingdom as a result of his deportation, expulsion or other removal by compulsion of law from another country to the United Kingdom;[³ . . .].

(j) [⁷ . . .]

(k) [⁷ . . .]

[¹⁰(5) In this regulation—

"EEA national" has the meaning given in regulation 2(1) of the Immigration (European Economic Area) Regulations 2016;

"family member" has the meaning given in regulation 7(1)(a), (b) or (c) of the Immigration (European Economic Area) Regulations 2016 except that regulation 7(4) of those Regulations does not apply for the purposes of paragraphs (3B) and (4)(zd);

"relevant person of Northern Ireland" has the meaning given in Annex 1 of Appendix EU to the immigration rules made under section 3(2) of the Immigration Act 1971.]

[¹¹(6) In this regulation references to the Immigration (European Economic Area) Regulations 2016 are to be read with Schedule 4 to the Immigration and Social Security Co-ordination (EU Withdrawal) Act 2020 (Consequential, Saving, Transitional and Transitory Provisions) Regulations 2020.]

AMENDMENTS

1. Social Security (Persons from Abroad) Amendment Regulations 2006 (SI 2006/1026) reg.9 (April 30, 2006).

2. Social Security (Persons from Abroad) Amendment (No.2) Regulations 2006 (SI 2006/2528) reg.4 (October 9, 2006).

3. Social Security (Habitual Residence) (Amendment) Regulations 2009 (SI 1009/362) reg.4 (March 18, 2009).

4. Treaty of Lisbon (Changes in Terminology or Numbering) Order 2012 (SI 2012/1809) art.3 and Sch. Pt 2 (August 1, 2012).

5. Social Security (Habitual Residence) (Amendment) Regulations 2012 (SI 2012/2587) reg.4 (November 8, 2012).

6. Social Security (Croatia) Amendment Regulations 2013 (SI 2013/1474) reg.4(2) (July 1, 2013).

7. Social Security (Miscellaneous Amendments) (No.3) Regulations 2013 (SI 2013/2536) reg.10(3) (October 29, 2013).

8. Social Security (Habitual Residence) (Amendment) Regulations 2014 (SI 2014/902) reg.4 (May 31, 2014).

9. Social Security (Income-related Benefits) (Updating and Amendment) (EU Exit) Regulations 2019 (SI 2019/872) reg.4(2) (May 7, 2019).

10. Social Security (Income-Related Benefits) (Persons of Northern Ireland—Family Members) (Amendment) Regulations 2020 (SI 2020/683) reg.4(2) (August 24, 2020).

11. Immigration and Social Security Co-ordination (EU Withdrawal) Act 2020 (Consequential, Saving, Transitional and Transitory Provisions) (EU Exit) Regulations 2020 (SI 2020/1309) reg.59 (December 31, 2020).

12. Immigration (Citizens' Rights etc.) (EU Exit) Regulations 2020 (SI 2020/1372) reg.13 (December 31, 2020).

13. Social Security (Habitual Residence and Past Presence) (Amendment) Regulations 2021 (SI 2021/1034) reg.2 (September 15, 2021).

14. Social Security (Habitual Residence and Past Presence) (Amendment) Regulations 2022 (SI 2022/344) reg.2 (March 22, 2022).

15. Social Security (Habitual Residence and Past Presence) (Amendment) (No.2) Regulations 2022 (SI 2022/990) reg.2(1) and (2)(c) (October 18, 2022).

GENERAL NOTE

It is a fundamental requirement of entitlement to the state pension credit that the claimant "is in Great Britain" (SPCA 2002 s.1(2)(a)). In this context note *EC v Secretary of State for Work and Pensions* [2010] UKUT 93 (AAC); [2010] AACR 39, where it was held that state pension credit is a special non-contributory benefit within art.10a of Regulation 1408/71 and so is payable only to those living in Great Britain. In its original form this provision simply adopted the habitual residence test from the income support scheme as a means of determining whether a person was "in Great Britain" for the purposes of pension credit. This was then supplemented by the addition of the right to reside test as from May 1, 2004. However, as from April 30, 2006, the provision was recast in its current form (and has subsequently also been further amended). The new reg.2 reflects the evolution of the right to reside test and in particular the coming into force of Directive 2004/38. Note also the special dispensation for those temporarily absent from Great Britain (reg.3) and those being treated abroad under NHS provisions (reg.4).

For a full analysis of both the habitual residence and the right to reside rules, see the commentary to reg.21AA of the Income Support (General) Regulations 1987 and the Immigration (European Economic Area) Regulations 2016 in Vol.V in this series. For detailed discussion of the position of persons subject to immigration control, see Part V of this Volume.

The pre-April 30, 2006 version of reg.2 was considered by Commissioner Jacobs in *CPC/3588/2006* and by Commissioner Rowland in *CPC/1072/2006*; the claimant's appeal in the latter case was dismissed by the Court of Appeal in *Patmalniece v Secretary of State for Work & Pensions* [2009] EWCA Civ 621 and then by the Supreme Court ([2011] UKSC 11; [2011] AACR 34). The Supreme Court held that s.1 of the Act and reg.2 had to be read as a whole. The test under reg.2(2) was constructed in such a way that it was more likely to be satisfied by a UK national than by a national of another Member State. In terms of EU law, that

3.10

meant that although it was not directly discriminatory on grounds of nationality, it was indirectly discriminatory and so had to be justified. The purpose of the right to reside test was to safeguard the UK's social security system from exploitation by those who wished to enter in order to live off income-related benefits rather than to work. That was a legitimate reason for the imposition of the test. It was independent of nationality, arising from the principle that only those who were economically or socially integrated with the host Member State should have access to its social assistance system. There was, therefore, sufficient justification for the discrimination arising from reg.2(2). The position of Irish nationals—who met the requirements of reg.2(2) even though they did not have a right to reside in the UK and were not habitually resident there—was protected by art.2 of the Protocol on the Common Travel Area. It was not discriminatory not to extend the same entitlement to the nationals of other Member States.

3.11   Commissioner Jacobs has analysed the post-April 30, 2006 version of reg.2 in *CPC/2134/2007* and *CPC/3764/2007*. In *CPC/2134/2007* the claimant, a Lithuanian national, arrived in the UK in 2000, and unsuccessfully claimed asylum. She abandoned her asylum appeal when Lithuania joined the EU in May 2004. She claimed state pension credit in January 2006 but her claim was not decided until October 2006, when it was refused on the basis that she had no right to reside. Commissioner Jacobs acknowledged that the claimant had been in the UK for more than five years but ruled that she had no permanent right of residence. Pre-accession periods of residence could not be taken into account (following *GN (EEA Regulations: five years' residence) Hungary* [2007] UKAIT 73). The claimant had not exercised any EU right either before or after accession.

In *CPC/3764/2007* Commissioner Jacobs likewise confirmed that a pre-accession period of residence by a Slovakian national between 1997 and 2004 could not be taken into account (see also *R(IS) 3/08*). The Commissioner also analysed in detail the argument of the claimant's representative based on proportionality, concluding that the circumstances were "not sufficiently exceptional to justify ignoring the terms of the legislation governing the right to reside" (at para.46).

See also *Secretary of State v AA* [2009] UKUT 249 (AAC), where the issue was whether the claimant had a right to reside where he was a dependant of his son, who was in employment and held both British and Spanish nationality and with whom he had gone to live on a rent-free basis. Upper Tribunal Judge Rowland distinguished *McCarthy v Secretary of State for the Home Department* [2008] EWCA Civ 641, ruling that on a literal construction of the Immigration (European Economic Area) Regulations 2006 (SI 2006/1003) "a Spanish national is therefore an EEA national to whom regulation 6 applies, even if he or she also holds British nationality" (at para.16). In *HG v Secretary of State (SPC)* [2011] UKUT 382 (AAC), a decision issued after the judgment of the ECJ in *McCarthy v Secretary of State for the Home Department* (C-434/09). [2011] All E.R. (EC) 729, it was accepted that the claimant, a Polish national, was dependent upon her daughter, Mrs D. Judge Jacobs, taking the same approach as Judge Rowland in *Secretary of State v AA* [2009] UKUT 249 (AAC), held that Mrs D had a right to reside in the UK under the Immigration (EEA) Regulations 2006:

"9. The claimant is a family member of Mrs D under regulation 7(1)(c) as a dependent direct relative in her ascending line. As such, she has a right to reside under regulation 14(2) if Mrs D has a permanent right to reside. Mrs D has resided for the requisite period of five years to acquire that right under regulation 15(1)(a), provided two conditions are satisfied. One is that she is 'an EEA national'. She satisfies that condition by virtue of the definitions in regulation 2(1), under which an EEA national is a national of an EEA State other than the United Kingdom. Mrs D, as I have said, is Polish. The other condition is that she has resided in the United Kingdom in accordance with the 2006 Regulations. She would do so if she has resided as a worker. Under regulation 4(1)(a) a worker means 'a worker within the meaning of Article 39 of the Treaty'. The Secretary of State accepts that the evidence shows that Mrs D was a worker within the case law of the European Court of Justice. Article 39 is a Treaty provision and so free of the limitations on the scope of Directive 2004/38. There is, therefore, no impediment to Mrs D relying on that status for the purposes of the 2006 Regulations."

The decision of the Deputy Commissioner in *CPC/1433/2008* has been reversed   **3.12**
by the Court of Appeal in *Pedro v Secretary of State for Work and Pensions* [2009] EWCA Civ 1358; [2010] AACR 18. The claimant was a 62-year-old Portuguese national who had come to the UK to live with her son, who worked here. She had largely been financially dependent upon him and had claimed JSA and later state pension credit. The Court of Appeal stressed that the aim of Directive 2004/38 was to strengthen the right of free movement in the EU. Furthermore, an EU citizen who wished to work in another state might be deterred from doing so if he knew that his elderly, but not then dependent, mother would not be regarded as his dependant for the purposes of art.2(2) were she to join him and later become dependent upon him. Thus no such impediment should be placed in his way (*Metock and Minister voor Vreemdelingenzaken en Integratie v Eind* (C-291/05) [2008] All E.R. (EC) 371). Whether someone had the status of a dependent family member was a question of fact (*Centre Public d'Aide Sociale, Courcelles v Lebon* (C-316/85) [1987] E.C.R. 2811). Article 2(2)(d) did not specify when the dependency had to have arisen, nor did it require that the relative had to be dependent in the country of origin. Accordingly, proof of the claimant's dependence on her son in the UK would suffice under art.2(2)(d), and as the tribunal had already found as a fact that she was dependent on him, she was entitled to state pension credit. On the importance of fact-finding where there is a claim of dependency on a relative, see also *LA v SSWP* [2010] UKUT 109 (AAC).

For a discussion of what may be needed to lose habitual residence, see *KS v SSWP* [2010] UKUT 156 (AAC), holding that a VSO volunteer who went to India for more than two years had not lost his UK habitual residence.

Secretary of State for Work and Pensions v LL (SPC) [2014] UKUT 136 (AAC), concerning a Belgian pensioner supported in the UK by her daughter, who was unemployed at the material time, confirms that the effect of para.(2) and (3) (b)(ii) is that a right to reside is excluded for the family member of a jobseeker. See also *Secretary of State for Work and Pensions v LZ (SPC)* [2014] UKUT 147 (AAC), holding that the lack of a registration certificate prevented the claimant (a 64-year-old Polish woman living with her brother in the UK) as an "extended family member" from being treated as the "family member" of her brother, with the consequence that she too had no right to reside.

CPC/3588/2006, referred to above in the context of the pre-April 2006 version of   **3.13**
the legislation, also decided that a residence permit is only evidence and does not of itself create a right to reside. This was confirmed by the ECJ in *Dias v SSWP (C-325/09)* [2012] AACR 36. See also *MD v SSWP (SPC)* [2016] UKUT 319 (AAC), in which a Turkish Cypriot had been wrongly issued with an EEA certificate of permanent residence. Judge Rowland held that the residence certificate "is capable of proving the right of permanent residence in the absence of adequate evidence to the contrary but it does not confer a right of permanent residence and was insufficient to prove such a right in the present case in the face of uncontested evidence that the claimant had not qualified for a right of permanent residence" (at para.15).

For an illustration of a case in which self-employed was found to be "marginal and ancillary" (the claimant was self-publishing his life story) rather than "genuine and effective", see *SSWP v HH (SPC)* [2015] UKUT 583 (AAC).

Paragraph (4)(i)
On the meaning of a "person subject to immigration control" within sub-   **3.14**
para.(4)(i), see *OO v Secretary of State for Work and Pensions (SPC)* [2013] UKUT 335 (AAC). A spouse who falls within that definition is not treated as

part of the claimant's household for SPC purposes, i.e. when calculating the claimant's applicable amount or income. The tribunal in this case had failed to distinguish between a spouse being "sponsored" for immigration purposes and a person being subject to a sponsorship undertaking (under immigration law, written sponsorship undertakings cannot apply to a spouse). The claimant's statement on his SPC claim form that his wife was sponsored to be in the UK was accurate (he had not stated that he had signed a written undertaking). The DWP, which had wrongly assumed that his wife was a person subject to immigration control (rather than having been given indefinite leave to remain, as in fact was the case), had failed to make proper enquiries as to her true immigration status. The resulting overpayment was, therefore, due to official error and was not recoverable. The entitlement decision was remitted to a new tribunal for detailed findings on the claimant's means which were required to determine his entitlement to SPC.

[¹ Persons temporarily absent from Great Britain

3.15

3.—(1) A claimant's entitlement to state pension credit while the claimant is temporarily absent from Great Britain is to continue but for no longer than—

(a) 4 weeks, provided the absence is not expected to exceed 4 weeks;

(b) 8 weeks, where paragraph (2) applies; or

(c) 26 weeks, where paragraph (3) applies,

provided the claimant continues to satisfy the other conditions of entitlement.

(2) This paragraph applies where the absence is not expected to exceed 8 weeks and is in connection with the death of—

(a) the claimant's partner or a child or qualifying young person normally living with the claimant; or

(b) a close relative of—

(i) the claimant;

(ii) the claimant's partner; or

(iii) a child or qualifying young person normally living with the claimant,

and the Secretary of State considers that it would be unreasonable to expect the claimant to return to Great Britain within 4 weeks.

(3) This paragraph applies where the absence is not expected to exceed 26 weeks and is solely in connection with—

(a) the claimant undergoing—

(i) treatment for an illness or physical or mental impairment by, or under the supervision of, a qualified practitioner; or

(ii) medically approved convalescence or care as a result of treatment for an illness or physical or mental impairment, where the claimant had that illness or impairment before leaving Great Britain; or

(b) the claimant accompanying his or her partner or a child or qualifying young person normally living with the claimant for treatment or convalescence or care as mentioned in sub-paragraph (a).

(4) In this regulation and in regulation 5—

"medically approved" means certified by a registered medical practitioner;

"qualified practitioner" means a person qualified to provide medical treatment, physiotherapy or a form of treatment which is similar to, or related to, either of those forms of treatment.]

DEFINITIONS

"close relative"—see reg.1(2).
"medically approved"—see para.(4).
"partner" —see reg.1(2).
"qualified practitioner"—see *ibid.*
"qualifying young person"—see reg.4A.

AMENDMENT

1. Housing Benefit and State Pension Credit (Temporary Absence) (Amendment) Regulations 2016 (SI 2016/624) reg.4(2) (July 28, 2016).

GENERAL NOTE

The generosity of the statutory provisions governing continuing entitlement to state pension credit for claimants temporarily absent from Great Britain has waxed and waned over the years. Initially, the general rule was that entitlement could only continue for up to four weeks. After October 2008, it became possible for pension credit to continue for up to 13 weeks during a temporary absence from GB, where the absence was unlikely to exceed 52 weeks. However, from 2008 there was no time limit in cases where the absence from GB was in order to receive medical treatment under NHS arrangements. But in November 2015, as part of the Spending Review and Autumn Statement, the Chancellor of the Exchequer announced that "The government will end the payment of Housing Benefit and Pension Credit to claimants who travel outside of Great Britain for longer than 4 weeks consecutively, from April 2016." **3.16**

In the event these changes did not come into force until July 28, 2016 (see further below on transitional protection). According to official statements, the temporary absence period was reduced (in most cases) from 13 weeks to four weeks so as to achieve fairness in the benefits system, balancing the burden on taxpayers with support for claimants on low incomes. The four-week rule also aligns the new provisions for both housing benefit and state pension credit with universal credit.

The starting point now is the rule in the new reg.(3)(1)(a) that entitlement to state pension credit while the claimant is temporarily absent from Great Britain continues but for no longer than four weeks, "provided the absence is not expected to exceed 4 weeks". This default rule is subject to two exceptions.

The first exception (reg.3(1)(b) and 3(2)) is in the case of temporary absence from GB in connection with the death of a partner, a child or young person (see the new reg.4A). In such a case the four-week period can be extended by a further four weeks, if it would be unreasonable to expect a return to GB within four weeks. This exception also applies where the temporary absence is in connection with the death of a "close relative" (on which see the definition in reg.1(1)) of the claimant, or of their partner or of a child or young person normally living with the claimant **3.17**

The second exception (reg.3(1)(c) and 3(3)) is in the event of temporary absence from GB due to the need to receive medical treatment or convalescence. In this type of case pension credit may continue for up to 26 weeks. Where the claimant is accompanying their partner or a child or a young person who lives with them for medical treatment or convalescence outside GB, then pension credit may also continue for up to 26 weeks. The effect of this amendment is simultaneously to broaden the range of circumstances where the medical exemption can apply (broadly equivalent to the position in universal credit) – so e.g. the exception is not confined to NHS arrangements – but to cap the previously indefinite period of continued entitlement at 26 weeks.

The new temporary absence from rules for pension credit claimants also apply to members of the claimant's household as well as the claimant (see amendments to reg.5 below).

Note also the transitional protection that may apply. Regulation 5(3) of the amending regulations provides that "Regulation 4 shall not apply in respect of a **3.18** person who is temporarily absent from Great Britain on 28th July 2016 until the day that person returns to Great Britain."

The amending regulations were the subject of a report by the SSAC, following an abridged consultation period (a report unhelpfully published in July 2016 under the same title as the regulations, namely *Housing Benefit and State Pension Credit (Temporary Absence) (Amendment) Regulations 2016 (S.I. 2016 No. 624)*. The Committee made a number of recommendations in respect of the new temporary absence provisions as they affected housing benefit claimants, some of which were accepted in part (e.g. a modification for housing benefit claimants who are victims of domestic violence). The government rejected a more general proposal that the default position be set at a temporary absence limit of eight weeks, rather than four weeks, which the SSAC had considered "would capture the hardest cases that are likely to be impacted by these proposals". The government also dismissed a proposal that decision makers be given discretion to extend the allowable period in individual cases where good cause was shown. This suggestion was rejected on the basis that it "would provide uncertainty for both customer and decision makers, as well as the potential for additional administrative costs".

[¹ Persons temporarily absent from Great Britain on 6th October 2008

3.19   **3A.** [² . . .]]

AMENDMENTS

1. Social Security (Miscellaneous Amendments) (No.4) Regulations 2008 (SI 2008/2424) reg.3(3) (October 6, 2008).
2. Housing Benefit and State Pension Credit (Temporary Absence) (Amendment) Regulations 2016 (SI 2016/624) reg.4(3) (July 28, 2016).

GENERAL NOTE

3.20   This regulation, repealed with effect from July 28, 2016, was in effect a spent provision giving transitional protection for those claimants who were already temporarily absent from Great Britain on October 6, 2008.

Persons receiving treatment outside Great Britain

3.21   **4.** [¹ . . .]

AMENDMENT

1. Housing Benefit and State Pension Credit (Temporary Absence) (Amendment) Regulations 2016 (SI 2016/624) reg.4(4) (July 28, 2016).

GENERAL NOTE

3.22   This regulation was repealed with effect from July 28, 2016. For the position of persons receiving treatment outside Great Britain, see now the new reg.3(3) above.

[¹ Meaning of "qualifying young person"

3.23   **4A.**—(1) A person who has reached the age of 16 but not the age of 20 is a qualifying young person for the purposes of these Regulations—

(a) up to, but not including, the 1st September following the person's 16th birthday; and

(b) up to, but not including, the 1st September following the person's 19th birthday, if the person is enrolled on, or accepted for, approved training or a course of education—

    (i) which is not a course of advanced education within the meaning of regulation 12(3) of the Universal Credit Regulations 2013;

   (ii) which is provided at a school or college or provided elsewhere but approved by the Secretary of State for the purposes of regulation 5 of the Universal Credit Regulations 2013; and

  (iii) where the average time spent during term time in receiving tuition, engaging in practical work or supervised study or taking examinations exceeds 12 hours per week.

(2) Where the young person is aged 19, he or she must have started the education or training or been enrolled on or accepted for it before reaching that age.

(3) The education or training referred to in paragraph (1) does not include education or training provided by means of a contract of employment.

(4) "Approved training" means training in pursuance of arrangements made under section 2(1) of the Employment and Training Act 1973 or section 2(3) of the Enterprise and New Towns (Scotland) Act 1990 which is approved by the Secretary of State for the purposes of regulation 5 of the Universal Credit Regulations 2013.

(5) A person who is receiving universal credit, a contributory employment and support allowance, a contribution-based jobseeker's allowance, an income-related employment and support allowance, an income-based jobseeker's allowance or income support is not a qualifying young person.]

AMENDMENT

1. Housing Benefit and State Pension Credit (Temporary Absence) (Amendment) Regulations 2016 (SI 2016/624) reg.4(5) (July 28, 2016).

DEFINITIONS

"approved training"—see para.(4).
"contribution-based jobseeker's allowance"—see reg.1(2).
"contributory employment and support allowance"—see *ibid.*
"income-related employment and support allowance"—see *ibid.*
"income-based jobseeker's allowance"—see *ibid.*
"universal credit"—see *ibid.*

Persons treated as being or not being members of the same household

5.—(1) A person is to be treated as not being a member of the same household as the claimant if—   3.24

  (a) he is living away from the claimant and—

    (i) he does not intend to resume living with the claimant; or

   (ii) his absence is likely to exceed 52 weeks except where there are exceptional circumstances (for example the person is in hospital or otherwise has no control over the length of his absence), and the absence is unlikely to be substantially more than 52 weeks;

  (b) he or the claimant is permanently in a care home [4or an independent hospital];

  (c) he or the claimant is, or both are—

    (i) detained in a hospital provided under [² the provisions of the Mental Health Act 1983, the [³ Mental Health (Care and Treatment) (Scotland) Act 2003], or the Criminal Procedure (Scotland) Act 1995; or]

    (ii) detained in custody pending trial or sentence upon conviction or under a sentence imposed by a court; or

    (iii) on temporary release in accordance with the provisions of the Prison Act 1952 or the Prison (Scotland) Act 1989;

  (d) the claimant is abroad and does not satisfy [² . . .] regulation 3 (persons [⁷ temporarily] absent from Great Britain);

  (e) [⁵ . . .]

[⁷ (f) except in circumstances where paragraph (1A) applies, he is absent from Great Britain;]

[¹(g) [². . .]

  (h) he is a person subject to immigration control within the meaning of section 115(9) of the Immigration and Asylum Act 1999.]

[⁵ [⁷ (1A) A person is to be treated as being a member of the same household as the claimant while he is absent from Great Britain but for no longer than—

  (a) 4 weeks, provided the absence is not expected to exceed 4 weeks;

  (b) 8 weeks, where paragraph (1B) applies; or

  (c) 26 weeks, where paragraph (1C) applies.

(1B) This paragraph applies where the absence is not expected to exceed 8 weeks and is in connection with the death of—

  (a) a child or qualifying young person normally living with the person; or

  (b) a close relative of—

    (i) the person;

    (ii) the person's partner; or

    (iii) a child or qualifying young person normally living with the person,

and the Secretary of State considers that it would be unreasonable to expect the person to return to Great Britain within 4 weeks.

(1C) This paragraph applies where the absence is not expected to exceed 26 weeks and is solely in connection with—

  (a) the person undergoing—

    (i) treatment for an illness or physical or mental impairment by, or under the supervision of, a qualified practitioner; or

    (ii) medically approved convalescence or care as a result of treatment for an illness or physical or mental impairment, where the person had that illness or impairment before leaving Great Britain; or

  (b) the person accompanying his partner or a child or qualifying young person normally living with the person for treatment or convalescence or care as mentioned in sub-paragraph (a).]

(2) Subject to [⁸paragraphs (1) and (5)], partners shall be treated as members of the same household notwithstanding that they are temporarily living apart.

[⁶. . .]

[⁸(3) Paragraph (5) applies where a claimant ("C"), who has attained the qualifying age, would otherwise not be entitled to either state pension credit or universal credit, because—

  (a) but for that paragraph, C would be a member of the same household as a partner who has not attained the qualifying age and therefore a

member of a mixed-age couple excluded from state pension credit by virtue of section 4(1A), and
- (b) C is neither entitled to universal credit jointly with that partner, nor entitled to universal credit as a single person, in one of the cases set out in paragraph (4).

(4) The cases are where C is not entitled to universal credit because C has attained the qualifying age and—
- (a) any of the following paragraphs of regulation 3 of the Universal Credit Regulations 2013 (couples) applies, and in the case of paragraph (ii) below, one of the following circumstances applies—
  - (i) paragraph (3) (treatment of certain couples—universal credit may only be claimed as a single person);
  - (ii) paragraph (4) (treatment of polygamous marriages), so that C is not entitled to universal credit because C may only claim universal credit either as one of two parties to a polygamous marriage to be treated as a couple where the other party has also attained the qualifying age, or as a remaining party to such a marriage to be treated as single;
  - (iii) paragraph (6) (absence from the household—universal credit may only be claimed as a single person); or
- (b) C lost joint entitlement to universal credit as part of a mixed-age couple due to one of the following changes of circumstances taking effect from a date (namely the first day of the universal credit assessment period in which the change occurred) that is earlier than when, but for paragraph (5), the same change would take effect for the purposes of state pension credit, those changes being where—
  - (i) C and their partner are no longer a couple; or
  - (ii) C is party to a marriage that is no longer polygamous and C's remaining spouse has attained the qualifying age.

(5) Where this paragraph applies—
- (a) C and their partner, who are to be treated as a non-polygamous couple in accordance with sub-paragraph (a)(ii) of paragraph (4), or who are no longer parties to a polygamous marriage in accordance with sub-paragraph (b)(ii), are to be treated as members of the same household as each other but not of that of any party (or parties) with whom they are not part of a couple in accordance with those provisions; or
- (b) C, who is to be treated as single in accordance with sub-paragraph (a)(i) to (iii) of paragraph (4), or is single in accordance with sub-paragraph (b)(i), is to be treated as though C is not a member of the same household as any party (or parties) with whom C is not part of a couple in accordance with those provisions,

where paragraph (4)(a) applies, with effect from the date on which the relevant paragraph of regulation 3 of the Universal Credit Regulations 2013 first applies to C, or, where paragraph (4)(b) applies, with effect from the date referred to in paragraph (4)(b) on which C lost entitlement to universal credit.

(6) In this regulation—
- (a) in relation to universal credit entitlement, "assessment period" has the meaning prescribed by regulation 21 of the Universal Credit Regulations 2013;
- (b) "mixed-age", in respect of a couple or a marriage, means where one member has attained the qualifying age and the other has not;

    (c) the definition in sub-paragraph (b) includes a polygamous marriage where at least one party to the marriage has attained the qualifying age and at least one has not; and

    (d) "polygamous marriage" means a marriage during which a party to it is married to more than one person and which took place under the laws of a country that permits polygamy.]

AMENDMENTS

1. State Pension Credit (Consequential, Transitional and Miscellaneous Provisions) (No.2) Regulations 2002 (SI 2002/3197) reg.2 and Sch. para.2 (October 6, 2003).

2. State Pension Credit (Transitional and Miscellaneous Provisions) Amendment Regulations 2003 (SI 2003/2274) reg.2(5) (October 6, 2003).

3. Mental Health (Care and Treatment) (Scotland) Act 2003 (Modification of Subordinate Legislation) Order 2005 (SSI 2005/445) art.2 and Sch. para.35(2) (October 3, 2005).

4. Social Security (Care Homes and Independent Hospitals) Regulations 2005 (SI 2005/2687) reg.6 and Sch.5 para.2 (October 24, 2005).

5. Social Security (Miscellaneous Amendments) (No.4) Regulations 2006 (SI 2006/2378) reg.14(2) (October 2, 2006).

6. Social Security (Miscellaneous Amendments) (No.4) Regulations 2008 (SI 2008/2424) reg.3(4) (October 6, 2008).

7. Housing Benefit and State Pension Credit (Temporary Absence) (Amendment) Regulations 2016 (SI 2016/624) reg.4(6) (July 28, 2016).

8. Universal Credit (Persons who have attained state pension credit qualifying age) (Amendment) Regulations 2020 (SI 2020/655) reg.2(2) (November 25, 2020).

MODIFICATION

The definition of "prisoner" in regulation 1(2) is modified as from April 8, 2020 by reg.3 of the Social Security (Coronavirus) (Prisoners) Regulations 2020 (SI 2020/409). For details of the modification, see the General Note to this regulation.

DEFINITIONS

    "appropriately qualified"—see para.(3) and reg.3(4).
    "care home"—see reg.1(2).
    "claimant"—see SPCA 2002 s.17(1).
    "close relative"—see reg.1(2).
    "medically approved"—see reg.3(4).
    "partner"—see reg.1(2).
    "qualified practitioner"—see reg.3(4).
    "qualifying young person"—see reg.4A.
    "young person"—see para.(3) and reg.3(4).

GENERAL NOTE

3.25   This provision is modelled on the parallel rule relating to income support (see Income Support (General) Regulations 1987 (SI 1987/1967) reg.16, in Vol.V of this series), although the drafting is a little more straightforward. The starting point is that partners (i.e. members of a married or unmarried couple) are treated as members of the same household "notwithstanding that they are temporarily living apart" (para.(2)). In other words, membership of the same household does not cease simply because one partner is temporarily living elsewhere. This basic rule is then subject to the exceptions set out in para.(1), which replicate in part those that apply to income support.

Note that para.(1)(c)(iii) is "to be read as if the words 'the Prison Act 1952 or' were omitted" (see Social Security (Coronavirus) (Prisoners) Regulations 2020 (SI 2020/409) reg.3). The purpose of this change was to make provision for those individuals on temporary release from a prison in England and Wales due to the outbreak of COVID-19 in Great Britain to access means-tested benefits during the period of that release. In particular, it enables a person temporarily released from a prison in England and Wales to be included as a member of a claimant's household. The regulations must be kept under review by the Secretary of State and ceased to have effect on August 31, 2021 (see SI 2021/476 reg.4(6) amending SI 2020/409 reg.6).

Amount of the guarantee credit

6.—(1) Except as provided in the following provisions of these Regulations, the standard minimum guarantee is—   3.26

    (a) [⁴£306.85] per week in the case of a claimant who has a partner;

    (b) [⁴£201.05] per week in the case of a claimant who has no partner.

(2) Paragraph (3) applies in the case of—

    (a) prisoners; and

    (b) members of religious orders who are fully maintained by their order.

(3) In a case to which this paragraph applies—

    (a) section 2(3) has effect with the substitution for the reference to the standard minimum guarantee in section 2(3)(a) of a reference to a [²nil] amount; and

    (b) except in the case of a person who is a remand prisoner, [² nil] is the prescribed additional amount for the purposes of section 2(3)(b).

(4) Except in a case to which paragraph (3) applies, an amount additional to that prescribed in paragraph (1) shall be applicable under paragraph (5) if the claimant is treated as being a severely disabled person in accordance with paragraph 1 of Part I of Schedule I.

(5) The additional amount applicable is—

    (a) except where paragraph (b) applies, [⁴£76.40] per week if paragraph 1(1)(a), (b) or (c) of Part I of Schedule I is satisfied; or

    (b) [⁴£152.80] per week if paragraph 1(1)(b) of Part I of Schedule I is satisfied otherwise than by virtue of paragraph 1(2)(b) of that Part and no one is entitled to and in receipt of an allowance under section 70 of the 1992 Act [¹, or has an award of universal credit which includes the carer element under regulation 29 of the Universal Credit Regulations 2013,] in respect of caring for either partner.

(6) Except in a case to which paragraph (3) applies, an amount additional to that prescribed in paragraph (1) shall be applicable—

    (a) if paragraph 4 of Part II of Schedule I is satisfied (amount applicable for carers);

    (b) in accordance with Part III of Schedule I (amount applicable for former claimants of income support or income-based jobseeker's allowance); [³ . . .]

    (c) except where paragraph (7) applies, in accordance with Schedule II (housing costs)[³; or]

    [³ (d) except where paragraph (11) applies, or entitlement ceases by virtue of paragraph (14), in accordance with Schedule IIA (additional amount applicable for claimants responsible for a child or qualifying young person).]

(7) This paragraph applies in the case of a person who has been detained in custody for more than 52 weeks pending trial or sentence following conviction by a court.

(8) The amount applicable if paragraph 4 of Part II of Schedule I is satisfied is [⁴ £42.75] per week, and in the case of partners, this amount is applicable in respect of each partner who satisfies that paragraph.

(9) In the case of a remand prisoner paragraph (6) shall apply as if sub-paragraphs (a) and (b) were omitted.

(10) In this regulation, "remand prisoner" means a person who, for a period not exceeding 52 weeks, has been detained in custody on remand pending trial or, as a condition of bail, required to reside in a hostel approved under section 27(1) of the Probation Service Act 1993 or, as the case may be, detained pending sentence upon conviction.

[³ (11) This paragraph applies in the case of a person who is awarded, or who is treated as having an award of, a tax credit under the Tax Credits Act.

(12) For the purposes of paragraph (11)—

(a) a person is to be treated as having an award of a working tax credit with effect from the start of the current tax year even though a decision has not been made under section 14 of the Tax Credits Act in respect of a claim for that tax credit for that tax year, if the person was awarded a working tax credit for the previous tax year and any of the cases specified in paragraph (13) applies; and

(b) a person is to be treated as having an award of a child tax credit with effect from the start of the current tax year even though a decision has not been made under section 14 of the Tax Credits Act in respect of a claim for that tax credit for that tax year, if the person was awarded a child tax credit for the previous tax year and any of the cases specified in paragraph (13) applies.

(13) The cases specified for the purposes of paragraph (12) are—

(a) a final notice has not been given to the person under section 17 of the Tax Credits Act in respect of the previous tax year;

(b) a final notice has been given which includes provision by virtue of subsection (2) or (4) of section 17, or a combination of those subsections and subsection (6), and—

(i) the date specified in the notice for the purposes of section 17(2) and (4) or, where different dates are specified, the later of them has not passed and no claim for a tax credit for the current tax year has been made or treated as made; or

(ii) a claim for a tax credit has been made or treated as made on or before the date mentioned in paragraph (i), but no decision has been made in relation to that claim under section 14 of that Act; or

(c) a final notice has been given, no claim for a tax credit for the current tax year has been made or treated as made, and no decision has been made under section 18(1) of the Tax Credits Act in respect of an award of a tax credit for the previous tax year.

(14) Entitlement to the additional amount specified in Schedule IIA ceases where a person is awarded a tax credit in the circumstances specified in paragraph (15) or (16).

(15) The circumstances specified in this paragraph are—

(a) the person was awarded a tax credit for the previous tax year which was not terminated by Her Majesty's Revenue and Customs under section 16 of the Tax Credits Act;

(b) a final notice has been given to the person under section 17 of the Tax Credits Act in respect of that tax year; and

(c) either—

    (i) the person makes a declaration during the period of 30 days following the cessation of payment of a tax credit made under section 24(4) of the Tax Credits Act; or

    (ii) the person makes a declaration after the end of the period of 30 days following the cessation of payment of a tax credit made under section 24(4) of the Tax Credits Act but before 31st January of the tax year following the period to which the notice relates, and, in the opinion of Her Majesty's Revenue and Customs, the person had good reason for not making the declaration by the date specified in paragraph (13)(b).

(16) The circumstances specified in this paragraph are that a decision under section 14(1), 15(1), 16(1), 18(1), (5), (6) or (9), 19(3) or 20(1) or (4) of the Tax Credits Act is revised in favour of the claimant following—

(a) a revision by virtue of section 21 of the Tax Credits Act;

(b) a request for a review under section 21A of the Tax Credits Act;

(c) an appeal under section 38 of the Tax Credits Act; or

(d) a revision, in any other circumstances, of a decision by Her Majesty's Revenue and Customs relating to an award of a tax credit under the Tax Credits Act.

(17) In this regulation—

"a tax credit" includes a child tax credit and a working tax credit;

"the Tax Credits Act" means the Tax Credits Act 2002;

"child tax credit" means a child tax credit under and by virtue of section 8 of the Tax Credits Act;

"working tax credit" means a working tax credit under and by virtue of section 10 of the Tax Credits Act and includes the child care element by virtue of section 12 of that Act.]

AMENDMENTS

1. Universal Credit and Miscellaneous Amendments Regulations 2015 (SI 2015/1754) reg.16(2) (November 4, 2015).

2. Social Security Benefits Up-rating Order 2017 (SI 2017/260) art.25(2) and Sch.13 (April 10, 2017).

3. State Pension Credit (Additional Amount for Child or Qualifying Young Person) (Amendment) Regulations 2018 (SI 2018/676), reg.2(2) and (3) (February 1, 2019).

4. Social Security Benefits Up-rating Order 2023 (SI 2023/316) art.30(2) (April 10, 2023).

DEFINITIONS

"the 1992 Act"—see reg.1(2).

"child tax credit"—see para.(17)

"claimant"—see SPCA 2002 s.17(1).

"partner"—see reg.1(3).

"prisoner"—see reg.1(2).

"remand prisoner"—see para.(10).

"a tax credit"—see para.(17).

"the Tax Credits Act"—see *ibid.*

"working tax credit"—see *ibid.*

GENERAL NOTE

Paragraph (1)

3.27   The general conditions of entitlement to state pension credit are set out in s.1 of the SPCA 2002, with the supplementary conditions for the guarantee credit component contained in s.2. The amount of the guarantee credit is the "appropriate minimum guarantee" for claimants with no income and the difference between that figure and the person's income in other cases (s.2(2)). The "appropriate minimum guarantee" is comprised of the "standard minimum guarantee" and such other amounts as may be prescribed. This provision sets out the amount of the "standard minimum guarantee" for individual claimants and couples respectively. The "standard minimum guarantee" therefore performs broadly the same function as the age-related personal allowance taken together with the former pensioner premium in the income support scheme before that was subject to amendments consequential upon the coming into force of the SPCA 2002. This figure is then aggregated together with other prescribed amounts as set out in the remaining paragraphs of this regulation and Sch.1 to these Regulations to produce the "appropriate minimum guarantee" (or applicable amount in income support terms). The calculation used to arrive at the final guarantee credit is then as provided for by s.2(2) of the SPCA 2002, as described above.

Paragraphs (2) and (3)

3.28   As with income support (see the Income Support (General) Regulations 1987 (SI 1987/1967) Sch.7 paras 7 and 8, in Vol.V of this series), prisoners and those fully maintained by their religious orders effectively have no entitlement to the guarantee credit, as their living costs are met from other sources. They also have a nil entitlement to the savings credit (reg.7(3)).

See further *CSPC/677/2007*, the lead case of several involving claims for state pension credit by nuns who were all members of a Carmelite closed order. Any income received by an individual nun was paid into a monastery account, which held the funds in common. Commissioner May QC held that in these circumstances the nuns were fully maintained by their order; no distinction could be made between those nuns who contributed their own income and those who had no income. Nor could any distinction be made between those orders which were self-maintaining and those which were not. The Commissioner also held that neither art.1 of Prot.1 nor art.8 of the European Convention on Human Rights was engaged.

Furthermore, in *Secretary of State for Work and Pensions v Sister IS and KM* [2009] UKUT 200 (AAC), where the claimants were Benedictine and Carmelite nuns, a three-judge panel of the Upper Tribunal ruled that: (1) the expression "religious order" in reg.6(2)(b) is to be read in the broader sense of that term found in dictionaries; it is not limited to those religious communities subject to a centralised authority or control; (2) the nuns in question were fully maintained from funds held by their orders, and that it did not matter from what source the funds originated (whether by their own work or any entitlement to benefits which contributed to the order's funds); and (3) it was possible to remove any element of religious discrimination (if there was one) in reg.6(2)(b) "by removing the reference to religion. That would leave the provision to apply to 'members of religious orders who are fully maintained by their order'."

The claimant's further appeal to the Court of Appeal was dismissed in *Scott v Secretary of State for Social Security* [2011] EWCA Civ 103; [2011] AACR 23. The Court held that the Upper Tribunal had not misdirected itself as to the proper construction of the phrase "fully maintained"; the proposition that "full maintenance" was only conceptually possible if the recipient of the funds was making no contribution could not be read into the Regulations. There was no doubt that the claimant was being "fully maintained" by her community when she made her claim. Her work was not for her own personal benefit, but exclusively for the trust, in return for which she received the benefit of bed and board under the trust arrangements in place. It followed that her maintenance was provided by the trust, rather than, as the Upper Tribunal had found, directly from her own efforts.

Paragraphs (4) and (5)

Section 2(7) of the SPCA 2002, which mirrors SSCBA 1992 s.135(5), requires an additional amount to be prescribed (for the purposes of calculating the "appropriate minimum guarantee") for severely disabled people. The qualifying criteria for this additional amount, which essentially performs the same function as the severe disability premium in the income support scheme, are set out in para.1 of Sch.1 to these Regulations. See further *DB (as executor of the estate of OE) v SSWP and Birmingham CC (SPC)* [2018] UKUT 46 (AAC). See *HT v SSWP (AA)* [2020] UKUT 57 (AAC) for an example of a case where receipt of an equivalent Polish disability benefit qualified for these purposes.

3.29

Paragraphs (6)–(10)

Further additional amounts for the purposes of calculating the "appropriate minimum guarantee" are prescribed for carers, former claimants of income support or income-based jobseeker's allowance, in respect of housing costs and for claimants entitled to the standard minimum guarantee who are responsible for a child or qualifying young person but do not have an award of a tax credit.

3.30

This last type of additional amount was introduced to compensate for the abolition of child tax credit by the Welfare Reform Act 2012. The amendment ensures that low income pensioners who are responsible for a child or young person continue to receive financial support akin to CTC. The criteria for the award of such an additional amount are set out in the new Sch.IIA. This Schedule applies to a claimant who is responsible for a "child" or "qualifying young person" (para.1); defines the terms "child" and "qualifying young person" (para.2); sets out the circumstances in which a person is, or is not, to be treated as responsible for a child or qualifying young person (paras 3 to 8); specifies the additional amount of benefit applicable to a claimant where he or she is responsible for a child or qualifying young person (the amount is increased if the child or qualifying young person is entitled to DLA or PIP or if they are certified as severely sight impaired or blind) (para.9); and provides for a higher amount to be payable where the eldest child or qualifying young person was born before April 6, 2017 (para.10).

Paragraphs (8)–(10)

The amount of the carer additional amount is set out in para.(8); the other additional amounts are detailed in Pt III of Sch.1, and Sch.2 to these Regulations respectively. Prisoners and fully maintained members of religious orders are not eligible for such additional amounts. Furthermore, those who have been detained in custody for more than 52 weeks pending trial or sentence following conviction are not eligible for housing costs. Note also that remand prisoners are in any event not eligible for the additional amounts prescribed for carers and for former claimants of income support or income-based jobseeker's allowance (paras (9) and (10)).

3.31

Paragraphs (11)–(17)

The effect of the addition of para.(6)(d) is to provide for the payment of an additional amount to a pension credit claimant who is entitled to the standard minimum guarantee, so long as that claimant is responsible for a child or qualifying young person and does not have an award of a tax credit (see paras (11) and (14)). Paragraph 11 provides for a person "who is awarded, or who is treated as having an award of, a tax credit" to be excluded from entitlement to the additional amount for a child or QYP. The relevant circumstances are as defined by paras (12) and (13). Paragraph (14) provides for a person to cease to be entitled to such an additional amount "where a person is awarded a tax credit in the circumstances specified in paragraph (15) or (16)".

3.32

Savings Credit

3.33 7.—(1) The percentage prescribed for the purposes of determining—
(a) the maximum savings credit is [² 60 per cent];
(b) "amount A" in section 3(4) is [² 60 per cent];
(c) "amount B" in section 3(4) is [² 40 per cent].

(2) The amount prescribed for the savings credit threshold is [³£174.49] for a claimant who has no partner and [³£277.12] for a claimant who has a partner.

(3) The maximum savings credit shall be taken to be [² nil] in the case of—
(a) prisoners; and
(b) members of religious orders who are fully maintained by their order.

[¹(4) If a calculation made for the purposes of paragraph (1)(b) or (c) results in a fraction of a penny, that fraction shall, if it would be to the claimant's advantage, be treated as a penny; otherwise it shall be disregarded.]

AMENDMENTS

1. State Pension Credit (Consequential, Transitional and Miscellaneous Provisions) Regulations 2002 (SI 2002/3019) reg.23(d) (October 6, 2003).
2. Social Security Benefits Up-rating Order 2017 (SI 2017/260), art.25(3) and (6) and Sch.13 (April 10, 2017).
3. Social Security Benefits Up-rating Order 2023 (SI 2023/316) art.30(3) (April 10, 2023).

DEFINITIONS

"claimant"—see SPCA 2002 s.17(1).
"partner"—see reg.1(3).
"prisoner"—see reg.1(2).

GENERAL NOTE

3.34 See annotations to s.3 of the SPCA 2002 for a full explanation as to the calculation of the savings credit. This regulation prescribes the relevant percentages (para.(1)) for the purposes of that calculation, specifies the savings credit threshold for individuals and couples (para.(2)) and excludes prisoners and fully maintained members of religious orders (para.(3)).

[¹ Limitation of savings credit for certain mixed-age couples

3.35 **7A.**—A person who is a member of a mixed-age couple, is not entitled to a savings credit unless one of the members of the couple—
(a) has been awarded a savings credit with effect from a day before 6th April 2016 and was entitled to a savings credit immediately before 6th April 2016, and
(b) remained entitled to a savings credit at all times since the beginning of 6th April 2016.]

AMENDMENT

1. Pension Credit (Amendment) Regulations 2015 (SI 2015/1529) reg.2(2) (April 6, 2016).

DEFINITION

"couple"—see reg.1(2).

3.36

The first requirement for entitlement to the savings credit element of pension credit, as originally enacted, was that the claimant (or their partner) was at least 65 (State Pension Credit Act 2002, s.3(1)). However, as a result of amendments made by the Pensions Act 2014, there is no longer access to the savings credit element for those claimants reaching state pension age on or after April 6, 2016 unless they are a member of a couple where their partner reached state pension age before that date (known as "a mixed-age couple"). Section 3ZA of the 2002 Act provides the enabling power for entitlement to the savings credit to be so restricted and defines what is meant by a "mixed-age couple". This regulation specifies the conditions which must be met for a mixed-age couple to qualify for savings credit. Although the drafting of the regulation suggests that there are only two pre-conditions, in reality there are three. First, one member must have attained state pension age before April 6, 2016. Secondly, that person must have been entitled to savings credit immediately before April 6, 2016. Thirdly, that individual must have been entitled to savings credit at all times since that date.

Special groups

3.37

8.—Schedule III shall have effect in the case of members of polygamous marriages and [1 persons serving a sentence of imprisonment detained in hospital].

AMENDMENT

1. Social Security (Persons Serving a Sentence of Imprisonment Detained in Hospital) Regulations 2010 (SI 2010/442) reg.4(2) (March 25, 2010).

GENERAL NOTE

3.38

Section 12 of the SPCA 2002 enables special provision to be made for members of polygamous marriages. Special provision for other persons is authorised by the general regulation-making powers in SSCBA 1992 s.175 which apply in this context by virtue of SPCA 2002 s.19(1).

Qualifying income for the purposes of savings credit

3.39

9.—For the purposes of section 3 (savings credit), all income is to be treated as qualifying income except the following which is not to be treated as qualifying income—
  (a) working tax credit;
  (b) incapacity benefit;
  (c) a contribution-based jobseeker's allowance [2 . . .]
  (d) severe disablement allowance;
  (e) maternity allowance;
  (f) payments referred to in regulation 15(5)(d) (maintenance payments).
[1 (g) contributory employment and support allowance.]

AMENDMENTS

1. Employment and Support Allowance (Consequential Provisions) (No.2) Regulations 2008 (SI 2008/1554) reg.4(3) (October 27, 2008).
2. Universal Credit (Consequential, Supplementary, Incidental and Miscellaneous Provisions) Regulations 2013 (SI 2013/630) reg.33(3) (April 29, 2013).

GENERAL NOTE

3.40   WTC and the other benefits and payments listed here are excluded from the definition of qualifying income for the purpose of calculating the savings credit under SPCA 2002 s.3.

In *CPC/4177/2005* Commissioner May QC dismissed a challenge to reg.9(d) based on Directive 79/7 (equal treatment). The Commissioner ruled that art.4 of the Directive was engaged for the purposes of the savings credit element of pension credit (but not for the guaranteed credit). The Commissioner then held that there was no discrimination and so no breach of art.4 of the Directive. However, the reasoning in this decision may be revisited in subsequent decisions–e.g. it is less than clear that it is permissible to "sever" pension credit into its constituent elements, given that jobseeker's allowance is treated as one benefit (see *Hockenjos v Secretary of State for Social Security* [2001] EWCA Civ 624; [2001] 2 C.M.L.R. 51). It should also be noted that in *CPC/4177/2005* the claimant did not attend the Commissioner's oral hearing and was unrepresented.

In *CPC/4173/2007* the claimant, aged 76, lived with her husband, aged 61, who received incapacity benefit. Her husband's incapacity benefit did not count as qualifying income for the purposes of savings credit by virtue of reg.9(b). The claimant argued that this was discriminatory as a woman of the same age as her husband would have received retirement pension (which does count as qualifying income). Commissioner Howell QC held that reg.9 does not contravene art.14 of the European Convention, as there was no differential treatment by reason of status. The Commissioner also ruled that there was no breach of Council Directive 79/7/EEC on equal treatment, as the circumstances fell squarely within the exclusion in art.7, which related to the determination of pensionable ages. Moreover, the Sex Discrimination Act 1975 had no application in this context.

Assessed income period

3.41   **10.**—(1) For the purposes of section 6(2)(b) (circumstances in which the Secretary of State is prevented from specifying an assessed income period), the circumstances are—

(a) in the case of partners, one partner is under the age of 60; or

(b) state pension credit is awarded, or awarded at a higher rate, because an element of the claimant's retirement provision which is due to be paid to the claimant stops temporarily.

[² (c) that—

(i) the Secretary of State has sent the claimant the notification required by regulation 32(6)(a) of the Claims and Payments Regulations; and

(ii) the claimant has not provided sufficient information to enable the Secretary of State to determine whether there will be any variation in the claimant's retirement provision throughout the period of 12 months beginning with the day following the day on which the previous assessed income period ends.]

(2) The circumstances prescribed for the purposes of section 7(4) (circumstances in which assessed amounts are deemed not to change) are that—

[⁴ (a) except where sub-paragraph (b) applies, the arrangements under which the assessed amount is paid contain no provision for periodic increases in the amount payable; or]

(b) the assessed income comprises income from capital other than income to which paragraph (7) applies.

(3) Paragraphs (4) and (5) do not apply where the assessed amount comprises income from capital.

(4) Where the Secretary of State is informed that the arrangements under which the assessed amount is paid contains provision—

(a) for the payment to be increased periodically;

(b) for the date on which the increase is to be paid; and

(c) for determining the amount of the increase, the assessed amount shall be deemed to increase from the day specified in paragraph (5) by an amount determined by applying those provisions to the amount payable apart from this paragraph.

[³ (5) The day referred to in this paragraph is—

(a) in a case to which paragraph (5A) applies—

   (i) where the first increased payment date is the day on which the benefit week begins, that day;

   (ii) where head (i) does not apply, the first day of the next benefit week which begins after that increased payment date;

(b) in a case to which paragraph (5A) does not apply—

   (i) where the second increased payment date is the day on which the benefit week begins, that day;

   (ii) where head (i) does not apply, the first day of the next benefit week following that increased payment date.

(5A) This paragraph applies where the period which—

(a) begins on the date from which the increase in the assessed amount is to accrue; and

(b) ends on the first increased payment date,

is a period of the same length as the period in respect of which the last payment of the pre-increase assessed amount was made.

(5B) In paragraphs (5) and (5A)—

"increased payment date" means a date on which the increase in the assessed amount referred to in paragraph (4) is paid as part of a periodic payment [⁴ . . .]; and

"pre-increase assessed amount" means the assessed amount prior to that increase.]

(6) Except where paragraph (4) applies, the assessed amount shall be deemed to increase—

[³ (a) on the day in April each year on which increases under section 150 (1)(c) of the Administration Act come into force if that is the first day of a benefit week but if it is not from the next following such day; and]

(b) by an amount produced by applying to the assessed amount the same percentage increase as that applied for the purposes of additional pensions under section 150(1)(c) and 151(1) of the Administration Act.

(7) Where the assessed amount comprises income from capital, it shall be deemed to increase or decrease—

(a) on the first day of the next benefit week to commence [¹on or after] the day on which the income increases or decreases; and

(b) by an amount equal to the change in the claimant's income produced by applying to his income changes made to the yields capital is deemed to produce, or to the capital amounts, specified in regulation 15(6), or to both if both are changed.

(8) [⁵ . . .]

AMENDMENTS

1. State Pension Credit (Consequential, Transitional and Miscellaneous Provisions) Regulations 2002 (SI 2002/3019) reg.23(e) (October 6, 2003).

2. State Pension Credit (Transitional and Miscellaneous Provisions) Amendment Regulations 2003 (SI 2003/2274) reg.2(6) (October 6, 2003).

3. State Pension Credit (Miscellaneous Amendments) Regulations 2004 (SI 2004/647) reg.3(2) and (3) (April 5, 2004).

4. State Pension Credit (Amendment) Regulations 2005 (SI 2005/3205) reg.2(2) (December 18, 2005).

5. Social Security (Miscellaneous Amendments) (No.4) Regulations 2006 (SI 2006/2378) reg.14(3) (October 2, 2006).

DEFINITIONS

"the Administration Act"—see SPCA 2002 s.17(1).
"assessed income period"—see *ibid.*
"benefit week"—see reg.1(2).
"claimant"—see SPCA 2002 s.17(1).
"increased payment date"—see para.(5B).
"partner"—see reg.1(3).
"pay day"—see para.(8).
"pre-increase assessed amount"—see para.(5B).
"retirement provision"—see SPCA 2002 ss.7(6) and 17(1).

GENERAL NOTE

3.42   The "assessed income period" was central to the original conception of the state pension credit. Recognising that the traditional weekly means test of income support has been an important factor in the relatively low take-up of that benefit amongst pensioners, the Government initially adopted a very different strategy for state pension credit. Section 6(1) of the SPCA 2002 imposed a duty on the Secretary of State to specify an assessed income period when making a decision on a state pension credit claim. In normal circumstances, the assessed income period was fixed at five years from the date that decision took effect (SPCA 2002 s.9(1)). The principle then was that changes in the pensioner's income during that period need not be reported and thus any increases in income did not, of themselves, result in disentitlement or run the risk of overpayments accruing. Instead, the claimant's income throughout the five-year period was deemed to be the same as the income at the outset (*ibid.*, and s.7(3)), subject to deemed cost of living increases (*ibid.* and s.7(4)).

See further *CPC/0206/2005*, discussed in the note to State Pension Credit Act 2002 s.7 and *CPC/1928/2005*, discussed in the note to s.9 of that Act.

However, as a result of the Pensions Act 2014, assessed income periods will be phased out as from April 2016. As a result, any change in retirement income will in future need to be reported to the Department when it occurs, triggering a review and change in benefit award where appropriate.

Paragraph (1)

3.43   Section 6(2) of the SPCA 2002 provides that the Secretary of State is prevented from specifying a standard assessed income period under s.6(1) in two categories of case. The first is where an assessed income period is already in force in the claimant's case by virtue of an earlier application of the s.6 rule. The second comprises "such other circumstances as may be prescribed" (SPCA 2002 s.6(2)(b)). This paragraph prescribes two such types of case. The first is where the claimant is a member of a couple and one partner is aged under 60. This inevitably increases the likelihood that they are in (or may re-enter) the labour market and so a five-year "deeming rule" may be inappropriate. The second is where there has been a temporary cessation of the claimant's retirement provision leading to an award (or higher award) of state pension credit.

Presumably the insertion of reg.10(1)(c) should be read as being preceded by the word "or" at the end of reg.10(1)(b).

Paragraph (2)
As explained in the General Note above, the normal rule is that the amount of income fixed at the date of claim (the "assessed amount") is deemed to be the claimant's income throughout the assessed income period, subject to cost of living increases (SPCA 2002 s.7(3) and (4)). The prescribed cost of living increases in a claimant's assessed income do not operate where there is no clause in the claimant's pension scheme or annuity contract which provides for such periodic increases in the amount payable. The assessed amount is also not periodically uprated where it comprises income from capital (except income covered by para. (7) below).   **3.44**

Paragraphs (3)–(5)
Many occupational and personal schemes will include provisions for periodic (typically annual) increases in the amount payable, which also specify when such increases are to be paid and how they are to be calculated. Where the Secretary of State is informed that such arrangements exist, then para.(4) enables the claimant's assessed income to be increased accordingly, reflecting such improvements in pension provision. The increase is deemed to apply from the start of the benefit week if the increase under the pension scheme is due to be paid on that day or, failing that, from the start of the next benefit week (para.(5)). For cases not covered by para.(4), see para.(6). These provisions do not apply where the assessed income comprises income from capital (para.(3); see further para (7)).   **3.45**

Paragraph (6)
In the event that the pension scheme does not include a provision which meets the criteria of para.(4), the default position is that the assessed amount is increased in line with the percentage increase stipulated by the Secretary of State as the amount by which additional pensions are to be increased.   **3.46**

Paragraph (7)
If the assessed amount comprises income from capital, it is deemed to increase (or decrease) in line with the tariff income rule under reg.15(6).   **3.47**

Retirement provision in assessed income period

11.—[1 (1) Where an element of a person's retirement provision ceases to be payable by one source but—   **3.48**
  (a) responsibility for that element is assumed by another source, income from both those sources shall be treated as income from the same source; or
  (b) in consequence of that element ceasing, income of a different description becomes payable from a different source, that income shall be treated as income of the same description from the same source as the element which ceased to be payable.
[1 (2) For the purposes of section 7(6) (meaning of retirement provision) of the Act, a foreign state retirement pension is to be treated as a benefit under the 1992 Act.]

AMENDMENT

1. Social Security (Miscellaneous Amendments) (No.2) Regulations 2010 (SI 2010/641) reg.6(4) (April 13, 2010).

The State Pension Credit Regs 2002

DEFINITION

"retirement provision"—see ss.7(6) and 17(1) of the SPCA 2002.

GENERAL NOTE

3.49   The purpose of this provision is to ensure that the assessed income period continues notwithstanding the fact that responsibility for a pensioner's retirement provision changes (e.g. from one pension provider to another). The addition of para. (2) was designed to reverse the effect of *CPC/571/2008*.

End of assessed income period

3.50   **12.**—An assessed income period shall end [² . . .]

(a) [² at such time as] the claimant no longer satisfies a condition of entitlement to state pension credit;

(b) [² at such time as] payments of an element of the claimant's retirement provision which is due to be paid to him stops temporarily or the amount paid is less than the amount due and in consequence his award of state pension credit is superseded under section 10 of the Social Security Act 1998;

(c) [² at such time as] a claimant who has no partner is provided with accommodation in a care home [¹ or an independent hospital] other than on a temporary basis [²;

(d) if, apart from this sub-paragraph, it would have ended on a date falling within the period specified in column 1 of the table in Schedule IIIA, on the corresponding date shown against that period in column 2 of that table.]

AMENDMENTS

1. Social Security (Care Homes and Independent Hospitals) Regulations 2005 (SI 2005/2687) reg.6 and Sch.5 para.3 (October 24, 2005).
2. State Pension Credit (Amendment) Regulations 2015 (SI 2015/1529) reg.2(3) (April 6, 2016).

DEFINITIONS

"assessed income period"—see SPCA 2002 ss.6, 9 and 17(1).
"care home"—see reg.1(2).
"claimant"—see SPCA 2002 s.17(1).
"partner"—see reg.1(3).
"retirement provision"—see ss.7(6) and 17(1) of the SPCA 2002.

GENERAL NOTE

3.51   The Assessed Income Period (AIP), a feature of pension credit from its introduction in 2003, removed the requirement for many recipients aged 65 and over to notify the DWP of changes to their retirement provision (i.e. savings and non-state pensions) during a set period. The maximum length of an AIP was five years in the case of recipients under the age of 75 when their AIP was set, but an indefinite period for those aged 75 or over. Changes which would increase the award could still be notified during an AIP and lead to a change in the award; changes that would reduce the award were assessed if they are notified, but the award itself was not changed until the end of the AIP.

Thus the normal rule was that the assessed income period would last for five years (SPCA 2002 s.9(1)). The primary legislation provides for various exceptions to this principle, namely where the claimant becomes (or ceases to be) a member

836

of a couple, reaches the age of 65 or (in the case of a couple) where their partner attains 65 (*ibid.*, and s.9(4)). The regulation originally provided for just three further and restricted circumstances in which that period will end before the expiry of five years—where the claimant no longer satisfies a condition of entitlement (para.12(a)), where there is a fall in income provided by way of retirement provision (para.12(b)), and where a single claimant goes into long-term care (para.12(c)). The underlying thinking is that instead of having to report the multitudinous changes of circumstances required under the income support scheme, state pension credit claimants will only have to report the sorts of significant life changes which have to be reported in any event for state pension purposes (e.g. bereavement, remarriage, moving into a care home).

As a result of the amendments made by the Pensions Act 2014 (see s.28), there is now a fourth and further situation in which assessed income periods will cease. This restriction is far more significant. The effect of the Pensions Act 2014 is to limit the application of the AIP legislation to decisions that took effect *before* April 6, 2016. Consequently, and as from April 6, 2016, no new AIPs have been or will be set. Where this change takes effect, any change in retirement provision must accordingly be reported by the claimant when it occurs, triggering an immediate review and (where appropriate) a change of the pension credit award. The position with AIPs already set before April 6, 2016 is that they will remain valid beyond that date, until such time as they end—whether through natural expiry, being phased out early, or under the existing rules on reporting changes of circumstances.

The effect of the new reg.12(d) is to bring to an end all pre-April 6, 2016 AIPs within three years (being the necessary time frame to achieve the annual expenditure savings agreed in the Government's 2013 Spending Round; the removal of the AIP is expected to generate savings of approximately £80 million per year by 2020/21). As a result, and as from April 2016, existing AIPs due to end on a date between April 2016 and March 2019 will run their course until they end (in whatever circumstances under the current rules); and existing AIPs that would otherwise be due to end after March 2019 will be brought forward to end on a specified date between July 2016 and March 2019. Consequently, by April 2019, the only AIPs still in existence should be those that were set indefinitely prior to April 6, 2016 (and where the claimants' circumstances have remained unchanged). The details of those AIPs which will be ended early are set out in a table to these Regulations, added as Schedule IIIA. Column 1 of the table in Sch.IIIA sets out the dates when these AIPs were originally due to be terminated, while Column 2 of Sch.IIIA provides the new dates on which they will now end. The Department's intention is that recipients with a fixed-term AIP which is to be ended early will receive a letter giving six months' advance notice of their revised end-date. The table contains several gaps between some of the months; the purpose of this which is to allow the Department's Operations branch to distribute and manage the prescribed volumes, including customer contact and explanation of benefit revision. As the fixed-term AIPs come to an end, the intention is that in future periodic case reviews will be conducted on those cases. These are generally conducted on a three-yearly basis, but the intervals for reviews are not set out in existing legislation and can therefore be applied more flexibly in practice.

The decision to abolish AIPs was taken as part of the 2013 Spending Round. The policy justification was that when AIPs were introduced, it was assumed that pensioners are more likely to have relatively stable income and capital. However, the Government has argued that this assumption has not proved to be correct. In particular, recent analysis suggests that pensioners' financial circumstances change more significantly than was anticipated (see DWP, *Abolition of Assessed Income Periods for Pension Credit; Impact Assessment*, October 2013, especially pp.10–11). As a result, fixing retirement provision for a long period has allowed some recipients to keep their benefit despite obtaining higher amounts of capital or new income streams—whereas if an AIP were not in place in these cases, the award would be either reduced or removed entirely.

3.52

Small amounts of state pension credit

3.53   **13.**—Where the amount of state pension credit payable is less than 10 pence per week, the credit shall not be payable unless the claimant is in receipt of another benefit payable with the credit.

DEFINITION

"claimant"—see SPCA 2002 s.17(1).

GENERAL NOTE

3.54   This applies the same de minimis rule as operates in the income support scheme (Social Security (Claims and Payments) Regulations 1987 (SI 1987/1968) reg.26(4)): see Vol.III).

[¹Part-weeks

3.55   **13A.**—(1) The guarantee credit shall be payable for a period of less than a week ("a part-week") at the rate specified in paragraph (3) if—
    (a) the claimant was entitled to [³ universal credit,] income support [², an income-related employment and support allowance] or an income-based jobseeker's allowance immediately before the first day on which the conditions for entitlement to the credit are satisfied; and
    (b) the claimant's entitlement to the credit is likely to continue throughout the first full benefit week which follows the part-week.
    (2) For the purpose of determining the amount of the guarantee credit payable in respect of the part-week, no regard shall be had to any income of the claimant and his partner.
    (3) The amount of the guarantee credit payable in respect of the part-week shall be determined—
    (a) by dividing by 7 the weekly amount of the guarantee credit which, taking into account the requirements of paragraph (2), would be payable in respect of a full week; and then
    (b) multiplying the resulting figure by the number of days in the part-week, any fraction of a penny being rounded up to the nearest penny.]

AMENDMENTS

1. State Pension Credit (Consequential, Transitional and Miscellaneous Provisions) Regulations 2002 (SI 2002/3019) reg.23(f) (October 6, 2003).
2. Employment and Support Allowance (Consequential Provisions) (No.2) Regulations 2008 (SI 2008/1554) reg.4(4) (October 27, 2008).
3. Universal Credit (Consequential, Supplementary, Incidental and Miscellaneous Provisions) Regulations 2013 (SI 2013/630) reg.33(4) (April 29, 2013).

DEFINITIONS

"a part-week"—see para.1.
"benefit week"—see reg.1(2).
"claimant"—see SPCA 2002 s.17(1).
"partner"—see reg.1(3).

GENERAL NOTE

3.56   This regulation provides for a simple means of ensuring continuity of payment for claimants transferring from income support or income-based jobseeker's allowance to state pension credit. Claimants in such circumstances are entitled to a part-week payment of the guarantee credit to take them up to the start of their first week on state pension credit. This part week payment is paid irrespective of the claimant's income (or that of their partner) (para.(2)). Note that there is no provision for part week payments of the savings credit.

[¹Date on which benefits are treated as paid

13B.—(1) The following benefits shall be treated as paid on the day of the week in respect of which the benefit is payable—

    (a) severe disablement allowance;

    (b) short-term and long-term incapacity benefit;

    (c) maternity allowance;

    (d) contribution-based jobseeker's allowance [⁴ . . .]

[³ (e) contributory employment and support allowance.]

    (2) All benefits except those mentioned in paragraph (1) shall be treated as paid on the first day of the benefit week in [² . . .] which the benefit is payable.]

3.57

AMENDMENTS

1. State Pension Credit (Consequential, Transitional and Miscellaneous Provisions) Regulations 2002 (SI 2002/3019) reg.23(f) (October 6, 2003).

2. State Pension Credit (Consequential, Transitional and Miscellaneous Provisions) (No.2) Regulations 2002 (SI 2002/3197) reg.2 and Sch. para.3 (October 6, 2003).

3. Employment and Support Allowance (Consequential Provisions) (No.2) Regulations 2008 (SI 2008/1554) reg.4(5) (October 27, 2008).

4. Universal Credit (Consequential, Supplementary, Incidental and Miscellaneous Provisions) Regulations 2013 (SI 2013/630) reg.33(5) (April 29, 2013).

DEFINITION

"benefit week"—see reg.1(2).

GENERAL NOTE

This provision is a good example of the topsy-turvy principle of statutory drafting. The general rule, as enshrined in para.(2), is that a social security benefit is treated as being paid on the first day of the benefit week in which the benefit is payable. The "benefit week" is the period of seven days beginning on the day in which, in the claimant's case, the state pension credit is payable (reg.1(2)). The exceptions to this general principle are then listed in para.(1). Employment and support allowance, incapacity benefit, severe disablement allowance and jobseeker's allowance are all normally paid fortnightly in arrears from the date of claim (Social Security (Claims and Payments) Regulations 1987 (SI 1987/1968) regs 24(1), 26A(1) and 26C(1)). Maternity allowance is usually payable on Fridays (Social Security (Claims and Payments) Regulations 1987 (SI 1987/1968) reg.24(4)).

3.58

PART III

Income

Calculation of income and capital

14.—The income and capital of—

    (a) the claimant; and

3.59

(b) any partner of the claimant,

shall be calculated in accordance with the rules set out in this Part; and any reference in this Part to the claimant shall apply equally to any partner of the claimant.

DEFINITIONS

"claimant"—see SPCA 2002 s.17(1).
"income"—see *ibid.*, and s.15.
"partner"—see reg.1(3).

GENERAL NOTE

3.60   On the definition of "income", see SPCA 2002 s.15(1) and regs 15–18 and reg.24 below. On the meaning of "capital", see regs 19–23 below. The normal rules on aggregating the income and capital resources of married and unmarried couples apply to state pension credit as to other means-tested benefits (SPCA 2002 s.5).

The approach to income is rather different to the income support scheme, under which claimants are required to report every element of their income and capital and any changes as they occur. For state pension credit purposes, the categories of income to be disclosed by claimants are set out in SPCA 2002 ss.15 and 16 and in this Part of the Regulations, taken together with Schs IV, V and VI, which deal with disregards and calculation. There is, therefore, no need to report forms of income which are not listed in these statutory provisions (e.g. charitable payments and compensation for personal injuries).

Income for the purposes of the Act

3.61   **15.**—(1) For the purposes of section 15(1)(e) (income), all social security benefits are prescribed except—

[³¹(za) universal credit;]

(a) disability living allowance;

[¹⁶(aa) personal independence payment;]

[¹⁷(ab) armed forces independence payment;]

(b) attendance allowance payable under section 64 of the 1992 Act;

(c) an increase of disablement pension under section 104 or 105 of the 1992 Act;

(d) a payment under regulations made in exercise of the power conferred by paragraph 7(2)(b) of Part II of Schedule 8 to the 1992 Act;

(e) an increase of an allowance payable in respect of constant attendance under paragraph 4 of Part I of Schedule 8 to the 1992 Act;

(f) any child special allowance payable under section 56 of the 1992 Act;

(g) any guardian's allowance payable under section 77 of the 1992 Act;

(h) any increase for a dependant, other than the claimant's partner, payable in accordance with Part IV of the 1992 Act;

(i) any social fund payment made under Part VIII of the 1992 Act;

(j) child benefit payable in accordance with Part IX of the 1992 Act;

(k) Christmas bonus payable under Part X of the 1992 Act;

[¹(l) housing benefit;

[¹⁵ . . .]

[²¹(n) bereavement support payment under section 30 of the Pensions Act 2014;]

(o) statutory sick pay;

(p) statutory maternity pay;

[¹⁴ (q) ordinary statutory paternity pay payable under Part 12ZA of the 1992 Act;

(qa) [¹⁹ . . .]

[¹⁸ (qb) statutory shared parental pay payable under Part 12ZC of the 1992 Act;]

[²⁶(qc) statutory parental bereavement pay payable under Part 12ZD of the 1992 Act;]

(r) statutory adoption pay payable under Part 12ZB of the 1992 Act;

[²³ (ra)carer's allowance supplement payable under section 81 of the Social Security (Scotland) Act 2018;]

[²⁴(rb) early years assistance given in accordance with section 32 of the Social Security (Scotland) Act 2018;]

[²⁵(rc) funeral expense assistance given in accordance with section 34 of the Social Security (Scotland) Act 2018;]

[²⁷(rd) any Scottish child payment assistance given in accordance with section 79 of the Social Security (Scotland) Act 2018;]

[²⁸(re) any assistance given in accordance with the Carer's Assistance (Young Carer Grants) (Scotland) Regulations 2019;]

[²⁹(rf) short-term assistance given in accordance with regulations made under section 36 of the Social Security (Scotland) Act 2018;]

[³⁰(rg) winter heating assistance given in accordance with regulations made under section 30 of the Social Security (Scotland) Act 2018;]

[³²(rh) disability assistance given in accordance with regulations made under section 31 of the Social Security (Scotland) Act 2018;]

(s) any benefit similar to those mentioned in the preceding provisions of this paragraph payable under legislation having effect in Northern Ireland.]

[¹³ (2) For the purposes of section 15(1)(f) (foreign social security benefits) of the Act, income includes—

(a) all foreign social security benefits which are similar to the social security benefits prescribed under paragraph (1), and

(b) any foreign state retirement pension.]

(3) Where the payment of any social security benefit prescribed under paragraph (1) [²², or retirement pension income to which section 16(1)(za) to (e)(2) applies,] is subject to any deduction (other than an adjustment specified in paragraph (4)) the amount to be taken into account under paragraph (1) [²², or section 16(1)(za) to (e),] shall be the amount before the deduction is made.

(4) The adjustments specified in this paragraph are those made in accordance with—

(a) the Social Security (Overlapping Benefits) Regulations 1979;

[⁸ (b) regulation 2 of the Social Security (Hospital In-Patients) Regulations 2005;]

(c) section 30DD or section 30E of the 1992 Act (reductions in incapacity benefit in respect of pensions and councillor's allowances);

[⁹ (d) section 3 of the Welfare Reform Act (deductions from contributory allowance);]

[²² (e) section 14 of the Pensions Act 2014 (pension sharing: reduction in the sharer's section 4 pension);

(f) section 45B or 55B of the Social Security Contributions and Benefits Act 1992 (reduction of additional pension in Category A retirement pension and shared additional pension: pension sharing)].

(5) For the purposes of section 15(1)(j) (income to include income of prescribed descriptions), income of the following descriptions is prescribed—
[¹⁰ (a) a payment made—
  (i) under article 30 of the Naval, Military and Air Forces Etc. (Disablement and Death) Service Pensions Order 2006, in any case where article 30(1)(b) applies; or
  (ii) under article 12(8) of that Order, in any case where sub-paragraph (b) of that article applies;]
[⁴(aa) a guaranteed income payment;
  (ab) a payment made under article 21(1)(c) of the Armed Forces and Reserve Forces (Compensation Scheme) Order 2005 [¹⁰, in any case where article 23(2)(c) applies];]
[¹⁰ (ac) any retired pay, pension or allowance granted in respect of disablement or any pension or allowance granted to a widow, widower or surviving civil partner in respect of a death due to service or war injury under an instrument specified in section 639(2) of the Income Tax (Earnings and Pensions) Act 2003, where such payment does not fall within paragraph (a) of the definition of "war disablement pension" in section 17(1) of the State Pension Credit Act 2002 or, in respect of any retired pay or pension granted in respect of disablement, where such payment does not fall within paragraph (b) of that definition;]
[²⁰(b) a pension paid by a government to victims of National Socialist persecution;]
  (c) payments under a scheme made under the Pneumoconiosis, etc. (Worker's Compensation) Act 1979;
  (d) payments made towards the maintenance of the claimant by his spouse [⁶, civil partner, former spouse or former civil partner] or towards the maintenance of the claimant's partner by his spouse [⁶, civil partner, former spouse or former civil partner], including payments made—
    (i) under a court order;
    (ii) under an agreement for maintenance; or
    (iii) voluntarily;
  (e) payments due from any person in respect of board and lodging accommodation provided by the claimant [⁵ . . .];
[¹¹ (f) royalties or other sums paid as a consideration for the use of, or the right to use, any copyright, design, patent or trade mark;] [². . .]
[¹¹ (g) any payment in respect of any—
    (i) book registered under the Public Lending Right Scheme 1982; or
    (ii) work made under any international public lending right scheme that is analogous to the Public Lending Right Scheme 1982;]
[² (h) any income in lieu of that specified in—
    (i) paragraphs (a) to (i) of section 15(1) of the Act, or
    (ii) in this regulation;
  (i) any payment of rent made to a claimant who—
    (i) owns the freehold or leasehold interest in any property or is a tenant of any property;
    (ii) occupies part of that property; and
    (iii) has an agreement with another person allowing that person to occupy that property on payment of rent.]
[³(j) any payment made at regular intervals under an equity release scheme;]

[⁷ (k) PPF periodic payments.]

[¹² (6) For the purposes of section 15(2) (deemed income from capital) and subject to regulation 17(8) (capital to be disregarded), a claimant's capital shall be deemed to yield a weekly income of—

(a) £1 for each £500 in excess of £10,000; and

(b) £1 for any excess which is not a complete £500.]

(7) [¹³ . . .]

(8) [¹³ . . .]

AMENDMENTS

1. State Pension Credit (Consequential, Transitional and Miscellaneous Provisions) Regulations 2002 (SI 2002/3019) reg.23(g) (October 6, 2003).

2. State Pension Credit (Transitional and Miscellaneous Provisions) Amendment Regulations 2003 (SI 2003/2274) reg.2(7) (October 6, 2003).

3. Social Security (Housing Benefit, Council Tax Benefit, State Pension Credit and Miscellaneous Amendments) Regulations 2004 (SI 2004/2327) reg.7(3) (October 4, 2004).

4. Social Security (Miscellaneous Amendments) Regulations 2005 (SI 2005/574) reg.2(2) (April 4, 2005).

5. Social Security (Miscellaneous Amendments) (No.2) Regulations 2005 (SI 2005/2465) reg.6(3) (October 3, 2005).

6. Civil Partnership (Pensions, Social Security and Child Support) (Consequential, etc. Provisions) Order 2005 (SI 2005/2877) art.2(3) and Sch.3 para.35(3) (December 5, 2005).

7. Social Security (Miscellaneous Amendments) Regulations 2006 (SI 2006/588) reg.4(2) (April 6, 2006).

8. Social Security (Hospital In-Patients) Regulations 2005 (SI 2005/3360) reg.8(3) (April 10, 2006).

9. Employment and Support Allowance (Consequential Provisions) (No.2) Regulations 2008 (SI 2008/1554) reg.4(6) (October 27, 2008).

10. Social Security (Miscellaneous Amendments) (No.7) Regulations 2008 (SI 2008/3157) reg.4(3) (January 5, 2009).

11. Social Security (Miscellaneous Amendments) Regulations 2009 (SI 2009/583) reg.5(2) (April 6, 2009).

12. Social Security (Deemed Income from Capital) Regulations 2009 (SI 2009/1676) regs 2 and 3 (November 2, 2009).

13. Social Security (Miscellaneous Amendments) (No.2) Regulations 2010 (SI 2010/641) reg.6(5) (April 13, 2010).

14. Social Security (Miscellaneous Amendments) Regulations 2012 (2012/757) reg.5(3) (April 1, 2012).

15. Council Tax Benefit Abolition (Consequential Provision) Regulations 2013 (SI 2013/458) reg.3 and Sch.1 (April 1, 2013).

16. Personal Independence Payment (Supplementary Provisions and Consequential Amendments) Regulations 2013 (SI 2013/388) reg.8 and Sch. para.27(3) (April 8, 2013).

17. Armed Forces and Reserve Forces Compensation Scheme (Consequential Provisions: Subordinate Legislation) Order 2013 (SI 2013/591) art.7 and Sch. para.23(3) (April 8, 2013).

18. Shared Parental Leave and Statutory Shared Parental Pay (Consequential Amendments to Subordinate Legislation) Order 2014 (SI 2014/3255) art.10(3)(b) (December 31, 2014).

19. Shared Parental Leave and Statutory Shared Parental Pay (Consequential Amendments to Subordinate Legislation) Order 2014 (SI 2014/3255) art.10(3)(a) (April 5, 2015).

20. Social Security (Income-Related Benefits) Amendment Regulations 2017 (2017/174) reg.4(2) (March 20, 2017).

21. Pensions Act 2014 (Consequential, Supplementary and Incidental Amendments) Order 2017 (SI 2017/422) art.21(2) (April 6, 2017).

22. Social Security (Miscellaneous Amendments) Regulations 2017 (SI 2017/1015) reg.10(2) and (3) (November 16, 2017).

23. Social Security (Scotland) Act 2018 (Consequential Modifications) Order 2018 (SI 2018/872), art.4 (September 3, 2018).

24. Social Security (Scotland) Act 2018 (Best Start Grants) (Consequential Modifications and Saving) Order 2018 (SI 2018/1138), art.7(2) (December 10, 2018).

25. Social Security (Scotland) Act 2018 (Funeral Expense Assistance and Early Years Assistance) (Consequential Modifications and Savings) Order 2019 (SI 2019/1060) art.11(2) (September 16, 2019).

26. Parental Bereavement Leave and Pay (Consequential Amendments to Subordinate Legislation) Regulations 2020 (SI 2020/354) reg.10(3) (April 6, 2020).

27. Social Security (Scotland) Act 2018 (Information-Sharing and Scottish Child Payment) (Consequential Provision and Modifications) Order 2020 (SI 2020/482) art.5(2) (November 9, 2020).

28. Social Security (Scotland) Act 2018 (Young Carer Grants, Short-Term Assistance and Winter Heating Assistance) (Consequential Provision and Modifications) Order 2020 (SI 2020/989) art.4(2) (November 9, 2020).

29. Social Security (Scotland) Act 2018 (Young Carer Grants, Short-Term Assistance and Winter Heating Assistance) (Consequential Provision and Modifications) Order 2020 (SI 2020/989) art.11(2) (November 9, 2020).

30. Social Security (Scotland) Act 2018 (Young Carer Grants, Short-Term Assistance and Winter Heating Assistance) (Consequential Provision and Modifications) Order 2020 (SI 2020/989) art.17(2) (November 9, 2020).

31. Universal Credit (Persons who have attained state pension credit qualifying age) (Amendment) Regulations 2020 (SI 2020/655) reg.2(3) (November 25, 2020).

32. Social Security (Scotland) Act 2018 (Disability Assistance, Young Carer Grants, Short-term Assistance and Winter Heating Assistance) (Consequential Provision and Modifications) Order 2021 (SI 2021/886) art.13(2) (July 26, 2021).

DEFINITIONS

"the 1992 Act"—see reg.1(2).
"attendance allowance"—see *ibid.*
"board and lodging accommodation"—see *ibid.*
"capital"—see SPCA 2002 s.17(1).
"care home"—see reg.1(2).
"claimant"—see SPCA 2002 s.17(1).
"income"—see *ibid.*
"partner"—see reg.1(2).

GENERAL NOTE

Paragraph (1)

3.62   The presumption under SPCA 2002 s.15(1)(e) is that social security benefits count as income for the purposes of calculating entitlement to state pension credit. There is, however, an extensive list of exceptions here. Note also that there are disregards that apply to certain forms of income, as specified in reg.17(7) and Sch.IV below.

Paragraph (2)

3.63   This provision was amended in order to reverse the effect of *SSWP v JK* [2009] UKUT 55 (AAC). If income is received in a currency other than Sterling, the value of any payment is determined by taking the Sterling equivalent on the date that payment is made (reg.17(6)).

Paragraph (3)

The effect of this rule is that payments of prescribed social security benefits are   **3.64**
taken into account gross, i.e. before any deductions are applied (e.g. under the
Social Security (Claims and Payments) Regulations 1987 (SI 1987/1968) reg.35
and Sch.9). This is subject to the exceptions specified in para.(4).

Paragraph (5)

Section 15(1)(j) is a catch-all provision that enables the Secretary of State to   **3.65**
prescribe other forms of income not caught by any of the other provisions. As
regards sub-para.(5)(b), the amended version gives effect to Judge Williams' decision in *MN v Bury Council and SSWP (HB)* [2014] UKUT 187 (AAC), where it
was held that compensation pension payments made by the Dutch Government to
victims of Nazi persecution should be treated in the same way as payments made
under schemes administered by the German and Austrian governments for the
purposes of calculating entitlement to housing benefit. The same disregard rules
now apply across all means-tested benefits to all those victims of Nazi persecution,
irrespective of the person's nationality and regardless of the national government
making the payments.

As regards board and lodging accommodation (sub-para.(5)(e)), and on the
importance of establishing the precise status of someone staying with the claimant
(e.g. as a sub-tenant, lodger or non-dependant), see *KC v Secretary of State for Work
and Pensions (SPC)* [2012] UKUT 114 (AAC).

Note that neither s.15 of the Act nor reg.15 seem to include as assessable income
for state pension credit purposes regular payments of income from a benevolent
institution (e.g. the Royal British Legion) or from a family member: see *AMS v
SSWP (PC) (final decision)* [2017] UKUT 381 (AAC) at para.13.

Paragraph (6)

The tariff income rule for state pension credit is markedly more generous to   **3.66**
claimants than that which applies in the income support scheme. In particular,
the assumed rate of return is halved. The rule for state pension credit is that the
claimant is assumed to receive £1 per week for every £500 or part thereof over
the threshold of £10,000. Thus a state pension credit claimant with £14,000 in
savings will have a deemed income of £8 per week from that capital. A person
of working age with £10,000 in capital is excluded from entitlement to income
support. Note also that there is no upper capital limit for state pension credit, and
that the threshold for the tariff income rule was raised to £10,000 for all claimants, and not just those in residential care and nursing homes, with effect from
November 2, 2009.

Retirement pension income

16.—There shall be added to the descriptions of income listed in section   **3.67**
16(1) (retirement pension income) the following [¹paragraphs]—

> "(k) any sum payable by way of pension out of money provided under the
> Civil List Act 1837, the Civil List Act 1937, the Civil List Act 1952, the
> Civil List Act 1972 or the [¹Civil List Act 1975];
> [¹(1) any payment, other than a payment ordered by a court or made in
> settlement of a claim, made by or on behalf of a former employer of a
> person on account of the early retirement of that person on grounds of
> ill-health or disability;]
> [²(m) any payment made at regular intervals under an equity release
> scheme;]"
> [⁴(n) any payment made under the Financial Assistance Scheme
> Regulations 2005.]

1. State Pension Credit (Consequential, Transitional and Miscellaneous Provisions) (No.2) Regulations 2002 (SI 2002/3197) reg.2 and Sch. para.3 (October 6, 2003).
2. Social Security (Housing Benefit, Council Tax Benefit, State Pension Credit and Miscellaneous Amendments) Regulations 2004 (SI 2004/2327) reg.7(4) (October 4, 2004).
3. State Pension Credit (Amendment) Regulations 2005 (SI 2005/3205) reg.2(3) (December 18, 2005).

DEFINITION

"income"—see SPCA 2002 ss.15 and 17(1).

GENERAL NOTE

3.68   Readers with republican tendencies will doubtless be reassured to see that pensions paid from the Civil List count as retirement pension income for the purposes of SPCA 2002 s.16(1). More prosaically, payments made by virtue of early retirement on ill-health grounds (other than those ordered by court or agreed under the settlement of a claim) also count.

Calculation of weekly income

3.69   **17.**—(1) Except where paragraph (2) and (4) apply, for the purposes of calculating the weekly income of the claimant, where the period in respect of which a payment is made—

    (a) does not exceed a week, the whole of that payment shall be included in the claimant's weekly income;

    (b) exceeds a week, the amount to be included in the claimant's weekly income shall be determined—

        (i) in a case where that period is a month, by multiplying the amount of the payment by 12 ad dividing the product by 52;

        (ii) in a case where that period is three months, by multiplying the amount of the payment by 4 and dividing the product by 52;

        (iii) in a case where that period is a year, by dividing the amount of the payment by 52;

        (iv) in any other case, by multiplying the amount of the payment by 7 and dividing the product by the number of days in the period in respect of which it is made.

(2) Where—

    (a) the claimant's regular pattern of work is such that he does not work the same hours every week; or

    (b) the amount of the claimant's income fluctuates and has changed more than once,

the weekly amount of that claimant's income shall be determined—

        (i) if, in a case to which sub-paragraph (a) applies, there is a recognised cycle of work, by reference to his average weekly income over the period of the complete cycle (including, where the cycle involves periods in which the claimant does no work, those periods but disregarding any other absences); or

        (ii) in any other case, on the basis of—

            (aa) the last two payments if those payments are one month or more apart;

            (bb) the last four payments if the last two payments are less than one month apart; or (cc) such other payments as may, in the particular circumstances of the case, enable the claimant's average weekly income to be determined more accurately.

(3) For the purposes of paragraph (2)(b) the last payments are the last payments before the date the claim was made or treated as made or, if there is a subsequent supersession under section 10 of the Social Security Act 1998, the last payments before the date of the supersession.

(4) If a claimant is entitled to receive a payment to which paragraph (5) applies, the amount of that payment shall be treated as if made in respect of a period of a year.

(5) This paragraph applies to—

[³ (a) royalties or other sums received as a consideration for the use of, or the right to use, any copyright, design, patent or trade mark;]

[³ (b) any payment in respect of any—

  (i) book registered under the Public Lending Right Scheme 1982; or

  (ii) work made under any international public lending right scheme that is analogous to the Public Lending Right Scheme 1982;]

  [¹ and

(c) any payment which is made on an occasional basis.]

(6) Where payments are made in a currency other than Sterling, the value of the payment shall be determined by taking the Sterling equivalent on the date the payment is made.

(7) Income specified in Schedule IV is to be disregarded in the calculation of a claimant's income.

(8) Schedule V shall have effect so that—

(a) the capital specified in Part I shall be disregarded for the purpose of determining a claimant's income; and

(b) the capital specified in Part II shall be disregarded for the purpose of determining a claimant's income under regulation 15(6).

[¹(9) The sums specified in Schedule VI shall be disregarded in calculating—

(a) the claimant's earnings; and

[³ (b) any amount to which paragraph (5) applies where the claimant is the first owner of the copyright, design, patent or trademark, or an original contributor to the book or work referred to in paragraph (5)(b).]

(9A) For the purposes of paragraph (9)(b), and for that purpose only, the amounts specified in paragraph (5) shall be treated as though they were earnings.]

(10) [¹Subject to regulation [²17B(6)] (deduction of tax and contributions for self-employed earners),] in the case of any income taken into account for the purpose of calculating a person's income, there shall be disregarded—

(a) any amount payable by way of tax;

(b) any amount deducted by way of National Insurance Contributions under the 1992 Act or under the Social Security Contributions and Benefits (Northern Ireland) Act 1992;

(c) [² . . .].

[¹(11) In the case of the earnings of self-employed earners, the amounts specified in paragraph (10) shall be taken into account in accordance with paragraph (4) or, as the case may be, paragraph (10) of regulation 13 of the Computation of Earnings Regulations, as having effect in the case of state pension credit.]

AMENDMENTS

1. State Pension Credit (Consequential, Transitional and Miscellaneous Provisions) Regulations 2002 (SI 2002/3019) reg.23(h) (October 6, 2003).

2. State Pension Credit (Consequential, Transitional and Miscellaneous Provisions) (No.2) Regulations 2002 (SI 2002/3197) reg.2 and Sch. para.5 (October 6, 2003).

3. Social Security (Miscellaneous Amendments) Regulations 2009 (SI 2009/583) reg.5(3) (April 6, 2009).

DEFINITIONS

"claimant"—see SPCA 2002 s.17(1).
"Computation of Earnings Regulations"—see reg.1(2).
"income"—see SPCA 2002 s.17(1).

GENERAL NOTE

Paragraph (1)

3.70   This follows the precedent of income support by providing for the same simple method of converting payments of income into weekly equivalents (Income Support (General) Regulations 1987 (SI 1987/1967) reg.32(1), in Vol.V of this series). This is subject to the special rules for irregular patterns of work (para.(2)) and for payments of royalties and other occasional payments (paras (4) and (5)).

In *R(PC) 3/08* the Commissioner rejected the Secretary of State's argument that "capital" has a special meaning in the state pension credit scheme. The Commissioner held that the general rule applied, namely that a payment of income (there state retirement pension, paid four-weekly) did not metamorphose into capital until the expiry of a period equal in length to the period in respect of which it was paid. The Commissioner applied the general principle to that effect as stated in *R(IS)3/93*, notwithstanding the absence in the state pension credit scheme of an equivalent provision to reg.29(2) of the Income Support (General) Regulations 1987. The Commissioner held that the state pension credit system "must operate on an assumed notion of a period of attribution" (para.24).

See also *PS v Secretary of State for Work and Pensions (SPC)* [2016] UKUT 21 (AAC), where the claimant had been paid arrears of his army pension in 2008, for a period going back to March 2006. The DWP subsequently sought to recover from the claimant an overpayment of pension credit, including the period from March 2006 to the date of receipt of the arrears. The First-tier Tribunal confirmed this decision. However, Judge Ward allowed the claimant's further appeal, ruling that for pension credit purposes income payable in arrears falls to be attributed *forward* from the date of receipt rather than *backwards* over the period in respect of which it was earned (see paras 14–17). In doing so Judge Ward followed *R(PC) 3/08* at para.24.

Paragraphs (2) and (3)

3.71   This is yet another variant on the various legislative measures devised to deal with the problematic question of accommodating those with irregular working patterns into a means-tested benefit system. The rule is modelled on but also departs from the traditional income support approach (see Income Support (General) Regulations 1987 (SI 1987/1967) reg.32(6)).

Paragraphs (4) and (5)

3.72   Royalties and other occasional payments are treated as paid in respect of a year, in contrast to the income support rule (Income Support (General) Regulations 1987 (SI 1987/1967) reg.30(2)).

Paragraph (6)

3.73   Any banking charges or commission payable when converting payments of income in other currencies into Sterling are disregarded (Sch.IV para.16).

Paragraph (7)
See the annotations to Sch.IV.   3.74

Paragraph (8)
Schedule V is divided into two Parts. Part I specifies those forms of capital   3.75
which are to be disregarded for the purpose of calculating the claimant's income.
This extensive list is modelled on Sch.10 to the Income Support (General)
Regulations 1987 (SI 1987/1967). Part II contains a more limited list of categories
of capital which are to be disregarded solely for the purposes of calculating
notional income.

Paragraph (9)
This links to Sch.VI, which carries forward the standard £5, £10 and £20 dis-   3.76
regards on earnings that apply in the income support scheme to the state pension
credit system. However, there is no hours rule for state pension credit, so it matters
not whether a pensioner is working under or over 16 hours a week.

Paragraph (10)
This is similar to the income support rule (see Income Support (General)   3.77
Regulations 1987 (SI 1987/1967) reg.36(3)). The principal difference is that the
income support rule applies to earnings, whereas this rule applies to all income.
The income support rule permits a deduction from earnings representing 50 per
cent of the amount of any occupational or personal pension scheme contributions. The parallel provision for state pension credit purposes is to be found in
reg.17A(4A) below.

Paragraph (11)
See also reg.17B.   3.78

[¹Treatment of final payments of income

17ZA.—(1) Save where regulation 13B applies, this regulation applies   3.79
where—
   (a) a claimant has been receiving a regular payment of income;
   (b) that payment is coming to an end or has ended; and
   (c) the claimant receives a payment of income whether as the last of the
        regular payments or following the last of them ("the final payment").
   (2) For the purposes of regulation 17(1)—
   (a) where the amount of the final payment is less than or equal to the
        amount of the preceding, or the last, regular payment, the whole
        amount shall be treated as being paid in respect of a period of the same
        length as that in respect of which that regular payment was made;
   (b) where the amount of the final payment is greater than the amount of
        that regular payment—
        (i) to the extent that it comprises (whether exactly or with an
             excess remaining) one or more multiples of that amount, each
             such multiple shall be treated as being paid in respect of a
             period of the same length as that in respect of which that regular
             payment was made; and
        (ii) any excess shall be treated as paid in respect of a further period
             of the same length as that in respect of which that regular
             payment was made.
   (3) A final payment referred to in paragraph (2)(a) shall, where not in fact
paid on the date on which a regular payment would have been paid had it
continued in payment, be treated as paid on that date.

(4) Each multiple and any excess referred to in paragraph (2)(b) shall be treated as paid on the dates on which a corresponding number of regular payments would have been made had they continued in payment.

(5) For the purposes of this regulation, a "regular payment" means a payment of income made in respect of a period—

(a) referred to in regulation 17(1)(a) or (b) on a regular date; or

(b) which is subject to the provisions of regulation 17(2).]

AMENDMENT

1. State Pension Credit (Miscellaneous Amendments) Regulations 2004 (SI 2004/647) reg.3(4) (April 5, 2004).

DEFINITIONS

"the final payment"—see para.(1)(c).
"regular payment"—see para.(5).

GENERAL NOTE

3.80 This regulation provides for the treatment of final payments of income. The rule applies whenever the claimant has been receiving a regular payment of income (a term which is wider than it first appears; see para.(5) and below), those payments come to an end and a final payment is made (para.(1)). The basic rule is that where the final payment of income is less than or equal to the previtous payment of income, then the whole of the final payment is attributed to the normal period for such payments (para.(2)(a); and see para.(3) for the date on which the final payment may be treated as paid). If, however, the final payment exceeds the usual or "regular payment", then it is treated as applying to a series of sequential periods, depending on the number of multiples involved (para.(2)(b); and see para.(4) for the dates on which such multiple payments may be treated as paid). Paragraph (5) defines "regular payment" by reference to reg.17(1) and (2); the effect of this is that irregular patterns of work may nevertheless give rise to a "regular payment" for the purpose of this provision (see reg.17(2)(b)(ii)).

[¹Earnings of an employed earner

3.81 **17A.**—(1) For the purposes of state pension credit, the provisions of this regulation which relate to the earnings of employed earners, shall have effect in place of those prescribed for such earners in the Computation of Earnings Regulations.

(2) Subject to paragraphs [²(3), (4) and 4(A)], "earnings" in the case of employment as an employed earner, means any remuneration or profit derived from that employment and includes—

(a) any bonus or commission;

(b) any payment in lieu of remuneration except any periodic sum paid to a claimant on account of the termination of his employment by reason of redundancy;

(c) any payment in lieu of notice;

(d) any holiday pay;

(e) any payment by way of a retainer;

(f) any payment made by the claimant's employer in respect of expenses not wholly, exclusively and necessarily incurred in the performance of the duties of the employment, including any payment made by the claimant's employer in respect of—

(i) travelling expenses incurred by the claimant between his home and place of employment;

 (ii) expenses incurred by the claimant under arrangements made for the care of a member of his family owing to the claimant's absence from home;

 (g) the amount of any payment by way of a non-cash voucher which has been taken into account in the computation of a person's earnings in accordance with Part V of Schedule 3 to the Social Security (Contributions) Regulations 2001;

 (h) statutory sick pay and statutory maternity pay payable by the employer under the 1992 Act;

[4 (i) [7 . . .] statutory paternity pay payable under Part 12ZA of the 1992 Act;

 (ia) [7 . . .];]

[6 (ib) statutory shared parental pay payable under Part 12ZC of the 1992 Act;]

[8 (ic) statutory parental bereavement pay payable under Part 12ZD of the 1992 Act;]

 (j) statutory adoption pay payable under Part 12ZB of the 1992 Act;

 (k) any sums payable under a contract of service—

 (i) for incapacity for work due to sickness or injury; or

 (ii) by reason of pregnancy or confinement.

(3) "Earnings" shall not include—

 (a) subject to paragraph (4), any payment in kind;

 (b) any payment in respect of expenses wholly, exclusively and necessarily incurred in the performance of the duties of the employment;

 (c) any occupational pension;

 (d) any lump sum payment made under the Iron and Steel Re-adaptation Benefits Scheme;

[2(e) any payment of compensation made pursuant to an award by an employment tribunal in respect of unfair dismissal or unlawful discrimination.]

[3 (f) any payment in respect of expenses arising out of the [5 claimant participating as a service user]

(4) Paragraph (3)(a) shall not apply in respect of any non-cash voucher referred to in paragraph (2)(g).

[2(4A) One half of any sum paid by a claimant by way of a contribution towards an occupational pension scheme or a personal pension scheme shall, for the purpose of calculating his earnings in accordance with this regulation, be disregarded.]

(5) In this regulation "employed earner" means a person who is gainfully employed in Great Britain either under a contract of service, or in an office (including elective office) with emoluments chargeable to income tax under Schedule E.]

AMENDMENTS

1. State Pension Credit (Consequential, Transitional and Miscellaneous Provisions) Regulations 2002 (SI 2002/3019) reg.23(i) (October 6, 2003).

2. State Pension Credit (Consequential, Transitional and Miscellaneous Provisions) (No.2) Regulations 2002 (SI 2002/3197) reg.3(1) (October 6, 2003).

3. Social Security (Miscellaneous Amendments) (No.4) Regulations 2009 (SI 2009/2655) reg.5(3) (October 26, 2009).

4. Social Security (Miscellaneous Amendments) Regulations 2012 (SI 2012/757) reg.5(4) (April 1, 2012).

5. Social Security (Miscellaneous Amendments) Regulations 2014 (SI 2014/591) reg.7(3) (April 28, 2014).

6. Shared Parental Leave and Statutory Shared Parental Pay (Consequential Amendments to Subordinate Legislation) Order 2014 (SI 2014/3255) art.10(4)(c) (December 31, 2014).

7. Shared Parental Leave and Statutory Shared Parental Pay (Consequential Amendments to Subordinate Legislation) Order 2014 (SI 2014/3255) art.10(4)(a) and (b) (April 5, 2015).

8. Parental Bereavement Leave and Pay (Consequential Amendments to Subordinate Legislation) Regulations 2020 (SI 2020/354) reg.10(4) (April 6, 2020).

DEFINITIONS

"claimant"—see para.(2)(a).
"Computation of Earnings Regulations"—see reg.1(2).
"employed earner"—see para.(5).
"occupational pension scheme"—see SPCA 2002 s.17(1).
"personal pension scheme"—see *ibid.*

GENERAL NOTE

3.82   This provides a comprehensive definition of "earnings" for employed earners who claim state pension credit which is independent of the rules contained in the Social Security (Computation of Earnings) Regulations 1996 (SI 1996/2745). In contrast, reg.17B below specifically applies the 1996 Regulations to the assessment of the earnings of *self*-employed earners, subject to certain modifications. The rules governing employed earners in this regulation follow closely (but do not entirely mirror) those that apply to the definition of an employed earner's earnings for the purposes of income support (see Income Support (General) Regulations 1987 (SI 1987/1967) reg.35, in Vol.V of this series).

[¹Earnings of self-employed earners

3.83   **17B.**—(1) For the purposes of state pension credit, the provisions of the Computation of Earnings Regulations in their application to the earnings of self-employed earners, shall have effect in so far as provided by this regulation.

(2) In their application to state pension credit, regulations 11 to 14 of the Computation of Earnings Regulations shall have effect as if—
[²(za) "board and lodging accommodation" has the same meaning as in [³ regulation 1(2)];]
   (a) "claimant" referred to a person claiming state pension credit and any partner of the claimant;
   (b) "personal pension scheme" referred to a personal pension scheme—
       (i) as defined in section 1 of the Pension Schemes Act 1993; or
       (ii) as defined in section 1 of the Pension Schemes (Northern Ireland) Act 1993.

(3) In regulation 11 (calculation of earnings of self-employed earners), paragraph (1) shall have effect, but as if the words "Except where paragraph (2) applies" were omitted.

(4) In regulation 12 (earnings of self-employed earners).
   (a) paragraph (1) shall have effect;
   (b) [⁵ the following paragraph shall be added after paragraph (1)]
   "(2) Earnings does not include—
   (a) where a claimant occupies a dwelling as his home and he provides in that dwelling board and lodging accommodation for which payment is made, those payments;

[⁵ (b) any payment made by a local authority to a claimant with whom a person is accommodated by virtue of arrangements made under—

   [⁹ (i) section 22C(2) of the Children Act 1989 (ways in which looked after children are to be accommodated and maintained),]

   [⁹ (ia) section 81(2) of the Social Services and Well-being (Wales) Act 2014 (ways in which looked after children are to be accommodated and maintained),]

   [⁸(ii) section 26 or 26A of the Children (Scotland) Act 1995 (manner of provision of accommodation to child looked after by local authority and duty to provide continuing care), or]

   (iii) regulations 33 or 51 of the Looked After Children (Scotland) Regulations 2009 (fostering and kinship care allowances and fostering allowances);]

(c) any payment made "by a voluntary organisation in accordance with section 59(1)(a) of the Children Act 1989 (provision of accommodation by voluntary organisations);

(d) any payment made to the claimant or his partner for a person ('the person concerned') who is not normally a member of the claimant's household but is temporarily in his care, by—

   (i) a health authority;

   (ii) a local authority;

   (iii) a voluntary organisation;

   (iv) the person concerned pursuant to section 26(3A) of the National Assistance Act 1948; [⁴ . . .]

   [⁶ (iva) [¹¹ an integrated care board established under Chapter A3 of Part 2 of the National Health Service Act 2006];

   (ivb) the National Health Service Commissioning Board; [⁷ . . .]]

   (v) [⁶ . . .]

   [⁴ (vi) a Local Health Board established under section 16BA of the National Health Service Act 1977 or established by an order made under section 11 of the Health Service (Wales) Act;] [⁷[⁹ . . .]

   (vii) the person concerned where the payment is for the provision of accommodation in respect of the meeting of that person's needs under section 18 or 19 of the Care Act 2014 (duty and power to meet needs for care and support);] [⁹ or

   (viii) the person concerned where the payment is for the provision of accommodation to meet that person's needs for care and support under section 35 or 36 of the Social Services and Well-being (Wales) Act 2014 (duty and power to meet care and support needs of an adult);]

[⁸(da) any payment or part of a payment made by a local authority in accordance with section 26A of the Children (Scotland) Act 1995 (duty to provide continuing care) to a person ("A") which A passes on to the claimant where A—

   (i) was formerly in the claimant's care;

   (ii) is aged 16 or over; and

   (iii) continues to live with the claimant;]

[¹⁰(db) any payment made to a claimant under section 73(1)(b) of the Children and Young People (Scotland) Act 2014 (kinship care assistance);]

(e) any sports award [² being an award made by one of the Sports Councils named in section 23(2) of the National Lottery etc.

Act 1993 out of sums allocated to it for distribution under that section]

(5) In regulation 13 (calculation of net profit of self-employed earners)—

(a) for paragraphs (1) to (3), the following provision shall have effect—

"(1) For the purposes of regulation 11 (calculation of earnings of self-employed earners), the earnings of a claimant to be taken into account shall be—

(a) in the case of a self-employed earner who is engaged in employment on his own account, the net profit derived from that employment;

(b) in the case of a self-employed earner whose employment is carried on in partnership, his share of the net profit derived from that employment less—

(i) an amount in respect of income tax and of social security contributions payable under the Contributions and Benefits Act calculated in accordance with regulation 14 (deduction of tax and contributions for self-employed earners); and

(ii) one half of any premium paid in the period that is relevant under regulation 11 in respect of a retirement annuity contract or a personal pension scheme";

(b) paragraphs (4) to (12) shall have effect.

(6) Regulation 14 (deduction of tax and contributions for self-employed earners) shall have effect.]

AMENDMENTS

1. State Pension Credit (Consequential, Transitional and Miscellaneous Provisions) Regulations 2002 (SI 2002/3019) reg.23(i) (October 6, 2003).

2. State Pension Credit (Consequential, Transitional and Miscellaneous Provisions) (No.2) Regulations 2002 (SI 2002/3197) reg.3(2) (October 6,2003).

3. Social Security (Miscellaneous Amendments) (No.2) Regulations 2005 (SI 2005/2465) reg.6(4) (October 3, 2005).

4. Social Security (Miscellaneous Amendments) (No.7) Regulations 2008 (SI 2008/3157) reg.4(4) (January 5, 2009).

5. Social Security (Miscellaneous Amendments) (No.5) Regulations 2010 (SI 2010/2429) reg.6 (November 1, 2010).

6. National Treatment Agency (Abolition) and the Health and Social Care Act 2012 (Consequential, Transitional and Saving Provisions) Order 2013 (SI 2013/235) art.11 and Sch.2 para.54(3) (April 1, 2013) (England and Wales only).

7. Care Act 2014 (Consequential Amendments) (Secondary Legislation) Order 2015 (SI 2015/643) reg.19(1) and (2) (April 1, 2015).

8. Children and Young People (Scotland) Act 2014 (Consequential Modifications) Order 2016 (SI 2016/732) art.4(2) (August 5, 2016).

9. Social Services and Well-being (Wales) Act 2014 and the Regulation and Inspection of Social Care (Wales) Act 2016 (Consequential Amendments) Order 2017 (SI 2017/901) regs.9(2) and 24 (November 3, 2017).

10. Social Security and Child Support (Care Payments and Tenant Incentive Scheme) (Amendment) Regulations 2017 (SI 2017/995) reg.4(2) (November 7, 2017).

11. Health and Care Act 2022 (Consequential and Related Amendments and Transitional Provisions) Regulations 2022 (SI 2022/634) reg.99 and Sch. (July 1, 2022).

DEFINITIONS

"board and lodging accommodation"—see para.(2)(za).
"claimant"—see para.(2)(a).
"Computation of Earnings Regulations"—see reg.1(2).
"dwelling occupied as the home"—see *ibid.*
"personal pension scheme"—see para.(2)(b).
"retirement annuity contract"—see SPCA 2002 s.16(3).

GENERAL NOTE

The earnings of self-employed earners for the purposes of state pension credit 3.84
are calculated in accordance with the Social Security (Computation of Earnings)
Regulations 1996 (SI 1996/2745) (on which see Vol.I in this series), subject to the
modifications made by this regulation. Thus the special rule relating to royalties
does not apply (para.(3)), as special provision is made for such payments for the
purposes of state pension credit (see reg.17(4) and (5)). There is also a more
extensive list of disregards to be applied when calculating earnings (para.(4)).

In *CPC/3373/2007* Deputy Commissioner Poynter held that the state pension
credit scheme does not permit a claimant to offset a loss from self-employment
income against his other sources of income. There is no equivalent within the state
pension credit scheme to what used to be s.380 of the Income and Corporation
Taxes Act 1988 (now Income Tax Act 2007 s.64). Accordingly, where a claimant
makes a loss on self-employed income, the net profit for the purposes of state
pension credit is nil, and not a negative figure. But note also that on the particular
facts of that case the Deputy Commissioner held that the Secretary of State had not
shown a relevant changes of circumstances such as to justify a supersession of the
award of benefit to the claimant.

Notional income

18.—[² (1) A claimant who has attained the qualifying age shall be 3.85
treated as possessing the amount of any retirement pension income—
   (a) to which section 16(1)[⁷(za)] to (e) applies,
   (b) for which no claim has been made, and
   (c) to which the claimant might expect to be entitled if a claim for it were
        made,
but only from the date on which that income could be expected to be
acquired if a claim for it were made.
   (1A) Paragraph (1) is subject to paragraphs (1B) [³, (1CA) and 1(CB)].
   (1B) Where a claimant—
   (a) has deferred entitlement to retirement pension income to which
        section 16(1)(a) to (c) applies for at least 12 months, and
   (b) would have been entitled to make an election under Schedule 5 or 5A
        to the 1992 Act or under Schedule 1 to the Graduated Retirement
        Benefit Regulations,
he shall be treated for the purposes of paragraph (1) as possessing the
amount of retirement pension income to which he might expect to be entitled if he were to elect to receive a lump sum.
   [³ (1C) Paragraphs (1CA) and (1CB) apply for the purposes of paragraph (1) (or, where applicable, paragraph (1) read with paragraph (1B)).
   (1CA) Where a benefit or allowance in payment in respect of the claimant would be adjusted under the Social Security (Overlapping Benefits)
Regulations 1979 if the retirement pension income had been claimed, he
shall be treated as possessing that income minus the benefit or allowance
in payment.

(1CB) Where a benefit or allowance in payment in respect of the claimant would require an adjustment to be made under the Social Security (Overlapping Benefits) Regulations 1979 to the amount of retirement pension income payable had it been claimed, he shall be treated as possessing that retirement pension income minus the adjustment which would be made to it.]

(1D) A claimant who has attained the qualifying age shall be treated as possessing income from an occupational pension scheme which he elected to defer, but only from the date on which it could be expected to be acquired if a claim for it were made.]

(2) Where a person, [⁵ who has attained the qualifying age], is a person entitled to money purchase benefits under an occupational pension scheme or a personal pension scheme, or is a party to, or a person deriving entitlement to a pension under, a retirement annuity contract, and—

  (a) he fails to purchase an annuity with the funds available in that scheme where—

    (i) he defers, in whole or in part, the payment of any income which would have been payable to him by his pension fund holder;

    (ii) he fails to take any necessary action to secure that the whole of any income which would be payable to him by his pension fund holder upon his applying for it, is so paid; or

    (iii) income withdrawal is not available to him under that scheme; or

  (b) in the case of a retirement annuity contract, he fails to purchase an annuity with the funds available under that contract,

the amount of any income foregone shall be treated as possessed by him, but only from the date on which it could be expected to be acquired were an application for it to be made.

(3) The amount of any income foregone in a case to which either head (i) or (ii) of paragraph (2)(a) applies shall be the [⁸ rate of the annuity which may have been purchased with the fund and is to be determined by the Secretary of State, taking account of information provided by the pension fund holder in accordance with regulation 7(5) of the Social Security (Claims and Payments) Regulations 1987].

(4) The amount of any income foregone in a case to which either head (iii) of paragraph (2)(a) or paragraph (2)(b) applies shall be the income that the claimant could have received without purchasing an annuity had the funds held under the relevant scheme or retirement annuity contract been held under a personal pension scheme or occupational pension scheme where income withdrawal was available and shall be determined in the manner specified in paragraph (3).

(5) In paragraph (2), "money purchase benefits" has the meaning it has in the Pensions Scheme Act 1993.

(6) [¹ Subject to [⁴ the following paragraphs],] a person shall be treated as possessing income of which he has deprived himself for the purpose of securing entitlement to state pension credit or increasing the amount of that benefit.

[¹ (7) Paragraph (6) shall not apply in respect of the amount of an increase of pension or benefit where a person, having made an election in favour of that increase of pension or benefit under Schedule 5 or 5A to the 1992 Act or under Schedule 1 to the Graduated Retirement Benefit Regulations, changes that election in accordance with regulations made under Schedule 5 or 5A to that Act in favour of a lump sum.

[⁷ (7ZA) Paragraph (6) shall not apply in respect of the amount of an increase of pension where a person, having made a choice in favour of that increase of pension under section 8(2) of the Pensions Act 2014, alters that choice in favour of a lump sum, in accordance with Regulations made under section 8(7) of that Act.

(7ZB) Paragraph (6) shall not apply in respect of the amount of an increase of pension where a person, having made a choice in favour of that increase of pension in accordance with Regulations made under section 10 of the Pensions Act 2014 which include provision corresponding or similar to section 8(2) of that Act, alters that choice in favour of a lump sum, in accordance with Regulations made under section 10 of that Act which include provision corresponding or similar to Regulations made under section 8(7).]

[⁴ (7A) Paragraph (6) shall not apply in respect of any amount of income other than earnings, or earnings of an employed earner, arising out of the [⁶ claimant participating as a service user]

(8) In paragraph (7), "lump sum" means a lump sum under Schedule 5 or 5A to the 1992 Act or under Schedule 1 to the Graduated Retirement Benefit Regulations.]

[⁷ (8A) In paragraph (7ZA), "lump sum" means a lump sum under section 8 of the Pensions Act 2014.

(8B) In paragraph (7ZB), "lump sum" means a lump sum under Regulations made under section 10 of the Pensions Act 2014.]

[² (9) For the purposes of paragraph (6), a person is not to be regarded as depriving himself of income where—

(a) his rights to benefits under a registered pension scheme are extinguished and in consequence of this he receives a payment from the scheme, and

(b) that payment is a trivial commutation lump sum within the meaning given by paragraph 7 of Schedule 29 to the Finance Act 2004.

(10) In paragraph (9), "registered pension scheme" has the meaning given in section 150(2) of the Finance Act 2004.]

AMENDMENTS

1. Social Security (Deferral of Retirement Pensions, Shared Additional Pension and Graduated Retirement Benefit) (Miscellaneous Provisions) Regulations 2005 (SI 2005/2677) reg.13(3) (April 6, 2006).

2. Social Security (Miscellaneous Amendments) (No.4) Regulations 2006 (SI 2006/2378) reg.14(4) (October 2, 2006).

3. Social Security (Miscellaneous Amendments) (No.5) Regulations 2007 (SI 2007/2618) reg.10(3) (October 1, 2007).

4. Social Security (Miscellaneous Amendments) (No.4) Regulations 2009 (SI 2009/2655) reg.5(4) (October 26, 2009).

5. Social Security (Miscellaneous Amendments) (No.2) Regulations 2010 (SI 2010/641) reg.6(6) (April 6, 2010).

6. Social Security (Miscellaneous Amendments) Regulations 2014 (SI 2014/591) reg.7(4) (April 28, 2014).

7. Pensions Act 2014 (Consequential, Supplementary and Incidental Amendments) Order 2015 (SI 2015/985) art.24(2) (April 6, 2016).

8. Social Security (Miscellaneous Amendments) Regulations 2017 (SI 2017/1015) reg.10(2)(a) (November 16, 2017).

DEFINITIONS

"claimant"—see SPCA 2002 s.17(1).
"income"—see *ibid.*
"lump sum"—see paras (8A) and (8B).
"money purchase benefits"—see para.(5).
"occupational pension scheme"—see SPCA 2002 s.17(1).
"pension fund holder"—see reg.1(2).
"personal pension scheme"—see SPCA 2002 s.17(1).
"qualifying age"—see SPCA 2002 s.1(6).
"retirement annuity contract"—see *ibid.*, and s.16(3).
"retirement pension income"—see SPCA 2002 ss.16 and 17(1).

GENERAL NOTE

3.86   This regulation provides for three types of notional income: certain forms of pension income which have not been applied for or have been deferred (para. (1)), income foregone under a money purchase benefits pension scheme or under a retirement annuity contract (paras (2)–(5)), and cases of income deprivation for the purpose of securing entitlement to (or increasing the amount of) state pension credit (para.(6)). Note also that Pt II of Sch.V lists various forms of capital which are to be disregarded in determining a person's notional income.

Paragraph (1)
3.87   The general rule is that pension income which the claimant could expect to receive on application is to be deemed to be notional income. The reference to SPCA 2002 s.16(1)(za)–(e) has the effect of confining this provision to various categories of state retirement pension income under the SSCBA 1992 or its Northern Ireland equivalent. The inclusion of the cross-reference to s.16(1)(za) in subs.(1)(a) means that for the purposes of pension credit a person is to be treated as receiving their new state pension while they are deferring it. Notional income also includes income from an occupational pension scheme which the claimant has chosen to defer. Other forms of income from private pension arrangements may be caught by paras (2)–(5).

Paragraphs (2)–(5)
3.88   These provisions mirror those that apply to income support (Income Support (General) Regulations 1987 (SI 1987/1967) reg.42(2A)–(2C), in Vol.V of this series; see further *BRG v SSWP (SPC)* [2014] UKUT 246 (AAC). The amendment to para.(3), made with effect from November 16, 2017, was designed to reverse the effect of Judge Humphrey's decision in *SSWP v IG (SPC)* [2018] UKUT 228 (AAC), where it was held that notional amounts from a personal pension scheme that had assets valued at less than the initial investment should be treated as payments of capital by instalments (and not income). However, in the event the Upper Tribunal's decision was reversed by the Court of Appeal in *SSWP v Goulding* [2019] EWCA Civ 839.

Paragraph (6)
3.89   This is expressed in the same terms as the notional income and notional capital rules for income support, and so the same principles apply ((Income Support (General) Regulations 1987 (SI 1987/1967) regs 42(1) and 51(1), in Vol.V of this series).

Paragraphs (7ZA) and (7ZB)
3.90   The effect of these provisions is that a person who changes their choice of a weekly increase to a lump sum in respect of the new state pension is not penalised by being treated as still possessing the extra income. See further paras.(8A) and (8B) for definitions.

[¹Calculation of capital in the United Kingdom

19.—Capital which a claimant possesses in the United Kingdom shall be **3.91**
calculated at its current market or surrender value less—
(a) where there would be expenses attributable to sale, 10 per cent; and
(b) the amount of any encumbrance secured on it.]

AMENDMENT

1. Social Security (Miscellaneous Amendments) (No.5) Regulations 2007 (SI
2007/2618) reg.10(4) (October 1, 2007).

DEFINITIONS

"capital"—see SPCA 2002 s.17(1).
"claimant"—see *ibid.*

GENERAL NOTE

This is in the same terms as the parallel provision in the income support scheme **3.92**
(see Income Support (General) Regulations 1987 (SI 1987/1967) reg.49, in Vol.V of
this series. See also *GE v Department for Communities (PC)* [2016] NICom 73, where
the claimant's capital consisted of a part ownership as tenant in common of a property which was her former matrimonial home. Commissioner Stockman observed
that "there is no market for the type of interest in property which the [claimant]
possesses. Where there is no market, it follows that the current market value of the
respondent's interest is likely to be, as the tribunal has found, nominal" (para.41).

Calculation of capital outside the United Kingdom

20.—Capital which a claimant possesses in a country outside the United **3.93**
Kingdom shall be calculated—
(a) in a case where there is no prohibition in that country against the
transfer to the United Kingdom of an amount equal to its current
market or surrender value in that country, at that value;
(b) in a case where there is such a prohibition, at the price which it
would realise if sold in the United Kingdom to a willing buyer,
less, where there would be expenses attributable to sale, 10 per cent, and the
amount of any encumbrance secured on it.

DEFINITIONS

"capital"—see SPCA 2002 s.17(1).
"claimant"—see *ibid.*

GENERAL NOTE

This is in the same terms as the parallel provision in the income support scheme **3.94**
(see Income Support (General) Regulations 1987 (SI 1987/1967) reg.50, in Vol.V
of this series).

Notional capital

21.—[²(1) A claimant shall be treated as possessing capital of which **3.95**
he has deprived himself for the purpose of securing entitlement to state
pension credit or increasing the amount of that benefit except to the extent
that the capital which he is treated as possessing is reduced in accordance
with regulation 22 (diminishing notional capital rule).]
[³ (2) A person who disposes of a capital resource for the purpose of—

(a) reducing or paying a debt owed by the claimant; or
(b) purchasing goods or services if the expenditure was reasonable in the circumstances of the claimant's case,

shall be regarded as not depriving himself of it.]

[¹(3) Where a claimant stands in relation to a company in a position analogous to that of a sole owner or partner in the business of that company, he shall be treated as if he were such sole owner or partner and in such a case—

(a) the value of his holding in that company shall, notwithstanding regulation 19 (calculation of capital), be disregarded; and
(b) he shall, subject to paragraph (4), be treated as possessing an amount of capital equal to the value or, as the case may be, his share of the value of the capital of that company and the foregoing provisions of this Chapter shall apply for the purposes of calculating that amount as if it were actual capital which he does possess.

(4) For so long as a claimant undertakes activities in the course of the business of the company, the amount which he is treated as possessing under paragraph (3) shall be disregarded.

(5) Where under this regulation a person is treated as possessing capital, the amount of that capital shall be calculated in accordance with the provisions of this Part as if it were actual capital which he does possess.]

AMENDMENTS

1. State Pension Credit (Consequential, Transitional and Miscellaneous Provisions) Regulations 2002 (SI 2002/3019) reg.23(j) (October 6, 2003).
2. State Pension Credit (Consequential, Transitional and Miscellaneous Provisions) (No.2) Regulations 2002 (SI 2002/3197) reg.2 and Sch. para.6 (October 6, 2003).
3. State Pension Credit (Miscellaneous Amendments) Regulations 2004 (SI 2004/647) reg.3(5) (April 5, 2004).

DEFINITIONS

"capital"—see SPCA 2002 s.17(1).
"claimant"—see *ibid.*

GENERAL NOTE

3.96   Readers who are well acquainted with the income support system will be familiar with the concept of notional capital, that is capital which the claimant is deemed to possess even though he or she does not actually have such resources. This is, therefore, essentially an anti-avoidance provision in the context of means-tested benefits. Section 15(6) of the SPCA 2002 (which mirrors SSCBA 1992 s.163(5)) provides the legislative authority for such a rule in the state pension credit scheme. The notional capital rule enshrined in this regulation contains some parallels with the equivalent rule in the income support scheme (Income Support (General) Regulations 1987 (SI 1987/1967) reg.51, in Vol.V of this series), but is also different. In particular, the state pension credit rule operates only where there is a deprivation of capital with a view to claiming or increasing entitlement to benefit (para.(1)) or where the claimant is a sole trader or a partner in a business which is a limited company (paras (3) and (4)). There is, therefore, no equivalent to the income support rules governing failures to apply for capital which is available, payments to third parties by someone else on the claimant's behalf or retention of capital received on behalf of a third party (Income Support (General) Regulations 1987 (SI 1987/1967) reg.51(2) and (3)).

See also *MC v SSWP* [2010] UKUT 29 (AAC) for guidance on how the presumption of a resulting trust may operate in the context of a transaction between family members.

Paragraph (1)

The general rule is expressed in similar terms to Income Support (General)   **3.97**
Regulations 1987 (SI 1987/1967) reg.51(1). The Secretary of State must accordingly show that: (1) the claimant has deprived him or herself of actual capital, and (2) this was done with the purpose of securing or increasing entitlement to state pension credit. As to (1), the traditional approach has been that "deprive" does not carry a special legal meaning and is a matter of ordinary English (*R(SB) 38/85, R(SB) 40/85*). However, these authorities will have to be applied with some care in the context of state pension credit as, unlike in the income support scheme, para.(2) below gives specific examples of what is not to be regarded as a deprivation. The supplementary benefit and income support case law on the claimant's purpose in making the deprivation will presumably apply equally here given the statutory language is the same in this respect (see commentary at para.2.419 in Vol.V of this series). There is, however, no express exception for capital for personal injuries compensation held in trust or administered by the court (contrast Income Support (General) Regulations 1987 (SI 1987/1967) reg.51(1)(a) and (c)).

Paragraph (2)

This is an interesting provision which has no direct parallel in the analogous   **3.98**
rule that applies under the income support scheme (Income Support (General) Regulations 1987 (SI 1987/1967) reg.51). That said, it appears to be an attempt to illustrate what is not to be regarded as an act of deprivation. Thus, a disposal for the purpose of either reducing or paying a debt owed by the claimant, or in purchasing goods or services "if the expenditure was reasonable in the circumstances of the claimant's case", is not to be seen as a deprivation. Under the income support scheme, such disposals would be seen as a deprivation and the argument would then revolve around the claimant's purpose in making such a disposal. Typically the claimant would argue that the payment was solely for some other purpose, and not with a view to claiming or increasing entitlement to benefit. The position under the state pension credit scheme would appear to be different and perhaps weighted more in favour of the claimant. If the claimant is able to demonstrate that one of the circumstances in para.(2) applies, then there has been no deprivation and the issue as to the claimant's purpose need not be explored. This construction is strengthened by the repeal of the qualifying phrase "Without prejudice to the generality of paragraph (1)" as from April 5, 2004. That amendment also repealed the provision which automatically deemed a disposal by way of a gift to a third party to be a deprivation. However, it remains open to decision-makers and tribunals to find that such a gift was a deprivation made with the intent of securing (or increasing) entitlement to pension credit.

Paragraphs (3) and (4)

These two paragraphs establish an artificial method for dealing with one person   **3.99**
companies and analogous enterprises. In summary, the value of the individual's shareholding itself is disregarded (para.(3)(a)) but the claimant is treated as possessing a proportionate share of the company's capital (para.(3)(b)). However, so long as the individual undertakes activities in the course of the business, the amount produced by para.(3)(b) is disregarded (para.(4)). See further the commentary on the parallel provisions in reg.51(4) and (5) of the Income Support (General) Regulations 1987 (SI 1987/1967).

Paragraph (5)

As the claimant's capital is to be calculated as though it were actual capital,   **3.100**
it follows that notional capital is assumed to yield a weekly income on the basis

set out in reg.15(6). It also means that any relevant capital disregards under reg.17(8) and Sch.V must be applied to the notional capital (by analogy with *CIS/231/1991*).

Diminishing notional capital rule

3.101   **22.**—(1) Where a claimant is treated as possessing capital under regulation 21(1) (notional capital), the amount which he is treated as possessing—

(a) in the case of a week that is subsequent to—

(i) the relevant week in respect of which the conditions set out in paragraph (2) are satisfied, or

(ii) a week which follows that relevant week and which satisfies those conditions,

shall be reduced by an amount determined under paragraph (2);

(b) in the case of a week in respect of which sub-paragraph (1)(a) does not apply but where—

(i) that week is a week subsequent to the relevant week, and

(ii) that relevant week is a week in which the condition in paragraph (3) is satisfied,

shall be reduced by the amount determined under paragraph (3).

(2) This paragraph applies to a benefit week where the claimant satisfies the conditions that—

(a) he is in receipt of state pension credit; and

(b) but for regulation [¹21(1)], he would have received an additional amount of state pension credit in that benefit week;

and in such a case, the amount of the reduction for the purposes of paragraph (1)(a) shall be equal to that additional amount.

(3) Subject to paragraph (4), for the purposes of paragraph (1)(b) the condition is that the claimant would have been entitled to state pension credit in the relevant week, but for regulation [¹21(1)], and in such a case the amount of the reduction shall be equal to the aggregate of—

(a) the amount of state pension credit to which the claimant would have been entitled in the relevant week but for regulation [¹21(1)];

(b) the amount of housing benefit (if any) equal to the difference between his maximum housing benefit and the amount (if any) of housing benefit which he is awarded in respect of the benefit week, within the meaning of regulation 2(1) of the Housing Benefit (General) Regulations 1987 (interpretation), which includes the last day of the relevant week;

(c) the amount of council tax benefit (if any) equal to the difference between his maximum council tax benefit and the amount (if any) of council tax benefit which he is awarded in respect of the benefit week which includes the last day of the relevant week, and for this purpose "benefit week" [² means a period of 7 consecutive days beginning on a Monday and ending on a Sunday].

(4) The amount determined under paragraph (3) shall be re-determined under that paragraph if the claimant makes a further claim for state pension credit and the conditions in paragraph (5) are satisfied, and in such a case—

(a) sub-paragraphs (a) to (c) of paragraph (3) shall apply as if for the words "relevant week" there were substituted the words "relevant subsequent week"; and

(b) subject to paragraph (6), the amount as re-determined shall have effect from the first week following the relevant subsequent week in question.

(5) The conditions are that—

(a) a further claim is made 26 or more weeks after—
   (i) the date on which the claimant made a claim for state pension credit in respect of which he was first treated as possessing the capital in question under regulation [¹21(1)]; or
   (ii) in a case where there has been at least one re-determination in accordance with paragraph (4), the date on which he last made a claim for state pension credit which resulted in the weekly amount being re-determined; or
   (iii) the date on which he last ceased to be in receipt of state pension credit, whichever last occurred; and

(b) the claimant would have been entitled to state pension credit but for regulation [¹21(1)].

(6) The amount as re-determined pursuant to paragraph (4) shall not have effect if it is less than the amount which applied in that case immediately before the re-determination and in such a case the higher amount shall continue to have effect.

(7) For the purpose of this regulation—

(a) "relevant week" means the benefit week in which the capital in question of which the claimant has deprived himself within the meaning of regulation [¹21(1)]—
   (i) was first taken into account for the purpose of determining his entitlement to state pension credit; or
   (ii) was taken into account on a subsequent occasion for the purpose of determining or re-determining his entitlement to state pension credit on that subsequent occasion and that determination or re-determination resulted in his beginning to receive, or ceasing to receive, state pension credit;
   and where more than one benefit week is identified by reference to heads (i) and (ii) of this sub-paragraph the later or latest such benefit week;

(b) "relevant subsequent week" means the benefit week which includes the day on which the further claim or, if more than one further claim had been made, the last such claim was made.

AMENDMENTS

1. State Pension Credit (Consequential, Transitional and Miscellaneous Provisions) (No.2) Regulations 2002 (SI 2002/3197) reg.2 and Sch. para.7 (October 6, 2003).

2. Council Tax Benefit Abolition (Consequential Provision) Regulations 2013 (SI 2013/458) reg.4 and Sch.2 para.6 (April 1, 2013).

DEFINITIONS

"benefit week"—see reg.1(2).
"capital"—see SPCA 2002 s.17(1).
"claimant"—see *ibid.*
"relevant week"—see para.(7)(a).
"relevant subsequent week"—see para.7(b).

GENERAL NOTE

3.102   This diminishing notional capital rule is, in all material respects, identical to that which operates under the income support scheme (Income Support (General) Regulations 1987 (SI 1987/1967) reg.51A, in Vol.V of this series). Thus if the amount of notional capital has the effect of removing entitlement to state pension credit altogether, owing to the application of the tariff income rule in reg.15(6) above, that notional capital is to be treated as reducing each week in accordance with para.(1)(b) and (3). In such a case the weekly reduction is by a sum representing the aggregate of the state pension credit which would have been received in the absence of such notional capital plus the proportion of rent and council tax not met by housing benefit and council tax benefit respectively. In other cases, the interaction of the notional capital rule and the tariff income rule will reduce rather than extinguish entitlement to state pension credit. In this type of situation the notional capital is to be treated as reducing each week by the amount by which the state pension credit would be increased in the absence of such notional capital (para.(1) (a) and (2)). Paragraphs (4)–(6) provide for redetermination and recalculation in the event of a fresh claim being made.

Capital jointly held

3.103   **23.**—Where a claimant and one or more persons are beneficially entitled in possession to any capital asset they shall be treated as if each of them were entitled in possession to the whole beneficial interest therein in an equal share and the foregoing provisions of this Part shall apply for the purposes of calculating the amount of capital which the claimant is treated as possessing as if it were actual capital which the claimant does possess.

DEFINITIONS

"capital"—see SPCA 2002 s.17(1).
"claimant"—see *ibid.*

GENERAL NOTE

3.104   This provision is essentially in the same terms as the parallel and notoriously problematic provision in the income support scheme (see Income Support (General) Regulations 1987 (SI 1987/1967) reg.52, in Vol.V of this series). For a valuable reminder that in cases where capital is held jointly "the market value of such an interest in circumstances such as these is not by any means the same thing as half the entire value of the freehold with vacant possession", see *AM v SSWP* [2010] UKUT 134 (AAC), para.5, applying *R(IS) 5/07*. However, its impact in the context of state pension credit is likely to be much less as there is no capital rule as such. It will, however, have effect for the purpose of calculating the value of the claimant's capital for the purpose of attributing the deemed tariff income under reg.15(6).

Income paid to third parties

3.105   **24.**—(1) Any payment of income, other than a payment specified in [¹ paragraphs (2) or (3)], to a third party in respect of the claimant shall be treated as possessed by the claimant.
    (2) Paragraph (1) shall not apply in respect of a payment of income made under an occupational pension scheme or in respect of a pension or other periodical payment made under a personal pension scheme where—
        (a) a bankruptcy order has been made in respect of the person in respect of whom the payment has been made or, to Scotland, the estate of that person is subject to sequestration or a judicial factor has been

appointed on that person's estate under section 41 of the Solicitors (Scotland) Act 1980;

(b) the payment is made to the trustee in bankruptcy or any other person acting on behalf of the creditors; and

(c) the person referred to in sub-paragraph (a) and his partner does not possess, or is not treated as possessing, any other income apart from that payment.

[[1] (3) Paragraph (1) shall not apply in respect of any payment of income arising out of the [[2] claimant participating as a service user.]

AMENDMENTS

1. Social Security (Miscellaneous Amendments) (No.3) Regulations 2011 (2011/2425) reg.15(4) (October 31, 2011).

2. Social Security (Miscellaneous Amendments) Regulations 2014 (SI 2014/591) reg.7(5) (April 28, 2014).

DEFINITIONS

"claimant"—see SPCA 2002 s.17(1).
"income"—see SPCA 2002 ss.15 and 17(1).
"occupational pension scheme"—see SPCA 2002 s.17(1).
"partner"—reg.1(3).
"personal pension scheme"—see *ibid.*

GENERAL NOTE

The claimant is deemed to possess income which is paid to a third party by   3.106
someone in respect of the claimant. This is subject to the exceptions set out in para. (2), which is in identical terms to regs 42(ZA)(d) and 51(3A)(c) of the Income Support (General) Regulations 1987 (SI 1987/1967), in Vol.V of this series, which apply to notional income and notional capital respectively for income support purposes.

See further *BL v SSWP (SPC)* [2018] UKUT 4 (AAC) (discussed in the commentary on s.15 of the 2002 Act), in which the claimant directed pension payments to his separated wife. Judge Farbey QC rejected a submission that payments to third parties should be discounted from income unless they are deployed for the alimentation of the claimant. In that case, "Standard Life paid the claimant's wife in lieu of the claimant; and the payments were treated as maintenance payments made by him. I do not regard the tribunal as having erred in law by concluding that, in these circumstances, Standard Life made the payments for the claimant's purposes and so 'in respect of' the claimant" (at para.48).

[[1]**Rounding of fractions**

24A.—Where any calculation under this Part results in a fraction of a   3.107
penny that fraction shall, if it would be to the claimant's advantage, be treated as a penny; otherwise it shall be disregarded.]

AMENDMENT

1. State Pension Credit (Consequential, Transitional and Miscellaneous Provisions) Regulations 2002 (SI 2002/3019) reg.23(k) (October 6, 2003).

GENERAL NOTE

This reflects the normal rule for means-tested benefits (see Income Support   3.108
(General) Regulations 1987 (SI 1987/1967) reg.27).

PART IV

Loss of benefit

Loss of benefit

3.109   **25.**—[*Omitted.*]

GENERAL NOTE

3.110   This regulation amends the Social Security (Loss of Benefits) Regulations 2001 (SI 2001/4022); the relevant changes are incorporated in Vol.III in this series.

SCHEDULES

Regulation 6(4)

SCHEDULE I

PART I

Circumstances in which persons are treated as being or not being severely disabled

Severe disablement

3.111   **1.**—(1) For the purposes of regulation 6(4) (additional amounts for persons severely disabled), the claimant is to be treated as being severely disabled if, and only if—

(a) in the case of a claimant who has no partner—
    (i) he is in receipt of attendance allowance [7, the care component of disability living allowance at the highest or middle rate prescribed in accordance with section 72(3) of the 1992 Act [12,] the daily living component of personal independence payment at the standard or enhanced rate in accordance with section 78(3) of the 2012 Act [12, the daily living component of adult disability payment at the standard or enhanced rate in accordance with regulation 5 of the Disability Assistance for Working Age People (Scotland) Regulations 2022] [8 or armed forces independence payment]];
    (ii) no person who has attained the age of 18 is normally residing with the claimant, nor is the claimant normally residing with such a person, other than a person to whom paragraph 2 applies; and
    (iii) no person is entitled to and in receipt of an allowance under section 70 of the 1992 Act ([2 carer's allowance]) [10, or has an award of universal credit which includes the carer element,] in respect of caring for him;
(b) in the case of a claimant who has a partner—
    (i) both partners are in receipt of attendance allowance [7, the care component of disability living allowance at the highest or middle rate prescribed in accordance with section 72(3) of the 1992 Act [12,] the daily living component of personal independence payment at the standard or enhanced rate in accordance with section 78(3) of the 2012 Act [12, the daily living component of adult disability payment at the standard or enhanced rate in accordance with regulation 5 of the Disability Assistance for Working Age People (Scotland) Regulations 2022] [8 or armed forces independence payment]]; and
    (ii) no person who has attained the age of 18 is normally residing with the partners, nor are the partners normally residing with such a person, other than a person to whom paragraph 2 applies;
    and either a person is entitled to, and in receipt of, an allowance under section 70 of the 1992 Act [10, or has an award of universal credit which includes the carer element,] in respect of caring for one only of the partners or, as the case may be, no person is entitled to, and in receipt of, such an allowance [10 under section 70, or has an award of universal credit which includes the carer element,] in respect of caring for either partner;
(c) in the case of a claimant who has a partner and to whom head (b) does not apply—

(i) either the claimant or his partner is in receipt of attendance allowance [⁷, the care component of disability living allowance at the highest or middle rate prescribed in accordance with section 72(3) of the 1992 Act [¹²,] or the daily living component of personal independence payment at the standard or enhanced rate in accordance with section 78(3) of the 2012 Act [¹², the daily living component of adult disability payment at the standard or enhanced rate in accordance with regulation 5 of the Disability Assistance for Working Age People (Scotland) Regulations 2022] [⁸ or armed forces independence payment]]; and

[⁹ (ii) the other partner is certified as severely sight impaired or blind by a consultant ophthalmologist; and.]

(iii) no person who has attained the age of 18 is normally residing with the partners, nor are the partners normally residing with such a person, other than a person to whom paragraph 2 applies; and

(iv) no person is entitled to and in receipt of an allowance under section 70 of the 1992 Act [¹⁰, or has an award of universal credit which includes the carer element, in] respect of caring for the person to whom head (c) (i) above applies.

(2) A person shall be treated—

(a) for the purposes of sub-paragraph (1) as being in receipt of attendance allowance or, as the case may be, [⁷, the care component of disability living allowance at the highest or middle rate prescribed in accordance with section 72(3) of the 1992 Act [¹²,] or the daily living component of personal independence payment at the standard or enhanced rate in accordance with section 78(3) of the 2012 Act [¹², the daily living component of adult disability payment at the standard or enhanced rate in accordance with regulation 5 of the Disability Assistance for Working Age People (Scotland) Regulations 2022] [⁸ or armed forces independence payment]], for any period—

(i) before an award is made but in respect of which the allowance [⁷or payment] is awarded; or

(ii) not covered by an award but in respect of which a payment is made in lieu of an award;

(b) for the purposes of sub-paragraph (1)(b) as being in receipt of attendance allowance or the care component of disability living allowance at the highest or middle rate prescribed in accordance section [¹72(3)] of the 1992 Act if he would, but for his being a patient for a period exceeding 28 days, be so in receipt;

[⁷ (ba) for the purposes of sub-paragraph (1)(b) as being in receipt of the daily living component of personal independence payment at the standard or enhanced rate in accordance with section 78 of the 2012 Act if he would, but for regulations made under section 86(1) (hospital in-patients) of that Act, be so in receipt;]

[¹² (bb) for the purposes of sub-paragraph (1)(b) as being in receipt of the daily living component of adult disability payment at the standard or enhanced rate in accordance with regulation 5 of the Disability Assistance for Working Age People (Scotland) Regulations 2022, if that person would, but for regulation 28 (effect of admission to hospital on ongoing entitlement to Adult Disability Payment) of those Regulations, be so in receipt;]

(c) for the purposes of sub-paragraph (1), as not being in receipt of an allowance under section 70 of the 1992 Act [¹⁰, or as having an award of universal credit which includes the carer element,] for any period before [⁵ the date on which the award is first paid].

[⁹ (3) For the purposes of sub-paragraph (1)(c)(ii), a person who has ceased to be certified as severely sight impaired or blind on regaining his eyesight shall nevertheless be treated as severely sight impaired or blind, as the case may be, and as satisfying the requirements set out in that sub-paragraph for a period of 28 weeks following the date on which he ceased to be so certified.]

[¹⁰ (4) For the purposes of this paragraph, a person has an award of universal credit which includes the carer element if the person has an award of universal credit which includes an amount which is the carer element under regulation 29 of the Universal Credit Regulations 2013.]

Persons residing with the claimant whose presence is ignored

2.—(1) For the purposes of paragraph 1(1)(a)(ii), (b)(ii) and (c)(iii), this paragraph applies to the persons specified in the following sub-paragraphs.

(2) A person who—

(a) is in receipt of attendance allowance [⁷, the care component of disability living allowance at the highest or middle rate prescribed in accordance with section 72(3) of the 1992 Act [¹²,] the daily living component of personal independence payment at the standard or enhanced rate in accordance with section 78(3) of the 2012 Act [¹², the daily living component of adult disability payment at the standard or enhanced rate in accordance with regulation 5 of the Disability Assistance for Working Age People (Scotland) Regulations 2022] [⁸ or armed forces independence payment]];

3.112

[⁹ (b) is certified as severely sight impaired or blind by a consultant ophthalmologist;

    (c) is no longer certified as severely sight impaired or blind in accordance with head (b) but was so certified not more than 28 weeks earlier;]

    (d) lives with the claimant in order to care for him or his partner and is engaged by a charitable or voluntary organisation which makes a charge to the claimant or his partner for the services provided by that person;

    (e) is a partner of a person to whom head (d) above applies; or

    (f) is a person who is [³ a qualifying young person [¹¹ within the meaning of regulation 4A] or] child [¹¹ as defined in section 40 of the 2012 Act].

(3) Subject to sub-paragraph (4), a person who joins the claimant's household for the first time in order to care for the claimant or his partner and immediately before he joined the household, the claimant or his partner was treated as being severely disabled.

(4) Sub-paragraph (3) applies only for the first 12 weeks following the date on which the person first joins the claimant's household.

(5) A person who is not a close relative of the claimant or his partner and—

    (a) who is liable to make payments on a commercial basis to the claimant or his partner in respect of his occupation of the dwelling;

    (b) to whom the claimant or his partner is liable to make payments on a commercial basis in respect of his occupation of that person's dwelling; or

    (c) who is a member of the household of a person to whom head (a) or (b) applies.

(6) Subject to paragraph 3(3), a person who jointly occupies the claimant's dwelling and who is either—

    (a) co-owner of that dwelling with the claimant or the claimant's [¹partner] (whether or not there are other co-owners); or

    (b) jointly liable with the claimant or the claimant's partner to make payments to a landlord in respect of his occupation of that dwelling.

(7) Subject to paragraph 3(3), a person who is a partner of a person to whom sub-paragraph (6) applies.

3.—(1) For the purposes of paragraphs 1 and 2, a person resides with another only if they share any accommodation except a bathroom, a lavatory or a communal area, but not if each person is separately liable to make payments in respect of his occupation of the dwelling to the landlord.

(2) In sub-paragraph (1), "communal area" means any area (other than rooms) of common access (including halls and passageways) and rooms of common use in sheltered accommodation.

(3) Paragraph 2(6) and (7) applies to a person who is a close relative of the claimant or his partner only if the claimant or his partner's co-ownership, or joint liability to make payments to a landlord in respect of his occupation, of the dwelling arose either before 11th April 1988, or, if later, on or before the date upon which the claimant or the claimant's partner first occupied the dwelling in question.

PART II

Amount applicable for carers

3.113

4.—(1) For the purposes of regulation 6(6)(a), this paragraph is satisfied if any of the requirements specified in sub-paragraphs (2) to (4) are met.

(2) A claimant is, or in the case of partners either partner is, or both partners are, entitled to an allowance under section 70 of the 1992 Act ([² carer's allowance]).

(3) Where an additional amount has been awarded under regulation 6(6)(a) but—

    (a) the person in respect of whose care the allowance has been awarded dies; or

    (b) the person in respect of whom the additional amount was awarded ceases to be entitled or ceases to be treated as entitled to the allowance,

this paragraph shall be treated as satisfied for a period of eight weeks from the relevant date specified in sub-paragraph (4).

(4) The relevant date for the purposes of [¹sub-paragraph (3) is]—

    (a) the Sunday following the death of the person in respect of whose care the allowance has been awarded (or beginning with the date of death if the death occurred on a Sunday);

    (b) where sub-paragraph (a) does not apply, the date on which the person who has been entitled to the allowance ceases to be entitled to that allowance.

5.—For the purposes of paragraph 4, a person shall be treated as being entitled to and in receipt of an allowance under section 70 of the 1992 Act for any period not covered by an award but in respect of which a payment is made in lieu of an award.

PART III

Amount applicable for former claimants of income support [⁶, income-based jobseeker's allowance or income-related employment and support allowance]

6.—(1) If on the relevant day the relevant amount exceeds the provisional amount, an additional amount ("the transitional amount") equal to the difference shall be applicable to a claimant to whom sub-paragraph (2) applies.

3.114

(2) This sub-paragraph applies to a claimant who, in respect of the day before the relevant day, was entitled to either income support [⁶, an income-based jobseeker's allowance or an income-related employment and support allowance.]

(3) The relevant day is the day in respect of which the claimant is first entitled to state pension credit.

(4) The provisional amount means the amount of the appropriate minimum guarantee applicable to the claimant on the relevant day but for this paragraph.

(5) The relevant amount means the amount which, on the day before the relevant day, was the claimant's applicable amount—

(a) for the purposes of determining his entitlement to income support; [⁶ . . .]

(b) for the purpose of determining his entitlement to an income-based jobseeker's allowance,

less any of the following amounts included in it—

    (i) any amount determined in accordance with paragraph 2 of Schedule 2 to the Income Support Regulations or paragraph 2 of Schedule 1 to the Jobseeker's Allowance Regulations;

    (ii) any amount by way of a residential allowance applicable in accordance with paragraph 2A of Schedule 2 to the Income Support Regulations or paragraph 3 of Schedule 1 to the Jobseeker's Allowance Regulations;

    (iii) any amount by way of family premium applicable in accordance with paragraph 3 of Schedule 2 to the Income Support Regulations or paragraph 4 of Schedule 1 to the Jobseeker's Allowance Regulations;

    (iv) any amount by way of disabled child premium applicable in accordance with paragraph 14 of Schedule 2 to the Income Support Regulations or paragraph 16 of Schedule 1 to the Jobseeker's Allowance Regulations; and

    (v) any amount in respect of a person other than the claimant or his partner by way of enhanced disability premium applicable in accordance with paragraph 13A of Schedule 2 to the Income Support Regulations [⁶, paragraph 7 of Schedule 4 to the Employment and Support Allowance Regulations] or paragraph 15A of Schedule 1 to the Jobseeker's Allowance Regulations [⁶; or

(c) for the purposes of determining his entitlement to income-related employment and support allowance.]

(6) In determining the relevant amount under sub-paragraph (5), the applicable amount shall be increased by an amount equal to the amount (if any) payable to the claimant in accordance with Part II of the Income Support (Transitional) Regulations 1987 (transitional protection) or regulation 87(1) of the Jobseeker's Allowance Regulations (transitional supplement to income-based jobseeker's allowance).

(7) If—

(a) paragraph 1 of Schedule 7 to the Income Support Regulations or paragraph 1 of Schedule 5 to the Jobseeker's Allowance [¹ Regulations] applied to the claimant or his partner on the day before the relevant day; but

(b) paragraph 2(2) of Schedule 3 does not apply to the claimant or his partner on the relevant day;

then for the purposes of this paragraph the relevant amount shall be determined on the assumption that the provision referred to in sub-paragraph (7)(a) did not apply in his case.

(8) Subject to sub-paragraph (9), the transitional amount shall—

(a) be reduced by a sum equal to the amount (if any) by which the appropriate minimum guarantee increases after the relevant day;

(b) cease to be included in the claimant's appropriate minimum guarantee from the day on which—

    (i) the sum mentioned in head (a) above equals or exceeds the transitional amount; or

    (ii) the claimant or the claimant's partner ceases to be entitled to state pension credit.

(9) For the purposes of sub-paragraph (8), there shall be disregarded—

(a) any break in entitlement not exceeding 8 weeks; and
[⁴ (b) any amount by which the appropriate minimum guarantee of a patient is increased on
10th April 2006 by virtue of the substitution of paragraph 2 of Schedule 3.]
[¹ (10) This sub-paragraph applies where the relevant amount included an amount in respect
of housing costs relating to a loan—
    (a) which is treated as a qualifying loan by virtue of regulation 3 of the Income Support
(General) Amendment and Transitional Regulations 1995 or paragraph 18(2) of
Schedule 2 to the Jobseeker's Allowance Regulation [⁶ or paragraph 20(2) of Schedule
6 to the Employment and Support Allowance Regulations]; or
    (b) the appropriate amount of which was determined in accordance with paragraph
7(6C) of Schedule 3 to the Income Support Regulations as in force prior to 10th
April 1995 and maintained in force by regulation 28(1) of the Income-related Benefits
Schemes (Miscellaneous Amendments) Regulations 1995.
(11) Where sub-paragraph (10) applies, the transitional amount shall be calculated or, as
the case may be, recalculated, on the relevant anniversary date determined in accordance with
paragraph 7(4C) of Schedule II ("the relevant anniversary date") on the basis that the provisional amount on the relevant day included, in respect of housing costs, the amount calculated
in accordance with paragraph 7(1) of Schedule II as applying from the relevant anniversary
date and not the amount in respect of housing costs determined on the basis of the amount of
the loan calculated in accordance with paragraph 7(4A) of that Schedule.
(12) The transitional amount as calculated in accordance with sub-paragraph (11) shall only
be applicable from the relevant anniversary date.]

AMENDMENTS

1. State Pension Credit (Consequential, Transitional and Miscellaneous Provisions) (No.2) Regulations 2002 (SI 2002/3197) reg.2 and Sch. para.8 (October 6,
2003).
2. State Pension Credit (Transitional and Miscellaneous Provisions) Amendment
Regulations 2003 (SI 2003/2274) reg.2(8) (October 6, 2003).
3. Social Security (Young Persons) Amendment Regulations 2006 (SI 2006/718)
reg.6(3) (April 10, 2006).
4. Social Security (Miscellaneous Amendments) Regulations 2006 (SI 2006/588)
reg.4(3) (April 10, 2006).
5. Social Security (Miscellaneous Amendments) Regulations 2007 (SI 2007/719)
reg.4 (April 2, 2007).
6. Employment and Support Allowance (Consequential Provisions) (No.2)
Regulations 2008 (SI 2008/1554) reg.4(7) (October 27, 2008).
7. Personal Independence Payment (Supplementary Provisions and Consequential Amendments) Regulations 2013 (SI 2013/388) reg.8 and Sch. para.27(4)
(a) (April 8, 2013).
8. Armed Forces and Reserve Forces Compensation Scheme (Consequential
Provisions: Subordinate Legislation) Order 2013 (SI 2013/591) art.7 and Sch.
para.23(4) (April 8, 2013).
9. Universal Credit and Miscellaneous Amendments (No.2) Regulations 2014 (SI
2014/2888) reg.3(4)(a) (November 26, 2014).
10. Universal Credit and Miscellaneous Amendments Regulations 2015 (SI
2015/1754) reg.16(3) (November 4, 2015).
11. Housing Benefit and State Pension Credit (Temporary Absence) (Amendment)
Regulations 2016 (SI 2016/624) reg.4(7) (July 28, 2016).
12. Social Security (Disability Assistance for Working Age People) (Consequential
Amendments) Order 2022 (SI 2022/177) art.8(3) (March 21, 2022).

GENERAL NOTE

3.115   Schedule I sets out the criteria for the award of additional guarantee credit
amounts, on the same basis as under the income support scheme, for severely
disabled pensioners (Pt I), for carers (Pt II) and for pensioners with entitlement
to transitional additions (Pt III). Regulation 6 is the principal provision governing
the guarantee credit and lists the actual weekly amounts for the principal additional
elements.

Paragraph 1
According to *CPC/2021/2008* (at paras 56–64), the reference to a person being **3.116** "in receipt of attendance allowance" is to be read as meaning "in actual receipt of attendance allowance" rather than being "entitled to but not actually in receipt of attendance allowance", notwithstanding the absence of a provision equivalent to para.14B of Sch.2 to the Income Support (General) Regulations 1987 (SI 1987/1967). See further *DB (as executor of the estate of OE) v SSWP and Birmingham CC (SPC)* [2018] UKUT 46 (AAC), in which Judge Mitchell concluded that the legislator "intended to link the additional amount for severe disability to factual receipt of attendance allowance rather than its payability" (at para.53). See *HT v SSWP (AA)* [2020] UKUT 57 (AAC) for an example of a case where receipt of an equivalent Polish disability benefit qualified for these purposes.

Paragraphs 2 and 3
In *CPC/1446/2008*, Deputy Commissioner Wikeley considered whether a claim- **3.117** ant was "residing with" a non-dependent within the meaning of Sch.1 paras 2 and 3. The Deputy Commissioner followed *CSIS/652/2003* in preferring *CSIS/2532/2003* to *CIS/185/1995* on the parallel income support rules. According to the Deputy Commissioner, a kitchen may therefore form part of shared accommodation even if the claimant personally does not visit the kitchen so long as he uses it in some other way (e.g. storage or for a third party to prepare meals). However, in *RK v SSWP* [2008] UKUT 34 (AAC) Judge Rowland was prepared to accept that a person does not necessarily share a kitchen merely because meals are prepared for him or her there. Judge Rowland also agreed with the outcomes of the appeals in *CSIS/185/1995*, *CIS/2532/2003*, *CSIS/652/2003* and *CPC/1446/2008* if not all of the reasoning. Judge Rowland took the view that "residing with" means "living in the same household as". On the facts a claimant who was confined to her bedroom in her son's house shared accommodation with her son and so normally resided with him, and so was not entitled to a severe disability premium. See further, *ST v Secretary of State for Work and Pensions* [2009] UKUT 269 (AAC).

Regulation 6(6)(c)

SCHEDULE II

HOUSING COSTS

Housing costs
1.—(1) Subject to the following provisions of this Schedule, the housing costs applicable to **3.118** a claimant in accordance with regulation 6(6)(c) are those costs—
   (a) which the claimant or, if he has a partner, his partner is, in accordance with paragraph 3, liable to meet in respect of the dwelling occupied as the home which he or his partner is treated as occupying; and
   (b) which qualify [[41] under paragraph 13].
   (2) [[41] . . .]
   (3) For the purposes of sub-paragraph (2)(a), a person shall not cease to be a disabled person on account of his being disqualified for receiving benefit or treated as capable of work by virtue of the operation of section 171E of the 1992 Act (incapacity for work, disqualification, etc.) [[19] or disqualified for receiving employment and support allowance or treated as not having limited capability for work in accordance with regulations made under section 18 of the Welfare Reform Act (disqualification)].
   (4) In this Schedule, "non-dependant" means any person, except someone to whom sub-paragraph (5), (6) or (7) applies, who normally resides with the claimant.
   (5) This sub-paragraph applies to—
   (a) a partner of the claimant or any person under the age of [[13] 20] for whom the claimant or the claimant's partner is responsible;
   (b) a person who lives with the claimant in order to care for him or for the claimant's partner and who is engaged for that purpose by a charitable or voluntary organisation

which makes a charge to the claimant or the claimant's partner for the care provided by that person;

(c) the partner of a person to whom head (b) above applies.

(6) This sub-paragraph applies to a person, other than a close relative of the claimant or the claimant's partner—

(a) who is liable to make payments on a commercial basis to the claimant or the claimant's partner in respect of his occupation of the claimant's dwelling; [²or]

(b) [² . . .]

(c) who is a member of the household of a person to whom head (a) [² . . .] above applies.

(7) This sub-paragraph applies to—

(a) a person who jointly occupies the claimant's dwelling and who is either—

(i) co-owner of that dwelling with the claimant or the claimant's partners (whether or not there are other co-owners); or

(ii) jointly liable with the claimant or the claimant's partner to make payments to a landlord in respect of his occupation of that dwelling;

(b) a partner of a person to whom head (a) above applies.

(8) For the purpose of sub-paragraphs (4) to (7) a person resides with another only if they share any accommodation except a bathroom, a lavatory or a communal area but not if each person is separately liable to make payments in respect of his occupation of the dwelling to the landlord.

(9) In sub-paragraph (8), "communal area" means any area (other than rooms) of common access (including halls and passageways) and rooms of common use in sheltered accommodation.

Remunerative work

3.119

2.—(1) Subject to the following provisions of this paragraph, a person shall be treated for the purposes of this Schedule as engaged in remunerative work if he is engaged, or, where his hours of work fluctuate, he is engaged on average, for not less than 16 hours a week, in work for which payment is made or which is done in expectation of payment.

(2) Subject to sub-paragraph (3), in determining the number of hours for which a person is engaged in work where his hours of work fluctuate, regard shall be had to the average of hours worked over—

(a) if there is a recognisable cycle of work, the period of one complete cycle (including, where the cycle involves periods in which the person does no work, those periods but disregarding any other absences);

(b) in any other case, the period of 5 weeks immediately prior to the date of claim, or such other length of time as may, in the particular case, enable the person's weekly average hours of work to be determined more accurately.

(3) Where, for the purposes of sub-paragraph (2)(a), a person's recognisable cycle of work at a school, other educational establishment or other place of employment is one year and includes periods of school holidays or similar vacations during which he does not work, those periods and any other periods not forming part of such holidays or vacations during which he is not required to work shall be disregarded in establishing the average hours for which he is engaged in work.

(4) Where no recognisable cycle has been established in respect of a person's work, regard shall be had to the number of hours or, where those hours will fluctuate, the average of the hours, which he is expected to work in a week.

(5) A person shall be treated as engaged in remunerative work during any period for which he is absent from work referred to in sub-paragraph (1) if the absence is either without good cause or by reason of a recognised, customary or other holiday.

(6) A person on income support or an income-based jobseeker's allowance for more than 3 days in any benefit week shall be treated as not being in remunerative work in that week.

(7) A person shall not be treated as engaged in remunerative work on any day on which the person is on maternity leave [⁴, paternity leave [³³, shared parental leave] [⁴², parental bereavement leave] or adoption leave,] or is absent from work because he is ill.

(8) A person shall not be treated as engaged in remunerative work on any day on which he is engaged in an activity in respect of which—

(a) a sports award has been made, or is to be made, to him; and

(b) no other payment is made or is expected to be made to him [², and for the purposes of this sub-paragraph, "sports award" means an award made by one of the Sports Councils named in section 23(2) of the National Lottery etc. Act 1993 out of sums allocated to it for distribution under that section.]

(9) In this paragraph "benefit week"—

(a) in relation to income support, has the same meaning as in regulation 2(1) of the Income Support Regulations;

(b) in relation to jobseeker's allowance, has the same meaning as in regulation 1(3) of the Jobseeker's Allowance Regulations.

Circumstances in which a person is liable to meet housing costs

3.—A person is liable to meet housing costs where—   **3.120**

(a) the liability falls upon him or his partner but not where the liability is to a member of the same household as the person on whom the liability falls;

(b) because the person liable to meet the housing costs is not meeting them, the claimant has to meet those costs in order to continue to live in the dwelling occupied as the home and it is reasonable in all the circumstances to treat the claimant as liable to meet those costs;

(c) he in practice shares the housing costs with other members of the household none of whom are close relatives either of the claimant or his partner, and—

(i) one or more of those members is liable to meet those costs, and

(ii) it is reasonable in the circumstances to treat him as sharing responsibility.

Circumstances in which a person is to be treated as occupying a dwelling as his home

4.—(1) Subject to the following provisions of this paragraph, a person shall be treated as   **3.121**
occupying as his home the dwelling normally occupied as his home by himself or, if he has a partner, by himself and his partner, and he shall not be treated as occupying any other dwelling as his home.

(2) In determining whether a dwelling is the dwelling normally occupied as the claimant's home for the purposes of sub-paragraph (1) regard shall be had to any other dwelling occupied by the claimant or by him and his partner whether or not that other dwelling is in Great Britain.

(3) Subject to sub-paragraph (4), where a claimant who has no partner is a full-time student or is on a training course and is liable to make payments (including payments of mortgage interest or, in Scotland, payments under heritable securities or, in either case, analogous payments) in respect of either (but not both) the dwelling which he occupies for the purpose of attending his course of study or his training course or, as the case may be, the dwelling which he occupies when not attending his course, he shall be treated as occupying as his home the dwelling in respect of which he is liable to make payments.

(4) A full-time student shall not be treated as occupying a dwelling as his home for any week of absence from it, other than an absence occasioned by the need to enter hospital for treatment, outside the period of study, if the main purpose of his occupation during the period of study would be to facilitate attendance on his course.

(5) Where a claimant has been required to move into temporary accommodation by reason of essential repairs being carried out to the dwelling normally occupied as his home and he is liable to make payments (including payments of mortgage interest or, in Scotland, payments under heritable securities or, in either case, analogous payments) in respect of either (but not both) the dwelling normally occupied or the temporary accommodation, he shall be treated as occupying as his home the dwelling in respect of which he is liable to make those payments.

(6) Where a person is liable to make payments in respect of two (but not more than two) dwellings, he shall be treated as occupying both dwellings as his home only—

(a) where he has left and remains absent from the former dwelling occupied as the home through fear of violence in that dwelling or of violence by a close relative or former partner and it is reasonable that housing costs should be met in respect of both his former dwelling and his present dwelling occupied as the home; or

(b) in the case of partners, where one partner is a full-time student or is on a training course and it is unavoidable that he or they should occupy two separate dwellings and reasonable that housing costs should be met in respect of both dwellings; or

(c) in the case where a person has moved into a new dwelling occupied as the home, except where sub-paragraph (5) applies, for a period not exceeding four benefit weeks [15 from the first day of the benefit week where the move takes place on that day, but if it does not, from the first day of the next following benefit week] if his liability to make payments in respect of two dwellings is unavoidable.

(7) Where—

(a) a person has moved into a dwelling and was liable to make payments in respect of that dwelling before moving in; and

(b) he had claimed state pension credit before moving in and either that claim has not yet been determined or it has been determined but—

(i) an amount has not been included under this Schedule; or

(ii) the claim has been refused and a further claim has been made within four weeks of the date on which the claimant moved into the new dwelling occupied as the home; and

(c) the delay in moving into the dwelling in respect of which there was liability to make payments before moving in was reasonable and—

(i) that delay was necessary in order to adapt the dwelling to meet the disablement needs of the claimant, his partner or a person under the age of [¹³ 20] for whom either the claimant or his partner is responsible; or

(ii) the move was delayed pending [²⁷ local welfare provision or] the outcome of an application under Part VIII of the 1992 Act for a social fund payment to meet a need arising out of the move or in connection with setting up the home in the dwelling; or

(iii) the person became liable to make payments in respect of the dwelling while he was a patient or was in a care home [¹¹ or an independent hospital],

he shall be treated as occupying the dwelling as his home for any period not exceeding four weeks immediately prior to the date on which he moved into the dwelling and in respect of which he was liable to make payments.

[¹¹ (8) This sub-paragraph applies to a person who enters a care home or an independent hospital—

(a) for the purpose of ascertaining whether that care home or independent hospital suits his needs, and

(b) with the intention of returning to the dwelling which he normally occupies as his home should, in the event that, the care home or independent hospital prove not to suit his needs,

and while in the care home or independent hospital, the part of the dwelling which he normally occupies as his home is not let, or as the case may be, sub-let to another person.]

(9) A person to whom sub-paragraph (8) applies shall be treated as occupying the dwelling he normally occupies as his home during any period (commencing with the day he enters the [¹¹ care home or independent hospital]) not exceeding 13 weeks in which the person is resident in the [¹¹ care home or independent hospital], but only in so far as the total absence from the dwelling does not exceed 52 weeks.

(10) A person, other than a person to whom sub-paragraph (11) applies, shall be treated as occupying a dwelling as his home throughout any period of absence not exceeding 13 weeks, if, and only if—

(a) he intends to return to occupy the dwelling as his home; and

(b) the part of the dwelling normally occupied by him has not been let or, as the case may be, sub-let to another person; and

(c) the period of absence is unlikely to exceed 13 weeks.

(11) This sub-paragraph applies to a person whose absence from the dwelling he normally occupies as his home is temporary and—

(a) he intends to return to occupy the dwelling as his home; and

(b) while the part of the dwelling which is normally occupied by him has not been let or, as the case may be, sub-let; and

(c) he is—

[⁸ (i) detained in custody on remand pending trial or, as a condition of bail, required to reside—

(aa) in a dwelling, other than the dwelling he occupies as his home; or

(bb) in premises approved under [²¹ section 13 of the Offender Management Act 2007]

or, detained pending sentence upon conviction; or]

(ii) resident in a hospital or similar institution as a patient; or

(iii) undergoing or, as the case may be, his partner or a person who has not attained the age of [¹³ 20] and who is dependent on him or his partner is undergoing, in the United Kingdom or elsewhere, medical treatment, or medically approved convalescence, in accommodation other than in a care home [¹¹ or an independent hospital]; or

(iv) following, in the United Kingdom or elsewhere, a training course; or

(v) undertaking medically approved care of a person residing in the United Kingdom or elsewhere; or

(vi) undertaking the care of a person under the age of [¹³ 20] whose parent or guardian is temporarily absent from the dwelling normally occupied by that parent or guardian for the purpose of receiving medically approved care or medical treatment, or

(vii) a person who is, whether in the United Kingdom or elsewhere, receiving medically approved care provided in accommodation other than a care home [¹¹ or an independent hospital]; or

(viii) a full-time student to whom sub-paragraph (3) or (6)(b) does not apply; or

(ix) a person, other than a person to whom sub-paragraph (8) applies, who is receiving care provided in a care home [¹¹ or an independent hospital]; or

(x) a person to whom sub-paragraph (6)(a) does not apply and who has left the dwelling he occupies as his home through fear of violence in that dwelling, or by a person who was formerly his partner or is a close relative; and

(d) the period of his absence is unlikely to exceed a period of 52 weeks or, in exceptional circumstances, is unlikely substantially to exceed that period.

(12) A person to whom sub-paragraph (11) applies is to be treated as occupying the dwelling he normally occupies as his home during any period of absence not exceeding 52 weeks beginning with the first day of that absence.

(13) In this paragraph—

(a) "medically approved" means certified by a medical practitioner;

(b) "training course" means such a course of training or instruction provided wholly or partly by or on behalf of or in pursuance of arrangements made with, or approved by or on behalf of [²² Skills Development Scotland], Scottish Enterprise, Highlands and Islands Enterprise, a government department or the Secretary of State.

Housing costs not met

5.—(1) No amount may be met under the provisions of this Schedule—   **3.122**

(a) in respect of housing benefit expenditure; or

(b) where the claimant is in accommodation which is a care home [¹¹ or an independent hospital] except where he is in such accommodation during a temporary absence from the dwelling he occupies as his home and in so far as they relate to temporary absences, the provisions of paragraph 4(8) to (12) apply to him during that absence.

[¹(1A) In paragraph (1), "housing benefit expenditure" means expenditure in respect of which housing benefit is payable as specified in regulation 10(1) of the Housing Benefit (General) Regulations 1987 but does not include any such expenditure in respect of which an additional amount is applicable under regulation 6(6)(c) (housing costs).]

(2)–(13) [⁴¹ . . .]

Apportionment of housing costs

6.—(1) Where the dwelling occupied as the home is a composite hereditament and—   **3.123**

(a) before 1st April 1990 for the purposes of section 48(5) of the General Rate Act 1967 (reduction of rates on dwellings), it appeared to a rating authority or it was determined in pursuance of subsection (6) of section 48 of that Act that the hereditament, including the dwelling occupied as the home, was a mixed hereditament and that only a proportion of the rateable value of the hereditament was attributable to use for the purpose of a private dwelling; or

(b) in Scotland, before 1st April 1989 an assessor acting pursuant to section 45(1) of the Water (Scotland) Act 1980 (provision as to valuation roll) has apportioned the net annual value of the premises including the dwelling occupied as the home between the part occupied as a dwelling and the remainder,

the additional amount applicable under this Schedule shall be such proportion of the amounts applicable in respect of the hereditament or premises as a whole as is equal to the proportion of the rateable value of the hereditament attributable to the part of the hereditament used for the purposes of a private tenancy or, in Scotland, the proportion of the net annual value of the premises apportioned to the part occupied as a dwelling house.

(2) Subject to sub-paragraph (1) and the following provisions of this paragraph, where the dwelling occupied as the home is a composite hereditament, the additional amount applicable under this Schedule shall be the relevant fraction of the amount which would otherwise be applicable under this Schedule in respect of the dwelling occupied as the home.

(3) For the purposes of sub-paragraph (2), the relevant fraction shall be obtained in accordance with the formula—

$$\frac{A}{A + B}$$

where—

"A" is the current market value of the claimant's interest in that part of the composite hereditament which is domestic property within the meaning of section 66 of the Act of 1988;

"B" is the current market value of the claimant's interest in that part of the composite hereditament which is not domestic property within that section.

(4) In this paragraph—

"composite hereditament" means—
(a) as respects England and Wales, any hereditament which is shown as a composite hereditament in a local non-domestic rating list;
(b) as respects Scotland, any lands and heritages entered in the valuation roll which are part residential subjects within the meaning of section 26(1) of the Act of 1987;
"local non-domestic rating list" means a list compiled and maintained under section 41(1) of the Act of 1988;
"the Act of 1987" means the Abolition of Domestic Rates, Etc. (Scotland) Act 1987;
"the Act of 1988" means the Local Government Finance Act 1988.

(5) Where responsibility for expenditure which relates to housing costs met under this Schedule is shared, the additional amounts applicable under this Schedule shall be calculated by reference to the appropriate proportion of that expenditure for which the claimant is responsible.

The calculation for loans
3.124   7.—[⁴¹ . . .]

General provisions applying to housing costs
3.125   8.—[⁴¹ . . .]

The standard rate
3.126   9.—[⁴¹ . . .]

Excessive Housing Costs
3.127   10.—[⁴¹ . . .]

Loans on residential property
3.128   11.—[⁴¹ . . .]

Loans for repairs and improvements to the dwelling occupied as the home
3.129   12.—[⁴¹ . . .]

[⁴¹ Housing costs]
3.130   13.—(1) Subject to the deduction specified in sub-paragraph (2) and the reductions applicable in sub-paragraph (5), there shall be met under this paragraph the amounts, calculated on a weekly basis, in respect of the following housing costs—
(a) payments by way of rent or ground rent relating to a long tenancy [¹⁴ . . .];
(b) service charges;
(c) payments by way of rentcharge within the meaning of section 1 of the Rentcharges Act 1977;
(d) payments under a co-ownership scheme;
(e) payments under or relating to a tenancy or licence of a Crown tenant;
(f) where the dwelling occupied as the home is a tent, payments in respect of the tent and the site on which it stands.

(2) Subject to sub-paragraph (3), the deductions to be made from the weekly amounts to be met under this paragraph are—
(a) where the costs are inclusive of any of the items mentioned in paragraph 5(2) of Schedule I to the Housing Benefit (General) Regulations 1987 (payment in respect of fuel charges), the deductions prescribed in that paragraph unless the claimant provides evidence on which the actual or approximate amount of the service charge for fuel may be estimated, in which case the estimated amount;
(b) where the costs are inclusive of ineligible service charges within the meaning of paragraph 1 of Schedule I to the Housing Benefit (General) Regulations 1987 (ineligible service charges) the amounts attributable to those ineligible service charges or where that amount is not separated from or separately identified within the housing costs to be met under this paragraph, such part of the payments made in respect of those housing costs which are fairly attributable to the provision of those ineligible services having regard to the costs of comparable services;

(c) any amount for repairs and improvements, and for this purpose the expression "repairs and improvements" has [⁴¹ the meaning in sub-paragraph (7)].

(3) Where arrangements are made for the housing costs, which are met under this paragraph and which are normally paid for a period of 52 weeks, to be paid instead for a period of 53 weeks, or to be paid irregularly, or so that no such costs are payable or collected in certain periods, or so that the costs for different periods in the year are of different amounts, the weekly amount shall be the amount payable for the year divided by 52.

(4) Where the claimant or the claimant's partner—

(a) pays for reasonable repairs or redecorations to be carried out to the dwelling he occupies; and

(b) that work was not the responsibility of the claimant or his partner; and

(c) in consequence of that work being done, the costs which are normally met under this paragraph are waived, then those costs shall, for a period not exceeding eight weeks, be treated as payable.

(5) Where in England and Wales an amount calculated on a weekly basis in respect of housing costs specified in sub-paragraph (l)(e) (Crown tenants) includes water charges, that amount shall be reduced—

(a) where the amount payable in respect of water charges is known, by that amount;

(b) in any other case, by the amount which would be the likely weekly water charge had the property not been occupied by a Crown tenant.

[¹(6) In this paragraph—

(a) "co-ownership scheme" means a scheme under which a dwelling is let by a housing association and the tenant, or his personal representative, will, under the terms of the tenancy agreement or of the agreement under which he became a member of the association, be entitled, on his ceasing to be a member and subject to any condition stated in either agreement, to a sum calculated by reference directly or indirectly to the value of the dwelling;

(b) "Crown tenant" means a person who occupies a dwelling under a tenancy or licence where the interest of the landlord belongs to Her Majesty in right of the Crown or to a government department or is held in trust for Her Majesty for the purposes of a government department except (in the case of an interest belonging to Her Majesty in right of the Crown) where the interest is under the management of the Crown Estate Commissioners [³⁴ or a relevant person];

(c) "housing association" has the meaning assigned to it by section 1(1) of the Housing Associations Act 1985;

(d) "long tenancy" means a tenancy granted for a term of years certain exceeding twenty one years, whether or not the tenancy is, or may become, terminable before the end of that term by notice given by or to the tenant or by re-entry, forfeiture (or, in Scotland, irritancy) or otherwise and includes a lease for a term fixed by law under a grant with a covenant or obligation for perpetual renewal unless it is a lease by sub-demise from one which is not a long tenancy[³⁴; and

(e) "relevant person", in relation to any property, rights or interests to which section 90B(5) of the Scotland Act 1998 applies, means the person who manages that property or those rights or interests.]]

[⁴¹ (7) For the purposes of sub-paragraph (2)(c), "repairs and improvements" means any of the following measures undertaken with a view to maintaining the fitness of the dwelling for human habitation or, where the dwelling forms part of a building, any part of a building containing that dwelling—

(a) provision of a fixed bath, shower, wash basin, sink or lavatory, and necessary associated plumbing, including the provision of hot water not connected to a central heating system;

(b) repairs to existing heating system;

(c) damp proof measures;

(d) provision of ventilation and natural lighting;

(e) provision of drainage facilities;

(f) provision of facilities for preparing and cooking food;

(g) provision of insulation of the dwelling occupied as the home;

(h) provision of electric lighting and sockets;

(i) provision of storage facilities for fuel or refuse;

(j) repairs of unsafe structural defects;

(k) adapting a dwelling for the special needs of a disabled person; or

(l) provision of separate sleeping accommodation for persons of different sexes aged 10 or over but under the age of 20 who live with the claimant and for whom the claimant or the claimant's partner is responsible.]

Persons residing with the claimant

3.131

14.—(1) Subject to the following provisions of this paragraph, the following deductions from the amount to be met under the preceding paragraphs of this Schedule in respect of housing costs shall be made—

(a) in respect of a non-dependant aged 18 or over who is engaged in any remunerative work, [⁴⁶£116.75];

(b) in respect of a non-dependant aged 18 or over to whom paragraph (a) does not apply, [⁴⁶£18.10].

(2) In the case of a non-dependant aged 18 or over to whom sub-paragraph [⁴(1)(a)] applies because he is in remunerative work, where the claimant satisfies the Secretary of State that the non-dependant's gross weekly income is—

(a) less than [⁴⁶£162.00], the deduction to be made under this paragraph shall be the deduction specified in sub-paragraph [(1)(b)];

(b) not less than [⁴⁶£162.00] but less than [⁴⁶£236.00], the deduction to be made under this paragraph shall be [⁴⁶£41.60];

(c) not less than [⁴⁶£236.00] but less than [⁴⁶£308.00], the deduction to be made under this paragraph shall be [⁴⁶£57.10];

(d) not less than [⁴⁶£308.00] but less than [⁴⁶£410.00], the deduction to be made under this paragraph shall be [⁴⁶£93.40];

(e) not less than [⁴⁶£410.00] but less than [⁴⁶£511.00], the deduction to be made under this paragraph shall be [⁴⁶£106.35].

(3) Only one deduction shall be made under this paragraph in respect of partners and where, but for this sub-paragraph, the amount that would fall to be deducted in respect of one partner is higher than the amount (if any) that would fall to be deducted in respect of the other partner, the higher amount shall be deducted.

(4) In applying the provisions of sub-paragraph (2) in the case of partners, only one deduction shall be made in respect of the partners based on the partners' joint weekly income.

(5) Where a person is a non-dependant in respect of more than one joint occupier of a dwelling (except where the joint occupiers are partners), the deduction in respect of that non-dependant shall be apportioned between the joint occupiers (the amount so apportioned being rounded to the nearest penny) having regard to the number of joint occupiers and the proportion of the housing costs in respect of the dwelling occupied as the home payable by each of them.

(6) No deduction shall be made in respect of any non-dependants occupying the dwelling occupied as the home of the claimant, if the claimant or any partner of his is—

[³² (a) certified as severely sight impaired or blind by a consultant ophthalmologist, or who is within 28 weeks of ceasing to be so certified; or]

(b) receiving in respect of himself either—

(i) an attendance allowance; or

(ii) the care component of the disability living allowance²⁷; [²⁹ ...]

(iii) the daily living component of personal independence payment];[²⁹ [⁴⁵ ...]

[⁴⁵(iiia) the daily living component of adult disability payment; or]

(iv) armed forces independence payment.]

(7) No deduction shall be made in respect of a non-dependant—

(a) if, although he resides with the claimant, it appears to the Secretary of State that the dwelling occupied as his home is normally elsewhere; or

(b) if he is in receipt of a training allowance paid in connection with [²¹ youth training] under section 2 of the Employment and Training Act 1973 or section 2 of the Enterprise and New Towns (Scotland) Act 1990; or

(c) if he is a full-time student during a period of study or, if he is not in remunerative work, during a recognised summer vacation appropriate to his course; or

[²(cc) if he is a full-time student and the claimant or his partner has attained the age of 65;]

(d) if he is aged under 25 and in receipt of income support or an income-based jobseeker's allowance; or

[¹⁴ (dd) in respect of whom a deduction in the calculation of a rent rebate or allowance falls to be made under regulation 55 (non-dependant deductions) of the Housing Benefit (Persons who have attained the qualifying age for state pension credit) Regulations 2006; or]

(e) if he is not residing with the claimant because he has been [¹² an in-patient residing in a hospital or similar institution] for a period in excess of [³52] weeks, or is a prisoner; and in calculating any period of [³52] weeks, any 2 or more distinct periods separated by one or more intervals each not exceeding 28 days shall be treated as a single period [¹⁰; or]

[¹⁰ (f) if he is in receipt of state pension credit;]

[19] (g) if he is aged less than 25 and is in receipt of [27 income-related] employment and support allowance which does not include an amount under section [20 . . .] 4(4) [35 . . .] of the Welfare Reform Act [35 (component) or is not a member of the work-related activity group]] [30; or

    (h) if he is aged less than 25 and is entitled to an award of universal credit which is calculated on the basis that he does not have any earned income;]

(8) In the case of a non-dependant to whom sub-paragraph (1) applies because he is in remunerative work, there shall be disregarded from his gross income—

    [45(a) any attendance allowance, disability living allowance, armed forces independence payment, personal independence payment or adult disability payment received by him;]

    (b) any payment from the Macfarlane Trust, the Macfarlane (Special Payments) Trust, the Macfarlane (Special Payments) (No.2) Trust ("the Trusts"), the Fund, the Eileen Trust [23, MFET Limited] [25, the Skipton Fund, the Caxton Foundation] [37, the Scottish Infected Blood Support Scheme][39, [40 an approved blood scheme], the London Emergencies Trust, the We Love Manchester Emergency Fund] [43, the National Emergencies Trust] or the Independent Living [20 Fund (2006)]; and

[43(ba) any Grenfell Tower payment;]

[44(bb) any child abuse payment;

    (bc) any Windrush payment;]

    (c) any payment in kind;

    [41 (d) any payment made under or by a trust, established for the purpose of giving relief and assistance to disabled persons whose disabilities were caused by the fact that during their mother's pregnancy she had taken a preparation containing the drug known as Thalidomide, and which is approved by the Secretary of State.]

    [30 (9) For the purposes of sub-paragraph (7)(h), "earned income" has the meaning given in regulation 52 of the Universal Credit Regulations 2013.]

Rounding of fractions

    15.—Where any calculation made under this Schedule results in a fraction of a penny, that fraction shall be treated as a penny.

3.132

AMENDMENTS

1. State Pension Credit (Consequential, Transitional and Miscellaneous Provisions) Regulations 2002 (SI 2002/3019) reg.23(l) (October 6, 2003).

2. State Pension Credit (Consequential, Transitional and Miscellaneous Provisions) (No.2) Regulations 2002 (SI 2002/3197) reg.2 and Sch. para.9 (October 6, 2003).

3. Social Security (Hospital In-Patients and Miscellaneous Amendments) Regulations 2002 (SI 2003/1195) reg.8(2) (May 21, 2003).

4. State Pension Credit (Transitional and Miscellaneous Provisions) Amendment Regulations 2003 (SI 2003/2274) reg.2(9)(a) (October 6, 2003).

5. Social Security (Housing Costs Amendments) Regulations 2004 (SI 2004/2825) reg.2(2) (November 28, 2004).

6. Social Security (Housing Costs Amendments) Regulations 2004 (SI 2004/2825) reg.2(3) (November 28, 2004).

7. Social Security (Housing Costs Amendments) Regulations 2004 (SI 2004/2825) reg.2(4) (November 28, 2004).

8. Social Security (Housing Benefit, Council Tax Benefit, State Pension Credit and Miscellaneous Amendments) Regulations 2004 (SI 2004/2327) reg.7(5)(a) (April 4, 2005).

9. Social Security (Housing Benefit, Council Tax Benefit, State Pension Credit and Miscellaneous Amendments) Regulations 2004 (SI 2004/2327) reg.7(5)(b)(i) (April 4, 2005).

10. Social Security (Housing Benefit, Council Tax Benefit, State Pension Credit and Miscellaneous Amendments) Regulations 2004 (SI 2004/2327) reg.7(5)(b)(ii) (April 4, 2005).

11. Social Security (Care Homes and Independent Hospitals) Regulations 2005 (SI 2005/2687) reg.6 and Sch.5 para.5 (October 24, 2005).

12. Social Security (Hospital In-Patients) Regulations 2005 (SI 2005/3360) reg.8(4) (April 10, 2006).

13. Social Security (Young Persons) Amendment Regulations 2006 (SI 2006/718) reg.6(4) (April 10, 2006).

14. Social Security (Miscellaneous Amendments) (No.4) Regulations 2006 (SI 2006/2378) reg.14(5) (October 2, 2006).

15. Social Security (Miscellaneous Amendments) (No.5) Regulations 2006 (SI 2006/3274) reg.4(1) (January 8, 2007).

16. Social Security (Miscellaneous Amendments) (No.5) Regulations 2007 (SI 2007/2618) reg.10(5) (October 1, 2007).

17. Social Security (Housing Costs and Miscellaneous Amendments) Regulations 2007 (SI 2007/3183) reg.5 (December 17, 2007).

18. Social Security (Miscellaneous Amendments) Regulations 2008 (SI 2008/698) reg.5 (April 14, 2008).

19. Employment and Support Allowance (Consequential Provisions) (No.2) Regulations 2008 (SI 2008/1554) reg.4(8) (October 27, 2008).

20. Employment and Support Allowance (Miscellaneous Amendments) Regulations 2008 (SI 2008/2428) reg.41(4) (October 27, 2008).

21. Social Security (Miscellaneous Amendments) (No.6) Regulations 2008 (SI 2008/2767) reg.5(4) (November 17, 2008).

22. Social Security (Miscellaneous Amendments) Regulations 2009 (SI 2009/583) reg.5(4) (April 6, 2009).

23. Social Security (Miscellaneous Amendments) (No.2) Regulations 2010 (SI 2010/641) reg.6(3)(b) (April 6, 2010).

24. Social Security (Housing Costs) (Standard Interest Rate) Amendment Regulations 2010 (SI 2010/1811) reg.2(1)(c) and (2) (October 1, 2010).

25. Social Security (Miscellaneous Amendments) (No.3) Regulations 2011 (2011/2425) reg.15(5) (October 31, 2011).

26. Employment and Support Allowance (Duration of Contributory Allowance) (Consequential Amendments) Regulations 2012 (SI 2012/913) reg.6 (May 1, 2012).

27. Social Security (Miscellaneous Amendments) Regulations 2013 (SI 2013/443) reg.6(3) (April 2, 2013).

28. Personal Independence Payment (Supplementary Provisions and Consequential Amendments) Regulations 2013 (SI 2013/388) reg.8 and Sch. para.27(5) (April 8, 2013).

29. Armed Forces and Reserve Forces Compensation Scheme (Consequential Provisions: Subordinate Legislation) Order 2013 (SI 2013/591) art.7 and Sch. para.23(5) (April 8, 2013).

30. Universal Credit (Consequential, Supplementary, Incidental and Miscellaneous Provisions) Regulations 2013 (SI 2013/630) reg.33(6) (April 29, 2013).

31. Social Security (Miscellaneous Amendments) Regulations 2014 (SI 2014/591) reg.7(6) (April 28, 2014).

32. Universal Credit and Miscellaneous Amendments (No.2) Regulations 2014 (SI 2014/2888) reg.3(4)(b) (November 26, 2014).

33. Shared Parental Leave and Statutory Shared Parental Pay (Consequential Amendments to Subordinate Legislation) Order 2014 (SI 2014/3255) art.10(5) (December 31, 2014).

34. Crown Estate Transfer Scheme 2017 (SI 2017/524) art.8 and Sch.5, para. 94 (April 1, 2017).

35. Employment and Support Allowance and Universal Credit (Miscellaneous Amendments and Transitional and Savings Provisions) Regulations 2017 (SI 2017/204) reg.7(1) and Sch.1, para.5(3) (April 3, 2017).

36. Employment and Support Allowance and Universal Credit (Miscellaneous Amendments and Transitional and Savings Provisions) Regulations 2017 (SI 2017/204) reg.7(1) and Sch.1, para.14 (April 3, 2017).

37. Social Security (Scottish Infected Blood Support Scheme) Regulations 2017 (SI 2017/329) reg.5(3)(a) (April 3, 2017).
38. Social Security Benefits Up-rating Order 2017 (SI 2017/260) art.25(4) and Sch.13 (April 10, 2017).
39. Social Security (Emergency Funds) (Amendment) Regulations 2017 (SI 2017/689) reg.4(3)(a) (June 19, 2017).
40. Social Security (Infected Blood and Thalidomide) Regulations 2017 (SI 2017/870) reg.5(3)(a) and (4) (October 23, 2017).
41. Loans for Mortgage Interest Regulations 2017 (SI 2017/725) reg.18 and Sch.5, para.4 (April 6, 2018).
42. Parental Bereavement Leave and Pay (Consequential Amendments to Subordinate Legislation) Regulations 2020 (SI 2020/354) reg.10(5) (April 6, 2020).
43. Social Security (Income and Capital) (Miscellaneous Amendments) Regulations 2020 (SI 2020/618) reg.4(3) (July 15, 2020).
44. Social Security (Income and Capital Disregards) (Amendment) Regulations 2021 (SI 2021/1405) reg.4(3) (January 1, 2022).
45. Social Security (Disability Assistance for Working Age People) (Consequential Amendments) Order 2022 (SI 2022/177) art.8(4) (March 21, 2022).
46. Social Security Benefits Up-rating Order 2023 (SI 2023/316) art.30(4) (April 10, 2023).

GENERAL NOTE

This Schedule, dealing with housing costs, follows the pattern of the income support scheme (Income Support (General) Regulations 1987 (SI 1987/1967) Sch.3), as now extensively amended (and substituted) by the Loans for Mortgage Interest Regulations 2017 (SI 2017/725). Note that although paras.7–12 were repealed by those Regulations (see Sch.5, para.4(c)), there are transitional rules for existing claimants—see regs 19, 19A and 20 of those Regulations and the commentary in Part IIA of this Volume.   3.133

Paragraph 3
On the application of para.3(b), see *Secretary of State for Work and Pensions v DP* [2009] UKUT 225 (AAC), confirming that "there had to be an immediate threat to the continued occupation of the home, not a theoretical possibility of this happening in the future" (agreeing with *CIS/14/1993*). See further *AH v SSWP* [2010] UKUT 353 (AAC).   3.134

Paragraph 4
The purpose of para.4 is to make it clear that "in general, for the purpose of entitlement to housing costs, a person is only occupying the dwelling normally occupied by him as his home if he is living there": *PJ v Secretary of State for Work and Pensions* (SPC) [2014] UKUT 0152 (AAC) at para.15. The claimant and his wife had moved out of their flat as they could no longer afford the council tax. One of their daughters lived in the flat for a while, and when she was ill the claimant and/or his wife would stay overnight at the flat to look after her. However, they were staying over to care for the daughter in *her* home, and not because it was the *claimant's* home.   3.135

The amendment to para.4(6)(c) made by Social Security (Miscellaneous Amendments) (No.5) Regulations 2006 (SI 2006/3274) reg.4(1) does not apply to any person covered by reg.36(6) of the State Pension Credit (Consequential, Transitional and Miscellaneous Provisions) Regulations 2002 (SI 2002/3019) (i.e. persons entitled to income support immediately before the appointed day). In such cases para.4(6) (c) is to be read as if after "four benefit weeks" there were inserted "from the first day of the benefit week in which the move occurs": Social Security (Miscellaneous Amendments) (No.5) Regulations 2006 (SI 2006/3274) reg.4(2) and (3).

Paragraphs 7–12
Paragraphs 7–12 were repealed by para.4(c) of Sch.5 to the Loans for Mortgage Interest Regulations 2017 (SI 2017/725) subject to transitional rules for existing   3.136

claimants—see regs 19, 19A and 20 of those Regulations and the commentary in Part IIA of this Volume.

Paragraph 13(1)(a): ground rent relating to a long tenancy

3.137   On the meaning of "long tenancy" (see para.(6)(d)) under Scots law, see *NR v Secretary of State for Work and Pensions* [2013] UKUT 0647 (AAC), dealing with the requirement that the tenancy be capable of registration (see also *R(H) 3/07*). Judge J.N. Wright QC held that in principle this requirement did not apply in Scotland, because although a lease for 20 years or more requires to be registered to be effectual against singular successors (i.e. successors in title), under Scots law a tenancy might be enforceable only against the granter. This did not assist the tenant on the facts, as there was no written agreement, and Scots law requires a lease for more than one year to be in writing. The decision also confirms that caravan park periodical fees for mobile homes will normally fall under the housing benefit scheme.

Paragraph 13(1)(b): service charges

3.138   The treatment of service charges for the purposes of entitlement to pension credit was considered by the Commissioner in *R(PC) 1/07*. Tribunals cannot assume that where a proportion of service charges are met by the Supporting People programme, the balance necessarily constitute eligible housing costs under para.13. In *R(PC) 1/07* the evidence before the tribunals lacked "any detail of what the scheme manager did other than in relation to general counselling and support, and nowhere was there any indication of what proportion of his time a scheme manager spent on activities said to relate to the provision of adequate accommodation" (at para.18). The Commissioner agreed:

"with the remark of the Commissioner in paragraph 9 of *CPC/968/2005* that a "broad approach" is called for: for example, a decision-maker or tribunal supplied with the terms of the lease relating to services and service charges, a breakdown of the service charges, details of what service charges (if any) are met by the Supporting People programme, and a statement from the scheme manager as to how his working time is usually divided up should normally be able to make a reasoned estimate of how much of the service charges in dispute are eligible or ineligible. Each case will, however, inevitably turn on its own facts and evidential requirements will vary" (at para.23).

See also *R(PC) 2/08*, which deals with several technical issues concerned with how an award of state pension credit should be adjusted for housing costs after estimated service charges have been finalised.

The case law on the treatment of eligible service charges was considered further in *DL v Secretary of State for Work and Pensions* [2013] AACR 22; [2013] UKUT 29 (AAC). This review of the authorities confirmed that charges for maintenance, repairs, cleaning, and utility charges for communal areas and gardens are eligible (*CIS/1459/1995*); charges for reserve fund contributions for accommodation costs are eligible (*CPC/968/2005* and *CIS/667/2002*); staffing costs fairly attributable to the provision of adequate accommodation based on what the staff actually do in the particular development or similar developments are eligible (*R(PC) 1/07* and *CPC/977/2007*); and other administrative costs, which cannot be neatly categorised, should be apportioned in the same ratio as eligible and non-eligible charges in the rest of the budget (*R(PC) 1/07* and *CPC/968/2005*), rather than in the same ratio as eligible and non-eligible charges in the staff costs budget only (as held in *R(IS) 2/07*).

Paragraph 13(2)(c) and (7): repairs and improvements

3.139   In practice the absence of documentation to support claims for loans taken out to pay for repairs and improvements is often a problem when the work in question was undertaken some years ago. As Judge Lane pointed out in *KWA v Secretary of State for Work and Pensions (SPC)* [2011] UKUT 10 (AAC), "the tribunal cannot pluck figures out of the air" (at para.7). Thus:

"There are two principles which come into play where there is a lack of evidence on an issue. The first is that parties to tribunal proceedings have a duty to cooperate with the tribunal. If a party has not done all that he could reasonably do to provide evidence which lies within his purview, a tribunal is entitled to determine an issue dependent upon that evidence against him: *Kerr v Department for Social Development* [2004] UKHL 23, per Lady Hale of Richmond [62, 63]. The second is that if, at the end of the day, an issue cannot be resolved because of the lack of evidence, it will be decided against the party who had the burden of proving it. In this case, the burden is on the claimant" (at para.8).

Judge Lane also observed that "'repairs and improvements' must be carried out with a view to maintaining fitness for human habitation. That is a low standard. It does not reflect the highest standards of living a person may wish to have. Moreover, the work done is only a repair and improvement if it falls within one of the categories (a)–(l). There is no discretion to award housing costs in relation to works which do not fall within the headings set out" (at para.12).

The scope of para.13(7)(l) (or rather its predecessor, para.12(2)(l), now repealed) was considered by Judge Jacobs in *CPC/2038/2008*. A loan taken out to provide separate sleeping accommodation may be taken out before a child reaches the age of 10 and still be covered by this provision; how far in advance will depend on the circumstances of the particular case (broadly following *CIS/14657/1996* and *CIS/5119/2001* and not following *CIS/1678/1999*).

Regulation 6(6)(d)

[¹ SCHEDULE IIA

ADDITIONAL AMOUNT APPLICABLE FOR CLAIMANTS RESPONSIBLE FOR A CHILD OR QUALIFYING YOUNG PERSON

General
1. This Schedule applies to a claimant who is responsible for a child or qualifying young person.   3.140
2.—(1) In this Schedule—
"child" means a person under the age of 16;
"qualifying young person" has the meaning given in regulation 4A.
(2) Whether a claimant is responsible for a child or qualifying young person for the purposes of this Schedule is determined in accordance with paragraphs 3 to 8.

Child or qualifying young person normally living with the claimant
3.—(1) Subject to sub-paragraph (2), a claimant is responsible for a child or qualifying young person who normally lives with the claimant.   3.141
(2) A claimant is not responsible for a qualifying young person if the two of them are living as a couple.
(3) Where a child or qualifying young person normally lives with two or more persons who are not a couple, only one of them is to be treated as responsible, and that is the person who has the main responsibility for that child or qualifying young person.
(4) The persons referred to in sub-paragraph (3) may jointly nominate for the purposes of this Schedule which of them has the main responsibility for the child or qualifying young person, but the Secretary of State may determine that question—
   (a) if there is no joint nomination; or
   (b) if a nomination or change of nomination does not, in the opinion of the Secretary of State, reflect the arrangements between those persons.

Child or qualifying young person looked after by a local authority
4.—(1) Except where sub-paragraph (3) applies, a claimant is to be treated as not being responsible for a child or qualifying young person during any period when the child or qualifying young person is looked after by a local authority.   3.142
(2) A child or qualifying young person is treated as looked after by a local authority for the purposes of sub-paragraph (1) if that child or qualifying young person is looked after by a local authority within the meaning of section 22 of the Children Act 1989, section 17(6) of the Children (Scotland) Act 1995 or section 74 of the Social Services and Well-being (Wales) Act 2014.

(3) This sub-paragraph applies to any period—

    (a) which is in the nature of a planned short term break, or is one of a series of such breaks, for the purpose of providing respite for the person who normally cares for the child or qualifying young person; or

    (b) during which the child or qualifying young person is placed with, or continues to live with, their parent or a person who has parental responsibility for them.

(4) For the purposes of sub-paragraph (3), a person has parental responsibility if they are not a foster parent and—

    (a) in England and Wales, they have parental responsibility within the meaning of section 3 of the Children Act 1989, or

    (b) in Scotland, they have any or all of the legal responsibilities or rights described in sections 1 or 2 of the Children (Scotland) Act 1995.

Prisoners

3.143   **5.** The claimant is to be treated as not being responsible for a child or qualifying young person during any period when the child or qualifying young person is a prisoner.

Temporary absence in Great Britain

3.144   **6.** A claimant is to be treated as not being responsible for a child or qualifying young person during periods of temporary absence of the child or qualifying young person in Great Britain if the period of absence is likely to exceed 52 weeks, except where there are exceptional circumstances (for example, the child or qualifying young person is in hospital), and the absence is unlikely to be substantially more than 52 weeks.

Temporary absence outside Great Britain

3.145   **7.**—(1) A claimant is to be treated as not being responsible for a child or qualifying young person if the child or qualifying young person is temporarily absent from Great Britain for longer than—

    (a) 4 weeks, or where the absence is expected to exceed 4 weeks;

    (b) where sub-paragraph (2) applies—

        (i) 8 weeks; or

        (ii) where the absence is expected to exceed 8 weeks; or

    (c) where sub-paragraph (3) applies—

        (i) 26 weeks; or

        (ii) where the absence is expected to exceed 26 weeks.

(2) This sub-paragraph applies where the absence of the child or qualifying young person is in connection with the death of—

    (a) the claimant's partner or a child or qualifying young person normally living with the claimant; or

    (b) a close relative of—

        (i) the claimant;

        (ii) the claimant's partner; or

        (iii) a child or qualifying young person normally living with the claimant,

and the Secretary of State considers that it would be unreasonable to expect the child or qualifying young person to return to Great Britain within 4 weeks.

(3) This sub-paragraph applies where the absence of the child or qualifying young person is solely in connection with—

    (a) the child or qualifying young person undergoing—

        (i) treatment for an illness or physical or mental impairment by, or under the supervision of, a qualified practitioner; or

        (ii) medically approved convalescence or care as a result of treatment for an illness or physical or mental impairment, where the child or qualifying young person had that illness or impairment before leaving Great Britain; or

    (b) the child or qualifying young person accompanying the claimant or the claimant's partner for convalescence or care as mentioned in sub-paragraph (a).

(4) In this paragraph—

"medically approved" means certified by a registered medical practitioner;

"qualified practitioner" means a person qualified to provide medical treatment, physiotherapy or a form of treatment which is similar to, or related to, either of those forms of treatment.

Death of child or qualifying young person

3.146   **8.**—(1) If a child or qualifying young person for whom a claimant is responsible dies, the claimant is to be treated as responsible for that child or qualifying young person until—

    (a) the end of the period of eight weeks starting with the day on which the child or qualifying young person dies; or

(b) in the case of a qualifying young person, the date on which he or she would have attained the age of 20, if earlier.

(2) The additional amount applicable to the claimant during the period in which they are treated as responsible for a child or qualifying young person under sub-paragraph (1) is to be calculated in accordance with paragraph 9 on the basis of the circumstances which existed on the day before the day on which the child or qualifying young person died.

Amount of additional payment
9.—(1) The additional amount applicable to a claimant to whom this Schedule applies is—   3.147
  (a) subject to paragraph 10, [⁴£61.88] for each child or qualifying young person; and
  (b) a further amount of—
    (i) [⁴£33.67] where sub-paragraph (2) applies; or
    (ii) [⁴£104.86] where sub-paragraph (3) applies.

(2) This sub-paragraph applies where the claimant is responsible for a child or qualifying young person who is entitled to a disability living allowance [², child disability payment (within the meaning given in regulation 2 of the Disability Assistance for Children and Young People (Scotland) Regulations 2021)] [³, adult disability payment] or personal independence payment.

(3) This sub-paragraph applies where the claimant is responsible for a child or qualifying young person who is—
  (a) entitled to the care component of disability living allowance at the highest rate [³, the daily living component of adult disability payment at the enhanced rate] or the daily living component of personal independence payment at the enhanced rate; or
[²(aa) entitled to the care component of child disability payment at the highest rate in accordance with regulation 11(5) of the Disability Assistance for Children and Young People (Scotland) Regulations 2021; or]
  (b) certified as severely sight impaired or blind by a consultant ophthalmologist.

Amount for the eldest child or qualifying young person born before 6th April 2017
10. In a case where the eldest child or qualifying young person for whom the claimant is   3.148
responsible was born before 6th April 2017, the amount prescribed in paragraph 9(1)(a) in respect of that child or qualifying young person is [⁴£72.31].

AMENDMENTS

1. State Pension Credit (Additional Amount for Child or Qualifying Young Person) (Amendment) Regulations 2018 (SI 2018/676), reg.2(4) (February 1, 2019).
2. Social Security (Scotland) Act 2018 (Disability Assistance for Children and Young People) (Consequential Modifications) Order 2021 (SI 2021/786) art.10 (July 26, 2021).
3. Social Security (Disability Assistance for Working Age People) (Consequential Amendments) Order 2022 (SI 2022/177) art.8(5) (March 21, 2022).
4. Social Security Benefits Up-rating Order 2023 (SI 2023/316) art.30(5) and (6) (April 10, 2023).

DEFINITIONS

"child"—see para.2(1).
"close relative"—see reg.1(2).
"couple"—see *ibid.*
"medically approved"—see para.7(4).
"personal independence payment"—see reg.1(2).
"prisoner"—see *ibid.*
"qualified practitioner"—see para.7(4).
"qualifying young person"—see para.2(1).

GENERAL NOTE

This Schedule sets out the criteria for the award of an additional amount to a state   3.149
pension credit claimant who qualifies for the guarantee credit and has responsibility for a child or qualifying young person (see reg.6(6)(d)). Claimants who receive tax

credits are excluded from entitlement, as this provision is designed to compensate for the abolition of CTC (see reg.6(11)–(17)).

Paragraph 2

3.150   This paragraph applies the standard definitions, so a "child" means someone under the age of 16, while "qualifying young person" (QYP) is a person who has reached the age of 16 but not the age of 20, and has enrolled or been accepted in full-time, non-advanced education or approved training before the age of 19 (see reg.4A).

Paragraph 3

3.151   A person is treated as responsible for a child or QYP who normally lives with them (but not if they are living together with a QYP as a couple). In cases where a child or QYP resides with two or more people who are not a couple, only one person can be treated as responsible for a child or QYP, namely the person who has the "main responsibility". They may nominate which of them has the main responsibility. If they cannot agree, or where it is considered that the nomination does not reflect the arrangements for the child or QYP, the Secretary of State has the discretion to decide who has main responsibility. These rules broadly reflect those that apply to universal credit, albeit with some minor drafting differences: see UC Regs 2013 reg.4(2)–(5).

Paragraph 4

3.152   A person is to be treated as *not* responsible for a child or QYP during any period for which the child or QYP is looked after by a local authority. This is subject to exceptions for planned short term breaks (or one of a series of such breaks) for the purpose of providing the responsible person with a respite period. There is also an exception for periods where the child or QYP is placed with (or continues to live with) their parent or a person who has parental responsibility for them. These rules reflect those that apply to universal credit: see UC Regs 2013 reg.4A.

Paragraph 5

3.153   A person cannot be treated as responsible for a child or QYP for any time that the child or QYP is a prisoner, as defined by reg.1(2).

Paragraphs 6 and 7

3.154   A claimant is treated as not responsible for a child or QYP if they are away from the claimant and the absence is likely to exceed a specified period. Paragraph 6 deals with temporary absences of the child or QYP *in* Great Britain while para.7 deals with temporary absences *outside* Great Britain.

Where a child or QYP is absent from the claimant but remains within Great Britain, the claimant can be treated as responsible for them as long as the absence is not expected to be for more than 52 weeks (para.6). If it was known at the start of the absence that it will exceed 52 weeks, responsibility ceases from the start of the absence, unless there are exceptional circumstances (e.g. that the child or QYP is in hospital and the absence is not expected to be substantially longer than 52 weeks).

If the absence is outside Great Britain, then the length of time for which a claimant is treated as responsible varies according to the circumstances as detailed by para.7.

Paragraph 8

3.155   Where a child or QYP dies, there is a run-on period of 8 weeks, to allow the claimant time to adjust to their new circumstances, thus aligning provision with the rules for housing benefit.

Paragraphs 9 and 10

3.156   These paragraphs set out the relevant weekly rates, depending on the circumstances of the child or QYP.

Regulation 8

SCHEDULE III

SPECIAL GROUPS

Polygamous marriages

1.—(1) The provisions of this paragraph apply in any case to which section 12 (polygamous marriages) applies if the claimant is taken to be "the person in question" for the purposes of that section.

(2) The following provision shall apply instead of section 3(1)—

"(1) The first condition is that, if the claimant is taken [¹ . . .] to be "the person in question" for the purposes of section 12 (polygamous marriages)—
(a) the case is one to which that section applies; and
(b) any one or more of the persons falling within subsection (1)(c) of that section [¹² has attained pensionable age before 6 April 2016 and] has attained the age of 65 [¹² (before, on or after that date)].".

(3) The following provision shall apply instead of section 4(1)—

"(1) A claimant is not entitled to state pension credit if, taking the claimant to be 'the person in question' for the purposes of section 12 (polygamous marriages)—
(a) the case is one to which that section applies; and
(b) any one or more of the other persons falling within subsection (1)(c) of that section is entitled to state pension credit.".

(4) The following provision shall apply instead of section 5—

"**5.**—**Income and capital of claimant, spouses, etc.**

(1) This section applies in any case to which section 12 (polygamous marriages) applies if the claimant is taken to be 'the person in question' for the purposes of that section.

(2) In any such case, the income and capital of each of the other persons falling within subsection (1)(c) of that section shall be treated for the purposes of this Act as income and capital of the claimant, except where regulations provide otherwise.".

(5) In regulation 6 (amount of the guarantee credit), for paragraph (1) there shall be substituted—

"(1) Except as provided in the following provisions of these Regulations, in a case to which section 12 (polygamous marriages) applies if the claimant is taken to be 'the person in question' for the purposes of that section the standard minimum guarantee is the sum of—
(a) [¹³£306.85] per week in respect of the claimant and any one spouse of the claimant's; and
(b) [¹³£105.80] per week in respect of for each additional spouse (whether of the claimant or that spouse) who falls within section 12(1)(c).".

(6) The maximum savings credit shall be determined on the assumption that the standard minimum guarantee is the amount prescribed for partners under regulation 6(1)(a).

(7) In regulation 7 (savings credit) for paragraph (2) there shall be substituted—

"(2) In any case to which section 12 (polygamous marriages) [²applies] if the claimant is taken to be 'the person in question' for the purposes of that section, the amount prescribed for the savings credit threshold is [¹³£277.12]."

[¹¹ (7A) The following provision shall apply instead of regulation 7A (limitation of savings credit for certain mixed-age couples)—

"**7A.**—(1) This regulation applies if, taking the claimant to be the person in question for the purposes of section 12 (polygamous marriages),—
(a) the case is one to which that section applies; and
(b) at least one of the persons falling within subsection (1)(c) of that section had attained pensionable age before 6 April 2016 and at least one of those persons had not.

(2) Where this regulation applies, the claimant is not entitled to a savings credit unless the claimant—

3.157

887

(a) has been awarded a savings credit with effect from a day before 6 April 2016 and was entitled to a savings credit immediately before that date; and
(b) remained entitled to a savings credit at all times since the beginning of 6 April 2016."]

(8) In regulations [¹⁰ 3, [⁶. . .],5, [¹6(8),] 10,12 and 14 and in paragraph [³6(5)(b)(v)] of Schedule 1 and in Schedule 2, any reference to a partner includes also a reference to any additional spouse to whom this paragraph applies.

(9) For the purposes of regulation 6(5)(a) and (b), paragraph 1(1)(b)(i) of Part I of Schedule I is satisfied only if both partners and each additional spouse to whom this paragraph applies are in receipt of attendance allowance [⁸, the care component of disability living allowance at the highest or middle rate prescribed in accordance with section 72(3) of the 1992 Act [¹²,] the daily living component of personal independence payment at the standard or enhanced rate in accordance with section 78(3) of the 2012 Act [¹², the daily living component of adult disability payment at the standard or enhanced rate in accordance with regulation 5 of the Disability Assistance for Working Age People (Scotland) Regulations 2022] [⁹ or armed forces independence payment]].

(10) For the purposes of regulation 6(5)(a), paragraph 1(1)(c) of Part I of Schedule 1 is only satisfied if—
    (a) both partners and each additional spouse to whom this paragraph applies all fall within either paragraph 1(1)(c)(i) or paragraph 1(1)(c)(ii); and
    (b) at least one of them falls within paragraph 1(1)(c)(i); and
    (c) at least one of them falls within paragraph 1(1)(c)(ii) but not paragraph 1(1)(c)(i); and
    (d) either paragraph 1(1)(c)(iv) is satisfied or a person is entitled to and in receipt of an allowance under section 70 of the 1992 Act in respect of caring for one or more, but not all, the persons who fall within paragraph 1(1)(c)(i).

(11) Any reference in this paragraph to an additional spouse to whom this paragraph applies is a reference to any person who is an additional spouse (whether of the claimant's or of a spouse of the claimant's) falling within subsection (1)(c) of section 12 if the claimant is taken to be "the person in question" for the purposes of that section.

Persons serving a sentence of imprisonment detained in hospital

3.158   [⁴2. —[⁷ (1) Sub-paragraph (2) applies in the case of a claimant ("C") who satisfies either of the following conditions.
    (1A) The first condition is that—
    (a) C is being detained under section 45A or 47 of the Mental Health Act 1983 (power of higher courts to direct hospital admission; removal to hospital of persons serving sentences of imprisonment etc.); and
    (b) in any case where there is in relation to C a release date within the meaning of section 50(3) of that Act, C is being detained on or before the day which the Secretary of State certifies to be that release date.
    (1B) The second condition is that C is being detained under—
    (a) section 59A of the Criminal Procedure (Scotland) Act 1995 (hospital direction); or
    (b) section 136 of the Mental Health (Care and Treatment) (Scotland) Act 2003 (transfer of prisoners for treatment of mental disorder).]
    (2) In the case of a claimant to whom paragraph (1) applies—
    (a) section 2(3) has effect with the substitution of a reference to a nil amount for the reference to the standard minimum guarantee in paragraph (a) [⁵, and [¹¹ nil] is the prescribed additional amount for the purposes of paragraph (b)] and
    (b) the maximum amount of savings credit shall be taken to be [¹¹ nil]].

AMENDMENTS

1. State Pension Credit (Consequential, Transitional and Miscellaneous Provisions) Regulations 2002 (SI 2002/3019) reg.23(m) (October 6, 2003).
2. State Pension Credit (Consequential, Transitional and Miscellaneous Provisions) (No.2) Regulations 2002 (SI 2002/3197) reg.2 and Sch. para.10 (October 6, 2003).
3. State Pension Credit (Transitional and Miscellaneous Provisions) Amendment Regulations 2003 (SI 2003/2274) reg.2(10) (October 6, 2003).
4. Social Security (Hospital In-Patients) Regulations 2005 (SI 2005/3360) reg.8(5) (April 10, 2006).
5. Social Security (Miscellaneous Amendments) Regulations 2006 (SI 2006/588) reg.4(4) (April 10, 2006).

6. Social Security (Miscellaneous Amendments) (No.4) Regulations 2008 (SI 2008/2424) reg.3(5) (October 6, 2008).

7. Social Security (Persons Serving a Sentence of Imprisonment Detained in Hospital) Regulations 2010 (SI 2010/442) reg.4(2) (March 25, 2010).

8. Personal Independence Payment (Supplementary Provisions and Consequential Amendments) Regulations 2013 (SI 2013/388) reg.8 and Sch. para.27(6) (April 8, 2013).

9. Armed Forces and Reserve Forces Compensation Scheme (Consequential Provisions: Subordinate Legislation) Order 2013 (SI 2013/591) art.7 and Sch. para.23(6) (April 8, 2013).

10. Housing Benefit and State Pension Credit (Temporary Absence) (Amendment) Regulations 2016 (SI 2016/624) reg.4(8) (July 28, 2016).

11. Social Security (Miscellaneous Amendments No. 5) Regulations 2017 (SI 2017/1187) reg.5(3) (December 21, 2017).

12. Social Security (Disability Assistance for Working Age People) (Consequential Amendments) Order 2022 (SI 2022/177) art.8(6) (March 21, 2022).

13. Social Security Benefits Up-rating Order 2023 (SI 2023/316) art.30(7) (April 10, 2023).

GENERAL NOTE

Paragraph 2
This paragraph was amended with effect from March 25, 2010 in response to the   3.159
Court of Appeal's decision in *R. (on the application of D & M) v Secretary of State for Work and Pensions* [2010] EWCA Civ 18. The Court of Appeal had held that the previous wording meant that a person subject to an indeterminate sentence of imprisonment who was being detained in hospital for treatment for mental disorder would be eligible for DWP benefits when the tariff part of the sentence had been served. This was regarded as contrary to Government policy. The amended paragraph provides a revised form of words which is intended to ensure that such a person continues to be excluded from benefits when the tariff date has passed.

Regulation 12

[¹ SCHEDULE IIIA

Date on which certain fixed length assessed income periods end

Column 1 *Period in which the assessed income period would end apart from regulation 12(d)*	Column 2 *Date on which assessed income period is to end*	3.160
1st April 2019 to 14th April 2019	14th July 2016	
15th April 2019 to 30th April 2019	28th July 2016	
1st May 2019 to 14th May 2019	14th August 2016	
15th May 2019 to 31st May 2019	28th August 2016	
1st June 2019 to 14th June 2019	14th October 2016	
15th June 2019 to 30th June 2019	28th October 2016	
1st July 2019 to 14th July 2019	14th November 2016	
15th July 2019 to 31st July 2019	28th November 2016	
1st August 2019 to 14th August 2019	14th December 2016	
15th August 2019 to 31st August 2019	28th December 2016	
1st September 2019 to 14th September 2019	14th February 2017	
15th September 2019 to 30th September 2019	28th February 2017	
1st October 2019 to 14th October 2019	14th March 2017	
15th October 2019 to 31st October 2019	28th March 2017	
1st November 2019 to 14th November 2019	14th April 2017	
15th November 2019 to 30th November 2019	28th April 2017	

Column 1 *Period in which the assessed income period would end apart from regulation 12(d)*	Column 2 *Date on which assessed income period is to end*
1st December 2019 to 14th December 2019	14th June 2017
15th December 2019 to 31st December 2019	28th June 2017
1st January 2020 to 14th January 2020	14th July 2017
15th January 2020 to 31st January 2020	28th July 2017
1st February 2020 to 14th February 2020	14th September 2017
15th February 2020 to 29th February 2020	28th September 2017
1st March 2020 to 14th March 2020	14th October 2017
15th March 2020 to 31st March 2020	28th October 2017
1st April 2020 to 14th April 2020	14th December 2017
15th April 2020 to 30th April 2020	28th December 2017
1st May 2020 to 14th May 2020	14th January 2018
15th May 2020 to 31st May 2020	28th January 2018
1st June 2020 to 14th June 2020	14th March 2018
15th June 2020 to 30th June 2020	28th March 2018
1st July 2020 to 14th July 2020	14th April 2018
15th July 2020 to 31st July 2020	28th April 2018
1st August 2020 to 14th August 2020	14th June 2018
15th August 2020 to 31st August 2020	28th June 2018
1st September 2020 to 14th September 2020	14th July 2018
15th September 2020 to 30th September 2020	28th July 2018
1st October 2020 to 14th October 2020	14th August 2018
15th October 2020 to 31st October 2020	28th August 2018
1st November 2020 to 14th November 2020	14th October 2018
15th November 2020 to 30th November 2020	28th October 2018
1st December 2020 to 14th December 2020	14th November 2018
15th December 2020 to 31st December 2020	28th November 2018
1st January 2021 to 14th January 2021	14th January 2019
15th January 2021 to 31st January 2021	28th January 2019
1st February 2021 to 14th February 2021	14th February 2019
15th February 2021 to 28th February 2021	28th February 2019
1st March 2021 to 14th March 2021	14th March 2019
15th March 2021 to 5th April 2021	28th March 2019]

AMENDMENT

1. State Pension Credit (Amendment) Regulations 2015 (SI 2015/1529) reg.2(4) (April 6, 2016).

GENERAL NOTE

3.161   See the notes to reg.12 above and to s.2(6) of the State Pension Credit Act 2002.

Regulation 17(7)

SCHEDULE IV

AMOUNTS TO BE DISREGARDED IN THE CALCULATION OF INCOME OTHER THAN EARNINGS

3.162   **1.**—In addition to any sum which falls to be disregarded in accordance with paragraphs 3 to 6, £10 of any of the following, namely—

(a) a war disablement pension (except insofar as such a pension falls to be disregarded under paragraph 2 or 3);

(b) a war widow's or war widower's pension;

[⁷ (ba) unless paragraph 1(a) or (b) applies, any payment described in regulation 15(5)(ac) (except insofar as such a payment falls to be disregarded under paragraph 2 or 3);]

(c) a pension payable to a person as a [⁶ widow, widower or surviving civil partner] under [⁷. . .]any power of Her Majesty other wise than under an enactment to make provision about pensions for or in respect of persons who have been disabled or have died in consequence of service as members of the armed forces of the Crown;

[⁴ (cc) a guaranteed income payment] [⁷ and, if the amount of that payment has been abated to less than £10 by a [⁸ pension or payment falling within article 31(1)(a) or (b) of the Armed Forces and Reserve Forces (Compensation Scheme) Order 2005], so much of [⁸ that pension or payment] as would not, in aggregate with the amount of [⁸ any] guaranteed income payment disregarded, exceed £10];

(d) a payment made to compensate for the non-payment of such a pension [⁴ or payment] as is mentioned in any of the preceding sub-paragraphs;

(e) a pension paid by the government of a country outside Great Britain which is analogous to any of the [⁴ pensions or payments mentioned in sub-paragraphs (a) to (cc) above];

[⁹ (f) a pension paid by a government to victims of National Socialist persecution.]

2.—The whole of any amount included in a pension to which paragraph 1 relates in respect of—

(a) the claimant's need for constant attendance;

(b) the claimant's exceptionally severe disablement.

3.—Any mobility supplement under [⁷ article 20 of the Naval, Military and Air Forces Etc. (Disablement and Death) Service Pensions Order 2006] (including such a supplement by virtue of any other scheme or order) or under article 25A of the Personal Injuries (Civilians) Scheme 1983 or any payment intended to compensate for the non-payment of such a supplement.

[⁷ **4.**—Any supplementary pension under article 23(2) of the Naval, Military and Air Forces Etc. (Disablement and Death) Service Pensions Order 2006 (pensions to surviving spouses and surviving civil partners) and any analogous payment made by the Secretary of State for Defence to any person who is not a person entitled under that Order.]

5.—In the case of a pension awarded at the supplementary rate under article 27(3) of the Personal Injuries (Civilians) Scheme 1983 (pensions to [⁶ widows, widowers or surviving civil partners]), the sum specified in paragraph 1(c) of Schedule 4 to that Scheme.

6.—(1) Any payment which is—

(a) made under any of the Dispensing Instruments to a [⁶ widow, widower or surviving civil partner] of a person—

(i) whose death was attributable to service in a capacity analogous to service as a member of the armed forces of the Crown; and

(ii) whose service in such capacity terminated before 31st March 1973; and

[⁷ (b) equal to the amount specified in article 23(2) of the Naval, Military and Air Forces Etc. (Disablement and Death) Service Pensions Order 2006.]

(2) In this paragraph "the Dispensing Instruments" means the Order in Council of 19th December 1881, the Royal Warrant of 27th October 1884 and the Order by His Majesty of 14th January 1922 (exceptional grants of pay, non-effective pay and allowances).

7.—£10 of any widowed parent's allowance to which the claimant is entitled under section 39A of the 1992 Act.

[²7A.—£10 of any widowed mother's allowance to which the claimant is entitled under section 37 of the 1992 Act.]

8.—(1) Where the claimant occupies a dwelling as his home and he provides in that dwelling board and lodging accommodation, an amount, in respect of each person for whom such accommodation is provided for the whole or any part of a week, equal to—

(a) where the aggregate of any payments made in respect of any one week in respect of such accommodation provided to such person does not exceed £20.00, 100 per cent of such payments; or

(b) where the aggregate of any such payments exceeds £20.00, £20.00 and 50 per cent of the excess over £20.00.

(2) [⁵ . . .]

9.—If the claimant—

(a) owns the freehold or leasehold interest in any property or is a tenant of any property; and

(b) occupies a part of that property; and

(c) has an agreement with another person allowing that person to occupy another part of that property on payment of rent and—

(i) the amount paid by that person is less than £20 per week, the whole of that amount; or

(ii) the amount paid is £20 or more per week, £20.

10.—Where a claimant receives income under an annuity purchased with a loan, which satisfies the following conditions—

(a) that the loan was made as part of a scheme under which not less than 90% of the proceeds of the loan were applied to the purchase by the person to whom it was made of an annuity ending with his life or with the life of the survivor of two or more persons

The State Pension Credit Regs 2002

(in this paragraph referred to as "the annuitants") who include the person to whom the loan was made;

(b) that at the time the loan was made the person to whom it was made or each of the annuitants had attained the age of 65;

(c) that the loan was secured on a dwelling in Great Britain and the person to whom the loan was made or one of the annuitants owns an estate or interest in that dwelling;

(d) that the person to whom the loan was made or one of the annuitants occupies the dwelling on which it was secured as his home at the time the interest is paid; and

(e) that the interest payable on the loan is paid by the person to whom the loan was made or by one of the annuitants,

the amount, calculated on a weekly basis, equal to—

(i) where, or insofar as, section 369 of the Income and Corporation Taxes Act 1988 (mortgage interest payable under deduction of tax) applies to the payments of interest on the loan, the interest which is payable after deduction of a sum equal to income tax on such payments at the applicable percentage of income tax within the meaning of section 369(1A) of that Act;

(ii) in any other case the interest which is payable on the loan without deduction of such a sum.

11.—(1) Any payment, other than a payment to which sub-paragraph (2) applies, made to the claimant by Trustees in exercise of a discretion exercisable by them.

(2) This sub-paragraph applies to payments made to the claimant by Trustees in exercise of a discretion exercisable by them for the purpose of—

(a) obtaining food, ordinary clothing or footwear or household fuel;

(b) the payment of rent, council tax or water charges for which that claimant or his partner is liable;

(c) meeting housing costs of a kind specified in Schedule 2;

(d) [¹. . .].

(3) In a case to which sub-paragraph (2) applies, £20 or—

(a) if the payment is less than £20, the whole payment; or

(b) if, in the claimant's case, £10 is disregarded in accordance with paragraph 1(a) to (f), [¹ or paragraph 7] [² or 7A] £10 or the whole payment if it is less than £10.

(4) For the purposes of this paragraph—

"ordinary clothing and footwear" means clothing or footwear for normal daily use, but does not include school uniforms, or clothing and footwear used solely for sporting activities; and

"rent" means eligible rent for the purposes of the Housing Benefit (General) Regulations 1987 less any deductions in respect of non-dependants which fall to be made under regulation 63 (non-dependant deductions) of those Regulations.

12.—Any increase in [⁷ pension or allowance under Part 2 or 3 of the Naval, Military and Air Forces Etc. (Disablement and Death) Service Pensions Order 2006] paid in respect of a dependent other than the pensioner's [⁷ . . .] [⁶ partner].

13.—Any payment ordered by a court to be made to the claimant or the claimant's partner in consequence of any accident, injury or disease suffered by [²the person] to whom the payments are made.

14.—Periodic payments made to the claimant or the claimant's partner under an agreement entered into in [² . . .] settlement of a claim made by [² that person] for an injury suffered by him.

15.—Any income which is payable outside the United Kingdom for such period during which there is a prohibition against the transfer to the United Kingdom of that income.

16.—Any banking charges or commission payable in converting to Sterling payments of income made in a currency other than Sterling.

17.—[⁷ . . .]

[³18. Except in the case of income from capital specified in Part II of Schedule V, any actual income from capital.]

AMENDMENTS

1. State Pension Credit (Consequential, Transitional and Miscellaneous Provisions) Regulations 2002 (SI 2002/3019) reg.23(n) (October 6, 2003).

2. State Pension Credit (Consequential, Transitional and Miscellaneous Provisions) (No.2) Regulations 2002 (SI 2002/3197) reg.2 and Sch. para.11 (October 6, 2003).

3. State Pension Credit (Transitional and Miscellaneous Provisions) Amendment Regulations 2003 (SI 2003/2274) reg.2(11) (October 6, 2003).

4. Social Security (Miscellaneous Amendments) Regulations 2005 (SI 2005/574) reg.2(7) and (8)(d) (April 4, 2005).
5. Social Security (Miscellaneous Amendments) (No.2) Regulations 2005 (SI 2005/2465) reg.6(5) (October 3, 2005).
6. Civil Partnership (Pensions, Social Security and Child Support) (Consequential, etc. Provisions) Order 2005 (SI 2005/2877) art.2(3) and Sch.3 para.35(4) (December 5, 2005).
7. Social Security (Miscellaneous Amendments) (No.7) Regulations 2008 (SI 2008/3157) reg.4(5) (January 5, 2009).
8. Social Security (Miscellaneous Amendments) (No.4) Regulations 2009 (SI 2009/2655) reg.5(5) (October 26, 2009).
9. Social Security (Income-Related Benefits) Amendment Regulations 2017 (2017/174) reg.4(2) (March 20, 2017).

GENERAL NOTE

This Schedule performs the same function in relation to state pension credit as Sch.9 to the Income Support (General) Regulations 1987 (SI 1987/1967) (see Vol.V of this series) does in the context of income support, although the list of disregards is much less extensive (reflecting the different nature of state pension credit).   **3.163**

Paragraph 1
See Income Support (General) Regulations 1987 (SI 1987/1967) Sch.9 para.16 (although that also includes widowed mother's allowance and widowed parent's allowance: see para.(7)).   **3.164**

Paragraph 3
See Income Support (General) Regulations 1987 (SI 1987/1967) Sch.9 para.8.   **3.165**

Paragraphs 4–6
See Income Support (General) Regulations 1987 (SI 1987/1967) Sch.9 paras 54–56.   **3.166**

Paragraphs 7–7A
See Income Support (General) Regulations 1987 (SI 1987/1967) Sch.9 para.16(g) and (h).   **3.167**

Paragraph 8
See Income Support (General) Regulations 1987 (SI 1987/1967) Sch.9 para.20.   **3.168**

Paragraph 9
This is a more generous provision than the nearest equivalent under the income support scheme. Income Support (General) Regulations 1987 (SI 1987/1967) Sch.9 para.19 provides that, for the purposes of income support, only the first £4 a week of income from a sub-tenant is disregarded (plus a slightly larger prescribed figure where the rent charged includes an amount for heating). This provision grants a state pension credit claimant in similar circumstances a disregard of up to £20 a week on payments from a sub-tenant or licensee.   **3.169**

Paragraph 10
See Income Support (General) Regulations 1987 (SI 1987/1967) Sch.9 para.17.   **3.170**

Paragraph 11
See Income Support (General) Regulations 1987 (SI 1987/1967) Sch.9 para.15 for the closest equivalent under the income support scheme.   **3.171**

Paragraphs 13–14
These are more generous rules than apply to income support. The rule there is that sums paid by way of personal injuries compensation and held under a trust are disregarded as capital (Income Support (General) Regulations 1987   **3.172**

(SI 1987/1967) Sch.10 para.12), but payments made out of the fund to the claimant count as income or capital in the normal way. The rule for state pension credit is that payments made in compensation for personal injuries under a court order or following a settlement do not count as income. The repeal of the word "final" in the first amendment to para.14 (so that it reads "in settlement of" and not "in final settlement of ") presumably ensures that the benefit of this provision will be gained by pensioners who receive provisional awards of personal injuries damages under the Supreme Court Act 1981 s.32A.

Paragraphs 15–16

3.173   See Income Support (General) Regulations 1987 (SI 1987/1967) Sch.9 paras 23–24.

Regulation 17(8)

SCHEDULE V

INCOME FROM CAPITAL

PART I

Capital disregarded for the purpose of calculating income

3.174   1.—Any premises acquired for occupation by the claimant which he intends to occupy as his home within 26 weeks of the date of acquisition or such longer period as is reasonable in the circumstances to enable the claimant to obtain possession and commence occupation of the premises.

[³ 1A.—The dwelling occupied by the claimant as his home but only one home shall be disregarded under this paragraph.]

2.—Any premises which the claimant intends to occupy as his home, and in respect of which he is taking steps to obtain possession and has sought legal advice, or has commenced legal proceedings, with a view to obtaining possession, for a period of 26 weeks from the date on which he first sought such advice or first commenced such proceedings whichever is the earlier, or such longer period as is reasonable in the circumstances to enable him to obtain possession and commence occupation of those premises.

3.—Any premises which the claimant intends to occupy as his home to which essential repairs or alterations are required in order to render them fit for such occupation, for a period of 26 weeks from the date on which the claimant first takes steps to effect those repairs or alterations, or such longer period as is necessary to enable those repairs or alterations to be carried out.

4.—Any premises occupied in whole or in part—

  (a)   by a [⁶ person who is a close relative, grandparent, grandchild, uncle, aunt, nephew or niece of the claimant or of his partner] as his home where that person [¹⁸ has attained the qualifying age for state pension credit or is incapacitated];

  (b)   by the former partner of the claimant as his home; but this provision shall not apply where the former partner is a person from whom the claimant is estranged or divorced [⁹ or with whom he had formed a civil partnership that has been dissolved].

5.—Any future interest in property of any kind, other than land or premises in respect of which the claimant has granted a subsisting lease or tenancy, including sub-leases or sub-tenancies.

6.—(1) Where a claimant has ceased to occupy what was formerly the dwelling occupied as the home following his estrangement or divorce from [⁹, or dissolution of his civil partnership with,] his former partner, that dwelling for a period of 26 weeks from the date on which he ceased to occupy that dwelling or, where the dwelling is occupied as the home by the former partner who is a lone parent, for so long as it is so occupied.

(2) In this paragraph—

  (a)   "dwelling" includes any garage, garden and outbuildings, which were formerly occupied by the claimant as his home and any premises not so occupied which it is impracticable or unreasonable to sell separately, in particular, in Scotland, any croft land on which the dwelling is situated;

  (b)   "lone parent" means a person who has no partner and who is responsible for, and a member of the same household as, a child; and

  (c)   "child" means a person [¹² who is a qualifying young person [³¹ within the meaning of regulation 4A] or] a child [³¹ as defined in section 40 of the 2012 Act].

7.—Any premises where the claimant is taking reasonable steps to dispose of the whole of his interest in those premises, for a period of 26 weeks from the date on which he first took such steps, or such longer period as is reasonable in the circumstances to enable him to dispose of those premises.

8.—All personal possessions.

9.—The assets of any business owned in whole or in part by the claimant and for the purposes of which he is engaged as a self-employed earner or, if he has ceased to be engaged, for such period as may be reasonable in the circumstances to allow for disposal of those assets.

[¹**9A.**—The assets of any business owned in whole or in part by the claimant if—
  (a) he is not engaged as a self-employed earner in that business by reason of some disease or bodily or mental disablement; but
  (b) he intends to become engaged (or, as the case may be, re-engaged) as a self-employed earner in that business as soon as he recovers or is able to become engaged, or re-engaged, in that business,
    [³ . . .].]

10.—The surrender value of any policy of life insurance.

11.—The value of any funeral plan contract; and for this purpose, "funeral plan contract" means a contract under which—
  (a) the claimant makes one or more payments to another person ("the provider");
  (b) the provider undertakes to provide, or secure the provision of, a funeral in the United Kingdom for the claimant on his death; and
  (c) the sole purpose of the plan is to provide or secure the provision of a funeral for the claimant on his death.

12.—Where an ex-gratia payment has been made by the Secretary of State on or after 1st February 2001 in consequence of the imprisonment or [²internment] of—
  (a) the claimant;
  (b) the claimant's partner;
  (c) the claimant's deceased spouse [⁹ or deceased civil partner]; or
  (d) the claimant's partner's deceased spouse [⁹ or deceased civil partner],
by the Japanese during the Second World War, an amount equal to that payment.

13.—(1) Subject to sub-paragraph (2), the amount of any trust payment made to a claimant or a claimant's partner [³ who is]—
  (a) [³ . . .] a diagnosed person;
  (b) [³a diagnosed person's partner or] was a diagnosed person's partner at the time of the diagnosed person's death;
  (c) [³ . . .] a parent of a diagnosed person, a person acting in place of the diagnosed person's parents or a person who was so acting at the date of the diagnosed person's death.

(2) Where [³ a trust payment is made to]—
  (a) [³ a person referred to in sub-paragraph (1)(a) or (b), that sub-paragraph] shall apply for the period beginning on the date on which the trust is made and ending on the date on which [³ that person] dies;
  (b) [³ a person referred to in sub-paragraph (1)(c), that sub-paragraph] shall apply for the period beginning on the date on which the trust payment is made and ending two years after that date.

(3) Subject to sub-paragraph (4), the amount of any payment by a person to whom a trust payment has been made or of any payment out of the estate of a person to whom a trust payment has been made, which is made to a claimant or a claimant's partner [³ who is]—
  (a) [³ . . .] the diagnosed person;
  (b) [³ a diagnosed person's partner or] was a diagnosed person's partner at the date of the diagnosed person's death; or
  (c) [³ . . .] a parent of a diagnosed person, a person acting in place of the diagnosed person's parents or a person who was so acting at the date of the diagnosed person's death.

(4) Where [³ a payment referred to in sub-paragraph (3) is made to]—
  (a) [³ a person referred to in sub-paragraph (3)(a) or (b), that sub-paragraph] shall apply for the period beginning on the date on which the payment is made and ending on the date on which [³ that person] dies;
  (b) [³ a person referred to in sub-paragraph (3)(c), that sub-paragraph] shall apply for the period beginning on the date on which the payment is made and ending two years after that date.

(5) In this paragraph, a reference to a person—
  (a) being the diagnosed person's partner;

(b) acting in place of the diagnosed person's parents,
at the date of the diagnosed person's death shall include a person who would have been such a person or a person who would have been so acting, but for the diagnosed person [⁸ residing in a care home or independent hospital].

(6) In this paragraph—

"diagnosed person" means a person who has been diagnosed as suffering from, or who, after his death, has been diagnosed as having suffered from, variant [³ Creutzfeldt]-Jakob disease;

"relevant trust" means a trust established out of funds provided by the Secretary of State in respect of persons who suffered, or who are suffering, from variant [³ Creutzfeldt]-Jakob disease for the benefit of persons eligible for payments in accordance with its provisions;

"trust payment" means a payment under a relevant trust.

14.—[¹⁶ (1)] The amount of any payment, other than a war disablement pension or a war widow's or widower's pension, to compensate for the fact that the claimant, the claimant's partner, the claimant's deceased spouse [⁹ or deceased civil partner] or the claimant's partner's deceased spouse [⁹ or deceased civil partner]—

(a) was a slave labourer or a forced labourer;

(b) had suffered property loss or had suffered personal injury; or

(c) was a parent of a child who had died, during the Second World War.

[¹⁶ (2) In sub-paragraph (1), "war disablement pension" and "war widow's or widower's pension" include any payment described in regulation 15(5)(ac).]

15.—(1) Any payment made under [²⁰ or by] the Macfarlane Trust, the Macfarlane (Special Payments) Trust, the Macfarlane (Special Payments) (No.2) Trust ("the Trusts"), the Fund, the Eileen Trust [¹⁹, MFET Limited] [⁴, the [¹⁵ Independent Living Fund (2006)] [¹⁰, the Skipton Fund [²¹, the Caxton Foundation] [³³, the Scottish Infected Blood Support Scheme] [³⁵, [³⁶ an approved blood scheme], the London Emergencies Trust, the We Love Manchester Emergency Fund] [⁴², the National Emergencies Trust] or the London Bombings Relief Charitable Fund]].

[⁴² (1A) Any Grenfell Tower payment [⁴⁸, child abuse payment, Windrush payment] or any payment made by the Child Migrants Trust (registered charity number 1171479) under the scheme for former British child migrants.]

(2) Any payment by or on behalf of a person who is suffering or who suffered from haemophilia or who is or was a qualifying person, which derives from a payment made under [²⁰ or by] any of the Trusts to which sub-paragraph (1) refers [⁴², or from a Grenfell Tower payment,] [⁴⁸, a child abuse payment or a Windrush payment] and which is made to or for the benefit of that person's partner or former partner from whom he is not, or where that person has died was not, estranged or divorced [⁹ or with whom he has formed a civil partnership that has not been dissolved or, where that person has died, had not been dissolved at the time of that person's death].

(3) Any payment by or on behalf of the partner or former partner of a person who is suffering or who suffered from haemophilia or who is or was a qualifying person provided that the partner or former partner and that person are not, or if either of them has died were not, estranged or divorced [⁹ or, where the partner or former partner and that person have formed a civil partnership, the civil partnership has not been dissolved or, if either of them has died, had not been dissolved at the time of the death], which derives from a payment made under [²⁰ or by] any of the Trusts to which sub-paragraph (1) refers [⁴², or from a Grenfell Tower payment,] [⁴⁸, a child abuse payment or a Windrush payment] and which is made to or for the benefit of the person who is suffering from haemophilia or who is a qualifying person.

(4) Any payment by a person who is suffering from haemophilia or who is a qualifying person, which derives from a payment under [²⁰ or by] any of the Trusts to which sub-paragraph (1) refers [⁴², or from a Grenfell Tower payment,] [⁴⁸, a child abuse payment or a Windrush payment] where—

(a) that person has no partner or former partner from whom he is not estranged or divorced [⁹ or with whom he has formed a civil partnership that has not been dissolved], nor any child who is or had been a member of that person's household; and

(b) the payment is made either—

(i) to that person's parent or step-parent, or

(ii) where that person at the date of the payment is a child or a student who has not completed his full-time education and has no parent or step-parent, to any person standing in the place of his parent,

but only for a period from the date of the payment until the end of two years from that person's death.

(5) Any payment out of the estate of a person who suffered from haemophilia or who was a qualifying person, which derives from a payment under [²⁰ or by] any of the Trusts to which

sub-paragraph (1) refers [^{42}, or from a Grenfell Tower payment,] [^{48}, a child abuse payment or a Windrush payment] where—

(a) that person at the date of his death (the relevant date) had no partner or former partner from whom he was not estranged or divorced [^{9} or with whom he has formed a civil partnership that had not been dissolved], nor any child who was or had been a member of his household; and

(b) the payment is made either—

    (i) to that person's parent or step-parent, or

    (ii) where that person at the relevant date was a child or a student who had not completed his full-time education and had no parent or step-parent, to any person standing in place his parent,

but only for a period of two years from the relevant date.

(6) In the case of a person to whom or for whose benefit a payment referred to in this paragraph is made, any capital resource which derives from any payment of income or capital made under or deriving from any of the Trusts [^{42}, or from a Grenfell Tower payment] [^{48}, a child abuse payment or a Windrush payment].

(7) For the purposes of sub-paragraphs (2) to (6), any reference to the Trusts shall be construed as including a reference to the Fund [^{5}, the Eileen Trust [^{19}, MFET Limited] [^{10}, the Skipton Fund [^{21}, the Caxton Foundation] [^{33}, the Scottish Infected Blood Support Scheme]][^{35}, [^{36} an approved blood scheme] the London Emergencies Trust, the We Love Manchester Emergency Fund] [^{42}, the National Emergencies Trust], and the London Bombings Relief Charitable Fund]].

(8) In this paragraph—

"child" means any person [^{12} who is a qualifying young person [^{31} within the meaning of regulation 4A] or] a child [^{31} as defined in section 40 of the 2012 Act];

"course of study" means any course of study, whether or not it is a sandwich course and whether or not a grant is made for undertaking or attending it;

"qualifying course" means a qualifying course as defined for the purposes of Parts II and IV of the Jobseeker's Allowance Regulations;

"sandwich course" has the meaning given in regulation 5(2) of the Education (Student Support) Regulations 2001, regulation 5(2) of the Education (Student Loans) (Scotland) Regulations 2000 or regulation 5(2) of the Education (Student Support) Regulations (Northern Ireland) 2000, as the case may be;

"student" means a person, other than a person in receipt of a training allowance, who is attending or undertaking—

    (a) a course of study at an educational establishment; or

    (b) a qualifying course;

"training allowance" means an allowance (whether by way of periodical grants or otherwise) payable—

    (a) out of public funds by a Government department or by or on behalf of the Secretary of State, [^{17} Skills Development Scotland,] Scottish Enterprise or Highlands and Islands Enterprise;

    (b) to a person for his maintenance or in respect of a member of his family; and

    (c) for the period, or part of the period, during which he is following a course of training or instruction provided by, or in pursuance of arrangements made with, that department or approved by that department in relation to him or so provided or approved by or on behalf of the Secretary of State, [^{17} Skills Development Scotland,] Scottish Enterprise or Highlands and Islands Enterprise,

but it does not include an allowance paid by any Government department to or in respect of a person by reason of the fact that he is following a course of full-time education, other than under arrangements made under section 2 of the Employment and Training Act 1973 or is training as a teacher [^{2}. . .].

[^{7} **15A.**—[^{10}. . . .]]

16.—[^{1}(1)] An amount equal to the amount of any payment made in consequence of any personal injury to the claimant or, if the claimant has a partner, to the partner.

[^{1}(2) Where the whole or part of the payment is administered—

    [^{13}(a) by the High Court or the County Court under rule 21.11(1) of the Civil Procedure Rules 1998, or the Court of Protection, or on behalf of a person where the payment can only be disposed of by order or direction of any such court;]

    (b) in accordance with an order made under [^{13} . . .] rule 36.14 of the Ordinary Cause Rules 1993 or under rule 128 of those Rules; or

    (c) in accordance with the terms of a trust established for the benefit of the claimant or his partner,

the whole of the amount so administered.]

17.—Any amount specified in paragraphs 18 to 20 [¹⁶ or 20B]—
   (a) in a case where there is an assessed income period, until the end of that period or until the expiration of one year from the date of payment, whichever is the later; or
   (b) in any other case, for a period of one year beginning with the date of receipt.

18.—Amounts paid under a policy of insurance in connection with the loss of or damage to the property occupied by the claimant as his home and to his personal possessions.

19.—So much of any amounts paid to the claimant or deposited in the claimant's name for the sole purpose of—
   (a) purchasing premises which the claimant intends to occupy as his home; or
   (b) effecting essential repairs or alterations to the premises occupied or intended to be occupied by the claimant as his home.

20.—(1) Any amount paid—
   (a) by way of arrears of benefit;
   (b) by way of compensation for the late payment of benefit; or
   (c) in lieu of the payment of benefit;
[³ (d) any payment made by a local authority (including in England a county council), or by the [¹⁶ Welsh Ministers], to or on behalf of the claimant or his partner relating to a service which is provided to develop or sustain the capacity of the claimant or his partner to live independently in his accommodation] [²³; or
   (e) by way of local welfare provision including arrears and payments in lieu of local welfare provision; or
   (f) in consequence of a reduction of council tax under section 13, 13A or 80 of the Local Government Finance Act 1992 (reduction of liability of [⁴² council tax;
   (g) to rectify, or to compensate for, an error made by an officer of the Department for Work and Pensions which was not caused or materially contributed to by any person outside the Department and which prevented or delayed an assessment of the claimant's entitlement to contributory employment and support allowance.]
   (2) In paragraph (1), "benefit" means—
   (a) attendance allowance under section 64 of the Contributions and Benefits Act;
   (b) disability living allowance;
[²⁴ (ba) personal independence payment;]
[²⁵ (bb) armed forces independence payment;]
   (c) income support;
   (d) income-based jobseeker's allowance;
   (e) housing benefit;
   (f) state pension credit;
   (g) [³ . . .]
   (h) [³ an increase of a disablement pension under section 104 of the Contributions and Benefits Act (increase where constant attendance needed), and any further increase of such a pension under section 105 of that Act (increase for exceptionally severe disablement)];
   (i) any amount included on account of the claimant's exceptionally severe disablement [³ or need for constant attendance] in a war disablement pension or [¹⁶ any other such amount described in regulation 15(5)(ac)].
[¹(j) council tax benefit;
   (k) social fund payments;
   (l) child benefit;
   (m) [³ . . .]
   (n) child tax credit under the Tax Credits Act 2002;]
[¹⁴ (o) income-related employment and support allowance] [²⁶;
   (p) universal credit;]
[³⁴ (q) bereavement support payment under section 30 of the Pensions Act 2014;]
[³⁹ (r) early years assistance given in accordance with section 32 of the Social Security (Scotland) Act 2018;]
[⁴⁰(s) funeral expense assistance given in accordance with section 34 of the Social Security (Scotland) Act 2018;]
[⁴¹(t) maternity allowance under section 35 of the 1992 Act (state maternity allowance for employed or self-employed earner).]
[⁴³(u) any Scottish child payment assistance given in accordance with section 79 of the Social Security (Scotland) Act 2018];
[⁴⁴(v) any assistance given in accordance with the Carer's Assistance (Young Carer Grants) (Scotland) Regulations 2019.]
[⁴⁵(w) short-term assistance given in accordance with regulations made under section 36 of the Social Security (Scotland) Act 2018;]

[⁴⁶(x) winter heating assistance given in accordance with regulations made under section 30 of the Social Security (Scotland) Act 2018.]

[⁴⁷(y) disability assistance given in accordance with regulations made under section 31 of the Social Security (Scotland) Act 2018.]

[³**20A.**—(1) Subject to sub-paragraph (3), any payment of £5,000 or more to which paragraph 20(1)(a), (b) or (c) applies, which has been made to rectify, or to compensate for, an official error [³⁸ or an error on a point of law] relating to a [⁴² relevant benefit, or to which paragraph 20(1)(g) applies, and which has been] received by the claimant in full on or after the day on which he became entitled to benefit under these Regulations.

(2) Subject to sub-paragraph (3), the total amount of any payment disregarded under—

(a) paragraph 7(2) of Schedule 10 to the Income Support (General) Regulations 1987;

(b) paragraph 12(2) of Schedule 8 to the Jobseeker's Allowance Regulations 1996;

[¹⁶. . .]

[¹⁴ or

(e) paragraph 11(2) of Schedule 9 to the Employment and Support Allowance Regulations,]

[¹⁶ (f) paragraph 9(2) [⁴² or 9A] of Schedule 6 to the Housing Benefit Regulations 2006;

(g) paragraph 22 of Schedule 6 to the Housing Benefit (Persons who have attained the qualifying age for state pension credit) Regulations 2006;

(h) paragraph 9(2) of Schedule 5 to the Council Tax Benefit Regulations 2006; [²⁶. . .]

(i) paragraph 22 of Schedule 4 to the Council Tax Benefit (Persons who have attained the qualifying age for state pension credit) Regulations 2006;] [²⁶ or

(j) [²⁷ paragraph 18] of Schedule 10 to the Universal Credit Regulations 2013;]

[⁴²(k) regulations 10A to 10C of the Universal Credit (Transitional Provisions) Regulations 2014;]

where the award during which the disregard last applied in respect of the relevant sum either terminated immediately before the relevant date or is still in existence at that date.

(3) Any disregard which applies under sub-paragraph (1) or (2) shall have effect until the award comes to an end.

(4) In this paragraph—

"the award", except in sub-paragraph (2), means—

(a) the award of State Pension Credit under these Regulations during which the relevant sum or, where it is received in more than one instalment, the first instalment of that sum is received; or

(b) where that award is followed immediately by one or more further awards which begins immediately after the previous award ends, such further awards until the end of the last award, provided that, for such further awards, the claimant—

(i) is the person who received the relevant sum;

(ii) is the partner of that person; or

(iii) was the partner of that person at the date of his death;

"official error"—

(a) where the error relates to housing benefit [²². . .] has the meaning given by regulation 1(2) of the Housing Benefit and Council Tax Benefit (Decisions and Appeals) Regulations 2001; and

(b) where the error relates to any other relevant benefit, has the meaning given by regulation 1(3) of the Social Security and Child Support (Decisions and Appeals) Regulations 1999;

"the relevant date" means the date on which the claimant became entitled to benefit under the Act;

"relevant benefit" means any benefit specified in paragraph 20(2); and

"the relevant sum" means the total payment referred to in sub-paragraph (1) or, as the case may be, the total amount referred to in sub-paragraph (2).]

[⁴⁹ **20AA.** Any payment of a widowed parent's allowance made pursuant to section 39A of the 1992 Act (widowed parent's allowance)—

(a) to the survivor of a cohabiting partnership (within the meaning in section 39A(7) of the 1992 Act) who is entitled to a widowed parent's allowance for a period before the Bereavement Benefits (Remedial) Order 2023 comes into force, and

(b) in respect of any period of time during the period ending with the day before the survivor makes the claim for a widowed parent's allowance,

but only for a period of 52 weeks from the date of receipt of the payment.]

[¹⁶ **20B.**—Any arrears of supplementary pension which is disregarded under paragraph 4 of Schedule 4 (amounts to be disregarded in the calculation of income other than earnings) or of any amount which is disregarded under paragraph 5 or 6 of that Schedule.]

21.—Where a capital asset is held in a currency other than sterling, any banking charge or commission payable in converting that capital into sterling.

22.—The value of the right to receive income from an occupational pension scheme or a personal pension scheme.

23.—The value of a right to receive income from a under a retirement annuity contract.

[¹¹ **23A.**—Where a person elects to be entitled to a lump sum under Schedule 5 or 5A to the 1992 Act or under Schedule 1 to the Graduated Retirement Benefit Regulations, or is treated as having made such an election, and a payment has been made pursuant to that election, an amount equal to—

   (a) except where sub-paragraph (b) applies, the amount of any payment or payments made on account of that lump sum;

   (b) the amount of that lump sum,

but only for so long as that person does not change that election in favour of an increase of pension or benefit.]

[³⁰ **23AA.** Where a person chooses a lump sum under section 8(2) of the Pensions Act 2014 or in accordance with Regulations made under section 10 of that Act which include provision corresponding or similar to section 8(2) of that Act, or fails to make a choice, and a lump sum payment has been made, an amount equal to—

   (a) except where sub-paragraph (b) applies, the amount of any payment or payments made on account of that lump sum;

   (b) the amount of that lump sum,

but only for so long as that person does not alter that choice in favour of an increase of pension.]

[¹⁷ **23B.**—Any payment made under Part 8A of the 1992 Act (entitlement to health in pregnancy grant).]

[²¹ **23C.**—Any payments made [²⁸ . . .]—

   (a) [²⁸ by virtue of regulations made under] section 57 (direct payments) of the Health and Social Care Act 2001;

   [²⁸ (b) as a direct payment as defined in section 4(2) of the Social Care (Self-directed Support) (Scotland) Act 2013; [²⁹ . . .]

   (c) [²⁸ by virtue of regulations made under] sections 12A to 12C (direct payments for health care) of the National Health Service Act 2006] [²⁹[³⁷ . . .]

   (d) under sections 31 to 33 of the Care Act 2014 [³⁷ (direct payments); or

   (e) by virtue of regulations made under section 50 or 52 of the Social Services and Wellbeing (Wales) Act 2014 (direct payments).].]

[³² **23D.**—(1) Any payment made by a local authority in accordance with section 26A of the Children (Scotland) Act 1995.

   (2) Subject to sub-paragraph (3), any payment or part of a payment made by a local authority in accordance with section 26A of the Children (Scotland) Act 1995 to a person ("A") which A passes on to the claimant.

   (3) Sub-paragraph (2) only applies where A—

   (a) was formerly in the claimant's care;

   (b) is aged 16 or over; and

   (c) continues to live with the claimant.]

[³⁴ **23E.** [⁴⁹ (1)] A payment of bereavement support payment in respect of the rate set out in regulation 3(2) or (5) of the Bereavement Support Payment Regulations 2017 (rate of bereavement support payment), but only for a period of 52 weeks from the date of receipt of the payment.]

[⁴⁹ (2) Where bereavement support payment under section 30 of the Pensions Act 2014 is paid to the survivor of a cohabiting partnership (within the meaning in section 30(6B) of the Pensions Act 2014) in respect of a death occurring before the day the Bereavement Benefits (Remedial) Order 2023 comes into force, any amount of that payment which is—

   (a) in respect of the rate set out in regulation 3(1) of the Bereavement Support Payment Regulations 2017, and

   (b) paid as a lump sum for more than one monthly recurrence of the day of the month on which their cohabiting partner died,

but only for a period of 52 weeks from the date of receipt of the payment.]

[³⁶ **23F.** Any payment made under or by a trust, established for the purpose of giving relief and assistance to disabled persons whose disabilities were caused by the fact that during their mother's pregnancy she had taken a preparation containing the drug known as Thalidomide, and which is approved by the Secretary of State.]

PART II

[¹Capital disregarded only for the purposes of determining deemed income]   3.175
24.—The value of the right to receive any income under a life interest or from a life rent.

25.—The value of the right to receive any rent except where the claimant has a reversionary interest in the property in respect of which rent is due.

26.—The value of the right to receive any income under an annuity or the surrender value (if any) of such an annuity.

27.—[³ . . .]

28.—Where property is held under a trust, other than—
  (a) a charitable trust within the meaning of the Charities Act 1993; or
  (b) a trust set up with any payment to which paragraph 16 of this Schedule applies, and under the terms of the trust, payments fall to be made, or the trustees have a discretion to make payments, to or for the benefit of the claimant or the claimant's partner, or both, that property.

AMENDMENTS

1. State Pension Credit (Consequential, Transitional and Miscellaneous Provisions) Regulations 2002 (SI 2002/3019) reg.23(o) (October 6, 2003).

2. State Pension Credit (Consequential, Transitional and Miscellaneous Provisions) (No.2) Regulations 2002 (SI 2002/3197) reg.2 and Sch. para.12 (October 6, 2003).

3. State Pension Credit (Transitional and Miscellaneous Provisions) Amendment Regulations 2003 (SI 2003/2274) reg.2(12) (October 6, 2003).

4. Social Security (Miscellaneous Amendments) (No.2) Regulations 2004 (SI 2004/1141) regs 3(3) and 3(4)(d) (May 12, 2004).

5. Social Security (Miscellaneous Amendments) (No.2) Regulations 2004 (SI 2004/1141) regs 3(5) and 3(6)(d) (May 12, 2004).

6. Social Security (Housing Benefit, Council Tax Benefit, State Pension Credit and Miscellaneous Amendments) Regulations 2004 (SI 2004/2327) reg.7(6) (October 4, 2004).

7. Income-related Benefits (Amendment) Regulations 2005 (SI 2005/2183) reg.6 (August 5, 2005).

8. Social Security (Care Homes and Independent Hospitals) Regulations 2005 (SI 2005/2687) reg.6 and Sch.5 para.6 (October 24, 2005).

9. Civil Partnership (Pensions, Social Security and Child Support) (Consequential, etc. Provisions) Order 2005 (SI 2005/2877) art.2(3) and Sch.3 para.35(5) (December 5, 2005).

10. Income-related Benefits (Amendment) (No.2) Regulations 2005 (SI 2005/3391) reg.7(3) (December 12, 2005).

11. Social Security (Deferral of Retirement Pensions, Shared Additional Pension and Graduated Retirement Benefit) (Miscellaneous Provisions) Regulations 2005 (SI 2005/2677) reg.13(4) (April 6, 2006).

12. Social Security (Young Persons) Amendment Regulations 2006 (SI 2006/718) reg.6(5) (April 10, 2006).

13. Social Security (Miscellaneous Amendments) (No.4) Regulations 2006 (SI 2006/2378) reg.14(6) (October 2, 2006).

14. Employment and Support Allowance (Consequential Provisions) (No.2) Regulations 2008 (SI 2008/1554) reg.4(9) (October 27, 2008).

15. Social Security (Miscellaneous Amendments) (No.6) Regulations 2008 (SI 2008/2767) reg.5(5) (November 17, 2008).

16. Social Security (Miscellaneous Amendments) (No.7) Regulations 2008 (SI 2008/3157) reg.4(6) (January 5, 2009).

17. Social Security (Miscellaneous Amendments) Regulations 2009 (SI 2009/583) reg.5(4) and (5) (April 6, 2009).

18. Social Security (Equalisation of State Pension Age) Regulations 2009 (SI 2009/1488) regs 22 and 23 (April 10, 2010).

19. Social Security (Miscellaneous Amendments) (No.2) Regulations 2010 (SI 2010/641) reg.6(3)(c) (April 6, 2010).

20. Social Security (Miscellaneous Amendments) (No.2) Regulations 2010 (SI 2010/641) reg.6(2) (April 6, 2010).

21. Social Security (Miscellaneous Amendments) (No.3) Regulations 2011 (2011/2425) reg.15(6) and (7) (October 31, 2011).

22. Council Tax Benefit Abolition (Consequential Provision) Regulations 2013 (SI 2013/458) reg.3 and Sch.1 (April 1, 2013).

23. Social Security (Miscellaneous Amendments) Regulations 2013 (SI 2013/443) reg.6(4) (April 2, 2013).

24. Personal Independence Payment (Supplementary Provisions and Consequential Amendments) Regulations 2013 (SI 2013/388) reg.8 and Sch. para.27(7) (April 8, 2013).

25. Armed Forces and Reserve Forces Compensation Scheme (Consequential Provisions: Subordinate Legislation) Order 2013 (SI 2013/591) art.7 and Sch. para.23(7) (April 8, 2013).

26. Universal Credit (Consequential, Supplementary, Incidental and Miscellaneous Provisions) Regulations 2013 (SI 2013/630) reg.33(7) (April 29, 2013).

27. Social Security (Miscellaneous Amendments) (No.3) Regulations 2013 (SI 2013/2536) reg.10(4) (October 29, 2013).

28. Social Care (Self-directed Support) (Scotland) Act 2013 (Consequential Modifications and Savings) Order 2014 (SI 2014/513) art.2 and Sch. para.7 (April 1, 2014).

29. Care Act 2014 (Consequential Amendments) (Secondary Legislation) Order 2015 (SI 2015/643) reg.19(1) and (2) (April 1, 2015).

30. Pensions Act 2014 (Consequential, Supplementary and Incidental Amendments) Order 2015 (SI 2015/1985) reg.24(2) (April 6, 2016).

31. Housing Benefit and State Pension Credit (Temporary Absence) (Amendment) Regulations 2016 (SI 2016/624) reg.4(9) (July 28, 2016).

32. Children and Young People (Scotland) Act 2014 (Consequential Modifications) Order 2016 (SI 2016/732) art.4(3) (August 5, 2016).

33. Social Security (Scottish Infected Blood Support Scheme) Regulations 2017 (SI 2017/329) reg.5(3)(b) (April 3, 2017).

34. Pensions Act 2014 (Consequential, Supplementary and Incidental Amendments) Order 2017 (SI 2017/422) art.21(3) (April 6, 2017).

35. Social Security (Emergency Funds) (Amendment) Regulations 2017 (SI 2017/689) reg.4(3)(b) (June 19, 2017).

36. Social Security (Infected Blood and Thalidomide) Regulations 2017 (SI 2017/870) reg.5(3)(b) and 5(5) (October 23, 2017).

37. Social Services and Well-being (Wales) Act 2014 and the Regulation and Inspection of Social Care (Wales) Act 2016 (Consequential Amendments) Order 2017 (SI 2017/901) reg.9(3) (November 3, 2017).

38. Social Security (Treatment of Arrears of Benefit) Regulations 2018 (SI 2018/932), reg.4 (September 11, 2018).

39. Social Security (Scotland) Act 2018 (Best Start Grants) (Consequential Modifications and Saving) Order 2018 (SI 2018/1138), art.7(3) (December 10, 2018).

40. Social Security (Scotland) Act 2018 (Funeral Expense Assistance and Early Years Assistance) (Consequential Modifications and Savings) Order 2019 (SI 2019/1060) art.11(2) (September 16, 2019).

41. Social Security (Capital Disregards) (Amendment) Regulations 2019 (SI 2019/1314) reg.4(2) (October 31, 2019, reg.4(2)).

42. Social Security (Income and Capital) (Miscellaneous Amendments) Regulations 2020 (SI 2020/618) reg.4 (July 15, 2020).

43. Social Security (Scotland) Act 2018 (Information-Sharing and Scottish Child Payment) (Consequential Provision and Modifications) Order 2020 (SI 2020/482) art.5 (November 9, 2020).

44. Social Security (Scotland) Act 2018 (Young Carer Grants, Short-Term Assistance and Winter Heating Assistance) (Consequential Provision and Modifications) Order 2020 (SI 2020/989) art.4(3) (November 9, 2020).

45. Social Security (Scotland) Act 2018 (Young Carer Grants, Short-Term Assistance and Winter Heating Assistance) (Consequential Provision and Modifications) Order 2020 (SI 2020/989) art.11(3) (November 9, 2020).

46. Social Security (Scotland) Act 2018 (Young Carer Grants, Short-Term Assistance and Winter Heating Assistance) (Consequential Provision and Modifications) Order 2020 (SI 2020/989) art.17(3) (November 9, 2020).

47. Social Security (Scotland) Act 2018 (Disability Assistance, Young Carer Grants, Short-term Assistance and Winter Heating Assistance) (Consequential Provision and Modifications) Order 2021 (SI 2021/886) art.13(3) (July 26, 2021).

48. Social Security (Income and Capital Disregards) (Amendment) Regulations 2021 (SI 2021/1405) reg.4(4) (January 1, 2022).

49. Bereavement Benefits (Remedial) Order 2023 (SI 2023/134) art.10 and Sch. para.5 (February 9, 2023).

GENERAL NOTE

This Schedule includes many of the same disregards as are to be found in Sch.10 to the Income Support (General) Regulations 1987 (SI 1987/1967) (see Vol.V of this series). However, the function of the two Schedules is conceptually different. The purpose of Sch.10 in the income support scheme is to provide for disregards to be applied in calculating the claimant's capital with a view to seeing whether the relevant capital threshold is exceeded. The purpose of this Schedule is to specify disregards which apply in the assessment of capital which is then used for calculating the claimant's income under the tariff income rule in reg.15(6), there being no capital rule as such in the state pension credit scheme. That said, the actual drafting of these provisions follows closely the parallel provisions in the income support schemes. But note also that the disregards in this Schedule are subdivided into two categories: those which are disregarded for the purpose of calculating income (Pt I) and those disregarded— which are fewer in number—for the purpose of calculating notional income (Pt II). **3.176**

Paragraph 1
See Income Support (General) Regulations 1987 (SI 1987/1967) Sch.10 para.2. The claimant's own home (Sch.2 para.1 of the 1987 Regulations) is disregarded for state pension credit purposes by para.1A below. **3.177**

Paragraphs 2–3
See Income Support (General) Regulations 1987 (SI 1987/1967) Sch.10 paras 27–28. **3.178**

Paragraphs 4–5
See Income Support (General) Regulations 1987 (SI 1987/1967) Sch.10 paras 4 and 5. **3.179**
Paragraph (4)(a) provides for the disregard of the value of a second property where that property is occupied by someone who is aged 60 or over or is incapacitated and who is a relative of the pension credit claimant or their partner. Note that the original drafting of para.(4) meant that the disregard applied only if the occupier of the property was a close relative of the pension credit claimant himself (or herself). The amended formulation applies the disregard equally where the occupier is a close relative of the claimant's partner. The original wording reflected a drafting oversight, and the Minister has indicated that extra-statutory payments will be considered to anyone who lost out (*Hansard*, HC Vol. 421, col. 140W, May 10, 2004).
Paragraph 4(b) makes similar provision where the claimant's former partner occupies the property. This disregard is not available if the claimant is divorced or estranged from their ex-partner (or a civil partnership has been dissolved). On the meaning of "estranged", see *CPC/0683/2007*, following *R(IS) 5/05* and *CH/0177/2005*.

Paragraph 6

3.180   This applies the more generous housing benefit disregard (see, e.g. Housing Benefit (General) Regulations 1987 (SI 1987/1971) Sch.5 para.24) in preference to the more limited disregard in the Income Support (General) Regulations 1987 (SI 1987/1967) Sch.10 para.25. Thus the disregard on a former family home is for 26 weeks where the claimant moves out following a relationship breakdown, and beyond that time if the remaining partner is a lone parent (until such time as that status ceases).

Paragraph 7

3.181   See Income Support (General) Regulations 1987 (SI 1987/1967) Sch.10 para.26.

Paragraph 8

3.182   See Income Support (General) Regulations 1987 (SI 1987/1967) Sch.10 para.10 (although the qualification in the income support provision is not repeated here).

Paragraphs 9–9A

3.183   See Income Support (General) Regulations 1987 (SI 1987/1967) Sch.10 para.6(1) and (2).

Paragraph 10

3.184   See Income Support (General) Regulations 1987 (SI 1987/1967) Sch.10 para.15. See further *AB v SSWP* [2010] UKUT 343 (AAC), where the claimant wrote to the DWP asking for a recalculation of his pension credit and for it to be backdated, as he now realised that on his claim form he had declared details of the surrender value of a life insurance policy which should not have been counted as part of his capital resources. His benefit was recalculated as from the date of the letter. Judge Ovey held that the tribunal had erred in treating the information supplied by the claimant as a notification of a change of circumstances rather than revelation of a mistake in the calculation of the original award, and had further failed to consider whether there had been an official error in the making of that award.

Paragraph 11

3.185   This has no direct parallel under the income support scheme.

Paragraph 12

3.186   See Income Support (General) Regulations 1987 (SI 1987/1967) Sch.10 para.61.

Paragraphs 13–14

3.187   See Income Support (General) Regulations 1987 (SI 1987/1967) Sch.10 paras 64–65.

Paragraph 15

3.188   *See Income Support (General) Regulations 1987 (SI 1987/1967) Sch.10 para.22.*

Paragraph 16

3.189   Payments in respect of compensation for personal injuries are disregarded for both capital and income purposes (see also Sch.IV paras 13 and 14). Paragraph 16(2) deals with the specific example of funds held in court: see Income Support (General) Regulations 1987 (SI 1987/1967) Sch.10 paras 44 and 45.

Paragraphs 17–19

3.190   These paragraphs are designed to fulfil broadly the same functions as the disregards Income Support (General) Regulations 1987 (SI 1987/1967) Sch.10 paras 3 and 8. These disregards, however, last for one year rather than the "26 weeks or such longer period as is reasonable in the circumstances" qualification that applies under the income support scheme. See *DH v SSWP* [2010] UKUT 241 (AAC), confirming that for the purposes of the disregard in paras 17(b) and 19 time runs from the actual date of receipt of the funds, regardless of whether the claimant is actually in the UK at the time in question.

Paragraph 20
See Income Support (General) Regulations 1987 (SI 1987/1967) Sch.10 para.7.　　**3.191**

Paragraph 21
See Income Support (General) Regulations 1987 (SI 1987/1967) Sch.10 para.21.　　**3.192**
See also reg.17(6).

Paragraph 22
See Income Support (General) Regulations 1987 (SI 1987/1967) Sch.10 para.(23).　　**3.193**

Paragraph 23AA
The effect of this provision is that an amount equal to the pre-tax amount of the　　**3.194**
lump-sum payment paid where a person changes their choice of payment of the new
state pension is to be disregarded for life, so long as that person does not change
their choice to a weekly increase.

Paragraphs 24–26
See Income Support (General) Regulations 1987 (SI 1987/1967) Sch.10 paras　　**3.195**
13, 24 and 11 respectively.

Regulation 17(9)

SCHEDULE VI

Sums Disregarded from Claimant's Earnings

1.—(1) In a case where a claimant is a lone parent, £20 of earnings.　　**3.196**
(2) In this paragraph—
 (a) "lone parent" means a person who has no partner and who is responsible for, and a
  member of the same household as, a child;
 (b) "child" means a person [⁴ who is a qualifying young person [¹¹ within the meaning of
  regulation 4A] or] a child [¹¹ as defined in section 40 of the 2012 Act].
2.—In a case of earnings from employment to which sub-paragraph (2) applies, £20.
(2) This paragraph applies to employment—
[⁹ (a) a part-time fire-fighter employed by a fire and rescue authority under the Fire and
  Rescue Services Act 2004 or by the Scottish Fire and Rescue Service established
  under section 1A of the Fire (Scotland) Act 2005;]
 (b) as an auxiliary coastguard in respect of coast rescue activities;
 (c) in the manning or launching of a lifeboat if the employment is part-time;
 [¹(d) a member of any territorial or reserve force prescribed in Part I of Schedule 6 to the
  Social Security (Contributions) Regulations 2001].
[¹2A.—Where a person is engaged in one or more of the employments specified in paragraph
2 but his earnings derived from those employments are less than £20 in any week and he is also
engaged in any other employment, so much of his earnings from that other employment as would
not in aggregate with the amount of his earnings disregarded under paragraph 2 exceed £20.]
[² 2B.—Where only one member of a couple is in employment specified in paragraph 2(2),
so much of the earnings of the other member of the couple as would not, in aggregate with the
earnings disregarded under paragraph 2, exceed £20.]
3.—(1) If the claimant or one of the partners is a carer, or both partners are carers, £20 of
any earnings received from his or their employment.
(2) In this paragraph the claimant or his partner is a carer if paragraph 4 of Part II of
Schedule I (amount applicable for carers) is satisfied in respect of him.
4.—(1) £20 is disregarded if the claimant or, if he has a partner, his partner—
 (a) is in receipt of—
  (i) long-term incapacity benefit under section 30A of the 1992 Act;
  (ii) severe disablement allowance under section 68 of that Act;
  (iii) attendance allowance;
  (iv) disability living allowance under section 71 to 76 of that Act;
  (v) any mobility supplement under [⁶ article 20 of the Naval, Military and Air
   Forces Etc. (Disablement and Death) Service Pensions Order 2006] (including

such a supplement by virtue of any other scheme or order) or under article 25A of the Personal Injuries (Civilians) Scheme 1983; [⁵ . . .]

[¹(vi) the disability element or the severe disability element of working tax credit under Schedule 2 to the Working Tax Credit (Entitlement and Maximum Rate) Regulations 2002; or]

[⁵ (vii) employment and support allowance; [⁷ . . .]]

[⁷ (viii) personal independence payment; [⁷ . . .]]

[¹² (viiia) adult disability payment;]

[⁸ (ix) armed forces independence payment; or]

[¹⁰ (b) is or are certified as severely sight impaired or blind by a consultant ophthalmologist.]

(2) Subject to sub-paragraph (4), £20 is disregarded if the claimant or, if he has a partner, his partner has, within a period of 8 weeks ending on the day in respect of which the claimant first satisfies the conditions for entitlement to state pension credit, had an award of income support [⁵, income-based jobseeker's allowance or income-related employment and support allowance] and—

    (a) £20 was disregarded in respect of earnings taken into account in that award;

    (b) the person whose earnings qualified for the disregard in employment after the termination of that award.

(3) Subject to sub-paragraph (4), £20 is disregarded if the claimant or, if he has a partner, his partner, immediately before attaining pensionable age—

    (a) had an award of state pension credit; and

    (b) a disregard under paragraph 4(1)(a)(i) or (ii) was taken into account in determining that award.

(4) The disregard of £20 specified in sub-paragraphs (2) and (3) applies so long as there is no break, other a break which does not exceed eight weeks—

    (a) in a case to which sub-paragraph (2) refers, in a person's entitlement to state pension credit or in employment following the first day in respect of which state pension credit is awarded; or

    (b) in a case where sub-paragraph (3) applies, in the person's entitlement to state pension credit since attaining pensionable age.

(5) [¹. . .].

[¹4A.—(1) £20 is the maximum amount which may be disregarded under any of paragraphs 1, 2, 3 or 4 notwithstanding that—

    (a) in the case of a claimant with no partner, he satisfies the requirements of more than one of those paragraphs or, in the case of paragraph 4, he satisfies the requirements of more than one of the sub-paragraphs of that paragraph; or

    (b) in the case of [³ couples], both partners satisfy one or more of the requirements of paragraphs 2, 3 and 4.

(2) Where, in a case to which sub-paragraph (1)(b) applies, the amount to be disregarded in respect of one of the partners ("the first partner") is less than £20, the amount to be disregarded in respect of the other partner shall be so much of that other partner's earnings as would not, in aggregate with the first partner's earnings, exceed £20.]

5.—Except where the claimant or his partner qualifies for a £20 disregard under the preceding provisions of this Schedule—

    (a) £5 shall be disregarded if a claimant who has no partner has earnings;

    (b) £10 shall be disregarded if a claimant who has a partner has earnings.

6.—Any earnings [¹, other than any amount referred to in regulation 17(9)(b),] derived from any employment which ended before the day in respect of which the claimant first satisfies the conditions for entitlement to state pension credit.

[¹7.—Any banking charges or commission payable in converting to Sterling payments of earnings made in a currency other than Sterling.]

AMENDMENTS

1. State Pension Credit (Consequential, Transitional and Miscellaneous Provisions) (No.2) Regulations 2002 (SI 2002/3197) reg.2 and Sch. para.13 (October 6, 2003).

2. State Pension Credit (Transitional and Miscellaneous Provisions) Amendment Regulations 2003 (SI 2003/2274) reg.2(13) (October 6, 2003).

3. Civil Partnership (Pensions, Social Security and Child Support) (Consequential, etc. Provisions) Order 2005 (SI 2005/2877) art.2(3) and Sch.3 para.35(6) (December 5, 2005).

4. Social Security (Young Persons) Amendment Regulations 2006 (SI 2006/718) reg.6(6) (April 10, 2006).
5. Employment and Support Allowance (Consequential Provisions) (No.2) Regulations 2008 (SI 2008/1554) reg.4(10) (October 27, 2008).
6. Social Security (Miscellaneous Amendments) (No.7) Regulations 2008 (SI 2008/3157) reg.4(7) (January 5, 2009).
7. Personal Independence Payment (Supplementary Provisions and Consequential Amendments) Regulations 2013 (SI 2013/388) reg.8 and Sch. para.27(8) (April 8, 2013).
8. Armed Forces and Reserve Forces Compensation Scheme (Consequential Provisions: Subordinate Legislation) Order 2013 (SI 2013/591) art.7 and Sch. para.23(8) (April 8, 2013).
9. Social Security (Miscellaneous Amendments) (No.3) Regulations 2013 (SI 2013/2536) reg.10(5) (October 29, 2013).
10. Universal Credit and Miscellaneous Amendments (No.2) Regulations 2014 (SI 2014/2888) reg.3(4)(c) (November 26, 2014).
11. Housing Benefit and State Pension Credit (Temporary Absence) (Amendment) Regulations 2016 (SI 2016/624) reg.4(10) (July 28, 2016).
12. Social Security (Disability Assistance for Working Age People) (Consequential Amendments) Order 2022 (SI 2022/177) art.8(7) (March 21, 2022).

DEFINITIONS

"attendance allowance"—see reg.1(2).
"child"—see para.1(2).
"claimant"—see SPCA 2002 s.17(1).
"lone parent"—see para.1(2).
"partner"—see reg.1(3).
"pensionable age"—see SPCA 2002 s.17(1).

GENERAL NOTE

This Schedule performs the same function in relation to state pension credit as Sch.8   **3.197**
to the Income Support (General) Regulations 1987 (SI 1987/1967) (see Vol.V of this series) does in the context of income support. Thus the standard disregard on earnings is £5 a week for a single claimant and £10 a week for a couple (para.5). There are then various special cases (e.g. lone parents, carers, disabled claimants and those active pensioners who are still involved in various emergency services in a part-time capacity) where the disregard is £20 a week. Note that the maximum weekly disregard is £20 even where both members of a couple satisfy one of the tests for the maximum disregard (para.(4A)).

There is, however, one significant difference from income support: although the same earnings disregards apply, there is no 16-hours rule in the context of state pension credit. On the other hand, the low level of the earnings disregards is hardly an incentive for pensioners (or their partners) to work extra hours.

The typographical error in para.4(2)(b) ("disegard" for "disregard") appears in the original version of the Regulations and, as at the time of writing, has not been corrected.

PART IV

THE SOCIAL FUND

The Social Fund Cold Weather Payments (General) Regulations 1988

(SI 1988/1724) (AS AMENDED)

Made by the Secretary of State under ss.32(2A) and 84(1) of the Social Security Act 1986 and s.166(1) to (3A) of the Social Security Act 1975

GENERAL NOTE

Section 138(2) of the Contributions and Benefits Act provides that payments may 4.1
be made out of the social fund "to meet expenses for heating, which appear to the
Secretary of State to have been or to be likely to be incurred in cold weather". That
power has been used to make these Regulations and also the Social Fund Winter
Fuel Payment Regulations 2000 (see below).

The cold weather payments scheme was introduced in April 1988 and, although
there have been subsequent technical changes, has had substantially the same structure since November 1, 1991. That structure is as follows:

- Every postcode in Great Britain is linked to a weather site accredited by the
  Met Office. Until October 31, 2016, the link was prescribed by Schedules 1
  and 2 to these Regulations. However, from November 1, 2016, those Schedules
  were revoked by SI 2016/876 and the link is instead designated by the Secretary
  of State under reg.2A. According to the Explanatory Memorandum to that SI,
  the aim of the change was "to enable the Secretary of State to vary weather
  station designations relevant to cold weather payments without the need for
  new legislation every time a variation is needed".
- If a period of cold weather (i.e. seven consecutive days during which the
  average daily temperature is below 0°C) is forecast for, or recorded by, the
  weather site that is linked to a postcode district then any claimant whose home
  is in that district and who satisfies the conditions in reg.1A is entitled to a cold
  weather payment of (currently) £25.
- There is no need for a claim. However, a cold weather payment cannot be
  made after September 28 following the winter which included the period of
  cold weather (26 weeks beginning with March 31) (see reg.2(6)).

The decision to make a payment is made by a decision-maker but there is no notification in cases where a payment is not made. As it is not possible to make a claim,
a person who does not receive a payment to which s/he thinks s/he is entitled must
request a negative decision before there is something to appeal against.

For a historical review of the Scheme see pp.338–353 of the 3rd edition of T. Buck,
The Social Fund—Law and Practice (3rd edn) (London: Sweet & Maxwell, 2009),
pp.338–353.

Citation, commencement and interpretation

1.—(1) These regulations may be cited as the Social Fund Cold Weather 4.2
Payments (General) Regulations 1988 and shall come into force on 7th
November 1988.

(2) In these Regulations, unless the context otherwise requires—

[¹¹ "the 2012 Act" means the Welfare Reform Act 2012;]

[⁹ "the Act" means the Social Security Contributions and Benefits Act 1992;]

[⁷ "the Welfare Reform Act" means the Welfare Reform Act 2007;]

"the General Regulations" means the Income Support (General)
   Regulations 1987;

[⁴[¹²"the Met Office" means the Met Office of the Department for Business, Energy and Industrial Strategy;]]

[⁹ . . .]

[²"claimant" means a person who is claiming or has claimed income support [⁶, state pension credit [⁷, income-based jobseeker's allowance [¹¹, income-related employment and support allowance or universal credit [¹⁵ or who is in receipt of owner-occupier loan payments]]]];]

[⁹"cold weather payment" means a payment to meet expenses for heating made out of the social fund under section 138(2) of the Act and these Regulations;

"family" has the meaning given to it in section 137 of the Act and the General Regulations;]

[²"forecast" means a weather forecast produced by the [¹² Met] Office [⁴. . .] and supplied to the [⁸ Department for Work and Pensions] on a daily basis [⁴ between 1st November in any year and 31st March in the following year,] which provides the expected average mean daily temperature for a period of 7 consecutive days;

"forecasted period of cold weather" means a period of 7 consecutive days, during which the average of the mean daily temperature for that period is forecasted to be equal to or below 0 degrees celsius; and for the purposes of this definition where a day forms part of a forecasted period of cold weather it shall not form part of any other such forecasted period;]

"home" means the dwelling, together with any garage, garden and outbuildings normally occupied by the claimant as his home, including any premises not so occupied which it is impracticable or unreasonable to sell separately [¹⁷ ...];

[⁴"income-based jobseeker's allowance" has the same meaning in these Regulations as it has in the Jobseekers Act 1995 by virtue of section 1(4) of that Act;]

[⁷"income-related employment and support allowance" means an income-related allowance under Part 1 of the Welfare Reform Act (employment and support allowance);]

[⁹"income support" means income support under Part 7 of the Act;]

[⁶ . . .]

"mean daily temperature" means, in respect of a day, the average of the maximum temperature and minimum temperature recorded at a [¹⁶ site] for that day;

[¹⁴ ¹³ "member of the support group" means a person who has or is treated as having limited capability for work-related activity under Part 6 of the Employment and Support Allowance Regulations 2008;]

[¹⁴ ¹³ "member of the work-related activity group" means a person who has or is treated as having limited capability for work under Part 5 of the Employment and Support Allowance Regulations 2008 other than by virtue of regulation 30 of the Employment and Support Allowance Regulations 2008;]

[²"overlap period" means any period of a day or days, where a day forms part of a recorded period of cold weather and also forms part of a forecasted period of cold weather;]

[¹⁵ "owner-occupier loan payments" means loan payments made under the Loans for Mortgage Interest Regulations 2017;]

[⁶ . . .]

[⁹ . . .]

[⁴"postcode district" means a Post Office postcode district [⁵except in the case of any postcode district which is identified with an alpha suffix which shall, for the purposes of these Regulations, be treated as if it forms part of a postcode district which is identified without that suffix]];

"recorded period of cold weather" means a period of 7 consecutive days, during which the average of the mean daily temperature recorded for that period was equal to or below 0 degrees celsius; and for the purposes of this definition where a day forms part of a recorded period of cold weather it shall not form part of any other such recorded period;

[⁶ "state pension credit" has the meaning given by section 1(1) of the State Pension Credit Act 2002]

[⁴. . .]

[⁴ [¹⁶ "site" means a site accredited by the Met Office in relation to which a period of cold weather may be forecasted or recorded for the purposes of these Regulations;]]

[¹¹ "universal credit" means universal credit under Part 1 of the 2012 Act;]

[⁹ "winter period" means the period beginning on 1st November in any year and ending on 31st March in the following year.]

[⁶ . . .]

[¹ (2A) [⁶ . . .]]]

(3) In these Regulations, unless the context otherwise requires, a reference to a numbered regulation is to the regulation in these Regulations bearing that number and a reference in a regulation to a numbered paragraph or sub-paragraph is to the paragraph or sub-paragraph in that regulation bearing that number.

AMENDMENTS

1. Social Fund (Miscellaneous Amendments) Regulations 1990 (SI 1990/580) reg.3 (April 9, 1990).

2. Social Fund Cold Weather Payments (General) Amendment No.2 Regulations 1991 (SI 1991/2238) reg.2 (November 1, 1991).

3. Social Fund Cold Weather Payments (General) Amendment (No.2) Regulations 1992 (SI 1992/2448) reg.2 (November 1, 1992).

4. Social Fund Cold Weather Payments (General) Amendment Regulations 1996 (SI 1996/2544) reg.2 (November 4, 1996).

5. Social Fund Cold Weather Payments (General) Amendment Regulations 1997 (SI 1997/2311) reg.2 (November 1, 1997).

6. Social Fund Cold Weather Payments (General) Amendment Regulations 2005 (SI 2005/2724) reg.3 (November 1, 2005).

7. Employment and Support Allowance (Consequential Provisions) (No.2) Regulations 2008 (SI 2008/1554) reg.6(1) and (2) (October 27, 2008).

8. Social Fund Cold Weather Payments (General) Amendment Regulations 2008 (SI 2008/2569) reg.2(1) and (2) (November 1, 2008).

9. Social Fund Cold Weather Payments (General) Amendment Regulations 2010 (SI 2010/2442) reg.2(1) and (2) (November 1, 2010).

10. Transfer of Functions (Her Majesty's Land Registry, the Meteorological Office and Ordnance Survey) Order 2011 (SI 2011/2436) art.6 and Sch.2 para.6 (November 9, 2011).

11. Social Fund Cold Weather Payments (General) Regulations 1988 (SI 2013/248) reg.2(1) and (2) (November 1, 2013).

12. Social Fund Cold Weather Payments (General) (Amendment) Regulations 2016 (SI 2016/876) reg.2(1) and (2) (November 1, 2016).

13. Employment and Support Allowance and Universal Credit (Miscellaneous Amendments and Transitional and Savings Provisions) Regulations 2017 (SI 2017/204) reg.7(1) and Sch.1, Pt.1, para.2(1) and (3) (April 3, 2017).

14. Employment and Support Allowance (Miscellaneous Amendments and Transitional and Savings Provision) Regulations 2017 (SI 2017/581) reg.2 (June 23, 2017, subject to the transitional and savings provision in reg.10).

15. Loans for Mortgage Interest Regulations 2017 (SI 2017/725) reg.18 and Sch.5 para.10(1) and (2) (April 6, 2018).

16. Social Fund and Social Security (Claims and Payments) (Amendment) Regulations 2020 (SI 2020/600) reg.3(1) and (2) (July 9, 2020).

17. Social Security (Scotland) Act 2018 (Winter Heating Assistance) (Consequential Modifications) Order 2022 (SI 2022/1018) art.2 (November 1, 2022).

GENERAL NOTE

4.3   Most of the definitions in reg.1 are self-explanatory. The following merit additional comment.

"Home": The definition is the same as the definition of "dwelling occupied as the home" in reg.2(1) of the Income Support General Regulations. See the notes to that regulation in Vol.V of this series.

"Forecasted period of cold weather": The definition covers any period of seven consecutive days (i.e. not necessarily a calendar week) during which the average of the mean daily temperature (as defined) for that period is forecasted to be equal to or less than 0°C. If a day falls into a forecasted period of cold weather it cannot count in any other forecasted period, but it can be part of a "recorded period of cold weather" (see the definition of that phrase and of "overlap period"). The possibility of relying on a forecast without having to wait until a period of cold weather has actually been recorded allows the cold weather payment to be made nearer to the time when the need to incur additional heating expenses arises.

4.4   *"Overlap period"*: On the assumption that weather forecasts are occasionally correct, a day that falls within a "forecasted period of cold weather" will sometimes also fall within a "recorded period of cold weather". Such a day (or days) form an "overlap period". For the treatment of overlap periods, see reg.2(3)–(5).

"Recorded period of cold weather": The definition covers any period of seven consecutive days (i.e. not necessarily a calendar week) during which the average of the mean daily temperature (as defined) recorded for that period was equal to or less than 0°C. If a day falls into a recorded period of cold weather it cannot count in any other recorded period, but it can be part of a "forecasted period of cold weather" (see the definition of that phrase and of "overlap period"). The possibility of relying upon recorded temperatures means that a cold weather payment can be made in respect of a period of cold weather that was not forecast.

[1 10 **Prescribed description of persons**

4.5   **1A.**—(1) A cold weather payment may be made in the circumstances prescribed by regulation 2 to a person who satisfies the following conditions.

(2) The first condition is that, in respect of at least one day during the recorded or the forecasted period of cold weather specified in regulation 2(1)(a), the person has been awarded—

(a) state pension credit;

(b) income support;

(c) an income-based jobseeker's allowance; [13 . . .]

(d) an income-related employment and support allowance [13; [19 ...]

(e) universal credit] [19; or

(f) owner-occupier loan payments and is treated as entitled to a benefit specified in sub-paragraphs [20 (b)] to (d).]
[20 (g) owner-occupier loan payments and is treated as entitled to state pension credit.]
(3) The second condition (which applies only if the person ("P") falls within paragraph (2)(b), [13 (c), [19 (d), (e) or (f)]] is that, in respect of the day to which paragraph (2) relates—
    (a) P's family includes a member aged less than 5;
    (b) where P has been awarded income support, P's applicable amount includes one or more of the premiums specified in paragraphs 9 to 14 of Part 3 of Schedule 2 to the General Regulations;
    (c) where P has been awarded a jobseeker's allowance, P's applicable amount includes one or more of the premiums specified in paragraphs 10 to 16 of Part 3 of Schedule 1 to the Jobseeker's Allowance Regulations 1996;
[17 (d) P's child tax credit includes a disability element within the meaning of section 9(3) of the Tax Credits Act 2002;] [13 . . .]
    (e) where P has been awarded an employment and support allowance, [15 and]—
        (i) [15 P's applicable amount includes] one or more of the premiums specified in paragraphs 5 to 7 of Schedule 4 to the Employment and Support Allowance Regulations 2008, or
        (ii) P is a member of the work-related activity group or is a member of the support group; [19 ...]]
[13 (f) where P has been awarded universal credit—
        (i) the award includes an amount under section 10(2) of the 2012 Act (child or qualifying young person who is disabled); or
        [16 (ii) P has limited capability for work or limited capability for work and work-related activity as construed in accordance with regulations 39 and 40 of the Universal Credit Regulations 2013]] [19; or
    (g) where P has been awarded owner-occupier loan payments, P's applicable amount, if P were entitled to a benefit specified in paragraph (2)(b) to (d), would include one or more of the premiums specified in—
        (aa) where P is treated as entitled to income support, paragraphs 9 to 14 of Part 3 of Schedule 2 to the General Regulations;
        (bb) where P is treated as entitled to jobseeker's allowance, paragraphs 10 to 16 of Part 3 of Schedule 1 to the Jobseeker's Allowance Regulations 1996;
        (cc) where P is treated as entitled to employment and support allowance, paragraphs 5 to 7 of Schedule 4 to the Employment and Support Allowance Regulations 2008.]
[19(3A) In [20 paragraphs (2) and (3)], a person being treated as entitled to a benefit has the meaning given to it in regulation 2(2)(aa) of the Loans for Mortgage Interest Regulations 2017.]
(4) The third condition (which does not apply to a person who comes [11 within] paragraph (3)(a) or (d)) is that the person does not reside in—
    (a) a care home;
    (b) an independent hospital;
    (c) an establishment run by the Abbeyfield Society or by a body corporate or incorporate which is affiliated to that Society; or

(d) accommodation provided under section 3(1) of, and Part 2 of the Schedule to, the Polish Resettlement Act 1s947 (provision by the Secretary of State of accommodation in camps).

[¹³ (4A) In relation to a person who has been awarded universal credit, the third condition applies as if paragraph (4)(d) were omitted.]

(5) In paragraph (4) —

(a) "care home" in England [¹⁸ ...] has the meaning assigned to it by section 3 of the Care Standards Act 2000, [¹⁸ in Wales means a care home service within the meaning of Part 1 of the Regulation and Inspection of Social Care (Wales) Act 2016 which is provided wholly or mainly to persons aged 18 or over] and in Scotland means a care home service as defined by [¹² paragraph 2 of schedule 12 to the Public Services Reform (Scotland) Act 2010];

(b) "independent hospital"—

   (i) in England, means a hospital as defined by section 275 of the National Health Service Act 2006 that is not a health service hospital as defined by that section;

   (ii) in Wales, has the meaning assigned to it by section 2 of the Care Standards Act 2000; and

   (iii) in Scotland, means an independent healthcare service as defined in [¹² section 10F(1)(a) and (b) of the National Health Service (Scotland) Act 1978].]

[¹³ (6) The fourth condition, which applies only where the person has been awarded universal credit and their award of universal credit does not include an amount under section 10(2) of the 2012 Act (child or qualifying young person who is disabled) is that—

(a) in a case where a cold weather payment is payable in relation to a recorded period of cold weather as mentioned in regulation 2(1)(a)(i), the person was not in employment or gainful self-employment on any day during that period; or

(b) in a case where a cold weather payment is payable in relation to a forecasted period of weather as mentioned in regulation 2(1)(a)(ii), the person is not in employment or gainful self-employment on the day when the [¹⁴ Met] Office supplies the Department for Work and Pensions with the forecast.

(7) For the purpose of paragraph (6)—

(a) "employment" means employment under a contract of service, or in an office, including an elective office;

(b) a person is in gainful self-employment where—

   (i) they are carrying on a trade, profession or vocation as their main employment;

   (ii) their earnings from that trade, profession or vocation are treated as self-employed earnings for the purpose of regulations made under section 8(3) of the 2012 Act; and

   (iii) the trade, profession or vocation is organised, developed, regular and carried on in expectation of profit.]

[²¹ (8) The fifth condition is that the person's home is in England or Wales.]

AMENDMENTS

1. Social Fund Cold Weather Payments (General) Amendment No.3 Regulations 1991 (SI 1991/2448) reg.2 (November 1, 1991).

2. Social Fund Cold Weather Payments (General) Amendment Regulations 1993 (SI 1993/2450) reg.2 (November 1, 1993).

3. Social Fund Cold Weather Payments (General) Amendment Regulations 1996 (SI 1996/2544) reg.3 (November 4, 1996).

4. State Pension Credit (Consequential, Transitional and Miscellaneous Provisions) Regulations 2002 (SI 2002/3019) reg.31 (October 6, 2003).

5. Social Security (Removal of Residential Allowance and Miscellaneous Amendments) Regulations 2003 (SI 2003/1121) reg.3 (October 6, 2003).

6. Social Fund Cold Weather Payments (General) Amendment Regulations 2004 (SI 2004/2600) reg.2 (November 1, 2004).

7. Social Security (Care Homes and Independent Hospitals) Regulations 2005 (SI 2005/2687) reg.9 (October 24, 2005).

8. Social Fund Cold Weather Payments (General) Amendment Regulations 2008 (SI 2008/2569) reg.2(1) and (3) (October 27, 2008).

9. Health and Social Care Act 2008 (Miscellaneous Consequential Amendments) Order 2010 (SI 2010/1881) regs 2 and 6 (October 1, 2010).

10. Social Fund Cold Weather Payments (General) Amendment Regulations 2010 (SI 2010/2442) reg.2(1) and (3) (November 1, 2010).

11. Social Fund Cold Weather Payments (General) Amendment Regulations (No.2) 2010 (SI 2010/2591) reg.3(1) November 1, 2010.

12. Public Services Reform (Scotland) Act 2010 (Consequential Modifications of Enactments) Order 2011(SI 2011/2581) art.2 and Sch.2 para.15 (October 28, 2011).

13. Social Fund Cold Weather Payments (General) Regulations 1988 (SI 2013/248) reg.2(1) and (3)–(6) (November 1, 2013).

14. Social Fund Cold Weather Payments (General) (Amendment) Regulations 2016 (SI 2016/876) reg.2(1) and (3) (November 1, 2016).

15. Employment and Support Allowance and Universal Credit (Miscellaneous Amendments and Transitional and Savings Provisions) Regulations 2017 (SI 2017/204) reg.7(1) and Sch.1, Pt.1, para.2(1) and (3) (April 3, 2017).

16. Employment and Support Allowance and Universal Credit (Miscellaneous Amendments and Transitional and Savings Provisions) Regulations 2017 (SI 2017/204) reg.7(1) and Sch.1, Pt.2, para.11 (April 3, 2017).

17. Social Fund (Amendment) Regulations 2017 (SI 2017/271) reg.2 (April 6, 2017).

18. Social Security and Child Support (Regulation and Inspection of Social Care (Wales) Act 2016) (Consequential Provision) Regulations 2018 (SI 2018/228) reg.3 (April 2, 2018).

19. Loans for Mortgage Interest Regulations 2017 (SI 2017/725) reg.18 and Sch.5 para.10(1) and (3) (April 6, 2018).

20. Loans for Mortgage Interest (Amendment) Regulations 2021 (SI 2021/131) reg.3 (March 15, 2021).

21. Social Security (Scotland) Act 2018 (Winter Heating Assistance) (Consequential Modifications) Order 2022 (SI 2022/1018) art.2 (November 1, 2022).

DEFINITIONS

"the Act"—see reg.1(2).
"the General Regulations"—*ibid.*
"claimant"—*ibid.*
"family"—*ibid.*
"forecasted period of cold weather"—*ibid.*
"income-based jobseeker's allowance"—*ibid.*
"income support"—*ibid.*
"recorded period of cold weather"—*ibid.*

GENERAL NOTE

4.6 Regulation 1A sets out the five conditions which a claimant must satisfy in order to receive a cold weather payment. The second, third and fourth conditions do not apply to all claimants. However, where they apply, the conditions are cumulative so failure to satisfy any of them means that no cold weather payment can be made.

The first condition is that the claimant must either actually have been awarded (i.e. an underlying entitlement will not suffice) SPC, IS, income-based JSA, income-related ESA or universal credit, or owner-occupier loan payments—defined in reg.1(2) as meaning loan payments made under the Loans for Mortgage Interest Regulations 2017: see above—and in that latter case be treated as entitled to IS, IBJSA, SPC or IRESA under reg.2(2)(a) and (aa) of those Regulations, for at least one day in the relevant (forecasted or recorded) period of cold weather.

The second condition is that, unless the claimant has been awarded SPC (or has been awarded owner-occupier loan payments and is treated as entitled to SPC), then—for that day—either:

• his or her family must include a child under five;
• the claimant has an award of child tax credit which includes an individual element for a disabled, or severely disabled, child or qualifying young person;
• (if the claimant has been awarded IS or income-based JSA) his or her applicable amount must include one of the pensioner or disability premiums;
• (if the claimant has been awarded income-related ESA) he or she is in the work-related activity group or the support group, or his or her applicable amount must include either one of the pensioner or disability premiums; or
• (if the claimant has been awarded universal credit) the award includes either the disabled child addition (i.e. the additional amount of the child element payable for a child or qualifying young person who is disabled); or the claimant has limited capability for work or limited capability for work-related activity. Those who qualify on the basis that their award includes the LCW element or the LCWRA element must also satisfy the fourth condition.
• (if the claimant has been awarded owner-occupier loan payments) but is treated as entitled to either IS, IBJSA or IRESA (see above), his or her applicable amount for that benefit would include one of the premiums specified in the third to fifth bullet points above.

4.7 The third condition applies to claimants who do not have a child under five in their family and who do not have an award of child tax credit which includes one of the individual elements specified above. It is that the claimant does not reside in a care home or independent hospital (as defined in each case in para.(5)) or (for claimants who are not in receipt of universal credit: see para.(4A)) in an Abbeyfield Home or accommodation provided under the specified provisions of the Polish Resettlement Act 1947.

The fourth condition applies to claimants who have an award of universal credit that does not include the disabled child addition (i.e. those who have limited capability for work or work-related activity (see above)). It is that the claimant is not in gainful employment or self-employment (as defined in para.(7)) during the period of cold weather in respect of which the cold weather payment is payable.

The fifth condition is that the person's home is in England or Wales.

Since no claim for a cold weather payment is possible, the decision maker will identify qualifying claimants from Departmental records and make a payment automatically.

[¹**Prescribed circumstances**

4.8 **2.**—(1) The prescribed circumstances in which [⁹ a cold weather payment may be made] are—

[⁷ (a) subject to paragraphs (1A), (1B) and (3) to (6)—

    (i) there is a recorded period of cold weather at a primary [⁸ site], or
    (ii) there is a forecasted period of cold weather at a primary [⁸ site], and]
  (b) the home of the claimant is, or by virtue of paragraph (2)[⁷ ...] is treated as, situated in a postcode district in respect of which the [⁸ site] mentioned in sub-paragraph (a)(i) or, as the case may be, (a)(ii) is the designated [⁸ site].]
  (c) [² ...]

[⁵ [⁷ (1A) For the purposes of paragraph (1)(a)(i), where a primary [⁸ site] is unable to provide temperature information in respect of a particular day, the mean daily temperature on that day—
  (a) at the secondary [⁸ site], or
  (b) where there is no secondary [⁸ site] designated, or where the secondary [⁸ site] is unable to provide temperature information in respect of that day, at the alternative [⁸ site],
is to be used to determine whether or not there is a recorded period of cold weather at the primary [⁸ site].]

[⁷ (1B) For the purposes of paragraph (1)(a)(ii), where the Met Office is unable to produce a forecast in respect of a particular period at a primary [⁸ site], the forecast in respect of that period produced—
  (a) at the secondary [⁸ site], or
  (b) where there is no secondary [⁸ site] designated, or where the secondary [⁸ site] is unable to produce a forecast in respect of that period, at the alternative [⁸ site],
is to be used to determine whether or not there is a forecasted period of cold weather at the primary [⁸ site].]]

[⁷ (2) For the purposes of this regulation, where the home of the claimant is not situated within a postcode district for which a primary [⁸ site] is designated, it is to be treated as situated within a postcode district—
  (a) which, in the opinion of the Met Office, is the most geographically and climatologically representative of that postcode district, and
  (b) for which a primary [⁸ site] is designated.]

(3) Subject to paragraphs (4) and (5) where a recorded period of cold weather is joined by an overlap period to a forecasted period of cold weather a payment under paragraph (1) may only be made in respect of the forecasted period of cold weather.

(4) Where—
  (a) there is a continuous period of forecasted periods of cold weather, each of which is linked by an overlap period; and
  (b) the total number of recorded periods of cold weather during that continuous period is greater than the total number of forecasted periods of cold weather,
a payment in respect of the last recorded period of cold weather may also be made under paragraph (1).

[⁶ (5) Where—
  (a) a claimant satisfies the conditions in regulation 1A and paragraph (1) in respect of a recorded period of cold weather, and
  (b) a payment in respect of the recorded period of cold weather does not fall to be made by virtue of paragraph (4), and
  (c) the claimant does not satisfy the conditions in regulation 1A in respect of the forecasted period of cold weather which is linked to the recorded period of cold weather by an overlap period,

a cold weather payment may be made in respect of that recorded period of cold weather.

(6) A cold weather payment may not be made after the end of the period of 26 weeks beginning with the last day of the winter period in which the period of cold weather concerned falls.]

[⁷ (7) For the purposes of this regulation—

"alternative [⁸ site]" means a [⁸ site]—

(a) which, in the opinion of the Met Office, is the most geographically and climatologically representative for the postcode district in which the home of the claimant is situated, and

(b) is able to provide temperature information—

    (i) for the purposes of paragraph (1A), for the relevant day, or

    (ii) for the purposes of paragraph (1B), for the production of a forecast for the relevant period;

"primary [⁸ site]" means a [⁸ site] designated for a postcode district in accordance with regulation 2A(1);

"secondary [⁸ site]" means a [⁸ site] designated for a postcode district in accordance with regulation 2A(2).]

AMENDMENTS

1. Social Fund Cold Weather Payments (General) Amendments No.2 Regulations 1991 (SI 1991/2238) reg.3 (November 1, 1991).
2. Social Fund Cold Weather Payments (General) Amendment No.3 Regulations 1991 (SI 1991/2448) reg.3 (November 1, 1991).
3. Social Fund Cold Weather Payments (General) Amendment (No.2) Regulations 1992 (SI 1992/2448) reg.3 (November 1, 1992).
4. Social Fund Cold Weather Payments (General) Amendment Regulations 1996 (SI 1996/2544) reg.4 (November 4, 1996).
5. Social Fund Cold Weather Payments (General) Amendment Regulations 1997 (SI 1997/2311) reg.3 (November 1, 1997).
6. Social Fund Cold Weather Payments (General) Amendment Regulations 2010 (SI 2010/2442) reg.2(1) and (4) (November 1, 2010).
7. Social Fund Cold Weather Payments (General) (Amendment) Regulations 2016 (SI 2016/876) reg.2(1) and (4) (November 1, 2016).
8. Social Fund and Social Security (Claims and Payments) (Amendment) Regulations 2020 (SI 2020/600) reg.3(1) and (3) (July 9, 2020).

DEFINITIONS

"the Act"—see reg.1(2).
"the General Regulations"—*ibid.*
"claimant"—*ibid.*
"family"—*ibid.*
"forecasted period of cold weather"—*ibid.*
"home"—*ibid.*
"income support"—*ibid.*
"overlap period"—*ibid.*
"postcode district"—*ibid.*
"recorded period of cold weather"—*ibid.*
"[⁸ site]"—*ibid.*

GENERAL NOTE

4.9   Regulation 2 prescribes the circumstances in which a cold weather payment is to be made. The principal rule is established by para.1(a) and (b): a period of cold weather (i.e. seven consecutive days) must be either recorded or forecast at the weather site relevant to the claimant's home. The two conditions are alternatives so that the cold weather payment is payable even if a forecasted period of cold weather does not materialise or if there is a recorded period of cold weather that was not forecast.

Under para.(1), the relevant weather site will normally be the one designated for the relevant postcode district pursuant to reg.2A(1). However, if that weather site is unable to provide temperature information, the relevant site is the secondary site designated pursuant to reg.2A(2): see para.(2)(a). If the secondary site is also unable to provide temperature information, or if no secondary site has been designated, the relevant weather site will be the alternative site as defined in para.(7): see para.(2)(b).

Paragraphs (3)–(5) are designed to prevent double payment. An individual day can only count as part of one recorded period of cold weather or one forecasted period of cold weather (see the definitions in reg.1(2)), although it can be part of both a recorded and a forecasted period. Where there is a recorded period of cold weather which coincides wholly or partly with the forecasted period, there is then an overlap period, again defined in reg.1(2). The general rule in those circumstances is that the cold weather payment is only payable for the forecasted period (para.(3)) because the policy is to make the payment before the extra heating is required if possible. That rule is subject to two exceptions:

• where there is a continuous series of overlapping forecasted periods and recorded periods which includes more recorded periods than forecasted periods, a cold weather payment can also be made for the final recorded period (para.(4)); and

• where para.(4) does not apply and the claimant does not satisfy the conditions in reg.1A for any day of the forecasted period, but does satisfy those conditions for at least one day of the recorded period, then a payment can be made for the recorded period (para.(5)).

[¹ Designation of primary and secondary [² sites]

2A.—(1) The Secretary of State must designate a primary [² site] for each postcode district.

(2) The Secretary of State may designate a secondary [² site] for each postcode district.]

4.10

AMENDMENT

1. Social Fund Cold Weather Payments (General) (Amendment) Regulations 2016 (SI 2016/876) reg.2(1) and (5) (November 1, 2016).
2. Social Fund and Social Security (Claims and Payments) (Amendment) Regulations 2020 (SI 2020/600) reg.3(1), (4) and (5) (July 9, 2020).

GENERAL NOTE

There were originally 55 primary weather stations. At the time of going to press, there are 101 designated primary sites. The increase is intended to improve the sensitivity of the scheme.

4.11

[¹ Publication of designations

2B.—(1) The Secretary of State must publish details of a designation under regulation 2A.

(2) Publication under paragraph (1) may be in such manner as the Secretary of State considers appropriate.]

4.12

AMENDMENT

1. Social Fund Cold Weather Payments (General) (Amendment) Regulations 2016 (SI 2016/876) reg.2(1) and (5) (November 1, 2016).

4.13   The Secretary of State must publish details of the designation "in such manner as [she] considers appropriate". The current list (which dates from February 2017) can be found in Chapter L4: *Universal Credit – Social Fund – Cold Weather Payments* of *Advice for Decision Making*. There is a cold weather payment postcode checker at *https://coldweatherpayments.dwp.gov.uk/*.

[¹ Review and variation of designations

4.14   **2C.**—(1) The Secretary of State must, in accordance with paragraph (2), review a designation under regulation 2A to determine if it remains appropriate.

(2) Each designation must be reviewed every 12 months, in the period beginning with 1st November and ending with 31st October.

(3) If, on review, or at any other time, the Secretary of State is of the opinion that a designation is no longer appropriate, the Secretary of State must—

(a) vary the designation in such manner as the Secretary of State considers expedient, and

(b) publish details of the varied designation.

(4) Publication under paragraph (3)(b) may be in such manner as the Secretary of State considers appropriate.

(5) When determining whether to vary a designation, the Secretary of State must have regard to any recommendation made by the Met Office.

(6) For the purposes of this regulation, whether a designation is appropriate includes, in particular, whether the [² site] designated—

(a) is geographically and climatologically representative for the relevant postcode district, and

(b) provides accurate temperature information.]

AMENDMENT

1. Social Fund Cold Weather Payments (General) (Amendment) Regulations 2016 (SI 2016/876) reg.2(1) and (5) (November 1, 2016).

2. Social Fund and Social Security (Claims and Payments) (Amendment) Regulations 2020 (SI 2020/600) reg.3(1) and (6) (July 9, 2020).

GENERAL NOTE

4.15   Designations under reg.2A must be reviewed annually taking into account the matters in para.(6) and any recommendation made by the Met Office (para.(5)). If, as a result of the review, the Secretary of State decides to vary the designation, he must publish details of the variation, again "in such manner as [he] considers appropriate" (paras (3)(b) and (4)).

Prescribed amount

4.16   **3.**—[¹ . . .] The amount of the payment in respect of each period of cold weather shall be [²³£25].

AMENDMENTS

1. Social Fund Cold Weather Payments (General) Amendment No.2 Regulations 1991 (SI 1991/2238) reg.4 (November 1, 1991).

2. Social Fund Cold Weather Payments (General) Amendment Regulations 1995 (SI 1995/2620) reg.2 (November 1, 1995).

3. Social Fund Cold Weather Payments (General) Amendment Regulations (No. 2) 2010 (SI 2010/2591) reg.2(1) November 1, 2010.

GENERAL NOTE

Payment is at the fixed rate of £25 for each week which counts under regs 1A and 2. The weekly rate was originally set at £5 in 1988. It was then increased to £6 in February 1991, to £7 in November 1994 and to £8.50 in November 1995. For the periods from November 1, 2008 to March 31, 2009, and from November 1, 2009 to March 31, 2010, reg.3 was modified by, respectively, reg.3 of the Social Fund Cold Weather Payments (General) Amendment Regulations 2008 (SI 2008/2569) and reg.3 of the Social Fund Cold Weather Payments (General) Amendment Regulations 2009 (SI 2009/2649). In each case, the effect of the modification was that the weekly amount of £8.50 increased to £25 for any period of cold weather which began during either of the above periods. That increase was made permanent with effect from November 1, 2010.   **4.17**

Effect and calculation of capital

4.—[¹ . . .]   **4.18**

AMENDMENT

1. Social Fund Cold Weather Payments (General) Amendment No.2 Regulations 1991 (SI 1991/2238) reg.5 (November 1, 1991).

GENERAL NOTE

There is no capital limit for cold weather payments.   **4.19**

SCHEDULES

Regulation 2(1), (1A) and (2)

[¹⁸ SCHEDULE 1

IDENTIFICATION OF STATIONS AND POSTCODE DISTRICTS

[¹⁹ . . .]]   **4.20**

AMENDMENTS

1. Social Security Cold Weather Payments (General) Amendment Regulations 2000 (SI 2000/2690) reg.2 (November 1, 2000).
2. The Social Fund Cold Weather Payments (General) Amendment Regulations 2002 (SI 2002/2524) reg.2 (November 1, 2002).
3. Social Fund Cold Weather Payments (General) Amendment Regulations 2003 (SI 2003/2605) reg.2 and Sch.1 (November 1, 2003).
4. Social Fund Cold Weather Payments (General) Amendment (No.2) Regulations 2003 (SI 2003/3203) reg.2 (November 28, 2003).
5. Social Fund Cold Weather Payments (General) Amendment Regulations 2004 (SI 2004/2600) reg.3 (November 1, 2004).
6. Social Fund Cold Weather Payments (General) Amendment Regulations 2005 (SI 2005/2724) reg.4 and Sch.1 (November 1, 2005).
7. Social Fund Cold Weather Payments (General) Amendment Regulations 2006 (SI 2006/2655) reg.3 and Sch.1 (November 1, 2006).
8. Social Fund Cold Weather Payments (General) Amendment Regulations 2007 (SI 2007/2912) reg.3 and Sch.1 (November 1, 2007).

9. Social Fund Cold Weather Payments (General) Amendment Regulations 2008 (SI 2008/2569) reg.2(1) and (4) (November 1, 2008).

10. Social Fund Cold Weather Payments (General) Amendment Regulations 2009 (SI 2009/2649) reg.2(1) and (2) and Sch.1 (November 1, 2009).

11. Social Fund Cold Weather Payments (General) Amendment Regulations 2010 (SI 2010/2442) reg.2(1) and (5) (November 1, 2010).

12. Social Fund Cold Weather Payments (General) Amendment Regulations 2011 (SI 2011/2423) reg.2(1) and Sch.2 (November 1, 2011).

13. Social Fund Cold Weather Payments (General) Amendment Regulations 2012 (SI 2012/2280) reg.2(1) (November 1, 2012).

14. Social Fund Cold Weather Payments (General) Amendment (No.2) Regulations 2012 (SI 2012/2379) reg.2 (November 1, 2012).

15. Social Fund Cold Weather Payments (General) Amendment (No.2) Regulations 2013 (SI 2538/2013) reg.2(1) and Sch.1 (November 1, 2013).

16. Social Fund Cold Weather Payments (General) Amendment Regulations 2014 (SI 2014/2687) reg.2(1) and Sch.1 (November 1, 2014).

17. Social Fund Cold Weather Payments (General) Amendment Regulations 2015 (SI 2015/183) reg.2 (March 23, 2015).

18. Social Fund Cold Weather Payments (General) Amendment (No.2) Regulations 2015 (SI 2015/1662) reg.2(1) and Sch.1 (November 1, 2015).

19. Social Fund Cold Weather Payments (General) (Amendment) Regulations 2016 (SI 2016/876) reg.2(1) and (6) (November 1, 2016).

Regulation 2(1A)(a) and 2(1B)(a)

[[13] SCHEDULE 2

SPECIFIED ALTERNATIVE STATIONS

4.21   [[14] . . .]]

AMENDMENTS

1. Social Fund Cold Weather Payments (General) Amendment Regulations 1999 (SI 1999/2781) reg.3 and Sch.2 (November 1, 1999).

2. Social Fund Cold Weather Payments (General) Amendment Regulations 2003 (SI 2003/2605) reg.3 and Sch.2 (November 1, 2003).

3. Social Fund Cold Weather Payments (General) Amendment Regulations 2005 (SI 2005/2724) reg.5 and Sch.2 (November 1, 2005).

4. Social Fund Cold Weather Payments (General) Amendment Regulations 2006 (SI 2006/2655) reg.4 and Sch.2 (November 1, 2006).

5. Social Fund Cold Weather Payments (General) Amendment Regulations 2007 (SI 2007/2912) reg.4 and Sch.2 (November 1, 2007).

6. Social Fund Cold Weather Payments (General) Amendment Regulations 2008 (SI 2008/2569) reg.2(1) and (6) (November 1, 2008).

7. Social Fund Cold Weather Payments (General) Amendment Regulations 2009 (SI 2009/2649) reg.2(1) and (3) and Sch.2 (November 1, 2009).

8. Social Fund Cold Weather Payments (General) Amendment Regulations 2010 (SI 2010/2442) reg.2(1) and (6) (November 1, 2010).

9. Social Fund Cold Weather Payments (General) Amendment Regulations 2011 (SI 2011/2423) reg.2(2) and Sch.2 (November 1, 2011).

10. Social Fund Cold Weather Payments (General) Amendment Regulations 2012 (SI 2012/2280) reg.2(2) (November 1, 2012).

11. Social Fund Cold Weather Payments (General) Amendment (No.2) Regulations 2013 (SI 2538/2013) reg.2(2) and Sch.2 (November 1, 2013).

12. Social Fund Cold Weather Payments (General) Amendment Regulations 2014 (SI 2014/2687) reg.2(2) and Sch.2 (November 1, 2014).
13. Social Fund Cold Weather Payments (General) Amendment (No.2) Regulations 2015 (SI 2015/1662) reg.2(2) and Sch.2 (November 1, 2015).
14. Social Fund Cold Weather Payments (General) (Amendment) Regulations 2016 (SI 2016/876) reg.2(1) and (6) (November 1, 2016).

The Social Fund Winter Fuel Payment Regulations 2000

(SI 2000/729)

Made by the Secretary of State under ss.138(2) and (4) and 175(1), (3) and (4) of the Social Security Contributions and Benefits Act 1992 and ss.5(1)(a) and (i), and 189(1) and (4) of the Social Security Administration Act 1992 and s.16(1) and s.79(1) and (4) of, and para.3 of Sch.5 to, the Social Security Act 1998 [In force April 3, 2000]

GENERAL NOTE

In November 1997, the Government announced that all pensioner house-   4.22
holds would receive a one-off payment in the winter of 1998 (and another in 1999) towards their fuel bills. These payments would be in addition to any cold weather payments which might be awarded under the Social Fund Cold Weather Payments (General) Regulations 1998 (above). As is the case under those regulations, no separate claim needs to be made for a winter fuel payment. Entitlement simply depends on the person being ordinarily resident in Great Britain and over the qualifying age on at least one day in the "qualifying week" (see reg.1(2)).
The qualifying age was originally pensionable age (i.e. 60 for a woman and 65 for a man). However, in *R. v Secretary of State for Social Security, Ex p. Taylor* (C–382/98)(ECJ, December 16, 1999), the ECJ held that the different qualifying ages for men and women constituted unlawful discrimination on the ground of sex contrary to Directive 79/7/EEC. The qualifying age was therefore equalised at 60 for both women and men from the winter of 2000–2001 and remained at that level until April 6, 2010 when the gradual process of increasing pensionable age for women began. The qualifying age is now the same as for state pension credit, i.e. pensionable age in the case of a woman, and in the case of a man, the age which is pensionable age for a woman born on the same day.

Citation, commencement and interpretation

1.—(1) These Regulations may be cited as the Social Fund Winter Fuel   4.23
Payment Regulations 2000 and shall come into force on 3rd April 2000.
(2) In these Regulations—
[⁵ "care home" in England [¹⁵ …] has the meaning assigned to it by section 3 of the Care Standards Act 2000, [¹⁵ in Wales, means a care home service within the meaning of Part 1 of the Regulation and Inspection of Social Care (Wales) Act 2016 which is provided wholly or mainly to persons aged 18 or over] and in Scotland means a care home service as defined by [¹¹ paragraph 2 of schedule 12 to the Public Services Reform (Scotland) Act 2010];]
[⁶ [¹² ¹³ "couple" means—
(a) two people who are married to, or civil partners of, each other and are members of the same household; or

(b) two people who are not married to, or civil partners of, each other but are living together [16 as if they were a married couple or civil partners];]]
"free in-patient treatment" shall be construed in accordance with regulation [7 2(4) and (5) of the Social Security (Hospital In-Patients) Regulations 2005];
[8 "income-related employment and support allowance" means an income-related allowance under Part 1 of the Welfare Reform Act (employment and support allowance);]
[14 . . .]
[5 10 "independent hospital"—
  (a) in England, means a hospital as defined by section 275 of the National Health Service Act 2006 that is not a health service hospital as defined by that section;
  (b) in Wales, has the meaning assigned to it by section 2 of the Care Standards Act 2000; and
  (c) in Scotland, means an independent healthcare service as defined in [11 section 10F(1)(a) and (b) of the National Health Service (Scotland) Act 1978];]
[9 "qualifying age for state pension credit" means—
  (a) in the case of a woman, pensionable age; or
  (b) in the case of a man, the age which is pensionable age in the case of a woman born on the same day as the man;]
"qualifying week" means in respect of any year the week beginning on the third Monday in the September of that year;
[5 . . .]
"partner" means a member of—
  (a) [6 a couple]; or
  (b) a polygamous marriage;
[5 . . .] and
[4 "state pension credit" has the meaning assigned to it by section 1 of the State Pension Credit Act 2002;]
[1 . . .]
[2 (3) [5 . . .] in these Regulations a person—
(a) is in residential care if, disregarding any period of temporary absence, he resides in—
    [5 (i) a care home;
    (ii) an independent hospital; or]
    (iii) accommodation provided under section 3(1) of the Polish Resettlement Act 1947 (provision by the Secretary of State of accommodation in camps),
    throughout the qualifying week and the period of 12 weeks immediately before the qualifying week;
(b) lives with another person if—
    (i) disregarding any period of temporary absence, they share accommodation as their mutual home; and
    (ii) they are not in residential care.
[5 . . .]
(4) In these Regulations, unless the context otherwise requires, a reference—
  (a) to a numbered regulation is to the regulation in these Regulations bearing that number; and

(b) in a regulation to a numbered paragraph is to the paragraph in that regulation bearing that number.

AMENDMENTS

1. Social Fund Winter Fuel Payment (Amendment) Regulations 2000 (SI 2000/2864) reg.2(a)(1) (November 13, 2000).
2. Social Fund Winter Fuel Payment (Amendment) Regulations 2001 (SI 2001/3375) reg.2(2) (November 2, 2001).
3. Social Security (Removal of Residential Allowance and Miscellaneous Amendments) Regulations 2003 (SI 2003/1121) reg.5 (October 6, 2003).
4. Social Fund Winter Fuel Payment (Amendment) Regulations 2004 (SI 2004/2154) reg.2(a) (September 20, 2004).
5. Social Security (Care Homes and Independent Hospitals) Regulations 2005 (SI 2005/2687) reg.8 (October 24, 2005).
6. Civil Partnership (Pensions, Social Security and Child Support) (Consequential, etc. Provisions) Order 2005 (SI 2005/2877) art.2(3) and Sch.3 para.32 (December 5, 2005).
7. Social Security (Hospital In-Patients) Regulations 2005 (SI 2005/3360) reg.7 (April 10, 2006).
8. Employment and Support Allowance (Consequential Provisions) (No.2) Regulations 2008 (SI 2008/1554) reg.7(1) and (2) (October 27, 2008).
9. Social Security (Equalisation of State Pension Age) Regulations 2009 (SI 2009/1488) reg.19 (April 6, 2010).
10. Health and Social Care Act 2008 (Miscellaneous Consequential Amendments) Order 2010 (SI 2010/1881) regs 2 and 5 (October 1, 2010).
11. Public Services Reform (Scotland) Act 2010 (Consequential Modifications of Enactments) Order 2011(SI 2011/2581) art.2 and Sch.2 para.29 (October 28, 2011).
12. Marriage (Same Sex Couples) Act 2013 (Consequential Provisions) Order 2014 (SI 2014/107) reg.2 and Sch.1 para.28 (March 13, 2014). The amendment extends to England and Wales only (see SI 2014/107 art.1(4)).
13. Marriage and Civil Partnership (Scotland) Act 2014 and Civil Partnership Act 2004 (Consequential Provisions and Modifications) Order 2014 (SI 2014/3229) art.29 and Sch.6 para.19 (December 16, 2014). The amendment relates only to Scotland (see SI 2014/3229, art.3(4)) but is in the same terms as the amendments made in relation to England and Wales by SI 2014/107 (see point 12 above).
14. Social Security (Miscellaneous Amendments) Regulations 2015 (SI 2015/67) reg.4(1)(a) (February 23, 2015).
15. Social Security and Child Support (Regulation and Inspection of Social Care (Wales) Act 2016) (Consequential Provision) Regulations 2018 (SI 2018/228) reg.6 (April 2, 2018).
16. Civil Partnership (Opposite-sex Couples) Regulations 2019 (SI 2019/1458) reg.41 and Sch.3 Pt.2 para.58 (December 2, 2019).

GENERAL NOTE

"qualifying age for state pension credit": As a result of the progressive increase in the retirement age for women, pensionable age for men and women is now the same for anyone born after December 5, 1953.

Social fund winter fuel payments

[¹**2.**—(1) Subject to paragraphs (2) [⁶ to (4)] and regulation 3 of these Regulations, and regulation 36(2) of the Social Security (Claims and Payments) Regulations 1987, the Secretary of State shall pay to a person who—   **4.24**
[⁶ (a) in respect of any day falling within the qualifying week is—

      (i) ordinarily resident in Great Britain; or

    (ii) habitually resident in [⁸ any of the countries listed in the Schedule to these Regulations]; and]

[⁵ (b) in or before the qualifying week has attained the qualifying age for state pension credit,]

a winter fuel payment of—

      (i) £200 unless he is in residential care or head (ii)(aa) applies; or

    (ii) £100 if [³ state pension credit] [⁴ , an income-based jobseeker's allowance or an income-related employment and support allowance] has not been, nor falls to be, paid to him in respect of the qualifying week and he is—

        (aa) in that week living with a person to whom a payment under these Regulations has been, or falls to be, made in respect of the winter following the qualifying week; or

        (bb) in residential care.

  (2) Where such a person has attained the age of 80 in or before the qualifying week—

    (a) in paragraph (1)(i), for the sum of £200 there shall be substituted the sum of £300; and

[²(b) in paragraph (1)(ii), for the sum of £100 there shall be substituted the sum of £200, except that—

      (i) where he is in that week living with a person to whom a payment under these Regulations has been, or falls to be, made in respect of the winter following that week who has also attained the age of 80 in or before that week, or

    (ii) where he is in residential care,

there shall be substituted the sum of £150.]

  (3) Where such a person has not attained the age of 80 in or before the qualifying week but he is a partner of and living with a person who has done so, in paragraph (1)(i) for the sum of £200 there shall be substituted the sum of £300.]

  [⁶ (4) A person does not qualify for a winter fuel payment by virtue of falling within paragraph [⁷ (1)(a)(ii)] above unless—

    (a) they are a person to whom Council Regulation (EC) No 1408/71 [⁹, as amended from time to time,] on the application of social security schemes to employed persons, to self-employed persons and to members of their families moving within the Community, or Regulation (EC) No 883/2004 [⁹, as amended from time to time,] of the European Parliament and of the Council on the coordination of social security systems, applies; and

    (b) they are able to demonstrate a genuine and sufficient link to the United Kingdom social security system.]

AMENDMENTS

  1. Social Fund Winter Fuel Payment (Amendment) Regulations 2003 (SI 2003/1737) reg.2 (September 1, 2003).

  2. Social Fund Winter Fuel Payment (Amendment) (No.2) Regulations 2003, (SI 2003/2192) reg.2 (September 3, 2003).

  3. Social Fund Winter Fuel Payment (Amendment) Regulations 2004 (SI 2004/2154) reg.2(b) (September 20, 2004).

  4. Employment and Support Allowance (Consequential Provisions) (No.2) Regulations 2008 (SI 2008/1554) reg.7(1) and (3) (October 27, 2008).

5. Social Security (Equalisation of State Pension Age) Regulations 2009 (SI 2009/1488) reg.20 (April 6, 2010).
6. Social Fund Winter Fuel Payment (Amendment) Regulations 2013 (SI 2013/1509) reg.2(1) and (2) (September 16, 2013).
7. Social Security (Miscellaneous Amendments) Regulations 2015 (SI 2015/67) reg.4(1)(b) (February 23, 2015).
8. Social Fund Winter Fuel Payment (Amendment) Regulations 2014 (SI 2014/3270) reg.2(1) and (2) (September 21, 2015).
9. Social Security (Updating of EU References) (Amendment) Regulations 2018 (SI 2018/1084) reg.4 and Sch. para.9 (November 15, 2018).

DEFINITIONS

"qualifying week"—see reg.1(2).
"residential care"—see reg.1(3).

GENERAL NOTE

Regulation 2 sets out the conditions of entitlement to a winter fuel payment. A person qualifies if: **4.25**

(a) He or she is either ordinarily resident in Great Britain, or in one of the countries listed in the Schedule to the Regulations, in the qualifying week (i.e. the week commencing on the third Monday in September (see reg.1(2)).

Claimants who qualify on the basis of habitual residence in a scheduled country must also fall within the personal scope of Regulation (EC) No. 1408/71 or of Regulation (EC) 883/2004 and have a "genuine and sufficient link to the United Kingdom social security system": see para.(4) and Vol.III of the 2020/21 edition (as updated in Vol.III).

Until the winter of 2015/16, winter fuel payments were payable to people who were habitually resident in any EEA state (or Switzerland) rather than only to those who were habitually in a scheduled country. The effect of the amendment made by SI 2014/3270 with effect from September 21, 2015 is that those who are habitually resident in Cyprus, France, Greece, Malta, Portugal and Spain no longer qualify. According to the explanatory memorandum to SI 2014/3270 the average winter temperature (November to March) in the warmest part of the United Kingdom is 5.6°C. The policy is to exclude from entitlement those who are habitually resident in EEA states where the average winter temperature is warmer. The memorandum goes on to state:

"7.7   DWP is aware there will be people who live in cold regions of "warm" countries who will not be eligible for a Winter Fuel Payment. However, we would have to implement the scheme on a regional basis throughout the EEA in order to make a Winter Fuel Payment for even some of these people. DWP considered this very carefully but concluded that it would introduce disproportionate complexity and administrative costs. Therefore, the scheme has to be administered on a countrywide basis using the average winter temperature for each EEA country to determine where Winter Fuel Payments will be payable."

For the winter of 2019/20 the qualifying week ran from Monday, September 16 to Sunday, September 22, 2019; for the winter of 2020/21, it ran from Monday, September 21 to Sunday, September 27, 2020; and for the winter of 2021/22, it will run from Monday, September 20 to Sunday, September 26, 2021.

(b) He attains the qualifying age for state pension credit before the end of the qualifying week. To have been eligible for the winter 2021/22, the claimant must have been born on or before October 5, 1954. To be eligible for the winter 2021/22 s/he must have been born on or before September 26, 1955.

People who meet these conditions may nevertheless be excluded from entitlement if reg.3 applies to them.

The drafting of reg.2 is quite unnecessarily opaque and must be read with reg.3 to be fully understood. Careful analysis discloses that, subject to what is said below about modification, it prescribes four rates of payment—£300, £200, £150 and £100—which apply as follows.

4.26
Claimants who live alone, or are the only person in their household who qualify for the winter fuel payment, receive either £200 (reg.2(1)(b)(i)) or £300 if they have reached the age of 80 by the end of the qualifying week (reg.2(2)(a)). Those rates do not apply to claimants in residential care.

For claimants who live with another person, who also qualifies for a winter fuel payment (described in this note as a "qualifying person"), the position is more complicated:

- If the qualifying person is the claimant's *partner* and has been awarded SPC, income-based JSA or income-related ESA, then the claimant is excluded from entitlement (reg.3(1)(a)(i)). The effect, at least in the normal case where the couple do not live with a third (or fourth, etc.) person who is also a qualifying person, is that, as the claimant has been excluded, the partner becomes the only person in the household who qualifies for the payment and therefore receives the £200 rate under reg.2(1)(b)(i), or, if the partner or the claimant is over 80, the £300 rate under reg.2(2)(a) or reg.2(3) respectively.

- The converse also applies. Where it is the *claimant* who has been awarded SPC, income-based JSA or income-related ESA, and he/she lives with a partner who would otherwise be a qualifying person, then his or her partner is excluded from entitlement by reg.3(1)(a)(i) and it is therefore the claimant who is entitled to receive the £200 rate under reg.2(1)(b)(i).

- Subject to that, claimants who have *not* been awarded SPC, income-based JSA or income-related ESA, receive £100 (reg.2(1)(b)(ii)(aa)). That appears to be the case even if the qualifying people have been awarded SPC, income-based JSA or income-related ESA, as long as they are not the claimant's partner. That rate is increased to £200 for a claimant aged 80 or over (reg.2(2)(b)), unless the qualifying person is also aged 80 or over, in which case it is increased to £150 reg.2(2)(b)(i).

- The rate payable where the claimant has been awarded SPC, income-based JSA or income-related ESA and lives with qualifying person, who is not his or her partner, and who has also been awarded SPC, income-based JSA or income-related ESA is unclear.

The point turns on the meaning of the words "or head (ii)(aa) applies" in reg.2(1)(b)(i). Does head (aa) apply whenever a claimant lives with a qualifying person, or does it only apply when the additional requirement that the claimant has not been awarded SPC, income-based JSA or income-related ESA is satisfied? The former interpretation is the more natural: the additional requirement is contained in the main body of subpara.(ii) but not in head (aa) itself, so if it was intended to refer to it why not refer to the whole subparagraph rather than just head (aa)? But on that view, neither the claimant, nor the qualifying person receives a payment: reg.2(1)(b)(i) does not apply (because head (ii)(aa) does) and no other rate has been prescribed that expressly covers the situation in the first sentence of this bullet point.

It cannot have been intended to leave two people, both of whom are reliant on income-related benefits, without a winter fuel payment that is paid to many people who are much better off financially. Therefore one is driven to the latter interpretation. On that view, head (ii)(aa) does not apply in the circumstances under discussion (because the claimant has an award of SPC, income-based JSA or income-related ESA for the qualifying week) and so the claimants (and the qualifying people) are entitled to £200 under reg.2(1)(b)(i) (if they are aged 79 or less) or £300 (if they are aged 80 or over).

The test for whether one person lives with another for these purposes, is established in reg.1(3)(b). It provides a person lives with another person if, disregarding any period of temporary absence, they share accommodation as their mutual home and are not in residential care (as defined below).

Claimants who are in residential care are only entitled if they have *not* been awarded SPC, income-based JSA or income-related ESA for the qualifying week, in which case they get £100 (reg.2(1)(b)(ii)(bb)) or, if they are 80 or over, £150 (reg.2(2)(b)(ii)). Claimants in residential care who do have an award of SPC, income-based JSA or income-related ESA for the qualifying week are excluded from entitlement. With effect from February 23, 2015, the new reg.3(1)(a)(iv)—which appears to have been introduced to address criticisms of the drafting made in previous editions—confirms that this is the case. People count as being in residential care if they have resided in a care home an independent hospital or a Polish Resettlement Home for a continuous period of at least 13 weeks ending with the last day of the qualifying week: see reg.1(3)(a). Temporary absences are disregarded when calculating the 13-week period. **4.27**

The position is further complicated by the fact that the above rates of payment were temporarily modified by:

- reg.2 of the Social Fund Winter Fuel Payment (Temporary Increase) Regulations 2008 (SI 2008/1778) during "the 2008–09 winter" (defined as "the winter which follows the qualifying week beginning on 15th September 2008");

- reg.2 of the Social Fund Winter Fuel Payment (Temporary Increase) Regulations 2009 (SI 2009/1489) during "the 2009–2010 winter" (defined as "the winter which follows the qualifying week beginning on 21st September 2009"); and

- reg.2 of the Social Fund Winter Fuel Payment (Temporary Increase) Regulations 2010 (SI 2010/1161) during "the 2010-2011 winter" (defined as the winter which follows the qualifying week beginning on September 20, 2010).

On each occasion, the modifications took the form of a temporary increase in so that the £100 rate in regs 2(1)(b)(ii) became £125; the £100 figure in reg.2(2)(b) became £125; the £200 rate in regs 2(1)(b)(i), (2)(a) and (3), became £250; the £200 rate in reg.2(2)(b) became £275; the £150 rate in reg.2(2)(b) became £200; and the £300 rate in regs 2(2)(a) and 2(3) became £400.

In respect of the winter of 2022/23, yet another temporary modification was made, but at different rates. For the winter that follows the qualifying week beginning on September 19, 2022, reg.2 of the Social Fund Winter Fuel Payment (Temporary Increase) Regulations 2022 (SI 2022/813) modified the 2000 Regulations as follows:

- the £100 rate in regs 2(1)(b)(ii) and 2(2)(b) became £250;

- the £200 rate in regs 2(1)(b)(i), (2)(a) and (3) became £500;

- the £200 rate in reg.2(2)(b) became £350;

- the £150 rate in reg.2(2)(b) became £300; and

- the £300 rate in regs 2(2)(a) and 2(3) became £600.

Those 2022/23 rates will be maintained for the winter of 2023/24: Social Fund Winter Fuel Payment (Temporary Increase) Regulations 2023 (SI 2023/549), coming into force on September 18, 2023.

Note that it is possible to be "ordinarily resident" in more than one country: see *CIS/1691/2014.*

Persons not entitled to a social fund winter fuel payment

4.28
3.—(1) Regulation 2 shall not apply in respect of a person who—
(a) is [⁵ throughout the qualifying week]—
  [⁴ (i) a partner of, and living with, a person who attained the qualifying age for state pension credit in or before the qualifying week and to whom state pension credit, an income-based jobseeker's allowance or an income-related employment and support allowance has been, or falls to be, paid in respect of the qualifying week;]
  (ii) receiving free in-patient treatment and has been receiving free in-patient treatment for more than 52 weeks; or
  (iii) detained in custody under a sentence imposed by a court; or
  [⁷ (iv) in residential care and is a person to whom state pension credit, an income-based jobseeker's allowance or an income-related employment and support allowance has been, or falls to be, paid in respect of the qualifying week; or]
(b) subject to paragraph (2), has not made a claim for a winter fuel payment [⁵ on or before the 31st March] following the qualifying week in respect of the winter following that week.
(2) Paragraph (1)(b) shall not apply where—
(a) a payment has been made by virtue of regulation 4(1) [⁵ on or before the 31st March] following the qualifying week in respect of the winter following that week; or
(b) regulation 4(2) applies.
[⁶ (3) No person is entitled to a winter fuel payment for the winter of 1997 to 1998, 1998 to 1999 or 1999 to 2000 unless they have made a claim for such a payment on or before 31st March 2014.]

AMENDMENTS

1. Social Fund Winter Fuel Payment (Amendment) Regulations 2000 (SI 2000/2864) reg.2(a)(ii) (November 13, 2000).
2. Social Fund Winter Fuel Payment (Amendment) Regulations 2004 (SI 2004/2154) reg.2(c) (September 20, 2004).
3. Employment and Support Allowance (Consequential Provisions) (No.2) Regulations 2008 (SI 2008/1554) reg.7(1) and (4) (October 27, 2008).
4. Social Security (Equalisation of State Pension Age) Regulations 2009 (SI 2009/1488) reg.21 (April 6, 2010).
5. Social Security (Miscellaneous Amendments) Regulations 2012 (SI 2012/757) reg.18 (April 1, 2012).
6. Social Fund Winter Fuel Payment (Amendment) Regulations 2013 (SI 2013/1509) reg.2(1) and (3) (September 16, 2013).
7. Social Security (Miscellaneous Amendments) Regulations 2015 (SI 2015/67) reg.4(1)(c) (February 23, 2015).

DEFINITIONS

"free in-patient treatment"—see reg.1(2).
"qualifying week"—*ibid.*

Regulation 3 excludes certain people from entitlement to a winter fuel payment **4.29** even if they fall within reg.2(a) and (b). There are five categories:

(a) partners of people who were entitled to state pension credit, income-based jobseeker's allowance or income-related employment and support allowance throughout the qualifying week (reg.3(1)(a)(i)). This is to prevent double payment;

(b) people who, throughout the qualifying week, have been receiving free in-patient treatment (see the notes to reg.21(3) of the Income Support Regulations) for more than 52 weeks (reg.3(1)(a)(ii));

(c) people serving a custodial sentence throughout the qualifying week (reg.3(1) (a)(iii)). Note that the reference to "a sentence imposed by a court" excludes those in prison on remand;

(d) people in residential care who were entitled to state pension credit, income-based jobseeker's allowance or income-related employment and support allowance during the qualifying week; and

(e) anyone who does not automatically receive a winter fuel payment under reg.4 and who fails to claim it by March 31 in the following year. There is an exception for refugees to whom reg.4(2) applies. In *CIS 2337/2004*, Commissioner Jacobs held that the time limit in reg.3(1)(b) does not infringe claimants' rights under art.1 of the First Protocol to the European Convention on Human Rights even when a payment has been made without a claim in respect of previous years. The time limit did not deprive claimants of any rights but merely defined the scope of those rights. In *Walker-Fox v Secretary of State for Work and Pensions* [2005] EWCA Civ 1441 (*R(IS) 3/06*), the Court of Appeal held (overruling the decision of the Deputy Commissioner in *CIS/488/2004*) that the March 31 time limit applied for the winters of 2000/01 and 2001/02 in cases in which the claimant had to rely on Regulation 1408/71, even though the UK Government did not accept that there was an entitlement in such cases until July 2002 (i.e. after those time limits had expired). In this context, see also *CIS/3555/2004*. The final time limit for claiming a winter fuel payment for the winters of 1997/1998, 1998/1999 and 1999/2000 is March 31, 2014 (see para.(3)).

A claim for a winter fuel payment may be made using one of the forms at *http:// www.gov.uk*. Typing the words "winter fuel payment claim" into the search box on the home page gives a link to the forms (one for those living in Great Britain and the other for those living in another EEA country or Switzerland). Proof of age will usually be required. Claiming in other ways may be acceptable, as long as it is done in writing, but—unless to do so would risk missing the absolute time limit for claiming—it is better to use the appropriate form, if possible.

Making a winter fuel payment without a claim

4.—(1) Subject to paragraph (2), the Secretary of State may [³ on or **4.30** before the 31st March] of the year following the year in which the qualifying week falls make a winter fuel payment under regulation 2 in respect of the preceding winter to a person who (disregarding regulation 3(b)) appears from official records held by the Secretary of State to be entitled to a payment under that regulation.

(2) Where a person becomes entitled to income support [¹[² , state pension credit or an income-related employment and support allowance]] in respect

of the qualifying week by virtue of a decision made after that week that section 115 of the Immigration and Asylum Act 1999 (exclusions) ceases to apply to him the Secretary of State shall make a winter fuel payment to that person under regulation 2 in respect of the winter following the qualifying week.

(3) Subject to paragraph (4), for the purposes of paragraphs (1) and (2) official records held by the Secretary of State as to a person's circumstances shall be sufficient evidence thereof for the purpose of deciding his entitlement to a winter fuel payment and its amount.

(4) Paragraph (3) shall not apply so as to exclude the revision of a decision under section 9 of the Social Security Act 1998 (revision of decisions) or the supersession of a decision under section 10 of that Act (decisions superseding earlier decisions) or the consideration of fresh evidence in connection with the revision or supersession of a decision.

AMENDMENTS

1. Social Fund Winter Fuel Payment (Amendment) Regulations 2004 (SI 2004/2154) reg.2(d) (September 20, 2004).
2. Employment and Support Allowance (Consequential Provisions) (No.2) Regulations 2008 (SI 2008/1554) reg.7(1) and (5) (October 27, 2008).
3. Social Security (Miscellaneous Amendments) Regulations 2012 (SI 2012/757) reg.18 (April 1, 2012).

DEFINITION

"qualifying week"—see reg.1(2).

GENERAL NOTE

4.31   Regulation 4 empowers (but does not oblige) the Secretary of State to make winter fuel payments on the basis of Benefits Agency records and without an express claim being made. At the outset, the information in those records is deemed to be sufficient evidence of entitlement or non-entitlement (see reg.4(3)) but reg.4(4) permits the initial decision to be revised or superseded in the normal way if further information comes to light. Those who consider themselves to be entitled to a winter fuel payment but do not receive one automatically may make a claim for it, provided they do so by March 31 in the year following the qualifying week (see reg.3(1)(b)). In cases where the Secretary of State does not make an automatic payment, there is no right of appeal against that omission. This is because omitting to make a payment does not give rise to a "decision" against which there is a right of appeal (see *CIS/751/2005* and *CIS/840/2005*, the latter decision doubting the decision of the Deputy Commissioner in *CIS/4088/2004*). In *CIS/840/2005*, the Commissioner explained the point as follows:

"9. . . . I do not consider that, where the Secretary of State does not decide to make a payment under regulation 4(1), he is obliged to issue a decision not to make a payment. Indeed, it seems to me that he is not entitled, before 31 March of the relevant year, to issue a decision not to make a payment to a person who may be entitled to one, because that person may still make a claim within the time allowed by regulation 3(1)(b) and might establish his entitlement on the claim. He can make a decision under regulation 4 to make a payment but otherwise it seems to me that he must leave matters open and await a possible claim."

And, of course, after March 31 the Secretary of State's power to make the payment ends in any event by virtue of reg.3(1)(b).

For the effect of reg.4(2) before June 14, 2007, see p.1246 of Vol.II of the 2007 edition. The paragraph now appears to be otiose following the revocation of reg.21ZB of the Income Support Regulations. However, it has not itself been revoked.

In *CIS 2497/2002* an argument was raised that the operation of reg.4 discriminated indirectly against men on the grounds of their sex contrary to Directive 79/7. The evidence was that those selected by the Secretary of State to receive a winter fuel payment without a claim had been identified from official records of those receiving social security benefits (including retirement pension) in the qualifying week. As the pensionable age for women is lower than that for men, it was argued that there would be significantly more women than men in that category. However, Commissioner Mesher rejected that argument on the basis that, even if the operation of the rules allowing the Secretary of State to make payments without a claim was discriminatory, the claimant had not been disadvantaged by reg.4 but by "the overall and identical time-limit [i.e. March 31, after the winter in question] set for claims and for the making of payments without a claim".

In *JE v Secretary of State for Work and Pensions (SF)* [2022] UKUT 12 (AAC), the appellant relied on discrimination arguments which were in substance quite similar to those rejected in *CIS 2497/2002*, but made them in the context of the Human Rights Act 1998 instead of EU law. Upper Tribunal Judge Wikeley dismissed the appeal.

Revocations

5.—The Social Fund Winter Fuel Payment Regulations 1998, the Social Fund Winter Fuel Payment Amendment Regulations 1998 and the Social Fund Winter Fuel Payment Amendment Regulations 1999 are hereby revoked.
   4.32

[¹ Regulation 2

SCHEDULE

Countries	4.33
Republic of Austria	
Kingdom of Belgium	
Republic of Bulgaria	
Republic of Croatia	
Czech Republic	
Kingdom of Denmark	
Republic of Estonia	
Republic of Finland	
Federal Republic of Germany	
Republic of Hungary	
Republic of Iceland	
Republic of Ireland	
Republic of Italy	
Republic of Latvia	
Principality of Liechtenstein	
Republic of Lithuania	
Grand Duchy of Luxembourg	
Kingdom of the Netherlands	
Kingdom of Norway	
Republic of Poland	
Republic of Romania	
Slovak Republic	
Republic of Slovenia	
Kingdom of Sweden	
Swiss Confederation.]	

AMENDMENT

1. Social Fund Winter Fuel Payment (Amendment) Regulations 2014 (SI 2014/3270) reg.2(1) and (3) (September 21, 2015).

The Social Fund Maternity and Funeral Expenses (General) Regulations 2005

(SI 2005/3061) (AS AMENDED)

Made by the Secretary of State under sections 138(1)(a) and (4) and 175(1), (3) and (4) of the Social Security Contributions and Benefits Act 1992, after agreement by the Social Security Advisory Committee that proposals in respect of these Regulations should not be referred to it

[In force December 5, 2005]

ARRANGEMENT OF REGULATIONS

PART I

GENERAL

PART II

PAYMENTS FOR MATERNITY EXPENSES

PART III

PAYMENTS FOR FUNERAL EXPENSES

GENERAL NOTE

4.35 With effect from December 5, 2005, these Regulations replaced the Social Fund Maternity and Funeral Expenses (General) Regulations 1987 in their entirety. However, with a few exceptions, the effect was intended to consolidate those regulations and to produce a (greatly needed) simplification in the structure and wording of the rules for funeral payments.

The main changes were:

- a new definition of "couple" in reg.3(1) to reflect the coming into force of the Civil Partnership Act 2004. The definition has since been amended to reflect the coming into force of the Marriage (Same Sex Couples) Act 2013;

- a cosmetic change to the definition of "family" in reg.3(1). The definition now refers to "polygamous marriage" rather than a "polygamous relationship";

- the exclusion from the "immediate family member test" in reg.8(1) of students aged less than 19 who are in non-advanced education. Previously only those in advanced education were excluded (see reg.8(4)(a) of the former regulations);

- a large increase in the categories of people that are excluded from the "closer contact" test in reg.8(6)–(8) so that those categories are now the same as the categories of people who are exempt from the "immediate family member test" (cf. reg.8(8)(b) with reg.7(7) of the former regulations); and

- the metrification of references to distance.

PART I

GENERAL

Citation and commencement

1.—(1) These Regulations may be cited as the Social Fund Maternity and Funeral Expenses (General) Regulations 2005 and shall come into force on 5th December 2005. **4.36**

Revocation

2.—The Regulations specified in the Schedule are revoked to the extent specified there. **4.37**

GENERAL NOTE

The Schedule has not been reproduced. Its effects are noted at paras 3.197 and 3.200–3.204 of the Supplement to the 2005 edition. **4.38**

Interpretation

3.—(1) In these Regulations— **4.39**
"the Act" means the Social Security Contributions and Benefits Act 1992;
[³ "the 1995 Act" means the Jobseekers Act 1995;
"the 2007 Act" means the Welfare Reform Act 2007;
"the 2012 Act" means the Welfare Reform Act 2012;]
[¹ "the Employment and Support Allowance Regulations" means the Employment and Support Allowance Regulations 2008;]
"the Income Support Regulations" means the Income Support (General) Regulations 1987;
"the Jobseeker's Allowance Regulations" means the Jobseeker's Allowance Regulations 1996;
"absent parent" means a parent of a child who has died where—
(a) that parent was not living in the same household with the child at the date of that child's death; and
(b) that child had his home, at the date of death, with a person who was responsible for that child for the purposes of Part IX of the Act;
[² "adoption agency" has the meaning given in section 2 of the Adoption and Children Act 2002;
"adoption order" means an order made under section 46 of the Adoption and Children Act 2002;]

937

"child" means a person under the age of 16 or a young person within the meaning of regulation 14 of the Income Support Regulations or, as the case may be, of regulation 76 of the Jobseeker's Allowance Regulations;

[⁵ "child arrangements order" means a child arrangements order as defined in section 8(1) of the Children Act 1989 which consists of, or includes, arrangements relating to either or both of the following—

(i) with whom the child is to live, and

(ii) when the child is to live with any person;]

"child tax credit" means a child tax credit under section 8 of the Tax Credits Act 2002;

"claimant" means a person claiming a social fund payment in respect of maternity or funeral expenses;

"close relative" means a parent, parent-in-law, son, son-in-law, daughter, daughter-in-law, step-parent, step-son, step-son-in-law, step-daughter, step-daughter-in-law, brother, brother-in-law, sister or sister-in-law;

"confinement" means labour resulting in the [² birth] of a living child, or labour after 24 weeks of pregnancy resulting in the [² birth] of a child whether alive or dead;

[⁴ ⁶ "couple" means—

(a) two people who are married to, or civil partners of, each other and are members of the same household; or

(b) two people who are not married to, or civil partners of, each other but are living together [¹¹ as if they were a married couple or civil partners];]

"family" means—

(a) a couple and any children who are members of the same household and for whom at least one of the couple is responsible;

(b) a person who is not a member of a couple and any children who are members of the same household and for whom that person is responsible;

(c) persons who are members of a polygamous marriage who are members of the same household and any children who are also members of the same household and for whom a member of the polygamous marriage is responsible [³ except where the claimant is in receipt of universal credit,];

[⁷ . . .]

[⁸ . . .]

"funeral payment" has the meaning given in regulation 7(1);

[² "guardian" means a person appointed as a guardian or special guardian under section 5 or 14A of the Children Act 1989;]

"health professional" means—

(a) a registered medical practitioner, or

(b) a registered nurse or registered midwife;

"immediate family member" means a parent, son or daughter;

"income-based jobseeker's allowance" has the same meaning as it has in the Jobseekers Act 1995 by virtue of section 1(4) of that Act;

[¹ "income-related employment and support allowance" means an income-related allowance under Part 1 of the Welfare Reform Act (employment and support allowance);]

"occupational pension scheme" has the same meaning as in the Pension Schemes Act 1993;

[⁹ "owner-occupier loan payments" means loan payments made under the Loans for Mortgage Interest Regulations 2017;]

[² "parental order" means an order made under section 30 of the Human Fertilisation and Embryology Act 1990 or section 54 [¹⁰ or section 54A] of the Human Fertilisation and Embryology Act 2008;]

"partner" means where a person—

(a) is a member of a couple, the other member of that couple;

(b) is married polygamously to two or more members of his household, any such member [³ except that paragraph (b) does not apply where the claimant is in receipt of universal credit,];

[² "placed for adoption" has the meaning given in section 18 of the Adoption and Children Act 2002;]

"person affected by a trade dispute" means a person—

(a) to whom section 126 of the Act applies; or

(b) to whom that section would apply if a claim for income support were made by or in respect of him;

"prescribed time for claiming" means the appropriate period during which a Sure Start Maternity Grant or, as the case may be, a funeral payment, may be claimed pursuant to regulation 19 of, and Schedule 4 to, the Social Security (Claims and Payments) Regulations 1987;

[² "qualifying order" has the meaning given in regulation 3A;

"residence order" means a residence order as defined in section 8, and made under section 10, of the Children Act 1989;]

[⁵ . . .]

"still-born child", in relation to England and Wales, has the same meaning as in section 12 of the Births and Deaths Registration Act 1926 and, in relation to Scotland, has the same meaning as in section 56(1) of the Registration of Births, Deaths and Marriages (Scotland) Act 1965;

"Sure Start Maternity Grant" is to be construed in accordance with regulation 5;

[³ "universal credit" means universal credit under Part 1 of the 2012 Act;]

"working tax credit" means a working tax credit under section 10 of the Tax Credits Act 2002.

[² (1A) References in these Regulations to—

(a) section 5, 8, 10 or 14A of the Children Act 1989,

(b) section 2, 18, 46 or 66 of the Adoption and Children Act 2002,

are to be construed as including a reference to a provision (if any) in legislation which has equivalent effect in Scotland, Northern Ireland, the Channel Islands or the Isle of Man.]

(2) For the purposes of Part III of these Regulations, persons shall be treated as members of the same household where—

(a) they are married to each other, or in a civil partnership with each other, and are living in the same care establishment, or

(b) they were partners immediately before at least one of them moved permanently into such an establishment,

and at least one of them is resident in a care establishment as at the date of death of the person in respect of whom a funeral payment is claimed.

(3) In paragraph (2), "care establishment" means—

(a) a care home,

(b) an Abbeyfield Home, or

(c) an independent hospital,

as defined in regulation 2(1) of the Income Support Regulations [¹ or regulation 2(1) of the Employment and Support Allowance Regulations].

(4) For the purposes of these Regulations—

(a) persons are to be treated as not being members of the same household in the circumstances set out in regulation 16(2) and (3)(a), (b) and (d) of the Income Support Regulations [¹ , in regulation 156 of the Employment and Support Allowance Regulations] or, as the case may be, in regulation 78(2) and (3)(a) to (c) of the Jobseeker's Allowance Regulations;

(b) [³ except where the claimant is in receipt of universal credit,] a person shall be treated as a member of a polygamous marriage where, during the subsistence of that marriage, a party to it is married to more than one person and the ceremony of marriage took place under the law of a country which permits polygamy.

[⁹ (5) For the purposes of these Regulations, a person being treated as entitled to a benefit has the meaning given to it in regulation 2(2)(aa) of the Loans for Mortgage Interest Regulations 2017.]

AMENDMENTS

1. Employment and Support Allowance (Consequential Provisions) (No.2) Regulations 2008 (SI 2008/1554) reg.8(1) and (2) (October 27, 2008).

2. Social Fund Maternity Grant Amendment Regulations 2010 (SI 2010/2760) reg.2 (December 13, 2010).

3. Social Fund (Maternity and Funeral Expenses) Amendment Regulations 2013 (SI 2013/247) reg.2 (April 1, 2013) (Note that the extraneous comma at the end of the definition of "partner" is required by SI 2013/247 and is not an editorial error).

4. Marriage (Same Sex Couples) Act 2013 (Consequential Provisions) Order 2014 (SI 2014/107) reg.2 and Sch.1 para.37 (March 13, 2014). The amendment extends to England and Wales only (see SI 2014/107, art.1(4)).

5. Child Arrangements Order (Consequential Amendments to Subordinate Legislation) Order 2014 (SI 2014/852) art.12(1) and (2) (April 22, 2014).

6. Marriage and Civil Partnership (Scotland) Act 2014 and Civil Partnership Act 2004 (Consequential Provisions and Modifications) Order 2014 (SI 2014/3229) art.29 and Sch.6 para.26 (December 16, 2014). The amendment relates only to Scotland (see SI 2014/3229 art.3(4)) but is in the same terms as the amendments made in relation to England and Wales by SI 2014/107 (see point 4 above).

7. Social Fund (Amendment) Regulations 2017 (SI 2017/271) reg.3 (April 6, 2017).

8. Social Fund Funeral Expenses Amendment Regulations 2018 (SI 2018/61) regs 3 and 4 (April 2, 2018).

9. Loans for Mortgage Interest Regulations 2017 (SI 2017/725) reg.18 and Sch.5 para.9(1) and (2) (April 6, 2018).

10. Human Fertilisation and Embryology Act 2008 (Remedial) Order 2018 (SI 2019/1413) art.3(2) and Sch.2 para.2 (January 3, 2019).

11. Civil Partnership (Opposite-sex Couples) Regulations 2019 (SI 2019/1458) reg.41 and Sch.3 Pt.2 para.81 (December 2, 2019).

GENERAL NOTE

Paragraph (1)

4.40   Regulation 3 defines the terms commonly used in these Regulations. Where relevant, these will be noted at the appropriate places in the commentary below. The following should, however, be noted:

"*Close relative*": The definition is narrower than the equivalent definitions in reg.2(1) of the Income Support Regulations and reg.1(3) of the Jobseeker's

Allowance Regulations because, although it includes a "step-son-in-law" and a "step-daughter-in-law", it does not specify that the partner of a close relative is also a close relative. So, for example, the unmarried partner or civil partner of the claimant's son (or a person with whom the claimant's son lives as if they were civil partners) is a "close relative" for the purposes of IS and JSA but not of maternity grants or funeral payments. For the position of "half-blood" and adoptive relationships, see the commentary to reg.2(1) of the Income Support Regulations.

"Confinement": Note that a payment can be made for a stillbirth only if it occurs after the 24th week of the pregnancy.

"Couple": The definition is the same as for IS and JSA—see the note to the definition in reg.2(1) of the Income Support Regulations in Vol.V of this series. In some circumstances where the members of a couple are living apart, they are deemed not to be members of the same household—see the note to para.(4)(a) below. For the position where at least one member of the couple lives in a "care establishment" see paras (2) and (3).

"Family": See the commentary on the definition of "family" in s.137(1) of the Contributions and Benefits Act in Vol.V of this series. The definition in para.(1) is differently worded from that definition (which applies for IS purposes) and the equivalent definition in s.35(1) of the Jobseekers Act. But, subject to the commentary to para.(4)(a) below, the consequences of the definition are the probably the same for all claimants other than those in polygamous marriages and their children (who are included in the definition for the purposes of maternity grants and funeral payments but not of IS or JSA). (For the circumstances in which a person is to be treated as a member of a polygamous marriage, see para.(4)(b).)

For the circumstances in which a person is "responsible" for a child see reg.4A below.

"Still-born child": The definition referred to is "a child which has issued forth from its mother after the 24th week of pregnancy and which did not at any time after being completely expelled from its mother draw breath or show any other signs of life."

Paragraphs (2) and (3)
For *"care home"*, *"Abbeyfield Home"* and *"independent hospital"*, see reg.2(1) of the Income Support Regulations and the commentary to that regulation in Vol.V of this series.   **4.41**

Paragraph 4(a)
See the commentary to reg.16 of the Income Support Regulations in Vol.V of this series. The general rule in that regulation (and reg.78 of the Jobseeker's Allowance Regulations and reg.156 of the ESA Regulations) is that family members are treated as continuing to be members of the same household even though one or more of them is temporarily living away from the others. That general rule is subject to the exceptions listed in paras (2) and (3) of reg.16. Previous editions of this work have expressed the view that the operation of para.(4)(a) is problematical because, whilst it incorporates the exceptions into the rules for maternity grants and funeral payments (other than the exceptions relating to residential care, which are dealt with in paras (2) and (3)) and goes further than reg.16 by deeming people within those exceptions *not* to be members of the same household, it does not incorporate the general rule. If that were correct, it would follow that, in cases that do not fall within the exceptions, the general law applies to the question of whether membership of a household endures through a temporary absence (see *England v Secretary of State for Social Services* [1982] 3 F.L.R. 222; *Taylor v Supplementary Benefit Officer (R(FIS) 5/85)*; *Santos v Santos* [1972] 2 All E.R. 246). However, in *SSWP v LD (IS)* [2010] UKUT 77 (AAC), the Upper Tribunal held that the general rule in reg.16(1) (or,   **4.42**

by implication, in regs 78 and 156) does apply to maternity grants and funeral payments. Judge Levenson stated:

"16. Regulation 3(4)(a) of the 2005 regulations refers to not being treated as a member of the same household in the circumstances set out in regulation 16(2) of the 1987 regulations. Those circumstances refer to paragraph 16(1) of the 1987 regulations not applying if paragraph 16(2) applies. The logic of this is that 16(1) is also incorporated into the story by the wording of regulation 3(4) (a). There is no doubt that before the deceased moved away from the claimant, they were partners living in the same household. The First-tier Tribunal was clearly satisfied, as am I, that the deceased was only temporarily living away from the claimant. Regulation 16(1) of the 1987 regulations requires that they continue to be treated as members of the same household. That being the case, they continued to be a couple for the purposes of regulation 7(8)(a) of the 2005 regulations."

In any event, the couple in that case continued to be members of the same household whilst living in different places.

Paragraph (4)(b)

4.43   This applies the usual social security rule regarding polygamous marriages (i.e. that the marriage is polygamous at any time during which it is actually, rather than potentially, polygamous) to maternity grants and funeral payments.

[¹ Provision against double payment: Sure Start Maternity Grants

4.44   **3A.**—(1) In this regulation—
(a) "C" is the child in respect of whom a Sure Start Maternity Grant has been claimed;
(b) "first grant" is a first Sure Start Maternity Grant [³ or a Best Start Grant] in respect of C;
[³ (c) "subsequent grant" is, in respect of C—
(i) a second or subsequent Sure Start Maternity Grant; or
(ii) if a Best Start Grant has been given, a first Sure Start Maternity Grant;
(d) "Best Start Grant" is a grant given to a qualifying individual under Regulations made under section 32 of the Social Security (Scotland) Act 2018 in connection with having, or expecting to have, a new baby in the family.]
(2) Subject to paragraph (3), a [³ subsequent] grant may not be awarded if a first grant has been awarded.
(3) A [³ subsequent] grant may be awarded to a person ("P") if the following conditions are satisfied.
(4) The first condition is that P—
(a) alone, or together with another person, has been granted a qualifying order; or
(b) falls within regulation 5(3)(b), (d), (e) or (f).
(5) The second condition is that P—
(a) has not already received a first grant; or
(b) was not, at the time a first grant was claimed, a member of the family of a person to whom a first grant has been paid.
(6) A qualifying order is one of the following types of order—
(a) an adoption order;
(b) a parental order;
(c) a [² child arrangements] order.]

AMENDMENTS

1. Social Fund Maternity Grant Amendment Regulations 2010 (SI 2010/2760) reg.2 (December 13, 2010).
2. Child Arrangements Order (Consequential Amendments to Subordinate Legislation) Order 2014 (SI 2014/852) art.12(1) and (3) (April 22, 2014).
3. Social Security (Scotland) Act 2018 (Best Start Grants) (Consequential Modifications and Saving) Order 2018 (SI 2019/1138) art.3(1) and (2) (December 10, 2018).

GENERAL NOTE

Paragraph (2) sets out the general rule is that only one maternity grant or Best   **4.45**
Start Grant (collectively in this Note, a "grant") may be paid for any individual child. That rule is subject to the exceptions set out in paras (3)–(5).

Those exceptions allow a second grant to be paid in circumstances where the claimant did not receive the first grant (and was not a family member of the person who received the first grant when that grant was claimed)—see para.(5)—and either:

- the claimant has been granted a "qualifying order" (defined by para.(6) as an adoption order, a parental order or a child arrangements order);

- the claimant is responsible for a child aged under 12 months in the circumstances set out in reg.5(3)(b) below;

- the claimant (or claimant's partner) has been appointed the guardian of a child under 12 months and is responsible for that child (i.e. where reg.5(3) (d) applies);

- the claimant (or claimant's partner) is responsible for a child aged under 12 months who has been "placed for adoption" by an "adoption agency" (i.e. where reg.5(3)(e) applies and see the commentary to that provision for the definition of the terms in quotation marks); or

- (in certain circumstances) the claimant (or claimant's partner) has adopted a child aged under 12 months under the laws of a country outside the UK (i.e. where reg.5(3)(f) applies).

The various types of "qualifying order" are defined further by reg.3(1). An "adoption order" is an order made under s.46 of the Adoption and Children Act 2002. A "parental order" is an order made under either s.30 of the Human Fertilisation and Embryology Act 1990 or s.54 of the Human Fertilisation and Embryology Act 2008 (which replaced s.30 with effect from April 6, 2010). Such an order provides for a child who has been born following a surrogate pregnancy to be treated in law as the child of the couple in whose favour it is granted. A "child arrangements order" is "a child arrangements order as defined in section 8(1) of the Children Act 1989 which consists of, or includes, arrangements relating to either or both of the following (i) with whom the child is to live, and (ii) when the child is to live with any person".

Note that, even if none of the above exceptions applies, only a lawful payment bars another payment—see *CG/30/1990*. So, where the first payment was made to the partner of the maternity grant claimant (who was the income support claimant) and not to her, this did not prevent her receiving a payment.

[¹ Provision against double payment: funeral payments

4.—(1) Subject to paragraph (2), no funeral payment shall be made under   **4.46**
these Regulations if such a payment [³ , or an award of funeral expense assistance given in accordance with regulations made under section 34 of the Social Security (Scotland) Act 2018,] has already been made in respect of any funeral expenses arising from the death of the same person.

(2) A further funeral payment may be made in respect of any funeral expenses arising from the death of a person in respect of which such a payment has already been made where—

(a) the decision pursuant to which the funeral payment was awarded has been revised; and

(b) the further amount of the award as revised, together with the amount of the funeral payment already paid in respect of the death of that person, does not exceed the amount of any funeral payment which may be awarded pursuant to regulation 9.]

[² (3) No funeral payment may be made under these Regulations for an item or service for which payment has been received under The Social Fund (Children's Funeral Fund for England) Regulations 2019, unless the amount paid under those Regulations is less that the total amount charged for the item or service, in which case a payment may be made for an amount not exceeding the remainder of the amount charged.]

AMENDMENTS

1. Social Fund Maternity Grant Amendment Regulations 2010 (SI 2010/2760) reg.2 (December 13, 2010).
2. Social Fund (Children's Funeral Fund for England) Regulations 2019 (SI 2019/1064) reg.6 (July 23, 2019).
3. Social Security (Scotland) Act 2018 (Funeral Expense Assistance and Early Years Assistance) (Consequential Modifications and Savings) Order 2019 (SI 2019/1060) art.3(1) and (2) (September 16, 2019, subject to the saving in art.4).

GENERAL NOTE

4.47 As amended, the effect of reg.4 is that only one of the following payments may be made in respect of any individual death:

- a funeral payment;
- a Children's Funeral Fund payment under SI 2019/1064 (see below); or
- Scottish funeral expense assistance under SSI 2019/292 (see Pt XIII of Vol.IV of this series).

There are two exceptions. The first is where the decision to award the funeral payment is revised so as to increase the amount of the claimant's entitlement after the original (smaller) payment has been made. In such a case, a further payment may be made (subject to the overall maximum prescribed by reg.9). The second is where the amount paid from the Children's Funeral Fund was less that the total charge for the item or service. In such a case, the balance can be met by a funeral payment: see para.(3).

PART II

PAYMENTS FOR MATERNITY EXPENSES [¹ IN ENGLAND AND WALES]

AMENDMENT

1. Social Security (Scotland) Act 2018 (Best Start Grants) (Consequential Modifications and Saving) Order 2018 (SI 2019/1138) art.3(1) and (3) (December 10, 2018).

[¹ Persons to be treated as responsible for children

4.48 **4A.**—(1) For the purposes of this Part, subject to paragraph (4), a person ("P") is to be treated as responsible for a child if paragraph (2) or (3) applies.

(2) This paragraph applies if—
(a) P is receiving child benefit in respect of the child, unless P is a child in respect of whom another person is receiving child benefit; or
(b) no one is receiving child benefit in respect of the child but the child usually lives with P.

(3) This paragraph applies where P is receiving child benefit in respect of a child who is in receipt of child benefit in respect of another child in which case P is to be treated as responsible for both children.

(4) P is not to be treated as responsible for a child if the child is—
(a) being looked after by a local authority within the meaning of section 22 of the Children Act 1989, or section 93 of the Children (Scotland) Act 1995, [² or section 74 of the Social Services and Well-being (Wales) Act 2014,] unless the child usually lives with P; or
(b) detained in custody pending trial or sentence upon conviction or under a sentence imposed by a court.]

AMENDMENTS

1. Social Fund Maternity Grant Amendment Regulations 2011 (SI 2011/100) reg.2 (January 24, 2011).
2. Social Services and Well-being (Wales) Act 2014 and the Regulation and Inspection of Social Care (Wales) Act 2016 (Consequential Amendments) Order 2017 (SI 2017/901) art.10 (November 3, 2017).

GENERAL NOTE

It is only possible for claimants to qualify for a maternity grant under regs.5(3) **4.49** (b)–(e) below if they (or, sometimes, their partners) are "responsible for" the child in respect of whom the grant is to be made. From January 24, 2011 reg.4A defines the circumstances in which a person is to be treated as responsible for a child for the purposes of these Regulations.

The general rule is that the person receiving child benefit for the child is responsible. But that does not apply where a person is receiving child benefit for a child who is herself the parent of, and receiving child benefit for, another child. In those circumstances, the first person mentioned is responsible for both children. If no-one receives child benefit for the child, then the person with whom the child usually lives is responsible.

Under para.(4), no-one is responsible for—and therefore reg.5(3)(b)–(e) do not apply with respect to—children who are looked after by a local authority or are detained in custody. The only exception is where a child who is looked after by a local authority nevertheless usually lives with another person. In those circumstances, the person with whom the child usually lives is responsible.

[² Entitlement

5.—(1) Subject to [³ regulations 5A and 6], a payment of £500 to meet **4.50** maternity expenses (referred to in these Regulations as a "Sure Start Maternity Grant") shall be made in respect of a child or still-born child where the following conditions are satisfied.

(2) The first condition is that the claimant or the claimant's partner has, in respect of the date of the claim for a Sure Start Maternity Grant, been awarded—
(a) income support;
(b) state pension credit;
(c) an income-based jobseeker's allowance;

(d) working tax credit where the disability element or the severe disability element of working tax credit as specified in regulation 20(1)(b) and (f) of the Working Tax Credit (Entitlement and Maximum Rate) Regulations 2002(11) is included in the award;

(e) child tax credit [⁵ which includes an individual element or a disability element referred to in section 9(3) of the Tax Credits Act 2002]; [⁴ ...]

(f) an income-related employment and support allowance [⁴; [⁶ ...]

(g) universal credit] [⁶; or

(h) owner-occupier loan payments and is treated as entitled to a benefit specified in sub-paragraphs (a) to (c) and (f).]

(3) The second condition is that—

(a) the claimant or, if the claimant is a member of a family, one of the family is pregnant or has given birth to a child or a still-born child;

[³ (b) the child's parents are not partners at the date of the claim and the claimant—

    (i) is the parent (but not the mother) of the child (who must not exceed the age of twelve months at the date of the claim), or is responsible for that parent, and

    (ii) is responsible for the child;]

(c) the claimant or the claimant's partner—

    (i) has been granted a qualifying order in respect of a child who does not exceed the age of twelve months at the date of the claim, and

    (ii) is responsible for the child;

(d) the claimant or the claimant's partner—

    (i) has been appointed the guardian of a child who does not exceed the age of twelve months at the date of the claim, and

    (ii) is responsible for the child;

(e) a child who does not exceed the age of twelve months at the date of the claim has been placed for adoption with the claimant or the claimant's partner by an adoption agency and the claimant or the claimant's partner is responsible for the child; or

(f) the claimant or the claimant's partner has adopted a child who does not exceed the age of twelve months at the date of the claim and that adoption falls within section 66(1)(c) to (e) of the Adoption and Children Act 2002 (meaning of adoption).

(4) The third condition is that the claimant or the claimant's partner has received advice from a health professional—

(a) on health and welfare matters relating to the child (but this requirement does not apply where the claim is made after the birth of a still-born child); and

(b) where the claim is made before the child is born, on health and welfare matters relating to maternal health.

(5) The fourth condition is that the claim is made within the prescribed time for claiming a Sure Start Maternity Grant.]

[⁷ (6) The fifth condition is that the claimant lives in England or Wales.]

AMENDMENTS

1. Employment and Support Allowance (Consequential Provisions) (No.2) Regulations 2008 (SI 2008/1554) reg.8(1) and (3) (October 27, 2008).

2. Social Fund Maternity Grant Amendment Regulations 2010 (SI 2010/2760) reg.2 (December 13, 2010).
3. Social Fund Maternity Grant Amendment Regulations 2011 (SI 2011/100) reg.2 (January 24, 2011).
4. Social Fund (Maternity and Funeral Expenses) Amendment Regulations 2013 (SI 2013/247) reg.2(4) (April 1, 2013).
5. Social Fund (Amendment) Regulations 2017 (SI 2017/271) reg.3 (April 6, 2017).
6. Loans for Mortgage Interest Regulations 2017 (SI 2017/725) reg.18 and Sch.5 para.9(1) and (3) (April 6, 2018).
7. Social Security (Scotland) Act 2018 (Best Start Grants) (Consequential Modifications and Saving) Order 2018 (SI 2018/1138) art.3(1) and (4) (December 10, 2018).

GENERAL NOTE

Regulation 5 sets out the five conditions of entitlement for a one-off lump sum payment of £500 per child (see para.(1)) called a "Sure Start Maternity Grant". Those conditions are: **4.51**

- the claimant (or the claimant's partner) must be in receipt of a qualifying benefit (para.(2));

- the claimant, (or, in some cases, the claimant's partner or a member of the claimant's family) must be either pregnant or, have given birth to a child, or have become responsible for a child aged less than 12 months in certain specified circumstances (para.(3));

- except in the case of a still-birth, the claimant (or the claimant's partner) must have received advice from a health professional (para.(4)); and

- the claim for the maternity grant must have been made within the time limit (para.(5)); and

- (from December 10, 2018) the claimant must live in England and Wales (para.(6)).

All five conditions must be satisfied to qualify for the grant. In addition there are restrictions on entitlement where the claimant (or the claimant's partner) is a person affected by a trade dispute (see reg.6) and, from January 24, 2011 (but subject to the transitional protection in reg.3 of SI 2011/100: see below) where another member of the claimant's family is under 16.

Qualifying benefits—para. (2)
These are listed in sub-paras (a)–(h) of para.(2) and are largely self-explanatory. **4.52**
For tax credits generally, see Vol.IV. In *GC v SSWP (SF)* [2010] UKUT 100 (AAC), it was accepted by the Secretary of State that the reference in reg.7 to "having an award" of CTC or WTC was to the award under s.14 TCA 2002, rather than the subsequent determination of entitlement under s.18 of that Act. Presumably the same is true of the requirement in para.(1) that the claimant should have "been awarded" tax credits.
WTC comprises seven separate elements, namely the basic, disabled, 30-hour, second adult, lone parent, childcare, and severe disability elements (see TCA s.11 2002 and reg.3 of the Working Tax Credit (Entitlement and Maximum Rate) Regulations 2002 ("the WTC Regulations")). WTC is a qualifying benefit for a maternity grant if either the disability element (under reg.9 of the WTC Regulations) or the severe disability element (under reg.17) is included in the calculation of the claimant's "maximum annual rate of working tax credit" under reg.20 of the WTC Regulations.
The rule for CTC looks equally straightforward but is problematic. Until April 5, 2017, para.(2)(e) provided that CTC was a qualifying benefit for a maternity grant if it was "payable at a rate higher than the family element". The effect of that rule was that CTC was only a qualifying benefit to the extent that the taper did not completely extinguish the individual element(s) paid in respect of each child or qualifying young **4.53**

person for whom the claimant (or one of joint claimants) was responsible (see the commentary under the hearing, *"Family element"* in para.5.32 of Vol.II of the 2016/17 edition). However, from April 6, 2017, SI 2017/271 amended para.(2)(e) to provide that CTC was a qualifying benefit if it "includes an individual element or a disability element referred to in section 9(3) of the Tax Credits Act 2002". On first impression therefore, it appears that the rule for CTC is being brought into line with that for WTC so that it is a qualifying benefit if certain elements are included in the calculation of the award and the rate at which the award is payable is no longer relevant. However, the problem arises when it is realised that the "individual element" (i.e. as defined by TCA 2002 s.9(3)) is included in *every* award of CTC. A claimant is (or joint claimants are) entitled to an individual element "in respect of each child or qualifying young person for whom the person is, or either of them is or are, responsible": see s.9(2)(b). It is inevitable that anyone who is awarded CTC will be responsible for at least one child or qualifying young person because otherwise the basic condition of entitlement to that tax credit in TCA 2002 s.8(1) will not be satisfied. On that basis, everyone who has been awarded CTC is in receipt of a qualifying benefit for a maternity grant.

The Explanatory Memorandum for SI 2017/271 says:

"This instrument amends the Social Fund Maternity and Funeral Expenses (General) Regulations 2005 in consequence of the changes to the family element of Child Tax Credit that will take effect from 6 April 2017. Entitlement to a Sure Start Maternity Grant and Funeral Expenses Payment from 6 April 2017 will be linked to the award of an individual element or disability element of Child Tax Credit, as from this date not all claimants awarded Child Tax Credit will be awarded the family element. The intention of this change is to ensure that all claimants who would have qualified for a Sure Start Maternity Grant or Funeral Expenses Payment prior to 6 April 2017 will continue to do so."

so it seems unlikely that the intention was to extend entitlement. However, what matters is the meaning of what the legislator has said, rather than what they meant to say. It is even difficult to argue that an award of CTC no longer includes the individual element where that element has been extinguished by the taper because that is not consistent with the use of the word "includes" in para.(2)(d).

The qualifying benefit must have been awarded to the claimant or to her partner. Whether or not a claimant has a partner is a matter of law, and her own views on the point are relevant factors to be taken into account but are not conclusive of that issue—see *CIS/2031/2003* in which the Commissioner advised tribunals that:

"... the question of whether a claimant has a partner is intrinsic to the very question of entitlement to a grant and in an appeal against a refusal of a grant which depends on the question of entitlement to a qualifying benefit, a tribunal should always enquire whether the person applying for the grant has a partner".

4.54   In that appeal, the claimant was entitled to a maternity grant because her (undisclosed) partner had been entitled to IS at the relevant date, albeit not in respect of her.

To meet the condition in para.(2), it is necessary for a qualifying benefit to have been awarded "in respect of the date of claim". It is not necessary that the qualifying benefit should actually have been paid by that date. Further, although para.(1) (a) appears to require that a qualifying benefit "has . . . been awarded", an award of made *after* the date of the claim for the maternity grant but which covers the date of claim will suffice (see *SSWP v FS (IS)* [2010] UKUT 18 (AAC) at para.27 and *GC v SSWP* [2010] UKUT 100 (AAC)). For what happens when a decision refusing a grant has been made and a qualifying benefit is subsequently awarded, see under *"Time limit for claims"* (below).

Pregnancy, birth and becoming responsible for a child under 12 months—para. (3)

4.55   When reg.5 was completely recast with effect from December 13, 2010, the main change was to extend the list of circumstances (now set out in para.(3)) in which a maternity grant can be made. That list now takes into account the decision of the Court of Appeal in *Francis v Secretary of State for Work and Pensions* [2005] EWCA Civ 1303, *R(IS) 6/06* (and see further p.1332 of Vol.II of the 2010/11 edition), which held that the refusal (under the former reg.5(1)(b)) of a maternity grant to a parent who had obtained a residence order (in circumstances in which a grant would have been made if she had obtained an adoption order) discriminated against her contrary to arts 8 and 14 of the ECHR. It also creates new entitlements to a maternity grant in the circumstances set out in sub-paras (b), (d), (e) and (f).

For the definitions of "family", "parent" and "still-born child" see reg.3 and the commentary to that regulation. For "qualifying order" see regs 3(1) and 3A(6) and the commentary to the latter. For "responsible for the child" see reg.4A.

Sub-paragraphs (a)–(f) are alternative rather than cumulative so it is sufficient to satisfy any one of them. The issues to which they give rise will normally be simple ones of fact.

Sub-paragraph (a)—The phrase "is pregnant" in sub-para.(a) means that an advance payment can be made where a child is to be born to the claimant or a member of her/his family. In other cases, entitlement can only arise after the event. **4.56**

Sub-paragraph (b)—was amended with effect from January 24, 2011 by SI 2011/100. Its original wording (which was in effect from December 13, 2010 to January 23, 2011) was as follows:

"(b) the claimant is the parent (but not the mother) of a child not exceeding the age of twelve months at the date of the claim and is responsible for the child and the child's parents are not partners at the date of the claim;".

The effect of that wording was to confer entitlement on a father of a child under 12 months who is responsible for that child and who is not the partner of the child's mother. The amended wording continues to cover those circumstances but also confers entitlement where:

- the child is less than 12 months old;

- the mother or father of the child is a child her/himself; and

- the claimant is responsible for the mother or father and is also responsible for the child.

The drafting would have been clearer if the amendment had dealt with those two, very different, cases by using different sub-paragraphs.

Sub-paragraph (d)—"Guardian" is defined by reg.3(1) as "a person appointed as a guardian or special guardian under section 5 or 14A of the Children Act 1989". **4.57**

Sub-paragraph (e)—"Adoption agency" is defined by reg.3(1) as having the meaning set out in s.2 of the Adoption and Children Act 2002. That Act provides that a local authority or a "registered adoption society" "may be referred to as an adoption agency". "Registered adoption society" is itself defined (subject to a proviso) as a "voluntary organisation which is an adoption society registered under Pt 2 of the Care Standards Act 2000 (c. 14). . .". Regulation 3(1) also defines "placed for adoption" by reference to s.18 of the 2002 Act which empowers an adoption agency to place a child for adoption with prospective adopters and, following such a placement, to leave the child with them as prospective adopters.

Sub-paragraph (f)—Section 66(1)(c)–(e) of the Adoption and Children Act 2002 covers:

- an adoption under the law of a country or territory outside the British Islands, in which the Hague Convention (i.e. the Convention on Protection of Children and Co-operation in respect of Intercountry Adoption, concluded at the Hague on 29th May 1993) is in force that has been certified in pursuance of Article 23(1) of that Convention (see also s.144 of the 2002 Act);

- an "overseas adoption" as defined by s.87 of the 2002 Act; and

● an adoption recognised by the law of England and Wales and effected under the law of any other country.

Double payments—Where sub-paras (b), (d), (e) or (f) apply, it will sometimes be possible for the claimant to be awarded a maternity grant even if such a grant has previously been paid to another person: see reg.3A.

Health and welfare advice—para. (4)

4.58   Under para.(4), either the claimant or her partner (if she has one) must have received advice on the health and welfare of the child from a "health professional" (as defined in reg.3) before a maternity grant can be paid. For obvious reasons, this requirement does not apply if the child is still-born (see sub-para.(a)). Where the claim is made before the birth of the child, advice must also have been given about the health of the mother.

Time limit for claims—para. (5)

4.59   Under para.(5), it is a condition of entitlement to a maternity grant that it should have been claimed within the time limit for doing so. That time limit is prescribed by reg.19(1) of, and Sch.4 para.8 to, the Claims and Payments Regulations as amended with effect from October 18, 2018, by reg.2 of the Social Security (Claims and Payments) (Social Fund Maternity Grant) (Amendment) Regulations 2018 (SI 2018/989) (see Vol.III). Before that date, each of the six-month time limits set out below were three-month time limits.

The time limit depends upon which sub-paragraph of reg.5(3) is the basis for the claim. Where the claim is based on pregnancy or the birth of a child (reg.5(3)(a)), the time limit is the period beginning 11 weeks before the first day of the expected week of confinement and ending six months after the actual date of confinement. A claim based on the grant of a qualifying order (reg.5(3)(c)) must be made within six months after the date the order is made. A claim based on appointment as a guardian (reg.5(3) (d)), or placement for adoption (reg.5(3)(e)) must be made within six months after the date on which the appointment took effect or the placement was made. A claim based on a foreign adoption (reg.5(3)(f)) must be made within six months after the date on which the adoption either took effect or was recognised under UK law.

The time limit for claims based on reg.5(3)(b) is six months from the date the claimant became responsible for the child.

4.60   The time limit in Sch.4 para.8 cannot be extended. However if a claim for a maternity grant is refused because (at the date of that claim) a qualifying benefit not yet been awarded then, as long as the qualifying benefit is claimed within 10 working days of the original claim for the maternity grant, a further claim made within three months of a subsequent award of the qualifying benefit is treated as made on the date of the original claim, or the date the qualifying benefit was awarded, whichever is later (Claims and Payments Regulations, regs 6(16)–(18) and (22)). There is no provision in the legislation to extend the 10 working days limit: see *MW v SSWP (IS)* [2017] UKUT 291 (AAC) at para.41.

When deciding whether the claim for the qualifying benefit was made within 10 working days time limit, it is the date on which the claim form was received by the relevant office that counts. A claim for council tax benefit (or housing benefit) that is backdated and therefore "treated as made" within the 10-day period will not suffice— see *CIS/3416/2004* (a case about funeral payments, for which the rules are identical).

Another way of dealing with the problem caused by a subsequent award of a qualifying benefit is by seeking a revision of the earlier decision to refuse the original claim. Under reg.3(3) of the Decisions and Appeals Regulations (see Vol.III). the Secretary of State has power to revise that decision where the application for a revision is made within one month of the notification of the original refusal, or within the six months' time limit, whichever is later. So far those time limits are less generous to claimants than the rules in reg.6(16)–(18) of the Claims and Payments Regulations. The potential advantage of this route is that the time limit may be extended under reg.4 of the Decisions and Appeals Regulations up to 13 months from the date of notification of the original decision. If the qualifying benefit was not awarded until after the expiry of the primary time limit, that might amount to "special circumstances . . . as a result of [which] it was not practicable for the application to be made within the time limit"—see reg.4(4)(c) of those Regulations. Note, however, that there is no right of appeal against a refusal by the Secretary of State to extend time under reg.4 (see *R(TC) 1/05*).

As this way around the time limit problem involves seeking a revision of the original decision, rather than a supersession, it cannot be used where the claimant is subsequently awarded but with effect from a date after the claim for the maternity grant: see *MW v SSWP (IS)* [2017] UKUT 291 (AAC) at paras 44–45.

Living in England and Wales—para. (6)

Until December 9, 2018 maternity grants were payable to anyone living in Great Britain who met the conditions of entitlement. However, as part of the devolution of social security to the Scottish Parliament, those living in Scotland became eligible to a pregnancy and baby grant paid under s.32 of, and Sch.6 to, the Social Security (Scotland) Act 2018 and the Early Years Assistance (Best Start Grants) (Scotland) Regulations 2018 (SSI 2018/370) (see Pt XIII of Vol.IV of this series). As a consequence, maternity grants are now only payable to those living in England and Wales.

There will presumably be cases in which a claimant could be said to be living in both England and Wales and Scotland. However, the provision against double payment in reg.3A (as amended), and in Sch.2 to SSI 2018/370, will prevent such a claimant receiving both a maternity grant and a pregnancy and baby grant in respect of the same child.

4.61

[¹ ² Entitlement where another member of the claimant's family is under the age of 16

5A.—(1) In this regulation—

(a) "C" means the child or still-born child in respect of whom a Sure Start Maternity Grant is claimed; and

(b) "existing member of the family" has the meaning given in paragraph (2) or, as the case may be, (3).

(2) Where a parent of C ("P") is under the age of 20 and a member of the claimant's family, "existing member of the family" means any member of the claimant's family who is also a child of P, apart from C or any other child born as a result of the same pregnancy as C.

(3) In any other case, "existing member of the family" means any member of the claimant's family apart from—

(a) C;

(b) any other child born as a result of the same pregnancy as C;

(c) any child whose parent is under the age of 20 and a member of the claimant's family [³;

(d) any child—

(i) who was not, at the time of the child's birth, a child of the claimant (or, where the claimant has a partner at the date of claim, the claimant's partner); and

(ii) whose age, at the time that the claimant (or, where the claimant has a partner at the date of claim, the claimant's partner) first became responsible for that child, exceeded 12 months.]

(4) Subject to the following provisions of this regulation, a Sure Start Maternity Grant shall not be awarded if, at the date of claim, any existing member of the family is under the age of 16.

(5) Where C is one of two or more children—

4.62

(a) born or still-born as a result of the same pregnancy, or

(b) (if the claim is made before the confinement in a case where regulation 5(3)(a) applies) who are expected to be born as a result of the same pregnancy,

(c) the number of Sure Start Maternity Grants to be awarded is to be determined in accordance with paragraphs (6) and (7).

(6) Where at the date of claim no existing member of the family is under the age of 16 a Sure Start Maternity Grant is to be awarded in respect of each of the children mentioned in paragraph (5).

(7) Where at the date of claim any existing member of the family is under the age of 16 then—

(a) where each of those existing members of the family under the age of 16 was born as a result of separate pregnancies, a Sure Start Maternity Grant is to be awarded for all but one of the children mentioned in paragraph (5); and

(b) where two or more of those existing members of the family under the age of 16 were born as a result of a single pregnancy, the number of Sure Start Maternity Grants to be awarded in respect of the children mentioned in paragraph (5) is the number of children mentioned in paragraph (5) minus the maximum number of existing members of the family born as a result of a single pregnancy.]

AMENDMENTS

1. Social Fund Maternity Grant Amendment Regulations 2011 (SI 2011/100) reg.2 (January 24, 2011).
2. Social Fund Maternity Grant Amendment Regulations 2012 (SI 2012/1814) reg.2 (August 13, 2012).
3. Loans for Mortgage Interest and Social Fund Maternity Grant (Amendment) Regulations 2018 (SI 2018/307) reg.3 (April 6, 2018).

GENERAL NOTE

4.63 From January 24, 2011, a maternity grant cannot generally be awarded if any "existing member of the family" is under the age of 16. That general rule is now stated in para.(4).

For the definition of "family" see the commentary to reg.3(1). "Existing member of the family" is defined by paras (2) and (3). The phrase normally means any member of the family apart from the child for whom the maternity grant is claimed ("C"), any other child born as a result of the same pregnancy as C and any child whose parent is under the age of 20 and a member of the claimant's family (para.(3)).

However, where C's parent ("P") is under 20 and the claim is made by another member of the family (i.e. normally, a grandparent), "existing member of the family" means any child of P, apart from C or any other child born as a result of the same pregnancy as C, who is also a member of the claimant's family (para.(2)). That definition has the effect that the a maternity grant can be awarded for C even if there are other members of the family (excluding children born as a result of the same pregnancy as C) who are under 16, as long as P is not the parent of those other family members.

4.64 Paragraph (6), taken together with para.(5), provides that where more than one child is born (or still born or expected to be born) as a result of the same pregnancy and there is no other family member under the age of 16, a maternity grant is payable for each child. Presumably this provision has been included out of an abundance of caution because the consequence appears to follow in any event. In those circumstances, the definition of "existing member of the family " in para.(3) would remove the other child born as a result of the same pregnancy from the scope of the restriction in para.(4) even if para.(6) did not exist.

Paragraph (7), taken together with para.(5), introduces a further exception the first time from August 13, 2012. Where more than one child is born (or still born or expected to be born) as a result of the same pregnancy, then a maternity grant is to be awarded in respect of the additional child or children born even if other existing members of the family are under 16. As the explanatory memorandum to SI 2012/1814 states:

"For example, if a claimant has an existing child but then has twins, one further [maternity grant] will be paid on the basis that the claimant already has existing baby items from the first child but needs additional baby items in respect of the second twin. If they have one existing child and then have triplets, two more grants will be paid and so on."

Paragraph (7)(b) modifies that principle where there have been previous multiple births in the family (or, more technically, where two or more of the existing members of the family under the age of 16 were born as a result of a single pregnancy).

Regulation 3 of SI 2012/1814 (see below) contains transitional provisions which mean that claimants cannot take advantage of the more generous terms of the new reg.5A where:

4.65

- the claim is based on reg.5(3)(a), was made before the birth and before August 13, 2012 and the expected date of confinement is before October 29, 2012;

- the claim is based on reg.5(3)(a), was made after the birth and the birth took place before October 29, 2012;

- the claim is based on reg.5(3)(c) and the qualifying order was made before October 29, 2012;

- the claim is based on reg.5(3)(d) and the appointment as guardian took effect before October 29, 2012;

- the claim is based on reg.5(3)(e) and the child is placed for adoption with the claimant or the claimant's partner before October 29, 2012; and

- the claim is based on reg.5(3)(f) and the adoption took effect before October 29, 2012.

For claims affected by the transitional provisions, the former version of reg.5A continues to apply: see pp.1393–1394 of Vol.II of the 2012/13 edition.

In *LS v SSWP (SF)* [2014] UKUT 298 (AAC), it was submitted that reg.5A is ultra vires on the ground that the Secretary of State had not complied with the public sector equality duty in s.71 of the Race Relations Act 1976 as amended when making it. The Upper Tribunal (Judge Levenson) rejected that submission.

In *SK and LL v SSWP* [2020] UKUT 145 (AAC), the Upper Tribunal (Judge Church) held that reg.5A discriminated unlawfully against:

- refugees with "pre-flight children" (i.e. those with an existing child but who were unlikely to have been able to bring that child's baby things to the UK when fleeing persecution) contrary to art.14 read with art.8 and A1P1 of the Convention; and

- those having their first biological child while already responsible for a child who came into their care after reaching 12 months old contrary to art.14 read with A1P1 of the Convention.

Judge Church disapplied reg.5A in the cases before him and, there being no dispute as to the other conditions of entitlement, awarded the claimants a Sure Start Maternity Grant.

Persons affected by a trade dispute

4.66   **6.**—(1) Where the claimant or the claimant's partner is a person affected by a trade dispute, a Sure Start Maternity Grant shall be made only if—
  (a) in the case where the claimant or the claimant's partner is in receipt of income support or income-based jobseeker's allowance, the trade dispute has, at the date of the claim for that payment, continued for not less than six weeks; or
  (b) in the case where the claimant or the claimant's partner is in receipt of—
    (i) working tax credit where the disability element or the severe disability element of working tax credit as specified in regulation 20(1)(b) and (f) of the Working Tax Credit (Entitlement and Maximum Rate) Regulations 2002 is included in the award, or
    (ii) child tax credit [¹ which includes an individual element or a disability element referred to in section 9(3) of the Tax Credits Act 2002]
  (2) In paragraph (1)(b), the relevant claim means the claim in respect of which a tax credit of the type referred to in head (i) or (ii) of that sub-paragraph was awarded.

AMENDMENT

  1. Social Fund (Amendment) Regulations 2017 (SI 2017/271) reg.3 (April 6, 2017).

GENERAL NOTE

4.67   Regulation 3 defines "person affected by a trade dispute" by reference to s.126 of the Social Security Contributions and Benefits Act 1992, which refers on to s.14 of the old style Jobseekers Act 1995 (see the notes to those provisions in Vol.V of this series).
    If the claimant (or her/his partner) is affected by a trade dispute then there is no entitlement to a maternity grant unless, either, that dispute is of at least six weeks' duration or the family is entitled to one of the tax credits specified in sub-para.(b) by virtue of a claim made before the trade dispute started. See the General Note to reg.5 for an argument that every award of CTC "includes" an individual element.
    It may sometimes be difficult to tell when a trade dispute started, since the dispute is to be distinguished from the stoppage of work due to it.

PART III

PAYMENTS FOR FUNERAL EXPENSES [¹ IN ENGLAND AND WALES]

AMENDMENT

  1. Social Security (Scotland) Act 2018 (Funeral Expense Assistance and Early Years Assistance) (Consequential Modifications and Savings) Order 2019 (SI 2019/1060) art.3(1) and (3) (September 16, 2019, subject to the saving in art.4).

Funeral payments: entitlement

4.68   **7.**—(1) In these Regulations—
  (a) "funeral payment" means a social fund payment to meet funeral expenses of a deceased person;
  (b) "responsible person" means the person who accepts responsibility for the funeral expenses.
  (2) Subject to regulation 8, a funeral payment shall be made where each of the conditions referred to in paragraphs (3) to [⁶ (9A)] is satisfied.

(3) The first condition is that, in respect of the date of the claim for a funeral payment, the responsible person or his partner is a person to whom paragraph (4) applies.

(4) This paragraph applies to a person—

(a) who has an award of—

    (i) income support,

    (ii) state pension credit,

    (iii) income-based jobseeker's allowance,

    (iv) working tax credit where the disability element or the severe disability element of working tax credit as specified in regulation 20(1)(b) and (f) of the Working Tax Credit (Entitlement and Maximum Rate) Regulations 2002 is included in the award,

    (v) child tax credit [⁴ which includes an individual element or a disability element referred to in section 9(3) of the Tax Credits Act 2002],

    (vi) housing benefit, or

    (vii) [³ . . .] [² . . .

    (viii) income-related employment and support allowance; [⁵ ...]]

[³ (ix) universal credit] [⁵; or

    (x) owner-occupier loan payments and is treated as entitled to a benefit specified in sub-paragraphs (i) to (iii) and (viii).]

(b) [³ . . .]

(5) The second condition is that the deceased was ordinarily resident in the United Kingdom at the date of his death.

(6) The third condition is that the claim is made within the prescribed time for claiming a funeral payment.

(7) The fourth condition is that the claimant is the responsible person or the partner of the responsible person.

(8) The fifth condition is that—

(a) the responsible person was the partner of the deceased at the date of death; or

(b) in a case where the deceased was a child and—

    (i) there is no absent parent, or

    (ii) there is an absent parent who, or whose partner, is a person to whom paragraph (4) applied as at the date of death,

the responsible person was the person, or the partner of the person, responsible for that child for the purposes of Part IX of the Act as at the date of death; or

(c) in a case where the deceased was a still-born child, the responsible person was a parent, or the partner of a parent, of that still-born child as at the date when the child was still-born; or

(d) in a case where the deceased had no partner and neither sub-paragraph (b) nor (c) applies, the responsible person was an immediate family member of the deceased and it is reasonable for the responsible person to accept responsibility for those expenses; or

(e) in a case where the deceased had no partner and none of sub-paragraphs (b), (c) and (d) applies, the responsible person was either—

    (i) a close relative of the deceased, or

    (ii) a close friend of the deceased,

and it is reasonable for the responsible person to accept responsibility for the funeral expenses.

(9) The sixth condition is that the funeral takes place—
(a) in a case where paragraph (10) applies, in a member State of the European Union, Iceland, Liechtenstein [¹, [⁸ Norway, Switzerland or the United Kingdom]];
(b) in any other case, in the United Kingdom.

[⁶ (9A) The seventh condition is that the claimant lives in England and Wales.]

[¹ [⁷ (10) This paragraph applies where the responsible person or the responsible person's partner is—
(a) a qualified person within the meaning of regulation 6(1)(b) (worker) or (c) (self-employed person) of the Immigration (European Economic Area) Regulations 2016 (the EEA Regulations);
(b) a person who retains the status referred to in sub-paragraph (a) pursuant to regulation 6(2) or (4) of the EEA Regulations;
(c) a person who is a family member of a person referred to in sub-paragraph (a) or (b) within the meaning of regulation 7(1) of the EEA Regulations; or
(d) a person who has a right to reside permanently in the United Kingdom by virtue of regulation 15(1)(c), (d) or (e) of the EEA Regulations;
(e) a person granted indefinite leave to enter, or remain in, the United Kingdom under the Immigration Act 1971 by virtue of Appendix EU to the immigration rules made under section 3(2) of that Act.]]

[⁷ (11) References in this regulation to the Immigration (European Economic Area) Regulations 2016 are to be read with Schedule 4 to the Immigration and Social Security Co-ordination (EU Withdrawal) Act 2020 (Consequential, Saving, Transitional and Transitory Provisions) Regulations 2020.]

AMENDMENTS

1. Social Security (Persons from Abroad) Amendment Regulations 2006 (SI 1026/2006) reg.8(2) (April 30, 2006).
2. Employment and Support Allowance (Consequential Provisions) (No.2) Regulations 2008 (SI 2008/1554) reg.8(1) and (4) (October 27, 2008).
3. Social Fund (Maternity and Funeral Expenses) Amendment Regulations 2013 (SI 2013/247) reg.2(5) (April 1, 2013).
4. Social Fund (Amendment) Regulations 2017 (SI 2017/271) reg.3 (April 6, 2017).
5. Loans for Mortgage Interest Regulations 2017 (SI 2017/725) reg.18 and Sch.5 para.9(1) and (4) (April 6, 2018).
6. Social Security (Scotland) Act 2018 (Funeral Expense Assistance and Early Years Assistance) (Consequential Modifications and Savings) Order 2019 (SI 2019/1060) art.3(1) and (4) (September 16, 2019, subject to the saving in art.4).
7. Immigration and Social Security Co-ordination (EU Withdrawal) Act 2020 (Consequential, Saving, Transitional and Transitory Provisions) (EU Exit) Regulations 2020 (SI 2020/1309) reg.62 (December 31, 2020 at 11.00 pm).
8. Social Fund Funeral Expenses Payment (Amendment) Regulations 2021 (SI 2021/65) reg.2 (February 15, 2021).

GENERAL NOTE

4.69   For the legislative history of funeral payments see pp.1229–1230 of Vol.II of the 2005 edition.

This regulation, together with reg.8, governs the right to funeral payments. Regulation 7 sets out the conditions of entitlement and reg.8 makes supplementary provision and contains two exclusory rules which disqualify some claimants who would otherwise have been entitled.

Regulation 7 specifies seven conditions of entitlement, all of which must be satisfied (para.(2)):

- the claimant (or her/his partner) must have an award of a qualifying benefit or be a person in respect of whom council tax benefit in the form of second adult rebate could be awarded (paras (3) and (4));

- the deceased must have been ordinarily resident in the UK (para.(5));

- a claim must have been made within the time limit (para.(6));

- the claimant (or her/his partner) must be a "responsible person" (para.(7));

- the responsible person must be sufficiently closely connected to the deceased (para.(8));

- the funeral must take place in the UK or (in certain circumstances) in an EEA state (paras (9)–(11)); and

- the claimant must live in England or Wales (para.(9A)).

Each of these conditions requires consideration in more detail.

Qualifying benefit
　　Under paras (3) and (4), the benefits that qualify a claimant for a funeral payment 　　**4.70**
include all those that are qualifying benefits for a sure start maternity grant (see the commentary to reg.5) with the addition of housing benefit.

For the family element of child tax credit, see the note to the relevant definition in reg.3.

Before April 1, 2013, the first condition was also satisfied if the claimant (or her/his partner) was a person in respect of whom a second adult rebate could be awarded: see the former sub-para.(4)(b). Secondly adult rebate was an alternative form of council tax benefit, which was abolished with effect from that date. For further details of the position before April 1, 2013, see p.1397 of Vol.II of the 2012/13 edition.

The award of the qualifying benefit must be in respect of the date of claim for the 　　**4.71**
funeral payment. See the notes to reg.5(1) and *GC v SSWP* (SF) [2010] UKUT 100 (AAC). Also note *CIS/2059/1995*. In that case the claimant's claim for a funeral payment had been rejected on the ground that he was not entitled to income support. However, the consequence of the Commissioner allowing his appeal against the decision refusing income support was that the basis for the rejection of his claim for a funeral payment had gone. Thus the tribunal's decision on that appeal, although sound when it was given, had become erroneous and it too had to be set aside.

A person "has an award" of income-based JSA (and therefore satisfies the condition in para.(4)(a)(iii)) while serving the waiting days (i.e. under Jobseekers Act 1995 Sch.1 para.4 and reg.46 of the JSA Regulations 1996) before entitlement to that benefit begins: *SSWP v SJ (IS)* [2015] UKUT 127 (AAC).

The requirement that claimants should be in receipt of a qualifying benefit has been held not to infringe their Convention rights under the Human Rights Act 1998, see *CIS/3280/2001*, *CIS/1722/2002* and *Faith Stewart v SSWP* [2011] EWCA Civ 907, [2012] AACR 9, upholding *SSWP v FS (SF)* [2010] UKUT 18 (AAC). It has also been held that failure of the scheme to provide for the personal representative of an insolvent estate to be eligible for a payment was neither irrational nor an infringement of the Convention: see *RM v SSWP (IS)* [2010] UKUT 220 (AAC).

Ordinary residence in the UK
　　The deceased must be ordinarily resident in the UK at the date of his death. 　　**4.72**
Ordinary residence "connotes residence in a place with some degree of continuity

and apart from accidental and temporary absences" (see *R(P) 1/78* at para.7). As the requirement is one of ordinary residence, not presence, a claim can be made in respect of a UK resident who dies, for example, while on holiday abroad for the cost of the funeral in the UK (although the cost of transporting the body back to the UK would not be covered, except possibly under reg.9(2)(g)).

The time limit

4.73   Under Claims and Payments Regulations, reg.19(1) and Sch.4 para.9, the time for claiming a funeral payment begins on the date of the death and ends six months after the date of the funeral. Otherwise the rules in this area are the same as for maternity grants—see the note to reg.5.

The six-month time limit begins to run on the day after the funeral and ends on the day six months later that corresponds to the day of the month on which the funeral took place: see *SSWP v SC (SF)* [2013] UKUT 607 (AAC) in which the funeral took place on July 26, 2011 and the time limit, which was then three months, ended on October 26, 2011 so that a claim made on October 27, 2011 was out of time.

Responsible person

4.74   The claimant (or her/his partner) must be a "responsible person", which is defined by para.(1)(b) as "the person who accepts responsibility for the funeral expenses".

In *CSB/488/1982*, it was held that the fact that someone else makes the arrangements does not mean that the claimant has not taken responsibility for the costs. The test is not who is responsible for arranging the funeral. The question is whether the claimant (or partner) has entered into a contractual relationship with the funeral director. Often the fact that the claimant's name appears on the funeral director's account will be sufficient evidence of that. But if someone else's name appears that does not necessarily mean that the claimant has not accepted responsibility because that person may, on a correct legal analysis, have been acting as the claimant's (or partner's) agent. In *CIS/12344/1996* the claimant's son made the funeral arrangements; his mother was unable to do so because of her age and the sudden death of her husband. The bill was in his name and he paid it before the claim for a social fund funeral payment was made. It is held that the son had been acting as agent for his mother and the fact that the account was addressed to him did not detract from this. The claimant had accepted responsibility for the funeral costs. In *R(IS) 6/98* the Commissioner retracts his statement in *CIS/12344/1996* that it was necessary for the undertakers to know of the agency. The concept of the "undisclosed principal" in the law of agency allowed an agency to exist even where this was not disclosed to the third party, provided that the agent had in fact had authority beforehand. But if there was no agency at the time the funeral debt was incurred, it was not open to a person to intervene later and claim to be legally responsible for the debt (although depending on the circumstances a novation may achieve that result, see below). In *VC v SSWP (IS)* [2010] UKUT 189 (AAC), the Upper Tribunal stressed the importance of making sufficient findings of fact as to the nature of any agreement between the claimant and any other putative responsible person.

Agency must be distinguished from a novation, or transfer, of the contract as occurred in *R(IS) 9/93*. The Commissioner follows *CSB/423/1989* in holding that if another person has initially made a contract with the undertakers the claimant may assume liability for the funeral costs by a novation of the contract under which the claimant assumes the other person's liability and the undertakers release the other person from his liability. The novation requires the consent of all three parties, but no consideration or further payment is necessary. Providing that the claimant comes within one of the heads of what is now sub-para.(e) and has assumed responsibility for the costs before the decision is made (or possibly before the claim is made) the condition is satisfied. Often, arrangements will be made without thinking about the legal niceties, and a commonsense view should be taken.

Legal issues can also arise if the closest relative lacks the legal capacity to accept a contractual liability to the undertakers. In *C1/01-02(SF)* the Commissioner had to decide whether a 16-year-old boy could legally "accept responsibility" for the expenses of his mother's funeral under the Northern Ireland equivalent of reg.7. She held that, in the particular circumstances of that case (where the claimant was the deceased's eldest child, 16-years old, had become the tenant of the family home and there was no other parent whose whereabouts were known) those expenses were a "necessary" for him so that he was obliged to pay a reasonable price for them under s.3 of the Sale of Goods Act 1979 even though he did not have capacity to make a binding contract to pay them.

Connection with the deceased

Paragraph 8 identifies the person who may claim a funeral expenses payment on the basis of how closely he or she was related to, or connected with, the deceased. There are two different hierarchies depending on whether the deceased was an adult or a child.   **4.75**

If the deceased was an adult then, under sub-para.(a), the claimant must be his or her partner. If the deceased had no partner at the date of death then, under sub-para.(d), the claim may be made by an "immediate family member" (i.e. a parent, son or daughter—see reg.3(1)) if it is reasonable for him or her to take responsibility for the funeral expenses. If the deceased dies without a partner or an immediate family member (or if there was an immediate family member but it is not reasonable for him or her to take responsibility for the funeral expenses), then, under subpara.(e), the claim may be made by a "close relative" (i.e. a parent, parent-in-law, son, son-in-law, daughter, daughter-in-law, step-parent, step-son, step-son-in-law, step-daughter, step-daughter-in-law, brother, brother-in-law, sister or sister-in-law—again see reg.3(1)) or a close friend. Again, a close relative or close friend, must show that it was reasonable for him or her to take responsibility for the funeral expenses. In the very rare case where the deceased's partner also dies before the deceased's funeral without making a claim for a funeral payment, then the deceased is treated as not having had a partner at the date of his or her death—see reg.8(4).

If the deceased was a child then the first question to ask is whether s/he was still-born. If so, then the claimant must be one of the child's parents or a person who was the partner of one of the child's parents at the date of the death (sub-para.(c)). If not, then the claimant must be the person responsible for the child at the date of death (or his or her partner), unless there is an absent parent (defined in reg.3(1)) who (or whose partner) was not receiving a qualifying benefit at the date of death (sub-para.(b)). If no-one qualifies under sub-paras (b) or (c) then, as for adults, the claimant must be an "immediate family member", or failing this, a "close relative" or a close friend. A person is responsible for a child if s/he is counted as such for the purposes of child benefit.

If there is more than one "immediate family member" then, unless the claimant is the deceased's partner, see also reg.8(1) and (2).   **4.76**

In any case where the claimant is a close relative (other than an immediate family member) or a close friend of the deceased, s/he must also establish that it was reasonable for him or her to accept responsibility for the funeral expenses. Regulation 8(5) states that this "shall be determined by the nature and extent of his contact with the deceased". *R(IS) 3/98* holds that in deciding this question, regard should be had to the person's relationship with the deceased as a whole and not just during the period immediately preceding the date of death. The claimant had claimed a funeral payment in respect of his late father whom he had not seen for 24 years. He was the only close relative. The Commissioner decided that the lack of contact over the previous 24 years did not automatically erase the contact they had had in the preceding 30 years. It was not unreasonable for a son to wish to pay his last respects to his father whatever the reasons for their estrangement. See also *CIS/13120/1996* (claimant divorced from the deceased only two weeks before his death after 40 years of marriage), a decision on the law as in force up to June 5, 1995 (although the actual result would be different on the current law). The fact that it is reasonable for one person to assume responsibility for the cost of a funeral does not mean that it is not reasonable for someone else to do so (*CIS/13120/196*). If there is more than one close relative then see reg.8(6)–(8).

It will be apparent from the above that an ex-partner (or someone who is no longer treated as a partner), or a relative who is not a close relative, will have to qualify under the category of close friend. According to the Decision Makers Guide, in considering whether a person was a close friend of the deceased, the depth of the relationship will be more important than its duration. In *CIS/788/2003* the deceased was a boy who had died at the age of three months. The child's mother was herself a minor and the funeral directors refused to enter into a contract with her for that reason. The child's grandmother therefore undertook responsibility for the expenses and claimed a funeral payment. Commissioner Turnbull held that the grandmother could be treated as a "close friend" of the deceased. The Secretary of State had argued that as child benefit had been paid to the child's mother, she would have satisfied what is now reg.7(8)(b)(ii) if she had accepted responsibility for the funeral expenses and therefore that the words equivalent to "none of sub-paragraphs (b), (c) and (d) applies" in sub-para.(e) were not satisfied. The Commissioner rejected that argument. The provision about the receipt of child benefit "did not apply" because there was no real possibility of the mother taking responsibility for the funeral expenses. Neither the existence of a family relationship between the grandmother and the child nor the child's very young age prevented her from being treated as his "close friend" for the purposes of the regulation.

Place of funeral

4.77   Paragraph (9) provides that the "funeral" must take place in the UK unless para. (10) (as qualified by para.(11)) applies. The effect is that funeral payments can still be made where the responsible person (or partner) has settled status under the EU Scheme or falls within one of the provisions of the 2016 Regulations that are listed in para.(10)(a)–(d), as those provisions are preserved and modified by Sch.4 to SI 2020/1309: see further Vol.V.

Until April 2, 2018, "funeral" was defined by reg.3(1) as "a burial or cremation". However, that definition was revoked by reg.4 of SI 2018/61, leaving the word undefined. The result must be that, for the purposes of the Regulations, "funeral" is to be treated as an ordinary word of the English language, rather than as a term of art (and reg.9(3)(ba) does contemplate that a funeral payment may be made in respect of one cost of "the disposal of the body of the deceased, whether by burial, cremation *or otherwise*" (emphasis added)). The most important funeral costs that are eligible for a funeral payment, however, remain those incurred as a result of burial or cremation (see reg.9(3)(a) and (b)), but not both (seer reg.9(5)).

In *JEC v Secretary of State for Work and Pensions (SF)* [2021] UKUT 243 (AAC), Upper Tribunal Judge Caldwell QC decides that in relation to the reg.7(9) requirement for a funeral to take place in the UK (or, in certain circumstances, an EU/ EFTA state), "for the purposes of the 2005 Regulations a 'funeral' is one event that involves disposal of the deceased's body" [para.37].

JEC does not address situations where there is no body, and the Secretary of State has subsequently issued guidance [ADM Memo 17/21, para.6]: "In the case where there is no body or remains of the deceased, a payment may be made for a single commemorative event."

In those cases in which a funeral that takes place in an EEA country remains eligible for a funeral payment, financial help with the funeral expenses is available that would not be available where the funeral takes place in other countries. This has led to a number of attempts to argue that the rule (and its predecessor which required the funeral to take place in the UK) were unlawfully discriminatory. Apart from the challenge in *O'Flynn v Adjudication Officer* (C–237/94) (R(IS) 4/98) in which the former absolute requirement that the funeral must take place in the UK was held to be contrary to EU law (as to which see pp.1231–1232 in Vol.II of the 2005 edition), these were all unsuccessful:

- In *R. v Secretary of State for Social Security, Ex p. Nessa, The Times*, November 15, 1994, the High Court rejected an argument that the predecessor rule was unlawful under the Race Relations Act 1976. Section 75 of that Act stated that it applied to acts done by ministers, as it applied to acts done by a private person. But Auld J held that acts of a governmental nature, such as the making of regulations, were not subject to the control of the 1976 Act as they were not acts of a kind that could be done by a private person.

- In *CIS/3150/1999* a challenge to the validity of the rule on the basis that it was ultra vires and irrational was rejected.

- In *CIS 4769/2001* the Commissioner rejected a challenge under the Human Rights Act: the rule was not directly discriminatory and the Commissioner was not persuaded either that there was any indirect discrimination against the claimant, a Muslim of Pakistani origin, or that, if there was such discrimination, it had not been established that it was not objectively justified.

- In *Esfandiari v SSWP* [2006] EWCA Civ 282 (*R(IS) 11/06*), the Court of Appeal also held the rule did not discriminate unlawfully against recent migrants. Giving the judgment of the Court, Carnwath LJ stated:

  "8. . . . I find it impossible to see this as a case of 'discrimination' in any relevant sense. The state made provision for a suitable burial in the UK for all those of inadequate means, regardless of personal characteristics or status. There was no obligation on the state to do so, and certainly no obligation to do more. It was open to each appellant to take advantage of this provision, but each chose not to do so for understandable, but entirely personal, reasons.

  9. The only way in which this can be represented as 'discriminatory' is by characterising them as members of a 'group', that of recent migrants to this country; and then finding 'indirect' discrimination, in that as a group (so it is assumed) they are more likely than other comparable groups to have retained family links with their countries of origin, and therefore more likely to want their loved ones to be buried there. Such reasoning seems to me, with respect, wholly artificial. Without demeaning the strength and sincerity of the wishes of these appellants as individuals, it is not obvious that recent migrants, as a group, are particularly likely to prefer a burial in their country of origin, rather than in the country they have made their home. In any event there may be many other categories of people resident in this country, who, given the choice, might elect for a burial abroad for themselves or their loved ones, whether for religious, family, social or purely sentimental reasons. They may have spouses from another country, who have retained their native family links; they may have spent large parts of their lives in another country; they may have children who have moved to another country. Such wishes are understandable and to be respected; but it is not the job of the state to satisfy them. Nor does the sharing of such desires render those who have them a 'group' requiring special protection under Article 14."

- Alternatively, if the rule was regarded as discriminatory then that discrimination was objectively justified.

In *CIS/1335/2004*, the claimant's husband died while they were on holiday in Spain. Because she could not afford to have his body flown back to the UK, he was cremated in Spain. His ashes were then interred in England. The Commissioner confirmed the Secretary of State's decision to refuse a funeral payment. The "funeral" was the Spanish cremation and not the subsequent burial of ashes in the

UK. Therefore, the actual cost of the burial did not qualify under reg.9(3)(a) and the other UK costs could only qualify as other funeral expenses under reg.9(3)(g) as incidental to, or consequential upon, the cremation in Spain if the claimant was in principle entitled to a funeral payment in respect of that cremation. That was not the case because the claimant was neither a migrant worker nor a family member of such a worker within the provisions set out in para.(10). The result was that the rule treated UK citizens less favourably than citizens of other Member States exercising rights in the UK under EU law. However, that discrimination was not unlawful under EU law or under ECHR art.14, taken together with art.1 of the First Protocol. From April 30, 2006 para.(10) applies to nationals of Switzerland as well as to nationals of Iceland, Liechtenstein and Norway—and to members of their families as defined by art.2 of the Rights of Residence Directive—as if those nationals were EU nationals (see reg.10(g) of SI 1026/2006).

Country where the claimant lives

4.78   From September 16, 2019, para.(9A) requires that a claimant must live in England or Wales to be entitled to a funeral payment. Claimants who live in Scotland must claim funeral expense assistance from the Scottish Ministers: see the Funeral Expense Assistance (Scotland) Regulations 2019 (SSI 2019/292) in Part XIII of Vol.IV of this series, particularly reg.9.

Funeral payments: supplementary

4.79   **8.**—(1) Subject to paragraph (2), the claimant shall not be entitled to a funeral payment where the responsible person is an immediate family member, a close relative or a close friend of the deceased and—

(a) there are one or more immediate family members of the deceased;

(b) one or more of those immediate family members or their partners are not persons to whom regulation 7(4) applied as at the date of death; and

(c) any of the immediate family members referred to in sub-paragraph (b) was not estranged from the deceased at the date of his death.

(2) Paragraph (1) shall not apply to disentitle the claimant from a funeral payment where the immediate family member who meets the description specified in sub-paragraph (c) of that paragraph is at the date of death—

(a) a person who has not attained the age of 18;

(b) [¹ a qualifying young person within the meaning of section 142 of the Act (child and qualifying young person);]

[² (bb) a qualifying young person under section 10(5) (prescription of qualifying young person) of the Welfare Reform Act 2012;]

(c) a person who has attained the age of 18 but not the age of 19 and who is attending a full-time course of advanced education, as defined in regulation 61 of the Income Support Regulations, or, as the case may be, a person aged 19 or over but under pensionable age who is attending a full-time course of study, as defined in that regulation, at an educational establishment;

(d) a person in receipt of asylum support under section 95 of the Immigration and Asylum Act 1999;

(e) a member of, and fully maintained by, a religious order;

(f) being detained in a prison, remand centre or youth custody institution and either that immediate family member or his partner is a person to whom regulation 7(4) applied immediately before that immediate family member was so detained;

[³(ff) a person resident in a care establishment within the meaning of regulation 3(3), whose accommodation and care costs are met in whole or in part by a local authority within the meaning of the Local Government Act 1972 or the Local Government etc (Scotland) Act 1994;]

(g) a person who is regarded as receiving free in-patient treatment within the meaning of the Social Security (Hospital In-Patients) Regulations 1975, or the Social Security (Hospital In-Patients) Regulations (Northern Ireland) 1975, and either that immediate family member or his partner is a person to whom regulation 7(4) applied immediately before that immediate family member was first regarded as receiving such treatment; or

(h) a person ordinarily resident outside the United Kingdom.

(3) Paragraphs (4) to (8) apply for the purposes of regulation 7(8)(d) and (e).

(4) The deceased shall be treated as having had no partner where the deceased had a partner at the date of death and—

(a) no claim for funeral expenses is made by the partner in respect of the death of the deceased; and

(b) that partner dies before the date upon which the deceased's funeral takes place.

(5) Whether it is reasonable for the responsible person to accept responsibility for meeting the expenses of a funeral shall be determined by the nature and extent of his contact with the deceased.

(6) Paragraph (7) applies (subject to paragraph (8)) in a case where the deceased had one or more close relatives.

(7) If, on comparing the nature and extent of any close relative's contact with the deceased and the nature and extent of the responsible person's contact with the deceased, any such close relative was—

(a) in closer contact with the deceased than the responsible person,

(b) in equally close contact with the deceased and neither that close relative nor his partner, if he has one, is a person to whom regulation 7(4) applies,

the claimant shall not be entitled to a funeral payment.

(8) However paragraph (7) shall not apply where the close relative who was in—

(a) closer contact with the deceased than the responsible person, or (as the case may be)

(b) equally close contact with the deceased,

is at the date of death of a description specified in any of sub-paragraphs (a) to (h) of paragraph (2).

(9) In a case where the responsible person is the partner of the person who was a close relative, immediate family member or (as the case may be) close friend of the deceased, references in the preceding provisions of this regulation, and in regulation 7(8)(d) and (e), to the responsible person are to be construed as references to the responsible person's partner.

AMENDMENTS

1. Social Security (Miscellaneous Amendments) Regulations 2006 (SI 2006/588) reg.6 (April 10, 2006).

2. Social Fund (Maternity and Funeral Expenses) Amendment Regulations 2013 (SI 2013/247) reg.2(6) (April 1, 2013).

3. Social Fund Funeral Expenses Amendment Regulations 2018 (SI 2018/61) regs 3 and 5 (April 2, 2018).

The Social Fund Maternity and Funeral Expenses (General) Regs 2005

GENERAL NOTE

4.80   Apart from making supplementary provision that has already been noted in the commentary to reg.7, reg.8 contains two important exclusory rules.
The first, in para.(1), disentitles a claimant who was not the deceased's partner if there are any immediate family members of the deceased (other than those excluded under para.(2)) who, or whose partners, have not been awarded a qualifying benefit, unless they were estranged from the deceased.
The second, in paras (6)–(8), disentitles a claimant who was not the deceased's partner if any close relative (other than one excluded under para.(2)) either had closer contact with the deceased or had equal contact and was not (or his or her partner was not) in receipt of qualifying benefit. This is a separate test from that in para.(1) so that estrangement from the deceased is not directly relevant in a claim where there are no immediate family members (*CIS/3534/2007* and *MS v SSWP* [2009] UKUT (AAC) 201).

4.81   To avoid confusion between the two rules, it is necessary to pay close regard to the distinction between "immediate family members" and "close relatives". In everyday language a brother or sister, for example, might be regarded as an immediate family member. As defined in reg.3(1), however, the *only* "immediate family members" are parents, sons and daughters. As people in those categories are also "close relatives", *both* exclusory rules apply to them.
Other relatives, however, (i.e. brothers, sisters, sons-in-law, daughters-in-law, parents-in-law, brothers-in-law, sisters-in-law, step-parents, step-children and step-children-in-law) are "close relatives only" and not "immediate family members". For the reasons given below, the first exclusory rule does not usually apply to them. Except where they have claimed in circumstances where there is an immediate family member (i.e. where the immediate family member has not claimed because it is not reasonable for him or her to take responsibility got the funeral expenses), they will be subject to the second exclusory rule only.

Immediate family members not in receipt of a qualifying benefit
4.82   The first exclusory rule will normally only apply to claims by an "immediate family member". This is because, where there is an "immediate family member", a claim by a "close relative" or "close friend" is only possible in circumstances where it is not reasonable for the immediate family member to take responsibility for the funeral expenses (see reg.7(8)(e) and, e.g. *CIS/788/2003*).
The meaning of the provision corresponding to para.(1) in the 1987 Regulations was considered in *CIS/2288/1998*. Read as a whole, the paragraph means that the claimant is not entitled to a funeral payment if there is at least one (other) immediate family member who not estranged from the deceased and neither that family member nor his or her partner was in receipt of a qualifying benefit.
A further point arose in *CIS/1218/1998*. The claimant had applied for a funeral payment in respect of his late mother. His sister was not in receipt of a qualifying benefit. The tribunal decided that what is now para.(1)(b) referred to *both* the claimant and his sister and since he was in receipt of a qualifying benefit the disentitlement imposed by the paragraph did not apply. The AO appealed, contending that if the tribunal's interpretation was correct, no claim would ever be caught by the provision since it was a requirement under what is now reg.7(3) and (4) that the responsible person be in receipt of a qualifying benefit. In addition, there would be no need to exempt those immediate family members now listed in para.(2) from the operation of the provision. The Commissioner agreed; in his view the immediate family members referred to in sub-paras (a) and (b) did not include the responsible person.

4.83   "Estrangement" has "connotations of emotional disharmony" (*R(SB) 2/87*) and may exist even though financial support is being provided. In *C1/01–02(SF)*, the Commissioner stated that "[m]ere disagreement is not sufficient to constitute estrangement, there must be something akin to treating as a stranger for a sufficient period of time". On the facts of that case estrangement had taken place between the claimant's grandparents and his mother (who had a drink problem) "in that there was a deliberate decision to sever relationships due to the strong disapproval and anger which the grandparents felt about the deceased's drinking and the strong desire which they felt that this lifestyle should change and had to change before any relationships could be resumed." In *CIS/4498/2001* the claimant's deceased mother had suffered from senile dementia as a result of which she could not communicate with anyone or recognise family members and his sister—the other "immediate family member"—had lived in Australia for 10 years but had returned to Britain on at least three occasions because of her mother's ill-health. Quoting his earlier decision in *CIS/5321/1998*, Commissioner Henty stated:

"The appropriate OED definition of 'estranged', accepted in *CIS/5119/97* is, 'to alienate in feeling or affection'. I might put a gloss on that such as 'not to be on speaking terms'. The evidence before the tribunal points, I think, not at so much as an alienation of feeling or affection—the emphasis being on 'alienation', a concept which involves some form of positive consideration—but a drifting apart which to my mind connotes something short of alienation. Of course a long period of 'drifting apart' may lead to the inference that there had been an alienation, but such is not, in my view, the case here'. Those considerations are equally applicable here. Had such a break down in relation occurred before the on set of the mother's incapacity, then estrangement there would have been. But the incapacity by itself is not estrangement, and neither is the fact that the sister had been in Australia for some 10 years."

In *CIS 1228/2004*, Commissioner Fellner held "that registering a death is [not] enough *in itself* to show that the person who does so *cannot* have been estranged from the deceased" (original emphasis).

In *CIS/4096/2005*, Commissioner Jupp reviewed the authorities on estrangement (in the context of reg.13(1)(d) of the Income Support Regulations) and concluded that there was no requirement of mutuality in feeling for estrangement to exist, as had been suggested by the Commissioner in *CIS/4498/2001*. Disharmony can arise from one person's attitude to another even though the other party may not wish the situation to be as it is. The position has to be judged from the point of view of (in the context of funeral payments) the surviving immediate family member who is being considered and not from the point of view of the deceased.

The concept of "estrangement" is also relevant to the capital disregard in para. (4) of Sch.10 to the Income Support Regulations, Sch.8 to the JSA Regulations and Sch.5 to the State Pension Credit Regulations. However, caution needs to be exercised when applying the case law on that provision to funeral payments. In *CPC/683/2007*, the Commissioner noted that "the language used in [that] legislation is attempting to identify those cases in which the relationship between the parties is such that it is appropriate for their finances to be treated separately for the purposes of benefit entitlement". That is not the same as the context in which estrangement needs to be considered on a claim for a funeral payment.   **4.84**

What happens if—as may well be the case even in relatively close families—the claimant simply does not know whether or not any of the other immediate family members or close relatives is in receipt of a qualifying benefit: where does the burden of proof lie? This was one of the issues considered by the House of Lords in *Kerr v Department for Social Development* [2004] UKHL 23 *(R 1/04 (SF))*. In that case, which concerned the Northern Ireland equivalent of the current reg.8, the claimant was the eldest of three brothers and a sister who, although living in the Belfast area, had not been in touch with each other for over 20 years. One of the brothers died and the claimant was traced by the police and agreed to accept financial responsibility for the funeral. He claimed a funeral payment which was refused without any enquiry by the Department into whether the surviving brother and sister had been awarded a qualifying benefit, an question which, of course, the Department was better placed to answer than the claimant. The issue was therefore whether Mr Kerr had to prove a negative—that neither his sister or brother were in receipt of a qualifying benefit—or whether the Department had to show that they were. Giving the judgment of the House, Baroness Hale said, in a passage which has profound implications for social security administration generally:

"61. Ever since the decision of the Divisional Court in *R. v Medical Appeal Tribunal (North Midland Region), Ex p Hubble* [1958] 2 QB 228, it has been accepted that the process of benefits adjudication is inquisitorial rather than adversarial. Diplock J. as he then was said this of an industrial injury benefit claim at p.240:

'A claim by an insured person to benefit under the Act is not truly analogous to a lis inter partes. A claim to benefit is a claim to receive money out of the insurance funds . . . Any such claim requires investigation to determine whether any, and if so, what amount of benefit is payable out of the fund. In such an investigation, the minister or the insurance officer is not a party adverse to the claimant. If analogy be sought in the other branches of the law, it is to be found in an inquest rather than in an action.'

62. What emerges from all this is a co-operative process of investigation in which both the claimant and the department play their part. The department is the one which knows what questions it needs to ask and what information it needs to have in order to determine whether the conditions of entitlement have been met. The claimant is the one who generally speaking can and must supply that information. But where the information is available to the department rather than the claimant, then the department must take the necessary steps to enable it to be traced.

63. If that sensible approach is taken, it will rarely be necessary to resort to concepts taken from adversarial litigation such as the burden of proof. The first question will be whether each partner in the process has played their part. If there is still ignorance about a relevant matter then generally speaking it should be determined against the one who has not done all they reasonably could to discover it. As Mr Commissioner Henty put it in decision *CIS/5321/1998*, 'a claimant must to the best of his or her ability give such information to the AO as he reasonably can, in default of which a contrary inference can always be drawn.' The same should apply to information which the department can reasonably be expected to discover for itself."

In this case, the claim was allowed because the Department had failed to ask Mr Kerr the necessary questions and could not "use its own failure to ask questions which would have led it to the right answer to defeat the claim" (at para.65). Baroness Hale also addressed the position which would have existed if both the claimant and the Department had done everything which was legally required of them but it had still not proved possible to ascertain the true position? In that case:

"66. This will not always be sufficient to decide who should bear the consequences of the collective ignorance of a matter which is material to the claim. It may be that everything which could have been done has been done but there are still things unknown. The conditions of entitlement must be met before the claim can be paid. . . It may therefore become relevant to ask whether a particular matter relates to the conditions of entitlement or to an exception to those conditions. In this case, the department argues that all the elements, including those in regulation 6(6) [equivalent to reg.8(7) of the current GB regulations], are conditions of entitlement, so that the claimant must bear the consequences of ignorance. The claimant argues that the conditions of entitlement are laid down in regulation 6(1), supplemented where relevant by paragraphs (2) and (5) [regs 7 and 8((4) and (5) of the current GB Regulations]. Paragraphs (3) and (4), which go together, and paragraph (6) [reg.8(1),(2) and (7) of the current GB regulations] are exceptions.

67. The structure and wording of the regulation support the claimant's case. Conditions (a), (b), (c) and (d) in regulation 6(1) are clearly established. The

claimant qualifies as a 'close relative' under condition (e)(iv)(aa) but this also requires that it be reasonable for him to accept responsibility. Under regulation 6(5) the question 'whether it is reasonable for a person to accept responsibility for meeting the expenses of the funeral shall be determined by the nature and extent of that person's contact with the deceased'. The tribunal decided that it was reasonable for the claimant, as the eldest son who had grown up with his brother, to accept that responsibility, despite the fact that they had not been in contact with one another for many years. That conclusion is not challenged in this appeal, in my view rightly. For the reasons given earlier, there is a strong public interest in encouraging families to take responsibility for the speedy and seemly burial of their deceased relatives.

68. Regulation 6(3) provides that the person who has made himself responsible 'shall not be entitled' if there is a more appropriate immediate family member. That this is a disentitling provision is made clear by regulation 6(4), which states that 'Paragraph (3) shall not apply to *disentitle* the responsible person' (my emphasis) in the circumstances there set out. In the same way, paragraph 6(6) provides that if there is a close relative who is either in closer contact or in equally close contact and not receiving benefits or having capital, the responsible person 'shall not be entitled' to the payment. These paragraphs are therefore worded in terms of exceptions rather than qualifying conditions. If anything, this interpretation is supported by the legislative history given earlier, as the existence of a more suitable relative was added as an exception or qualification to the basic rule.

69. This, therefore, is a case in which the department should bear the burden of the collective ignorance and pay the claim."

Paragraph (2) sets out the circumstances in which the claimant may remain entitled to a funeral payment even if s/he has an immediate family member who is not in receipt of a qualifying benefit. These are largely self-explanatory and include where the immediate family member is under 18, a qualifying young person for child benefit purposes, in certain types of full-time education, in receipt of asylum support, ordinarily resident outside the UK or—in some circumstances—in hospital or in prison.

Closer contact

Under paras (6)–(8), if the responsible person is an immediate family member,   **4.85** another close relative or a close friend (see para.(3)), and the deceased had one or more close relatives (para.(6)), the nature and extent of their contact with the deceased will be compared (para.(7)).

This is a separate test from deciding whether it is reasonable for the person to have accepted responsibility for the funeral costs (see para.(5)), as confirmed in *R(IS)* 3/98. If any close relative had closer contact, the claimant will not be entitled to a funeral payment (para.(7)(a)). If the contact was equally close, a payment will also be refused if the close relative (or their partner) is not getting a qualifying benefit (see para.(7)(b)). But this rule does not apply if at the date of death the close relative concerned came within any of the categories listed in para.(2) (see above).

Close contact will be a question of fact in each case. It should be noted that the test involves having regard to the nature as well as the extent of the contact. Thus this will bring in issues of quality as well as quantity. *CIS/8485/1995* states that, when considering the question of contact with the deceased, tribunals should adopt a broad brush, commonsense approach. The amount of time spent with the deceased is only one factor, and the nature of the contact should be judged not just by visits, letters, etc. but also by the quality of the contact. So if the claimant's half-brother's unpredictable nature had affected his relationship with his late mother, that should have been taken into account in assessing the nature of his contact with her. The guidance given to decision-makers by the Decision Makers Guide is that they "should consider the overall nature and extent of the contact with the deceased given the circumstances of the individual. For example, domestic or work responsibilities may prevent a close relative from keeping in regular contact with the deceased but the nature of the contact may be equally as close as a close friend who visited every day." The guidance suggests that factors to be considered include the nature of the relationship, frequency of contact, type of contact, domestic or caring assistance given to the deceased, social outings and holidays, domestic or work responsibilities and estrangements or arguments with the deceased (paras 39181–39182).

4.86   As the Deputy Commissioner pointed out in *CIS/3534/2007*, whether or not the close relative was estranged from the deceased is not legally relevant to the test in para.(7). However, the existence of estrangement may be relevant as a matter of fact. It is suggested that a close relative who was not estranged from the deceased will normally have been in closer contact with the deceased than a close relative who was so estranged.

The question of how para.(7)(b) applies in the situation where none of the close relatives was in contact with the deceased at all—i.e. whether the phrase "in equally close contact" includes circumstances in which there was an equal lack of contact—was considered, obiter, by three members of the House of Lords in the *Kerr* case (above). Lord Scott was of the view that it did not. To read "equally close contact" as meaning "equal contact" was to rewrite the statutory language and to ignore the significance of the words "close" and "in"—one cannot be "in" a "close" lack of contact. Where there was no contact at all, then none of the sub-paras of what is now para.(7) was applicable. Further, the question was not whether any of the close relatives "had had close contact with the deceased in the past" but "whether they were 'in equally close contact' with him at the time of his death" (paras 26–35). By contrast Lord Hope held (at para.9) that the test in what is now para.(7)(b) was not necessarily limited to the state of affairs which existed at the time of the deceased's death:

> "Regulation [8(7)] assumes that where there is 'contact' the question of 'closeness' is put in issue, however slight or remote in time that may be. I do not find anything in the regulation to indicate that the contact must have been current at, or immediately before, the date of the deceased's death. The period of time during which a comparison of the nature and extent of the contact is to be undertaken is not specified. The conclusion which I would draw from this is that there is no restriction as to the time of this contact. In my opinion the first question which the adjudicator must ask himself is whether the relevant person had any 'contact' with the deceased at all at any time. If he did, the question of the relative 'closeness' of that contact in comparison with the contact of the responsible person can and must be asked and answered."

> Baroness Hale (at para.70), whilst agreeing with Lord Scott that it was "harder to see how 'was . . . in equally close contact' can cover contact which ended 20 years earlier", preferred not to express any view on the issue. It is disappointing that when the regulations were re-drafted in 2005, the opportunity was not taken to clarify the point one way or another.

Amount of funeral payment

4.87   **9.**—(1) A funeral payment shall be an amount sufficient to meet any relevant expenditure less any amount which falls to be deducted under regulation 10.

(2) In paragraph (1), "relevant expenditure" means any costs to which paragraph (3) applies which fall to be met or have been met by the responsible person (or a person acting on behalf of the responsible person), inclusive of any available discount on those costs allowed by the funeral director or by any other person who arranges the funeral.

(3) This paragraph applies to the following costs—

(a) where the deceased is buried—

[¹ (i) the necessary costs of obtaining a new burial plot for the deceased and a right of burial in that plot, whether or not that right is exclusive]

(ii) the fees levied in respect of a burial by the authority or person responsible for the provision and maintenance of cemeteries for the area where the burial takes place, [³ and] the fees levied by a private grave-digger, in so far as it is necessary to incur those fees;

(b) where the deceased is cremated—

(i) the fees levied in respect of a cremation by the authority or person responsible for the provision and maintenance of crematoria for the area where the cremation takes place in so far as it is necessary to incur those fees;

(ii) [¹ ...]

(iii) [¹ ...]

(iv) the fee payable for the removal of any device as defined for the purposes of the Active Implantable Medical Devices Regulations 1992 save that, where that removal is carried out by a person who is not a registered medical practitioner, no more than £20 shall be met in respect of that fee;

[¹(ba) the cost of obtaining any medical reference, report or other documentation required in connection with the disposal of the body of the deceased, whether by burial, cremation or otherwise;]

(c) the cost of obtaining any documentation, production of which is necessary in order to release any assets of the deceased which may be deducted from a funeral payment pursuant to regulation 10;

(d) where the deceased died at home or away from home and it is necessary to transport the deceased within the United Kingdom in excess of 80 kilometres (approximately 50 miles) to the funeral director's premises or to the place of rest, the reasonable cost of transport in excess of 80 kilometres;

(e) where transport is provided by a vehicle for the coffin and bearers and by one additional vehicle, from the funeral director's premises or the place of rest to the funeral and—

(i) the distance travelled, in the case of a funeral which consists of a burial where no costs have been incurred under sub-paragraph (a)(i) above, exceeds 80 kilometres; or

(ii) the distance travelled, in the case of any other funeral, necessarily exceeds 80 kilometres,

the reasonable cost of the transport provided, other than the cost in respect of the first 80 kilometres of the distance travelled;

(f) the necessary cost of one return journey for the responsible person, either for the purpose of making arrangements for, or for attendance at, the funeral; and

(g) any other funeral expenses which shall not exceed [² £1,000] in any case.

(4) Paragraphs (2) and (3) have effect subject to the following provisions.

(5) Paragraph (3)(a) does not apply to costs in connection with burial of the deceased's ashes (where he was cremated).

(6) All references to 80 kilometres shall be construed as applying to—

(a) in a case to which paragraph (3)(d) applies, the combined distance from the funeral director's premises or the deceased's place of rest to the place of death and of the return journey;

(b) in a case to which paragraph (3)(e) applies, the combined distance from the funeral director's premises or the deceased's place of rest to the funeral and of the return journey.

(7) The cost of items and services referred to in paragraph (3)(a), (b), (d) and (e) shall not include any element in the cost of those items and services which relates to a requirement of the deceased's religious faith.

(8) Paragraph (3)(e)(i) includes costs only to the extent that, together with the costs referred to under paragraph (3)(a)(ii), they do not exceed the costs which would have been incurred under—

(a) paragraph (3)(a)(i) and (ii), and

(b) where appropriate, paragraph (3)(e)(ii),

if it had been necessary to purchase for the deceased a new burial plot [¹ with a right of burial in that plot, whether or not that right is exclusive].

(9) Paragraph (3)(f) includes costs only to the extent that they do not exceed the costs which would have been incurred in respect of a return journey from the home of the responsible person to the location where the necessary costs of a burial or, as the case may be, cremation referred to in paragraph (3)(a) or (b) would have been incurred.

(10) Where items and services have been provided on the death of the deceased under a pre-paid funeral plan or under any analogous arrangement—

(a) no funeral payment shall be made in respect of items or services referred to in paragraph (3) which have been provided under such a plan or arrangement; and

(b) paragraph (3)(g) shall have effect in relation to that particular claim as if for the sum [² £1,000], there were substituted the sum "£120".

AMENDMENTS

1. Social Fund Funeral Expenses Amendment Regulations 2018 (SI 2018/61) regs 3 and 6 (April 2, 2018).
2. Social Fund Funeral Expenses Payment (Coronavirus) (Amendment) Regulations 2020 (SI 2020/405) reg.2 (in relation to deaths occurring on or after April 8, 2020: see reg.3).
3. Social Fund and Social Security (Claims and Payments) (Amendment) Regulations 2020 (SI 2020/600) reg.2 (July 9, 2020).

GENERAL NOTE

4.88   Regulation 9 defines "relevant expenditure", i.e. the expenses that are eligible to be met by a funeral payment. Under para.(1) the amount of the funeral payment is the total relevant expenditure less any deduction that falls to be made under reg.10.

A payment can be made for the expenses that are listed in para.(3)(a)–(f) (except for those that have been met by a pre-paid funeral plan or similar arrangement (para.(10)(a)), together with up to £700 for other funeral expenses, or £120 if some of the funeral costs have been met under a pre-paid funeral plan or similar arrangement, (paras (3)(g) and (10)(b)). For funeral plans, see also reg.10(e) and the commentary on that provision.

It will be noted that some of sub-paras (a)–(f) in para.(3) contain an express limitation to "reasonable" costs and some do not (in others the word "necessary" is used). On a previous form of this provision *R(IS) 14/92* considered that the word "reasonable" should be read into the listed categories even where it was not expressed. But in *CIS/6818/1995* the Commissioner concluded that what was said about reasonableness in *R(IS) 14/92* was not an essential part of the decision. He expressed the view (which was also not necessary to his decision) that each sub-paragraph in what is now reg.8(3) contained its own complete test and that there was no room for any further conditions to be implied. In view of the quite specific nature of the items or services covered by para.(3)(a)–(f) it is suggested that the approach of *CIS/6818/1995* is to be preferred.

Any element in the burial or transport costs that relates to a requirement of the deceased's religious faith will not be met (para.(7))—see *CSIS/42/1996*, which held that a vigil is a requirement of the Roman Catholic faith.

Burial and cremation—paras 3(a) and (b)

Paragraph (3)(a)(i) allows "the necessary costs of purchasing a new burial plot   **4.89** for the deceased". The meaning of the word "necessary" in a predecessor of this paragraph was considered in *R(IS) 18/98*. The Commissioner decided that it implied that any expense over that which was properly required was to be excluded. However, its effect was not to require the purchase of the cheapest possible plot without regard to any other consideration. Account should be taken of the proximity to the deceased's residence while he was alive and of the deceased's religion, so that, for example a person of the Greek Orthodox faith was entitled to be buried in an area set aside for people of that faith.

A funeral payment may be awarded for the cost of either a cremation or a burial but not both. Costs in connection with the burial of cremated ashes are not eligible (para.(5)).

See also in this context *CIS/1335/2004* discussed in the commentary to reg.7(10) (above).

Transport costs—paras (3)(d)–(f)

Paragraphs (3)(d) and (e) allow certain transport costs for distances (i.e. the   **4.90** combined distance of the outward and return journey (para.(3)), in excess of 80km (about 50 miles) to be met. For the calculation of the 80km, see para.(6).

R(IS) 11/91 decided that the deceased's "home" in para.(3)(d) was the accommodation where he normally lived prior to his death, as opposed to his "home town".

Where the costs of transport and burial in an existing plot (i.e. usually away from where the deceased lived) exceed the purchase and burial costs of a new plot, plus any necessary transport costs (i.e. the costs of burying locally), para.(3)(e)(i) provides that such costs will be met up to the level of the local burial costs (para.(8))

Paragraph (3)(f) covers the necessary costs of one return journey for the responsible person for arranging the funeral or attending it. The journey is not restricted to a journey within the UK but see para.(9) which limits the costs that will be met to those of a return journey from the responsible person's home to the place where the "necessary" funeral costs would have been incurred (although the drafting is not entirely clear, it is understood that the intention is to restrict payment of travel costs to those that would have been incurred if the funeral had taken place in the UK). *CIS 16957/1996* decides that although sub-para.(f) refers to a "return journey" it did also apply where the claimant only undertook a single journey (her husband had died away from home and she had travelled home to attend the funeral). Others who are relatives of the deceased may be eligible for a community care grant for the cost of travel to and from a funeral in the UK (see Social Fund direction 4(b)(ii)). The applicant must be a member of a family containing a claimant in receipt of income support or income-based JSA.

Other expenses

The expenses to be covered by para.(3)(g) are not specified but will include items   **4.91** such as a funeral director's fees (including the cost of a coffin which cannot be met under either para.(3)(a) or (b)—see *CIS/2651/2003* and *CIS 2607/2003*), church fees or flowers. But there is no definition of funeral expenses and so any expense that is a funeral expense should be allowed. Thus, in *CIS/1345/2004*, Commissioner Williams held that "suitable funeral attire" might amount to a funeral expense within sub-para. (g). The test was not, as had been suggested by the Secretary of State, whether the expense was "wholly exclusively and necessarily required for the funeral". There was no basis in law for restricting the scope of the paragraph beyond the words actually used in the sub-para. The only tests for applying sub-para.(g) were:

"(i) Were the expenses in fact funeral expenses that took into account any relevant discounts?

(ii) If so, were the expenses met by the claimant or partner (or will they be)?

(iii) If so, were they of a nature covered by any of the provisions in regulation [9(3)(a) to (f)]?

(iv) If not, do they exceed the set sum?

If they do not, they are allowable."

It should be noted, however, that in *CIS/1924/2004*, Commissioner Fellner held that, although flowers were capable of amounting to a funeral expense within the sub-para., obituary notices and the cost of a memorial stone and flower container were not. There is a clear tension between these two decisions: if the *CIS/1345/2004* test had been applied to the items disallowed in *CIS/1924/2004*, it seems probable that some, at least, would have been allowed.

Under para.(3)(g) there is no limit on the funeral expenses that are to be met, other than the £1,000 ceiling. There is therefore nothing to prevent para.(3)(g) being used to pay for the cost of items or services in para.(3)(a)–(f) that have not been fully met or—as para.3(g) is not mentioned in para.(7)—to cover the cost of a religious requirement.

Payment of funeral expenses

4.92   A funeral payment will be made even if the costs have already been met by the claimant, his partner, or a person acting on their behalf. If the funeral costs have not been paid any funeral payment is to be made direct to the creditor—see reg.35(2) of the Claims and Payments Regulations.

Deductions from an award of a funeral payment

4.93   **10.**—(1) There shall be deducted from the amount of any award of funeral payment which would otherwise be payable—

(a) [⁴ subject to paragraph (1A)] the amount of any assets of the deceased which are available to the responsible person (on application or otherwise) or any other member of his family without probate or letters of administration, or (in Scotland) confirmation, having been granted;

(b) the amount of any lump sum due to the responsible person or any other member of his family on the death of the deceased by virtue of any insurance policy, occupational pension scheme or burial club, or any analogous arrangement;

[⁸ (c) . . .]

(d) the amount of any funeral grant, made out of public funds, in respect of the death of a person who was entitled to a war disablement pension;

(e) in relation to a pre-paid funeral plan or any analogous arrangement—

(i) where the plan or arrangement had not been paid for in full prior to the death of the deceased, the amount of any sum payable under that plan or arrangement in order to meet the deceased's funeral expenses;

(ii) where the plan or arrangement had been paid for in full prior to the death of the deceased, the amount of any allowance paid under that plan or arrangement in respect of funeral expenses.

[⁴ (1A) For the purposes of regulation 10(1)(a), arrears of the following benefits payable to the deceased as at the date of death are excluded from the assets of the deceased—

972

(a) attendance allowance under Part 3 of the Act;
(b) bereavement allowance under Part 2 of the Act;
(c) carer's allowance under Part 3 of the Act;
(d) child benefit under Part 9 of the Act;
(e) child tax credit under section 8 of the Tax Credits Act 2002(8);
(f) council tax benefit under Part 7 of the Act;
(g) disability living allowance under Part 3 of the Act;
(h) employment and support allowance under—
    (i) Part 1 of the 2007 Act as amended by Schedule 3, and Part 1 of Schedule 14, to the 2012 Act (to remove references to an income-related allowance); or
    (ii) Part 1 of the 2007 Act as it has effect apart from the amendments made by Schedule 3, and Part 1 of Schedule 14, to the 2012 Act;
(i) exceptionally severe disablement allowance under Part 5 of the Act;
(j) guardian's allowance under Part 3 of the Act;
(k) housing benefit under Part 7 of the Act;
(l) incapacity benefit under Part 2 of the Act;
(m) income support under Part 7 of the Act;
(n) industrial death benefit under Part 5 of the Act;
(o) industrial injuries disablement benefit under Part 5 of the Act;
(p) jobseeker's allowance under—
    (i) the 1995 Act as amended by Part 1 of Schedule 14 to the 2012 Act (to remove references to an income-based allowance); or
    (ii) the 1995 Act as it has effect apart from the amendments made by Part 1 of Schedule 14 to the 2012 Act;
(q) maternity allowance under Part 2 of the Act;
(r) personal independence payment under Part 4 of the 2012 Act;
(s) reduced earnings allowance under Part 5 of the Act;
(t) severe disablement allowance under Part 3 of the Act;
(u) state pension credit under section 1 of the State Pension Credit Act 2002;
(v) state retirement pension under Parts 2 or 3 of the Act;
[6 (va) a state pension under Part 1 of the Pensions Act 2014;]
(w) universal credit under Part 1 of the 2012 Act;
(x) war disablement pension under an instrument specified in section 639(2) of the Income Tax (Earnings and Pensions) Act 2003(10) in respect of the death or disablement of any person;
(y) war widow's pension under an instrument specified in section 639(2) of the Income Tax (Earnings and Pensions) Act 2003 in respect of the death or disablement of any person;
(z) war widower's pension under an instrument specified in section 639(2) of the Income Tax (Earnings and Pensions) Act 2003 in respect of the death or disablement of any person;
(aa) widowed mother's allowance under Part 2 of the Act;
(bb) widowed parent's allowance under Part 2 of the Act;
(cc) widow's pension under Part 2 of the Act;
(dd) winter fuel payment under Part 8 of the Act;
(ee) working tax credit under section 10 of the Tax Credits Act 2002] [5;
(ff) armed forces independence payment under the Armed Forces and Reserve Forces (Compensation Scheme) Order 2011.]
[8 (2) . . .]
[8 (3) . . .]

AMENDMENTS

1. Income-related Benefits (Amendment) (No.2) Regulations 2005 reg.8 (December 12, 2005).
2. Social Security (Miscellaneous Amendments) (No.2) Regulations 2010 (SI 2010/641) reg.7 (April 6, 2010).
3. Social Security (Miscellaneous Amendments) (No.3) Regulations 2011 (SI 2011/2425) reg.18 (October 31, 2011).
4. Social Fund (Maternity and Funeral Expenses) Amendment Regulations 2013 (SI 2013/247) reg.2 (April 1, 2013).
5. Armed Forces and Reserve Forces Compensation Scheme (Consequential Provisions: Subordinate Legislation) Order 2013 (SI 2013/591) art.7 and Sch. para.32 (April 8, 2013).
6. Pensions Act 2014 (Consequential, Supplementary and Incidental Amendments) Order 2015 (SI 2015/1985) art.27 (April 6, 2016).
7. Social Security (Emergency Funds) (Amendment) Regulations 2017 (SI 2017/689) reg.5 (June 19, 2017).
8. Social Fund Funeral Expenses Amendment Regulations 2018 (SI 2018/61) regs 3 and 7 (April 2, 2018).

GENERAL NOTE

4.94   The amounts listed in reg.10 are deducted from the amount calculated under reg.9. Those amounts do not include the value of the deceased's estate but, by virtue of s.78(4) of the Administration Act any funeral payment from the social fund may be recovered from the estate (i.e. not just those assets available to the responsible person without a grant of probate or letters of administration: see para.(1)(a)) as if it were a funeral expense—see further the commentary to s.78 in Vol.III.

Paragraph (1) specifies the amounts that are to be deducted.

4.95   *Sub-paragraph (a)*: Under the Administration of Estates (Small Payments) Act 1965 certain sums can be distributed from the estate to beneficiaries without a grant of probate or letters of administration. The current limit is £5,000. In addition many statutes regulating Post Office and building society accounts, savings certificates, etc. (but not, after privatisation, Trustee Savings Bank accounts) allow payment to be made after the owner's death. There is a similar power for most social security benefits. One problem is that these provisions are generally merely permissive, so that payment cannot be demanded as of right. In *R(IS) 14/91* the Commissioner indicates that in straightforward cases it may be concluded that such an amount is available on application. However, the circumstances (e.g. some dispute between next of kin of equal status) may point to the opposite conclusion. *R(IS) 14/91* also decides that evidence of availability of assets from the date of death up to the date of the decision on the claim is relevant. Thus where the claim was made on the date of death, a sum of £1300 in the deceased's building society account was available, although the claimant did not obtain the money until a week later. Nor was that conclusion defeated by the fact that before the decision the claimant had distributed or spent most of the money.

In *PA v SSWP (SF)* [2010] UKUT 42 (AAC), the deceased left no partner or surviving close relatives. The funeral was arranged by his carer, who claimed a funeral payment as a close friend. That claim was refused, ultimately because he did not provide evidence of the deceased's estate, the Secretary of State drawing the inference that the amount available to the claimant was sufficient to extinguish any entitlement. Allowing the appeal, Judge Mesher pointed out that reg.10(1)(a) "does not contain a rule that the value of the deceased's estate or of any assets within the estate is always to be set against the amount of a funeral payment that would otherwise be awarded". It only applies where those assets are "available" and available "to the claimant or some member of this family". There was some evidence that the claimant had approached the deceased's bank to try to obtain the balance standing to the credit of his account. According to that evidence, Judge Mesher remarked (at para.11):

"The bank said that if there was money in the account a cheque would be sent to the funeral directors. There was not in fact an indication that money would have been paid over to the claimant, a person apparently not entitled to any share of Mr O's estate and not an executor under a will or an administrator on intestacy. Nor was there a clear indication that such a person would be provided with a copy of the closing bank statement."

As there was no other evidence to suggest that the deceased had (or had in the past had) significant capital, and as the burden of proof on the issue was on the Secretary of State (para.14), Judge Mesher awarded the claimant a funeral payment on the basis that reg.10(1)(a) did not apply.

Funeral expenses are a first charge on the estate *(R(SB) 18/84)*. If there are liquid assets in the estate, these may be immediately available for funeral expenses regardless of other debts. In *R(IS) 12/93* arrears of attendance allowance for the deceased were paid to the claimant as next of kin. The Commissioner holds that the arrears were available. Since they exceeded the cost of the funeral, no award was made.   **4.96**

However, from April 1, 2013, arrears of the benefits listed in para.(1A) (including attendance allowance) do not form part of the deceased's assets for these purposes and therefore no deduction can be made in respect of them under para.(1)(a).

In *TG v SSWP (SF)* [2015] UKUT 571 (AAC), the claimant made an internet transfer of £2,500 from his late mother's bank account to his own shortly before his mother died on a Sunday afternoon. However, as Sunday was not a business day, the deceased's bank statements did not show the money leaving her account until the following day. Whether or not the claimant was entitled to a funeral payment depended upon whether the sum of £2,500 was an asset of the deceased at the time of her death.

Judge Rowley accepted the Secretary of State's submission in support of the appeal that ". . . where a transfer is ordered prior to death, notwithstanding that the transaction does not clear until after the death, the funds which are the subject of the transfer are, generally speaking, no longer 'assets of the deceased' available to the responsible person". That proposition was subject to any contrary provision in the contractual arrangements between the deceased and her bank. However, there was no such provision in *TG*. Rather, the evidence from the bank was that when one of its customers transferred funds using internet banking the funds would be applied to the payee's account within minutes even if the transfer were made on a non-business day, and even though, in those circumstances, the payment would only show on the customer's statement as being paid on the next following business day.   **4.97**

The claimant said that his mother had owed him the money and that he had made the transfer on her instructions. However, the First-tier Tribunal did not accept that the transfer represented a genuine reimbursement of money owed to the claimant. Rather, it viewed the transaction as a means of reducing the mother's estate prior to her death. Judge Rowley held that the motivation behind the transfer was irrelevant. The question to be determined was whether there were assets of the deceased that were available to the responsible person. If the transfer was validly made, then the transferred assets did not fall within reg.10(1)(a).

Sub-paragraph (b): For this sub-paragraph to apply, the amount must be due to the claimant or a member of his family (defined in reg.3(1)). Due must mean legally due. Sometimes such a member will have a clear legal entitlement under an insurance policy or a pension scheme. Sometimes trustees may have a discretion as to who should be paid a lump sum. In these circumstances no amount can be legally due until the trustees have exercised that discretion.   **4.98**

In *PA v SSWP* [2010] UKUT 157 (AAC), the deceased's daughter had taken out insurance policies on her mother's life. In England and Wales children do not have an insurable interest in the lives of their parents and it was therefore arguable that the proceeds of those policies were not "due" within the meaning of subpara. (b). However, Judge Levenson held that the insurance company had accepted the premiums and a court (or the regulatory institutions of the insurance industry) would have enforced payment. Even if what the daughter had entered into could not technically be an "insurance policy" it was an "analogous arrangement" within the subparagraph.

Where a policy has become fully-paid up, and could have been, but was not, encashed before the deceased's death the test is whether the proceeds of the policy were due and paid on a triggering event other than the death: see *PA* (above) and *SSWP v GB (IS)* [2020] UKUT 316 (AAC).

4.99   *Sub-paragraph (c):* Until April 1, 2018, any contribution towards funeral expenses which had been actually been received by the claimant or a family member from a charity or a relative of the claimant or the deceased was deducted from any funeral payment. See pp.1566-1567 of Vol.II of the 2017/18 edition for commentary on the former provision. The rule was revoked by SI 2018/61 with effect from April 2, 2018. The fact that no charitable payments are now deducted from a funeral payment means that it is no longer necessary to have specific disregards for payments from the charities formerly listed in para.(2) and defined in para.(3). Those paragraphs were therefore also revoked.

4.100   *Sub-paragraph (d):* This paragraph is straightforward.

4.101   *Sub-paragraph (e):* Any amount payable under a pre-paid funeral plan or similar arrangement will be deducted. In order to avoid a double deduction, it is necessary to interpret this deduction as applying when a funeral plan pays a cash benefit to the responsible person or other relative of the deceased and reg.9(10) as applying where payment under the plan has been made direct to the funeral director. This interpretation is supported by the use of the words "[w]here items and services have been provided . . . under a pre-paid funeral plan . . ." in reg.9(10).

4.102   *Paragraph (1A):* Arrears of these benefits that had not been paid to the deceased at the date of her/his death do not count as "assets of the deceased" for the purposes of the rule in para.(1)(a).

The Social Fund Maternity Grant Amendment Regulations 2012

(SI 2012/1814)

Made by the Secretary of State for Work and Pensions under ss.138(1)(a) and (4) and 175(1), (3) and (4) of the Social Security Contributions and Benefits Act 1992, the Social Security Advisory Committee having agreed that proposals in respect of these regulations should not be referred to it.

GENERAL NOTE

4.103   See the commentary to reg.5A of the Social Fund Maternity and Funeral Expenses (General) Regulations 2005 (above).

Citation, commencement and interpretation

4.104   **1.**—(1) These Regulations may be cited as the Social Fund Maternity Grant Amendment Regulations 2012.

(2) They come into force on 13th August 2012.

(3) In these Regulations, "the principal Regulations" means the Social Fund Maternity and Funeral Expenses (General) Regulations 2005 and expressions defined in those Regulations have the same meaning in these Regulations.

Amendment of the principal Regulations

2.—*[For the amendments made by reg. 2, see reg. 5A of the Social Fund Maternity and Funeral Expenses (General) Regulations 2005]* 4.105

Transitional provisions

3.—(1) The substitution made by regulation 2 does not apply in a case 4.106
where any of paragraphs (2) to (7) apply.

(2) This paragraph applies in a case where—
(a) the claimant falls within regulation 5(3)(a) of the principal Regulations;
(b) the claim is made before C's birth;
(c) the claim is made before 13th August 2012; and
(d) the expected date of confinement is before 29th October 2012.

(3) This paragraph applies in a case where—
(a) the claimant falls within regulation 5(3)(a) or (b) of the principal Regulations;
(b) the claim is made after C's birth; and
(c) C is born before 29th October 2012.

(4) This paragraph applies in a case where—
(a) the claimant falls within regulation 5(3)(c) of the principal Regulations; and
(b) the qualifying order is made before 29th October 2012.

(5) This paragraph applies in a case where—
(a) the claimant falls within regulation 5(3)(d) of the principal Regulations; and
(b) the appointment as guardian takes effect before 29th October 2012.

(6) This paragraph applies in a case where—
(a) the claimant falls within regulation 5(3)(e) of the principal Regulations; and
(b) C is placed for adoption with the claimant or the claimant's partner before 29th October 2012.

(7) This paragraph applies in a case where—
(a) the claimant falls within regulation 5(3)(f) of the principal Regulations; and
(b) the adoption referred to in that provision takes effect before 29th October 2012.

(8) In this regulation, "C" means the child or still-born child in respect of whom a Sure Start Maternity Grant is claimed.

The Social Security (Scotland) Act 2018 (Best Start Grants) (Consequential Modifications and Saving) Order 2018

(SI 2018/1138)

Made by the Secretary of State under sections 104 and 113(4) and (5) of the Scotland Act 1998(1).

[In force December 10, 2018]

PART 1

INTRODUCTORY

Citation, commencement and extent

4.107   **1.**—(1) This Order may be cited as the Social Security (Scotland) Act 2018 (Best Start Grants) (Consequential Modifications and Saving) Order 2018.

(2) This Order comes into force immediately after the coming into force of the first Regulations made under section 32 of the Social Security (Scotland) Act 2018.

(3) Each amendment made by this Order has the same extent as the provision to which it relates.

GENERAL NOTE

4.108   The first Regulations made under s.32 of the Social Security (Scotland) Act 2018 were the Early Years Assistance (Best Start Grants) (Scotland) Regulations 2018 (SSI 2018/370)—see Pt XIII of Vol.IV of this series—which came into force on December 10, 2018.

PART 2

AMENDMENTS AND SAVING IN RELATION TO SURE START MATERNITY GRANTS

Interpretation

4.109   **2.** In this Part, "the 2005 Regulations" means the Social Fund Maternity and Funeral Expenses (General) Regulations 2005(3).

Amendment of the 2005 Regulations

4.110   **3.** *[Omitted]*

Saving in relation to the amendment of the 2005 Regulations

4.111   **4.**—(1) The amendments made to the 2005 Regulations in article 3 are of no effect in relation to a claim for Sure Start Maternity Grant made before the date on which the first Regulations made under section 32 of the Social Security (Scotland) Act 2018 come into force.

(2) In paragraph (1), "Sure Start Maternity Grant" has the meaning given in the 2005 Regulations.

(SI 2019/1060)

The Social Security (Scotland) Act 2018 (Funeral Expense Assistance and Early Years Assistance) (Consequential Modifications and Savings) Order 2019

(SI 2019/1060)

Made by the Secretary of State under sections 104 and 113(2), (4) and (5) of the Scotland Act 1998.

[In force September 16, 2019]

ARTICLES REPRODUCED

PART 1

INTRODUCTORY

PART 2

AMENDMENTS AND SAVINGS IN RELATION TO FUNERAL PAYMENTS

PART 1

INTRODUCTORY

Citation, commencement and extent

1.—(1) This Order may be cited as the Social Security (Scotland) Act 2018   4.113
(Funeral Expense Assistance and Early Years Assistance) (Consequential
Modifications and Savings) Order 2019.

(2) This Order comes into force as follows:

(a) [*Omitted as relating to Northern Ireland*]

(b) all other provisions, immediately after the coming into force of
the first Regulations made under section 34 of the Social Security
(Scotland) Act 2018.

(3) Each amendment made by this Order has the same extent as the provision being amended.

GENERAL NOTE

4.114   The first Regulations made under s.34 of the Social Security (Scotland) Act 2018 were the Funeral Expense Assistance (Scotland) Regulations 2019 (SSI 2019/292) which came into force on September 16, 2019 (see Pt XIII of Vol.IV of this series).

PART 2

AMENDMENTS AND SAVINGS IN RELATION TO FUNERAL PAYMENTS

Interpretation

4.115   **2.** In this Part:
(a) the "2005 Regulations" means the Social Fund Maternity and Funeral Expenses (General) Regulations 2005;
(b) [*Omitted as relating to Northern Ireland*]

Amendment of the 2005 Regulations

4.116   **3.** [*Omitted: see the amended text of reg. 4 and reg. 7 of the 2005 Regulations (above)*]

Saving in relation to the amendments of the 2005 Regulations

4.117   **4.**—(1) The amendments made to the 2005 Regulations in article 3 are of no effect in relation to a claim for a funeral payment made before the date on which the first Regulations made under section 34 of the Social Security (Scotland) Act 2018 come into force.

(2) In paragraph (1), "funeral payment" has the meaning given in regulation 7(1)(a) of the 2005 Regulations.

The Social Fund (Children's Funeral Fund for England) Regulations 2019

(SI 2019/1064)

[In force July 23, 2019]

Made by the Secretary of State under sections 138(1)(a) and (4) and 175(1), (3), (4) and (5) of the Social Security Contributions and Benefits Act 1992, and sections 1(1) and (1C), and 5(1)(a), (i) and (j), and (1A), and 189(1), (4), (5), (5A) and (5B) of the Social Security Administration Act 1992, the Social Security Advisory Committee having agreed under section 173(1)(b) of the Social Security Administration Act 1992, that the proposals in respect of these Regulations should not be referred to it.

GENERAL NOTE

These Regulations establish a "Children's Funeral Fund payment" (a "CFF   4.119
payment"), which is a new type of funeral payment from the social fund. It is
payable if the person who has died was under the age of 18 at the date of his or
her death (reg.3(1)(a)(i), or a stillborn child as defined (reg.3(1)(a)(ii)), and the
funeral takes place in England on or after 23 July 2019 (reg.3(1)(b)). The payment
is to be the amount of any fees charged by a burial or cremation authority or of any
associated expenses (reg.3(4)). "Fees charged by a burial or cremation authority"
are defined in reg.4 and "associated expenses" in reg.5. Both regulations contain
an anti-abuse provision that restricts the amount payable to "what the Secretary of
State considers to be reasonable in the circumstances" (regs 4(2) and 5(2)) Further,
no payment can be made in respect of "any element which relates exclusively to a
requirement of the religious faith of the deceased or the family of the deceased"
(regs 4(3) and 5(3)).

CFF payments have two notable new features. First, there is no means-testing.
A payment can be made if the requirements of regs 3-6 are met irrespective of the
income and assets of the person who has died and of his or her parents. Second,
a claim for fees charged by a burial or cremation authority may *only* be made by
the burial or cremation authority that charges those fees. Claims for "associated
expenses" may be made by a burial authority, a cremation authority, a funeral
director, or "the person responsible for the purchase of a listed item". Given the
nature of associated expenses, the person responsible for the purchase is likely
to be the funeral director unless the funeral is arranged privately. The time limit
for making a claim is the same as for a funeral payment under the Social Fund
Maternity and Funeral Expenses (General) Regulations 2005 (see reg.2(1) of the
Claims and Payments Regulations 1979 as amended by reg.7).

Regulation 6 contains provisions against double payment. Under para.(1),
there is an absolute bar on more than one CFF payment being made for the same
listed item. Para.(2), together with the amended reg.4 of the 2005 Regulations
and reg.8(5) of the Funeral Expense Assistance (Scotland) Regulations 2019 (SSI
2019/292, Part XIII of Vol.IV of this series), govern how the main funeral expenses
scheme for England and Wales and the funeral expense assistance scheme in
Scotland interrelate.

Note, finally, that in Wales a contribution of £500 towards the funeral costs of a
child can be claimed when registering the child's death: see further *https://gov.wales/
child-funeral-and-other-related-costs-information-html.*

Citation, commencement and extent

1.—(1) These Regulations may be cited as the Social Fund (Children's   4.120
Funeral Fund for England) Regulations 2019 and come into force on 23rd
July 2019.

(2) Subject to paragraph (3), these Regulations extend to England and
Wales only.

(3) Regulations 7 and 8 extend to England and Wales, and Scotland.

Interpretation

4.121   **2.** In these Regulations—

"associated expenses" means the expenses referred to in regulation 5;

"burial authority" means a person responsible for the management of a burial ground;

"claimant" means—

(a) with respect to claims in relation to fees charged by a burial or cremation authority, the burial authority or cremation authority in question;

(b) with respect to claims in relation to associated expenses, a burial authority, a cremation authority, a funeral director, or the person responsible for the purchase of a listed item;

"cremation authority" means a person responsible for the management of a crematorium;

"fees charged by a burial or cremation authority" means the fees referred to in regulation 4;

"funeral" means erecting a memorial in a case where there is no body, or the burial or cremation of a body (whether or not the burial or cremation is accompanied by the erection of a memorial);

"listed item" means an item or service referred to in regulation 4(1) or regulation 5(1);

"qualifying age" means an age less than 18 years old.

Entitlement

4.122   **3.**—(1) A claimant is entitled to a Children's Funeral Fund payment in relation to a funeral, where—

(a) the deceased was—

(i) of qualifying age at the time of death; or

(ii) a stillborn child as defined in section 41 of the Births and Deaths Registration Act 1953, born after the 24th week of pregnancy;

(b) the funeral takes place in England on or after 23rd July 2019; and

(c) were it not for these Regulations, those fees or expenses would be chargeable to a person involved in the organisation of the funeral.

(2) Section 1(1A) of the Social Security Administration Act 1992 (the requirement to provide evidence of a national insurance number in order to make a claim) is disapplied in relation to a claim for a Children's Funeral Fund payment.

(3) Subject to regulation 6, a claimant may be awarded more than one Children's Funeral Fund payment in relation to a funeral.

(4) In this regulation, a "Children's Funeral Fund payment" means a payment out of the social fund in the amount of any fees charged by a burial or cremation authority or of any associated expenses.

DEFINITIONS

"claimant"—see reg.2.

"cremation authority"—*ibid.*

"fees charged by a burial or cremation authority"—see regs 2 and 4.

"funeral"—see reg.2.

"qualifying age"—*ibid.*

Fees charged by a burial or cremation authority

4.—(1) Fees charged by a burial or cremation authority are— $\qquad$ **4.123**
(a) where the deceased is buried—
 (i) the fees for obtaining a burial plot and a right of burial for the deceased in that plot, whether or not that right is exclusive;
 (ii) the fees levied in respect of a burial by the burial authority or the person responsible for the provision and maintenance of cemeteries for the area where the burial takes place;
(b) where the deceased is cremated—
 (i) the fees levied in respect of the cremation by the cremation authority or person responsible for the provision and maintenance of crematoria for the area where the cremation takes place;
 (ii) fees levied for a private post mortem examination where this is necessary for the cremation to be authorised;
(c) the fees levied for the scattering of ashes;
(d) the fees levied for the burial of ashes;
(e) the fees levied for the storage of ashes in a columbarium or similar receptacle until the point where the deceased, if alive, would have ceased to be of qualifying age;
(f) the fees levied in respect of obtaining permission to erect a memorial;
(g) where it is a condition of the right of burial, the maintenance fees of the place of burial until the point where the deceased, if alive, would have ceased to be of qualifying age;
(h) fees levied for renewal of the right of exclusive use of the burial plot until the point where the deceased, if alive, would have ceased to be of qualifying age;
(i) any other fees the Secretary of State considers to be appropriate.
(2) Fees charged by a burial or cremation authority are limited to what the Secretary of State considers to be reasonable in the circumstances.
(3) Fees charged in accordance with paragraph (1) must not include any element which relates exclusively to a requirement of the religious faith of the deceased or the family of the deceased.

DEFINITIONS

"burial authority"—see reg.2.
"cremation authority"—*ibid.*
"qualifying age"—*ibid.*

Associated expenses

5.—(1) Associated expenses are— $\qquad$ **4.124**
(a) where the deceased is buried, the fees levied by a private grave-digger, inclusive of the fees levied for the removal and replacement of headstones and kerbing;
(b) where the deceased is cremated—
 (i) the fees payable for the removal of any active implantable medical device as defined in regulation 2 of the Medical Devices Regulations 2002 save that, where that removal is carried out by a person who is not a registered medical practitioner no more than £20 may be met in respect of that removal;
 (ii) the fees levied for the completion of cremation certification;

(c) the price of a coffin, shroud, or casket in which the deceased is buried or cremated;

(d) the price of an appropriate receptacle for storage of cremated remains where the receptacle in which the cremated remains are returned is unsuitable for this purpose.

(2) Associated expenses are limited to what the Secretary of State considers to be reasonable in the circumstances.

(3) Associated expenses charged in accordance with paragraph (1) must not include any element which relates exclusively to a requirement of the religious faith of the deceased or the family of the deceased.

Provisions against double payment

4.125   **6.**—(1) No payment may be made for a listed item under these Regulations where a payment has already been made under these Regulations for that listed item in relation to the same funeral.

(2) No payment may be made for a listed item under these Regulations if—

(a) a payment for the listed item has been made in respect of funeral expenses arising from the death of the same person under the Social Fund Maternity and Funeral Expenses (General) Regulations 2005; or

(b) a payment for the listed item has been made in respect of funeral expenses arising from the death of the same person under Regulations made under section 34 of the Social Security (Scotland) Act 2018,

unless the amount paid under those Regulations is less than the total amount charged for the listed item, in which case a payment may be made for an amount not exceeding the remainder of the amount charged for the listed item.

Amendment of the Social Fund Maternity and Funeral Expenses (General) Regulations 2005

4.126   **7.** [*Omitted: see reg. 4 (Provision against double payment: funeral expenses) of the 2005 Regulations, above.*]

Amendment of the Social Security (Claims and Payments) Regulations 1987

4.127   **8.** [*Omitted: see reg. 2(1) (Interpretation) of the 1987 Regulations in Vol. III.*]

PART V

PERSONS SUBJECT TO IMMIGRATION CONTROL

The Social Security (Immigration and Asylum) Consequential Amendments Regulations 2000

(SI 2000/636) (AS AMENDED)

Made by the Secretary of State under ss.115(3), (4) and (7), 123S) and (6), 166(3) and 167 of the Immigration and Asylum Act 1999, ss.64(1), 68(4), 70(4), 71(6), 123(1)(a), (d) and (e), 135(1), 136(3) and (4), 137(1) and (2) (i) and 175(1), (3) and (4) of the Social Security Contributions and Benefits Act 1992, ss.5(1)(a) and (b), 189(1) and (4) and 191 of the Social Security Administration Act 1992, ss.12(1) and (2), 35(1) and 36(2) and (4) of the Jobseekers Act 1995

[In force April 3, 2000]

GENERAL NOTE

The United Kingdom's withdrawal from the European Union

The United Kingdom left the European Union on January 31, 2020 at 11.00 pm and the transitional "Implementation Period" during which EU law continued to apply ended on December 31, 2020 at 11.00 pm. These Regulations are reproduced below as they are worded with effect from January 1, 2021. For the law that applied during the Implementation Period, see pp.913–926 of Vol.V of the 2020/21 edition.

Persons subject to immigration control 5.1
These regulations are made under s.115 of the Immigration and Asylum Act 1999 (see Part I above), which excludes "persons subject to immigration control" from entitlement to specified non-contributory benefits (including universal credit). Regulation 2 and the Schedule provide for exceptions to that exclusion. The combined effect of those provisions is as follows.

"*Person subject to immigration control*" is defined by s.115(9). Note first of all that a British citizen can never be a person subject to immigration control for social security purposes—R(PC)2/07. Until December 31, 2020 at 11.00 pm, neither could EEA nationals, but that is no longer the case. Except for those EEA nationals with transitional protection under SI 2020/1209 (see further Vol.V), the rules for EEA nationals are the same as for nationals of any other country outside the Common Travel Area.

Nationals of such countries are subject to immigration control if they are within one of the following four categories:

(a) A person who requires leave to enter or remain in the UK but does not have it
This category (s.115(9)(a)) covers illegal entrants, overstayers, people who are 5.2
subject to a deportation order, those allowed temporary admission to the UK and, subject to R(SB) 11/88 (below), anyone whose immigration status has yet to be determined (other than those EEA nationals with transitional protection under SI 2020/1209 (see further Vol.V)). It does not apply to EEA nationals who have settled or pre-settled status because both groups have leave to remain which does not fall within s.115(9)(b)–(d) (albeit for a limited period in the case of those with pre-settled status).

The practice of the Home Office is to grant temporary admission to asylum seekers (except those who are detained) pending investigation of their claims (see CIS/3108/97). Section 115 therefore has the effect of excluding all asylum seekers from benefit. Asylum seekers who are destitute will instead receive support from a Home Office agency, the National Asylum Support Service, under ss.95–100 of the Immigration and Asylum Act.

For social security purposes, whether or not a person requires leave to enter or remain in the UK is a matter for the decision-maker (or, on appeal, for the First-tier Tribunal or Upper Tribunal) to determine and any decision by the Home Office is not binding (*R(SB) 11/88* but see *R(SB) 2/85* and *R(SB) 25/85* as to the terms on which leave is granted).

By s.3ZA(1) of the Immigration Act 1971, an Irish national does not require leave to enter or remain in the UK unless directions have been given under section 3ZA(2) (which permits exclusion where the Home Secretary decides it is "conducive to the public good") or s/he is an "excluded person" for the purposes of section 8B. Nationals of the Isle of Man and the Channel Islands have freedom of travel within the UK and do not require leave to enter (Immigration Act 1971 s.1(3)).

For the position where leave to enter or remain-or British citizenship-is obtained by fraud, see the decisions of the Upper Tribunal in *R v HMRC and Kirklees Metropolitan BC (CH & CTC)* [2020] UKUT 379 (Judge Hemingway) and *ED v SSWP* [2020] UKUT 352 (AAC) (Judge Perez).

(b) A person who has leave to enter or remain but subject to a condition that he does not have recourse to public funds

5.3   Limited leave to enter or remain subject to there being no recourse to public funds is given under s.33(1) of the Immigration Act 1971. From April 6, 2016, "public funds" are defined by rule 6 of the Immigration Rules as attendance allowance, severe disablement allowance, carer's allowance, disability living allowance, income support, (the former) council tax benefit and housing benefit, a social fund payment, child benefit, income-based JSA, income-related ESA, state pension credit, child tax credit, working tax credit, universal credit, personal independence payment, council tax reduction, certain publicly funded housing, and payments from local welfare funds under s.1 of the Localism Act 2011, the Welfare Funds (Scotland) Act 2015, or regulations made under art.135 of the Welfare Reform (Northern Ireland) Order 2015. Note however the clarifications of that definition in rules 6A–6C, as follows:

"6A.   For the purpose of these Rules, a person (P) is not to be regarded as having (or potentially having) recourse to public funds merely because P is (or will be) reliant in whole or in part on public funds provided to P's sponsor unless, as a result of P's presence in the United Kingdom, the sponsor is (or would be) entitled to increased or additional public funds (save where such entitlement to increased or additional public funds is by virtue of P and the sponsor's joint entitlement to benefits under the regulations referred to in paragraph 6B).

6B.   Subject to paragraph 6C, a person (P) shall not be regarded as having recourse to public funds if P is entitled to benefits specified under section 115 of the Immigration and Asylum Act 1999 by virtue of regulations made under subsections (3) and (4) of that section or section 42 of the Tax Credits Act 2002. For an example of this principle, see *OD v SSWP (JSA)* [2015] UKUT 0438 (AAC).

6C.   A person (P) making an application from outside the United Kingdom will be regarded as having recourse to public funds where P relies upon the future entitlement to any public funds that would be payable to P or to P's sponsor as a result of P's presence in the United Kingdom, (including those benefits to which P or the sponsor would be entitled as a result of P's presence in the United Kingdom under the regulations referred to in to paragraph 6B)."

The circumstances in which a "no recourse to public funds" condition will be imposed are set out in Appendix FM to the Immigration Rules. In *R. (on the application of W (A Child)) v Secretary of State for the Home Department* [2020] EWHC 1299 (Admin), the Divisional Court (Bean LJ and Chamberlain J) summarised the provisions of that Appendix as follows:

"16.   As a result [*i.e.*, of the events set out earlier in the judgment], the criteria for deciding whether to impose or lift the NRPF condition were included in the

Immigration Rules. That was done by way of amendment to Appendix FM to the Immigration Rules. Appendix FM provides a number of bases on which a person may be granted LTR with a view to eventual settlement by virtue of a connection with a family member who is a British citizen, settled in the UK or a refugee or person entitled to humanitarian protection. There are separate provisions governing applications for entry clearance or LTR as a partner (D-ECP and D-LTRP), a child (D-ECC and DLTRC) and a parent (D-ECPT and D-LTRPT) of such a person. The rules for those applying as partners and parents stipulate that entry clearance or LTR, if granted, will be subject to a condition of NRPF "unless the decision-maker considers, with reference to paragraph GEN 1.11A, that the applicant should not be subject to such a condition". The rules for those applying as children provide that the child will be subject to the same condition as the parent.

17.　　Paragraph GEN 1.11A provides as follows:

"Where entry clearance or leave to remain as a partner, child or parent is granted under paragraph D-ECP.1.2., D-LTRP.1.2., D-ECC.1.1., DLTRC.1.1., D-ECPT.1.2. or D-LTRPT.1.2., it will normally be granted subject to a condition of no recourse to public funds, unless the applicant has provided the decision-maker with:
(a)　satisfactory evidence that the applicant is destitute as defined in section 95 of the Immigration and Asylum Act 1999; or
(b)　satisfactory evidence that there are particularly compelling reasons relating to the welfare of a child of a parent in receipt of a very low income."

In *Re W*, the Divisional Court held (at [73]) that:

"The NRPF regime ... [does] not adequately recognise, reflect or give effect to the Secretary of State's obligation not to impose, or to lift, the condition of NRPF in cases where the applicant is not yet, but will imminently suffer inhuman or degrading treatment [*i.e.*, by becoming destitute] without recourse to public funds. In its current form the NRPF regime is apt to mislead caseworkers in this critical respect and gives rise to a real risk of unlawful decisions in a significant number of cases. To that extent it is unlawful."

It is suggested, however, that it is not open to a tribunal to decide on an appeal against a decision refusing a social security benefit on the basis that the claimant is a person subject to immigration control, that a no recourse to public funds condition that has in fact been imposed, should not have been: see *R(SB) 2/85* and *R(SB) 25/85* below. Such an argument must be pursued by an appeal against the immigration decision or by judicial review. However, different considerations potentially apply following the decision of a Divisional Court of the Queen's Bench Division in *ST and VW v Secretary of State for the Home Department* [2021] EWHC 1085 (Admin) which declared that the No Recourse to Public Funds Scheme as a whole does not comply with s.55 of the Borders, Citizenship and Immigration Act 2009.

For this category (s.115(9)(b)) and the following two (s.115(9)(c) and (d)) to apply, it is necessary that the person should actually require leave to enter or remain in the UK. So, for example, if the Home Office mistakenly grants conditional leave to a person who is in fact a British citizen and does not require leave at all, the mistake does not cause that person to become subject to immigration control for social security purposes (see *R(SB) 11/88*). However, where leave is required, the decision of the Home Office as to the terms on which leave is granted is conclusive (see *R(SB) 2/85* and *R(SB) 25/85*). A proper statement of the terms of leave should be obtained from the Home Office (*CSSB/137/82*).

Until October 28, 2013 there was one exception to the exclusion from benefit in s.115(9)(b). However, that exception was abolished with effect from October

29, 2013, by reg.9(1) and (3) of the Social Security (Miscellaneous Amendments) (No.3) Regulations 2013 (SI 2013/2536). For details of the law as it stood before that date, see pp.375, 800–801 and 809–810 of Vol.II of the 2013/14 edition.

(c) A person who has leave to enter or remain which was given as a result of a maintenance undertaking

5.4   "Maintenance undertaking" is defined by s.115(10) as "a written undertaking given by another person in pursuance of the immigration rules to be responsible for [the claimant's] maintenance and accommodation". Under r.35 of the Immigration Rules such undertakings may be demanded from "a sponsor of a person seeking leave to enter or variation of leave to enter or remain in the United Kingdom" but are normally only required from the sponsors of elderly or other dependent relatives.

Rule 6 defines "sponsor" as meaning:

"the person in relation to whom an applicant is seeking leave to enter or remain as their spouse, fiancé, civil partner, proposed civil partner, unmarried partner, same-sex partner or dependent relative, as the case may be, under paragraphs 277 to 295O or 317 to 319 or the person in relation to whom an applicant is seeking entry clearance or leave as their partner or dependent relative under Appendix FM."

A promise of support given by someone who is not a "sponsor" as so defined cannot amount to a "maintenance undertaking" for the purposes of s.115(10) or para.3 of the Schedule: see *Leeds City Council v EO (HB)* [2019] UKUT 96 (AAC).

The purpose of the undertaking is to reinforce a condition that the person seeking leave to enter or remain should not have recourse to public funds by

- demonstrating that the sponsor has sufficient resources to maintain and accommodate the relative without the latter claiming public funds; and

- making the sponsor legally "liable to maintain" the relative. This has the effect that, if the Secretary of State does for any reason have to pay income support to the relative (and, in most cases, the mere existence of an undertaking will mean that the relative has no such entitlement), the sponsor may, in certain circumstances, be subject to a criminal penalty and the Secretary of State may recoup the benefit paid by making a complaint in a magistrates' court (see, respectively ss.105 and 106 of the SSAA 1992 in Vol.III).

The requirement in the definition that the undertaking has been given "in pursuance of the immigration rules" cannot mean "in pursuance of a requirement in the immigration rules" because the decision whether to ask for an undertaking is a discretionary one. Rather, it means "under" or "further to" the immigration rules, see *CIS/1697/2004*, paras 41 and 42. In that case, the Deputy Commissioner held that it was sufficient that the sponsor was making a promise in furtherance of the claimant's application for indefinite leave to remain.

It is not necessary that the undertaking should be given on one of the official Home Office forms (either Form RON 112 or the Form SET(F) that replaced it)—see *R. (Begum) v Social Security Commissioner* [2003] EWHC 3380 (QB), QBD (Sir Christopher Bellamy), November 6, 2003 confirming *CIS/2474/1999*, *CIS/2816/2002* and, on this point, *CIS/47/2002*. Those forms "are expressly in the language of undertaking and emphasise the significance of such undertakings" (see Rix LJ at [36] of *Ahmed v Secretary of State for Work & Pensions* [2005] EWCA Civ 535, CA (May, Rix and Jacob LJJ), April 19, 2005 (reported as *R(IS) 8/05*). But if an official form is not used, consideration may need to be given to whether the document signed by the sponsor amounts to an "undertaking" at all. In *Ahmed* the Court of Appeal held (upholding the Commissioner in *CIS/426/2003* and disagreeing, on this point, with the Commissioner in *CIS/47/2002* in which the disputed document was in similar terms) that the issue is one of substance rather than form and that the legal test is whether or not the document contains a promise or agreement about what the sponsor will do in the future rather than a statement about his or her present abilities and intentions:

"47. . . . It seems to me that an undertaking has to be something in the nature of a promise or agreement and the language that 'I am able and willing to maintain and accommodate' is language which has reference, essentially, to current ability and intention and does not amount to a promise for the future. The essence of an undertaking is a promise as to the future, as typically found in the language 'I will.'

48. I accept that the use of any particular language is not a condition precedent. The absence of an express reference to 'I undertake', such as is found in the Home Office's forms, or to 'I promise' or 'I agree', will not necessarily be critical if it is still clear that the substance of what is said is a promise for the future." (per Rix LJ)

So, the declaration in the *Ahmed* case that the sponsor was "able and willing to maintain and accommodate the applicant without recourse to public funds and in suitable accommodation" was not an undertaking because it only related to present facts and intentions. For a further example (in which the opposite conclusion was reached on the facts) see *CIS/1697/2004*. That decision also holds that neither a Commissioner, nor (by necessary implication) a tribunal, has any power to grant rectification of a defective maintenance undertaking .

In *CIS 3508/2001* it was held that leave to enter or remain was given "as a result of" a maintenance undertaking if the existence of that undertaking was a factor in the decision to grant leave. It does not have to be the only, or even a major, factor. It is sufficient that it was of some relevance. It seems that that will almost always be the case if the immigration decision-maker acts within the Immigration Rules. In *Shah v Secretary of State for Work and Pensions* [2002] EWCA Civ 285 (reported as *R(IS) 2/02*), the Court of Appeal held that a maintenance undertaking should be regarded as a continuing obligation and therefore applied even if the claimant had left the UK (thereby causing his or her indefinite leave to remain to lapse) and had been made a fresh grant of indefinite leave to remain as a returning resident on his or her return. *Shah* was decided under the pre-April 2000 law, but it is suggested that the same principles also apply to s.115(9)(c).

Under the principles set out by the House of Lords in *Kerr v Department for Social Development* [2004] UKHL 23; *R1/04 (SF)*, it is for the Secretary of State to show that the maintenance undertaking was a factor in the decision to grant leave: see *R(PC) 1/09*. In that case, where the decision to grant leave was made outside the Immigration Rules, the causal connection could not be inferred and had not been established: see also *SSWP v SS (SPC)* [2010] UKUT 485 (AAC) and *SJ v SSWP* [2015] UKUT 505 (AAC).

People who are granted leave to enter or remain as a result of a maintenance undertaking are not entitled to income support or income-based JSA until they have been resident in the UK for a period of at least five years from the date of entry or the date on which the undertaking was given, whichever is later. The only exceptions are where the sponsored immigrant becomes a British citizen during the five-year period (see *R(PC) 2/07*) and where the person (or all the people if there was more than one) who gave the maintenance undertaking has died before the end of the five-year period. See para.3 of Pt I of the Schedule. The five years' residence need not be continuous: it can be made up of shorter periods (see paras 74–75 of the Commissioner's decision in *R(IS) 2/02*). In *CPC/1035/2005* the Commissioner considered the position of a Pakistani national who had been given leave to enter the UK under a maintenance undertaking. Since entering the UK in October 1996, she had returned to Pakistan for periods of 17 months, nearly 14 months and 21 months in order to look after her parents. In July 2004, over 7½ years after she first entered, she claimed—and, in August 2004, was refused—SPC. The Commissioner upheld that refusal. Although it was not necessary for the claimant to be physically present

5.5

in the UK in order to be resident here, "whether a person is or is not resident in a particular place during a period of physical absence depends on a calculus consisting of the duration and circumstances of the absence". Some absences affect residence simply on account of their length. Each period of absence had to be considered individually but none of the periods listed above, not even the shortest, was compatible with the claimant remaining resident in the UK. It followed that as the claimant had not been resident in the UK for nearly 58 months (4 years and 10 months) of the period between October 1996 and August 2004, she had not been resident for a total of five years since the date of her entry and was therefore still excluded from benefit.

Sponsored immigrants are not excluded from social fund payments (see para.4 of Pt II of the Schedule) but in practice are unlikely to be eligible for anything other than a winter fuel payment. This is because, as persons subject to immigration control, they are excluded from the qualifying benefits for maternity and funeral expenses payments, budgeting loans and cold weather payments. Sponsored immigrants are also not excluded from entitlement to attendance allowance, severe disablement allowance, (the former) health in pregnancy grants, carer's allowance, disability living allowance, personal independence payment or child benefit.

(d) A person who has leave to enter or remain only because he is appealing against certain immigration decisions

5.6   Section 115(9)(d) provides that a person who "has leave to enter or remain in the United Kingdom only as a result of paragraph 17 of Schedule 4 [*i.e.,* Sch.4 to the Immigration and Asylum Act 1999 itself]" is a person subject to immigration control. Para.17 of Sch.4 was repealed by Sch.9, para.1 to the Nationality, Immigration and Asylum Act 2002 with effect from 1 April 2003. However, *EE v City of Cardiff (HB)* [2018] UKUT 418 (AAC) the Upper Tribunal held that s.17(2) of the Interpretation Act 1978 has the effect that the reference to para.17 of Schedule 4 in s.115(9)(d) must be read as a reference to that provision as re-enacted in section 3C(1) and (2)(b) and (c) of the Immigration Act 1971.

Under s.82 of the 2002 Act (the successor to s.61 of the 1999 Act referred to in to para.17 of Sch.4 to that Act), a person with limited leave to enter or remain in the UK has a right of appeal against a decision to vary, or to refuse to vary, his leave. Section 3C of the Immigration Act 1971 provides that while such an appeal is pending, the leave to which the appeal relates and any conditions subject to which it was granted continue to have effect. *EE* holds that of s.115(9)(d) is therefore now that those whose leave has automatically been extended by s.3C are persons subject to immigration control. (See the General Note to s.115 of the Immigration and Asylum Act 1999, earlier in this volume, for a brief analysis of why *EE* may not be correctly decided.)

The former section 3D of the Immigration Act 1971 (which was in force from 31 August 2006 to 30 November 2016) is also potentially relevant. It applied where a person's leave to enter or remain in the United Kingdom is "varied with the result that he has no leave to enter or remain in the United Kingdom, or ... is revoked" and had the effect that the former leave to enter or remain was extended during any period when the person was appealing against it. The reference in s.115(9)(d) to paragraph 17 of Schedule 4 is not to be treated as a reference to section 3D—see *EE* (above) at paras 37-40—so anyone within s.3D was not a person who "requires leave to enter or remain in the United Kingdom but does not have it" within s.115(9)(a): see *GO v HMRC (CHB)* [2018] UKUT 328 (AAC).

The ECSMA Agreement and the European Social Charter

5.7   Nationals of those countries that have ratified the European Convention on Social and Medical Assistance ("the ECSMA Agreement") or the European Social Charter (both of which are treaties concluded under the auspices of the Council of Europe (ETS Nos 14 and 35 respectively) are not excluded from income support, income-based jobseeker's allowance, income-related ESA, housing benefit, social fund payments or (before April 1, 2013) council tax benefit: see *OD v SSWP (JSA)*

(SI 2000/636) (as amended)

[2015] UKUT 438 (AAC). Until the amendment of reg.2(1A) by SI 2020/1505 with effect from January 1, 2021 there was no exclusion from universal credit either. This affects EEA Nationals and nationals of Turkey (ECSMA Agreement and Social Charter), Switzerland (Social Charter) and the Republic of Northern Macedonia (Social Charter). Turkey ratified the Social Charter on November 24, 1999 and the ECSMA Agreement on December 2, 1996. Switzerland ratified the Social Charter on May 6, 1976 and Northern Macedonia ratified it on March 31, 2005. Records of which States have ratified a Council of Europe treaty are maintained by the Council's Treaty Office and are available from its website at *http://www.conventions.coe.int/*.

Note, finally, that there are two European Social Charters. For the purposes of these regulations it is the original Charter (which was opened for signature in Turin on October 18, 1961) that is relevant, not the Revised Social Charter (ETS 163) (which was opened for signature in Strasbourg on May 3, 1996).

The meaning of "lawfully present" was considered by the House of Lords in *Szoma v Secretary of State for Work and Pensions* [2005] UKHL 64 (reported as *R(IS) 2/06*). That appeal was a challenge to the decision of the Court of Appeal in *Kaya v Haringey LBC* [2001] EWCA Civ 677, in which it had been held, following the decision of the House of Lords in *In re Muisi* (reported *sub nom. R. v Home Secretary Ex p. Bugdaycay* [1987] A.C. 514), that a person granted temporary admission to the UK could not be "lawfully present" because he or she was deemed by s.11 of the Immigration Act 1971 not to be present in the UK at all. In *Szoma*, their Lordships overruled *Kaya* and held that lawful presence did not require

". . . more by way of positive legal authorisation for someone's presence in the UK than that they are at large here pursuant to the express written authority of an immigration officer provided for by statute."

Note that an ECSMA national who is not excluded from benefit by virtue of para.4 of Pt I of the Schedule, may nevertheless be excluded by virtue of the habitual residence and right to reside tests—see *Yesiloz v Camden LBC and SSWP* [2009] EWCA Civ 415 *(R(H) 7/09)*.

Spouses and family members of EEA nationals

Until December 31, 2020 at 11.00 pm, a person who was not an EEA national but who was a family member of such a national was not excluded from social fund payments (and certain non-contributory, non-means-tested benefits covered by Vol.I: see para.1 of Pt II of the Schedule). In *CDLA/708/2007*, the Deputy Commissioner held that para.1 only applied where the EEA national is "exercising his or her rights or freedoms under the EEA Agreement (whether or not he or she also has equivalent rights under EC law) and where the family member is a person who has rights under the EEA Agreement as a family member. However, in *JFP v DSD (DLA)* [2012] NI Com 267, the Chief Commissioner of Northern Ireland declined to follow *CDLA/708/2007*. In his view, there was no reason not to give para.1 of Pt II of the Schedule its natural meaning so that s.115 did not exclude any family member of any EEA national from entitlement to attendance allowance, disability living allowance, carer's allowance, child benefit, a social fund payment or any of the other benefits set out in the heading to that Part of the Schedule. In *MS v SSWP (DLA)* [2016] UKUT 42 (AAC) a judge of the Upper Tribunal in Great Britain considered the reasoning in both decisions and preferred that in *CDLA/708/2007*. The judge's views on this point were *obiter* because he had already decided that the claimant did not satisfy the conditions of entitlement to DLA. However, in *SSWP v AS (CA)* [2021] UKUT 24 (AAC), the Upper Tribunal (Judge Ward) also followed the decision of the Deputy Commissioner (albeit for additional reasons) in an appeal that turned on the point. The decision in *SSWP v AS* creates a conflict of precedent between Great Britain and Northern Ireland. The strict position has always been that the FTT in Great Britain was bound to follow

5.8

CDLA/708/2007 and appeal tribunals in Northern Ireland were bound by the decision of the Chief Commissioner. However, most tribunals in Great Britain would in practice have regarded themselves as free to follow *JFP v DSD* because, although it was given in another jurisdiction, it was of considerable persuasive authority, had considered *CDLA/708/2007* in detail, and disapproved it. That line of argument is no longer open following *MS v SSWP* and *SSWP v AS*.

However, that conflict of precedent is unlikely to have much practical effect: para.1 of Pt II of the Schedule was revoked with effect from December 31, 2020 at 11.00 pm, by reg.57 of the Immigration and Social Security Co-ordination (EU Withdrawal) Act 2020 (Consequential, Saving, Transitional and Transitory Provisions) (EU Exit) Regulations 2020 (SI 2020/1309), so the issue will no longer arise in the future.

As regards entitlement to social fund payments, see the note on sponsored immigrants (above) as to the practical restrictions on eligibility.

Reciprocal agreements

5.9   Under art.217 (ex-238 TEC) of the Treaty on the Functioning of the European Union, the EU "may conclude with one or more States or international organisations agreements establishing an association involving reciprocal rights and obligations, common action and special procedure".

Before the end of the Implementation Period, paras 2 and 3 of Pt II of the Schedule applied to "association agreements" under art.217 that provided for equal treatment in the field of social security of workers who are nationals of the signatory State and their families. In those circumstances, nationals of the non-EU State who were lawfully working in the UK and members of their families who were living with them were not excluded by s.115 from entitlement to social fund payments, attendance allowance, SDA, the former health in pregnancy grants, carer's allowance, DLA and child benefit. For further details, see p.920 of Vol.V of the 2020/21 edition.

From January 1, 2021 (and see below for the position for the final hour of December 31, 2020), A person who is lawfully working in Great Britain and is a national of a State with which the UK has concluded an agreement which replaces in whole or in part a former association agreement under art.217 is not excluded from entitlement to the above benefits.

The habitual residence test and the right to reside

5.10   Note that, even if claimants are not excluded from benefit as a person subject to immigration control, entitlement to universal credit, IS, IBJSA, IRESA, HB and SPC is also dependent upon their being (or treated as being) habitually resident (including, where appropriate, satisfying the right to reside test: see Vol.V).

Citation, commencement and interpretation

5.11   **1.**—(1) These Regulations may be cited as the Social Security (Immigration and Asylum) Consequential Amendments Regulations 2000.

(2) These Regulations shall come into force on 3rd April 2000.

(3) In these Regulations—

"the Act" means the Immigration and Asylum Act 1999;

"the Attendance Allowance Regulations" means the Social Security (Attendance Allowance) Regulations 1991;

"the Claims and Payments Regulations" means the Social Security (Claims and Payments) Regulations 1987;

"the Contributions and Benefits Act" means the Social Security Contributions and Benefits Act 1992;

[¹ . . .];

"the Disability Living Allowance Regulations" means the Social Security (Disability Living Allowance) Regulations 1991;
[² "the Employment and Support Allowance Regulations" means the Employment and Support Allowance Regulations 2008;]
[¹ . . .];
"the Income Support Regulations" means the Income Support (General) Regulations 1987;
"the Invalid Care Allowance Regulations" means the Social Security (Invalid Care Allowance) Regulations 1976;
"the Jobseeker's Allowance Regulations" means the Jobseeker's Allowance Regulations 1996;
[³ "personal independence payment" means personal independence payment under Part 4 of the Welfare Reform Act 2012;]
"the Persons from Abroad Regulations" means the Social Security (Persons from Abroad) Miscellaneous Amendments Regulations 1996;
"the Severe Disablement Allowance Regulations" means the Social Security (Severe Disablement Allowance) Regulations 1984.
[² "income-related employment and support allowance" means an income-related allowance under Part 1 of the Welfare Reform Act 2007 (employment and support allowance) [⁴ ;
"universal credit" means universal credit under Part 1 of the Welfare Reform Act 2012].]
(4) In these Regulations, unless the context otherwise requires, a reference—
(a) to a numbered regulation or Schedule is to the regulation in, or the Schedule to, these Regulations bearing that number;
(b) in a regulation or Schedule to a numbered paragraph is to the paragraph in that regulation or Schedule bearing that number.

AMENDMENTS

1. Housing Benefit and Council Tax Benefit (Consequential Provisions) Regulations 2006 (SI 2006/217) reg.3 and Sch.1 (March 6, 2006).
2. Employment and Support Allowance (Consequential Provisions) (No.2) Regulations 2008 (SI 2008/1554) reg.69(1) and (2) (October 27, 2008).
3. Personal Independence Payment (Supplementary Provisions and Consequential Amendments) Regulations 2013 (SI 2013/388) reg.8 and Sch. para.23(1) and (2) (April 8, 2013).
4. Universal Credit (Consequential, Supplementary, Incidental and Miscellaneous Provisions) Regulations 2013 (SI 2013/630) reg.31(1) and (2) (April 29, 2013).

GENERAL NOTE

With effect from April 7, 2003 the definition of "the Claims and Payments Regulations" was revoked in so far as it related to child benefit and guardian's allowance (reg.43 of and Pt I of Sch.3 to the Child Benefit and Guardian's Allowance (Administration) Regulations 2003). The definition remains in force for the purposes of other benefits. 5.12

Persons not excluded from specified benefits under section 115 of the Immigration and Asylum Act 1999

2.—(1) For the purposes of entitlement to income-based jobseeker's allowance, income support, a social fund payment, [¹¹ or] [³ income-related 5.13

employment and support allowance] [¹¹ ...] as the case may be, a person falling within a category or description of persons specified in Part I of the Schedule is a person to whom section 115 of the Act does not apply.

[⁸ (1A) For the purposes of entitlement to [¹¹ housing benefit under the Contributions and Benefits Act, state pension credit under the State Pension Credit Act 2002, or] universal credit [¹¹ , as the case may be,] a person falling within a category or description of persons specified in [¹⁰ paragraphs 2 and 3] of Part I of the Schedule is a person to whom section 115 of the Act does not apply.]

(2) For the purposes of entitlement to attendance allowance, severe disablement allowance, [¹ carer's allowance], disability living allowance, a social fund payment [⁴ , health in pregnancy grant] or child benefit under the Contributions and Benefits Act [⁷ or personal independence payment], as the case may be, a person falling within a category or description of persons specified in Part II of the Schedule is a person to whom section 115 of the Act does not apply.

(3) For the purposes of entitlement to child benefit, attendance allowance or disability living allowance under the Contributions and Benefits Act [⁷ or personal independence payment], as the case may be, a person in respect of whom there is an Order in Council made under section 179 of the Social Security Administration Act 1992 giving effect to a reciprocal agreement in respect of one of those benefits, as the case may be, is a person to whom section 115 of the Act does not apply.

[¹⁰ (3A) For the purposes of entitlement to child benefit under the Contributions and Benefits Act, a person—
(a) who is lawfully working in Great Britain; and
(b) who is a national of a State with which the United Kingdom has concluded an agreement which replaces, in whole or in part, an agreement under Article 217 of the Treaty on the Functioning of the European Union which makes provision for the receipt of family allowances for members of their family who are legally resident in the United Kingdom,
is a person to whom section 115 of the Act does not apply.]

(4) For the purposes of entitlement to—
(a) income support, a social fund payment, housing benefit [⁶ . . .] under the Contributions and Benefits Act, [³ or income-related employment and support allowance,] as the case may be, a person who is entitled to or is receiving benefit by virtue of paragraph (1) or (2) of regulation 12 of the Persons from Abroad Regulations is a person to whom section 115 of the Act does not apply;

(b) attendance allowance, disability living allowance, [¹carer's allowance, severe disablement allowance, a social fund payment or child benefit under the Contributions and Benefits Act, as the case may be, a person who is entitled to or is receiving benefit byvirtue of paragraph (10) of regulation 12 is a person to whom section 115 of the Act does not apply.

[²(c) state pension credit under the State Pension Credit Act 2002, a person to whom sub-paragraph (a) would have applied but for the fact that they have attained the qualifying age for the purposes of state pension credit, is a person to whom section 115 of the Act does not apply.]

[⁵ (5) For the purposes of entitlement to [⁸ universal credit,] income support, [⁸ an income-based jobseeker's allowance under the Jobseekers

Act 1995], an [⁸ income-related] employment and support allowance or a social fund payment under the Contributions and Benefits Act, as the case may be, a person who is an asylum seeker within the meaning of paragraph (4) of regulation 12 who has not ceased to be an asylum seeker by virtue of paragraph (5) of that regulation is a person to whom section 115 of the Act does not apply.]

(6) For the purposes of entitlement to housing benefit [⁶ . . .] or a social fund payment under the Contributions and Benefits Act, as the case may be, a person to whom regulation 12(6) applies is a person to whom section 115 of the Act does not apply.

[² (7) For the purposes of entitlement to state pension credit under the State Pension Credit Act 2002, a person to whom paragraph (5) would have applied but for the fact that they have attained the qualifying age for the purposes of state pension credit, is a person to whom section 115 of the Act does not apply.

(8) [⁹ . . .]]

AMENDMENTS

1. Social Security Amendment (Carer's Allowance) Regulations 2002 (SI 2002/2497) reg.3 and Sch.2 (April 1, 2003).
2. State Pension Credit (Transitional and Miscellaneous Provisions) Amendment Regulations 2003 (SI 2003/2274) reg.6 (October 6, 2003).
3. Employment and Support Allowance (Consequential Provisions) (No.2) Regulations 2008 (SI 2008/1554) reg.69(1) and (3) (October 27, 2008).
4. Health in Pregnancy Grant (Entitlement and Amount) Regulations 2008 (SI 2008/3108) reg.8(2) (January 1, 2009).
5. Social Security (Miscellaneous Amendments) (No.5) Regulations 2009 (SI 2009/3228) reg.3(5) (January 25, 2010).
6. Council Tax Benefit Abolition (Consequential Provision) Regulations 2013 (SI 2013/458) reg.3 and Sch.1 (April 1, 2013).
7. Personal Independence Payment (Supplementary Provisions and Consequential Amendments) Regulations 2013 (SI 2013/388) reg.8 and Sch. para.23(1) and (3) (April 8, 2013).
8. Universal Credit (Consequential, Supplementary, Incidental and Miscellaneous Provisions) Regulations 2013 (SI 2013/630) reg.31(1) and (3) (April 29, 2013).
9. Social Security (Miscellaneous Amendments) (No.3) Regulations 2013 (SI 2013/2536) reg.9(2) (October 29, 2013).
10. Social Security and Tax Credits (Miscellaneous and Coronavirus Amendments) Regulations 2021 (SI 2021/495) reg.4 (May 13, 2021).
11. Social Security and Council Tax Reduction Schemes (Amendment) Regulations 2022 (SI 2022/449) reg.2 (May 3, 2022).

Transitional arrangements and savings

12.— *Omitted*   5.14

GENERAL NOTE

Reg.12 makes transitional provision for those who claimed asylum before April   5.15
3, 2000 (when the Immigration and Asylum Act 1999 came into force) and whose
claims have not subsequently been decided or abandoned. The regulation remains
in force but has not been reproduced because, more than 21 years after April 3,

2000, it is doubtful whether it now applies to anyone and, even if it does, it has not given rise to a significant number of appeals for many years.
For the text of the regulation, and commentary, see pp.923–925 of Vol.V of the 2020/21 edition.

Regulation 2

SCHEDULE

PERSONS NOT EXCLUDED FROM CERTAIN BENEFITS UNDER SECTION 115
OF THE IMMIGRATION AND ASYLUM ACT 1999

PART I

5.16   *Persons not excluded under section 115 of the Immigration and Asylum Act from entitlement to [⁵ universal credit,] income-based jobseeker's allowance, income support, [³ income-related employment and support allowance,] a social fund payment, housing benefit or council tax benefit.*

1. [⁹ ...]
[⁸ 2. A person who is lawfully working in Great Britain and is a national of a State with which—
   (a) [¹⁰ ...]
   (b) the United Kingdom has concluded an agreement which replaces in whole or in part [¹⁰ an agreement under Article 217 of the Treaty on the Functioning of the European Union] which has ceased to apply to, and in, the United Kingdom, providing, in the field of social security, for the equal treatment of workers who are nationals of the signatory State and their families.]
3. A person who—
   (a) has been given leave to enter or remain in, the United Kingdom by the Secretary of State upon an undertaking by another person or persons pursuant to the immigration rules within the meaning of the Immigration Act 1971, to be responsible for his maintenance and accommodation; and
   (b) has been resident in the United Kingdom for a period of at least five years beginning on the date of entry or the date on which the undertaking was given in respect of him, whichever date is the later.
4. A person who is a national of a state which has ratified the European Convention on Social and Medical Assistance (done in Paris on 11th December 1953) or a state which has ratified the Council of Europe Social Charter (signed in Turin on 18th October 1961) and who is lawfully present in the United Kingdom.

PART II

5.17   *Persons not excluded under section 115 of the Immigration and Asylum Act from entitlement to attendance allowance, severe disablement allowance, [¹carer's allowance], disability living allowance, [⁴ personal independence payment,] a social fund payment [² , Health in Pregnancy Grant] or child benefit.*

1. [⁹ ...]
[⁸ 2. A person who is lawfully working in Great Britain and is a national of a State with which—
   (a) [¹⁰ ...]
   (b) the United Kingdom has concluded an agreement which replaces in whole or in part [¹⁰ an agreement under Article 217 of the Treaty on the Functioning of the European Union] which has ceased to apply to, and in, the United Kingdom, providing, in the field of social security, for the equal treatment of workers who are nationals of the signatory State and their families.]
3. A person who is a member of a family of, and living with, a person specified in paragraph 2.

4. A person who has been given leave to enter, or remain in, the United Kingdom by the Secretary of State upon an undertaking by another person or persons pursuant to the immigration rules within the meaning of the Immigration Act 1971, to be responsible for his maintenance and accommodation.

AMENDMENTS

1. Social Security Amendment (Carer's Allowance) Regulations 2002 (SI 2002/2497) reg.3 and Sch.2 (April 1, 2003).
2. Health in Pregnancy Grant (Entitlement and Amount) Regulations 2008 (SI 2008/3108) reg.8(3) (January 1, 2009).
3. Employment and Support Allowance (Consequential Provisions) (No.2) Regulations 2008 (SI 2008/1554) reg.69(1) and (5) (October 27, 2008).
4. Personal Independence Payment (Supplementary Provisions and Consequential Amendments) Regulations 2013 (SI 2013/388) reg.8 and Sch. para.23(1) and (4) (April 8, 2013).
5. Universal Credit (Consequential, Supplementary, Incidental and Miscellaneous Provisions) Regulations 2013 (SI 2013/630) reg.31(1) and (4) (April 29, 2013).
6. Social Security (Croatia) Amendment Regulations 2013 (SI 2013/1474) reg.8 (July 1, 2013).
7. Social Security (Miscellaneous Amendments) (No.3) Regulations 2013 (SI 2013/2536) reg.9(3) (October 29,2013).
8. Social Security, Child Benefit and Child Tax Credit (Amendment) (EU Exit) Regulations 2019 (SI 2019/1431) reg.2 (December 31, 2020 at 11.00 pm).
9. Immigration and Social Security Co-ordination (EU Withdrawal) Act 2020 (Consequential, Saving, Transitional and Transitory Provisions) (EU Exit) Regulations 2020 (SI 2020/1309) reg.57 (December 31, 2020 at 11.00 pm).
10. Social Security, Child Benefit and Child Tax Credit (Amendment) (EU Exit) Regulations 2020 (SI 2020/1505) reg.2(1) and (3) (January 1, 2021).

GENERAL NOTE

See under the heading, *Reciprocal agreements*, above. 5.18
For the period of one hour between December 31, 2020 at 11.00 pm (when SI 2020/1309 came into effect) and January 1, 2021 (when it was further amended by SI 2020/1505), para.2 read as follows:

"2. A person who is lawfully working in Great Britain and is a national of a State with which—

(a) the European Union has concluded an agreement under Article 217 of the Treaty on the Functioning of the European Union (an "EU Agreement") providing, in the field of social security, for the equal treatment of workers who are nationals of the signatory State and their families; or

(b) the United Kingdom has concluded an agreement which replaces in whole or in part an EU Agreement in sub-paragraph (a) which has ceased to apply to, and in, the United Kingdom, providing, in the field of social security, for the equal treatment of workers who are nationals of the signatory State and their families."

SOCIAL SECURITY VOLUME V SUPPLEMENT 2023/2024

General Editor
Nick Wikeley, M.A. (Cantab)

Commentary by

John Mesher, B.A., B.C.L. (Oxon), LL.M. (Yale)
Retired Judge of the Upper Tribunal
Emeritus Professor of Law, University of Sheffield

Tom Royston, M.A. (Cantab)
Barrister

Nick Wikeley, M.A. (Cantab)
Judge of the Upper Tribunal,
Emeritus Professor of Law, University of Southampton

Consultant Editor
Child Poverty Action Group

SWEET & MAXWELL

THOMSON REUTERS

PREFACE

This is the Cumulative Supplement to Volume V in this series, *Income Support and the Legacy Benefits 2021/22*. For more detail on the background to this initiative, we refer readers to the separate Note on Restructuring the *Social Security Legislation* series which follows the main Preface in this volume (i.e. the preface to Volume II). We urge all readers, and especially seasoned readers of these Volumes (who may now not find material where they expected it to be), to read that Note. It explains the process of restructuring the series to reflect the fact that universal credit has now become the default working-age means-tested benefit for new claims in the social security system. This has resulted in some re-ordering of material across the volumes to provide readers with a clear and coherent explanation (at least so far as we can) of the various social security benefits.

A specific part of this restructuring process is that no new edition of Volume V has been published since 2021/22. This is because there were then estimated to be only (sic) about 1.5 million households still in receipt of income support and old style ESA and JSA, a number that will continue to fall with the combined effect of "natural migration" and "managed migration" to universal credit, so giving rise to a diminishing number of appeals that are likely to involve any of the legacy benefits. Instead, this Cumulative Supplement incorporates the up-dating for Volume V contained in the 2021/22 Supplement, the Supplement contained in Volume II 2022/23 and the 2022/23 Supplement, as well as subsequent amendments up to April 10, 2023. The internal structure of the Cumulative Supplement for Volume V, *Income Support and the Legacy Benefits 2021/22*, follows the same model as the main volume. It is anticipated that the same approach will be followed in succeeding years, although this will be kept under review. Readers are therefore advised not to dispose of their copies of the 2021/22 Volume V, which will in the future most probably only be up-dated by way of such Supplements.

As to the content of this Supplement, there have, of course, been the usual routine amendments to primary legislation and to regulations since the 2022/23 Supplement, including the April 2023 up-rating of benefits and the flawed provisions aimed at providing a disregard as capital of payments made in consequence of the Bereavement Benefits (Remedial) Order 2023. Important new case law discussed includes the decision of the Court of Appeal in *R. (T) v Secretary of State for Work and Pensions* [2023] EWCA Civ 24 that the failure to give recipients of legacy benefits the same £20 coronavirus uplift as universal credit recipients did not constitute unlawful discrimination against disabled people and the decision of a three-judge panel in *SSWP v AT (UC)* [2022] UKUT 330 (AAC) (on the continuing effect of the Charter of Fundamental Rights of the European Union on the right to reside rules – under appeal to the Court of Appeal), as well as other Upper Tribunal decisions on the right to reside.

We renew our thanks for the flexibility and forbearance of the publishers and for a great deal of help from a number of sources. Those include in particular the Child Poverty Action Group as advisory editor to this series in this 40th anniversary year of the publication of the ancestor of Volumes II and V in the form of Mesher, CPAG's *Supplementary Benefit Legislation Annotated*, which would never have got off the ground without the Group's support. We remain grateful for this assistance in our task of providing an authoritative reflection on the current state of the law. Users of the series, and its predecessor works, have over the years contributed to their effectiveness by providing valuable comments on our commentary, as well as pointing out where the text of some provision has been omitted in error, or become garbled, or not been brought fully up to date. In providing such feedback, users of the work have helped to shape the content and ensure the accuracy of our material, and for that we continue to be grateful. That is all the more important given the major restructuring that has taken place. We therefore hope that users of the work will continue to provide such helpful input and feedback. Please write to the General Editor of the series, Professor Nick Wikeley, c/o School of Law, University of Southampton, Highfield, Southampton SO17 1BJ, email: njw@soton.ac.uk, and he will pass on any comments received to the appropriate commentator.

Our gratitude also goes to the President of the Social Entitlement Chamber of the First-tier Tribunal and her colleagues there for continuing the now long tradition of help and encouragement in our endeavours.

August 2023   John Mesher
                                                         Tom Royston
                                                         Nick Wikeley

CONTENTS

PAGES OF MAIN VOLUMES AFFECTED BY MATERIAL
IN THIS SUPPLEMENT

PART VI

No updates

PART VII

TABLE OF CASES

Table of Cases

TABLE OF COMMISSIONERS' DECISIONS

TABLE OF EUROPEAN LEGISLATION

TABLE OF STATUTES

TABLE OF STATUTORY INSTRUMENTS

PART I

SOCIAL SECURITY STATUTES

p.15, *amendment to the Social Security Contributions and Benefits Act 1992 s.126(7) (Trade disputes)*

With effect from April 10, 2023, art.23 of the Social Security Benefits   **5.001**
Up-rating Order 2023 (SI 2023/316) substituted "£47.00" for "£42.50"
(as had been in effect from April 11, 2022) in subs.(7).

p.18, *annotation to the Social Security Contributions and Benefits Act 1992 s.126(5)(b) (Trade disputes—relevant sum)*

Note that the amount of the "relevant sum" for the purposes of s.126(5)   **5.002**
(b) is specified in subs.(7), not (6). With effect from April 10, 2023 the sum
was increased to £47 (see the entry for p.15).

pp.19–20, *annotation to the Social Security Contributions and Benefits Act 1992 s.134(1) (Exclusions from benefit)*

In the Institute for Government and the Social Security Advisory   **5.003**
Committee's 2021 joint report *Jobs and benefits: The Covid-19 challenge* it
was noted that if the capital limit had risen in line with prices since 2006 it
would be close to £23,500 (or £25,000: different figures are given) and recommended that the limit should be increased to £25,000 and subsequently
automatically indexed to maintain its real value (pp.22 and 31). That recommendation was summarily rejected in the Government's response of
March 22, 2022.

p.33, *annotation to the old style Jobseekers Act 1995 GENERAL NOTE*

The two remaining prohibitions on claiming universal credit have now been   **5.004**
removed. The former exception for "frontier workers" was removed with effect
from March 30, 2022 by the Welfare Reform Act 2012 (Commencement
No.34 and Commencement No.9, 21, 23, 31 and 32 and Transitional
Provisions (Amendment)) Order 2022 (SI 2022/302) and the discretion
given to the Secretary of State under reg.4 of the Transitional Provisions
Regulations 2014 (SI 2014/1230) to determine (for the safeguarding of
efficient administration or ensuring the efficient testing of administrative
systems) that no claims for universal credit were to be accepted in an area or
category of case was removed with effect from July 25, 2022 by reg.2 of the
Universal Credit (Transitional Provisions) Amendment Regulations 2022 (SI
2022/752). There is thus now no exception, however remote, to the proposition that any new claim for JSA can only be for new style JSA.

p.72, *annotation to the Jobseekers Act 1995 s.13(1) (Income and capital: income-based jobseeker's allowance)*

In the Institute for Government and the Social Security Advisory   **5.005**
Committee's 2021 joint report *Jobs and benefits: The Covid-19 challenge* it was
noted that if the capital limit had risen in line with prices since 2006 it would be
close to £23,500 (or £25,000: different figures are given) and recommended
that the limit should be increased to £25,000 and subsequently automatically
indexed to maintain its real value (pp.22 and 31). That recommendation was
summarily rejected in the Government's response of March 22, 2022.

p.81, *annotation to the old style Jobseekers Act 1995 s.15(2) (Effect on other claimants—trade disputes)*

5.006   With effect from April 10, 2023 the "prescribed sum" for the purposes of s.15(2)(d) was increased to £47 (see the entry for p.1086).

p.124, *correction to the old style Jobseekers Act 1995 s.20E (Contracting out)*

5.007   The text in s.20E(1)–(3) should be replaced with the following:

"(1) The following functions of the Secretary of State may be exercised by, or by employees of, such person (if any) as the Secretary of State may authorise for the purpose, namely—
   (a) [^{2}...]
   (b) [^{2}...]
   (c) [^{2}...]
   (d) [^{3}...]
   (e) [^{3}...]
   (f) [^{3}...]
(2) The following functions of officers of the Secretary of State may be exercised by, or by employees of, such person (if any) as the Secretary of State may authorise for the purpose, namely—
   (a) specifying places and times, and being contacted, under section 8;
   (b) entering into or varying any jobseeker's agreement under section 9 or 10 and referring any proposed agreement or variation to the Secretary of State under section 9 or 10;
   (c) giving notifications under section 16[^{2}...];
   (d) [^{2}...].
(3) Regulations may provide for any of the following functions of the Secretary of State to be exercisable by, or by employees of, such person (if any) as the Secretary of State may authorise for the purpose—
   (a) any function under regulations under section 8,[^{2}...] 17A[^{2}...][^{3}...], except the making of an excluded decision (see subsection (4));
   (b) the function under section 9(1) of the 1998 Act (revision of decisions) so far as relating to decisions (other than excluded decisions) that relate to any matter arising under any such regulations;
   (c) the function under section 10(1) of the 1998 Act (superseding of decisions) so far as relating to decisions (other than excluded decisions) of the Secretary of State that relate to any matter arising under any such regulations;
   (d) any function under Chapter 2 of Part 1 of the 1998 Act (social security decisions), except section 25(2) and (3) (decisions involving issues arising on appeal in other cases), which relates to the exercise of any of the functions within paragraphs (a) to (c)."

p.133, *annotation to the old style Jobseekers Act 1995 s.35 (Interpretation— definition of "employment officer")*

5.008   Note in relation to the schemes whose providers have been designated as employment officers that the Work Programme has ceased to operate and that reg.8(3) of the SAPOE Regulations has been revoked with effect from March 22, 2022 (see the entry for p.1187).

PART II

INCOME SUPPORT REGULATIONS

p.229, *amendments to the Income Support (General) Regulations 1987 (SI 1987/1967) reg.2 (Interpretation)*

With effect from July 26, 2021, Sch.1 para.2 of the Social Security (Scotland) Act 2018 (Disability Assistance for Children and Young People) (Consequential Modifications) Order 2021 (SI 2021/786) inserts the following definitions: **5.009**

"child disability payment" has the meaning given in regulation 2 of the DACYP Regulations;
"DACYP Regulations" means the Disability Assistance for Children and Young People (Scotland) Regulations 2021;

With effect from January 1, 2022, reg.2(2) of the Social Security (Income and Capital Disregards) (Amendment) Regulations 2021 (SI 2021/1405) inserts the following definitions:

"child abuse payment" means a payment from a scheme established or approved by the Secretary of State for the purpose of providing compensation in respect of historic institutional child abuse in the United Kingdom;"
"Windrush payment" means a payment made under the Windrush Compensation Scheme (Expenditure) Act 2020;"

With effect from January 1, 2022, reg.2(2) of the Social Security (Income and Capital Disregards) (Amendment) Regulations 2021 (SI 2021/1405) inserts ", a child abuse payment or a Windrush payment" into the definition of "qualifying person", after "Grenfell Tower payment".

With effect from March 21, 2022, art.2(2) of the Social Security (Disability Assistance for Working Age People) (Consequential Amendments) Order 2022 (SI 2022/177) inserts the following definition:

"adult disability payment" has the meaning given in regulation 2 of the Disability Assistance for Working Age People (Scotland) Regulations 2022;

p.275, *amendments to the Income Support (General) Regulations 1987 (SI 1987/1967) reg.4 (Temporary absence from Great Britain)*

With effect from July 26, 2021, Sch.1 para.3 of the Social Security (Scotland) Act 2018 (Disability Assistance for Children and Young People) (Consequential Modifications) Order 2021 (SI 2021/786) makes the following amendment: **5.010**

In reg.4(2)(c)(v)(aa) after "allowance", insert ", the care component of child disability payment at the highest rate in accordance with the DACYP Regulations (see regulation 11(5) of those Regulations)".

With effect from March 21, 2022, art.2(3) of the Social Security (Disability Assistance for Working Age People) (Consequential Amendments) Order 2022 (SI 2022/177) makes the following amendment:

In reg.4(2)(c)(v)(aa) (temporary absence from Great Britain):
(a) for "or" after "armed forces independence payment" substitute ",";
(b) after "personal independence payment" insert "or the enhanced rate of the daily living component of adult disability payment".

p.314, *annotation to the Income Support (General) Regulations 1987 (SI 1987/1967) reg.17 (Applicable amounts)*

5.011   The Social Security (Coronavirus) (Further Measures) Regulations 2020 (SI 2020/371), followed by the Universal Credit (Extension of Coronavirus Measures) Regulations 2021 (SI 2021/313), had the effect that for the 18 months to October 2021, the standard allowances of UC were uplifted by £20 per week. Similar measures were employed for working tax credit: the Coronavirus Act 2020 s.77, followed by the Coronavirus Act 2020 Functions of Her Majesty's Revenue and Customs (Covid-19 support scheme: working households receiving tax credits) Direction (7 April 2021).

Recipients of IS, ESA and JSA did not receive an uplift. In *R(T) v Secretary of State for Work and Pensions*, the legality of this differential treatment was challenged (unsuccessfully) as being unlawfully discriminatory contrary to the ECHR.

In [2022] EWHC 351 (Admin) (18 February 2022) the High Court: (i) rejected the claim that there was unlawful discrimination against people with the status of being a legacy benefit claimant, on the basis that being a legacy benefit claimant was not a status within the scope of ECHR art.14 (paras 22–24); and (ii) rejected the claim that there was unlawful discrimination against disabled people, on the basis that the discrimination was justified (paras 30–38). Permission to appeal to the Court of Appeal was refused on point (i) but given on point (ii). In [2023] EWCA Civ 24 (17 January 2023), the Court of Appeal confirmed that the disability discrimination was justified. The Secretary of State's focus was on prioritising people likely to be facing a recent reduction in income, and on adopting an approach she considered technically practicable (paras 53–54). In that context, the High Court did not err by deciding that the limitation of uplift to UC and WTC was a proportionate means of achieving a legitimate aim.

pp.329–331, *amendment to the Income Support (General) Regulations 1987 (SI 1987/1967) reg.21AA (Special cases: supplemental—persons from abroad)*

5.012   The text in the main volume at para.2.167 should be replaced with the following:

"[¹ Special cases: supplemental—persons from abroad

21AA.—(1) "Person from abroad" means, subject to the following provisions of this regulation, a claimant who is not habitually resident in the United Kingdom, the Channel Islands, the Isle of Man or the Republic of Ireland.

(2) No claimant shall be treated as habitually resident in the United Kingdom, the Channel Islands, the Isle of Man or the Republic of Ireland unless he has a right to reside in (as the case may be) the United Kingdom, the Channel Islands, the Isle of Man or the Republic of Ireland other than a right to reside which falls within paragraph (3) [¹² or (3A)].

(3) A right to reside falls within this paragraph if it is one which exists by virtue of, or in accordance with, one or more of the following—

(a) regulation 13 of the [¹² Immigration (European Economic Area) Regulations 2016];

(b) regulation 14 of those Regulations, but only in a case where the right exists under that regulation because the claimant is—

  (i) a jobseeker for the purpose of the definition of "qualified person" in regulation 6(1) of those Regulations, or
  (ii) a family member (within the meaning of regulation 7 of those Regulations) of such a jobseeker; [14 or]
[7[12(bb) regulation 16 of those Regulations, but only in a case where the right exists under that regulation because the claimant satisfies the criteria in paragraph (5) of that regulation;]]
[14 (c)–(e) . . .]
  [12 (3A) A right to reside falls within this paragraph if it exists by virtue of a claimant having been granted limited leave to enter, or remain in, the United Kingdom under the Immigration Act 1971 by virtue of—
  (a) Appendix EU to the immigration rules made under section 3(2) of that Act; [15 . . .]
  (b) being a person with a Zambrano right to reside as defined in Annex 1 of Appendix EU to the immigration rules made under section 3(2) of that Act.] [15; or
  (c) having arrived in the United Kingdom with an entry clearance that was granted under Appendix EU (Family Permit) to the immigration rules made under section 3(2) of that Act.]
  [13 (3B) Paragraph (3A)(a) does not apply to a person who—
  (a) has a right to reside granted by virtue of being a family member of a relevant person of Northern Ireland; and
  (b) would have a right to reside under the [12 Immigration (European Economic Area) Regulations 2016] if the relevant person of Northern Ireland were an EEA national, provided that the right to reside does not fall within paragraph (3).]
  (4) A claimant is not a person from abroad if he is—
[17(zza) a person granted leave in accordance with the immigration rules made under section 3(2) of the Immigration Act 1971, where such leave is granted by virtue of—
  (i) the Afghan Relocations and Assistance Policy; or
  (ii) the previous scheme for locally-employed staff in Afghanistan (sometimes referred to as the ex-gratia scheme);
(zzb) a person in Great Britain not coming within sub-paragraph (zza) or [18 (h)] who left Afghanistan in connection with the collapse of the Afghan government that took place on 15th August 2021;]
[18(zzc) a person in Great Britain who was residing in Ukraine immediately before 1st January 2022, left Ukraine in connection with the Russian invasion which took place on 24th February 2022 and—
  (i) has been granted leave in accordance with immigration rules made under section 3(2) of the Immigration Act 1971; [19 . . .]
  (ii) has a right of abode in the United Kingdom within the meaning given in section 2 of that Act;] [19 or
  (iii) does not require leave to enter or remain in the United Kingdom in accordance with section 3ZA of that Act;]
[10(za) a qualified person for the purposes of [16 regulation 6 of the Immigration (European Economic Area) Regulations 2016] as a worker or a self-employed person;
  (zb) a family member of a person referred to in sub-paragraph (za) [13 . . .];

(zc) a person who has a right to reside permanently in the United Kingdom by virtue of regulation 15(1)(c), (d) or (e) of those Regulations;]

[¹³(zd)a family member of a relevant person of Northern Ireland, with a right to reside which falls within paragraph (3A)(a), provided that the relevant person of Northern Ireland falls within sub-paragraph (za), or would do so but for the fact that they are not an EEA national;]

[¹⁴(ze) a frontier worker within the meaning of regulation 3 of the Citizens' Rights (Frontier Workers) (EU Exit) Regulations 2020;

(zf) a family member, of a person referred to in sub-paragraph (ze), who has been granted limited leave to enter, or remain in, the United Kingdom by virtue of Appendix EU to the immigration rules made under section 3(2) of the Immigration Act 1971;]

(g) a refugee within the definition in Article 1 of the Convention relating to the Status of Refugees done at Geneva on 28th July 1951, as extended by Article 1(2) of the Protocol relating to the Status of Refugees done at New York on 31st January 1967;

[³[⁹(h)a person who has been granted leave or who is deemed to have been granted leave outside the rules made under section 3(2) of the Immigration Act 1971 [¹⁸ . . .];

(hh) a person who has humanitarian protection granted under those rules;] [⁹ or]

(i) a person who is not a person subject to immigration control within the meaning of section 115(9) of the Immigration and Asylum Act and who is in the United Kingdom as a result of his deportation, expulsion or other removal by compulsion of law from another country to the United Kingdom; [⁵ . . .] [⁹ . . .]

[¹³ (5) In this regulation—

"EEA national" has the meaning given in regulation 2(1) of the Immigration (European Economic Area) Regulations 2016;

"family member" has the meaning given in regulation 7(1)(a), (b) or (c) of the Immigration (European Economic Area) Regulations 2016 except that regulation 7(4) of those Regulations does not apply for the purposes of paragraphs (3B) and (4)(zd);

"relevant person of Northern Ireland" has the meaning given in Annex 1 of Appendix EU to the immigration rules made under section 3(2) of the Immigration Act 1971.]

[¹⁴ (6) In this regulation references to the Immigration (European Economic Area) Regulations 2016 are to be read with Schedule 4 to the Immigration and Social Security Co-ordination (EU Withdrawal) Act 2020 (Consequential, Saving, Transitional and Transitory Provisions) Regulations 2020.]"

AMENDMENTS

1. Social Security (Persons from Abroad) Amendment Regulations 2006 (SI 1026/2006) reg.6(3) (April 30, 2006).

2. Social Security (Lebanon) Amendment Regulations 2006 (SI 2006/1981) reg.2 (July 25, 2006). The amendment ceased to have effect from January 31, 2007.

3. Social Security (Persons from Abroad) Amendment (No. 2) Regulations 2006 (SI 2006/2528) reg.2 (October 9, 2006).

4. Social Security (Bulgaria and Romania) Amendment Regulations 2006 (SI 2006/3341) reg.2 (January 1, 2007).
5. Social Security (Habitual Residence) (Amendment) Regulations 2009 (SI 2009/362) reg.2 (March 18, 2009).
6. Social Security (Miscellaneous Amendments) (No. 3) Regulations 2011 (SI 2011/2425) reg.7(1) and (3) (October 31, 2011).
7. Social Security (Habitual Residence) (Amendment) Regulations 2012 (SI 2012/2587) reg.2 (November 8, 2012).
8. Social Security (Croatia) Amendment Regulations 2013 (SI 2013/1474) reg.2 (July 1, 2013).
9. Social Security (Miscellaneous Amendments) (No. 3) Regulations 2013 (SI 2013/2536) reg.4(1) and (5) (October 29, 2013).
10. Social Security (Habitual Residence) (Amendment) Regulations 2014 (SI 2014/902) reg.2(1) (May 31, 2014).
11. Social Security (Updating of EU References) (Amendment) Regulations 2018 (SI 2018/1084) reg.4 and Sch. para.6 (November 15, 2018).
12. Social Security (Income-related Benefits) (Updating and Amendment) (EU Exit) Regulations 2019 (SI 2019/872) reg.2 (May 7, 2019).
13. Social Security (Income-Related Benefits) (Persons of Northern Ireland—Family Members) (Amendment) Regulations 2020 (SI 2020/683) reg.2 (August 24, 2020).
14. Immigration and Social Security Co-ordination (EU Withdrawal) Act 2020 (Consequential, Saving, Transitional and Transitory Provisions) (EU Exit) Regulations 2020 (SI 2020/1309) reg.53 (December 31, 2020 at 11.00pm).
15. Immigration (Citizens' Rights etc.) (EU Exit) Regulations 2020 (SI 2020/1372) reg.8 (December 31, 2020 at 11.00 pm).
16. Social Security (Income-related Benefits) (Updating and Amendment) (EU Exit) Regulations (SI 2019/872) reg.2 (May 7, 2019).
17. Social Security (Habitual Residence and Past Presence) (Amendment) Regulations 2021 (SI 2021/1034) reg.2 (September 15, 2021).
18. Social Security (Habitual Residence and Past Presence) (Amendment) Regulations 2022 (SI 2022/344) reg.2 (March 22, 2022).
19. Social Security (Habitual Residence and Past Presence) (Amendment) (No. 2) Regulations 2022 (SI 2022/990) reg.2 (October 18, 2022).

p.355, *annotation to the Income Support (General) Regulations 1987 (SI 1987/1967) reg.23 (Calculation of the income and capital of members of claimant's family and of a polygamous marriage)*

In line 4 of p.355, for "on the exclusion of", substitute "so as to exclude" and in line 5 for "s.11", substitute "ss.11 and 12".

5.013

p.412, *annotation to the Income Support (General) Regulations 1987 (SI 1987/1967) reg.40(1) (Calculation of income other than earnings)*

Add to the non-exhaustive list of benefits disregarded as income under Sch.9, various Scottish benefits (paras 81–85 of Sch.9).

5.014

p.421, *amendment to the Income Support (General) Regulations 1987 (SI 1987/1967) reg.42(4ZB) (Notional income—exceptions)*

With effect from January 1, 2022, reg.2(3) of the Social Security (Income and Capital Disregards) (Amendment) Regulations 2021 (SI 2021/1405) amended para.(4ZB) by substituting the following for "a payment of income which is a Grenfell Tower payment":

5.015

"any of the following payments of income—
(a) a Grenfell Tower payment;
(b) a child abuse payment;
(c) a Windrush payment."

All of those payments are defined in reg.2(1). See the entry for p.684 for discussion of the nature of child abuse and Windrush payments.

pp.431–433, *annotation to the Income Support (General) Regulations 1987 (SI 1987/1967) reg.42(4) and (4ZA) (Notional income—third parties)*

5.016   Note the extended exception to the operation of para.(4) (see the entry for p.421).

p.438, *annotation to the Income Support (General) Regulations 1987 (SI 1987/967) reg.45 (Capital limit)*

5.017   In the Institute for Government and the Social Security Advisory Committee's 2021 joint report *Jobs and benefits: The Covid-19 challenge* it was noted that if the capital limit of £16,000 had risen in line with prices since 2006 it would be close to £23,500 (or £25,000: different figures are given) and recommended that the limit should be increased to £25,000 and subsequently automatically indexed to maintain its real value (pp.22 and 31). That recommendation was summarily rejected in the Government's response of March 22, 2022.

p.439, *annotation to the Income Support (General) Regulations 1987 (SI 1987/1967) reg.46 (Calculation of capital)*

5.018   At some point, the valuation of digital assets, such as non-fungible tokens, cryptocurrency etc., may have to be addressed, including how they fit into the notions of capital and of personal possessions. There is extensive discussion of the existing legal framework in the Law Commission's *Digital Assets: Consultation Paper* (Law Com. No.256, July 28, 2022). Now see *Digital Assets: Final report* (Law Com. No.412, June 27, 2023).

pp.440–441, *annotation to the Income Support (General) Regulations 1987 (SI 1987/1967) reg.46 (Calculation of capital)*

5.019   The text in the paragraph starting "See also" on p.440 to the paragraph ending "had ceased." on p.441 should be deleted.
         Insert the following text on p.441 between the paragraph starting "However" and the heading "*Beneficial ownership*":

Interests under a will or intestacy when someone has died
         The DMG (paras 29169-29175) contains guidance adopting in para.29174 the general principle that a beneficiary under a will or intestacy has no legal or equitable interest in any specific property while the estate remains unadministered. The personal representative in those circumstances has full ownership of the assets of the estate. That principle was applied by the Tribunal of Commissioners in *R(SB) 5/85*, relying on the foundational Privy Council decision in *Commissioner of Stamp Duties (Queensland) v Livingston* [1965] A.C. 694.

However, there are two important qualifications. The first is that, even where the *Livingston* principle applies, the beneficiary has a right to have the deceased's estate properly administered. That is a chose in action that has a market value. It can be transferred and can be borrowed against. Depending on the particular circumstances, the market value can be considerable and not far off the value that would be put on the asset(s) in question if owned outright. That point was made clearly by Commissioner Howell in para.28 of his decision in *R(IS) 1/01* and nothing to the contrary was said in the Court of Appeal in *Wilkinson v Chief Adjudication Officer*, reported as part of *R(IS) 1/01*, in upholding the Commissioner's decision. Nor is *R(SB) 5/85* to the contrary: the Commissioners there expressly noted that the claimant had a chose in action (para.7). It is submitted that that is the basis on which the later decision of Commissioner Howell in *CIS/1189/2003* is to be supported. The claimant there was the sole residuary beneficiary under her mother's will and the estate, whose main asset was a property that the claimant did not live in, remained unadministered for several years, so that the property had not actually vested in the claimant. In para.11, the Commissioner said that the claimant was beneficially entitled to the property from the date of her mother's death subject only to the formalities needed to perfect her title, so that for all practical purposes she had an entitlement equivalent to full beneficial ownership. That proposition can easily be misinterpreted, but in para.12, the Commissioner noted that as the claimant was the sole *residuary* beneficiary, it was para.28 of *R(IS) 1/01* that was applicable. So the valuation was of the claimant's chose in action, but in the circumstances the difference in value from that of full beneficial ownership was negligible.

The second qualification is that the position may be different where there has been a specific gift of some asset, as was the case in *R(IS) 1/01*, where the will of the claimant's mother gave the claimant and her brother equal shares in some income bonds and other money in a bank account and in a property. The matter was put very strongly by Commissioner Howell in para.27 of his decision, where he said that the *Livingston* principle had:

"never had any application to property specifically devised or bequeathed by a will. Such property becomes in equity the property of the legatee as soon as the testator dies, subject only to the right of the personal representative to resort to it for payment of debts if the remainder of the estate is insufficient for this purpose [citations omitted]."

No specific comment on that proposition was made in the judgments of the Court of Appeal in *Wilkinson*, but Mummery LJ did note generally that the evidence did not suggest that there was any question of the executors needing to have recourse to the property for payment of debts or that there was any other legal obstacle to the immediate completion of the administration of the estate and to an assent by the executors vesting the property in the names of the claimant and her brother as joint owners. That strongly suggests that what was being considered was a valuation of the claimant's chose in action, rather than of some equitable interest. It is submitted that that is the proper approach. The valuation would therefore be sensitive to the possibilities mentioned by Mummery LJ in the particular case, as well as to the value of the underlying asset. That approach would hold also for personal property or money, although there it should be noted that the process of the personal representative giving an assent, i.e. an indication that a certain asset is not required for administration purposes and may pass under the will or (possibly) an intestacy into the ownership of the beneficiary, does not need to be in writing and may be implied from conduct.

p.443, *annotation to the Income Support (General) Regulations 1987 (SI 1987/967) reg. 46 (Calculation of capital—claimant holding as trustee)*

5.020   In line 10 of the paragraph starting "One particular", insert the following between "return it" and the full stop:

"(a result most recently confirmed by the decision of the Privy Council in the *Prickly Bay* case)"

p.446, *annotation to the Income Support (General) Regulations 1987 (SI 1987/967) reg. 46 (Calculation of capital—claimant holding as trustee)*

5.021   Note, in relation to the discussion of cases in which the *Quistclose* principle has or has not been applied, that the Privy Council in *Prickly Bay Waterside Ltd v British American Insurance Co Ltd* [2022] UKPC 8; [2022] 1 W.L.R. 2087, while accepting the value of summaries of principles, in particular of those established by the judgment of Lord Millett in *Twinsectra Ltd v Yardley* [2002] 2 A.C. 164, warned against not going back to the "core analysis" in that judgment. It was emphasised again that it is not enough that money is provided for a particular purpose. The question is whether the parties intended that the money should be at the free disposition of the recipient. An intention that it should not be need not be mutual, in the sense of being shared or reciprocated, but could be imposed by one party and acquiesced in by the other. A *Quistclose* trust is a default trust, so can be excluded or moulded by the terms of the parties' express agreements. In the particular case, involving complex commercial transactions in which a sum was loaned to a bank that contracted to guarantee payment of the purchase price of a property on future completion, it was significant to the outcome that a *Quistclose* trust had not been established that there had been no requirement that the sum be segregated by the bank from its other funds. It is submitted that in other contexts, such as family or other relatively informal arrangements more likely to be encountered in the social security context, a lack of segregation, say into a separate account, would not carry nearly such weight.

p.451, *annotation to the Income Support (General) Regulations 1987 (SI 1987/967) reg. 46 (Calculation of capital—claimant holding as trustee)*

5.022   Note the decision of the Supreme Court, by a majority of three to two, in *Guest v Guest* [2022] UKSC 27; [2022] 3 W.L.R. 911 on proprietary estoppel and the nature of the remedies available in equity. Lord Briggs, giving the majority judgment, conducted an exhaustive survey of the English and Australian case law, as well as academic debate, and rejected the theory that the aim of the remedy was to compensate the person given a promise or assurance about the acquisition of property for the detriment suffered in reliance on the promise or assurance, rather than primarily to hold the person who had given the promise or assurance to the promise or assurance, which would usually prevent the unconscionability inherent in the repudiation of the promise or assurance that had been detrimentally relied on (paras 71 and 61). However, the remedy was a flexible one dependent on the circumstances. Lord Briggs summarised the principles as follows:

"74. I consider that, in principle, the court's normal approach should be as follows. The first stage (which is not in issue in this case) is to determine whether the promisor's repudiation of his promise is, in the light of the promisee's detrimental reliance upon it, unconscionable at all. It usually will be, but there may be circumstances (such as the promisor falling on hard times and needing to sell the property to pay his creditors, or to pay for expensive medical treatment or social care for himself or his wife) when it may not be. Or the promisor may have announced or carried out only a partial repudiation of the promise, which may or may not have been unconscionable, depending on the circumstances.

75. The second (remedy) stage will normally start with the assumption (not presumption) that the simplest way to remedy the unconscionability constituted by the repudiation is to hold the promisor to the promise. The promisee cannot (and probably would not) complain, for example, that his detrimental reliance had cost him more than the value of the promise, were it to be fully performed. But the court may have to listen to many other reasons from the promisor (or his executors) why something less than full performance will negate the unconscionability and therefore satisfy the equity. They may be based on one or more of the real-life problems already outlined. The court may be invited by the promisor to consider one or more proxies for performance of the promise, such as the transfer of less property than promised or the provision of a monetary equivalent in place of it, or a combination of the two.

76. If the promisor asserts and proves, the burden being on him for this purpose, that specific enforcement of the full promise, or monetary equivalent, would be out of all proportion to the cost of the detriment to the promisee, then the court may be constrained to limit the extent of the remedy. This does not mean that the court will be seeking precisely to compensate for the detriment as its primary task, but simply to put right a disproportionality which is so large as to stand in the way of a full specific enforcement doing justice between the parties. It will be a very rare case where the detriment is equivalent in value to the expectation, and there is nothing in principle unjust in a full enforcement of the promise being worth more than the cost of the detriment, any more than there is in giving specific performance of a contract for the sale of land merely because it is worth more than the price paid for it. An example of a remedy out of all proportion to the detriment would be the full enforcement of a promise by an elderly lady to leave her carer a particular piece of jewellery if she stayed on at very low wages, which turned out on valuation by her executors to be a Faberge worth millions. Another would be a promise to leave a generous inheritance if the promisee cared for the promisor for the rest of her life, but where she unexpectedly died two months later."

Thus, in circumstances where proprietary estoppel might be in play (as would probably now be the case on similar facts to *R(SB) 23/85* and *R(SB) 7/87*), great care would be needed in establishing the primary facts and, outside the clearest cases, in a deeper investigation of the principles of law governing the nature of any remedy available. And would a repudiation of a promise when the promisor would otherwise be forced to rely on a means-tested benefit be unconscionable? However, even if it were to be concluded that the claimant did not hold the property in question on trust for someone else, the possibility of a claim in equity, e.g. for some monetary compensation, may well affect the valuation of the property.

p.457, *amendment to the Income Support (General) Regulations 1987 (SI 1987/1967) reg.48(10) (Income treated as capital—exceptions)*

5.023   With effect from January 1, 2022, reg.2(4) of the Social Security (Income and Capital Disregards) (Amendment) Regulations 2021 (SI 2021/1405) amended para.(10) by inserting the following after sub-para.(ab):

> "(ac) which is a child abuse payment;
> (ad) which is a Windrush payment; or"

Both of those payments are defined in reg.2(1). See the entry for p.684 for discussion of their nature. The "or" following sub-para.(ab), omitted in error in the main volume, has also been removed.

p.467, *amendment to the Income Support (General) Regulations 1987 (SI 1987/1967) reg.51(3B) (Notional capital—exceptions)*

5.024   With effect from January 1, 2022, reg.2(5) of the Social Security (Income and Capital Disregards) (Amendment) Regulations 2021 (SI 2021/1405) amended para.(3B) by substituting the following for "a payment of capital which is a Grenfell Tower payment":

> "any of the following payments of capital—
> (a) a Grenfell Tower payment;
> (b) a child abuse payment;
> (c) a Windrush payment."

All of those payments are defined in reg.2(1). See the entry for p.684 for discussion of the nature of child abuse and Windrush payments.

pp.520–523, *annotations to the Income Support (General) Regulations 1987 (SI 1987/1967) reg.61 (Interpretation—students—meaning of "Full-time course")*

5.025   The principles derived from the case law, taking into account Court of Appeal decisions not all of which are discussed in the main volume, have recently very helpfully been summarised by Judge Rowley in para.19 of *BK v SSWP (UC)* [2022] UKUT 73 (AAC) (some references added by annotator):

> "a. Whether or not a person is undertaking a full-time course is a question of fact for the tribunal having regard to the circumstances in each particular case (*R/SB 40/83* at [13]; *R(SB) 41/83* at [12]). Parameters have been set, as appear below:
> b. The words 'full-time' relate to the course and not to the student. Specifically, they do not permit the matter to be determined by reference to the amount of time which the student happens to dedicate to their studies (*R/SB 40/83* at [14], [15]; *R(SB) 2/91* at [7]; *R(SB) 41/83* at [11]).
> c. Evidence from the educational establishment as to whether or not the course is full-time is not necessarily conclusive, but it ought to be

accepted as such unless it is inconclusive on its face, or is challenged by relevant evidence which at least raises the possibility that it ought to be rejected (*R/SB 40/83* at [18]), and any evidence adduced in rebuttal should be weighty in content (*R/SB 41/83* at [12]). See also *Flemming v Secretary of State for Work and Pensions* [2002] EWCA Civ 641; [2002] 1 W.L.R. 2322 [also reported as *R(G) 2/02*] at [21]–[22] and [38]; and *Deane v Secretary of State for Work and Pensions* [2010] EWCA Civ 699; [2011] 1 W.L.R. 743 [also reported at [2010] AACR 42] where the Court of Appeal repeated an earlier statement in *Flemming* that:

> "38 . . . A tribunal of fact should, I think be very slow to accept that a person expects or intends to devote—or does, in fact, devote—significantly less time to the course than those who have conduct of the course expect of him, and very slow to hold that a person who is attending a course considered by the educational establishment to be a part-time course is to be treated as receiving full-time education because he devotes significantly more time than that which is expected of him . . . "

d. If the course is offered as a full-time course, the presumption is that the recipient is in full-time education. There may be exceptions to the rule, such where a student is granted exemptions from part of the course: *Deane* [51]."

In *BK* itself, the claimant was on a one-year MA course at Goldsmiths, University of London, described by that institution as full-time and involving more than 24 hours of study per week. Letters from the Department concerned confirmed six contact hours of teaching in two terms, with an expectation of at least six hours per week in independent study. A dissertation was to be written in the third term. The First-tier Tribunal rejected the claimant's argument that those letters, and the fact that he could arrange his time to be available for work, showed that the course was not full-time. Judge Rowley held that it did not err in law in doing so and that in saying that Goldsmiths' description was "determinative" of the nature of the course it had not strayed into regarding the description as conclusive, but had applied the test in para.19(c) above.

p.526, *annotation to the Income Support (General) Regulations 1987 (SI 1987/1967) reg.61 (Interpretation—"postgraduate loan")*

The value of a postgraduate loan under the English scheme described (there are different schemes for other UK countries) has been increased to £11,836 for courses starting on or after August 1, 2022 and to £12,167 for courses starting on or after August 1, 2023.   5.026

p.550, *amendments to the Income Support (General) Regulations 1987 (SI 1987/1967) Sch.1B (Prescribed categories of persons)*

With effect from July 26, 2021, Sch.1 para.4 of the Social Security (Scotland) Act 2018 (Disability Assistance for Children and Young People) (Consequential Modifications) Order 2021 (SI 2021/786) makes the following amendments: 5.027

- In para.4(a) of Sch.1B (persons caring for another person):
  - in para.(i), after "Contributions and Benefits Act" insert ", the care component of child disability payment at the highest or

middle rate in accordance with the DACYP Regulations (see regulation 11(5) of those Regulations),";

- in para.(iii), after "disability living allowance", insert ", child disability payment";
- after para.(iiia), insert "(iiib) the person being cared for ("P") has claimed entitlement to the care component of child disability payment in accordance with regulation 24 (when an application is to be treated as made and beginning of entitlement to assistance) of the DACYP Regulations, an award at the highest or middle rate has been made in respect of P's claim, and where the period for which the award is payable has begun, P is in receipt of that payment;".

With effect from March 21, 2022, art.2(4)–(5) of the Social Security (Disability Assistance for Working Age People) (Consequential Amendments) Order 2022 (SI 2022/177) makes the following amendments:

- In para.4(a) (persons caring for another person) of Sch.1B (prescribed categories of person):
  - in sub-para.(i):
    - for "or" after "(see regulation 11(5) of those Regulations)," substitute ",";
    - after "2012 Act" insert "or the daily living component of adult disability payment at the standard or enhanced rate in accordance with regulation 5 of the Disability Assistance for Working Age People (Scotland) Regulations 2022";
  - in sub-para.(iii):
    - for "or" after "armed forces independence payment" substitute ",";
    - after "personal independence payment" insert "or adult disability payment";
  - after sub-para.(iv) insert "(v)the person being cared for has claimed entitlement to the daily living component of adult disability payment in accordance with regulation 35 (when an application is to be treated as made and beginning of entitlement to assistance) of the Disability Assistance for Working Age People (Scotland) Regulations 2022, an award at the standard or enhanced rate has been made in respect of that claim and, where the period for which the award is payable has begun, that person is in receipt of the payment;".

- In para.7A (certain persons in receipt of the daily living component of personal independence payment) of Sch.1B:
  - in the heading, after "personal independence payment" insert "or adult disability payment";
  - after "at the enhanced rate" insert "or the daily living component of adult disability payment at the enhanced rate".

pp.571–572, *amendments to the Income Support (General) Regulations 1987 (SI 1987/1967) Sch.2 (Applicable amounts)*

5.028   The text in the main volume at paras 2.606–2.626 should be replaced with the following:

Regulations 17 [³ (1)] and 18

"SCHEDULE 2

APPLICABLE AMOUNTS

[³⁵ PART I

PERSONAL ALLOWANCES

1.—The weekly amounts specified in column (2) below in respect of each person or couple specified in column (1) shall be the weekly amounts specified for the purposes of regulations 17(1) and 18(1) (applicable amounts and polygamous marriages).

2.606

Column (1) Person or Couple	Column (2) Amount
(1) Single claimant aged— 　(a) except where head (b) or (c) of this sub-paragraph applies, less than 18; [²⁸(b) less than 18 who falls within any of the circumstances specified in paragraph 1A;] 　(c) less than 18 who satisfies the condition in [⁶⁵ paragraph 11(1)(a)] 　(d) not less than 18 but less than 25; 　(e) not less than 25.	(1) 　(a) [⁸⁵ £67.20]; 　(b) [⁸⁵ £67.20]; 　(c) [⁸⁵ £67.20]; 　(d) [⁸⁵ £67.20]; 　(e) [⁸⁵ £84.80].
(2) Lone parent aged— 　(a) except where head (b) or (c) of this sub-paragraph applies, less than 18; [²⁸(b) less than 18 who falls within any of the circumstances specified in paragraph 1A;] 　(c) less than 18 who satisfies the condition in [⁶⁵ paragraph 11(1)(a)] 　(d) not less than 18.	(2) 　(a) [⁸⁵ £67.20]; 　(b) [⁸⁵ £67.20]; 　(c) [⁸⁵ £67.20]; 　(d) [⁸⁵ £84.80].
[²⁸(3) Couple— 　(a) where both members are aged less than 18 and— 　　(i) at least one of them is treated as responsible for a child; or 　　(ii) had they not been members of a couple, each would have qualified for income support under regulation 4ZA [⁷¹ or income-related employment and support allowance]; or 　　(iii) the claimant's partner satisfies the requirement of section 3(1)(f)(iii) of the Jobseekers Act 1995 (prescribed circumstances for persons aged 16 but less than 18); or 　　(iv) there is in force in respect of the claimant's partner a direction under section 16 of the Jobseekers Act 1995 (persons under 18: severe hardship); 　(b) where both members are aged less than 18 and head (a) does not apply but one member of the couple falls within any of the circumstances specified in paragraph 1A;	(3) 　(a) [⁸⁵ £101.50]; 　(b) [⁸⁵ £67.20];

Column (1) Person or Couple	Column (2) Amount
(c) where both members are aged less than 18 and heads (a) and (b) do not apply;	(c) [⁸⁵ £67.20];
(d) where both members are aged not less than 18;	(d) [⁸⁵ £133.30];

(e) where one member is aged not less than 18 and the other member is a person under 18 who—(2)
   (i) qualifies for income support under regulation 4ZA [⁷¹ or income-related employment and support allowance], or who would so qualify if he were not a member of a couple; or
   (ii) satisfies the requirements of section 3(1)(f)(iii) of the Jobseekers Act 1995 (prescribed circumstances for persons aged 16 but less than 18); or
   (iii) is the subject of a direction under section 16 of the Jobseekers Act 1995 (persons under 18: severe hardship);
	(e) [⁸⁵ £133.30];

(f) where the claimant is aged not less than 18 but less (f) than 25 and his partner is a person under 18 who—
   (i) would not qualify for income support under regulation 4ZA [⁷¹ or income-related employment and support allowance] if he were not a member of a couple; and
   (ii) does not satisfy the requirements of section 3(1)(f)(iii) of the Jobseekers Act 1995 (prescribed circumstances for persons aged 16 but less than 18); and
   (iii) is not the subject of a direction under section 16 of the Jobseekers Act 1995 (persons under 18: severe hardship);
	(f) [⁸⁵ £67.20];

(g) where the claimant is aged not less than 25 and his (g) partner is a person under 18 who—
   (i) would not qualify for income support under regulation 4ZA [⁷¹ or income-related employment and support allowance] if he were not a member of a couple; and
   (ii) does not satisfy the requirements of section 3(1)(f)(iii) of the Jobseekers Act 1995 (prescribed circumstances for persons aged 16 but less than 18); and
   (iii) is not the subject of a direction under section 16 of the Jobseekers Act 1995 (persons under 18: severe hardship).]]
	(g) [⁸⁵ £84.80].

2.607   [²⁸ **1A.**—(1) The circumstances referred to in paragraph 1 are that—
   (a) the person has no parents nor any person acting in the place of his parents;
   (b) the person—
      (i) is not living with his parents nor any person acting in the place of his parents; and
      (ii) in England and Wales, was being looked after by a local authority pursuant to a relevant enactment who placed him with some person other than a close relative of his; or in Scotland, was in the care of a local authority under a relevant enactment and whilst in that care was not living with his parents or any close relative, or was in custody in any institution to which the Prison Act 1952 or the Prisons (Scotland) Act 1989 applied immediately before he attained the age of 16;
   (c) the person is in accommodation which is other than his parental home, and which is other than the home of a person acting in the place of his parents, who entered that accommodation—
      (i) as part of a programme of rehabilitation or resettlement, that programme being under the supervision of the probation service or a local authority; or

  (ii) in order to avoid physical or sexual abuse; or

  (iii) because of a mental or physical handicap or illness and needs such accommodation because of his handicap or illness;

(d) the person is living away from his parents and any person who is acting in the place of his parents in a case where his parents are or, as the case may be, that person is, unable financially to support him and his parents are, or that person is—

  (i) chronically sick or mentally or physically disabled; or

  (ii) detained in custody pending trial or sentence upon conviction or under sentence imposed by a court; or

  (iii) prohibited from entering or re-entering Great Britain; or

(e) the person of necessity has to live away from his parents and any person acting in the place of his parents because—

  (i) he is estranged from his parents and that person; or

  (ii) he is in physical or moral danger; or

  (iii) there is a serious risk to his physical or mental health.

(2) In this paragraph—

(a) "chronically sick or mentally or physically disabled" has the same meaning it has in regulation 13(3)(b) (circumstances in which persons in relevant education are to be entitled to income support);

(b) in England and Wales, any reference to a person acting in place of a person's parents includes a reference to—

  (i) where the person is being looked after by a local authority or voluntary organisation who place him with a family, a relative of his, or some other suitable person, the person with whom the person is placed, whether or not any payment is made to him in connection with the placement; or

  (ii) in any other case, any person with parental responsibility for the child, and for this purpose "parental responsibility" has the meaning it has in the Children Act 1989 by virtue of section 3 of that Act;

(c) in Scotland, any reference to a person acting in place of a person's parents includes a reference to a local authority or voluntary organisation where the person is in their care under a relevant enactment, or to a person with whom the person is boarded out by a local authority or voluntary organisation whether or not any payment is made by them.]

[^{35} 2.—[^{59} . . .]]   2.608

[^{17} 2A.—[^{55} . . .]]   2.609

PART II

Regulations 17[^{3} (1)](c) [^{3} and 18(1)](d)

FAMILY PREMIUM

3.—[^{59} . . .]   2.610

PART III

Regulations 17[^{3} (1)](d) [^{3} and 18(1)](e)

PREMIUMS

4.—Except as provided in paragraph 5, the weekly premiums specified in Part IV of this Schedule shall, for the purposes of regulations 17[^{3}(1)](d)[^{3} and 18(1)](e), be applicable to a claimant who satisfies the condition specified in [^{42} paragraphs 8A] [^{10} to 14ZA] in respect of that premium.

           2.611

5.—Subject to paragraph 6, where a claimant satisfies the conditions in respect of more than one premium in this Part of this Schedule, only one premium shall be applicable to him and, if they are different amounts, the higher or highest amount shall apply.

[⁵⁸ **6.**—(1) Subject to sub-paragraph (2), the following premiums, namely—
   (a) a severe disability to which paragraph 13 applies;
   (b) an enhanced disability premium to which paragraph 13A applies;
   (c) [⁵⁹ . . .]; and
   (d) a carer premium to which paragraph 14ZA applies,
may be applicable in addition to any other premium that may apply under this Schedule.
   (2) An enhanced disability premium in respect of a person shall not be applicable in addition to—
   (a) a pensioner premium under paragraph 9 or 9A; or
   (b) a higher pension premium under paragraph 10.]
   7.—[¹⁰(1) Subject to sub-paragraph (2)] for the purposes of this Part of this Schedule, once a premium is applicable to a claimant under this Part, a person shall be treated as being in receipt of any benefit—
   (a) in the case of a benefit to which the Social Security (Overlapping Benefits) Regulations 1979 applies, for any period during which, apart from the provisions of those Regulations, he would be in receipt of that benefit; and
   (b) for any period spent by a claimant in undertaking a course of training or instruction provided or approved by the [¹² Secretary of State [⁶⁸ . . .]] under section 2 of the Employment and Training Act 1973 [¹¹, or by [⁶⁹ Skills Development Scotland,] Scottish Enterprise or Highlands and Islands Enterprise under section 2 of the Enterprise and New Towns (Scotland) Act 1990,] [⁷ or for any period during which he is in receipt of a training allowance].
   [¹⁰(2) For the purposes of the carer premium under paragraph 14ZA, a person shall be treated as being in receipt of [⁴⁹ carer's allowance] by virtue of sub-paragraph (1)(a) only if and for so long as the person in respect of whose care the allowance has been claimed remains in receipt of attendance allowance [¹⁵ , [⁷⁵ . . .] the care component of disability living allowance at the highest or middle rate prescribed in accordance with section 37ZB(3) of the Social Security Act [SSCBA, s.72(3)]] [⁸² , the care component of child disability payment at the highest or middle rate prescribed in accordance with the regulation 11(5) of the DACYP Regulations] [⁷⁵ or the daily living component of personal independence payment at the standard or enhanced rate in accordance with section 78(3) of the 2012 Act] [⁸³ , the daily living component of adult disability payment at the standard or enhanced rate in accordance with regulation 5 of the Disability Assistance for Working Age People (Scotland) Regulations 2022] [⁷⁶ or armed forces independence payment].]

Lone Parent Premium
2.612   **8.**—[²⁹ . . .].

[⁴² Bereavement Premium
2.613   **8A.**—[⁶⁷ . . .]]

[Pensioner premium for persons under 75
2.614   [⁵⁴ **9.**—The condition is that the claimant has a partner aged [⁷⁰ not less than the qualifying age for state pension credit] but less than 75.]

Pensioner premium for persons 75 and over
2.615   [⁵⁴ **9A.**—The condition is that the claimant has a partner aged not less than 75 but less than 80.]]

Higher Pensioner Premium
2.616   **10.**—[⁵⁴ (1) [⁶⁵ Subject to sub-paragraph (6), the] condition is that—
   (a) the claimant's partner is aged not less than 80; or
   (b) the claimant's partner is aged less than 80 but [⁷⁰ not less than the qualifying age for state pension credit] and either—
       (i) the additional condition specified in [⁵⁸ paragraph 12(1)(a), (c) or (d)] is satisfied; or
       (ii) the claimant was entitled to, or was treated as being in receipt of, income support and—
           (aa) the disability premium was or, as the case may be, would have been, applicable to him in respect of a benefit week within eight weeks of [⁷⁰ the day his partner attained the qualifying age for state pension credit]; and

(bb) he has, subject to sub-paragraph (3), remained continuously entitled to income support since his partner attained [⁷⁰ the qualifying age for state pension credit].]

(2) [. . .]

(3) For the purposes of this paragraph and paragraph 12—

  (a) once the higher pensioner premium is applicable to a claimant, if he then ceases, for a period of eight weeks or less, to be entitled to [⁴¹or treated as entitled to] income support, he shall, on becoming re-entitled to income support, thereafter be treated as having been continuously entitled thereto;

  (b) in so far as [⁵⁴ sub-paragraph (1)(b)(ii) is] concerned, if a claimant ceases to be entitled to [⁴¹or treated as entitled to] income support for a period not exceeding eight weeks which includes [⁷⁰ the day his partner attained the qualifying age for state pension credit], he shall, on becoming re-entitled to income support, thereafter be treated as having been continuously entitled thereto.

[³³ (4) In the case of a claimant who is a welfare to work beneficiary, references in sub-paragraphs (1)(b)(ii) [⁶⁵ . . .] and (3)(b) to a period of 8 weeks shall be treated as references to a period of [⁶⁴ 104 weeks].]

[⁴¹ (5) For the purposes of this paragraph, a claimant shall be treated as having been entitled to and in receipt of income support throughout any period which comprises only days on which he was participating in an employment zone programme and was not entitled to income support because, as a consequence of his participation in that programme, he was engaged in remunerative work or had income in excess of his applicable amount as prescribed in Part IV.]

[⁶⁵ (6) The condition is not satisfied if the claimant's partner to whom sub-paragraph (1) refers is a long-term patient.]

Disability Premium

11.—[⁶⁵ (1) Subject to sub-paragraph (2), the] condition is that—   **2.617**

  (a) where the claimant is a single claimant or a lone parent, [⁵⁴ . . .] the additional condition specified in paragraph 12 is satisfied; or

  (b) where the claimant has a partner, either—

    [⁵⁴ (i) the claimant satisfies the additional condition specified in paragraph [⁵⁸ 12(1) (a), (b), (c) or (d)]; or]

    (ii) his partner [⁷⁰ has not attained the qualifying age for state pension credit] and the additional condition specified in [⁵⁸ paragraph 12(1)(a), (c) or (d)] is satisfied by his partner.

[⁶⁵ (2) The condition is not satisfied if—

  (a) the claimant is a single claimant or a lone parent and (in either case) is a long-term patient;

  (b) the claimant is a member of a couple or polygamous marriage and each member of the couple or polygamous marriage is a long-term patient; or

  (c) the claimant is a member of a couple or a polygamous marriage and a member of that couple or polygamous marriage is—

    (i) a long-term patient; and

    (ii) the only member of the couple or polygamous marriage to whom sub-paragraph (1)(b) refers.]

Additional condition for the Higher Pensioner and Disability Premiums

12.—(1) Subject to sub-paragraph (2) and paragraph 7 the additional condition referred to   **2.618**
in paragraphs 10 and 11 is that either—

  (a) the claimant or, as the case may be, his partner—

    (i) is in receipt of one or more of the following benefits: attendance allowance, [¹⁵ disability living allowance, [⁷⁶ armed forces independence payment,] [⁷⁵ personal independence payment,] [⁸³ adult disability payment,] [⁵⁰ the disability element or the severe disability element of working tax credit as specified in regulation 20(1)(b) and (f) of the Working Tax Credit (Entitlement and Maximum Rate) Regulations 2002]], mobility supplement, [²⁵ long-term incapacity benefit] under [²² Part II of the Contributions and Benefits Act or severe disablement allowance under Part III of that Act] [¹but, in the case of [²⁵ long-term incapacity benefit] or severe disablement allowance only where it is paid in respect of him]; or

    (ii) is provided by the Secretary of State with an invalid carriage or other vehicle under section 5(2) of the National Health Service Act 1977 (other services) or, in Scotland, under section 46 of the National Health Service (Scotland) Act 1978 (provision of vehicles) or receives payments by way of grant from the Secretary of State under paragraph 2 of Schedule 2 to that 1977 Act (additional provisions as to vehicles) or, in Scotland, under that section 46; or

[77 (iii) is certified as severely sight impaired or blind by a consultant ophthalmologist; or]

[26 (b) the claimant—
    (i) is entitled to statutory sick pay or [27 is, or is treated as, incapable of work,] in accordance with the provisions of Part XIIA of the Contributions and Benefits Act and the regulations made thereunder (incapacity for work), and
    (ii) has been so entitled or so incapable [27, or has been treated as so incapable,] for a continuous period of not less than—
        (aa) 196 days in the case of a claimant who is terminally ill within the meaning of section 30B(4) of the Contributions and Benefits Act; or
        (bb) [63 subject to [65 paragraph 2A] of Schedule 7] 364 days in any other case; and for these purposes any two or more periods of entitlement or incapacity separated by a break of not more than 56 days shall be treated as one continuous period; or]

[54 (c) the claimant's partner was in receipt of long-term incapacity benefit under Part II of the Contributions and Benefits Act when entitlement to that benefit ceased on account of the payment of a retirement pension under that Act [81 or a state pension under Part 1 of the Pensions Act 2014] and—
    (i) the claimant has since remained continuously entitled to income support;
    (ii) the higher pensioner premium or disability premium has been applicable to the claimant; and
    (iii) the partner is still alive;
(d) except where paragraph [63 2A [65 . . .]] of Schedule 7 (patients) applies, the claimant or, as the case may be, his partner was in receipt of attendance allowance [75, disability living allowance [83, personal independence payment or adult disability payment]]—
    (i) but payment of that benefit has been suspended under the [60 Social Security (Attendance Allowance) Regulations 1991 [75, the Social Security (Disability Living Allowance) Regulations 1991 or regulations made under section 86(1) (hospital in-patients) of the 2012 Act]] or otherwise abated as a consequence of the claimant or his partner becoming a patient within the meaning of regulation 21(3); and
    (ii) a higher pensioner premium or disability premium has been applicable to the claimant.]

[34(1A) In the case of a claimant who is a welfare to work beneficiary, the reference in sub-paragraph (1)(b) to a period of 56 days shall be treated as a reference to a period of [64 104 weeks].]

[77 (2) For the purposes of sub-paragraph (1)(a)(iii), a person who has ceased to be certified as severely sight impaired or blind on regaining his eyesight shall nevertheless be treated as severely sight impaired or blind, as the case may be, and as satisfying the additional condition set out in that sub-paragraph for a period of 28 weeks following the date on which he ceased to be so certified.]

(3) [26 . . .]

(4) For the purpose of [58 sub-paragraph (1)(c) and (d)], once the higher pensioner premium is applicable to the claimant by virtue of his satisfying the condition specified in that provision, if he then ceases, for a period of eight weeks or less, to be entitled to income support, he shall on again becoming so entitled to income support, immediately thereafter be treated as satisfying the condition in [58 sub-paragraph (1)(c) and (d)].

[4(5) For the purposes of sub-paragraph (1)(b), once the disability premium is applicable to a claimant by virtue of his satisfying the additional condition specified in that provision, he shall continue to be treated as satisfying that condition for any period spent by him in undertaking a course of training provided under section 2 of the Employment and Training Act 1973 [7 or for any period during which he is in receipt of a training allowance].]

[25(6) For the purposes of [58 sub-paragraph (1)(a)(i) and (c)], a reference to a person in receipt of long-term incapacity benefit includes a person in receipt of short-term incapacity benefit at a rate equal to the long-term rate by virtue of section 30B(4)(a) of the Contributions and Benefits Act (short-term incapacity benefit for a person who is terminally ill), or who

would be or would have been in receipt of short-term incapacity benefit at such a rate but for the fact that the rate of short-term incapacity benefit already payable to him is or was equal to or greater than the long-term rate.]
[⁴⁰ [⁶¹ . . .]]

Severe Disability Premium
13.—(1) The condition is that the claimant is a severely disabled person.   2.619

(2) For the purposes of sub-paragraph (1), a claimant shall be treated as being a severely disabled person if, and only if—

    (a) in the case of a single claimant[¹⁹, a lone parent or a claimant who is treated as having no partner in consequence of sub-paragraph (2A)]—
        (i) he is in receipt of attendance allowance [¹⁵ [⁷⁵ . . .] the care component of disability living allowance at the highest or middle rate prescribed in accordance with section 37ZB(3) of the Social Security Act [SSCBA, s.72(3)]] [⁷⁵ or the daily living component of personal independence payment at the standard or enhanced rate in accordance with section 78(3) of the 2012 Act] [⁸³ , the daily living component of adult disability payment at the standard or enhanced rate in accordance with regulation 5 of the Disability Assistance for Working Age People (Scotland) Regulations 2022] [⁷⁶ or armed forces independence payment], and
       (ii) subject to sub-paragraph (3), he has no non-dependants aged 18 or over [²³ normally residing with him or with whom he is normally residing,] and
      (iii) [⁴¹ no person is entitled to, and in receipt of, [⁴⁹ a carer's allowance] under section 70 of the Contributions and Benefits Act [⁸⁰ or has an award of universal credit which includes the carer element] in respect of caring for him;]

    (b) [⁴² in the case of a claimant who] has a partner—
        (i) he is in receipt of attendance allowance [¹⁵, [⁷⁵ . . .] the care component of disability living allowance at the highest or middle rate prescribed in accordance with section 37ZB(3) of the Social Security Act [SSCBA, s.72(3)]] [⁷⁵ or the daily living component of personal independence payment at the standard or enhanced rate in accordance with section 78(3) of the 2012 Act] [⁸³ , the daily living component of adult disability payment at the standard or enhanced rate in accordance with regulation 5 of the Disability Assistance for Working Age People (Scotland) Regulations 2022] [⁷⁶ or armed forces independence payment]; and
       (ii) his partner is also in receipt of such an allowance or, if he is a member of a polygamous marriage, all the partners of that marriage are in receipt thereof; and
      (iii) subject to sub-paragraph (3), he has no non-dependants aged 18 or over [²³ normally residing with him or with whom he is normally residing,]
and either [⁴¹ a person is entitled to, and in receipt of, [⁴⁹ a carer's allowance] [⁸⁰ or has an award of universal credit which includes the carer element] in respect of caring for only one of the couple or, in the case of a polygamous marriage, for one or more but not all the partners of the marriage or, as the case may be, no person is entitled to, and in receipt of, such an allowance] [⁸⁰ or has such an award of universal credit] in respect of caring for either member of the couple or any partner of the polygamous marriage.

[¹⁹ (2A) Where a claimant has a partner who does not satisfy the condition in sub-paragraph (2)(b)(ii), and that partner is [⁷⁷ severely sight impaired or blind or treated as severely sight impaired or blind] within the meaning of paragraph 12(1)(a)(iii) and (2), that partner shall be treated for the purposes of sub-paragraph (2) as if he were not a partner of the claimant.]

(3) For the purposes of sub-paragraph (2)(a)(ii) and (2)(b)(iii) no account shall be taken of—

    (a) a person receiving attendance allowance [¹⁵, [⁷⁵ . . .] the care component of disability living allowance at the highest or middle rate prescribed in accordance with section 37ZB(3) of the Social Security Act [SSCBA, s.72(3)]] [⁷⁵ or the daily living component of personal independence payment at the standard or enhanced rate in accordance with section 78(3) of the 2012 Act] [⁸³ , the daily living component of adult disability payment at the standard or enhanced rate in accordance with regulation 5 of the Disability Assistance for Working Age People (Scotland) Regulations 2022] [⁷⁶ or armed forces independence payment]; or
    (b) [²¹ . . .]

(c) subject to sub-paragraph (4), a person who joins the claimant's household for the first time in order to care for the claimant or his partner and immediately before so joining the claimant or his partner was treated as a severely disabled person; [¹⁹ or (d) a person who is [⁷⁷ severely sight impaired or blind or treated as severely sight impaired or blind] within the meaning of paragraph 12(1)(a)(iii) and (2).]

[¹(3A) For the purposes of sub-paragraph (2)(b) a person shall be treated [⁴¹ . . .]

(a) [⁴¹ as being in receipt of] attendance allowance [¹⁵, or the care component of disability living allowance at the highest or middle rate prescribed in accordance with section 37ZB(3) of the Social Security Act [SSCBA, s.72(3)]] if he would, but for his being a patient for a period exceeding 28 days, be so in receipt;

(b) [⁴¹ as being entitled to and in receipt of [⁴⁹ a carer's allowance] [⁸⁰ or having an award of universal credit which includes the carer element] if he would, but for the person for whom he was caring being a patient in hospital for a period exceeding 28 days, be so entitled and in receipt [⁸⁰ of carer's allowance or have such an award of universal credit].]]

[⁷⁵ (c) as being in receipt of the daily living component of personal independence payment at the standard or enhanced rate in accordance with section 78(3) of the 2012 Act if he would, but for a suspension of benefit in accordance with regulations under section 86(1) (hospital in-patients) of the 2012 Act, be so in receipt [⁸³ ;

(d) as being in receipt of the daily living component of adult disability payment at the standard or enhanced rate in accordance with regulation 5 of the [⁸⁴ Disability Assistance for Working Age People (Scotland) Regulations 2022], if they would, but for regulation 28 (effect of admission to hospital on ongoing entitlement to Adult Disability Payment) of those Regulations, be so in receipt.]]

[²²(3ZA) For the purposes of sub-paragraph (2)(a)(iii) and (2)(b), no account shall be taken of an award of [⁴⁹ a carer's allowance] [⁸⁰ or universal credit which includes the carer element] to the extent that payment of such an award is back-dated for a period before [⁶⁶ the date on which the award is first paid].]

(4) Sub-paragraph (3)(c) shall apply only for the first 12 weeks following the date on which the person to whom that provision applies first joins the claimant's household.

[⁴⁵ (5) In sub-paragraph (2)(a)(iii) and (b), references to a person being in receipt of [⁴⁹ a carer's allowance] [⁸⁰ or as having an award of universal credit which includes the carer element] shall include references to a person who would have been in receipt of that allowance [⁸⁰ or had such an award] but for the application of a restriction under section [⁷² 6B or] 7 of the Social Security Fraud Act 2001 (loss of benefit provisions).]

[⁸⁰ (6) For the purposes of this paragraph, a person has an award of universal credit which includes the carer element if the person has an award of universal credit which includes an amount which is the carer element under regulation 29 of the Universal Credit Regulations 2013.]

[⁴³ **Enhanced disability premium**

2.620   **13A.**—[⁷⁵ ⁷⁶ (1) Subject to sub-paragraph (2), the condition is that—

(a) the claimant; or

(b) the claimant's partner, if any, who has not attained the qualifying age for state pension credit, is a person to whom sub-paragraph (1ZA) applies.

(1ZA) This sub-paragraph applies to the person mentioned in sub-paragraph (1) where—

(a) armed forces independence payment is payable to that person;

(b) the care component of disability living allowance is, or would, but for a suspension of benefit in accordance with regulations under section 113(2) of the Contributions and Benefits Act or but for an abatement as a consequence of hospitalization, be payable to that person at the highest rate prescribed under section 72(3) of that Act; [⁸² . . .

(ba) the care component of child disability payment is payable to that person at the highest rate in accordance with the DACYP Regulations (see regulation 11(5) of those Regulations); [⁸³ . . .]]

(c) the daily living component of personal independence payment is, or would, but for regulations made under section 86(1) (hospital in-patients) of the 2012 Act, be payable to that person at the enhanced rate in accordance with section 78(2) of that Act [⁸³]; or

(d) the daily living component of adult disability payment is, or would, but for regulation 28 (effect of admission to hospital on ongoing entitlement to Adult Disability Payment) of the [⁸⁴ Disability Assistance for Working Age People (Scotland) Regulations 2022], be payable to that person at the enhanced rate in accordance with regulation 5 of those Regulations.]]

[[73] (1A) Where the condition in sub-paragraph (1) ceases to be satisfied because of the death of a child or young person, the condition is that the claimant [[74] or partner] is entitled to child benefit in respect of that person under section 145A of the Contributions and Benefits Act (entitlement after death of child or qualifying young person).]

[[65] (2) The condition is not satisfied if the person to whom sub-paragraph (1) refers is—
  (a) [[50] . . .]
  (b) a single claimant or a lone parent and (in either case) is a long-term patient;
  (c) a member of a couple or polygamous marriage and each member of the couple or polygamous marriage is a long-term patient; or
  (d) a member of a couple or polygamous marriage who—
      (i) is a long-term patient; and
      (ii) is the only member of the couple or polygamous marriage to whom sub-paragraph (1) refers.]

Disabled Child Premium
14.—[[59] . . . [65]]   **2.621**

[[10] Carer premium
14ZA.—(1) [[13] Subject to sub-paragraphs (3) and (4),] the condition is that the claimant or   **2.622**
his partner is, or both of them are, [[41] entitled to [[49] a carer's allowance] under section 70 of the Contributions and Benefits Act]
(2) [[57] . . .]
[[41] [[48] (3) Where a carer premium is awarded but—
  (a) the person in respect of whose care the [[49] carer's allowance] has been awarded dies; or
  (b) in any other case the person in respect of whom a carer premium has been awarded ceases to be entitled [[57] . . .] to [[49] a carer's allowance], the condition for the award of the premium shall be treated as satisfied for a period of eight weeks from the relevant date specified in sub-paragraph (3A) below.
(3A) The relevant date for the purposes of sub-paragraph (3) above shall be—
  (a) [[57] where sub-paragraph (3)(a) applies,] the Sunday following the death of the person in respect of whose care [[49] a carer's allowance] has been awarded or the date of death if the death occurred on a Sunday;
  (b) [[57] . . .]
  (c) in any other case, the date on which the person who has been entitled to [[46] a carer's allowance] ceases to be entitled to that allowance.]
(4) Where a person who has been entitled to an invalid care allowance ceases to be entitled to that allowance and makes a claim for income support, the condition for the award of the carer premium shall be treated as satisfied for a period of eight weeks from the date on which—
[[48] (a) the person in respect of whose care the [[49] carer's allowance] has been awarded dies;
  (b) [[57] . . .]
[[57] (c) in any other case, the person who has been entitled to a carer's allowance ceased to be entitled to that allowance.]]]]

[[3] Persons in receipt of concessionary payments
14A.—For the purpose of determining whether a premium is applicable to a person [[12]   **2.623**
under paragraphs 12 to 14ZA], any concessionary payment made to compensate that person for the non-payment of any benefit mentioned in those paragraphs shall be treated as if it were a payment of that benefit.]

[[8] Person in receipt of benefit
14B.—For the purposes of this Part of this Schedule, a person shall be regarded as being in   **2.624**
receipt of any benefit if, and only if, it is paid in respect of him and shall be so regarded only for any period in respect of which that benefit is paid.]

WEEKLY AMOUNTS OF PREMIUMS SPECIFIED IN PART III

Column (1) Premium	Column (2) Amount
15.—(1) [²⁹ . . .] [⁴²(1A) [⁶⁷ . . .]] [⁵⁴(2) Pensioner premium for persons to whom paragraph 9 applies. (2A) Pensioner premium for persons to whom paragraph 9A applies. (3) Higher pensioner premium for persons to whom paragraph 10 applies.]	(1) [²⁹ . . .]. [⁴² (1A) [⁶⁷ . . .]] (2) [⁵⁴ . . .] (2A) [⁵⁴ . . .] (3) [⁵⁴ . . .]

(4) Disability Premium—
  (a) where the claimant satisfies the condition in [⁶⁵ paragraph 11(1)(a)];
  (b) where the claimant satisfies the condition in [⁶⁵ paragraph 11(1)(b)].
	(4)
	
	  (a) [⁸⁶ £39.85].
	  (b) [⁸⁶ £56.80].

(5) Severe Disability Premium—
  (a) where the claimant satisfies the condition in paragraph 13(2)(a);
  (b) where the claimant satisfies the condition in paragraph 13(2)(b).
    (i) if there is someone in receipt of [⁴⁹ a carer's allowance] or if he or any partner satisfies that condition only by virtue of paragraph 13(3A);
    (ii) if no-one is in receipt of such an allowance.
	(5)
	
	  (a) [⁸⁶ £76.40];
	
	  (b)
	
	    (i) [⁸⁶ £76.40];
	
	    (ii) [⁸⁶ £152.80];

(6) [⁵⁹ . . .]	(6) [⁵⁹ . . .]
(7) Carer Premium—	(7) [⁸⁶ £42.75] in respect of each person who satisfied the condition specified in paragraph 14ZA.]

[⁴³ (8) Enhanced disability premium where the conditions in paragraph 13A are satisfied—	(8)
	  (a) [⁵⁹ . . .]
	  (b) [⁸⁶ £19.55] in respect of each person who is neither—
	    (i) a child or young person; nor
	    (ii) a member of a couple or a polygamous marriage, in respect of whom the conditions specified in paragraph 13A are satisfied:
	  (c) [⁸⁶ £27.90] where the claimant is a member of a couple or a polygamous marriage and the conditions specified in paragraph 13A are satisfied in respect of a member of that couple or polygamous marriage.]

Income Support Regulations

PART V

ROUNDING OF FRACTIONS

16. Where income support is awarded for a period which is not a complete benefit week and   **2.626**
the applicable amount in respect of that period results in an amount which includes a fraction
of a penny that fraction shall be treated as a penny."

AMENDMENTS

1. Income Support (General) Amendment Regulations 1988 (SI 1988/663)
reg.29 (April 11, 1988).
2. Income Support (General) Amendment No. 3 Regulations 1988 (SI 1988/1228)
reg.9 (September 12, 1988).
3. Income Support (General) Amendment No. 4 Regulations 1988 (SI 1988/1445)
reg.19 (September 12, 1988).
4. Income Support (General) Amendment No. 5 Regulations 1988 (SI 1988/2022)
reg.17(*b*) (December 12, 1988).
5. Income Support (General) Amendment No. 5 Regulations 1988 (SI 1988/2022)
reg.17(*a*) (April 10, 1989).
6. Income Support (General) Amendment Regulations 1989 (SI 1989/534) reg.5
(October 9, 1989).
7. Income Support (General) Amendment No. 3 Regulations 1989 (SI 1989/1678)
reg.6 (October 9, 1989).
8. Income Support (General) Amendment Regulations 1990 (SI 1990/547)
reg.17 (April 9, 1990).
9. Income Support (General) Amendment No. 2 Regulations 1990 (SI 1990/1168)
reg.2 (July 2, 1990).
10. Income Support (General) Amendment No. 3 Regulations 1990 (SI
1990/1776) reg.8 (October 1, 1990).
11. Enterprise (Scotland) Consequential Amendments Order 1991 (SI
1991/3870) art.9 (April, 1991).
12. Income Support (General) Amendment Regulations 1991 (SI 1991/236)
reg.2 (April 8, 1991).
13. Income Support (General) Amendment No. 4 Regulations 1991 (SI 1991/236)
reg.15 (August 5, 1991).
14. Income Support (General) Amendment No. 4 Regulations 1991 (SI
1991/1559) reg.15 (October 7, 1991).
15. Disability Living Allowance and Disability Working Allowance (Consequential
Provisions) Regulations 1991 (SI 1991/2742) reg.11(4) (April 6, 1992).
16. Income Support (General) Amendment Regulations 1992 (SI 1992/468)
reg.6 (April 6, 1992).
17. Social Security Benefits (Amendments Consequential Upon the Introduction
of community Care) Regulations 1992 (SI 1992/3147) reg.2 (April 1, 1993).
18. Social Security Benefits (Miscellaneous Amendments) Regulations 1993 (SI
1993/518) reg.5 (April 1, 1993).
19. Income-related Benefits Schemes (Miscellaneous Amendments) (No. 2)
Regulations 1993 (SI 1993/1150) reg.3 (May 25, 1993).
[20.]
21. Income-related Benefits Schemes (Miscellaneous Amendments) (No. 4)
Regulations 1993 (SI 1993/2119) reg.18 (October 4, 1993).
22. Income-related Benefits Schemes (Miscellaneous Amendments) (No. 5)
Regulations 1994 (SI 1994/2139) reg.30 (October 3, 1994).
23. Income-related Benefits Schemes (Miscellaneous Amendments) (No. 6)
Regulations 1994 (SI 1994/3061) reg.2(3) (December 2, 1994).
24. Income-related Benefits Schemes (Miscellaneous Amendments) Regulations
1995 (SI 1995/516) reg.24 (April 10, 1995).

25. Disability Working Allowance and Income Support (General) Amendment Regulations 1995 (SI 1995/482) reg.16 (April 13, 1995).
26. Disability Working Allowance and Income Support (General) Amendment Regulations 1995 (SI 1995/482) reg.17 (April 13, 1995).
27. Income-related Benefits Schemes and Social Security (Claims and Payments) (Miscellaneous Amendments) Regulations 1995 (SI 1995/2303) reg.6(8) (October 2, 1995).
28. Income Support (General) (Jobseeker's Allowance Consequential Amendments) Regulations 1996 (SI 1996/206) reg.23 and Sch.2 (October 7, 1996).
29. Child Benefit, Child Support and Social Security (Miscellaneous Amendments) Regulations 1996 (SI 1996/1803) reg.39 (April 7, 1997).
30. Income-related Benefits and Jobseeker's Allowance (Personal Allowances for Children and Young Persons) (Amendment) Regulations 1996 (SI 1996/2545) reg.2 (April 7, 1997).
31. Income-related Benefits and Jobseeker's Allowance (Amendment) (No. 2) Regulations 1997 (SI 1997/2197) regs 7(5) and (6)(a) (October 6, 1997).
32. Social Security Amendment (Lone Parents) Regulations 1998 (SI 1998/766) reg.12 (April 6, 1998).
33. Social Security (Welfare to Work) Regulations 1998 (SI 1998/2231) reg.13(3)(a) (October 5, 1998).
34. Social Security (Welfare to Work) Regulations 1998 (SI 1998/2231) reg.13(3)(b) (October 5, 1998).
35. Social Security Benefits Up-rating Order 1999 (SI 1999/264) art.18(3) and Sch.4 (April 12, 1999).
36. Social Security Benefits Up-rating Order 1999 (SI 1999/264) art.18(4)(b) (April 12, 1999).
37. Social Security Benefits Up-rating Order 1999 (SI 1999/264) art.18(5) and Sch.5 (April 12, 1999).
38. Social Security Amendment (Personal Allowances for Children and Young Persons) Regulations 1999 (SI 1999/2555) reg.2(1)(b) and (2)(April 10, 2000).
39. Social Security and Child Support (Tax Credits) Consequential Amendments Regulations 1999 (SI 1999/2566) reg.2(2) and Sch.2 Pt II (October 5, 1999).
40. Social Security (Miscellaneous Amendments) (No. 2) Regulations 1999 (SI 1999/2556) reg.2(8) (October 4, 1999).
41. Social Security (Miscellaneous Amendments) Regulations 2000 (SI 2000/681) reg.4 (April 3, 2000).
42. Social Security Amendment (Bereavement Benefits) Regulations 2000 (SI 2000/2239) reg.2(3) (April 9, 2001).
43. Social Security Amendment (Enhanced Disability Premium) Regulations 2000 (SI 2629) reg.2(c) (April 9, 2001).
44. Social Security Amendment (Residential Care and Nursing Homes) Regulations 2001 (SI 2001/3767) reg.2 and Sch. Pt I para.14 (April 8, 2002).
45. Social Security (Loss of Benefit) (Consequential Amendments) Regulations 2002 (SI 2002/490) reg.2 (April 1, 2002).
46. Social Security Amendment (Residential Care and Nursing Homes) Regulations 2001 (SI 2001/3767) reg.2 and Sch. Pt I para.14 (as amended by Social Security Amendment (Residential Care and Nursing Homes) Regulations 2002 (SI 2002/398) reg.4(2)) (April 8, 2002).
47. Social Security Amendment (Personal Allowances for Children and Young Persons) Regulations 2002 (SI 2002/2019) reg.2 (October 14, 2002).
48. Social Security Amendment (Carer Premium) Regulations 2002 (SI 2002/2020) reg.2 (October 28, 2002).
49. Social Security Amendment (Carer's allowance) Regulations 2002 (SI 2002/2497) reg.3 and Sch.2 (April 1, 2003).
50. Social Security (Working Tax Credit and Child Tax Credit) (Consequential Amendments) Regulations 2003 (SI 2003/455) regs 1(5) and 2 and Sch.1 para.20(b) (April 7, 2003).

51. Social Security Benefits Up-Rating Order 2003 (SI 2003/526) art.17(3) and Sch.2 (April 7, 2003).

52. Social Security Benefits Up-Rating Order 2003 (SI 2003/526) art.17(5) and Sch.3 (April 7, 2003).

53. Social Security Benefits Up-Rating Order 2003 (SI 2003/526) art.17(4) (April 7, 2003).

54. State Pension Credit (Consequential, Transitional and Miscellaneous Provisions) Regulations 2002 (SI 2002/3019) reg.29(5) (October 6, 2003).

55. Social Security (Removal of Residential Allowance and Miscellaneous Amendments) Regulations 2003 (SI 2003/1121) reg.2 and Sch.1 para.6 (October 6, 2003).

56. Social Security (Hospital In-Patients and Miscellaneous Amendments) Regulations 2003 (SI 2003/1195) reg.3 (May 21, 2003).

57. Social Security (Miscellaneous Amendments) (No. 2) Regulations 2003 (SI 2003/2279) reg.2(3) (October 1, 2003).

58. Income Support (General) Amendment Regulations 2003 (SI 2003/2379) reg.2 (October 6, 2003).

59. Social Security (Working Tax Credit and Child Tax Credit) (Consequential Amendments) Regulations 2003 (SI 2003/455) reg.2 and Sch.1 para.20 (April 6, 2004, except in "transitional cases" and see further the note to reg.17 of the Income Support Regulations).

60. Social Security (Miscellaneous Amendments) (No. 2) Regulations 2004 (SI 2004/1141) reg.6 (May 12, 2004).

61. Social Security (Back to Work Bonus and Lone Parent Run-on) (Amendment and Revocation) Regulations 2003 (SI 2003/1589) reg.2(d) (October 25, 2004).

62. Civil Partnership (Pensions, Social Security and Child Support) (Consequential, etc. Provisions) Order 2005 (SI 2005/2877) art.2(3) and Sch.3 para.13(3) (December 5, 2005).

63. Social Security (Hospital In-Patients) Regulations 2005 (SI 2005/3360) reg.4 (April 10, 2006).

64. Social Security (Miscellaneous Amendments) (No. 4) Regulations 2006 (SI 2006/2378) reg.5(7) (October 2, 2006).

65. Social Security (Miscellaneous Amendments) Regulations 2007 (SI 2007/719) reg.2(7) (April 9, 2007). As it relates to paras 13A(2)(a) and 14, the amendment only affects "transitional cases". See further the note to reg.17 of the Income Support Regulations and the commentary below.

66. Social Security (Miscellaneous Amendments) Regulations 2007 (SI 2007/719) reg.2(7)(e) (April 2, 2007).

67. Social Security (Miscellaneous Amendments) (No. 5) Regulations 2007 (SI 2007/2618) reg.2 and Sch. (October 1, 2007).

68. Social Security (Miscellaneous Amendments) Regulations 2008 (SI 2008/698) reg.2(12) (April 14, 2008).

69. Social Security (Miscellaneous Amendments) Regulations 2009 (SI 2009/583) reg.2(1) and (3) (April 6, 2009).

70. Social Security (Equalisation of State Pension Age) Regulations 2009 (SI 2009/1488) reg.3 (April 6, 2010).

71. Social Security (Miscellaneous Amendments) (No. 2) Regulations 2010 (SI 2010/641) reg.2(1) and (9) (April 13, 2010).

72. Social Security (Loss of Benefit) Amendment Regulations 2010 (SI 2010/1160) reg.10(1) and (3) (April 1, 2010).

73. Social Security (Miscellaneous Amendments) Regulations 2011 (SI 2011/674) reg.3(5) (April 11, 2011).

74. Social Security (Miscellaneous Amendments) (No. 3) Regulations 2011 (SI 2011/2425) reg.7(1) and (7) (October 31, 2011).

75. Personal Independence Payment (Supplementary Provisions and Consequential Amendments) Regulations 2013 (SI 2013/388) reg.8 and Sch. para.11(1) and (5) (April 8, 2013).

76. Armed Forces and Reserve Forces Compensation Scheme (Consequential Provisions: Subordinate Legislation) Order 2013 (SI 2013/591) art.7 and Sch. para.4(1) and (5) (April 8, 2013).
77. Universal Credit and Miscellaneous Amendments (No. 2) Regulations 2014 (SI 2014/2888) reg.3(2)(a) (November 26, 2014).
78. Welfare Benefits Up-rating Order 2015 (SI 2015/30) art.6 and Sch.1 (April 6, 2015).
79. Social Security Benefits Up-rating Order 2015 (SI 2015/457) art.14(5) and Sch.3 (April 6, 2015).
80. Universal Credit and Miscellaneous Amendments Regulations 2015 (SI 2015/1754) reg.14 (October 28, 2015).
81. Pensions Act 2014 (Consequential, Supplementary and Incidental Amendments) Order 2015 (SI 2015/1985) art.8(1) and (3) (April 6, 2016).
82. Social Security (Scotland) Act 2018 (Disability Assistance for Children and Young People) (Consequential Modifications) Order 2021 (SI 2021/786) Sch.1 para.5 (July 26, 2021).
83. Social Security (Disability Assistance for Working Age People) (Consequential Amendments) Order 2022 (SI 2022/177) art.2(6) (March 21, 2022).
84. Social Security (Disability Assistance for Working Age People) (Consequential Amendments) (No. 2) Order 2022 (SI 2022/530) art.2(2) (June 6, 2022).
85. Social Security Benefits Up-rating Order 2023 (SI 2023/316) art.21(1) and (3) and Sch.2 (April 10, 2023).
86. Social Security Benefits Up-rating Order 2023 (SI 2023/316) art.21(1) and (5) and Sch.3 (April 10, 2023).

DEFINITIONS

"adult disability payment"—see reg.2(1).
"attendance allowance"—*ibid.*
"benefit week"—*ibid.*
"child"—see SSCBA s.137(1).
"child disability payment"—see reg.2(1).
"claimant"—*ibid.*
"close relative"—*ibid.*
"couple"—*ibid.*
"the DACYP Regulations"—*ibid.*
"disability living allowance"—*ibid.*
"family"—see SSCBA s.137(1).
"invalid carriage or other vehicle"—see reg.2(1).
"lone parent"—*ibid.*
"mobility supplement"—*ibid.*
"non-dependent"—see reg.3.
"partner"—see reg.2(1).
"personal independence payment"—*ibid.*
"polygamous marriage"—*ibid.*
"preserved right"—see reg.2(1) and reg.19.
"single claimant"—see reg.2(1).
"Social Security Act"—*ibid.*
"welfare to work beneficiary"—*ibid.*
"young person"—*ibid.*, reg.14.
For the General Note to Sch.2, see Vol.V paras 2.627–2.650.

p.605, *amendments to the Income Support (General) Regulations 1987 (SI 1987/1967) Sch.3 para.18 (Housing costs—non-dependant deductions)*

5.029   With effect from April 10, 2023, art.21 of the Social Security Benefits Up-rating Order 2023 (SI 2023/316) makes the following amendments:

- in sub-para.(1)(a) for "£102.85" substitute "£115.75";
- in sub-para.(1)(b) for "£15.95" substitute "£18.10";
- in sub-para.(2)(a) for "£149.00" substitute "£162.00";
- in sub-para.(2)(b):
    (i) for "£35.65" substitute "£41.60";
    (ii) for "£149.00" substitute "£162.00"; and
    (iii) for "£217.00" substitute "£235.00";

- in sub-para.(2)(c):
    (i) for "£50.30" substitute "£57.10";
    (ii) for "£217.00" substitute "£235.00"; and
    (iii) for "£283.00" substitute "£308.00";

- in sub-para.(2)(d):
    (i) for "£82.30" substitute "£93.40";
    (ii) for "£283.00" substitute "£308.00"; and
    (iii) for "£377.00" substitute "£410.00"; and

- in sub-para.(2)(e):
    (i) for "£93.70" substitute "£105.35";
    (ii) for "£377.00" substitute "£410.00"; and
    (iii) for "£469.00" substitute "£511.00".

p.606, *amendments to the Income Support (General) Regulations 1987 (SI 1987/1967) Sch.3 para.18 (Housing costs—non-dependant deductions)*

With effect from July 26, 2021, para.6 of Sch.1 to the Social Security (Scotland) Act 2018 (Disability Assistance for Children and Young People) (Consequential Modifications) Order 2021 (SI 2021/786) inserts into sub-paragraph (6)(b), after paragraph (ii), "(iia) the care component of child disability payment;" and inserts into sub-paragraph (8)(a), after "disability living allowance", ", child disability payment". 5.030

With effect from January 1, 2022, reg.2(6) of the Social Security (Income and Capital Disregards) (Amendment) Regulations 2021 (SI 2021/1405) inserts into para.18(8)(b), after "Grenfell Tower payment", ", child abuse payment or Windrush payment".

With effect from March 21, 2022, art.2(7) of the Social Security (Disability Assistance for Working Age People) (Consequential Amendments) Order 2022 (SI 2022/177) makes the following amendments:

in para.18(6)(b)(iii) omit "or" at the end;
after para.18(6)(b)(iii) insert "(iiia) the daily living component of adult disability payment; or"; and
in para.18(8)(a), for "or personal independence payment" substitute ", personal independence payment, adult disability payment".

p.642, *amendments to the Income Support (General) Regulations 1987 (SI 1987/1967) Sch.9 paras 6 and 9 (Sums to be disregarded in the calculation of income other than earnings—mobility component and AA, care component and daily living component)*

With effect from March 21, 2022, art.2(8)(a) of the Social Security (Disability Assistance for Working Age People) (Consequential Amendments) Order 2022 (SI 2022/177) amended para.6 to read as 5.031

follows (square brackets indicate only the present amendment, those indicating previous amendments having been omitted):

"**6.**—The mobility component of disability living allowance[,] the mobility component of personal independence payment [or the mobility component of adult disability payment]."

With effect from March 21, 2022, art.2(8)(b) of the same Order amended para.9 to read as follows (square brackets indicate only the present amendment, those indicating previous amendments having been omitted):

"**9.**—Any attendance allowance, the care component of disability living allowance[,] the daily living component of personal independence payment [or the daily living component of adult disability payment]."

"Adult disability payment" is defined in reg.2(1) by reference to reg.2 of the Disability Assistance for Working Age People (Scotland) Regulations 2022 (SSI 2022/54) (see Vol.IV of this series).

p.644, *amendment to the Income Support (General) Regulations 1987 (SI 1987/1967) Sch.9 para.21(2) (Sums to be disregarded in the calculation of income other than earnings—income in kind)*

5.032   With effect from January 1, 2022, reg.2(7)(a) of the Social Security (Income and Capital Disregards) (Amendment) Regulations 2021 (SI 2021/1405) amended sub-para.(2) by inserting ", a child abuse payment or a Windrush payment" after "Grenfell Tower payment". All of those payments are defined in reg.2(1). See the entry for p.684 for discussion of the nature of child abuse and Windrush payments.

p.646, *amendment to the Income Support (General) Regulations 1987 (SI 1987/1967) Sch.9 para.27(da) (Sums to be disregarded in the calculation of income other than earnings—payments for persons temporarily in care of claimant)*

5.033   With effect from July 1, 2022, reg.99 of and Sch. to the Health and Care Act 2022 (Consequential and Related Amendments and Transitional Provisions) Regulations 2022 (SI 2022/634) amended para.27(da) by substituting the following for the text after "(da)":

"an integrated care board established under Chapter A3 of Part 2 of the National Health Service Act 2006;"

p.648, *amendment to the Income Support (General) Regulations 1987 (SI 1987/1967) Sch.9 para.39(1A) (Sums to be disregarded in the calculation of income other than earnings)*

5.034   With effect from January 1, 2022, reg.2(7)(b) of the Social Security (Income and Capital Disregards) (Amendment) Regulations 2021 (SI 2021/1405) amended para.39 by substituting the following for sub-para.(1A):

"(1A) Any—
(a)   Grenfell Tower payment;
(b)   child abuse payment;
(c)   Windrush payment."

In addition, reg.2(7)(c) amended sub-paras (2) to (6) by inserting ", a child abuse payment or a Windrush payment" after "Grenfell Tower payment" in each place where those words occur. All of those payments are defined in reg.2(1).

See the entry for p.684 (Sch.10 (Capital to be disregarded) para.22) for some technical problems arising from the date of effect of these amendments. Because all the payments so far made from the approved historic institutional child abuse schemes and from the Windrush Compensation Scheme have been in the nature of capital, the question of disregarding income has not yet arisen.

p.665, *annotations to the Income Support (General) Regulations 1987 (SI 1987/1967) Sch.9 paras 6 and 9 (Sums to be disregarded in the calculation of income other than earnings—mobility component and AA, care component and daily living component)*

Note the amendments to paras 6 and 9 on p.642 to take account of the introduction of Scottish adult disability payment (see Vol.IV of this series).   5.035

p.676, *annotation to the Income Support (General) Regulations 1987 (SI 1987/1967) Sch.9 para.34 (Sums to be disregarded in the calculation of income other than earnings—payments by trade unions during trade disputes)*

The relevant sum was increased to £47 with effect from April 10, 2023 (see the entries for pp.15 and 18).   5.036

p.677, *annotation to the Income Support (General) Regulations 1987 (SI 1987/1967) Sch.9 para.39 (Sums to be disregarded in the calculation of income other than earnings—payments from certain funds)*

See the entries for pp.648 and 684 for the extension in a new sub-para. (1A) of the funds covered to child abuse compensation payments from certain schemes and to payments under the Windrush Compensation Scheme.   5.037

p.682, *amendment to the Income Support (General) Regulations 1987 (SI 1987/1967) Sch.10 para.7A (Capital to be disregarded—widowed parent's allowance)*

With effect from February 9, 2023, para.1(a) of the Schedule to the Bereavement Benefits (Remedial) Order 2023 (SI 2023/134) inserted the following after para.7 of Sch.10:   5.038

"7A. Any payment of a widowed parent's allowance made pursuant to section 39A of the Contributions and Benefits Act (widowed parent's allowance)—
(a)   to the survivor of a cohabiting partnership (within the meaning in section 39A(7) of the Contributions and Benefits Act) who is entitled to a widowed parent's allowance for a period before the Bereavement Benefits (Remedial) Order 2023 comes into force, and

(b)   in respect of any period of time during the period ending with the
        day before the survivor makes the claim for a widowed parent's
        allowance,
but only for a period of 52 weeks from the date of receipt of the
payment."

The legislation on widowed parent's allowance (WPA), and bereavement
support payment (BSP) that replaced it for deaths after April 5, 2017, was
declared incompatible with the ECHR by discriminating against children
whose parents were cohabiting but not married to each other or in a civil
partnership (see *Re McLaughlin's Application for Judicial Review* [2018]
UKSC 48; [2018] 1 W.L.R. 4250 and *R(Jackson) v Secretary of State for
Work and Pensions* [2020] EWHC 183 (Admin); [2020] 1 W.L.R. 1441 in
Vol.I of this series). The Remedial Order allows retrospective claims to be
made for those benefits from August 30, 2018 onwards and accordingly for
arrears of benefit to be paid if the conditions of entitlement are met. The
new para.7A, and the amended para.72 on BSP, deal with the consequences
of such payments on income support entitlement, although with somewhat
differing outcomes.

The Explanatory Memorandum misleadingly asserts in para.7.15 that
the Remedial Order provides for payments of arrears under the Order to
be treated as capital and disregarded for the purposes of income-related
benefits, in line with assurances that had been given by the government to
the Joint Committee on Human Rights and in its response to public consultation on a draft of the Order (see *Draft Bereavement Benefits (Remedial
Order 2022: Second Report* (HC 834, HL Paper 108) (December 6, 2022),
para.61). However, it is absolutely plain that the amendments made by the
Order do nothing to deem any payment of arrears to be capital. The new
provisions like para.7A merely provide for a disregard of the payment for
52 weeks in so far as it is properly to be regarded as capital. It has been
firmly established at least since the decision in *R(SB) 4/89* (see para.2.245
of the 2021/22 main volume) that cumulative arrears of social security
benefits that would have been income if paid on time retain their nature
as income though paid as a lump sum. Then, as a result of regs 29 and 31
the periodical payments are to be treated for income support purposes as
paid on the date on which they were due to be paid (i.e. in the past) for
the payment period starting with that date. Thus, if a claimant receiving a
sum of arrears of WPA had been in receipt of income support (or another
"legacy" income-related benefit) for some part of the period to which the
WPA is properly to be attributed as income (subject to the £10 per week
disregard under Sch.9 para.16(h)) that would trigger the Secretary of
State's power to revise the decision(s) awarding income support (Social
Security and Child Support (Decisions and Appeals) Regulations 1999
(SI 1999/991) reg.3(7) and SSA 1998 s.9(3) in Vol.III of this series) and,
if exercised, the creation of an overpayment that would be recoverable
under the SSAA s.74, either by abatement of the amount payable by way
of arrears of WPA or, if that was not exercised by recovery from the claimant.

That that is the legal position was effectively conceded by Viscount
Younger, the Minister for Work and Pensions in the House of Lords, in a
letter of February 2, 2023 to Baroness Sherlock (deposited in the Library
of the House of Lords), in which he said this:

"It is right that usual rules apply in these cases, to ensure that we don't treat cohabitee claimants differently to those claimants who were in a legal union with the deceased. WPA is taken into account as income when assessing entitlement to other means-tested benefits. Where a claimant was in receipt of a legacy income-related benefit during the period of entitlement for WPA, we will offset any overpayment of the relevant benefit from the retrospective lump sum of WPA and pay a net WPA award. Where a claimant was in receipt of Universal Credit during the period of WPA entitlement, the claimant may incur an overpayment of Universal Credit as a consequence of receiving a retrospective WPA award. We will make this clear to claimants, so that they are able to make an informed choice about making a claim."

The Explanatory Memorandum appears not so far to have been corrected and DMG Memo 2/23 makes no mention of this issue.

There remains something for the new para.7A to bite on. Because of the £10 weekly disregard, even if the abatement process is applied over the entire period to which the arrears of WPA are attributed, there will be some amount of arrears payable, which according to accepted principle would metamorphose from income into capital at the end of the period to which it is properly attributable as income (see *R(IS) 3/93* and paras 2.208 and 2.209 of the 2020/21 main volume). Such capital is to be disregarded for 52 weeks, as would capital deriving from weeks in the past in which no income-related benefit was in payment. If the abatement process had been available but did not take place, it is arguable that the arrears of income would only metamorphose into capital after deduction of the liability to recovery of the overpayment (*R(SB) 2/83* and *R(SB) 35/83*).

Note that the outcome for BSP (see the amendment to para.72) is different because BSP is disregarded entirely as income for income support purposes (Sch.9 para.80).

p.684, *amendment to the Income Support (General) Regulations 1987 (SI 1987/1967) Sch.10 para.22 (Capital to be disregarded)*

With effect from January 1, 2022, reg.2(8)(a) of the Social Security (Income and Capital Disregards) (Amendment) Regulations 2021 (SI 2021/1405) amended sub-para.(1A) by inserting ", child abuse payment, Windrush payment" after "Grenfell Tower payment" and amended sub-paras (2) to (6) by inserting ", a child abuse payment or a Windrush payment" after "Grenfell Tower payment" in each place where those words occur. All of those payments are defined in reg.2(1).   5.039

There are some technical problems with the addition only with effect from January 1, 2022 of the disregards of payments from approved schemes providing compensation in respect of historic institutional child abuse in the UK (para.(1)(a)(vii)) and from the Windrush Compensation Scheme. All the schemes so far in existence provide payments in the nature of capital.

The Explanatory Memorandum to the amending regulations reveals that four child abuse compensation schemes had been approved by the Secretary of State as at January 1, 2022: under the Historical Institutional Abuse (Northern Ireland) Act 2019; under the Redress for Survivors (Historical Child Abuse in Care) (Scotland) Act 2021; the London Borough of Lambeth Redress Scheme and the London Borough of Islington's proposed support payment scheme. All provide one-off capital payments. The Memorandum also reveals that payments under the Northern Ireland and Lambeth schemes could have been made prior to January 1, 2022. The application of the disregards provided under SI 2021/1405 to such pre-January 2022 payments has been authorised by a ministerial direction from the Secretary of State, acting under "common law powers" (see the letters of December 3, 2021 between the Permanent Secretary and the Secretary of State, published on the internet). The Windrush Compensation Scheme has also been making payments for some time. The correspondence above states that extra-statutory arrangements agreed with HM Treasury provided for the disregard in practice of such payments in means-tested benefits from the outset. It might be thought that the delay in putting that outcome on a proper statutory basis is symptomatic of the way in which the victims of that scandal have been treated.

Those arrangements raise questions as to what a tribunal on appeal should do if it has evidence of receipt prior to January 1, 2022 of a payment that would have been disregarded under the amendments if it had been received on or after that date. The legislation that a tribunal is bound to apply would not allow a disregard of such a payment unless it fell within an existing "personal injury" disregard in para.12 or 12A (possible for some historic institutional child abuse payments, though not for payments to next of kin or those who had merely been in "harm's way" or for Windrush Compensation Scheme payments). However, if an express submission from the DWP recorded the practical result of the application of the disregard either on the basis of a ministerial direction or an extra-statutory arrangement, it would appear that the issue of the treatment of the payment would not arise on the appeal (see SSA 1998 s.12(8)(a)) and it is submitted that it would then be irrational for the tribunal to exercise its discretion to consider the issue nonetheless. If evidence of a payment that had not been taken into account as capital emerged in the course of an appeal, but there was no express DWP submission to explain that outcome, it is submitted that a tribunal with knowledge of the matters mentioned above could still legitimately conclude that the issue did not arise on the appeal and decline to exercise its discretion under s.12(8)(a). Memo DMG 15/21 on the effect of the amendment to Sch.10 says nothing about these questions, although it does name the currently approved historic institutional child abuse schemes and give the date of approval (December 10, 2021).

p.685, *amendment to the Income Support (General) Regulations 1987 (SI 1987/1967) Sch.10 para.29 (Capital to be disregarded—payments in kind)*

5.040   With effect from January 1, 2022, reg.2(8)(b) of the Social Security (Income and Capital Disregards) (Amendment) Regulations 2021 (SI 2021/1405) amended para.29 by inserting ", child abuse payment or Windrush payment" after "Grenfell Tower payment". All of those payments are defined in reg.2(1). See also the entry for p.684.

p.689, *amendment to the Income Support (General) Regulations 1987 (SI 1987/1967) Sch.10 para.72 (Capital to be disregarded—bereavement support payment)*

5.041   With effect from February 9, 2023, para.1(b) of the Schedule to the Bereavement Benefits (Remedial) Order 2023 (SI 2023/134) amended para.72 by making the existing text sub-para.(1) and inserting the following:

"(2) Where bereavement support payment under section 30 of the Pensions Act 2014 is paid to the survivor of a cohabiting partnership (within the meaning in section 30(6B) of the Pensions Act 2014) in respect of a death occurring before the day the Bereavement Benefits (Remedial) Order 2023 comes into force, any amount of that payment which is—
(a)   in respect of the rate set out in regulation 3(1) of the Bereavement Support Payment Regulations 2017, and
(b)   paid as a lump sum for more than one monthly recurrence of the day of the month on which their cohabiting partner died,
but only for a period of 52 weeks from the date of receipt of the payment."

See the entry for p.682 for the general background. The operation of this amendment is much more straightforward than that of the new para.7A on widowed parent's allowance. Although a payment of arrears of bereavement support payment (BSP) is in its nature a payment of income and attributable to the past period in respect of which it is due, the payment could not affect any entitlement to income support in that past period because it would be disregarded entirely as income (Sch.9 para.80). The amount of the arrears would thus immediately metamorphose into capital, which would then be disregarded under para.72(2) subject to the 52 week limit.

p.695, *annotation to the Income Support (General) Regulations 1987 (SI 1987/1967) Sch.10 (Capital to be disregarded)*

In the list of categories of disregards of capital, insert the following between the entry for para.7 and the entry for para.8:   5.042

"*Para.7A*   Arrears of widowed parent's allowance;"

p.697, *annotation to the Income Support (General) Regulations 1987 (SI 1987/1967) Sch.10 (Capital to be disregarded)*

With effect from June 28, 2022 "Cost of living payments" under the Social Security (Additional Payments) Act 2022 (see Part I of Vol.II of this series), both those to recipients of specified means-tested benefits and "disability" payments, are not to be taken into account for any income support purposes by virtue of s.8(b) of the Act. The same effect was achieved with effect from March 23, 2023 in relation to payments under the Social Security (Additional Payments) Act 2023 (s.8(b) of that Act). See Pt I of Vol.II for the text of both Acts.   5.043

p.709, *annotation to the Income Support (General) Regulations 1987 (SI 1987/1967) Sch.10 para.7A (Capital to be disregarded—arrears of widowed parent's allowance)*

Insert the following before the note to para.8:

"*Paragraph 7A*   5.044
This new disregard as capital of arrears of widowed parent's allowance was introduced with effect from February 9, 2023. See the entry for p.682 for the text and discussion of its effect."

p.711, *annotation to the Income Support (General) Regulations 1987 (SI 1987/1967) Sch.10 para.12 (Capital to be disregarded—trusts derived from payments made in consequence of personal injury)*

5.045   Note that *R(IS) 15/96*, mentioned in para.2.819, holds that payments made under the Criminal Injuries Compensation Scheme are in consequence of personal injury.

p.714, *annotation to the Income Support (General) Regulations 1987 (SI 1987/1967) Sch.10 para.18A (Capital to be disregarded—local welfare provision)*

5.046   There has been no specific provision made under Sch.10 (or the equivalent old style ESA or JSA provisions) to disregard 2022 Energy Rebate Scheme payments as capital, as has been done for universal credit in the Universal Credit (Energy Rebate Scheme Disregard) Regulations 2022 (SI 2022/257) (see Pt II of Vol.II). That is because the payments to be administered by local authorities (the £150 council tax rebate for properties in bands A–D and under the discretionary scheme for the vulnerable) are considered already to be covered by para.18A.

p.721, *annotation to the Income Support (General) Regulations 1987 (SI 1987/1967) Sch.10 para.72 (Capital to be disregarded—bereavement support payments)*

5.047   See the entry for p.689 for the text of the amendment with effect from February 9, 2023 extending this disregard to arrears of payments made under the Bereavement Benefits (Remedial) Order 2023 (SI 2023/134) and discussion of its effect.

p.742, *amendment to the Fines (Deductions from Income Support) Regulations 1992 (SI 1992/2182) reg.4 (Deductions from offender's income support, universal credit, state pension credit or jobseeker's allowance)*

5.048   With effect from October 29, 2021, reg.2 of the Fines (Deductions from Income Support) (Miscellaneous Amendments) Regulations 2021 (SI 2021/1077) substitutes a new reg.4(1B):

"(1B) The amount that may be deducted under paragraph (1A) is 5 per cent. of the appropriate universal credit standard allowance for the offender for the assessment period in question, as specified under regulation 36 of the UC Regulations."

This amendment follows the decision of Kerr J in *R. (Blundell) v SSWP* [2021] EWHC 608 (Admin); [2021] P.T.S.R. 1342, where the Secretary of State's policy on deductions was found to be unlawfully fettering her discretion about the amount to deduct under reg.4(1B). The new regulation removes that discretion, by limiting deductions to the smallest amount which could previously have been deducted.

PART III

OLD STYLE JOBSEEKER'S ALLOWANCE REGULATIONS

p.787, *annotation to the Jobseeker's Allowance Regulations 1996 (SI 1996/207)*

Insert the following text at the end of the GENERAL NOTE as a new paragraph:

5.049

Note that after July 25, 2022, there are no longer any circumstances in which it is possible to make a new claim for old style JSA: see the entry for p.33.

p.787, *amendments to the Jobseeker's Allowance Regulations 1996 (SI 1996/207), reg.1 (Citation, commencement, interpretation and application)*

With effect from July 26, 2021, Sch.3 para.2 of the Social Security (Scotland) Act 2018 (Disability Assistance for Children and Young People) (Consequential Modifications) Order 2021 (SI 2021/786) inserts the following definitions:

5.050

"child disability payment" has the meaning given in regulation 2 of the DACYP Regulations;
"DACYP Regulations" means the Disability Assistance for Children and Young People (Scotland) Regulations 2021;

With effect from January 1, 2022, reg.3(2) of the Social Security (Income and Capital Disregards) (Amendment) Regulations 2021 (SI 2021/1405) inserts the following definitions:

"child abuse payment" means a payment from a scheme established or approved by the Secretary of State for the purpose of providing compensation in respect of historic institutional child abuse in the United Kingdom;"
"Windrush payment" means a payment made under the Windrush Compensation Scheme (Expenditure) Act 2020;"

With effect from January 1, 2022, reg.3(2) of the Social Security (Income and Capital Disregards) (Amendment) Regulations 2021 (SI 2021/1405) inserts ", a child abuse payment or a Windrush payment" into the definition of "qualifying person", after "Grenfell Tower payment".
In the definition of "qualifying person", after "Grenfell Tower payment" inserts ", a child abuse payment or a Windrush payment".
With effect from March 21, 2022, art.5 of the Social Security (Disability Assistance for Working Age People) (Consequential Amendments) Order 2022 (SI 2022/177) inserts the following definition:

"adult disability payment" has the meaning given in regulation 2 of the Disability Assistance for Working Age People (Scotland) Regulations 2022;

pp.851–852, *Jobseeker's Allowance Regulations 1996 (SI 1996/207) reg.16 (Further circumstances in which a person is to be treated as available: permitted period)*

Note that there has been no amendment to reg.16, equivalent to that made for universal credit and new style JSA purposes by SI 2022/108 (see the notes to reg.97(4) and (5) of the Universal Credit Regulations 2013 in Pt II of Vol.II of this series and to reg.14(3) of the JSA Regulations 2013 in

5.051

Vol.I of this series), to reduce the maximum length of a "permitted period" from 13 weeks to four.

pp.872–873, *Jobseeker's Allowance Regulations 1996 (SI 1996/207) reg.20 (Further circumstances in which a person is to be treated as actively seeking employment: permitted period)*

5.052   Note that there has been no amendment to reg.20, equivalent to that made for universal credit and new style JSA purposes by SI 2022/108 (see the notes to reg.97(4) and (5) of the Universal Credit Regulations 2013 in Pt II of Vol.II of this series and to reg.14(3) of the JSA Regulations 2013 in Vol.I of this series), to reduce the maximum length of a "permitted period" from 13 weeks to four.

pp.910–912, *amendments to the Jobseeker's Allowance Regulations 1996 (SI 1996/207) reg.51 (Remunerative work)*

5.053   The text in the main volume at para.3.166 should be replaced with the following:

"Remunerative work

51.—(1) For the purposes of the Act "remunerative work" means—
(a) in the case of [⁵ a claimant], work in which he is engaged or, where his hours of work fluctuate, is engaged on average, for not less than 16 hours per week; and
(b) in the case of any partner of the claimant, work in which he is engaged or, where his hours of work fluctuate, is engaged on average, for not less than 24 hours per week; [¹ and
(c) in the case of a non-dependant, or of a child or young person to whom paragraph 18 of Schedule 6 refers, work in which he is engaged or, where his hours of work fluctuate, is engaged on average, for not less than 16 hours per week,]
and for those purposes, [³ "work" is work] for which payment is made or which is done in expectation of payment.
(2) For the purposes of paragraph (1), the number of hours in which [⁵ a claimant] or his partner is engaged in work shall be determined—
(a) where no recognisable cycle has been established in respect of a person's work, by reference to the number of hours or, where those hours are likely to fluctuate, the average of the hours, which he is expected to work in a week;
(b) where the number of hours for which he is engaged fluctuate, by reference to the average of hours worked over—
(i) if there is a recognisable cycle of work, and sub-paragraph (c) does not apply, the period of one complete cycle (including, where the cycle involves periods in which the person does not work, those periods but disregarding any other absences);
(ii) in any other case, the period of five weeks immediately before the date of claim or the date of [⁴ supersession], or such other length of time as may, in the particular case, enable the person's average hours of work to be determined more accurately;
(c) [⁷ . . .]

(3) In determining in accordance with this regulation the number of hours for which a person is engaged in remunerative work—

(a) that number shall include any time allowed to that person by his employer for a meal or for refreshments, but only where the person is, or expects to be, paid earnings in respect of that time;

(b) no account shall be taken of any hours in which the person is engaged in an employment or scheme to which any one of paragraphs (a) to (h) of regulation 53 (person treated as not engaged in remunerative work) applies;

(c) no account shall be taken of any hours in which the person is engaged otherwise than in an employment as an earner in caring for—

(i) a person who is in receipt of attendance allowance [¹ . . .] [⁹ , the care component of disability living allowance at the highest or middle rate [¹¹ the care component of child disability payment at the highest or middle rate in accordance with regulation 11(5) of the DACYP Regulations] [¹⁰ , armed forces independence payment] [¹² . . .] the daily living component of personal independence payment at the standard or enhanced rate] [¹² , or the daily living component of adult disability payment at the standard or enhanced rate]; or

(ii) a person who has claimed an attendance allowance [¹ . . .] [⁹, disability living allowance [¹¹ child disability payment] [¹⁰ , armed forces independence payment] [¹² . . .] personal independence payment] [¹² or adult disability payment], but only for the period beginning with the date of claim and ending on the date the claim is determined or, if earlier, on the expiration of the period of 26 weeks from the date of claim; or

(iii) another person [² and] is in receipt of [⁶ carer's allowance] under Section 70 of the [¹ Benefits Act; or

(iv) a person who has claimed either attendance allowance or disability living allowance and has an award of attendance allowance or the care component of disability living allowance at one of the two higher rates prescribed under section 72(4) of the Benefits Act for a period commencing after the date on which that claim was made] [⁹ ; or

[¹¹ (iva) a person who has claimed child disability payment and has an award of the care component of child disability payment at the highest or middle rate in accordance with regulation 11(5) of the DACYP Regulations for a period commencing after the date on which the claim was made;] or

(v) a person who has claimed personal independence payment and has an award of the daily living component at the standard or enhanced rate under section 78 of the 2012 Act for a period commencing after the date on which that claim was made] [¹⁰ ; or

[¹² (va) a person who has claimed adult disability payment and has an award of the daily living component at the standard or enhanced rate under regulation 5 of the Disability Assistance for Working Age People (Scotland) Regulations 2022 for a period commencing after the date on which that claim was made;] or

(vi) a person who has claimed and has an award of armed forces independence payment for a period commencing after the date on which that claim was made.]
[8 . . .]"

AMENDMENTS

1. Jobseeker's Allowance (Amendment) Regulations 1996 (SI 1996/15160) reg.9 (October 7, 1996).
2. Jobseeker's Allowance (Amendment) Regulations 1996 (SI 1996/1516) reg.20 and Sch. (October 7, 1996).
3. Social Security (Miscellaneous Amendments) Regulations 1997 (SI 1997/454) reg.2(5) (April 7, 1997).
4. Social Security Act 1998 (Commencement No. 11, and Savings and Consequential and Transitional Provisions) Order 1999 (SI 1999/2860 (C.75)) art.3(1) and (12) and Sch.12 para.5 (October 18, 1999)
5. Jobseeker's Allowance (Joint Claims) Regulations 2000 (SI 2000/1978) reg.2(5) and Sch.2 para.14 (March 19, 2001).
6. Social Security (Miscellaneous Amendments) Regulations 2003 (SI 2003/511) reg.3(4) and (5) (April 1, 2003).
7. Social Security (Miscellaneous Amendments) Regulations 2009 (SI 2009/583) reg.4(1) and (4) (April 6, 2009).
8. Social Security (Miscellaneous Amendments) (No. 3) Regulations 2011 (SI 2011/2425) reg.10(1) and (3) (October 31, 2011).
9. Personal Independence Payment (Supplementary Provisions and Consequential Amendments) Regulations 2013 (SI 2013/388) reg.8 and Sch. para.16(1) and (3) (April 8, 2013).
10. Armed Forces and Reserve Forces Compensation Scheme (Consequential Provisions: Subordinate Legislation) Order 2013 (SI 2013/591) art.7 and Sch. para.10(1) and (3) (April 8, 2013).
11. Social Security (Scotland) Act 2018 (Disability Assistance for Children and Young People) (Consequential Modifications) Order 2021 (SI 2021/786) Sch.3 para.3 (July 26, 2021).
12. Social Security (Disability Assistance for Working Age People) (Consequential Amendments) Order 2022 (SI 2022/177) art.5(3) (March 21, 2022).

DEFINITIONS

"the Act"—see reg.1(3).
"adult disability payment"—*ibid.*
"attendance allowance"—*ibid.*
"the Benefits Act"—see Jobseekers Act s.35(1).
"child"—*ibid.*
"child disability payment"—see reg.1(3).
"claimant"—see Jobseekers Act s.35(1).
"date of claim"—see reg.1(3).
"DACYP Regulations"—*ibid.*
"disability living allowance"—*ibid.*
"earnings"—*ibid.*
"employment"—see reg.3.
"partner"—see reg.1(3).
"payment"—*ibid.*
"personal independence payment"—*ibid.*
"week"—*ibid.*
"young person"—*ibid.*, reg.76.
For the General Note to reg.51, see Vol.V paras 3.167–3.169.

p.923, *amendment to the Jobseeker's Allowance Regulations 1996 (SI 1996/207) reg.55ZA(2)(a) (Extended period of sickness)*

With effect from July 1, 2022, reg.4(1) of the Social Security (Medical Evidence) and Statutory Sick Pay (Medical Evidence) (Amendment) (No. 2) Regulations 2022 (SI 2022/630) omitted the words "a doctor's" between "form of" and "statement".

5.054

p.970, *annotation to the Jobseeker's Allowance Regulations 1996 (SI 1996/207) reg.83 (Applicable amounts)*

On the lawfulness of not uplifting the amounts paid in IS, JSA and ESA by £20 per week (as was done with UC for 18 months during the coronavirus pandemic), see the annotation to the Income Support (General) Regulations 1987 (SI 1987/1967) reg.17 (Applicable amounts), above.

5.055

pp.974–977, *amendments to the Jobseeker's Allowance Regulations 1996 (SI 1996/207) reg.85A (Special cases: supplemental—persons from abroad)*

The text in the main volume at para.3.278 should be replaced with the following:

5.056

"**85A.**—(1) "Person from abroad" means, subject to the following provisions of this regulation, a claimant who is not habitually resident in the United Kingdom, the Channel Islands, the Isle of Man or the Republic of Ireland.

[¹⁰ (2) No claimant shall be treated as habitually resident in the United Kingdom, the Channel Islands, the Isle of Man or the Republic of Ireland unless—
   (a) [¹² subject to the exceptions in paragraph (2A),] the claimant has been living in any of those places for the past three months; and
   (b) the claimant has a right to reside in any of those places, other than a right to reside which falls within paragraph (3) [¹³ or (3A)].]

[¹² (2A) The exceptions are where the claimant has at any time during the period referred to in paragraph (2)(a)—
   (a) paid either Class 1 or Class 2 contributions by virtue of regulation 114, 118, 146 or 147 of the Social Security (Contributions) Regulations 2001 or by virtue of an Order in Council having effect under section 179 of the Social Security Administration Act 1992; or
   (b) been a Crown servant posted to perform overseas the duties of a Crown servant; or
   (c) been a member of Her Majesty's forces posted to perform overseas the duties of a member of Her Majesty's forces.]

(3) A right to reside falls within this paragraph if it is one which exists by virtue of, or in accordance with, one or more of the following—
   (a) regulation 13 of the [¹³ Immigration (European Economic Area) Regulations 2016]; [¹⁵ or]
[⁷[¹³(aa) regulation 16 of those Regulations, but only in a case where the right exists under that regulation because the claimant satisfies the criteria in paragraph (5) of that regulation;]]
   (b) [¹⁵ . . .]
   (c) [¹⁵ . . .]

[¹³ (3A) A right to reside falls within this paragraph if it exists by virtue of a claimant having been granted limited leave to enter, or remain in, the United Kingdom under the Immigration Act 1971 by virtue of—
  (a) Appendix EU to the immigration rules made under section 3(2) of that Act; [¹⁶ . . .]
  (b) being a person with a Zambrano right to reside as defined in Annex 1 of Appendix EU to the immigration rules made under section 3(2) of that Act.] [¹⁶; or
  (c) having arrived in the United Kingdom with an entry clearance that was granted under Appendix EU (Family Permit) to the immigration rules made under section 3(2) of that Act.]
[¹⁴ (3B) Paragraph (3A)(a) does not apply to a person who—
  (a) has a right to reside granted by virtue of being a family member of a relevant person of Northern Ireland; and
  (b) would have a right to reside under the Immigration (European Economic Area) Regulations 2016 if the relevant person of Northern Ireland were an EEA national, provided that the right to reside does not fall within paragraph (3A).]
  (4) A claimant is not a person from abroad if he is—
[¹⁶(zza) a person granted leave in accordance with the immigration rules made under section 3(2) of the Immigration Act 1971, where such leave is granted by virtue of—
  (i) the Afghan Relocations and Assistance Policy; or
  (ii) the previous scheme for locally-employed staff in Afghanistan (sometimes referred to as the ex-gratia scheme);
(zzb) a person in Great Britain not coming within sub-paragraph (zza) or [¹⁷ (h)] who left Afghanistan in connection with the collapse of the Afghan government that took place on 15th August 2021;]
[¹⁷(zzc) a person in Great Britain who was residing in Ukraine immediately before 1st January 2022, left Ukraine in connection with the Russian invasion which took place on 24th February 2022 and—
  (i) has been granted leave in accordance with immigration rules made under section 3(2) of the Immigration Act 1971; [¹⁸ . . .]
  (ii) has a right of abode in the United Kingdom within the meaning given in section 2 of that Act;] [¹⁸ or
  (iii) does not require leave to enter or remain in the United Kingdom in accordance with section 3ZA of that Act;]
[¹¹(za) a qualified person for the purposes of regulation 6 of the [¹³ Immigration (European Economic Area) Regulations 2016] as a worker or a self-employed person;
  (zb) a family member of a person referred to in sub-paragraph (za) [¹⁴ . . .];
  (zc) a person who has a right to reside permanently in the United Kingdom by virtue of regulation 15(1)(c), (d) or I of those Regulations;]
[¹⁴(zd) a family member of a relevant person of Northern Ireland, with a right to reside which falls within paragraph (3A)(a), provided that the relevant person of Northern Ireland falls within sub-paragraph (za), or would do so but for the fact that they are not an EEA national;]
[¹⁵(ze) a frontier worker within the meaning of regulation 3 of the Citizens' Rights (Frontier Workers) (EU Exit) Regulations 2020;

(zf) a family member, of a person referred to in sub-paragraph (ze), who has been granted limited leave to enter, or remain in, the United Kingdom by virtue of Appendix EU to the immigration rules made under section 3(2) of the Immigration Act 1971;]

(g) a refugee within the definition in Article 1 of the Convention relating to the Status of Refugees done at Geneva on 28th July 1951, as extended by Article 1(2) of the Protocol relating to the Status of Refugees done at New York on 31st January 1967;

[³[⁹(h) a person who has been granted leave or who is deemed to have been granted leave outside the rules made under section 3(2) of the Immigration Act 1971 [¹⁷ . . .]]

(hh) a person who has humanitarian protection granted under those rules;] [⁹ or]

(i) a person who is not a person subject to immigration control within the meaning of section 115(9) of the Immigration and Asylum Act and who is in the United Kingdom as a result of his deportation, expulsion or other removal by compulsion of law from another country to the United Kingdom; [⁵ . . .]

[⁹ . . .]

[¹⁴ (5) In this regulation—

"EEA national" has the meaning given in regulation 2(1) of the Immigration (European Economic Area) Regulations 2016;

"family member" has the meaning given in regulation 7(1)(a), (b) or (c) of the Immigration (European Economic Area) Regulations 2016 except that regulation 7(4) of those Regulations does not apply for the purposes of paragraphs (3B) and (4)(zd);

"relevant person of Northern Ireland" has the meaning given in Annex 1 of Appendix EU to the immigration rules made under section 3(2) of the Immigration Act 1971.]

[¹⁵ (6) In this regulation references to the Immigration (European Economic Area) Regulations 2016 are to be read with Schedule 4 to the Immigration and Social Security Co-ordination (EU Withdrawal) Act 2020 (Consequential, Saving, Transitional and Transitory Provisions) Regulations 2020.]"

AMENDMENTS

1. Social Security (Persons from Abroad) Amendment Regulations 2006 (SI 1026/2006) reg.7(3) (April 30, 2006).

2. Social Security (Lebanon) Amendment Regulations 2006 (SI 2006/1981) reg.3 (July 25, 2006). The amendment ceased to have effect from January 31, 2007.

3. Social Security (Persons from Abroad) Amendment (No. 2) Regulations 2006 (SI 2006/2528) reg.3 (October 9, 2006).

4. Social Security (Bulgaria and Romania) Amendment Regulations 2006 (SI 2006/3341) reg.3 (January 1, 2007).

5. Social Security (Habitual Residence) (Amendment) Regulations 2009 (SI 2009/362) reg.3 (March 18, 2009).

6. Social Security (Miscellaneous Amendments) (No. 3) Regulations 2011 (SI 2011/2425) reg.10(1) and (7) (October 31, 2011).

7. Social Security (Habitual Residence) (Amendment) Regulations 2012 (SI 2012/2587) reg.3 (November 8, 2012).

8. Social Security (Croatia) Amendment Regulations 2013 (SI 2013/1474) reg.3 (July 1, 2013).

9. Social Security (Miscellaneous Amendments) (No. 3) Regulations 2013 (SI 2013/2536) reg.6(1) and (8) (October 29, 2013).

10. Jobseeker's Allowance (Habitual Residence) Amendment Regulations 2013 (SI 3196/2013) reg.2 (January 1, 2014).
11. Social Security (Habitual Residence) (Amendment) Regulations 2014 (SI 2014/902) reg.3 (May 31, 2014).
12. Jobseeker's Allowance (Habitual Residence) Amendment Regulations 2014 (SI 2014/2735) reg.3 (November 9, 2014).
13. Social Security (Income-related Benefits) (Updating and Amendment) (EU Exit) Regulations 2019 (SI 2019/872) reg.3 (May 7, 2019).
14. Social Security (Income-Related Benefits) (Persons of Northern Ireland— Family Members) (Amendment) Regulations 2020 (SI 2020/683) reg.3 (August 24, 2020).
15. Immigration and Social Security Co-ordination (EU Withdrawal) Act 2020 (Consequential, Saving, Transitional and Transitory Provisions) (EU Exit) Regulations 2020 (SI 2020/1309) reg.55 (December 31, 2020 at 11.00 pm).
16. Social Security (Habitual Residence and Past Presence) (Amendment) Regulations 2021 (SI 2021/1034), reg.2 (September 15, 2021).
17. Social Security (Habitual Residence and Past Presence) (Amendment) Regulations 2022 (SI 2022/344) reg.2 (March 22, 2022).
18. Social Security (Habitual Residence and Past Presence) (Amendment) (No. 2) Regulations 2022 (SI 2022/990) reg.2 (October 18, 2022).

p.1014, *amendment to the Jobseeker's Allowance Regulations 1996 (SI 1996/207) reg.105(10A) (Notional income—exceptions)*

5.057   With effect from January 1, 2022, reg.3(3) of the Social Security (Income and Capital Disregards) (Amendment) Regulations 2021 (SI 2021/1405) amended para.(10A) by inserting the following after sub-para.(ab):

"(ac) a child abuse payment;
(ad) a Windrush payment;"

Those payments are defined in reg.1(3). See the entry for p.684 for discussion of the nature of those payments.

p.1021, *annotation to the Jobseeker's Allowance Regulations 1996 (SI 1996/207) reg.107 (Capital limit)*

5.058   In the Institute for Government and the Social Security Advisory Committee's 2021 joint report *Jobs and benefits: The Covid-19 challenge* it was noted that if the capital limit of £16,000 had risen in line with prices since 2006 it would be close to £23,500 (or £25,000: different figures are given) and recommended that the limit should be increased to £25,000 and subsequently automatically indexed to maintain its real value (pp.22 and 31). That recommendation was summarily rejected in the Government's response of March 22, 2022.

p.1023, *amendment to the Jobseeker's Allowance Regulations 1996 (SI 1996/207) reg.110(10) (Income treated as capital—exceptions)*

5.059   With effect from January 1, 2022, reg.3(4) of the Social Security (Income and Capital Disregards) (Amendment) Regulations 2021 (SI 2021/1405) amended para.(10) by inserting the following after sub-para.(ab):

"(ac) which is a child abuse payment;
(ad) which is a Windrush payment; or"

Those payments are defined in reg.1(3). See the entry for p.684 for discussion of the nature of those payments. The "or" following sub-para.(ab), omitted in error in the main volume, has also been removed.

p.1027, *amendment to the Jobseeker's Allowance Regulations 1996 (SI 1996/207) reg.113(3B) (Notional capital—exceptions)*

With effect from January 1, 2022, reg.3(5) of the Social Security (Income and Capital Disregards) (Amendment) Regulations 2021 (SI 2021/1405) amended para.(3B) by substituting the following for "a payment of capital which is a Grenfell Tower payment":

5.060

"any of the following payments of capital—
(a) a Grenfell Tower payment;
(b) a child abuse payment;
(c) a Windrush payment."

All of those payments are defined in reg.1(3). See the entry of p.684 for discussion of the nature of child abuse and Windrush payments.

pp.1059–1060, *amendments to the Jobseeker's Allowance Regulations 1996 (SI 1996/207) reg.140 (Hardship payments)*

With effect from July 26, 2021, Sch.3 para.4 of the Social Security (Scotland) Act 2018 (Disability Assistance for Children and Young People) (Consequential Modifications) Order 2021 (SI 2021/786) makes the following amendments to reg.140(1)(h):

5.061

- in para.(i), after "Benefits Act", insert ", the care component of child disability payment at the highest or middle rate in accordance with regulation 11(5) of the DACYP Regulations";
- in para.(ii), after "disability living allowance", insert ", child disability payment";
- after para.(iii), insert "(iiia) has claimed child disability payment and has an award of the care component of child disability payment at the highest or middle rate in accordance with regulation 11(5) of the DACYP Regulations for a period commencing after the date on which the claim was made; or".

With effect from March 21, 2022, art.5 of the Social Security (Disability Assistance for Working Age People) (Consequential Amendments) Order 2022 (SI 2022/177) makes the following amendments to reg.140(1)(h):

- in para.(i):
  - after "DACYP Regulations" for "or" substitute ",";
  - after "the 2012 Act" insert ", the daily living component of adult disability payment at the standard or enhanced rate in accordance with regulation 5 of the Disability Assistance for Working Age People (Scotland) Regulations 2022";
- in para.(ii):
  - after "armed forces independence payment" for "or" substitute ",";
  - after "personal independence payment" insert "or adult disability payment";

- after para.(iv) insert "(iva) has claimed adult disability payment and has an award of the daily living component of adult disability payment at the standard or enhanced rate in accordance with regulation 5 of the Disability Assistance for Working Age People (Scotland) Regulations 2022 for a period commencing after the date on which that claim was made; or".

pp.1071–1072, *amendments to the Jobseeker's Allowance Regulations 1996 (SI 1996/207) reg.146A (Meaning of "couple in hardship")*

5.062 With effect from July 26, 2021, Sch.3 para.5 of the Social Security (Scotland) Act 2018 (Disability Assistance for Children and Young People) (Consequential Modifications) Order 2021 (SI 2021/786) makes the following amendments to reg.146A(1)(e):

- in para.(i), after "Benefits Act", insert ", the care component of child disability payment at the highest or middle rate in accordance with regulation 11(5) of the DACYP Regulations";
- in para.(ii), after "disability living allowance", insert ", child disability payment";
- after para.(iii), insert "(iiia) has claimed child disability payment and has an award of the care component of child disability payment at the highest or middle rate in accordance with regulation 11(5) of the DACYP Regulations for a period commencing after the date on which the claim was made; or".

With effect from March 21, 2022, art.5(5) of the Social Security (Disability Assistance for Working Age People) (Consequential Amendments) Order 2022 (SI 2022/177) makes the following amendments to reg.146A(1)(e):

- in para.(i):
  - after "armed forces independence payment", for "or" substitute ", ";
  - after "the 2012 Act" insert ", or the daily living component of adult disability payment at the standard or enhanced rate in accordance with regulation 5 of the Disability Assistance for Working Age People (Scotland) Regulations 2022";
- in para.(ii):
  - after "armed forces independence payment", for "or" substitute ",";
  - after "personal independence payment" insert "or adult disability payment";
- after para.(iv) insert "(iva) has claimed adult disability payment and has an award of the daily living component at the standard or enhanced rate in accordance with regulation 5 of the Disability Assistance for Working Age People (Scotland) Regulations 2022 for a period commencing after the date on which that claim was made; or".

p.1086, *amendment to the Jobseeker's Allowance Regulations 1996 (SI 1996/207) reg.172 (Trade disputes: prescribed sum)*

5.063 With effect from April 10, 2023, art.28 of the Social Security Benefits Up-rating Order 2023 (SI 2023/316) substituted "£47.00" for "£42.50" (as had been in effect from April 11, 2022).

pp.1087–1088, *amendments to the Jobseeker's Allowance Regulations 1996 (SI 1996/207) Sch.A1 (Categories of members of a joint-claim couple who are not required to satisfy the conditions in section 1(2B)(b))*

With effect from July 26, 2021, Sch.3 para.6 of the Social Security (Scotland) Act 2018 (Disability Assistance for Children and Young People) (Consequential Modifications) Order 2021 (SI 2021/786) makes the following amendments to para.3(a) (member caring for another person):

5.064

- in para.(i), after "Benefits Act", insert ", the care component of child disability payment at the highest or middle rate in accordance with regulation 11(5) of the DACYP Regulations";
- in para.(iv), after "disability living allowance", insert ", child disability payment";
- after para.(v), insert "(va) the person being cared for ("P") has claimed entitlement to the care component of child disability payment in accordance with regulation 24 (when an application is to be treated as made and beginning of entitlement to assistance) of the DACYP Regulations, an award at the highest or middle rate has been made in respect of P's claim, and where the period for which the award is payable has begun, P is in receipt of that payment;"

With effect from March 21, 2022, art.5(6) of the Social Security (Disability Assistance for Working Age People) (Consequential Amendments) Order 2022 (SI 2022/177) makes the following amendments to para.3(a) (member caring for another person):

- in para.3(a)(i) (member caring for another person):
  - after "armed forces independence payment" for "or" substitute ", ";
  - after "the 2012 Act" insert "or the daily living component of adult disability payment at the standard or enhanced rate in accordance with regulation 5 of the Disability Assistance for Working Age People (Scotland) Regulations 2022";
- in para.3(a)(iv):
  - after "armed forces independence payment" for "or" substitute ", ";
  - after "personal independence payment" insert "or adult disability payment";
- in para.3(a)(vi) omit "or" at the end; and
- after para.3(a)(vi) insert "(via) the person being cared for has claimed entitlement to the daily living component of adult disability payment in accordance with regulation 35 (when an application is to be treated as made and beginning of entitlement to assistance) of the Disability Assistance for Working Age People (Scotland) Regulations 2022, an award of the standard or enhanced rate of the daily living component has been made in respect of that claim and, where the period for which the award is payable has begun, that person is in receipt of that payment; or"

p.1091, *amendments to the Jobseeker's Allowance Regulations 1996 (SI 1996/207) Sch.1 (Applicable amounts)*

Substitute the following for paras 3.479–3.508

5.065

1077

Regulations 83 and 84(1)

"SCHEDULE 1

APPLICABLE AMOUNTS

[⁹ PART I

PERSONAL ALLOWANCES

3.479   1.—The weekly amounts specified in column (2) below in respect of each person or couple specified in column (1) shall be the weekly amounts specified for the purposes of regulations 83 [²⁸ 84(1), 86A and 86B] (applicable amounts and polygamous marriages).

Column (1) *Person or Couple*	Column (2) *Amount*

(1) Single claimant aged—
(a) except where head (b) or (c) of this sub-paragraph applies, less than 18;
(b) less than 18 who falls within paragraph (2) of regulation 57 and who—
   (i) is a person to whom regulation 59, 60 or 61 applies [¹ . . .]; or
   (ii) is the subject of a direction under section 16;
(c) less than 18 who satisfies the condition in [³³ paragraph 13(1)(a)] of Part 3;
(d) not less than 18 but less than 25;
(e) not less than 25.
	1.
	(a) [⁵⁵ £67.20];
	(b) [⁵⁵ £67.20];
	
	(c) [⁵⁵ £67.20];
	
	(d) [⁵⁵ £67.20];
	(e) [⁵⁵ £84.80];

(2) Lone parent aged—
(a) except where head (b) or (c) of this sub-paragraph applies, less than 18;
(b) less than 18 who falls within paragraph (2) of regulation 57 and who—
   (i) is a person to whom regulation 59, 60 or 61 applies [¹ . . .]; or
   (ii) is the subject of a direction under section 16;
(c) less than 18 who satisfies the condition in [³³ paragraph 13(1)(a)] [² of Part 3];
(d) not less than 18.
	2.
	(a) [⁵⁵ £67.20];
	(b) [⁵⁵ £67.20];
	
	(c) [⁵⁵ £67.20];
	
	(d) [⁵⁵ £84.80].

(3) Couple—
(a) where both members are aged less than 18 and—
   (i) at least one of them is treated as responsible for a child; or
   (ii) had they not been members of a couple, each would have been a person to whom regulation 59, 60 or 61
(circumstances in which a person aged 16 or 17 is eligible for a jobseeker's allowance) applied or
   (iii) had they not been members of a couple, the claimant would have been a person to whom regulation 59, 60 or 61 (circumstances in which a person aged 16 or 17 is eligible for a
	3.
	(a) [⁵⁵ £101.50];

Column (1) Person or Couple	Column (2) Amount
jobseeker's allowance) applied and his partner satisfies the requirements for entitlement to income support [³⁶ or an income-related employment and support allowance] other than the requirement to make a claim for it; or	
[¹(iv) they are married [³¹ or civil partners]and one member a of the couple is person to whom regulation 59, 60 or 61 applies and the other member is registered in accordance with regulation 62; or	
(iva) they are married [³¹ or civil partners] and each member of the couple is a person to whom regulation 59, 60 or 61 applies; or]	
(v) there is a direction under section 16 (jobseeker's allowance in cases of severe hardship) in respect of each member; or	
(vi) there is a direction under section 16 in respect of one of them and the other is a person to whom regulation 59, 60 or 61 applies [¹ . . .], or	
(vii) there is a direction under section 16 in respect of one of them and the other satisfies requirements for entitlement to income support [³⁶ or an income-related employment and support allowance] other than the requirement to make a claim for it;	
(b) where both members are aged less than 18 and sub-paragraph (3)(a) does not apply but one member of the couple falls within paragraph (2) of regulation 57 and either— (i) is a person to whom regulation 59, 60 or 61 applies [¹ . . .]; or (ii) is the subject of a direction under section 16 of the Act;	(b) [⁵⁵ £67.20];
(c) where both members are aged less than 18 and neither head (a) nor (b) of sub-paragraph (3) applies but one member of the couple— (i) is a person to whom regulation 59, 60 or 61 applies [¹ . . .]; or (ii) is the subject of a direction under section 16;	(c) [⁵⁵ £67.20];
(d) where both members are aged less than 18 and none of heads (a), (b) or (c) of sub-paragraph (3) apply but one member of the couple is a person who satisfies the requirements of [³³ paragraph 13(1)(a)];	(d) [⁵⁵ £67.20];
[³⁵ (e) where— (i) both members are aged not less than 18; or (ii) one member is aged not less than 18 and the other member is a person who is— (aa) under 18, and (bb) treated as responsible for a child;]	(e) [⁵⁵ £133.30];
(f) where [³⁵ paragraph (e) does not apply and] one member is aged not less than 18 and the other member is a person under 18 who— (i) is a person to whom regulation 59, 60 or 61 applies [¹ . . .]; or (ii) is the subject of a direction under section 16; [³⁸ or	(f) [⁵⁵ £133.30];

Column (1) Person or Couple	Column (2) Amount

(iii) satisfies requirements for entitlement to income support or who would do so if he were not a member of a couple, other than the requirement to make a claim for it; or
    (iv) satisfies requirements for entitlement to an income-related employment and support allowance other than the requirement to make a claim for it;]
  (g) where one member is aged not less than 18 but less than 25 and the other member is a person under 18—
    (i) to whom none of the regulations 59 to 61 applies; or
    (ii) who is not the subject of a direction under section 16; and
    (iii) does not satisfy requirements for entitlement to income support [36 or an income-related employment and support allowance] disregarding the requirement to make a claim for it;
  (h) where one member is aged not less than 25 and the other member is a person under 18—
    (i) to whom none of the regulations 59 to 61 applies; or
    (ii) is not the subject of a direction under section 16; and
    (iii) does not satisfy requirements for entitlement to income support [36 or an income-related employment and support allowance] disregarding the requirement to make a claim for it.
	(g) [55 £67.20];
	
	(h) [55 £84.80].

2.—[30 . . .]	
3.—[29 . . .]	

PART II

FAMILY PREMIUM

3.480   **4.**—[30 . . .]

PART III

PREMIUMS

3.481   **5.**—Except as provided in paragraph 6, the weekly premiums specified in Part IV of this Schedule shall for the purposes of regulations 83(e) and 84(1)(f), be applicable to a claimant who satisfies the condition specified in [4 15 paragraphs 9A] to 17 in respect of that premium.

    6.—Subject to paragraph 7, where a claimant satisfies the conditions in respect of more than one premium in this Part of this Schedule, only one premium shall be applicable to him and, if they are different amounts, the higher or highest amount shall apply.

    [16 **7.**—(1) Subject to sub-paragraph (2), the following premiums, namely—
  (a) a severe disability premium to which paragraph 15 applies;
  (b) an enhanced disability premium to which paragraph 15A applies;
  (c) [30 . . .]; and
  (d) a carer premium in which paragraph 17 applies,

may be applicable in addition to any other premium which may apply under this Part of this Schedule.

(2) An enhanced disability premium in respect of a person shall not be applicable in addition to—
  (a) a pensioner premium under paragraph 10 or 11; or
  (b) a higher pensioner premium under paragraph 12.]

8.—(1) Subject to sub-paragraph (2) for the purposes of this Part of this Schedule, once a premium is applicable to a claimant under this Part, a person shall be treated as being in receipt of any benefit—
  (a) in the case of a benefit to which the Social Security (Overlapping Benefits) Regulations 1979 applies, for any period during which, apart from the provisions of those Regulations, he would be in receipt of that benefit; and
  [³(b) for any period spent by a claimant in undertaking a course of training or instruction provided or approved by the Secretary of State [³⁵ . . .] under section 2 of the Employment and Training Act 1973, or by [³⁷ Skills Development Scotland,] Scottish Enterprise or Highlands and Islands Enterprise under section 2 of the Enterprise and New Towns (Scotland) Act 1990 or for any period during which he is in receipt of a training allowance.]

(2) For the purposes of the carer premium under paragraph 17, a person shall be treated as being in receipt of [²⁴ carer's allowance] by virtue of sub-paragraph (1)(a) only if and for so long as the person in respect of whose care the allowance has been claimed remains in receipt of attendance allowance, [⁴⁶ the care component of disability living allowance at the highest or middle rate prescribed in accordance with section 72(3) of the Benefits Act [⁵², the care component of child disability payment at the highest or middle rate prescribed in accordance with regulation 11(5) of the DACYP Regulations] [⁴⁷ , armed forces independence payment] [⁵³ ,] the daily living component of personal independence payment at the standard or enhanced rate prescribed in accordance with section 78(3) of the 2012 Act] [⁵³ , or the daily living component of adult disability payment at the standard or enhanced rate prescribed in accordance with regulation 5 of the Disability Assistance for Working Age People (Scotland) Regulations 2022].

Lone Parent Premium
9.—[⁴ . . .]   3.482

[¹⁵ Bereavement Premium
9A.—[³⁴ . . .]]   3.483

Pensioner premium for persons [⁴⁰ over the qualifying age for state pension credit]
10.—The condition is that the claimant—   3.484
  (a) is a single claimant or lone parent who has attained [⁴⁰ the qualifying age for state pension credit]; or
  (b) has attained [⁴⁰ the qualifying age for state pension credit] and has a partner; or
  (c) has a partner and the partner has attained [⁴⁰ the qualifying age for state pension credit] but not the age of 75.

Pensioner premium where claimant's partner has attained the age of 75
11.—The condition is that the claimant has a partner who has attained the age of 75 but   3.485
not the age of 80.

Higher Pensioner Premium
12.—(1) [³³ Subject to sub-paragraph (5), the] condition is that—   3.486
  (a) the claimant is a single claimant or lone parent who has attained [⁴⁰ the qualifying age for state pension credit] and either—
    (i) satisfies one of the additional conditions specified in paragraph 14(1)(a), (c), [⁵¹ (ca), (cb),] (e), (f) [⁵¹, (fa)] or (h); or
    (ii) was entitled to either income support or income-based jobseeker's allowance [¹², or was treated as being entitled to either of those benefits and the disability premium was or, as the case may be, would have been,] applicable to him in respect of a benefit week within 8 weeks of [⁴⁰ the date he attained the qualifying age for state pension credit] and he has, subject to sub-paragraph (2), remained continuously entitled to one of those benefits since attaining that age; or
  (b) the claimant has a partner and—
    (i) the partner has attained the age of 80; or

(ii) the partner has attained [40 the qualifying age for state pension credit] but not the age of 80, and the additional conditions specified in paragraph 14 are satisfied in respect of him; or

(c) the claimant—
(i) has attained [40 the qualifying age for state pension credit];
[3(ii) satisfies the requirements of either sub-head (i) or (ii) of paragraph 12(1)(a); and]
(iii) has a partner.

(2) For the purposes of this paragraph and paragraph 14—

(a) once the higher pensioner premium is applicable to a claimant, if he then ceases, for a period of eight weeks or less, to be entitled to either income support or income-based jobseeker's allowance [12 or ceases to be treated as entitled to either of those benefits], he shall, on becoming re-entitled to either of those benefits, thereafter be treated as having been continuously entitled thereto;

(b) in so far as sub-paragraphs (1)(a)(ii) and (1)(c)(ii) are concerned, if a claimant ceases to be entitled to either income support or an income-based jobseeker's allowance [12 or ceases to be treated as entitled to either of those benefits] for a period not exceeding eight weeks which includes [40 the date he attained the qualifying age for state pension credit], he shall, on becoming re-entitled to either of those benefits, thereafter be treated as having been continuously entitled thereto.

[8(3) In this paragraph where a claimant's partner is a welfare to work beneficiary, sub-paragraphs (1)(a)(ii) and (2)(b) shall apply to him as if for the words "8 weeks" there were substituted the words "[32 104 weeks]".]

[12 (4) For the purposes of this paragraph, a claimant shall be treated as having been entitled to income support or to an income-based jobseeker's allowance throughout any period which comprises only days on which he was participating in an employment zone programme and was not entitled to—

(a) income support because, as a consequence of his participation in that programme, he was engaged in remunerative work or had income in excess of the claimant's applicable amount as prescribed in Part IV of the Income Support Regulations; or

(b) a jobseeker's allowance because, as a consequence of his participation in that programme, he was engaged in remunerative work or failed to satisfy the condition specified in section 2(1)(c) or in section 3(1)(a).]

[33 (5) The condition is not satisfied if—

(a) the claimant is a single claimant or a lone parent and (in either case) is a long-term patient;

(b) the claimant is a member of a couple or polygamous marriage and each member of the couple or polygamous marriage is a long-term patient; or

(c) the claimant is a member of a couple or a polygamous marriage and a member of that couple or polygamous marriage is—
(i) a long-term patient; and
(ii) the only member of the couple or polygamous marriage to whom sub-paragraph (1)(b) or (c) refers.]

Disability Premium

3.487   **13.** [33 —(1) Subject to sub-paragraph (2), the] condition is that the claimant—

(a) is a single claimant or lone parent who has not attained [40 the qualifying age for state pension credit] and satisfies any one of the additional conditions specified in paragraph 14(1)(a), (c), [51 (ca), (cb),] (e), (f) [51, (fa)] or (h); or

(b) has not attained [40 the qualifying age for state pension credit], has a partner and the claimant satisfies any one of the additional conditions specified in paragraph 14(1)(a), (c), [51 (ca), (cb),] (e), (f) [51, (fa)] or (h); or

(c) has a partner and the partner has not attained [40 the qualifying age for state pension credit] and also satisfies any one of the additional conditions specified in paragraph 14.

[33 (2) The condition is not satisfied if—

(a) the claimant is a single claimant or a lone parent and (in either case) is a long-term patient;

(b) the claimant is a member of a couple or polygamous marriage and each member of the couple or polygamous marriage is a long-term patient; or

(c) the claimant is a member of a couple or polygamous marriage and a member of that couple or polygamous marriage—
(i) is a long-term patient; and

(ii) is the only member of the couple or polygamous marriage to whom the condition in sub-paragraph (1)(b) or (c) refers.]

Additional conditions for Higher Pensioner and Disability Premium

14.—(1) The additional conditions specified in this paragraph are that— **3.488**

(a) the claimant or, as the case may be, his partner, is in receipt [²⁵ the disability element or the severe disability element of working tax credit as specified in regulation 20(1) (b) and (f) of the Working Tax Credit (Entitlement and Maximum Rate) Regulations 2002] or mobility supplement;

(b) the claimant's partner is in receipt of severe disablement allowance;

(c) the claimant or, as the case may be, his partner, is in receipt of attendance allowance or disability living allowance or is a person whose disability living allowance is payable, in whole or in part, to another in accordance with regulation 44 of the Claims and Payments Regulations (payment of disability living allowance on behalf of third party);

[⁴⁶ (ca) the claimant or, as the case may be, his partner, is in receipt of personal independence payment or is a person whose personal independence payment is payable, in whole or in part, to another in accordance with regulation 58(2) of the Universal Credit etc. Claims and Payments Regulations (payment to another person on the claimant's behalf);]

[⁵³ (caa) the claimant or, as the case may be, the claimant's partner, is in receipt of adult disability payment or is a person whose adult disability payment is payable, in whole or in part, to another in accordance with regulation 33 of the Disability Assistance for Working Age People (Scotland) Regulations 2022 (making payments);]

[⁴⁷ (cb) the claimant or, as the case may be, the claimant's partner, is in receipt of armed forces independence payment or is a person whose armed forces independence payment is payable, in whole or in part, to another in accordance with article 24D of the Armed Forces and Reserve Forces (Compensation Scheme) Order 2011;]

(d) the claimant's partner is in receipt of long-term incapacity benefit or is a person to whom section 30B(4) of the Benefits Act (long term rate of incapacity benefit payable to those who are terminally ill) applies;

(e) the claimant or, as the case may be, his partner, has an invalid carriage or other vehicle provided to him by the Secretary of State under section 5(2)(a) of and Schedule 2 to the National Health Service Act 1977 or under section 46 of the National Health Service (Scotland) Act 1978 or provided by the Department of Health and Social Services for Northern Ireland under article 30(1) of the Health and Personal Social Services (Northern Ireland) Order 1972, or receives payments by way of grant from the Secretary of State under paragraph 2 of Schedule 2 to the Act of 1977 (additional provisions as to vehicles) or, in Scotland, under section 46 of the Act of 1978;

(f) the claimant or, as the case may be, his partner, is a person who is entitled to the mobility component of disability living allowance but to whom the component is not payable in accordance with regulation 42 of the Claims and Payments Regulations (cases where disability living allowance not payable);

[⁴⁶ (fa) the claimant or, as the case may be, his partner, is a person who is entitled to the mobility component of personal independence payment but to whom the component is not payable in accordance with regulation 61 of the Universal Credit etc. Claims and Payments Regulations (cases where mobility component of personal independence payment not payable);]

[⁵³ (fb) the claimant or, as the case may be, the claimant's partner, is a person who is entitled to the mobility component of adult disability payment but to whom the component is not payable in accordance with regulation 34(6) of the Disability Assistance for Working Age People (Scotland) Regulations 2022 (amount and form of adult disability payment);]

(g) the claimant's partner was either—

(i) in receipt of long term incapacity benefit under section 30A(5) of the Benefits Act immediately before attaining pensionable age and he is still alive;

(ii) entitled to attendance allowance or disability living allowance but payment of that benefit was suspended in accordance with regulations under section 113(2) of the Benefits Act or otherwise abated as a consequence of [² the partner] becoming a patient within the meaning of regulation 85(4) (special cases), [⁵³ ; . . .]

(iii) entitled to personal independence payment but no amount is payable in accordance with regulations made under section 86(1) (hospital in-patients) of the 2012 Act] [⁵³ ; or

(iv) entitled to adult disability payment but no amount is payable in accordance with regulation 28 (effect of admission to hospital on ongoing entitlement to Adult Disability Payment) of the Disability Assistance for Working Age People (Scotland) Regulations 2022;]
and [53 in any of the cases described in sub-paragraphs (i) to (iv),]the higher pensioner premium or disability premium had been applicable to the claimant or his partner;
[48 (h) the claimant or, as the case may be, his partner, is certified as severely sight impaired or blind by a consultant ophthalmologist.]
[48 (2) For the purposes of sub-paragraph (1)(h), a person who has ceased to be certified as severely sight impaired or blind on regaining his eyesight shall nevertheless be treated as severely sight impaired or blind, as the case may be, and as satisfying the additional condition set out in that sub-paragraph for a period of 28 weeks following the date on which he ceased to be so certified.]

Severe Disability Premium

3.489   **15.**—(1) In the case of a single claimant, a lone parent or a claimant who is treated as having no partner in consequence of sub-paragraph (3), the condition is that—
(a) he is in receipt of attendance allowance [46 , the care component of disability living allowance at the highest or middle rate prescribed in accordance with section 72(3) of the Benefits Act [47 , armed forces independence payment] [53 ,] the daily living component of personal independence payment at the standard or enhanced rate in accordance with section 78(3) of the 2012 Act] [53 , or the daily living component of adult disability payment at the standard or enhanced rate in accordance with regulation 5 of the Disability Assistance for Working Age People (Scotland) Regulations 2022]; and
(b) subject to sub-paragraph (4), there are no non-dependants aged 18 or over normally residing with him or with whom he is normally residing; and
[11(c) no person is entitled to, and in receipt of, [24 a carer's allowance] under section 70 of the Benefits Act [50 or has an award of universal credit which includes the carer element] in respect of caring for him;]
(2) Where the claimant has a partner, the condition is that—
(a) the claimant is in receipt of attendance allowance [46 , the care component of disability living allowance at the highest or middle rate prescribed in accordance with section 72(3) of the Benefits Act [47 , armed forces independence payment] [53 ,] the daily living component of personal independence payment at the standard or enhanced rate in accordance with section 78(3) of the 2012 Act] [53 , or the daily living component of adult disability payment at the standard or enhanced rate in accordance with regulation 5 of the Disability Assistance for Working Age People (Scotland) Regulations 2022]; and
(b) the partner is also in receipt of a qualifying benefit, or if he is a member of a polygamous marriage, all the partners of that marriage are in receipt of a qualifying benefit; and
(c) subject to sub-paragraph (4), there is no non-dependant aged 18 or over normally residing with him or with whom he is normally residing; and (d) either—
(i) [11 no person is entitled to, and in receipt of, [24 a carer's allowance] under section 70 of the Benefits Act [50 or has an award of universal credit which includes the carer element] in respect of] caring for either member of the couple or all the members of the polygamous marriage; or
(ii) a person is engaged in caring for one member (but not both members) of the couple, or one or more but not all members of the polygamous marriage, and in consequence is [11 entitled to] [24 a carer's allowance] under section 70 of the Benefits Act [50 or has an award of universal credit which includes the carer element].
(3) Where the claimant has a partner who does not satisfy the condition in sub-paragraph (2)(b), and that partner is [48 severely sight impaired or blind or treated as severely sight impaired or blind] within the meaning of paragraph 14(1)(h) and (2), that partner shall be treated for the purposes of sub-paragraph (2) as if he were not a partner of the claimant.
(4) The following persons shall not be regarded as a non-dependant for the purposes of sub-paragraphs (1)(b) and (2)(c)—
(a) a person in receipt of attendance allowance [46 , the care component of disability living allowance at the highest or middle rate prescribed in accordance with section 72(3) of the Benefits Act [47 , armed forces independence payment] [53 ,] the daily living component of personal independence payment at the standard or enhanced rate in accordance with section 78(3) of the 2012 Act] [53 , or the daily living component of adult disability payment at the standard or enhanced rate in accordance with regulation 5 of the Disability Assistance for Working Age People (Scotland) Regulations 2022];

(b) subject to sub-paragraph (6), a person who joins the claimant's household for the first time in order to care for the claimant or his partner and immediately before so joining the claimant or his partner satisfied the condition in sub-paragraph (1) or, as the case may be, (2);

(c) a person who is [⁴⁸ severely sight impaired or blind or treated as severely sight impaired or blind] within the meaning of paragraph 14(1)(h) and (2).

(5) For the purposes of sub-paragraph (2), a person shall be treated [¹¹ . . .] (a) [¹¹ as being in receipt of] attendance allowance, or the care component of disability living allowance at the highest or middle rate prescribed in accordance with section 72(3) of the Benefits Act if he would, but for his being a patient for a period exceeding 28 days, be so in receipt;

[⁴⁶ (aa) as being in receipt of the daily living component of personal independence payment at the standard or enhanced rate in accordance with section 78 of the 2012 Act if he would, but for regulations made under section 86(1) (hospital in-patients) of the 2012 Act, be so in receipt;]

[⁵³ (ab) as being in receipt of the daily living component of adult disability payment at the standard or enhanced rate in accordance with regulation 5 of the Disability Assistance for Working Age People (Scotland) Regulations 2022 if they would, but for regulation 28 (effect of admission to hospital on ongoing entitlement to Adult Disability Payment) of those Regulations be so in receipt;]

[¹¹(b) as being entitled to and in receipt of [²⁴ a carer's allowance] [⁵⁰ or having an award of universal credit which includes the carer element] if he would, but for the person for whom he was caring being a patient in hospital for a period exceeding 28 days, be so entitled and in receipt [⁵⁰ of carer's allowance or have such an award of universal credit].]

(6) Sub-paragraph (4)(b) shall apply only for the first 12 weeks following the date on which the person to whom that provision applies first joins the claimant's household.

(7) For the purposes of sub-paragraph (1)(c) and (2)(d), no account shall be taken of an award of [²⁴ carer's allowance] [⁵⁰ or universal credit which includes the carer element] to the extent that payment of such an award is backdated for a period before [³⁴ the date on which the award is first paid].

(8) A person shall be treated as satisfying this condition if he would have satisfied the condition specified for a severe disability premium in income support in paragraph 13 of Schedule 2 to the Income Support Regulations by virtue only of regulations 4 to 6 of the Income Support (General) Amendment (No. 6) Regulations 1991 (savings provisions in relation to severe disability premium) and for the purposes of determining whether in the particular case regulation 4 of those Regulations had ceased to apply in accordance with regulation 5(2)(a) of those Regulations, a person who is entitled to an income-based jobseeker's allowance shall be treated as entitled to income support.

[²⁰ (9) In sub-paragraphs (1)(c) and (2)(d), references to a person being in receipt of [²⁴ a carer's allowance] [⁵⁰ or as having an award of universal credit which includes the carer element] shall include references to a person who would have been in receipt of that allowance [⁵⁰ or had such an award] but for the application of a restriction under section [³⁹ 6B or] 7 of the Social Security Fraud Act 2001 (loss of benefit provisions).]

[⁵⁰ (10) For the purposes of this paragraph, a person has an award of universal credit which includes the carer element if the person has an award of universal credit which includes an amount which is the carer element under regulation 29 of the Universal Credit Regulations 2013.]

[¹⁶ **Enhanced disability premium**

15A.—[⁴⁶ (1) Subject to sub-paragraph (2), the condition is that—   3.490

(a) the claimant; or

(b) the claimant's partner (if any), is a person who has not attained the qualifying age for state pension credit and is a person to whom sub-paragraph (1ZA) applies.

(1ZA) This sub-paragraph applies to the person mentioned in sub-paragraph (1) where—

(a) the care component of disability living allowance is, or would, but for a suspension of benefit in accordance with regulations under section 113(2) of the Benefits Act or but for an abatement as a consequence of hospitalisation, be payable to that person at the highest rate prescribed under section 72(3) of the Benefits Act; or

[⁵² (aa) the care component of child disability payment is payable to that person at the highest rate in accordance with regulation 11(5) of the DACYP Regulations; or]

(b) the daily living component of personal independence payment is, or would, but for a suspension of benefits in accordance with regulations under section 86(1) (hospital in-patients) of the 2012 Act, be payable to that person at the enhanced rate in accordance with section 78(2) of the 2012 Act] [⁴⁷ ; or

[53 (ba)   the daily living component of adult disability payment is, or would, but regulation 28 (effect of admission to hospital on ongoing entitlement to Adult Disability Payment) of the Disability Assistance for Working Age People (Scotland) Regulations 2022, be payable to that person at the enhanced rate in accordance with regulation 5 of those Regulations]

(c)   armed forces independence payment is payable to that person.]

[42 (1A) Where the condition in sub-paragraph (1) ceases to be satisfied because of the death of a child or young person, the condition is that the claimant is entitled to child benefit in respect of that person under section 145A of the Benefits Act (entitlement after death of child or qualifying young person).]

[33 (2) The condition is not satisfied where the person to whom sub-paragraph (1) refers is—

(a)   a child or young person—

    (i)   whose capital if calculated in accordance with Part 8 of these Regulations in like manner as for the claimant, except as provided in regulation 106(1), would exceed £3,000; or

    (ii)   who is a long-term patient;

(b)   a single claimant or a lone parent and (in either case) is a long-term patient;

(c)   a member of a couple or polygamous marriage and each member of the couple or polygamous marriage is a long-term patient; or

(d)   a member of a couple or polygamous marriage who is—

    (i)   a long-term patient; and

    (ii)   the only member of the couple or polygamous marriage to whom sub-paragraph (1) refers.]]

Disabled Child Premium

3.491   **16.**—[30 . . . 33]

Carer Premium

3.492   **17.**—(1) Subject to sub-paragraphs (3) and (4), the condition is that the claimant or his partner is, or both of them are, [11 entitled to] [24 a carer's allowance] under section 70 of the Benefits Act.

(2) [28 . . .]

[23 (3) Where a carer premium is awarded but—

(a)   the person in respect of whose care the [24 carer's allowance] has been awarded dies; or

(b)   in any other case the person in respect of whom a carer premium has been awarded ceases to be entitled [28 . . .] to [24 a carer's allowance], the condition for the award of the premium shall be treated as satisfied for a period of eight weeks from the relevant date specified in sub-paragraph (3A) below.

(3A) The relevant date for the purposes of sub-paragraph (3) above shall be—

(a)   [28 where sub-paragraph (3)(a) applies,] the Sunday following the death of the person in respect of whose care [24 a carer's allowance] has been awarded or the date of death if the death occurred on a Sunday;

(b)   [28 . . .]

(c)   in any other case, the date of which the person who has been entitled to [24 a carer's allowance] ceases to be entitled to that allowance.]

(4) Where a person who has been entitled to an invalid care allowance ceases to be entitled to that allowance and makes a claim for a jobseeker's allowance, the condition for the award of the carer premium shall be treated as satisfied for a period of eight weeks from the date on which—

[23(a)   the person in respect of whose care the [24 carer's allowance] has been awarded dies;

(b)   [28 . . .]

[28 (c)   in any other case, the person who has been entitled to a carer's allowance ceased to be entitled to that allowance.]]

Persons in receipt of concessionary payments

3.493   **8.**—For the purpose of determining whether a premium is applicable to a person under paragraphs 14 to 17, any concessionary payment made to compensate that person for the non-payment of any benefit mentioned in those paragraphs shall be treated as if it were a payment of that benefit.

Person in receipt of benefit

3.494   **19.**—For the purposes of this Part of this Schedule, a person shall be regarded as being in receipt of any benefit if, and only if, it is paid in respect of him and shall be so regarded only for any period in respect of which that benefit is paid.

PART IV

WEEKLY AMOUNTS OF PREMIUMS SPECIFIED IN
PART III

Premium	Amount
20.—(1) [⁴ . . .]	(1) [⁴ . . .]
(1A) [³⁴ . . .];	(1A) [³⁴ . . .];
(2) Pensioner premium for persons [⁴⁰ who have attained the qualifying age for state pension credit]— (a) where the claimant satisfies the condition in paragraph 10(a); (b) where the claimant satisfies the condition in paragraph 10(b). (c) where the claimant satisfies the condition in paragraph 10(c).	(2) (a) [⁵⁶ £116.25]; (b) [⁵⁶ £173.55]; (c) [⁵⁶ £173.55];
(3) Pensioner premium for claimants whose partner has attained the age of 75 where the claimant satisfies the condition in paragraph 11;	(3) [⁵⁶ £173.55];
(4) Higher Pensioner Premium— (a) where the claimant satisfies the condition in paragraph 12(1)(a); (b) where the claimant satisfies the condition in paragraph 12(1)(b) or (c).	(4) (a) [⁵⁶ £116.25]; (b) [⁵⁶ £173.55];
(5) Disability Premium— (a) where the claimant satisfies the condition in [³³ paragraph 13(1)(a)]; (b) where the claimant satisfies the condition in [³³ paragraph 13(1)(b) or (c)].	(5) (a) [⁵⁶ £39.85]; (b) [⁵⁶ £56.80].

(6) Severe Disability Premium—
 (a) where the claimant satisfies the condition in paragraph 15(1);
 (b) where the claimant satisfies the condition in paragraph 15(2)—
   (i) if there is someone in receipt of [²⁴ a carer's allowance] or [² if any partner of the claimant] satisfies that condition by virtue of paragraph 15(5);
   (ii) if no-one is in receipt of such an allowance.
	(6)
	 (a) [⁵⁶ £76.40];
	
	 (b)
	
	   (i) [⁵⁶ £76.40]
	
	   (ii) [⁵⁶ £152.80]

(7) [³⁰ . . .]	(7) [³⁰ . . .]
(8) Carer Premium.	(8) [⁵⁶ £42.75] in respect of each person who satisfied the condition specified in paragraph 17.

[¹⁶ (9) Enhanced disability premium where the conditions in paragraph 15A are satisfied.]	[¹⁶ (9) (a)[³⁰ . . .]
	 (b) [⁵⁶ £19.55] in respect of each person who is neither—
	   (i) a child or young person; nor
	   (ii) a member of a couple or a polygamous marriage, respect of whom the in conditions specified in paragraph 15A are satisfied;

Premium	Amount
	(c) [^{56} £27.90] where the claimant is a member of a couple or a polygamous marriage and the conditions specified in paragraph 15A are satisfied in respect of a member of that couple or polygamous marriage.]

[^{14} PART IVA

PREMIUMS FOR JOINT-CLAIM COUPLES

3.497   **20A.**—Except as provided in paragraph 20B, the weekly premium specified in Part IVB of this Schedule shall, for the purposes of regulations 86A(c) and 86B(d), be applicable to a joint-claim couple where either or both members of a joint-claim couple satisfy the condition specified in paragraphs 20E to 20J in respect of that premium.

20B.—Subject to paragraph 20C, where a member of a joint-claim couple satisfies the conditions in respect of more than one premium in this Part of this Schedule, only one premium shall be applicable to the joint-claim couple in respect of that member and, if they are different amounts, the higher or highest amount shall apply.

[^{16} **20C.**—(1) Subject to sub-paragraph (2), the following premiums, namely—
     (a) a severe disability premium to which paragraph 20I applies;
     (b) an enhanced disability premium to which paragraph 20IA applies; and
     (c) a carer premium to which paragraph 20J applies,
may be applicable in addition to any other premium which may apply under this Part of this Schedule.

(2) An enhanced disability premium in respect of a person shall not be applicable in addition to—
     (a) a pensioner premium under paragraph 20E; or
     (b) a higher pensioner premium under paragraph 20F.]

20D.—(1) Subject to sub-paragraph (2) for the purposes of this Part of this Schedule, once a premium is applicable to a joint-claim couple under this Part, a person shall be treated as being in receipt of any benefit—
     (a) in the case of a benefit to which the Social Security (Overlapping Benefits) Regulations 1979 applies, for any period during which, apart from the provisions of those Regulations, he would be in receipt of that benefit; and
     (b) for any period spent by a person in undertaking a course of training or instruction provided or approved by the Secretary of State under section 2 of the Employment and Training Act 1973, or by [^{37} Skills Development Scotland,] Scottish Enterprise or Highlands and Islands Enterprise under section 2 of the Enterprise and New Towns (Scotland) Act 1990, or for any period during which he is in receipt of a training allowance.

(2) For the purposes of the carer premium under paragraph 20J, a person shall be treated as being in receipt of [^{24} carer's allowance] by virtue of sub-paragraph (1)(a) only if and for so long as the person in respect of whose care the allowance has been claimed remains in receipt of attendance allowance, [^{46} the care component of disability living allowance at the highest or middle rate prescribed in accordance with section 72(3) of the Benefits Act [^{52} or the care component of child disability payment at the highest or middle rate in accordance with regulation 11(5) of the DACYP Regulations]or the daily living component of personal independence payment at the standard or enhanced rate in accordance with section 78(3) of the 2012 Act [^{53}, the daily living component of adult disability payment at the standard or enhanced rate in accordance with regulation 5 of the [^{54} Disability Assistance for Working Age People (Scotland) Regulations 2022] [^{47} or armed forces independence payment]].

Pensioner premium where one member of a joint-claim couple has attained [^{40} the qualifying age for state pension credit]
3.498   **20E.**—The condition is that one member of a joint-claim couple has attained [^{40} the qualifying age for state pension credit]but not the age of 75.

Higher Pensioner Premium

20F.—(1) [³³ Subject to sub-paragraph (5), the] condition is that one member of a joint   **3.499**
claim couple—

  (a) has attained [⁴⁰ the qualifying age for state pension credit] but not the age of 80, and either the additional conditions specified in paragraph 20H are satisfied in respect of him; or

  (b) has attained [⁴⁰ the qualifying age for state pension credit] and—

    (i) was entitled to or was treated as entitled to either income support or an income-based jobseeker's allowance and the disability premium was or, as the case may be, would have been applicable to him in respect of a benefit week within 8 weeks of [⁴⁰ the date he attained the qualifying age for state pension credit] and he has, subject to sub-paragraph (2), remained continuously entitled to one of those benefits since attaining that age; or

    (ii) was a member of a joint-claim couple who had been entitled to, or who had been treated as entitled to, a joint-claim jobseeker's allowance and the disability premium was or, as the case may be, would have been applicable to that couple in respect of a benefit week within 8 weeks of [⁴⁰ the date either member of that couple attained the qualifying age for state pension credit] and the couple have, subject to that sub-paragraph (2), remained continuously entitled to a joint claim jobseeker's allowance since that member attained that age.

(2) For the purpose of this paragraph and paragraph 20H—

  (a) once the higher pensioner premium is applicable to a joint-claim couple, if that member then ceases, for a period of 8 weeks or less, to be entitled or treated as entitled to either income support or income-based jobseeker's allowance or that couple cease to be entitled to or treated as entitled to a joint-claim jobseeker's allowance, he shall or, as the case may be, that couple shall, on becoming re-entitled to any of those benefits, thereafter be treated as having been continuously entitled thereto;

  (b) in so far as sub-paragraph (1)(b)(i) or (ii) is concerned, if a member of a joint-claim couple ceases to be entitled or treated as entitled to either income support or an income-based jobseeker's allowance or that couple cease to be entitled to or treated as entitled to a joint-claim jobseeker's allowance for a period not exceeding 8 weeks which includes [⁴⁰ the date either member of that couple attained the qualifying age for state pension credit], he shall or, as the case may be, the couple shall, on becoming re-entitled to either of those benefits, thereafter be treated as having been continuously entitled thereto.

(3) In this paragraph, where a member of a joint-claim couple is a welfare to work beneficiary, sub-paragraphs (1)(b)(i) and (2)(b) shall apply to him as if for the words "8 weeks" there were substituted the words "[³²104 weeks]".

(4) For the purposes of this paragraph, a member of a joint-claim couple shall be treated as having been entitled to income support or to an income-based jobseeker's allowance or the couple of which he is a member shall be treated as having been entitled to a joint-claim jobseeker's allowance throughout any period which comprises only days on which a member was participating in an employment zone scheme and was not entitled to—

  (a) income support because, as a consequence of his participation in that scheme, he was engaged in remunerative work or had income in excess of the claimant's applicable amount as prescribed in Part IV of the Income Support Regulations; or

  (b) a jobseeker's allowance because, as a consequence of his participation in that scheme, he was engaged in remunerative work or failed to satisfy the condition specified in section 2(1)(c) or the couple of which he was a member failed to satisfy the condition in section 3A(1)(a).

[³³ (5) The condition is not satisfied if the member of the joint-claim couple to whom sub-paragraph (1) refers is a long-term patient.]

[³³ Disability Premium

20G.—(1) Subject to sub-paragraph (2), the condition is that a member of a joint-claim   **3.500**
couple has not attained [⁴⁰ the qualifying age for state pension credit] and satisfies any one of the additional conditions specified in paragraph 20H.

(2) The condition is not satisfied if—

  (a) paragraph (1) only refers to one member of a joint-claim couple and that member is a long-term patient; or

  (b) paragraph (1) refers to both members of a joint-claim couple and both members of the couple are long-term patients.]

Additional conditions for Higher Pensioner and Disability Premium

3.501   **20H.**—(1) The additional conditions specified in this paragraph are that a member of a joint-claim couple—

(a) is in receipt of [²⁶ the disability element or the severe disability element of working tax credit as specified in regulation 20(1)(b) and (f) of the Working Tax Credit (Entitlement and Maximum Rate) Regulations 2002] or mobility supplement;

(b) is in receipt of severe disablement allowance;

(c) is in receipt of attendance allowance or disability living allowance or is a person whose disability living allowance is payable, in whole or in part, to another in accordance with regulation 44 of the Claims and Payments Regulations (payment of disability living allowance on behalf of third party);

[⁴⁶ (ca) is in receipt of personal independence payment or is a person whose personal independence payment is payable, in whole or in part, to another in accordance with regulation 58(2) of the Universal Credit etc. Claims and Payments Regulations (payment to another person on the claimant's behalf);]

[⁵³ (caa) is in receipt of adult disability payment or is a person whose adult disability payment is payable, in whole or in part, to another in accordance with regulation 33 of the Disability Assistance for Working Age People (Scotland) Regulations 2022 (making payments);]

[⁴⁷ (cb) is in receipt of armed forces independence payment or is a person whose armed forces independence payment is payable, in whole or in part, to another in accordance with article 24D of the Armed Forces and Reserve Forces (Compensation Scheme) Order 2011;]

(d) is in receipt of long-term incapacity benefit or is a person to whom section 30B(4) of the Benefits Act (long-term rate of incapacity benefit payable to those who are terminally ill) applies;

(e) has been entitled to statutory sick pay, has been incapable of work or has been treated as incapable of work for a continuous period of not less than—

(i) 196 days in the case of a member of a joint-claim couple who is terminally ill within the meaning of section 30B(4) of the Benefits Act; or

(ii) 364 days in any other case,

and for these purposes, any two or more periods of entitlement or incapacity separated by a break of not more than 56 days shall be treated as one continuous period;

[³⁶ (ee) has had limited capability for work or has been treated as having limited capability for work for a continuous period of not less than—

(i) 196 days in the case of a member of a joint-claim couple who is terminally ill within the meaning of regulation 2(1) of the Employment and Support Allowance Regulations; or

(ii) 364 days in any other case,

and for these purposes any two or more periods of limited capability for work separated by a break of not more than 12 weeks is to be treated as one continuous period;]

(f) has an invalid carriage or other vehicle provided to him by the Secretary of State under section 5(2)(a) of, and Schedule 2 to, the National Health Service Act 1977 or under section 46 of the National Health Service (Scotland) Act 1978 or provided by the Department of Health and Social Services for Northern Ireland under article 30(1) of the Health and Personal Social Services (Northern Ireland) Order 1972, or receives payments by way of grant from the Secretary of State under paragraph 2 of Schedule 2 to the Act of 1977 (additional provisions as to vehicles) or, in Scotland, under section 46 of the Act of 1978;

(g) is a person who is entitled to the mobility component of disability living allowance but to whom the component is not payable in accordance with regulation 42 of the Claims and Payments Regulations (cases where disability living allowance not payable);

[⁴⁶ (ga) is a person who is entitled to the mobility component of personal independence payment but to whom the component is not payable in accordance with regulation 61 of the Universal Credit etc. Claims and Payments Regulations (cases where mobility component of personal independence payment not payable);]

[⁵³ (gb) is a person who is entitled to the mobility component of adult disability payment but to whom the component is not payable in accordance with regulation 34(6) of the Disability Assistance for Working Age People (Scotland) Regulations 2022 (amount and form of adult disability payment);]

(h) was either—

(i) in receipt of long-term incapacity benefit under section 30A(5) of the Benefits Act immediately before attaining pensionable age and he is still alive; or

    (ii) entitled to attendance allowance or disability living allowance but payment of that benefit was suspended in accordance with regulations under section 113(2) of the Benefits Act or otherwise abated as a consequence of either member of the joint-claim couple becoming a patient within the meaning of regulation 85(4) (special cases), [⁴⁶ [⁵³ . . .]

    (iii) entitled to personal independence payment but no amount is payable in accordance with regulations under section 86(1) (hospital in-patients) of the 2012 Act,] [⁵³ or

    (iv) entitled to adult disability payment but no amount is payable in accordance with regulation 28 (effect of admission to hospital on ongoing entitlement to Adult [⁵⁴ Disability Payment) of the Disability Assistance for Working Age People (Scotland) Regulations 2022,]

    and [⁵³ in any of the cases described in paragraphs (i) to (iv)], the higher pensioner premium or disability premium had been applicable to the joint-claim couple; or

[⁴⁸ (l) is certified as severely sight impaired or blind by a consultant ophthalmologist.]

(2) [⁴¹ . . . [³² . . .]]

[⁴⁸ (3) For the purposes of sub-paragraph (1)(i), a person who has ceased to be certified as severely sight impaired or blind on regaining his eyesight shall nevertheless be treated as severely sight impaired or blind, as the case may be, and as satisfying the additional condition set out in that sub-paragraph for a period of 28 weeks following the date on which he ceased to be so certified.]

Severe Disability Premium

20I.—(1) The condition is that—

    (a) a member of a joint-claim couple is in receipt of attendance allowance [⁴⁶ , the care component of disability living allowance at the highest or middle rate prescribed in accordance with section 72(3) of the Benefits Act [⁴⁷ , armed forces independence payment] [⁵³ ,] the daily living component of personal independence payment at the standard or enhanced rate in accordance with section 78(3) of the 2012 Act] [⁵³ , or the daily living component of adult disability payment at the standard or enhanced rate in accordance with regulation 5 of the Disability Assistance for Working Age People (Scotland) Regulations 2022]; and

    (b) the other member is also in receipt of such an allowance, or if he is a member of a polygamous marriage, all the partners of that marriage are in receipt of a qualifying benefit; and

    (c) subject to sub-paragraph (3), there is no non-dependant aged 18 or over normally residing with the joint-claim couple or with whom they are normally residing; and

    (d) either—

        (i) no person is entitled to, and in receipt of, [²⁴ a carer's allowance] under section 70 of the Benefits Act [⁵⁰ or has an award of universal credit which includes the carer element] in respect of caring for either member or the couple or all the members of the polygamous marriage; or

        (ii) a person is engaged in caring for one member (but not both members) of the couple, or one or more but not all members of the polygamous marriage, and in consequence is entitled to [²⁴ a carer's allowance] under section 70 of the Benefits Act [⁵⁰ or has an award of universal credit which includes the carer element].

(2) Where the other member does not satisfy the condition in sub-paragraph (1)(b), and that member is [⁴⁸ severely sight impaired or blind or treated as severely sight impaired or blind] within the meaning of paragraph 20H(1)(i) and (2), that member shall be treated for the purposes of sub-paragraph (1) as if he were not a member of the couple.

(3) The following persons shall not be regarded as non-dependant for the purposes of sub-paragraph (1)(c)—

    (a) a person in receipt of attendance allowance [⁴⁶ , the care component of disability living allowance at the highest or middle rate prescribed in accordance with section 72(3) of the Benefits Act [⁴⁷ , armed forces independence payment] [⁵³ ,] the daily living component of personal independence payment at the standard or enhanced rate in accordance with section 78(3) of the 2012 Act] [⁵³ , or the daily living component of adult disability payment at the standard or enhanced rate in accordance with regulation 5 of the Disability Assistance for Working Age People (Scotland) Regulations 2022];

    (b) subject to sub-paragraph (5), a person who joins the joint-claim couple's household for the first time in order to care for a member of a joint claim couple and immediately before so joining, that member satisfied the condition in sub-paragraph (1);

3.502

(c) a person who is [⁴⁸ severely sight impaired or blind or treated as severely sight impaired or blind] within the meaning of paragraph 20H(1)(i) and (2).

(4) For the purposes of sub-paragraph (1), a member of a joint-claim couple shall be treated—

(a) as being in receipt of attendance allowance, or the care component of disability living allowance at the highest or middle rate prescribed in accordance with section 72(3) of the Benefits Act if he would, but for his being a patient for a period exceeding 28 days, be so in receipt;

(b) as being entitled to and in receipt of [²⁴ a carer's allowance] [⁵⁰ or having an award of universal credit which includes the carer element] if he would, but for the person for whom he was caring being a patient in hospital for a period exceeding 28 days, be so entitled and in receipt [⁵⁰ of carer's allowance or have such an award of universal credit].

[⁴⁶ (c) as being in receipt of the daily living component of personal independence payment at the standard or enhanced rate in accordance with section 78 of the 2012 Act if he would, but for regulations made under section 86(1) (hospital in-patients) of the 2012 Act, be so in receipt.]

[⁵³ (d) as being in receipt of the daily living component of adult disability payment at the standard or enhanced rate in accordance with regulation 5 of the [⁵⁴ Disability Assistance for Working Age People (Scotland) Regulations 2022], if he would, but for regulation 28 (effect of admission to hospital on ongoing entitlement to Adult Disability Payment) of those Regulations, be so in receipt]

(5) Sub-paragraph (3)(b) shall apply only for the first 12 weeks following the date on which the person to whom that provision applies first joins the joint-claim couple's household.

(6) For the purposes of sub-paragraph (1)(d), no account shall be taken of an award of [²⁴ carer's allowance] [⁵⁰ or universal credit which includes the carer element] to the extent that payment of such an award is back-dated for a period before [³⁴ the date on which the award is first paid].

[²⁰ (7) In sub-paragraph (1)(d), the reference to a person being in receipt of [²⁴ a carer's allowance] [⁵⁰ or as having an award of universal credit which includes the carer element] shall include a reference to a person who would have been in receipt of that allowance [⁵⁰ or had such an award] but for the application of a restriction under section [³⁹ 6B or] 7 of the Social Security Fraud Act 2001 (loss of benefit provisions).]

[⁵⁰ (8) For the purposes of this paragraph, a person has an award of universal credit which includes the carer element if the person has an award of universal credit which includes an amount which is the carer element under regulation 29 of the Universal Credit Regulations 2013.]

[¹⁶ Enhanced disability premium

3.503   **20IA.**—[⁴⁶ (1) Subject to sub-paragraph (2), the condition is that in respect of a member of a joint-claim couple who has not attained the qualifying age for state pension credit—

(a) the care component of disability living allowance is, or would, but for a suspension of benefit in accordance with regulations under section 113(2) of the Benefits Act or but for an abatement as a consequence of hospitalisation, be payable at the highest rate prescribed under section 72(3) of the Benefits Act; or

(b) the daily living component of personal independence payment is, or would, but for regulations made under section 86(1) (hospital in-patients) of the 2012 Act, be payable at the enhanced rate in accordance with section 78(2) of the 2012 Act [⁵³ , the daily living component of adult disability payment is, or would, but for regulation 28 (effect of admission to hospital on ongoing entitlement to Adult Disability Payment) of the [⁵⁴ Disability Assistance for Working Age People (Scotland) Regulations 2022], be payable at the enhanced rate under those Regulations,] [⁴⁷ or armed forces independence payment is payable].]

[³³ (2) The condition is not satisfied if—

(a) paragraph (1) only refers to one member of a joint-claim couple and that member is a long-term patient; or

(b) paragraph (1) refers to both members of a joint-claim couple and both members of the couple are long-term patients.]]

Carer Premium

3.504   **20J.**—(1) Subject to sub-paragraphs (3) and (4), the condition is that either or both members of a joint-claim couple are entitled to [²⁸ . . .] [²⁴ a carer's allowance] under section 70 of the Benefits Act.

(2) [²⁸ . . .]

[²³ (3) Where a carer premium is awarded but—
(a) the person in respect of whose care the [²⁴ carer's allowance] has been awarded dies: or
(b) in any other case the member of the joint-claim couple in respect of whom a carer premium has been awarded ceases to be entitled [²⁸ . . .] to [²⁴ a carer's allowance], the condition for the award of the premium shall be treated as satisfied for a period of eight weeks from the relevant date specified in sub-paragraph (3A) below.
(3A) The relevant date for the purposes of sub-paragraph (3) above shall be—
(a) [²⁸ where sub-paragraph (3)(a) applies,] the Sunday following the death of the person in respect of whose care [²⁴ a carer's allowance] has been awarded or beginning with the date of death if the death occurred on a Sunday;
(b) [²⁸ . . .]
(c) in any other case, the date on which that member ceased to be entitled to [²⁴ a carer's allowance].]
(4) Where a member of a joint-claim couple who has been entitled to an invalid care allowance ceases to be entitled to that allowance and makes a claim for a jobseeker's allowance jointly with the other member of that couple, the condition for the award of the carer premium shall be treated as satisfied for a period of eight weeks from the date on which—
[²³(a) the person in respect of whose care the [²⁴ carer's allowance] has been awarded dies;
(b) [²⁸ . . .]
(c) [²⁸ in any other case, the person who has been entitled to a carer's allowance ceased to be entitled to that allowance.]]

Member of a joint-claim couple in receipt of concessionary payments
20K.—For the purpose of determining whether a premium is applicable to a joint-claim couple under paragraphs 20H to 20J, any concessionary payment made to compensate a person for the non-payment of any benefit mentioned in those paragraphs shall be treated as if it were a payment of that benefit.   3.505

Person in receipt of benefit
20L.—For the purposes of this Part of this Schedule, a member of a joint-claim couple shall be regarded as being in receipt of any benefit if, and only if, it is paid in respect of him and shall be so regarded only for any period in respect of which that benefit is paid.   3.506

PART IVB

Premium	Amount
20M.—	
(1) Pensioner premium where one member of a joint-claim couple [⁴⁰ has attained the qualifying age for state pension credit] and the condition in paragraph 20E is satisfied.	(1) [⁵⁷ £173.55].
(2) Higher Pensioner Premium where one member of a joint-claim couple satisfies the condition in paragraph 20F.	(2) [⁵⁷ £173.55].
(3) Disability Premium where one member of a joint-claim couple satisfies the condition in paragraph [³³ 20G(1)].	(3) [⁵⁷ £56.80].
(4) Severe Disability Premium where one member of a joint-claim couple satisfies the condition in paragraph 20I(1)— (i) if there is someone in receipt of [²⁴ a carer's allowance] or if either member satisfies that condition only by virtue of paragraph [¹⁶ 20I(4)]; (ii) if no-one is in receipt of such an allowance.	(4) (i) [⁵⁷ £76.40]; (ii) [⁵⁷ £152.80].

Income Support and the Legacy Benefits: Cumulative Supplement

Premium	Amount
(5) Carer Premium.	(5) [57 £42.75] in respect of each person who satisfied the condition specified in paragraph 20J.]
[16 (6) Enhanced disability premium where the conditions specified in paragraph 20IA are satisfied.	(6) [57 £27.90] where the conditions in paragraph 20IA are satisfied in respect of a member of a joint-claim couple.]

PART V

ROUNDING OF FRACTIONS

3.508   21.—Where an income-based jobseeker's allowance is awarded for a period which is not a complete benefit week and the applicable amount in respect of that period results in an amount which includes a fraction of one penny that fraction shall be treated as one penny."

AMENDMENTS

1. Jobseeker's Allowance (Amendment) Regulations 1996 (SI 1996/1516) reg.18 (October 7, 1996).

2. Jobseeker's Allowance (Amendment) Regulations 1996 (SI 1996/1516) reg.20 and Sch. (October 7, 1996).

3. Social Security and Child Support (Jobseeker's Allowance) (Miscellaneous Amendments) Regulations 1996 (SI 1996/2538) reg.2(11) (October 28, 1996).

4. Child Benefit, Child Support and Social Security (Miscellaneous Amendments) Regulations 1996 (SI 1996/1803) reg.44 (April 7, 1997).

5. Income-related Benefits and Jobseeker's Allowance (Personal Allowances for Children and Young Persons) (Amendment) Regulations 1996 (SI 1996/2545) reg.2 (April 7, 1997).

6. Income-related Benefits and Jobseeker's Allowance (Amendment) (No. 2) Regulations 1997 (SI 1997/2197) reg.7(5) and (6)(b) (October 6, 1997).

7. Social Security Amendment (Lone Parents) Regulations 1998 (SI 1998/766) reg.14 (April 6, 1998).

8. Social Security (Welfare to Work) Regulations 1998 (SI 1998/2231) reg.14(3) (October 5, 1998).

9. Social Security Amendment (Personal Allowances for Children and Young Persons) Regulations 1999 (SI 1999/2555) reg.2(1)(b) and (2) (April 10, 2000).

10. Social Security and Child Support (Tax Credits) Consequential Amendments Regulations 1999 (SI 1999/2566) reg.2(2) and Sch.2 Pt III (October 5, 1999).

11. Social Security (Miscellaneous Amendments) Regulations 2000 (SI 2000/681) reg.4(3) (April 3, 2000).

12. Social Security Amendment (Employment Zones) Regulations 2000 (SI 2000/724) reg.4 (April 3, 2000).

13. Social Security Amendment (Personal Allowances for Children) Regulations 2000 (SI 2000/1993) reg.2 (October 23, 2000).

14. Jobseeker's Allowance (Joint Claims) Regulations 2000 (SI 2000/1978) reg.2(5) and Sch.2 para.53 (March 19, 2001).

15. Social Security Amendment (Bereavement Benefits) Regulations 2000 (SI 2000/2239) reg.3(2) (April 9, 2001).

16. Social Security Amendment (Enhanced Disability Premium) Regulations 2000 (SI 2629) reg.5(c) (April 9, 2001).

17. Social Security Amendment (Joint Claims) Regulations 2001 (SI 2001/518) reg.2(7) (March 19, 2001).

18. Social Security Amendment (Bereavement Benefits) Regulations 2000 (SI 2000/2239) reg.3(2)(c) (April 9, 2001).

19. Social Security Amendment (Residential Care and Nursing Homes) Regulations 2001 (SI 2001/3767) reg.2 and Sch. Pt II para.18 (April 8, 2002).

20. Social Security (Loss of Benefit) (Consequential Amendments) Regulations 2002 (SI 2002/490) reg.2 (April 1, 2002).

21. Social Security Amendment (Residential Care and Nursing Homes) Regulations 2001 (SI 2001/3767) reg.2 and Sch. Pt II para.18 (as amended by Social Security Amendment (Residential Care and Nursing Homes) Regulations 2002 (SI 2002/398) reg.4(3)) (April 8, 2002).

22. Social Security Amendment (Personal Allowances for Children and Young Persons) Regulations 2002 (SI 2002/2019) reg.2 (October 14, 2002).

23. Social Security Amendment (Carer Premium) Regulations 2002 (SI 2002/2020) reg.3 (October 28, 2002).

24. Social Security (Miscellaneous Amendments) Regulations 2003 (SI 2003/511) reg.3(4) and (5) (April 1, 2003).

25. Social Security (Working Tax Credit and Child Tax Credit) (Consequential Amendments) Regulations 2003 (SI 2003/455) regs 1(9), 3 and Sch.2 para.20(b) (April 7, 2003).

26. Social Security (Working Tax Credit and Child Tax Credit) (Consequential Amendments) Regulations 2003 (SI 2003/455) regs 1(9), 3 and Sch.2 para.20(e) (April 7, 2003).

27. Social Security (Hospital In-Patients and Miscellaneous Amendments) Regulations 2003 (SI 2003/1195) reg.6 (May 21, 2003).

28. Social Security (Miscellaneous Amendments) (No. 2) Regulations 2003 (SI 2003/2279) reg.3(3) (October 1, 2003).

29. Social Security (Removal of Residential Allowance and Miscellaneous Amendments) Regulations 2003 (SI 2003/1121) reg.4 and Sch.2 para.9 (October 6, 2003).

30. Social Security (Working Tax Credit and Child Tax Credit) (Consequential Amendments) Regulations 2003 (SI 2003/455) reg.3 and Sch.2 para.20 (April 6, 2004, except in "transitional cases" and see further the note to regs 83 and to 17 of the Income Support Regulations).

31. Civil Partnership (Pensions, Social Security and Child Support) (Consequential, etc. Provisions) Order 2005 (SI 2005/2877) art.2(3) and Sch.3 para.26(11) (December 5, 2005).

32. Social Security (Miscellaneous Amendments) (No. 4) Regulations 2006 (SI 2006/2378) reg.13(10) (October 1, 2006).

33. Social Security (Miscellaneous Amendments) Regulations 2007 (SI 2007/719) reg.3(8) (April 9, 2007). As it relates to paras 15(2)(a) and 16, the amendment only affects "transitional cases". See further the note to reg.17 of the Income Support Regulations and the commentary below.

34. Social Security (Miscellaneous Amendments) (No. 5) Regulations 2007 (SI 2007/2618) reg.2 and Sch. (October 1, 2007).

35. Social Security (Miscellaneous Amendments) Regulations 2008 (SI 2008/698) reg.4(14) (April 14, 2008).

36. Employment and Support Allowance (Consequential Provisions) (No. 2) Regulations 2008 (SI 2008/1554) reg.3(1) and (24) (October 27, 2008).

37. Social Security (Miscellaneous Amendments) Regulations 2009 (SI 2009/583) reg.4(1) and (3) (April 6, 2009).

38. Social Security (Students and Miscellaneous Amendments) Regulations 2009 (SI 2009/1575) reg.3 (August 1, 2009).

39. Social Security (Loss of Benefit) Amendment Regulations 2010 (SI 2010/1160) reg.11(1) and (3) (April 1, 2010).

40. Social Security (Equalisation of State Pension Age) Regulations 2009 (SI 2009/1488) reg.13 (April 6, 2010).

41. Employment and Support Allowance (Transitional Provisions, Housing Benefit and Council Tax Benefit) (Existing Awards) (No. 2) Regulations 2010 (SI 2010/1907) reg.26(1) and Sch.4 para.1A(3) (as amended by the Employment and Support Allowance (Transitional Provisions, Housing Benefit and Council Tax Benefit) (Existing Awards)

(No. 2) (Amendment) Regulations 2010 (SI 2010/2430) reg.15) (November 1, 2010).

42. Social Security (Miscellaneous Amendments) Regulations 2011 (SI 2011/674) reg.7(7) (April 11, 2011).

43. Social Security Benefits Up-rating Order 2012 (SI 2012/780) art.25(3) and Sch.13 (April 9, 2012).

44. Social Security Benefits Up-rating Order 2012 (SI 2012/780) art.25(5) and Sch.14 (April 9, 2012).

45. Social Security Benefits Up-rating Order 2012 (SI 2012/780) art.25(6) and Sch.15 (April 9, 2012).

46. Personal Independence Payment (Supplementary Provisions and Consequential Amendments) Regulations 2013 (SI 2013/388) reg.8 and Sch. para.16(1) and (7) (April 8, 2013).

47. Armed Forces and Reserve Forces Compensation Scheme (Consequential Provisions: Subordinate Legislation) Order 2013 (SI 2013/591) art.7 and Sch. para.10(1) and (7) (April 8, 2013).

48. Universal Credit and Miscellaneous Amendments (No. 2) Regulations 2014 (SI 2014/2888) reg.3(3) (November 26, 2014).

49. Welfare Benefits Up-rating Order 2015 (SI 2015/30) art.9 and Sch.3 (April 6, 2015).

50. Universal Credit and Miscellaneous Amendments Regulations 2015 (SI 2015/1754) reg.15 (October 28, 2015).

51. Universal Credit and Jobseeker's Allowance (Miscellaneous Amendments) Regulations 2018 (SI 2018/1129) reg.2 (November 28, 2018).

52. Social Security (Scotland) Act 2018 (Disability Assistance for Children and Young People) (Consequential Modifications) Order 2021 (SI 2021/786) Sch.3 paras 7–8 (July 26, 2021).

53. Social Security (Disability Assistance for Working Age People) (Consequential Amendments) Order 2022 (SI 2022/177) art.7 (March 21, 2022).

54. Social Security (Disability Assistance for Working Age People) (Consequential Amendments) (No. 2) Order 2022 (SI 2022/530) art.3(2) (June 6, 2022).

55. Social Security Benefits Up-rating Order 2023 (SI 2023/316) art.27(1) and (3)(a), and Sch.8 (April 10, 2023).

56. Social Security Benefits Up-rating Order 2023 (SI 2023/316) art.27(1) and (5), and Sch.9 (April 10, 2023).

57. Social Security Benefits Up-rating Order 2023 (SI 2023/316) art.27(1) and (6), and Sch.10 (April 10, 2023).

DEFINITIONS

"adult disability payment"—see reg.1(3).
"attendance allowance"—*ibid.*
"the Benefits Act"—see Jobseekers Act s.35(1).
"child"—*ibid.*
"child disability payment"—*ibid.*
"claimant"—*ibid.*
"couple"—see reg.1(3).
"DACYP Regulations"—*ibid.*
"disability living allowance"—*ibid.*
"family"—see Jobseekers Act s.35(1).
"invalid carriage or other vehicle"—see reg.1(3).
"lone parent"—*ibid.*
"mobility supplement"—*ibid.*
"non-dependent"—see reg.2.
"partner"—see reg.1(3).
"personal independence payment"—*ibid.*
"polygamous marriage"—*ibid.*
"preserved right"—*ibid.*

"single claimant"—*ibid.*
"welfare to work beneficiary"—*ibid.*
"young person"—see reg.76.
For the General Note to Sch.1, see Vol.V paras 3.509–3.518.

p.1120, *amendments to the Jobseeker's Allowance Regulations 1996 (SI 1996/207) Sch.2 para.17 (Non-dependant deductions)*

With effect from April 10, 2023, art.27 of the Social Security Benefits Up-rating Order 2023 (SI 2023/316) makes the following amendments to para.17 of Sch.2:   5.066

- in sub-para.(1)(a) for "£102.85" substitute "£115.75";
- in sub-para.(1)(b) for "£15.95" substitute "£18.10";
- in sub-para.(2)(a) for "£149.00" substitute "£162.00";
- in sub-para.(2)(b):
  (iv) for "£35.65" substitute "£41.60";
  (v) for "£149.00" substitute "£162.00"; and
  (vi) for "£217.00" substitute "£235.00";
- in sub-para.(2)(c):
  (iv) for "£50.30" substitute "£57.10";
  (v) for "£217.00" substitute "£235.00"; and
  (vi) for "£283.00" substitute "£308.00";
- in sub-para.(2)(d):
  (iv) for "£82.30" substitute "£93.40";
  (v) for "£283.00" substitute "£308.00"; and
  (vi) for "£377.00" substitute "£410.00"; and
- in sub-para.(2)(e):
  (iv) for "£93.70" substitute "£105.35";
  (v) for "£377.00" substitute "£410.00"; and
  (vi) for "£469.00" substitute "£511.00".

pp.1120–1122, *amendments to the Jobseeker's Allowance Regulations 1996 (SI 1996/207) Sch.2 para.17 (Housing costs—non-dependant deductions)*

With effect from July 26, 2021, Sch.3 para.9 of the Social Security (Scotland) Act 2018 (Disability Assistance for Children and Young People) (Consequential Modifications) Order 2021 (SI 2021/786) makes the following amendments to Sch.2 para.17:   5.067

- in sub-para.(6)(b), at the end of para.(ii), insert "or (iia) the care component of child disability payment;"
- in sub-para.(8)(a), after "disability living allowance", insert ", child disability payment".

With effect from January 1, 2022, reg.3(6) of the Social Security (Income and Capital Disregards) (Amendment) Regulations 2021 (SI 2021/1405) inserts into para.17(8)(b), after "Grenfell Tower payment", ", child abuse payment or Windrush payment".

With effect from March 21, 2022, art.5(8) of the Social Security (Disability Assistance for Working Age People) (Consequential Amendments) Order 2022 (SI 2022/177) makes the following amendments to Sch.2 para.17:

- after para.17(6)(b)(iii) (non-dependant deductions), insert "(iiia) the daily living component of adult disability payment;";
- in para.17(8)(a):
  - after "armed forces independence payment" for "or" substitute ",";
  - after "personal independence payment" insert "or adult disability payment".

p.1146, *amendment to the Jobseeker's Allowance Regulations 1996 (SI 1996/207) Sch.7 para.7 (Sums to be disregarded in the calculation of income other than earnings—mobility component)*

5.068   With effect from March 21, 2022, art.5(9)(a) of the Social Security (Disability Assistance for Working Age People) (Consequential Amendments) Order 2022 (SI 2022/177) amended para.7 to read as follows (square brackets indicate only the present amendment, those indicating previous amendments having been omitted):

"**7.**—The mobility component of disability living allowance[,] the mobility component of personal independence payment [or the mobility component of adult disability payment]."

"Adult disability payment" is defined in reg.1(3) by reference to reg.2 of the Disability Assistance for Working Age People (Scotland) Regulations 2022 (SSI 2022/54) (see Vol.IV of this series).

p.1147, *amendment to the Jobseeker's Allowance Regulations 1996 (SI 1996/207) Sch.7 para.10 (Sums to be disregarded in the calculation of income other than earnings—attendance allowance, care component of DLA or daily living component)*

5.069   With effect from March 21, 2022, art.5(9)(b) of the Social Security (Disability Assistance for Working Age People) (Consequential Amendments) Order 2022 (SI 2022/177) amended para.10 to read as follows (square brackets indicate only the present amendment, those indicating previous amendments having been omitted):

"**10.**—Any attendance allowance, the care component of disability living allowance[,] the daily living component of personal independence payment [or the daily living component of adult disability payment]."

"Adult disability payment" is defined in reg.1(3) by reference to reg.2 of the Disability Assistance for Working Age People (Scotland) Regulations 2022 (SSI 2022/54) (see Vol.IV of this series).

p.1149, *amendment to the Jobseeker's Allowance Regulations 1996 (SI 1996/207) Sch.7 para.22(2) (Sums to be disregarded in the calculation of income other than earnings—income in kind)*

5.070   With effect from January 1, 2022, reg.3(7)(a) of the Social Security (Income and Capital Disregards) (Amendment) Regulations 2021 (SI 2021/1405) amended sub-para.(2) by inserting ", a child abuse payment or a Windrush payment" after "Grenfell Tower payment". All of those payments are defined in reg.1(3). See the entry for p.684 for discussion of the nature of child abuse and Windrush payments.

p.1151, *amendment to the Jobseeker's Allowance Regulations 1996 (SI 1996/207) Sch.7 para.28(da) (Sums to be disregarded in the calculation of income other than earnings—payments for persons temporarily in care of claimant)*

With effect from July 1, 2022, reg.10 of the Health and Care Act 2022 (Consequential and Related Amendments and Transitional Provisions) Regulations 2022 (SI 2022/634) amended para.28 by substituting the following for sub-para.(da): **5.071**

"(da) an integrated care board established under Chapter A3 of Part 2 of the National Health Service Act 2006;"

Note that sub-para.(dzb) seems to be out of the proper order in the 2021/22 main volume.

p.1153, *amendments to the Jobseeker's Allowance Regulations 1996 (SI 1996/207) Sch.7 para.41 (Sums to be disregarded in the calculation of income other than earnings)*

With effect from January 1, 2022, reg.3(7)(b) of the Social Security (Income and Capital Disregards) (Amendment) Regulations 2021 (SI 2021/1405) amended para.41 by substituting the following for sub-para. (1A): **5.072**

"(1A) Any—
(a) Grenfell Tower payment;
(b) child abuse payment;
(c) Windrush payment."

In addition, reg.3(7)(c) amended sub-paras (2) to (6) by inserting ", a child abuse payment or a Windrush payment" after "Grenfell Tower payment" in each place where those words occur. All of those payments are defined in reg.1(3).

See the entry for p.684 (Income Support Regulations, Sch.10 (capital to be disregarded) para.22) for some technical problems arising from the date of effect of these amendments. Because all the payments so far made from the approved historic institutional child abuse compensation schemes and from the Windrush Compensation Scheme have been in the nature of capital, the question of disregarding income has not yet arisen.

p.1166, *amendment to the Jobseeker's Allowance Regulations 1996 (SI 1996/207) Sch.8 para.12A (Capital to be disregarded—widowed parent's allowance)*

With effect from February 9, 2023, para.3(a) of the Schedule to the Bereavement Benefits (Remedial) Order 2023 (SI 2023/134) inserted the following after para.12: **5.073**

"12A. Any payment of a widowed parent's allowance made pursuant to section 39A of the Contributions and Benefits Act (widowed parent's allowance)—
(a) to the survivor of a cohabiting partnership (within the meaning in section 39A(7) of the Contributions and Benefits Act) who is entitled

to a widowed parent's allowance for a period before the Bereavement Benefits (Remedial) Order 2023 comes into force, and
   (b) in respect of any period of time during the period ending with the day before the survivor makes the claim for a widowed parent's allowance,
but only for a period of 52 weeks from the date of receipt of the payment."

The legislation on widowed parent's allowance (WPA), and bereavement support payment (BSP) that replaced it for deaths after April 5, 2017, was declared incompatible with the ECHR by discriminating against children whose parents were cohabiting but not married to each other or in a civil partnership (see *Re McLaughlin's Application for Judicial Review* [2018] UKSC 48; [2018] 1 W.L.R. 4250 and *R(Jackson) v Secretary of State for Work and Pensions* [2020] EWHC 183 (Admin); [2020] 1 W.L.R. 1441 in Vol.I of this series). The Remedial Order allows retrospective claims to be made for those benefits from August 30, 2018 onwards and accordingly for arrears of benefit to be paid if the conditions of entitlement are met. The new para.12A, and the amended para.65 on BSP, deal with the consequences of such payments on old style JSA entitlement, by providing for them to be disregarded as capital for 52 weeks from receipt. See the entry for p.682 on income support for the effect of the payment of arrears of WPA being in its nature a payment of income to be taken into account (subject to a £10 per week disregard under para.17(i) of Sch.7 to the JSA Regulations 1996) against entitlement in past periods (allowing revision and the creation of an overpayment) and the misleading state of para.7.15 of the Explanatory Memorandum to the Order.

pp.1167–1168, *amendments to the Jobseeker's Allowance Regulations 1996 (SI 1996/207) Sch.8 para.27 (Capital to be disregarded)*

5.074   With effect from January 1, 2022, reg.3(8)(a) of the Social Security (Income and Capital Disregards) (Amendment) Regulations 2021 (SI 2021/1405) amended sub-para.(1A) by inserting ", child abuse payment, Windrush payment" after "Grenfell Tower payment" and amended sub-paras (2) to (6) by inserting ", a child abuse payment or a Windrush payment" after "Grenfell Tower payment" in each place where those words occur. All of those payments are defined in reg.1(3).
   See the entry for p.684 (Income Support Regulations Sch.10 (Capital to be disregarded) para.22) for some technical problems with the addition only with effect from January 1, 2022 of the disregards of payments from approved schemes providing compensation in respect of historic institutional child abuse in the UK and from the Windrush Compensation Scheme. All the schemes so far in existence provide payments in the nature of capital. That entry also contains information about the nature of the schemes involved, including the child abuse compensation schemes so far approved.

p.1168, *amendment to the Jobseeker's Allowance Regulations 1996 (SI 1996/207) Sch.8 para.31 (Capital to be disregarded—payments in kind)*

5.075   With effect from January 1, 2022, reg.3(8)(b) of the Social Security (Income and Capital Disregards) (Amendment) Regulations 2021 (SI 2021/1405) amended para.31 by inserting ", a child abuse payment or a

Windrush payment" after "Grenfell Tower payment". All of those payments are defined in reg.1(3). See also the entry for p.684.

p.1172, *amendment to the Jobseeker's Allowance Regulations 1996 (SI 1996/207) Sch.8 para.65 (Capital to be disregarded—bereavement support payment)*

With effect from February 9, 2023, para.3(b) of the Schedule to the Bereavement Benefits (Remedial) Order 2023 (SI 2023/134) amended para.65 by making the existing text sub-para.(1) and inserting the following:　　　5.076

"(2) Where bereavement support payment under section 30 of the Pensions Act 2014 is paid to the survivor of a cohabiting partnership (within the meaning in section 30(6B) of the Pensions Act 2014) in respect of a death occurring before the day the Bereavement Benefits (Remedial) Order 2023 comes into force, any amount of that payment which is—
(a) in respect of the rate set out in regulation 3(1) of the Bereavement Support Payment Regulations 2017, and
(b) paid as a lump sum for more than one monthly recurrence of the day of the month on which their cohabiting partner died,
but only for a period of 52 weeks from the date of receipt of the payment."

See the entry for p.682 on income support for the general background. The operation of this amendment is much more straightforward than that of the new para.12A on widowed parent's allowance. Although a payment of arrears of bereavement support payment (BSP) is in its nature a payment of income and attributable to the past period in respect of which it is due, the payment could not affect any entitlement to old style JSA in that past period because it would be disregarded entirely as income (Sch.7 para.76). The amount of the arrears would thus immediately metamorphose into capital, which would then be disregarded under para.65(2) subject to the 52 week limit.

p.1177, *annotation to the Jobseeker's Allowance Regulations 1996 (SI 1996/207) Sch.8 (Capital to be disregarded)*

With effect from June 28, 2022 "Cost of living payments" under the Social Security (Additional Payments) Act 2022, both those to recipients of specified means-tested benefits and "disability" payments are not to be taken into account for any old style JSA purposes by virtue of s.8(b) of the Act. The same effect was achieved with effect from March 23, 2023 in relation to payments under the Social Security (Additional Payments) Act 2023 (s.8(b) of that Act). See Pt I of Vol.II for the text of both Acts.　　5.077

p.1184, *annotation to the Jobseeker's Allowance (Schemes for Assisting Persons to Obtain Employment) Regulations 2013 (SI 2013/276)*

Note the doubts expressed in the note to reg.3 in the 2021/22 main volume about the validity of the prescription of the Work and Health Programme in reg.3(8C) and in the entry below for p.1187 about the validity of the prescription of the Restart Scheme in reg.3(8D).　　5.078

p.1187, *amendment to the Jobseeker's Allowance (Schemes for Assisting Persons to Obtain Employment) Regulations 2013 (SI 2013/276) reg.3 (Schemes for assisting persons to obtain employment)*

5.079   With effect from March 14, 2022, reg.2(3) of the Jobseeker's Allowance (Schemes for Assisting Persons to Obtain Employment) (Amendment) Regulations 2022 (SI 2022/154) amended reg.3 by omitting para.(8) and by inserting the following after para.(8C):

"(8D) The Restart Scheme is a scheme which provides support for a period of up to 12 months for claimants who have been unemployed for 9 months or more and reside in England and Wales."

The Explanatory Memorandum to SI 2022/154 (note that a revised Memorandum, not labelled as such in its heading but with an additional "001" in the version online, was issued on April 13, 2022) explains that the Work Programme no longer exists. There is therefore no controversy about the removal of para.(8), which described that scheme.

However, the introduction of the new para.(8D) is of very doubtful validity. That is because s.17A(1) of the old style Jobseekers Act 1995 only allows claimants to be required to participate in schemes designed to assist them to obtain employment that are of a "prescribed description". The Supreme Court in *R. (Reilly and Wilson) v SSWP* [2013] UKSC 68; [2014] 1 A.C. 453 held that the Jobseeker's Allowance (Employment, Skills and Enterprise Scheme) Regulations 2011 (SI 2011/917) reg.2 did not satisfy that test because it did not add anything to the description of the schemes in the Act itself, which was necessary for the requirement for a prescribed description to have any point. Regulation 2 had provided that the Employment, Skills and Enterprise Scheme (ESES) meant a scheme of that name within s.17A and provided pursuant to arrangements by the Secretary of State that was designed to assist claimants to obtain employment or self-employment and which might include for any individual work-related activity, including work experience or job search. The Supreme Court must therefore have regarded the reference to the possible inclusion of work-related activity as too vague to constitute any kind of description of what the scheme involved. The Court agreed that it was not necessary in the case of the ESES to explore how much detail needed to be included in the regulations to comply with s.17A(1), as no description at all was given.

The amendment contained in SI 2022/154 may therefore not be on all fours with the ESES Regulations reg.2, because the new para.(8D) could be said to contain *some* description of the Restart Scheme, in identifying the categories of claimants who could be directed to the Restart Scheme, the maximum length of the scheme and that it would provide support (although arguably that word, in conjunction with the other specified elements, is also so vague as not to constitute any meaningful description at all). If it is accepted that there is *some* description, the question then, as in *R. (Smith) v SSWP* [2015] EWCA Civ 229 on the Jobseeker's Allowance (Mandatory Work Activity Scheme) Regulations 2011 (SI 2021/688), would be whether there is sufficient description for the purposes of s.17A(1). In *Smith*, Underhill LJ suggested at para.25 that the natural reading of "prescribed description" connoted "no more than an indication of the character of the scheme provided for, such as a scheme in which the claimant was required to undergo training or education or to work with a mentor, or—as here—to do work or work-related activity". So the CA held that the mention of work or work-related activity, with the specification of maximum weekly hours and length of participation, was enough for the MWAS Regulations to be valid. Although the present amendment specifies which claimants fall into the scope of the Restart Scheme and the maximum length, it says nothing worthwhile about the nature of the scheme. All it says is that it "provides support", nothing about what kind of support or who it will be provided by. Equally, if not more, important, it says nothing about what a claimant is to be expected to do by way of participation. What does it mean to have "support" thrust on a claimant? The argument that the new para.(8D) provides an insufficient description seems very strong. It might be thought that the Explanatory Memorandum betrays the faulty approach in paras 7.8 and 7.9, where it is said that the current legislation "lists" the employment schemes claimants can be required to participate in and that the amendment adds the Restart Scheme to the list. To be valid, and to carry the requirement to participate backed by sanctions, a regulation must not merely "list" a scheme, but must describe it.

The Explanatory Memorandum records that the Restart Scheme was already in existence through 12 providers in England and Wales, initially for universal credit claimants who had spent 12 to 18 months uninterrupted time in the Intensive Work Search Regime (i.e. subject to all work-related requirements), but now with the time reduced to nine months. Because of improved labour market conditions the opportunity arose to widen the eligibility criteria to provide intensive employment support for old style JSA claimants that had previously only been available to limited groups. The Scheme is still only available in England and Wales. The emphasis is said to be on positive engagement with the claimant to encourage participation, with the requirement to participate being "used as a backstop where reasonable attempts at engagement fail without good reason" (para.6.7). However, it is stated that claimants who fail to comply with the requirement to participate in compulsory activities may be issued with a low-level sanction (para.6.6). It is far from clear that "compulsory activities" are adequately described by the term "support" in para.(8D).

The policy paper *How the Restart Scheme will work* (January 18, 2022, updated April 26, 2022, available on the gov.uk website) states:

"Through regular contact with all participants, providers will develop a strong understanding of individuals' employment history, skills, aspirations and support needs to develop the right package of support to help each participant succeed.

For some this might be bespoke training to take advantage of opportunities in a growth sector or to succeed in a major recruitment exercise, for others it might be support to get the right certificate to take up a job in a different industry such as construction or transport or to update skills such as IT."

That document thus gets to a description of the scheme, but as there is no reference to it in para.(8D) there can be no reliance on its description merely by use of the label "Restart Scheme".

Providers will be given letters of empowerment under reg.17 authorising them to exercise the functions of the Secretary of State to issue notices requiring participation (reg.5) or that that requirement has ceased (reg.6(3) (a)) (Explanatory Memorandum, para.6.3). It is understood that providers and employees will not be designated as "employment officers" under s.35 of the old style Jobseekers Act 1995, so that they will have no power to issue jobseeker's directions under s.19A(2)(c).

p.1188, *annotation to the Jobseeker's Allowance (Schemes for Assisting Persons to Obtain Employment) Regulations 2013 (SI 2013/276) reg.3 (Schemes for assisting persons to obtain employment)*

5.080   Note, in addition to the points made in the entry for p.1187, that in the last paragraph of the existing note the reference to s.19(2)(c) should be to s.19A(2)(c).

PART IV

OLD STYLE EMPLOYMENT AND SUPPORT ALLOWANCE REGULATIONS

p.1209, *amendments to the Employment and Support Allowance Regulations 2008 (SI 2008/794) reg.2 (Interpretation)*

With effect from January 1, 2022, reg.7(2) of the Social Security (Income and Capital Disregards) (Amendment) Regulations 2021 (SI 2021/1405) inserts the following definitions:

5.081

"child abuse payment" means a payment from a scheme established or approved by the Secretary of State for the purpose of providing compensation in respect of historic institutional child abuse in the United Kingdom;"
"Windrush payment" means a payment made under the Windrush Compensation Scheme (Expenditure) Act 2020;"

With effect from January 1, 2022, reg.7(2) of the Social Security (Income and Capital Disregards) (Amendment) Regulations 2021 (SI 2021/1405) inserts ", a child abuse payment or a Windrush payment" into the definition of "qualifying person", after "Grenfell Tower payment".

p.1209, *amendments to the Employment and Support Allowance Regulations 2008 (SI 2008/794) reg.2 (Interpretation)*

With effect from July 26, 2021, Sch.9 para.2 of the Social Security (Scotland) Act 2018 (Disability Assistance for Children and Young People) (Consequential Modifications) Order 2021 (SI 2021/786) adds the following definitions:

5.082

"child disability payment" has the meaning given in regulation 2 of the DACYP Regulations;
"the DACYP Regulations" means the Disability Assistance for Children and Young People (Scotland) Regulations 2021;

With effect from March 21, 2022, art.11 of the Social Security (Disability Assistance for Working Age People) (Consequential Amendments) Order 2022 (SI 2022/177) adds the following definition:

"adult disability payment" has the meaning given in regulation 2 of the Disability Assistance for Working Age People (Scotland) Regulations 2022;

With effect from April 4, 2022, reg.2(1) of the Universal Credit and Employment and Support Allowance (Terminal Illness) (Amendment) Regulations 2022 (SI 2022/260) amends the definition of "terminally ill" by substituting for "6 months", "12 months".

p.1220, *amendment to the Employment and Support Allowance Regulations 2008 (SI 2008/794) reg.2 (Interpretation)*

With effect from April 4, 2022, reg.2(1) of the Universal Credit and Employment and Support Allowance (Terminal Illness) (Amendment) Regulations 2022 (SI 2022/260) substituted "12 months" for "6 months" in the definition of "terminally ill".

5.083

p.1230, *revocation of the Employment and Support Allowance Regulations 2008 (SI 2008/794) reg.6 (The assessment phase—a claimants appealing against a decision)*

5.084 Strictly speaking, reg.6 was *revoked* by reg.9(5) of the Social Security (Miscellaneous Amendments) (No. 3) Regulations 2010/840 (rather than *omitted* by the annotator).

pp.1238–1239, *amendment of the Employment and Support Allowance Regulations 2008 (SI 2008/794) reg.18 (Circumstances in which the condition that the claimant is not receiving education does not apply)*

5.085 Regulation 18 now reads, as amended, as follows:

"Paragraph 6(1)(g) of Schedule 1 to the Act does not apply where the claimant is entitled to a disability living allowance [³, child disability payment] [², armed forces independence payment] [⁴,] [¹ personal independence payment] [⁴ or adult disability payment]."

In addition, the following notes should be added to the list of

AMENDMENTS:

3. Social Security (Scotland) Act 2018 (Disability Assistance for Children and Young People) (Consequential Modifications) Order 2021 (SI 2021/786) Sch.9 para.3 (July 26, 2021).
4. Social Security (Disability Assistance for Working Age People) (Consequential Amendments) Order 2022 (SI 2022/177) art.11(3) (March 21, 2022).

p.1250, *amendment to the Employment and Support Allowance Regulations 2008 (SI 2008/794) reg.21 (Information required for determining capability for work)*

5.086 With effect from July 1, 2022, reg.4(2) of the Social Security (Medical Evidence) and Statutory Sick Pay (Medical Evidence) (Amendment) (No. 2) Regulations 2022 (SI 2022/630) omitted the words "a doctor's" between "form of" and "statement".

p.1260, *annotation to the Employment and Support Allowance Regulations 2008 (SI 2008/794) reg.24 (Matters to be taken into account in determining good cause in relation to regs 22 or 23)*

5.087 See, however, the successful application for a new inquest in *Dove v HM Assistant Coroner for Teesside and Hartlepool, Rahman and SSWP* [2023] EWCA Civ 289. Mrs Dove's daughter, Jodey, had died of an overdose shortly after her ESA award had been stopped. Jodey, who had been in receipt of ESA for several years, had a history of mental health problems, suicidal ideation and overdoses, as well as physical ill-health. In 2016, on a periodic review, she asked the DWP for a home visit. The DWP neglected to deal with that request and required her to attend an HCP assessment, which she failed to do. The DWP decided that Jodey had shown neither good cause for the failure to attend nor that she had limited capability for work. Jodey's ESA was duly stopped on February 7, 2017, and she died a fortnight later. Mrs Dove believed that the withdrawal of benefit had created extra stress and contributed to her daughter's death. The coroner ruled that questioning the DWP's decisions was beyond her remit under the Coroners and Justice Act 2009.

Mrs Dove applied to the High Court under the Coroners Act 1988 s.13, seeking two remedies: (a) to quash the coroner's suicide verdict; and (b) to order a new inquest covering the circumstances surrounding her daughter's death. Mrs Dove submitted that (1) the coroner's inquiry was insufficient in scope and should have covered the DWP's failings; (2) those failings meant that the state was in breach of ECHR art.2, so requiring a wider inquiry; (3) fresh evidence (in the form of an expert psychiatrist's report, obtained after the inquest, which concluded it was likely that Jodey's mental state would have been substantially affected by the decision to stop her benefits and an ICE report on a complaint about the DWP's handling of Jodey's claim) showed that a new inquest was necessary. At first instance the Divisional Court ([2021] EWHC 2511 (Admin); Warbey LJ, Farbey J and HH Judge Teague QC) dismissed the application on all three grounds.

However, the Court of Appeal allowed Mrs Dove's appeal and directed a fresh inquest ([2023] EWCA Civ 289: Lewis LJ, William Davis LJ and Whipple LJ). The Court ruled that the psychiatrist's report (but not the ICE report) was fresh evidence making it desirable in the interests of justice to hold a fresh inquest (*R v HM Coroner for North Humberside and Scunthorpe Ex p. Jamieson* [1995] Q.B. 1). Thus, "it is in the interests of justice that Mrs Dove and her family should have the opportunity to invite a coroner, at a fresh inquest, to make a finding of fact that the Department's actions contributed to Jodey's deteriorating mental health and, if that finding is made, to invite the coroner to include reference to that finding in the conclusion on how Jodey came by her death" (per Whipple LJ at [72]). One of the reasons for the Court reaching this conclusion was that "there is a public interest in a coroner considering the wider issue of causation raised on this appeal. If Jodey's death was connected with the abrupt cessation of benefits by the Department, the public has a legitimate interest in knowing that. After all, the Department deals with very many people who are vulnerable and dependent on benefits to survive, and the consequences of terminating benefit payments to such people should be examined in public, where it can be followed and reported on by others who might be interested in it."

p.1302, *annotation to the Employment and Support Allowance Regulations 2008 (SI 2008/794) reg.35 (Certain claimants to be treated as having limited capability for work-related activity)*

For further examples of the need for sufficient fact-finding and adequate reasons in appeals where reg.35 is in issue, see *MH v SSWP (ESA)* [2021] UKUT 90 (AAC) and *CT v SSWP (ESA)* [2021] UKUT 131 (AAC). On the importance of tribunals in universal credit appeals (that turn on the equivalent provision to reg.35 in Sch.9 para.4) ensuring they have been provided with an accurate list of work-related activities, see *KS v SSWP (UC)* [2021] UKUT 132 (AAC). Secretary of State appeal responses on such appeals may not have included accurate lists of work-related activities until after July 2020.

5.088

pp.1334–1335, *amendment of the Employment and Support Allowance Regulations 2008 (SI 2008/794) reg.64D (The amount of a hardship payment)*

5.089   The text in the main volume at para.4.174 should be replaced with the following:

"[¹ The amount of a hardship payment

64D.—[² (1) A hardship payment is either—
(a) 80% of the prescribed amount for a single claimant as set out in paragraph (1)(a) of Part 1 of Schedule 4 where—
  (i) the claimant has an award of employment and support allowance which does not include entitlement to a work-related activity component under section 4(2)(b) of the Welfare Reform Act 2007 as in force immediately before 3rd April 2017; and
  (ii) the claimant or any other member of their family is either pregnant or seriously ill; or
(b) 60% of the prescribed amount for a single claimant as set out in paragraph (1)(a) of Part 1 of Schedule 4 in any other case.]
(2) A payment calculated in accordance with paragraph (1) shall, if it is not a multiple of 5p, be rounded to the nearest such multiple or, if it is a multiple of 2.5p but not of 5p, to the next lower multiple of 5p.]"

AMENDMENTS

1. Employment and Support Allowance (Sanctions) (Amendment) Regulations 2012 (SI 2012/2756) reg.6 (December 3, 2012).
2. Employment and Support Allowance (Exempt Work Hardship Amounts) (Amendment) Regulations 2017 (SI 2017/205) reg.5 (April 3, 2017).

p.1336, *annotation to the Employment and Support Allowance Regulations 2008 (SI 2008/794) reg.67 (Prescribed amounts)*

5.090   On the lawfulness of not uplifting the amounts paid in IS, JSA and ESA by £20 per week (as was done with UC for 18 months during the coronavirus pandemic), see the annotation to the Income Support (General) Regulations 1987 (SI 1987/1967) reg.17 (Applicable amounts), above.

pp.1341–1342, *amendment to the Employment and Support Allowance Regulations 2008 (SI 2008/794) reg.70 (Special cases: supplemental—persons from abroad)*

5.091   The text in the main volume at para.4.187 should be replaced with the following:

"Special cases: supplemental—persons from abroad

70.—(1) "Person from abroad" means, subject to the following provisions of this regulation, a claimant who is not habitually resident in the United Kingdom, the Channel Islands, the Isle of Man or the Republic of Ireland.

(2) A claimant must not be treated as habitually resident in the United Kingdom, the Channel Islands, the Isle of Man or the Republic of Ireland unless the claimant has a right to reside in (as the case may be) the United

1110

Kingdom, the Channel Islands, the Isle of Man or the Republic of Ireland other than a right to reside which falls within paragraph (3) [⁸ or (3A)].

(3) A right to reside falls within this paragraph if it is one which exists by virtue of, or in accordance with, one or more of the following—

(a) regulation 13 of the [⁸ Immigration (European Economic Area) Regulations 2016];

(b) regulation 14 of those Regulations, but only in a case where the right exists under that regulation because the claimant is—

(i) a jobseeker for the purpose of the definition of "qualified person" in regulation 6(1) of those Regulations; or

(ii) a family member (within the meaning of regulation 7 of those Regulations) of such a jobseeker; [¹⁰ or]

[⁴[⁸(bb) regulation 16 of those Regulations, but only in a case where the right exists under that regulation because the claimant satisfies the criteria in paragraph (5) of that regulation;]]

(c) [¹⁰ . . .]

(d) [¹⁰ . . .]

(e) [¹⁰ . . .]

[⁸ (3A) A right to reside falls within this paragraph if it exists by virtue of a claimant having been granted limited leave to enter, or remain in, the United Kingdom under the Immigration Act 1971 by virtue of—

(a) Appendix EU to the immigration rules made under section 3(2) of that Act; [¹¹ . . .];

(b) being a person with a Zambrano right to reside as defined in Annex 1 of Appendix EU to the immigration rules made under section 3(2) of that Act.] [¹¹; or

(c) having arrived in the United Kingdom with an entry clearance that was granted under Appendix EU (Family Permit) to the immigration rules made under section 3(2) of that Act.]

[⁹ (3B) Paragraph (3A)(a) does not apply to a person who—

(a) has a right to reside granted by virtue of being a family member of a relevant person of Northern Ireland; and

(b) would have a right to reside under the Immigration (European Economic Area) Regulations 2016 if the relevant person of Northern Ireland were an EEA national, provided that the right to reside does not fall within paragraph (3).]

(4) A claimant is not a person from abroad if the claimant is—

[¹²(zza) a person granted leave in accordance with the immigration rules made under section 3(2) of the Immigration Act 1971, where such leave is granted by virtue of—

(i) the Afghan Relocations and Assistance Policy; or

(ii) the previous scheme for locally-employed staff in Afghanistan (sometimes referred to as the ex-gratia scheme);

(zzb) a person in Great Britain not coming within sub-paragraph (zza) or [¹³ (h)] who left Afghanistan in connection with the collapse of the Afghan government that took place on 15th August 2021;]

[¹³(zzc) a person in Great Britain who was residing in Ukraine immediately before 1st January 2022, left Ukraine in connection with the Russian invasion which took place on 24th February 2022 and—

(i) has been granted leave in accordance with immigration rules made under section 3(2) of the Immigration Act 1971; [¹⁴ . . .]

    (ii) has a right of abode in the United Kingdom within the meaning given in section 2 of that Act;] [^{14} or

   (iii) does not require leave to enter or remain in the United Kingdom in accordance with section 3ZA of that Act;]

[^{7}(za) a qualified person for the purposes of regulation 6 of the [^{8} Immigration (European Economic Area) Regulations 2016] as a worker or a self-employed person;

  (zb) a family member of a person referred to in sub-paragraph (za) [^{9} . . .];

  (zc) a person who has a right to reside permanently in the United Kingdom by virtue of regulation 15(1)(c), (d) or (e) of those Regulations;]

[^{9}(zd) a family member of a relevant person of Northern Ireland, with a right to reside which falls within paragraph (3A)(a), provided that the relevant person of Northern Ireland falls within sub-paragraph (za), or would do so but for the fact that they are not an EEA national;]

[^{10}(ze) a frontier worker within the meaning of regulation 3 of the Citizens' Rights (Frontier Workers) (EU Exit) Regulations 2020;

  (zf) a family member of a person referred to in sub-paragraph (ze), who has been granted limited leave to enter, or remain in, the United Kingdom by virtue of Appendix EU to the immigration rules made under section 3(2) of the Immigration Act 1971;]

   (g) a refugee within the definition in Article 1 of the Convention relating to the Status of Refugees done at Geneva on 28th July 1951, as extended by Article 1(2) of the Protocol relating to the Status of Refugees done at New York on 31st January 1967;

[^{6}(h) a person who has been granted leave or who is deemed to have been granted leave outside the rules made under section 3(2) of the Immigration Act 1971 [^{13} . . .]

   (i) a person who has humanitarian protection granted under those rules; [^{6} or]

   (j) a person who is not a person subject to immigration control within the meaning of section 115(9) of the Immigration and Asylum Act and who is in the United Kingdom as a result of deportation, expulsion or other removal by compulsion of law from another country to the United Kingdom; [^{1} . . .]

  (k) [^{6} . . .]

  (l) [^{1} [^{6} . . .]]]

[^{9} (5) In this regulation—

"EEA national" has the meaning given in regulation 2(1) of the Immigration (European Economic Area) Regulations 2016;

"family member" has the meaning given in regulation 7(1)(a), (b) or (c) of the Immigration (European Economic Area) Regulations 2016 except that regulation 7(4) of those Regulations does not apply for the purposes of paragraphs (3B) and (4)(zd);

"relevant person of Northern Ireland" has the meaning given in Annex 1 of Appendix EU to the immigration rules made under section 3(2) of the Immigration Act 1971.]

[^{10} (6) References in this regulation to the Immigration (European Economic Area) Regulations 2016 are to be read with Schedule 4 to the Immigration and Social Security Co-ordination (EU Withdrawal)

Act 2020(Consequential, Saving, Transitional and Transitory Provisions) Regulations 2020.]"

AMENDMENTS

1. Social Security (Habitual Residence) (Amendment) Regulations 2009 (SI 2009/362) reg.9 (March 18, 2009).
2. Social Security (Miscellaneous Amendments) (No. 3) Regulations 2011 (SI 2011/2425) reg.23(1) and (7) (October 31, 2011).
3. Treaty of Lisbon (Changes in Terminology or Numbering) Order 2012 (SI 2012/1809) art.3(1) and Sch.1 Pt.2 (August 1, 2012).
4. Social Security (Habitual Residence) (Amendment) Regulations 2012 (SI 2012/2587) reg.2 (November 8, 2012).
5. Social Security (Croatia) Amendment Regulations 2013 (SI 2013/1474) reg.7 (July 1, 2013).
6. Social Security (Miscellaneous Amendments) (No. 3) Regulations 2013 (SI 2013/2536) reg.13(1) and (24) (October 29, 2013).
7. Social Security (Habitual Residence) (Amendment) Regulations 2014 (SI 2014/902) reg.7 (May 31, 2014).
8. Social Security (Income-related Benefits) (Updating and Amendment) (EU Exit) Regulations 2019 (SI 2019/872) reg.7 (May 7, 2019).
9. Social Security (Income-Related Benefits) (Persons of Northern Ireland – Family Members) (Amendment) Regulations 2020 (SI 2020/638) reg.7 (August 24, 2020).
10. Immigration and Social Security Co-ordination (EU Withdrawal) Act 2020 (Consequential, Saving, Transitional and Transitory Provisions) (EU Exit) Regulations 2020 (SI 2020/1309) reg 73 (December 31, 2020 at 11.00 pm).
11. Immigration (Citizens' Rights etc.) (EU Exit) Regulations 2020 (SI 2020/1372) reg.23 (December 31, 2020 at 11.00 pm).
12. Social Security (Habitual Residence and Past Presence) (Amendment) Regulations 2021 (SI 2021/1034) reg.2 (September 15, 2021).
13. Social Security (Habitual Residence and Past Presence) (Amendment) Regulations 2022 (SI 2022/344) reg.2 (March 22, 2022).
14. Social Security (Habitual Residence and Past Presence) (Amendment) (No. 2) Regulations 2022 (SI 2022/990) reg.2 (October 18, 2022).

MODIFICATION

Regulation 70 is modified by Sch.1 para.10A of the Employment and Support Allowance (Transitional Provisions, Housing Benefit and Council Tax Benefit) (Existing Awards) (No. 2) Regulations 2010 (SI 2010/1907) as amended for the purposes specified in reg.6(1) of those Regulations. For the details of the modification, pp.1410–1452 of Vol.I of the 2020/21 edition.

DEFINITION

"Immigration and Asylum Act"—reg.2(1).

p.1373, *amendment to the Employment and Support Allowance Regulations 2008 (SI 2008/794) reg.107(10A) (Notional income—exceptions)*

With effect from January 1, 2022, reg.7(3) of the Social Security (Income and Capital Disregards) (Amendment) Regulations 2021 (SI 2021/1405) amended para.(10A) by substituting the following for "a payment of income which is a Grenfell Tower payment":

5.092

"any of the following payments of income—
(a)   a Grenfell Tower payment;

(b)   a child abuse payment;
(c)   a Windrush payment."

All of those payments are defined in reg.2(1). See the entry for p.684 for discussion of the nature of child abuse and Windrush payments.

p.1377, *annotation to the Employment and Support Allowance Regulations 2008 (SI 2008/794) reg.110 (Capital limit)*

5.093   In the Institute for Government and the Social Security Advisory Committee's 2021 joint report *Jobs and benefits: The Covid-19 challenge* it was noted that if the capital limit of £16,000 had risen in line with prices since 2006 it would be close to £23,500 (or £25,000: different figures are given) and recommended that the limit should be increased to £25,000 and subsequently automatically indexed to maintain its real value (pp.22 and 31). That recommendation was summarily rejected in the Government's response of March 22, 2022.

p.1378, *amendment to the Employment and Support Allowance Regulations 2008 (SI 2008/794) reg.112(8) (Income treated as capital—exceptions)*

5.094   With effect from January 1, 2022, reg.7(4) of the Social Security (Income and Capital Disregards) (Amendment) Regulations 2021 (SI 2021/1405) amended para.(8) by substituting the following for sub-para.(b):

"any—
(a)   Grenfell Tower payment;
(b)   child abuse payment;
(c)   Windrush payment."

All of those payments are defined in reg.2(1). See the entry for p.684 for discussion of the nature of child abuse and Windrush payments.

p.1382, *amendment to the Employment and Support Allowance Regulations 2008 (SI 2008/794) reg.115(5A) (Notional capital—exceptions)*

5.095   With effect from January 1, 2022, reg.7(5) of the Social Security (Income and Capital Disregards) (Amendment) Regulations 2021 (SI 2021/1405) amended para.(5A) by substituting the following for "a payment of capital which is a Grenfell Tower payment":

"any of the following payments of capital—
(a)   a Grenfell Tower payment;
(b)   a child abuse payment;
(c)   a Windrush payment."

All of those payments are defined in reg.2(1). See the entry for p.684 for discussion of the nature of child abuse and Windrush payments.

p.1413, *annotation to the Employment and Support Allowance Regulations 2008 (SI 2008/794) reg.145 (Linking rules)*

5.096   For more detailed analysis see the commentary on SSCBA 1992 s.30C(1)(c) in Vol.I of the 2011/12 edition of this work (at paras 1.67–1.77).

pp.1431–1432, *amendments to the Employment and Support Allowance Regulations 2008 (SI 2008/794) reg.158 (Meaning of "person in hardship")*

With effect from July 26, 2021, Sch.9 para.4 of the Social Security 5.097
(Scotland) Act 2018 (Disability Assistance for Children and Young People)
(Consequential Modifications) Order 2021 (SI 2021/786) makes the following amendments to reg.158:

- In para.(3):
  - in sub-para.(c), after "disability living allowance", insert ", child disability payment";
  - in sub-para.(d)(ii), after "disability living allowance", insert ", child disability payment".
- For para.(7), substitute:
  "(7) In this regulation, "care component" means—
  (a) the care component of disability living allowance at the highest or middle rate prescribed under section 72(3) of the Contributions and Benefits Act; or
  (b) the care component of child disability payment at the highest or middle rate provided for in regulation 11(5) of the DACYP Regulations.".

With effect from March 21, 2022, art.11(4) of the Social Security (Disability Assistance for Working Age People) (Consequential Amendments) Order 2022 (SI 2022/177) makes the following amendments to reg.158(3):

- in sub-para.(b):
  - after "armed forces independence payment" for "or" substitute ",";
  - after "daily living component" insert "or the daily living component of adult disability payment";
- in sub-para.(c):
  - after "armed forces independence payment" for "or" substitute ",";
  - after "personal independence payment", insert "or adult disability payment";
- in sub-para.(d):
  - in para.(i):
    - after "armed forces independence payment" for "or" substitute ",";
    - after "daily living component" insert "or the daily living component of adult disability payment";
  - in para.(ii):
    - after "armed forces independence payment" for "or" substitute ",";
    - after "personal independence payment", insert "or adult disability payment".

pp.1494–1496, *annotation to the Employment and Support Allowance Regulations 2008 (SI 2008/794) Sch.2 Activity 17 (Appropriateness of behaviour with other people, due to cognitive impairment or mental disorder)*

Consideration of Activity 17 may require the disclosure of Unacceptable 5.098
Customer Behaviour (UCB) forms as provided in confidence by the DWP
to HMCTS: *MH v SSWP (ESA)* [2021] UKUT 90 (AAC).

pp.1507–1514, *amendments to the Employment and Support Allowance Regulations 2008 (SI 2008/794) Sch.4 (Amounts)*

5.099   Substitute the following for paras 4.420–4.429

Regulations 67(1)(a) and (2) and 68(1)(a) and (b)

"SCHEDULE 4

AMOUNTS

PART 1

PRESCRIBED AMOUNTS

4.420   1. The weekly amounts specified in column (2) in respect of each person or couple specified in column (1) are the weekly amounts specified for the purposes of regulations 67(1) and 68 (prescribed amounts and polygamous marriages).

(1) *Person or Couple*	*(2)* *Amount*

(1) *Single claimant*—
  (a) who satisfies the conditions set out in section 2(2) [¹² . . .] or 4(4) [¹² . . .] of the Act [¹³ or who is a member of the work-related activity group];
  (b) aged not less than 25
  (c) aged less than 25.
	(1)
	
	  (a) [¹⁵ £84.80];
	
	  (b) [¹⁵ £84.80];
	  (c) [¹⁵ £67.20];

(2) Lone parent [⁶ or a person who has no partner and who is responsible for and a member of the same household as a young person]—
  (a) who satisfies the conditions set out in section 4(4) [¹² ...] of the Act[¹³ or who is a member of the work-related activity group and satisfies the conditions set out in Part 2 of Schedule 1 to the Act];
  (b) aged not less than 18;
  (c) aged less than 18.
	(2)
	
	  (a) [¹⁵ £84.80];
	
	  (b) [¹⁵ £84.80];
	  (c) [¹⁵ £67.20];

(3) Couple—
  (a) where both members are aged not less than 18;
  (b) where one member is aged not less than 18 and the other member is a person under 18 who—
    (i) [³ if that other member had not been a member] of a couple, would satisfy the requirements for entitlement to income support other than the requirement to make a claim for it; or
    (ii) [³ if that other member had not been a member] of a couple, would satisfy the requirements for entitlement to an income-related allowance; or
    (iii) satisfies the requirements of section 3(1) (f)(iii) of the Jobseekers Act (prescribed circumstances for persons aged 16 but less than 18); or
	(3)
	  (a) [¹⁵ £133.30];
	  (b) [¹⁵ £133.30];

(1) Person or Couple	(2) Amount

(iv) is the subject of a direction under section 16 of that Act (persons under 18: severe hardship);
(c) where the claimant satisfies the conditions set out in section 4(4) [¹² . . .] of the Act [¹³ or the claimant is a member of the work-related activity group and satisfies the conditions set out in Part 2 of Schedule 1 to the Act] and both members are aged less than 18 and—
    (i) at least one of them is treated as responsible for a child; or
    (ii) had they not been members of a couple, each would have qualified for an income-related allowance; or
    (iii) had they not been members of a couple the claimant's partner would satisfy the requirements for entitlement to income support other than the requirement to make a claim for it; or
    (iv) the claimant's partner satisfies the requirements of section 3(1)(f)(iii) of the Jobseekers Act (prescribed circumstances for persons aged 16 but less than 18); or
    (v) there is in force in respect of the claimant's partner a direction under section 16 of that Act (persons under 18: severe hardship);
(d) where both members are aged less than 18 and—
    (i) at least one of them is treated as responsible for a child; or
    (ii) had they not been members of a couple, each would have qualified for an income-related allowance; or
    (iii) had they not been members of a couple the claimant's partner satisfies the requirements for entitlement to income support other than a requirement to make a claim for it; or
    (iv) the claimant's partner satisfies the requirements of section 3(1)(f)(iii) of the Jobseekers Act (prescribed circumstances for persons aged 16 but less than 18); or
    (v) there is in force in respect of the claimant's partner a direction under section 16 of that Act (persons under 18: severe hardship);
(e) where the claimant is aged not less than 25 and the claimant's partner is a person under 18 who—
    (i) would not qualify for an income-related allowance if the person were not a member of a couple;
    (ii) would not qualify for income support if the person were not a member of a couple;
    (iii) does not satisfy the requirements of section 3(1)(f)(iii) of the Jobseekers Act (prescribed circumstances for persons aged 16 but less than 18); and
    (iv) is not the subject of a direction under section 16 of that Act (persons under 18: severe hardship);
	(c) [¹⁵ £133.30];
	
	(d) [¹⁵ £101.50];
	
	(e) [¹⁵ £84.80];

(1) Person or Couple	(2) Amount
(f) where the claimant satisfies the conditions set out in section 4(4) [¹² . . .] of the Act [¹³ or the claimant is a member of the work-related activity group and satisfies the conditions set out in Part 2 of Schedule 1 to the Act] and the claimant's partner is a person under 18 who— 　(i) would not qualify for an income-related allowance if the person were not a member of a couple; 　(ii) would not qualify for income support if the person [¹ were] not a member of a couple; 　(iii) does not satisfy the requirements of section 3(1)(f)(iii) of the Jobseekers Act (prescribed circumstances for persons aged 16 but less than 18); and 　(iv) is not the subject of a direction under section 16 of that Act (persons under 18: severe hardship);	(f) [¹⁵ £84.80];
(g) where the claimant satisfies the conditions set out in section 4(4) [¹² . . .] of the Act [¹³ or the claimant is a member of the work-related activity group and satisfies the conditions set out in Part 2 of Schedule 1 to the Act] and both members are aged less than 18 and paragraph (c) does not apply;	(g) [¹⁵ £84.80];
(h) where the claimant is aged not less than 18 but less than 25 and the claimant's partner is a person under 18 who— 　(i) would not qualify for an income-related allowance if the person were not a member of a couple; 　(ii) would not qualify for income support if the person were not a member of a couple; 　(iii) does not satisfy the requirements of section 3(1)(f)(iii) of the Jobseekers Act (prescribed circumstances for persons aged 16 but less than 18); and 　(iv) is not the subject of a direction under section 16 of that Act (persons under 18: severe hardship);	(h) [¹⁵ £67.20];
(i) where both members are aged less than 18 and paragraph (d) does not apply.	(i) [¹⁵ £67.20].

Regulations 67(1)(b) and 68(1)(c)

PART 2

PREMIUMS

4.421　2. Except as provided in paragraph 4, the weekly premiums specified in Part 3 of this Schedule are, for the purposes of regulation 67(1)(b) and 68(1)(c), to be applicable to a claimant who satisfies the condition specified in paragraphs 5 to 8 in respect of that premium.

　3. An enhanced disability premium in respect of a person is not applicable in addition to a pensioner premium.

4.—(1) For the purposes of this Part of this Schedule, once a premium is applicable to a claimant under this Part, a person is to be treated as being in receipt of any benefit—

(a) in the case of a benefit to which the Social Security (Overlapping Benefits) Regulations 1979 applies, for any period during which, apart from the provisions of those Regulations, the person would be in receipt of that benefit; and

(b) for any period spent by a person in undertaking a course of training or instruction provided or approved by the Secretary of State under section 2 of the Employment and Training Act 1973, or by [³ Skills Development Scotland] or Highlands and Islands Enterprise under section 2 of the Enterprise and New Towns (Scotland) Act 1990, or for any period during which the person is in receipt of a training allowance.

[⁷ (2) For the purposes of the carer premium under paragraph 8, a claimant is to be treated as being in receipt of a carer's allowance by virtue of sub-paragraph (1)(a) only if and for so long as the person in respect of whose care the allowance has been claimed remains in receipt of—

(a) attendance allowance;

(b) the care component of disability living allowance at the highest or middle rate prescribed in accordance with section 72(3) of the Contributions and Benefits Act; [⁸ . . .]

(c) the daily living component of personal independence payment at the standard or enhanced rate in accordance with section 78(3) of the 2012 Act [⁸ [¹⁴ . . .

(ca) the daily living component of adult disability payment at the standard or enhanced rate in accordance with regulation 5 of the Disability Assistance for Working Age People (Scotland) Regulations 2022; or]

(d) armed forces independence payment.]]

Pensioner premium

5. The condition is that the claimant or the claimant's partner has attained the qualifying age for state pension credit.

4.422

Severe disability premium

6.—(1) The condition is that the claimant is a severely disabled person.

(2) For the purposes of sub-paragraph (1), a claimant is to be treated as being a severely disabled person if, and only if—

4.423

(a) in the case of a single claimant, a lone parent [⁶ , a person who has no partner and who is responsible for and a member of the same household as a young person] or a claimant who is treated as having no partner in consequence of sub-paragraph (3)—

   (i) the claimant is in receipt of the care component [⁷ , the daily living component] [¹⁴ , the daily living component of adult disability payment] [⁸ , armed forces independence payment] [⁵ or attendance allowance];

   (ii) subject to sub-paragraph (4), the claimant has no non-dependants aged 18 or over normally residing with the claimant or with whom the claimant is normally residing; and

   (iii) no person is entitled to, and in receipt of, [¹¹ a carer's allowance or has an award of universal credit which includes the carer element] in respect of caring for the claimant;

(b) in the case of a claimant who has a partner—

   (i) the claimant is in receipt of the care component [⁷ , the daily living component] [¹⁴ , the daily living component of adult disability payment] [⁸ , armed forces independence payment] [⁵ or attendance allowance];

   (ii) the claimant's partner is also in receipt of the care component [⁷ , the daily living component] [¹⁴ , the daily living component of adult disability payment] [⁸ , armed forces independence payment] or attendance allowance or, if the claimant is a member of a polygamous marriage, all the partners of that marriage are in receipt of the care component [⁷ , the daily living component] [¹⁴ , the daily living component of adult disability payment] [⁸ , armed forces independence payment] or attendance allowance; and

   (iii) subject to sub-paragraph (4), the claimant has no non-dependants aged 18 or over normally residing with the claimant or with whom the claimant is normally residing, and,

   either a person is entitled to, and in receipt of, a carer's allowance [¹¹ or has an award of universal credit which includes the carer element] in respect of caring for only one of the couple or, in the case of a polygamous marriage, for one or more but not all

1119

the partners of the marriage or, as the case may be, no person is entitled to, and in receipt of, such an allowance [¹¹ or has such an award of universal credit] in respect of caring for either member of the couple or any partner of the polygamous marriage.

(3) Where a claimant has a partner who does not satisfy the condition in sub-paragraph (2) (b)(ii) and that partner is blind or severely sight impaired or is treated as blind or severely sight impaired that partner is to be treated for the purposes of sub-paragraph (2) as if the partner were not a partner of the claimant.

(4) For the purposes of sub-paragraph (2)(a)(ii) and (b)(iii) no account is to be taken of—
   (a) a person receiving attendance allowance, [⁷ the daily living component] [¹⁴ , the daily living component of adult disability payment] [⁸ , armed forces independence payment] or the care component;
   (b) subject to sub-paragraph (7), a person who joins the claimant's household for the first time in order to care for the claimant or the claimant's partner and immediately before so joining the claimant or the claimant's partner was treated as a severely disabled person; or
   (c) a person who is blind or severely sight impaired or is treated as blind or severely sight impaired.

(5) For the purposes of sub-paragraph (2)(b) a person is to be treated—
   (a) as being in receipt of attendance allowance or the care component if the person would, but for the person being a patient for a period exceeding 28 days, be so in receipt;
   (b) as being entitled to, and in receipt of, a carer's allowance [¹¹ or having an award of universal credit which includes the carer element] if the person would, but for the person for whom the person was caring being a patient in hospital for a period exceeding 28 days, be so entitled and in receipt [¹¹ of carer's allowance or have such an award of universal credit] .
   [⁷(c) as being in entitled to, and in receipt of, the daily living component if the person would, but for regulations under section 86(1) (hospital in-patients) of the 2012 Act, be so entitled and in receipt.]
   [¹⁴ (d) as being in entitled to, and in receipt of, the daily living component of adult disability payment if the person would, but for regulation 28 (effect of admission to hospital on ongoing entitlement to Adult Disability Payment) of the Disability Assistance for Working Age People (Scotland) Regulations 2022, be so in receipt.]

(6) For the purposes of sub-paragraph (2)(a)(iii) and (b), no account is to be taken of an award of carer's allowance [¹¹ or universal credit which includes the carer element] to the extent that payment of such an award is backdated for a period before the date on which the award is first paid.

(7) Sub-paragraph (4)(b) is to apply only for the first 12 weeks following the date on which the person to whom that provision applies first joins the claimant's household.

(8) In sub-paragraph (2)(a)(iii) and (b), references to a person being in receipt of a carer's allowance [¹¹ or as having an award of universal credit which includes the carer element] are to include references to a person who would have been in receipt of that allowance [¹¹ or had such an award] but for the application of a restriction under section [⁴ 6B or] 7 of the Social Security Fraud Act 2001 (loss of benefit provisions).

(9) [¹¹ (a)] In this paragraph—

[⁹ "blind or severely sight impaired" means certified as blind or severely sight impaired by a consultant ophthalmologist and a person who has ceased to be certified as blind or severely sight impaired where that person's eyesight has been regained is, nevertheless, to be treated as blind or severely sight impaired for a period of 28 weeks following the date on which the person ceased to be so certified;]

"the care component" means the care component of disability living allowance at the highest or middle rate prescribed in accordance with section 72(3) of the Contributions and Benefits Act.

[¹¹ (b) A person has an award of universal credit which includes the carer element if the person has an award of universal credit which includes an amount which is the carer element under regulation 29 of the Universal Credit Regulations 2013.]

Enhanced disability premium

4.424   7.—(1) Subject to sub-paragraph (2), the condition is that—
   (a) the claimant's applicable amount includes the support component; [⁷ . . .]
   (b) the care component of disability living allowance is, or would, but for a suspension of benefit in accordance with regulations under section 113(2) of the Contributions and Benefits Act or, but for an abatement as a consequence of

hospitalisation, be payable at the highest rate prescribed under section 72(3) of that Act in respect of—
  (i) the claimant; or
  (ii) the claimant's partner (if any) who is aged less than the qualifying age for state pension credit [7 ; [8 . . .]
  (c) the daily living component is, or would, but for regulations made under section 86(1) (hospital in-patients) of the 2012 Act, be payable at the enhanced rate under section 78(2) of that Act in respect of—
    (i) the claimant; or
    (ii) the claimant's partner (if any) who is aged less than the qualifying age for state pension credit"]; [14 . . .
  (ca) the daily living component of adult disability payment is, or would, but for regulation 28 (effect of admission to hospital on ongoing entitlement to Adult Disability Payment) of the Disability Assistance for Working Age People (Scotland) Regulations 2022, be payable at the enhanced rate under section 78(2) of those Regulations in respect of—
    (i) the claimant; or
    (ii) the claimant's partner (if any) who is aged less than the qualifying age for state pension credit; or]
  (d) armed forces independence payment is payable in respect of—
    (i) the claimant; or
    (ii) the claimant's partner (if any) who is aged less than the qualifying age for state pension credit.]
(2) An enhanced disability premium is not applicable in respect of—
  (a) a claimant who—
    (i) is not a member of a couple or a polygamous marriage; and
    (ii) is a patient within the meaning of regulation 69(2) and has been for a period of more than 52 weeks; or
  (b) a member of a couple or a polygamous marriage where each member is a patient within the meaning of regulation 69(2) and has been for a period of more than 52 weeks.

Carer premium
8.—(1) Subject to sub-paragraphs (2) and (4), the condition is that the claimant or the   4.425
claimant's partner is, or both of them are, entitled to a carer's allowance under section 70 of
the Contributions and Benefits Act.
(2) Where a carer premium is awarded but—
  (a) the person in respect of whose care the carer's allowance has been awarded dies; or
  (b) in any other case the person in respect of whom a carer premium has been awarded ceases to be entitled to a carer's allowance, the condition for the award of the premium is to be treated as satisfied for a period of 8 weeks from the relevant date specified in sub-paragraph (3).
(3) The relevant date for the purposes of sub-paragraph (2) is—
  (a) where sub-paragraph (2)(a) applies, the Sunday following the death of the person in respect of whose care a carer's allowance has been awarded or the date of death if the death occurred on a Sunday; or
  (b) in any other case, the date on which the person who has been entitled to a carer's allowance ceases to be entitled to that allowance.
(4) Where a person who has been entitled to a carer's allowance ceases to be entitled to that allowance and makes a claim for an income-related allowance, the condition for the award of the carer premium is to be treated as satisfied for a period of 8 weeks from the date on which—
  (a) the person in respect of whose care the carer's allowance has been awarded dies; or
  (b) in any other case, the person who has been entitled to a carer's allowance ceased to be entitled to that allowance.

Persons in receipt of concessionary payments
9. For the purpose of determining whether a premium is applicable to a person under para-   4.426
graphs 6, 7 and 8, any concessionary payment made to compensate that person for the non-
payment of any benefit mentioned in those paragraphs is to be treated as if it were a payment
of that benefit.

Persons in receipt of benefit
10. For the purposes of this Part of this Schedule, a person is to be regarded as being in   4.427
receipt of any benefit if, and only if, it is paid in respect of the person and is to be so regarded
only for any period in respect of which that benefit is paid.

PART 3

WEEKLY AMOUNT OF PREMIUMS SPECIFIED IN PART 2

4.428   **11.—**

Premium	Amount

(1) Pension premium for a person to whom paragraph 5 applies who—
  (a) is a single claimant and—
    (i) [^{12} . . .];
    (ii) is entitled to the support component;
    or
  [^{12}(iii) is not entitled to the support component;]
  (b) is a member of a couple and—
    (i) [^{12} . . .]
    (ii) is entitled to the support component;
    or
  [^{12} (iii) is not entitled to the support component;]
	(1)
	
	  (a)
	    (i) [^{12} . . .];
	    (ii) [^{16} £71.55];
	
	    (iii) [^{16} £116.25];
	
	  (b)
	    (i) [^{12}];
	    (ii) [^{16} £128.85];
	    (iii) [^{16} £157.65];

(2) Severe disability premium—
  (a) where the claimant satisfies the condition in paragraph 6(2)(a);
  (b) where the claimant satisfies the condition in paragraph 6(2)(b)—
    (i) if there is someone in receipt of a carer's allowance or if the person or any partner satisfies that condition only by virtue of paragraph 6(5);
    (ii) if no-one is in receipt of such an allowance.
	(2)
	  (a) [^{16} £173.65];
	  (b)
	
	    (i) [^{16} £76.40];
	
	    (ii) [^{16} £152.80].

(3) Carer premium.	(3) [^{16} £42.75]; in respect of each person who satisfies the condition specified in [^{1} paragraph 8(1)].

(4) Enhanced disability premium where the conditions in paragraph 7 are satisfied.	(4)(a) [^{16} £19.55]; in respect of each person who is neither—
	    (i) a child or young person; nor
	    (ii) a member of a couple or a polygamous marriage, in respect of whom the conditions specified in paragraph 7 are satisfied;
	  (b) [^{16} £27.90]; where the claimant is a member of a couple or a polygamous marriage and the conditions specified in [^{1} paragraph 7] are satisfied in respect of a member of that couple or polygamous marriage.

Regulation 67(3)

PART 4

[¹²THE COMPONENT]

12. [¹² . . .].   4.429

13. The amount of the support component is [¹⁷ £44.70]."

AMENDMENTS

1. Employment and Support Allowance (Miscellaneous Amendments) Regulations 2008 (SI 2008/2428) reg.14 (October 27, 2008).
2. Social Security (Miscellaneous Amendments) Regulations 2009 (SI 2009/583) reg.10(2) (April 6, 2009).
3. Social Security (Miscellaneous Amendments) (No. 4) Regulations 2009 (SI 2009/2655) reg.11(1) and (16) (October 26, 2009).
4. Social Security (Loss of Benefit) Amendment Regulations 2010 (SI 2010/1160) reg.12(1) and (3) (April 1, 2010).
5. Social Security (Miscellaneous Amendments) (No. 3) Regulations 2011 (SI 2011/2425) reg.23(14) (October 30, 2011).
6. Social Security (Work-focused Interviews for Lone Parents and Partners) (Amendment) Regulations 2011 (SI 2011/2428) reg.5(5) (October 30, 2011).
7. Personal Independence Payment (Supplementary Provisions and Consequential Amendments) Regulations 2013 (SI 2013/388) reg.8 and Sch. para.40(1) and (5) (April 8, 2013).
8. Armed Forces and Reserve Forces Compensation Scheme (Consequential Provisions: Subordinate Legislation) Order 2013 (SI 2013/591) art.7 and Sch. para.37(1) and (5) (April 8, 2013).
9. Universal Credit and Miscellaneous Amendments (No. 2) Regulations 2014 (SI 2014/2888) reg.3(7)(a) (November 26, 2014).
10. Welfare Benefits Up-rating Order 2015 (SI 2015/30) art.11(1) and Sch.4 (April 6, 2015).
11. Universal Credit and Miscellaneous Amendments Regulations 2015 (SI 2015/1754) reg.19 (November 4, 2015).
12. Employment and Support Allowance and Universal Credit (Miscellaneous Amendments and Transitional and Savings Provisions) Regulations 2017 (SI 2017/204) reg.2(1) and (4) (April 3, 2017).
13. Employment and Support Allowance (Miscellaneous Amendments and Transitional and Savings Provision) Regulations 2017 (SI 2017/581) reg.7(1) and (4) (June 23, 2017, subject to the transitional and savings provision in reg.10).
14. Social Security (Disability Assistance for Working Age People) (Consequential Amendments) Order 2022 (SI 2022/177) art.11(5) (March 21 2022).
15. Social Security Benefits Up-rating Order 2023 (SI 2023/316) art.31(1) and (2) and Sch.11 (April 10, 2023).
16. Social Security Benefits Up-rating Order 2023 (SI 2023/316) art.31(1) and (4) and Sch.12 (April 10, 2023).
17. Social Security Benefits Up-rating Order 2023 (SI 2023/316) art.21(6)(b) (April 10, 2023).

For the General Note to Sch.4, see Vol.V para.4.430.

pp.1525–1532, amendments to the Employment and Support Allowance Regulations 2008 (SI 2008/794) Sch. 6 (Housing costs)

5.100   With effect from July 26, 2021, Sch.9 para.5 of the Social Security (Scotland) Act 2018 (Disability Assistance for Children and Young People) (Consequential Modifications) Order 2021 (SI 2021/786) makes the following amendments to Sch.6:

- In para.15(11)(b) (linking rule), after "disability living allowance", insert ", child disability payment".
- In para.19(6)(b) (non-dependent deductions), after sub-para.(ii), insert "(iia) the care component of child disability payment;".

With effect from January 1, 2022, reg.7(6) of the Social Security (Income and Capital Disregards) (Amendment) Regulations 2021 (SI 2021/1405) inserts into para.19(8)(b), after "Grenfell Tower payment", ", child abuse payment or Windrush payment".

With effect from March 21, 2022, art.11(5) of the Social Security (Disability Assistance for Working Age People) (Consequential Amendments) Order 2022 (SI 2022/177) makes the following amendments to Sch.6:

- in para.15(11)(b) (linking rule):
  - after "armed forces independence payment" for "or" substitute ",";
  - after "personal independence payment", insert "or adult disability payment";
- in para.19(8)(a) (non-dependent deductions):
  - after "armed forces independence payment" for "or" substitute ",";
  - after "personal independence payment", insert "or adult disability payment";
- at the end of para.19(6)(b)(iii) omit "or";
- after para.19(6)(b)(iii) insert "(iiia) the daily living component of adult disability payment; or".

With effect from April 10, 2023, art.31 of the Social Security Benefits Up-rating Order 2023 (SI 2023/316) makes the following amendments to para.19 of Sch.6::

- in sub-para.(1)(a) for "£102.85" substitute "£115.75";
- in sub-para.(1)(b) for "£15.95" substitute "£18.10";
- in sub-para.(2)(a) for "£149.00" substitute "£162.00";
- in sub-para.(2)(b):
  (vii) for "£35.65" substitute "£41.60";
  (viii) for "£149.00" substitute "£162.00"; and
  (ix) for "£217.00" substitute "£235.00";
- in sub-para.(2)(c):
  (vii) for "£50.30" substitute "£57.10";
  (viii) for "£217.00" substitute "£235.00"; and
  (ix) for "£283.00" substitute "£308.00";
- in sub-para.(2)(d):
  (vii) for "£82.30" substitute "£93.40";
  (viii) for "£283.00" substitute "£308.00"; and
  (ix) for "£377.00" substitute "£410.00"; and

- in sub-para.(2)(e):
  (vii) for "£93.70" substitute "£105.35";
  (viii) for "£377.00" substitute "£410.00"; and
  (ix) for "£469.00" substitute "£511.00".

p.1540, *amendments to the Employment and Support Allowance Regulations 2008 (SI 2008/794) Sch.8 paras 8 and 11 (Sums to be disregarded in the calculation of income other than earnings—mobility component and AA, care component and daily living component)*

With effect from March 21, 2022, art.11(7)(a) of the Social Security   5.101
(Disability Assistance for Working Age People) (Consequential Amendments) Order 2022 (SI 2022/177) amended para.8 to read as follows (square brackets indicate only the present amendment, those indicating previous amendments having been omitted):

"**8.**—The mobility component of disability living allowance[,] the mobility component of personal independence payment [or the mobility component of adult disability payment]."

With effect from March 21, 2022, art.11(7)(b) of the same Order amended para.11 to read as follows (square brackets indicate only the present amendment, those indicating previous amendments having been omitted):

"**9.**—Any attendance allowance, the care component of disability living allowance[,] the daily living component of personal independence payment [or the daily living component of adult disability payment]."

"Adult disability payment" is defined in reg.2(1) by reference to reg.2 of the Disability Assistance for Working Age People (Scotland) Regulations 2022 (SSI 2022/54) (see Vol.IV of this series).

p.1542, *amendment to the Employment and Support Allowance Regulations 2008 (SI 2008/794) Sch.8 para.22(2) (Sums to be disregarded in the calculation of income other than earnings—income in kind)*

With effect from January 1, 2022, reg.7(7)(a) of the Social Security   5.102
(Income and Capital Disregards) (Amendment) Regulations 2021 (SI 2021/1405) amended sub-para.(2) by inserting ", a child abuse payment or a Windrush payment" after "Grenfell Tower payment". All of those payments are defined in reg.2(1). See the entry for p.684 for discussion of the nature of child abuse and Windrush payments.

p.1544, *amendment to the Employment and Support Allowance Regulations 2008 (SI 2008/794) Sch.8 para.29(da) (Sums to be disregarded in the calculation of income other than earnings—payments for persons temporarily in care of claimant)*

With effect from July 1, 2022, reg.99 of and Sch. to the Health and   5.103
Care Act 2022 (Consequential and Related Amendments and Transitional Provisions) Regulations 2022 (SI 2022/634) amended para.29(da) by substituting the following for the text after "(da)":

"an integrated care board established under Chapter A3 of Part 2 of the National Health Service Act 2006;"

p.1546, *amendments to the Employment and Support Allowance Regulations 2008 (SI 2008/794) Sch.8 para.41 (Sums to be disregarded in the calculation of income other than earnings)*

5.104   With effect from January 1, 2022, reg.7(7)(b) of the Social Security (Income and Capital Disregards) (Amendment) Regulations 2021 (SI 2021/1405) amended para.41 by substituting the following for sub-para.(1A):

"(1A) Any—
(a)   Grenfell Tower payment;
(b)   child abuse payment;
(c)   Windrush payment."

In addition, reg.7(7)(c) amended sub-paras (2) to (6) by inserting ", a child abuse payment or a Windrush payment" after "Grenfell Tower payment" in each place where those words occur. All of those payments are defined in reg.2(1).

See the entry for p.684 (Income Support Regulations Sch.10 (capital to be disregarded) para.22) for some technical problems arising from the date of effect of these amendments. Because all the payments so far made from the approved historic institutional child abuse compensation schemes and from the Windrush Compensation Scheme have been in the nature of capital, the question of disregarding income has not yet arisen.

p.1556, *amendment to the Employment and Support Allowance Regulations 2008 (SI 2008/794) Sch.9 para.11A (Capital to be disregarded—widowed parent's allowance)*

5.105   With effect from February 9, 2023, para.11(a) of the Schedule to the Bereavement Benefits (Remedial) Order 2023 (SI 2023/134) inserted the following after para.11:

"**11A.** Any payment of a widowed parent's allowance made pursuant to section 39A of the Contributions and Benefits Act (widowed parent's allowance)—
(a)   to the survivor of a cohabiting partnership (within the meaning in section 39A(7) of the Contributions and Benefits Act) who is entitled to a widowed parent's allowance for a period before the Bereavement Benefits (Remedial) Order 2023 comes into force, and
(b)   in respect of any period of time during the period ending with the day before the survivor makes the claim for a widowed parent's allowance,
but only for a period of 52 weeks from the date of receipt of the payment."

The legislation on widowed parent's allowance (WPA), and bereavement support payment (BSP) that replaced it for deaths after April 5, 2017, was declared incompatible with the ECHR by discriminating against children whose parents were cohabiting but not married to each other or in a civil partnership (see *Re McLaughlin's Application for Judicial Review* [2018] UKSC 48; [2018] 1 W.L.R. 4250 and *R(Jackson) v Secretary of State for Work and Pensions* [2020] EWHC 183 (Admin); [2020] 1 W.L.R. 1441 in Vol.I of this series). The Remedial Order allows retrospective claims to be made for those benefits from August 30, 2018 onwards and accordingly for arrears of benefit to be paid if the conditions of entitlement are met.

The new para.11A, and the amended para.60 on BSP, deal with the consequences of such payments on old style ESA entitlement, by providing for them to be disregarded as capital for 52 weeks from receipt. See the entry for p.682 on income support for the effect of the payment of arrears of WPA being in its nature a payment of income to be taken into account (subject to a £10 per week disregard under para.17(i) of Sch.8 to the ESA Regulations 2008) against entitlement in past periods (allowing revision and the creation of an overpayment) and the misleading state of para.7.15 of the Explanatory Memorandum to the Order.

pp.1558–1559, *amendments to the Employment and Support Allowance Regulations 2008 (SI 2008/794) Sch.9 para.27 (Capital to be disregarded)*

With effect from January 1, 2022, reg.7(8)(a) of the Social Security (Income and Capital Disregards) (Amendment) Regulations 2021 (SI 2021/1405) amended sub-para.(1A) by inserting ", child abuse payment, Windrush payment" after "Grenfell Tower payment" and amended sub-paras (2) to (6) by inserting ", a child abuse payment or a Windrush payment" after "Grenfell Tower payment" in each place where those words occur. All of those payments are defined in reg.2(1). 5.106
See the entry for p.684 (Income Support Regulations Sch.10 (Capital to be disregarded) para.22) for some technical problems with the addition only with effect from January 1, 2022 of the disregards of payments from approved schemes providing compensation in respect of historic institutional child abuse in the UK and from the Windrush Compensation Scheme. All the schemes so far in existence provide payments in the nature of capital. That entry also contains information about the nature of the schemes involved, including the child abuse compensation schemes so far approved.

p.1559, *amendment to the Employment and Support Allowance Regulations 2008 (SI 2008/794) Sch.9 para.31 (Capital to be disregarded—payments in kind)*

With effect from January 1, 2022, reg.7(8)(b) of the Social Security (Income and Capital Disregards) (Amendment) Regulations 2021 (SI 2021/1405) amended para.31 by inserting ", a child abuse payment or a Windrush payment" after "Grenfell Tower payment". All of those payments are defined in reg.2(1). See also the entry for p.684. 5.107

p.1563, *amendment to the Employment and Support Allowance Regulations 2008 (SI 2008/794) Sch.9 para.60 (Capital to be disregarded—bereavement support payment)*

With effect from February 9, 2023, para.11(b) of the Schedule to the Bereavement Benefits (Remedial) Order 2023 (SI 2023/134) amended para.60 by making the existing text sub-para.(1) and inserting the following: 5.108

"(2) Where bereavement support payment under section 30 of the Pensions Act 2014 is paid to the survivor of a cohabiting partnership (within the meaning in section 30(6B) of the Pensions Act 2014) in respect of a death occurring before the day the Bereavement Benefits (Remedial) Order 2023 comes into force, any amount of that payment which is—

(a) in respect of the rate set out in regulation 3(1) of the Bereavement Support Payment Regulations 2017, and

(b) paid as a lump sum for more than one monthly recurrence of the day of the month on which their cohabiting partner died,

but only for a period of 52 weeks from the date of receipt of the payment."

See the entry for p.682 on income support for the general background. The operation of this amendment is much more straightforward than that of the new para.111A on widowed parent's allowance. Although a payment of arrears of bereavement support payment (BSP) is in its nature a payment of income and attributable to the past period in respect of which it is due, the payment could not affect any entitlement to old style ESA in that past period because it would be disregarded entirely as income (Sch.8, para.68). The amount of the arrears would thus immediately metamorphose into capital, which would then be disregarded under para.60(2) subject to the 52 week limit.

pp.1565–1566, *annotation to the Employment and Support Allowance Regulations 2008 (SI 2008/794) Sch.9 (Capital to be disregarded)*

5.109   With effect from June 28, 2022 "Cost of living payments" under the Social Security (Additional Payments) Act 2022, both those to recipients of specified means-tested benefits and "disability" payments are not to be taken into account for any old style ESA purposes by virtue of s.8(b) of the Act. The same effect was achieved with effect from March 23, 2023 in relation to payments under the Social Security (Additional Payments) Act 2023 (s.8(b) of that Act). See Pt I of Vol.II for the text of both Acts.

PART V

UNIVERSAL CREDIT COMMENCEMENT ORDERS

p.1613, *amendment of the Welfare Reform Act 2012 (Commencement No.9 and Transitional and Transitory Provisions and Commencement No.8 and Savings and Transitional Provisions (Amendment)) Order 2013 (SI 2013/983) art.5A (Transitional provision where Secretary of State determines that claims for universal credit may not be made: effect on claims for employment and support allowance and jobseeker's allowance)*

With effect from March 30, 2022, art.5 and Sch.1 para.1(2) of the Welfare Reform Act 2012 (Commencement No. 34 and Commencement No. 9, 21, 23, 31 and 32 and Transitional and Transitory Provisions (Amendment)) Order 2022 (SI 2022/302) omitted the phrase "or article 4(11) of the Welfare Reform Act 2012 (Commencement No. 32 and Savings and Transitional Provisions) Order 2019 (no claims for universal credit by frontier workers)" in art.5A(1). But note also the next entry. **5.110**

p.1613, *revocation of the Welfare Reform Act 2012 (Commencement No.9 and Transitional and Transitory Provisions and Commencement No.8 and Savings and Transitional Provisions (Amendment)) Order 2013 (SI 2013/983) art.5A (Transitional provision where Secretary of State determines that claims for universal credit may not be made: effect on claims for employment and support allowance and jobseeker's allowance)*

With effect from July 25, 2022, reg.11 of, and Sch. para.2(2) to, the Universal Credit (Transitional Provisions) Amendment Regulations 2022 (SI 2022/752) revoked art.5A. **5.111**

p.1615, *amendments to the Welfare Reform Act 2012 (Commencement No. 9 and Transitional and Transitory Provisions and Commencement No. 8 and Savings and Transitional Provisions (Amendment)) Order 2013 (SI 2013/983) art.6 (Transitional provision: where the abolition of income-related employment and support allowance and income-based jobseeker's allowance is treated as not applying)*

With effect from March 30, 2022, art.5 and Sch.1 para.1(3) of the Welfare Reform Act 2012 (Commencement No. 34 and Commencement No. 9, 21, 23, 31 and 32 and Transitional and Transitory Provisions (Amendment)) Order 2022 (SI 2022/302) omitted the phrase "or article 4(11) of the Welfare Reform Act 2012 (Commencement No. 32 and Savings and Transitional Provisions) Order 2019 (no claims for universal credit by frontier workers)" in art.6(1)(e)(ii). **5.112**

With effect from July 25, 2022, reg.11 of, and Sch. para.2(3) to, the Universal Credit (Transitional Provisions) Amendment Regulations 2022 (SI 2022/752) omitted para.(1)(e)(ii) in art.6 and the "or" preceding it.

pp.1663–1664, *annotation to the Welfare Reform Act 2012 (Commencement No.20 and Transitional and Transitory Provisions and Commencement No.9 and Transitional and Transitory Provisions (Amendment)) Order 2014 (SI 2014/3094)*

Article 6 of SI 2014/3094 (Transitory provision: claims for housing benefit, income support or a tax credit) was revoked with effect from July **5.113**

25, 2022, by reg.11 of, and Sch. para.5 to, the Universal Credit (Transitional Provisions) Amendment Regulations 2022 (SI 2022/752).

pp.1670–1672, *amendment of the Welfare Reform Act 2012 (Commencement No.21 and Transitional and Transitory Provisions) Order 2015 (SI 2015/33) art.6 (Transitional provision: claims for housing benefit, income support or a tax credit)*

5.114   With effect from March 30, 2022, art.5 and Sch.1 para.2 of the Welfare Reform Act 2012 (Commencement No. 34 and Commencement No. 9, 21, 23, 31 and 32 and Transitional and Transitory Provisions (Amendment)) Order 2022 (SI 2022/302) omitted the phrase "or by virtue of article 4(11) of the Welfare Reform Act 2012 (Commencement No. 32 and Savings and Transitional Provisions) Order 2019" in art.6(11). But note also the next entry.

pp.1670–1672, *revocation of the Welfare Reform Act 2012 (Commencement No.21 and Transitional and Transitory Provisions) Order 2015 (SI 2015/33) art.6 (Transitional provision: claims for housing benefit, income support or a tax credit)*

5.115   With effect from July 25, 2022, reg.11 of, and Sch. para.3 to, the Universal Credit (Transitional Provisions) Amendment Regulations 2022 (SI 2022/752) revoked art.6.

p.1674, *annotation to the Welfare Reform Act 2012 (Commencement No.23 and Transitional and Transitory Provisions) Order 2015 (SI 2015/634) (General Note)*

5.116   Delete the letter "a" after "These" in line 3 of the General Note at para.5.116.

p.1681, *amendment of the Welfare Reform Act 2012 (Commencement No.23 and Transitional and Transitory Provisions) Order 2015 (SI 2015/634) art.7 (Transitional provision: claims for housing benefit, income support or a tax credit)*

5.117   With effect from March 30, 2022, art.5 and Sch.1 para.3 of the Welfare Reform Act 2012 (Commencement No. 34 and Commencement No. 9, 21, 23, 31 and 32 and Transitional and Transitory Provisions (Amendment)) Order 2022 (SI 2022/302) omitted the phrase "or by virtue of article 4(11) of the Welfare Reform Act 2012 (Commencement No. 32 and Savings and Transitional Provisions) Order 2019" in art.7(2). But note also the next entry.

pp.1681–1683, *revocation of the Welfare Reform Act 2012 (Commencement No.23 and Transitional and Transitory Provisions) Order 2015 (SI 2015/634) art.7 (Transitional provision: claims for housing benefit, income support or a tax credit)*

5.118   With effect from July 25, 2022, reg.11 of, and Sch. para.6 to, the Universal Credit (Transitional Provisions) Amendment Regulations 2022 (SI 2022/752) revoked art.7.

p.1732, *amendment to the Welfare Reform Act 2012 (Commencement No. 31 and Savings and Transitional Provisions and Commencement No. 21 and 23 and Transitional and Transitory Provisions (Amendment)) Order 2019 (SI 2019/37) art.2 (Interpretation)*

With effect from July 25, 2022, reg.11 of, and Sch. para.4(2) to, the   5.119
Universal Credit (Transitional Provisions) Amendment Regulations 2022 (SI 2022/752) omitted "and article 8(2)(b)" in art.2(3).

p.1734, *amendment to the Welfare Reform Act 2012 (Commencement No. 31 and Savings and Transitional Provisions and Commencement No. 21 and 23 and Transitional and Transitory Provisions (Amendment)) Order 2019 (SI 2019/37) art.6 (Transitional provision: termination of awards of housing benefit)*

With effect from July 25, 2022, reg.11 of, and Sch. para.4(3) to,   5.120
the Universal Credit (Transitional Provisions) Amendment Regulations 2022 (SI 2022/752) substituted "in regulation 2 of the Universal Credit (Transitional Provisions) Regulations 2014" for "respectively in sub-paragraphs (h) and (l) of article 7(11) of the No.23 Order" in art.6(4).

p.1734, *amendment to the Welfare Reform Act 2012 (Commencement No. 31 and Savings and Transitional Provisions and Commencement No. 21 and 23 and Transitional and Transitory Provisions (Amendment)) Order 2019 (SI 2019/37) art.7 (Transitional provision: application to housing benefit of the rules in universal credit for treatment of couples and polygamous marriages)*

With effect from July 25, 2022, reg.11 of, and Sch. para.4(4) to,   5.121
the Universal Credit (Transitional Provisions) Amendment Regulations 2022 (SI 2022/752) substituted "regulation 6A of the Universal Credit (Transitional Provisions) Regulations 2014" for "article 6 of the No. 21 Order or article 7 of the No. 23 Order" in art.7(1)(a)(i).

p.1735, *amendment of the Welfare Reform Act 2012 (Commencement No. 31 and Savings and Transitional Provisions and Commencement No. 21 and 23 and Transitional and Transitory Provisions (Amendment)) Order 2019 (SI 2019/37) art.8 (Transitional provision: where restrictions on claims for universal credit are in place)*

With effect from March 30, 2022, art.5 and Sch.1 para.4 of the Welfare   5.122
Reform Act 2012 (Commencement No. 34 and Commencement No. 9, 21, 23, 31 and 32 and Transitional and Transitory Provisions (Amendment)) Order 2022 (SI 2022/302) inserted "or" at the end of art.8(1)(a) and omitted both art.8(1)(c) and the "or" preceding it. But note also the next entry.

pp.1735–1736, *revocation of the Welfare Reform Act 2012 (Commencement No. 31 and Savings and Transitional Provisions and Commencement No. 21 and 23 and Transitional and Transitory Provisions (Amendment)) Order 2019 (SI 2019/37) art.8 (Transitional provision: where restrictions on claims for universal credit are in place)*

With effect from July 25, 2022, reg.11 of, and Sch. para.4(5) to, the   5.123
Universal Credit (Transitional Provisions) Amendment Regulations 2022 (SI 2022/752) revoked art.8.

p.1738, *amendment of the Welfare Reform Act 2012 (Commencement No. 32 and Savings and Transitional Provisions) Order 2019 (SI 2019/167) art.1 (Citation and interpretation)*

5.124   With effect from March 30, 2022, art.4(3) of the Welfare Reform Act 2012 (Commencement No. 34 and Commencement No. 9, 21, 23, 31 and 32 and Transitional and Transitory Provisions (Amendment)) Order 2022 (SI 2022/302) omitted art.1(3).

p.1742, *amendment of the Welfare Reform Act 2012 (Commencement No. 32 and Savings and Transitional Provisions) Order 2019 (SI 2019/167) art.4 (Appointed day—coming into force of universal credit provisions and abolition of income-related employment and support allowance and income-based jobseeker's allowance: persons resident outside Great Britain)*

5.125   With effect from March 30, 2022, art.4(4) of the Welfare Reform Act 2012 (Commencement No. 34 and Commencement No. 9, 21, 23, 31 and 32 and Transitional and Transitory Provisions (Amendment)) Order 2022 (SI 2022/302) omitted art.4(11).

p.1745, *insertion of new Commencement Order at para.5.188 onwards.*

The Welfare Reform Act 2012 (Commencement No. 34 and Commencement No. 9, 21, 23, 31 and 32 and Transitional and Transitory Provisions (Amendment)) Order 2022

SI 2022/302 (C.12)

5.126   *The Secretary of State makes the following Order in exercise of the powers conferred by section 150(3) and (4)(a), (b)(i) and (c) of the Welfare Reform Act 2012:*

ARRANGEMENT OF ARTICLES

1.   Citation

2.   Interpretation

3.   Full commencement of universal credit

4.   Removal of restriction preventing frontier workers from claiming universal credit

5.   Consequential amendments

Schedule: Consequential amendments

Citation

5.188   **1.** This Order may be cited as the Welfare Reform Act 2012 (Commencement No. 34 and Commencement No. 9, 21, 23, 31 and 32 and Transitional and Transitory Provisions (Amendment)) Order 2022.

Interpretation

2. In this Order—   5.189

"the No. 9 Order" means the Welfare Reform Act 2012 (Commencement No. 9 and Transitional and Transitory Provisions and Commencement No. 8 and Savings and Transitional Provisions (Amendment)) Order 2013; "the No. 32 Order" means the Welfare Reform Act 2012 (Commencement No. 32 and Savings and Transitional Provisions) Order 2019.

Full commencement of universal credit

3. 30th March 2022 ("the appointed day") is the appointed day for the   5.190
coming into force of the provisions of the Welfare Reform Act 2012 listed in Schedule 2 (universal credit provisions coming into force in relation to certain claims and awards) to the No. 9 Order, in so far as they are not already in force.

Removal of restriction preventing frontier workers from claiming universal credit

4.—(1) The amendments of the No. 32 Order set out in paragraphs (3)   5.191
and (4) have effect from the appointed day.
(2) The No. 32 Order is amended as follows.
(3) In article 1 (citation and interpretation), omit paragraph (3).
(4) In article 4 (appointed day—coming into force of universal credit provisions and abolition of income-related employment and support allowance and income-based jobseeker's allowance: persons resident outside Great Britain), omit paragraph (11).

Consequential amendments

5. The consequential amendments set out in the Schedule have effect   5.192
from the appointed day.

Article 5

SCHEDULE

CONSEQUENTIAL AMENDMENTS

1.—(1) The No. 9 Order is amended as follows.   5.193
(2) In article 5A (transitional provision where Secretary of State determines that claims for universal credit may not be made: effect on claims for employment and support allowance and jobseeker's allowance), in paragraph (1) omit "or article 4(11) of the Welfare Reform Act 2012 (Commencement No. 32 and Savings and Transitional Provisions) Order 2019 (no claims for universal credit by frontier workers)".
(3) In article 6 (transitional provision: where the abolition of income-related employment and support allowance and income-based jobseeker's allowance is treated as not applying), in paragraph (1)(e)(ii) omit "or article 4(11) of the Welfare Reform Act 2012 (Commencement No. 32 and Savings and Transitional Provisions) Order 2019 (no claims for universal credit by frontier workers)".

2.—(1) The Welfare Reform Act 2012 (Commencement No. 21 and Transitional and Transitory Provisions) Order 2015 is amended as follows.

(2) In article 6 (transitional provision: claims for housing benefit, income support or a tax credit), in paragraph (11) omit "or by virtue of article 4(11) of the Welfare Reform Act 2012 (Commencement No. 32 and Savings and Transitional Provisions) Order 2019".

3.—(1) The Welfare Reform Act 2012 (Commencement No. 23 and Transitional and Transitory Provisions) Order 2015 is amended as follows.

(2) In article 7 (transitional provision: claims for housing benefit, income support or a tax credit), in paragraph (2) omit "or by virtue of article 4(11) of the Welfare Reform Act 2012 (Commencement No. 32 and Savings and Transitional Provisions) Order 2019".

4.—(1) The Welfare Reform Act 2012 (Commencement No. 31 and Savings and Transitional Provisions and Commencement No. 21 and 23 and Transitional and Transitory Provisions (Amendment)) Order 2019 is amended as follows.

(2) In article 8 (transitional provision: where restrictions on claims for universal credit are in place)—

(a) at the end of paragraph (1)(a) insert "or"; and

(b) omit subparagraph (1)(c) and the "or" preceding it.

PART VI

TRANSITIONAL, SAVINGS AND MODIFICATIONS PROVISIONS

PART VII

IMMIGRATION STATUS AND THE RIGHT TO RESIDE

p.1793, *annotation to the Immigration (European Economic Area) Regulations 2016 (SI 2016/1052) (General Note—EEA nationals and their family members with pre-settled status)*

In *R. (Fratila) v SSWP* [2021] UKSC 53; [2022] P.T.S.R. 448 the   5.127
Supreme Court allowed the appeal by the Secretary of State against a decision of the Court of Appeal which had found reg.9(3)(c)(i) unlawfully discriminatory contrary to art.18 of the TFEU for treating EU nationals with pre-settled status differently to UK nationals. The judgment of the Court of Appeal had become unsustainable following the decision of the CJEU, in *CG v Department for Communities* (C-709/20) [2021] 1 W.L.R. 5919, that such a provision is not contrary to art.18 of the TFEU, or Directive 2004/38.

However, what the Supreme Court elected not to address (since it was a new point, which would have required new evidence) was the implications for the domestic Regulations of what had also been said in *CG* about the Charter of Fundamental Rights of the European Union (the Charter). The Court of Justice had stated:

"[93] . . . [Where] a Union citizen resides legally, on the basis of national law, in the territory of a Member State other than that of which he or she is a national, the national authorities empowered to grant social assistance are required to check that a refusal to grant such benefits based on that legislation does not expose that citizen, and the children for which he or she is responsible, to an actual and current risk of violation of their fundamental rights, as enshrined in Articles 1, 7 and 24 of the Charter. Where that citizen does not have any resources to provide for his or her own needs and those of his or her children and is isolated, those authorities must ensure that, in the event of a refusal to grant social assistance, that citizen may nevertheless live with his or her children in dignified conditions. In the context of that examination, those authorities may take into account all means of assistance provided for by national law, from which the citizen concerned and her children are actually entitled to benefit."

Important questions arising from *CG* are:

- whether the Charter has any ongoing application, since the end of the transition period in December 2020, for EU nationals resident in the UK on the basis of pre-settled status; and
- what if any substantive or procedural requirements are imposed on the Secretary of State by the obligation to 'check' that Charter rights will not be breached.

In *SSWP v AT (UC)* [2022] UKUT 330 (AAC) (December 12, 2022), a three-judge panel addressed those questions. It dismissed the Secretary of State's appeal against a decision that a destitute parent who was also a victim of domestic violence was entitled to UC. Though her only right of residence was on the basis of her pre-settled status, the refusal of UC would breach her Charter rights. The panel decided that by virtue of the Withdrawal Agreement, the Charter does indeed continue to apply following the end of the transition period where a person is residing in the UK with pre-settled status. It also decided that *CG* does indeed impose a requirement on the Secretary of State (and by extension the FTT) to check in individual cases that there is no breach of Charter rights. It gives guidance on how that check should be conducted. The Secretary of State has been given permission to appeal to the Court of Appeal.

p.1798, *annotation to the Immigration (European Economic Area) Regulations 2016 (SI 2016/1052) (General Note—Overview)*

5.128 In *FN v SSWP (UC)* [2022] UKUT 77 (AAC), Judge Ward records an example of the evidential problems which can arise for claimants seeking to demonstrate a right of residence under these Regulations:

"[4] . . . On the (erroneous) basis that it was necessary to demonstrate that the husband was a 'qualified person', the claimant, by her social worker, had informed the DWP that she and her daughter had fled the family home due to domestic violence and that the claimant had obtained a non-molestation order against her husband. His name, date of birth, national insurance number and details of his then current and previous employers were provided to the DWP, who were asked to contact them, as although the social worker had had some contact with the husband, he had been uncooperative in providing the information necessary.

[5] On mandatory reconsideration, the DWP upheld the original decision saying that the Data Protection Act prevented them from providing the information relating to the husband that had been requested.

[6] On appeal, the DWP indicated they could provide information if in response to a tribunal or court order. The claimant's representatives emailed the FtT on 6 February 2020 explaining this and asking for an order to be made. The email did not on its face identify that the claimant and her husband were estranged due to domestic violence and that may have contributed to why the District Tribunal Judge (DTJ) refused the application, saying, put shortly, that the husband should get them and send them to the DWP and that the FtT would only become involved if the parties had exhausted their own efforts. This prompted a follow-up email on 16 March 2020 explaining the background of domestic abuse and providing a copy of the non-molestation order. The DTJ remained adamant, indicating that the order did not prevent the claimant from contacting her husband through solicitors and until there was evidence that an attempt had been made to do so and had been unsuccessful the decision remained unaltered. Subsequently, on 26 May 2020 a registrar did make an order for the evidence to be supplied by DWP but it was not, despite the representative sending a follow-up email. The case was then listed as a paper hearing, without further notification to the claimant or her representative, and decided [adversely to the claimant]."

As the facts of *FN* indicate, problems are particularly likely where a right of residence may derive from a family member from whom the claimant is estranged. A Tribunal's failure to exercise the FTT's inquisitorial duty to seek evidence of a right of residence, including by establishing details about a relative's identity and possible rights of residence, may constitute an error of law. See, e.g. *AS v SSWP (UC)* [2018] UKUT 260 (AAC); *ZB v SSWP* CIS/468/2017 unreported April 25, 2019 ([21]: "an award of benefit is not a prize rewarding only the most adept"), and *PM v SSWP (IS)* [2014] UKUT 474 (AAC). It is clear from those decisions that the Tribunal can direct the Secretary of State to provide information she holds about an estranged family member. Further, while the Secretary of State appears to consider that due to her data protection obligations she can provide information about such a third party only if ordered to do so by a court or tribunal, there is room for doubt about whether that view is in fact correct, as noted in *ZB* at [19].

pp.1826–1829, *annotation to the Immigration (European Economic Area) Regulations 2016 (SI 2016/1052) reg.4 ("Worker", "self-employed person", "self-sufficient person" and "student")*

Self-sufficient persons

In *VI v Commissioners for HMRC* (C–247/20 O) (September 30, 2021) at [56]–[64], AG Hogan's opinion described a "fundamental question" in that case as "probably" being whether free access to the NHS satisfies the requirement to have CSI, and lamented that the UK Government had not made any submissions about that issue. However, the AG did not express an opinion on the answer, and advised the Court not to do so either.   5.129

Surprisingly, the court's judgment ([2022] EUECJ C–247/20 [2022] 1 W.L.R. 2902) did give an answer, and the answer was that free access to the NHS does satisfy the CSI requirement:

"[68] In the present case, it is apparent from the documents before the Court that VI and her son were affiliated during the period in question, namely from 1 May 2006 to 20 August 2006, to the United Kingdom's public sickness insurance system offered free of charge by the National Health Service.

[69] In that regard, it must be recalled that, although the host Member State may, subject to compliance with the principle of proportionality, make affiliation to its public sickness insurance system of an economically inactive Union citizen, residing in its territory on the basis of Article 7(1)(b) of Directive 2004/38, subject to conditions intended to ensure that that citizen does not become an unreasonable burden on the public finances of that Member State, such as the conclusion or maintaining, by that citizen, of comprehensive private sickness insurance enabling the reimbursement to that Member State of the health expenses it has incurred for that citizen's benefit, or the payment, by that citizen, of a contribution to that Member State's public sickness insurance system (judgment of 15 July 2021, *A (Public health care)* (C–535/19) EU:C:2021:595 at [59]), the fact remains that, once a Union citizen is affiliated to such a public sickness insurance system in the host Member State, he or she has comprehensive sickness insurance within the meaning of Article 7(1)(b).

[70] Furthermore, in a situation, such as that in the main proceedings, in which the economically inactive Union citizen at issue is a child, one of whose parents, a third-country national, has worked and was subject to tax in the host State during the period at issue, it would be disproportionate to deny that child and the parent who is his or her primary carer a right of residence, under Article 7(1)(b) of Directive 2004/38, on the sole ground that, during that period, they were affiliated free of charge to the public sickness insurance system of that State. It cannot be considered that that affiliation free of charge constitutes, in such circumstances, an unreasonable burden on the public finances of that State."

That decision is obviously inconsistent with a long line of domestic authority, cited in the main volume commentary: for example *Ahmad v Secretary of State for the Home Department* [2014] EWCA Civ 988; *FK (Kenya) v Secretary of State for the Home Department* [2010] EWCA Civ 1302; *W (China) and X (China) v Secretary of State for the Home Department* [2006] EWCA Civ 1494 and *VP v SSWP (JSA)* [2014] UKUT 32 (AAC) and *SSWP v GS (PC) (European Union law: free movement)* [2016] UKUT 394 (AAC); [2017] AACR 7.

VI falls within the scope of art.89 of the Withdrawal Agreement (as a CJEU reference made before the end of the Transition Period). As such, it so far appears to be uncontentious that *VI* is directly binding, in relation to periods before December 31, 2020, and that the old domestic authorities should no longer be followed. See *WH v Powys County Council and SSWP* [2022] UKUT 203 (AAC), para.3.

In *SSWP v WV (UC)* [2023] UKUT 112 (AAC) the Upper Tribunal shows one way in which *VI* may have practical application for a person reliant on benefit income. A Belgian national was a carer for his disabled wife who received income-related ESA. The amount of social assistance decreased due to the claimant's presence in the household: the loss of some premiums, and the inclusion of carer's allowance (which is social security not social assistance), more than offset the increase to couple rates. UTJ Ward decided the claimant had a right to reside at that time as a self-sufficient person. Until *VI*, the claimant's argument would have foundered on the comprehensive sickness insurance requirement, but *VI* meant that the claimant met it. When the couple then claimed universal credit, the relatively modest additional cost which awarding that benefit to the couple rather than just awarding it to his UK national spouse as a single person (and only for the 23 months until the claimant qualified for settled status), along with the cost of similar such claims which would also now fall to be allowed, was not an "unreasonable burden" on the UK social assistance system. Consequently, the claimant did not lose his right to reside as a self-sufficient person, and was therefore entitled to a joint award of universal credit.

p.1890, *erratum—Immigration (European Economic Area) Regulations 2016 (SI 2016/1052), reg.16 (Derivative right to reside)*

5.130   There is an error in the first of the two parallel versions of reg.16(12) (i.e. the version stated as now applying to those with pre-settled status). The words "unless that decision" should be deleted from that version.

pp.1891–1892, *annotation to the Immigration (European Economic Area) Regulations 2016 (SI 2016/1052) reg.16 (Derivative right to reside)*

Primary carers of self-sufficient children

5.131   The main volume General Note discusses a pending reference to the CJEU in *Bajratari v Secretary of State for the Home Department* [2017] NICA 74. The Court's judgment (C-93/18) was delivered on October 2, 2019 ([2020] 1 W.L.R. 2327). It agreed with AG Szpunar and held (at [53]), that a Union citizen minor can meet the requirement to have sufficient resources not to become an unreasonable burden on the social assistance system of the host Member State during his period of residence, "despite his resources being derived from income obtained from the unlawful employment of his parent, a third-country national without a residence card and work permit".

pp.1892–1893, *annotation to the Immigration (European Economic Area) Regulations 2016 (SI 2016/1052) reg.16 (Derivative right to reside)*

Primary carer of children of migrant workers in education
The main volume General Note asserts: "Where primary carers are also jobseekers (in the EU sense of that term), they cannot be denied social assistance on the basis of the derogation in art.24(2) of the Citizenship Directive". There is now domestic authority for that proposition: *Sandwell MBC v KK and SSWP (HB)* [2022] UKUT 123 (AAC).   **5.132**

p.1893, *annotation to the Immigration (European Economic Area) Regulations 2016 reg.16 (SI 2016/1052) (Derivative right to reside)*

Primary carers of previously self-sufficient children with a right of permanent residence
Regulation 16(2) and reg.16(5) address the position of carers of *Chen* children and of *Zambrano* children respectively (*Zhu and Chen v Home Secretary* (C-200/02); *Zambrano v Office national de l'emploi (ONEm)* (C-34/09)). It might be thought that both groups are in essentially the same position, insofar as the carer's right of residence does not generate a right to reside triggering social security entitlement. However, the difference is that the *Chen* child may eventually acquire a right of permanent residence under Directive 2004/38 art.16. The situation of primary carers of *previously* self-sufficient children who *now* have a right of permanent residence is not recognised in domestic law. But in *FE v HMRC (CHB)* [2022] UKUT 4 (AAC) the Upper Tribunal decides that it is necessary to treat that category differently, and recognise their right of access to social assistance.   **5.133**

INDEX TO VOLUME II

This index has been prepared using Sweet and Maxwell's Legal Taxonomy. Main index entries conform to keywords provided by the Legal Taxonomy except where references to specific documents or non-standard terms (denoted by quotation marks) have been included. These keywords provide a means of identifying similar concepts in other Sweet & Maxwell publications and online services to which keywords from the Legal Taxonomy have been applied. Readers may find some minor differences between terms used in the text and those which appear in the index. Suggestions to *sweetandmaxwell.taxonomy@thomson.com*.

(All references are to paragraph number)

"Approved blood scheme"
state pension credit, 3.2
Armed forces
entitlement to universal credit,
2.40–2.41
Armed forces independence payments
state pension credit
definition, 3.2
generally, 3.61
Assessed income period
circumstances in which Secretary of
State prevented from specifying,
3.41–3.47
end of period, 3.50–3.52
retirement provision, and, 3.48–3.49
Assessment periods
See Awards
Asylum seekers
exclusion from benefits
exceptions, 5.1–5.18
persons not excluded from benefits
general provision, 5.13
schedule, 5.16–5.18
Attendance allowance
state pension credit, 3.2
universal credit
benefit cap, 2.306
meaning, 2.6
Awards
amounts
generally, 2.136–2.137
run-on after death, 2.138–2.140
apportionment
re-claim delayed after loss of
employment, where, 2.88–2.89
assessment periods
Regulations, 2zy.74–2z7.81
statutory provisions, 1.133–1.134
basis, 1.133–1.134
calculation, 1.135–1.136
capability for work and work-related
activity
generally, 2.111–2.112
period for which element not to be
included, 2.113–2.114
Regulations, 2.111–2.114
statutory provisions, 1.143–1.144
carer element
amount, 2.136–2.137
generally, 2.115–2.116
'regular and substantial caring
responsibilities for a severely
disabled person', 2.117–2.118
Regulations, 2.115–2.118
statutory provisions, 1.143–1.144
child element
adoptions, 2.100, 2.555
exceptions, 2.98–2.103, 2.553–2.559
from April 2017, 2.829–2.830
generally, 2.94–2.96
multiple births, 2.99, 2.554
non-consensual conception, 2.102,
2.557

non-parental caring arrangements,
2.101, 2.556
step-parents, 2.103, 2.558
subsequent awards, 2.103, 2.558
transitional protection, 2.97
transitionally protected children,
2.829
childcare costs element
amount, 2.136–2.137
calculation, 2.127–2.129
charges attributable to an assessment
period, 2.130–2.131
childcare costs condition, 2.123–2.126
introduction, 2.90–2.91
generally, 2.119–2.120
Regulations, 2.119–2.135
'relevant children', 2.132–2.135
statutory provisions, 1.139–1.140
work condition, 2.121–2.122
deduction of income, 2zy.82–2zy.86
elements
amounts, 2.136–2.140
carers, 2.115–2.118
child, 2.92–2.106
childcare costs, 2.119–2.135
housing costs, 2.107–2.110
introduction, 2.90–2.91
LCWRA, 2.111–2.114
particular needs or circumstances,
2.111–2.135
statutory provisions, 1.137–1.144
entitlement to other benefits, and,
2.73–2.74
entitlement period, 2.76
general note
Regulations, 2.72
statutory provisions, 1.114
'having an award of universal credit', and,
2.74
housing costs element
amount, 2.109–2.110, 2.136–2.137
calculation, 2.109–2.110
generally, 2.107–2.108
introduction, 2.90–2.91
miscellaneous, 2.406–2.517
owner-occupiers, 2.109–2.110
Regulations, 2.107–2.110
renters, 2.109–2.110
statutory provisions, 1.141–1.142
in-work allowance, 2zy.82–2zy.86
introduction, 2.71
limited capability for work and work-
related activity element
amount, 2.136–2.137
generally, 2.111–2.112
period for which element not to be
included, 2.113–2.114
Regulations, 2.111–2.114
statutory provisions, 1.143–1.144
maximum amount
generally, 2.91
introduction, 2.72
statutory provisions, 1.135–1.136

reduction of benefits
  generally, 2.389–2.390
  miscellaneous, 2.548–2.552
sanctions
  escalation, 2.812–2.813
  generally, 2.814–2.815
social fund
  cold weather payments, 4.2
  funeral expenses, 4.39
  maternity expenses, 4.39
  winter fuel payments, 4.23
transitional provisions
  before end of assessment period,
    2.788–2.789
  escalation of sanctions, 2.812–2.813
  generally, 2.786–2.787
  sanctions, 2.814–2.815
two week run-on, 2.756–2.757
"Energy Bills Support Sheme"
  additional payments, 1.310
"Energy Rebate Sheme"
  disregard for universal credit,
    2.728–2.730
Entitlement
armed forces personnel, 2.40–2.41
arrears disregarded as capital
  general, 2.762–2.763
  maternity allowance, 2.764
basic conditions
  generally, 1.119–1.126
  minimum age, 2.26–2.28
capital limit, 2.62–2.63
cases where minimum age is 16,
    2.26–2.28
claimant commitment
  acceptance date and method,
    2.53–2.58
  exceptions, 2.59–2.60
  generally, 1.147–1.151
compensatory payment disregarded as
    capital, 2.765–2.766
'confinement', 2.26
'course of advanced education', 2.48
Crown servants, 2.40–2.41
education
  'course of advanced education', 2.48
  exceptions to the requirement not to be,
    2.51–2.52
  'receiving education', 2.46–2.48
  'undertaking a course', 2.49–2.50
  'undertaking a full-time course of
    advanced education', 2.48
existing benefits
  appeals, 2.773–2.774
  arrears disregarded as capital,
    2.762–2.764
  compensatory payment disregarded as
    capital, 2.765–2.766
  exclusion, 2.742–2.743
  generally, 2.746
  housing benefit, and, 2.747
  income support, and, 2.747
  maternity allowance arrears, 2.764

ongoing entitlement, 2.758–2.759
overpayments, 2.760–2.761
persons entitled to severe disability
    premium, 2.740–2.741
restriction on claims, 2.747
Secretary of State's discretion, 2.739
tax credits, and, 2.747
termination of awards for, 2.748–2.753
financial conditions
  capital limit, 2.62–2.63
  generally, 1.127–1.130
  minimum amount, 2.61
funeral payments
  conditions, 4.69–4.77
  generally, 4.68
  residence of claimant, 4.78
  restrictions, 4.79–4.86
generally, 1.117–1.118
habitual residence
  appreciable period, 2.33–2.38
  introduction, 2.30
  meaning, 2.31
  overview, 2.31–2.32
  right to reside, and, 5.10
  'settled intention', 2.33–2.34
  viability, 2.39
in Great Britain
  excluded persons, 2.29–2.30
  habitual residence, 2.31–2.39
  overseas postings, 2.40–2.41
  temporary absence, 2.42–2.45
introduction, 2.25
maternity allowance
  arrears disregarded as capital, 2.764
maternity expenses, 4.50–4.61
members of religious orders, 2.64–2.67
minimum age, 2.26–2.28
minimum amount, 2.61
overseas postings, 2.40–2.41
persons entitled to severe disability
    premium
  general provision, 2.740–2.741
  miscellaneous provisions, 2.882–2.883
persons treated as not being in Great
    Britain, 2.29–2.30
prisoners, 2.64–2.67
receiving education
  'course of advanced education', 2.48
  exceptions to the requirement not to be,
    2.51–2.52
  meaning, 2.46–2.48
  'undertaking a course', 2.49–2.50
  'undertaking a full-time course of
    advanced education', 2.48
Regulations, 2.25–2.67
restrictions
  generally, 1.131–1.132
  members of religious orders, 2.64–2.67
  prisoners, 2.64–2.67
service personnel, 2.40–2.41
severe disability premium
  general provision, 2.740–2.741
  miscellaneous provisions, 2.882–2.883

entitlement
  conditions, 4.69–4.77
  generally, 4.68
  residence of claimant, 4.78
  restrictions, 4.79–4.86
  expenses, 4.91
  'family', 4.40
  'family element', 4.40
  'funeral', 4.77
  general note, 4.35
  immediate family members not in receipt
      of qualifying benefit, 4.82–4.84
  ordinary residence in UK, 4.72
  payment, 4.92
  place of funeral, 4.77
  polygamous marriages, 4.43
  qualifying benefit, 4.70–4.71
  residence of claimant, 4.78
  responsible person, 4.74
  restrictions, 4.79–4.86
  Scotland, in
      Order (2019), 4.112–4.117
  'still-born child', 4.40
  supplementary, 4.79–4.86
  time limits, 4.73
  transport costs, 4.90
Gainful self-employment
  See Earned income
"Grenfell Tower payment"
  state pension credit, 3.2
Guarantee credit
  amount, 3.26–3.32
  carers, 3.113
  housing costs, 3.118–3.139
  pensioners with entitlement to transitional
      additions, 3.114–3.117
  severe disablement, 3.111–3.112
Habitual residence
  appreciable period
      duration, 2.35–2.38
      generally, 2.33–2.34
  entitlement, 2.30
  meaning, 2.31
  overview, 2.31–2.32
  right to reside, and, 5.10
  'settled intention', 2.33–2.34
  viability, 2.39
Hardship payments
  amount, 2.402–2.403
  conditions, 2.396–2.399
  duration, 2.400–2.401
  generally, 1.211–1.212
  introduction, 2.395
  period, 2.400–2.401
  recoverability, 2.404–2.406
  Regulations, 2.395–2.406
  statutory provisions, 1.211–1.212
Higher sanctions
  See Reduction of benefits
"Household Support Fund"
  additional payments, 1.310
Housing benefit
  generally, 1.112

improvement loans
  state pension credit, 3.127
  state pension credit, 1.221–1.222
  transitional provisions, 2.746–2.747
Housing costs
  state pension credit, 3.127
  transitional provisions, 2.808–2.809
Housing costs element
  amount
      generally, 2.109–2.110
      rates, 2.136–2.137
  calculation, 2.109–2.110
  claimant aged 18 to 21, 2.897–2.898
  claimant treated as liable to make
      payments
      generally, 2.419–2.422
      introduction, 2.430
  claimant treated as not liable to make
      payments
      generally, 2.423–2.428
      introduction, 2.431–2.435
  claimant treated as not occupying
      accommodation
      general note, 2.452
      generally, 2.444
      introduction, 2.445
  claimant treated as occupying
      accommodation
      general note, 2.445–2.452
      generally, 2.436–2.443
      introduction, 2.445
  claimants aged 18 to 21, 2.897–2.898
  definitions, 2.406–2.418
  generally, 2.107–2.108
  introduction, 2.90–2.91
  meaning, 2.6
  miscellaneous
      claimant treated as liable or not liable,
          2.419–2.435
      claimant treated as not occupying,
          2.444–2.452
      claimant treated as occupying,
          2.436–2.452
      definitions, 2.406–2.418
      owner-occupiers, 2.502–2.517
      renters, 2.453–2.501
  owner-occupiers, for
      calculation of amount, 2.509–2.517
      definitions, 2.503
      exception to inclusion, 2.505
      generally, 2.109–2.110
      introduction, 2.502
      miscellaneous, 2.502–2.517
      payments, 2.411–2.413
      qualifying period, 2.506–2.508
      'relevant payments', 2.504
  payment condition
      definitions, 2.406
      general note, 2.416–2.418
      owner-occupier payments,
          2.411–2.413
      rent payments, 2.407–2.410
      service charge payments, 2.414–2.415

Regulations, 2.107–2.110
rent payments
  generally, 2.407–2.410
  introduction, 2.417
renters, for
  additional room, 2.467
  calculation of amount, 2.460–2.474
  cap rent, 2.500
  contributions, 2.468–2.471
  core rent, 2.499
  definitions, 2.454
  18 but under 22, 2.457–2.459
  extended benefit unit, 2.464
  general note, 2.493–2.501
  generally, 2.109–2.110
  housing cost contributions,
    2.468–2.471
  inclusion, 2.456–2.459
  introduction, 2.453
  miscellaneous, 2.453–2.501
  more than one accommodation,
    2.472–2.474
  number of bedrooms allowed, 2.465
  payments taken into account,
    2.461–2.462
  private rented sector, 2.475–2.484
  'relevant payments', 2.455
  room allocation, 2.463–2.467
  16 or 17 year old care leavers, 2.456
  size criteria, 2.463
  social rented sector, 2.485–2.492
  temporary absence of extended benefit
    unit, 2.466
  temporary accommodation,
    2.475–2.484
service charge payments
  generally, 2.414–2.415
  introduction, 2.418
statutory provisions, 1.141–1.142
temporary accommodation
  generally, 2.475–2.484
  rent payments, 2.410
terminology, 2.406–2.418
Housing costs element (state pension
  credit)
amendments, 3.132
apportionment, 3.123
calculation for loans, 3.124
excessive, 3.127
general note, 3.133–3.139
general provisions, 3.125
generally, 3.118
ground rent, 3.137
improvement loans, 3.129
improvements, 3.139
liability to meet, 3.120
loans for repairs and improvements,
  3.129
loans on residential property, 3.128
not met, 3.122
occupying dwelling as home, 3.121
other, 3.130
persons residing with claimant, 3.131

Regulations
  amendments, 3.132
  general note, 3.133–3.139
  schedule, 3.118–3.132
remunerative work, 3.119
repair loans, 3.129
repairs and improvements, 3.139
rounding, 3.132
service charges, 3.138
standard rate, 3.126
Housing credit element
consequential amendments,
  1.263–1.268
generally, 1.221–1.222
Immigrants
'person subject to immigration control',
  1.112
persons not excluded from benefits
  definitions, 5.11–5.12
  ECSMA Agreement, 5.7
  European Social Charter, 5.7
  family member of EEA national, 5.8
  general note, 5.1–5.10
  general provision, 5.13
  habitual residence test, 5.10
  has leave to enter or remain only
    because appealing against
    decision, 5.6
  has leave to enter or remain but subject
    to condition not to have recourse
    to public funds, 5.3
  has leave to enter or remain given as
    result of maintenance
    undertaking, 5.4–5.5
  reciprocal agreements, 5.9
  requires leave to enter or remain but
    does not have it, 5.2
  scheduled persons, 5.16–5.18
  spouse of EEA national, 5.8
  statutory provision, 1.6–1.7
  transitional amendments, 5.14–5.15
Regulations
  persons not excluded from benefits,
    5.1–5.18
Immigration and Asylum Act 1999
See also Immigrants
arrangement of sections, 1.5
consequential amendments Regulations
  citation, 5.11
  commencement, 5.11
  definitions, 5.11–5.12
  general note, 5.1–5.10
  general provision, 5.13
  schedule, 5.16–5.18
  transitional amendments, 5.14–5.15
general provisions
  exclusion from benefits, 1.6–1.7
Imprisonment
state pension credit, 3.6
Incapacity benefit
transitional provisions
  assessment under 2010 Regulations,
    2.796–2.797

ndex to Volume II

information requirement, 2.151–2.152
introduction, 2.140–2.141
medical examinations, 2.153–2.154
miscellaneous provisions, 2.518–2.520
relevance, 2.141
statutory provisions, 1.227–1.231
transitional provisions
  credits only cases, 2.792–2.793
  universal credit, 2.885–2.896
work capability assessments
  relevant circumstances, 2.146–2.149
  supplementary, 2.150
Limited capability for work and work-related activity
assessment
  generally, 2.146–2.150
  miscellaneous, 2.521–2.522
awards, and, 1.143–1.144
circumstances in which claimant is treated as having, 2.530–2.535
'couple', 1.230–1.231
elements of award
  amount, 2.136–2.137
  generally, 2.111–2.114
  introduction, 2.90–2.91
  Regulations, 2.111–2.114
  statutory provisions, 1.143–1.144
generally
  Regulations, 2.144–2.145
  statutory provisions, 1.227–1.228
information requirement
  Regulations, 2.151–2.152
  statutory provisions, 1.229
introduction, 2.140–2.141
medical examinations, 2.153–2.154
Regulations
  assessment, 2.146–2.150
  generally, 2.144–2.145
  information requirement, 2.151–2.152
  introduction, 2.140–2.141
  medical examinations, 2.153–2.154
  miscellaneous provisions, 2.521–2.522
  relevance, 2.141
statutory provisions, 1.227–1.231
transitional provisions
  credits only cases, 2.792–2.793
  universal credit, 2.885–2.896
work capability assessments
  relevant circumstances, 2.146–2.149
  supplementary, 2.150
Loans (mortgage interest)
acceptance of offer, 2.597–2.601
adapting accommodation for disabled person, 2.624
alternative finance payments, 2.631–2.632
calculation of loan payment
  alternative finance payments, as to, 2.631–2.632
  generally, 2.614–2.615
  insurance payment deduction, 2.637–2.638
  method, 2.619–2.630

non-dependent deductions, 2.635–2.636
qualifying loans, as to, 2.616–2.630
standard rate, 2.633–2.634
capital limit, 2.618
'claimant', 2.596
conditions of offer
  generally, 2.602–2.603
  information, 2.604–2.605
consequential amendments
  Regulations, 2.699–2.700
  statutory provision, 1.304–1.305
deductions
  insurance payment, 2.637–2.638
  non-dependent, 2.635–2.636
direct payments to qualifying lenders
  general provision, 2.644–2.645
  miscellaneous provision, 2.690–2.698
duration of loan payment, 2.612–2.613
further provision, 1.302–1.303
general provision, 1.300–1.301
insurance payment deduction, 2.637–2.638
interest, 2.639–2.640
'legacy benefit claimants', 2.596
loan payments
  calculation, 2.614–2.638
  direct payments, 2.644–2.645
  duration, 2.612–2.613
  interest, 2.639–2.640
  offer, 2.598–2.601
  period covered, 2.608–2.611
  pre-conditions, 2.602–2.605
  repayment, 2.641–2.642
  timing, 2.606–2.607
  transfer between properties, 2.643
non-dependent deductions, 2.635–2.636
occupying accommodation
  general, 2.671
  legacy benefit claimants, 2.672–2.680
  SPC claimants, 2.672–2.680
  UC claimants, 2.681–2.689
offer of loan payments
  acceptance, 2.597–2.601
  conditions, 2.602–2.605
  generally, 2.598–2.596
  made before 6th April 2018, 2.648–2.649
  made on or after 6th April 2018, 2.650–2.651
'owner-occupier payments'
  circumstances in which claimant liable, 2.664–2.670
  general provision, 2.596
  meaning, 2.658–2.663
payments
  calculation, 2.614–2.638
  direct payments, 2.644–2.645
  duration, 2.612–2.613
  interest, 2.639–2.640
  offer, 2.598–2.601
  period covered, 2.608–2.611
  pre-conditions, 2.602–2.605

1160

employment support allowance
  escalation, 2.812–2.813
  reduction, 2.389–2.390
escalation
  old style ESA, 2.812–2.813
  old style JSA, 2.816–2.817
higher-level sanctions
  ceasing paid work for no good reason,
    1.198–1.203
  leaving employment voluntarily without
    just cause, 1.198–1.203
  loss of employment as employed earner,
    1.193
  misconduct, 1.192–1.197
  Regulations, 2.370–2.371
  Regulations (2019), 2.708–2.712
  statutory provisions, 1.185–1.206
jobseeker's allowance
  escalation, 2.816–2.817
  reduction, 2.389–2.390
leaving employment voluntarily without
  just cause
  domestic circumstances, 1.203
  generally, 1.198
  grievances about work, 1.202
  onus of proof, 1.199
  personal circumstances, 1.203
  'voluntarily leaves', 1.200
old style ESA
  escalation, 2.812–2.813
  general provision, 2.810–2.811
old style JSA
  escalation, 2.816–2.817
  general provision, 2.814–2.815
other, 1.207–1.210
reduction of benefits
  amount, 2.385–2.388
  calculation, 2.368–2.377
  commencement, 2.378–2.379
  continuation where award terminates,
    2.380–2.381
  daily rate, 2.387–2.388
  ESA, and, 2.389–2.390
  failure for which no reduction is
    applied, 2.391–2.392
  fraud, and, 2.382–2.383
  higher-level sanction, 2.370–2.371
  introduction, 2.367
  JSA, and, 2.389–2.390
  low-level sanction, 2.374–2.375
  lowest-level sanction, 2.376–2.377
  'mandatory work activity',
    2.393–2.394
  medium-level sanction,
    2.372–2.373
  miscellaneous, 2.389–2.392
  periods, 2.368–2.377
  start, 2.378–2.379
  statutory provisions, 1.185–1.206
  suspension, 2.382–2.383
  termination, 2.383–2.384
  'trade dispute', 2.392
  work placements, 2.393–2.394

statutory provisions
  higher-level sanctions, 1.185–1.206
  other sanctions, 1.207–1.210
  temporary return to existing benefits,
    2.818–2.819
transitional provisions
  old style ESA, 2.810–2.811
  old style JSA, 2.814–2.815
  loss of benefit penalties, 2.820–2.827
  temporary return to existing benefits,
    2.818–2.819
Savings credit
  amount, 3.33–3.34
  limitation for certain mixed-age couples,
    3.35–3.36
  qualifying income, 3.39–3.40
Scotland
  best start grants
    background, 4.61
    Order (2018), 4.107–4.111
  early years assistance
    background, 4.61
    Order (2018), 4.107–4.111
  funeral expense assistance
    Order (2019), 4.112–4.117
Self-employed earnings
  See Earned income
Self-employed workers
  state pension credit, 3.83–3.84
Service charges
  housing costs element
    generally, 2.414–2.415
    introduction, 2.418
Service personnel
  entitlement to universal credit, 2.40–2.41
Severe disability premium
  universal credit
    general provision, 2.740–2.741
    miscellaneous provisions, 2.882–2.883
Severe disablement allowance
  state pension credit, 3.111–3.112
Single member companies
  universal credit, 2.297–2.302
Small amounts
  See State pension credit
Social fund
  Children's Funeral Fund payments
    associated expenses, 4.124
    definitions, 4.121
    double payment, 4.125
    entitlement, 4.122
    fees charged by burial or cremation
      authority, 4.123
    general note, 4.119
  cold weather payments
    capital limits, 4.18–4.19
    definitions, 4.2–4.4
    introduction, 4.1
    prescribed amount, 4.16–4.17
    prescribed circumstances, 4.8–4.9
    prescribed description of persons,
      4.5–4.7
    weather stations, 4.20–4.21

third parties, to, 3.105–3.106
weekly income, 3.69–3.78
interpretation, 1.68–1.69
local welfare provision, 3.2
loss of benefit, 3.109–3.110
members of same household, 3.24–3.25
national insurance numbers, 3.7–3.8
notional capital
    diminishing rule, 3.101–3.102
    generally, 3.95–3.100
notional income, 3.85–3.90
overview, 1.9–1.13
part-weeks, 3.55–3.56
patients
    definition, 3.5
    generally, 3.37–3.38
payment date, 3.57–3.58
pension fund holder, 3.2
pensioners with entitlement to transitional
        additions, 3.114–3.117
persons not in Great Britain, 3.9–3.14
pilot schemes, 1.70–1.71
policy of life insurance, 3.2
polygamous marriages
    generally, 3.37–3.38
    miscellaneous provisions, 3.157–3.159
    statutory provisions, 1.57–1.58
prisoner, 3.6
prisoners detained in hospital, 3.37–3.38
qualifying age, 1.19
qualifying income
    generally, 3.39–3.40
    meaning, 1.27
'qualifying young person', 3.23
receiving treatment outside Great Britain,
        3.21–3.22
responsibility for child or young person,
        3.140–3.156
retirement pension income
    generally, 3.67–3.68
    meaning, 1.66–1.67
retirement provision
    assessed income period, 1.42–1.41
rounding, 3.107–3.108
savings credit
    amount, 3.33–3.34
    Amount A, 1.29
    Amount B, 1.30
    generally, 1.22–1.32
    limitation for certain mixed-age
        couples, 3.35–3.36
    power to limit, 1.33–1.34
    qualifying income, 1.27, 3.39–3.40
    threshold, 1.28
self-employed earner's earnings, 3.83–
        3.84
severe disablement, 3.111–3.112
small amounts, 3.53–3.54
temporary absence
    generally, 3.15–3.18
    on 6 October 2008, 3.19–3.20
voluntary organisation, 3.2
water charges, 3.2

weekly income, 3.69–3.78
Windrush payment, 3.2
young person responsibilities,
        3.140–3.156
State Pension Credit Act 2002
See also State pension credit
arrangement sections, 1.8
citation, 1.77–1.78
commencement
    generally, 1.77–1.78
    introduction, 1.14
consequential amendments, 1.61–1.62
financial provisions, 1.74
general note, 1.9–1.14
general provisions
    aggregation, 1.40–1.41
    entitlement and amount, 1.15–1.39
    retirement provision, 1.42–1.54
interpretation
    general provision, 1.68–1.69
    income and capital, 1.63–1.65
    retirement pension income, 1.66–1.67
miscellaneous provisions
    administration, 1.55–1.56
    pilot schemes, 1.70–1.71
    polygamous marriages, 1.57–1.58
    regulations and orders, 1.72–1.73
overview, 1.9–1.13
repeals, 1.75–1.76
schedules, 1.79
transitional provisions, 1.59–1.60
State Pension Credit Regulations 2002
See also State pension credit
arrangement, 3.1
citation, 3.2
commencement, 3.2
definitions, 3.2–3.6
general provisions
    entitlement and amount, 3.7–3.58
    income, 3.59–3.108
    loss of benefit, 3.109–3.110
    national insurance numbers, 3.7–3.8
schedules
    disregarded sums, 3.196–3.197
    end date for fixed length assessed
        income periods, 3.160–3.161
    guarantee credit, 3.111–3.117
    housing costs, 3.118–3.139
    income from capital, 3.174–3.195
    special groups, 3.157–3.159
    sums disregarded, 3.196–3.197
    weekly income, 3.162–3.173
State retirement pension
state pension credit
    generally, 3.67–3.68
    meaning, 1.66–1.67
universal credit
    general note, 2.257
    generally, 2.271–2.272
Statutory adoption pay
universal credit, 2.6
Statutory maternity pay
universal credit, 2.6

Index to Volume II

weather stations
 generally, 4.20
 specified alternatives, 4.21
winter fuel payments
 amount, 4.24
 definitions, 4.23
 eligibility, 4.24–4.29
 introduction, 4.22
 payment without claim, 4.30–4.31
"Weekly earnings"
 universal credit, 2.6
Welfare Reform Act 2012
 abolition of benefits
  consequential amendments,
   1.251–1.262
  generally, 1.218–1.226
 arrangement of sections, 1.80–1.83
 background
  challenges of transition, 1.88
  disincentives to work, 1.85
  incentivising work, 1.89
  introduction, 1.85
  proposed solution, 1.86
  simplification of system, 1.87
 challenges of transition, 1.88
 citation, 1.247
 commencement, 1.245
 consequential amendments
  abolition of benefits, 1.251–1.262
  generally, 1.216
 definitions, 1.232
 extent, 1.245
 final provisions, 1.242–1.247
 financial provision, 1.244
 general note
  amount, 1.99
  assessment periods, 1.97
  background, 1.85–1.89
  benefit cap, 1.105
  calculation of entitlement,
   1.98–1.100
  calculation of income, 1.101–1.103
  claimant commitment, 1.107
  claimant responsibilities, 1.108
  conditions, 1.95–1.96
  connected requirements, 1.109
  couples, 1.94
  deductions, 1.100
  earned income, 1.101–1.102
  employment, 1.101
  existing claimants, 1.92
  financial conditions, 1.96
  housing costs, 1.106
  introduction, 1.84
  maximum amount, 1.99
  new claims, 1.91
  sanctions, 1.110
  self-employment, 1.102
  structure, 1.93
  transitional issues, 1.90–1.92
  treatment of capital, 1.104
  unearned income, 1.103
  work-related requirements, 1.108

general provisions
 abolition of benefits, 1.218–1.226
 awards, 1.133–1.144
 benefit cap, 1.237–1.242
 claimant responsibilities, 1.145–1.214
 delegation, 1.213–1.214
 entitlement, 1.117–1.132
 introductory, 1.111–1.116
 miscellaneous, 1.227–1.231
 reduction of benefit, 1.185–1.212
 regulations, 1.233–1.236
 requirements, 1.145–1.184
 supplementary, 1.215–1.217
long title, 1.83
miscellaneous provisions,
regulations
 generally, 1.233–1.236
 supplementary powers, 1.248–1.250
repeals, 1.243
schedules, 1.248–1.293
short title, 1.247
supplementary provisions, 1.215–1.217
Welfare Reform and Work Act 2016
 arrangement of sections, 1.294
 consequential provisions, 1.308
 general note, 1.295
 general provisions
  loans for mortgage interest, 1.300–1.307
  welfare benefits, 1.296–1.299
Widowed mother's allowance
 universal credit, 2.6
Widowed parent's allowance
 universal credit, 2.6
Widow's pension
 universal credit, 2.6
"Windrush payment"
 state pension credit, 3.2
Winter fuel payments
 additional payments, 1.310
 amount, 4.24
 definitions, 4.23
 eligibility
  excluded persons, 4.28–4.29
  generally, 4.24–4.27
 introduction, 4.22
 payment without claim, 4.30–4.31
Work allowance
 See Awards
Work availability requirements
 See also Work-related requirements
 able and willing immediately to take up
  paid work, 2.344–2.348
 Coronavirus, and
  able and willing, 2.345
  exempt claimants, 2.326
  general note, 1.161
  restrictions, 2.359
 domestic violence, 2.355–2.357
 exempt claimants
  earnings thresholds, 2.328–2.329
  generally, 2.325–2.327
  Regulations, 2.325–2.329
  statutory provisions, 1.160–1.163

1178